COUNTER THE COUNTER... FOUNDATION FOR SUCC...

Books are our best friends, is the adag... the pirates of piracy are continuously ... and their supplementary online resources are copyrighted, and we don't lend any right-to-copy. Piracy is synonymous to stealing books.

Knowledge comes real, let's not encourage its counterfeit. Therefore, we appeal all our readers to discourage pirated books and **choose authentic ones**.

HOW TO IDENTIFY THE PIRATED BOOKS?

1 Cover and Spine

- Look and feel (new or used book)
- Blurred images on the cover
- Hologram pasted on front
- Defective spine (wrinkles) or air pocket at its bottom
- Unclear ISBN/bar codes
- Missing/non-operational access codes for supplemental online or e-learning materials

2 Text/Printing/Binding

- Uneven inking of pages
- Poor quality or blurred photographs/images/charts
- Substandard paper quality and opacity
- Misaligned pages
- Missing pages
- Inferior binding quality

You can further watch this video on How to identify a pirated book

For more information about identifying piracy, visit **https://www.mheducation.co.in/piracy**

To report a pirated book, send 'Hi' on WhatsApp code given on the back cover or write to us at **support.india@mheducation.com**.

Reported pirated books are examined to combat their piracy.

Let's fight the Pirates of Piracy and resolve to go for original!

About the Author

Pavneet Singh is an educator for civil services examination at Unacademy and Prepladder. He is also the author of best-selling title on Internal Security published by McGraw Hill Education.

FOURTH EDITION

INTERNATIONAL RELATIONS

FOR GENERAL STUDIES PRELIMINARY AND MAIN EXAMINATION

PAVNEET SINGH

McGraw Hill

McGraw Hill Education (India) Private Limited

Published by McGraw Hill Education (India) Private Limited
Registered Office: Anjana Complex No: 5/90 A, Butt Road, St. Thomas Mount, Chennai – 600016

International Relations, 4e

ISBN (13): 978-93-5532-210-4
ISBN (10): 93-5532-210-0

1 2 3 4 5 6 7 8 9 D103074 26 25 24 23 22

Printed and bound in India.

Typeset at APS Compugraphics, 4G, PKT 2, Mayur Vihar Phase-III, Delhi 96 & printed at Rajkamal Electric Press, Kundli (Hr.)

Cover Image Source: Shutterstock

Cover Designer: Neeraj Dayal

Visit us at: www.mheducation.co.in
Write to us at: info.india@mheducation.com
CIN: U80302TN2010PTC111532
Toll Free Number: 1800 103 5875

Words of Appreciation

The original syllabus of UPSC Mains General Studies Paper-II contained only two topics of International Relations (IR) viz. (1) India and the World and (2) India's Economic Interaction with the World. In 2013, the syllabus was expanded to introduce many new topics. Consequently, the nature, depth and difficulty of the IR questions have greatly changed.

For example, before the change of syllabus, the UPSC asked: *Do you agree with the view that Israel is a natural ally of India*? (Asked in 2010). After the syllabus changed in 2013, the nature of the question changed to: *Too little cash, too much politics, leaves UNESCO fighting for life. Discuss the statement in the light of the US withdrawal and its accusation of the cultural body as being 'anti-Israel bias.* (Asked in 2019)

Sadly, nowadays, the newspaper editorials are too much centred on selective coverage of Pakistan/China/USA/Sri Lanka etc. to cater particular masses of audience on nationalism, visa and immigration only. So, *why did the USA exit from UNESCO*? You may not even have heard about this news in the newspaper. Gone are the days when newspaper editorials alone were sufficient to prepare IR.

In this situation, Pavneet Singh saves your time and trouble. Because if you are going through his book, then you will **not** have to manually wade through:

1. 2500+ pages of BA and MA Political Science material to learn about the evolution of India's bilateral relations, Indian foreign policy and contribution of Indian diaspora.
2. 1000+ pages worth MEA brief given for India's relations with individual countries.
3. Three dozen+ websites of the international organisations and their notable agreements.
4. Websites like IDSA, EPW, ORF, TIME Magazine and other supplementary readings required to learn about the economic and strategic interests of India.

Pavneet Singh's experience as a teacher of International Relations has helped a lot in the right articulation of this book. He has kept the content inside crisp, compact and highly UPSC exam-oriented. Further, he updates this book on an annual basis with new development in the foreign policy and diplomacy.

In his magnificent 4th edition, Pavneet Singh has added completely new material, innovative mind maps, analysis of issues like Ukraine crisis, Takeover by Taliban, Ladakh standoff with China, Developments with all neighbours; to a new chapter like 'Ethical Dilemmas in Indian Foreign Policy'; re-written chapters of the US, Russia, Africa, Indo-Pacific, QUAD and its impact on India's global diplomacy to Indo-EU Summit etc.; and topic-wise analysis of questions from 1979 onwards, as well as practice questions with suggested answer writing approach for future examinations.

The content is also helpful for other areas of the syllabus like topics of GS Mains Paper-I (Globalisation and Its Impact on Indian Society), GS Mains Paper-III (International Economy, Internal Security and Challenges in Border Management), IR-related Essay and Political Science as an optional subject. Even college students and researchers pursuing BA/MA/UGC-NET/JRF in Political Science and International Relations will also find this book very useful.

I wish the best of luck to Pavneet Singh and the esteemed readers of this comprehensive and succinct textbook for International Relations.

Mrunal Patel

Foreword

An ex-US President, no less a Republican taking on a pro-Russia hue, Pakistan kowtowing to Russia, Arab world reconfiguring its ties with the Zionist state, India becoming a part of the QUAD which notwithstanding potentials to the contrary cannot seem to shed the perception of being in an anti-China alliance with the potential of becoming a military bloc; these are some of the important developments in the international arena that appear to shock and stump the best and most perspicacious foreign policy experts, let alone amateur observers or students of international politics. The extant global order is well and truly on its way out but a new balance of power is yet to emerge to take its place. The global system is in a state of flux like never before. The new tech game that has thrown up in the post-pandemic world has added another layer of complexity to the already chaotic global scenario. The upshot of the foretasted developments is likely to challenge and shake the very foundation of the fundamentals that have long influenced the foreign policy of the nation states and have formed the basis of our understanding of the same. The contemporary scenario thus leaves a student of International Relations (IR) in a bit of quandary and state of confusion. Making sense of foreign policy, an already complex area thus becomes a burdensome and onerous endeavour. In this context, 'International Relations', a text prepared with immense labour and intellect by my colleague and dear friend Pavneet Singh comes as a breath of fresh air. This meticulously designed and succinct textbook is designed to fill the critical gaps and help the Civil Services aspirants alike. The text begins with basic fundamentals, including a glimpse of world history, and gradually takes the reader into more complex aspects and imparts a contextual background that enables the readers to appreciate and absorb the contemporary developments. Furthermore, the students get insights about the real workings of the strategic policy and the pulls and pressures that are characteristic of bilateral and multilateral relations. I hope and believe that the students would relish reading this singular, exam-oriented text for International Relations.

Good luck to all students and aspirants.

M. Puri

Preface

This work on International Relations (IR) is a mandatory text for the students/aspirants preparing for the General Studies papers. This book acts as a foundation builder for any Civil Services aspirant because it serves as a primary source to prepare for Current Affairs of International Importance (Item 1 of Part-A, Paper-I General Studies, Preliminary examination) and International Relations (Items 17, 18, 19, 20 of Part-B, Paper-III General Studies-II, Mains examination).

Each chapter in this book is meticulously written with an intention to enhance the understanding of the reader on the topic discussed. The chapters adopt multidimensional analysis paradigm and start with basic background and history of diplomatic relations and then covers different dimensions involved in diplomatic relations. This holistic coverage from background till the present-day diplomacy enhances the overall understanding of the reader. Once the reading of the entire book is over, the reader shall have complete command on the subject.

The readers would be able to analyse the events related to Indian Foreign Policy. This book will thereby equip the readers with adequate knowledge for Current Affairs of International Importance (part of Preliminary examination syllabus of the UPSC), International Relations (part of GS Mains examination paper) and Civil Services Personality Test. The most interesting feature of the book is that I have incorporated plenty of diagrams and case studies. Each diagram will help to summarise the core discussion. These diagrams not only facilitate revision but can also be used directly in the Mains examination while writing answers. Such diagrams will certainly fetch additional marks in this paper. The case studies in the chapters add on to the existing understanding and are designed to provide the readers a completely fresh perspective on the dimension being discussed, along with providing applications for the policies that are under scrutiny.

I welcome constructive feedback from the readers for further improvements. Please feel free to reach out to me for any clarifications.

Email: pavneet.unacademy@gmail.com

YouTube: https://www.youtube.com/c/PavneetSinghUPSC

Telegram: https://t.me/currentaffairsbypavneetsingh

Regards,

Pavneet Singh

Acknowledgements

I would like to convey my deepest thanks to Shivani Shingte for her valuable guidance in strategising this book and her constant support in planning and reviewing the chapters of the book from time to time. A special thanks to the people who have transformed my thoughts through deep interactions and they include Shri Rajiv Mehrishi, IAS (Comptroller and Auditor General of India); Mrs. Meera Mehrish, IAS; Shri Sanjeev Tripathi, IPS (Secretary, Research and Analysis Wing—RAW); Shri Tilak Devasher, IPS (Special Secretary, Research and Analysis Wing—RAW); Shri Rakesh Bansal, IAS (Additional Chief Secretary, Government of Madhya Pradesh); Shri Y. K. Chaudhary, IRS (Chief Commissioner, Income Tax); Shri Shishir Priyadarshi, IAS (India's Representative to WTO, Geneva); and Shri M. K. Dhar, IPS (Joint Director, Intelligence Bureau). Many thanks to my friends and well-wishers that include M. Puri sir, Mrunal Patel, Pratik Nayak, Varun Khullar, Bhagwat Rathore, Minister Ashok Kumar, Dipika Goyal, IFS, Neha Bhatia, Neeta Tripathi mam, Trinity, Sonali Bansal, Dr. Happymon Jacob, Dr. Vinay and Preeti Mishra.

I would also like to thank my family members for their understanding and patience. A special thanks to members of my family, K. J. Singh, Sarita Singh, Jasbir Singh, Moneesha Singh, Little Dizzy, Robinder Singh, Sasha Singh, Sukanya Singh, Shishir Deo, Manjit Kochar, Devnita Bakshi, Amar, Param, Kaushik and Kavleen.

Pavneet Singh

What is New in the 4th Edition?

Every chapter is reconstructed with policy updates since global pandemic, making it the only updated book in the market for the time being. Instead of theory, this book is written on the basis of conversation of author with serving intelligence officials and diplomats. It is a practical guide that takes you on an exhilarating journey of India's foreign policy. Considering that diplomats and university professors evaluate IR answers in GS Mains Paper-II, such insights in each chapter will fetch more marks to the aspirant.

The book, at the first step, covers India's relation with its neighbours, the prime ministers and their policies. It further covers India's bilateral relation with countries like Afghanistan, Pakistan, China, Sri Lanka, Nepal, Bhutan, Myanmar and Bangladesh.

Starting with India's relation with its neighbours, the Prime ministers and their policies to India's relation with countries like Pakistan. Afghanistan, Sri Lanka, Bangladesh ... this book covers a wide range of topic, step by step.

How to Study International Relations for Civil Services Examination

In any competitive examination, the key to success is to understand the syllabus thoroughly. This write up, as an introductory one, precisely does the same for International Relations (IR) for the UPSC Civil Services Examination.

RELEVANCE OF IR IN CIVIL SERVICES EXAMINATION

First, let us try to understand the sections of IR in the vast syllabus prescribed by the UPSC. IR is crucial for all the three stages of the examination. It is directly mentioned in the syllabus of the Prelims (the first stage) and the Mains (the second stage). Third stage is the interview of civil services examination.

In the Prelims examination, IR comes under the heading of the syllabus mentioned as "Current Affairs of National and International Importance". A simple analysis of the previous year Prelims papers will help understand any aspirant that the above-mentioned section is one of the most important sections of the syllabus, contributing nearly 35 to 40 questions per year. A further breakdown of the above section of the syllabus gives us a better picture. As per that, one can infer that on an annual basis, there are 10 to 12 questions in the Prelims examination that can be directly related to IR.

Number of questions from IR in Mains examination: 4 to 5

Number of questions from IR in Prelims examination: 10 to 12

EXAMPLES OF QUESTIONS IN THE PRELIMINARY EXAMINATION

The nature of the questions in the Prelims is simple and straightforward. The questions normally range from International organisations in which India participates or is affected by its dynamics; bilateral and multilateral diplomatic agreements and accords signed by India or affecting interests and diplomatic values of India; geopolitical changes in India's neighbourhood or extended neighbourhood affecting India.

Preliminary Examination Question in 2018

In 2018, India was diplomatically striving to join the Nuclear Suppliers Group (NSG). The joining of NSG has tremendous implications on India's nuclear programme (covered in chapter on Indian Nuclear Diplomacy). The UPSC asked question related to NSG in the Prelims asking the consequences of India joining NSG.

Preliminary Examination Question in 2019

Israel–Palestine issue was in news throughout 2019 due to conflict between Palestinians in Gaza Strip and Israel. The UPSC asked the question related to the "two-state solution" in 2019 Prelims.

Seeing the instances of the two questions, one thing can be safely inferred. The Prelims examination revolves around the current happenings.

HOW TO APPROACH IR FOR THE PRELIMINARY EXAMINATION?

3-Point Strategy for Prelims Examination

Strategy Point 1: An aspirant should read the newspaper carefully.

Strategy Point 2: One should analyse what are the major events happening on the international front in the newspaper. This means you need to look out for all the news related to IR on editorial, op-editorial and international pages of the newspaper.

Strategy Point 3: The aspirants should try to study different dimensions related to the items in the news from the book here. For instance, if India joined the NSG—this as a news item will be found in every newspaper. What is expected from the aspirant is that after seeing this news item, one should go to the chapter on India's nuclear programme and try to study about NSG and associated multilateral export control regimes and India's diplomatic stance. Similarly, if Israel and Palestinian people are having a conflict, then the aspirants need to read Israel–Palestine dispute from the book here. One must note that reading the entire Israel–Palestine issue is important as it is a broad issue. If in 2019, the UPSC has asked about the two-state solution; and if the issue continues in news in 2019 (which it is), then, the UPSC can ask any other dimension from the issue ranging from HAMAS to Palestinian Authority to the policy of Khaled Mashal and Mohammad Abbas etc.

Thus, read the newspaper. Identify the IR-specific issue in the news. Read its background from the relevant chapters in the book. Add from the news whatever tit-bits you get. The dimension is ready for the Prelims examination.

HOW TO APPROACH FOR THE MAIN EXAMINATION?

The IR is a part of General Studies Mains Paper-II. There are four topics mentioned by the UPSC in the syllabus.

Topic 1: The first topic in the syllabus is called *India and neighbourhood relations*. By far, this is the most important topic. It encompasses all are land and maritime neighbours. The neighbours of India stretch from Afghanistan to Myanmar to China to Maldives. This book has covered the bilateral relations with all the neighbours from ancient times till 2020–21. Any developments between India and its neighbours have to be carefully analysed. For instance, if India and Pakistan decided to open Kartarpur Corridor in 2019, the aspirants should know all the consequences related to it.

Topic 2: *Bilateral, regional and global groupings and agreements involving India and/or affecting India's interests* is the second topic. This broad topic literally includes India's relation with all the countries from regional to the international level.

Topic 3: The third topic is *Effect of Policies and politics of developed and developing countries on India's interests, Indian diaspora.* For instance, If Sri Lanka comes out with a policy that affects Indian Tamils in Sri Lanka, then it comes under this heading.

Topic 4: The last topic of the syllabus is *Important International institutions, agencies and fora, their structure, mandate.* The examiner tests the aspirants' command over India's international diplomatic negotiation style at international institutions and agencies. Therefore, the aspirants need to study carefully the various meetings where India participates and its style of negotiation.

Answer Writing Technique for the Mains Examination for International Relations

For Mains examination, three things are to be followed that constitute the basic structure of any answer.

Step 1: Introduction of the answer and Five Golden Points

Writing an effective and a powerful introduction will act as a force multiplier to overall score. Please note that as you are writing answers for the UPSC Civil Services Main examination, your answers should reflect the same maturity. Also, keep in mind the Five Golden Points while writing an introduction.

Point 1: Introduction is a snapshot of the answer. The idea is to give a glimpse to the examiner of what to expect in the answer ahead.

Point 2: Please refrain from using definitions and quotations in the introduction, as introduction is a summary of the answer in short.

Point 3: It has to be short and crisp.

Point 4: The standard practice is that in a 150 words question, introduction should be in not more than 2 lines and in a 250 words question, the introduction should not be more than 3 lines.

Point 5: By default, introduction should always be in a paragraph and never ever in bullets points.

Step 2: Key Points to Design a Powerful Body of the Answer

Body of an answer helps to communicate the core ideas to the examiner. Key Points are:

Point 1: An aspirant can be innovative here. One can use diagrams to give information. Throughout the book you will come across many diagrams. They will help you understand how to create diagrams in IR to fetch surplus marks.

Point 2: One can use bullets points but bullets are used only for writing factual points in the answer. If there is nothing factual in your answer, then the body of the answer should better be in a paragraph.

Step 3: Three Power Points for a Powerful Conclusion of the Answer

Most of the aspirants neglect this and end up in losing marks. Please note the following points.

Power Point 1: Answer needs to be concluded always and it cannot be abruptly ended. Conclusion of an answer should always be on a positive note. This is universal fact.

Power Point 2: It is always a futuristic suggestion. This means that the examiner should know the future ahead and how to achieve the future.

Power Point 3: It should be non-repetitive. One should be careful to note that conclusion should never consist of any point that one has already mentioned in the body above.

Final Summary to Remember

Structure	Design
Introduction	Summary of the answer/150 words = 2 lines/250 words = 3 lines/always in a paragraph/no definitions ever.
Body	Always in a paragraph/Diagram and bullet points if needed
Conclusion	Positive point/Futuristic suggestion/Non-repetitive point

APPROACH FOR THE ESSAY PAPER

Basic Idea

Essay in Civil Services is a full-fledged paper of 250 Marks. The UPSC normally asks two essays which an aspirant needs to attempt. A lot of essays have been asked by the UPSC from topics of international relations and this book can be very beneficial to develop content that one needs for the essay paper. To attempt any essay, one needs to remember that there is a defined approach. First, an essay is nothing but a very long answer of general studies (GS). So, if you master the art of writing GS answers then you are not likely to have any difficulty in attempting an essay. In essay, you need to organise and articulate your thoughts in the form of an introduction, body and conclusion. The contents of these three remain the same as for GS answers, with three exceptions. Firstly, the introduction should have a glimpse of your entire essay/your position you intend to take/your core points of the body and conclusion. So, it is not wrong to say that an introduction to the essay is a miniature snapshot of the essay itself. Secondly, the body should have well-defined and well-articulated arguments, logically designed in a coherent flow. Thirdly, the conclusion should present 'your views and opinion' with respect to the stand you have taken.

Topic 1: The emerging global order, political and economic (**1993**)

Topic 2: Restructuring of UNO to reflect present realities (**1996**)

Topic 3: The world of the 21st century (**1998**)

Topic 4: India's contribution to the world wisdom (**1998**)

Topic 5: My vision of an ideal world order (**2000**)

Topic 6: India's role in promoting ASEAN cooperation (**2004**)

Topic 7: Terrorism and world peace (**2005**)

Topic 8: Importance of India–US Nuclear deal (**2006**)

Topic 9: Are we a soft state? (**2009**)

Topic 10: Good fences make good neighbours (**2009**)

Topic 11: In the Indian context, both human intelligence and technical intelligence are crucial in combating terrorism (**2011**)

Topic 12: Has the non-alignment lost its relevance in a multi-polar world? (**2017**)

Topic 13: Technology as a silent factor in International Relations (**2021**)

HOW WILL THIS BOOK HELP IN ANSWERING THESE TOPICS?

These topics are easy to attempt if an aspirant has conceptual clarity. This is where the relevance of this book enters. It equips you with potential fodder base to write these essays. If you look at the topic number 8, this topic is dealt in depth in the chapter of India and the USA relations. It is explained there why did the US sign the deal with India? What was the need of the deal? How did it help India? What were its implications on Indian strategy of great power politics? What were the implications of the deal on China/Pakistan/regional Asian security/and global nuclear proliferation order?

So, all that I am trying to convey to you here is that in order to attempt any essay, you need to have in-depth fundamental clarity of the topic. I urge you to read all the chapters in the book carefully. Once done, I would urge you to come back to these topics once again and then attempt these essays. Please send these 13 topics to me for evaluation at my email when you are done with them.

"An infallible method of conciliating a tiger is to allow oneself to be devoured."

Contents

SECTION 5: INDIA'S RELATIONSHIP WITH CENTRAL ASIA 205

SECTION 6: INDIA'S RELATIONSHIP WITH AFRICA 227

SECTION 11: INDIA'S RELATIONSHIP WITH AMERICA 417

SECTION 12: IMPORTANT INTERNATIONAL INSTITUTIONS, AGENCIES AND FORA—THEIR STRUCTURE, MANDATE 453

SECTION 1

Building Blocks of International Relations

1. The Fundamentals of International Relations
2. Basics of World History and International Relations
3. Multipolarity, Crisis of Multilateralism and India in the Post-Pandemic World

AN OVERVIEW

The World History for International Relations is regarded as building blocks section. This topic is not directly mentioned in the UPSC syllabus, but a few questions were asked in the past. In 2000, question came on the difference between collective security and cooperative security. In 2002, a question was asked, "What is meant by unipolar world"? In 2003, a question on the concept of veto in the United Nations was asked. Similarly, in 2007, a question was based on the meaning of global governance. In 2011, a very conceptual question was asked, "Is there still a role of concept of balance of power in contemporary international politics"?

Potential foresight On the basis of the above-mentioned questions asked by the UPSC, we should note that the commission can ask questions pertaining to the World History section in future. For instance, with the presence of Covid-19 pandemic, a question on the crisis of multilateralism may be asked. A thought related to this could be that why India has faith in multilateralism or has India lost faith? Because a question on unipolarity had already been asked previously, now a question on multipolarity might be asked. The commission can also ask a question on why India advocates for multipolarity and what role can India play strengthening multilateralism. This chapter is constructed succinctly with a foresight in mind that will equip one with the knowledge for answering such questions.

CHAPTER 1

The Fundamentals of International Relations

THE NEED FOR BUILDING BLOCKS

Whenever an aspirant studies International Relations (IR), they often struggle with some fundamental terms and concepts. These terms come repeatedly in the newspapers and the aspirants struggle to find their succinct meanings. In this chapter, our endeavor is to enable the aspirants develop a basic understanding of some of the most commonly used terms and concepts in IR. The aspirants are expected to master these terms and develop a conceptual grasp over them so that these terms can enable better understanding of the subject and the textbook.

CONCEPT OF STATE, SOVEREIGNTY AND SECURITY

'State' is a creation of man and not a creation of mother earth or nature. Further to it, State is a political association that has a defined territory with a permanent population to be governed by a government, which is sovereign. Sovereignty entails hierarchy within the state. It means, state has the freedom to take independent decisions in domestic and international affairs without being answerable to any authority above it. Security ensures the absence of any threat. Security at a micro level, is called human security, at state level is called national security and at a global level is known as international security.

UNDERSTANDING DIPLOMACY, FOREIGN POLICY AND INTERNATIONAL RELATIONS

In simple language, diplomacy is communication between strangers. The strangers here are states, so, diplomacy is communication between states and other actors. At times, diplomacy was called honorable spying. It is not just formal communication, it also includes negotiations, information gathering and image management. In this sense, we can say that diplomacy is an instrument of statecraft for implementation of interests of state through communication. International Relations is a study of state's relationship with other countries, and it is an interdisciplinary field that includes the study of history, international law and security. Foreign policy is what a country does, and International Relations is how a country does what it does. International Relations is a political marketplace where a state can sell its foreign policy. The interests of a state are known as 'national interests'. National interest is used as an analytical tool to identify the objectives of foreign policy of a state. National interest is always those basic determinants used by a state to guide state policy in relation to other states in an international system. According to Charles Beard, the term 'national interest' gained momentum in political lexicon during sixteenth century in Europe, when it replaced *raison d'état* during the gradual development of the idea of nationalism. The idea expressed was of development of interest of the whole of the society. Later, it was used in International Relations as an exercise of state power.

WOLF WARRIOR DIPLOMACY

In recent times, wolf warrior diplomacy has been attributed to China. It is a term that has its origin to the Chinese movie 'Cut the Clutter', released in 2015, where the plot depicts Chinese soldiers fighting and teaching a hard lesson to the enemies of the state. The diplomats of China are quite prosaic and conventional, but since 2019, we have seen changes in their language. Chinese diplomats and Foreign Ministers have used phrases like '*pushing back countries that deliberately insult China*', '*refute groundless slander with facts*' (when an opinion is given to China which they do not prefer to hear) and in response to Chinese handling of COVID-19, Xi Jinping sent a message to his internal constituency stating, "*The whole world is against us, I am fighting back*". This recent change in the behavior of Chinese diplomats has led the world leaders and the global diplomatic community to draw parallels with the Chinese film 'Cut the Clutter'. Put simply, the global diplomatic circles have given this new term to imply the **harsh diplomacy** being practiced by China, called wolf warrior diplomacy.

PERIODIZATION OF WORLD AFFAIRS

For the simplicity of understanding chronology, it is expected that the aspirants remember the following periodization of world affairs. The period from 1914 to 1918 is the period of World War I and the period from 1939 to 1945 is the period of World War II. The period between 1918 and 1945 is known as Inter-War period. The time between 1947 and 1989 is broadly called as the period of Cold War and the period since 1989 till now is the period of post-Cold War.

Age of Uncertainty

Certain scholars often refer the period of post-cold war as an age of uncertainty. They do so because this period of the history of the world has seen uncertain and unpredictable behaviors by states. Indian Ambassador Rakesh Sood is also one of the vocal champions of this term in his writings.

BASICS OF COLD WAR AND POST-COLD WAR

For the time being, till we undertake a deeper elaboration in the subsequent chapters, we must note that Cold War is a period that began after the World War II ended. This period saw the world being ideologically divided between communist and capitalist ideologies. The world also witnessed geopolitical tensions between US (for promoting capitalism in the world) and USSR (for promoting socialism in the world), thereby making the world bipolar (meaning two poles, US and USSR, spreading their own ideologies globally). In 1989, the USSR disintegrated and the world witnessed a rapid transformation. The world became unipolar (means only one pole, namely the US) and the world slipped into post-Cold War period. However, today, it is stated that the world is multipolar, which means there is an international system with multiple power centers. This gives an assertion that multiple countries in the world exist in the international system that can exercise power.

Polarity Thesis

The word 'pole' comes from polarity, which implies the way power is distributed in the international system. The period of Cold War saw the power distributed between US and USSR, thus, making the world bipolar.

CONCEPT OF ALLIANCE

Alliance is a written formal agreement between two states with common values where one state intends to offer security protection to the other; while the other state receiving the security protection offers its market access to security provider. It is an agreement where both parties gain mutual benefits. For instance, in 1949, the US created an alliance called North Atlantic Treaty Organisation (NATO). Similarly, in 1955, the Soviet Union created a Warsaw Pact as an alliance.

The above-mentioned view is one way of looking an alliance, which is seen through a security lens. The alliance can also be seen in a more generic sense, which can imply a grouping of like-minded nations to achieve a common goal. For instance, the International Solar Alliance is a generic alliance, not a security one, having a group of like-minded states brought together by India and France to develop solar potential and clean energy.

Challenges for NATO

NATO was formed for tackling Cold War but since the post-Cold War period, new challenges confront NATO and they include the challenges of climate change, cyber war attacks, threats to energy supplies and global commerce.

CONCEPT OF STRATEGIC PARTNERSHIP AGREEMENT

The strategic partnership agreement is a written formal agreement between two states with common values where the states decide to cooperate with each other on multiple dimensions and deepen their relationships. These dimensions are limitless and it is the individual prerogative of states define the end lines of cooperation. They could range from economic cooperation, trade and cultural cooperation to energy diplomacy and technological cooperation etc. It is important to note that in a strategic partnership agreement, the parties concluding the agreement have the necessary security capabilities to protect themselves and would not undertake offering or receiving of any security protection. The states shall utilise their existing security capacities to defend themselves from adversaries. However, due to possession of common values that bind the two states, the states will cooperate and deepen their ties further where strategic partnership agreement offers them a framework for better cooperation. But we must note that a strategic partnership agreement may include the security dimension as one of the dimensions in the multidimensional cooperation. This security dimension, however, shall not be security protection but commercial defence sales. For instance, India and Japan are strategic partners since 2006 and the strategic partnership agreement includes cooperation in multiple dimensions including defence, where Japan has been undertaking commercial defence sales of defence products to India as a privileged partner.

Global Partners, Special Global Partners, or Strategic Partners ... all are similar terms. The difference in nomenclature asserts the symbolic significance the states intend to attach to their special partners.

DIFFERENTIATING CONFLICT AND WAR

Why was 1962 a conflict between India and China?

India and China had difference of opinion over the boundary, which was a colonial inheritance. The two sides, since 1949, tried to find a mutually acceptable solution for the border, but failed. This led to an un-intentional violent clash in 1962.

In IR, conflict and war are two important terms that have special significance. Just like two people can have differences, so can two countries. The countries can have differences because of any issues, be it different interpretation of boundaries or different interpretation of trade policies (often called by economists as a 'trade war', but in reality, it is a conflict over difference of opinion on trade policy) or different interpretation in conduct of states. The best way to resolve differences is dialogue. However, at times, there could be a possibility that the dialogue between the two states may not give the intended results. In case the dialogue fails to deliver, the two states can become insecure and this insecurity may manifest as a violent clash. This clash, however, will be accidental, unintentional and non-deliberate. The conflicting parties will again take the recourse of dialogue to resolve the differences. However, in war, there is a deliberate attempt by one nation to violate the sovereignty of another nation. As war involves a deliberate attack, the country under attack reserves the right to retaliate in self-defence. The war is always intentional and deliberate. There is another situation, called civil war, which is a fight between two political groups within the borders of a country, primarily with the objective of capturing state power. The core differences between conflict and war can be summed up in the table given below.

Conflict	Unintentional	Non-deliberate
War	Intentional	Deliberate

In India, we have had our own instances of conflicts and wars. India and China had a conflict in 1962; however, India and Pakistan had a war in 1971.

CONCEPT OF IMPERIALISM AND COLONIALISM

Imperialism is a phenomenon where one country tries to control and subordinate another country. This phenomenon involves a capitalist country, which uses its economic and military power, to subordinate a pre-capitalist country. When the capitalist country subordinates the pre-capitalist country, they use their resources for their own welfare. One way of doing imperialism is known as colonialism. In colonialism, one country militarily and politically annexes the other and the country annexed loses its sovereignty and eventually gets exploited. Once a country is colonised, its resources are taken by the coloniser, its people are subjugated and the political and economic systems are also controlled by the coloniser. The country that gets colonised resorts to resistance against the coloniser. The resistance can be peaceful or violent, but is aimed at de-colonisation.

Neo-Colonialism

In neo-colonialism, the country that gets decolonised comes under indirect pressure by erstwhile coloniser or other powerful countries. The attempt is now to use indirect pressures like economic levers and conditionalities to subjugate the weak countries.

CONCEPT OF GEOPOLITICS

Geopolitics, in a simple language, means the role of geographical factors in foreign policy. In other words, geopolitics is concerned about how a country leverages its geographical location or resources, its core geographical factors, in doing relationship with others. A country can have a favourable location and may leverage its location in engagement with others. For instance, the location of Iran, when seen from Indian point of view, is favourable because the location of Iran allows India an access to Central Asia and Afghanistan. This makes Iran a geopolitically significant country for India. Similarly, Saudi Arabia possess a natural resource called oil and they use it in their relationship with other countries. India is their customer and uses oil for its domestic economic development. This makes Saudi Arabia geopolitically important for India. We also observe an interesting phenomenon that both Saudi Arabia and Iran are geopolitically important for India, for different reasons, as given in the table below.

Geopolitical significance of Saudi Arabia for India	Oil (resource)
Geopolitical significance of Iran for India	Access to different countries (location)

HYPHENATION AND DE-HYPHENATION

Let us understand this concept through an example. During the Cold War, the US would always do diplomacy with Pakistan by looking at its implications on India. This was because during the Cold War, the US was concerned that their diplomacy with Pakistan should not 'provoke' India to balance Pakistan by engaging with someone else. This is known as hyphenation. In this way, one country does diplomacy with another country by looking at implications of its diplomacy on the other country, thus hyphenating the two. So, we can say that during the Cold War, the US hyphenated India and Pakistan. This implies that US's diplomacy, during Cold War, with Pakistan was done with keeping in mind how India would react to such diplomacy. The reaction, US aimed, should not provoke India to counter Pakistan by engaging with an adversary of the US. The concept of de-hyphenation is exactly opposite to hyphenation. Here, the focus is to engage with two states independently and not get concerned about the implications. Since the end of the Cold War, the US has de-hyphenated India and Pakistan. The US is not concerned about the diplomatic implications of their engagement with Pakistan on India and vice versa.

CONCEPT OF GREAT POWERS

The concept of great powers is used in the theory of realism by realist scholars and it signifies the ranking of the global states in terms of their economic and military capabilities they possess.

The term 'great powers' found its first written mention in the Treaty of Chaumont in 1817, as, by the Congress of Vienna in 1815, Austria, Britain, France, Prussia and Russia were granted the great power status for the first time. In 1944, a foreign policy and IR scholar named William Thornton Rickert Fox replaced the term 'great powers' with 'superpowers' and since then, the US, Britain, France, Russia and China have been given the status of superpowers. The hierarchy that is established on the basis of capabilities is as follows:

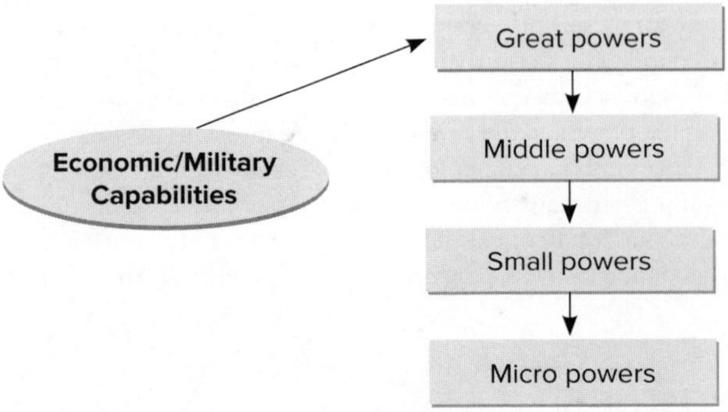

CONCEPT OF TREATY, CONVENTIONS AND PROTOCOLS

A treaty is a written agreement which is signed by countries or international organisations, making it obligatory for the signatory parties to accept certain rules that have been consensually agreed upon in the contract. On signature of the treaty, the signatory parties agree to follow the written obligations while agreeing to accept liabilities on failure to follow said obligations. The treaties are governed through the Vienna Convention (1969), which is also known as the laws of treaties or the treaty of treaties. We must note that when a state signs a treaty, it remains a party to the treaty even if domestically, after signing a treaty, the state government changes. On the other hand, a convention is a special treaty that concludes the discussion of an issue of global significance leading to the creation of an agreement to be ratified by the member states discussing the global issue. For instance, climate change and its consequences are discussed in conventions attended by several global member states. A protocol is also a kind of a treaty but a specialised one as it allows amendments and alterations in the main text of the treaty. If a state undertakes a signature to a treaty, it means that the state has an interest in following the points mentioned in the treaty. Signature is a legal process and is of two types—simple signature and definitive signature. In a simple signature, a state is not bound to follow the points of the treaty until it ratifies the treaty. Thus, a simple signature involves no obligation on the state as the state reserves the option of putting the treaty before the domestic national parliament allowing its people to have a say in the external matters of the state. On the other hand, in a definitive signature of a treaty, the state expresses its willingness to be bound by all the points of the treaty without the need for ratification of the treaty. When a state ratifies a treaty, it gives its consent to be bound by the treaty. In the ratification of a treaty, the state agrees to get the treaty approved by its national parliament and also indicates its willingness to be bound to other contracting parties in the treaty. In ratification, it gives the national parliament of state a much bigger role to direct state's external affairs.

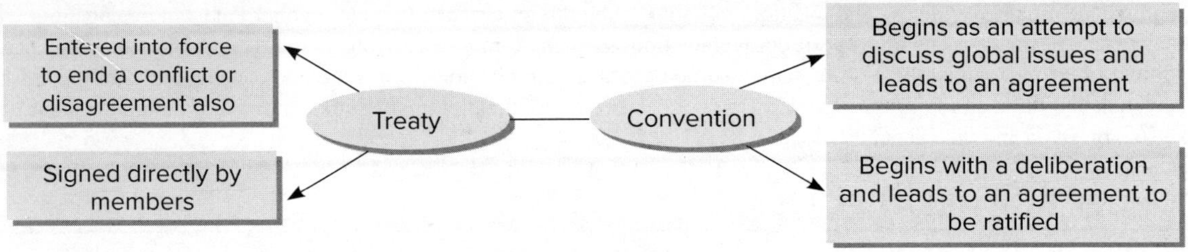

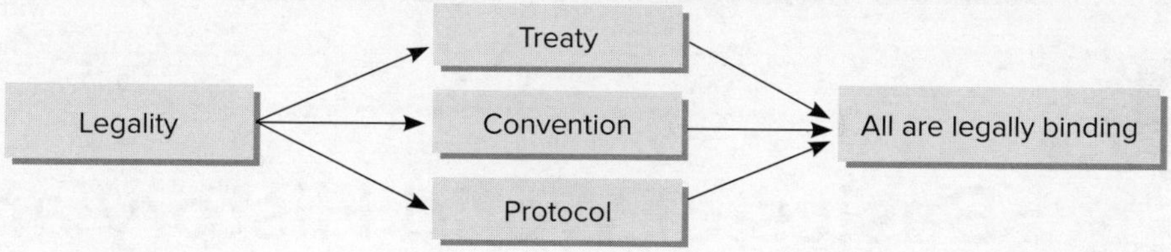

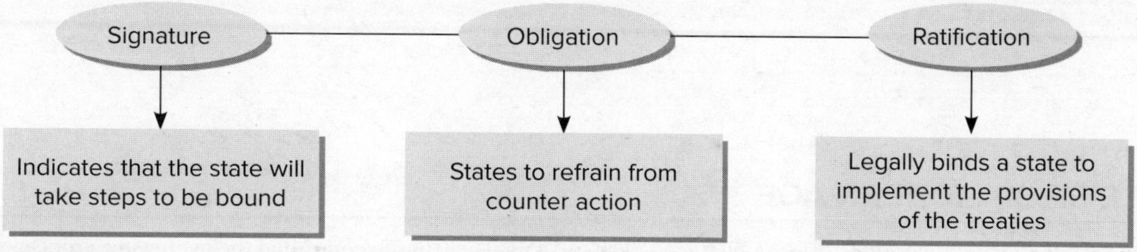

KEY TERMS

1.	State	Defined territory with a permanent population to be governed by a government, which is sovereign
2.	Diplomacy	An instrument of statecraft for implementation of interests of state through communication
3.	Wolf Warrior Diplomacy	Harsh diplomacy practiced by China while communicating with countries in the international system
4.	Cold War	A situation of no war, yet no peace
5.	Alliance	Written formal agreement offering security protection in return for market access
6.	Strategic Partnerships	Written formal agreements to deepen cooperation in multiple dimensions other than security protection owing to existing capabilities to protect
7.	Imperialism and Colonialism	Subordinating a pre-capitalist country is imperialism and colonialism is exploiting the resources for augmenting own power

CHAPTER 2

Basics of World History and International Relations

THE RISE OF MODERN AGE

The study of the modern world history can be traced back to 1453. The Church controlled the medieval European society and was the most important institution in the medieval era. It controlled the behaviour of men (including what and how will men think) and also politics (that is, who will be the king and who will not) in the society.

The medieval Europeans did commercial trade with Asian states. This trade was managed by the Ottomans, who acted as intermediaries. They purchased commodities from Asia and sold them to Europe, thereby making a huge commission in the process.

The economic wealth accumulated by the Ottomans sparked political expansionist ambitions. They began to expand westwards, towards Europe. On 29th May 1453, they captured the city of Constantinople (the capital of the European Byzantine Empire) and established control over the key trade gateway to Europe and Asia.

This led the Europeans to search for alternative trade routes, compelling them to explore alternatives in the sea. As the Europeans went to the sea, they discovered distant lands and new people. As they intermingled with distant cultures and people, their perception of the outside world changed.

They began to think differently and rationally. They refused to accept the notions popularised by the Church and preferred to accept things that could be rationally and empirically verified. This new scientific, rational and empirical thought process which people developed emerged as a new movement known as Renaissance.

The invention of Press popularised renaissance. Instead of being dependent upon the sermons from the priests, people began to read the religious scriptures on their own. Bible was translated into languages people could understand.

As people read Bible and other scriptures, they found the discrepancies in the written texts and the existing narrative. People began to question the authority of Church and sought reforms in the functioning of it. Thus, the renaissance paved way for the rise of reformation. As it affected the authority of Church, it led to massive crisis in the society.

A natural consequence was civil war, which lasted for many decades, and eventually ended in 1648 with the Peace of Westphalia. This not only separated the religion from politics but also paved way for stability, and thus, the rise of nation states.

The nation states that eventually began to rise were strong monarchies. The Monarchs continued to support scientific thoughts, rationalism and modernism. This led to the rise of a new intellectual movement known as Enlightenment in Europe, which became the foundation for Industrial Revolution. The Monarchs also continued the commercial trade with Asia.

As Europe entered the dawn of industrial age, it needed resources, which were not enough in Europe to fulfil the growing appetites. The need for resources compelled the Europeans to colonise distant lands of Asia, Africa and Far East, thus began the era of colonisation.

POWER POLITICS, ALLIANCE FORMATION AND EVENTS LEADING TO WORLD WAR I

As the European states colonised distant lands for access to resources to fuel their industrial revolution, their insecurities with each other grew. To mitigate these insecurities, they formed alliances.

Till 1870, Germany was a broken and fragmented territory. Otto Von Bismarck unified it in 1870 and began to colonise territories in Asia, Africa and Far East (like Micronesia islands). The German unification sent shivers down the spine of Britain and France, who were to then confront a territorially and economically strong Germany.

In 1870, Germany resorted to power politics and Franco-German war happened, where Germany defeated France and snatched away Alsace Loraine from the latter. Knowing that French would retaliate, in 1879, Germany entered into an alliance with Austria–Hungary.

The Austria–Hungary Empire was on the fringes of Europe, bordering the Balkan lands. The Balkan land was under the imperial control of Russia and the Balkans fiercely resisted Russian imperialism.

The Balkan lands were not economically important but strategically significant as they were located as a bridge between Asia and Europe. The Balkan lands were an ethnic port of different races and cultures. The Russians always wanted to develop an imperial control over Austria–Hungary. Thus, Austria–Hungary, in order to mitigate the threat of imperial Russia, joined an alliance with Germany in 1879, thereby giving birth to the Dual Alliance.

What are the Balkans?

The lands between Adriatic Sea, Aegean Sea, Baltic Sea and Mediterranean Sea comprising of states such as Bulgaria, Romania, Greece, and Serbia.

In 1882, Italy joined the Dual Alliance making it the Triple Alliance or Central Powers. The Italians had ambitions to acquire Libya, which was neighbour of French-controlled Algeria and Morocco. Italy knew that France would act as an irritant to Italians. Thus, it joined the Dual Alliance to mitigate the threat of France for their African foray.

Even though the Triple Alliance was formed to maintain status quo, it generated sense of insecurity amongst the British, French and the Russians, leading to formation of counter alliances.

In 1893, France initiated the alliance formation and joined an alliance with Russia. France did not enter into alliance with Britain because it had colonial disputes with the latter and by signing an alliance with Russia, it tried to isolate the British. It had the desired effect.

The British resolved their colonial disputes and in 1904, the British and French signed an alliance, isolating Russia. The reason was that the British were not happy to join an alliance with autocratic Russia. The Russians realised their isolation, compelling the Russian Czar to provide for freedom of speech to the Russian people and also carry out partial democratic reforms. This was appreciated by the British, and in 1907 the British, Russians and the French established an alliance of Allies. By 1907, Europe was divided between Allies and Central Powers.

Who are Czars?

Russia was led by rulers known as Czars, who were autocratic and the British found engagement with Russia repugnant to democratic Britain.

THE INTERNATIONAL HISTORY OF THE WORLD WAR I

The Balkan states were developing intense nationalism, driven against imperial tendencies, by developing secret organisations. In Serbia, a secret organisation called Black Hand gave responsibility to Gavrillo Principe to assassinate Archduke Francis Ferdinand (who was about to become the ruler of Hapsburg Empire, which was under larger control of Austria–Hungary).

In 1914, when Archduke Francis Ferdinand was assassinated, Austria–Hungary told Serbia to clamp down upon these secret organisations, investigate the assassination and allow it to participate in the investigation. Serbia refused to allow it to join investigation, as doing so would have threatened the secret societies that existed in the Balkans. Thus, Austria–Hungary declared a war on Serbia. Because Serbia was under imperial control of Russia, the Russian came to the rescue of Serbia. Seeing this, Germany joined Austria–Hungary and declared a war on Russia and France. As Germany attacked France and Austria–Hungary attacked Russia, the British declared a war on the Germans and Austria–Hungarians.

In 1914, Central Powers were at war with Allies. Italy was a part of Central Powers and was debating whether it should participate in the war or not. France made a proposal to Italy and stated that if the Italians support the Allies, the Allies on victory would allow Italy to have access to Libya, South Tyrol, Fiume and Dalmatian Islands. This was much more than Italians had aspired for. Thus, Italy deflected from the Central Powers and joined the Allies.

On the other hand, Japan in the East had colonial ambitions over China. But it could not materialise its ambitions, as it was not interested to upset British in India and French in Cambodia, Laos and Vietnam. It decided to support the Allies in the war, thinking that after the war, Japan could get concessions to acquire lands in China. Initially, the Central Powers were able to defeat Allies in the ongoing battles.

In 1915, the Allies sought the help of the US. As the negotiations materialised, the US began to provide monetary assistance and arms to the Allies. The American ships with armament sailed via Atlantic to reach the shores of Britain and France, which increased the power of the Allies.

Why did the US Enter World War I?

The US entered the World War I in 1917–1918 when Germans attacked American ships, which was perceived by the US as an attack on its sovereignty.

1916 onwards, with the American support, the Allies were able to hit Central Powers and finally defeated them in 1918, thereby ending the World War I. After their victory, the Allies began the post-war settlements at the Paris Peace Conference through various treaties with defeated powers (such as Treaty of Versailles for Germany, Treaty of St. Germaine for Austria–Hungary and it created Poland, Treaty of Neuilly for Bulgaria, Treaty of Trianon for Hungary and Treaty of Severs in 1920 for Turkey).

What are Administered Territories?

This concept was advocated by Jan Smuts and George Louis Beer under Article XXII of the covenant of the League of Nations to control and administer the colonial possessions of Germany in Africa, Pacific and Turkey in the Middle East. It was a system that did not involve direct annexation and traditional imperialism. The 'responsible' states in 'sacred trust' of the League of Nations would provide guidance and support to the powers incapable of self-governing themselves.

The US President Woodrow Wilson announced the creation of League of Nations as a body, which would strive to alter the behaviour of the states by modifying the environment in which the states exist, so that it could display positive and 'good' behaviour, thereby preventing another world war. The concept of right to self-determination (RTSD) was applied, though selectively in Balkans and territories of the defeated powers, but not in the colonies.

A concept of administered territories was proposed by the League for the lands of defeated powers and especially for the Ottoman lands and it led to the birth of Mandate System (under which the British and France became mandatory powers, who were to provide guidance and support to the defeated Ottoman lands).

The Mandate System was unique because without officially colonising the Ottoman lands, the British got the control of Iraq, Trans-Jordan and Palestine; whereas France got the control of Syria and Lebanon, for guidance and support (an indirect attempt by the British and French to hijack the oil reserves in Middle East and establish monopoly).

At the end of the World War I, the US did emerge as a rising power (through display of its capabilities), but still allowed the British and French to assert dominance in the international system. Japan got the control of lands in the Far East and some concessions in China, only at the apprehension of British and French, which was perceived negatively by Japan (Japan perceived that British and French would do everything possible to prevent the rise of Japan).

But the defeated Central Powers were not invited in the Paris Peace Conference held in 1919. Also, due to selective application of RTSD, the image of Europeans in colonies declined and it intensified nationalist struggles in the colonies, thereby, shifting the nationalism to Asia.

INTERNATIONAL RELATIONS IN THE INTER-WAR PERIOD

The Treaty of Versailles (which was imposed upon the Germans by the British and French) restricted the German economic growth and domestic production, military expansion and attempts towards colonisation. Not only Germany consequently became economically and militarily weak but also, the treaty hurt the psyche of the German people.

The 1929 Great Depression pushed the German economy on the verge of collapse. This created an ideal condition for the rise of Hitler, who launched his Fascist campaign based on Nordic superiority (that Germans are the purest Aryans and all other who are impure need to be killed) and Lebensraum theory (that superior Nordic Aryan Germans need more living space, thus Germany will acquire more lands).

Italy, which deflected to the Allies on the promises of territory, saw the rise of Fascist Mussolini as the Allies refused to give the promised lands to Italy. Russia, as stated earlier, was a feudalistic and agrarian society under the Czars. In 1853, when British and French were busy colonising, the Russians colonised the Danube region (which was under Ottoman rule), near Crimea.

This sent alarm bells to the British, who perceived that southward expansion of Russia would be a threat to the British in the Jewel in the Crown, India. In 1854, British, Ottoman and French collectively attacked Russia near Crimea, leading to the outbreak of the Crimean war. The Russians, after their defeat in the Crimean war, decided to match British and French. So, they began to industrialise and adopted the policy to capitalise and colonise.

The Czars remained suppressive while the newly emerging Russian capitalists became exploitative, crushing the Russian people anyway. This, in 1898, paved way for the rise of socialists in Russia, who established the Russian Socialist Democratic Labor Party (RSDLP).

Why did Great Depression occur in 1929?

It occurred because the US stopped providing monetary support to the Europeans for post-war reconstruction, pushing the British and French economies into depression, as they were taking American support since 1920 to rebuild their economies that were devastated by war.

They wanted to remove Czars, but were divided on how to, as Bolsheviks in the RSDLP wanted to use peasants and labour to fight Czars while the Mensheviks favoured the support of capitalists to remove Czars. In 1917, during World War I, the Bolsheviks succeeded (led by Vladimir Lenin) in a revolution against the Czars thorough guerilla warfare.

Due to Russian revolution (which gave birth to modern day USSR and created the Communist Party of Soviet Union—CPSU), Lenin through the Treaty of Brest–Litovsk, in 1917, withdrew Russia from World War I and later announced a new form of international relations based on equality, non-exploitation and suppression and RTSD, which sent deep shivers down the capitalist world (Britain, France and the US, who perceived Communism as a threat to Capitalism).

The Russian revolution at one place inspired Nehru in India (who was motivated by state-led industrialisation model) and Dr. San Yet San in China (to fight Japanese suppression).

What is Revolution?

A revolution means a sudden change in the system of governance of a state through violence. A revolution also signifies a change in the value system of the state.

The League of Nations failed to check the rise of Hitler and Mussolini. It also failed to contain Italian annexation of Abyssinia and Japanese invasion of Manchuria in 1935. The rising insecurities in the world again paved way for alliance formation.

British and French again became allies; Italy and Germany came together. Japan realised that its rise as a power in the East bothered Britain and France. Thus, Japan joined Germany and Italy and a Fascist Axis was born again. Russians wanted Britain and France to sign a military pact against Germany. But the British and the French knew that Communist Russia was a bigger threat than the Germans. So, they did not favour the Russian proposed military pact. This compelled Russia to sign a non-aggression pact with Germany in 1939, which came as a shock to the British and the French.

THE INTERNATIONAL HISTORY OF WORLD WAR II

Poland was a territory sandwiched between Russia and Germany. The Polish people knew that due to their location, they witnessed a threat from Russia and Germany. Thus, Poland sought a security guarantee from British and French. In 1936, Hitler signed a non-aggression pact with Poland, which Polish people appreciated thinking that they had mitigated one serious threat.

In 1939, when Russia and Germany signed the non-aggression pact, Hitler secretly proposed to Russia that both of them would attack Poland and take away territories bilaterally (based on Lebensraum of Hitler). The Russians accepted the proposal of Hitler as they got the control of territory of Poland. The Russia–Germany non-aggression pact in reality became a pact for aggression in Poland.

In 1939, Russia attacked Poland from the East and Germany from the West, compelling Britain and France (security granters of Poland) to wage a war on Germany. While Germany came under attack, Russians used this as a shield to annex Finland, Latvia, Lithuania and Estonia. The Germans began to counter attack Britain and France, compelling the two to seek assistance from the US.

The US (through Cash and Carry Act 1939 and Lend and Lease Act 1941) aided the Allies in Europe to use American support and lease land bases and attack the Axis. In 1941, to the surprise of Russia, Germans attacked them. Germany asserted that the need to attack Russia (despite a non-aggression pact in 1939) was because the Russians were acquiring bases to attack the Germans in Baltics and Finland. However, the claim was vehemently refuted by Russia.

The Russians immediately joined the Allies and sought help of Britain and France, both of whom were devastated due to German attacks. The Allies (Britain, France and Russia) now sought the help of the US to target the Axis, but it was Japan that brought the US in the World War II. Japan, since the end of the World War I, had imperial ambitions over China (it also got German colony of Micronesia Island, located close to Hawaii, the US).

For its domestic industrialisation, Japan was seeking oil from South East Asian states (Indonesia, Brunei and South China Sea) and was simultaneously developing dominance over the region, leading to serious concerns for British, French and America. In 1935, when Japan attacked China; the US imposed sanctions on Japan and prevented Japan to seek oil. This drastically affected Japan, compelling Japan in 1941 to attack the American naval base at Pearl Harbor in Hawaii.

The US declared a war on Japan and entered the World War II on behalf of the Allies, eventually crushing them in 1945. The war quickly ended in Europe with Russia, France and British emerging victorious. As per the Potsdam Conference in 1945 (the conference related to post-war settlement in Europe), Germany was divided into four zones (one zone each for Britain, France, Russia and the US).

The British, French and the US zones in Germany were merged as West Germany (capitalist) and Russia renamed its zone as East Germany (communist), both divided by the Berlin wall (which eventually fell in 1989, marking the end of the Cold War). But the war was still going on in 1945 in the East, as Japan had not surrendered.

The Allies built bases in China to attack Japan (the US used this opportunity to condemn the rising red star in China), but the US surprised all by dropping atomic bombs on Hiroshima and Nagasaki, leading to instant surrender of Japan.

The use of atomic bombs by the US (coupled with the secrecy of the Americans in developing the bombs) sent shivers down the spine of Russia, which feared that the Americans could use them against Russia if they did not acquire the similar capability.

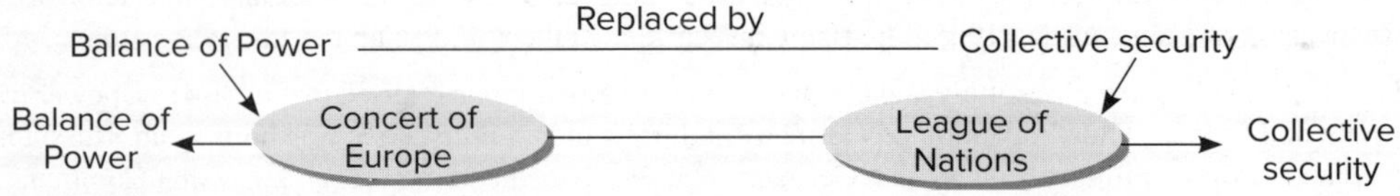

RISE OF STRATEGIC BIPOLARITY, IDEOLOGICAL BIPOLARITY AND COLD WAR

> **What is Veto?**
>
> Veto means an ability or power to stop an undesirable outcome unilaterally. A state needs to possess capabilities to exercise veto.

At the end of World War II, the US, due to use of atomic bombs, emerged as a global superpower. Even though the British and French were victorious, but both were economically and militarily devastated. However, they were accommodated by the Americans in the new international global order through permanent membership seats in a new institution known as United Nations. The UN Security Council was conceptualised with veto power that accepted their status as Middle Powers (countries that accept an existence of a superpower above them, the US here).

The three post-war settlement conferences, such as Potsdam Conference 1945, London Conference 1945 and Paris Conference 1946, gave a huge territory to Russia in Europe. This made Russia not only territorially the largest power in Europe but also ideologically opposite to the US in the world, thereby emerging as a superpower.

However, Russia was determined to seek parity with the Americans and speeded up the development of their nuclear bomb. By 1949 (though the US by now developed hydrogen bomb), after giving the US four years of unbridled atomic power supremacy, the USSR emerged as a challenger (by developing atomic bomb in 1949 and hydrogen bomb by 1953) to the US.

The USSR was now territorially and economically strong along with absolute strategic parity with the US. The ideological bipolarity was cemented by the Greek crisis and Turkish crisis. During the World War II, Greece was under the control of Germany. The Greeks had monarchy, but due to the Russian revolution, by 1940s there was a growing Communist movement in Greece. At the end of the World War II, the Greek monarchy wanted to get rid of the Germans, and hence, they sought the support of the Communists, who in turn sought support of the USSR. The USSR saw this as an opportunity to make Greece communist and plunged to help.

The Germans were ousted by 1946 and now the USSR compelled the monarchy to accept communism, which the monarchy and the Greek people vehemently opposed. They favoured monarchy to be in power. This is where the US saw an opportunity (where it perceived that the USSR was trying to 'impose communism') and stepped in to support the Greek people and monarchy, and eventually helped them to oust the Communists by 1949.

The Greek crisis compelled the US to think about a strategy to protect the 'freedom' of the people from totalitarian communism. The US Congress, under the 'Freedom Agenda' empowered the American President to militarily intervene to protect the 'freedom' of the people anywhere endangered in the world, which manifested as the Truman Doctrine (named after the US President Harry S. Truman, the then American President who sought such powers from the Congress).

This military doctrine gradually developed an economic component known as Marshall Plan (proposed by the US Secretary of State George S. Marshall, also known as the European Recovery Plan), where the core idea was to provide economic assistance for post-war recovery in the European continent (though, in reality was designed to prevent post-war European states to fall into the orbit of communism).

The Truman Doctrine and the Marshall Plan, born out of the Greek crisis, became the ideological tools of the American strategy in the Cold War. The Russians responded by creating Council for Mutual Economic Assistance (CMEA).

Turkey was a part of the Ottoman Empire. At the end of World War I, through the Treaty of Severs 1920 and the Treaty of Lausanne 1923, the modern day Turkey was born, and it continued to have good ties with Britain. In 1947, the USSR asked Turkey to provide them with access of Turkish straits (the area near Black Sea and Mediterranean Sea) for commercial trade with the world.

The Turks refused (as they feared that after access, the Russians would demand a base and eventually spread communism in Turkey) to comply with the Russian demand and sought British help to check Russia. This angered the Russians, who responded through gunboat diplomacy. The Americans, seeing this, came to the rescue of Turkey, and responded with counter gunboat diplomacy, leading to escalation.

What is Cold War?

The term was coined by H. B. Scope, who was an American journalist. Walter Lipmann, a scholar, popularised the term and stated that Cold War describes a situation where there is no war, yet no peace. It is a term that signified the global ideological tensions in the world created in the aftermath of the World War II by the US and the Soviet Union.

To de-escalate, the two immediately came on the table for talks to find a diplomatic solution. The Americans bargained that if the USSR guarantees that they would not spread communism, they could be allowed access to the Turkish straits. The Russians agreed and the crisis was de-escalated, with Russians getting the strategic access demanded, but the US deployed Jupiter and Thor missiles (directed at the USSR) in Turkey.

However, after the Turkish crisis, the Americans were concerned, thinking that they would be able to intervene, but in future, the USSR can again resort to these hard tactics against states. The US decided a need to work out a security architecture, which would be an alliance, where the US could provide a security umbrella to states, and thereby protecting them from Soviet assertion.

In 1949, the US established North Atlantic Treaty Organization (NATO) as a tool of strategic bipolarity and a transatlantic alliance. The USSR responded to NATO by establishing Warsaw Treaty Organization or Warsaw Pact (Warsaw, the capital of Poland, where the agreement was signed) in 1954.

The American tools of ideological bipolarity were Truman Doctrine and the Marshall Plan whereas the Russian one was Council for Mutual Economic Assistance (CMEA). The American tool of strategic bipolarity was NATO and the Russian one was Warsaw Pact. These tools finally paved way for the official onset of the Cold War and creation of bases.

NATO and Collective Security

Collective security is equivalent to the doctrine of 'one for all and all for one'. The idea is to create mechanisms legally to prevent an aggression by any state in the system against other states. In a system of collective security, the states remain sovereign but relinquish the quest of using force to settle disputes among themselves to maintain peace among the members of the system. NATO is a collective defence system. In the post-Cold War times, the idea of cooperative security has become more popular than the idea of collective security.

THE COLD AND HOT WARS FROM 1945 TO 1988

With the rise of ideological and strategic bipolarity between the USSR and the US, the world slipped into a Cold War. It was a situation where there was no war, yet there was no peace. There was no war as the two superpowers had a moral obligation to maintain world peace and prevent another world war.

There was no peace because the two superpowers continued to have the urge to fight, if not militarily, then ideologically (where both superpowers decided to market their respective ideologies and tried to convince states to accept their ideologies as an attempt to seek ideological dominance in the world). This ideological battle, between communism and capitalism, manifested in different theatres of the world and at times, because of this, the Cold War did turn into a hot war as well. In 1954, the US created South East Asia Treaty Organization (SEATO). Its members were USA, Britain, France, Australia, New Zealand, Thailand, Philippines and Pakistan. In 1957, the US also created ANZUS or Australia, New Zealand and US alliance. It is important to analyse the two specific hot wars in the region. In 1955, Iran, Iraq, Pakistan, Turkey and United Kingdom created CENTO or Central Treaty Organization, also known as Baghdad Pact as a military alliance (dissolved in 1979). In 1958, Iraq left the Baghdad pact due to Baathist Revolution (a pro-socialist revolution), and thus, the Baghdad Pact was renamed as Central Treaty Organization or CENTO. After the failure of the US in Vietnam, they along with Saudi Arabia and Pakistan played out the Cold War in Afghanistan from 1979 to 1988.

What is a Base?

In the context of international relations, it is a term that signifies a point of military supply and troop concentration. Bases are strategically located and during the Cold War, both the US and the USSR established points of troop concentration in the territory of their allies.

Base

Base signifies a point of military supply and troop concentration. Bases are strategically located. During the Cold War, both the US and the USSR established points of troop concentration in the territory of their allies.

THE RISE OF COMMUNISM IN CHINA

Till 1644, China was ruled by the Ming dynasty. In 1644, tribals from North China, known as Manchus, crossed the Great Wall of China, invaded the Ming dynasty and removed it from power and established the rule of Manchus or Qing Dynasty. The rulers of Qing Dynasty followed Buddhism and discriminated the local Han Chinese. By 1800s, when the British established rule in India, they began to seek trade ties with China and Tibet.

Who are Han Chinese?

The name Han comes from the Han dynasty which ruled China in 202 AD and followed Han synthesis—Confucianism and Legalism.

The rulers of the Qing Dynasty perceived that the British had no trade motive and were here to spread Christianity. The rulers of Qing dynasty adopted a closed foreign policy and decided to shun engagement with the British.

The British decided to carry out illegal trade with Tibet and also adopted the policy of corrupting the Chinese youth through drug trade. This led the Chinese and the British to fight Opium wars. After the Opium War II (1860), where the British defeated the Chinese, they got trade concessions and access to strategic Chinese ports like Hong Kong.

In Hong Kong, the British tried to outmaneuver the Qing Dynasty by legalising Christianity and also supported the Han Chinese (who were discriminated by the rulers in China). This led to constant interference by the British into the affairs of China and eventually led to the collapse of Qing Dynasty in 1911. The collapse was rejoiced by the Chinese people, who now, inspired by nationalistic urges, established a nationalist party known Kuomintang Party (KMT) under the leadership of Chiang Kai Shek.

The Russian Revolution of 1917 inspired Dr. Sun Yet San, who in 1920 established the Communist Party of China (CPC), under the leadership of Mao Zedong. After the end of World War I, as noted previously, Japan became aggressive in China and began to occupy areas in China.

The KMT and CPC, despite divergent ideologies, often united together against Japan. However, the KMT and CPC had serious differences regarding China, as CPC wanted to focus on rural areas first and then capture urban areas; whereas the KMT only focused on urban areas, neglecting the rural areas completely. Due to these growing differences, in 1927, China descended into a civil war. Japan took opportunity of the civil war and attacked Manchuria in 1935 and again attacked China in 1937.

The CPC and KMT did unite against Japan, but both were crushed by Japan. From 1937 onwards, they again began their civil war, which however remained suspended from 1939 to 1945, owing to the World War II. After the surrender of Japan in 1945, the US tried to negotiate peace between CPC (supported by the USSR by now) and KMT (supported by the US this time) but failed.

The CPC was able to mobilise Chinese people by branding the KMT as anti-nationalists for they are seeking support of the US. The public sympathy increased with the CPC and by 1949, the CPC was able to oust KMT and established the People's Republic of China (PRC), thereby China emerged as a Communist state. The KMT fled away to Taiwan and established the Republic of China (ROC), with ideological differences with PRC. To keep a check upon communist China, in 1951, the US and Japan entered into an alliance through the Treaty of San Francisco.

THE CRISIS IN VIETNAM

In 1800s, when the British colonised India and Burma, this compelled France to colonise Cambodia, Laos and Vietnam (which eventually came to be known as Indochina region). The French not only got access to South China Sea (via Vietnam) but also tea, rubber, oil and rice from the region.

After the World War II, a movement of decolonisation, with the help of USSR, began in North Vietnam, led by Ho Chi Minh, against France. The US supported the French, but by 1953–54, the French were ousted from North Vietnam. The French decided to decolonise Vietnam, but decided to divide Vietnam into two parts, where North Vietnam came under the communists (Ho Chi Minh, who ousted the French) but not the South Vietnam.

In fact, the people in South Vietnam were anti-communists, which was the only saving grace for France. After the French left, Ho Chi Minh stated that the French had divided the territory but could not divide the people of Vietnam. Ho Chi Minh began to construct a system of rail and road networks (called Ho Chi Minh trails) to provide connectivity to the people. These trails were used by Ho Chi Minh to spread communist ideas to the South.

To keep a check upon Vietnam, after the resolution of Korean crisis (explained separately later), the US and South Korea entered into a mutual defence treaty. The US was concerned and it started sending advisors (who in reality were Central Intelligence Agency [CIA] spies) to assist South Vietnam.

As Ho Chi Minh continued to spread communist ideas overtly and covertly, the insecurity of the US grew and it began to think that South Vietnam too would fall to communism (since 1949, birth of PRC, the US was always concerned about the 'domino effect' of communism in Asia, that is, spread of communism from China to other states). In 1964, the US began to deploy naval ships in Gulf of Tonkin (a gulf near North Vietnam which witnessed extreme rainfall and lightening in the sea).

In 1964, the lightening at the sea damaged some American naval ships, but the US began to assert that its ships were targeted by torpedo fired by North Vietnam. The US used this instance, known as Gulf of Tonkin crisis, where the US Congress passed a Gulf of Tonkin Resolution, which empowered the US President to send massive military force to South Vietnam against the North Vietnam.

Ho Chi Minh began to attack the massive US military on ground with guerilla warfare tactics, something that puzzled the Americans, as they never knew about guerilla warfare. The US resorted to use of chemical weapon known as 'Agent Orange', leading to thousands of deaths. This led to massive negative sentiment against the US and the American people too demanded that the US need to withdraw from Vietnam.

Under public pressure, in 1972, Ho Chi Minh and the US concluded the Paris Accord, leading to the US withdrawal. In 1973, Ho Chi Minh declared a war on South Vietnam and unified Vietnam in 1975. The British and French enjoyed a historical presence in the Middle East. This made it easy for the US to enter the region.

THE CUBAN MISSILE CRISIS AND WORLD ON THE BRINK OF NUCLEAR WAR

America and Spain fought a war in 1898. Since the war, Cuba had been under American control. At the onset of the Cold War, America had a proxy in Cuba known as Fulgencio Batista, who was gradually growing unpopular. A lot of American businesses flourished in Cuba.

Taking advantage of the weakened rule of Batista, Fidel Castro, on 26th July 1953, led an attack on the Moncada army barracks. He was imprisoned for this assault. By the time he was released, Batista's rule diminished as it faced financial bankruptcy. Thus, there was a vacuum to be filled and Castro undertook this successfully.

One thing to be noted was that Cuba, at the time of the power transition, did not witness a civil war. As Castro strengthened his rule, he initiated the programme of nationalisation of property owned by the US business houses. Castro gave the logic of sovereignty and nationalism to justify his move.

The US retaliated by closing down its markets for import of sugarcane from Cuba. A lot of Cubans were affected due to this. Some even left Cuba for the US to settle in Florida. As the economy of Cuba got badly hit, Castro domestically fuelled nationalism and internationally requested help from Russia. Perceiving this, the then US President Kennedy gave the task of solving Cuban menace to CIA.

The CIA drew up a plan of using Cuban exiles in Florida to be airdropped on Cuban beaches (Bay of Pigs). The idea was that exiles would be dropped on the beaches, and as per the plan they would intermingle with the Cuban population to create unrest for Castro.

The CIA assumed that Castro did not enjoy popular support of the Cuban people and the plan was executed. The exiled Cubans were dropped in Bay of Pigs. Within a span of three days the local Cubans overpowered them. The exiled Cubans requested help from the CIA.

The US did not help them, as they were not prepared for this. Observing the matter thus unfolding, Nikita Khrushchev of the USSR decided to defend the small range missiles in Cuba, since this would not only defend Cuba, but also ensure his presence in Cuba, which would be at a proximate destination to launch attacks on the US on the East Coast.

The CIA got the photographic evidence of sites of Russians creating missile-launching sites in Cuba, after which the US ordered quarantine and a blockade for incoming Russian ships and began to scan for nuclear weapons. Russia, in the meanwhile, backed out. Diplomatically, a huge nuclear crisis was averted. The Russian seemed to teach the US how it feels to have missiles nearby (The US had stationed Jupiter and Thor in Turkey).

The issue concluded by the acceptance of the US not to militarily invade Cuba and the subsequent removal of its missiles from Turkey. Both the USSR and the US realised that how quickly a small issue like Cuba could have escalated conflicts. They took a step towards disarmament namely, the 1963 Partial Test Ban Treaty (PTBT). The PTBT became a step towards subsequent Nuclear Non-Proliferation Treaty (NPT) in 1970 and Comprehensive Test Ban Treaty (CTBT) in 1996.

DISINTEGRATION OF SOVIET UNION AND RISE OF UNIPOLARITY

The disintegration of the USSR occurred because of many factors. Firstly, the regimes in the USSR consisted of Russia and fifteen other satellite states. These regimes were tightly controlled by Moscow and states had no breathing space.

The frustration of the people increased. Winston Churchill pointed out to the descendants of the 'iron curtain' in Europe. This iron curtain was between the West Europe (capitalist) and the East Europe (communist). This created a huge difference in the developmental strategies adopted by the ideologically different regimes. As people of East Europe travelled to West Europe, they saw the differences, which also contributed to the rising resentment.

What are Glasnost and Perestroika?

Glasnost means openness in state affairs and Perestroika means rebuilding of political and economic system of Russia.

In 1988, Gorbachev introduced changes in the USSR through Glasnost and Perestroika and democratisation and eventually reversed the Brezhnev doctrine. Czechoslovakia was one of the Russian satellite states headed by Alexander Dubcek. In 1968, he introduced freedom of speech and travel and other changes.

This event came to be known as Prague Spring. The USSR, which was ruled by Leonid Brezhnev, militarily intervened to halt the Prague Spring. In 1968, Brezhnev announced 'The Sovereignty and International Obligations of Soviet People and the Soviet Union', where he stated that the Soviet people in the satellite states had a right for RTSD provided they did not alter or damage the principles of socialism and Soviet Union, else, the USSR had the right to military intervention.

Gorbachev in 1988 reversed this and enabled Soviet people to manifest their destiny. This created a spark in the satellite states, which began to seek RTSD from the USSR, contributing to the disintegration of the USSR, leading to the rise of unipolar US. The US again enjoyed a decade of unipolar power, from 1991 to around 2001. It remained the sole military superpower in the world. The US proved their unipolar power in the Gulf War I, when Saddam Hussein attacked Kuwait and the US along with a coalition defeated Iraq.

CHRONOLOGICAL FLOW OF THE EVENTS

Fall of Constantinople → Geographical discoveries → Renaissance → Reformation → Civil wars → Peace of Westphalia → Modern states → Trade → Enlightenment → Inventions → Fusion created Industrial Revolution → Created need for resources → Led to rise of imperial ambitions → Manifested as colonialism → Colonialism generated insecurities → To mitigate insecurity, alliances formed → Formation of alliances generated more insecurity → Conditions created for World War I → World War I is won → League of Nations → Ottoman Empire is disintegrated → Italians, Germans and Japanese are given step brotherly treatment → Clouds build up for World War II → World War II occurs → League of Nations is replaced with United Nations → World enters into Cold War → Bipolar world and Cold War becomes Hot war in certain instances → Soviet Union disintegrates → World enters post-Cold War Period

3

CHAPTER

Multipolarity, Crisis of Multilateralism and India in the Post-Pandemic World

FROM UNIPOLARITY TO MULTIPOLARITY

Since 2001, the world has witnessed multiple challenges. Firstly, there is a rise in Islamic radicalisation, which ranged from Al Qaeda to ISIS, and is a manifestation of what Samuel Huntington called as the 'clash of civilisations'. Secondly, the economic supremacy of the US has been challenged since 2008 economic crisis and also by the meteoric economic rise of China. Thirdly, the hegemony of the US is challenged by a resurgent Russia and a rising India. Fourthly, the globe is witnessing new challenges that range from poverty and unemployment to climate change and hunger. All these require innovative diplomacy and global cooperation. How the world will resolve them is uncertain. A global consensus is elusive on all these challenges, from terrorism to climate change. All these challenges have pointed out that there is no country in the world which is in a position to offer solutions to such problems.

INDIAN FOREIGN POLICY PARADIGM OF MULTIPOLARITY

Today, with rising ambitions of various countries such as India, China, Brazil, Turkey and UAE; there is growing discomfort amongst the countries to accept the US as the sole unipolar power. Many countries, especially India, favour a multipolar world. India favours a multipolar world on the premise that such a world will have multiple power centres (as opposed to just one, the US) and all countries in the world will be able to have a say in the shaping of the new world order. In this backdrop, it is easier for us to understand that because the global challenges are such that they require cooperation, a world which is multipolar, than unipolar, is more suitable. This is why when India advances the idea of a multipolar world, it advocates that global institutions must reform. The global institutions, like the United Nations today, constitute the multilateralism architecture.

CRISIS OF MULTILATERALISM

Multilateralism is a diplomatic practice which is based on cooperation between several states on issues that confront the world, like climate change for instance. The concept of multilateralism, in modern times, can be traced to League of Nations. The League was the first international institution that brought countries on a common platform to maintain peace and foster cooperation. Subsequently, the League was replaced by the United Nations (UN) in 1945, as the fulcrum of multilateralism architecture. The UN was able to perform its duties as per its charter in the international history but the system was based on giving power only to the permanent five members of the Security Council, who acted as the torchbearers of the world. The UN played an important role in facilitating a liberal international order, which facilitated the spread of globalisation and enabled the creation of an integrated world based on global governance.

Far from being flawless, the multilateralism began to witness endemic structural impairments since the disintegration of the Soviet Union. Today, multilateralism is more akin to a faltering hot air balloon, as it has entered a serious situation of crisis. The crisis is driven by rising economies like India which seek their rightful place in the comity of nations.

The UN as an institution is at the heart of criticism for its lack of efficiency, institutional sclerosis, ideological infighting and denying rising economies.

The crisis such as climate change, promotion of free trade and management of the coronavirus pandemic have exposed that multilateral institutions have faced global governance crisis. All these crisis have only strengthened the notion, which is also advocated by India, that such problems require global cooperation and that is possible only when countries like India are given a say to shape international events. India continues to have belief in multilateralism but asserts that the global governance architecture requires a massive re-haul. Increased participation and inclusiveness are the heart of India's argument to strengthen multilateralism.

What is Global Governance?

Global governance means a set of international institutions that coordinate behaviour of states, resolve their conflicts/disputes, alleviate collective action programmes and enforce international rules.

It is also noted that India has reposed faith in multilateralism because international history has proven that multilateralism has ensured global peace. In this sense, India is not against multilateralism but favours reforms in multilateralism so that the multilateralism can be strengthened.

PANDEMIC AND CRISIS OF MULTILATERALISM

The Coronavirus pandemic has recently exposed the phenomena of weaponised interdependence. Since the end of the Cold War, the globalisation has brought the world closer. Many countries have used the theory of comparative advantage and engaged in global trade. Some countries have emerged as a pioneer in producing global goods. China, owing to its labour sector, government policy and vision, has emerged as a global producer of goods. To ensure the free flow of goods for mutual global growth, the countries in the last three decades had established interdependent supply chains.

However, with this interconnected growth of the last three decades, many countries achieved significant progress and improved their economic prowess. This led to some countries developing insecurities seeing the prosperity of others. The insecurity was driven more by competition and power rivalry. For instance, India in the last three decades has made tremendous economic progress and same is the case with Chinese. However, the Chinese are not very comfortable to see a rising and a powerful India in its neighbourhood, as it perceives India as a rival in world power.

The pandemic has exposed the phenomena of weaponised interdependence. Because of the pandemic, the world witnessed a global lockdown to curtail the spread of the Coronavirus. The global lockdown broke the global supply chains also. As the lockdowns were lifted and vaccination drive paced up, the supply chains were brought back on track. But it is at this juncture that countries like China tried to weaponise the interdependence by exploiting the control they had over the hubs of production networks in an era of globally integrated supply chains.

This weaponisation of interdependence also exposed how the multilateralism architecture failed to offer any solutions. The failure of World Health Organization (WHO) to ensure global cooperation in pandemic prevention and failure of World Trade Organization (WTO) to ensure equitable distribution and manufacturing of vaccines for ensuring human welfare of all have exposed the vulnerabilities of multilateralism.

In this backdrop, India's assertion of making multilateralism work through an inclusive order by reforms of multilateral institutions makes sense. The weaponisation of supply chains by a few handful countries have reasserted the need to create new minilaterals that would foster cooperation and resilient supply chains.

INDIA'S FOREIGN POLICY IN THE POST-PANDEMIC GLOBAL ORDER

On the basis of the above analysis, it is clear that India, which for decades, had been advancing the idea of reforms in global institutions has now an important responsibility to shape the post-pandemic global order. India must adopt a four-point foreign policy framework.

Firstly, it must be realised that any reform in multilateralism cannot be driven by efforts of India alone. This explains why since the pandemic, India has displayed a new thrust in establishing a coalition with like-minded countries to form minilateral groupings. These groupings will give India the power to collectively amplify India's voice for reforms.

Secondly, while keeping a global eye, India should not neglect its immediate neighbourhood. As Chinese have weaponised the supply chains and affected the global recovery, this is where India needs to join hands with European Union, Japan and South Korea to ensure that a niche is created where India and the like-minded countries emerge as key suppliers of global goods and foster regional growth and well-being.

Thirdly, it must be noted from the above analysis that India's stance on reforms in multilateralism are pragmatic and driven by pragmatism, but India needs to go one step ahead. It needs to realise that it must enhance its global and regional presence by emphasising on values. While pragmatism is always the key driver of foreign policy, the values are the glue. While seeking the reforms of the multilateralism architecture, India must advocate the values such as democracy, rule of law, freedom of speech and pluralism; which it stands for. The attention to values and its fusion with pragmatism will give India an edge over China.

Fourthly, none of the above-mentioned strategies will work unless India rectifies its domestic front. This implies that the most crucial determinant to achieve the above strategies will be a strong domestic economy. The importance of this helps us to understand that India has launched the Atmanirbhar Bharat campaign to achieve self-reliance in cooperation with like-minded countries. A sustainable economic growth, fused with democracy, rule of law, freedom of speech and pluralism will give India more persuasive power and an economic clout to shape the multilateral architecture.

CHRONOLOGICAL FLOW OF EVENTS

Post-Cold War world order begins from 1991 → US asserts unipolar power → World witnesses globalisation → Rise of interconnected world → Global governance takes shape → Multilateral institutions shape globalisation and one world → Centre of gravity shifts to Asia → Globalisation spreads to Asia and propels its growth → Asian countries become part of global supply chains → World begins to witness new crisis → Climate change, poverty, unemployment, drug trafficking, migration and inequality emerge new challenges → Existing multilateral institutions fail to offer credible solutions → Multilateral institutions unable to foster global cooperation to solve these problems → Multilateralism and global governance comes under stress → Multilateralism centric stress aggravated when countries taking advantage of globalisation seek multipolarity in international relations → Unipolar status of the US, multilateralism and global governance are stressed and call for reforms grow → World witnesses COVID-19 pandemic → WHO fails to ensure prevention of pandemic and WTO fails to ensure vaccine equity → Crisis of multilateralism amplifies when countries weaponise supply chains → India takes the lead in calling out need for reforming multilateralism → India articulates its policy to seek reform of multilateralism through minilaterals → The world is still evolving and age of uncertainty continues.

QUESTIONS FOR PRACTICE

1.	"Nuclearisation of the world after 1945 helped in maintaining a stable Europe." Analyse.
2.	"In the wake of changing world order due to COVID-19, India should neither permit capsizing of the world order nor allow it to be captured by any superpower". Analyse how can India resuscitate drowning multilateralism in the global order today?
3.	The US exit from Afghanistan in 2021 proves that Afghanistan ended up in being the next Vietnam for USA. Explain.
4.	"China and the US are locked in a Thucydides Trap". Explain.
5.	Examine the role Indian foreign policy that can play rescuing multilateralism from the crisis.

SECTION 2

Historical Origins and Making of Indian Foreign Policy

1. Historical Genesis and Values of Indian Foreign Policy
2. Institutions Involved in Making Indian Foreign Policy

AN OVERVIEW

This section is also not directly mentioned in the syllabus but again, as is the case of previous section. UPSC has taken an implied meaning of the defined syllabus and asked questions from this chapter. In 1981, the UPSC asked a question on how does tradition influence Indian foreign policy. In 1996, a question was asked on Kautilya's Mandala Theory. In 2013, a question on the identification of the elements of change in India's foreign policy was asked. In 2014, a question was asked on the role of MEA and PMO in Indian foreign policy making. In 2015, a question was asked on how does the Parliament determine and influence the making of India's foreign policy.

Potential foresight On the basis of the above-mentioned questions asked by the UPSC, we can draw a few learnings. The UPSC can potentially ask questions on Mandala Theory with an example. Recently Afghanistan is in news again and India has often used Mandala Theory in engagement with Afghanistan. This theory can also be applied to Indian engagement with Philippines and Vietnam. Similarly, the UPSC can probably ask questions pertaining to values of Indian foreign policy. In the crisis like Ukraine, South China Sea and China–US–Russia Cold War, the response of India to all these emerging situations would be determined by the values that India stands for. Thus, keeping the potential foresight in mind, the section is designed to give the content to enable one to have adequate thoughts and knowledge to answer any such questions ahead.

1 CHAPTER

Historical Genesis and Values of Indian Foreign Policy

RELEVANCE OF HISTORY IN INDIAN FOREIGN POLICY

India is a civilisational country, which had a glorious past. India's values trace their origin from the history. The behaviour in the foreign policy India displays, is also influenced by the past. It is not wrong to argue that India's foreign policy is deeply influenced by tradition, history and geography. Let us try to understand the genesis of Indian foreign policy through one example of tradition and history and one of geography.

Lessons from Ramayana – What do diplomats do today?

In modern times, diplomats are known as information agents. They carry information from one state and convey it to their own parent state. As the diplomats carry sensitive information, when they deliver it, the diplomats must provide a truthful account. They must not distort or manipulate the fact. This is precisely what Hanuman did. He carried the information to Ram and delivered the message without distortion.

How is Power Projection done Today?

Today, when Indian PM visits a foreign state, he highlights the economic prowess of India and positions of India as a lucrative destination for investments and trade.

RAMAYANA AND INDIAN FOREIGN POLICY

If we study the Ramayana, we get to know that there are many principles of modern diplomacy owe their origin to the text.

Sita, wife of Ram, was kidnapped by Ravana, the king of Lanka. Ram entrusted on Hanuman the responsibility to locate Sita. Hanuman, who was able to locate Sita in Lanka, first tried to convince her that he was a messenger of Ram and not that of Ravana. Once he convinced Sita that he had been sent by Ram, she too conveyed a message to Hanuman to deliver it to Ram. From this situation, we may infer that Hanuman, who delivers Sita's message to Ram, was seen to be doing what a diplomat does in modern times.

The next scene that is important for us is the court scene where Hanuman argued with Ravana to liberate Sita. He initiated his dialogue by telling Ravana about the power of Ram. He intimated Ravana of how popular Ram was back in Ayodhya, Ravana about his leadership and his followership. He was thereby indulging in something known as 'power projection'. He was projecting the power of Ram in front of Ravana. During the ancient and medieval times in the world history, power projection was always individual in nature. The diplomats, during this time, undertook power projection of an individual personality, who was invariably their own king. For instance, if a South Indian king sent a diplomat in a mission to another state, say in West Asia or East Africa, the diplomat used to project the might of his king in the court of the other king. The diplomat would glorify his own king's power, and his military prowess and his territorial extent. During the early modern times of colonial rule, the coercive elements of power projection diplomacy emerged.

In a situation, in Ramayana, Hanuman told Ravana that it was against ethics to keep Sita in captivity over a long period of time and if Ravana did not liberate Sita, Ram might burn Lanka into ashes. To this, Ravana reacted angrily and ordered that Hanuman should be put to death. But Ravana's brother Vibheeshana said that Hanuman who had come to Lanka as an emissary from a foreign state could not be put to death.

CHANAKYA'S MANDALA THEORY AND INDIAN FOREIGN POLICY

Geography is the most important determinant of our foreign policy. In the Hindu cosmology, the location of India is on the southern petal floating on the cosmic ocean. The lotus petal resembles the shape of the subcontinent as it is narrow at the tip and broad when it emerges or blossoms from the central axis. The Indian foreign policy and its worldview are based on the concept of Mandala, where the entire cosmos has a vast circle. This circle has seven concentric oceans. The oceans separate six regions, also known as Vanshas. Certain geographical features separate the Vanshas. At the centre of all these is a lotus, which has four petals, and it features Bharata, which is also known as Jambudvipa. As mandala radiates out, each radiating circle outside is superior to preceding circle and India is just one of the Dvipas with peculiar and different values. This is different from Chinese worldview. They saw Hans at core being the most advanced and the larger circles as barbaric and uncivilised. This is why Chinese suffered from the middle kingdom complex.

What is the Middle Kingdom Complex?

The ancient Chinese perceived themselves at the centre of the universe. They were at the centre of the civilised world and all other countries outside were perceived as barbarians and uncivilised. This perception of Chinese, continues to dominate their foreign policy thinking, thus making others around China believe that this is a complex world view as it hinders cooperation, thus, middle kingdom complex.

NITISARA OF KAMANDAKI AND INDIAN FOREIGN POLICY

Nitisara, the famous ancient Indian treatise on politics and statecraft, influences India's foreign worldview. It mentions in detail a great theory of diplomacy. Kamandaki, the writer of Nitisara was a disciple of Chanakya. In this book, he talks about three types of ambassadors—diplomats, envoys and plenipotentiaries. It further says that any diplomat needs to have the following qualities:

- Should have ability to be an expert debater
- Should have possess a good memory
- Should be eloquent
- Should have knowledge of military science
- Should have the ability to bear adversary's abusive language, anger and impulses
- Should always keep his own plan of actions secret
- Should have knowledge of psychology to ascertain other people's feelings

KAUTILYA'S ARTHASHASTRA AND INDIAN FOREIGN POLICY

It is important to understand Kautilya's Arthashastra as it is an Indian treatise on statecraft and diplomacy and also gives valuable insights into international relations and foreign policy. Kautilya is India's own realist as his ideas resonate with realism.

For Kautilya, the state is the most important and legitimate instrument that enjoys sovereignty. The responsibility of the king is to guard his subjects and ensure their protection and survival. This should be the primary national interest of any state. The core objective of a state is to acquire wealth, deliver justice and undertake expenditure. A state has to be strong and for this, it needs good administration, stability and justice. This results in a situation conducive for wealth creation and leads to military expeditions for conquests. The wealth in the state is generated by elaborate taxation machinery.

What is Realism?

Realism is a view in international politics, which argues that states in the international system must focus on ensuring their own security and pursue their own national interests.

The primary duty of a king is the welfare of the people. If the king is unable to make the people prosper, it is inevitable that people will become restless and finally rebel. The rebellion can take any form, including that of violence.

The Kautilyan idea of national interest is based on welfare of people. If people prosper, so will the state. Kautilya's concept of power begins from society. His grand strategy is based on the idea that the king needs to be a conqueror. He needs to aim to increase his power over neighbours. The king is envisaged as a 'Chakravartin'.

'Chakravartin' is an ancient Indian term used to refer to an ideal universal ruler, who rules ethically and benevolently over the entire world. Such a ruler's reign is known as sarvabhauma. The goal of such a king is to promote national economy and ensure national security and social order. The state is primarily agrarian in nature. Cattle rearing and agriculture are primary activities. This leads to production of surplus, which leads to trade. As trade is undertaken, economy is strengthened.

A strong economy sustains the state and the army. To develop this kind of a state, which is based on powerful agrarian economy, the state needs to conquer new lands. The king undertakes expeditions to conquer new lands. The new lands conquered would allow citizens to expand opportunities to earn livelihood. The goal of the ruler is a stable state, which needs to be achieved for the welfare of citizens and to achieve such a state; the ruler is responsible for good governance.

Governance is a means to achieve the aforementioned goals, as well as to achieve social harmony. At the foreign policy level, Kautilya had a different thought. If the ruler has to be a conqueror, then war is a natural outcome of his foreign policy. Kautilya said that the ruler had to be careful because his immediate neighbours were enemy states, jealous of the social harmony and progress of the king and the kingdom.

Thus, conflicts with neighbours are likely to be natural and to resolve the conflict, the king has to decide if he would resort to conciliation and give gifts to another state to make it an ally, or sow dissension and use force, if needed. This depends upon the power of the king and options for war available to discussion and use of force when the need arises. Kautilya propounded that the power exuded by the state were of three types.

The first is individual power. This is the power and courage of the king. This is psychological in nature. The second is hard power. This is the military and economic capacity of the ruler and the state. The third is soft power. This is the diplomatic power of the ruler.

Kautilya said that before a ruler declares war on an enemy state, he should measure his power. He should ensure that he possesses superiority over all three levels, i.e., terrain of warfare (place), season and his own counsellors. Hence, if a ruler is morally intelligent and has good counsel, he will win diplomatically.

If a ruler has adequate economic and military strength, he will win on the basis of physical power and achieve physical success (application of hard power). The ruler, Kautilya said, should strive for soft power rather than hard power. Depending upon the situation, he has three types of war to wage—

First one is Dharma-yudha, which is outright, righteous war, fought while following certain predetermined rules. The second option is alternative to Dharama-yudha, which is war by deception. There is no lawful framework governing this war. The third one is silent warfare, where a state undertakes war without public attention. Kautilya also said that aim of the state should be to expand national power. This can be done by conquests or alliances. The components of national power are called Prakritis. There are seven components—political leadership, administration, resources, infrastructure, economy, security forces and alliances. So, shakti and prakriti, if used prudently, leads to rise of comprehensive national power.

SOME VALUES OF INDIAN FOREIGN POLICY

Value	Preference for the middle way
Philosophy	This is based on the Sanskrit saying *Ati Sarvatra Varjaye*, which means "let us eschew excess at all times". This is based on the Indian philosophical idea that we should not look things as extremes and should not have a tendency to look at stuff as black and white.
Advocacy	It advocates a focus on the middle path, which is reflected in the synthesis of Dharma, Artha, Karma and Moksha. Even Bhagwat Geeta favours a middle path be followed and also advocates for divine sanctions for desires which are against model order.

Opinion	Michael Brecher, the renowned political scientist, says that Indian philosophy of golden middle path of compromise and tolerance of opposites is reflected in Indian foreign policy.

Value	Blend of idealism and realism
Philosophy	Since ancient times, war has always been an option of last resort. The Upanishads clearly mentioned non-violence as they assert that the spirit is undivided and universe is an expression of the spirit and universe is where all humans are a part. The Buddhist/Jain texts clearly assert non-violence. Asoka, post-Kalinga battle, preached non-violence, so did Gandhi. The ancient royal policy from Arthashastra, Bharadwaj in manusmriti to the teachings of Panchtantra, all have advocated for realist thinking but the royal policy has always been of the idea that there should be peace in the beginning and war at the end.
Advocacy	The entire thought has been that war is just, not immoral, but be used as a last resort because war is expensive, troublesome and victory is not certain.

Value	Value of tolerance
Philosophy	The value of tolerance is based on the ancient idea of *Vade, Vade, Jayte Tattava Siddhih*, which means enlightenment is achieved through debate. All throughout ancient times, there has been focus on paramountcy of reason. The Mahabharata notes Dharma to be judged on the basis of expression and reason. The value of tolerance is based on the idea of human mind that has limited range and power. This is clearly visible even in Upanishads that assert that all different parts lead to same goals, that is, cows of different colours yield the same milk. Tolerance, in India, is not just seen in philosophy, but is a social reality.
Advocacy	In 47 AD, Christians came to Kerala and in 70 AD Jews came. Both were allowed to preach, practice and propagate their religions. The Akbar's policy of universal harmony, i.e., Sulh i Kul and Dara Sikhon or Shajahan's translation of Upanishad in Persian, is a testimony to historical tolerance.

Value	Absence of imperialistic traditions
Philosophy	India has not been imperialist. Historically, there has been an assertion of the value of not being imperialist. Mahabharata notes that Indian Empire should not extend beyond its geographical limits. Even Kautilya, Bodhayan and Manusmriti assorted against the extension of Empire of India beyond the geographical boundary of Bharat—that is from Himalayas to south sea and West sea to East. The Buddhists (who have a world view of rule by love) and Hindus who went to South East Asia, went as traders for business and not as warriors to conquer. The Mughals also unified India—Akbar had a policy of tolerance, conciliation and diplomacy. No attempt towards imperialism was ever visible.
Advocacy	When the British came to India as imperialists, India's developing anti-imperialism was a natural manifestation. The entire national movement of India was anti-imperialistic in tone and tenor and this became a feature of foreign policy subsequently.

Value	Expression of positive ideas through negative terms
Philosophy	India will not use the word 'peace' but uses 'non-violence'.
Advocacy	India will not use the word 'defeat' but uses 'non-victory'; 'non-idleness' against exertion and 'non-grudge' against tolerance.
Opinion	K. P. Mishra, the renowned author, says that the Indian language at the foreign policy level is to use negative terms to express positive ideas of profound importance.

KEY POINTS

- History influences foreign policy. In India, history, tradition and geography have influenced foreign policy.
- Ramayana has contributed to influence Indian foreign policy and influenced global diplomatic history.
- The practice of diplomats as information agents, power projection by states and diplomatic immunity are Indian contribution to global diplomatic history.
- India is different in global perception from Chinese and perceives every country equal, a thought since ancient times.
- Chinese have called themselves a middle kingdom and perceived others as barbarians, creating complex relations.
- Nitisara of Kamandaki was a treatise defining qualities, a diplomat must possess for effective diplomacy.
- The Nitisara of Kamandaki is one of the core training modules used for grooming Indian Foreign Service officials.
- Kautilya is India's realist who favoured economic development as a strategy to assert regional and global power.
- Kautilya emphasised that when countries grow in power, they will generate insecurity around.
- The rise of China, insecurity of the US that China could replace them as a superpower today is explained by Kautilya.
- Kautilya gave the first explanation of Thucydides trap, that a rising power will generate insecurity in established power.
- Indian foreign policy stands for certain values such as expression of positive ideas through negative terms, absence of imperialistic traditions, preference for the middle way, blend of idealism and realism and value of tolerance.

CHAPTER

2

Institutions Involved in Making Indian Foreign Policy

CORE INSTITUTIONS IN INDIA INVOLVED IN MAKING FOREIGN POLICY

The making of foreign policy (FP) is a complex process. Initially in European countries, the FP was formed by the foreign office but the entire process was shrouded in secrecy. The public was not a participant in the process of formulation of FP or debate. In a democratic society like India, the decision-making in the FP involves multiple agencies but the overall policy always bears the stamp of ideological underpinnings of the Prime Minister (PM).

Thus, the Prime Minister's Office (PMO), Ministry of External Affairs (MEA) and the political party in power at the centre always have a deep sense of influence on the Indian Foreign Policy (IFP). Thus, it is not wrong to say that FP formulation in India involves a blend of actors, personality politics, neurological impulses and institutional support. K. Subramanyam asserted that IFP was always leadership driven which often lacked consensus. However, today as globalisation has led to creation of a global village, the internal and external boundaries between states have been erased. The foreign policy matters are no longer just under the MEA but also involve other actors. Now, we will have a look at various institutions or actors involved briefly.

ROLE OF MINISTRY OF EXTERNAL AFFAIRS IN MAKING INDIAN FOREIGN POLICY

It is the primary institution on matters related to external affairs. It is responsible to gather, process and analyse information, which is done by the diplomatic corps through embassies abroad for decision-making. Siuli Sarkar, the eminent educationist, mentioned that origin of MEA can be traced back to 1783 when the British established the first ever foreign office to manage India's relations abroad along with internal affairs. J. Bandopadhyay, the famous diplomat and scholar of IR, said that the Charter Act of 1833 finally separated internal and external functions of East India Company and established a foreign department. Initially, the MEA remained under the control of the PM and the PM, as the Minister of External Affairs, directly exercised influence.

Over a period of time, we have had independent ministers in MEA. As per J. Bandopadhyay, until 1962, MEA had no policy formulation wing or section but after 1962 Sino-Indian conflict, a new policy planning and research division was created. The division was concerned with strategic and foreign policy formulation. In 1965, N. R. Pillai Committee was appointed by Lal Bahadur Shastri to suggest remedies to the problems faced by IFS. The committee found that the strength of IFS has been quite less in contrast to the requirements of the diplomatic corps. It also pointed out the lack of coordination between foreign bureaucracy and other foreign policy formulation departments.

In 2009, a scholar named Daniel Markey in an essay titled '*Developing India's Foreign Policy Software*' asserted that the IFS cadre is very small in contrast to the required numbers. He also said that the Foreign Service bureaucracy has inadequate mid-career training programmes and is quite reluctant to explore outside expertise in policy formulation. He suggested that there is an urgent need to expand the IFS cadre and also provide a mixture of better pay and incentives to retain the efficiency.

Markey, the eminent lawyer and politician, advocated that on the limited term engagement policy, the MEA should bring non-career foreign policy experts and enhance its intellectual bank. The present day crisis in MEA of IFS is such that even Shashi Tharoor asserted that as India undertakes a global stretch, its frugal staffing pattern of IFS reveals a country punching well below its weight on the global stage. As per R. B. Jain, the political writer, the MEA has not undergone any massive structural change since 1947 till today.

STRUCTURAL CHANGES IN THE MINISTRY OF EXTERNAL AFFAIRS BY MODI GOVERNMENT

In 2020, the MEA, under the leadership of a diplomat-turned foreign minister, S. Jaishankar, decided to undergo massive structural changes. The new foreign secretary of India, Harsh Vardhan Shringla explained the rationale behind the changes. As per him, the objective of MEA and Indian Foreign Service (IFS) is to advance the national interests of India and serve the people of India all over the world. To achieve this objective, the MEA has decided to undertake the needed changes.

The prime focus of the change is to make the ministry more nimble and responsive to strategic issues. To make routine foreign policy matters separate from strategic projects, the MEA has decided to create multiple verticals. An IFS officer of the rank of Additional Secretary (equivalent to a political director) will head each of these verticals. This will allow the Additional Secretaries to focus on the vertical policy and the Secretaries to focus more on strategising foreign policy. The MEA has identified the need to create a corporate-like vertical for the following:

- Economic diplomacy vertical
- Trade diplomacy vertical
- Development partnership vertical
- Emerging technology vertical
- External publicity vertical
- Cultural diplomacy vertical
- Indian Ocean and Indo-Pacific vertical

ROLE OF PRIME MINISTER'S OFFICE IN MAKING OF INDIAN FOREIGN POLICY

The PMO initially was known as the PM Secretariat (PMS). When Nehru was the PM, the PM Secretariat became the nerve centre in foreign policy decision making. J. Bandopadhyay says that PMS was so influential during Nehruvian era that it eclipsed the role of cabinet in foreign policy. Bandopadhyay justifies his view by giving an example of Kashmir where he asserted that Nehru had taken many decisions on Kashmir without consulting even senior cabinet colleagues like Patel.

Roxane Sismanidis, an IR expert, asserts that as the time progressed, the successors of Nehru ensured that PMO became a de facto coordinator and a supra ministry of the government. Till today, PMO remains the centre of gravity in foreign policy establishment. In fact, Harish Kapoor in his book '*Foreign Policies of Indian PMs*' clearly asserts that India has never seen an independent and a powerful foreign minister, who has left an imprint on Indian foreign policy despite its exclusive jurisdiction and existence. It remains a body that follows dictates from PMO.

With the creation of National Security Advisor (NSA) post, the NSA continues to play an important role in advising PM on foreign and security policy by virtue of being an important stakeholder of PMO. Many times we have seen a customised PM and PMO centric foreign policy in India. The PM also deserves an exclusive privilege of appointing special envoys for matters close to the heart of PM. K. Subramananyam, the famous international strategic affairs analyst, had rightly said that IFP is leadership-specific - certain PMs have left an imprint on the foreign policy like Indira Gandhi's USSR policy, Nehru's Disarmament policy, Gujral Doctrine on the neighbourhood policy, Rajiv Gandhi's China policy, Vajpayee's Nuclear policy, Manmohan Singh's India–US relations policy and Modi's greater power politics.

ROLE OF THE PARLIAMENT IN MAKING INDIAN FOREIGN POLICY

The Constitution of India has accorded the Parliament of India the status of supreme legislative body to make policies on union list matters that include foreign policy. As the government is accountable to the Parliament, the Parliament can use the two houses as a platform to influence the foreign policy of the government.

The Standing Committee on External Affairs offers the Parliament to keep a track of policies at foreign level. The item number 10 of the Union List and items from number 9 to 21 empower the Parliament to make laws on subjects ranging from foreign affairs, war, peace, UN matters and international treaties. Over a period of time, in response to the legislative authority guaranteed by the Constitution to the Parliament, it has formed various laws that include—the Emigration Act 1983, Civil Liability for Nuclear Damages Act 2010, the Extradition Act, UN (Security Council) Act etc. It has created institutions such as NSC (National Security Council), RAW (Research and Analysis Wing) etc. to guide foreign policy.

Naheed Murtaza asserts that till the 1962 Sino-Indian conflict, the foreign policy of Nehru was not subjected to parliamentary scrutiny in a big way. It was Shastri who revolutionised the concept and introduced the increased role of Parliament in scrutinising foreign policy through debates and discussions and motions. This led to discussion on issues such as India and NPT, India and CTBT, Tibetan policy, major power relations etc. Paul Martin, an eminent politician, has studied that in India, parliamentary debates on foreign policy matters are interlinked to international situation and world behaviour. Some instances are as follows:

S. No.	Instances of debates on foreign policy in Parliament
1.	A. Appadorni's talks of Parliament influence India's China policy. After 1962 conflict, India decided to go for high-powered voice of American transmitter to match Chinese propaganda. The leftist rhetoric in Parliament of anti-Americanism forced government to cancel it.
2.	When the US invaded Iraq in 2003, Vajpayee did not favour offending the US invasion by condemning it in the Parliament despite the growing rhetoric of opposition to show solidarity with Iraq. The PM used the 'middle path' and chose to use the Hindi word 'Ninda' over 'condemn'.
3.	During Gulf War-1, the Chandra Shekhar government allowed the US planes to refuel in Mumbai. The Congress party, through intense parliamentary debate, compelled a change in policy.

KEY POINTS

- Foreign policy making is a complex task and multiple institutions play important roles in the process.
- In India, MEA plays an important role because it is staffed by career diplomats.
- The MEA, as many studies have pointed out, witness serious shortage of staff and trained experts.
- In recent times, Government of India has created new verticals in MEA to sync the foreign policy with challenges.
- Creation of a new vertical on the Indo-Pacific is an example of how Indian foreign policy is dynamic towards institutional changes.
- The Prime Ministers and National Security Advisors always leave a deep imprint on the foreign policy.
- The Parliament plays an important role in ensuring that legislations are passed to ensure smooth functioning of foreign policy.

QUESTIONS FOR PRACTICE

S. No.	Questions for Practice
1.	How does the Parliament determine and influence the making of India's foreign policy?
2.	Examine how geographical location of India is a key determinant of India's foreign policy?
3.	Is India a historically conscious nation with respect to foreign policy? Explain with examples.
4.	Increasing comprehensive national power will manifest as Thucydides trap. Suggest remedial measures.

SECTION 3

How Prime Ministers Shaped Indian Foreign Policy

- 1. The Foreign Policy of Jawaharlal Nehru
- 2. The Foreign Policy from Indira Gandhi to Manmohan Singh
- 3. The Foreign Policy of Narendra Modi and the Modi Doctrine
- 4. The Ethical Dilemmas of Indian Foreign Policy

AN OVERVIEW

This is a foundational section that helps us understand the subsequent chapters by placing the things in a context. The UPSC has asked many questions from this chapter in the past. In 1980, question was asked on how fruitful has been the policy of non-alignment. In 2000, there was a question that required the aspirants to explain non-alignment is a need and not a creed. In 2002, the commission asked questions on the Gujral Doctrine and on India's contribution to the growth of non-alignment. In 2007, there was a question on relevance of non-alignment. In 2013, a question was asked on relevance of Gujral doctrine. In 2015, a question was asked on how non-alignment is the basic principle of Indian foreign policy. In 2017, there was a question about the era of rise of multiple organisations, and the relevance of non-alignment. In 2018, a question was asked on how India's current foreign policy marks a qualitative shift from that of previous regimes.

Potential foresight A clear analysis of the above-mentioned questions suggests that the UPSC has been asking repeated questions on Gujral doctrine and non-alignment. An interesting observation is that in 2018, the UPSC asked a subtle question on the comparative analysis of the foreign policy of Modi and others. We can now build a foresight that in future, the UPSC will diversify this and ask questions on how Gujral doctrine is different from Neighbourhood First policy; how is non-alignment relevant in the post-pandemic world order; what role can India play in using non-alignment as a tool in the post-pandemic world order and how are retail diplomacy, faith diplomacy and summit style diplomacy new trends in India's foreign policy. One would not be surprised if the UPSC may ask a question on comparison between non-alignment and strategic autonomy. Keeping the above threads in mind, this chapter has been constructed to give an analytical edge over all the elements of potential foresight.

CHAPTER 1

The Foreign Policy of Jawaharlal Nehru

GRAND STRATEGY, STRATEGIC THOUGHT AND INDIA'S STRATEGIC CULTURE

A grand strategy is an aggregation of national resources and national capacity of a country. It includes a combination of military, diplomatic, political, economic, cultural and moral capabilities that a nation deploys in the service of national security. A grand strategy is all about protection of domestic values. Every state has certain values and to uphold those values are the primary goals of every state. But as a state cannot protect all values, it resorts to satisfactorily protecting the few it holds most sacred. In case the values of a state are threatened, either by a non-state actor or by an act of nature such as an earthquake or tsunamis, how the state manages to restore the value threatened, is the main concern. To protect its internal and external security, a state may deploy its capabilities combined, known as grand strategy.

This takes us to strategic thought. Strategic thought signifies the resources a government has (such as diplomacy, military, economic strength, cultural values, etc.) and the way it uses these resources to achieve security for the society. For India, strategic thought means certain values and preferences, which leads to the state evolving some ideas and using these ideas in its policies and approaches in foreign policy.

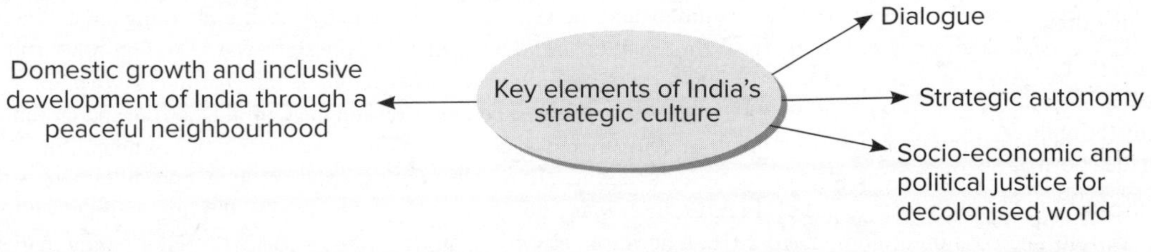

INDUSTRIAL DEVELOPMENT AS A TOOL OF INTERNATIONAL POWER

After India became independent in 1947, it initiated the process of developing its foreign policy. The Indian Foreign Policy (IFP) that came to be developed was under the leadership of Nehru. He did not invent the IFP but had nurtured it and gave it a shape. The IFP has its roots in India's past and its traditions.

When India became independent, the world witnessed Cold War and Asia and Africa witnessed reawakening. The national reawakening, which manifested as aggressive nationalist struggles in Asia and Africa, were driven by the urge of the colonised people of Africa and Asia to manifest their own destiny in an independent manner. This led to the development of an idea where the people of Asia and Africa decided to develop an independent world view based on their historical legacies, national interests and social milieu.

Nehru was confronted with the challenge of articulating how India would conduct its international relations. But, India also confronted the challenge of how to manage its domestic development. At this juncture, Nehru fused domestic development with Indian foreign policy and articulated that India would develop industrially at the domestic level and that would help in advancing India's international image.

India had to make a choice of either developing the state militarily or economically. Nehru realised that states such as Pakistan and Thailand focused on developing their military establishments at the cost of developing their nations economically; these states thereby had unstable politics. In this context, Nehru understood that the foundation of social coherence lies in economic strength. The Nehruvian perspective was that economic strength is the guarantee of security of a state and a strong economic base could also enable India to develop a robust military. Nehru, therefore, shifted India's focus on industrial development.

DESIGNING THE STRATEGY OF NON-ALIGNMENT

Though the origin of IFP is traced back to ancient texts and leaders, its immediate roots lay in the Indian struggle for independence against the British. It was during the Indian National Movement (INM) that India developed certain principal elements to its foreign policy that were used by India throughout the Cold War. It was during the INM that India declared its commitment to fight imperialism and colonialism and support the unity of all nations struggling to fight imperialism and colonialism. The period after the World War II saw the decline of imperialism but also led to the economic and military dominance of the USA.

This led to an arms race between the USA and the USSR, which ultimately became nuclear in nature during the Cold War. It was against such a backdrop, with an arms race and an ideological war waging across the world, that India had to evolve its foreign policy. India, being a non-communist country, was not welcomed in the Soviet bloc and nor did India developed any intention of joining the Communist bloc either.

Joining the US bloc was out of the question, as India perceived the USA as a mouthpiece for capitalism, which it believed to be a form of neo-imperialism. Joining the US bloc would have meant that India would go against the entire tradition of its national movement. The Nehruvian idea was very clear.

Joining any bloc would lead to lessening of the sovereign space for decision making that India fought for during the INM. Because the priority for Nehru was to promote global peace and support anti-colonial struggles while adopting independence in deciding domestic, foreign, economic and military policy; it needed an independent sovereign space.

At the heart of our foreign policy was an urge to advance our national interests and ensure our space for, strategic autonomy to take decisions independently. An independent foreign policy involved interactions with all players of the system while retaining the ability to make one's own decisions regarding one's own issues. Thus, it is not wrong to say that non-alignment was an idea born out of the genius of the Indian people because this idea of maintaining the autonomy to take independent decisions evolved as the spirit of non-alignment.

Non-alignment was born out of a coordinated effort of Nehru (India), Nasser (Egypt) and JB Tito (Yugoslavia). In 1947, Asian Relations Conference was held in New Delhi, which highlighted the dangers of the neo-imperialism for the first time. Subsequently, in 1955, the Bandung Conference brought together states of Asia and Africa, which highlighted the rising threats of rising military alliances in the world.

After the Bandung conference, there was a need felt by the states to adopt common principles that these states would stand for in the era of bipolarity. It was in 1956 that JB Tito, along with Nehru and Nasser, laid the embryo of non-alignment and it finally manifested in the Non-Aligned Conference in Belgrade in 1961.

What exactly does non-alignment mean?

Non-alignment is used in international relations to describe the foreign policy followed by states that did not align to the USSR or the US during the period of the Cold War. These states pursued the policy of an independent foreign policy with a focus of engaging all states to achieve their national interests.

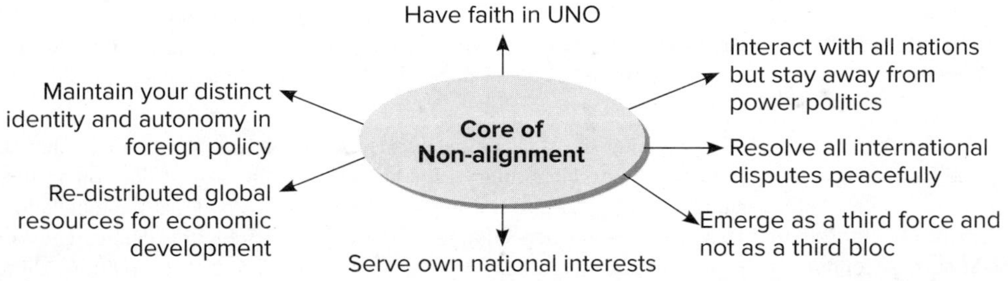

NON-ALIGNMENT AND NEUTRALITY IN INTERNATIONAL RELATIONS

When these states, following an independent course of action in foreign policy, came together on a common platform, it led to the rise of the Non-Aligned Movement or NAM. It is important to note that non-alignment and neutrality are two different things. Firstly, neutrality is a legal concept whereas non-alignment is a political one. Non-alignment is not written in the constitution of a state as a law, but neutrality is written.

Secondly, neutrality is a negative concept whereas non-alignment is a positive concept. This is because non-alignment stands for engagement with all states in the world through active cooperation in the affairs of the world. The beauty of non-alignment is that it seeks to promote friendship with all the states in the world irrespective of the ideology followed by any state of the world. Its core focus was to develop peace areas in the world.

EIGHT FOREIGN POLICY GOALS OF NON-ALIGNED STATES

The non-aligned states agreed to follow the following goals:

1. These states will chart out an independent course of action in foreign policy during Cold War.
2. All the states will commonly oppose colonialism, apartheid, racialism and imperialism.
3. The non-aligned states will not join military blocs and not conclude military-specific treaties with superpowers in the Cold War.
4. The territories of the non-aligned states shall not be used as military bases by superpowers for their superpower rivalry.
5. States following non-alignment will strive for world peace to promote their economic well-being.
6. States following non-alignment will not resort to any form of arms race. They will save their resources from irrelevant arms race and channelise the same of economic development.
7. Collectively the states following non-alignment will put up a common cause of the third world in the United Nations.
8. States following non-alignment will restructure the international order by striving for a New International Economic Order (NIEO). The NIEO will enhance the bargaining power of the global south over the global north.

PHILOSOPHICAL BASIS OF NON-ALIGNMENT

The philosophical basis of non-alignment was the ancient Indian philosophy of looking at reality from different prisms and recognising that reality is not merely black and white and that it could have many shades of grey. For the US, during the Cold War, the world was a completely polarised affair, with a clear demarcation of black and white and no other shade in between. Thus, the US found it very difficult to reconcile with the Indian concept of NAM all throughout the Cold War.

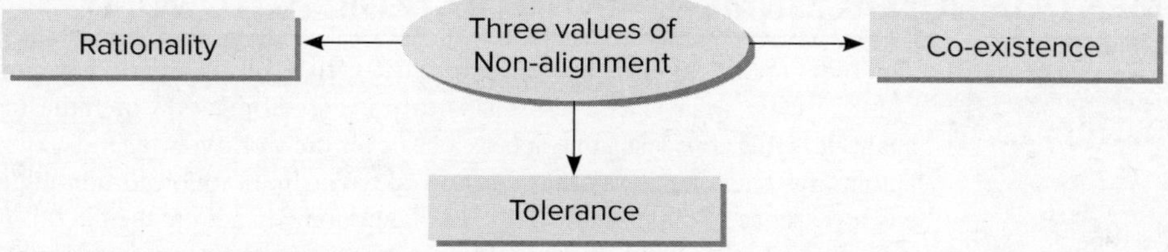

RELEVANCE OF NON-ALIGNMENT IN THE 21st CENTURY

In fact, since the end of the Cold War, despite opposition to the use of the term non-alignment, the essence of non-alignment remains unchanged. In this unipolar-cum-multipolar world order of today, the essence of non-alignment still remains relevant. In author's discussion with Mr. K. P. Fabian, Indian ambassador to Iraq, the idea was very succinctly put. Mr. Fabian asserted that one should look at non-alignment through the prism of Hinduism. Just like Hinduism is a way of life, non-alignment was also a way of conducting foreign policy. In Hinduism, when an individual dies, it is believed that the body is dead but the soul or the spirit remains alive. This is the same prism through which one should view non-alignment.

It is said that non-alignment is dead (as the Cold war is over), but its soul or spirit remains alive as it stood for independence, autonomy and national interests. This very aptly applies to the Indian foreign policy today. The Indian foreign policy in the post-Cold War period continues to be guided by the spirit or essence of non-alignment. Today, India practices a foreign policy of alignment, which is not ideological, but issue-based.

This clarity gives India tremendous operational flexibility in maintaining 'strategic autonomy'.

Why is India reluctant to sign alliances?

India is still reluctant to enter alliances because it still perceives that alliances are a 'permanent wedlock' that would snatch India's independence (or now we can say strategic autonomy) to take decisions.

What is the meaning of Strategic Autonomy?

It is a new metaphysical construct in Indian foreign policy debate and a recent term for non-alignment where the foreign policy continues to follow the essence of non-alignment in conduct of international relations with priority towards national interests, independence and autonomy.

CAN INDIA REVIVE NON-ALIGNMENT?

In the post-Cold War period, India can take the following four steps to revive the spirit of non-alignment again in the post-Cold War period.

1. Today, the emerging market economies are being pressurised by the West to liberalise their intellectual property laws. This may affect the overall development of these states. Non-alignment can become a new tool of all emerging market economies to have a consensus on the intellectual property rights (IPR) issue.
2. The West has been constantly blaming the Global South for polluting the world and causing climate change problems because of its developmental strategy. This is at a time when the West itself has been the biggest polluter historically. Non-alignment can become a new platform for the emerging market economies to evolve a consensus on environmental policy. India can be a lead state here.
3. The world continues to be divided and faces a nuclear apartheid. The permanent five members of the UN Security Council continue to monopolise the nuclear weapons and associated technologies. They have denied the larger world the opportunity to use nuclear resource. The non-alignment can become a platform to seek a better bargain in the post-Cold war era. With exceptionally strong nuclear non-proliferation track record of India, it can emerge as a bridge between the West and the rest.
4. The world continues to remain imbalanced in its global representation at the United Nations. The emerging markets such as India, Brazil, Germany and Japan collectively represent a huge chunk of rising economic power. Non-alignment can become a powerful platform for seeking restructuring the United Nations.

ASSESSMENT OF NON-ALIGNMENT AND STRATEGIC AUTONOMY

Henry Kissinger on Non-alignment

According to Henry Kissinger, the strategy of non-alignment enabled India to elevate a bargaining tactic into a principle of ethics. In his book, 'World Order' he mentions that India's non-alignment during cold war had a unique parallel to the US history. If India had accepted the bipolar politics; it would have been relegated as a secondary ally in superpower camps and would have had very less influence in international affairs.

The Indian political class has perceived the British rule as a period of humiliation. The political class today has a consensus to prevent subjugation of India to foreign rule again. It is this consensus that acts as a basis for the worldview of India and its search for autonomy. Thus, if we say that during Cold War India followed non-alignment, which had an essence of maintaining a degree of autonomy in action; then in this foreign policy behaviour, that guided India's worldview, can be traced to India's historical subjugation by the British. During the Cold War, the non-alignment allowed India to blend righteous moralism and psychologies of major powers.

The strategy of non-alignment enabled India to seek developmental support of the USSR and the US. This enabled India to exercise more influence in the world than it could have otherwise exercised, had it been a camp follower in the Cold War cosmos. Preservation of peace became an integral part of our own foreign policy because only with peace in the world was consistent economic development possible.

KEY POINTS

- The strategy of non-alignment was rooted in India's past and historical tradition.
- India advocated for non-alignment during the Cold War period because it wanted to resist imperialism and colonialism, which it could not had it been a camp follower.
- India's non-alignment was not about antagonising any state but engaging with all on the principle of national interests.
- The core of non-alignment was to advance national interests without compromising the autonomy and independence to take decisions.
- The autonomy and independence would have been compromised had India become a camp follower during bipolar politics.
- Since the end of Cold War, while the term non-alignment may not be relevant, but its essence guides our foreign policy, which is called strategic autonomy.
- India can champion the cause of third world in climate change, poverty and clean energy by using non-alignment as a strategy today.
- The reforms of the multilateralism, as advanced by India today, can also be facilitated by non-alignment.

2

CHAPTER

The Foreign Policy from Indira Gandhi to Manmohan Singh

EQUALITY AS BASIS OF DIPLOMATIC ENGAGEMENT

After the death of Nehru, Lal Bahadur Shastri succeeded him as the next Prime Minister but Shastri passed away on 10 January 1966 and Indira Gandhi became the PM on 24 January 1966. Indira Gandhi brought about a recalibration in the way India would approach its international relations. She stated that equality would become the basis for India's global engagement. It was during the 1970 Lusaka NAM summit where scholars were able to get an insight into the essential tenets of foreign policy as was being adopted by Indira Gandhi. For the first time, she emphasised that India wished to be friends with all nations but on the basis of equality. She asserted that no state could look at India as an inferior state and India would conduct its diplomacy with all states (read the USA and the USSR) on equal footing. Her most important contribution was to make India into a brand equal to the great powers.

MILITARY AND FOREIGN POLICY FUSION

Indira Gandhi undertook the Peaceful Nuclear Explosion (PNE) in 1974 (contextually explained later in a separate chapter). It is a testimony to the fact that her foreign policy was determined to make India a military power.

FOREIGN POLICY SHOULD BE BASED ON MERIT OF EACH SITUATION

Indira Gandhi stated that foreign Policy should be based on merit of each situation. In 1979, due to internal political chaos in Afghanistan, Soviet Union invaded them. They did so because the neighbour of Afghanistan was Pakistan (which during Cold War was an ally of the USA) and Soviet Union thought that the US might take advantage of political crisis in Afghanistan and invade them and expand their rule. The Soviet Union's invasion of Afghanistan led the US to counter it. The US collaborated with Pakistan and Saudi Arabia to train the Afghani people to wage a proxy war against Soviet Union in Afghanistan. The US wanted to use the Afghani people as a proxy in their indirect fight against USSR. They, in support with Pakistan and Saudi Arabia, created insecurity in the Afghan people that Soviet Union is an enemy of Islam and it has invaded Afghanistan to eliminate Islam.

This generated insecurity in the Afghani people and they wanted to protect their religion, which they perceived, was in danger. The USA along with Pakistan trained these Afghan men to wage a Jihad (a holy war to protect the religion when it is in danger). From 1979 to1988, a Mujahedeen campaign (a campaign of jihad) was launched in Afghanistan, where Afghan people fought Soviet army in Afghanistan. The USA supported these Mujahedeen with arms, ammunition and money till 1988, when Soviet Union finally decided to withdraw from Afghanistan.

India, being a friend of USSR, did not condemn the invasion and the USA asserted that non-condemnation by India is a sign of Indian support to the Soviet policy. But India stood upright stated that its policy is based on the merit of the situation and it considers invasion of Soviet as something beneficial for the stability and development of Afghanistan.

DIFFERENTIATING NEHRUVIAN FOREIGN POLICY FROM INDIRA GANDHI'S FOREIGN POLICY

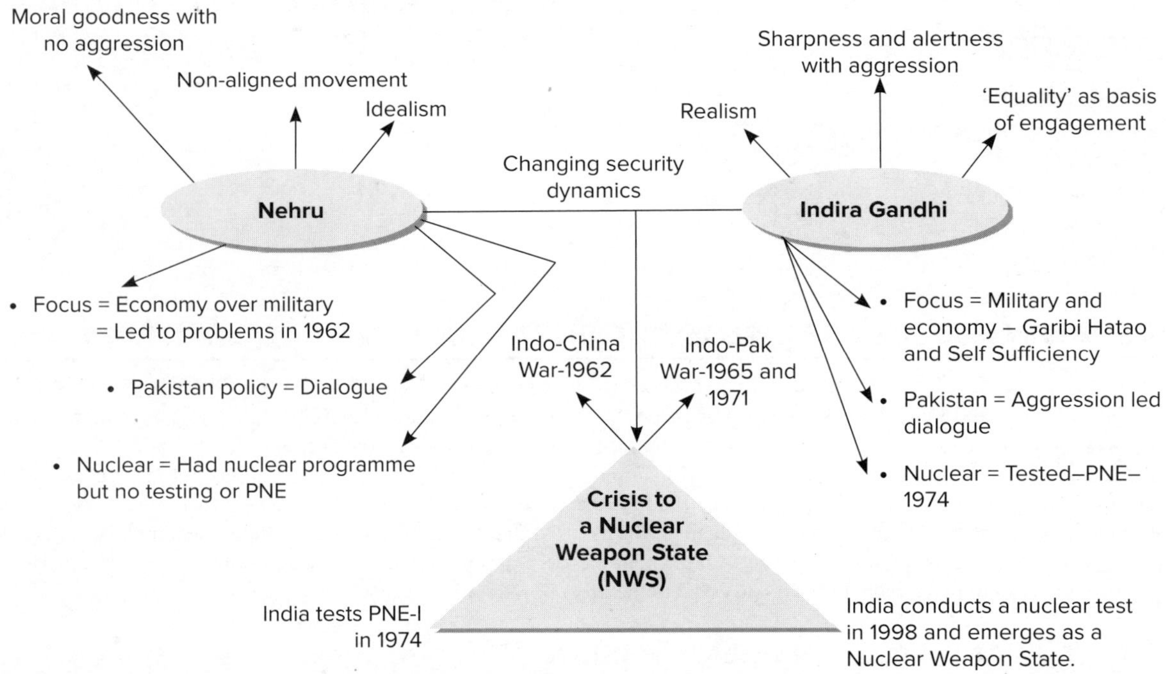

BLENDING IDEALISM AND REALISM AND POLICY OF 'ENLIGHTENED SELF-INTERESTS'

Foreign policy under Rajiv Gandhi had a fine blend of idealism and realism. This is visible in his Pakistan and USA policy. Since the 1962 conflict with China, the relations were frozen. India was insistent that unless the border issue is resolved, no other dimension of relationship can be explored. The ice was broken by Rajiv Gandhi. His visit to China in 1989 and meeting with Deng Xiaoping, urging to separate the border issue from economic diplomacy proved that he followed the policy of 'enlightened self-interests'. He also used Non-aligned Movement as a tool to promote the economic interests of India.

ECONOMIC REFORMS AND RISE OF ECONOMIC DIPLOMACY

By 1990, following the complete disintegration of Soviet Union, the erstwhile USSR was now succeeded by Russian Federation, which meant that India had now lost the patronage of the erstwhile USSR. What was worrisome for India was the future supply of defence products.

During the Cold War, Russia was one of the major defence suppliers to India. Now after the end of Cold War, India had to renegotiate all contracts and at certain places, even sign new contracts. However, the greater dilemma was with whom were these new contracts to be negotiated.

There was a vacuum and not much clarity. At this juncture, many in Russia felt the need to end the special favour for India. However, things normalised when Boris Yeltsin visited India in 1993. During his visit, the 1971 India–Russia Treaty of Friendship and Cooperation was revised with 14 additional clauses and was signed to mark a new era in bilateral relationship post-Cold War.

At the same time Narsimha Rao also developed new contacts with the five Central Asian Republics that emerged after the breakup of USSR. During the time, Rao reached out to the USA, China, Russia and Central Asia to explore economic-centric foreign relations.

THE GUJRAL DOCTRINE AND ITS RELEVANCE

In 1997, Gujral became the PM and evolved a fresh approach vis-à-vis the foreign policy that is now known as the Gujral doctrine. The basic foreign policy ideas of Gujral doctrine are as follows:

- India is a dominant power in the South Asian region.
- India should not look for arithmetical reciprocity.
- The core of the idea was to give more than what you may take from a foreign state.
- In a simpler language, the Gujral doctrine meant that if a neighbour moved an inch, India should move a yard.
- This policy would enable India, according to him, to pursue a new quality of relationship with its neighbours, leading to sober and constructive responses from the neighbourhood.
- He even instructed Research and Analysis Wing (RAW) to dismantle all human assets it had established in Pakistan for covert operations, as he perceived them as tools that would hinder constructive engagement with neighbours.

SEEKING INDIA'S RIGHTFUL PLACE IN COMITY OF NATIONS

After the withdrawal of support by the Congress party, the Gujral government was replaced by that of Atal Bihari Vajpayee. From 11 to 13 May 1998, the government carried out nuclear tests. These tests were significant because one of the tests conducted in Pokhran was a thermonuclear test, which indicated hydrogen bomb capability.

India reached the sub-critical level in the tests, which meant that it generated enough data in these experiments where further improvements could be carried out through computer simulation. Thus, after the operation Shakti I-V (the code name for the tests), India declared itself a nuclear state. India thus declared a voluntary moratorium on further nuclear testing. Vajpayee in a letter to Clinton asserted that India faced threats from China and Pakistan and that these were compelling reasons for India to undertake nuclear tests. The letter to Clinton was leaked to the *New York Times* and these aggravated tensions further between India and China.

INDIAN DIASPORA AS BRAND AMBASSADORS OF INDIA

In 2000, the US President Bill Clinton visited India. He became the fourth USA President after Eisenhower, Nixon and Carter to visit the country. Clinton's visit saw a push towards bilateral economic diplomacy as deals worth three billion dollars were signed, ranging from broadband connectivity to energy dimensions.

The emerging economic opportunities for the USA in India and a presence of a vibrant Indian diaspora in the USA that played a pivotal role in US politics proved instrumental factors in creating a new bridge in the bilateral relationship. The Clinton administration was replaced by the Bush administration. The momentum of establishing a new relationship with India gained strength with the coming of Bush. The 9/11 attack bolstered some major changes in the subcontinent. Immediately after the 9/11 attack, India went ahead to put on record that it was willing to enter into military alliance with the US and work with it in its global war on terrorism (GWOT).

THE INDIAN FOREIGN POLICY'S GREAT POWER ASPIRATIONS

The relationship with China under Manmohan Singh took a momentous step ahead and the two sides decided to boost bilateral trade and reopened the Nathu La Pass in 2006, apart from many positive frameworks. In 2004, Manmohan Singh and Putin met at the India–Russia Annual PM Summit. The two sides decided to resolve their long pending disputes related to defence. India was concerned about the supply of defence spares and their timely delivery and pricing. Russia was concerned about India's IPR laws. During the 2004 summit meeting, India conveyed its assurance to Russia that it would respect IPR laws of all equipment supplied to India by Russia and ensured they were neither copied nor secretly stolen by any state. The two sides subsequently strengthened cooperation in defence and energy in the years ahead. The next steps in strategic partnership launched during the Vajpayee regime between India and the USA (explained in the US–India chapter) ultimately culminated into the India–USA civilian nuclear cooperation deal in 2005. The nuclear deal between India and the USA not only opened up a new chapter in bilateral relationships but also signified that the USA had come to accept India as a major power of the future.

INDIA'S DEVELOPMENT DIPLOMACY AND GREAT POWER ASPIRATIONS

Manmohan Singh continued to deepen India's relationship with the ASEAN states, which had started with a sectoral dialogue partnership between India and ASEAN at the end of the Cold War. During Manmohan Singh's regime as the PM, India and ASEAN concluded a free trade agreement (FTA) in goods (2010) and services (2012). Singh also invested tremendous diplomatic capital to strengthen ties with Japan. The two sides, under the leadership of Manmohan Singh and Shinzo Abe, concluded an agreement to establish a single seamless whole envisaging free movement of navy, capital and people. Besides India and Japan, Manmohan Singh also strengthened Indian ties with Africa. India launched multiple initiatives, ranging from Focus Africa Programme to Pan-Africa-e-Network Projects, to enhance people-to-people ties.

INDIAN FOREIGN POLICY'S ENERGY DIPLOMACY

The ties with West Asia saw resurgence based on the theme of oil diplomacy. It was during Manmohan Singh's regime that India and Saudi Arabia concluded a strategic partnership agreement. Our cooperation with UAE, Kuwait, Qatar and Oman continued. India and Qatar signed an agreement on Liquefied Natural Gas (LNG) and Qatar decided to supply India LNG for energy security. The foreign policy of Manmohan Singh saw India emerge as one of the lead players in the reconstruction of Afghanistan.

KEY POINTS

- Indira Gandhi ensured that no country in the world perceives India as an inferior state.
- The foreign policy responses were based on independent merit that each situation demanded and Indian response to Soviet invasion of Afghanistan is an example of the same.
- Rajiv Gandhi was a disrupter and a moderniser. He chose to focus on economic self-interests and decided to engage with Chinese.
- Narsimha Rao built upon the legacy of Rajiv Gandhi and infused economics deep into the foreign policy.
- The Look East Policy and renewed economic diplomacy of Rao with central Asia and the US were his notable achievements.
- However, most of India's neighbours looked at India with a pejorative sense, compelling Rao to adopt a hands-off approach.
- To improvise the ties with the neighbours, Gujral adopted Gujral doctrine and emphasised the need to engage with neighbours without reciprocity.
- Vajpayee resorted to initiation of great power politics and brought diaspora on Indian foreign policy centre-stage.
- Manmohan Singh leveraged the great power politics and eventually articulated nuclear deal, development diplomacy and energy diplomacy.

CHAPTER 3

The Foreign Policy of Narendra Modi and the Modi Doctrine

THE CULTURE OF SAMVAD IN FOREIGN POLICY

The year 2014 saw Modi coming to power as the Prime Minister of India. He won his second term in 2019. The earliest signs of Modi's diplomacy date back to his tenure as the Chief Minister (CM) of Gujarat. During his decade-long stint as the CM, he travelled to various countries to get investment for his state. During his foreign visits, he developed a style of personal diplomacy where he emphasised building of strong personal relationships with leaders of the states he visited. This style of personal diplomacy is now recognised as the hallmark of Modi's way of engaging with the world. Modi's diplomatic skills were further strengthened when Vajpayee, as the PM, deputed Modi to travel abroad for party work where he always displayed avid interest in learning how foreign states solved problems related to infrastructure, roads, rivers etc. and applying that learning to Indian situations. This ability of learning from the foreign states and to replicate the same in India is visible in his style. Modi's background in RSS has also inculcated in him a sense of a wider engagement with people of all walks of life for suggestions. In fact, during his RSS days in 1970s and 1980s, Modi effectively worked upon the RSS pillar, *Samvad*. *Samvad* also eventually emerged as a key pillar of his foreign policy.

THE 'INDIA FIRST' DOCTRINE

When he travels abroad, he does not restrict his engagement with merely the heads of states but widens his reach to include private sector firms to monks, to students, to workers in factories. His idea of foreign policy or diplomacy is that it should not just be perceived as the art of government-to-government interaction but more as a leader-to-people interaction.

RETAIL DIPLOMACY AND MODI DOCTRINE

Diplomacy involving leader-to-people interactions is called retail diplomacy. In retail diplomacy, the state leader interacts, meets and shakes hands with a wide spectrum of scholars to monks to workers. Retail diplomacy not only enhances the perceived approachability of the leader in the eyes of the public but also helps in developing very strong interpersonal relationships.

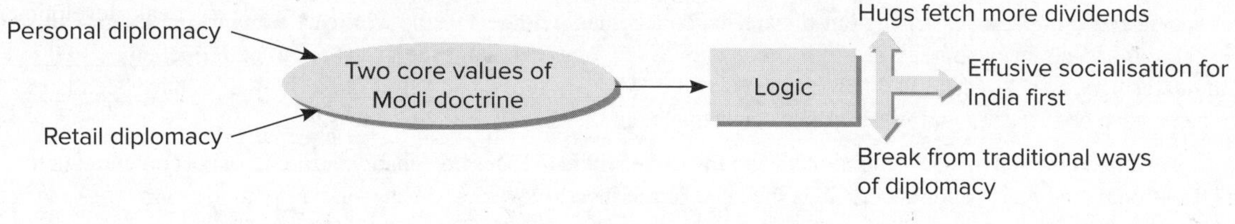

INDIAN DIASPORA AND TRANSFORMATIVE DIPLOMACY

The Modi doctrine is defined by his emphasis on 4D's:

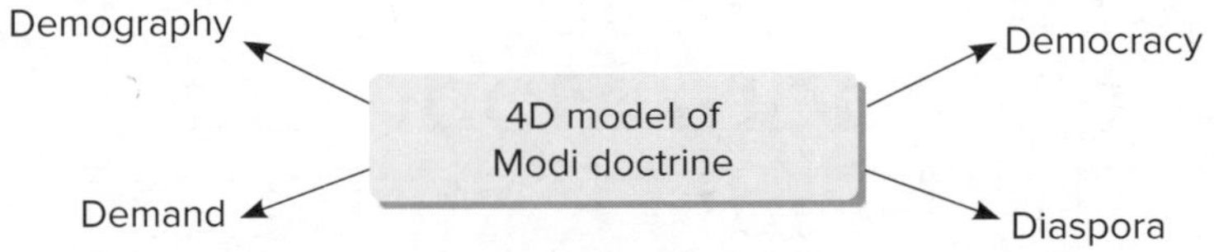

Modi has adopted Democracy, Demography and Demand as key drivers to highlight India's economic power abroad. However, Diaspora is the oxygen to his foreign policy. Modi has, from day one, addressed concerns related to the Indian diaspora. On any foreign tour, Modi makes it a point to address a gathering of the Indian diaspora. There are two purposes for the same. First, he addresses the diaspora to not only reconnect with their homeland but also to convey them the problems India faces in the twenty-first century. In most of his addresses to the diaspora, Modi outlines domestic issues of India and government initiatives to tackle them. He often discusses issues such as lack of manufacturing base in India, issues related to cleanliness and so on. In the address, he appraises the diaspora of initiatives the government has taken, ranging from Make in India to Swachch Bharat and so forth.

The intention of this exercise is to convince the diaspora that they can emerge as effective stakeholders in the problems faced by India. He intends to convey to the diaspora that their contribution is imperative for India's development story and its rise as a global power. Second, his address to the Indian diaspora in foreign countries is a message to the governments of those countries—'if you take care of this constituency, they will take care of your governments in elections'. This diaspora diplomacy is a classic example of how the diaspora can be a catalyst for transformative diplomacy in the era of globalisation. His focus, in the long run, is to use the diaspora for domestic development.

His intention is to attract the interests of the diaspora back home and affect a reversal from brain drain to brain gain. Thus, it is not wrong to say that Modi knows that the diaspora is a part of the great Indian family, which will be a partner to India's emergence as a global player. This is also in sync with the BJP's perception of the importance of the diaspora. An important thing to note here is that in his addresses to the diaspora, he would link the past, present and the future in such an array that the diaspora gets galvanised, energised and enthusiastic to play a role in India's future. His addresses to the diaspora in the USA (Howdy Modi in 2019), Australia and the UK reflect the intermixing of past, present and future. The doctrine of the diaspora here aims to attract foreign direct investment (FDI) to India and use it for domestic development. Modi's idea of diaspora diplomacy is to ensure a collective Indian voice in the countries of their residence where they are simultaneously loyal citizens.

ECONOMIC DIPLOMACY AS A KEY TO GREAT POWER STATUS

Another very crucial dimension of Modi doctrine is his thrust on economic diplomacy. All diplomatic engagements undertaken by Modi till date are driven by the economic thrust of making India a leading commercial power. Modi from Gujarat imbibed the value of economic diplomacy. Gujarat had been an important port of international trade during the peak of trade via the ancient silk route. Trade was natural to Gujarat and this had emerged as a crucial element of the Modi doctrine. Modi understood well that domestic growth rates cannot be boosted by domestic initiatives alone and that geo-strategic imperatives arising out of external engagement with rest of the world are a key to India's growth story. The economic diplomacy strategy of Modi is based on a model where domestic growth is to be propelled by FDI in the manufacturing sector. To make FDI absorption easy, the 'Make in India' and 'Skill India' initiatives have been launched and steps have been taken to improve India's performance in the ease of doing business.

In 2019, Modi addressed the IFS probationers and instructed them to focus on enhancing India's export potential in textile and traditional medicine. Modi understands the need of the investors well and has worked upon government-to-business contacts. During an address at a business lunch in Tokyo, in 2014, Modi said that while he had been the CM of Gujarat, he had invited Japanese investments. As Japanese businesses came, he began to study Japanese culture and found that the Japanese like to play golf. This led Modi to establish world-class golf courses in Gujarat, thereby showing what a proactive government can do for investors. For Modi, economic diplomacy is about marketing, streamlining, downsizing and modernisation brought about in a seamless manner within a global economy.

Media Diplomacy

Indian diplomats face two constraints. First is a cultural constraint. Many are neither attuned to nor professionally trained to deal with the highly opinionated opinion makers. Second is financial. The government does not provide adequate funds to diplomats to conduct such outreach in an adequately suitable and subtle manner. Media outreach is not conducting a press conference. It requires systematic relationship building that requires considerable investment of time and money. The government is trying to address these concerns.

Soft Power is India's Power

His usage of India's soft power capabilities has taken primacy in the Modi doctrine. For instance, the intense diplomacy to get 21 June declared as the International Day of Yoga at the UN General Assembly is an example of soft power diplomacy. Thus, one may conclude that the Modi doctrine is all about putting India into a higher international orbit and for achieving the same; tasks have been clearly cut out for the future. Modi believes that a joint co-action of all the neighbours can also help each one of us to tackle problems collectively. In April 2020, Modi emphasised upon the SAARC as a platform to be used by all states in the region to tackle the novel COVID-19.

> **Vaccine Maitri and COVID-19**
>
> During the Covid-19 pandemic, India seized the opportunity to project itself as a global saviour by exporting Hydroxy chloroquine (a drug required for the treatment of the virus) to the US, Brazil and Maldives. Thus, by assisting others in an unfortunate situation, India established 'India Model'. China too exported relief assistance following 'China Model' but the quality for those were poor and some conditions were applied to it.

THE NEIGHBOURHOOD FIRST DOCTRINE

Under the new Neighbourhood First policy, Modi's key focus vis-à-vis India's relation with its neighbours is economic trade. Modi believes that aggressive economic trade with neighbours will benefit all and the benefits will percolate deep down in the society. This will bring about a radical shift in the way its neighbours perceive India. The erstwhile image of India, projected to its neighbours as a 'Big Brother', will transform into one of a collaborative ally and shall prove positive spill over for the entire region. At the neighbourhood level, connectivity has emerged as an inbuilt dimension of economic diplomacy. Our understanding of the foreign policy of Modi helps us to analyse few goals the IFP intends to achieve in the future. Modi has clarified that India is not going to be a balancing power but intends to aspire to be a leading power. India needs to have a three-step foreign policy:

Observe and react to international events
If needed, infuse energy to shape international events
Occasionally, play a role to drive the events

Modi focuses on the following three core points in diplomacy.

Personal energy with pragmatism
Focus on problem solving based diplomacy
Prioritising national interests with economic diplomacy

DOCTRINE OF CIVILISATIONAL AND FAITH DIPLOMACY

While interacting with world leaders, Modi ensures that he develops a strong personal chemistry with them. Modi's idea is that a strong personal bond helps India to bargain its national interests at the highest level possible. One of the most important influences of RSS on Modi's foreign policy has been his interest in spearheading India's culture and values and promotion of the same at a global level. The RSS background has infused this value in Modi who practises the same with much vigour in the foreign policy. His cultural and civilisational diplomacy is clearly reflected in his visits to temples in foreign states.

In the recent times, Modi has taken steps to bridge a link between faith and diplomacy. In India's Asian policy, Buddhism has acquired a new focus. When Modi went to Mongolia, he delivered a lecture in their Parliament where he highlighted the importance of Buddhism to solve contemporary Asian and global challenges. The IFP has always emphasised upon cultural, historical and civilisational ties and has tried to keep religion out of foreign policy engagements. Modi has initiated a new diplomatic path of using religion, as a tool to promote global harmony. Globally there is a trend of using religion as a diplomatic tool. The US have an office of Religious and Global Affairs in the Department of State, which assists the US Secretary of State on religious issues. European Union does so in case of West Asia while China has been doing so since long. India is trying to put its IFP in line with this global trend. It has begun with Buddhism, which helps India reinforce its leadership in South East Asia.

OMNI-ALIGNMENT AND STRATEGIC AUTONOMY DIPLOMACY

Indian PM participated in the Shangri-La Dialogue in 2019. This is the first time the Indian PM outlined a foreign policy framework that will remain as a dominant doctrine in Indian policy for long. Some core ideas can be ascertained from the speech of the Indian PM. He stated that the world is witnessing tremendous uncertainty. There is a competition over various geopolitical ideas and political models in the world. At this juncture, the Indian PM stated that India would position itself as an independent actor and an independent power across Asia. For the first time, he stated that the USA and Russian Federation are India's partners. With these partners, India's relationship is based on geopolitics in Asia and overlapping interests globally. He asserted that the relation with China is complex and has 'many layers'. But, still the relation with China has an undertone of stability and is crucial for the world. Importantly, India asserted that it would not be a part of any closed group of nations or even any aggregate power or any bloc. In fact, India asserted that based on its own power, capacity and ideas, India will chart out its own course. Some asserted the revival of non-alignment, though the PM used the term 'strategic autonomy'.

DIPLOMACY OF MINILATERALS, INDO-PACIFIC AND QUADRILATERAL SECURITY DIALOGUE

India asserted that Indo-Pacific is not perceived by India as a China-centric or a club of limited members.

India perceives Indo-Pacific as an inclusive bloc of pluralism and co-existence. India continues to assert that it looks the world as free, inclusive and open rules based on global order where these rules are to be centred upon the consent of all and not just a few. Indian PM categorically stated that the rivalry in Asia will descend into conflict but cooperation of rivals will be conducive for stability. In conclusion, India positioned itself to seek a multi-polar world with capability for making its own destiny. Reflecting its own unique geography, India has asserted that it wants to leverage its position in the Pacific and Eurasia. India, now, is a leading power with strategic intent of 'Omni-alignment'. If India intends to play the leadership role in the world, India would have to advocate for more global investment and trade flows.

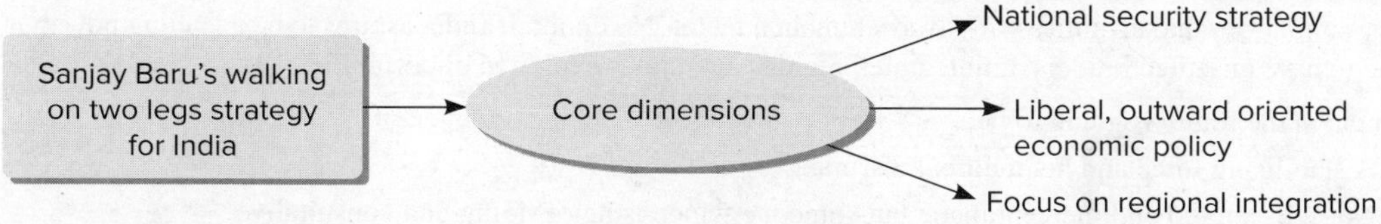

PRACTICING DOCTRINE OF STRATEGIC AUTONOMY

The foreign policy of Modi believes that long-held assumptions and alignments rooted in the legacies of colonialism and the ideology of the Cold War are making way for new configurations and partnerships but India remains committed to the principles and objectives of the non-aligned movement, including its long-standing solidarity and support for the Palestinian cause. The question that arises is that does the government's decision to send Vice President Venkaiah Naidu to the 2019 NAM Summit represented a "downgrade" of India's representation? The answer is no. It may not be possible for PM Modi to attend all multilateral events, given the huge demands on his time. In fact in the past, many Prime Ministers attended the UN General Assembly, but PM Modi has not followed that tradition and spoken at the General Assembly only on three occasions. There are some scholars and analysts who are of the opinion that as non-alignment was a tool of the Cold War, it has lost relevance in the post-Cold War period. Some scholars also argue that whatever non-alignment aspired for, it has achieved as the countries are now decolonised and there is no more apartheid etc. However, it is important to remember that non-alignment was only an independent choice of foreign policy. It has nothing to do with the existence or absence of the Cold War. No doubt decolonisation was one of the central tenets of non-alignment as it coincided with Cold War, but its essence remains relevant till today.

What is Strategic Autonomy in Indian Foreign Policy?

The essence of non-alignment, called by Modi as strategic autonomy, can be seen in three points as follows: Looking at every issue through the prism of merit. States reserving the right to take actions against an issue they perceive as wrong by any major power. States reserving the right to take actions in their foreign policy on the basis of their independence, national interest and thereby reserving their autonomy.

INDIA AS A RISING POWER AND AVOIDING THE KINDLEBERGER TRAP

In the past 20 years, there have been three clear instances when India's actions have not only forced its diplomacy out of South Block and to the rest of the world, but have been inflexion points in its larger foreign policy, forcing India to articulate its way forward. One was the nuclear tests of 1998 and the second, the India–US nuclear deal of 2008. The third was India's decision to nullify Article 370 and reorganise Jammu and Kashmir. In an unnoticed remark, India's Foreign Minister, Jaishankar informed the UN's new grouping on multilateralism. "The Kindleberger trap on the shortage of global goods is far more serious than the Thucydides Trap." Basically he was saying China's mercantilism rendered it a selfish superpower because it disregarded existing international norms (like UNCLOS) without helping to create a new order. It was the clearest indictment of the Chinese view of power, as well as an excoriation of the US's withdrawal from its traditional role of being the provider of global goods (defined as "stable climate, financial stability or freedom of the seas" by Joseph Nye). That is the space India sees for itself in the coming decades, a middle power raising by sharing the global burdens in providing for global goods in coalition with large powers such as the US. Indian Foreign Minister, in 2020, outlined India's foreign policy mantras as greater pluralism, pragmatic cooperation, convergence with many, congruence with none, not pure transnationalism, but accommodation, nationalism and internationalism to co-exist.

What is Kindleberger Trap?

The term Kindleberger trap was coined by Joseph Nye, which signifies the dangers inherent when world witnesses changing balance of power. The Kindleberger trap is similar to the concept of weaponisation of supply chains analysed in Section 1 and here the idea is that when balance of power changes, some countries will leverage their power and deny others' public goods.

He rightly stated that in this intensely competitive world India's goal should be to move closer towards the strategic sweet spot. Even India looks at an era of more dispersed power and sharper competition, the way forward is more likely to be new forms of accommodation rather than pure transactions. While nations will, naturally, strive to advance their particular interests, similarities and affinities will always remain a factor. No doubt, if India aspires to be a leading power, it cannot continue to have unsettled borders, unintegrated regions and under-exploited opportunities.

Thus, India in the future is going to be:

1. A stabilising force and not a global disrupter.
2. Not self-centred and mercentalistic but someone which is law abiding and consultative.
3. A nation that is a net security provider, net development provider, connectivity provider, firm in dealing with terrorism, one, which has values in place, and one that will address global issues.
4. A nation that will remain a voice of the global South (means developing states and emerging market economies) and connects uniquely to the diaspora to project 'Brand India'.

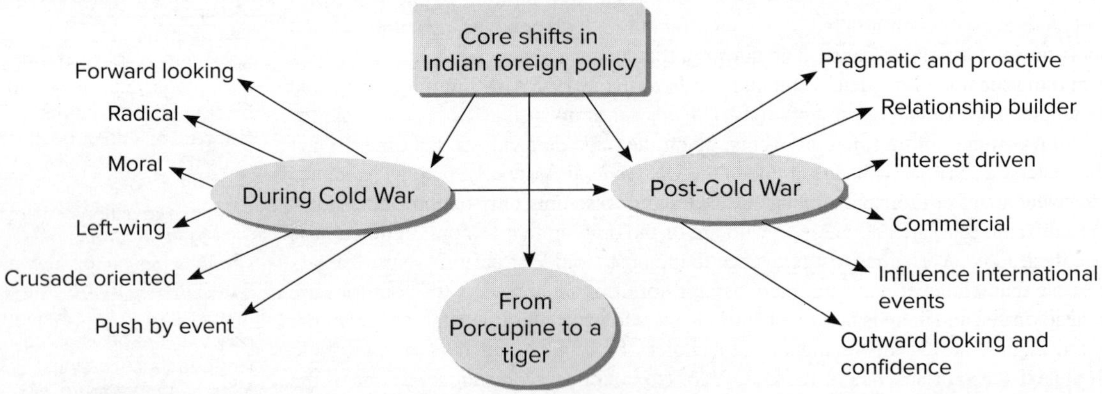

KEY POINTS

- The foreign policy under Modi has adopted many new paradigms.
- Development of India is at the heart of Indian foreign policy goals now.
- The focus is on faith diplomacy to leverage India's civilisational strengths.
- India favours summit style diplomacy to give emphasis on great power politics.
- India is more interested in shaping international events now than merely reacting to them.
- The focus is on emerging to as a rising power by display of capabilities.

CHAPTER

4 The Ethical Dilemmas of Indian Foreign Policy

INDIA'S MIDDLE PATH

When India became independent, we were wooed by the Americans to join their capitalist camp. But, had India joined the US camp, what could have been the result? Probably, a mini Marshall Plan for India, settlement of Kashmir issue in the UN and a powerful India to take on Chinese in 1962. The leap into the lap of the US would have definitely transformed India but India chose self-respect by articulating non-alignment, wisely because aligning would have meant accepting a subservient status, which would have been akin to centuries of humiliation we had already faced. India chose the middle path, a difficult choice, but foreign policy is seldom easy because the gains are incremental and reverses are common. India chose the third way in a bipolar world and found non-alignment as a low-cost influence enhancer in the world. However, the non-alignment as a brand punched far above its weight during the Cold War and was shorn of moralistic hyperbole and lacked any solid foundation on which it could flaunt its muscles, nothing but an ethical dilemma.

INDIA'S EMERGING WORLDVIEW

Since the end of the Cold War, India has moved away from non-alignment. Diplomatic practitioners argue that non-alignment is dead and India today follows strategic autonomy. However, as argued in the chapters previously, the strategic autonomy is an old wine in the new bottle. There is a growing belief amongst the global diplomatic community that India has shed off old beliefs, but it is yet to clearly articulate an effective doctrine for the future. While strategic autonomy is the blunt answer, but the question is, how can India exercise strategic autonomy when it has a weak indigenous defence industry? This is an ethical dilemma because if India is to rely on foreign players for military equipments, it will continue to remain strategically dependent. Also, presently, India needs a strong economic heft to advance the notion of strategic dilemma. The economic and military dimensions are not the only dilemma because chains around India's machinations also include Pakistan and China. Pakistan continues to bleed India and chip away its territorial integrity, thereby acting as an irritating bee that does not go away. Afterall, it is rightly said that history is to nations what character is to people.

INDIA AS A MINI GLOBAL POWER OR A SWING STATE

The global commentators have often debated on whether India has done well for itself! Is India rising as a power and on way to become a global power? This is a serious ethical dilemma that Indian foreign policy mandarins are unable to explain because there is a lot of ambiguity about India's ambitions for itself and the envisaged global role. Whatever be the status, one fact that has remained constant is that India counts in the world affairs today. This has been the case since Nehruvian times of moral leadership to present quest for a leadership role in shaping world events.

INDIA'S STATECRAFT OR STAGECRAFT

What will determine our global presence is contingent upon how we deal with our neighbours and the major powers. A key determinant would be on how India will ensure peace and security. Existing theories argue that a blend of coercion, payment and attraction are good optics of a national strategy. Put simply, great power politics is a mixture of soft power, hard power and smart power. The dilemma that confronts India is that does India have the capacity to absorb this wisdom? Can India manage the challenges in the neighbourhood through a doctrinal approach of 'speaking softly but carrying a big stick' to ensure that its national interests and territorial integrity is not challenged? It has been argued that India has found use of 'sharp power' more conducive as a strategy where the focus is on playing spy games that use manipulative diplomatic practices to influence and undermine the political systems of the adversaries because the strategy has the ability to pierce, penetrate and perforate the political and information systems that the adversaries have used against India.

INDIA AS A CONFUSED POWER

The biggest contribution of globalisation to the society of Asia has been the spectacular rise of China. The Chinese were born in 1949, after the civil war ended. Initially they remained a communist economy till 1978 but owing to their frictions with the Soviet Union, the Chinese switched the gears and embraced capitalism. In 1978, Deng Xiaoping made the embrace and propelled Chinese on path of economic growth via capitalism. Since then, till today, the Chinese have not only grown but have acquired tremendous economic and military power. The power acquired by the Chinese is such that they have disturbed the balance of power in Asia today. At the systemic level, Asia faces a regional order threat centred either on the US or China, leaving India in the foray. Secondly, Asia today is confronted with several powers of varying sizes and capabilities that are contending for primacy and influence to maximise their individual interests, a pattern which is quite similar to what was seen in Europe in the nineteenth century. The question that arises is that in this geopolitically contested and crowded Asia, what is India's strategy? Though India asserts that our approach is of multipolarity but multipolarity can only lead to crisis management and confidence building but not give strength to shape international events. The dilemma for India is, at one place it aspires to be a great power and at the other place, the assertion of multipolarity limits its ability to shape and influence global events. How will India find the answer to this?

INDIA'S FUTURE FOREIGN POLICY TASKS

India is witnessing a challenging global order where it needs to articulate a response to three challenges. The first is an intellectual challenge, where it has to develop a coherent understanding of present world and place India in it. Secondly, it has to define policies that are going to sustain the transformation India has embarked in foreign policy. Thirdly, India has to generate the core tenets of its grand strategy. Today, India is unable to intellectually understand its present state in the world because of the partition. Till India was a British colony, it was a coherent unit that exercised geopolitical significance and was the ultimate pivot state. However, since the partition, India is not a single geopolitical unit anymore and Indian borders do not conform to the geographic borders of the subcontinent. This is the heart of India's continental dilemma because Pakistan and China are today robbing India of political energy which India could have harnessed to display power in Eurasia and Indian Ocean. While it is good to argue that 'India will be a great power', 'India is a rising power'; the problem is that we lack any defined tangible matrices to assess how we make such assertions. In the absence of the matrices, these narratives are then merely ideas of hierarchy and perception and reduce the international relations in the minds of the people to a macho contest. India is and will remain an important player in world affairs but the power of India will not be asserted through how many countries it can outdo or push down but how well can it uplift its own people from ambitious poverty. The desire for a great power status has to be driven by quest for a great power status and not by a desire to be recognised by few states in joint statements.

MANIFESTING INDIA'S DESTINY IN THE WORLD

The future of India resides in the hands and heads of the citizens of India. How the citizens will perceive India and build the narrative will affect the destiny of India. When India became independent, it sought no apology from the British but used the national confidence of the national movement to build our future, our way. The confidence was seen in our national narrative which accepted history for what history was and did not focus attention on exaggerated boasts. Today, India requires a similar confidence and objectivity if it aspires to be a great power because emotions and sentiments do not make a country a great power but logic, reason and clarity does. Bravado and extravagant statements might enthuse some domestic elements but do not auger well for a country that claims global power status on civilisational strengths. India should not accept simulacrum of leadership or prejudices masquerading as ideas but allow India to stand for a message with a universal appeal of peace, harmony, tolerance and growth for all.

CHALLENGES FOR INDIAN FOREIGN POLICY IN POST-PANDEMIC WORLD

A common theme that has dominated our foreign policy is an understanding that ideas matter more than material power. This is why the bigger challenge for the foreign policy today is to conceptualise the ideas that we should stand for. There is a consensus in Indian strategic community that India's power is different and its power is the 'power of example'. This implies that India today does domestically what it speaks internationally. For instance, if India today intends to promote a healthy living and spirituality, then it is promoting use of Yoga domestically and internationally as International Yoga Day. However, there are a few proponents in the foreign policy establishment who argue that in a changed global environment, India must not neglect material or hard power. This itself is at the heart of Indian dilemma, that how does it find a balance between material power and power of ideas. The second challenge for Indian foreign policy is that it is unable to articulate an idea whether it should promote democracy abroad or not. While India is proud of its democratic credentials and has been advancing democracy as a soft power through multiple diplomatic and academic initiatives. However, what India lacks is a clear vision and an institutional architecture to promote democracy as a foreign policy goal. The dilemma in policy makers is whether the Election Commission of India, which has been a temple of Indian democracy, should collaborate with Ministry of External Affairs or not, for promoting democracy internationally. In the current post-pandemic age which is witnessing democratic recession, it is imperative for India to robustly assert democracy. Come what may, India must resolve this challenge by developing a coherent response. The third challenge for India is to clarify what exactly it stands for as a value in foreign policy. This is crucial because India though asserts 'strategic autonomy' but has often been identified as a 'camp follower of the US'. For a nation in transition that is witnessing multitude of challenges, it is important that India clarifies what it means by strategic autonomy and defines the policy underpinnings to avoid uncalled for criticism.

QUESTIONS FOR PRACTICE

S. No.	Questions for Practice
1.	How to blend ideas and material power ambition?
2.	Should India use democracy as a value of foreign policy and promote democracy in international relations.
3.	Defining what are India's national interests and the underpinnings of what is meant by strategic autonomy.
4.	Turning statesmanship to salesmanship is a new phenomenon in Indian foreign policy. Examine.
5.	Does India's hyper-activism on the foreign policy front enable it to be a system-shaper and a global rule-maker or is it still a rule-taker?
6.	Do you observe a fundamental foreign policy shift or is it just a large number of optics-friendly acts that are well choreographed but not visionary? Analyse.
7.	When the world is struggling to manage the most pressing existential risk, is it any surprise that other international regimes are equally gridlocked? Analyse.
8.	Is India's current foreign policy guided more by economic than strategic interests? Examine.
9.	Is there any significance of religion in shaping Indian foreign policy making or its discourse in the past or today?
10.	Does India's religious demographic profile play any role in framing foreign policy towards Islamic states?

S. No.	Questions for Practice
11.	Is India always on the wrong side of geo-strategic and geo-economic evolution that we get caught on the wrong foot all the time?
12.	Whether promoting democracy abroad, like strengthening the opposition in other states, will always serve India's self-interest?
13.	Can a state interfere in another country's domestic matter by avoiding the allegation of being imperialistic?
14.	Can India have the moral claim to preach democracy where its essential democratic institutions and political discourse are in tatters? Examine.
15.	Why else would India promote cultural soft power if it has no practical consequence in international politics? Analyse.

SECTION 4

INDIA AND NEIGHBOURHOOD RELATIONS

AN OVERVIEW

Neighbourhood is an area mentioned in the syllabus. The nature of questions, if analysed carefully, clearly gives an indication that current happenings are fused with the background of neighbourhood studies and a question is constructed. In 2013, five questions on neighbourhood were asked and they ranged from Sri Lanka, protests in Maldives, String of Pearls to protests in Bangladesh. In 2014, when the US announced that they would move their troops out of Afghanistan, a question was asked on its implications on India. Similarly, in 2015, when Pakistan resorted to the use of terrorism as a state policy to destabilise India, a question on the use of soft power as a tool was asked. In 2017, a question on China was asked when the use of Chinese economic power status to alter regional power equations after its BRI became a destabilising force.

Potential foresight On the basis of the insights developed from the questions visible, we can be certain that if a major event happens in our neighbourhood, then a potential question can be asked on its implications in India. In the next two years, the author feels questions on implications of debt crisis of Sri Lanka on India, Indian ability to manage the art of balancing military Junta and democracy in Myanmar, rentier state politics of Pakistan and possibilities of state failure on security of India, implications of Bhutan's tilt towards China on India, role of India in development of Nepal, Nepali map machinations, Chinese attempts of salami slicing, its utilisation of sub-conventional tactics in Ladakh and great power rivalry between India and China in tech diplomacy and marine realm are prominent areas of questions.

CHAPTER 1

India and Neighbourhood Policy – Key Drivers of the Relationship

HISTORICAL BACKGROUND OF INDIA'S RELATIONSHIP WITH NEIGHBOURS

The entire South Asian subcontinent was unified under the British for the first time after the decline of the Mughal Empire in India. The British established a double line of defence, on the basis of the policy of reverse slopes. Under this policy, China and Russia were to have no presence in the subcontinent and the British tried to ensure this through the subordination of individual states. The British established a buffer state fences on reverse Himalayan slopes. The partition of India and Pakistan in 1947 saw a reversal of the reverse slope policy and opened up the possibility of foreign intervention in the region, which India did not favour. After the partition, despite a loss of territory in borders of the West and the East, India emerged as a pre-eminent regional power since a huge amount of land still came to India. Because of a huge territory and its geographical importance in the subcontinent, the subsequent security conception of India was not national but geopolitical and regional in nature. India realised that, due to its geopolitical location, it would witness a threat first from powers of the region than powers outside the region. India felt that it might witness a threat from the neighbours who may be weak or unstable because such a weak neighbour would always invite a powerful foreign player to intervene on its behalf against India. This would bring external powers to a zone; India felt fell in its own sphere of influence, where India can be the only power that can intervene. Thus, for India, security of South Asia is based on stability of South Asia. Jawaharlal Nehru propounded this view and some scholars have referred to it as the Indian Monroe Doctrine (drawing a parallel from the 19th century where the US President James Monroe exercised a similar influence of power in the Western hemisphere to prevent the European colonisation of America) as Nehru, after independence, resonated with similar views when he advocated that foreign colonial powers should stay out of South Asia. During the Cold War, India followed this foreign policy of trying to limit the influence of foreign powers in Asia, but such an attempt proved difficult for India as India lacked both the resources and the experience in governance to extend security to its neighbouring states. However, India today tries to extend this security to its neighbours and has tried to position itself as a Net Security Provider.

NEIGHBOURHOOD POLICY OF INDIA FROM NEHRU TO MANMOHAN SINGH

India, during Nehru's times, followed a global strategy of non-alignment to keep India away from the Cold War politics. The neighbourhood policy did not receive the same attention as India tried to position itself as a neutral force in the era of bipolarity.

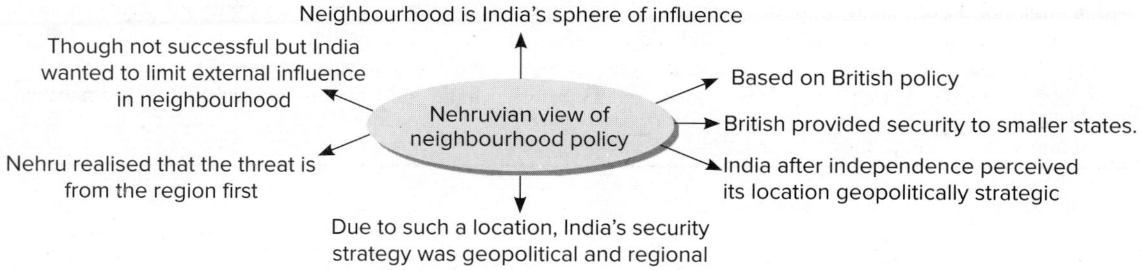

The coming of Indira Gandhi brought about a change in India's neighbourhood policy. She added a new component of bilateralism in the neighbourhood policy. This means that Indira Gandhi insisted that India should bilaterally resolve issues of the region without any intervention from external powers. Indira ensured that external powers have no role when matters are resolved bilaterally by India. The Indian neighbourhood policy, for that matter, was always fraught with contradictions. Regionally, in South Asia, India clung to the precepts of the balance of power and sphere of influence, while rejecting the same internationally. Regionally, under Indira Gandhi, India provided security to small nations while internationally opposing the intervention of the great powers in the affairs of the weak states. India, under Indira Gandhi, preached bilateralism at a time when it globally advocated for multilateralism. Another feature of Indira's neighbourhood policy was that she resorted to military interventions with a neighbour if it threatened India's security. India's intervention in 1971 during the East Pakistan crisis is a testimony to the fact. Many of the neighbours began to perceive India's military strategy as an interventionist approach.

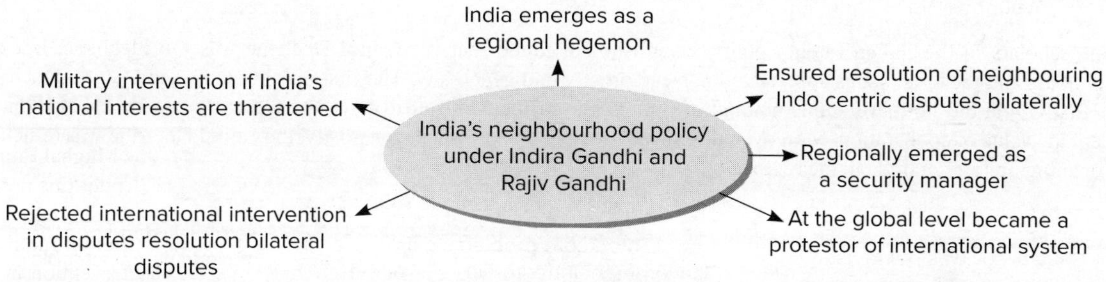

When Rajiv Gandhi assumed control, the Indian intervention in Maldives and Sri Lanka in 1980s (explained in the subsequent chapters) transformed India into a perceptual regional hegemon. Many scholars raised issues with India establishing itself as a regional hegemon. They asserted that India, during Indira and Rajiv's times (under Indira Doctrine and Rajiv Doctrine), did not provide economic and security benefits to the neighbours (as the definition of a regional hegemon warranted) but intervened militarily to assert hegemony.

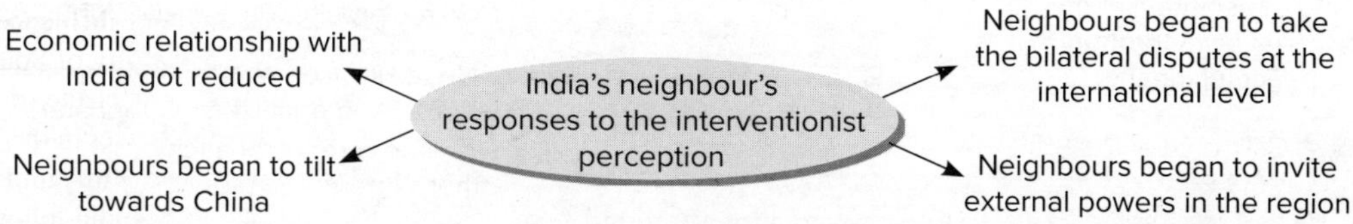

When the Cold War ended, India began to realise that the interventionist approach had become unsustainable. India was visibly upset by this rising anti-Indian sentiment. When P. V. Narsimha Rao became the Prime Minister, he evolved a fresh approach to the neighbourhood policy. He followed a hands-off approach. His idea was that India should not interfere in the functioning of the neighbouring states. If the hands-off policy did not create new tensions, it also did not contribute to reducing old problems. Later the, approach of Rao was carried forward by the then Prime Minister I. K. Gujral. He introduced a proper doctrine for the neighbourhood for the first time and tried to reduce the problems.

I. K. Gujral's foreign policy doctrine was based upon the logic of non-reciprocity and generosity. Under Gujral, India re-evaluated its self-interests and decided to be more generous towards its neighbours. Under the Gujral Doctrine, India's avowed aim was to build goodwill amongst its neighbours instead of leaving space for the development of anti-India sentiments. India, though its non-reciprocity and generosity, wanted to show to the neighbours that there lay a huge economic and political benefit in cooperating with India.

The "Gujral Doctrine" enunciated in September 1996, sought to assert that no South Asian country would allow its territory to be used against the interests of another country of the region; that none would interfere in the internal affairs of another; that all South Asian countries must respect each other's territorial integrity and sovereignty; and that they would settle disputes through peaceful bilateral negotiations. For India specifically, Gujral also declared that it "does not ask for reciprocity but gives all it can in good faith and trust".

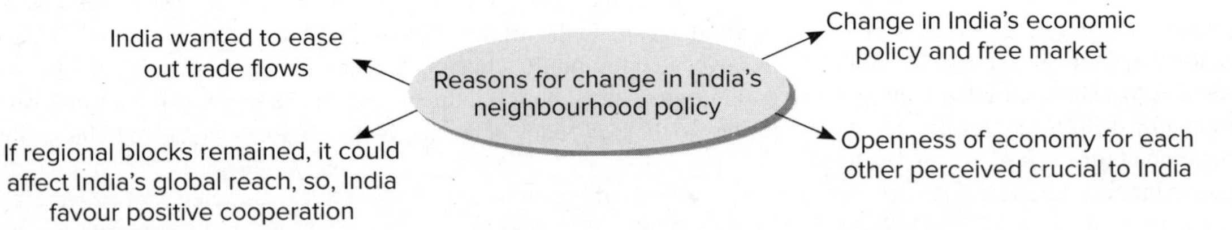

Some scholars in the Indian foreign policy establishment found that the Gujral Doctrine was too idealistic, but the neighbours and the other states appreciated non-reciprocity and generosity. The first missing link in the Gujral Doctrine was that Gujral did not have ample amount of time as the Prime Minister to force the foreign bureaucracy of India to accept the value of cooperation. Moreover, despite advocating openness and generosity, the Gujral Doctrine was reluctant on opening up foreign trade in the region.

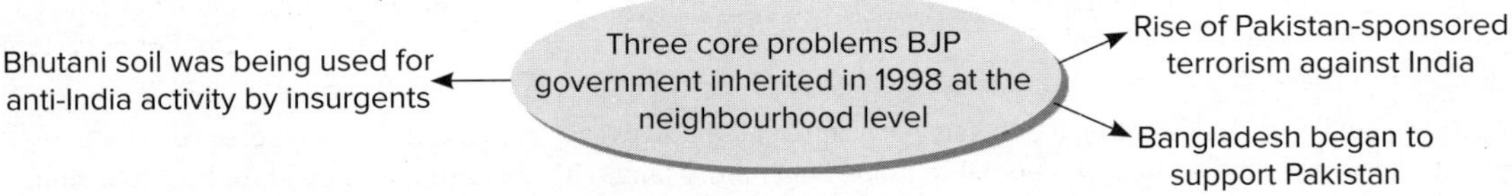

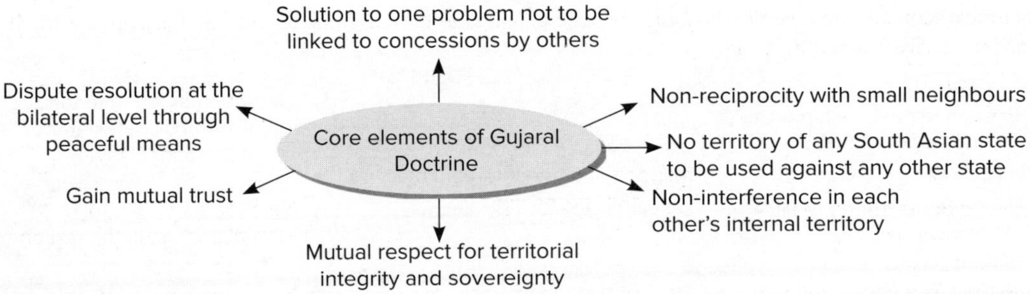

When the Atal Bihari Vajpayee-led Bharatiya Janata Party came to power in 1998, it became busy in managing the fallout of the Pokhran-II test at the global level. As the BJP government began to shift its focus to its neighbours, it decided to use SAARC (South Asian Association for Regional Cooperation) as platform for regional cooperation. The Vajpayee government wanted a kind of South Asian Union by upgrading the SAARC where there was a free trade amongst states and a very small negative list. India had a grand vision of using the South Asian Union under SAARC not only for economic cooperation but also as a political union on the lines of the European Union. However, one reason why the idea failed was that India, under the BJP, insisted on a security guarantee for economic cooperation. However, the government was also not able to achieve much success in using SAARC as a platform due to problems caused by Pakistan.

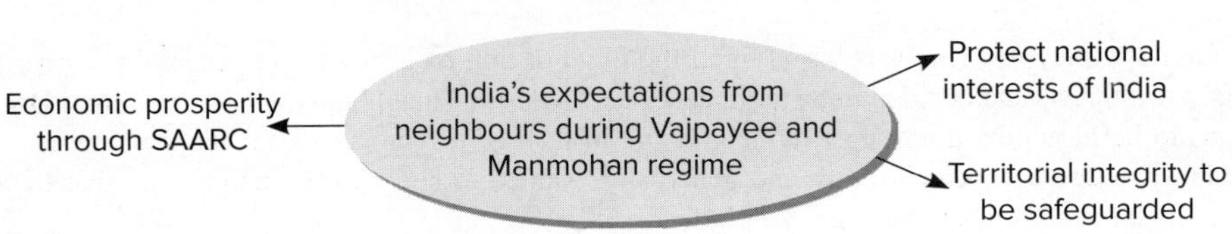

The Manmohan Singh government too tried to use SAARC as a platform to further integration amongst the neighbouring states. The UPA government favoured political dialogue with neighbours. It almost followed all dimensions of the Gujral Doctrine without publicly accepting the same.

INDIA'S NEIGHBOURHOOD FIRST POLICY AND MODI DOCTRINE

India has realised the need to be a leading power in the post-Cold War times, which, many scholars read as India's tendency to behave like a proto-imperialist power. India, according to such scholars, has not been able to enhance its influence in South Asia and has instead been perceived as a second-tier imperialist power by the South Asian states. Since the beginning of the Cold War till the present, the societies of South Asia, instead of working with each other to enhance cooperation at the regional level, have preferred to look towards the North for technology and resources. Because of this, economic interaction and integration of the South Asian region has remained largely neglected. Some scholars assert that India has tried to emerge as the regional hegemon, but this may not be a genuine assessment of India's neighbourhood policies because a regional hegemon provides economic and security benefits to other states while India has not done any such thing in South Asia. It is in this context, to rectify its earlier shortcomings in the neighbourhood policy, that India announced its 'Neighbourhood First' policy in 2014. India now tries to provide those economic and security benefits to the neighbours that range from resources to technology, and is trying to position itself as a Net Security Provider and a Net Development Provider, the core goals of 'Neighbourhood First' policy.

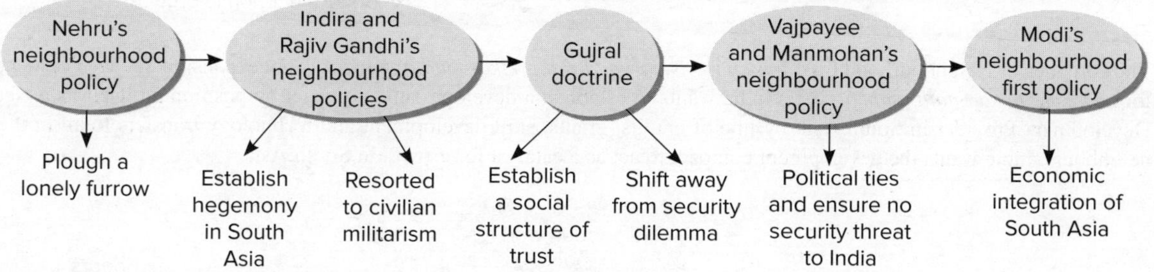

The idea of the neighbourhood first policy is to link India's development to the development of South Asia. In order to realise this vision, a special focus is given to SAARC and the idea is to transform the entire South Asian region into an integrated economic union with enhanced connectivity. The neighbourhood first policy has picked up grains from the Gujral Doctrine without publicly accepting the same. A special thrust is laid upon improving connectivity within South Asia so that all the states in the region can benefit from mutual cooperation leading to shared prosperity for all. India believes that the economic integration can create a conclusive environment for political negotiations to resolve pending disputes (Pakistan remains the slowest camel in the caravan) and end up in stabilising the South Asian region as a whole.

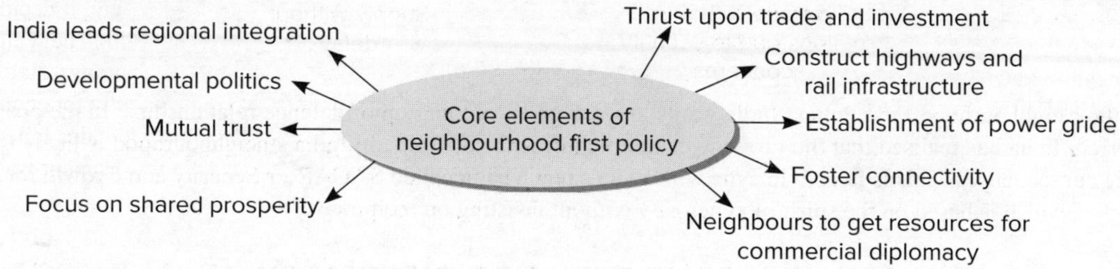

The Indian Space Research Organisation (ISRO) launched the SAARC satellite in May 2017 for India's neighbours so that they would take advantage of telemedicine and e-learning.

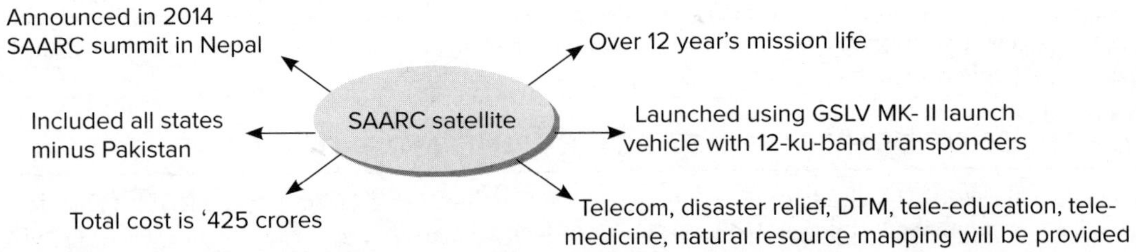

The basic idea of the neighbourhood first policy is that India would shape events in its neighbourhood rather than merely reacting to them. Such an attempt to shape events is in sync with India's quest to play an important role in global affairs. It also signified that India is now willing to shoulder responsibilities in its neighbourhood. India wants to use the neighbourhood first policy to expand India's influence in South Asia through commercial, cultural, connectivity and cooperative diplomacy. The essence of India's new policy is to build up a new geo-economic constituency in the neighbourhood.

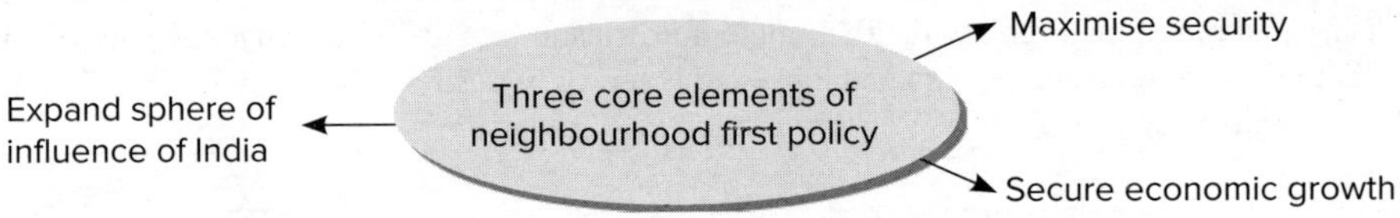

The core idea of Neighbourhood First Policy is *Vistaarvaad Nahi, Vikasvaad* (the focus is not expansion but development for all) and *Sabka Saath, Sabka Vikas*. India wants to establish a developmental compact by positioning itself as a Net Development Provider in South Asia by line of credits, grants, skill development and technology transfers to all in the neighbours. India wants the development compact to act as a catalyst for growth in South Asia.

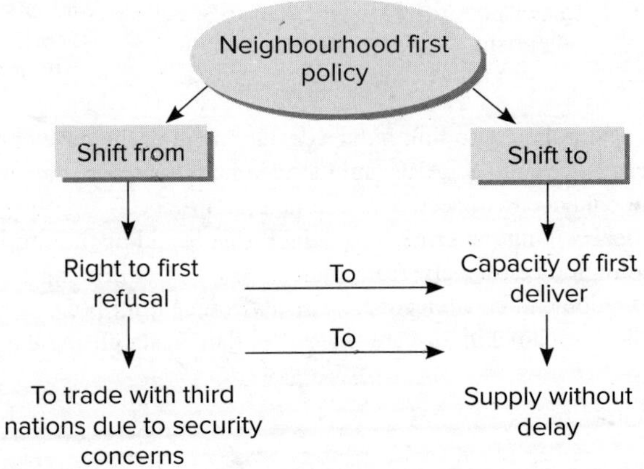

Under the Neighbourhood First Policy, India wants to work upon building up of defence relationships. In the post-Cold War period, India has realised that the growing economic influence of China in India's neighbourhood is likely to have strategic consequences. This is largely in sync with India's new vision called SAGAR or Security and Growth for All in the Region, which is based on the spirit of generosity without insisting on reciprocity.

CONSTRAINTS IN INDIA'S NEIGHBOURHOOD DIPLOMACY

Firstly, inadequate resources create a constraint. Secondly, most of the diplomatic scholars assert that even if India is able to commit projects, it fails to invest proportional diplomatic capital to pursue the projects. Because of this, the projects get delayed and lags are imminent. Thirdly, the strategic diffidence in the strategic culture of India is aggravated due to its insistence on going solo for such engagements. To address such issues, India needs to evolve a multilateral approach based upon global consensus on core challenges. In fact, developing a loose multilateral coalition driven by the strategic objectives and interests of India can help in mitigating the self-imposed unilateral biases we have in engaging with our neighbourhood.

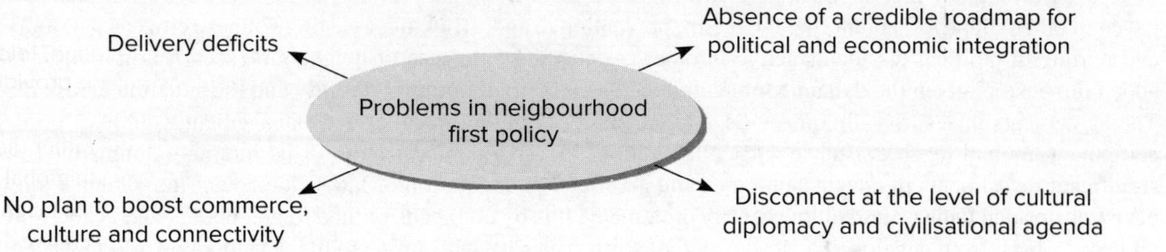

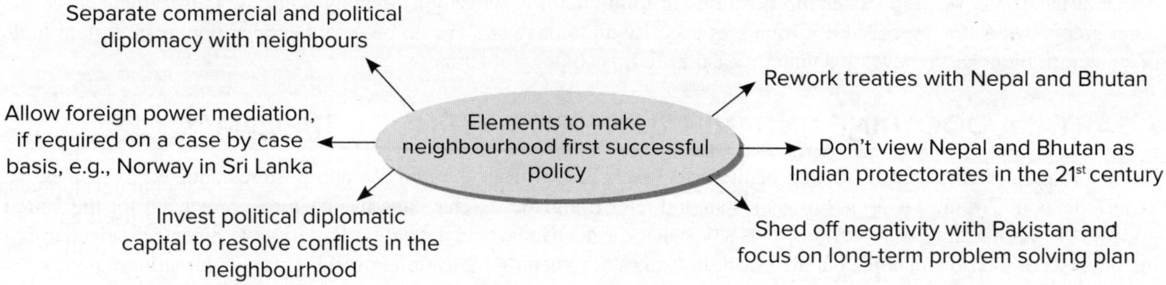

India has to embed deep that it cannot compete with China. China has deep pockets due to which it is able to sponsor massive infrastructure projects. India does not have such material capabilities like China as of now. So, India must focus on identifying the weaknesses of China and make them its strength. For instance, India can play an important role in institution building and soft power. India should open new vistas of two plus one format of cooperation (a minilateral coalition as explained above) and open up Para diplomacy.

INDIAN CITIZENSHIP AMENDMENT ACT AND IMPLICATIONS ON INDIA'S NEIGHBOURS

In 2019, Indian government passed the Citizenship Amendment Act. The act aims to legalise religious discrimination as a basis for citizenship. It aims to amend the definition of illegal immigrants from Afghanistan, Pakistan and Bangladesh for Hindus, Sikhs, Christians, Buddhists and Parsis, who have lived without documentation and aims to provide them fast-track citizenship in six years. The logic of the government is that these groups have faced persecution in Muslim-majority nations and have escaped to India and need protection. The logic is not sound because it does not apply to all neighbours and does not protect all religious minorities. The opinion of the government is that Muslims can seek refuge in Islamic nations while these other groups can seek refuge in India. Such a rationale of the government has caused angst amongst Pakistan, Sri Lanka and Bangladesh. The government has mitigated the concerns through its diplomatic approach that we have explained in the chapters on India and Sri Lanka, India and Bangladesh and India and Pakistan subsequently.

SECURITY DIPLOMACY OF CHINA AND ITS IMPACT ON INDIA'S RELATIONS WITH NEIGHBOURS

In the recent times, China has started undertaking bilateral security cooperation with states in South Asia. By bilateral security cooperation, we are not referring to military and defence exchanges but to the expanding engagement between the police forces, intelligence agencies, border management organisations and law-enforcement authorities of the two nations. Chinese "security diplomacy" is separate from "defence diplomacy". The globalisation and digitalisation of the Chinese economy, the growing movement of people across Chinese borders and expanding capital and human assets beyond borders have made law enforcement cooperation with the rest of the world a major priority for China. The range of issues involved in security diplomacy include tracking down fugitives from Beijing's anti-corruption campaign, criminals seeking safe haven in other countries, countering terrorism, preventing drug trafficking, assisting Chinese citizens and tourists abroad and reining in political dissidents active in other countries. In the case of neighbours, security diplomacy takes on an added dimension, given the dynamic interaction between internal political stability and the situation across the frontiers. The agreements in security diplomacy have touched areas ranging from border management, supply of border security equipment, mutual legal assistance and collaboration. Massive modernisation of its internal administrative structures, significant investments in new technologies and an effective integration of law enforcement into China's foreign policy have transformed China's pursuit of security diplomacy. It is by no means limited to neighbours and is now spread across all geographies, from developed countries in the North America and Europe to the developing world in Asia and Africa. China is also participating in the development of new international rules on law enforcement, shaping the discourse on issues at hand, and seeking leadership positions in multilateral organisations dealing with law enforcement. Like the other great powers that preceded it, China sees security diplomacy and law enforcement cooperation as important tools of statecraft. India has to develop counter measures to this strategy of Chinese.

AGARTALA DOCTRINE AND INDIAN NEIGHBOURHOOD DIPLOMACY

The Agartala Doctrine is a distillation of the principles derived from the policies and postures adopted by successive governments in Tripura vis-à-vis East Pakistan and later Bangladesh. The same has been recommended for the Union government's consideration. According to its advocates, the doctrine would not only help state governments in safeguarding the interests of their own people but also work towards strengthening the Union government's neighbourhood policy.

The three most basic components of the doctrine are: (a) states should have a greater say in foreign policy matters involving neighbours so that their core interests are protected; (b) states should act as responsible stake holders and not as spoilers seeking narrow domestic electoral gains; and (c) states should take the initiative to improve relations with neighbouring countries while keeping in mind the broader national interest. The conception of the doctrine, which emerged from the deliberations at the first Tripura Conclave, held in Agartala in July 2014. In essence, this doctrine highlights Tripura's seemingly "appropriate, proactive and befitting response" to challenges arising from East Pakistan/Bangladesh with a view to protect its own core security and economic interests.

CHAPTER 2

India's Relationship with Bhutan

HISTORICAL BACKGROUND OF INDIA AND BHUTAN

The ancient kingdom of Bhutan was originally the State of Monyul. The traditional name of Bhutan is Drukyul, that is, the country of Drukpas or the 'land of thunder dragons'. India's relations with Bhutan go back to 747 AD when a Buddhist monk Padmasambhava went from India to Bhutan and led the Nyingmapa sect of Buddhism. Thus, India contributed to the cultural growth of Buddhism in Bhutan. In the modern times, there were Anglo-Bhutan wars and Bhutan became a part of British Empire. In 1910, as per the Treaty of Punakha, between China–Tibet and Bhutan, Bhutan was not officially annexed but the legal status of Bhutan remained undefined during the period of the British. Bhutan also preferred India to China as, in 1949, when China took over Tibet, it did create tensions and fears of annexation in Bhutan. In fact, in 1949, China snatched away some villages of Bhutan on the China–Bhutan border. This upset Bhutan to the extent that they decided not to have diplomatic relations with the Chinese. In 2014, after the swearing in of the new government, the thrust towards neighbourhood first policy saw the Indian Prime Minister, Narendra Modi, visiting Bhutan. During his visit, the Prime Minister inaugurated the Supreme Court building in Bhutan, made with Indian assistance. He addressed a joint session of the Bhutanese Parliament. Normally, the people of Bhutan do not use clapping as a congratulatory gesture as they find clapping inauspicious and evil. However, when the Prime Minister delivered a speech, the Bhutanese legislators in the house clapped to him.

INDIA AND BHUTAN TREATY OF FRIENDSHIP AND TREATY-RELATED ISSUES

When India became independent in 1947, Nehru went on a horseback to Bhutan to build relations and advised King J. D. Wangchuk to build relations with India. In 1949, India and Bhutan concluded a Treaty of Friendship. The treaty discussed peace, trade, commerce and equal justice between India and Bhutan, which became the bedrock of India and Bhutan relationship. India in 1971 took up the matter of the UN membership for Bhutan and succeeded in making Bhutan a member of the UN.

As per the Treaty of Friendship in 1949, India and Bhutan agreed to extend national treatment to the citizens of each other's states. As per the precepts of national treatment, Indian citizens have same right for employment in Bhutan as Bhutanese nationals do in India. Under the treaty, India and Bhutan have agreed to have an open border. Under the open border system, citizens of India and Bhutan have a right to move into each other's territory without a visa. However, to preserve the fragile environment of the state, Bhutan from 2020 has imposed a visa fees on tourist travels. The treaty has a special mention of a clause of extradition. In the treaty, as per Article 2, India accepted the sovereign and independent status of Bhutan but advised that Bhutan, in matters of external affairs, seek assistance from India. In 2007, Bhutan raised the issue of Article 2 with India and advocated the modification of Article 2. India, immediately agreeing to revise the treaty, modified Article 2 in the treaty. Under the revised treaty of 2007, India and Bhutan would cooperate with each other on matters of 'national security'. This instilled confidence in Bhutan about its broad relations with India and made an impression that India is a partner in Bhutani progress. India recognises the sovereignty, independence and territorial integrity of Bhutan. The treaty also talks about cultural cooperation, sports development, cooperation in science and technology and healthcare.

INDIA AND BHUTAN COMMERCIAL DIPLOMACY

The origin of commercial diplomacy goes back to 1961 when India began to provide assistance to the First and the Second Five-Year Plans of Bhutan. In 1971, when Bhutan became a UN member, the external aid it received got diversified as other nations in the world began to contribute. Bhutan has 80% of its trade with India and it majorly happens through the Kolkata port. There is a Phuentsholing to Paro road that facilitates Indo-Bhutan trade. Indian banks, such as the State Bank of India and Bank of Baroda, have presence in Bhutan. Indian firms are undertaking work related to hydroelectric power, minerals exploration and construction in Bhutan. India imports from Bhutan, minerals, hydropower, wood and chemicals while it exports machinery and food products. The trade is governed by the Agreement on Trade and Commerce, 2006, which also provides for duty free trade and use of territory for third-country transit.

INDIA AND BHUTAN DEVELOPMENT PARTNERSHIP

India and Bhutan also have a developmental partnership and India has assisted Bhutan in development administration, as can be seen in three phases. In the first phase, from 1960 to 1980, initially, India provided support for physical infrastructure creation. The second phase, from 1980 to 2000, was a period when Bhutan explored the dimension of a transition to democracy. During this period, India provided assistance for development of democratic values and provided capacity support for decentralisation. In this period, institutional sharing of the best democratic and decentralisation-related practices were encouraged for exchange. The third phase, which is ongoing from 2000 till present, is where Indian developmental assistance has been diversified. Today, the assistance ranges from hydroelectricity generation to IT services including support in education and skill development.

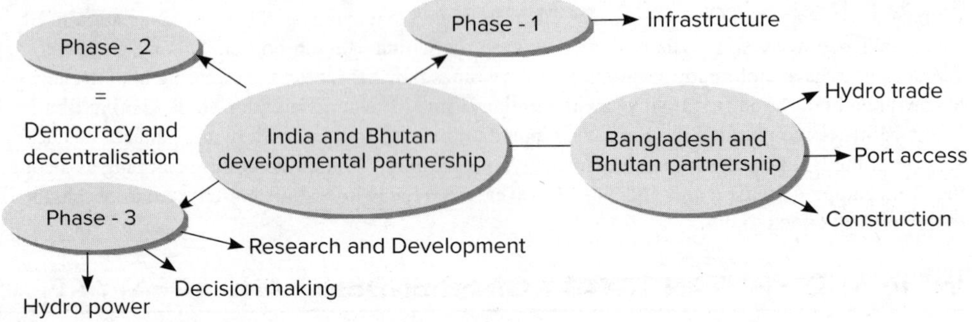

INDIA AND BHUTAN RELATIONS DURING PANDEMIC

> **Ahlay Trade Route**
>
> Ahlay is located in Pasakha Industrial Estate of Bhutan and is a hub of industrial activities. This route is an alternative to Jaigaon–Phuentsholing route. When Bhutan decided to seal international borders owing to the pandemic, This route has been used to seek international aid.

It is often stated that difficult times are true reminiscent of true character of the relationships of two countries. The pandemic has unfolded multitude challenges for the globe but India and Bhutan have exhibited robust ties during pandemic. The wisdom of the monarchs of Bhutan, the Neighborhood First policy of India and a win-win partnership throughout the historical past have sustained the 'special ties' between India and Bhutan. When the pandemic affected the world in March 2020, the Bhutanese decided to seal their international border. India decided, based on the core tenet of Neighborhood First policy of being responsive to the needs of the neighborhood, to supply Bhutan with essential supplies, medicines and Covid-19 toolkits. India also opened a new trade route through Ahlay and issued a notification to allow import of potatoes grown by farmers of Bhutan, who were distressed as they did not have a market to sell as the pandemic shut down tourism. The two sides are working closely to ensure that they both tide away the pandemic by being on the side of each other.

BHUTAN AND BANGLADESH RELATIONS AND IMPACT ON INDIA AND BHUTAN

A comparison with Bangladesh–Bhutan trade is warranted at this stage. The relationship between Bhutan and Bangladesh is at three levels viz., trade, culture and environment. Bangladesh is very keen on purchasing power from Bhutan and allows Bhutan to use their seaports for third-country trade. A lot of Bangladeshi workers have been significantly present in Bhutanese construction companies. This also upset Bhutan because this deprives their local people of job opportunities, as most of the Bhutanese construction companies prefer to recruit the cheap labour from Bangladesh.

INDIA AND BHUTAN HYDROPOWER DIPLOMACY

Bhutan is a Himalayan state with tremendous hydropower potential. It is an upper riparian state where rivers originate. Bhutan exports around 45% of its hydropower to India. Surprisingly, the electricity generation in Bhutan was developed in 1960s with Indian assistance itself. India in the 1960s had provided Bhutan with diesel sets, which helped in providing electricity in towns. During this period, Bhutan lacked capacity to generate electricity and in 1967 Bhutan began to replace Indian diesel sets with import of electricity from Jaldakha plant in Bengal. In 1989, India helped Bhutan with the establishment of a 33-megawatt electricity plant in Chukha.

It is only in the 1980s that, with Indian assistance, Bhutan realised the potential of hydropower. Bhutan also became convinced that hydropower generation is safe and is environment-friendly. Bhutan realised that if it succeeds in developing hydropower, it can also emerge as a net exporter of the same which can eventually help Bhutan generate foreign exchange. They began to seek Indian assistance, which can be broadly seen in two phases.

Phase 1—1987 to 2007 In this initial phase, India helped Bhutan in the establishment of specific site-based plants at Chukha, Kurichu and Tala. India provided monetary assistance in the form of 60% grant and 40% loan for these projects. Meanwhile, India domestically worked to establish grid infrastructure in its territory. As these plants became operational, they supplied electricity to India and this electricity from Bhutan fed the Northern and North Eastern power grid in India.

Phase 2—2007 to 2020 In this phase, India has committed to undertake creation of mega hydro plants in India primarily to harness the targeted 10,000 megawatt electricity by 2020.

Over a period of time, due to the existence of hydro diplomacy between India and Bhutan, some issues have erupted on both sides. The Indian side witnessed massive flooding in the downstream state of Assam in 2014. Bhutan alleges today that due to hydro cooperation with India, there is a dominance of Indian firms in Bhutan. It feels that an overwhelming presence of Indian firms in Bhutan has restricted the space of growth for the Bhutanese corporate sector. Moreover, Bhutan feels that the Indian firms end up recruiting cheap Bangladeshi labour, as a result of which Bhutanese do not stand to benefit from the hydro diplomacy. To pacify fears of Bhutan related to dominance of Indian firms in hydropower sector, the Indian Prime Minister has agreed to establish a Power Training Institute in Bhutan to provide its youth skilled training to ensure they contribute to the Bhutanese workforce. The hydropower generation of Bhutan is basically seasonal in nature. In the recent times, domestic consumption of power in Bhutan is on the rise. In the winter season, Bhutan imports electricity from India while in summers it exports electricity to us. To address the problem, India has agreed to establish a power bank in Bhutan in future. The Prime Minister also laid a foundation for a 600 megawatt Kholongchu Hydroelectric power plant in 2014.

INDIA AND BHUTAN DEFENCE AND SECURITY DIPLOMACY

Since the 1962 Sino-Indian conflict, India has been focusing on forward access to the upper reaches of Himalayas to keep an eye on China. In this respect, Bhutan becomes strategically significant from the Indian point of view. India has strategic presence in Bhutan. Bhutan, due to its border skirmishes, does not have a diplomatic relation with China. An absence of diplomatic relation with China enhances India's chance to exercise its sphere of influence in Bhutan. India has established the IMTRAT, that is, the Indian Military Training Team unit, in Haa district of Bhutan. Under a bilateral agreement, India also provides training to army officers of Bhutan in India. The Border Roads Organisation has, since 1961, run Project Dantak. Under this project, the BRO provides for roads construction, telecom works, colleges, schools and other infrastructure. Under the project, there have been notable achievements too.

CHINA FACTOR IN INDIA AND BHUTAN RELATIONS AND CHUMBI VALLEY ISSUE

Chumbi valley is a tri-junction between Bhutan, India and China. It is close to the chicken's neck (the Siliguri corridor) and a gateway to India's northeast. Chumbi valley holds significance for China as it connects Tibet and Sikkim and China wants to expand its manoeuvres here. The Bhutan–China border problem began in 1950 when China published a map and claimed the West Bhutan area. This map also included Chinese claims on North Bhutan. China and Bhutan began negotiations on border issue in 1984. China, in West Bhutan, claims Doklam, Charithang, Sinchulimpa and Dramana pastures. This brings China close to Chumbi Valley, between Sikkim and Bhutan. The Chumbi Valley has one artery running from the Tibetan city of Shigaste to Yatung. By claiming area in West Bhutan, China can widen its land and in the eventuality of war, it can have more space on their side as otherwise, the size of Chumbi Valley is less for the stationing of any number of troops. For India, any such claim is dangerous as Chumbi Valley is barely 500 km from the Siliguri corridor, which is a narrow strip of Indian Territory connecting the Indian northeast to the rest of India.

Even in the recent times, the border issue between Bhutan and China has not been resolved and China has undertaken tremendous intrusions into the border areas around Bhutan. These intrusions deprive the people of Bhutan of forest produce and create uncertainty about their resources and livelihood. Since 2012, China has begun to engage in cultural and religious diplomacy with Bhutan. China has gifted the tallest statue of Buddha in Bhutan, in Thimpu. It is investing in the telecom sector of Bhutan as well. There is rising tourism between Bhutan and China and a lot of Chinese tourists have been visiting Bhutan in the recent times.

BHUTANESE PERCEPTION OF INDIA AND KEY LESSONS TO MATERIALISE BHARAT TO BHUTAN VISION

Why does Bhutan want to go digital?

Bhutan wants to reduce its dependency on hydropower due to its lack of sustainability in the long run. Being armed with a youthful population, digital and IT and IT-Enabled Services is a natural choice for Bhutan. With India being a global leader in IT, it becomes a natural 'pull' factor for the two nations to explore in the future and India will be able to realise the Bharat to Bhutan Vision.

Today, Bhutan has 60% of its population as youth. The youth of Bhutan is the key driver of the destiny of the nation. It is imperative for India to understand the pulse of this youth because they will be the determinant of how India and Bhutan will shape the narrative. While the older generation people of Bhutan have appreciated India for the role India played in security, economic development and infrastructure building in Bhutan, the same is not the feelings of the youth. There is a growing disenchantment in the youth on over reliance on India and they feel that Bhutan seems to be 'dependent' on India. Today, there is 10.6% unemployment and high external debt in Bhutan, which has compelled the youth to question the 'loans and grants' model. The youth today favours 'investments' over 'aid' and want the leadership of their nation to adopt an open door policy because some segments of youth believe that India is hampering the development of relations of Bhutan with other states. By skillfully using non-diplomatic levers, Chinese are trying to position themselves amongst the youth as new job, revenue and growth creator. It is at this juncture that India needs to re-orient the relationship with Bhutan and enter the digital and space domains and fulfil the aspirations of the youth.

CHAPTER 3

India's Relationship with Afghanistan

THE EMOTIONAL AND HISTORICAL BOND BETWEEN INDIA AND AFGHANISTAN

The relation of India with Afghanistan is a mixture of an emotional and historical bond. The emotional bond is because of Rabindranath Tagore's famous Kabuliwalla (a short story). The generations of people in India are still aware of those old Afghans who used to settle down as Kabuliwallas. Historically, the relations between the two go back to the Indus Valley Civilisation. Afghanistan has been noted in empires of Maurya, Asoka, Kushans and Indo-Scythians. The medieval period's Grant Trunk road captures the depth historically. The British fought the Anglo-Afghan wars. They tried to keep Afghanistan as a buffer between India and Russia. Modern India and Afghanistan relations are traced back to India and Afghanistan Treaty of Friendship in 1950. The treaty laid down the foundation of diplomatic ties and enabled the foundational relationship in culture and trade. During the World War II, an agreement was signed between the British India and Afghanistan. As per the 1945 agreement, British India would supply arms and train the Afghan soldiers. After Indian independence, India asserted that it can continue to train Afghan soldiers but it will not go ahead with arms supply, as it would contradict India's non-alignment credentials and its quest for international peace. Afghanistan was an important participant in the Bandung Conference. Both India and Afghanistan used the non-alignment as a platform to criticise states (namely Pakistan) that had joined military alliances such as CENTO and SEATO.

THE EVOLUTION OF INDIA AND AFGHAN RELATIONS IN THE COLD WAR AND CHANGING POLICY CONTOURS

In the initial years, Afghanistan continued to favour Pakistan. Afghanistan had a reason for this. It is important to note that the British created Durand Line in 1893. This line artificially divided Pakistan and Afghanistan. This line has never been accepted by Afghanistan as a border (even till today) as Afghanistan has asserted that the line has artificially divided the families on both sides of the boundary. Afghanistan still claims the Baluchistan, Khyber Pakhtunkhwa (KP) region, both of which have been forcibly acquired by Pakistan. The Afghanistan government thought that by siding Pakistan and not upsetting it, Afghanistan could seek a solution for Baluchistan and North West Frontier Province (NWFP). The 1965 India and Pakistan war was a testing time for India and Afghanistan relations. In 1965 war, Pakistan attacked India by launching Operation Gibraltar and Operation Grand Slam. Through them, Pakistan tried to create an anti-India uprising in Kashmir. Pakistan thought that they would incite Indian Kashmiri people and once they revolt against India, Pakistan would send its army to support them and militarily snatch away Kashmir from India. As the war began, India used its military power and gave a befitting response to Pakistan and eventually defeated Pakistan. At the UN, Pakistan subsequently raised the idea that India is suppressing the people of Kashmir and is not giving Right To Self-Determination (RTSD) for Kashmiri people. India countered the Pakistani narrative by raising the RTSD denied by Pakistan for the people of KP, Baluchistan and East Pakistan. This Indian narrative was not perceived well by Afghanistan as they claimed the area of KP and Baluchistan. Afghanistan thought that the India raising the RTSD for KP and Baluchistan contradicts the Afghan claims. After Indo-Pakistan war 1965, India publicly supported Pashtun nationalism in KP and Baluchistan.

In return, Afghanistan began to support Pakistan. Thus, the bilateral ties got affected. But, when Afghanistan saw that the entire international public opinion was against Pakistan for their initiation of 1965 war, Afghanistan immediately did a U-turn and started asserting the RTSD for Baloch and Pashtuns in KP. The Afghans thought that their support to Pakistan in 1965 war with India would compel Pakistan to go for revisionism and peacefully handover the disputed territories to Afghanistan. This did not happen. In the late 1960s, West Pakistan began to suppress the Bengali Muslims in East Pakistan. Afghanistan became very concerned about the fate of its own ethnic community in KP and Baluchistan in Pakistan. After creating Bangladesh in 1971, India covertly supported Baluchistan people and ensured the victory of a pro-India aggressive and a nationalist party in Baluchistan. This led to massive suppression of the Baloch people by the regime of Pakistan. This Pakistani suppression of Baloch and Pashtun people in 1974 led to the birth of a new resistance group called Baloch Peoples Liberation Front (BPLF). The BPLF began to target Pakistani establishment. Pakistan army began to suppress the BPLF. This led the BPLF to shift their cadres from Pakistan to Afghanistan. Throughout 1970s, Afghanistan tilted to the USSR. This was similar to the tilt by India. This enabled both India and Afghanistan to use the USSR as a shield to balance Pakistan. In 1968, Research and Analysis Wing (RAW) was created. A secret alliance was established between RAW, KHAD (Khadamat-e Aetla'at-e Dawlati, the intelligence agency of Afghanistan) and KGB (Komitet Gosudarstvennoy Bezopasnosti, the intelligence agency of USSR). Indian RAW began to provide BPLF with arms, ammunition and money to fight Pakistan. In 1973, in a bloodless coup, the Afghan king Zahir Shah was removed and Mohammad Doud Khan acquired power. He was very aggressive towards Pakistan and wanted a military solution to the KP and Baluchistan issue. Even though India was appreciative of Doud Khan's policy, but it feared the Balkanisation of Pakistan, if Doud succeeded in the military solution. As Doud began to initiate a covert war on Pakistan for KP and Baluchistan issue, two things happened. Firstly, the US lifted the arms embargo on Pakistan and supplied them with arms. Secondly, ISI started supporting the opponents of Doud in Afghanistan. This led the ISI to create an organisation called Jamat-e-Islami (JEI), which consisted of Ahmed Shah Masood, Burhanuddin Rabbani and Gulubuddin Hikmatyar. In 1975, the JEI, with the support of the ISI, attempted a coup against Doud. The coup failed. This led to a split in the JEI. Hekmatyar and another Qazi Mohammad Amin Waqad came out and formed Hizb-E-Islami Afghan.

INDIA'S AFGHAN POLICY AFTER SOVIET INVASION, 1979

In 1978, there was a coup again in Afghanistan and this created a massive political crisis in Afghanistan, which only ended with the Soviet invasion in 1979. The Soviet began to think that as Pakistan is behind these multiple coups in Afghanistan, the US might use Pakistan to expand influence in Afghanistan. Thus, to prevent the US to gain advantage in Afghanistan, the Soviet invaded it and installed their own puppet government. The Soviet installed a government led by Babrak Kramal. In 1985, Babrak Karmal was replaced by the Soviet in Afghanistan and they installed another puppet ruler named Najibullah. When Soviet invaded Afghanistan, India had a caretaker government led by Charan Singh. The government criticised the Soviet invasion. In 1980, Indira Gandhi came to power. She initiated a new strategy. She decided to credibly offer a pro-USSR stand on Afghanistan. This happened because the US, Saudi and Pakistan began to initiate a Mujahedeen campaign to counter the Soviets in Afghanistan. The strategy of the US was simple. They would use Pakistan and Saudi to radicalise the Afghani people and use them in a jihad against the Soviet in Afghanistan. In 1979, Pakistan began to mobilise Afghani people and brought them to Pakistan. Saudi sent their religious clerics to Pakistan and they launched a narrative amongst the Afghani people in Pakistan that Soviet has invaded Afghanistan to eliminate Islam, thus, Islam is in danger in Afghanistan. This Saudi narrative frustrated and alienated the Afghani people and they wanted to do something to protect their religion. As a solution, Pakistan suggested the need to wage a jihad against Soviet and Saudi also supported the jihad. This motivated the alienated Afghani people to pick up arms and resist the Soviet. This is where the Americans stepped in and supported these Afghani people by giving them arms, ammunition and money. Saudi Arabia radicalised the Afghani people while Pakistan trained them in violence and the Americans gave them the support for the Jihad. Thus, in 1979, Afghani people launched the Jihad against Russia in Afghanistan. To make the Jihad more virulent and stronger the Americans also falsely promised the Mujahedeen that once they succeed in removing Soviet from Afghanistan, the US would help the Mujahedeen to acquire power in Afghanistan and if the Afghani people have their own government in Afghanistan, they can also safeguard their religion in Afghanistan. This motivated the Mujahedeen to fight more aggressively.

INDIA'S RELATIONSHIP WITH MUJAHEDEEN FIGHTERS AND EARLY TALIBS IN AFGHANISTAN

Indira Gandhi revived the RAW–KHAD and KGB axis to covertly establish links with the Mujahedeen in Afghanistan. The Indian support to the Soviet in Afghanistan alienated India from the aspirations of the Afghan people. This also alienated Indian Muslims and gave CIA and ISI an opportunity to incite troubles in India. Indira Gandhi's decision of not respecting the sovereignty of the people of Afghanistan was criticised domestically. It was believed that India had compromised its non-alignment credentials by not respecting the sovereignty of the people. A common statement was that India's non-alignment was not genuine and tilted like the leaning tower of Pisa. This policy of Indira Gandhi fractured India's long-term approach and created a crevasse in seeking 'friends'. Since the debacle of Indira Gandhi, India's policy in Afghanistan has been to search for 'friends' in Afghanistan who would sympathise with the national interests of India. However, one question always haunted Indira Gandhi. It was, what if Soviets withdrew from Afghanistan? Her fear was that if this happens, it will strengthen the US–Pakistan axis and leave India in out in the cold. To bring back India as a credible player on the scene again and to mitigate India's fears, Rajiv Gandhi brought about the shift in Indian policy on Afghanistan. He adopted the policy of peaceful equilibrium with Pakistan, which on the face was peaceful but he covertly activated RAW to create havoc in Pakistan. The RAW created the Counter-Insurgency Team-X which planted bombs across different cities of Pakistan. The objective was to destabilise Pakistan and make their attempts to sponsor terrorism in Punjab costlier. He also launched a Grand dialogue to engage with America and Russia. In 1980s, Russia was looking for options to exit Afghanistan. India asserted that if Russia leaves Afghanistan and then there has to be an independent and non-aligned government in Afghanistan. Russia thought that India wants to free ride the Russians and wants to use the Russian withdrawal to assert its own hegemony in South Asian. This caused a fracture between the relationship of Russia and India. Russia in return began to court Pakistan. When India communicated its concerns to the US, the US too rejected the demand of India for a non-aligned government in Afghanistan that would be favourable to India. As the USSR and the US sidelined India, the RAW began to court Zahir Shah. He was living in Rome. Teams of RAW operatives from Geneva were dispatched to deal with Zahir Shah and other exiles. The RAW wanted to play the Zahir Shah card before the USSR withdrawal from Afghanistan. Indian RAW hoped of bringing Zahir Shah back to Afghanistan and this upset the US, the USSR and Pakistan. Thus, at the insistence of Pakistan, India was not allowed to take part in the Geneva Accord, 1987 (signed by Americans, Soviets and Pakistanis seeking the Soviet withdrawal from Afghanistan) even as an observer state. The Zahir Shah episode proved that India punched much above its weight and this was the reason for it being sidelined at the Geneva Accord. The Zahir Shah gambit of India failed. India was unable to contemplate a post-Najibullah scenario.

INDIA'S AFGHAN POLICY AFTER THE END OF THE COLD WAR

Despite covert links of RAW with the Mujahedeens, India was not able to build concrete links with them for post-Soviet withdrawal. From 1988, Soviet began to initiate their withdrawal. The Mujahedeen perceived this as a victory against 'evil' Russia that had threatened Islam. The Mujahedeen now told the Americans to assist them to acquire power as they had promised. But the Americans too retreated from Afghanistan. The US never had any genuine motive to assist the Mujahedeen to acquire power, as they only wanted to use the Afghani people to resist and remove Soviet. The US succeeded in achieving their objectives. This angered the Mujahedeen. One group of them wanted to take revenge against the US for using them. They came together and formed an extremist group called Al Qaeda in 1988 and Abdullah Azam and Osama Bin Laden-led Al-Qaeda. The Al-Qaeda began to use the territory of Afghanistan to train extremists for seeking revenge against the US. The other group of Mujahedeen favoured a political solution and was not interested in seeking revenge against the US. They took support of Pakistan to form a government. After the Soviet left Afghanistan finally in1989, Najibullah continued till 1992 while the other group of Mujahedeen sought support of Pakistan to form a government. In 1992, Mujahedeens, with support of Pakistan, eventually replaced Najibullah. The US too provided the needed legitimacy to the Afghan Mujahedeen government and asserted that they fulfilled their old promise.

INDIA'S DIPLOMATIC RECOGNITION OF MUJAHEDEEN GOVERNMENT UNDER PESHAWAR ACCORDS

In 1992, India was compelled to recognise the Mujahedeen government. Pakistan played a very crucial role in brokering the Peshawar Accord (which brought the Mujahedeen to power in Afghanistan) in 1992. India led by Narsimha Rao as the Prime Minister initiated a new policy for Afghanistan. He asserted that India would engage with the Mujahedeens. India would not distinguish whether the Mujahedeen is a Wahhabi or he is supported by Pakistan. It would engage with all factions in Afghanistan. It would maintain people to people ties in Afghanistan and focus on the reconstruction of Afghanistan. In 1992, the Indian government recognised the government of Mujahedeen, which was then led by Burhanuddin Rabbani.

EVOLUTION IN INDIA'S AFGHAN POLICY NULLIFYING THE ISI'S K-2 PROGRAMME IN KASHMIR

Thus, India adopted a conciliatory approach. There were many reasons for the shift in the Indian policy. Firstly, during the era of Indira Gandhi and Rajiv Gandhi, even though India supported Najibullah, but now, as per the changed ground realities, Najibullah too accepted the Mujahedeen government. In 1991, Najibullah changed the name of the communist party (called PDPA in the Cold War) to Hizb-E-Watan Party. The new party was symbolically Islamic now. As the international community too accepted the new Afghan realities, so did India. Secondly, even though India favoured the government of Najibullah (also called as 'Najib Model' in the corridors of RAW), but it failed due to the rise of Mujahedeens. India also had concerns regarding Indian diaspora in Afghanistan; thereby, India agreed to support Mujahedeen government. Thirdly, India realised that as Pakistan was heavily supporting the Mujahedeens; allowing Pakistan and Afghanistan to strengthen at the cost of India would end up in undermining India's interests. India did not look at Afghanistan from the context of South Asia only but the larger context of geopolitical significance of Central Asia, which had resources that India sought via Afghanistan. Fourthly, not engaging with the Mujahedeen's would give ISI the leverage to exploit fertile ground of Afghanistan to wage a jihad against India in Kashmir. The RAW was able to identify that HEI did train a few Kashmiri Muslims. JEI was anyway sympathetic to the Kashmiri cause, but the RAW, through their intelligence network spanning Afghanistan to Kashmir, ensured that they did not end up in supporting the cause of ISI-sponsored terrorism in Kashmir. The Afghan Mujahedeens were also never interested in meddling in between the rivalry of India and Pakistan. Thus, to prevent the micromanagement of Mujahedeen government by Pakistan, the Mujahedeen too balanced Pakistan by favouring a dialogue with India. Even though Pakistan tried to micromanage Mujahedeen government, it failed to understand that there were serious intra-Mujahedeen differences. India, on the other hand, played well between Rabbani, Ahmed Shah Masood and Hekmatyar, to safeguard its own interests. However, the internal differences descended Afghanistan into a civil war in 1992. ISI was also alarmed to see the growing proximity of India and the role of RAW in supporting the Mujahedeen government. This is why at the end of the Cold War; ISI of Pakistan initiated the K-2 programme. It was the brainchild of Brigadier Imtiaz of ISI and Brigadier Badam of ISI. They began to infiltrate in Afghanistan to search for Kashmiri looking Afghan Pashtuns, train them and send them to Kashmir. This strategy was deliberately followed by the ISI to break India's ties with Mujahedeen government. This was so because if the Kashmiri looking Afghan Pashtuns begin to carry out attacks in Kashmir, then India would think that Afghan Mujahedeen government is supporting Kashmir Jihad. This would create acrimony between India and Afghanistan and give Pakistan leverage in Afghanistan. The RAW was able to counter-infiltrate K-2 and weakened it from within by assassinating ISI officers involved in the programme. The influence of Pakistan outweighed India amongst the Mujahedeen government.

INDIA'S RELATIONSHIP WITH TALIBAN FROM 1996 TO 2001

As Afghanistan descended into a civil war after the breakdown of Mujahedeen government, Pakistan realised that it would find it difficult to bring these Mujahedeen together again in the future. So, from 1994 to 1996, Pakistan began to knit together the radicalised educated students to come together to establish a group to provide leadership to their country. This group was called Taliban. Taliban comes from the first few letters of the word called TALIB, which means educated students. In 1996, ISI was able to successfully bring the Taliban to power in Afghanistan. To counter Taliban, India along with Russia and Iran began to support the United Islamic Front for the Salvation of Afghanistan or Northern Alliance (a group of Pashtuns, Tajiks, Uzbeks and Hazaras). The Taliban, led by Mullah Omar, removed Rabbani from power and Rabbani then became a part of Northern Alliance. Taliban killed Najibullah in public display. His death sent shock waves down the spine of the entire world. The Al-Qaeda found an ally in Taliban. The Al-Qaeda provided the needed legitimacy for Taliban to unleash a Sharia rule in Afghanistan and Taliban provided Al-Qaeda a breeding sanctuary of people in Afghanistan to radicalise and seek revenge against the US.

INDIAN PM, MULLAH MUTTAWAKIL OF TALIBAN AND INDIA'S TALIBAN POLICY

In 1997, Taliban sent a direct feeler to India. In a secretly arranged and covert meeting of an Indian RAW officer in Indian embassy in Afghanistan, with Mullah Omar, he conveyed to him that if India is willing to stop its engagement with Rabbani and help Taliban, then Taliban is willing to engage with India. One Indian RAW officer in Indian embassy in Afghanistan had a covert meeting with 'Mullah Muttawakil', the Foreign Minister of Taliban and he communicated to the RAW officer that India should stop engaging with Rabbani, Northern Alliance and halt its policy of interfering in the internal affairs of Afghanistan. Doing so, as per Mullah Muttawakil would create a condition for negotiation with the Taliban for India. On the basis of the inputs from the ground intelligence, hectic meetings were organised between RAW Chief, Indian Military Intelligence Chief, Indian Chief of the Army Staff, Director of Intelligence Bureau, Research Secretary and Indian Prime Minister. The above officials did a very deep analysis of Taliban. A senior RAW officer who met Mullah Muttawakil, met the Indian Prime Minister and informed him of her ground analysis. She informed the Prime Minister that Taliban is a Pashtun movement. Most of its members are Pashtun tribals from rural areas. Taliban, wanted to seek international recognition, for which they sought India's support. This was because that Taliban was not sure as to how much time will it be in power and how much control would it be able to yield over non-Pashtun in Afghanistan. More importantly, she told the Prime Minister that, contrary to the narrative, a massive segment of Taliban is not pro-Pakistan. Prime Minister was informed that Pakistan and Taliban have very serious differences on Durand Line issue, Khyber-Pakhtunkhwa and Baluchistan issues. The Prime Minister was informed in 1999 that India should seriously consider giving Taliban the political recognition if not diplomatic recognition. However, the MEA (Ministry of External Affairs) bureaucracy overpowered the RAW and MEA mandarins told the Prime Minister that Taliban is a creation of ISI and thus, India should have no business with Taliban. The MEA told the Prime Minister that any recognition to Taliban would only be a certificate to them to do Jihad. The MEA said that Taliban is an extremist group that is designed by Pakistan to harm Indian interests in Afghanistan. For the MEA, terrorism meant Taliban. However, the RAW officials who spent time talking to Taliban leaders convinced the Prime Minister that all Pashtuns are not Talibanis and fundamentalists. The MEA countered this in front of the Prime Minister by stating that as per some reports they have, Taliban and Harkat-ul-Ansar share facilities where ISI trains militants for Kashmir. The Prime Minister finally took a decision. He stated that India should continue to follow the MEA and support Northern Alliance. But the Prime Minister told RAW to do two things. Firstly, they would provide covert military support and overt moral and diplomatic support to the Northern Alliance. Secondly, RAW would work on the ground covertly and maintain, nurture and strengthen the links with Taliban. India followed this overt and covert policy till 2001 and mitigated the Taliban dilemma. Covertly, Taliban was also very happy to engage with India because they knew that India was the only country that could balance Pakistan on issues related to Afghanistan.

WHY TALIBAN WAS NOT INVOLVED IN THE HIJACKING OF IC-814 AND INDIA'S NEW PERCEPTION OF TALIBAN

In 1994, Masood Azhar was travelling in an auto rickshaw with Sajjad Afghani. At that time, Masood was a part of a group called Harkat-ul-Ansar while Sajjad Afghani was a part of Harkat-ul-Mujahedeen (HuM). The Military Intelligence was intercepting both of them. Both were arrested after a small chase at the Khannabal Chowk, Anantnag in Kashmir. Both were sent to Jammu for interrogation. Later it was stated that Masood was initially very rigid and unwilling to speak out to the Indian army regarding any information after his arrest. Senior Officials intervened to interrogate Masood at Kot Bhalwal Jail in Jammu. He showed him the picture of Omar Saeed Shaikh and Illyas Kashmiri. Both of them had a relationship with Masood. Masood opened up in front of him. During interrogation, he told him that he had landed in India through a fake Portuguese passport and ISI had instructed him to carry out the merger of HuM and Harkat-ul-Jihad-E-Islami (HuJI), led by Nasarullah Mansoor Langriyal, who was also in the Indian custody. When asked about Abdul Hamid al-Turki, Masood said that Turki was a man of low intellect and one who had been a Turkish national and presently living in Anantnag. The army used this input and on 4th December 1995, killed Turki in an operation in Anantnag. However, throughout his interrogation, Masood always asserted that India is underestimating his popularity. He used to say that ISI would do anything and everything to secure his release. The words of Azhar proved out to be prophetic. On 31st December 1999, an Indian Airlines aircraft was hijacked by the terrorist (sent by ISI) from Kathmandu in Nepal and taken to Kandahar in Afghanistan. The Taliban, which controlled Afghanistan, was reluctant to allow IC-814 to even land in Kandahar, but the ISI put its foot down and began to threaten the Taliban leaders that not allowing the IC-814 to land in Afghanistan will have serious consequences for the family members of Taliban living in Pakistan. In the process of negotiations to get the passengers of the IC-814 released, Masood was released in exchange. The moment Masood reached Pakistan, he was declared the ultimate 'Ghazi' against India and ISI handed over to him all the training camps cadre of HuM. The cadre was now merged into a new group called Jaish-e-Mohammad. The IC-814 incident not only cemented the Pakistan–Taliban nexus but also was an eye opener for India. India realised its strategic failure of not being able to establish contacts with Taliban. But the IC-814 incident also softened India's stand on Taliban as India realised that Taliban had no role to play in executing the IC-814 incident, which was solely the brain of ISI. This also helped India realise that Taliban was not a threat to India. All these helped India to gradually change their perception of Taliban.

INDIA–TALIBAN RELATIONS AFTER 9/11 AND GLOBAL WAR ON TERRORISM

In 2001, Al-Qaeda finally took their revenge against the US and attacked the World Trade Centers on 11th September. The 9/11 attacks were executed by Al-Qaeda and planned by them in Afghanistan with support of Taliban. This led the US to officially invade Afghanistan and remove Taliban and Al-Qaeda. The US responded to the 9/11 by launching the Operation Enduring Freedom and Operation Anaconda and unleashed Global War on Terrorism (GWOT). In 2001, a Bonn Conference was organised by the US to seek political reconstruction of Afghanistan through a democratic government. In 2003 Afghanistan witnessed their first ever-democratic election and elected Hamid Karzai as their first President. India also saw this conference as an opportunity to rectify its past errors and used the conference as an opportunity to go to Afghanistan and broaden its engagement with each constituency in Afghanistan. The Bonn also provided India an opportunity to deepen ties with Pashtuns, which India till now was unable to build because of Taliban. India finally accepted that Afghanistan is a potpourri of different ethnic groups. The RAW were told to develop strong links with all groups of Afghanistan (while maintaining links with Taliban) that can help in advancing Indian national interests. A strong covert architecture was laid down by RAW in Afghanistan. This also enabled India, with the help of Pashtuns, to expand its covert footprint in Baluchistan. The US continued their GWOT and tried to dismantle Taliban and Al-Qaeda. The Taliban and Al-Qaeda immediately shifted over to Pakistan. The ISI of Pakistan gave shelter to Taliban, as it was their baby that they had created and nurtured. They also gave shelter to Al-Qaeda in Pakistan. The RAW kept on covertly engaging with Taliban even while it was taking shelter in Pakistan.

ROLE OF INDIA IN THE RECONSTRUCTION OF AFGHANISTAN AFTER 2001

India launched a massive humanitarian programme with a strong developmental component to rebuild war-torn Afghanistan. The new diplomatic presence not only enhanced India's developmental diplomacy, but also its consulates and Indian embassy in Kabul were used to reach out to Pashtuns and other factions. They also enabled India to keep a strong watch on Pakistan in Afghanistan and their activities. The US was also happy to see the development work of India and the US often used to call India as a 'nice big brother' that is here to stay in Afghanistan. The RAW and Indian Council of Cultural Relations (ICCR) played an important role in constituency building amongst different political and ethnic factions in Afghanistan. The ICCR decided to provide scholarships to Afghan students to study in India. The Indian consulates in Afghanistan based upon the diplomatic officials independent political judgment would provide the scholarships. This enabled the local politicians to nurture their constituencies by sponsoring candidates and widening their political base. Whenever a local politician came up with names of students, a deal was stuck that he would have to safeguard Indian national interests and build a reputation in his area that India is 'helping' the constituents through education and development. It was a win-win situation where India was able to develop micro level contacts with Afghan politicians. The constituency-specific Small

Development Projects (SDPs) were designed by India to win hearts and minds of local people, enabling India to generate goodwill. India also began to provide medical assistance to Afghan citizens by allowing them to visit Delhi for medical treatments. The Indian government also provides funds to Afghan politicians and gives them the freedom to use the funds. There is no accounting of these funds done by India. India has also not established a vast developmental bureaucracy like the US AID or DFID of the UK and prefers to go for a hands-free approach where Afghan people decide for themselves. The developmental work by India in Afghanistan is such that today even Taliban is highly appreciative of India in Afghanistan.

INDIA'S POWER POLITICS FOR STABILISING AFGHANISTAN

Central Asia is crucial for India's energy security. India is deepening its proximity with Iran to reach Central Asia. India is developing the Chabahar port of Iran for this purpose. By accessing Central Asia, India will be able to tap a vast energy and resource market. The access to Central Asia will also enable India to reach Eurasia region. (Refer the chapter of Central Asia and Europe for more details.)

AFGHANISTAN IS A LITMUS TEST FOR INDIA'S REGIONAL POWER

India, today, successfully uses Afghanistan as classic case to assert its regional hegemony. As India's economic and military profiles grow, India is trying to use Afghanistan to establish its own credentials as a regional security provider and a regional stabiliser and a committed developmental provider. India knows that its ability to emerge as a great power in the near future hinges upon its strategic capacity exercised in dealing with its own region. Afghanistan has a pivotal place in this regard to Indian Foreign Policy's goal of power play.

Since 2001, Bonn-I conference, India has provided almost 3 billion dollars for the reconstruction of the Afghan society and has pledged 3 billion dollars for overall development. Indian assistance has been largely focused on infrastructure, irrigation and defence.

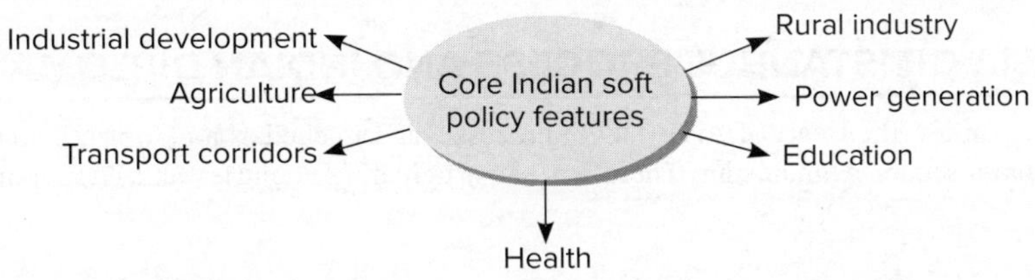

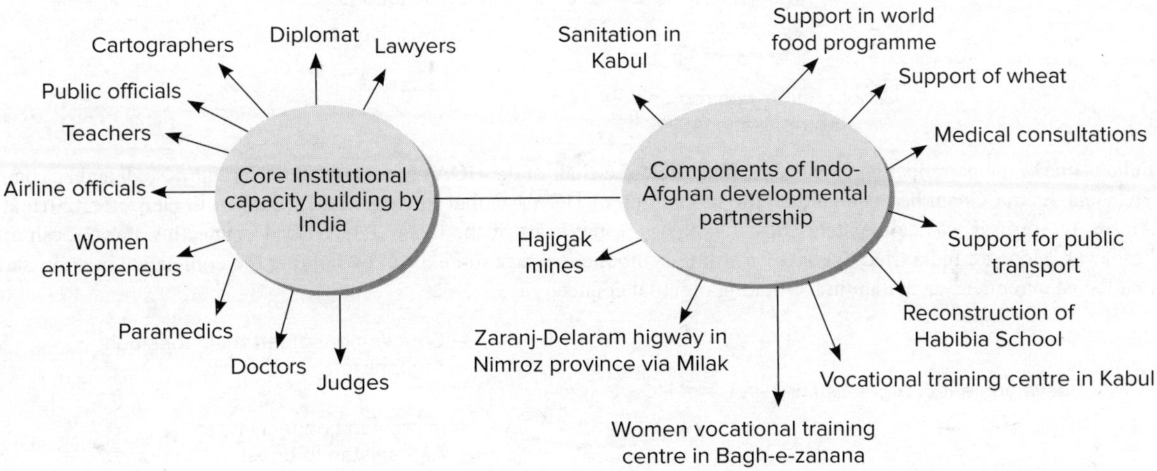

In 2011, India and Afghanistan concluded a Strategic Partnership Agreement (SPA).

The Indian has built the parliament building of Afghanistan in 2015. India had also decided to open a new consulate in Hyderabad of Afghanistan in 2015 to further development diplomacy. In June 2016, the Prime Minister again visited Afghanistan. India constructed the Salma Dam (called as Afghan–India Friendship dam). The project would irrigate fields of 640 villages in Chiste, Obe, Koshan, Karokh, Pashtun, Zarghun, Gozura, Injil, Zindijan and Ghoryan. It will generate 42 megawatt and irrigate 75,000-hectare land on Hari Rud River. The two countries in June 2017 established an Air Corridor, which was envisaged, by Ashraf Ghani and Modi in 2016. The air corridor will be a big enabler to the bilateral trade and will send a strong message to Pakistan that despite its obstructionist behaviour, India will continue to engage with Afghanistan. In 2010, Pakistan and Afghanistan concluded an Afghanistan–Pakistan Trade and Transit Agreement (APTTA). Under the APTTA, Afghanistan could send goods in trucks till India (at the Wagah border near Amritsar, Punjab) but its trucks had to return back to Afghanistan empty. Also in APTTA, Pakistan could send its trucks via Afghanistan to Uzbekistan and the Pakistani trucks were allowed to carry goods back from Central Asia, thus the Air corridor.

HEART OF ASIA OR ISTANBUL PROCESS AND INDIAN DIPLOMACY

In 2011, in Istanbul, Turkey, the Heart of Asia (HOA) process was launched as a platform involving regional players to ensure a stable and a secure Afghanistan. There are 14 participating countries and I7 supporting countries in the HOA process.

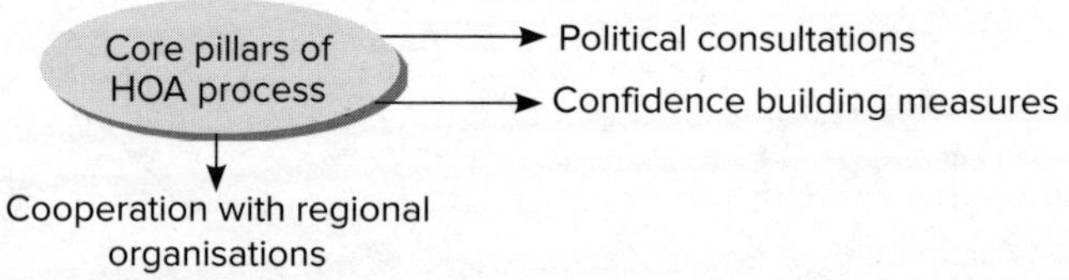

India is one of the participating countries and has held the chair of the HOA process in 2016. Narendra Modi and Afghan President Ashraf Ghani had inaugurated the 6th edition of HOA Istanbul Process of Afghanistan in December 2016 at Amritsar. Amritsar was deliberately chosen as it lies at the heart of the Grant Trunk Road connecting Bangladesh to Peshawar. More so, India tried to convey a strong symbolic message to Pakistan by holding the conference in Amritsar that Pakistan remains an irritant in facilitating regional connectivity.

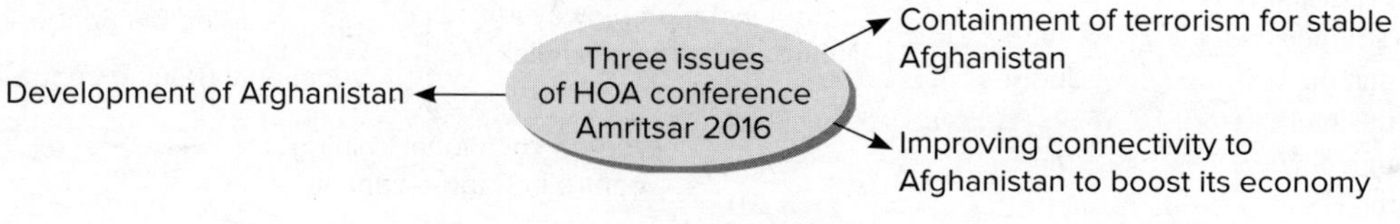

REGIONAL POLICIES OF IRAN, TURKEY, QATAR, CHINA AND RUSSIA IN AFGHANISTAN

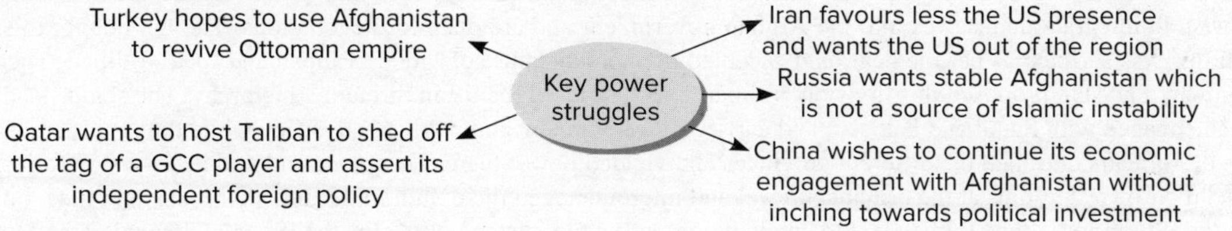

AFGHAN TALIBAN AND PAKISTAN TALIBAN—CIA AND ISI DEAL

From 2001 to 2008, India overtly tilted to engage with Pashtuns and engaged with Taliban in Pakistan covertly. Such a policy neglected the non-Pashtuns. The RAW often told the government that India is losing the plot in Afghanistan if it keeps tilting only in favour of Pashtuns. The US too by 2008 realised that they only succeeded in ousting Taliban and not eliminating Taliban. Since 2007, ISI supported Taliban in Afghanistan to violently snatch power in Afghanistan. The ISI and the US stuck a deal in 2007. The deal was that ISI would give intelligence to the US on the cells of Al-Qaeda and allow the US to target the Al-Qaeda. The US in return would allow the ISI to nurture Taliban and later, when required, help them to acquire power in Afghanistan. The reason why the US had no problem with Taliban was because the Taliban was not involved directly in 9/11. Also, the US wanted to act against Al-Qaeda because they had to show to their domestic American public that the US is acting against the perpetrators of 9/11. The ISI too had realised that they could not bring Taliban back to Afghanistan through brute force now and needed the US support in future. The only option was political reconciliation of Taliban in Afghanistan, which can happen when the US seriously helps them. However, the US were more interested in hunting down and killing Osama and were not interested in Taliban for the time being. This is where ISI and CIA differed. For ISI, Taliban was crucial while for CIA, Osama and Al-Qaeda was. In 2007, Al-Qaeda created Pakistan Taliban. The Pakistan Taliban was created to hit Pakistan internally. Its members were of Al-Qaeda. Pakistan Taliban is distinct from Afghan Taliban, as Afghan Taliban was the Taliban that ISI nurtured with American support. The Pakistan Taliban did not position itself as a monolithic organisation. Rather, it adopted a fragmented and decentralised strategy to hit Pakistan internally. They created multiple groups that ranged from SWAT Taliban, Punjabi Taliban, Bajaur Taliban and Tehreek-E-Taliban Pakistan. The ISI on the other hand played it cool and successfully initiated reconciliation with Afghan Taliban in 2008.

LONDON CONFERENCE AND INSTITUTIONALISATION OF TALIBAN AS CORE ACTOR OF AFGHANISTAN

In 2010, there was a London Conference, where ISI was successfully institutionalised a dialogue with Taliban (note that we refer to Afghan Taliban here). But this was also the time period when RAW told Afghan President Hamid Karzai that excluding non-Pashtuns in the Afghan government will only increase their resentment and will create a trouble for Karzai in the future. The anti-Karzai brigade kept growing. Karzai was informed that the Americans are plotting for his removal by taking help of alienated non-Pashtuns. The CIA and ISI began to carry out attacks in Afghanistan to put pressure on Karzai to accommodate non-Pashtuns. This compounded the problem for Karzai.

But, in 2011, in a surgical strike, the US killed Osama Bin Laden in Pakistan. To show the world, this incident of Osama eventually strained the US–Pakistan ties forever. The US, to show the world, became sceptical of Pakistan for it harbouring a terrorist that the US wanted for a decade. The US created a global narrative that they were very upset with Pakistan. But, internally, the intelligence community of the US was happy as they demonstrated to the US public that Obama Administration and his 'tough' terrorism policy eliminated Osama. Problem for Karzai grew further with the US under Obama deciding to announce the US troop withdrawal from Afghanistan in 2012. The Obama administration announced this because Obama had made a poll promise back home that he would end the Afghan war and bring back the US soldiers home. Thus, Obama administration signed a Strategic Partnership Agreement with Afghanistan to facilitate the troop withdrawal.

THE RISE OF 'GOOD' TALIBAN AND 'BAD' TALIBAN

Pakistan saw that this is the best time to integrate Taliban into Afghanistan. In 2012, Pakistan proposed to the US and the world that there are some 'good' and 'bad' elements of Taliban. Pakistan proposed that 'good' Taliban are those members who wish to integrate themselves into the Afghan government and are open for negotiations. The US bought this logic (as all this was scripted as per the deal) and accepted the nomenclature of 'good' Taliban and 'bad' Taliban. There is a reason why Pakistan proposed this division. Taliban operated in Afghanistan through a hierarchy. The senior leaders of Taliban engaged with Saudi and Pakistan and carried out diplomacy and political advocacy while the junior and middle layers of Taliban controlled the different provinces and yielded power there. The junior and middle layers of Taliban had created their own fiefdoms at the provincial level and micromanaged the opium trade and other local activities. In 2012, when the ISI proposed that Taliban would be integrated into Afghanistan politically, the ISI and CIA understood that the senior level of Taliban would only be accommodated and the junior and middle levels of Taliban would resist that because they cannot be politically accommodated. They would resist any change in the status quo and would also not favour the senior level to play a role that may affect their fiefdoms. The ISI and CIA knew that there would be resistance by many in Taliban hierarchy and such elements had to be eliminated. To prepare for this eventuality in advance, the ISI created this nomenclature where the senior Taliban would automatically fall into the 'Good' Taliban category and the opponents of political integration of Taliban would be put in 'Bad' Taliban category, who can be eventually eliminated later through this 'bad' justification. As the ISI and CIA began a dialogue with the 'Good' Taliban, the CIA in 2014, with support of Israeli Mossad, created Islamic State of Iraq and Syria (ISIS) under the leadership of a trained Mossad operative named Elliot Shimon, who came in front of the world as Dr. Abu Bakr Al Baghdadi. The creation of ISIS also gave an opportunity to the middle and junior levels of Taliban to join ISIS as they thought that this ISIS would give them arms and ammunition. They thought that they could use these arms and ammunition to resist the senior leaders of Taliban and threaten them by unleashing violence in the fiefdoms. They joined ISIS to safeguard their fiefdoms but their joining ISIS gave the US an opportunity to eliminate them eventually. Thus, in 2020, we were only left with the 'Good Taliban' and the 'Bad Taliban' was eliminated successfully and that is why ISIS too was wrapped up (in 2019 when the US showed to the world that Abu Bakr Al Baghdadi was eliminated). To show the world, India officially rejected this divergent nomenclature and stated that all terrorists are bad terrorists and there cannot be such artificial perceptual division. This was done officially, but covertly India had been engaging with Taliban (good Taliban) and was not very affected with this division. As the civil unrest in Afghanistan grew, in 2013, Karzai presented a wish list of military hardware from India. The RAW too asserted that India should arm Afghanistan and this should be done to control ISI's strategic depth in Afghanistan. The RAW presented a case for strong India and Afghanistan defence ties. A senior RAW official told the Indian Prime Minister that India should instil fear in the minds of Pakistan by arming Afghanistan. However, MEA asserted that a strong India in Afghanistan would instil a fear in Pakistan that India is trying to support Afghan revanchist designs. MEA said that once the US troops withdraw, there could be a possibility that these arms supplied by India can fall in wrong hands. Also, the MEA said that India has no law that permits transfer of lethal arms to foreign states. Thus, in the absence of a law, in 2015, India 'gifted' four MI-35 attack helicopters to Kabul. Today, India says that there are two concerns in deepening defence ties with Afghanistan. Firstly, the Afghan National Security Force (ANSF) is trained to use American weapons. If India gives arms, there will be interoperability issues. Secondly, the list of weapons from Afghanistan keep changing and this has confused the leadership in India.

THE FIVE STAGES OF EVOLUTION OF INDIA'S AFGHAN POLICY

India's Taliban policy has witnessed five stages of denial in 1996, anger in 1997, bargaining in 1998, depression in 1999 and finally acceptance from 2002. Initially, as we have analysed previously, there have been various factors that have prevented India to engage with Taliban. One of the biggest problems India faced with Taliban was epistemic limitation and knowledge about Taliban. This was also coupled with political conservatism in India. But India always covertly maintained a link with Taliban. In fact, in 2006 Fazlur Rehman, a senior Taliban leader visited India on a four-day state visit. He even had the meeting with the Indian Prime Minister and the RAW Chief. But since 2011, India has shed off its perception of looking at Taliban as a monolith controlled by Pakistan. India understands that Taliban is a very diverse organisation. Its main fight is against Western forces on the soil of Afghanistan and not India or Kashmir. India has also understood that it is not possible to militarily defeat Taliban. India today believes that the Afghan government will depend upon external support for financial and military needs. So, India is of the opinion that Afghanistan should not be dependent upon Pakistan for the same, as that will affect Indian national interests. India has understood that there are various groups in Afghanistan, which also include Taliban, which are dependent upon Pakistan. Non-engagement with such groups is unviable now because this would only isolate them from India and make them gravitate towards Pakistan. India knows that because of its developmental diplomacy, which is even highly appreciated by Taliban, it wants to use this goodwill and broaden its engagement with Afghanistan and Taliban. Engagement with Taliban will only help in India to secure its core interests in the region. Even though India knows that the cost of reconciliation of Afghan government and Taliban is not going to be an easy task, it still favours engagement with Taliban because the cost of non-engagement is higher than the cost of engagement. Even though Taliban is entrenched in drugs, violence and extortions, they are still not at odds with India and we have repeated time and again in this chapter that Taliban have never targeted India or Kashmir. Since 2011, India has officially accepted that Afghan led reconciliation with Taliban will be supported by India.

INDIA'S RELATIONSHIP WITH TALIBAN 2.0

The Indian strategy is that it is trying to be in touch with all key stakeholders to bolster a wide range of coalition. One suggestion for India is to launch an India–Afghan Dialogue (on lines of India and Central Asia Dialogue) with various regional players as key stakeholders. It is important for India to engage with China and use China to convince Pakistan to loosen its grip on anti-India Jihad factions like Haqqani networks. If China in return demands a dilution of Indo-US military partnership, India should display open mindedness to such a grand bargain. More so, India can engage with Central Asia and deploy boots on the ground in Central Asia to ensure that ceasefire between the US and Taliban is respected. Iran also enjoys influence (despite Iranians being Shias and Taliban Sunnis) on Taliban (because both do not want foreign troops in Afghanistan, thus Iran bedfellowing Taliban) and is willing to allow India to step in to open a channel for talks. The Tajiks in Afghanistan are Persian speaking (close to Iran) and are in the Afghan bureaucracy, thus, being another asset for India to leverage. The good offices of Russia with Taliban are also used by India at the covert level to engage. India and China (RAW has set up a covert military base in Wakhan corridor, connecting Badakshan Province of Afghanistan and Xinjiang) along with Russia and Iran can evolve a model of regional concert cooperation for Afghanistan. The reality is that Taliban actively supports India's works in rural Afghanistan. To take the dialogue further, in 2018, India even allowed 'non-official' participation through its retired diplomats in a multilateral meeting in Russia. The next logical step for India will be to go for MAGA (Make Afghanistan Great Again) campaign. It is the Pakistani-sponsored Haqqani networks that target India in Afghanistan. Thus, India does not have an Afghan problem, but a Pakistan problem. Since 2021, when Taliban acquired power in Afghanistan, India has adopted the policy of engaging with Taliban but not endorsing the Taliban.

INDIA AND TALIBANI FACTION OF MULLAH ABDUL SALAM ROCKETI

In the present times, India knows that not all factions of Taliban are anti-India. There are certain factions of Taliban that are supported by Pakistan to target Indians in Afghanistan. There is a faction of Taliban in Afghanistan led by Mullah Abdul Salam Rocketi, who is pro-India. It is stated that Rocketi has a good knowledge of ISI and has deep penetration within the ISI. Through Rocketi, RAW knows that ISI has given responsibility to its officials like Major Nadeem Taj, Brigadier Sher Zamin and Captain Khan Zamin to target India in Afghanistan. The RAW often uses Rocketi to gather ground intelligence on ISI and their activities in Afghanistan and Pakistan. Thus, RAW has embarked upon a new journey in Afghanistan where Taliban and RAW gather tactical intelligence on the ground together.

INDIA AND ITS RELATIONSHIP WITH THE HAQQANI NETWORKS

As of now, India engages with all of Taliban minus Haqqani networks. The Haqqani networks (created by the US in Afghanistan as part of Afghan Mujahedeen campaign in 1980 under the leadership of Jalaluddin Haqqani) are good to be used by Pakistan. The common belief is that the Haqqani networks are a veritable arm of the ISI. It is true that ISI played a very important role in creating the Haqqani networks in 1980s during the Afghan Jihad. Sirrajuddin Haqqani (son of Jalaluddin Haqqani) leads the Haqqani networks and is also the number two in Taliban and they are present in the areas of Durand line in South and East Afghanistan. They also enjoy a considerable hold over the local economy. However, the RAW has infiltrated inside the Haqqani networks. The Haqqani networks operate purely with a monetary motive and they do not have any ideology. The ISI uses them via money and gets them to target Indians in Afghanistan. Thus, if Haqqani networks take money from ISI, they are open to take money from others also. This is where Indian RAW is working today with Haqqani networks. With the Taliban majorly pro-India today, if Haqqani networks are financially neutralised, the ISI will lose the plot in Afghanistan completely in the future.

INDIA'S FUTURE STRATEGY FOR ENGAGING WITH TALIBAN

The Taliban has asked for India's help on how to integrate Taliban in Afghanistan and assistance on counterinsurgency. India has suggested that Taliban should first end violence and secondly should accept any negotiation under the Afghan constitution. Today, India has been talking to senior Taliban leaders that range from Tayyab Agha, Abdal Salam Zaeef and Muttawakil. India has been regularly inviting them to Delhi and having intense negotiations with them. The Taliban Chief, Maulvi Hebatullah Akhundzda, covertly visited Delhi for negotiations many times. The RAW is also talking to Taliban leaders like Agha Jan Mutasim, Abdul Ghani Baradar and Zabinullah Mujahid to see the possibility if they can help internally weaken Pakistan. Taliban is not anti-India and will not allow Pakistan to use Afghanistan to target India anywhere, from Kashmir to Afghanistan. But India continues to deepen ties with Taliban to wean them away from Pakistan. RAW was sceptical about India opening a dialogue with HEI and Hekmatyar as Pakistani ISI trained him. But since 2017 ceasefire, HEI is more pro-India than Pakistan. Today, India is able to break into Taliban effectively because of Pakistan. Pakistan has often shown their back to Taliban. In fact, the RAW officer says that whenever Taliban did not toe down to the line of ISI, the ISI used Haqqani networks to target Taliban. This has made Taliban more anti-Pakistan today and this is a positive point for RAW and India. At times, a proposal is made in the media that India should deploy military in Afghanistan. If Indian troops get involved in Afghanistan, India would be sucked into a vicious proxy war with huge financial and strategic costs. Pakistan will perceive that Indian troops in Afghanistan would be used for supporting revanchist designs in KP and Baluchistan, thus, the Afghan situation does not favour an Indian security intervention.

QUADRILATERAL COORDINATION GROUP IN AFGHANISTAN AND INDIA–TALIBAN DIPLOMACY

The US in January 2016 established the QCG (Quadrilateral Coordination Group), which had the US, Afghanistan, Pakistan and China. The QCG established a roadmap where Pakistan was made a key player to bring Taliban on the table for talks with the US. But the hopes for peace were dashed when Mullah Mansoor (head of Taliban) did not relinquish violence and kept on insisting that the US leave Afghanistan. Frustrated with Mansoor, the US in May 2016, through a drone strike eliminated Mansoor. This led to Maulvi Hebatullah Akhundzda become the successor in Taliban. On insistence of Russian intelligence, in 2018, the Islamic Movement of Uzbekistan (active in North and East Afghanistan) announced their decision to join Islamic State (ISIS). The IS logic was created by Russia (which asserted IS could become a threat to Russia) to open up its dialogue with Taliban directly. All this gave Taliban a new legitimacy, something that Pakistan always craved for. The US have tacitly understood that the only thing ISI wants is Taliban in Afghanistan at any cost. Pakistan prefers a controlled (through their control over Taliban) instability in Afghanistan that keeps the Taliban in power but also keeps it dependent upon the ISI. The US cannot take any harsh measures against Pakistan that range from designating it as a state sponsorer of terrorism to cancelling the status of 'major non-NATO ally'. The US apparently remains committed to this unhappy marriage with Pakistan. Thus, all that the US wanted was an honourable exit from Afghanistan. Over a period of time, Taliban has also changed its stance. From being an armed militia that destroyed schools, courts and medical clinics, today it is supporting them. Taliban is also allowing them to be managed by government servants. It has adopted this strategy of co-opting development to display its governance skills, so that it can present itself as a credible player in the future of Afghanistan.

THE 'US–TALIBAN PACKAGE DEAL' AND 'TALK AND FIGHT' STRATEGY OF TALIBAN

It is in the backdrop of issues analysed above that the US in 2018 appointed Zalmay Khalizad as its chief negotiator and special representative with Taliban. Trump had thrown Afghanistan into an epic scrum by his logic that great nations do not fight endless wars. The ground situation in 2020 was that Taliban controlled 15% Afghan lands, the Afghan government held 56% while 39% was contested between Afghan government and Taliban. The US have followed a three-way negotiation strategy. First, they opened up the Doha track with the Taliban; a second was with Islamabad/Rawalpindi track and the third was with Kabul government to ensure that the Afghan government would accept the outcome of the deal. The dice was loaded because Taliban and Pakistan negotiated as a team with the US. Within six months of 2018, Taliban presented four objectives to the US and they were: a ceasefire, an intra-Afghan peace dialogue, cutting ties with terrorist organisations such as Al-Qaeda, and finally, the US troop withdrawal from Afghanistan. However, the strategy of Taliban was that at one place it would continue to fight foreign troops and simultaneously talk to the US. This is called the 'talk and fight' approach. The Taliban and the US reached a deal in March 2020, which is pregnant with positivity. *Agreement for Bringing Peace to Afghanistan between the Islamic Emirate of Afghanistan, which is not recognised by the United States as a state and is known as the Taliban and the United States of America* is the title of the 'deal'. The deal has five core components:

Troops withdrawal: The US will withdraw 8,600 troops in 135 days and the NATO or coalition troop numbers will also be brought down, proportionately and simultaneously. The US will withdraw 'all' troops will be out within 14 months where the word "all" would include "non-diplomatic civilian personnel" (which in reality are "intelligence" personnel of CIA). The US withdrew from Afghanistan in 2021 and Taliban established there presence.

Taliban commitment: The deal says that Taliban will not allow any of its members, other individuals or groups, including Al-Qaeda, to use the soil of Afghanistan to threaten the security of the United States and its allies. The pact is silent on anti-India groups like Lashkar-e-Toiba or Jaish-e-Mohammed. Also, India, not being an US ally, is not covered under this pact for the time being.

Sanctions removal: The UN sanctions on Taliban leaders to be removed by three months, that is by 29th May 2020 and the US sanctions by 27th August 2020.

Prisoner release: The joint declaration says the US will facilitate "discussion with Taliban representatives on confidence building measures, to include determining the feasibility of releasing significant numbers of prisoners on both sides". While there are no numbers or deadlines in the joint declaration, the US–Taliban pact says up to 5,000 imprisoned Taliban and up to 1,000 prisoners from "the other side" held by Taliban "would be released" by 10th March 2020, which was the date when intra-Afghan negotiations started, in Oslo. However, the prisoner exchange witnessed a snag when on 10th March 2020, the Afghan government refused to release the prisoners. The Oslo talks were suspended due to the outbreak of COVID-19 and eventually occurred in 2021.

Ceasefire: The agreement states ceasefire will be simply "an item on the agenda" when intra-Afghan talks start and indicates actual ceasefire will come with the "completion" of an Afghan political agreement. Ideally, the intra-Afghan talks should have preceded the deal, but that did not happen, making the entire future complicated now.

PRIVATISATION OF WARS AND CONFLICT THEATRES

The US has in a way lost the game in Afghanistan. It is rightly said that Afghanistan for the US has become their next Vietnam. It is determined to carry out an honourable exit from Afghanistan. It is in this context, a debate has initiated of privatising the Afghan war. In the present context of hybrid wars, the roles of private armies have drastically increased. In the US, most of its retired defence personnel have floated private security companies, which have a private army ready to be deployed in a situation. In the US, the idea to privatise the war in Afghanistan is made by Erik Prince, a former US Navy seal and head of a private security firm called Frontier Resource Group. He has proposed that a private army of 6000, 90 private army planes along with 2000 troops of the US Special Forces on ground in Afghanistan can make a big difference on the ground operations, apart from a fraction cost to the treasury of the US (4 billion USD in contrast to 50 billion USD per annum at present). Prince asserts that with a right strategy on the ground, the private army can defeat

Taliban if they go violent. Prince also asserted that a small private army in Afghanistan could give the US a leverage to reduce its dependence on Pakistan and simultaneously put pressure on Pakistan if it continues to support extremism. There have been concerns raised about the outsourcing of the war that range from issues of accountability to human right abuses. Anyway, the concept of the US resorting to privatisation is not new because for many years thousands of 'contractors', also called 'non-governmental personnel' have been performing military duties from logistics to translation etc. The US Central Command (which has the responsibility to carry out wars in Middle East) has employed more than 50000 contractors. For that matter, even Russia has been using a private army in Syria presently. The above debate proves that the concept of private armies are now a part of modern battlefields, but whether Pakistan will allow the US the liberty to do this in Afghanistan is a question mark.

THE NARRATIVE OF TALIBAN AS A THREAT IN KASHMIR AND THREAT TO INDIA

There is a belief that after abrogation of Article 370, which was done unilaterally by India without consulting Kashmiri people, there is a lot of disenchantment against the Indian government in the valley. Pakistan feels that it can exploit a vast segment of people in tans-Pir Panjal region and alienated Kashmiri people against India. The consequence of the US–Taliban deal will be more psychological. The people in the valley may perceive the deal this way. They will feel that if Taliban could defeat a mighty superpower like the US, then defeating Indian forces in Kashmir will not be difficult too. The Kashmiri youth might pick up arms and ISI may fuel the violence to create Kashmir Militancy 2.0. However, one thing that even Pakistan's deep state will acknowledge is that the situation in J&K is not even remotely akin to what it was in 1989–90. At that juncture, Kashmir Valley had a single Indian division strength force, with a couple of independent brigades. India's 15 Corps was stretched in its responsibility from Demchok in Eastern Ladakh to the Pir Panjal, all along the LAC and LoC; a deployment which only changed after Kargil 1999. Indian Army's 15 Corps and Jammu and Kashmir Police (JKP) now have 30 years of experience handling intense hybrid war. In the rear in second and third tiers is deployed the Rashtriya Rifles (RR), India's finest military experiment. In addition there is the CRPF, which is far more confident and well-integrated with the RR. Pakistan could aim to employ four facets to make the situation simmer; mass infiltration, terror acts, people's agitation and influence operations through various means including social media and mosque power. Indian capability to limit infiltration received a boost since 2004 with the LoC fence and induction of modern surveillance technology. The effectiveness of successfully infiltrated terror groups is contingent upon the support of over ground workers and availability of finance networks. Surge in local recruitment is contingent upon success of the Foreign Terror (FT) groups of Afghanistan and the penetration of influence operations by Pakistan's ISI. The degree of success to counter Pakistan thus depends upon our capability to initiate a slew of development and outreach measures in the valley. The victory of Taliban with the US here is not just a victory of a puritanical religious outfit but an act of legitimisation of religious fundamentalism. The only saving grace here is that when India abrogated Article 370 in August 2019, Taliban issued a statement saying that there is no link between the issues of Kashmir and Afghanistan. This proves that Taliban has never supported the ISI-sponsored violence in Kashmir and in future will also not do the same. Thus, for India, the challenge is only to manage the situation of psychological alienation of the people in the valley.

THE POLICY OF STRATEGIC DEPTH OF PAKISTAN IN AFGHANISTAN AND INDIA'S TALIBAN COUNTERBALANCING

India's diplomatic energy in Afghanistan is invested primarily in enhancing its own interests in Afghanistan. To understand India's interest, it is important to understand the concept of strategic depth. Let us understand the concept of Strategic Depth through an example. Suppose that there are three hypothetical states—A, B and C. Strategic depth is a policy whereby state A may try to enhance its influence in state B to the extent that it emerges in a position to prevent the state C to exercise political influence in the state B. For instance, Pakistan has enhanced its presence in Afghanistan to ensure that there is a favourable regime in Afghanistan since a regime favourable to Pakistan in Afghanistan will allow Pakistan to limit the political influence of India in Afghanistan. Thus, Pakistan pursues a policy of strategic depth against India in Afghanistan.

India's first interest is to ensure that Pakistan does not gain an edge within governing structures of Afghanistan. India feels that if Pakistan succeeds in installing Taliban in Afghanistan, it will be detrimental to the cause of the regional security of India because Taliban will not be able to prevent ISI to use the territory of Afghanistan to train terrorists for unleashing terrorism in the Kashmir valley. In the post-2001 period, India decided to deepen its engagement with Afghanistan by opening consulates in Herat, Mazar-e-sharif, Kandahar and Jalalabad. These consulates provided India the needed base in Afghanistan to carry out development diplomacy (explained this above). Pakistan alleges that India uses these consulates to contain Pakistan as these consulates have officers of Indian RAW and they have used these consulates to create a deep covert network to gather intelligence from across the border and create terrorism in Pakistan. Pakistan also alleges that India aids Baluchistan rebels through these consulates.

INDIAN POLICY TO PREVENT OF SPILLOVER OF EXTREMISM TO KASHMIR

Pakistan even continues to use Jihad as a part of its grand strategy as it gives them the power to influence the region. India has been a victim of state-sponsored terrorism from Pakistan and India engages with Afghanistan to ensure no spillover of extremism or Islamic radicalism happens to India. At present, the extremists fighting in Kashmir owe their patronage mostly to Pakistan's ISI and have drawn inspiration from the resistance offered by Afghan mujahedeen against the Soviets during the Cold War. The test for India will be that how it tries to convince Taliban to not let Afghan lands be used by ISI to train anti-India elements.

THE KEY DRIVERS OF INDIA'S TALIBAN POLICY

In final conclusion of India's policy on Afghanistan, we can say that firstly, there is no one approach adopted by India for Afghanistan because Afghanistan has been rightly called the 'graveyard of Empires'. Its approach to Afghanistan vacillates from a partisan approach to a conciliatory approach. The Partisans are those people in the Indian establishment who favour an anti-engagement strategy. It means that they assert that India should build ties with all those who factions in Afghanistan who are at odds with Pakistan. They say that by deepening ties with them, India can weaken Pakistani strategic depth. Conciliators are those people in the Indian establishment who favour that India should favour a policy where it speaks to all those factions which are in power in Afghanistan and with whom India enjoys a goodwill. They favour engage all axiom and assert that the India needs to be open to even the pro-Pakistan constituency in Afghanistan. India uses an effective mixture of conciliators and partisans to achieve the goal of a sovereign, stable and a united Afghanistan. To achieve this, Indian foreign policy in Afghanistan is driven by finding official, unofficial and covert friends in Afghanistan, who will be supportive of India's interests and further the national interests of India. If they do so, India can reciprocate with infrastructure, aid or a mix of politico-military and international support for Afghanistan. Thus, the partition of India, which caused a geographical disconnect of India to Central Asia, did indeed become India's weakness but, it also became the pillar of cardinal strength of India and Afghanistan.

CHAPTER 4

India's Relationship with Pakistan

THE BASIS OF THE RIVALRY OF INDIA AND PAKISTAN

India and Pakistan, since their inception in 1947, have had sharp rivalries with each other. Peter T. Coleman rightly pointed out that 95% of the most serious disputes in the world can be resolved, but India and Pakistan come under the irresoluble 5%. The conflict between the two has vacillated from a clash of national identities to territorial disputes. In the 21st century, the two have become lethal nuclear rivals of each other. The relations have always been locked in a vicious cycle. They begin with much optimism and fanfare but soon get engulfed by uncertainties, generating complications that lead to the suspension of dialogue, only for the cycle to continue again with a fresh round of optimism the next time. Though the acquisition of nuclear capabilities by both countries has prevented a major conflict, small-scale conflicts such as Kargil crisis of 1999, localised attacks such as Pulwama attack of 2019 and subsequent Balakot strike of 2019 did take place. General Monty Palit has rightly stated that, over a certain period of time, the Indo-Pak relations have become, in a sense, a sort of communal riot disguised in armour. Krishna Kumar aptly states that the two sides have an iron curtain that prevents them from building a pool of common knowledge about each other. Today, the Jamaat-i-Islami in Pakistan believes that Pakistan has to emerge as the forerunner of an idea of Islamist awakening, and such an awakening would also absorb Indian Muslims and thereby India will become a part of Pakistan. The Indian RSS (Rashtriya Swayamsevak Sangh) on the other hand believes that Pakistan as an independent state is an unacceptable entity and a civilisational challenge to the existence of India and they advocate the idea of 'Akhand Bharat', which as an idea includes India's boundary up till Central Asia. Since its inception, Pakistan has sought to build a link between its religious identity and its geostrategic location. For Jinnah, Islamic Pakistanis, being followers of monotheistic Islam, were naturally more allied to the monotheistic Christians than Hindus. Using the religious angle, he favoured a deeper alliance with the US. Jinnah articulated that only monotheistic people could resist the godless communist Russia in the world. Jinnah asserted that Hindus and Indians could not be trusted in the fight against communism because the Hindu Indians were more sympathetic towards Soviets. Jinnah tried to market Pakistan as a Muslim Israel to America, which shared the same values and a belief in no god but god. The Pakistani establishment has a feeling that India has never accepted the idea of allowing Pakistan to exist as a state and they believe that India wants to militarily crush Pakistan. Pakistan uses an analogy with Israel to explain India's position with respect to itself. Pakistan feels that communities who perceived an impending threat of persecution by a majority state, as they constituted a minority, created both Pakistan and Israel. Both remained under threat from neighbours. Pakistan feels that after the Partition, the Hindus wanted to take revenge by attacking a minority-constituted Pakistan. Pakistan further maintains that to meet this threat, both countries (Pakistan and Israel) used a common strategic policy of building up of alliances with the West as a security guarantee. However, Pakistan alleges that neither Israel nor Pakistan got adequate support from the West for their security (Pakistan uses 1971 crises as an explanation), which compelled them to go nuclear for their own security and survival. In Pakistan, the army had dominated its national security and foreign policy discourse since the 1950s and the army has an upper hand in dictating diplomacy with India. Both sides feel that fear, hatred and a sense of persecution are the key drivers of the conflict. The conflict not only revolves around the disparity in size between India and Pakistan but Kashmir, water sharing and the Siachen Glacier issue also constitute the three core geostrategic issues affecting the two. The Pakistani army feels that the RAW (Research and Analysis Wing) has entrenched itself deeply in conflicts internal to Pakistan and has unleashed an inner leviathan in Pakistan to destabilise it from within.

KASHMIR ISSUE IN INDIA AND PAKISTAN RELATIONS

During the British times, Kashmir was one of the princely states under British suzerainty. In 1946, the memorandum of the Cabinet Mission to India defined the status of such princely states. As per the Cabinet Mission plan, once the British paramount ceases, the crown would no longer hold paramount power and such power would be transferred to the states of India and Pakistan. There will be an end to political arrangements between the states, crown and British India. The princely state will fill the void by establishing a relationship with India, Pakistan or would remain independent. Two instruments, namely, Mountbatten proposed Instrument of Accession and a Standstill Agreement. Jinnah interpreted that, as per Cabinet Mission Plan, the situation post-lapse of paramountcy would be such that princely states would gain independent status of being sovereign in nature. Congress, through a resolution on 15th June 1947, held that on lapse of paramountcy, the will of the people of concerned princely states would be required to ascertain their choices, as lapse of paramountcy did not tantamount to the independence of a state. With this interpretation, the Congress raised objections when the Maharaja of Junagadh began to negotiate an accession with Pakistan. India insisted its interpretation in case of Junagadh. A referendum on Junagadh happened and its population voted in favour of India.

THE GAMES OF HARI SINGH AND PAKISTANI MAXIMALIST OPTION OF TRIBAL RAIDS

Kashmir was a princely state and it posed some difficulty because it was a Muslim majority state ruled by a Hindu monarch, Maharaja Hari Singh. Initially, Hari Singh was reluctant to join either India or Pakistan. Meanwhile, Pakistan launched a campaign by sending its troops disguised as tribesmen to forcefully annex the state of Kashmir. A revolt against the rule of Hari Singh was fomented by Pakistan. Hari Singh had his own fears. He never wanted to accede to Pakistan, as he feared that a Muslim state of Pakistan would soon integrate the Muslims of Kashmir thereby relegating him to a minority status. He also had similar concerns for India, as he thought that if he acceded to India, a socialist Jawaharlal Nehru would strip him of the privileges he enjoyed. In September 1947, there was a communal trouble in Poonch province in the state. Simultaneously, Pakistani tribesmen had started pouring in and had unleashed a campaign of carnage in other areas reaching up till Srinagar.

THE FIRST INDIA AND PAKISTAN WAR

On 24th October 1947, Hari Singh requested arms and troop support from India to stop the Pakistani-sponsored menace. As Hari Singh had not acceded either to India or Pakistan, troops from India could not be sent. Mountbatten asserted that the accession should be determined by a plebiscite after the tribesmen have been driven out of Kashmir. Nehru accepted the views of Mountbatten. Mountbatten contended that, as India has not signed a formal accession treaty with Kashmir, if it sends troops to Kashmir, Pakistan would do the same and this may lead to a war. It was decided by Nehru to inform Hari Singh that only if Hari Singh acceded to India would there be any troop commitment. Nehru, however, clarified that such an accession is conditioned and once law and order is restored, the will of the Kashmiri people about their future would hold sacrosanct. Hari Singh signed the instrument of accession and sent a letter to Nehru to that effect. In the letter Hari Singh stated that Kashmir had signed a standstill agreement with Pakistan. As per the agreement, Pakistan provided postal and telegraph services in the state. Hari Singh also complained that Pakistan had put a lot of pressure on him and one of the pressure tactics was the tribal raid. He wrote that in this emergency, instead of allowing Pakistan to destroy his state, he preferred concluding an instrument of accession with India. The Indian government accepted the accession and decided to provide military help to Kashmir. Pakistan immediately declared that the accession was an act of fraud and it summarily rejected the accession. The challenging of the legality of the accession by Pakistan was an unsound political move. The Indian troops were able to stop the onslaught by Pakistani forces but by then, one-third of Kashmir had fallen into the hands of the invaders.

THE KASHMIR ISSUE IN UNITED NATIONS AND INDIAN DIPLOMACY

Nehru, heeding the advice of Mountbatten, referred the case of Kashmir to the United Nation in 1948. Mountbatten urged Nehru that an international agency such as the UN can ensure impartiality in the plebiscite. Once law and order would be restored, there would be a plebiscite under the observation of the UN. The UN subsequently established a UN Commission for India and Pakistan with power to exercise mediatory influence. In January 1948, the Security Council adopted Resolution 39, establishing the United Nations Commission for India and Pakistan (UNCIP) to investigate and mediate the dispute. As the UNCIP came to the subcontinent, there arose disagreements over de-militarisation in Kashmir. The UNCIP was instructed to work jointly with the two states and create a condition conducive for a plebiscite. In April 1948, by its Resolution 47, the Council decided to enlarge the membership of UNCIP and to recommend various measures including the use of observers to create conditions for peace. At the recommendation of UNCIP, the Secretary-General appointed the Military Adviser to support the Commission on military aspects and provided for a group of military observers to assist him. The first team of unarmed military observers, which eventually formed the nucleus of the United Nations Military Observer Group in India and Pakistan (UNMOGIP), arrived in the mission area in January 1949 to supervise, in the State of Jammu and Kashmir, the ceasefire between India and Pakistan and to assist the Military Adviser to UNCIP. The tasks of the observers, as defined by the Military Adviser, were to accompany the local authorities in their investigations, gather as much information as possible, and report as completely, accurately and impartially as possible. To immediately halt the hostilities due to the invasion of the tribesmen, the UNCIP, through negotiations, helped India and Pakistan sign an agreement in 1949 in Karachi.

THE KARACHI AGREEMENT AND CEASEFIRE LINE

As per the Karachi Agreement, a ceasefire line was drawn as a temporary arrangement to divide the line between Kashmiri territory left with India and Pakistan-occupied Kashmir (PoK), which they called Azad Kashmir. The Karachi Agreement specified that UNCIP would station observers where it deemed necessary, and that local commanders on each side would verify the ceasefire line mutually on the ground with the assistance of the UN military observers. Disagreements were to be referred to the UNCIP Military Adviser, whose decision would be final. The Pakistani army decided to take over the operational control of the PoK and stationed its troops in the region. India alleged that this troop presence of Pakistan was one of the reasons why a condition conducive for a plebiscite had not been created. The ceasefire line officially came into effect from 1st January 1949. India alleged that the stalemate over Kashmir could not end and a plebiscite could not happen, as Pakistan did not withdraw its troops from the PoK, which was a necessary condition for restoration of peace leading to a future plebiscite.

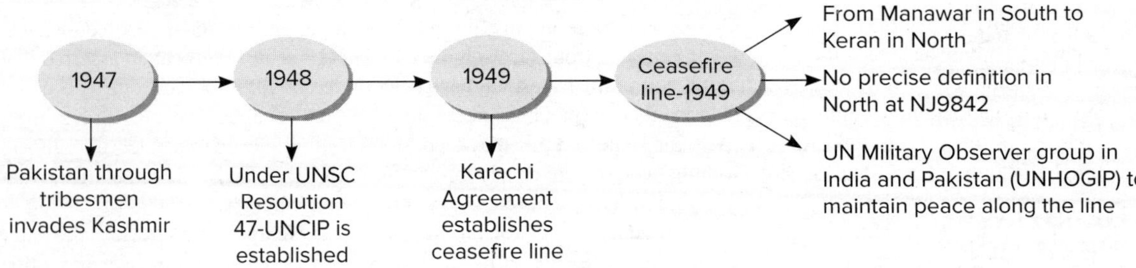

The UNCIP yet again tried under McNaughton's leadership to create a condition for plebiscite by advocating demilitarisation in 1950. However, the UNCIP failed and the UNSC terminated the UNCIP in 1950 and appointed Sir Owen Dixon as the UN Representative to the Security Council. Owen Dixon again proposed the idea of a plebiscite after demilitarisation. On 30 March 1951, following the termination of UNCIP, the Security Council, by its Resolution 91 decided that UNMOGIP should continue to supervise the ceasefire in Jammu and Kashmir. India, by 1960, began to assert that it would not accept international mediation and would resort to a bilateral dialogue with Pakistan over

Kashmir but continue to support plebiscite. India advocated a shift of treating the Kashmir problem as a world question to treating it as a domestic issue.

AGREEMENT ON BOUNDARY BETWEEN CHINESE XINJIANG AND THE CONTIGUOUS AREAS, THE DEFENCE OF WHICH IS UNDER THE CONTROL OF PAKISTAN (1963)

In 1962, India had a border conflict with China. After its defeat in the conflict, it decided to upgrade its military with assistance from the USA, Russia and the UK. After the 1962 conflict, the Pakistanis 'gifted' parts of Ladakh and Aksai Chin (called 5180 square kilometre Shaksgam Valley) to Chinese in 1963 by an agreement called "Agreement on Boundary Between Chinese Xinjiang and the contiguous areas, the defence of which is under the control of Pakistan 1963". For China, these territories they got from Pakistan as a gift were never a part of Jammu and Kashmir, but part of Tibet and Xinjiang under the British rule. (*In the recent times, Chinese have tried to show that even the Hunza region was in union with Xinjiang till 1947–48 and this is because the Hunza ruler Jamal Khan had been negotiating with officials of Xinjiang before he eventually acceded to Pakistan. This does not mean that Chinese have given up their claims for Hunza, though they have just allowed Pakistan to keep it for the time being, but in future, the CPEC enters Pakistan through Hunza, the larger Chinese economic influence in Gilgit–Baltistan will compel them to restart their claims*).

THE 1965 WAR AND TASHKENT AGREEMENT

The British and Americans too used this opportunity to induce bilateral dialogue between the two states. The US sent its Secretary of State, Dean Rusk, to persuade Nehru to initiate a dialogue with Pakistan on the Kashmir issue. From 1962 to 1963, though there was dialogue between the two sides, nothing favourable was achieved. As the talks between the two could not yield any results, it motivated Pakistan to launch yet another offensive in 1965. In 1965, Pakistan launched an offensive based on certain assumptions. Firstly, Pakistan perceived that the 1962 Sino-Indian conflict has proven that Indian Army is very weak and can be defeated easily. Secondly, they perceived that Lal Bahadur Shastri, who succeeded Nehru as the Indian Prime Minister after his death in 1964, is a weak Prime Minister and does not enjoy any international support. Pakistan believed that with the US fully on the side of Pakistan, they could attack India and snatch away Kashmir. In 1965, when Pakistan attacked India, Indian forces gave a befitting response to Pakistan. This happened as Pakistan had miscalculated the fact that India had initiated military modernisation. The Indian response in 1965 led to the miserable defeat of Pakistan. The USA did not want to be involved in the resolution of conflict between the two, as the previous US attempt had not yielded any result. This allowed the USSR to broker peace after the 1965 conflict through the Tashkent Agreement as it saw the bleak US interest as an opportunity to expand its Asian influence. The Tashkent Agreement stated that the Indian and Pakistani forces would pull back to their pre-conflict positions (pre-August 1965 lines), no later than 25 February 1966. Further, the nations would not interfere in each other's internal affairs, economic and diplomatic relations would be restored, there would be an orderly transfer of prisoners of war, and the two leaders would work towards improving bilateral relations. The Tashkent Agreement led to maintenance of status quo by the two sides. After 1965, India was amply frustrated with Pakistan for their repeated territorial aggression.

THE 1971 WAR, SIMLA AGREEMENT AND CEASEFIRE LINE TO LINE OF CONTROL

Indira Gandhi authorised the creation of a lethal covert spy agency called Research and Analysis Wing (RAW) in 1968 and instructed them to teach a lesson to Pakistan for their territorial aggression. In December 1970, Pakistani held a general election. As per the result, the Awami League (led by Sheikh Mujibur Rehaman) won the election in East Pakistan while Pakistan People's Party (PPP) swept the polls in West Pakistan. The PPP and Awami League began negotiating a power sharing agreement but by March 1971, the two reached a more severe deadlock. The Awami League protestors, on failure to reach a power sharing agreement, initiated a massive protest to seek autonomy. The Pakistani army began to suppress the Awami League supporters in Dacca city from March 1971. As the suppression continued, the supporters of the Awami

League began to leave their country and started a migration to the Indian state of West Bengal. As this refugee influx began, India took up the issue diplomatically. As the matter was being negotiated diplomatically, India's RAW began to design a plan to invade East Pakistan and break it away from the control of West Pakistan. The RAW began to train and support the Mukti Bahini movement. The Mukti Bahini movement was a liberation force trained for covert capabilities. Witnessing renewed unrest, on 6th December 1971, Pakistani Air Force launched pre-emptive strikes on Indian air bases in North India. India perceived the attacks on its air bases as attack on the sovereignty of India and decided to militarily retaliate. The Indian forces entered deep inside East Pakistan and captured around 90,000 Prisoners of War (POWs). India subsequently supported Sheikh Mujibur Rehaman and succeeded in seceding East Pakistan from the West. Bangladesh was finally born out of the war. After the 1971 war, in 1972, the two sides decided to sign Simla Agreement. Under the Simla Agreement of 1972, as mentioned above, the ceasefire line was now renamed as LoC and thereby the tenure of UNMOGIP to maintain peace on the ceasefire line came to an end. The Simla agreement of 1972 gave India an opportunity to put the conversion of the Kashmir issue from an international to a bilateral issue on paper. In 1972, under the Simla Agreement, Pakistan agreed to resolve Kashmir bilaterally without any third-party intervention. Though India gained at this point in 1972, however, critics point out that India lost an opportunity in 1972 to make the LoC as an international border.

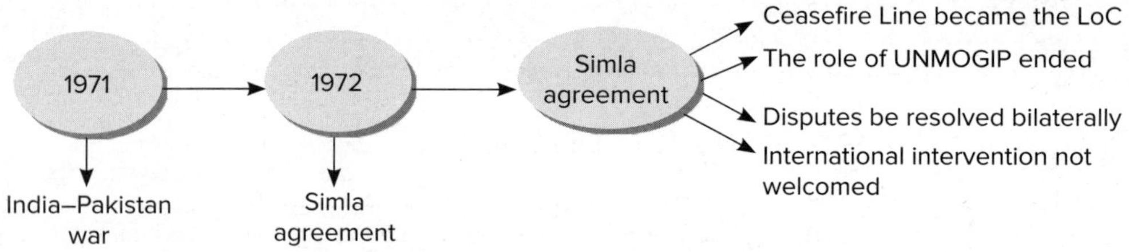

The Simla Agreement of 1972 could not solve all the problems and proved unable to stabilise Kashmir.

After East Pakistan seceded, the US and China began to use Pakistan to create troubles for India. The CIA of the USA, along with Pakistani ISI, began to create unrest in Punjab by supporting terrorism in the form of the Khalistan movement in 1980s. In 1984, the Indian RAW came to know that Pakistan had purchased specialised clothing for very low temperatures for its army from a supplier in London.

OPERATION MEGHDOOT, OPERATION BRASSTACKS, OPERATION SLEDGEHAMMER AND FLYING HORSE

Under the Karachi Agreement, the demarcation in the North at point NJ9842 was not clear. The two sides had no disagreement in the glacier area, as the terrain was uninhabitable. In 1984, Pakistan undertook expeditions in the region near NJ9842 in an area called the Siachen Glacier. The RAW alerted the Indian army and during there one of the operations, the army found a Pakistani expedition team in a place near Siachen. India too launched an expedition in the Siachen Glacier. Pakistan eventually tried to occupy the glacier. In 1984, Indian army, under Operation Meghdoot, thwarted Pakistan's efforts and successfully occupied the Siachen Glacier. India considers Siachen strategically crucial. The Indian army, since then, has favoured a policy of status quo on Siachen while it is the only issue where Pakistan seeks an agreement. The strategic significance of Siachen for India is control of the Karakoram region that Pakistan and China have expanded into, under the pretext of developing a Karakoram highway. India feels that its presence in Siachen can keep the China–Pakistan activities under check. The roots of the Siachen occupation for India, thus, are not embedded in topography but the higher geopolitics of the region. General K. Sundarji led Indian army at that time. To intimidate Pakistan for their role in Khalistan terrorism, Sundarji chose the state of Rajasthan to launch a massive military exercise codenamed as Operation Brasstacks in 1987. The sheer magnitude of the exercise, involving around 1,50,000 soldiers, generated anxieties in Pakistan. The Pakistanis too responded with their own military exercises, codenamed as Operation Sledgehammer and Flying Horse.

THE OPERATION TOPAC EXECUTED IN KASHMIR

As the situation became tensed, the Soviet and the US diplomats and officials of CIA and KGB swung into action and began to work with RAW and ISI officials to reduce tensions. As the crises de-escalated, in an interview to Kuldip Nayar, Pakistan's Abdul Qadeer Khan resorted to nuclear signalling by arguing that Pakistan was on the way to have a nuclear weapon. Rajiv Gandhi authorised the nuclear scientists of Indian to begin work on Indian nuclear bomb. As the crisis defused, General Zia died in a plane crash in 1988 and subsequently, under the US pressure, the Pakistani army decided to go for elections, with Benazir Bhutto assuming power. Bhutto began to initiate a new round of dialogues with Rajiv Gandhi but as the military in Pakistan began to create unrest in Kashmir from 1989, the newly launched peace process was jeopardised. In 1987, Kashmir held elections. After the death of Sheikh Abdullah, Farooq Abdullah, his son, decided to form an alliance with the Congress for the elections. In the 1980s, various social and religious organisations that wanted to resolve the Kashmir issue peacefully formed Muslim United Front (MUF). The MUF too wanted to use the 1987 elections to put forth Kashmiri grievances peacefully at the legislative forum. Farooq Abdullah won the elections. The MUF alleged that the elections were rigged, after which the MUF candidate Mohmmad Yusuf Shah was imprisoned. This led to mass protests in the valley. The 1987 elections and the suppression of MUF had given Pakistan a fertile ground to fuel unrest in the valley. After the elections of 1987, when MUF cadres reached Pakistan for support, the ISI began to train them with arms and ammunition. A Pakistani militant outfit leader Syed Salahuddin too fuelled the protestors through his group, known as the Hizbul Mujahideen (HM), which had been originally founded by Muhammad Ahsan Dar in 1989.

THE CREATION OF COMPETITIVE TANZEEM INDUSTRY AND EXODUS OF KASHMIRI PANDITS

The HM group mobilised Abdul Hamid Sheikh, Ashfaq, Majid Wani, Javed Ahmed Mir and Yasin Malik and formed the Jammu and Kashmir Liberation Front (JKLF). As the JKLF received support and training from Pakistan, in 1989, they attacked a Hindu Kashmiri Pandit, Tika Lal Taploo. The assassination of Taploo created fear amongst the Kashmiri Pandits. The HM too vocally began to assert that Kashmiri Pandits immediately leave the valley, and this led to the exodus of the Kashmiri Pandits in 1989. Kashmir, which had been home to Sufi Islam and Hinduism, who had always coexisted peacefully, witnessed communal crisis. Lashkar-e-Taiba (LeT) was created by Hafiz Saeed in 1989.

AHL-I-HADITH, WAHABISM IN KASHMIR VALLEY AND OPERATION CHANAKYA

The LeT is ideologically linked to the Ahl-i-Hadith interpretations of Islam. Since 1990s, the ISI of Pakistan launched a campaign that sought to infiltrate Kashmir with the Ahl-i-Hadith ideology. The Ahl-i-Hadith interpretation is interlinked with the Wahabism school of Islam, which is one of the most orthodox and stringent forms of Islam practised in the world. Since 1990s, attempts have thus been made to Wahabise the Kashmiri society, which has always practised a softer, Sufi ideology-oriented Islam. Through a dedicated department known as the Joint Intelligence North (JIN), the ISI began to provide support to separatists and terrorist groups to encourage infiltration into Kashmir. They carry out clandestine activities in the Kashmir region. In 1990s, to counter the ISI campaign, RAW stepped in and launched Operation Chanakya. The basic idea of Operation Chanakya was to neutralise ISI groups using Indian counter-insurgency groups. The RAW began to form 'political cells' in Kashmir to counter the separatists. In South Kashmir, Kuka Parray alias Jamsheed Sheraji, in association with RAW formed, the pro-India counter-insurgency outfit called Ikwan-ul-Musalmeen. The Ikwan group neutralised Pakistani groups in South Kashmir. Jamsheed was a member of state assembly of Kashmir. The RAW also created the Muslim Mujahideen to neutralise Pakistani groups in Kashmir. In 1993, 26 social and religious organisations united to form the All Parties Hurriyat Conference (APHC). The APHC began to raise the call for the independence of Kashmir. The USA too had given tacit support to APHC leaders in India and the CIA financially backed it. As violence against the Hindus unfolded in the valley in 1990, the central government decided to appoint Jagmohan Malhotra as the new governor of Kashmir. By 1996, HM and JKLF were severely weakened.

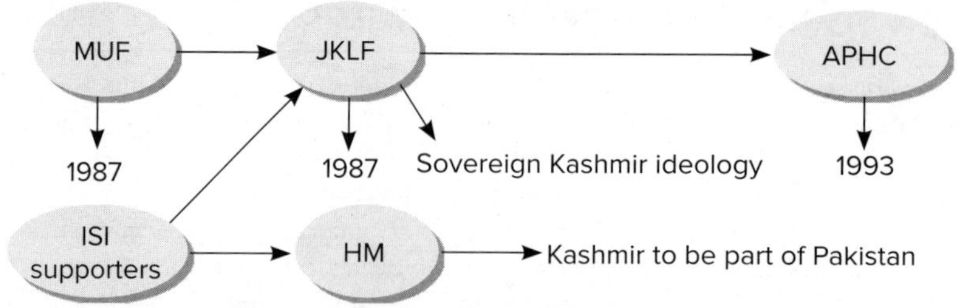

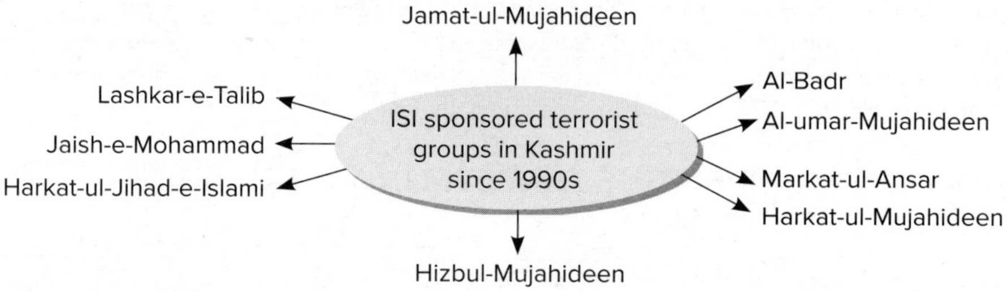

JIHAD UNDER THE NUCLEAR UMBRELLA

The test of nuclear weapons by India and Pakistan in 1998 led to a new dimension of conflict. We have already explained nuclear dimension separately. To defuse rising tensions, Indian Prime Minister Vajpayee, initiated a dialogue by visiting Lahore in February 1999. Vajpayee launched new bus diplomacy between Amritsar and Lahore. During his meeting with Nawaz Sharif, Vajpayee launched a series of Confidence Building Measures (CBMs).

The visit of Vajpayee to Lahore was a watershed event. Vajpayee also visited Minar-e-Pakistan where he publicly asserted that a stable Pakistan is in India's interest. This was the most important statement ever by an Indian head of the state on Pakistani soil, as Vajpayee endorsed the idea of the existence of Pakistan, which had been a long-standing concern for Pakistan. The Minar-e-Pakistan was chosen as a venue to announce this because it was the same place where the Lahore Declaration was passed to establish Pakistan in 1940. Vajpayee appointed a journalist, R. K. Mishra, as an interlocutor for the dialogues on the Kashmir crisis. Nawaz responded by appointing Pakistani diplomat Niaz Naik. For the first time, India decided to bypass official diplomatic channels for talks on Kashmir as Vajpayee, by appointing R. K. Mishra, injected new blood into the negotiations.

THE KARGIL CONFLICT 1999 AND DOCTRINE OF NUCLEAR PROVOCATION

As the dialogue was brought back on track, it got abruptly suspended as from May 1999, the Pakistani army intruded into Kargil and launched an offensive. India and Pakistan had an agreement in 1994, which stated that the two sides would mutually retreat from Kargil and Drass sectors of the LoC in December every year and would re-occupy the posts in March. Pakistan tried to provoke India after the 1998 nuclear tests and in December 1998, they refused to withdraw from the LoC even while the Indian side withdrew. In March 1999, when Indian troops went back to LoC, they found that Pakistan had occupied the peaks on Indian side of the LoC (a breach of Simla Agreement). Despite negotiations to convince Pakistan to withdraw from the occupied peaks, they refused. The Northern Light Infantry (NLI), armed with surface-to-air missiles was the Pakistani force that penetrated inside the LoC and occupied Indian-favoured posts that were vacant. Pakistan occupied the vacant Indian posts and occupied Batalik, Turtuk and Dras in Kargil. In May 1999, the Indian Air force (IAF) launched Operation Safed Sagar, which was a sustained air strike meant to support the ground troops and was aimed to flush out regular and irregular troops of the Pakistani Army from vacated Indian positions in the Kargil sector along the line of control. This air strike came as a big blow to Pakistan as it was never a part of the planned calculations. The innovative airstrikes by India also caused an extremely detrimental psychological impact on Pakistan who found extremely difficult to retaliate. The IAF used innovative bombing mechanisms to cause landslides and avalanches. A massive strike by IAF on a logistical camp in Muntho Dhalo in Batalik sector caused havoc for Pakistan, as it was the sole supply depot for the forces of the Northern Light Infantry Regiment (NLI). By the end of July 1999, the intruders were completely driven out from the posts. Pakistan, alarmed by the Indian response, immediately sought to seek partial de-escalation and an end to air and ground strikes from Indian. In the course of conflict, diplomatically, China favoured a neutral stance, but the ground reality was different. During the crisis, Sharif went to the US and met Clinton on 4th July 1999 in the belief that the US support would help control the crisis. However, Sharif was surprised and shocked to his core when Clinton asserted that the conflict had been initiated by Pakistan and that they had no right to violate the sanctity of the LoC. Pakistan was defeated in Kargil and now wanted an opportunity to seek revenge for Kargil.

THE IC-814 HIJACKING, ATTACK ON INDIAN PARLIAMENT, JAISH-E-MOHAMMAD AND OPERATION PARAKRAM

The Indo-Pak relationship took a severe plunge in December 1999 when IC-814 was hijacked and taken to Kandahar. The IC-814 was a routine flight from Kathmandu to Lucknow. The negotiations led to the release of Maulana Masood Azhar, Mushtaq Ahmed Zarg and Ahmed Umar Syed. This was followed by attacks by terrorists on Amaranath Yatris in 2000. Despite these issues, Musharraf was yet again invited for a dialogue in 2001. The talks again did not occasion in any material success as Musharraf wanted to accomplish some tangible progress on the Kashmir dispute in a single meeting. On 13th December 2001, while the Parliament was in session, terrorists of Lashkar-e-Taiba (LeT) and Jaish-e-Mohammad (JeM) stormed the Parliament complex in New Delhi and began to fire indiscriminately. The Indian security officials swung into action and eliminated the terrorists. After the Parliament attack, there were calls for strong military action on Pakistan. The Indian government, however, resorted to coercive diplomacy. India broke off existing diplomatic ties with Pakistan and recalled its High Commissioner. India closed its airspace for civilian aircrafts of Pakistan while sending Indian jets at forward positions. The army was asked for a timeline for a possible strike on Pakistan. The Indian army stated that any substantial operation against Pakistan would require a minimum of three weeks. To create a deterrent to Pakistan, the Indian government authorised troop mobilisation under Operation Parakram in 2002. In the meantime, Musharraf went public and announced a host of measures to ensure that none of the terror groups use Pakistani soil to wage terrorist attacks against any state. Such announcements in public made it more difficult for India to launch a military offensive. As the ISI received a setback, they initiated a new campaign of violence with a new tactic from 2002.

THE FIDAYEEN PHASE OF TERRORISM AND INDIA AND PAKISTAN CEASEFIRE AGREEMENT 2003

The ISI resorted to a new *fidayeen* phase of the campaign. The idea was to attack army camps, zero down on targets and terrorise the Kashmiri population. The logic behind ISI-sponsored *fidayeen* attacks were to cause a psychological blow to the Indian forces, Indian people, and the Indian state. The ISI used Lashkar-e-Taiba and Jaish-e-Mohammad for the campaign. Because of enormous pressure on Pakistan from the US, Musharraf finally declared a unilateral ceasefire with India along with LoC in 2003 and the two sides signed the India and Pakistan Ceasefire Agreement 2003 under which both sides decided to maintain tranquillity at the LoC and undertake no cross-border firing at the LoC. In 2003, Vajpayee visited Srinagar and announced fresh dialogues with Pakistan called the Composite Dialogues from 2004.

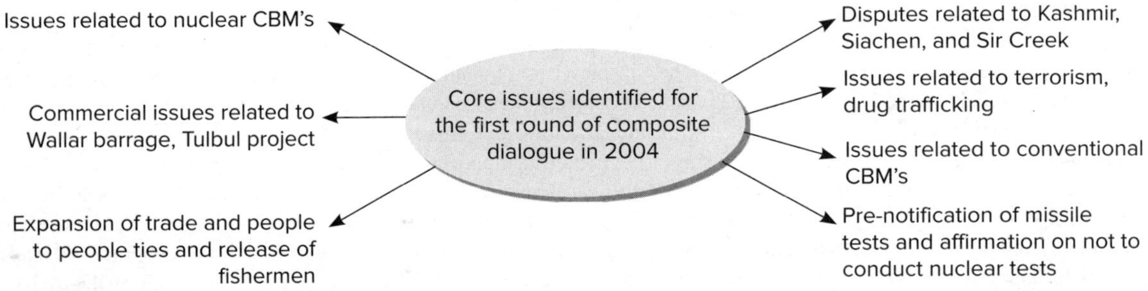

THE COLD START DOCTRINE OF INDIA AND RISE OF SUB-CONVENTIONAL DOCTRINE

The Indian army, on the other hand, after Kargil, began to search for a new doctrine. This led India to toy with the idea of the Cold Start doctrine in 2004, as a doctrine for limited war. Under the Cold Start doctrine, it has been decided to break the large 'strike corps' into division-sized integrated battle groups, which, with thorough speed, will resort to rapid mobilisation. Such mobilisation will resort to swift manoeuvre over Pakistan and capture a limited strip of land through air, ground and naval action. Such captured territory is to be used as a bargaining chip with Pakistan. In 2004, the Vajpayee government was replaced with the government of Manmohan Singh. Manmohan Singh decided to carry forward the idea of Composite Dialogue. Manmohan Singh stressed the idea of negotiating with Pakistan, as he strongly believed that India would not be able to position itself as a global player if it remained mired in conflict with Pakistan. The diplomatic ties were re-established, and a process of normalisation began. It decided to reduce troop presence in Kashmir and decided to help in establishing a channel for negotiations with Kashmiri separatists. Satinder Lambah led the back-channel diplomacy launched by India. It resulted in start of Srinagar–Muszaffarabad bus service. Musharraf paid a one-day visit to India and attended an Indo-Pak cricket match. However, a crisis erupted again as terrorists struck the Srinagar–Muzaffarabad bus service. The negotiations continued in 2006 and Manmohan Singh even offered a new Treaty of Peace, Security and Friendship to Pakistan. However, Pakistan responded to the offer of the treaty by asserting that Kashmir remained their central question. The peace process was derailed in July 2006, when LeT cadres orchestrated the blasts in local trains in Mumbai. The peace process moved at an extremely slow pace after the blasts. In September 2006, the two sides established a Joint Mechanism for Investigation and Countering Terrorism. In December 2006, Musharraf announced a four-step package approach for the Kashmir problem.

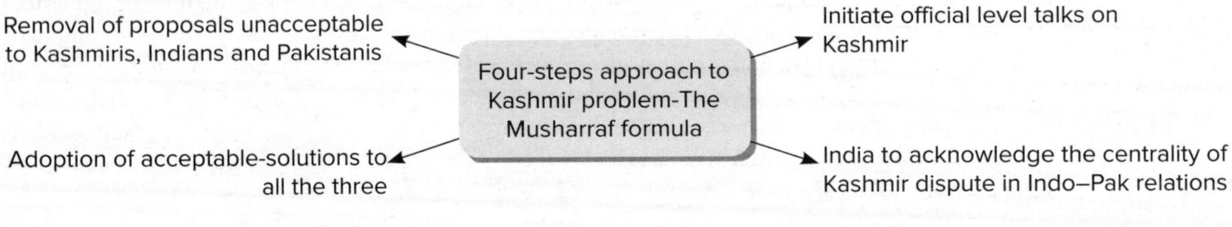

In February 2007, the Samjhauta Express was bombed. As any Pakistani group did not take the responsibility of this bombings, the talks continued. The Mumbai blasts (26/11) in 2008 altogether halted the peace process.

THE AMARNATH VIOLENCE, MACHIL ENCOUNTER AND STONE-PELTING PHASE OF UPRISING IN KASHMIR

In 2008, the Indian government, along with the government of Kashmir, decided to undertake a land transfer of 99 acres to the Sri Amarnath Shrine Board (SASB). Such a land transfer immediately assumed a communal dimension and Hindu–Muslim violence broke out. After intense and heated debates, the government decided to stall the transfer to the SASB. However, the political parties had already begun to believe that Islam was under threat in Kashmir and violence unfolded. In 2010, the Indian army carried out an encounter of terrorists in the Machil Sector in the district of Kupwara. Investigation found that instead of militants, the army had killed civilians living in Rafiabad area and had done a fake encounter. A month later, in June 2010, during a police crackdown, the police killed some innocents in the Srinagar area. This led to massive protests. The protestors began to pelt stones at the security forces. The protestors demanded the Indian troops to 'quit Kashmir'. The ISI saw an opportunity to revive their support to the protestors in the valley. The RAW found evidence that the ISI had begun to use social media platforms to mobilise the Kashmiri youth against India. The Indian government announced measures to curtail tensions. Apart from an all-party meeting, the government decided to appoint interlocutors to Kashmir. The army, too, brought the perpetrators of Machil fake encounter to task. As the situation turned to normalcy, again sparks erupted. In 2013, the government hanged Afzal Guru. His hanging for his role in the Parliament attack caused a massive unrest in the valley.

MODI DOCTRINE AND STRATEGY OF DENIAL

In 2014, Modi government came to power and Modi tried to break the ice with Pakistan, but terrorist attacks in Pathankot, Pampore, Uri, Kupwada and Pulwama in 2019 have again led to the suspension of the composite dialogue.

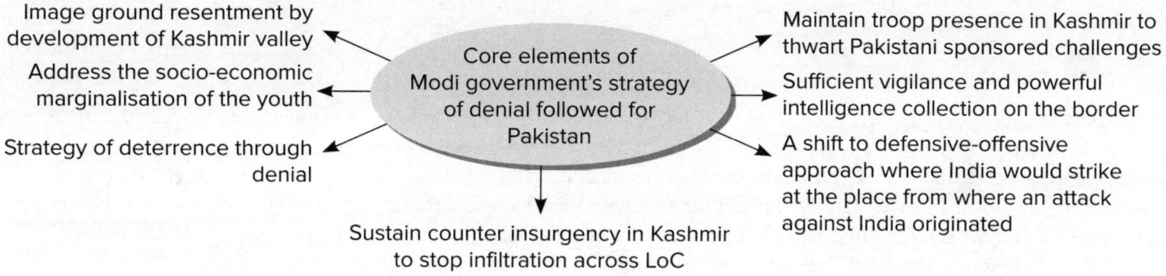

In 2015, the PDP decided to form a government in Kashmir in alliance with the BJP. The people of the valley did not favour such an alliance. This angered the youth and certain sections of the youth again found solace in extremism.

BURHAN WANI AND HYBRID TERRORISM IN KASHMIR

Burhan Wani was a classic example as he joined the Hizbul Mujahideen (HM). The HM, adequately supported by the ISI, aggressively used the social media for radicalisation and indoctrination. The HM made him the commander of South Kashmir. His youthful age and sincerity found immense resonance amongst alienated Kashmiri youth. On 8th July 2016, the Indian armed forces killed Wani in an encounter. His death led to an upsurge in the valley. Lakhs of people attended his funeral. The ISI and HM, through social media, instigated the youth to resort to stone pelting against the Indian forces. Prem Shankar Jha has called the 2016 unrest in the valley as a Kashmiri intifada. This radical suicidal stone pelting, in the face of pellet guns and other armed forces ammunition, is an outcome of Pakistan-sponsored radical Wahabi indoctrination amongst the youth. The ISI of Pakistan, according to RAW, has earmarked 1000 crores to be given to groups in Kashmir to create stone-pelting led unrest.

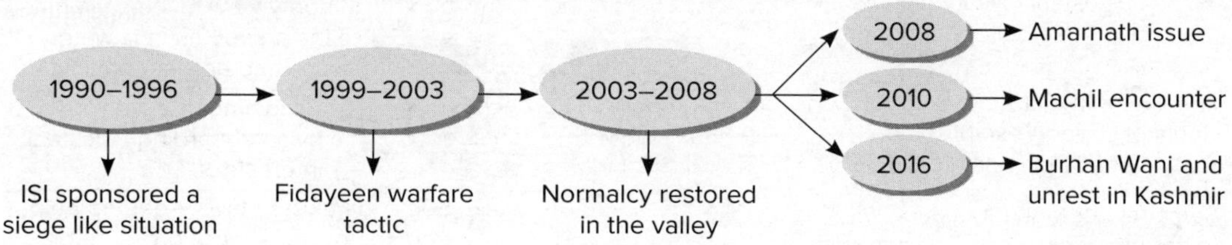

The RAW has found that Pakistani strategy is to instigate Kashmiri youth to obstruct forces and pelt stones at them, which will inevitably lead to forces using fire upon youth. The more youth are killed, the more it would alienate the Kashmiri population further from India. Such alienation will provide the ISI to activate HM and other groups to radicalise youth by preaching Wahabism. The radicalised Wahabi youth would resort to Jihad to create more unrest in the valley. However, an understanding of deeper dynamics of protestors and stone pelters point out different factors for the uprising. Apart from the anger against the security forces, the protestors were also frustrated due to lack of employment as there were no jobs for the youth, with instances of violence arbitrarily perpetrated by security personnel alienating Kashmiri youth further. A lot of suggestions have been put forward for resolving the crises. The most important, however, is that the government should address the alienation of the Kashmiri youth and bring them into the mainstream society. There should be immediate job creation and political mobilisation of the youth and efforts should be taken to connect the youth to the political processes in the country. Taking advantage of the void created by the failure of institutional mechanisms by the state and the central government's side, Pakistan is back in the valley with a vengeance.

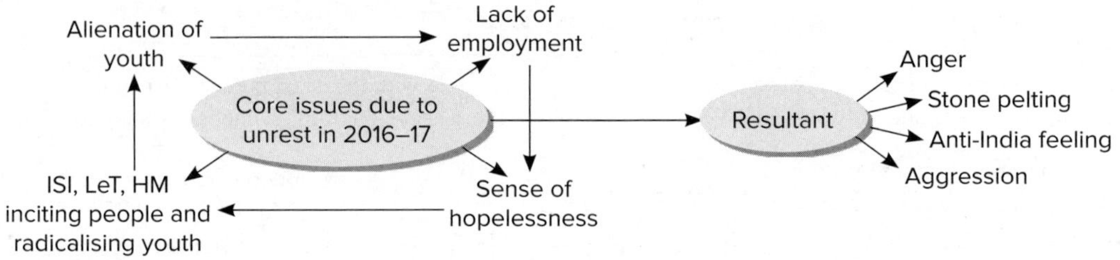

In 2019, the Union Government abrogated Article 370. Since 2019, the Union government has clarified that talks and terrorism cannot go together. The government has stated that till the time Pakistan does not stop sponsoring terror, India would not resume a dialogue and the talks remain suspended till 2020. Though both states have nuclear weapons and have ruled out a possibility of a fully-fledged nuclear war, they have resorted to continuing a sub-conventional war by using the ISI and the RAW. Only a few options remain in bringing about normalisation. One is that both sides resort to a 'do-nothing' approach. India has largely followed the idea of 'masterly inactivity' under Modi.

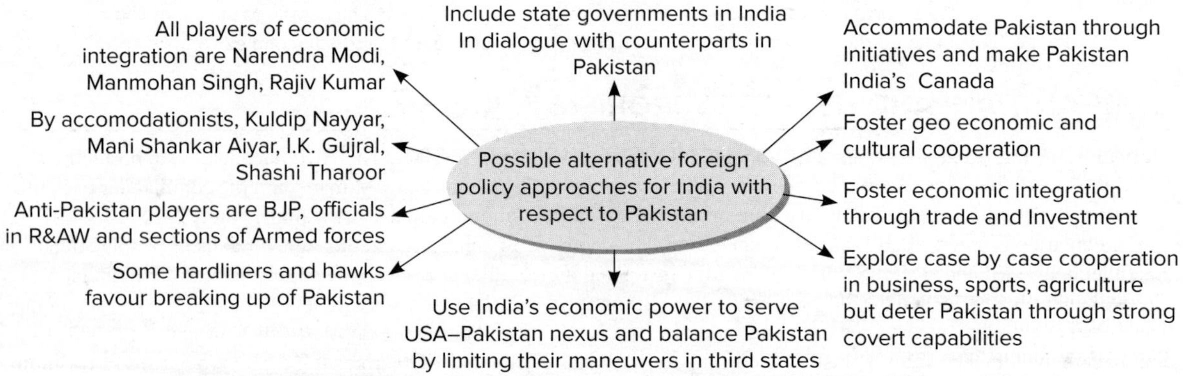

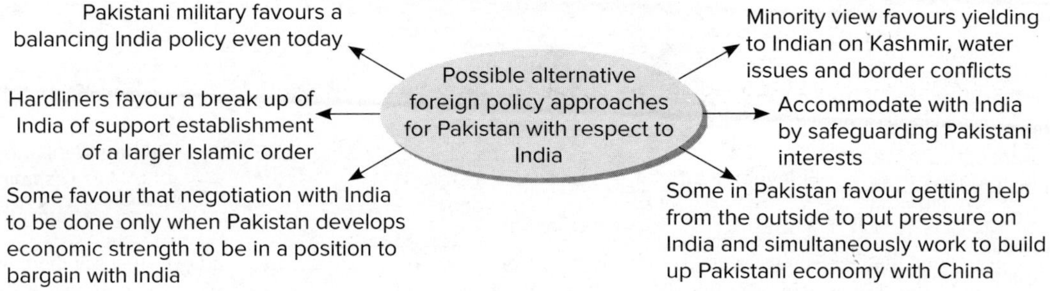

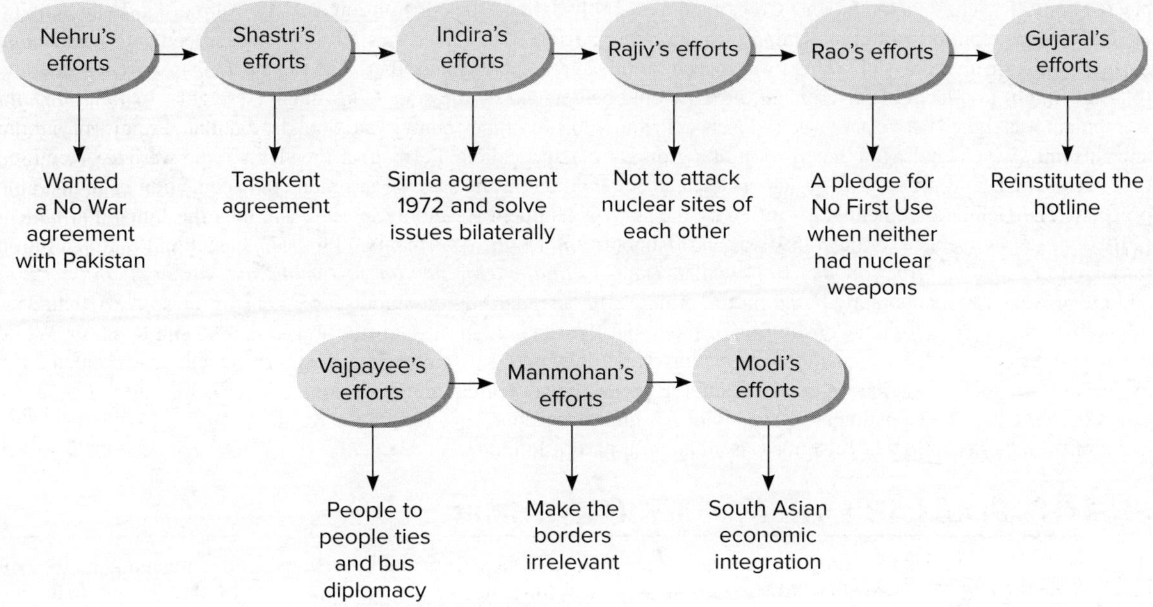

HISTORICAL ORIGIN OF ARTICLE 370

India may be a very ancient civilisation, but the modern-day India and Pakistan are political creations of the British, created through political agreement called the Partition Plan of 3rd June 1947, which was announced by the British for partitioning the subcontinent. The political agreement above was crystallised in law and the British Parliament amended the Government of India Act of 1935 and later enacted the Indian Independence Act of 1947. On the 15th August 1947, Jammu and Kashmir was a sovereign princely state under Hari Singh and was not part of India or Pakistan. Then, in 1947, a strategy was employed by the British and Pakistan called the tribal invasion to get Jammu and Kashmir to accede to Pakistan, which eventually boomeranged because the ruler, Hari Singh, acceded to India on 26th October 1947. With the accession of Kashmir, entire state of Kashmir became an integral part of India. The Accession Instrument was a model template that was given by India to all the princely states to accede to Union of India. It enabled the Union of India to exercise control over external affairs, communications, defence and ancillary matters of the princely states. The princely states eventually executed supplementary instruments to the Instrument of Accession to cede further powers to the Union of India, which eventually enabled them to adopt the future Constitution of India. The princely states executed instruments of merger and merged their territories to the Union of India, but the Princely State of Jammu and Kashmir refused to do so. The Princely State of Jammu and Kashmir sent four representatives to the Constituent Assembly of India. They stated that Princely State of Jammu and Kashmir wants to limit the accession of the state to the terms Kashmir of the accession. This means that the four representatives stated that the Kashmir would be giving only external affairs, communications and defence to the Union of India. The four also stated that if India wishes to talk about matters other than the ones mentioned above in the Instrument of Accession, then they need the consent of the state of Kashmir. This position of the four representatives was reflected in Article 370, which was drafted by the Indian Constituent Assembly. The provision of Article 370 stated that the President of India could apply powers of the Indian Constitution to the state in respect of matters mentioned in the Instrument of Accession after consulting the state of Kashmir and on matters outside the Instrument of Accession, only with the consent of the state. Article 370 stated that the state Constituent Assembly would frame the Constitution of Jammu and Kashmir. The state Constituent Assembly would further define the constitutional relationship of the state of Kashmir with India. But, as the state Constituent Assembly was yet to be set up and the constitutional relationship was yet to be decided. Dr. Ambedkar decided to keep the provisions of Article 370 under Part XXI of the Indian Constitution as "Temporary Transitional and Special Provisions". In 1951, the State Constituent Assembly of Jammu and Kashmir was set up as an elected body. The chairperson of state Constituent Assembly defined the constitutional relationship of Kashmir as being an autonomous republic within the Union of India. After Article 370, a need was felt for a new agreement, which came as the Delhi Agreement of 1952. There was a need for this agreement because there had to be a transition from monarchy (of Hari Singh) to a form of government, which would be decided by the state Constituent Assembly. In 1952, a Delhi Agreement was signed between Jawaharlal Nehru, Prime Minister of the country, and Sheikh Abdullah, Premier of Jammu and Kashmir, which envisaged the creation of a group of persons called "Permanent Residents" who were to be entitled to "special rights and privileges" in matters such as employment in the state government and acquisition of immovable property. The Delhi Agreement was ratified by the state Constituent Assembly in 1952 and then the Indian Parliament ratified it in the same year. Article 35A was an offshoot of the Delhi Agreement and it was included in the Constitution through a Presidential Order of May 1954 [called *The Constitution (Application to Jammu and Kashmir) Order, 1954*] and the provision was apparently based on the principle of safeguarding the interests of "sons of the soil". Article 35A did not figure in the text of the Constitution of India, but figured only in the Constitution of Jammu and Kashmir. While the 1954 Presidential Order constituted a founding legal document for Jammu and Kashmir, Article 35A protected the exclusive laws, such as the bar on outsiders buying property and women marrying non-Kashmiris losing their property rights of the State. The Constituent Assembly of Kashmir adopted a Constitution for Kashmir on 17th November 1956. The Constitution declared that Kashmir was an integral part of India.

SHEIKH ABDULLAH'S TREACHERY IN KASHMIR

It is important to note that the abrogation of the 'Article 370' and those 'Special Provisions' had no meaning at all when they were abrogated. When Article 370 was introduced, it was introduced only at the insistence of Sheikh Abdullah, who wanted to keep a possibility open to seek independence for Kashmir. His aim was to seek independence for the entire state, even from the non-Muslim people and from non-Kashmiri regions. His administration tried his level best to keep the Hindus, Sikhs and Buddhists in Kashmir as second-class citizens. The logic of Sheikh Abdullah was that Kashmir is a Muslim-majority state. The majority of the Muslims are Kashmiris and they want independence. He wanted complete centralisation of power in his hands (by asserting 'azadi') because he wanted to seek a revenge that how could a Hindu-minority ruler yielded power on Muslims in the state. In 1952, Sheikh Abdullah had greeted Prime Minister Jawaharlal Nehru at Lal Chowk in Srinagar, with a couplet from the Sufi poet, Amir Khusro: *"Mun tu shudam tu mun shudi, mun tun shudam tu jaan shudi; Taakas na guyad baad azeen, mun deegaram tu deegari* (I have become you, and you me, I am the body, you soul; So, that no one can say hereafter, that you are someone, and me someone else.) This couplet captures why he wanted to use his friendship with Nehru to seek the concessions he had in his mind, which he succeeded, as we have explained previously in the 1952 New Delhi Agreement. However, his ambitions were cut short during the regime of Nehru itself when he was imprisoned in 1953, as Nehru believed that Sheikh Abdullah was displaying secessionist tendencies. After Nehru, his successors virtually brought all autonomy of Kashmir to zero by amending Article 370 time and again. The successors of Sheikh Abdullah, Bakshi Ghulam Mohammad and Mir Qasim ensured that Union government could spread their tentacles by amending Article 370. What was eventually left after 44 such amendments to Article 370 was just a myth of Kashmiri autonomy. Article 370 was now a symbol without any real content of Jammu and Kashmir's autonomy and special status. The parties in Kashmir to mollify the Muslims of Kashmir under the current called 'Kashmiri sentiment' often used this myth. The real issue was Article 35A which did not allow the people of Jammu and Ladakh to settle in Kashmir, even though the Kashmiri people could freely reside in Jammu and Ladakh. This is what the abrogation seeks to rectify. Historically, there is an argument that Article 370 was brought in a very notorious background. Article 370 was being negotiated in the Indian Constituent Assembly as Article 306A. On 27th May 1949, a discussion took place in the Indian Constituent Assembly to nominate members from Jammu and Kashmir to the Indian Constituent Assembly. As per the rules at that time, if a Princely state was to send four members to the Indian Constituent Assembly, then out of the four members, two were to be nominated by the ruler of the Princely State and the other two would be from the provincial legislatures (Praja Sabha) in the Princely States that were in existence prior to Indian independence. This rule was religiously followed for all other princely states except Jammu and Kashmir. The reason was because Nehru stated that Praja Sabha elections that happened in Jammu and Kashmir in 1946 were fraudulent elections and they have no legal validity to send nominations to Indian Constituent Assembly. Nehru even asserted that Hari Singh would also not nominate any members.

Nehru advanced an idea that all four members from Jammu and Kashmir would be nominated in consultation with Sheikh Abdullah only. Ironically, Sheikh Abdullah had not only boycotted the Praja Sabha elections in Jammu and Kashmir in 1946 but, while the rest of the country was busy fighting the British, Sheikh Abdullah had launched Quit Kashmir agitation against Hari Singh. Surprisingly, this was the man in whom Nehru had reposed his trust. Abdullah eventually got the four members nominated, which included Abdullah himself and Mirza Afzal Baig, Maulana Masoodi and Moti Ram Baigra. Thorough this discriminatory provision, the political parties of the state kept the myth of 'special status to Kashmir' alive and robbed the people of the state of any development and putting an end to this propaganda was the need of the hour.

ACQUIRE, INTERNATIONALISE AND CRY

We have already explained that the state of Kashmir acceded unconditionally to India in three areas and ancillary matter and India stated that they accept this accession provisionally and asserted that they would let the people of the state decide the future of the accession. But this is where the issue began. After the tribal invasion by Pakistan, India took the matter to the United Nations. India urged the world community to comment on the happenings of the state. India complained to the United Nations of Pakistani aggression and eventually committed to a plebiscite in Kashmir. India is the only country on earth which went to the United Nations and asserted that there was aggression in our territory and come back from the United Nations by promising to conduct a plebiscite to see whether territory under externally sponsored aggression part of our territory is even or not. Thus, it was India, which made Kashmir a disputed territory in front of the international community. Despite our repeated assertions that Kashmir is an integral part of India, if we look at the situation of Kashmir outside the borders of India, it is till date marked as a disputed territory by countries in the maps they have. All this happened because Indian government itself casted a doubt on the title to the state by accepting the accession provisionally and then internationalising the same. Surprisingly later India began to follow a policy of territorial status quo by asserting that Kashmir is a bilateral issue and that the United Nations has nothing to do with the Kashmir dispute. What we ironically forget is that each time we assert that Kashmir is a bilateral issue, we end up in conferring a standing on Pakistan other than that of an aggressor. This clearly proves that the 'Kashmir issue' is not an issue of Article 370 but the real Kashmir issue is about getting back the territory of Kashmir not with us, the PoK. The real Kashmir issue is also about getting back the Kashmiri citizens back into the mainstream of the society. The real Kashmir issue is about getting rid of the 'disputed territory' tag on Kashmir and this is what the abrogation of Article 370 initiates to do.

POLITICAL CONSENSUS TO REVOKE ARTICLE 370

Politically speaking, Dr. Ambedkar himself was not in favour of limited powers to the Union on Kashmir and he even called the proposal as a treacherous thing against the national interests of India. On 27th November 1963, Nehru pointed out in the parliament that Article 370 is only a temporary provision and is a part of the constitution as long as it remains so. In 1964, a Private Members Bill in the Parliament got near-unanimous support seeking the abrogation of Article 370. In fact, a non-official resolution to seek the revocation of the article was moved by Prakash Vir Shastri in the Lok Sabha and it had the support of Ram Manohar Lohiya and K. Hanumanthaiya. K. Hanumanthaiya, the Congress stalwart, went on to say that Article 370 in no way fulfills the dream of national integration. The fact that Home Minister of Nehru, Gulzari Lal Nanda stated that Article 370 is nothing more than a shell emptied of its contents proves that this dysfunctional provision had limited utility.

BREAKING THE INVISIBLE BERLIN WALL OF ARTICLE 370

Political royalty over the last few decades have ensured that Kashmiri democracy lived up to Iqbal's warning that "*Jamhuriyat ik tarz-e-hukumat hai ki jis mein bandon ko gina karte hain taula nahin karte*" (democracy is a system where people are counted but not weighed). This wall of Article 370, which existed as an invisible Berlin Wall was made tyrannical and diabolical by separatists and local politics. The abrogation of Article 370 is the first step towards the fall of this invisible Berlin Wall. Zubin Mehta had rightly stated that all those people who scream about Kashmir being an armed camp are in fact responsible for keeping it that way.

FAILURE OF GUPKAR MODEL

Since 1952, Kashmir became a victim to Gupkar model. In Srinagar, there is a street named Gupkar road. It houses not only the political, business and security elite of the valley, but the haunted guesthouses that had become the interrogation centres. Gupkar road was the Union Government's approach to Kashmir. In Gupkar road what had unleashed in the last 70 years was a network of patronage and power that had been gamed by friends and adversaries of the valley. The Gupkar model had incentivised bad politics and rent seeking bureaucracy. Shorn of its ideological fervour, it was imperative for the Union government to bring a new plan of directly reaching out to the people of Kashmir without the mediation of separatists and mainstream politicians of the valley who had been demanding more autonomy as the only solutions. This is what Modi government wanted to achieve.

ISLAMIC CALIPHATE IN KASHMIR

Since 2016, when Burhan Wani, the Hizbul commander was shot down, there was a new security threat in the valley. The Internet space was widely used by the extremist groups to carry out large-scale radicalisation. Surprisingly, this radicalisation was not for Azadi or merger with Pakistan but was a call for a Caliphate in Kashmir. The Kashmiri youth were being indoctrinated with the Islamic State videos, which tried to convince the youth that Azadi was overwhelmed by Jihadi. The political space in the valley was drying up because the mainstream parties still held on to the idea that engagement with the separatists is the only solution, despite the separatist model of engagement having outlived its utility. Thus, there was a space to break from the past and bring a new wave of engagement, which abrogation of Article 370 strived to seek.

GEOPOLITICAL INFLUENCE OF TALIBAN

The move to abrogate Article 370 was also based on immediate geopolitics in the region. In Afghanistan, the Americans have concluded a deal with Taliban (explained in India and Afghanistan chapter). Even though India has a deep relationship with Taliban and knows that Taliban will never target or attack India or Kashmir; but India had a fear that Taliban may not be in a position to prevent ISI of Pakistan to use Afghanistan under Taliban to train jihadi elements for the valley, thereby necessitating the abrogation and ramp up security. Rising unilateralism in global politics, decline in multilateral arrangements and immediate geopolitics drove Indian moves.

DONALD TRUMP'S MEDIATION FACTOR

The American President Donald Trump, non-professional managing global affairs, made statements that India wanted the US to mediate between India and Pakistan on Kashmir. The irony is that the Indian Prime Minister mentioned to Trump that he could help to reduce tensions in the subcontinent, which was perceived by Trump as Indian Prime Minister asserting the need for him to act as a mediator between India and Pakistan on Kashmir. The fact is that when Trump starts speaking, it is a freewheeling fact-free stream of consciousness performance where each of his sentences leads to something more fantastical until it all ends in a mind-numbing spaghetti soup.

DISCRIMINATION ANGLE IN KASHMIR

There was a widespread allegation that Articles 370 and 35A were discriminatory to women of the valley. This was so because if Kashmiri women married outside the state, she would be deprived of the permanent residency rights and would end up losing property and employment rights. In 2002, the Jammu and Kashmir High Court gave a judgment where it upheld the rights to the Kashmiri women but deprived the rights to their children. This would not be the case anymore post-abrogation. Article 35A also prevented outsiders to purchase land, property, set up manufacturing industries or take up government jobs. All these led to shortages of qualified doctors, professional educational institutions and arrested industrial growth of the state. The Dalits in the state were denied reservation and permanent residency certificates. To keep the Scheduled Castes away from political power, the state had decided not to increase political seats in the legislature till 2031. The fundamental rights of PoK refugees, Kashmiri Pandits, Sikhs, West Pakistan refugees, Valmiki members, communities displaced by firing from LoC, people of Ladakh and descendants of Gorkha soldiers were denied.

PREVENTION OF NATIONAL INTEGRATION THEORY

The provisions of Right to Information, Right to Education and Comptroller and Auditor General of India did not apply to Kashmir. The root causes of youth angst and alienation of people of the valley are deep-rooted corruption embedded in the administrative structures of the state. Corruption is not addressed at the fringes but has to be tackled at the core of the rotten system and this is what probably Article 370 aims to address.

UNDERSTANDING THE PROCESS FOR EK DESH EK VIDHAN EK SAMVIDHAN

The Union Home Minister introduced two statutory resolutions on 5th August 2019. The first was to recommend that the President issue a notification rendering Article 370 inoperative, and the second was to accept the Jammu and Kashmir Reorganisation Bill. The passage of the former resolution enabled the President to declare that Article 370 is inoperative. The bill, that is now an act, has converted Jammu and Kashmir into a Union Territory with a legislature, and Ladakh region as another Union Territory, but without a legislature. It is on 5th August 2019 that the Indian President Ram Nath Kovind issued a presidential order under Article 370(1) of the Constitution, which enabled the President to specify the matters that are applicable to Jammu and Kashmir. As it could be issued only with the Jammu and Kashmir government's concurrence, the notification used the words "with the concurrence of the Government of the State of Jammu and Kashmir". This meant that the Governor of Kashmir, who was administering the State under President's Rule after the fall of the state government since 2018, has given his concurrence on behalf of the State government. The Order of the President also superseded the 1954 Presidential Order. This effectively means that all the provisions that formed the basis of a separate "Constitution" for Jammu and Kashmir stood abrogated. The Order declared that all the provisions of the Constitution of India would now apply to Jammu and Kashmir. However, some special measures were still needed for the scrapping of Article 370. This is why a few separate clauses were added to Article 367 of the Constitution, which contained "Interpretations". The provisions of Article 367 contain guidance on how to read or interpret some provisions of the Constitution. The new clauses now added say that all references to the 'Sadar-i-Riyasat' earlier, acting on the aid and advice of the Council of Ministers will now be construed as references to the Governor of Jammu and Kashmir and all references to the State government now shall mean "the Governor". The reference to the "Constituent Assembly" present in Article 370(3) has been amended and now it is read as "Legislative Assembly of the State". Article 370(3) is the provision that stated that the President could declare that Article 370 is no more operative only on the recommendation of the Constituent Assembly. But as of 5th August 2019, since there was no Constituent Assembly, it means that there was no body to "recommend" the demise of Article 370 and this is why the State Assembly had to play that role because the government had made use of the fact that Jammu and Kashmir is under President's Rule.

THE INTEGRITY CRITIQUE TO ABROGATION

We have seen wide level of criticism of the decision to abrogate Article 370. The critics argue that BJP has asserted that abrogation of Article 370 was a step towards integration of India but they say that BJP conflated 'integrity' with 'integration'. The Indian effort was to preserve the integrity of the nation. Integrity was a quality to be honoured and an attack on the integrity of the nation was an attack on its honour and was not to be tolerated. Kashmir was an integral part of India. An integer was a whole and India was an integer and fractions were illegal. Fractions caused fractures in the integer and were thus not integral. When truth and integrity conflicted it was integrity that was to be given precedence. Integration may involve forced homogenisation but integrity is moral disposition towards truth and honesty.

THE CONSTITUTIONAL CRITICISM TO ABROGATION

The logic here is that there are serious legal infirmities in the manner in which the abrogation has been carried out. The critics argue that Article 370 is a kind of royalty and was the only article of the Indian Constitution that had the privilege of choosing the mechanism of its own review. Though the matter is already in the Supreme Court, but the question to ponder is that can the will of an extinct Constituent Assembly prevail over the will of the Indian Parliament, as the Indian Parliament had successfully passed the changes?

THE DEMOCRATIC ARGUMENT TO ABROGATION

The criticism is based on a democratic argument that the will of the people of Kashmir was not ascertained before the abrogation. Both the houses of the Indian parliament have passed the changes brought by the Union of India and the changes have received the assent of the President of India also. In no way does the democratic argument hold true anymore. However, the question to ponder is that can the purported wishes of the valley override the wishes of the people of India (represented in the Parliament)? If so, then it is nothing short of an extraordinary claim of democratic entitlement. Democracy is firstly a system of electoral power. In 2019 general elections, the BJP received 229 million votes and the party during the election had committed to abrogate Article 370. Having received the electoral majority, it does fulfil the democratic criteria.

THE HISTORICAL ARGUMENT TO ABROGATION

The criticism revolves around the historical argument. It asserts that even if the articles are modified, the constitutional guarantees given by Nehru to Kashmir at the time of its accession remain valid and should continue to be honoured. It is very hard to believe the idea that Nehru offered any blank cheque to Kashmir with no expiry date. He designed Article 370 to ensure assimilation of Kashmir to the 'idea of India'.

THE POLITICAL ETHICS ARGUMENT TO ABROGATION

The criticism is that the abrogation has led to harsh security measures and a complete lockdown in the valley. This argument is based on the logic of morality and civil liberties of the people. This argument says that democracy is a system of political ethics, which states that in a democracy, those affected by a decision are given a chance to speak up even if they are destined to lose by the decision. They also assert that the Kashmiri people were not allowed to speak and their leaders were arrested and Kashmir witnessed emergency-type situation. Considering that the changes brought about were far reaching and historic, there was a possibility of large-scale unprecedented violence. The question to ponder is that is trying to prevent mass violence immoral or a duty of a responsible government?

THE BILATERALISM FAILURE THESIS

The criticism is regarding India's policy that India has always asserted that Kashmir is a bilateral dispute (basing it on understanding achieved with Pakistan in the 1971 Simla Agreement) but India cannot have a duality in its policy of maintaining that it is a bilateral issue to resolve and yet rejecting bilateral dialogue with Pakistan. This criticism remains valid for the time being but the abrogation has an impact on Pakistan policy. Now, in the future diplomatic relations between India and Pakistan, Kashmir will no longer be the 'unresolved agenda' or 'unresolved issue'. This means that any resumption of dialogue with Pakistan is no longer based on 'past parameters'.

INTERNAL COLONIALISM CHALLENGE

The criticism is that the government will now try to study the records of policies of Israel and China on restive areas. The government will deliberately promote migration of people from other states to Kashmir and such a policy reeks of internal colonialism.

INDIA WANTS TO BE CHINA AND NOT BE CHINA

There is a criticism that asserts the manner in which Article 370 was abrogated, shrouded in secrecy, with no democratic consultations, arrests, crackdowns and shutdown of communications is a strategy that India has apparently borrowed from Chinese. Even though India has had a schizophrenic relationship with China, but this divergence seems to be patching up. Today, India wants to be China and not be China. It wants to be recognised for its six-lanes highways and would love to be called a manufacturing powerhouse but would also want to be praised for yoga and political swiftness. Both have a common problem of how to tackle with their restive ethno-nationalist populations demanding independence and higher autonomy (for China, it is Hong Kong, Xinjiang and Tibet and for India it is Kashmir and the Northeast). Same way, both, thorough display of aggressive nationalism, in the recent times have declared the border regions as integral to the country and refuse to accept the presence of any dispute in the region (with China now claiming that Tibet has been a part of Chinese territory for 700 years) and the periphery being labelled as lands crucial for national security. The dissenters are labelled as "splittists" in China and "separatists" in India. In China, the regime of Xi Jinping has created propaganda that these regions of Tibet and Xinjiang have always been given special privileges and special sops. They have always misused those special sops for ulterior motives, rent seeking and corruption. They have prevented the application of national laws and have prevented the Han Chinese to settle down in these areas, thereby depriving the nationalist masses of their due rights. We do not need to draw a parallel on Kashmir narrative of the BJP here, as the things are crystal clear. It has been argued that both India and China are 'postcolonial informal empires', whose anti-imperialist rhetoric disguises their imperialistic attempts to "consolidate and discipline their borderlands." But what used to distinguish India from the more common charges of colonialism faced by China was the fact that the people of Jammu and Kashmir had been provided guarantees under Articles 370 and 35A of the Indian Constitution, along with a strong foundation to build a system of local governance. The ban on non-locals buying land, and permanently settling in the State, also prevented demographic engineering like the large-scale Han migration into Tibet and Xinjiang. Independent India's crowning achievement till date had been the development of institutional mechanisms for negotiating large-scale diversity and accommodating frequent, aggressive disagreements. This is an achievement that deserves as much awe and respect as China's economic miracle since 1978. It might be less shiny and more chaotic, but it is, in its own way, quite spectacular. Debate and contestation are not a discardable option for India but an existential necessity. Historically, India has been a civilisational rather than territorial entity, more metaphysical than geographic. It is a nation held together not by language, religion or geography, but by an idea. Multiplicity is foundational to this idea. It is what has allowed India to persist and flourish as a political unit, despite the once widespread belief in the West that an independent India would inevitably Balkanise. The abrogation of Article 370 by the Indian government may well help cover up some of the cracks that its relatively liberal history was unable to weld. It may also fail to do so and lead to complete rupture. But the risk of India forsaking its own sources of strength of pluralism and debate and to emerge as a second rate copy of its muscular, nationalist neighbour to the north is clear.

PAKISTAN'S MUSLIM UMMAH SUPPORT TACTIC

First, it sought the support of Muslim Ummah (namely the Gulf states led by Kingdom of Saudi Arabia) to condemn the step of Indian. The Ummah pledged support for a bilateral solution than one against India. This has happened due Indian economic diplomacy. Thus, Pakistan got deprived of the Ummah option.

PAKISTAN'S WAR AGAINST INDIA TACTIC

Second, Pakistan initiated rhetoric of an attack on India and even threatened to wage a full-fledged nuclear war. This option was ruled out as despite all efforts of Pakistan to seek military parity with India, it had understood and internalised that conventional military war with India was not an option anymore. It also realised the futility of the nuclear rhetoric as no country in the world even responded to such rhetorical show of Pakistan.

PAKISTAN'S EATING FLESH OF AMERICA STRATEGY

Third, Pakistan pressurises the US knowing that the Americans were seeking support of Pakistan to move out of the mess in Afghanistan. Pakistan tried to assert to the US that bloodletting in Kashmir and peace in Afghanistan cannot go hand in hand. But, the US dismissed the political rhetoric because Pakistan was asking for something that was of no interest to the US. It is important to understand that the US focuses only on its national interests. Kashmir issue has never been a national interest of the US and this is the reason why they have never spent diplomatic or military capital to seek any solution or 'assist' in solving Kashmir. If Kashmir ever becomes a national interest of the US, then US will invest all its might to 'assist' in resolving the issue. But, that does not seem to be an option ever in the future.

REVIVAL OF JIHAD THEORY

The fourth option for Pakistan was to revive the jihad. It was possible as an option but very difficult to execute. The reason was that in the recent times, the Indian security forces have brought about a massive radical shift in their approach to tackling terrorism. Till now, if the Indian forces tried to seize the weapons of the terrorists, now they have adopted the American model. The Americans have always tackled the financing of the terrorists. Thus, India has adopted the strategy to economically blacklist Pakistan at the Financial Action Task Force (FATF). This economic diplomatic isolation of Pakistan makes it very difficult for them to sustain a jihad, especially at a level they did in 1990s.

FINANCIALLY VIABLE HYBRID TERRORISM AND HUMAN RIGHTS NARRATIVE

In the recent times, the strategy of Pakistan in Kashmir is that it has focused on carrying out targeted individual acts of violence. This is a financially viable low cost-terrorism approach. By individual acts of violence, we mean to say that since the abrogation of Article 370, the ISI of Pakistan has used the strategy of targeting the minorities in Kashmir. There are two minorities, the first are the Kashmiri Pandits (as not all of them left Kashmir in 1989) and the second are the Sikhs. The ISI deliberately adopted this strategy since 5th August 2019 and by targeting the minorities, the ISI tried to convey four things. Firstly, such attacks keep the ISI in the limelight and give an indication that nothing in the valley has changed and Pakistan still retains control over the security space of the valley. Secondly, this strategy enables ISI to propagate that return of normalcy in the valley is a distant dream. Thirdly, such a strategy also ensures that economic activity in the valley does not pick up while Pakistan gets immunity from the charge of unleashing high terror. Fourthly, such kind of a restrained terror activity allows Pakistan the space to make a case on violation of human rights in Kashmir. The abrogation of Article 370 and the subsequent security tightening in the valley has provided the security forces with a 'tactical pause'. This has happened because the terrorist infiltration and activities have drastically declined in comparison to the past. This tactical pause is being used by India to develop strategies for neutralising the larger ecosystem of state sponsorship of terrorism by Pakistan.

PAKISTAN AND UNITED NATIONS ON ABROGATION OF ARTICLE 370

After the abrogation of Article 370, Pakistani ISI designed an approach to internationalise the issue. The last time Kashmir was raised in the UNSC was in 1971 and after that, in 2019 and 2020. The ISI got support of Turkey, Malaysia and China. China being a permanent member of the UNSC and an ally of Pakistan assisted Pakistan to launch an apoplectic tirade against India at the UN General Assembly. Pakistan is nothing but a colonial outpost of China that is aimed at checkmating India. Pakistani Prime Minister Imran Khan wrestled with India at the UNGA meeting in 2019 to raise the matter of 'human rights' violation by India in Kashmir. He went on to assert that the condition in Kashmir was such that the citizens of the valley were threatened with genocide and there is a need for Pakistan's deterrent to cover them. This statement was embedded in his habitual resort to nuclear rattling and showed the international community the gap between a sensible nuclear power and the actual behaviour of Pakistan. This policy of human rights violation is raised by Pakistan at all other international forums and Pakistan is also getting positive support of China in internationalisation of this narrative. China has supported resolutions against India in the UN Security Council asserting that India's abrogation of Article 370 has altered the dynamics of the dispute and the abrogation is an illegal move. No doubt, Chinese are working at the behest of Pakistan even while majority of the other countries in the world believe that the 5th August decision of India was a step in their domestic affair over which the world has no interest. The duplicity of Pakistan in their narrative at the UN became more visible when Alice Wells, the US State Department Representative for South Asia, asserted that Pakistan was more concerned about the Muslims of Kashmir, who are far better off than Uyghur Muslims of China. He also stated that the fact that Pakistan preferred to remain mum on suppression of Uyghur Muslims demonstrated that Pakistan had no concern for the human rights of real sufferers but was more interested in hypocritical rhetoric over 'bilateral matters'. Pakistan also raised the issue at the United Nations that India's decision to abrogate Article 370 would endanger peace and security in the region. The peace and security in the region would not be endangered by an internal Indian decision but would be if Pakistan uses Jihadi elements to create mayhem in the valley. The international community today very well knows the track record of Pakistan in orchestrating violence in Kashmir.

CHINESE STRATEGY AT UNITED NATIONS

China has long played the Kashmir card against India. For example, in 2010, it started the practice of issuing stapled visas to Indian citizens from J&K and denied a visa to the Indian army's Northern Command chief for a bilateral defence dialogue on grounds that he commanded "a disputed area called J&K". It also officially shortened the length of the border it shares with India by purging the line separating Indian J&K from Chinese-held J&K. Although J&K is divided among three countries, only India was maintaining special powers and privileges for its portion. China shields Pakistan's proxy war by terror against India, even though it has locked up more than a million Muslims in the name of cleansing their minds of extremist thoughts. In fact, like Pakistan, China wages asymmetric warfare against India. This is in the form of a "salami slicing" strategy of furtive, incremental territorial encroachments in Ladakh and elsewhere. Turning Ladakh into a Union territory will advance India's effort to counter China's hostile manoeuverings, including increasing military forays and incursions. The J&K constitutional change also compartmentalises India's territorial disputes with Pakistan and China centred in that region, although India today faces Chinese troops on both flanks of its portion of J&K because of Chinese military presence in the Pakistan-occupied areas. China had raised criticisms over Indian decision to abrogate Article 370 because China considers itself to be a party in claiming Ladakh. India has categorically asserted that Ladakh was and would always be a part of India. India has also conveyed to Chinese that the abrogation of Article 370 was not about India making any territorial claims but was about promoting better governance and socio-economic development of the entire region.

BRITAIN AND CLOSED-DOOR MEETINGS OF UNSC AND PAKISTAN TILTING

In October 2019, a closed-door meeting of the UNSC was organised by China and Britain, supported by Pakistan, to discuss the Kashmir issue. The meeting resulted in no formal outcome or a formal statement. In fact, 14 out of the 15 members at the UNSC in the meeting stated that Indian decision to abrogate the article was an internal matter. This was no doubt a victory of India's diplomacy, but India should be careful to watch the changing international dynamics because economic pressures, demographic changes and parochial politics have now emerged as a new diplomatic currency. These factors explain why British supported the resolution to have this discussion. India, however, has never raised the rhetoric over Brexit and has always called the Brexit an internal issue of Britain. However, to tackle British tilt to Pakistan, owing to rising Pakistani Muslim diaspora in London, India has multiple options that range from raising Brexit to that of British occupation of Ireland and in extremity, preventing the British to access Indian markets in the post-Brexit period.

INDIA'S STRATEGY AT THE UN ON ABROGATION OF ARTICLE 370

Despite Malaysia, Turkey, Britain and China, no other country in the world has been supportive of Pakistan's policy on Kashmir. This clearly proves that it is a diplomatic victory for India that most of the states in the world have branded the abrogation as "an internal affair of India". All this has been only possible because of India's growing economic heft that offer unlimited business opportunities to the world. India must continue the policy of aggressive economic growth and stay away from protectionist headwinds and insular mindsets because policies that undermine economic growth can also undermine diplomatic heft.

MEDIATION, CONFLICT RESOLUTION AND CRISIS MANAGEMENT ON KASHMIR AND INDIAN POLICY

India happens to refuse the logic for mediation on Kashmir. There are reasons why India displays this behaviour. Indian establishment follows a traditional logic, third-party mediation in Jammu and Kashmir might not be a useful idea simply because third parties typically come with their own agenda. Second, it might do more harm than good in Kashmir. More so, past instances of third-party mediation have had mixed results. At this juncture it is important to note that the reason why India has favoured the idea that it seeks no mediation in Kashmir is because of a belief that mediation favours the weaker parties by levelling the playing field and with a strong conventional and non-conventional prowess, India sees no significant gain in bringing a third party into the dispute. Here, let us make a conceptual distinction between conflict resolution and crisis management. While both involve some amount of mediation, the former is focused on a specific issue, like Kashmir in this case, and seeks to address and resolve the root causes of the conflict. The latter involves mediation during an ongoing crisis with a potential for escalation. Crisis mediation unlike conflict resolution does not seek to resolve the political or root causes of a conflict. India has traditionally been averse to mediation in the form of conflict resolution while accepting more than once third-party mediation during crisis events. Kargil is an example when India accepted third-party mediation by the Clinton administration in the US. This was also evident during the post-Pulwama military standoff in 2019. While both Kargil and the February 2019 Pulwama standoff were directly linked to Kashmir, mediation by the third party did not seek to address anything beyond the immediate diffusion of tensions. Then there are other instances where third-party crisis mediation took place even though they had no direct links to Kashmir such as the post-26/11 terror attacks. For sure, crisis management is different from conflict resolution. And yet even when the focus is on crisis management, the larger conflict, which has given rise to the crisis comes into focus and become part of the conversations between the mediator and the conflicting parties. Thus, India accepts crisis management, and not conflict resolution in the context of Kashmir because it is not easy to separate the two either during a crisis or when the conflict is crisis prone. Put differently, given that crisis, at least in this context, is the function of a pre-existing conflict, crisis management by third parties and the attendant focus on the broader conflict is not easy to avoid. More so, while India is loath to having third-party discussions on Kashmir, especially on the human rights situation, it actively seeks third-party attention on terror emanating from Pakistan as well as the latter's sponsorship of violence in the Valley. While this might be a desirable distinction to India's mind, it is not easy to get a third party to focus on one part of the problem and ignore the other. What further ensures third-party involvement in Kashmir is the lack of a conflict resolution process between India and Pakistan. By not resolving conflicts between themselves, India and Pakistan are effectively outsourcing crisis management, and thereby conflict resolution, albeit in a limited manner, to third parties.

WHY CHINA WANTS KASHMIR?

China aims to become the world's leading microchip manufacturer. Microchip manufacturing needs two raw materials, sand and freshwater. It is interesting to know that a 30-cm silicon wafer needs 10,000 litres of fresh water. While China's Taklamakan Desert provides a lot of sand, its own water resources are already under pressure. Here is where Kashmir comes in for China. The Shaksgam valley, which is a part of the old Gilgit Agency, which came under Pakistani control in 1947, when they illegally snatched it away from India, has 242 glaciers and is the world's most glaciated region. In 1963, Pakistan transferred the Shaksgam valley to China (Pakistan deliberately 'gifted' 5180 kilometre square territory to the Chinese in 1963 to further humiliate India after its defeat in the 1962 conflict with china when they transferred the land as a part of 1963 China–Pakistan Boundary Agreement) to facilitate the construction of the Karakorum Highway. China's annexation of Aksai Chin in Jammu and Kashmir from India since 1947 has provided it with a convenient route to the water-rich valley. This quest for water by China, explains the tightening of Sino-Pakistan ties through the China–Pakistan Economic Corridor (CPEC). Among other projects, this includes the construction of five dams, constituting the North Indus River Cascade that China has undertaken to construct in Pakistan and PoK, thus ensuring its water requirements for the microchip manufacture project.

WHY PAKISTAN WANTS KASHMIR?

Pakistan has tried to fight a sub-conventional proxy war in Kashmir for decades. It has sponsored terrorism in the valley as a part of the strategy but has not gained anything out of the endeavour. It still continues to raise the boogey of Kashmir because it is perceived to be an ideal distraction from an arduous task of governing Pakistan's restive population. The fact that the country has gone to IMF every few years to seek a bailout economic passage proves that it has nothing worthwhile to offer for development of Kashmir, which it seeks as an 'unfinished business of partition'. Pakistan has no affinity for the Muslims of Kashmir. It has no interest in their welfare. Pakistan solely wants Kashmir for its water. The water of rivers from Kashmir is used by Punjabis of Pakistan to do agriculture. The rich feudal Punjabi Pakistani agrarian class dominates the Pakistani politics, bureaucracy and armed forces. This is the reason why all the three agencies of the state work in tandem to keep up the Kashmir narrative. For Pakistan, the reason for Kashmir is water, nothing else. The ISI has used militant organisations such as Lashkar and Jaish to bring about a shift in their tactics. The Pakistan-based militant organisations have often initiated mass protests in Pakistan alleging that India is resorting to water terrorism. Most of these mass protests happen in the Punjab part of Pakistan where agrarian economy demands water. A new wave of anti-India sentiment had been generated by Pakistani terrorist organisation. The fact that Hafeez Saeed and Masood Azhar also belong to Pakistan Punjab help ISI establishes affinity with local population. Water-related issues between the two states would always generate emotionalism, as there is no regional level institution today that can capably solve the problem.

RICARDO HAUSMANN THESIS ON KASHMIR QUESTION

Professor Ricardo Hausmann at Harvard's Centre for International Development suggested that the only predictor of sustained economic success is economic complexity, and development was like a game of scrabble; the more letters you have, not only can you make more words, but you can make longer words. The government provides vowels. So, development is about creating new letters and vowels. Hausmann believes that new letters in the private sector come from migration, diaspora, venture capital, inbound investment, skills, studying overseas, business travel. Professor James Robinson suggested that inclusive economic systems need vowels from inclusive political systems that distribute political power broadly rather than concentrate, monopolies or hoard it. On the basis of these thoughts, it is imperative for the government to facilitate cross LoC trade. Such trade has the potential of offering business opportunities to Kashmiri citizens and will promote business and employment in the valley because Deng Xiaoping rightly said that development is the hard truth. The Srinagar airport should develop capabilities that would enable Kashmir to export its products to the world, as this will have a positive diplomatic repercussion as well. Similarly, the government should positively speed up rehabilitation of Kashmiri Pandits back in the valley.

CURZON'S INSIGHT AND INDIA'S NEW KASHMIR POLICY

In 1907, Lord Curzon had given Romanes Lecture at the Oxford University. These lectures continue to offer insight into the contemporary problems of colonial frontiers. In those lectures, Curzon stated that a precondition for national development was to have a stable frontier. He asserted that frontiers are razor edges on which hang suspended the modern issues of war, peace, life and death of nations. He was convinced that the problems of frontiers may never disappear from the politics of the world but could be managed through tools of political accommodation and scientific demarcations. The abrogation of Article 370 is all about rectifying the unfinished colonial mess by extending effective territorial sovereignty over lands that India has claimed historically. By confronting the Pakistani terrorism and reorganising the political status of the valley, the government has established a new foreign policy template and the key to its success now depends upon two factors. The first is political reconciliation in the valley and this is crucial because BJP may have carried out the decision because it may have had the numbers in the Parliament. But, democracy is not about parliamentary majority, but much more than that. Lech Walesa rightly stated that it is hardly possible to build anything if frustration, bitterness and a mood of helplessness prevail. The second is persuading the army of Pakistan to accept that their interests are also served better by accepting a stable, peaceful and a legitimate frontier with India.

POPULISM THEORY AND ARTICLE 370

In his treatise "What is Populism?" Princeton professor Jan-Werner Müller asserts how populist regimes frequently frame their actions as representing the will of the "real people", a group they exclusively represent. By extension and example, those who dissent are deemed to be not "Real Poles" (prawdziwi Polacy) in Poland or "Real Hungarians" in Hungary. In the same vain was the retort by Turkish President Recep Tayyip Erdoğan to his opponents in 2020 "We are the people. Who are you?" In populist moves worldwide, such actions are "authorised by the people", and therefore no blame accrue to the government if anything goes wrong. By contrast, Müller says that democratic accountability would actually mean that the burden is on the government to justify just how it uses its political judgment to ensure desired outcomes. The "Modi's vivendi" on Kashmir was aimed at his domestic base and it mirrors the prevailing trend of populism worldwide and this is why one of his Cabinet Ministers stated that till the abrogation of Article 370, Kashmir witnessed Kautilya and now will witness the post-Kalinga Asoka.

FROM CENTRALITY TO PERIPHERY MODEL OF PAKISTAN

Pakistan has always kept the centrality of Kashmir in its bilateral talks with India and has seen shifts from being a "developmental state" in 1960s to a "security state" in 1980's to a "jihadi state" since 2001. They began the rhetoric of Kashmir with "unfinished agenda of Partition", then "Kashmir banega Pakistan", then "Pakistan's jugular" to "core issue with India". The obsession of Pakistan with Kashmir is so entrenched in their psyche that it is visible from a book written by Z. A. Bhutto called "The myth of independence". Bhutto states in the book that till the time a Muslim majority province remains a part of India, the sole reason for existence of Pakistan would remain incomplete; thus, Pakistan should continue to support her struggle. Bhutto went on to say that if Pakistan ever fails to get back Kashmir, it will imply that idea of Pakistan would collapse.

MAXIMALIST FOREIGN POLICY OPTIONS

As Donald Trump rightly said, "Leverage, don't make a deal without it", this now seems to be the dictum guiding the maximalist foreign policy option adopted by India. India's new position on Pakistan is that if a dialogue happens with Pakistan, when it stops sponsoring terrorism, then it will happen only on PoK. No doubt it will take a long time for Pakistan to understand that Kashmir is no more a bilateral issue. From the Pakistani viewpoint, accepting the abnormal as the new normal would require a massive shift in the psyche of Pakistan. Pakistani army would no longer be able to claim the supremacy on foreign policy anymore and would also not be able to garner majority of the resources in name of a fictional Kashmir issue. With India isolating Pakistan economically at the FATF and Kashmir issue no longer a bilateral issue; Pakistan would not require the jihadi elements and the jihadi sanctuary it had nurtured. The jihadi sanctuary would eventually dissolve and the dissolution will enable the Pakistani society to reclaim the space it had lost to the jihadis. By diverting the scarce resources from sponsoring terrorism in future, it would do well to use the resources for its own development and peace with India. All this is easier said than done, as it requires serious quality of leadership to understand the gravity of the situation. It also requires hard choices be made by an exceptionally thought provoking leadership (short in supply at the moment in Pakistan) in the army to jettison its leverage over foreign and security policy of terrorism, for their own welfare and existence. Otherwise, time is not far when the state of Pakistan would march to its own abyss and Pakistan would eventually collapse on its own weight.

INDIA AND PAKISTAN TRADE AND COMMERCIAL RELATIONS

A study by Nisha Taneja and Eugenia Baroncelli has found that India and Pakistan collectively constitute 90% of the GDP of the region and peace between the two states could yield a 405% rise in trade at the bilateral level. It is important to note here is that both states have a collusion of interests on items of international trade, signifying the possibility of a tacit cooperation in existence between the two states. Instead of using this to leverage South Asian integration, ironically, the South Asian states have explored the global markets of North America, Europe and China. The intraregional trade in South Asia is so low today that, at times, it is described as inverse regionalism. Weak trade facilitation mechanisms, protectionism, lack of transit facilities and mutual suspicion are major factors in deterring trade practices. Though there is a call for the expansion of bilateral Indo-Pak trade, some Pakistani firms do fear that Indian firms could dominate Pakistan if free trade is facilitated. However, many in Pakistan do believe that the opening up of trade between the two states could lead to greater material gains for both. The two states together have a great potential to emerge as a net exporter of ferrochrome to the world. Indian companies have the potential to export trucks, tires to Pakistan as the same commodity is imported by Pakistan from third countries via Dubai.

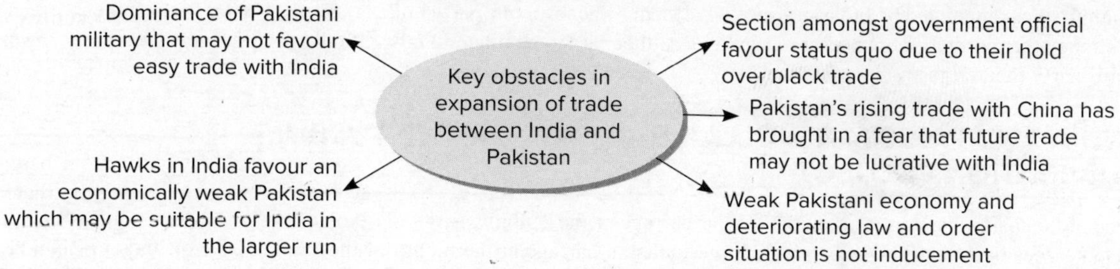

Despite the obstructive behaviour of Pakistan to allow trade to materialise, the two sides have a tremendous potential for bilateral trade. In 1996, India gave MFN status to Pakistan, which it reciprocated in 2012 only. The bilateral trade is around 2.5 billion USD despite a potential of 20 billion USD. It is imperative for the two to explore cooperation in trade and establish a regional value chain in the globalised and integrated world. Some experts have suggested that the two can explore product-specific regional value chains in sectors such as textiles, sports goods and surgical instruments. For instance, in Surat (Gujarat) and Tiruppur (Tamil Nadu), there is production of raw materials of textiles that can be linked to production centres in Lahore and Faisalabad. Similarly, in India, there is a huge demand of Pakistani salwaar-kameez and wedding attire, which can be explored as a sector. Similarly, Pakistan is gradually emerging as a global supplier of sports goods. Sialkot in Pakistan is a manufacturing hub for sports goods from football to cycling gloves. The footballs manufactured here have been used in the FIFA world cup also. However, the manufactures of these products in Sialkot need high-quality raw materials and semi-finished products, which at present they import from Thailand. This is where India can step in. India has high-quality latex, rubber and football bladders, which it can directly provide to Sialkot. Again, Sialkot is known for its expertise in surgical instruments and is a global supplier to the US and major powers in Europe. India is a major importer of surgical instruments. At present, it imports them from developed states of the world at very high prices. A direct import from Sialkot is economically and logistically conducive for India. For instance, India can enhance the supply of stainless steel to Pakistan, which in turn will be a ready raw material available to manufacturers in Sialkot. Sialkot enjoys a historical edge because till 1947, Jalandhar and Sialkot were integrated manufacturing hubs. After the partition, the skilled labour moved to Sialkot. The hope of the trade is that it will help to create a constituency of peace, which will enable Pakistan to relinquish terror and join the economic race. But, the ISI finds no merit in the argument of trade with India and is keen to skilfully use its geographical position to harm India. After the Pulwama attack in 2019, India has also hiked the duties for bilateral trade and withdrawn the MFN status with Pakistan. Thus, the politics has again taken over economics in the bilateral ties.

INDIA AND PAKISTAN INDUS WATER TREATY

Before Partition, the water of Indus River the Indus system was jointly used by India and Pakistan. After 1947, the two sides concluded an Inter-Dominion Accord where it was decided that on annual payments from Pakistan, India would release enough water to Pakistan. It was decided in the Inter-Dominion Accord that the two sides in future would negotiate a permanent solution. In 1951, the former chairman of Tennessee Valley Authority, David Lilienthal visited the region and recommended joint operation and development of Indus basin. On the basis of the idea propounded by Lilienthal, the then chairman of World Bank Eugene Black convinced India and Pakistan to negotiate a settlement for water sharing. The meetings began from 1954 and finally concluded in 1960 with Indus Water Treaty (IWT) signed between Nehru and Ayub Khan. The Indus basin has three eastern-flowing rivers (Sutlej, Beas and Ravi) and three western-flowing rivers (Indus, Jhelum and Chenab). As per the IWT, 1960, India got control over the Eastern rivers while Pakistan got control of the Western rivers. India, however, as per the IWT was allowed to use the water from the Western rivers for the purpose of consumption with restricted use of the river water for storage. On the Western rivers, except for specific cases, India was not to build storage and irrigation systems on the rivers. In the IWT, if there were to be a disagreement between India and Pakistan, there was a provision to seek mediation and arbitration. As per Article XII of the IWT, a modification is permissible when both parties agree for the need of the same. To make sure that neither of the parties is violating any of the provisions of the IWT, the treaty provides for a Permanent Indus Commission (PIC) where there would be one commissioner appointed by India and one by Pakistan. Whenever one party initiates a project, it has to share the information with the other party. If there is ever a dispute, first there are to be bilateral talks. If talks fail, the aggrieved party can seek third-party (neutral party) intervention.

INDIA AND PAKISTAN WULLAR BARRAGE OR THE TULBUL NAVIGATION PROJECT

One of the major disputes is about the Wullar barrage or the Tulbul Navigation Project on Jhelum River in Kashmir. The dispute goes back to 1984. India wanted to establish a barrage at the mouth of the Wullar Lake on Jhelum River. That the project entailed the creation of a 439 feet long and 40 feet wide barrage which would store 0.30 million acres feet of water which would make the river navigable during summer season. Pakistan had taken the matter to Indus Water Commission (since 1986) as it alleged that the Wullar barrage violated the Indus Water Treaty of 1960 and the creation of the barrage would be used by India as a geostrategic weapon to restrict water supplies to Pakistan. India uses the term Tulbul Navigation Project while Pakistan uses the term Wullar barrage to refer to the project. Since 1986, there have been negotiations between the two sides to resolve the dispute, but it still persists.

INDIA AND PAKISTAN BAGHLIAR DAM ISSUE

In 2005, Pakistan again objected to India's 450 megawatt Baglihar Dam constructed on the Chenab River. Pakistan invoked provisions of the Indus Water Treaty and sought arbitration from the World Bank. A neutral expert was appointed for arbitration. The verdict was announced in 2011 in favour of India.

INDIA AND PAKISTAN KISHANGANGA HYDROELECTRIC PLANT ISSUE

Jhelum is a west-flowing river, one of its tributaries is Kishanganga. The Kishanganga in Pakistan is called Neelam River. India authorised the National Hydropower Corporation to establish a dam named Gurez on the Kishanganga River. To generate electricity, the National Hydropower Corporation envisaged the creation of a 20-kilometre-long tunnel to divert water. The water through the tunnel could be diverted through the tunnel to generate 300+ megawatt electricity at Kishanganga Hydroelectric Plant (KHEP) in Bonar Nallah. Pakistan objected to the KHEP project alleging that the diversion of the water will reduce the availability of water Pakistan requires for the Neelum–Jhelum hydropower plant and thereby also reduces the original share of river water due to Pakistan under the IWT by 15%. Thus, in 2010, Pakistan approached the International Court of Arbitration (ICA). The ICA gave a final decision in December 2013. As per the ICA, Pakistan will need at least 9 cubic metre per second water flow in the river which shall be maintained by India and India would be able to, after ensuring 9 cubic metre per second flow in the river, go ahead with KHEP project. Pakistan had also raised four design-related issues at the ICA, but out of the four, only one was settled while the rest could not settle at the bilateral level between the two. In June 2013, India initiated a new 850-hydropower station to be constructed as the Ratle plant on the Chenab River. Pakistan raised objection to the Ratle plant and took up the issue for arbitration by the court of arbitration at the World Bank. Pakistan, on 19th August 2013, requested the World Bank to constitute a court of arbitration. India, as per the IWT, had to respond to the request on 19th October 2013. On 4th October 2013, India requested that a neutral expert be appointed. If state requests a neutral expert be appointed, then such a request has to be accepted immediately. The World Bank, however, chose to sit on India's request. On 19th October 2013, when the Pakistani request matured, the World Bank advocated both the setting up of a court of arbitration and appointment of a neutral expert. India objected to the proposal, observing that it would complicate the process. India threatened that it may not participate in the court of arbitration as it had requested for a neutral expert's appointment, which had to be accepted immediately, but it was not. The World Bank exercised a pause to the two processes and urged the two states to find an alternative resolution mechanism. The matter was taken up at the level of the Permanent Indus Commission. After the Uri attack in September 2016, India decided not to hold the PIC meetings with Pakistan till it stopped funding terrorists. However, in March 2017, the suspension was lifted and the meetings were resumed.

INDIA AND PAKISTAN AND THE ISSUE OF KULBHUSHAN JADHAV

Kulbhushan Jadhav was a retired Indian Navy officer. He was involved in marine trade when members of Jaish Ul-Adl group saw Jadhav near the Iranian border. Jadhav was kidnapped and traded by Jaish Ul-Adl group, linked to the Jundullah, to the Directorate of Inter-Services Intelligence of Pakistan for a monetary transaction. Jaish Ul-Adl group is a Sunni militant group and has been floated by Directorate of Inter-Services Intelligence of Pakistan. They operate in Baluchistan region and have been created to prevent any Iranian influence on Baluchistan. The Directorate of Inter-Services Intelligence of Pakistan rewarded Jaish Ul-Adl group with some arms subsequently. The Directorate of Inter-Services Intelligence of Pakistan uses the group as a front organisation to gather intelligence on Iranian activities and feeds them to American Central Intelligence Agency. The group has some junior-level officers of Directorate of Inter-Services Intelligence of Pakistan and Pakistan army working for them too. Jadhav was charged for espionage as an agent of India's RAW and sentenced to death on 10th April 2017. Since his custody, twenty-six times India demanded consular access to Kulbhushan Jadhav under the Vienna Convention (1963), all of which were rejected by Pakistan. Thus, on 26th April 2017, India decided to move the case to the International Court of Justice (ICJ). The first priority of India was to save him from death sentence. On 18th May 2017, the ICJ passed an interim order ordering Pakistan not to execute Kulbhushan Jadhav. The order of the ICJ relied upon powers from its cases of Ukraine versus Russia (2017) and Article 41 of the statute. The case of India is based on Article 36(1) of the statute of the ICJ. India has asserted that Pakistan is bound by the Vienna Convention to provide consular access and not by the India–Pakistan Consular Agreement of 2008, where Pakistan has tried to carve out its own space of limiting the applicability to spies. India has also asserted that the death sentence be annulled as Kulbhushan Jadhav has not been provided any fair trial. The ICJ has no powers to comment upon the death penalty awarded by a sovereign state. But, the ICJ examined the fair trial that paved way for the death penalty. Indian argument was that the military courts in Pakistan have powers for awarding death penalty. They derive these powers under the Army Act 1952 and Official Secret Act 1923. India has stated that these military courts perform as executive courts under a military command and operate without any elementary rights or public hearing for the accused. India has stated that Kulbhushan Jadhav has been facing a media trial in Pakistan, which is based on the narrative created by the Pakistan army that he was caught for espionage, sabotage and treason. India says that this kind of trial is akin to the trial of the gladiators in Rome, who too were awarded death penalty based upon the roaring of the crowds. The real aim of Pakistan is to use Kulbhushan Jadhav to create a frenzy that India is interfering in Baluchistan. It wants to feed a narrative in the society that India is behind destabilisation of Pakistan. This will help them to sustain and reinforce anti-India narrative. The treatment of Kulbhushan Jadhav and his entire case is a clear example of misdirected diplomacy of Pakistan. Such diplomatic adventurism is not based on the principles of justice but egregious untruths. In a recent hearing on the matter in 2019, the Indian Joint Secretaries in the MEA did not shake hands with the Attorney General of Pakistan, Anwar Mansoor Khan. They rather greeted him with folded hands, a sign of new diplomatic triumph of India. In the hearing, India again reiterated that Pakistan has amended its laws related to the military courts. These laws now allow civilians to be tried by the military courts. The ICJ rejected Pakistan's objections to the admissibility of the application of India with a 15-1 votes. The only dissenting judge of the ICJ was ad hoc Judge Jillani, who is from Pakistan. India got major victories in the ICJ ruling on three counts. First, the ICJ suspended the death penalty awarded to Kulbhushan Jadhav by the Pakistani military court. Secondly, the ICJ ruled that Pakistan would have to review the entire process of trial and conviction of Kulbhushan Jadhav. It directed Pakistan to take all measures at its disposal to ensure that Mr. Jadhav is not executed pending the final decision in the present proceedings. The court considers that a continued stay of execution constitutes an indispensable condition for the effective review and reconsideration of the conviction and sentence of Mr. Jadhav. Thirdly, the ICJ noted that Pakistan breached the obligation incumbent upon it under Article 36 of the Vienna Convention on consular relations. This means that Pakistan has now to provide India consular access to Kulbhushan Jadhav. Though India succeeded in securing a stay on the death sentence of Kulbhushan Jadhav, its argument to annul the military court verdict was not accepted. The Indian side also sought a direction to Pakistan for providing a safe passage for Kulbhushan Jadhav to return home. The ICJ ruled, it is not the conviction and sentence of Mr. Jadhav which are to be regarded as a violation of Article 36 of the Vienna Convention.

INDIA AND PAKISTAN GURUDWARA DIPLOMACY

The Kartarpur Gurudwara holds immense religious significance for the Sikh community. The Gurudwara is in Narowal district of Pakistan, just across Gurdaspur district in Punjab, India. It is located on the bank of river Ravi. Guru Nanak lived in the Gurudwara for 18 years before his death at the same place in 1539. The two countries in 2018 decided to establish a Kartarpur Gurudwara corridor that will facilitate pilgrims to visit the historic Gurudwara without a visa and return the same day. As per the plan, the Kartarpur Gurudwara corridor was opened in 2019 to commemorate the 550th birth anniversary of Guru Nanak. The two sides decided to keep the corridor open from 8 a.m. to 5 p.m. everyday. There is a consensus on point of crossings, identity documents, security procedures and bilateral guarantees by both sides. Had the Kartarpur Gurudwara corridor been established when the ties were good, it would have been a confidence building measure, which could have helped the strengthening of the relationship. But, as the Kartarpur Gurudwara corridor was opened at a time of a sour relationship between the two sides, it should not be conflated with the larger Indo-Pak relation and should be seen as a separate initiative, which emerges, as a sore thumb when the relationship is going down. So, here there are no India and Pakistan relations at work, but rather Pakistan's own strategic and tactical objectives at work as from the Pakistan side, it is the ISI, which is managing the project. There are various reasons for the announcement of the corridor in 2018. First, Pakistan for long is witnessing growing isolation. The proposal of the corridor with India was one of the attempts to break this isolation. Secondly, in India, in the rural areas of Punjab, there has been a long pending demand for the corridor as the rural folks have strong panthic leanings. Thirdly, the corridor is a low octane attempt by Pakistan to initiate a dialogue with India, which has been insisting that terror and dialogue cannot go together. Pakistan aims to base the corridor on the example of France and Germany, both of whom had an acrimonious past and eventually buried their differences to seek an economic union. But what Pakistan forgets is that Germany renounced the use of militarist ultra-nationalist groups is what compelled France to come forward. Some feel that the establishment of the corridor can be as momentous as the fall of the Berlin wall. In this event, Pakistan is unwilling to forgo the use of terrorism as a sub-conventional option against India. There is a belief that Pakistan could position the corridor as a 'gift' to the Sikhs. This will allow Pakistan to continue to foment terrorism in India and then hold the Kartarpur Gurudwara corridor a hostage to 'good behaviour' of India in reciprocity. The ISI–army complex planned the corridor with ulterior motives because they want India to confront the Hobson's choice. According to the senior officer of RAW, in 1980, the ISI assassinated the guru of the Nirankari sect and subsequently the other Nirankaris in Punjab. The Nirankaris are at odds with the mainstream Sikh population. This is so as they believe in a living guru, which the mainstream Sikhs do not believe as for them the living guru is the guru Granth Sahib. The 1980 assassination was used by the ISI to unleash the Punjab militancy. In 2018, the ISI attacked the Nirankari worshippers in Amritsar thorough a grenade attack on the Nirankari Bhawan. Thus, as per a senior officer of RAW, the event of Kartarpur Gurudwara corridor groundbreaking ceremony and the attack on the Nirankari Bhawan have to be seen in totality. It suggests that ISI is planning to revive its old strategy and open a 'second' front in Punjab. It wants to open up the corridor and use the Sikhs pilgrims for radical indoctrination, which will revive the Khalistani militancy. The ISI has established a slow attritional policy of reviving separatism thorough recruitment, indoctrination and radicalisation method. The Khalistani groups operating in Pakistan are the diaspora and they have been stationed all across the corridor (they are also being trained by the ISI at Muridke, Shakargarh and Narowal in the Punjab province of Pakistan). They have been trained by the ISI to keep a watch on potential recruits from amongst the visitors and establish contacts with them. Once the contacts are established with the pilgrims, they can be subsequently used for carrying out propaganda of the revival of separatism. Therefore, the senior officer of RAW says that India has to thwart the attempts of Pakistan to revive the militancy. The senior officer of RAW says that caution is important because the 'Pakistani Gurudwara Prabandhak Committee' is controlled by the army of Pakistan and its first chief was the brainchild of 1993 Mumbai blasts—Lieutenant General Javed Nasir of ISI. The officer of RAW also told the author of the book that one reason why Pakistan wanted to seek the corridor is because it wanted to cool off its "eastern front" (read as the border with India) because the things are going out of control for Pakistan on their 'western front' (read as the border with Afghanistan) as Pakistan Taliban and Al-Qaeda have been repeatedly attacking Pakistani army at the Durand Line. The pilgrim fees of 20 USD and the charities by the Sikhs in the Gurudwara during the visit will be siphoned off by however, in some ways, the Kartarpur Agreement resembles the Indus Water Treaty (IWT), which too was negotiated in an inflamed backdrop of Kashmir. It is hoped that the Kartarpur Agreement too would eventually withstand the repeated shocks witnessed in the bilateral relationship and would eventually become a template for India and Pakistan to initiate a wider process of constructive engagement. For that to happen, Pakistan must eschew the knack of asking for engagement and then sabotaging the same if the ties sour in the future. This means that Pakistan should delink the corridor from political developments and not terminate the corridor in case of any exigency. Even when the recent political past of the two states divide, the history has still united the two.

KHALISTAN REFERENDUM AND REVIVAL TENDENCIES OF KHALISTAN MOVEMENT 2.0

The campaign of Khalistan Referendum 2020 was a brainchild of ISI of Pakistan. The man behind this was Lt. Col Shahid Mehmood Malhi. In ISI, he is known as Chaudhary Sahib. He is a part of Lahore detachment of ISI based in Lahore for Punjab-specific activities. He was born in Wapda, Lahore, Pakistan. Shahid Mehmood Malhi has service number PA 35043 in the Pakistani army. On 13th October 1995, he was commissioned into the Pakistani army in the 25th regiment of the Baloch regiment. On 10th August 2012, he joined the ISI and the same day he was promoted to the rank of Lt. Col in the army and appointed as the station officer of the Lahore detachment. The Khalistan plan is called by the ISI as Operation Express. Major Danish of the ISI of Pakistan, on a covert mission, posted, as an undercover diplomat in Pakistani mission to London, was involved in orchestrating the Khalistan protest in London in 2018. He is constantly tailed by RAW in London. The attempt of RAW is to retaliate to Pakistan for Khalistan. The strategy of RAW is called engineered subversion and hybrid war. There are three areas RAW counters Pakistan at the hybrid war level by engineering deep subversive strategy. The RAW reminds Pakistan that any aggressive act of Pakistan against Indian side can lead to vivisection of three areas—Pasthun region, Sindh region and Baluchistan, as prospective steps to an Akhand Bharat.

INDIA AND PAKISTAN NUCLEAR DIPLOMACY AND JIHAD UNDER THE NUCLEAR UMBRELLA

In 1998, the two tested their nuclear weapons. A new combustible mixture has emerged due to the nuclear option. Let us have a look at the optimistic view. In India, Sumit Ganguly propounds this view. He opines that the leaders of India and Pakistan are interested in their national survival. Both leaders realise that either party has adequate capabilities to inflict harm on its adversaries. Thus, if there were a crisis, both sides would strive to exercise caution with an intention to ensure that crises are not escalated to the nuclear level. This, as per the deductive logic propounded by Thomas Schelling and Kenneth Waltz, would lead to the prevention of escalation of conflict to a nuclear level and would bring about stability. Ganguly adds further details to his argument. He observes that the Partition has had a profound impact on both India and Pakistan. Pakistani leadership continues to feel, despite losses inflicted upon them in 1965 and 1971, that Kashmir is an unfinished agenda. Though, since 1971, the South Asian region has not witnessed a war it has witnessed limited conflicts in 1999 and Pakistani-sponsored ethno-religious insurgency in Kashmir. It is well accepted that the overt acquisition of nuclear weapons in 1998 has played an important role in preventing escalation of conflicts, including the Kargil intrusion, into a full-fledged war. Despite further escalation of tensions during 2006 Mumbai attacks, then the 26/11 attacks and the localised attacks in 2016 and 2017 from Pathankot, Pampore, Uri, Kupwara and Pulwama, both sides have exhibited restraint and have not violated thresholds, despite the nuclear rhetoric of Pakistan. Ganguly asserts that Pakistan may resort to a proxy war but knows its limitation. Pakistan knows that if it initiates any conventional conflict with India, India too would resort to retaliation and this could push both towards a nuclear war. India, however, has followed a mixture of resolve and restraint. It has given Pakistan substantial responses to Pakistani provocation. Yet the nuclear deterrence between India and Pakistan would remain a robust tool to avert full-scale wars in future.

There is also a pessimistic view advanced by S. Paul Kapur. Firstly, the pessimists agree with the optimists on the fact that if players have nuclear weapons; they would behave strategically and strive for international stability. Instead of challenging the optimistic school on this account, the pessimists argue that organisations that are given the responsibility to manage nuclear weapons could go rogue and indulge in destabilising strategies. For pessimists, organisational pathologies would short circuit the adoption of stabilising strategies. Paul Kapur adds further that if a state acquires nuclear weapon, it may create incentives for a state to create destabilisation. He observes that there could be a possibility that there is a weak state in the scenario, say, which is not satisfied with the territorial boundaries with a neighbouring strong state. The neighbouring strong state is a status quo power with stronger military while the weaker state may position itself as a revisionist state. The weaker state may want to alter the boundaries to seek a boundary favourable to itself but knows that if it resorts to a conventional conflict against the strong state, the strong state would inflict heavy damage in retaliation and thereby, the weak state prefers to live with undesirable boundaries. Kapur asserts that acquisition of nuclear weapons will change the scenario. Let us say that the weaker state acquires nuclear weapons. Now, through them, the weaker state has tried to overcome strong state's conventional military might with actuation of nuclear arsenal. Now let us assume that the strong state threatens the weaker one with a military catastrophe. The weaker state, to mitigate the threat by the stronger state, could launch a nuclear strike. On first strike by the weaker state, the stronger state could resort to massive and unacceptable retaliation. But, the stronger state, in such a scenario, would not prefer to launch a full-scale attack or resort to a conventional war against a weak for the fear of nuclear escalation. The strong state may resort to strategic restraint and at times, if needed, resolve to a limited extent with no possibility of crossing the nuclear threshold. If the weaker state develops the understanding that the stronger state would exercise strategic restraint, then, it may embolden the weaker state to resort to tactics to attempt to alter boundaries because it would know that the stronger state would not employ its full military power in its response to the opponent. More importantly, the weaker state may try to indulge in destabilising behaviour due to availability of diplomatic incentives for itself. The weaker state may provoke the adversary. Such provocation will push the stronger state to respond, which could push the conflict towards nuclear escalation. As the tensions rise, the international community would intervene. Such intervention to defuse crises could lead to a territorial settlement that may prove profitable for the weaker state. The weaker state would eventually, through international intervention, seek to get a territorial settlement that it may not have been in a position to get bilaterally with the stronger state. Thus, the weaker state could also deliberately resort to provoking the stronger state to push crisis towards nuclear escalation. If the provocation by the weaker state increases, there could be retribution by the stronger state. If the weaker state, after provocation, say happens to alter the boundaries by capturing some territory, it could invite a strong action from the adversary. The stronger state may not only inflict tremendous harm through a conventional military attack but may try to breach the nuclear threshold. The conventional military attack by the stronger state could be stronger than what the weaker state could anticipate. There could be a possibility that the response by the stronger state could weaken the weaker state's nuclear controls. To prevent such a possible fear, the weaker state could hand over its nuclear launching authority to the armed forces (a shift in organisation managing the arsenal or shift in the organisational pathologies) with a hope that if the stronger state retaliates, the nuclear command does not lose the ability to respond. Thus, apart from just the organisational pathologies, the insulation from full-scale retaliation and possibility of international intervention can also lead to destabilising behaviour. Therefore, a dissatisfied state with a weaker military could acquire nuclear weapons to cause destabilisation. This is a situation of strategic pessimism, which advocates that having nuclear weapons will not always lead to rational calculations but, at times, can create incentives to cause destabilisation and escalation.

Now, let us apply the two views in the context of the nuclear weapons of India and Pakistan. Though, India and Pakistan tested their weapons in 1998, but the idea of acquiring such weapons goes back to the 1970s. After India defeated Pakistan in the 1971 war, in 1974, it demonstrated its capabilities through a Peaceful Nuclear Explosion or PNE. The Pakistani defeat in 1971 war and subsequent Indian PNE brought about a major shift in Pakistani strategic thinking and it began working on the development of its own nuclear weapon. The development, in a covert manner, continued by both states in 1980s. By the end of 1980s, the two had capabilities to develop their weapons at a short notice. If we apply strategic pessimism here, then some more factors can help us understand Pakistan's bid for the acquisition of nuclear weapons. Pakistan was not happy with the partition in 1947. It wanted to alter the boundaries with India in Kashmir, as analysed in the chapter. After Kashmir signed the Instrument of Accession with India in 1947, Pakistan tried to alter the boundaries through 1947–48 wars and 1965 war. With the Pakistani territory of East Pakistan also lost in the form of an independent state (Bangladesh) in 1971, Pakistan realised that it would not be able to fight a war with India over Kashmir ever again. But, Pakistan did not give up the cause of Kashmir fully. It decided to challenge territorial boundaries in Kashmir after it acquired capabilities that could alter the strategic situation. This compelled Pakistan to acquire nuclear weapons. As the acquisition of weapons was going on, the Soviet invasion of Afghanistan in 1979 and subsequent mujahedeen campaign by the US gave Pakistan a new idea on how to resort to a proxy model to alter the status quo in Kashmir. As the Cold War ended in 1989, bolstered with arms, training and knowledge from the mujahedeen campaign, coupled with a capability to produce a nuclear weapon at a short notice, Pakistan unleashed proxy insurgency in Kashmir in 1989. Pakistan began to realise that it could use the nuclear option if India resorted to a conventional attack upon Pakistan due to provocation in Kashmir. Pakistani strategic elite clearly knows that it can continue to support terrorism in Kashmir as the acquisition of nuclear capabilities has neutralised the Indian option of conventional conflict with Pakistan. Therefore, as the Pakistani side began to support terrorists in Kashmir, the Indian side immediately enhanced its security presence in Kashmir to suppress the terrorists. The Pakistani side responded by enhancing their presence along the international border. Indian side responded by deploying armoured units from the international border till the LoC. As the crises escalated, Pakistan feared a full-scale attack from India while India feared an attack on Kashmir. To defuse the crisis, the US government sent its Deputy National Security Adviser Robert Gates to the region. The Gates Mission succeeded in defusing the crises by warning Pakistan that in case of an attack from India, it would be defeated. As the crisis de-escalated, both sides announced normalcy again.

One view that explains why the two sides did not go for a war in 1990s is the view by Sumit Ganguly. According to him, despite massive infiltration by Pakistan in Kashmir, India exercised caution because it was aware of Pakistan's nuclear capabilities. In 1965, when Pakistan had undertaken infiltration, Indian troops had crossed over the ceasefire line and destroyed the assembly points used by the infiltrators in Pakistan. In 1990s, when this massive infiltration happened again, the Indian side enhanced force presence at the LoC but did not undertake any forceful measures. The Indian officials at that time offer a different perspective. They argue that India never wanted to escalate the 1990 crisis into a war, as India did not perceive the situation at that time volatile enough to occasion a full-fledged war. The then Indian Foreign Secretary S. K. Singh stated clearly that assuming that the 1990s crisis could lead to war is a mere conjecture.

Again, in 1998, Pakistani army men carried out an intrusion in Kargil. They crossed over the LoC and entered into the Indian side. When the Indian side observed these intrusions, in 1999, Indian forces carried out an intense air and ground offensive and drove out the intruders. As the Indian side had suppressed the terrorism in Kashmir by 1996, the international attention on Kashmir too began to decline. Pakistan wanted to make an incursion in the region again without harming vital its security interests of India. The prime intention of making an intrusion in Kargil was to slice off a part of the National Highway 1-A as doing so would make it difficult for India to supply logistics to the Indian troops in the Siachen Glacier. India launched an offensive to dislodge intruders but ensured that neither the ground troops nor its air force crosses the LoC India exercised tremendous restraint. Pakistan thought that its nuclear capabilities would prevent an Indian conventional response and also the international attention in case of crisis between two nuclear-armed players would be beneficial to Pakistan.

The optimists argue that the nuclear weapons in the context of Kargil prevented escalation. However, the Indian officials argue differently. Indian Army Chief during Kargil conflicts, V. P. Malik, asserts that India did not cross over the LoC as it wanted international support and had cared for the world's opinion. Even G. Parthasarathy asserts that India did not cross the LoC to ensure that the world would accept that Kargil had happened because of Pakistani provocation. Indian response was rooted in self-defence. V. P. Malik further states that as the political leaders wanted the forces to eject the intruders, they exercised fluidity and flexibility by granting the forces the authorisation to cross over the LoC if need be. He asserts that there was no nuclear threat in the picture and if the tactical operation did not go well, India could have crossed the LoC. Even Brajesh Mishra asserted that if army would have requested the need to cross over the LoC and the political leadership would have accepted the request if circumstances had necessitated thus. According to the official view, crossing the LoC would not have triggered any nuclear backlash from Pakistan. As the crises of Kargil ended, new situations erupted and now the Indo-Pakistan conflict was at an all-new level. India demanded that Pakistan hand over terrorists responsible for attacks on India, failing which India would strike Pakistan and snatch their territories. In January 2002, Pakistan declared LeT and Jaish-e-Mohammed illegal and banned their activities. Musharraf asserted that Pakistani territory would not be used against India by terrorists. The US Secretary of State, Colin Powell, visited India to assure India of serious steps taken by Pakistan to dismantle terrorist infrastructures. India, in the wake of visit of Colin Powell, decided not to strike but did not remove its forces from the borders. In May 2002, Pakistan ambushed Indian troops in Kuluchak in Jammu. India decided to attack Pakistan from Rajasthan across the LoC and seize territory and destroy Pakistani forces. Consequently, Musharraf assured the world that Pakistan would permanently end infiltration. The USA Deputy Secretary of State, Richard Armitage, visited India and assured India once again of Musharraf's pledge. India began to withdraw the plan and decided to end Operation Parakram. Why did India not resort to attacking Pakistan despite escalation of conflicts in 2001–2002? One view is that the nuclear weapons prevented any serious conflict escalation and India exercised restraint. The other view is that Indian officials did not feel the need to attack Pakistan, as they believed that Operation Parakram had delivered the desired results. Indian officials observe that there was no point attacking Pakistan because they received assurances from the US that Pakistan would dismantle its terrorist infrastructure. They further clarify that their goal was to ensure that terrorism does not emanate from Pakistan and Operation Parakram and the USA assurances achieved this goal. Since the standoff, the two sides have not witnessed any form of major crises escalation. India's use of coercive diplomacy has sent a strong message to Pakistan. Nuclear weapons have played a considerable role in crises prevention strategy. Despite Pakistani provocations in the form of 2006 Mumbai train attacks, 26/11 Mumbai attack, localised attacks in Pathankot (2016), Pampore (2016), Uri (2016), Kupwara (2017), Krishna Ghati (2017) and Pulwama (2019); India has resorted to a strategy of diplomatic isolating Pakistan and on provocation, has followed a mixture of resolve and restraint (explained below separately). Our discussion in the preceding section has proven that the Pakistani nuclear weapons are India-specific. The potential motivation for Pakistan to develop nuclear weapons began with its perceived asymmetry with India in conventional warfare. The response of the USA in not fully supporting Pakistan outright in the 1965 and 1971 wars aggravated Pakistan's fear that the US would not be able to function as a long-term security guarantor. The secession of East Pakistan in 1971 made Pakistan perceive India as an existential threat. It therefore decided that acquisition of nuclear weapon would provide it with a tool to face India equally. For Pakistan, the nuclear weapons are not just a response to conventional superiority of India but also a tool to ensure the stability and survivability of Pakistan. Though India advocates a No First Use (NFU) policy, Pakistan has stated that it does not have any confidence on India's NFU and they have, therefore, not accepted the NFU as a viable policy.

Pakistan's idea of strategic deterrence is based upon the logic of developing conventional capabilities first. Pakistan believes that developing conventional capabilities will help them ward off a conventional attack from India. On the basis of this logic, Pakistan has sought to buy the F-16 fighter jets from the US. This is driven by the logic that Pakistan should not allow India to exploit any Pakistani fault lines—from sub-conventional to conventional to nuclear level—as this may endanger the security of Pakistan. Pakistan further believes that if India ever resorts to a full-scale conventional attack, Pakistan would resist the same through conventional preparedness, but, if the survivability of Pakistan is under a threat, then it may exercise a nuclear option.

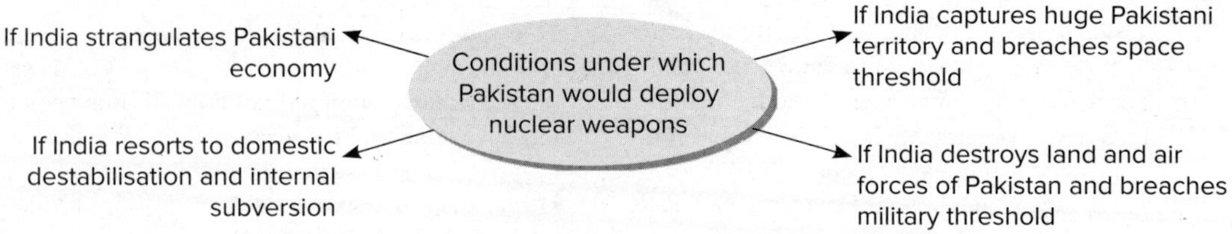

The four conditions are not officially mentioned by Pakistan. In fact, they believe that the essence of deterrence is ambiguity and some amount of uncertainty will create dissonance amongst Indians about the extent they can they push Pakistan. Pakistan deliberately favours stability–instability paradox as a central element of their security competition with India. The stability–instability paradox is an international relations theory regarding the effect of nuclear weapons and mutually assured destruction. It states that when two countries each have nuclear weapons, the probability of a direct war between them greatly decreases, but the probability of minor or indirect conflicts between them increases. To aggravate matters further, Pakistan strives for developing a large nuclear stockpile. Pakistan believes that the Indo-USA nuclear deal, the NSG waiver for India and a potential NSG membership for India will allow India to buy uranium globally and use its own uranium for its weapons programme, which might contribute yet again to an existential threat to Pakistan. This has compelled Pakistan to explore the idea of developing an offensive deterrence posture.

Nuclear weapons by Pakistan have allowed them an umbrella to facilitate a proxy war in Kashmir. Pakistan has also developed an understanding that because of its nuclear weapons, it can continue to resort to a proxy war, and if conflict escalates, international intervention will pressurise India not to wage a war against Pakistan. Such international intervention legitimises the Pakistani idea of inflicting a low-intensity conflict on India. Pakistan also knows that even if the US and others may become critical about Pakistan, no power would abandon a freelancing nuclear power like Pakistan for the fear of a nuclear conflict in Asia and the possibility of proliferation of nuclear weapons to terrorists or other rogue states. Thus, today, it is not a nuclear capable Pakistan that deters India, but an ambiguity that allows Pakistan to indulge in the risk-seeking behaviour of supporting terrorists and proxies. The nuclear weapons offer a shield to Pakistan's adventurism and offer them immunity in the long run. Pakistan uses terrorism as a rational strategy as it is designed to generate security and survivability for Pakistan. This kind of militancy has been nurtured by Pakistan to hide its domestic, economic and political weaknesses and the state uses it as a tool of asymmetric warfare (through non-state actors) to confront India. Nuclear weapons, its augmentation of conventional forces and use of militant proxies today form a combined grand strategy of Pakistan. Therefore, jihad today forms a core of grand strategy of Pakistan.

PAKISTAN'S SEVEN-CARD STRATEGY TO POSITION ITSELF AN INTERNATIONAL INSURGENT

A basic analysis of strategic calculus of Pakistan tells us that maintaining a controlled degree of hostility with India is an essential component of the Pakistani army and its grand strategy. Such a hostile relationship with India enables the army of Pakistan to create an ecosystem to allow safe existence of state-sponsored terror groups. These groups also provide a cheaper alternative to conventional war and help bleed India. The Pakistan has always played its seven cards to position itself as an international insurgent:

1. Kashmir card (low-intensity war)
2. Afghanistan card (strategic depth against India)
3. Muslim Ummah card (preventing India in the OIC)
4. Russia card (encouraging it to open talks with Taliban and positioning itself as a new market for defence)
5. China card (the sweeter than honey partnership)
6. Terrorism card (bleeding India by a thousand cuts) and
7. Nuclear card (nuclear rhetoric for low-cost proxy war)

INDIAN DOCTRINE OF STRATEGIC PATIENCE FOR PAKISTAN

India and Pakistan fought direct bilateral wars in 1947, 1965 and 1971. The 1971 war was a trigger point for Pakistan to establish a nuclear weapon. Pakistan in 1971 realised that its allies China and the US did nothing to prevent India from slicing off Pakistan in 1971. However, the 1974 'PNE' by India only affirmed the fear of Pakistan that India might use a nuke to hit them in future. Throughout 1970s, Pakistan worked hard to acquire a nuclear weapon and announced the completion of its atomic mission in 1987. By this time, India too acquired its arsenal, though officially announced it in 1998 only.

There were optimists who thought that the acquisition of nuclear weapons will enable the two behaves responsibly. But, Pakistan has used the nuclear umbrella to unleash a low-intensity war through state-sponsored terrorism. Since 1998, Pakistan began to assert that it would use a nuclear weapon if India attacks Pakistan at the conventional level. They believed that the nuclear rhetoric has shattered the conventional military superiority of India and given it an opportunity for a low-cost low-intensity war through Lashker-Taiba and Jaish-e-Mohammad to target military and civilian installations of India. The response of nuclear rhetoric of Pakistan by India was the doctrine of 'strategic patience', where it was stated that the LoC is sacrosanct and cannot be breached at any cost. This doctrine was implemented by India in 1999 during Kargil crisis. The forces were instructed not to breach the LoC. The UPA government from 2004 to 2014 also believed that there are going to be no political gains for any military confrontation with Pakistan. It believed that any military confrontation with Pakistan is neither going to solve political disputes nor going to end cross-border terrorism. Thus, post-1998, India began to follow nuclear restraint and asserted the 'sanctity of the LoC'.

INDIAN DOCTRINE OF OFFENSIVE DEFENCE FOR PAKISTAN

There is a change in the strategy for managing Pakistan today. The ISI is using the Lashkar-e-Taiba to counter ISIS and Pakistan Taliban in Pakistan. Thus, it has used Jaish-e-Mohammad as a principle vehicle against India. The JeM today diverts the members of Pakistan Taliban and uses them to fight in India. In 2014, with the coming of the NDA government, a new interpretation for Pakistan was born. The new approach had two elements. The first was that India would need to strengthen its deterrent capabilities to tackle any threat of Pakistan. The second was that India would have to devise an approach to break the nuclear buff of Pakistan. Both these points were based on the premise that there is no need for acceptance of a myth that the LoC is sacrosanct. The logic for this was that if Pakistan is resorting to cross-border terrorism, it means that Pakistan does not respect the LoC.

The new doctrine aims to explore where the nuclear brink is rather than just resorting to mere speculation that it exists in breaching the LoC.

So, under the new doctrine, the idea is to give Pakistan a befitting response in a graded manner to see where nuclear brink is located. As part of the graded strategy applied, in 2016 Indian forces first targeted the launch pads of terrorists across the LoC.

This did not provoke nuclear rhetoric of Pakistan. This affirmed to the strategic community that an operation along the LoC on terror camps could be one option that can be explored again. In 2019, the Balakot air strike (non-military preemptive strike based on credible ground intelligence of possible terror strike by JeM) was deep inside Pakistan (which Pakistan branded as eco-terrorism by India as it destroyed the pine trees). This strike again did not yield a nuclear rhetoric by Pakistan. The two strikes have affirmed that if India is attacked through a non-state actor, it will not shy away to go to the spot of the origin of offence (be it across LoC or inside Pakistan) and hit Pakistan hard.

However, quite unfortunately, Pakistan through Pulwama attack in 2019 has again presented itself as a master of terrorism. The Indian response to Pulwama in the Balakot air strikes has added to the muscular image of Modi. This easily ensured his electoral victory within India in 2019 general elections. This is what precisely Pakistan wanted. Because, if Modi became the Prime Minister again, Pakistan started to use the 'Hindu India' tag to position itself as a voice of suppression of Indian Muslims at the hands of Hindu government. This has allowed Pakistan to easily mobilise Indian Muslims and continue to give Pakistan the needed source to recruit Indian Muslims for its jihad against India. This strategy of Pakistan was visible in the protests that Pakistan was able to mobilise all over India (from Kerala to Shaheen Bagh) over the Citizenship Amendment Act 2019.

PAKISTANI BIO-WEAPON WAR AGAINST INDIA

In 1345, Jani Baig was a Mongol General whose army was fighting to capture the Citadel at Cafa (present day Feodosia) when his army soldiers were infected with bubonic plague. Unable to overrun the Citadel at Cafa, he began to cut down the bodies of his soldiers (infected with bubonic plague) and began to load them on catapults and lobbed them into the city. This apocryphal incident is often known as the world's first bio-weapon attack. Since the outbreak of COVID-19, Pakistan has started following General Baig's strategy. Pakistan has started pushing COVID-19-infected terrorists across the border into India and trying to play a bio-weapons war with India.

FOUR-POINT STRATEGY OF INDIA TO TACKLE PAKISTAN

India has adopted a 4-point strategy to tackle Pakistan:

1. *Military component*: India has demonstrated that it can swiftly retaliate to any such misadventures of Pakistan via surgical strike operations.
2. *Diplomatic component*: A new element in Indian diplomatic strategy is to constantly isolate Pakistan. The objective here is to demonstrate to the entire world that Pakistan is a state sponsorer of terrorism. This in the long run will ensure that the foreign states gradually disassociate to engage with Pakistan. Such strategy will make it difficult for Pakistani diaspora to seek jobs and reside in foreign states, thus affecting the state remittances. This will economically weaken Pakistan and make it tough for Pakistan to sustain the Jihad factory. Diplomatically, India

should use its good foreign relations with major powers to block the bank accounts of Pakistani army officials in Europe. These will economically breakdown the financing of the Pakistani army. The Financial Action Task Force has put Pakistan in the grey list in 2019. This is because of failure of Pakistan to curb terror financing. It will hurt the economy and international standing of Pakistan.

3. *Political component*: It is important to understand that any Jihad in a foreign state can only be sustained by taking advantage of a political vacuum. In Kashmir, there is intense alienation of people. The people of the society are disconnected from the grass root politics and do not have any mechanism to vent out their political grievances. This creates dissonance in the society and allows ISI to use local support as oxygen for radicalisation. Thus, within the political framework of the Indian Constitution, it is imperative to connect the masses to the mainstream politics and cut the supply of oxygen to ISI. The abrogation of Article 370 strives for this.
4. *Covert component*: The RAW is capable of demonstrating success in covert activity on the deep state of Pakistan (army and ISI). The RAW has been carrying out deep subversion and sabotage internally in Pakistan. Such kinds of covert operations are carried out round the year in Pakistan. They have deeply internally bleeded Pakistan every day to make life difficult for the common citizens. The RAW is creating an Indian version of 'counter non-state actors' to cause deep subversion in Pakistan in 2020.

FUTURE OF INDIA AND PAKISTAN RELATIONS

Firstly, the frequent changes in the geopolitics of the region leave a lasting impact on the bilateral ties of India and Pakistan. It is important to understand that the Western powers are no more interested in isolating Pakistan beyond a limit, even though it may be a diplomatic strategy for India. The world today feels that Pakistan is taking steps to improve their socio-economic architecture. This is the reason why Chinese, Americans and Russians continue to do business with Pakistan and have even prevented blacklisting of Pakistan at the FATF (where it remains in the grey-list while Iran and North Korea being the only two in blacklist). Secondly, the Western powers, led by the US, also do not wish to antagonise Pakistan beyond an extent because they wish to counter the growing Russian and Chinese clout in Eurasia, for which Pakistan may be crucial. Thirdly, the international community has understood that since 26/11, there has been no terror strike on Indian soil and most of the attacks in Kashmir during the Modi government's time have been 'locally staged' by the two parties. This does weaken Indian case on isolating Pakistan diplomatically. Pakistan has successfully ensured that the US exits from Afghanistan and power eventually flows in the hands of Taliban. There is a growing pressure within Pakistan to dismantle their terror networks and Pakistan has around 30,000 terrorists in their territory. To show the world of concrete action against the terrorist of Pakistani soil, Pakistan will try to offload them to Taliban-controlled Afghanistan and eventually train them in the territory of Afghanistan to unleash a proxy war against India. It will be imperative for India to ensure Taliban does not allow ISI to use Afghanistan to wage a proxy war against India. In this backdrop, there is a need for some creating rethinking on India's Pakistan policy now.

CHAPTER 5

India's Relationship with Bangladesh

HISTORICAL BACKGROUND OF INDIA AND BANGLADESH RELATIONS

Bangladesh is closely linked to India through its shared culture and ethnicity with West Bengal. The language, a slightly varied dialect of Bengali, acts as a bridge between East India, North East India and Bangladesh. The piece of land where Bangladesh exists has undergone three partitions. It began in October 1905, when the British, as per their 'divide-and-rule' policy, divided the Bengal Presidency on Hindu–Muslim lines. The Muslims, in majority in the state, landed in the area that later became East Pakistan. Because of massive mobilisation and political protests that eventually came to be known as the 'Banga Bhanga Andolan', the territory was reunited on 12th December 1911. However, as far as the national movement was concerned, the seeds for partition were already sown by the initial decision of the British to divide the region along religious lines. The Muslim League, which was established on 30th December 1906 in Dhaka, later demanded that the area be under East Pakistan during the Partition of India in 1947. As the partition took place in 1947, it led to the formation of East Pakistan with large-scale riots preceding the event in Calcutta and Noakhali. The territory again witnessed a split in 1971 to become Bangladesh. The factors that led to divisions of East Pakistan in 1971 emerged in the period after 1947. East Pakistan always had inadequate representation; it got access to fewer resources and, despite the popularity of the Bengali language, Urdu was imposed as the administrative language. This led to confrontation between the government and the masses and violence erupted in East Pakistan. In 1970, when elections took place, the Awami League won the elections. The regime in West Pakistan refused to recognise the mandate of the election and unleashed violence, disallowing Sheikh Mujibur Rehman, who had legally won the election in East Pakistan, to take power. The subsequent planning of a pre-emptive attack on India by Pakistan forced India to militarily retaliate and support the formation of independent Bangladesh as a new nation. The confrontation between India and Pakistan finally led to emergence of Bangladesh in December 1971. In 1972, India and Bangladesh signed a Treaty of Friendship and Cooperation, which became the foundation of the modern India–Bangladesh relations. Today, in Bangladesh, there are two key parties. Awami League, headed by Sheikh Hasina, is a party, which has stood up for secular ideals and is favourable towards India while Bangladesh Nationalist Party (BNP), which is headed by Begum Khaleda Zia, is a party that favours Bengali nationalism and is not favourably inclined towards India. Since 2009, the relations between the two have focused on the three C's of Cooperation, Coordination and Consolidation and in a neighbourhood full of distrust and cynicism; the Bangladesh and India ties have emerged as a template of optimism which is pregnant with trust and hope. The numbers of illegal immigrants from Bangladesh in India have declined from 3.7 million in 2001 to 2.7 million in 2011 and are likely to be lesser in 2021 census. Thus, it is imperative for the government in India to ensure that the National Register of Citizens (NRC) exercise in India does not emerge as an irritant.

The 50th Anniversary of India and Bangladesh Relations

In 2021, the two sides celebrated the 50th anniversary of their bilateral relationship. The two sides appreciated that the relations acquired considerable depths that today there exist more than fifty institutional mechanisms on issues ranging from peaceful use of nuclear energy, artificial intelligence, big data to youth developments through Swarna Jayanti Scholarships.

INDIA AND BANGLADESH DEFENCE DIPLOMACY

At the defence level, India prefers Bangladesh as a defence market, though, in recent times, Bangladesh has preferred to receive arms imports and defence equipment from the US, Russia and China. China had provided submarines to Bangladesh in 2019. A unique point for India's advantage is that Bangladesh is a leading contributor to the UN Peace Keeping Mission (UNPKM). This allays India's fears as the dominant theory is that the more Bangladesh participates in UNPKM, the lesser would be the idle availability of its armed forces to control polity and hence, the lesser would be the chance of Bangladesh becoming an active threat like Pakistan. India firmly supports Bangladesh to evolve fully as a democracy on the lines of Turkey and Indonesia. Both nations have regularly undertaken joint exercises at the army and navy level.

In 2013, the two nations also signed an Extradition Treaty. Shiekh Hasina paid a state visit to India in April 2017. The two nations signed India–Bangladesh Defence Cooperation Agreement to Combat Terrorism. The agreement would enhance cooperation in prevention of human and drug trafficking and illegal narcotics traded across the border. The two sides have also concluded a Defence Cooperation Framework and to promote strategic studies, a pact has been concluded between the Defence Services Staff College, Tamil Nadu and the National Defence College, Dhaka. The two have an Agreement on Peaceful Use of Nuclear Energy and Outer Space. In 2015, during the visit of Indian Prime Minister to Bangladesh, Agreement on Coastal Shipping was signed. The agreement enables merchant vessels of India to use Chattogram port, Chittagong port and Mangla port to ship goods to Bangladesh and this would boost cooperation on regional waters and promote blue economy. The vulnerability of Bangladesh as a centre of terror is not new. Since 9/11, the vulnerability of Bangladesh to terror attacks has increased manifold. Bangladesh is a secular republic. The Islamic NGOs of foreign nations have been promoting Wahhabism in Bangladesh. Pakistan has links with many such NGOs in Bangladesh, which it uses to target India. Since 1990, in Bangladesh, religion as a card in politics has been largely used to garner power. There is growing Al-Qaeda and ISIS presence in Bangladesh. The political compulsion to act against terror is a constraint for the present government as the opposition uses it as a tool against radical organised religion and ends up creating a possibility of a severe backlash. In Bangladesh, there has been a systematic attempt to target rationalists, atheists and bloggers. For India, it is worrisome as ISIS is at its very doorstep.

Bangladesh Armed Forces Contingent at Republic Day in India

In the 2022 Republic Day celebrations in India, a contingent of soldiers from army, navy and air force of Bangladesh participated and Bangladesh became the third foreign-friendly country to have their contingent in India after France in 2016 and UAE in 2017. This event showcases the recognition of contribution of India to the creation of Bangladesh and the depth in defence ties.

Hefazat-e-Islami

The Hefazat is emerging as a new space in Bangladesh where the Jamat-e-Islami existed earlier. These are the same people who are perpetually anti-India and rooted in revivalist Islamic tendencies. They are even unhappy with rising progress made by Bangladesh in aspects such as textiles and growth and intend that Bangladesh must focus on revival of Islamic practices than accepting a liberal order.

INDIA AND BANGLADESH COMMERCIAL DIPLOMACY

Bangladesh had been an agrarian economy but today has emerged as a South Asian dynamo. It has a strong demand for goods and India has emerged as an important trade partner in this context. It has also benefitted from the ongoing US–China trade war and has enhanced its exports in the global value chains. India provides duty-free and quota-free access for Bangladeshi exports to India. The trade is tilted in favour of India. India also gives line of credits and loans to Bangladesh and provides developmental aid. Tata is establishing a three billion USD steel plant in Bangladesh and there are other Indian firms in power generation, linking of power grids, telecom and transport, which are setting up presence in Bangladesh. However, India's steps to integrate Bangladeshi economy with India may be perceived with some suspicious by Bangladesh. It has also steadfastly refused India transit to North East, which, in reality, might have proved beneficial for both. In 2020, India had signed Bangladesh–India Professional Skill Development Agreement to undertake skill development for the people of Bangladesh.

Border Haats between India and Bangladesh

The first border haat was inaugurated in 2011, in the West Garo Hills district of the Indian state of Meghalaya while the other three border haats are at Balat (India)–Dolora (Bangladesh) in 2012; Srinagar (India)–Chhagalnaiya (Bangladesh); and Kamalasagar (India)–Kasba (Bangladesh) in 2015.

INDIA AND BANGLADESH LAND BOUNDARY AGREEMENT

When India became independent, Sir Radcliffe demarcated the boundary between India and Pakistan as well as India and East Pakistan (now Bangladesh). While dividing the territory in East Pakistan, Radcliffe did not pay attention to small patches of land called 'enclaves'. These enclaves were, in the pre-independence era, called Chitmahals and the Raja of Cooch Behar used them and Maharaja of Rangpur as stakes in the game of chess. After independence, Radcliffe drew a line to divide the territory. Efforts were made by Jawaharlal Nehru in 1958 to divide the territories through an agreement with Feroz Khan Noon called Nehru–Noon agreement. As per the agreement, India got the enclave of Dahagram and Angarpota while half of Berubari enclave was to be given to East Pakistan. The origin of the Berubari territory also goes back to the time of Radcliffe. Radcliffe tried to demarcate the boundary on the basis of *thanas* but he accidently omitted the Berubari number-12 *thana*. As the Berubari number-12 *thana* was within the Jalpaigudi *thana*, half of it was given to East Pakistan as they laid claims over it. To give effect to the Nehru–Noon agreement 1958, an amendment under Article 368 of Indian Constitution was made under the 9th Amendment Act of 1960. When Bangladesh was created in 1971, Indira Gandhi decided to resolve the pending disputes with Mujibur Rehman. In 1974, a Land Boundary Agreement (LBA) was designed (also called Indira–Mujib Pact) which clarified the need to exchange 111 Indian enclaves in Bangladesh and 51 Bangladeshi enclaves in India. In these enclaves, citizens were living with no available rights and facilities. On 16th May 1974, the agreement was signed but was not ratified by India and thereby the exchange under the LBA could not proceed successfully. According to the LBA, Bangladesh was to get Dahagram and Angarpota while India would get the other half of Berubari. Dahagram and Angarpota were to be connected through a corridor called Tin Bigha and India was to lease out the Tin Bigha corridor to Bangladesh in perpetuity. Because of strong internal resistance, the Indian government was finally only able to grant Bangladesh access to the corridor in 1992, and that too, for a limited number of hours per day. Full access to the corridor was finally granted in 2011. In 2006, the Hasina government in Bangladesh assumed power and in 2007 established a consultative mechanism in the area demarcated in the LBA. The people in the consultative mechanism asserted that they would not leave their areas. The rights of the people inhabiting the region of the LBA now came in stark incongruence to the precepts of the LBA, which advocated territorial relocations. In 2010, Hasina visited India and in 2011, a protocol to the LBA was agreed to. As per the protocol, it was decided that status quo was to be maintained in the regions and the wishes of the people would be respected. Thus in 2011, the procedural acceptance was completed on ground and the national exchange was agreed to. Since there was to be no cession of territory, the Indian Parliament ratified the bill in May 2016 and the entire process got completed by June 2016.

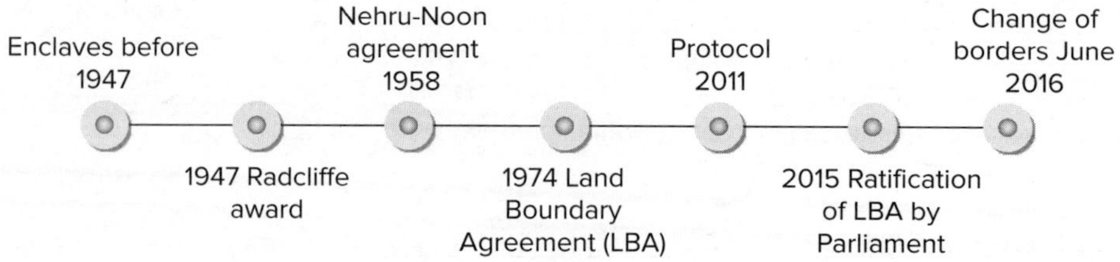

INDIA AND BANGLADESH MARITIME ISSUE

In 1970, the region of Bay of Bengal witnessed the Bhola cyclone. Because of the intensity of the cyclone, an offshore sandbar island called New Moore Island got created in 1970. Since then it became a disputed island between the two states because even though the island was uninhabited, the island had proven oil and gas reserves. India and Bangladesh have followed the Thalweg Doctrine, which is based on 'mid-channel flow' as per which the middle of Haribhanga River is taken as a boundary of the two states. The problem here was that the island was in the Sundarban Delta and kept on shifting its position due to deposition of silt and as a result of that, the two parties could not resolve the location dispute as per the Thalweg Doctrine. The failure to achieve success on negotiations related to New Moore Island in 2009 led Bangladesh to approach the Permanent Court of Arbitration under UNCLOS. The UNCLOS, under Annex-7 of the Convention for Delimitation of Maritime Boundary between India and Bangladesh, handed over the case to a five-member arbitration tribunal. The tribunal gave an award on 7th July 2014 and upheld Indian sovereignty over the New Moore islands and enabled India to have access to Haribhanga River. Bangladesh has been granted an additional access to 19,000 square kilometres Exclusive Economic Zone (EEZ). India shall continue to hold rights over its continental shelf but Bangladesh is allowed an outlet to the extended continental shelf. Bangladesh also now gets access to open sea and shall no more be a sea-locked nation due to overlap of EEZ.

THE HYDRO-DIPLOMACY FACTOR IN INDIA–BANGLADESH RELATIONS AND TEESTA RIVER ISSUE

Of the 57 transboundary rivers, Bangladesh shares 54 of them with India. Teesta is the 4th largest river in Bangladesh (after Ganga, Brahmaputra and Meghna). The flood plain of Teesta is 2750 square kilometres. In 1972, a Joint River Commission was established to share resources of 54 rivers. However, till now the only success is on an agreement related to Ganga River signed in 1996 for 30 years for water sharing. A key irritant is the issue related to the river Teesta. This river originates from Khangtse Glacier in Charamullake in Sikkim and drains in the Bay of Bengal. In 1983, both nations agreed an ad-hoc agreement where India received 39% of Teesta water while 36% was allocated to Bangladesh. Around 25% water was unallocated. In 2011, an agreement to establish a Joint Hydro Observation Station was evolved which proposed an interim agreement for the next 15 years under which India was to get 42.5% of the Teesta water while Bangladesh was to get 37.5% of water flow during the dry season. The key problem relates to a barrage at Gajoldoba in India and another at Dalia in Bangladesh. Using the barrages, both nations draw water for irrigation. India diverts water through the Teesta–Mahananda irrigation canal to meet the growing urban requirements of Siliguri and Jalpaiguri. Bangladesh complains that this water diverted by India is used for irrigating paddy fields in the region. The problem arises due to the severe shortage of water in the dry months. Bangladesh has been consistently demanding 50% share of the water because it says that in the absence of the stipulated flow it demands, its paddy crops and fishing are affected, thereby affecting critical livelihoods. The agreement has not been adopted due to opposition of the Chief Minister of West Bengal. The issue remains unresolved up to 2020 because in Indian Constitution, water is a state subject and the federal structure of our governance has created an institutional void at the basin level, by bridling the central government from taking an integrated approach to water governance that can lead to a cooperative outcome. A solution often proposed by hydrological experts is establishing a link canal between Manas–Ganga–Teesta and Sankosh but the issue remains. Today, due to divergent views of centre and states, the Teesta has emerged as a classic case of 'conflictual federalism'.

> **Climate Change Threats between India and Bangladesh**
>
> The analysis of water sharing in this section tells us how availability of fresh water has emerged as a serious threat for existence of populations. Because of rising population density and land pressures, the ecology of Sundarbans is witnessing decline and a joint conservation strategy is imperative. The climate-induced displacements are likely to emerge as new threats for the region and a joint collaboration for tackling marine pollution, river pollution and development-induced threats can be of help. In this backdrop, SAARC and BIMSTEC can emerge as core pillars.

A Joint River Commission in 1978 was established to explore possibility of a dam on Barak River. Because of regular flooding of Barak, a dam was proposed at junction of Mizoram, Assam and Manipur. It was decided to use water for irrigation also. Bangladesh says that the dam will affect water supply downstream and affect flow of water in summers. A 1500 MW dam is proposed where Manipur being the host state will get 15% free electricity.

INDIA AND BANGLADESH HYDROCARBON PARTNERSHIP

In 1997, the Bangladeshi firm Mahana Holdings proposed the idea of supplying gas from Sittwe fields in South Myanmar to India via Bangladesh. In 2005, Bangladesh, Myanmar and India reached an agreement that Myanmar would be supplying around 90 tonnes cubic feet gas. However, the Khaleda Zia government backed out of the agreement, citing as its reason, the fact, that India does not allow Bangladesh access to hydropower from Bhutan and Nepal. As the project got stuck, Myanmar signed a deal with China to supply gas to China from Kyaukpyu port to Ruili city in Yunnan province. Since 2015, with the coming back of Sheikh Hasina to power, the negotiations have begun anew. In 2017, the two sides concluded

India and Bangladesh Hydrocarbon Partnership. In 2020, Bangladesh decided to supply gas to Tripura. In 2020, India, Bangladesh and Bhutan started engaging on establishing a Regional Trilateral Energy Sharing Arrangement. India is also purchasing LPG from Bangladesh now.

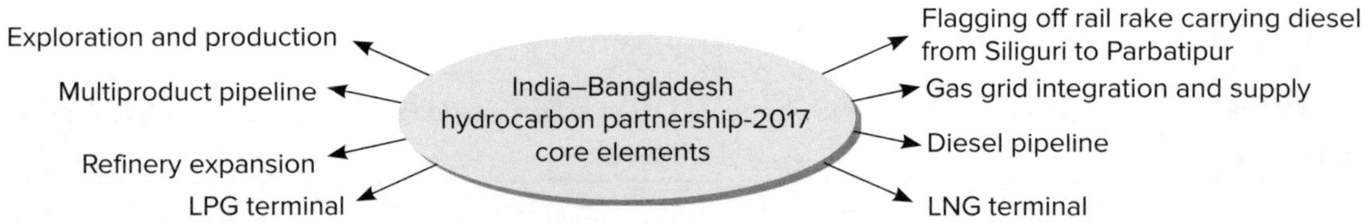

CHINA FACTOR IN INDIA–BANGLADESH TIES

Bangladesh is an active partner of Chinese BRI and has also received substantial support at the defence level. They have been recipients of a submarine from China in 2019. India may not be very comfortable to see growing strategic and economic collaboration of China and Bangladesh. But, India has to accept this as part of evolving regional strategic calculus, which is enabled by economic, trade and fiscal clout of China. India also should understand that Bangladesh is forging an economic partnership with China, which is purely to address its developmental aspirations and in no way is Bangladesh trying to use China as a hedge in its engagement with India. In this backdrop, it is crucial for India to chart out its own course on deepening its ties with Bangladesh.

FUTURE AREAS OF COOPERATION FOR INDIA AND BANGLADESH

1. Resolution of Teesta issue and concluding frameworks on Manu, Muhuri, Khowai, Gumti, Dharla, Feni and Dudkhumar rivers.
2. India can learn from Bangladesh how it has emerged a leader in export of readymade garments by integrating itself to the global value chains. The export dynamism is indeed a lesson for India ahead.
3. There has been a decline in cattle trafficking owing to stronger patrolling by both sides. However, there is occasional firing done by the border guarding forces. It is important for both sides to respect the international rules of engagement, which entail military action to be proportionate to provocation.

CHAPTER 6

India's Relationship with Myanmar

LOCATING MYANMAR IN INDIAN FOREIGN POLICY THOUGHT

International Relations (IR) is an ever-evolving discipline that focuses on global, regional and sub-regional issues. The most basic segment in the discipline of IR remains the study and analysis of neighbours because not only are the neighbours linked socially, economically and historically but also strategically. The relationship with neighbourhood has to be seen in the light of regional security and well-being of people. In this context, the study of Myanmar's relationship with India makes a pertinent case study because at the root lies a shared geographical congruity, linkages of civilisation, cultural interactions and shared political experiences. The commonality of strategic, political and developmental perspectives of India and Myanmar have made the relations linked with a common destiny. In recognition of the historical legacy and status of Myanmar as an immediate neighbour of India, the Ministry of External Affairs (MEA) has created the Bangladesh, Sri Lanka, Maldives and Myanmar division and the division is directly supervised by the Foreign Secretary himself. The above discussion amply makes it clear that Myanmar is important to India and the religion and ethnicity are considered the core binders of the two states. The most important connecting link between India and Myanmar (previously known as Burma) is Buddhism. In the ancient times, Gautama Buddha sent the two monks, Tapussa and Bhallika, with eight strands of his own hair to promote Buddhism in the Myanmar region. Tapussa and Bhallika built a pagoda in Shwedagon, which is now known as the Shwedagon Zedi Daw. Ashoka, during his reign, also sent missionaries to Burma. The people of Burma, since the ancient times, have been majorly Kshatriyas and their origins can be traced back to India, in the Gangetic valley. The 17th century Pyu dynasty used Indian titles like Hari Vikramaditya and Surya Vikramaditya. In modern times, the British had exiled Bahadur Shah Zafar, the last Mughal Emperor of India, to Yangon in Myanmar and the Konbaung King of Myanmar to Ratnagiri. A collective philosophical, spiritual, cultural and commercial interaction between the two states continues to persist and respect for India as a rising power and a growing economy is accepted by Myanmar.

INDIA'S STRATEGIC PERCEPTION OF MYANMAR

Indian foreign policy has evolved a perspective to view Myanmar and its significance for India. India asserts that Myanmar is a land bridge to ASEAN states. India looks at Myanmar as a state that can assist in controlling secessionism in India's northeast. This is because the Chinese have established many listening posts in Myanmar and have allowed the Pakistanis to supply arms to Myanmar. India looks at Myanmar as a state which is rich in natural gas and oil and thereby crucial for our energy security. India also believes that engagement with Myanmar can help us in balancing Chinese in the region. Lastly, for India, Myanmar is a gateway to the Southeast Asia and thereby land connectivity is the dominant paradigm to engage. These views represent the truisms of India and Myanmar relations today.

What is ASEAN?

ASEAN is an economic grouping of ten states of Southeast Asia, formed in 1967, that aspire to strengthen economic cooperation, keeping political differences and controversies aside.

THE SOCIO-CULTURAL PORTRAIT OF MYANMAR AND ITS IMPLICATIONS ON INDIA

Is Myanmar a Buddhist Society?

Myanmar is perceived as a Buddhist society and this assertion is correct and flawed both. While there does exist a strong Buddhist majority, Myanmar also has a powerful minority that displays allegiance to different religions. In a holistic way, Myanmar is a complex society which has multiple ethnic dimensions.

Myanmar has five neighbours and the shores being washed by Andaman Sea and Bay of Bengal. The location of the nation helps in understanding the socio-cultural character of Myanmar. The immediate neighbours of Myanmar include India, China, Bangladesh, Thailand and Laos. A unique feature of Myanmar is that it is able to effectively balance its two large-friendly neighbours, India and China. Let us delve as how is it possible. A basic study of history tells us that people who inhabit Myanmar today have come from China, India and Thailand. The Chinese moved southwards from Tibet and Yunnan and glued along Mizos and Kachin groups from India to migrate towards the fertile plains washed by the Irrawaddy River. Over the ages, Myanmar showed a remarkable genius of absorbing and synthesising influences and developed a unique style of its own. It is this feature of the national psyche that explains the dual inclinations of Myanmar to be friendly with India and China and yet assert independence in dealing with the two. Myanmar is a country with 145 national races and eight main ethnic groups that Bamar (68% population), Shan, Kachin, Chin, Karen, Kayah, Mon and Rakhine. The rest of the groups, other than Bamar, constitute 32% of the population and a power to reckon with, when we view it from the prism of accepted democratic norms.

MYANMAR'S FLIRTATION WITH DEMOCRACY AND IMPLICATIONS ON INDIA

Why is Myanmar unable to become Completely Democratic?

A very special feature of the Burmese people is that they conceal their feelings and views. They express their views in a limited sense, more limited to the foreigners, until they trust them. Over the ages, it has become a culture of the people to think first and then speak or sometimes think more and speak less. This factor also explains why military rule has been more dominant in Myanmar because the people of Myanmar often lived in a fear that if they express their views, they might be reported to the authorities and that may cause bodily harm to them.

The position of Myanmar is rightly known as hemmed in like a tender gourd amongst the cacti. In 1951, India and Burma established diplomatic relations through a Treaty of Friendship but the foundation of the Indo-Myanmar relations was laid down by the visit of Rajiv Gandhi in 1987. After the victory of Ne Win in Burma in 1948, he undertook aggressive nationalisation, which led to lot of discrimination to the Indian diaspora present in Burma. The Indian diaspora in Burma had British origins. Burma was an erstwhile British colony that gained independence in 1948 and the British had taken a large number of Indians belonging to Chettiar community to work in Burma as plantation workers. In 1988, Ne Win's resignation led to a referendum on whether or not multi-party democracy needed to be adopted in Myanmar. In 1988, the '8888 revolt' started in Burma. (It began on 8-8-1988 and is hence called 8888.) Aung San Suu Kyi led the revolt. Suu Kyi fought for democracy and won the election in Myanmar, but the military junta rejected the polls and launched massive crackdown on the activists. General Saw Haung took control of Myanmar and established the State Law and Order Restoration Council (SLOC). In 1990, SLOC announced elections. However, as per the SLOC, the election was to be held only for the purpose of redrafting the Constitution of the Myanmar. In the elections, the National League for Democracy (NLD) won 392 of 485 seats and the National Unity Party (backed by the army) won the rest. The NLD demanded immediate transfer of power on the basis of popular vote. This led to a confrontation based on the political values of democracy and autocracy. India has always been a supporter of NLD whereas China was a supporter of SLOC. Subsequently, Aung San Suu Kyi, the founder of NLD, was put under house arrest. The military-backed party was called Union Solidarity and Development Party, or USDP. During this period, because India had always focused on engaging with democratic forces, India was now suddenly isolated when Tatmadaw, the military regime of Myanmar, acquired power. The Chinese and Pakistanis were courting the military regime in Myanmar and Chinese were showing more interests in junta because the military had supported the Chinese in the suppression in 1989 in Tiananmen Square. While India was struggling to articulate a policy at a time when Chinese and Pakistanis were endangering Indian security in Myanmar; the problem was aggravated further when in the same time period, India struggled to even find an ambassador for Myanmar. India's inability to find a suitable ambassador was because India wanted a very seasoned officer to manage the complex challenges. However, the delay for appointing an ambassador was seen by the Tatmadaw negatively and they thought that India sides with democratic forces and is reluctant to accept the Tatmadaw in Myanmar. This perception was not true because India's dilemma, as explained, was to find a seasoned officer. In fact, the then External Affairs Minister I. K. Gujral even went to assert that considering the importance of Myanmar, if India is unable to find a diplomat, then probably a politician might be eventually sent to Myanmar as the ambassador. The difference in perceptions over the ambassadorship only strained India's relationship with Tatmadaw and India only got more isolated for its failure to act swiftly. Post-1992, Myanmar decided to head towards an open economy and joined ASEAN as a member and ended martial law. Since 1993, Indo-Myanmar relations have prospered as there were economic complementarities.

THE TATMADAW IN MYANMAR AND THE FOUR POLES OF POWER IN MYANMAR

Since the independence of Myanmar, the army, political parties and ethnic groups constitute the arm of the triangle which maintains a complex and the changing relationship with each other. While the three arms have differences and tensions with each other, none has political weight and power to be equal with each other. There are some who argue that there is a fourth element that exercises influence and that includes the exiled refugees and activists of Myanmar that live in India, Norway, the US and the UK and they too have close links with two poles, namely, political parties and ethnic groups but are hostile to the third pole, the army. In the political triangle explained here, the Tatmadaw or the army constitutes the base of the power pyramid because the army claims the credit for making significant contributions to seek independence of Myanmar. It is important to understand that the military in Myanmar has its own conception of its significance in the country. The Tatmadaw argues that they have got independence for Myanmar, ceaselessly safeguarded the unity and territorial integrity of their country and have played a role of guide for the well-being of the people. In effect, their argument, though never explicitly asserted, is that power stems from the military and not the people.

General Aung San

He is the most loved military man in Myanmar and he enjoys respect and aura in the hearts of the people. Even Suu Kyi, his daughter, often invokes his name in speeches, though with the motive of communicating the intent that even though she maybe a proponent of democracy, but she loves military as an institution and would love to work with them in an apolitical manner hoping that someday they would return to the barracks.

INDIA'S CORE STRATEGIC INTERESTS IN MYANMAR

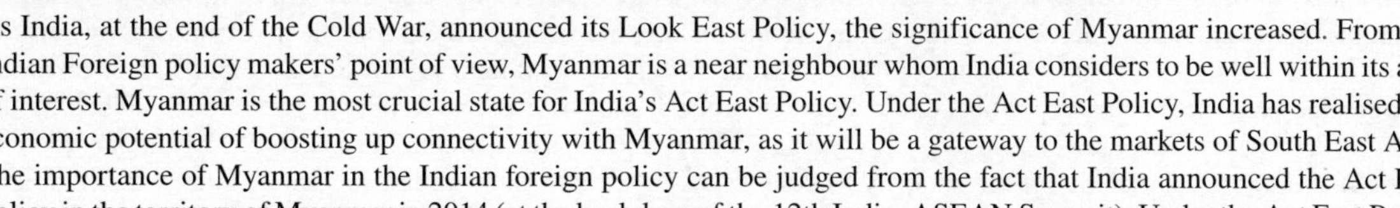

MYANMAR AS THE LYNCHPIN OF INDIA'S ACT EAST POLICY

As India, at the end of the Cold War, announced its Look East Policy, the significance of Myanmar increased. From the Indian Foreign policy makers' point of view, Myanmar is a near neighbour whom India considers to be well within its area of interest. Myanmar is the most crucial state for India's Act East Policy. Under the Act East Policy, India has realised the economic potential of boosting up connectivity with Myanmar, as it will be a gateway to the markets of South East Asia. The importance of Myanmar in the Indian foreign policy can be judged from the fact that India announced the Act East Policy in the territory of Myanmar in 2014 (at the backdrop of the 12th India–ASEAN Summit). Under the Act East Policy India has decided to leverage the geographical proximity and strengthen security relations. The connectivity with Myanmar can be a gateway to South East Asia, as envisaged under the India–Myanmar–Thailand Highway. In 2014, India–Myanmar signed a pact on border cooperation and intelligence sharing. India is also connecting with Myanmar to leverage Buddhism through the Buddhist circuit where India intends to use Buddhism's cultural heritage to promote tourism and create job.

THE ROHINGYA ISSUE IN MYANMAR

Since the 19th Century, people from various parts of India migrated to Myanmar. Over a period of time, they became prosperous and asserted their economic strength in the society. The local people of Myanmar were not happy and felt insecure. From 1920s to 1940s, there were violent revolts. During Ne Win's time, the non-Buddhist people were also targeted. Many of them left Myanmar during Ne Win's time. From Bengal, the Britishers took a lot of Muslims to Burma from 1823 onwards when the British occupied the Rakhine state of Myanmar. After the independence of Burma in 1948, these Muslims stayed back in Burma. Many of them are settled in South West Burma, which is known as the Rakhine area. The Rakhine area is in Arakan Yoma Mountains. From 'Rakhine' a word has originated for these Muslims in Myanmar's language and the word is Rohangs. These Muslims are therefore called Rohingyas (the people of Rakhine). In 1982 Citizenship law, a constitutional order, of Myanmar was passed by the government and the Rohingyas were not recognised as an official ethnic group and since then have become stateless in Myanmar. In the 1990s, a 969 movement began in Myanmar. The movement was a brainchild of Kyaw Lwin. Under the 969 movement the government used Lwin's ideas to win over people by preaching the good practices of Buddhism. In the 2000s, another movement called the 786 movement began. The origin of the 786 concept is in Arabic Abjad numerical system and is inspired from the opening passage of Quran. In Myanmar, 786 usually demarcate an area as belonging to Muslims. Normally, Muslims outside their homes and shops write 786. The Arabic meaning of 786 is Bismillah Al Rehman Al Rahim (in the name of god, most gracious and most merciful). The Buddhists of Myanmar began to misinterpret the 786 movement and they began to think the movement is aimed to dominate 21st century ($7 + 8 + 6 = 21$) as the Islamic century. The 9/11 attacks in 2001 cemented this fear amongst the Buddhists that Islam is going to dominate the 21st century. The insecurity of the Buddhists began to grow. The Buddhist insecurity manifested as riots in 2011 in the Sittwe–Rakhine region and the brain behind this ethnic violence was Ashin Wirathu. The rise of the radical and rightist Ashin Wirathu has brought out the face of radical Buddhism. This has led to the mass exodus of Rohingyas to Indonesia and Thailand in 2015.

THE ROHINGYAS AND OPERATION PIN CODE OF ISI OF PAKISTAN

According to RAW, ISI of Pakistan has created the cadres of the Harakah-al-Yaqin (HaY) group and uses it to create unrest in the region as part of their Operation Pin Code. RAW has found that ISI used the Arakan Rohingya Salvation Army (ARSA) and HaY to mastermind the attacks on military posts in the Rakhine state. The leader of ARSA is Hafiz Tohar who is an asset of the ISI. Tohar has created Aqa Mul Mujahedeen (AMM), which has been trained by the Lashkar group. As the HaY and ARSA unleash violence, Myanmar army retaliates by carrying out counter operations. These counter operations by the army of Myanmar lead to exodus of the Rohingya Muslims to Bangladesh and India, which the ISI, through their information war portrays to the world as a humanitarian crisis. There are around 10 lakh Rohingya Muslims in Myanmar and around 40,000 in India. These illegal immigrants, living majorly in Kashmir, are susceptible to recruitment by terrorist groups of ISI and thus constitute a security threat to India. The influx of Rohingya Muslims to India also disturbs the demographic pattern and social, political and cultural stability of the society. The Rohingya problem, described by the UN, is a classical textbook case of ethnic cleansing. The Rohingya crisis is a symptom of modern-day Myanmar where at heart of the crisis is the inability of the majority Buddhist state to accept a multi-religious society. Firstly, the Rohingya Muslims end up at a disadvantage because of deep conflict in Myanmar with respect to the civil–military divide and military positioning itself as the protector of the nation. Secondly, because of them being Muslims, the majority Bamar–

Buddhist community refuses to accept the Rohingya primacy in Rakhine area. Thirdly, the ultra-nationalists Buddhists have resorted to fuel Islamophobia against the Rohingya Muslims, which has caused their further alienation in the society.

INDIA'S ROHINGYA POLICY

India's response to Rohingya crisis has evolved over three distinct phases. In the first phase of India's policy, in 2012, when violent conflicts began in Rakhine area between the Buddhists and Rohingya Muslims, India asserted that it is an 'internal' problem of Myanmar. India adopted a two-point policy. Firstly, it provided a 1-million USD package to assist in development and rehabilitation of Rohingya Muslims. Secondly, India, as part of its age-old tradition of tolerance in welcoming refugees allowed the Rohingya refugees to settle in India (based on the principle of non-refoulement and voluntary repatriation, explained later).

In 2015, the Rohingya crisis assumed a regional dimension for the first time. In the same year, the Rohingya refugees tried to enter into Malaysia and Thailand. They tried to reach these areas via the sea when their boats were turned around. At that time there were calls made to India to rescue the people in the boats. India did not respond to any such requests. There were various factors that went into this shift in Indian perception of Rohingya Muslims. Firstly, India was not interested in upsetting Myanmar by taking up the Rohingya Muslims issue at a time when Myanmar was trying to make a shift towards democracy. India rightly believed that if Myanmar is pushed too much on the Rohingya Muslims issue, it might be compelled to go close to China, which India could not afford strategically. Secondly, India has been deeply involved in Shwe gas field, Kaladan project and Sittwe port development and did not want to upset Myanmar at a time when it was involved with Myanmar at this developmental and strategic level. India followed a careful balance between geo-politics, geo-strategic and geo-economic concerns in the first phase. The origin of the second phase of India's Rohingya Muslims policy can be traced back to 2017. On 9th August 2017, in a response to a Parliamentary question, Indian Home Minister asserted that the government is planning to deport the Rohingya Muslims who are settled in different parts of the country, as they are 'illegal immigrants'. Even though the minister did clarify that the plan to deport the Rohingya Muslims is still being planned. In September 2017, there was a huge inflow of Rohingya Muslims from Myanmar to Bangladesh. This heightened Indian concerns of the possibility of the outflow of the Rohingya Muslims from Bangladesh to India. India immediately responded by launching Operation Insaniyat. Under this operation, the government provided economic assistance to Bangladesh to provide relief to the Rohingya Muslims in the refugee camps in Myanmar. This is an important element of the Indian strategy in the second phase. The core logic is to de-incentivise the refugees to enter into India by incentivising Bangladesh. Thus, as we infer, that in the second phase, apart from geopolitical constraints, India adopted a policy with a mixture of humanitarian elements and non-interference in the internal affairs with adequate diplomatic capital invested in balancing Bangladesh and Myanmar. By the end of the second phase, India was able to achieve clarity regarding how to eventually approach the Rohingya Muslims problem and this led to the rise of the third phase. India developed clarity over three things. First, India stated that the situation could be normalised only when the displaced persons are returned to the Rakhine state. This policy stance meant that Rohingya Muslims needed to return to Myanmar not only from Bangladesh but also from India. This is where the catch lies. India calls the Rohingya Muslims in Myanmar as 'displaced persons' but calls the Rohingya Muslims in India as 'illegal immigrants'. Second, India believes rightly that the only long-term solution to the problem of the Rohingya Muslims is the development of the Rakhine state for which India needs to use its own resources and also mobilise the resources from the international community. Third, India has asserted that it will maintain a healthy and a constructive engagement with both Myanmar and Bangladesh while at the same time will convince the international community to handle the situation of Rohingya Muslims with restraint, owing to the welfare of the Rohingya Muslims. The analysis of third phase proves that India's approach to the Rohingya Muslims problem was driven by an urge to find a resolution to the Rohingya Muslims crisis. This is a perfect case of quiet Indian diplomacy at work. The ulterior reason for India to resort to the third phase was to counter the proactive and assertive role that China began to play in the resolution of Rohingya Muslims crisis. China had announced a three-step strategy to solve the Rohingya Muslims crisis. China asserted that firstly their needs to be a ceasefire to ensure people do not run around and live in peace. Secondly, China asserted that there needs to intense consultations on the basis of equality. Thirdly, China asserted the need for the international community to develop the Rakhine state. Indian perception was that if it does not step in into the issue of Rohingya Muslims immediately, then it would end up in providing strategic space to China to decide on issues in Indian neighborhood. This would enable China to take geopolitical gains in India's own backyard. This is the reason why India decided to step up its developmental engagement with the government of Myanmar and ended up in concluding agreements to undertake housing development, medicine support etc. for the Rohingya Muslims in the Rakhine area. As the countries in the West are busy in mitigating their own challenges, India has taken the Western vacuum to place itself in a comfortable position in developing its own strategy for the problem of Rohingya Muslims. There are two schools of thought that help us to analyse the conceptual prism of India's Rohingya policy. According to the first school, India has hesitation in designating any asylum seekers as refugees. Because of this thought in the strategic community of India, India creates disincentives for asylum seekers to stay permanently in India. According to the first school, the reason why India does not favour permanent settlement of refugees in India is because of an absence of a national policy for refugees. The second school of thought tries to explain the Indian approach to Rohingya Muslims by looking at the concept of implications. This school tries to explain the Rohingya Muslims problem through the implications Rohingya Muslims will have on India. As per this school, the government's approach of the Rohingya Muslims problem is explained through a security lens. This school asserts that the government in India is looking at the Rohingya Muslims problem as problem of radicalisation, which can lead to a spillover on the Muslim population of India. As per the second school, this policy of the government is a shortsighted policy because it puts thousands of members of Indian diaspora in Myanmar under a serious risk while allowing other states to take lead in proposing solutions to Rohingya Muslims problem (Chinese three-step solution). The second school assets that the Indian government's policy on Rohingya Muslims negates India's own past of being a democratic society with an open door for refugees.

INDIA, REFUGEE CONVENTION, NON-REFOULMENT AND ROHINGYA ISSUE

In 1951, a Refugee Convention relating to the status of refugees was proposed. At that time, Nehru stated that India was committed to follow its principles without any legal obligation of ratifying it. The Convention defines refugees as person fleeing persecution on grounds of race, religion, nationality, social group or political opinion. The refugees, under the Convention, get legal rights, which include the 'non-refoulement', which prevents the states from sending them back to the states from where the persecution originated. They also get secondary rights that range from work, property and education etc. India is not a signatory to 1957 UN Refugee Convention and nor to the 1967 Protocol, but the Indian government on case-to-case basis accepts asylum in India. If Indian government permits a seeker with asylum in India, the person in concern is provided with a Long-Term Visa (LTV). The LTV is renewed annually and allows a holder to work in private sector in India along with access to education and basic banking services. The UN has urged India to follow customary law while trying to deport Rohingya. This means that as in Myanmar, Rohingya Muslims are stateless, under the customary law; the principle of non-refoulement is applied where refugees cannot be returned forcibly to a place where there is a threat to their life or freedom. The Indian government has legal right to deport immigrants who may pose a security threat. Though selective targeting of Rohingya Muslims may be morally incorrect but places no legal limitations on the government. Three issues emerge in conclusion. Firstly, the way the government has handled the Rohingya Muslims problem has certainly raised questions on the democratic credentials in India. Secondly, India's initial reluctance to take a lead initially and reacting only after India saw the Chinese enter has raised questions on India's regional leadership question. Thirdly, the concentration of desperate people in Bangladesh and Myanmar only provide a fertile ground for breeding forms of radicalisation. One thing is clear. Instead of resorting to megaphone diplomacy to solve the Rohingya Muslims problem, India has preferred quiet diplomacy. As a future strategy, India should ensure that Rohingya Muslims are not deported back to Myanmar until it is safe for the Rohingya Muslims to reside in Myanmar. India can always prioritise national security but such prioritisation should not be imprudent and self-defeating. India should strive to establish cooperative agreements with Myanmar and Bangladesh to facilitate intelligence sharing that can prevent rise of radicalisation. A long-term strategy India should adopt is to try making Rohingya Muslims problem a core diplomatic agenda at various regional forums such as BIMSTEC and ASEAN. A 'regional diplomatic approach' can be a fruitful strategy in the long run. At the global level, India can play a role in convincing the West that sanctions on Myanmar will not work and eventually push Myanmar closer to China. Thus, the international community should constructively engage with Myanmar and help carve a developmental discourse. Such a strategy can help sharpen India's global credentials and help position India as a state with diplomatic capital for crisis management. In 2018, the Indian Supreme Court also stayed the deportation of seven Rohingya by the Indian government as they asserted that the Union Government in an affidavit had claimed that the Government of Myanmar accepted the refugees as citizens and the seven persons too orally agreed for their deportation. In 2020, an African state Gambia, took Myanmar to the International Court of Justice (ICJ) over the Rohingya crisis. The ICJ concluded that Rohingya face genocide by the Myanmar army. As a rising power which possess global aspirations coupled with a tradition-based history on dealing with refugees, India is duty bound to shape a narrative on Rohingya Muslims problem. Only then can India become a country, which Swami Vivekananda envisaged, a haven to the persecuted of the world, untainted by discrimination based on religion or nation.

INDIA AND MYANMAR BORDER COOPERATION

Myanmar and India share both land and maritime borders but since the 1990s, there has also been a growing proximity between China and Myanmar, who also share a land border. Myanmar continues to witness sea piracy and ethnic crises. Nagas have been living in the North East since time immemorial. After the decolonisation of Myanmar, new boundaries were created with India. This led to a division between India and Myanmar and affected the Nagas, who became ethnic minorities on both sides. To resolve the issue, the governments of both countries decided to establish a Free Movement Regime (FMR), which could allow Nagas greater interaction either side of the border. As per the FMR, the Nagas can travel 16 km across either side of the border without a visa. This FMR facilitated interaction between Konyaks, Khiamniungans and Yimchungar Nagas living in Eastern districts of Nagaland. The border crossing was possible only with a valid border pass, costing 20 rupees. India and Myanmar signed a Border Trade Agreement in 1994, which got operationalised in 1995. As per the agreement, the two sides will undertake border trade through designated check posts. Around 1% of the India–Myanmar trade happens through the border. The present duty is 5% for the 40 identified select items traded at the border.

INDIA–MYANMAR LAND BORDER CROSSING AGREEMENT 2018

In 2018, the two sides established a new border regime under which a citizen with a valid Indian or Myanmar passport and visa can now cross over to either side. There will no requirement of any special permit anymore. The two sides have identified Moreh in Manipur–Tamu in Myanmar (in Sagiang division) and Zokhawthar in Mizoram–Rhiikhawdar in Myanmar (in Chin state) as the crossing points. This will facilitate Buddhist tourists, medical tourists and students of Myanmar to travel to India with ease. There are many Manipuri people in Mandalay. Earlier they had to take a flight to Kolkata from Yangon. Now, the distance gets shortened and will facilitate people-to-people ties.

INDIA AND MYANMAR DEFENCE AND SECURITY COOPERATION

India, way back in 1950, had provided Myanmar with six Dakota aircrafts to aid in its fight against insurgency. The important dimension of the defence relationship is that India has been an important arms supplier to Myanmar. India has supplied T-55 tanks, transport planes and naval crafts to Myanmar, to name just a few. The broad contours of our defence engagement include border training, intelligence sharing and the training of Myanmar forces. In 1994, India and Myanmar signed a pact on Maintenance and Tranquility in Border Areas. Since then, India and Myanmar have been cooperating in the area of counter insurgency. Indian army chiefs regularly interact with their Myanmari counterparts. In 2006, both concluded a pact on intelligence sharing and training, where India envisages training of Myanmar's military to boost their military capabilities. Another driver of defence cooperation has been drug smuggling. Myanmar is a part of the Golden Triangle (Myanmar, Thailand and Laos) and has become an important transit country for illegal drug trafficking. In 2010, India and Myanmar established Mutual Legal Assistance Treaty on criminal matters, which have emerged as the core legal instrument to address issues related to drug smuggling and gun running. In 2012, both established Joint Working Group on Terrorism. In 2014, they signed a pact on border cooperation. India assists Myanmar in building Offshore Patrol Vehicles under Coordination Protocol (CORPAT). Recently, India also carried out a surgical strike on the Indian side of the border to shoot down insurgents operating in the region in 2016. Another key driver of defence cooperation is maritime security because India undertakes oil exploration in Myanmar. As Myanmar faces piracy and illegal fishing problems, India has been providing training to Myanmar's forces and especially navy. At the maritime level, the two sides in 2016 concluded a Standard Operating Procedure for Joint Naval Portal. India also signed a Maritime Security Agreement with Myanmar in 2017. Under the agreement, India and Myanmar would be sharing data related to non-classified merchant ships with each other. India would also provide coastal surveillance system to Myanmar. In 2020, India handed over INS Sindhuvir, a Kilo-class submarine, which India purchased from Russia in 1980. This makes India counter China in Myanmar, which was trying to sell Ming-class submarines.

INDIA–MYANMAR COMMERCIAL DIPLOMACY

There has been steady gradual improvement in the trade ties between India and Myanmar. India imports beans, pulses and forest products from Myanmar while it exports steel and pharmaceutical products. Myanmar stands to be the second largest supplier of pulses to India. There is a rising cooperation in the field of IT and plantation products.

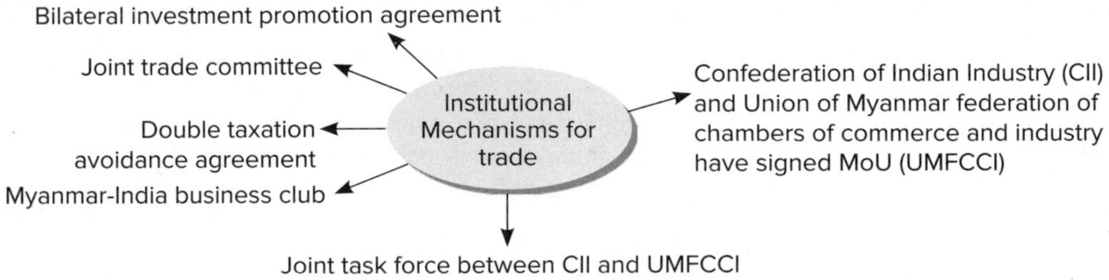

INDIA–MYANMAR HYDROCARBON PARTNERSHIP

At the level of hydrocarbons, India and Myanmar signed a pact in 2006 on cooperation in the petroleum sector. Since then India's ONGC Videsh Limited and GAIL have been present in exploration and development activities. India has acquired stakes in Shwe development and production area. Jubilant Energy and Reliance are also working in shallow water blocks in Myanmar. Both sides identified new areas of cooperation, which include construction of LPG terminals, railway cooperation and petroleum cooperation.

STRATEGIC SIGNIFICANCE OF KALADAN MULTI-MODAL TRANSIT TRANSPORT PROJECT ON INDIA–MYANMAR RELATIONS

The detailed project report was prepared in 2003 and a framework was agreed upon in 2008. The project was expected to be operational for shipment from 2020. It was conceived as an idea to have multi-modal transit transport for shipments from ports on India's east coast and North East through Myanmar. The project aimed to develop North East economy and integrate India's northeast to South East Asia. Through this, North East would be open to sea connectivity. It is a combination of rail, road and river transport. There are no land acquisition issues or environmental concerns, but security threats from insurgents and cost overrun are recurring issues. It would connect Kolkata to Sittwe by sea; from Sittwe to Paletwa by river transport and then a highway to Zorinpuri, Mizoram. The project will boost employment and helps lower the food prices in the region but the intrusion into the region will create a threat to local heritage.

CHINA FACTOR IN INDIA AND MYANMAR RELATIONS

China and Myanmar have deep relations, which are aptly called the "pauk-phaw" or fraternal ties. China is undertaking port construction in Myanmar. India felt that China would probably encircle India. In fact, from Myanmar point of view, the deepening of its relations with China compelled it to diversify and it became natural for Myanmar to look towards India to counter the dominating influence exerted by China. India certainly wants to limit Chinese assertion in Myanmar, as it constitutes Myanmar to be region of the Indian spear of influence. India asserts this because it supported democracy in Myanmar since the 1980s. However, to lay down a foundation for political reform, India, since the beginning of

21st century, had to support the Military Junta. Burmese scholars believe that the reason India became unsuccessful in challenging rising Chinese influence in Myanmar was its support to the Junta. The scholars also believe that when India began to support the Junta, it began to lose goodwill amongst the Burmese population. At present, India's influence is missing in the two camps of Myanmar—one camp that supports democracy and that which is supported by not only the ethnic minorities of Myanmar but also the USA, Japan and South Korea; while other camp is dominated by China and Tatmadaw or the Myanmar military. Though India has favoured the democracy camp, the views of the reformists hardly match with India. Drug trafficking across the borders is viewed by the reformists as a source of income but perceived as major threat by India. Since 2011, the coming of Thein Sein government has initiated a policy of global engagement. This has been beneficial for India, as Chinese influence in Myanmar will gradually diminish as Myanmar searches for new friends. The USA too has opened up to Myanmar, as it knows that a deeper engagement with Myanmar favours the USA in its attempt to keep the rise of China in check. The Chinese, on the other hand, began to support the United DWA State Army (UWSA). The UWSA has been getting arms and ammunition from China to fight the Myanmar government. The future depends on how Myanmar and the USA shall evolve and strengthen their relationship and whether the USA will provide military and defence supplies to Myanmar to counter China.

AREAS OF FUTURE COOPERATION BETWEEN INDIA AND MYANMAR

India has decided to support cooperation in identified areas. India will support Myanmar in livelihood creation, capacity building, construction of roads, tourism promotion, healthcare, education, telecom, renewable energy and fast moving consumer goods. In 2016, a motor vehicle agreement was concluded for Thailand–Myanmar–India roadways. The India–Myanmar–Thailand Highway shall be the next game changer. Not only Myanmar is the lynchpin for India's Act East Policy but also a gateway for a stable Indo-Pacific of the future.

Three Critical Gaps in India and Myanmar

Three areas need immediate intervention in India and Myanmar relations: security and connectivity at borders, connectivity with Indian northeast and expansion of bilateral border trade.

CHAPTER 7

India's Relationship with Nepal

HISTORICAL RELATIONSHIP BETWEEN INDIA AND NEPAL

The relationship between India and Nepal goes back to the times of the rule of the Sakya clan and Gautama Buddha. Feudalism in Nepali society owes its origin to Licchavis. From 750 AD to 1750 AD was a period when Nepal came under Newari rule and they consolidated their presence in Kathmandu. This time period also saw a shift from Buddhism to Hinduism in Nepal and witnessed widespread cultural diffusion. In the 12th century, during the Malla period and the rule of Yakshamala in Nepal, the two nations reached their cultural zenith. The early 1700s witnessed a change in the Nepalese power structure. The subsequent period witnesses both monarchical and prime ministerial rule. In 1846, Jung Bahadur Kunwar established a dynastic rule for the Prime Minister, known as the 'Rana'. The Rana rule took hold and continued in Nepal till 1951. Though the Rana regime was not very efficient, it did contribute to social developments in the field of schools and education. In the 1920s, as the Indian freedom struggle progressed, many educated Nepalese people came to India and partook in the struggle and with inspiration from Indian National Congress, they formed the Nepali Congress (NC). The Nepali elite and Nepali Congress subsequently launched a movement in Nepal and succeeded in ousting the Rana rule.

Is Buddhism a problem between India and Nepal?

It is a globally accepted fact that Buddha was born in Lumbini, Nepal. However, India often claims that Buddha is an apostle of peace and Buddhism is a philosophy about which India is proud of. Nepal perceives these assertions of India as an attempt to hijack their heritage. This is incorrect because the objective of India is to emphasise on a common shared heritage of India and Nepal.

INTERNAL GOVERNANCE OF NEPAL AND PERCEPTION OF INDIA

In 1951, after the ousting of the Rana rule, the monarchy continued to dominate Nepalese politics. Three important kings with respect to this period of Nepalese history are King Tribhuvan, Mahendra and Birendra. In the elections that were held in Nepal in 1951, Nepali Congress party (hereafter referred to as NC) won. The period from 1951 to 1959 witnessed the King, Tribhuvan Bir Bikram Shah, and thereafter, his successor, Mahendra Bir Bikram Shah, and the NC struggle to control Nepal. The situation was not stable due to the insecurity of the king as the king wanted to retain his power and was not keen on sharing power with new democratic elements such as the NC. In 1959, the confrontation between the King, Mahendra Bir Bikram Shah, and the NC reached a level where the king declared NC as corrupt, removed it from power and subsequently installed a party-less Panchayat system. This system was such where people would elect their representatives but the King would wield actual power. Thus, a highly centralised rule began from 1960. The period of party-less Panchayat system witnessed protests from NC and other sections of society. The protests finally culminated in the first Jan Andolan-I in Nepal in 1990.

The RSS in Nepal

It is interesting to know that Mahendra Bir Bikram Shah made Nepal a Hindu state under the 1962 constitution he gave for the country and subsequently assumed the title of Vishwa Hindu Samrat or Hindu emperor of the world. Tulsi Giri, the first Prime Minister under the party-less Panchayat system and a member of Indian RSS was instrumental in making Nepal a Hindu Rashtra.

During this time, the King Birendra Bir Bikram Shah, divested of any other options, brought back democracy and a new government under the NC was formed. During the rule of the NC in Nepal in the period after 1990, there was not much progress witnessed on the developmental front. In 1994 Unified Marxist Leninist Party (UML) which had got support from China tried to generate an anti-India feeling in Nepal. The UML began to assert that the NC is in reality controlled by Congress party of India. This led to a perception amongst the Nepali people about India's control and interference over Nepal and its internal affairs through the NC. The anti-India plan worked in favour of UML and they succeeded in capturing power for a short period of 9 months in Nepal. The UML was removed and the NC assumed power again in 1994. The subsequent period not only saw civil unrest but also witnessed the development projects of Nepal suffer. The civil unrest was fuelled by China, which, over a period of time, evolved into civil uprising and took an ideological turn to Maoism. The Maoist movement in Nepal became fully manifested by 2005. Perceiving the unrest and violence in society, King Gyanendra dissolved the Parliament again. This dissolution of the Parliament caused massive protests, ultimately leading to the second Jan Andolan-II in 2005.

FORMATION OF NEPALI CONSTITUTION 2015

The Jan Andolan-II led to a signing of a Peace Accord in 2006. An interim constitution was prepared in 2007.

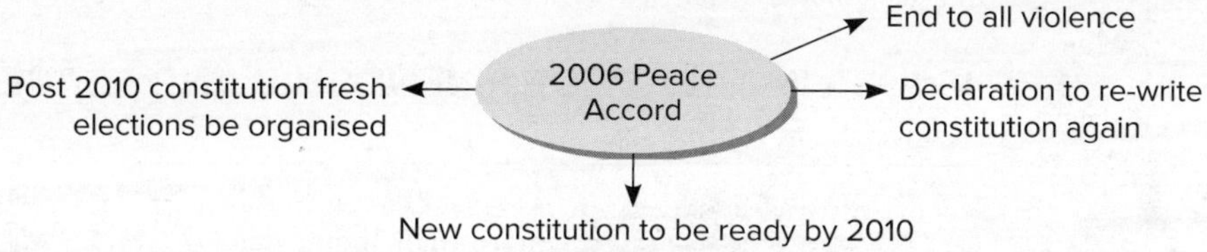

As mentioned, the 2006 Peace Accord planned that Nepal would establish the new constitution by 2010. However, by 2010, the constitution was not ready. It got delayed due to two key issues. The first related to the disagreement about the succeeding form of government. Maoists favoured the Presidential system while others favoured Parliamentary system. The second issue related to federalism. Maoists favoured ethnic federalism while others rejected the idea. Another important factor that delayed the constitutional development was Madhesi assertion. Madhesis are people living in South of Nepal in the region of Terai. They are people living close to the border of India. Pahadis or the people living in the upper reaches of Nepal have always discriminated the Madhesis. In fact, the discrimination against Madhesis at one point of time, was so intense by Pahadis that if a Madhesi citizen wanted to visit Kathmandu, they had to apply for a permit. The Muluki Ain or national code has established the practice to the extent that there was a time when a brahmin could not be given a death sentence but only exiled. The Madhesis, through their representation, demanded rights in the new constitution. After tremendous delays, Nepal finally accepted a constitution in September 2015.

The Nepalis Identity

In Nepal, the brahmins and chettris are the two divine groups that regulate the society. The two collectively dominate the army and politics of the state.

ASSESSMENT OF NEPALESE CONSTITUTION 2015 AND INDIA'S APPROACH TO THE NEW CONSTITUTION

Nepal is governed according to the Constitution of Nepal, which came into effect on 20 September 2015, replacing the Interim Constitution of 2007. The then constitution, which was its seventh, took almost nine years in the making. Nepal has alleged that India did not " welcome" the Nepali Constitution promulgated by the Constituent Assembly but merely "noted" it. What makes this 2015 constitution different from the previous six constitutions is that monarchs wrote old constitutions and an elected Constituent Assembly (CA) writes this seventh one. The new Constitution has been written by politicians and not by Jurists and legal luminaries. It has adopted a rights-based framework, which is high on promises. The CA mechanism was adopted to ensure that the diverse social and ethnic groups of Nepal come together on a platform and work on rules to be made for the entire society. The CA aimed to have an inclusive order with all groups on board.

However, the idea of a collective ownership to a constitution has not evolved as Madhesi people, an ethic group was not given adequate representation.

INDIA AND NEPAL TREATY OF FRIENDSHIP AND PEACE

India and Nepal, on 31st July 1950, signed a Treaty of Friendship and Peace. This treaty acts as the bedrock of the relation between the two nations. The treaty extends mutual peace, friendship and sovereignty to each other while it accepts non-interference in each other's territory. The treaty lets the nations extend national treatment to each other. The national treatment clause also extends for industrial and economic development. Basically, under Indo-Nepal national treatment, their citizens are empowered to the same privileges for property, trade and residence and movement in both countries. That means, a Nepali citizen can buy property in India while an Indian citizen can do so in Nepal if he/she so chooses. Also, an Indian citizen can reside anywhere in Nepal and a Nepali citizen too enjoys the right to residence in India under national treatment. Another important point of the treaty is open borders. As per this point, Indian citizens can move to Nepal without the need of a visa and vice versa.

Does India interfere in Nepal?

In one instance, Nepal had to appoint an IGP and the Home Minister of Nepal sent a name he intended to select to the Indian Ambassador in Kathmandu, even though the Ambassador never requested such a name. The Chair of House was supporting his own candidate and eventually a list of four candidates were shared with the Indian Ambassador, even though India never asked the same. The four candidates for IGP visited the Indian Ambassador to push their case and sought to extend cooperation with India, thereby the Indian Ambassador shared his views to the Nepalese Home Minister on a certain candidate for the post. However, after an internal political bickering, the candidate supported by the Chair of the House was made IGP. This instance clearly proves that India has no such intentions of micro-managing any events, despite repeated allegation that India tries to micro-manage Nepal through its intelligence agency, RAW.

ISSUES IN TREATY OF FRIENDSHIP AND PEACE RAISED BY NEPAL

Real Context of Signing the Treaty

In 1950, Nepal has alleged that India signed the treaty with an autocratic ruler, the Rana. However, the treaty was negotiated at a time when communists had taken control of China and were on way to annex Tibet. The rulers of Nepal were worried that in the absence of British from India and an aggressive Chinese in the north, there could be an existential threat to Nepal. It is in this context that the Rana signed the treaty to ensure his survival.

The treaty favours Nepal more than India, but Nepal still has certain issues with it. Nepal initially complained that when the treaty was concluded in 1950, India concluded the treaty with a Rana ruler. Nepal alleges that India signed the treaty with the Rana who had become unpopular. Certain sections in Nepal also alleged that the way treaty was signed signified that India considered Nepal as a small state and not an equal state because at the time of conclusion of the treaty, India sent its Indian ambassador to Nepal and Jawaharlal Nehru himself did not come to sign the treaty, signifying an unequal status of the countries. As mentioned earlier, in 1994, the UML had successfully generated an anti-India plank in the election. Since then, raising anti-India slogans and alleging that the Indo-Nepal Treaty of 1950 favours India more than Nepal has become a norm for gaining political mileage. Many times, Nepali political parties have demanded a change in the treaty. As per Article X in the treaty, either party can ask for a change in the treaty whenever demanded. Under Article X of the treaty, Nepal can ask India to bring change and India has to establish a mechanism for the same. Whenever Nepal has asked for a change in the treaty, India has accepted the Nepali request, but, absence of consensus in Nepal on issues that need revision prevents any meaningful engagement about the issue. In 2014, the two sides established an Eminent Persons Group (EPG) to review the treaty.

India and Nepal Bhai–Bhai?

Nepal always gets emotional when India asserts that India and Nepal have a bhai–bhai relationship. Nepal argues that they favour a relationship based on equality with India. However, when India asserts a bhai–bhai relationship, Nepal perceives that in such a relationship, there is always an elder brother and one younger brother and India aspires to be the elder one, thus big brother dilemma. The reality is that India genuinely cares for Nepal and when it asserts a bhai–bhai relationship, the objective is a genuine affection, which they find patronising.

ISSUES IN ARTICLE 2 AND ARTICLE 5 OF THE INDIA–NEPAL TREATY

Article 2 of the Treaty states that the two governments will inform each other of any serious friction or misunderstanding with any neighbouring state if it is likely to cause any breach in friendly relations between India and Nepal. A careful reading of Article 2 clearly suggests that there exists a veiled reference to Chinese. The Nepalese side, however, argues that India had never informed them of India's wars with Pakistan in 1965 and 1971, thus India has violated the treaty. Article 5 argues that Nepal is free to import arms, ammunition, war-like material and equipment necessary to secure Nepal from any country through India or from India but the procedure to give effect to this arrangement shall be worked out by consultation of the two governments. The objective of this point was to ensure that Nepal remains under the security umbrella of India and India consequently respects the sovereignty and independence of Nepal. A similar provision existed for Bhutan and over time, the clause with Bhutan has been also amended respecting their interests. Article 5, however, is an irritant for Nepal because Nepal has undertaken activities that undermine India's security interests.

MANAGEMENT OF INDIA AND NEPAL OPEN BORDER

India and Nepal have an open border with each other—a practice that dates back to the British times. Even the British had continued to maintain an open border between India and Nepal. The British and Nepal, after the Anglo-Nepal wars in 1814, concluded the Treaty of Sagauli in 1816. The British had drafted the Treaty of Sagauli on 2nd December 1815. The treaty was to be signed by Nepal by the deadline of 17th December 1815. Nepal refused to sign it by the date declared. The British subsequently threatened an invasion of Kathmandu and after a 92 days stalemate, a courtier, C. S. Upadhyay, signed the treaty. The Treaty of Sagauli was not signed by the King and thus led to troubles in later times The Treaty of Sagauli established Mahakali River (or Kali River) as a dividing line in the western sector. The open border has helped domestic Nepalese people to take advantage. The people of Nepal, through the open border, also entered into India for economic opportunities. The Nepalese who come to India for work are well accepted in India and are not treated as aliens. Nepali citizens have important contribution in India's security setup as well. The entire border is demarcated by border pillars but at various stretches, due to natural calamities and lack of maintenance, the border pillars have gone missing, necessitating a proper demarcation of the border to ensure that an absence of the same does not lead to escalation of tensions. In 1981, India and Nepal established a Joint Technical level Boundary Committee to survey the boundary again. The Committee in 2007 submitted 182 strip maps, which were to be ratified by both nations. The ratification of the 182 strip maps was still pending as of 2022. In July 2014, both countries established a Boundary Working Group (BWG) to resolve the Kalapani and Susta issues. The main issue related to the border management between India and Nepal is that the borders have been demarcated on the basis of a flowing river. The problem is that the rivers shift their courses over a period of time. This impacts the border, which gets affected due to shifting rivers. No doubt the boundary of the river is also based on a principled fixed border but if the river shifts, it results in creation of adverse possessions. The shifting of the rivers has led to the destruction of boundary pillars. The BWG will use GPS observations and generate data. The foreign secretaries of both nations, to solve pending border issues, will use the data.

How Sensitive is Nepal to India?

After the hijacking of IC-814, the Indian Airlines aircraft, which was hijacked from Kathmandu and taken to Kandahar; the Indian agencies decided to frisk passengers boarding flights with destination to India twice at Kathmandu. The agencies deployed their men in Kathmandu to frisk the passengers again. This created an outrage in Nepal that how can foreign troops do this on sacred soil of Nepal. A compromise was worked out and now Indian troops frisk the passengers two steps before they board a flight to India, at the tarmac! This is why Nepal cries of violation of sovereignty and favours repeated assurances from India that India does not intend to violate their sovereignty.

CHALLENGES AT THE INDIA AND NEPAL OPEN BORDER AND MITIGATION STRATEGIES

Intelligence reports of IB and RAW suggest that Pakistan has been taking advantage of the open border to infiltrate into India and that it uses the Nepal border route to pump fake currency into India with an intention to destabilise the Indian economy. The open border has given rise to criminality. Today, criminals of both nations use each other's territory for refuge making it tough for law enforcement agencies to track and catch criminals. There have been numerous cases of drug trafficking, gold smuggling, human trafficking and illegal arms trade that have been reported. Though closing the border is no solution, better management of the border areas are required. A Cross Border Crime Control Action Plan can be prepared and jointly enforced. Sashastra Seema Bal (SSB) can be empowered with modern technology and also empowered under the Passport Act to arrest criminals. In July 2017, the Government of India had given the approval to SSB to establish its own intelligence wing.

> **Why Nepal does not like India?**
>
> Ironically, Nepal and India are similar in identity, religion, culture, tradition, language and kinship. Yet, Nepal resists us because they are surrounded on three sides by India and they have developed a siege mentality. They have a desire to break away from this; therefore, they try to resist and fight the geography.

FOUNDATION OF HYDRO-DIPLOMACY BETWEEN INDIA AND NEPAL

Nepal is an upper riparian state which has more than two hundred rivers and has a hydropower generation potential of around 80,000 MW power. However, it has installed a capacity of around 800 MW only. On an average, 15 to 18 hours of power cuts are common throughout the country. Unfortunately, Nepal has not developed its hydropower potential due to a fear that if they undertake hydropower generation, India will assert dominance over the generated hydroelectricity. Despite the fact that India always cites the example of Bhutan–India hydro diplomacy as a successful case to Nepal. Nepal is still reluctant to improve its generation capacity. There are three treaties to regulate our water sharing today.

KOSI, GANDAK AND MAHAKALI RIVER WATER TREATIES BETWEEN INDIA AND NEPAL

Let us examine each treaty individually. In 1954, India and Nepal signed the India and Nepal Kosi River Treaty. Kosi River causes tremendous flooding and has been also called the Sorrow of Bihar. As per the treaty, the two sides agreed to cooperate to manage Kosi flooding. India, under the treaty, committed to create a low head diversion or a barrage dam, which, through gates, can regulate Kosi's water flow. India constructed the barrage in Nepal and Nepal agreed to give its management rights to India for 199 years. Over a period of time, certain sections in Nepal have brought up some issues pertaining to the Kosi treaty. A section in Nepal feels that barrages have a normal life of 50 years and India getting a lease of 199 years has given India rights to control it for long beyond the need. Certain sections in Nepal also allege that India, while managing the barrage, does not release adequate water for irrigation and during floods, opens the gates, leading to many villages getting submerged completely. A solution to this issue may come forth if both sides undertake a multi-stakeholder negotiation and resolve the issues. In 1959, India and Nepal also signed the India and Nepal Gandak River Treaty. The treaty has 13 Articles and under the treaty, both sides are to utilise water from the Gandak River to generate 20,000 MW electricity. In 1996, both concluded India and Nepal Mahakali Treaty. Under this treaty, India has agreed to undertake the creation of three dams at Sarda, Tanakpur and Pancheshwar. Both sides have agreed to share costs for the dam creation. However, there has been no progress on these projects owing to pending social and environmental impact assessment. Nepal has agreed to complete a Detailed Project Report for the Pancheshwar project in 2023.

SUSTA RIVER IRRITANT BETWEEN INDIA AND NEPAL

Similarly, Susta is an issue between the two states. The problem in Susta arises due to shifting of the course of the river. India has often asserted that Nepali people have illegally occupied the lands of Susta and Narsahi in Bihar. The Nepali people have encroached these two areas by resorting to construction activities and also settling own Nepali population here. The best mechanism to deal with Susta is to accept shifting border as the river shifts or agree on a fixed border despite the shifting course of the river.

POWER COOPERATION AGREEMENT BETWEEN INDIA AND NEPAL

In 2014, India and Nepal concluded a Power Cooperation Agreement (PCA; also called Power Trading Agreement or PTA). Under the PCA, nine articles are concluded and it has been decided to have a review of PCA after 10 years. The agreement shall be valid for 50 years. Under the PCA, Nepal would give license to Indian firms to undertake 28 surveys in Nepal to explore 8000 MW power generations. By 2021, GMR would establish a plant in Karnali to export 900 MW electricity to India.

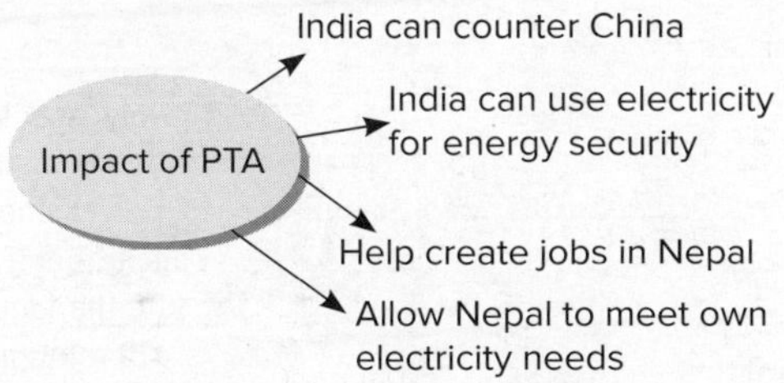

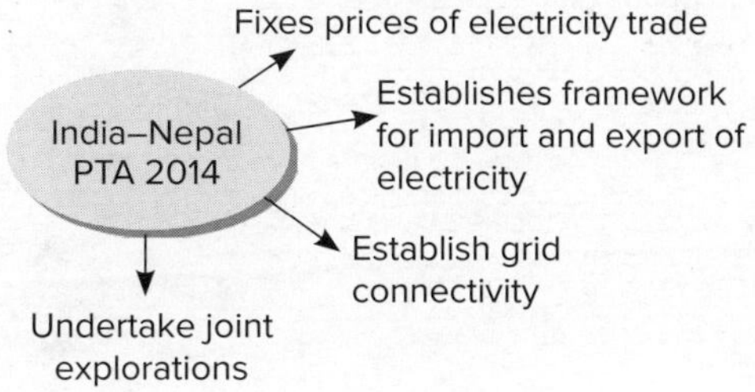

THE ROTI–BETI KA RISHTA AND THE CIVILISATIONAL CONNECT

The people of India and Nepal have roti–beti ka rishta. This term, used by Indian political class for Nepal, signifies the deep people-to-people ties between the two sides. In 1952, Nepal Citizenship Act was passed and it allowed the citizens of India to take up citizenship of Nepal with much ease. The law was later amended in 1962. The Indian women hailing from Uttrakhand, Sikkim, Uttar Pradesh and Bihar, have a long tradition of matrimonial ties, with people of Nepal. Upon the marriage, when the Indian woman renounces her Indian citizenship, she would automatically acquire a Nepali citizenship. But a cold Himalayan breeze seems to be blowing over the Indian and Nepal relations in 2020 and is likely to put the relations into a deep freeze. Under the new law now, the women would have to wait for a period of seven years before acquiring the Nepali citizenship. While the law is not discriminatory for Indian woman because it is universally applicable to all foreigners, but its impact would be felt the most amongst the Indians because they constitute the largest chunk in the foreigner category. If an Indian woman now marries a Nepali man, then with a seven year wait for citizenship, she will be deprived of opening a bank account in Nepal, get a job and inherit property, if need arises. This particular mindset revealed in the amended law is a reflection of distrust in the minds of communist leaders of Nepal who believe that India is driven with a motive to change the demography of Nepal and Nepal is on the path of becoming another Fiji. In fact, this distrust is deeply visible within Nepal also where the Nepali Pahadi people consider the Madhesi people as the fifth column of India. In 1974, when Sikkim was merged with Indian Union, Sikkim had a referendum where even the Nepali people, who had migrated to Sikkim in earlier decades, voted in favour of the merger. This incident too has cemented fears of certain Nepali political elite that India might try to Sikkimise Nepal.

The Civilisational Touch

Nepal is famous for the Pashupatinath Temple and the Head Priest of the temple is an Indian and as per tradition, he is the only person authorised to touch the holy Shivalinga. Such is the civilisational connect.

TRADE AND COMMERCIAL DIPLOMACY BETWEEN INDIA AND NEPAL

India and Nepal signed a Trade Treaty in 1996, which was revised in 2009. Ninety-five per cent of Nepali trade happens with India. Open border and 22 transit routes facilitate the trade. Raxaul, Tanakpur and Brahmandandi are prominent

Nepal–India Financial Diplomacy

In 2022, Nepal decided to launch RuPay card, thus opening a new chapter of financial connectivity with India. The launch of the card will now enable the tourists from India to access the ATMs and POS terminals across the nation, thereby adding a new layer to people-to-people relationship.

transit routes. There are more than 150+ Indian firms in Nepal working in manufacturing and services sectors. In 2013, both sides agreed to an Inter-Governmental Commission on Trade under which India has allowed the use of Kolkata port by Nepal for third-country trade and designated customs points have been established. The trade is imbalanced as India exports a majority of things ranging from food products to petroleum products while imports, being negligible, primarily include wood and traditional medicines. Since 1973, as per India and Nepal Petroleum Supply Agreement, India used to supply oil to Nepal via tankers. In 2020, India inaugurated 69-kilometre Barauni–Amlekhgunj oil pipeline, the first South Asian cross-border pipeline, which will carry two million tons of petroleum products annually and replace tanker trade.

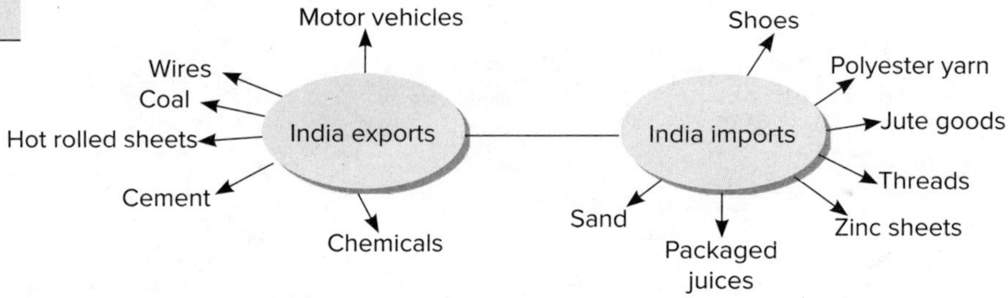

THE CHINESE RELATIONS WITH NEPAL

Contrasting the conventional wisdom, the Chinese have been a dominant player in the international relations of Nepal for a long time. When the British acquired control of India and East India Company began to trade from Calcutta, the Nepali rulers courted China to act as a frontline against British expansion into Nepal. The rulers of Nepal, in their desire to control the British in the plains, and preventing them from acquiring the control of Himalayas, also tried to build an alliance of native Indian rulers. After 1842, when the British won the Opium Wars with the Chinese, the rulers of Nepal realised the changing geopolitics and began to court the British. But, after the 1857 revolt, when the Raj took over the affairs of the company, the Nepali rulers began to enjoy being a British protectorate. It is this dynamic framework that India inherited and has found it difficult to manage till date.

STRATEGIC AND COMMERCIAL INTERESTS OF CHINA IN NEPAL AND IMPLICATIONS ON INDIA

In 1770, King Prithvi Narayan Shah had rightly called Nepal as a root vegetable between two big boulders and called for balance and equidistance. This has apparently never happened. The basic reason of Chinese presence in Nepal is to ensure that Tibetans (some 20,000 in Nepal) do not use Nepalese territory for breeding of discontent. In the initial years, from 1950s to 1980s, the Chinese tried to build an economic presence in Nepal, which got enhanced tremendously post-1990s. Initially, Chinese remained focused on engaging with Monarchy, but after the dissolution of Monarchy, Chinese have adopted an approach of penetrating every aspect of Nepali public life, from politics to army to bureaucracy. China has increased participation with Nepal at the economic front. For that matter, China has opened up many Mandarin language training schools in the Terai region. Chinese are providing Mandarin language training to Madhesis to ensure that in the near future, the Madhesis emerge as potential labours to work in the ever-expanding Chinese economy. China has made inroads into Nepal in infrastructure, education and health sectors. India feels that the Chinese inroads into Nepal are necessarily to counterbalance the Indian influence in Nepal. Certain sections in the Indian intelligence establishment feel that Maoism in Nepal has been encouraged by China and they have potential links with the Indian Naxalite movement, though this is not an officially-accepted view by the Indian government today. In the recent times, Nepal has made a strong tilt towards China. China is helping Nepal to fill their infrastructure gaps and is trying to position itself as a security provider to Nepal.

Nepal wants to take advantage of the rail infrastructure built by China in Tibet. Nepal has asserted that its relationship with China is purely economic and will not be hurting the Indian strategic interests in any way. The rising Nepal and China cooperation also signals that Himalayas are not a barrier anymore and for India, a strategy to check the Chinese engagements is required rather than reactions. Chinese strategy is to directly engage with the Nepali politicians and this has led China to build more trust. The China–Nepal relations can be judged from the following facts. At the developmental level, China has unleashed multiple projects. They include Nepal–China Agreement on Transit and Trade, Nepal–China Rail link agreement, Joint Military Exercise Pact, Rasuwagadhi–Syabrubesi Road link. Nepal is a part of Chinese Belt and Road Initiative with an SEZ promised, 1200 MW project on Budhi River by Gezhouba group.

NEPALESE PARTICIPATION IN BELT AND ROAD INITIATIVE AND ITS IMPLICATIONS ON INDIA

In 2019, Xi Jinping visited Nepal and asserted that China would assist Nepal to become a land-linked country from being a land-locked country. In 2020, China had proposed to create a rail link connecting Shigatse on Tibet border to Kathmandu. As China and Nepal are working on Nepal China Economic Corridor, which will bring railway of China till Lumbini; Indian intelligence believes that such a rail link will make Chinese covert and overt presence over Indo-Gangetic plain and will breach the red lines security between India and Nepal. It is important to remember that if China has gained an economic and strategic foothold in Nepal, it is because India has focused too much on geopolitics with Nepal than geo-economics. India has to shed of the mentality of looking at Nepal as a protectorate of a British. It should also allow Nepal to decide what they need and what is good for them and should tune its strategy appropriately than asserting that New Delhi knows what is good for Nepal. Nepal and China relations are not that smooth also. Nepal is not keen on letting China establish a National Defence University in Kathmandu. There are two reasons for this. Firstly, Nepalese Army has a deep relation with Indian Army and they are not comfortable in developing this security proximity with China. Secondly, Nepal army feels that establishing this university is a matter of pride and Nepalese would establish the university themself. Similarly, Nepal is reluctant to sign an Extradition Treaty, which China eagerly wants as they can use it to extradite Tibetans.

TENETS OF INDIA'S DEVELOPMENTAL DIPLOMACY WITH NEPAL

In May 2018, when the Indian Prime Minister visited Nepal, he announced a new vision for Nepal–India relations. India announced that the future of the bilateral ties include India to develop agriculture, railways links and inland waterways in Nepal. The trinity is going to be the future guiding tenets of India's diplomacy with Nepal where connectivity will be playing a catalytic role to enhance people-to-people ties and economic growth. During the visit, both leaders of the two states jointly inaugurated an Integrated Check Post at Birgunj in Nepal. This will be an important milestone in facilitating people and cargo movement. They also carried out the ground-breaking ceremony for Motihari–Amlekhgunj petroleum pipeline. However, the Raxaul–Kathmandu electrified rail link is the real game changer. This rail link once established can provide a channel to travel from Rameswaram to Mansarover. This will be a great push to the model of regional integration and India will be able to put up an alternative to the Belt and Road Initiative for the states.

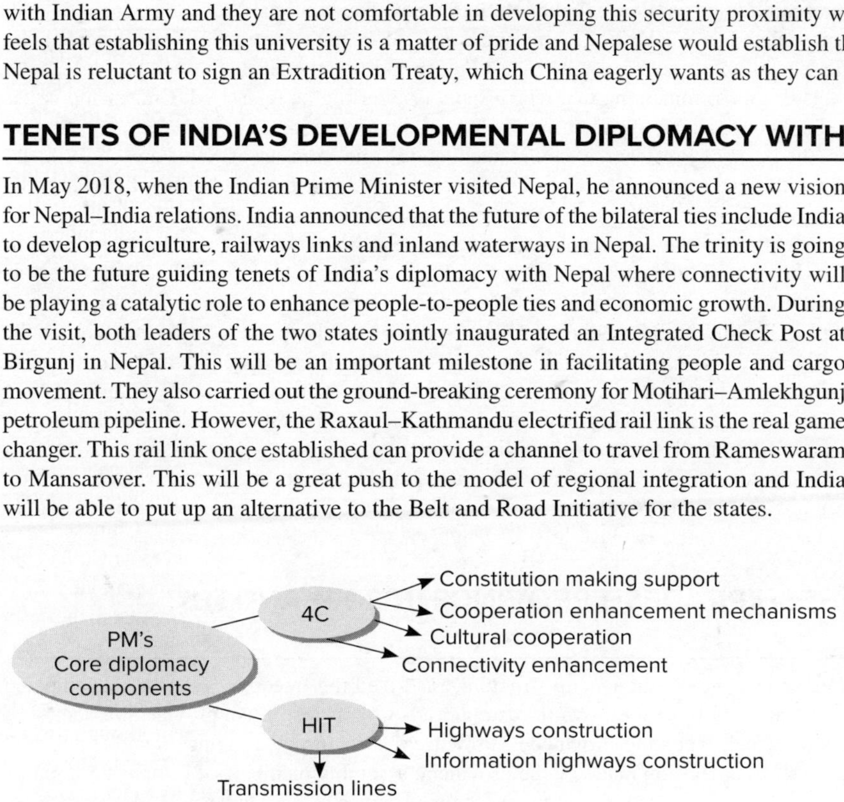

Can Civil Society act as a Bridge?

In 2015, Nepal witnessed a massive earthquake. India was the first immediate neighbour to extend assistance. However, many Indian NGOs played a role to assist the people of Nepal but faced bureaucratic hurdles. For instance, an Indian NGO that has raised resources in India cannot transfer money to a foreign state for NGO activity. This is in contrast to Chinese NGOs that operate globally. Considering that the core strength of India is not just its democracy but also its vibrant civil society; it is time that India establishes a framework on the role its civil society can play in diplomacy.

UNDERSTANDING THE MADHESIS OF NEPAL, THEIR DISCORD AND STRATEGIC IMPORTANCE IN NEPAL

The Constitution of Nepal conceptualised in 2015 has not given representation to the Madhesis on the basis of population. In the Pahadi region, there is one representative for every 5000 people while in the Terai region, it is one representative for every one lakh people. In the new constitution, the Madhesis and Tharus (who constitute 70% of the population of Terai) were left out. Madhesis consist of Maithili, Bhojpuri, Awadhi, Hindi and Urdu speaking people. The people in the hills or Pahadis consist of Limbus, Khambus, Magurs, Gurungs, Tamangs, Khasas and Nepali Aryans. Nepal has faced severe problems in accommodating people of South Terai. The Pahadis, in the new constitution, have reasserted their dominant role. The new constitution does not have equal representation of all groups in the Parliament. The total number of seats planned for the Parliament is 165. More than 50% of the Nepali population lives in the Terai region. The total seats allotted to people of Terai are just 65 in number. The Pahadi region has got 100 seats at a time when they had less than 50% of the population. India has requested Nepal to go for an inclusive constitution with equal representation. The Madhesis argue that by demarcating the Terai region differently, the Pahadis intend to destroy the roti–beti character. Under the roti–beti characteristic concept, women from Uttar Pradesh and Bihar if marry a Madhesi will be treated as a foreigner for up to five years from now. The Madhesis protests this and want Ek Madhesh, Ek Pradesh. As mentioned in 2007, there was an interim constitution that had, since then, been governing Nepal. In the interim constitution, as per Article 63(3), it was stated that geographical position and special characteristics would guide the electoral constitution. Article 63(3) also stated that Madhesis would be given representation as per their population. In the new constitution, Article 84, which talks of representation, has dropped the point related to Madhesis. The interim constitution, under Article 21 had advocated that various Nepali groups would participate in state structure on the basis of the proportional inclusion principle, while under Article 42 of the new constitution, is dropped, something that which India is asserting be reinserted. Citizenship issues are also at the forefront. Many Madhesis have acquired citizenship by birth or naturalisation. As per the new constitution under Article 282, it mandates that the posts of President, Vice President and Prime Minister of Nepal and so forth, are to be reserved exclusively for those with citizenship by descent. India has been pitching for the addition of citizens who have acquired citizenship by birth and naturalisation also to be considered for higher posts. Over a period of time, some amendments were made by Nepal in Articles 42, 84 and 286 (dealing with the delimitation process). Some sections of Nepali groups, in the Terai region, who opposed the new constitution, in Southern Nepal for long undertook a blockade of Birgunj border in Raxaul. As a result of this, basic supplies could not reach Nepal. There was subsequently a severe shortage of commodities, including LPG cylinders in Pahadi region. The Nepali people have a perception that through the blockade (in which India categorically denies any role), India has imposed its own version of economic sanctions in Nepal. Even in case of the Terai region, due to the blockade, there was a strong anti-India sentiment. The major businessmen community in the Terai region consists of Marwaris. They have good relations with the people of the hills but are not very comfortable with the Madhesis. India annually supplies 1.3 million tonnes petroleum products to Nepal. Because of the blockade, Nepali people had to resort to cutting of trees to meet the fuel shortages, there was a massive deforestation and this led to a huge layer of smog in Kathmandu and other areas. Despite immense poverty, Nepali people now had to face health-related issues due to the smog.

> **Why Pahadis hate Madhesis?**
>
> The origin can be traced back to Treaty of Sagauli, where under the point 7 of the Memorandum of Approval, the Raja of Nepal would not inhabitants of Terai or Madhesi people. Since this provision, the Pahadis have a fear of dual loyalties of Madhesis and perceive them more Indian than Nepalese.

FORMATION OF MADHESH PRADESH PROVINCE IN 2021 AND ITS IMPLICATIONS

As per the Constitution of Nepal, each province in the federal structure was given the freedom to decide its name and its capital and the names were to be endorsed by at least two-thirds majority of their respective provincial assemblies. Accordingly, all the five provinces of Nepal, including Province 3, Province 4, Province 5, Province 6 and Province 7 were successfully given names in 2021. The decision made by the provincial assembly members of Province 2 to name the province as 'Madhesh Pradesh' has been applauded by the people of the province as the Madhesh Pradesh has given an identity to the Madhesi people for the first time in Nepal's history. The naming of Province 2 as Madhesh Province is based on cultural identity and the naming has sent ripple effects in Nepalese political circles because other Nepalese provinces have been given the name either based on the name of the rivers or geographical locations. Since there are different ethnic groups or nationalities residing in Nepal, the naming of Madhesh Pradesh could compel people of other provinces to seek names based on ethnicity as well. However, the naming or formation of provinces on ethnic lines is not important because the real test of Nepal lies in creating an enabling environment in the federal structure where the different provinces get adequate autonomy at the financial and administrative levels. It is imperative for the political leaders of Nepal to consider this dimension seriously and contribute to strengthening federalism, democracy and republican system by granting due power to the provincial and local units.

THE HISTORY OF KALI RIVER, KALAPANI ISSUE AND TREATY OF SAGAULI

After the Anglo-Nepal war ended in 1814, the British and Nepal signed the Treaty of Sagauli on 2nd December 1815 (the treaty was eventually ratified on 4th March 1816).* Article V of the Treaty of Sagauli, as explained in the book says, "The Rajah of Nepal renounces for himself, his heirs and successors, all claims to or connection with countries lying west of the Kali River and engages never to have any concern with those countries or inhabitants thereof". The problem with the Treaty of Sagauli was that it never attached a map to demarcate authoritatively the alignment and source of the Kali River. The framers of the treaty (where W. J. Webb did the demarcation as the surveyor) were in no way aware of the geography of the region and based on their understanding on the fact that Hindus while going to Mansarover consider Kalapani, which is located at the base of Lipulekh Pass, as a source of the River Kali. The British Surveyor W. J. Webb toured the entire Byans region. The people of Byans are called Byansis. This was the region where the Kali River was located. He surveyed the territories in the west and east of the river. He stated that Kali River is a part of Kumaon region traditionally. Kumaon region historically, prior to the coming of British, was a part of Nepal. In 1817, the Nepali people made a representation to the British and claimed areas that were east of the Kali River. The Nepali people claimed the areas called Tinkar, Chaggru, Nabhi and Kuthi. The Governor-General in Council accepted the demand of the Nepali people. The Byans area was subsequently divided and Tinkar and Chaggru villages were transferred to Nepal, while the British kept Nabhi and Kuthi. The same ruling of the Governor-General in Council British also settled the question that arose related to the origin of the Kali River. The Governor-General in Council stated that the drainage of Kalapani and Lipulekh will remain with the Empire and Kali River shall form the boundary between the two states. Few years later, the Himalayan Gazetteer mentions that Bam Shah, the Governor of Doti (a local ruler of Nepal region), stated that Nepal boundary should be extended up to Kuthi Valley because Kuthi–Yankti streams are the western branches of the headwaters of Kali River. He asserted that the springs that were flowing from Kalapani had some smaller springs and one of the branches is Kali. On 4th February 1817, the first British Resident to Nepal, Edward Gardner told the Nepal Durbar that lowland areas between Kali and Gorakhpur were ceded by Nepal to the British in 1815 but these areas were given back to Nepal in 1860. The British clarified this to Bam Shah and kept Limpiyadhura Pass and Kuthi valley as part of Empire. After 1860, it was decided that the Deputy Commissioner of Almora would travel to Lipulekh Pass each year and open up the trade through the pass. The decision arrived was that the northern boundary of Byans would be the line of water passing between India and Hundes which was located in the settlement of Trail in 1828 (and Batten in 1840). Later in 1905, Charles Sherring was the Deputy Commissioner of Almora. He visited the Liplekh Pass and mentioned that he camped at Kalapani. He observed that Kalapani had half a dozen springs and also stated that Tinkar Pass formed the boundary of Nepal.

INDIA'S CONTENTIONS OVER KALAPANI

Nepal has two tri-junctions with India. One is at Lipulekh Pass and Kalapani in the western sector and Jhinsang Chuli in the eastern sector. The origin of the Kalapani issue goes back to Treaty of Sagauli. As per the treaty, Kali River is designated as the western part of the boundary. In between the two streams of the Kali River lies Kalapani. Kalapani is located at the tri-junction of Nepal–China and India near the Lipulekh Pass. The issue arises as the segments to the west of Kalapani of Kali River are claimed by Nepal while India claims segments to the east of Kalapani of Kali River area,

* The author has referred CU Aitcheson's "A Collection of Treaties, Engagements and Sanads Relating to India and Neighboring Countries" Volume II, published by the Superintendent Government Printing India, Calcutta in 1909.

thereby making a claim to entire Kalapani itself. In 1962, when India had a conflict with the Chinese, Nepal was under the rule of King Mahindra. He was of the opinion that India might resort to forcible occupation of Kalapani. This motivated him to handover Kalapani to India for security. Indian strategic community does not accept this Nepali version. The Indian strategic community asserts that aggressive Chinese tactics worried India in 1950s over Tibet. This motivated the Indian leadership to negotiate with King Mahindra and as per the negotiations, it was decided to build 18 military outposts in northern frontier of Nepal, including a military outpost at Kalapani. In 1969, the Nepali Prime Minister was Kirti Nidhi Bisht. He was advised by the monarchy to speak with the Indian Prime Minister and urge India to withdraw from the posts. The Nepali side sent a list to India that mentioned the posts India should withdraw from in the northern frontiers. Ironically Kalapani and the post at Lipulekh were not in the list because the Prime Minister of Nepal stated that the King of Nepal is concerned about India's security concerns with Chinese and as an act of generosity, the posts at Lipulekh and Kalapani may remain. India and China have also been carrying out trade through the Lipulekh area and the trade agreement does not include Nepal, making it furious. The main issue between the two is that Nepal asserts that Kali River originates in the higher Himalayas from Limpiyadhura. This point of origin allows Nepal to claim access to Limpiyadhura, Lipulekh and Kalapani triangular land. India, on the other hand, opposes the point of origin claimed by Nepal and asserts that the river originates further down. The Indian claim about the origin of the river reduces the territorial claims of Nepal. The issue that Indian and Nepali government should negotiate is the area that lies in the south of the Kali River, where Indian (and earlier the British) cartographers have taken the watershed principle and land revenue records of Gunji village into account. The issue of the origin of Kali River was taken up Nepal in 1997 for the first time. This happened after the two sides signed the Mahakali Treaty of 1996 that envisaged Pancheshwar Project. In 1981, India and Nepal had created Joint Technical Level Boundary Commission to resolve border issues and remained in practice till 2008. So, in 1997, when Nepal raised the Kali issue, it was taken up for discussion in the Joint Technical Level Boundary Commission. Since 2008, when the Joint Technical Level Boundary Commission was dissolved, these matters are now taken up at the Foreign Secretary Levels.

WRITTEN RECORDS ON KALAPANI, KALI AND LIPULEKH

In 1954, India and China signed a trade agreement and mentioned that Lipulekh Pass is a pass that can be used for trade and pilgrimage to Mansarover. In 1954, after signing the trade agreement, India established a police post in Kalapani in 1956. On 5th October 1961, China and Nepal also signed a Boundary Treaty called Boundary Treaty between the People's Republic of China and Kingdom of Nepal. They mentioned in Article 1 that the boundary between China and Nepal originates at a point where there is a watershed between Kali River and Tinkar Pass that meets the watershed that exists between the tributary of Mapchu River (also called the Karnali River) and Tinkar River. The beauty of this agreement is that it also shows the location of Kali River similar to the location as mentioned in Indian map of 1954. While the pillar number 1 at the boundary is placed at the Tinkar Pass, the Nepali diplomats assert that pillar number 0 could be at the tri-junction of India, Nepal and China (could be mean that in the 1961 agreement, it was left for demarcation in future). On 20th January 1963, China and Nepal signed a Boundary Protocol. In the Protocol, they created permanent border markers. These markers were numbered from 1 to 79 and the boundary marker 1 was located at Tinkar. The tri-junction, claimed by India (though not formally delineated) was based on the 1879 map of the British. But the subsequent maps of India show tri-junction 5-kilometre southeast of Lipulekh and Limpiyadhura Pass. In 1991, when Chinese Premier Li Peng visited India, the two sides concluded an Agreement on Resumption of Border Trade between India and China and this agreement clearly asserts that Lipulekh is a mutually agreed reading point. The Protocol of Entry and Exit Procedure for Border Trade between India and China of 1992 also mentions the same about Lipulekh. In 2005, India and China concluded the Agreement on Confidence Building on LAC. Article V of this agreement states that Lipulekh Pass in the middle sector of the LAC will be a route for trade.

SLEDGEHAMMER TACTICS, HYPERSENSITIVE SOVEREIGNTY AND MAP MACHINATIONS BY NEPAL

In November 2019, India published a new political map, approved by its Parliament, it showed Kalapani, Lipulekh and Limpiyadhura as a part of Indian Territory. The new Indian map of 2019 is ironically the exact replica of the map the India has published in 1954 in Atlas of Northern Frontiers. This Atlas, till date, remains, India's official map for the frontier regions. Nepal objected to the same by asserting that as per the Treaty of Sagauli, Kalapani, Lipulekh and Limpiyadhura belonged to Nepal and India should not resort to unilateral measures to hurt sentiments of Nepali citizens. The ties between India and Nepal further deteriorated after 8th May 2020 when India inaugurated the Dharchula–Lipulekh road. In 2009, it was decided to construct this road. Nepal did not object at that time. It is an 80-kilometre long road. This road will shorten the travel time for pilgrims travelling to Mansarover. Nepal raised a protest that the road passes through their territory, a claim that has been rejected by India. Nepal, in return, in 2020, amended their Constitution (by bringing a second Amendment to Nepali Constitution that will change Schedule 3 of the Nepali Constitution) to publish a new political map and made claims to Lipulekh, Kalapani and Limpiyadhura as territories belonging to Nepal. In fact, after showing Lipulekh, Kalapani and Limpiyadhura as part of Nepal, they have also shown three villages, belonging to India, in Pithoragarh District of Uttrakhand—Gunji, Kuti and Nabhi—as belonging to Nepal (thereby adding 335 sq km area in Nepal). Gunji is a historic village, which is last village in India, located on Indian border and Tibetan people often come to Mandi in Gunji. The new map shown by Nepal is based on the maps of Nepali scholars such as Mangal Sidhi Manandar and Hriday Lal Koirala. They have shown the origin of Kali River at Limpiyadhura. These scholars of Nepal have asserted that the British deliberately manipulated the maps after 1850 and showed the Nepal boundary from Lipu Khola (the British showed Lipu Gad as the boundary in 1857 and Pankha Gad in 1879) which they assert is a sign of incompetence of the British and a sinister plot. This is in contrast to the maps of India, of 1954 and 2019 that have shown the origin of Kali River being not at Limpiyadhura but Lipulekh. Nepal, however, maintains the Kali River as Kuti-Yangti River itself. India rightly asserted that under Article V of the Treaty of Sagauli, Nepal had renounced all claims on the areas west of Kali River. India has asserted that the issue related to Kali and Kalapani has been discussed in detail during the Joint Working Groups established in 1997 and 1998; thus, the recent attempts of K. P. Oli to resort to artificial map making serves no purpose. Nepal is right to assert that they have asked for talks on boundary issue for a long time and India has behaved as "big brother" and often refused talks, thus compelling Nepal to take the drastic step of going for a constitutional amendment.

INDIA'S 'NOTING' AND NOT 'REGRETTING' OR 'DEPLORED' POLICY STANCE

Ironically, after the constitutional Amendment was passed, Mr. Oli stated that he is ready to talk with India and sort out the issue. This is not a right time to talk to Nepal because the dialogue should have happened prior to the amendment. If India talks now, Mr. Oli will try to position himself in a situation of strength and will present India with political fait accompli. The resolution of the problem has become more intractable after the amendment. A dialogue is no doubt the only solution but can happen only in a conducive atmosphere. India has done right in "noting" the second constitutional Amendment and has not "regretted" or "deplored" the same.

CHINESE AND TWO AND A HALF 'NEPAL FRONT' EXPERIMENT AGAINST INDIA

The present issue is a symptom of a deeper malaise that afflicts India and Nepal ties where the Nepali Communist party has a deep rooted suspicion of India and wishes to enlarge its space by breaking free from what it perceives to be a claustrophobic embrace of India. It is this that has compelled Nepal to adopt a policy of balance, which manifests as the China card. It is very clear that the way K. P. Oli government has responded to Kalapani issue, Citizenship amendment issues, that they enjoy the backing of China. In fact, it is now clear to Indian strategic community that the Chinese have tried experiment opening of Nepal as a front against India at a time when they are themselves in a standoff with India in Ladakh. The Communist Party of China and Communist K. P. Oli sync well with each other and Oli seems to have used the deep pockets filled by the Chinese to offset any influence of India. The determination with which Oli has transformed a relationship based on roti–beti ka rishta clearly proves that his alignment to Chinese have given him the needed backing. In fact, it is also clear that the Chinese backing to Oli has come at an opportune time when Oli is witnessing massive backlash in his domestic political constituency, including his abject failure in tackling COVID-19 in Nepal and failure to fulfil the aspirations of the Nepali people. While the Indian government has steadfastly tried to build a relation with Nepal on Hinduness (which had the potential of opening up a civilisational and cultural alliance), but Oli seems to have preferred to use the boundary issue to politically save himself for his domestic failures, while distancing himself from India. While Oli may go for a tighter embrace of China, the Chinese smartly have occupied 33 hectares of Nepali land. The Survey

Department of Nepali Agriculture Ministry published a report in 2020 which asserts that 10 places out 11 have been encroached upon by the Chinese. The fact that Nepal has stated, "they were forced to act when India unilaterally created Lipulekh Dharchula road" is clearly in sync with the Chinese objection of "India unilaterally altering LAC by creating DSDBO road". The Chinese have carefully played with Nepal as a front and have succeeded in putting pressure on India at a time when they already choking India in Ladakh. India needs to prepare for a two-front war (China and Pakistan) and multi-front diplomatic stress in the future (Nepal today, which could bring Sri Lanka and Bangladesh in future as well).

BANGLADESH, BHUTAN, INDIA AND NEPAL MOTOR VEHICLES AGREEMENT AND CONNECTIVITY DIPLOMACY

In June 2015, the four SAARC nations, Bangladesh, Bhutan, India and Nepal (BBIN) concluded a sub-regional MVA for regulation of passenger personnel and cargo vehicular traffic. The MVA will not only facilitate economic development and integration of the region but also, will simultaneously facilitate seamless movement of goods and people amongst the four signatory states. The governments will boost regional connectivity.

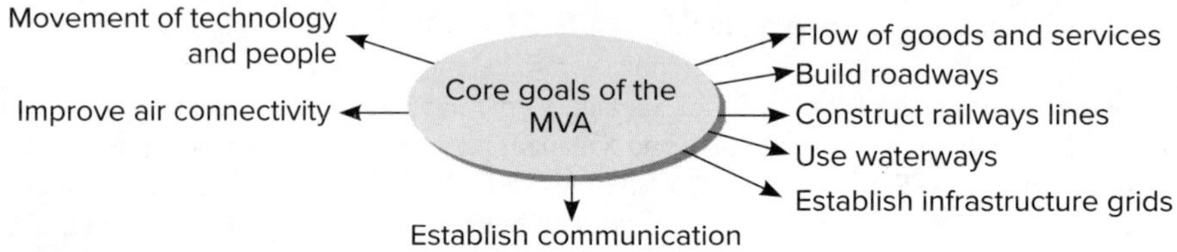

One of the major aims of the BBIN member states is to enhance connectivity and ensure seamless passenger traffic up to Thailand. The BBIN states are contemplating an MVA with Myanmar and Thailand as well. This would allow BBIN access to the ASEAN states. In the 2014 SAARC Summit in Kathmandu, there was a proposal to establish an MVA amongst all SAARC states. Because of reservations by Pakistan, the idea was dropped and a sub-regional MVA was envisaged which finally got concluded in 2015 in Thimpu. By 2016, all the states ratified the agreement, thereby paving way for seamless connectivity in South Asia. India and Bangladesh at the bilateral level have taken a number of steps to improve connectivity. In June 2016, the two concluded a Trans-Shipment Operation Agreement, enabling India the access to Ashuganj port of Bangladesh to be used for transporting goods to Tripura and other North Eastern States. There is an ongoing Kolkata–Dhaka–Agartala and Dhaka–Shillong–Guwahati Bus service already operational. One of the biggest achievements of the MVA would be that it would enable the establishment of regional South Asian supply chains, especially in textiles, yarn and readymade garments. Thus, it may not be wrong to say that the agreement indeed is a force multiplier that may boost economic integration in the region. The BBIN clearly is a positive step forward in India's neighbourhood first policy.

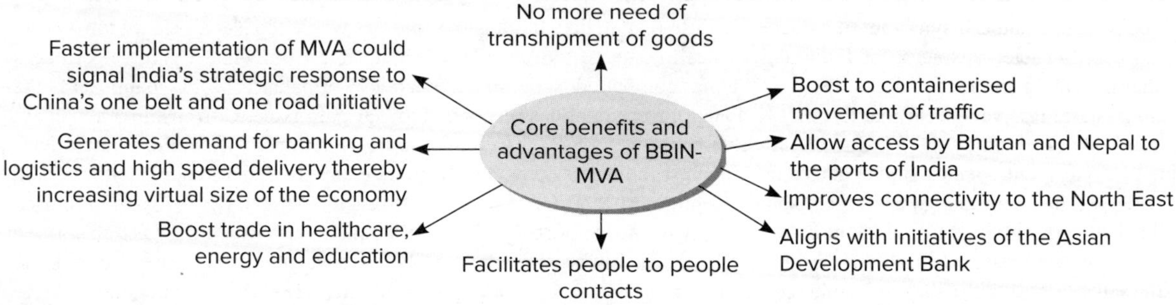

Bhutan had been a little hesitant with the MVA as it feared that an increase in the vehicular traffic in Bhutan due to the MVA from other states could lead to adverse environmental impacts on Bhutan. But studies have proven that regional MVA boosts not only economic integration but tourism as well. However, the truck and taxi operators of Bhutan have been quite critical of the MVA as they feel that the Bhutanese road infrastructure may not be able to sustain incoming vehicular traffic. The National Council of Bhutan, in November 2016, rejected the MVA. India, since then, has hopes that the Royal

Bhutanese government will take steps to ensure that all internal issues would be sorted out soon and the agreement would be operationalised. The issue raised by Bhutan has emerged as a key challenge to the implementation of the BBIN–MVA.

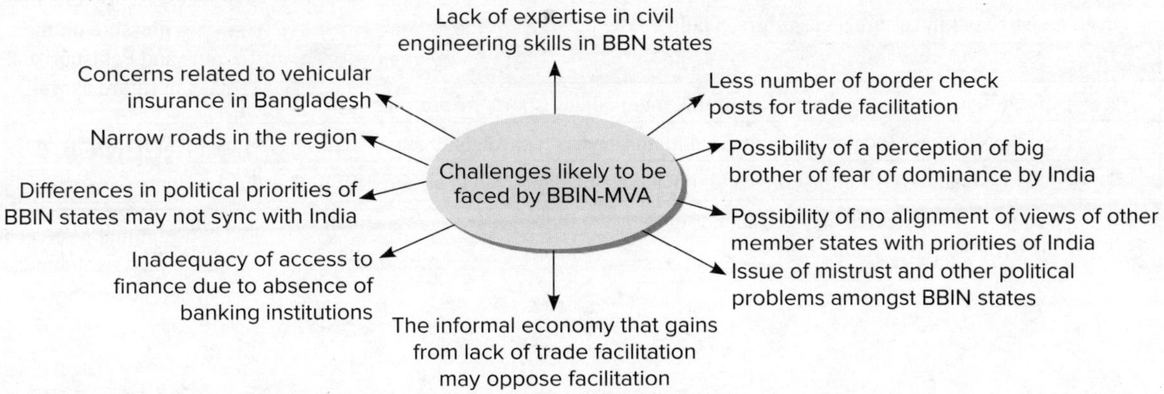

VARANASI TO BENGALURU SPECTRUM AND FUTURE OF INDIA AND NEPAL RELATIONS

Varanasi has been a keystone city for India and Nepal. From the Nepali doyen of democracy B. P. Koirala to Pushpalal Shreshta, the founder of Nepali Communist Party, both have been residents of Varanasi. Up to 1990s, the easiest way to reach Kathmandu was from Varanasi. However, with the onset of globalisation, the Varanasi–Kathmandu route witnessed a downturn and Bangalore–Kathmandu has now become the most profitable sector with Nepali programmers coming to Bangalore for creating software India supplies to the world. This reflects the changing dynamic of India and Nepal relations today. Even though the globalisation has influenced Nepal, its politicians, academia, bureaucracy remains ingrained with an anti-India sentiment as a plank of nationalism. This is why India feels that Nepal is incorrigible while Nepali attitude is a reflection of its angst as a small state against a civilisational giant. While globalisation may have improved the penetration of technology in Nepal, and given its people a cosmopolitan outlook, but this cosmopolitanism is without metropolitanism. Even though Nepal may try to diversify globally, its roots with India remain strong. This is why it is imperative for India to re-write its story for Nepal by focusing on what the Nepali youth wants, be it good infrastructure or even more shopping malls. Only by creating economic plusses can India and Nepal happen to keep their people-to-people ties stronger. The natural corollary of this would also be a much needed image makeover for the two. Because of cultural and ethnic commonalities in India and Nepal, it befuddles when anything goes awry between the two. While Varanasi may remain a key stone of the past, it is imperative to look at Bangalore as a contemporary reality.

I Wish to Change My Neighbours

Several Nepalese politicians have often stated in private communication that if Nepal had Maharashtra or some south Indian states as its neighbour, then Nepal would have witnessed prosperity. It is time for India to position Uttar Pradesh and Bihar as economic dynamos so that economic prosperity flows across the borders.

THE ECONOMIC PARTNERSHIP WE CAN GROW TOGETHER

The future of India and Nepal relationship is based on the paradigm of how Nepal will leverage India's economic dynamism for its own benefit? An assessment of the tenets in the chapter previously clearly argue that till now Nepal has followed the policy of arbitrage and differential custom duties, both of which have benefitted only a limited section of traders and politicians. Nepal has to firstly understand that the relationship with India has to move beyond the current 'politics only' and should draw up specific policies to enhance economic cooperation so that the political spheres and economic sphere are kept separate. This even requires India to develop a vision on how it sees Nepal, beyond just civilisational neighbour.

FUTURE AREAS WHERE INDIA CAN HELP IN CREATING A 'SAMRIDDHA NEPAL, SUKHI NEPAL'

India can assist Nepal in certain areas as given below.

S. No.	Areas where India can help in creating a 'Samriddha Nepal, Sukhi Nepal'
1.	Investments in high-quality educational, medical and sports institutions
2.	Assist Nepal to globally sell medicinal plants such as ashwagandha and shatavari in post-COVID world
3.	Assist Nepal to position itself as a global leader of Ilam tea and coffee, two high-value products they grow
4.	Set up training centres in Nepal that train their youth for jobs of caregivers in Israel and Gulf, thus leveraging the demographic dividend of Nepal

CHAPTER 8

India's Relationship with Sri Lanka

HISTORICAL RELATIONS BETWEEN INDIA AND SRI LANKA

The relations between India and Sri Lanka go back to the times of the advent of Buddhism. Buddhism as a movement spread over Sri Lanka some 2000 years ago. The earliest mention of Sri Lanka dates back to the time of the *Ramayana*. Ravana, the king of Lanka, who held Sita captive, was rescued by Ram with the help of Hanuman, who was in a way India's first diplomat, and who built the Adams Bridge (without L&T) to help Ram reach Lanka. The north and northeast region of Lanka has been economically integrated to India. The native people of Sri Lanka (then Ceylon) were colonially under the British, but were not a part of British India Empire, being administered separately. From the 1830s onwards, British acquired indentured labour from India, especially from Tamil Nadu, and took them to Ceylon. The Tamils who were transported by the British settled in the northern part of Ceylon. The northern region was relatively dry and lacked resource. The British used a well-planned policy of sending out missionaries to the northern part where the Tamils were residing. The Tamils were a mixture of Buddhists, Muslims, Hindus and Christians. They look advantage of the missionary education provided by the British. They sent their children in Ceylon to schools and later on these children contributed to the education system started of the British. India became independent in 1947 while Ceylon in 1948. In 1948, India advocated the idea of a federation based on a mutual defence agreement with India; Ceylon became extremely suspicious of India. India, time and again, did try to convey to Ceylon that it had no expansionist agenda and acknowledged its respect for Ceylon's independence and sovereignty. Ceylon was renamed as Sri Lanka in 1972, and later, in 1978, was officially named the Democratic Socialist Republic of Sri Lanka. As an autonomous federation, based on mutual defence alignment with the British, Sri Lanka signed a Defence Treaty with Britain and the British continued using Ceylon for naval and air activity.

THE TAMIL REFUGEE PROBLEM BETWEEN INDIA AND SRI LANKA

As previously mentioned, the British took Indian Tamils to Ceylon to work as plantation workers. After Ceylon became independent, the Sri Lankan government, called Sinhalese government, discriminated against Tamils against local natives called Sinhalese, thereby deepening the void in Indo-Ceylon relations. During Jawaharlal Nehru, no attempt was made to bring any Tamils back as, for generations, these Tamils had lived in Ceylon and were more citizens of that state than of India. Ceylon, on the other hand, devised a mechanism to make it tough for Tamils to acquire state citizenship. They also wanted to ensure they put an end to Tamil dominance in public services. Because of the British missionary work, the children of the Tamils grew up to hold positions in Ceylon's administrative departments. Post-independence, through the Sinhalese language barrier (by making Sinhalese language mandatory), they made it tough for Tamil administrators. However, in 1964, there was a Lal Bahadur Shastri–Sirimavo Bandaranaike pact that was signed whereby Ceylon agreed to give three lakh Indian Tamils in Ceylon citizenship and India also agreed to repatriate a sizeable number to India. In 1975, Sirimavo Bandaranaike had imposed emergency in Sri Lanka while in 1977 Indira Gandhi did this in India.

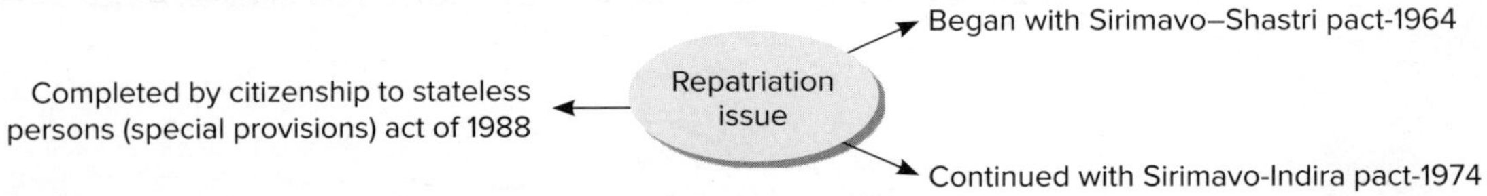

Jayewardene J. R., who succeeded Sirimavo Bandaranaike, did not promote Indo-Sri Lanka relations despite his coming to India for a state visit after being elected. Jayewardene continued to marginalise Tamils and Tamil subjugation continued unabated in Sri Lanka. Jayewardene tilted the foreign policy of Sri Lanka towards the US.

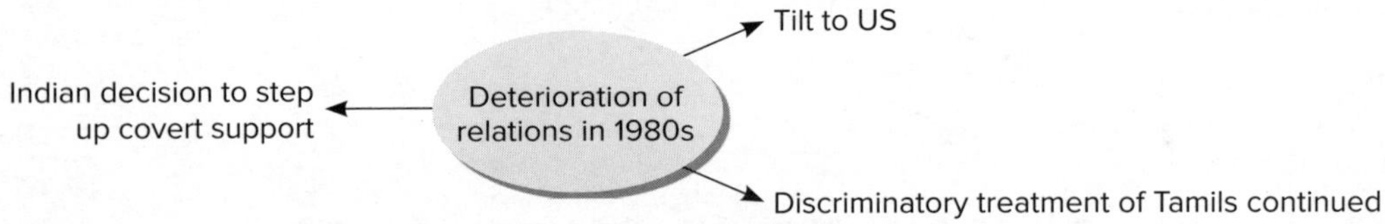

THE LIBERATION OF TAMIL TIGERS EELAM ISSUE

During the 1971 Indo-Pak war, Indian allegiance shifted towards the USSR as Sri Lanka gradually drifted towards the US. Jayewardene advanced a liberal and open economy and positioned Sri Lanka westward. Jayewardene not only allowed deeper presence of the US firms in Lanka but also granted refueling permit for the nuclear powered US aircraft carrier Kitty Hawk during India–Pakistan War of 1971. The situation especially deteriorated in 1977 and 1981 due to Tamil riots. The ruling party of Tamil Nadu, the All India Anna Dravida Munnetra Kazhagam (AIDMK) was an ally of the Congress Party at the centre, and Indira Gandhi, in 1981, warned Jayewardene that India would not tolerate the persecution meted out to Tamils and advocated him to be cautious. Post-1980, India adopted a very delicate policy. It wanted to take a revenge for the harsh treatment meted out to Tamils in Sri Lanka and also the Sri Lankan support to the US in 1971 when India was fighting a war. India used the Research and Analysis Wing (RAW) to train Tamil rebels in Sri Lanka. The aim was to use Tamil rebels to destabilise the Jayewardene regime. While arming the Tamils, RAW had to ensure that the Tamil rebels do not succeed in creating a separate state. The RAW supported Tamil Eelam Liberation Organisation. It was in 1976 that V. Prabhakaran formed the Liberation of Tamil Tigers Eelam (LTTE), a separatist and insurgent militant force, under the guidance of RAW. The RAW also supported TELO and LTTE and both began to seek support from Tamil political leaders in Tamil Nadu. As the RAW had gradually succeeded in destabilising the Sri Lankan government, it slowly stopped supporting the rebels as its objectives were achieved. But by this time, the LTTE had emerged as a powerful force and began to assert itself as the sole representative of Tamils in Sri Lanka. When Indira Gandhi died, Jayewardene took the help of Pakistan and the US to get Sri Lankan forces trained to counter the LTTE rebels. This move on the part of Sri Lanka was not well received by India. In 1987, Sri Lanka launched an operation against LTTE in the northern area of the state where Tamils lived. They imposed a blockade in the area. This led to massive humanitarian crisis because the Sri Lankan government imposed a blockade where Tamils were living in Jaffna region. The Indian Air Force airdropped food and other essentials to Tamils in the northern region. India warned Sri Lanka that if the blockade were not removed, India would militarily attack Sri Lanka. This warning had the desired effect and Sri Lanka advocated the need to resolve the matter through dialogue.

INDIA–SRI LANKA ACCORD 1987

After a dialogue of the two states, India–Sri Lanka Accord (ISLA) had been signed on 29 July 1987. As per ISLA, the LTTE was to give up their weapons to the Indian Peace Keeping Force (IPKF) and Sri Lanka was to accommodate the Tamils and go for devolution. The Accord assigned a certain amount of autonomy to Tamil areas with Eelam People's Revolutionary Liberation Front (EPRLF) controlling the regional council and called for the Tamil militant groups, including LTTE, to lay down their arms.

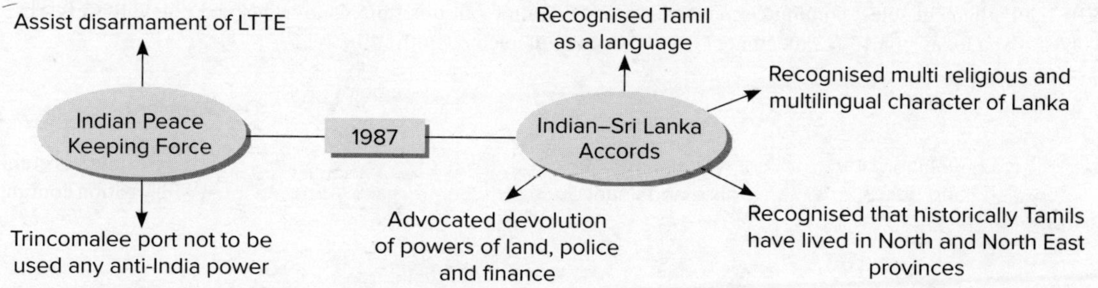

As the ISLA was executed, a large number of LTTE cadres avoided surrendering weapons to the IPKF and consumed cyanide. Many even began to fight the IPKF. The violence unleashed post the ISLA in Sri Lanka created renewed tensions in the minds of Sinhalese who began to perceive India's role as an undue interference in Sinhalese internal affairs that was not in Sri Lanka's best interests. The Indian government increased the IPKF numbers from 6,000 to one lakh and justified the raise by citing national security reasons. The ISLA was an attempt to conclude the ethnic war of Sri Lanka through constitutional and political means. The basic idea of Rajiv Gandhi while concluding the Accord was that the ISLA would provide India an opportunity to shape the post-war political trajectory of Sri Lanka. The ISLA had two goals. Firstly, the idea was to persuade the conflicting ethnic groups to join mainstream politics and secondly, seek political devolution in Sri Lanka by altering the constitution of the state to get autonomy for the Tamil community. The ISLA was rejected by the LTTE and it resorted to violence against both India and Sri Lanka and violence continued till 2009, when LTTE was finally crushed.

13th AMENDMENT ISSUE—13th PLUS AMENDMENT AND 13th MINUS AMENDMENT

In 1987, the Sri Lankan government, through the 13th Amendment, resorted to the devolution of power by creating provincial councils. In 1987, the Sri Lankan Parliament also passed the 13th Amendment Act to the 1978 Sri Lankan Constitution. The Provincial Councils Act No. 42 of 1987 established provincial councils. On September 2 and 8, 1988, President Jayewardene issued proclamations enabling the Northern and Eastern provinces to be one administrative unit administered by one elected Council. In 1988, elections were organised in North East Provincial Councils (NEPC) and A. V. Perumal of EPRLF won the elections, becoming the first Chief Minister of the North Eastern Provincial Council. India, under Rajiv Gandhi, linked the IPKF's withdrawal to the implementation of the 13th Amendment to the Constitution of Sri Lanka that granted councils in Tamil regions. In November 1989, in the Indian elections, V. P. Singh won and in March 1990, it ended the IPKF mission and delinked the IPKF's withdrawal from the 13th Amendment. The IPKF was recalled to India and the entire idea of NEPC devolution collapsed. In May 1991, the LTTE assassinated Rajiv Gandhi (or RAW!) and then was subsequently designated as a terrorist organisation. After the death of Rajiv Gandhi, many Tamil groups also began to stop supporting the LTTE. As India realised the failure of its mission, it also felt the need to go for a fresh look at India's Sri Lanka policy. After the defeat of the LTTE in 2009, Sri Lanka has announced the execution of the 13th Plus Amendment Act where the idea is to devolve more powers to its provinces. The members of Provincial Councils have consistently complained about their dependence on the central government of Sri Lanka for finances, with no powers to the highly restricted Provincial Councils to raise finances.

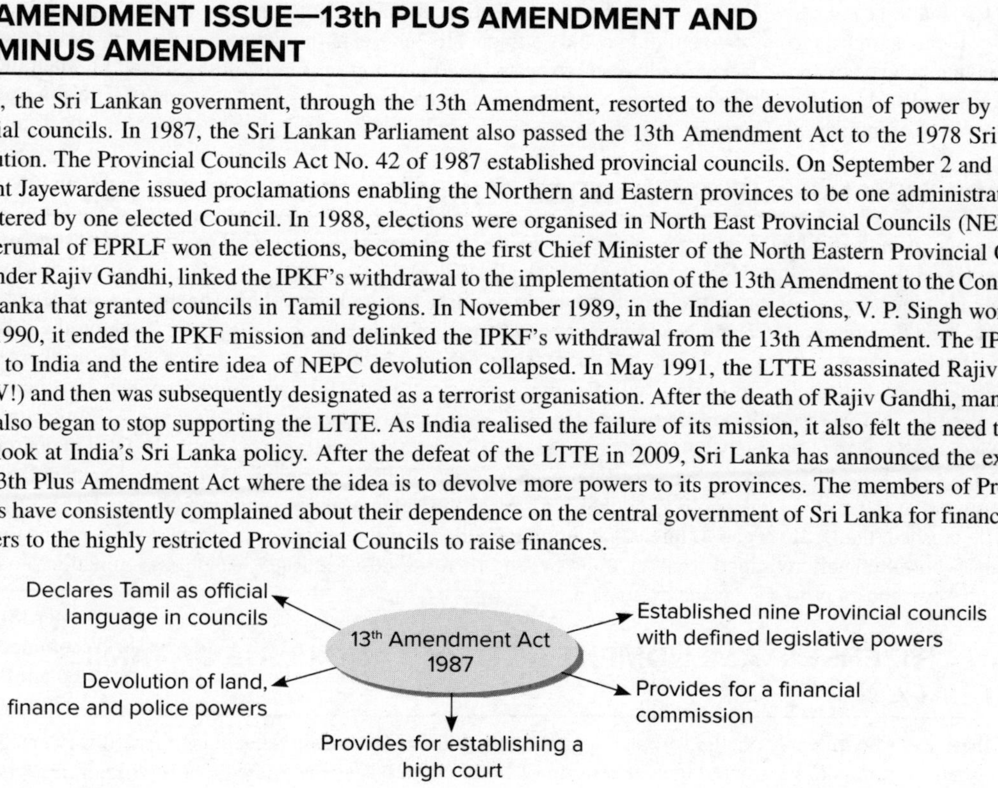

In 2013, a Parliament select committee met to discuss devolution but this time, land rights and police powers were not devolved. Even today, the 13th Amendment has not been implemented with full force.

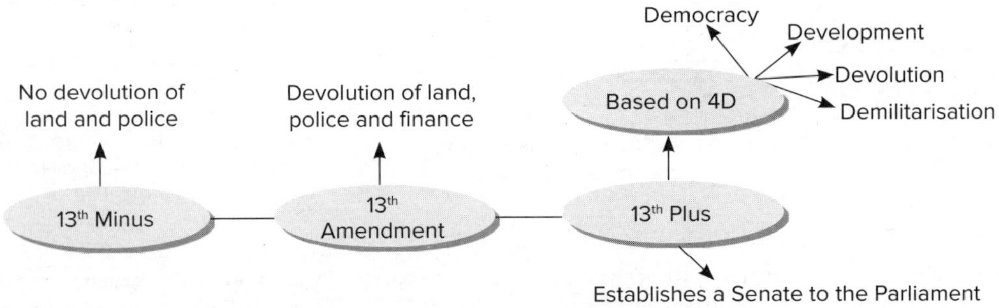

The basic issue is the reluctance of Sri Lanka to devolve policing powers fearing that active insurgent sleeper cells need centralised control. Though the councils have been created, but an analysis of the present state of the councils proves that they have become an extension of the ruling political party in power at the Centre. Corruption and patronage politics has slid the councils into complete decay and institutional paralysis. India has always followed the logic of national unity being the foundation of internal and external security. It is a key driver behind India's Sri Lanka policy. It has always felt that if there were a revival of separatist demands in Sri Lanka, it would have a spillover effect in India. Ironically, way back in 1963, Dravida Munnetra Kazhagam (DMK) had advocated for the secession of Tamil Nadu, but did not take up the issue after 1963. India has always followed the policy that positive nation building can always lead to greater nation unity and this may happen only if inclusive policies are followed. Sri Lanka, however, since its inception, has been driven by Sinhalese majority policy, which was instrumental in creating alienation in the minds of the Tamils residing in Sri Lanka. For India, an imbalance in state building could consequently have external fallout and could disturb the strategic-cum-economic balance of India. Hence, India had advocated the inclusion of Tamils in the nation building process of Sri Lanka since ISLA, as the psychological unity with Sri Lanka could have proven to be beneficial for the long-term national security of India itself.

ROLE OF INDIAN POLITICAL PARTIES IN INDIA AND SRI LANKA RELATIONS

Any discussion of India–Sri Lanka relations obviously needs a mention of role of political parties of Tamil Nadu. We also need to understand, however, that while the influence of the DMK and the AIDMK has been detected in India's attitude to the Tamil Eelam question, their instigation was not the sole deciding factor of our policy. The main reason of influence in the past has been the presence of Tamil Nadu-based parties as part of the coalition at the centre. When Rajiv Gandhi had gone to Sri Lanka to sign the ISLA in 1987, he had even taken DMK and AIDMK into confidence despite such concurrence not being mandated constitutionally. After Rajiv Gandhi's assassination in 1991, when the Congress government came back to power, the AIDMK supported Congress and in 1992, when it moved to ban the LTTE, the AIDMK was not only supportive of the demand but actively helped the process. In UPA-1 (2004–2009) government, the DMK was a supporter of the Congress Party and advocated a hands-off approach. In 2006, India accepted the DMK's Sri Lanka policy as what the Government of India's Sri Lanka policy should be in case of the Eelam war-IV. When in 2008, the LTTE were almost about to be crushed, the DMK began to threaten quitting the alliance if the Indian government took no steps to stop the Elam war-IV but ultimately refrained from anything beyond rhetoric. Post-the Rajiv Gandhi assassination, none of the Tamil parties ever took a pro-LTTE stand ever again.

INDIAN CITIZENSHIP AMENDMENT ACT, 2019 AND ISSUE OF TAMILS REPATRIATION

In 2020, there was a controversy that had erupted regarding the Indian Citizenship Amendment Act. It was stated that the Act did not allow Tamils to be granted the Citizenship of India. India has always stated that it will not allow the Tamil refugees in India because it follows the principle of non-refoulement and voluntary repatriation. In India, the government allows the United Nations High Commissioner for Refugees (UNHCR) to screen the refugees' incoming and ascertain the voluntary nature of repatriations. The UNHCR undertakes counselling of refugees and helps them obtain documents and provide reintegration grants and support. Also, with respect to Sri Lanka, it is important to understand that even the Indian government does not want Tamils to come to India because Sri Lanka follows the principle of proportional representation and if Tamils come to India, their numerical strength to seek political integration in Tamil-dominated areas of Sri Lanka will decrease. This is the reason why India has not included them in Citizenship Amendment Act as India favours voluntary repatriation of Tamils. Today, even India does not want too much pressure on Sri Lanka from the Western countries on Tamil question, as that will only push Sri Lanka to gravitate towards China. Thus, bilateral reconciliation and repatriation are good as a solution.

INDIA AND SRI LANKA DEFENCE DIPLOMACY

The defence relations between the two have not evolved deeply and are mired since 1990s. However, in recent times, cooperation has begun in the areas of maritime security and joint training. India has been training Sri Lankan officials at the Defence University of India and is constantly undertaking intelligence sharing. In fact, intelligence sharing has been a key area of cooperation since the Eelam War-IV. Indian Navy has regularly shared naval intelligence with the Lankan navy and the Coast guards of the two nations regularly cooperate. However, India does not supply any major arms to Lanka and has limited this defence cooperation to the use of defensive and non-lethal equipment and tactics.

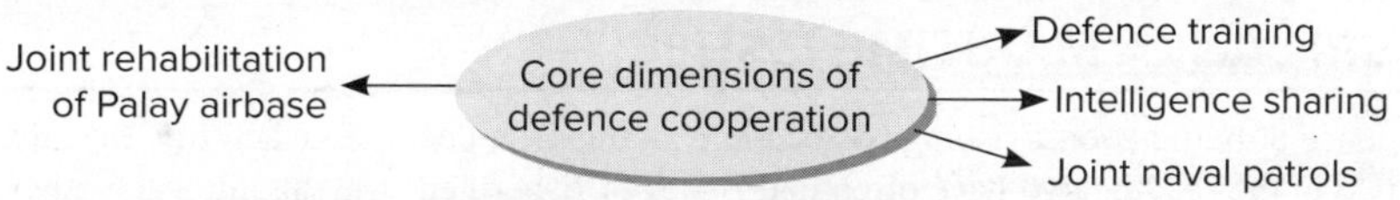

INDIA AND SRI LANKA FREE TRADE AGREEMENT

The economic relations between the two countries have opened up only since the end of the Cold War. Sri Lanka was, as a matter of fact, the first South Asian economy to go for liberalisation way back in 1978. By the end of the Cold War, trade began to increase with India as India liberalised its economy. Sri Lanka also perceives India as a potential for FDI supplier. There has been, moreover, a steady flow of tourists from India. The trade has gradually shifted in favour of India, as Sri Lankan exports to India are lesser than their imports. Both have tried to rectify trade practices through a Free Trade Agreement (FTA). India and Sri Lanka signed the FTA in 1998, which finally became operational in 2001. The India–Sri Lanka FTA gives duty-free preferential access to each other's goods in a time-bound manner. India exports petro products, pharmaceuticals, two wheelers and vegetables while importing rubber products, spices and electric wires. Indian firms operational in Sri Lanka include Tata, Jet Airways, Ashok Leyland, CEAT, Apollo, and so forth. In 2003, a joint working group was established for a comprehensive economic partnership agreement (CEPA). This was done to enhance the FTA and envisage the promotion of cooperation in the service sector. India is also undertaking development of the Trincomalee port, as this will boost its strategic presence vis-à-vis Sri Lanka. Indian Oil Corporation (IOC) has invested six million tonne per annum Grandfield refinery be established in Sri Lanka through direct investment. At present, Sri Lanka has only one 2.5 million tonne refinery.

INDIA AND SRI LANKA ECONOMIC AND TECHNICAL COOPERATION AGREEMENT

India envisages services-based cooperation in CEPA. However, Sri Lanka has had expressed some reservations, it hopes for more economic and technical cooperation rather than increased movement of Indian professionals in Sri Lanka as expressed in the CEPA. Sri Lanka favours an Economic and Technical Cooperation Agreement (ETCA) over the CEPA. In the CEPA, India had decided to open up 80 sectors for Sri Lanka and advised that Sri Lanka open up IT and marine ship building sectors. As the proposed CEPA would liberalise investment and trade in services, goods and facilitate movement of people, Sri Lanka feared that Indian firms may ultimately come to dominate the Sri Lankan economic space and might eventually lead to loss of jobs for the Sri Lankan native population. The movement of people's clause is highly resented by

Sri Lanka. In 2020, India had signed the ETCA for cooperation in services, investment and technology dimensions. The ETCA would provide Indian states in south India access to Sri Lankan markets. The ETCA has made Sri Lanka the new geo-economic pole of South Asia. Under the ETCA, India would focus on development of Trincomalee as a hydrocarbon hub for the region of Bay of Bengal.

INDIA AND SRI LANKA KACHCHATHEEVU ISLAND ISSUE

Kachchatheevu is a small island located about 10 miles northeast of Rameshwaram. The fishermen used it to dry their nets and catch fish. It has been a part of Raja of Ramnand's territory who was controlling it as the lead Zamindar. When the Zamindari system was abolished, Kachchatheevu became a part of the Presidency of Madras. When India became independent and initiated a boundary negotiation at the maritime level with Sri Lanka, Kachchatheevu was a disputed territory between Ceylon and the British and there was never an agreement on boundary ever. In 1947 and 1976, as per agreements, the issue was bilaterally resolved between India and Sri Lanka, and the resultant maritime agreement has allowed Indians to visit Kachchatheevu for pilgrimage for which no visa is required. The Indian government has maintained that the right of access to Kachchatheevu does not cover any fishing rights. In 2008, the AIDMK filed a petition in the Supreme Court (SC) asking that the SC declare the 1974 and 1976 agreements as unconstitutional. The Indian government produced the facts in the highest court and clarified the issue of Kachchatheevu, stating that the island has not been ceded. Consequently, the court disposed of the AIDMK's petition.

INDIA AND SRI LANKA MARITIME ISSUES

After the independence of both nations, fishing has become an important economic activity. Because of a large common area between the two in the sea, the two have often had issues of fishermen straying into each other's waters. In the last few decades, fish and aquatic life in the Indian continental shelf has depleted. As a result, more fishermen enter Sri Lankan waters and also resort to the use of modern fishing trolleys which Lankan fishermen are unable to match. The Indian fishermen saw a golden business opportunity during the LTTE era as the Sri Lankan government had disallowed the easy movement of Sri Lankan fishermen in waters owing to military operations. However, with the LTTE war over, since 2010, there is a resurgence of Sri Lankan fishermen in Palk Bay. They were trying to reclaim their legitimate lost base and, in the process, became engaged in conflict. In order to solve the issue, understanding the importance of ocean economy becomes significant. The Department of Ocean Development and Ministry of Agriculture have to ensure assistance to the states so that fishermen are able to find alternative livelihood to fishing in Palk Bay. The Indian government has renewed the thrust on ocean economy in recent times with the Prime Minister signing an Agreement on Ocean Economy with Sri Lanka, Mauritius and Maldives in 2015. There is an immediate need to sign a protocol for joint patrolling. In 2017, the two had agreed to adopt a humanitarian approach to the fishermen's issue and expanded defence cooperation in trilateral format with Maldives.

INDIA AND SRI LANKA NUCLEAR COOPERATION

The two concluded Agreement on Civilian Nuclear Cooperation in 2017 when Indian Prime Minister visited Sri Lanka.

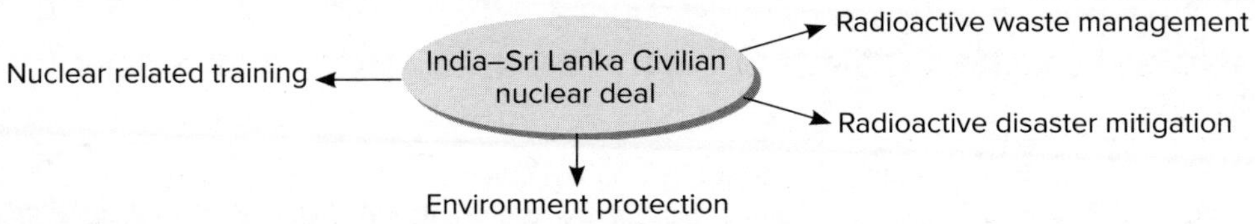

CHINA FACTOR IN INDIA AND SRI LANKA RELATIONS

In the recent times, China and Sri Lanka have deepened their ties. Sri Lanka is a part of Belt and Road Initiative. China has taken Hambantota port on lease for 99 years by erasing 1 billion dollar debt of Sri Lanka (which RAW says will be used by Chinese warships and submarines to refuel during war in Indian Ocean) while it has refurbished Colombo port to make it a transshipment hub and has created the Lotus Tower infrastructure project. This is despite the fact that India and Sri Lanka have no such major infrastructure project in the history. To counter this rising port diplomacy of China, India has adopted a two-point strategy. Firstly, it has decided to undertake direct strategic investments in Sri Lanka. Secondly, it has adopted the two plus one developmental model, where India and Japan have come together to offer infrastructure support as a challenge to the BRI. India has aided the development of Kankesanthurai port, Palay and Rajapakse International airport, Trincomalee oil storage facility and Jaffna–Colombo railway. India and Japan have also come together to work on East Container Terminal building at Colombo. The relationship of Colombo and Beijing is purely economic and some have asserted that China has magnified the debt to Sri Lanka to the extent that Sri Lanka has fallen into a debt trap. This is where India gains and India's former High Commissioner Taranjit Singh Sandhu rightly stated that *India's aid to Sri Lanka is not to raid or invade because our focus is co-prosperity of our neighbour.* Despite the growing China–Sri Lanka ties, Sri Lanka has often stated that while Beijing is a good friend of the Lankan people; India is a relative of Lankan people. In the future, it is imperative for India to understand that Sri Lanka is geopolitically located at the heart of Indo-Pacific, so China will have engagement with them. Rather, India should sit down with Sri Lanka and identify the red lines where Chinese projects can be a threat to the national security of India. At the political level, it is imperative for India to identify the orange zones of cooperation.

THE ECONOMIC AND POLITICAL CRISIS IN SRI LANKA AND INDIA'S POSITION: AN IN-DEPTH ANALYSIS

Majority of the countries in South Asia are witnessing economic and political upheavals. While Myanmar is witnessing crisis on refugee front, the Pakistanis are witnessing political and economic turmoil and Sri Lanka has had mass protests on streets and political altering. Sri Lankans are facing the most devastating economic crisis since their modern existence in 1948. The Sri Lankan civil war, analysed in preceding sections, had already caused a drain on the resources of the country for 26 years before coming to an end in 2009. What followed after 2009 was a series of economic mismanagements by successive governments that caused budgetary shortfalls and deficits in balance of payments. From 2010, the GDP of the country too fell drastically from 8.01% to (–) 3.56% in 2020. Because of aggressively falling GDP before the pandemic, the government had resorted to a massive tax cut in the economy to fulfil its electoral promises and between 2020 and 2022, this caused a shortfall of one million taxpayers at a time when economy was plummeting. The economic theory argues that any reduction in tax rates increases the disposable incomes in the hands of the people and increases the money circulation in the economy. However, this did not occur in the case of Sri Lanka because the people already paid a severe price owing to increased healthcare expenditures in the pandemic phase. As the resource mobilisation weakened and budgetary deficits widened, in the period from 2020 to 2022, the government resorted to massive inflow of external debt to manage the economy. As the external debt kept accumulating, the Central Bank of Sri Lanka kept printing more money and with almost negligible ways to put the money for productive economic use, the surplus money in the system ended up in spilling over inflation and worsened the exchange rates. Because of absolute mismanagement of economic situation, the government failed to bolster revenues, generate employment and boost public welfare; thus, plunging the state into an economic abyss. Because of shortages of essential medicines, food and fuel, the public distrust began to rise when government defaulted on 51 billion USD foreign debt. With International Monetary Fund insisting on a conditionality-centric bailout and Chinese, the traditional supporters of Sri Lanka in the post-2009 recovery period pumping half-baked financial assistance, the angst in the public rose to the extent that its first victim became the ruling political class. In this backdrop, the Indian government has adopted a Sri Lanka policy based on the Neighbourhood First Doctrine. While commenting on the political changes, India has maintained that what is happening inside Sri Lanka is an internal issue and India stands with the people of Sri Lanka, thus strengthening the people's dimension in its conduct of foreign policy. India has extended all possible help to the Sri Lankans, ranging from monetary to humanitarian aid, and striving to seek support of as many other donors as possible to ensure that Sri Lanka receives a multi-vector support. It is in India's interest to see a stable and prosperous Sri Lanka because any upheaval in Sri Lanka, economically and politically, will only end up in bringing more foreign powers in India's strategic lake and impinge on India's strategic autonomy. This thinking of India explains why India has taken a lead in providing support to Sri Lanka to help the state tide over the tough times.

CHAPTER 9

India's Relationship with China

LOCATING INDIA IN THE CHANGING NATURE OF CHINESE DIPLOMACY

The seventh century Buddhist monk, Xuanzang, described that India and China have a relationship based on soulful intimacy (aatmiata), closeness (nikatata) and solidarity (bhaichara). Today, the Sino-Indian relations are a mixture of cooperation, competition and rivalry.

When India became independent, three broad events influenced the formation of India's China policy. In 1949, there was a revolution in China and the Chinese Communist Party (CCP) was formed, establishing the People's Republic of China (PRC). The newly established PRC accepted the Leninist–Stalinist style of state administration. If we trace the history of China, we understand one thing that they do not believe in tracing their existence to a system based on sovereign equality but they trace their origin on the divine and boundless reach with Central authority of divine Chinese emperor, with focus on establishing tianxia (which in Mandarin means "all under heaven"), that is a Middle Kingdom guided by heaven. In 2012, when Xi Jinping acquired power, he gave the goal of "qiang zhounggou meng", which meant a dream of a strong nation to be at the centre of the earth, which he intends to achieve by 2049 (which Xi envisages as a "community of shared future of mankind").

Early 1950s was a period of decolonisation. Because new countries were born in the region, the question that emerged was what role India and China would play in this newly emerging postcolonial world order. India propounded its NAM (non-aligned movement) for the decolonised world and used NAM to position itself as a third force in the era of bipolarity. However, India realised that success or failure of its position in a new international order would depend upon the support or opposition to its efforts by China. Jawaharlal Nehru wanted to win the support of China and Nehru believed that an East led by India and China could guide the world morally at a time when the Western thought process was being guided by polarised ideological underpinnings. Thus, Nehru's idea of China was based on cooperation than containment. This is the reason why Nehru even invited Zhou Enlai to the Bandung Conference. Nehru wanted to build India's relationship with Chinese on the enduring historical connections of the two as civilisational states. (*It is important to note that we may emphasis that India and China have civilisational links, but, a study by Prabodh Chandra Bagchi rightly points out that the cultural relations between India and China have been a one-way traffic primarily with no attempts ever made to discover the influence of China on the life and thought of India. Also, the cross-Himalayan links have primarily concentrated around Tibet. Tibet has been one region that remained non-existent in the thoughts of Han Chinese historically. This means that the soul of China has been majorly untouched by the civilisation of India.*)

THE 24 CHARACTER STRATEGY OF CHINA AND ITS GLOBAL OUTLOOK

The Chinese tactic was called "united front". Under this tactic, the Chinese aimed to avoid their isolation by building solidarity with the non-aligned world and dividing the West. The Chinese played a consummate game of isolating the main threat by building unity with all other forces against the West. The Chinese diplomats kept the Chinese state steady in a churning sea that was full of storms. Whenever the storm tide rose in the sea, these diplomatic fishermen aptly gathered the fish and expanded the global presence of the Chinese and gained rightful international acceptability. Whenever the ship ebbed, these diplomatic fishermen of China ensured that the Chinese ship (the state) remained firmly moored. Vallabhbhai Patel, in contrast, had been a keen advocate of a more cautious approach and he advocated for a military build-up for India and creation of roads near the China border, along with other vital infrastructure. He even favoured the US cooperation to balance China if needed, but Nehru was not in favour of any US cooperation to contain China as he found it to be a Cold War tactic, which could weaken non-alignment. But the death of Patel in 1950 gave Nehru the steering wheel of India's China policy and Nehru could not be challenged by anyone thereafter. Throughout the Cold War, the Chinese played their cards well and ensured that they do not upset either Henry Kissinger or Alexei Kosygin. In 1972, when Chinese decided to open up their economy, Zhou persuaded Nixon to abandon Taiwan (which he did in 1978), a staggering act of diplomacy, considering, Chinese had not even exercised a single day of sovereignty over Taiwan. The high noon for Chinese diplomacy was the period of 1980s and 1990s. The American people became fascinated with the Chinese when the Protestant Missionaries in the 1990s began to assert that god wanted to bring salvation to the Chinese. In the 1980s, when Deng Xiaoping took over China, he decided to supplement the strategy of diplomacy adopted by Zhou till date with his own "24-Character Strategy". The basic premise of Deng Xiaoping was to observe calmly, secure the position of China, hide the capacities of China and bide time, maintain a low profile deliberately and do not claim leadership. These thoughts eventually became the Chinese diplomatic paradigms and the Chinese diplomats measured their words, maintained their dignity, projected their power but never blustered. The Chinese diplomats became masters of their briefs and were ingrained by Zhou that core advantage in any negotiation is to know more than the other side knows. This is why, a classical tactic of Chinese diplomats is that they flatter their acquaintances till today by calling them "old friends" and they deliberately built stronger relationships with interlocutors of less friendly states than friendly ones while behind the doors, they would skilfully put the blame of failure on their opponent. So seductive was the Chinese diplomacy that the Americans ironically lifted their sanctions within four weeks after the Tiananmen incident of 1989. After the death of Deng Xiaoping in 1997, arrogance began to replace the humility hallmark of Chinese diplomacy. The new diplomats, trained in English language and born with a careerist mindset quickly dropped persuasion and replaced it with a stick when a country took an action contrasting the Chinese wishes. The Chinese diplomacy in South China Sea asserts that the dominant diplomatic tactic of China is to pursue unilateralism and not compromise. Now the new tactic of China is to seek a revenge for the 'Century of Humiliation from 1839 to 1949' where China has developed an uncaring attitude towards the rest of the world as if the world has done nothing for China till today and rather, has shared a similar historical experience of humiliation only. In the international community, if a statement of fact or some reasoned opinion is presented to Chinese today, they perceive that as an insult or a humiliation, clearly reflecting that the veneer of humility has thinned down. This is a clear indication of depleting goodwill and the ship being adrift at the sea. If the Chinese do not take corrective measures in a post-COVID-19 world, then the ship could be soon dragged from the shore by a receding tide. The Chinese may do well to recall what Kissinger told the White House staff in July 1971 after his trip to China, something that they seem to have forgotten today: "The Chinese style is impressive. The Russians will fight you for every nickel and dime, and elbow you at every level, and lose a million dollars of goodwill in the process. The Chinese have a sense of the longer trends and focus on that, not on ploymanship."

CLOUDS SIGNIFYING THE RISE OF A NEW COLD WAR

All American Presidents, from Nixon, who gave international recognition to Chinese in 1978, to George H. W. Bush who washed the Chinese sins of Tiananmen Square in 1989, to Bill Clinton who ushered the Chinese entry in WTO (World Trade Organization), have been 'responsible stakeholders' in the rise of China. In contrast, the Chinese have always behaved as hard-nosed people who pursued engagements with the US on a selfish note, although couched in high principles always. They have always disguised their real purpose of thwarting the American hegemony by speaking the words that Americans always wanted to hear; from anti-Soviet rhetoric that was music to the American ears in the Cold War to that of market economy in the age of post-ideology. This was because the Chinese since Mao to Xi Jinping have always feared that Americans by deception wish to change communist regimes and keep their capitalist order intact and this view was reinforced to the Chinese when the Soviet Union collapsed in 1991. This strengthened the resolve of the Chinese to create a parallel universe of their own to resist the capitalistic America and since then Chinese have been building an alternative trading system (the Belt and Road Initiative), an alternative banking system (the New Development Bank), their own

GPS (Beidou), digital payment platforms (like Alipay and WeChat Pay) to that of cutting edge digital network of 5G, all under the nose of the Americans, despite voices of caution from eminent political scientists like John Mearsheimer, who rightly stated that Hu Jintao's 'peaceful rise' would not be 'peaceful'. While American diplomats like Steve Bannon may say that the US is already at a war with Chinese, others like Richard Hass and Robert Zoellick might warn that starting a new cold war with the Chinese could be a grave mistake. The recent literature emerging from China like an essay called "The Chinese Reassessment of Interdependence" by Julian Gewirtz asserts that if Trump is determined to disentangle China from the global supply chains, then, Xi Jinping too is determined to break the US chokehold on technology. As the de-coupling is inevitable now, India will suffer the collateral damages. In the post-COVID world, Hong Kong will emerge as a new game changer between the US and China because the rivalry, which till now was purely material between the two, is shifting now to the ideological realm, where the US has condemned the Chinese assaults on human freedoms. The reason being that Hong Kong remains the bastion of capitalism of the West in the East, because many in the US had looked at Honk Kong as a statue of liberty, holding a torch of freedom and democracy, for those who enter China, thus it is an assault on American beliefs. As the time will progress and world will see more information suppressed and errors of omission by China related to COVID-19, there would be more questions raised on the future model of China in contrast to democracy. This divergence could become the seed of a new Cold War of the 21st century.

THE WEI QUI AND BORDER ISSUE

While Indians may have invented chess, the Chinese version of chess is Wei Qui. Henry Kissinger gave an apt explanation of Wei Qui when he said, *If chess is about decisive battle, wei qui is about a protracted campaign and 'strategic encirclement' where opponents seek to occupy empty spaces and then surround and capture opposing pieces. While chess encourages single-mindedness, wei-qui generates guile and strategic flexibility.*

Let us try to understand the border problem by analysing the historical past. To explain the complex border issue, we have divided the study of the border into four phases.

INDIA AND CHINA BOUNDARY ISSUE DURING THE BRITISH TIMES

Firstly, let us understand some historical aspects about the Tibetan people, Nepal, Assam and Kashmir and then we will link the four collectively.

Let us start our study with Tibet. China was under the rule of Ming dynasty till 1644. The Ming Dynasty controlled the entire mainland of China but never defined their rule over Tibet. It is believed by the historians that Tibet was independent at the time of Ming Dynasty. In 1644, Qing dynasty came to power in China. During the rule of Qing dynasty also, the Tibetans preferred to stay in isolation and as they had different beliefs from Han Chinese. The spiritual head of Tibetans is called Dalai Lama and he is also called as the political head of Tibetan people. Tibetans have never owed any allegiance to rulers of China unlike rulers of Korea and Vietnam historically. In 1717, Dzungar tribesman came from Mongolia and invaded Tibet via Aksai Chin. This invasion was perceived by the rulers of Qing Dynasty as a potential threat to China in future. So, the rulers of the Qing Dynasty in China responded to this invasion by sending a military governor to Lhasa called as Ambans in 1728. The Chinese instructed the Tibetans to respect Ambans (the military governor) in Lhasa. But Qing Dynasty rulers neither annexed Tibet nor did it alter Tibetan independence. Qing Dynasty encouraged the Tibetan people to respect the Ambans through a priest patron relation where Tibet was the priest and Qing Dynasty sent Ambans were the patrons. In 1792 Qing Dynasty and Tibet rule got transformed as Qing Dynasty issued a 29-point decree to Ambans that gave Chinese Ambans powers equivalent to Dalai Lama. The Tibetan people who began to fear the motives of China behind the 29-point decree resented this. We will come back to Tibet after some time. Let us turn our attention to Nepal now.

In 1769, British had established presence in India. Nepal at that time was under Hindu rulers who were called Newars. In 1769, there was a conflict in Nepal between Newars and Gurkhas. The Gurkhas were inhabitants of the hilly areas of Nepal. The British supported Newars (Hindus) against Gurkhas but, in the conflict of 1769, the Gurkhas defeated Newars and established a Hindu Gorkha Kingdom in Nepal. This upset the British for two reasons because firstly, they thought that the Gurkhas could undermine the authority of the British in India and secondly, since 1775 Gurkhas were attacking Sikkimese people, which affected the British trade with Tibet through Sikkim. To prevent any potential Gorkha aggression,

Anglo-Nepal war began, between the British and Gurkhas in 1814. British won the war by defeating the Gurkhas in 1816. The British concluded Treaty of Sagauli at the end of the war in 1816 and gained access to Tibet via Kumaon and Garhwal regions, which at that time were a part of Nepal. In 1817, after British defeated Gurkhas again and signed Treaty of Titalia with Sikkim in 1817. As per the treaty Sikkim enjoyed British protection by becoming a British protectorate (which enabled the British to deploy a company of troops) and Sikkim became a safer trade route to Lhasa. The Treaty also gave British a platform in Sikkim to watch Gurkhas in future. The Treaty of Titalia was replaced in 1861 and the new treaty gave British larger say in domestic and internal affairs of Sikkim.

Let us look at Assam region now.

Assam was under Ahom Kingdom rule. The Ahom rulers established power in Assam in 1212 AD. The Ahom kingdom began to become weak by 1820s. Burma saw a week Ahom rule as an opportunity to expand to Assam. The British decided to check Burma and as a result in 1824 Anglo-Burma war took place. Burma got defeated in Anglo-Burma war in 1824. In 1826, Burma and British concluded a peace treaty in Yandabo, known as the Treaty of Yandabo. As per the treaty British got Assam under their control and Burma threat was nullified. Assam now gave British an easy access to trade with Tibet via Lohit Valley region of Assam. The British in Assam saw a bright spot in oil and tea plantations and this led the British to undertake massive investments in Assam.

When British began to undertake tea plantations, the local Assam tribes opposed British. They were not in favour of their areas to be exploited for commercial gains. The tribal groups of Assam also resented the British to use Lohit valley for commercial trade with Tibet. To tackle the obstructionist behaviour of tribals of Assam, the British decided to create inner line and outer line permits system with tribals. The rationale behind this system was to ensure that the British continue with their investments and trade without disturbing the tribals. The British succeeded in establishing the system with tribal rulers where they would do commercial acts in inner line areas while the outer line areas would remain with the tribals and British would not enter in those areas. Geographically, the region adjoining Assam was called Tawang (modern-day Arunachal Pradesh) and it was a part of Tibet or South Tibet. The region of Arunachal or Tawang was under the control of Monpas of Tawang (non-Tibetans). The Monpas of the Tawang were ethnically different people from Tibetan people but the region was a part of Tibet.

Let us look at Kashmir now.

THE JOHNSON LINE BETWEEN INDIA AND CHINA

Kashmir was a part of Punjab when Maharaja Ranjit Singh ruled Punjab. Maharaja Gulab Singh Jamwal was the founder of the Dogra dynasty of Jammu and he was under the suzerainty of Punjab. Ladakh was an independent region. Gulab Singh had sent his armies in 1830s to acquire Ladakh and he succeeded. From Ladakh, Gulab Singh tried to make attack Tibet but was unsuccessful. Thus, in 1840, the rulers of Tibet and Gulab Singh signed a treaty and decided to respect "old, established frontiers". This means that they decided to maintain a status quo and left the boundary unspecified. Ranjit Singh died in 1839. After his death, there were two camps that strived for power in Punjab. The first were Punjabi Sindhanwallias and the second were Hindu Dogras. While the Punjabi Sindhanwallias were the natives of Punjab, the Hindu Dogras belonged to Jammu region (and lived in Punjab). The Dogras, living in Punjab, succeeded in supporting Sher Singh, the eldest son of Ranjit Singh to power. As a result, the Punjabi Sindhanwallias took refuge in the British territory. Sher Singh was unable to control his empire and eventually, in 1845–46 there was an Anglo-Sikh war. The British defeated the Sikhs in the war and annexed Punjab. After the war, the British concluded Treaty of Lahore with the Sikhs and asked the Sikhs to pay 15 million rupees as war indemnity. The Sikhs could not pay the amount. The British decided that if Sikhs are unable to pay the amount, then they have to cede Ladakh and Kashmir (under the control of Gulab Singh, who lived under suzerainty of Punjab), or the area between Indus and Sutlej. Thus, the British got Ladakh and Kashmir as per the Treaty of Lahore. To formalise the Treaty of Lahore, the British signed Treaty of Amritsar in 1846. The Treaty of Amritsar was signed between the British and Gulab Singh of Jammu. Under the treaty, Gulab Singh purchased Kashmir and Ladakh region from the British by paying 7.5 million Nanakshai rupees (the currency of the Sikh empire) and became the Maharaja of Jammu and Kashmir. The Dogra rule in Jammu, Kashmir and Ladakh eventually began after the Treaty of Amritsar. Under the Treaty of Amritsar, the British told Gulab Singh two things. Firstly, they said that British transferred the region east of Indus and Eastern boundary hills to Gulab Singh but told him that the British will carry out survey and then define to Gulab Singh the purpose of this transfer. This line means that the British told Gulab Singh that he would only administer the territories that he is receiving from the British but the boundary of the territory he administers ends in the East (near China at Pangong lake), which for the time is being undefined and the British will carry out a survey to define the boundary sometime in future. The reason why the British maintained an ambiguous boundary in the east (near China at Pangong Lake) was because it never wanted to upset China. China always maintained that there was no need for a boundary in the east because since ancient times, the Karakorum Mountains acted as a natural border. So under the Treaty of Lahore, Gulab Singh was to manage Jammu, Kashmir and Ladakh and would not alter boundaries on his own until the British did a survey to define the border. Gulab Singh was instructed to maintain a balance of power and status quo on territorial boundaries.

THE JOHN ARDAGH LINE AND MCCARTNEY–MCDONALD LINE BETWEEN INDIA AND CHINA

On the East of the Kashmir, there was a boundary with China. The boundary was undefined. This boundary of Kashmir with China was with a territory called Kashgar.

In 1864, the local ruler of Kashgar was Yakub Baig and he was a good friend of Gulab Singh. Beg decided to rebel against the Qing Dynasty of China and sought help from Gulab Singh. During Yakub Baig's rebellion, Gulab Singh sent his forces and helped Yakub Baig against China. After he rebelled successfully, Yakub Baig established an independent kingdom of Kashgaria. In return for his help, Baig allowed Gulab Singh to select an area of his choice in his kingdom and establish for himself a private retreat. Gulab Singh built a fort in Aksai Chin region of Kashgaria. To protect his fort, he even deployed a small army at the fort permanently. Now under treaty of Amritsar, British had told Gulab Singh that they would carry out a survey to the East to establish a boundary. So in 1865, the British sent William Johnson to carry out a survey. Johnson carried out a survey of the East region as mandated under Treaty of Amritsar. Johnson published a map and in that map, he showed the areas from Shahidullah, Aksai Chin to Kunlun as part of Kashmir, and eventually under the British India. The Johnson line map was published in 1868 and when it was published, the world got to know about this area of Aksai Chin for the first time. Johnson showed Aksai Chin region as a part of Kashmir because he found the retreat or fort (and some troops) of Gulab Singh in Aksai Chin. So, Johnson concluded that Aksai Chin area belongs to Kashmir. In 1868 when the Johnson line was published, the then Surveyor General of British India, Colonel Walker rejected the fact that Aksai Chin belongs to Gulab Singh as depicted by Johnson because most of the Chinese maps at that time had shown Aksai Chin as part of China. One thing to be noted is that it is the same Johnson line, which is used by India since 1947 to claim Aksai Chin as a part of India till today. In 1877, the Chinese army of Qing Dynasty captured Kashgaria and defeated Yakub Beg and renamed Kashgaria as Xinjiang. In 1856, there were Crimean wars. Russia, after the Crimean wars, had begun to industrialise. The Russian Czars also expanded power to Central Asia. The British feared Russian expansionism and they perceived that the Russians might advance from Central Asia to North Kashmir and eventually acquire India through the North. To check Russian advances, the British decided to keep a watch in Kashmir. In Kashmir, there were two important regions called Hunza valley and Gilgit region. Both these regions were in the North of Kashmir. So in 1892, the British established the military post in Gilgit and acquired control of Hunza and Nagar regions. This led to some confrontation with the Chinese because China had been making claims over Hunza. The ruler of Hunza too was tilted towards China and the British were concerned about this because they wanted the Hunza well under their control to check Russian advancements. In 1893, Huang Te Chen, a Chinese military official in St. Petersburg published the Huang Te Chen line and this line showed Aksai Chin as a part of Kashmir. In 1896, the British instructed John Ardagh, the Chief of Military Intelligence, to demarcate a border. John Ardagh proposed a line called Ardagh line based on a 'forward school' thought. This means that Ardagh wanted the boundary to be as far as possible in Kashmir so that the boundary can act as a defence against the Russian advances. This line was nothing but a strategic adoption of Johnson line of 1865. The line proposed a boundary in the crust of Kunlun ranges and incorporated Karakash and Yarkand river area as part of Kashmir. To check Russian advancement, the British wanted a permanent solution on the border. They decided to bury Johnson line and John Ardagh line and decided to propose a new solution. The British minister in Pecking sir Claude McDonald proposed to British minister in Kashgar Charles McCartney in 1899 to finally solve the Kashmir China boundary. The British wanted that China renounce their claim over Hunza. As most of the Chinese map showed Aksai Chin as part of China, the British decided to do a trade-off. In 1899, McCartney–McDonald line was proposed. The proposal was that

China relinquishes its claim over Hunza and gets Aksai Chin in return. This line had the potential to resolve the issue. The proposal was sent to Peking but Peking remained silent on the same and did not respond to the McCartney–McDonald line. The British continued their control over Hunza and status of Aksai Chin, since Johnson line, remained unclear. In 1890, British and Chinese Qing Dynasty signed a trade treaty to do trade via Sikkim–Tibet border. The treaty did not include the Tibetans. The Tibetan became upset and decided to protest for their exclusion from the treaty. They destroyed the trade markers set up by the Britishers for passage in the area. The British and Chinese did not pay any importance to demand of the Tibetans. In 1893, the British and Chinese now signed a Convention to the 1890 Trade treaty and this convention gave the British the right to do trade via Chumbi valley. This again upset the Tibetan as Tibetan were again not involved in the Convention. The then Dalai Lama, Thubten Gyatso, now began to realise that Tibet will need third-party support as the British and Qing Dynasty are resorting to unilateral measures, that endanger the sovereignty of Tibet. Thubten Gyatso had an advisor named Agvan Dorzhiev. Dorzhiev was a Khori–Buryar Mongol. He guided Gyatso to seek help of Russia. From 1898 to 1901, Thubten and his men regularly visited Russia and Dorzhiev acted as a mediator.

THE SHIMLA CONVENTION AND CONSTRUCT OF MCMAHON LINE BETWEEN INDIA AND CHINA

In 1899, Lord Curzon became the next viceroy of British India and he replaced Lord Elgin. Curzon had intense hatred for Russians and became aware of Gyatso and his Russian support. Lord Curzon sent a mission to Lhasa. He wanted to inform through the mission to the Dalai Lama to respect the 1893 convention. A British named Younghusband led the mission. The mission of Younghusband reached Lhasa in 1904. The moment the mission reached Lhasa, Thubten and Dorzhiev fled Lhasa and Tibet came under the control of Ambans, who by now had become quite autonomous and powerful as parallel to Dalai Lama because the power Qing Dynasty in China was declining. Younghusband mission now directly dealt with the Ambans. A new treaty was concluded between British and Ambans on Tibet. As per the treaty, Tibet would no longer enter into third-party treaties including with Russians without the permission of British. The British would get access to all trading posts in the region of Tibet. A British agent will be stationed in South Tibet. As visible in the treaty, the British did not make Tibet a British protectorate nor fully established their presence in Tibet but allowed Ambans to continue a low-level administrative presence in Tibet. Thus, the 1904 Lhasa Convention ensured that the Tibet became a buffer between China and British India. Taking advantage of 1904 Lhasa Convention, the Chinese Qing Dynasty proposed that there be a new convention. In 1906, China proposed the new convention asserting that British also accept that neither the British nor the Qing Dynasty would interfere in Tibet nor will they annex Tibet. The British agreed to these demands and concluded the 1906 Convention. It is important to note that as per the 1906 Convention also, Qing Dynasty never attempted to annex Tibet and asserted its autonomous character. Anglo-Russian Convention now followed this in 1907 where Britain and Russia agreed not to negotiate with Tibet without the presence of Chinese. In 1909, Dalai Lama tried to come back to Tibet but as Ambans had already been taking care of Tibet, Dalai Lama fled to India in 1909. The British were prohibited to carry out any expeditions also in the outer line areas of Assam, as these areas were restricted for tribals. In 1911, a British officer Noel Williamson happened to cross the banks of river Dihang and entered into the area occupied by Abor tribe, which was in the outer line. This led to an aggression by the Abor tribe against Williamson and the Abor tribes massacred the entire team of Williamson. The British decided to retaliate to this. They crossed over into the Abor tribe region, massacred the tribals and reached up to Chinese boundary. They now asserted to the Chinese to establish a border in the East. What also motivated the British to design this Noel Williamson episode was the fall of Qing dynasty in 1911–12. As the Chinese were weak, due to the fall of Qing Dynasty, the British used the Noel Williamson episode to seek boundary solution. The collapse of Qing dynasty in China lead to a mutiny in Tibet and Tibetans revolted against the Ambans. This lead to collapse of the Ambans and Dalai Lama returned back to Lhasa in 1912. The British now got the right opportunity to keep Chinese and Russian route of Tibet and make Tibet a truly autonomous buffer state. The British played their cards. In 1912, the British minister in Peking short of a letter to Chinese administration. He asserted that China is interfering in Tibet and this is a violation of Lhasa convention 1906. He asserted that Chinese suzerainty is recognised by British over Tibet but that does not entitle the Chinese to interfere in Tibet. He asserted that China has violated Lhasa convention so they should now come for fresh negotiations. All this was just a game played by the British. Their ultimate aim was to take advantage of a weak Chinese Central government (due to fall of Qing Dynasty) and convince China to go for a fresh round of negotiations. The Chinese agreed to it and decided to go for talks. It is in this context that on 23rd May 1913 the British invited China, Dalai Lama for a three-party talk. They decided to hold a conference on 13th October 1913 in Shimla under the leadership of British foreign Secretary Sir Arthur Henry McMahon as the chairman of the conference. In 1913, the Shimla conference began. McMahon represented the British in the conference; the Chinese by Ivan Chen and Tibetan representative was Lonchen Shatra. The moment the conference began, China protested that why is Tibet given an equal status. The British downplayed their protests. During the conference, McMahon unveiled the plan of British called the McMahon plan. As per the plan, British India would get Tawang region. The plan stated that Tibet would be divided into outer Tibet (depicted by a Red line) and inner Tibet (depicted by a Blue line). The outer Tibet would have a boundary with India and outer Tibet will have the authority of Dalai Lama. The Tibetan delegation led by Lonchen Shatra urged the British to keep Tibetan states in red line area as they were and also if Tso Karpo and Tsari Sarpa (two sacred Tibetan sites) be inside Tibet. McMahon agreed to it and as per the Shimla Convention, Tibet became an autonomous buffer. Ivan Chen, the Chinese representative, refused to accept the Shimla Convention and also the division of Tibet and eventually China did not sign the Shimla Convention. Thus, the British concluded the Shimla Convention in 1914 bilaterally with Lonchen Shatra of Tibet.

The British did not publish the Shimla Convention of 1914 till 1937. This was done to ensure that Russia did not become angry with the British. This was possible because in 1907 both Britain and Russia had agreed upon a treaty where they stated that neither would negotiate with Tibet without the presence of Chinese while in the Shimla Convention, British had bilaterally concluded the Convention in 1914 without China. The British finally published the Shimla Convention in 1937 and showed the McMahon line as the border. Chinese maintained Tawang cannot be a part of India as it was a part of South Tibet but the British however continued to assert that McMahon line would be the boundary in the East. Thus, during the British times, neither the boundary in the Western sector (Aksai Chin and Ladakh area) could be fixed and nor the boundary in East (Tawang) could be fixed and a border which was mutually acceptable to both British and China could never be demarcated and the fixing and re-fixing of the boundaries during British times was primarily done to suit their colonial interests. The British approach to the entire border issue was fluid and more driven by geopolitics than basic requirements of a nation state.

THE ANNEXATION OF TIBET AND NORTHEASTERN FRONTIER AGENCY

After India became independent in 1947, there was a civil war in China at that time. The Chinese civil war ended in 1949 and the PRC was born. The PRC announced in 1950 that People's Liberation Army of China (PLA) should liberate Tibet. In 1950, PLA entered into Tibet through Aksai Chin. It is at this juncture, India wrote to China asserting that China should respect the autonomy of Tibet. China responded back by saying that Tibet is an internal issue of China and it will resolve it as per Chinese laws and it does not favour Indian interference in its internal affairs. In 1951, China entered into a 17-point Sino-Tibet Agreement. In the agreement, China stated that Tibet is one of the nationalities living in China since historical times and Tibet is an integral part of China. After the Sino-Tibet agreement, India accepted that it will not be able to deal with Tibet directly and will have to deal Tibet through China. In 1912, the British established Northeast Frontier Tracts

(NEFT) agency to administer Tawang. The NEFT officials negotiated with the leaders of tribes in Tawang and shifted the outer line further to the north but still Tawang remained a part of Tibet. Subsequently in 1914, the British signed the Shimla Convention and now Tibet was dissected as inner Tibet and outer Tibet. The outer Tibet was under the control of the Dalai Lama and China was to respect the autonomy of outer Tibet. However, the maps clearly did not demarcate Tibet and Tawang. Inner Tibet was the area in east and ended almost at the Bhutan, India, and Tibet tri-junction at Tawang. The British never labeled Tawang as a part of British India in the maps of Shimla Convention. In 1938, British Captain G. S. Lightfoot reached Tawang and informed the monastery leadership (Monpas) that Tawang is Indian Territory. The Tibetans and Monpas resented this and therefore British decided to restore Tawang to Tibet. In 1944, NEFT established control over Tawang during World War II but at the end of the war, Tawang was restored to the Tibet again. After India became independent, in 1947, Tibet wrote a letter to India to give back the lands under NEFT back to Tibet. India wrote back to Tibet saying that the areas are Indian Territory as per McMahon line and Tawang is a part of India. In 1954, The NEFT was renamed as NEFA or Northeast Frontier Agency.

THE ROAD TO PANCHSHEEL AND DIFFERING PERCEPTIONS ON BORDER

In 1952, China informed India about its willingness to discuss 'all inherited rights and specific problems' including the issue of Tibet through negotiations. Nehru thought that whenever the dialogue will happen, India will not raise the issue of McMahon line as doing that may push China to seek fresh negotiations on the border and India is not keen on fresh negotiations as it considers McMahon line as the boundary. The talks between India and China happened in 1954 and India did not raise McMahon line issue in the discussion. There are reasons why India decided not to discuss McMahon line issue. Firstly, Nehru thought that since 1954, India has been administering the territories up to the McMahon line. China has not raised any objection till 1954. India perceived that as China invited India to discuss "specific problems related to inherited right", the McMahon line does not fit into the criteria of "specific problems" as China never raised any objection. Secondly, Nehru thought that if China had any problem with the McMahon line, they should have raised the issue. But as China did not raise the issue, it proved that China had accepted the de facto border in the East. In 1954, the two sides signed the Panchsheel agreement and one of the principles of Panchsheel was "mutual respect for each other's territory".

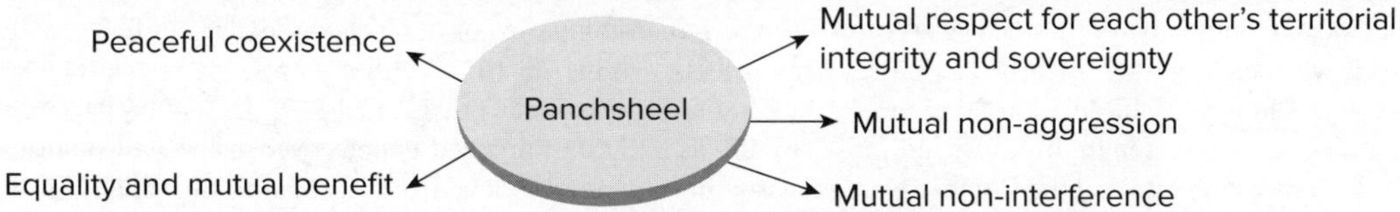

Thus, India thought that Panchsheel proves that India has a right to make McMahon line as a boundary in the East and China would respect Indian sovereignty on the border in the East. It is imperative to understand that why did China not raise the issue of McMahon line? Chinese always believed in deliberately not taking up the McMahon line border issue in 1954 with India because the Chinese were shrewd as they were constructing a road in Aksai Chin region to reach Tibet. They never wanted to raise the issue of any border with India as doing so would have exposed the Aksai Chin road to India and that could have complicated the Chinese plans in Tibet. In the Panchsheel, India however officially accepted that Tibet is a part of China.

INDIA AND CHINA BOUNDARY ISSUE FROM PANCHSHEEL ONWARDS

After the Panchsheel agreement, the dream of Nehru to work with China at the global level to emerge as a global players and guiding light of the East began to take shape. Nehru was of the view that the success of Panchsheel meant that the border question was also settled. Little did Nehru know that his actions would lead to a crisis in future. There were a lot of factors that led to the situation of 1962.

In 1950, the Survey of India had created a boundary between India and China. The Eastern sector of the boundary was designated as McMahon line but was stated as "un-demarcated". The western and Central sector boundary was demarcated as "undefined" and a colour-wash was used. After Panchsheel in 1954, Nehru ordered the Survey of India to publish new maps and show the boundary demarcated clearly. In the new maps, the words "un-demarcated" and "undefined" were dropped. The boundary in the East was now firmly established as per McMahon line. The colour-wash on the boundary in the Western and Central sector was also removed and a firm line was established. The boundary in the Western Sector in Kashmir was based on Johnson line and India showed Aksai Chin as a part of Indian Kashmir (as per Johnson line) and it is this that acted as the first seed for the conflict. Through these new map issued in 1954, Nehru indirectly conveyed that India's territorial integrity is non-negotiable. Even when India published these maps, China did not respond. In 1954, China published their maps. In the Chinese maps, they showed Aksai Chin and NEFA region, including Tawang, as a part of China. Nehru took up this issue with China in 1954. China responded by saying that the Chinese maps are old maps and the PRC has not yet revised those maps and Chinese government needs time to revise those maps. This response by China came as a surprise to India. After India came out with new maps in 1954, Nehru asserted that India established check posts along the entire Frontier with China and the check posts would act as symbols of India's territorial integrity. After China issued maps in 1954, China strongly protested the creation of Indian check posts. China asserted that Indians have transgressed deep inside Chinese territory. India responded by asserting that Indian posts were within the Indian Territory and not in China. China even complained that the boundary line in Middle or Central sector shown by India is not accurate as the boundary passes in Central sector through Himalayan passes and all these passes are located inside China. This issue emerged as the second point of friction. The border issue emerged in full proportion after 1957. In 1957, China officially announced the construction of Xinjiang–Tibet road that passed via Aksai Chin. India was shocked that China had secretly constructed a road in Aksai Chin, in an area that was claimed by India as per Johnson line of 1865. The 1957 Aksai Chin road was the third point of friction.

NEHRU, KRISHNA MENON AND THEIR BETRAYAL TO THE NATION

After the People's Liberation Army entered Lhasa, the Chinese made plans to improve communications and built new roads on a war-footing. The only way to consolidate and 'unify' the Middle Kingdom was to construct a large network of roads. One of these roads was the Tibet–Xinjiang Highway (today infamously known as the Aksai Chin road). The first surveys were done at the end of 1951–52 and construction began in 1953. The official report of the 1962 China War prepared by ministry of defence gave a few examples showing that the construction of the road cutting across Indian soil on the Aksai Chin plateau of Ladakh was known to the Indian ministries of defence and external affairs, and this long before it was made public. In early 1957, the Army selected an officer to go with a patrol and physically confirm the reports that China was building a road in the Aksai Chin area; the officer was Lt. Col R. S. Basera of 1 Kumaon Rifles. His mission was to be tough, exciting and most unique, as he had to proceed under cover to the vast plateau of Aksai Chin and confirm reports that the Chinese were constructing a motorable road from Kashgar to Lhasa. Disguised as a yak herder, Basera was accompanied by Havildar Diwan Singh from the Corps of Engineers. They were to move with three genuine Ladakhi yak herders. During a briefing at the Headquarters in Leh, Basera was told that it was crucial to maintain utmost secrecy about the mission. The Military Intelligence (MI) instructed them not to carry any documents that could disclose their identities and ordered them that no notes should be taken by them. They were asked to memorise the map and the route. They had to move in the easterly direction from Leh for about 250–300 km, till they reached the expected location of the new Chinese built road, in Aksai Chin. Initially, they would pass over difficult, undulating terrain, till they crossed the Karakoram Mountain Range and Shyok River. Their mission was of national importance, said their handlers in the MI. After a long and adventurous journey, they finally entered Aksai Chin. On the third day, one of the herders suddenly pulled Basera's shoulder and showed him a dark line on the horizon; it was the road. The next morning, they walked in the direction of the road: The otherwise sluggish yaks too moved forward with renewed energy, matching the sudden spring in the step of their handlers. At noon, they were now near the raised road, they mentally noted every detail of the road that was not yet tarred. They immediately decided to return and inform the authorities of their discovery. They were asked to report in Delhi. At the end of the day one Lt. Col told them from MI, that their report would be sent to Defence Minister Krishna Menon, who would then discuss it with the Prime Minister. When the Defence Minister saw the report, he surprisingly supported the Chinese side, and even called it a friendly neighbour. He asked the MI director, if the area through which the road passed had been confirmed on a map. The DMI told him the patrol had not carried a map for security reasons. But that was not all, the Prime Minister Nehru and the Defence Minister, more or less rebuked the DMI for sending the patrol. The Prime Minister told the Defence Minister that no more such patrols were to be sent to

Aksai Chin till the matter had been thoroughly investigated, as such patrols could easily vitiate the good relations between friendly neighbours. When Lt. Col Basera was informed of the review of the report by the Prime Minister and Defence Minister, he felt utterly disgusted because the long and difficult patrol they had undertaken, now appeared to have been a futile, month-long exercise. After all, for Nehru, Aksai Chin was an area where not even a blade of grass could grow.

BUILDING CLOUDS OF IMPENDING 1962 CONFLICT

In 1958, a Chinese magazine called *China Pictorial* printed a Chinese map on page 20 and 21. In the map, the NEFA (including Tawang) and Aksai Chin was shown by china as a part of Chinese territory. India protested strongly and asserted that China should not show Indian regions as a part of Chinese territory. The MEA of India sent a note to China asserting that China cannot show such a map as Zhou Enlai had asserted that the maps used by China are old maps and PRC has not revised them and a fresh survey was needed and only after that could the maps be changed. This was entirely a new approach by China and it had never said this point of a fresh survey earlier that it announced now. This came as a big blow to India as India had assumed since 1954 that Indian boundary was non-negotiable and the boundaries were fixed. Nehru took up the matter directly with China in 1958 to which China responded and clarified their position in January 1959. China expressed tremendous dissatisfaction in the way India unilaterally demarcated the borders. China reiterated that they had earlier informed India in 1954 that the Chinese maps are old and China needs time to revisit those old maps. China asserted that the Indians have unilaterally shown Aksai Chin as a part of India without consulting the Chinese. The Chinese asserted for the first time in 1959 in their response that they consider the McMahon line as an illegal line because the Chinese representative Ivan Chang never ratified the Shimla Convention and therefore, the Chinese had rejected the McMahon line. China asserted that the McMahon line is an imperialistic design of the British and as China did not accept the Shimla Convention, McMahon line cannot be considered legally acceptable by China. China indirectly conveyed that they could accept the McMahon line provided India displays 'accommodating attitude' on Aksai Chin (Chinese were looking for a land swap). The Chinese response was a big blow to India as India had assumed that McMahon line is the border. This response emerged as the fourth point of friction.

TIBET, THE CIA AND SINO-INDIAN CONFLICT

In 1724, Chinese had sent the Ambans after tribal invasions. That was the time when China also incorporated two regions of Tibet named Amdo and Kham into western China and renamed the areas as Qinghai. In 1912, when Qing dynasty collapsed, Dalai Lama left India from Darjeeling and went back to Lhasa. The Tibetans crushed Ambans and Dalai Lama resumed control again and ruled Tibet till 1933. In 1935, Tenzin Gyatso became the new Dalai Lama and he continues till today. In 1951, China and Tibet signed a 17-point agreement. Under this agreement it was decided that the land, which is held privately by Tibetans, would be taken away by the state. This upset the Tibetans as the Tibetans had owned a lot of private estate in the region. The Socialist revolution in Tibet began from peripheral areas of Kham and Amdo. Thus China said that Kham (in Sichuan province after 1949) and Amdo (in Qinghai province after 1949) would be from where the Communist system began. Here the farmers would act on Communist lands. All barley and crops produced would be acquired by state and some would be redistributed as per communist principles. Unfortunately, the grains acquired by Chinese state left Tibetans with no grains and this upset the people of Amdo and Kham to this extent that in 1956 they began to form resistance groups to arm themselves to fight back China. The CIA of the US, using Indian Territory as a base, assisted these rebels covertly to wage a war against China. As the rebels fought Chinese government, there was a huge exodus of people from Amdo and Kham to Lhasa. The Chinese PLA continued to suppress these warring rebels. In 1956, Dalai Lama on his visit to India told Nehru about his desire to put up an asylum in India. This visit generated suspicion in China as China began to think that India and CIA are working together to destabilise Tibet. By 1958, the number of resistance fighters and rebels grew almost to one lakh. Dalai Lama sent delegates to convince these guerrillas to not fight. The guerrillas convinced the Dalai Lama delegates to join the resistance and eventually the delegates ended up joining the resistance. By 1959, a lot of religious leaders from Amdo and Kham began to go missing. The people of Tibet began to feel that the Chinese were killing their leaders secretly and wanted to target Dalai Lama. The suspicion of Tibetans increased on 10 March 1959 when Chinese invited Dalai Lama to watch a Chinese drama in military barracks without bodyguards. Tibetans thought that this was a Chinese trap to kill the Dalai Lama. On 10th March 1959, lakhs of

Tibetans formed a human cordon around the Dalai Lama summer Palace called Norbulingka to protect the Dalai Lama from possible abduction by China. The crowd kept on protesting and asked the PLA to leave Tibet while Chinese thought India and CIA are fueling these protesters. As tensions grew in Tibet, on 15 March 1959, the PLA fired shells into Norbulingka and this forced Dalai Lama to exit and the Dalai Lama began to secretly trek to India. As Dalai Lama left, Tibet was burnt down and PLA killed around 80,000 plus Tibetans. As, Dalai Lama reached India; the Indian government gave refuge to Dalai Lama. In February 1960, Nehru invited Zhou Enlai for talks. Zhou decided to come to India for seven days. On 19th April 1960, Zhou arrived in India. On his arrival, Zhou rightly asserted, "I have come here to seek a solution and not to repeat arguments". China stated that they are willing to demonstrate 'practical attitude' to McMahon line and can accept McMahon line as a boundary as they have done with Myanmar, but provided India displays a similar 'accommodative attitude' on Aksai Chin. India insisted that Western, Central and Eastern sectors cannot be put on an equal footing and the three sectors need to be negotiated separately. Also, India rejected a bilateral swap of Aksai Chin and McMahon line and insisted that McMahon line be the boundary in east while Aksai Chin be a part of India. Chinese rejected Nehru's offer and were alarmed to see India claim Aksai Chin, an area that never belonged to India. The Chinese began to think that India's claim to Aksai Chin is a deliberate attempt by India to undermine Chinese authority in Tibet. The talks reached a deadlock and no concrete proposal on a border solution ever emerged. After the talks failed, Zhou Enlai returned.

IF I GIVE THEM AKSAI CHIN, I SHALL NO LONGER BE THE PM

The question is why did the talks fail? The answer lies in Nehru's jingoistic followers who sold him the idea that India should not concede any territory to China and should adopt the "no compromise" approach on Aksai Chin. The jingoistic followers suggested Nehru to accept a formula acceptable to 'Political Marketplace' (meant the opposition and the public). Traditional wisdom says that had India accepted the 'offer' of the Chinese, the border issue could have been permanently resolved. Later, Nehru himself voiced the fear by stating once "If I give them Aksai Chin, I shall no longer be the PM". Had Nehru accepted the offer, it would have had four consequences. First, there would have been no 1962 clash. Second, there would have been a solved border. Third, there would have been no face-offs on the boundary as the one in 2020 (explained in detailed later in this chapter); and fourth, something that India's intelligence community knows and which they never disclosed but we would do so here that Chinese even told India that they would accept India's sovereignty on Jammu and Kashmir vis-à-vis Pakistan.

FORWARD POLICY OF INDIA AND ARMED COEXISTENCE STRATEGY OF MAO

In 1960, China replaced their 1956 maps and issued new maps. In the new maps of 1960, China did cartographic aggression and claimed additional 5000 square km Indian Territory of Sirijap and Spanggur Lake. The Spanggur gap is a mountain pass in the South of mountains in the Pangong Lake. On 2nd November 1961, a meeting happened in PMO in New Delhi and a forward policy was announced. It was decided to establish forward posts in all areas claimed by China by Indian Army. The government ordered that Indian army should first establish posts in Western and Central sectors where China has no posts. Doing so would ensure that India has an upper hand. The army was told to avoid physical clashes with China. The army was instructed to first establish logistical and supply stations. Then from these stations, close to the boundary, the military would establish posts (forward posts) at the border. The army began to establish forward posts at the border without establishing logistic stations. The Indian concept of forward policy was to establish forward posts on the border and India believed that if the forward post is created, China would not establish their post or destroy Indian posts and the area would be under Indian control. As India began to create posts November 1961, it was in April 1962 that Mao ordered the armed coexistence strategy. Under this strategy, Mao ordered PLA to counter-encircle the Indian posts to outmanoeuvre Indian posts. The Panchsheel Agreement was signed in 1954 and was valid for 8 years. In the Panchsheel Agreement, there was a clause that either of the party could seek extension to the agreement. On 3rd December 1961, China informed India that it would seek a fresh agreement and would not like to continue with the existing agreement. India communicated that an essential condition for fresh negotiation is that China should reverse the aggressive tactics on the border. As India remained insistent on a pre-condition for fresh talks, the negotiation did not proceed and on 3rd June 1962, Panchsheel Agreement collapsed. As the agreement collapsed, India closed the trading marts in Gyantse, Tarung and Gartok while China closed their trading marts at Calcutta and Kalimpong.

THE NAMKA CHU, DHOLA POST AND 1962 SINO-INDIAN CONFLICT

In June 1962, the Indian army had established a forward post near the Namka Chu River in Tawang and named that post as Dhola, based on the name of the mountain near the river. China objected to the post saying that the post is located in the North of McMahon line and is deep inside China and India has no right of territorial occupation in this area. India insisted that the post was in proper Dhola region only and not in China. As the Chinese objected, the GOC of Army in the area suggested that the post be relocated to Thagala Ridge. By the time Army HQ granted the permission, Chinese established their post in Thagala Ridge. On 13th September 1962, Chinese troops made an announcement from other side of Namka Chu River that India should retreat from the post. As India ignored the advice, on 20th September 1962, Chinese dropped a grenade on the Indian post. The grenade was thrown by China to compel India to subdue and withdraw by inculcating a sense of fear. The government decided to respond to the grenade attack by deciding to evict China from Namka Chu. The Indian side sent a patrol team on 9th October 1962 near Namka Chu. As the patrol team reached close, China vehemently fired back on India. The entire dream and assumption of forward policy collapsed as Chinese resorted to aggression. Nehru was in Colombo when the Chinese fired and from Colombo he addressed the press asserting that India has ordered the army to evict the Chinese from Namka Chu. This address of Nehru from a foreign soil was perceived as aggressive by China. Mao decided to teach a painful military lesson to India. On 20th October 1962, Chinese attacked from Namka Chu and crossed over and reached Tezpur, Bomdi La and Tawang. The Chinese launched attacks on Western front at Galwan Post near Daulat Beg Oldi. Seeing the Chinese aggression, India sought American military help. President Kennedy dispatched an aircraft carrier to Bay of Bengal and squadrons of the US air force were dispatched. Seeing the American support, the Chinese on 21st November 1962 declared a unilateral ceasefire and retreated to 20 km of the Line of Actual Control (LAC). On 24th November 1962, Zhou Enlai told Nehru to settle the border peacefully. He urged that till the time both parties do not settle the border peacefully, neither of the sides should undertake patrolling up to 20 km of LAC. The term LAC was used for the first time by China here. Zhou Enlai asserted that LAC meant the customary line in Western and Central sector and Eastern line of LAC as per McMahon line. LAC was described only in general terms on maps not to scale by the Chinese. As per Zhou, the Eastern sector coincides with McMahon line and the Western and Middle sector coincides with the traditional customary line that has consistently been pointed out by China. Nehru insisted that China should go back to its position as it held on the 8th September 1962, which was the position before Chinese had occupied Namka Chu post. Nehru rejected the Chinese use of term LAC because he stated that the Chinese line called LAC is nothing but a disconnected series of points on a map that could be joined up in many ways. Nehru was adamant that Chinese should retreat from the positions they held on 8th September 1962. Zhou rejected this proposal of Nehru. China did not demand Indian retreat but asserted that China may strike back if India fires on posts in Chinese territory. However, Chinese continued to occupy Aksai Chin in Ladakh in the Western sector illegally after the end of the conflict. The Indian diplomat, Vasant Vasudeo Paranjpe, aptly described Chinese advances when he remarked that the PLA went through Indian army in 1962 like knife through butter. In November 1962, China went 20 km behind their 1959 position, thus creating two versions of LAC, the 1959 version (mentioned by Zhou to Nehru in a letter) and 1962 version (which they advocated after the conflict).

INDIA AND CHINA BOUNDARY ISSUE FROM 1962 CONFLICT ONWARDS

Since 1962 conflict, India maintained a simple approach to the border question. In 1976, the government in India formed China Study Group. The aim of the group was to study the limits to patrolling and rules of engagement at the border. This was needed because Chinese patrols were coming quite frequently in the disputed regions. Diplomatically, India favoured a sector-by-sector approach and till 1979, maintained the position that resolution of border dispute was the precondition for all diplomatic talks. It was in 1979 that when Atal Bihari Vajpayee visited China and broke the ice. China under Deng Xiaoping proposed a 'package approach' to Vajpayee. Under the package deal, Deng Xiaoping asserted that if India accepts status quo on Western sector, China would accept McMahon line in the East. India rejected the deal and asserted that sector-by-sector approach be adopted and border talks are a precondition for any other talks. Throughout this period, tranquility at border was maintained with minor skirmishes, including one at Sumdorongchu in 1988.

AGREEMENT ON MAINTENANCE OF PEACE AND TRANQUILITY AT THE LAC

In 1988, during Rajiv Gandhi's visit to China, a Joint Working Group (JWG) was established and the border as a precondition for further negotiation point was dropped. Rajiv Gandhi maintained that India and China should start diplomatic cooperation on all other fronts minus the border and the border talk should not affect the bilateral ties. In 1991, Chinese Premier Li Peng visited India and this was the time when Li Peng and Narsimha Rao developed an understanding to maintain some peace and tranquility at the LAC. This was the first times the Indian side began to display some positivity on the term called LAC, which till now they refused to accept. China accepted the growing pragmatism and this paved way in 1993 for Agreement on Maintenance of Peace and Tranquility at the LAC (signed when Narsimha Rao paved a visit to China in 1993). As per the agreement, the two sides decided to avoid military conflicts on the border by reducing troops and decided to establish a Military Expert Group (MEG) to determine differences over the LAC. At that time there was no attempt made to solve the border question but it was decided to maintain tranquility at the border. This was also in sync with what China as they too favoured tranquility and peace at the border and allow bilateral economic cooperation. It is important to note that the two sides in the 1993 Agreement agreed that LAC was unqualified and neither of the parties referred to the LAC of 1959 version or 1962 version.

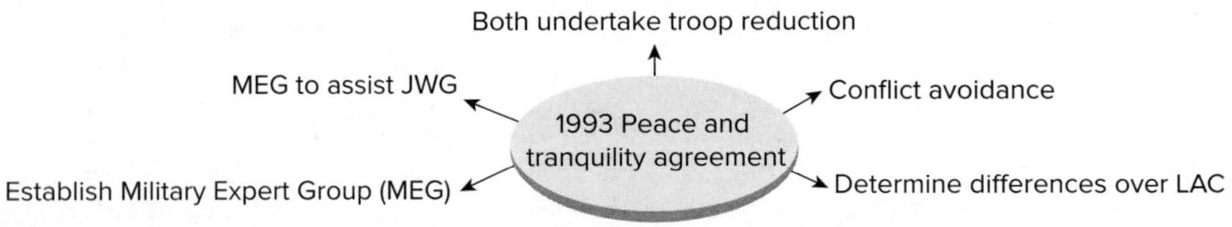

CONFIDENCE BUILDING MEASURE AGREEMENT 1996

Till 1993, China maintained two personnel for each one personnel from India. In 1993, as a part of Confidence Building Measure (CBM), China proposed one for one cutback where each will reduce equal numbers. But India said that geography favours China and on the side of India there is a difficult terrain, so the adjusted ratio formula was adopted under which both sides decided to maintain mutual and equal security and decided to cut troops mutually of equal numbers to equalise total troop presence on the border. Subsequently in 1996, India and China concluded a CBM Agreement and agreed for a no war in future, no fly zone at the LAC, ceiling of military exercises and minimum military at LAC. The 1996 CBM also talked about exchange of LAC maps to reduce potential conflicts.

The approach since 2002 shifted from earlier one package deal to mutual understanding and mutual accommodation. The architect of this approach was Chinese Premier Zhu Ronghji. The objective of Mutual accommodation approach meant a give and take solution to resolve border. In 2002, India and China exchanged maps for the Middle sector. They also 'shared' the maps for Western sector but never formally exchanged them. Till today, there is no publicly available map depicting the version of India's LAC.

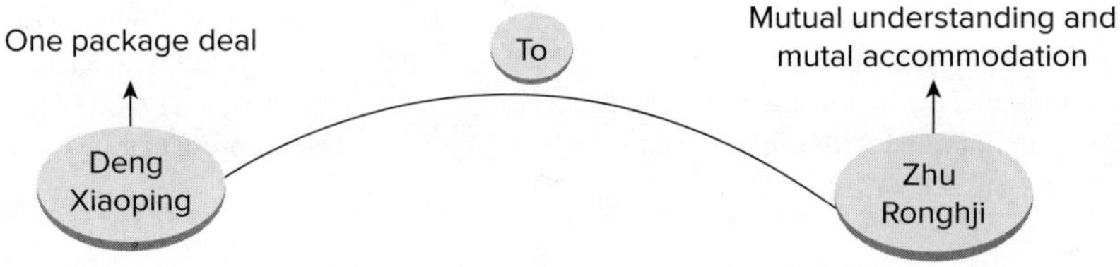

SPECIAL REPRESENTATIVE TALK MECHANISM

In 2003, Vajpayee initiated Special Representative Talk Mechanism (SRM) where higher political leadership is involved to resolve border issues on a sector-by-sector basis and announce an agreement only when all sectors are negotiated. The SRM aims to find a methodology to resolve border and device effective frameworks based on political parameters and guiding principles. In SRM, the negotiations were to be conducted by higher political representatives who would explore a framework solution. The focus was shifted to identifying common principles for resolving the border issues. The concept of the Special Representative Talk (SRT) was that both sides should not see the border issue through history alone but through the prism of political negotiations. The approach here was to first accept a territorial concession and then demarcate the border on the ground.

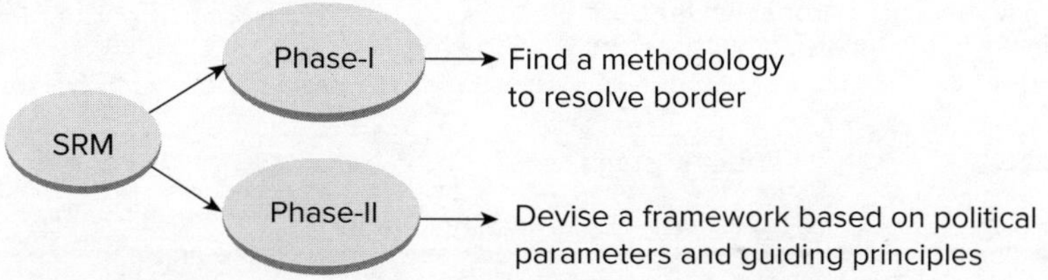

SIKKIM FACTOR IN INDIA–CHINA BOUNDARY QUESTION

Sikkim, as an issue, persisted till 2005. China always questioned the status of Sikkim and raised the issue of its merger with India. China maintained Sikkim could be resolved only as a part of package deal but soon realised that if it continues to hold the Sikkim rhetoric, India will open up the Tibetan issue. In 2005, during Wen Jiabao's visit to India, the Chinese presented a new map showing India with Sikkim as a part of India. In 2006, they opened Nathu La pass but incursions in Sikkim continued to be an issue till date. In 2005, the two sides also signed the Political Parameters and Guiding Principles for Settlement of the India and China Boundary Question. Under this agreement, the two decided to accept prominent geographical features to determine the basis of the border. This means that India asserted a principle that the border should be the Himalayan watershed was accepted. Secondly, there was an agreement that while solving the border, both parties will acknowledge the interests of the settled populations.

WORKING MECHANISM FOR CONSULTATION AND COORDINATION AND BDCA AGREEMENT

In 2012, India and China established a Working Mechanism for Consultation and Coordination on India–China Border Affairs. This mechanism is led by Joint Secretary level officers on both sides.

On 23rd October 2013, Manmohan Singh government concluded the Border Defence Cooperation Agreement (BDCA). The BDCA has brought an end to tailing by two sides. Now tell and tail signs (which were used by both parties till now in the Western sector to manage the border) were not used and this would enhance security of the border as absence of tell and tail signs would lead to avoidance of face-offs and reduction of tensions. The BDCA has initiated a concept of regular flag meetings of defence forces and regular meetings of defence ministers.

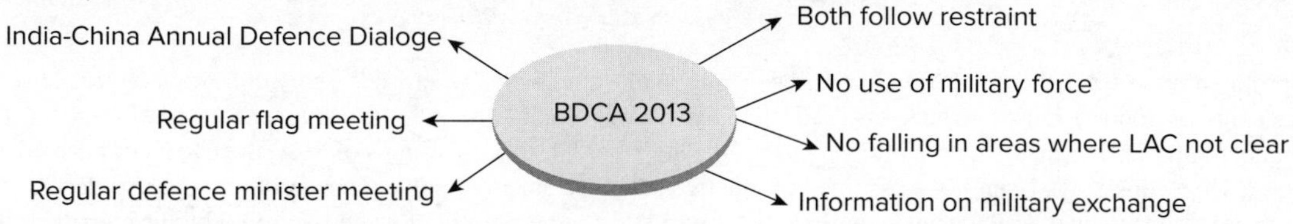

India–China border is divided into three sectors. The Middle sector or Central sector is relatively peaceful, unlike the Western and Eastern sectors. In Western sector, India alleges that China has occupied part of the Kashmir region and also an area gifted in 1963 by Pakistan to China, along with the Aksai Chin area of Ladakh, occupied as Xinjiang. In the Eastern sector, China insists that the 90,000 square kilometre Arunachal Pradesh is part of China and refuses to accept the McMahon line.

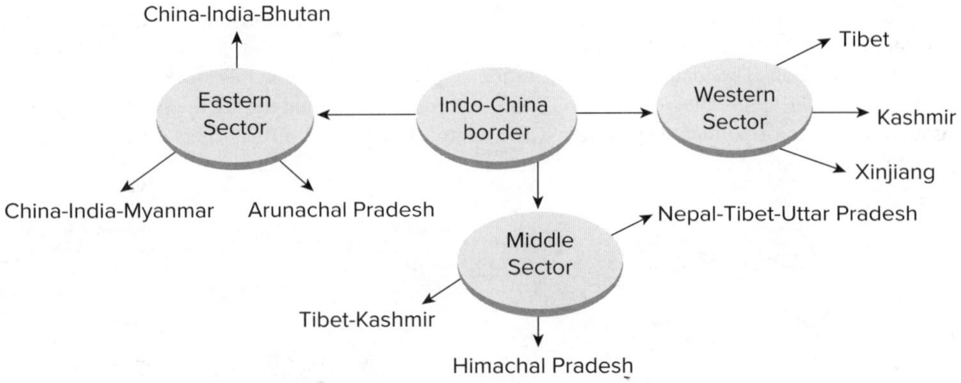

CHINESE NEGOTIATION ON BORDER QUESTION WITH INDIA

In 2015, Modi government tried to clarify maps for the LAC. The Chinese rejected the proposal and stated that they did try earlier to clarify the LAC, but that had let to difficulties, thus, they asserted that both sides should strive to maintain peace and tranquillity and not make things complicated. Thus, LAC till today remains a conceptual construct, which is neither demarcated on the map, nor on the ground and nor agreed mutually by both countries. Recently, Indian intelligence agencies have studied Chinese negotiational behaviour. The studies say that China can negotiate fast if it has a favourable solution in sight, but delays and advises patience in case it senses an unfavourable solution for itself. In case of Central Asia and Russia, China solved borders disputes quickly, while with India it knows that the border dispute has little or no possibility to be resolved in terms favourable to it. Consequently, there is a kind of freeze and the conspicuous lack of any sense of urgency. China claims Tawang saying it was a part of Mongul district and sixth Dalai Lama was born in Tawang. China has courted trouble in the Eastern sector by refusing IAS officers of Arunachal visa, saying residents of Arunachal need no visa to visit their own country. Even today China maintains the same policy. Thus, today, even under the Modi government, the border negotiations go on, and are carried out on the same framework.

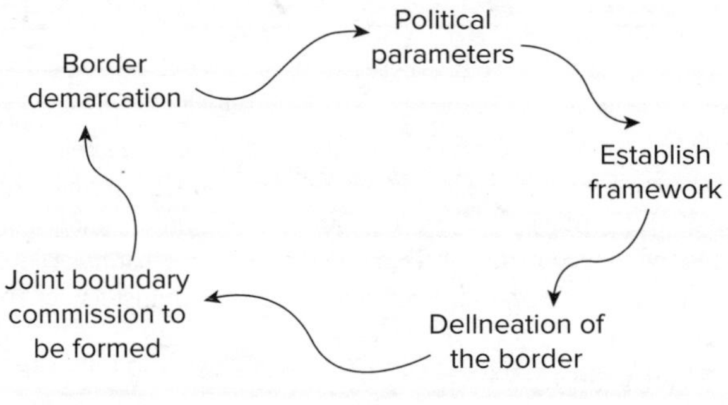

The problem however is that for China, the border issue is more of India–Tibet issue and China wants to make serious concessions in South Tibet or Arunachal Pradesh. This is unacceptable to India as Arunachal sends Members to the Parliament in India. The major source of contestation is thus Tibet. Despite 22 rounds of SRT, the two sides have not been able to reach a consensus. Even if we assume that the two sides are able to resolve their acrimony over border issue and minimise their tensions over Pakistan as an irritant, it will still not be possible for the two to end their overall conflict.

This is because the two are civilisational giants and both see each other as aspirational great powers. Such an aspiration is bound to create a space for the contest for China by India in Tibet, Xinjiang, Yunan, Hong Kong, Taiwan and Mongolia and by China for India in Kashmir, Punjab and North East. Despite the contest of power, China knows very well that it cannot antagonise India beyond a limit as doing so will compel India to develop proximity to the US, which is something China will never want. Thus, the two will remain strategic adversaries and still maintain confidence that they can cooperate.

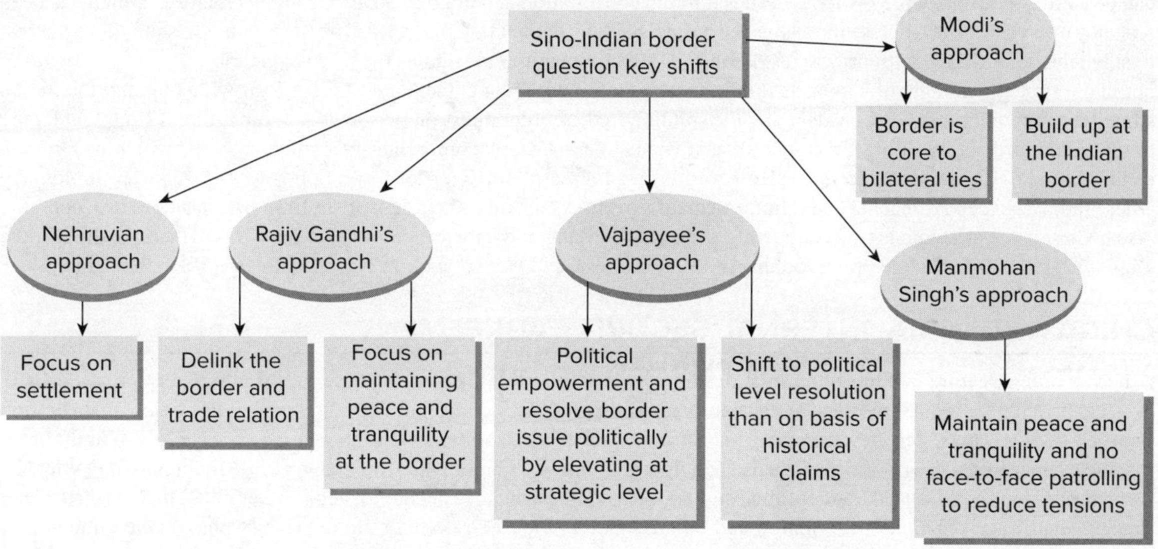

India and China do not have a strategic partnership yet but they have a tactical engagement. However, the tactical engagement is with depth and not a short-term foreign policy adjustment. It is important to note that today China follows the strategy of neutralisation with India. This means that China will try to inhibit India by pursuing a policy, which may be inimical to interests of China but will not accept any constraint on its own polices that, may undermine the security interests or sensitivities of India. This proves that the relationship is complex, which is not a threat to each other, but one that is best defined as a bivalent relationship. In this context, India needs a diplomatic strategy with China, which is a harmonious mixture of imaginative diplomacy, firmness, defence preparedness and a readiness to explore options that may allow India to benefit from technological and economic strength of Chinese.

DIPLOMATIC AND MILITARY MECHANISMS BETWEEN INDIA AND CHINA

China continues to believe in Mao's articulation of what they call as Five Fingers of the Tibetan Palm. This construct implies that Tibet and Xinjiang are the Chinese palm and they need to liberate the fingers of the palm, which were Ladakh, Nepal, Sikkim, Bhutan and Arunachal Pradesh.

The LAC often becomes a flashpoint between India and China. Both nations have a plethora of mechanisms that include

1. India and China Border CBM
2. India and China Border Personnel Meeting
3. India and China Meetings of the Working Mechanism for Consultation and Coordination on Border Affairs (WMCC)
4. India and China Strategic Guidance Route

To tackle various aspects of the boundary, the two sides have negotiated under the 22 rounds of SRT.

THE 22ND ROUND OF SPECIAL REPRESENTATIVE TALKS: AN ANALYSIS

The 22nd SRT happened in New Delhi in 2019. The discussions were constructive and forward looking where both sides decided to intensify the efforts to conclude a fair, reasonable and mutually acceptable solution to the LAC. In the 22nd meeting, India asserted that there is a need to view the boundary question from a strategic perspective. China asserted that a mutually acceptable solution could be a positive signal to the world that the two ancient and historic civilisations can peacefully coexist, while resolving issues through consultation and dialogue. Despite all this rhetoric, which has been repeated every time, the Chinese intransigence has delayed the delineation of the LAC on the ground. It is in India's interest to solve the border issue with priority as doing so leaves India with Pakistan as the sole adversaries, probably something not in the strategic thought of China, as it may disturb their own Asian game plan. There is a growing belief in the Indian strategic community that China is delaying the solution to the border question (as Deng Xiapoing said in 1988 that let the border issue be dealt by future generations), as it wants to enhance its comprehensive national power, which would then enable China to dictate terms to India. However, to be pragmatic, the long-term solution is to go for 'swap' diplomacy where India can keep Arunachal and relinquish claims over Aksai Chin. The pragmatism from Indian side is to accept that Aksai Chin is the strategic artery connecting China to Xinjiang and Tibet, the two most restive provinces of the Middle Kingdom. In 2020, both sides were looking at 'early harvest' and were discussing 'proposals' to resolve the matter.

CHINA AND INDIA: INTERNAL SECURITY AGREEMENT

A new evolving feature of Sino-India relationship was visible in the form of the two sides signing an Internal Security Agreement in 2018 (as an important de-escalatory measure post Doklam crisis). This agreement is a source of cooperation between the two states despite elements of constraints that range from Pakistan, abrogation of Article 370 and border dispute (Samar Lungpa, Trig Heights, Depsang bulge, Kongka La, Pangong Tso, Spanggur Gap, Mount Sajun, Dumchele, Demchok, Chumur in Eastern Ladakh; and Namka Chu, Sumdrong Chu, Yangste, Asaphilla, Long Ju, Dichu in Arunachal Pradesh; and Kaurik, Shipki La, Barahoti and Pulan Sunda in the Central sector are the twenty places where the border overlaps) and opposition of China to Indian membership of NSG. This new internal security agreement (which was being negotiated since 2015) is a continuation of the Wuhan spirit of 2018 (where there was a consensus to establish an umbrella agreement) and an unorthodox new diplomacy India has initiated (with patience ingrained as a diplomatic virtue) to seek behavioural change of China. The new agreement has identified four themes of cooperation. They include terrorism, narcotics and human trafficking, intelligence sharing and disaster management. Significance of the agreement signed is that it can yield results related to cross-border infiltration matters. It will establish a mechanism for forewarning in case of floods and help in better planning of disaster management. As terrorism is one of the components of the new agreement, it shows the rising awareness of China in tackling terrorism as a threat it may face to its ambitious Belt and Road Initiative.

DOLAM CRISIS 2017, CHINESE THREE WARFARE STRATEGIES AND SALAMI SLICING

The issue between India and China happened in the Dolam plateau (which is in Doklam area), which is different from the Doklam plateau (which is located 30 km to the North East of the Dolam plateau and is called Donglang by China). The Sino-Indian standoff happened in a tri-junction where borders of Sikkim, Bhutan and Tibet meet, which is disputed. The Sino-Indian boundary in Sikkim (not a part of India-China LAC), though settled, is not demarcated on a map. The disputed claims on the tri-junction are based on the individual interpretation of China and India on the basis of 1890 Calcutta Convention. The disputed tri-junction is claimed by India at a place called Batang La while China claims the tri-junction at 6.5 km to the South of Batang La at a place called Gymochen. In 2012, under the SRT mechanism, India and China decided to maintain status quo in this disputed area to their competing claims and resolve the dispute in consultation with Bhutan. A ridgeline runs from the Batang La in the North to Gymochen in the South where there is a pass known as the Doka La. One ridge line, 500 metres high, runs eastward from Batang La till Amo Chu river while the other runs eastwards from Gymochen to Amo Chu river and is called the Jampheri ridge. In the centre of the two ridges is 89 square kilometres bowl called Dolam plateau. Indian Army has a post in Doka La. The Batang La is the de-jure border while Doka La is the de-facto border. China has a motorable road called state highway S-204 that comes from Shigatse in Tibet to the northeast of the Nathu-La at a point called Yatung. From Yatung to Asam are unmettaled roads that come to Doka-La, which is a

20 km long Class-5 Track (capable of carrying a load vehicles like a jeep, etc.). At the end of 20 km point of the Class-5 Track in the Dolam plateau, near Doka La, is a turning point (barely few hundred metres away from an Indian Army post in Doka La) from where vehicles can reverse and traverse back.

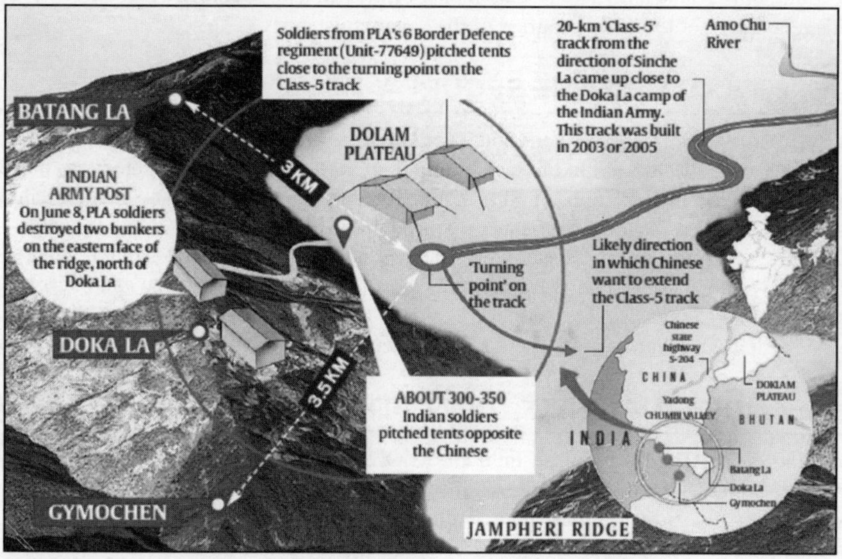

Picture Courtesy: Indian Express

THE CHINESE AND THEIR ROAD DILEMMAS

On 16th June 2017, a Chinese road construction party, consisting of some 100 men with earth moving equipment, came to the turning point and started surveys to extend the road towards Jampheri ridge. Seeing this, the Indian Army troops at the camp from Doka La came down in the Dolam Plateau near the turning point (in the territory of Bhutan) and formed a human chain, preventing the Chinese to make the road and the standoff began. Subsequently, the Indian and Chinese troops (PLA's 6 Border Defence Regiment Unit-77649) established tents in the area. India asserted that the creation of the road alters the status quo of 2012 (as established by the SRT) and if China created a road to Jampheri ridge, it would reduce the distance of China to access India's chicken's neck by 50 km. Doing so would not bring China in India's artillery range but it will affect India's offensive deployments in the area. As the standoff continued, China insisted that Indian troops withdraw from Dolam plateau (as it belonged to Bhutan and was not a territory in dispute with India) and go back to Doka La while India insisted on pre 16th June 2017 position (and decided to stay in the area to assist Bhutan as per Article 2 of India–Bhutan Friendship Treaty).

CHINESE THREE-WARFARE STRATEGY AT WORK

As the two sides got embroiled in an eyeball-to-eyeball confrontation, India began to build up troops along the LAC fearing that China could open up a new front elsewhere. At the same time China unleashed a psychological warfare with a strong verbal barrage driven with a motive to back off Indian troops unilaterally. This Chinese approach was very much in sync with Chinese Three Warfare Strategy (comprising media war, psychological war and legal war) developed by Chinese Central Military Commission in 2003 and reinforced in 2010. For India, the idea was not to back off (despite the fact that India for the first time was in the territory of a third nation—Bhutan, making this standoff different from the standoffs in Depsang in 2013 and Chumar in 2014, both of which happened on Indian territory) as doing so would have affected India's credibility in the neighborhood and ASEAN region where it is trying to position itself as a Net Security Provider. After a gap of 72 days, both sides diplomatically defused the crises by an agreement where both mutually decided to disengage the troops from the region and re-establish the status quo ante. Indian troops have retreated to Doka La but continue to occupy the vantage points on the top areas of the ridge while China has decided to halt the road construction activity but will continue to patrol the region. Both sides have moved out 'under verification' and China has agreed to 'make adjustments with the situation on the ground'. Xi Jinping demonstrated maturity while defusing the issue and succeeded in saving the BRICS Summit in Xiamen in 2017 (where Indian Prime Minister eventually met the Xi) while also succeeded in safeguarding his reputation for the 19th Congress of the Communist Party.

SALAMI SLICING AND CHINESE SECURITY POLICY

An analysis of the Dolam standoff proves that China again resorted to Salami Slicing (a term coined by Hungarian Communist Matyaas Rakosi in 1940s and in military terminology known as cabbage strategy) to make territorial grabs in the Himalayas (similar to its previous grabs of Aksai Chin, Tibet and Paracel Islands). Salami Slicing means a strategy of carrying out small actions in a clandestine manner that eventually accumulate into a larger action. China, to execute Salami Slicing, initiates territorial claims by staking claims to a territory. Then, carries out an intensive propaganda of all three types (in sync with Chinese Three Warfare Strategy) at all platforms (domestic and international) to claim the territory. The propaganda by China is so intense that it positions the territory in concern as a 'dispute'. Then China uses all its diplomatic and military might to resolve the dispute by avoiding a forceful intervention.

CHINESE 'DO-AND-BE DAMNED', 'DON'T-DO-AND-BE DAMNED' QUANDARY

Xi Jinping masterminded the standoff to punish India for its OBOR Lèse-majesté by weaning Bhutan away from India but eventually ended up in a situation of 'do-and-be damned, don't-do-and-be damned' quandary. Though the Sino-Indian standoff is resolved (however the border infrastructure built by Chinese was not removed or dismantled), positioning India as a mature and responsible status-quo power, India created a template for other countries to check China. The Dolam standoff presented to the world, the new border doctrine of India of "proactive diplomacy with firm ground positioning".

India needs to strengthen its critical border infrastructure, demarcate maps on settled sectors of the border and resolve pending border disputes with China to avoid future standoffs of this nature ahead. India needs to undertake some countermeasures at Siliguri corridor. As the corridor is just 22 km in width at its narrowest point, India should firstly enter into a treaty with Bangladesh to secure transit of military equipment during military times. This is possible by first negotiating a civilian traffic and trade activities to start with. Doing so would add a layer of strategic depth in the region and alleviate severance concerns in the Northeast. The next step is to strengthen the Doka La tri-junction by creating a blacktop road that will reduce the travel time to reach the area in future. Thirdly, India should construct underground tunnels, which allow multi-modal transit at the Siliguri corridor. Underground tunnelling is going to be costly but will give the military more room to take hard military options. During peacetime, the same can be used for trade and tourism to the Northeast.

LADAKH STANDOFF-2020: A RIDDLE WRAPPED IN A MYSTERY

We need to understand four concepts of geography to understand the Ladakh standoff better.

First is the concept of a ridge. In a simple language, when there is a continuous elevated terrain with sloping sides, we call it a ridge. So imagine the ridge as a long but narrow continuous top of a mountain, where the sides of the mountain tend to slope away from the narrow top on either side.

The second concept is of mountainous spurs. A mountainous spur is a long but a gentle sloping tongue of ground. This spur runs down from a hill to the lower ground and provide access to and from the ground to the hill for the walkers.

The third concept is of a valley. A valley is a depression of land that is scoured and washed out by a combination of forces of gravity, water and snow.

The fourth concept is related to Pangong Lake. The Pangong Lake is also called Pangong Tso. It is an endorheic lake. This means that the water of the lake remains in the basin area. It has no outflow and the water either seeps in the ground of the lake or it evaporates. The water in the lake comes from the glaciers in the nearby mountain melt and keep feeding the Pangong Lake. The Pangong Lake is a salt-water lake and it gets water from the melting of the glaciers, meaning it is fresh water. Since the lake has no outflow, the water gradually turns saline. The water of the lake is not fully saline, but brackish in nature (not as salty as sea water but saltier than the fresh water).

S. JAISHANKAR'S ACTION–REACTION THEORY

Since the Chinese Revolution of 1949, the leaders of China articulated their vision for their country, which rested upon making China an ambitious superpower with nuclear arsenal. This ambitious vision, realistic in scope, saw no Asian rival. Thus, neutralising India became a policy priority for Chinese, for which a partnership with Pakistan was built in 1963. Since then, Pakistan has played a valuable role in the strategic calculus of China by sustaining a 'hot' war on its borders with India and keeping the option of a two front war open. In Chinese Grand Strategy, an undefined LAC is a core instrument to embarrass India and keep India off the balance by repeatedly created transgressions on the border because it allows China to define the LAC as per their own interests. The Chinese land grabs are pre-mediated and blunt messages of dominance and a political pressure point for India. It is in this backdrop that we need to note that it is time for India to respond to Chinese by not being tied down in a defensive mode.

After the Dolam crisis in 2017, the matter related to India and China was raised in the Standing Committee on External Affairs (chaired by Shashi Tharoor) in the 16th Lok Sabha. The committee asserted that there is always a need to have healthy scepticism in dealing with China because of the 'deliberate encirclement policy of India' by China. Appearing before the Committee at that time was the then Foreign Secretary and now Foreign Minister S. Jaishankar. He asserted that India and China have a lot of transgressions and one of the most contested areas in the Western sector is the Pangong Lake. He stated that the lake is a contested region because the lake is too big (135 km) and both sides have a different perception as to where does the LAC pass in the lake. This is when S. Jaishankar informed the committee that India and China are likely to have a relationship based on 'action–reaction' as India builds border infrastructure at the LAC.

THE HEART OF THE LADAKH ISSUE

India's border in Ladakh is 857 square kilometres and the International Boundary is 368 square kilometres while the LAC is 489 square kilometres. The two have differing perceptions at LAC at Samar Lungpa, Depsang Plains, Hot Springs, Changlung, Kungkala–Phobrang, Sarjap, Spanguur and Dhumtsele.

Picture Courtesy: Indian Express

In the month of May 2020, the Chinese increased their number of troops at the LAC at many specific locations. The first is Patrol Point 14 in Galwan, Patrol Points 15 and 17 in Gogra at Ladakh, Naku La in Sikkim, Hot Springs and Finger-4 in Pangong Lake, Ladakh. There seems to be an enlargement of dispute by the Chinese because they entered the Indian territory of Galwan and Naku La for the first time in 2020.

CHINESE GOLD RUSH IN LADAKH

In 2020, the Chinese built a blacktopped road near the Indian post of Gogra in Ladakh. It is believed that this road near the Indian post would provide China with valuable access to gold because the mountain ranges at Gogra have this valuable mineral in abundance and Gogra is often called as 'Gold Mountain' amongst the Ladakhi people. This road would also enable the Chinese to mobilise men and material resources quickly.

THE CONFLICTUAL GEOGRAPHY OF PANGONG TSO

The situation began in May 2020 when China began to build structures from Finger-4 to Finger-8 along the Pangong Lake.

Pangong Lake is a huge lake at an altitude of 13,900 feet in Ladakh Union Territory of India. Two-thirds of the lake is under the control of the Chinese and the Chinese control extends from Tibet to India. On the northern bank of the lake is Sirijap Range from where several cliffs come out and are called "Finger series". The area adjoining the lake has mountainous spurs. These protrusions or mountainous spurs in security terminology are called 'fingers' by both sides. India and China have eight fingers or spurs all along the lake. These fingers allow the troops to create fortifications and bunkers for patrolling. India and China have a different perspective of LAC because the LAC is not demarcated on any map and has also become a source of friction between both sides in the recent times. As per India, when it comes to the Pangong Lake, the LAC runs North to South and Indian perception of the LAC is that it runs till Finger-8 and is at the South of Finger-8 (though Indian actual control is till Finger-4 only, but India has been patrolling up to Finger-8 for decades). However, the Chinese claim that the LAC (as per their perception), runs in between Finger-2 and Finger-3. India has a physical presence in the region till Finger-4 and also has one ITBP post between Finger-3 and Finger-4. However, for many decades, India has been patrolling from West to East. This means, historically, India has been patrolling from Finger-1 to Finger-8 (till the point where it perceives the LAC located between Finger-7 and Finger-8). The Chinese on the other hand claim that the LAC lies between Finger-2 and Finger-3 and they assert that India's legal claims are only at a place till Finger-4 and the rest, from Finger-4 to Finger-8 and beyond is an area belonging to the Chinese.

Picture Courtesy: Indian Express

Though the problem erupted now, it can be traced back to 1999. When India was undertaking operations against Pakistan for their intrusion in Kargil, the Chinese took advantage of Indian forces diverted to Kargil and began to build up a 4.5-km dirt track (imagine this like a rudimentary jogging track around a park we see in urban areas or what is called in rural areas as a "pakdandi") till Huangyangtan Base near National Highway G-219. This dirt track of the Chinese began from their rear bases from their side of the LAC and reached up to Finger-4 area (an area claimed by India) and crossed till Finger-8 and subsequently reached East at places called Sirijap-1 and Sirijap-2 (both areas on the Chinese side of the LAC and located on the rear sides of Finger-8). The Research and Analysis Wing (RAW) had pointed out the construction of the dirt track to the then Vajpayee Government, but the government chose to maintain a convenient blind eye. This lack of response by the Vajpayee government gave impetus to China and slowly over time, they blacktopped the dirt track and made it a permanent road. After the road became permanent, the PLA began to patrol the area from Sirijap to Finger-8 and from Finger-8 till Finger-2. However, the PLA used to only patrol the area with their vehicles but they never physically occupied the area despite their claims up to Finger-2. The problem is that now, the Chinese have built a series of defences all along from Finger-4 to Finger-8 and have also occupied their successive regional heights. This is what India called as the *change in status quo* in the disputed area. The Chinese are firm that the LAC is at Finger-4, which is around 8 km to the West of the LAC at Finger-8, which has always been patrolled by India. This means that the Chinese have been camping 8 km inside the Indian Territory. These defences led to a troop confrontation between Indian and Chinese on 5th and 6th May 2020. Since 6th May 2020, the Chinese have blocked all Indian patrols from Finger-4 to Finger-8 region. The Chinese have also been resorting to use of high-speed motorboats to deter India to patrol the region and denied patrolling to India in 50 square kilometres area which they have claimed.

THE STRATEGIC INTERESTS OF CHINA IN PANGONG TSO

We have to note that the dominance of China in the Pangong Tso is not just a territorial dominance but dominance of a resource-rich lake. Chinese design suggests that they aim to snatch the Pangong Lake through a three-step design by snatching the lake from Sirijap in the North, Chuchul in the South and Pangong Lake in the middle. Doing so will enable Chinese to cutoff India from Chip Chap Plains, Aksai Chin (in the east side) and Shyok valley to North. This will lead to India be pushed South of Indus and West of Shyok and will allow Chinese to push India to accept Shyok and Indus as natural boundaries, thereby allowing China to get access to Siachen (because of south side of Karakoram in their control) from Depsang corridor till Tashkurgan junction, from where the CPEC crosses the Gilgit Baltistan region. This will make the Nubra valley and Indian presence at Siachen vulnerable and the Chinese access to Changala Pass via Lukung and Tangste would threaten the region of Indus valley. By doing this, Chinese can divert the waters of Shyok, Galwan and Chang Chemo Rivers to Aksai Chin and Ali regions successfully in the future.

THE GALWAN VALLEY GRAND RIVALRY

During the colonial times, the British and the Chinese were very busy in a Great Game which unfolded not only in Afghanistan and Central Asia, but also from Leh to Karakoram Pass into Xinjiang. Today, the two aspirational powers of India and China happen to play the tail of the rivalry at strategic pivot all along their disputed mountainous boundaries.

The Galwan River was named after a Ladakhi explorer, Ghulam Rasool Galwan, who had assisted the British in various missions, including the ones led by Younghusband in 1890 and 1896. In 1892, Rasool once helped the British explorers who had lost their way during an expedition. Rasool paved path for the lost British explorers from a new way called Galwan Nala and brought them safely to Leh. After knowing this, the British government, in a reward, named the Nala (the valley) as Galwan valley.

Galwan River originates in Aksai Chin, on the Chinese side of the LAC and flows from east into India (in Ladakh) to meet Shyok River at the Indian side of the LAC. Galwan valley is located strategically between Ladakh on the west side and Aksai Chin on the east side and controlled by China. However, on the west of the Galwan valley are DSDBO road and Shyok River and on its east is Chinese National Highway G-219. The location of the LAC at Galwan valley is in the east of confluence of Galwan and Shyok rivers. It is up to the point of confluence where both parties have patrolled.

In 1962, under the Nehruvian 'Forward Policy', India built a post at Galwan Valley on 4th July 1962 and deployed 5 Jat regiment at Galwan. This post became a point of contention because this Indian post threatened communication of China in Samzungling in the Eastern side of Karakoram. This is why, on 10th July 1962, as part of Chinese policy of 'armed coexistence', the Chinese deployed a battalion 100 metres to the Indian post at Galwan. The Chinese began to identify a few 'strongholds' (or areas that had the potential to threaten the Chinese communications) and the 5 Jat regiment was in occupation of one of the strongholds. India, in 1962, took up the matter with Chinese envoy and asserted that any aggression at Galwan will be treated as an act of aggression. On 19th October 1962, the Galwan post was one of the first to be attacked by the Chinese (as it was a 'stronghold' under 5 Jat Regiment) and the Chinese lost 10 soldiers in the scuffle while they inflicted a damage of 120 on the Indian side. Within 24 hours after the 19th October 1962 incident, India decided to remove seven stronghold areas and this enabled the Chinese to secure communication to three key posts of China at Galwan. Since 1962, Chinese maps have claimed Galwan valley, but the maps shown by Zhou in 1956 had shown the correct alignment where Galwan valley was shown as a part of India.

THE DARBHUK-SHYOK-DAULET BEG OLDI (DS-DBO) ROAD FLASHPOINT

Earlier, India had an old road that connected Daulat Beg Oldi (an Indian post in Aksai Chin) to Ladakh via 17,500 feet high Sasser Pass, and this road was a part of Ancient Silk Road that connected Leh to Yarkand, but for most of the year, this road remained under snow. As an alternative to this Sasser Pass road, the Border Roads Organisation, decided to work upon two projects. The first was a "glaciated road" from Nubra Valley to Sasser Pass leading to Daulat Beg Oldi and the second is the DSDBO road.

India has been working on the Darbhuk–Shyok–Daulet Beg Oldi road for last fifteen years. This road was conceptualised after the Kargil conflict with Pakistan in 1999. India has a presence in the Daulat Beg Oldi (DBO) region, which is just 10 km west from the LAC at Aksai Chin, where India has a military post after Chinese occupied Aksai Chin in 1962. The DBO is a strategic area also because on its west is the Gilgit–Baltistan Area, from where the China–Pakistan Economic Corridor (CPEC) passes. Till now, the only way to reach out to DBO was through air support and use of CJ 130 aircrafts at the DBO airstrip. The DS-DBO road is a 255 km long road that connects Leh to Karakoram pass. The road was finally constructed in 2019 and is critical lifeline to the Sub-Sector North (SSN) of the Indian army. This road enables India to supply its troops with logistical support, which in its absence was dependent by air as stated above. This road also enables the logistical support with ease to be supplied to the troops deployed at Siachen Glacier. The DSDBO road provides the Indian Army an access to a small section of Tibet–Xinjiang Highway that passes via Aksai Chin (as the road runs parallel to the LAC at Aksai China). The DSDBO is an all-weather road because it also has 37 prefabricated military truss bridges.

Along with the road, in 2019, India also constructed a 430 meters bridge (called Colonel Chewang Rinchen Bridge, named after a local Ladakhi military hero) on the Shyok River (Shyok, that flows in northern Ladakh and Gilgit–Baltistan, itself is a tributary of Indus, and is also called river of Death by locals with tributaries that include Chip Chap, Galwan River, Chang Chenmo) at an altitude of 15,000 feet in the Galwan area (sandwiched between the Chang Chemo range and Karakoram range) to facilitate troop movement and assist local population. The construction of the bridge and DSDBO road compelled the Chinese to build 80 tents and temporary defence positions for faster reinforcements at the Galwan River. The PLA also has resorted to deliberately outnumber Indian troops whenever a face-off occurs.

The Chinese are upset with the DSDBO (Darbhuk–Shyok–Daulet Beg Oldi) road and the Galwan area bridge because they want to dominate this zone of LAC as they believe that any such infrastructure by India along the LAC can improve their access and patrolling at Aksai Chin, something that is perceived detrimental by China. So, the Chinese here have no difference of perception with respect to the LAC. This is so because the DSDBO road is 8 km within Indian Territory. For Chinese, their National Highway G-219 passes through the Aksai Chin and is the core link for Xinjiang and Tibet. The issue is that the Chinese want to maintain a military dominance and retain a tactical advantage against India, which they tend to lose, if the DSDBO is used by India. It is surprising that Chinese want to make Galwan a political fight by laying claim to a territory they never owned and whose claim was articulated by a military officer of China in 2020.

Picture Courtesy: Indian Express

THE MOONLIGHT MASSACRE AND IMPLICATIONS ON BILATERAL RELATIONS

The Indian satellite images in June 2020 had shown that the Chinese had deployed a Brigade-sized force at Galwan and this ipso facto points out to their intent of staying on long. Since June it was seen that the Chinese PLA had crossed into the Indian side and were putting up in tents on the Indian side. This led to initiation of a disengagement process. On 6th June 2020, as part of the ongoing disengagement process, it was decided in a meeting of Corps Commanders that there will be a mutually agreed disengagement process and a buffer zone would be created between the LAC and at the junction of Shyok and Galwan Rivers (which the Chinese call the Y-Nala). Such a buffer zone would prevent future face-offs and the armies were to move back by kilometre as a first step of the disengagement process. On 15th June 2020, Colonel Santosh Babu of Bihar Battalion saw that there was still one tent left in the area. Being a Corps Commander, he decided to get the tent removed and during this time, a scuffle broke out, which led to severe casualties, in the moonlight. The Chinese General Zhao Zongqi, the commander of WTC, had approved the assault that took place. After the moonlight massacre, the Commander of PLA Colonel Zhang Shuli of Western Theatre Command of PLA, raised many red flags in India when on 15th June 2020, he asserted that China owns sovereignty over Galwan Valley region. Since then, China has staked a claim to the entire Galwan valley.

2020 GALWAN VALLEY INCIDENT

The soldiers, at the site on 15th June 2020, were carrying personal weapons but they did not use them because of a long-standing practice, governed by 1996 and 2005 agreements, of not using arms during a face-off or standoff.

Article VI (1) of the 1996 Agreement on Confidence-Building Measures in the Military Field Along the LAC in the India–China Border Areas says,

With a view to preventing dangerous military activities along the line of actual control in the India–China border area. Neither side shall open fire, cause biodegradation, use hazardous chemicals, conduct blast operations or hunt with guns or explosives within two kilometres from the line of actual control. This prohibition shall not apply to routine firing activities in small arms firing ranges.

However, Article VI(4), more applicable in the current instance of moonlight massacre, says, *If the border personnel of the two sides come in a face-to-face situation due to differences on the alignment of the line of actual control of any other reason, they shall exercise self-restraint and take all necessary steps to avoid an escalation of the situation. Both sides shall also enter into immediate consultations through diplomatic and/or other available channels to review the situation and prevent any escalation of tension.* But the 1996 agreement comes with a provision in Article X(1) which says that *the full implementation of some of the provisions of the present Agreement will depend on the two sides arriving at a common understanding of the alignment of the line of actual control in the India–China border areas, the two sides agree to speed up the process clarification and confirmation of the line of actual control.* Article 1 of the 2005 agreement, *the two sides will resolve the boundary question through peaceful and friendly consultations. Neither side shall use or threaten to use force against the other by any means.* The 2013 Border Defence Cooperation Agreement categorically stated that neither side shall use its military capability against the other.

THE DISREGARD AT NAKU LA BY CHINESE

The Chinese skirmish and standoff at Naku La in May 2020 is a blatant disregard of Chinese commitments at Naku La. The Chinese in their designs at Naku La have violated the Sikkim–Tibet Convention of 1890. According to the Convention, the boundary in the area is based on the watershed principles. Its Article 1 states, *The boundary of Sikkim and Tibet shall be the crest of the mountain range separating the waters flowing into the Sikkim Teesta and its effluents from waters flowing into the Tibetan Mochu and northwards into other rivers of Tibet follows the above mentioned water-parting to the point where it meets Nipal Territory.* The Gazetteer of Sikkim in 1894, describes the physical features of Sikkim, and mentions the boundary that runs along Naku La–Chorten Nyima La and there is no ambiguity with respect to the location of the pass because the geographic realities cannot be altered.

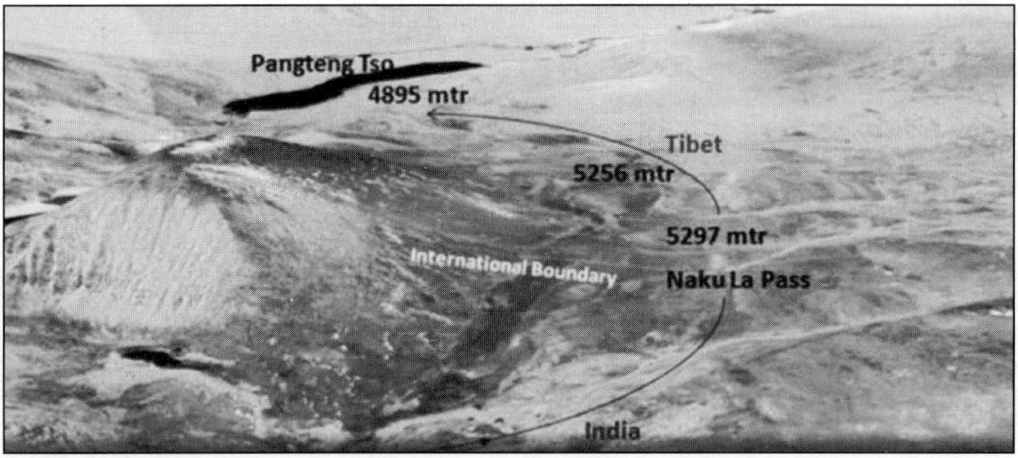

Picture Courtesy: Indian Express

DIFFERENCE BETWEEN TERRITORIAL CLAIMS AND LAC CLAIMS

It is at this juncture, we need to note, that territorial claims and LAC claims are two different things and regardless of the Chinese claims on Galwan, the reality is that both parties till now have agreed that LAC of both the countries ran through the Galwan valley. Sometimes, the distinction between LAC claims and territorial claims often gets blurred. The difference here lays in the fact that LAC claims means those areas that are effectively under the control of each side but not the territorial claim. Let us explain this. It means that even though the territorial claim of India lays 38,000 square kilometres across the LAC over entire Aksai Chin, but the LAC claims run through the Galwan Valley only. So, by claiming the Galwan Valley, China is trying to alter the LAC unilaterally which India calls as "exaggerated and untenable".

According to the 1993 Border Peace and Tranquility Agreement (BPTA), India and China agreed to *strictly respect and observe the LAC between the two sides.* This referred to the LAC at the time, rendering irrelevant the LAC of 1959 or 1962. The 1993 Border Peace and Tranquility Agreement say, *when necessary, the two sides shall jointly check and determine the segments of the line of actual control where they have different views as to its alignment.* Clarifying, the LAC has also been explicitly codified in the 1996 Agreement on Confidence-Building Measures and subsequent agreements. China, however, has refused to exchange maps in the Western sector to take this process forward. The BPTA also said, *the two sides agree that references to the line of actual control in this agreement do not prejudice their respective positions on the boundary question.*

THE TEMPLATE OF TWO-FRONT WAR

While India and China were involved in a standoff in Ladakh in 2020, the Chinese began to collaborate with the Pakistanis to pressurise India. Indian intelligence agencies informed the Indian government that Chinese compelled Pakistan to deploy 20,000 soldiers in the Gilgit–Baltistan region. These Pakistani troops had been deployed at the Line of Control with India with the sole objective to divert the attention of India on the Western front. According to the Indian intelligence agency assets, the Chinese also engaged in several meetings with a terrorist group called Al-Badr. The ISI of Pakistan created the Al-Badr in 1998. The ISI decided to use Al Badr independent of Hizbul Mujahedeen in the Kashmir valley. Along with Lashkar-e-Toiba, the Al Badr is the only group of the ISI that practices suicide terrorism. The Indian intelligence agency assets informed the Indian government that the Chinese in 2020 established links with Al Badr. There is a possibility that the Chinese could, in future, fund the Al Badr to resort to suicide terrorism in the Kashmir valley. The larger tactic of the Chinese in the Ladakh standoff has become clear. They want to pressurise India though alternative fronts. A military front with Pakistan and a diplomatic front with Nepal (explained in India and Nepal chapter) were used by China in 2020.

INDIA'S NEW NON-LINEAR OPTIONS

After the moonlight massacre, the government proposed the creation of Emergency Procurement Procedure. Under this project, the three armed forces can add additional firepower to their arsenal, in consultation with Department of Military Affairs, by purchasing any new weapon up to 500 crores for each project under the procedure. After the Galwan valley incident, the government has deployed 3-Infantry Division based at Leh (with 10,000 to 12,000 soldiers in each division) to the operational alert areas while also activating air force bases all across the LAC. The government has also stated that the forces on the ground are given liberty to act, "in an extraordinary situation". India has to articulate more non-linear options. Chinese always favour bilateralism and they do so because the stronger party always benefits. India need not to play with Chinese tactics anymore and remain stuck with bilateralism. As a possible non-linear option, India should strive to stand up and support Japan, Vietnam and Taiwan, whenever they are bullied by Chinese expansionism.

INDIAN DEMANDS OF RESTORATION OF STATUS QUO ANTE

Since the standoff has begun, India has resorted to a four-pronged strategy in discussion.

Firstly, India has insisted upon the *restoration of status quo ante* of the position that existed in April 2020 (and not status quo, because acceptance of status quo would mean accepting Chinese occupation of the territory).

Secondly, India has asked for mutual de-induction of troops at Pangong, Gogra, Hot springs and Galwan region. This means, India wants a withdrawal of all troops and artillery equipment (including tanks and guns), armoured vehicles, artillery units and infantry combat vehicles on Chinese side (which shall also be reciprocated by India) as a CBM.

Thirdly, India has advocated that Chinese should not obstruct the Indian road-building infrastructure at the LAC. This is so because India is carrying out all activities within their side of the boundary, over which it has a legal right.

Fourthly, Chinese have to restore the trust deficit by advocating restraint and advising their troops to observe the laid down protocols during face-to-face patrols.

CHINESE STRATEGY OF WINNING WITHOUT FIGHTING

As the two sides got embroiled in an eyeball-to-eyeball confrontation, India has built up troops along the LAC fearing that China could open up a new front elsewhere. At the same time China unleashed a psychological warfare with a strong verbal barrage driven with a motive to back off Indian troops unilaterally. This Chinese approach was very much in sync with Chinese Three Warfare Strategy (comprising Media war, Psychological war and Legal war) developed by Chinese Central Military Commission in 2003 and reinforced in 2010. The basic principle of Chinese psychological war is clear that if it wants India to not take a decision that might be contrary to the interests of China, then it will do so by raising the risk of a kinetic conflict. Chinese government's media house Global Times has launched an all-out media war by asserting that by deploying troops at Galwan Valley, "India has harmed military relations between two countries" and they have accused Indian side of "purposefully instigating conflicts". The Global Times has stated that the "Chinese troops have tightened control in Galwan Valley after India trespasses Chinese territory and has built defensive fortifications and obstacles to unilaterally change the current border fortifications".

MOONLIGHT MASSACRE—AN INTELLIGENCE FAILURE OF RAW AND CHIEF OF DEFENCE STAFF

Though the government may not display acceptance to the fact that the intelligence community miserably failed in providing adequate inputs for action, but it has come to fore that Defence Intelligence Agency, Research and Analysis Wing, National Technical Research Organisation and Special Frontier Force, all collectively failed in giving adequate inputs to the armed forces on the ground about PLA troop movement. In May 2020, more than 5000 Chinese PLA troops had carried out an exercise in hinterland of China and these troops were instantly mobilised by the Western Theatre Command (WTC) of Chinese army (that looks after India) to Tibetan Theatre Command. These troops, some 5000 of them, were unaware of the laid down protocols between India and China for border affairs. Their lack of knowledge of restraint was visible in the 15th June 2020 Galwan Valley clash. This certainly proves that these 5000 plus troops of the PLA were not regular WTC troops and probably belonged to some other command. Some deep assets of RAW in China now confirm that there is a possibility that PLA wanted to acquaint the 'new' troops into mountain warfare and this Galwan valley incident, which went out of control, was an exposure incident. The bigger question is that why did RAW fail to provide this input about 5000 troops coming from hinterland to the Western sector to the army? The officials of the RAW have countered the allegations by asserting that they did provide detailed human and technical intelligence to the army since February 2020 about troop built up by the PLA. If this is so and if the army was provided with adequate intelligence, then does the Galwan Valley incident prove that it is the first biggest failure of the Chief of Defence Staff (CDS)? The question is that if the Research and Analysis Wing provided Defence Intelligence Agency with inputs, then why was Bihar Battalion not replaced with infantry division from Leh? As always, since Kargil, why was there no synchronisation between armed forces and intelligence? Does the buck stop at the Chief of Defence Staff for the killing of 20 Indian troops? Instead of trying to blame the opposition as "Chinese agents" and using the media with 'BJP affiliated retired army officials and diplomats' to cover up yet again a massive failure (with others being Uri, Pulwama and Pathankot), the government ought to answer these grave charges of absolute failure of national security. India needs to pay heed to the advice of Sun Tzu, *If you know neither the enemy nor yourself, you will succumb in every battle. If you know yourself but not the enemy, for every victory gained you will also suffer a defeat. If you know the enemy and know yourself, you need not fear the result of a hundred battles.*

SALAMI SLICING AND CHINESE SECURITY POLICY

An analysis of the Ladakh standoff proves that China again resorted to Salami Slicing (a term coined by Hungarian Communist Matyaas Rakosi in 1940s and in military terminology known as cabbage strategy) to make territorial grabs in the Himalayas (similar to its previous grabs of Aksai Chin, Tibet and Paracel Islands in South China Sea). Salami Slicing means a strategy of carrying out small actions in a clandestine manner that eventually accumulate into a larger action. China, to execute Salami Slicing, initiates territorial claims by staking claims to a territory. Then, carries out an intensive propaganda of all three types (in sync with Chinese Three Warfare Strategy explained previously) at all platforms (domestic and international media) to claim the territory. The propaganda by China is so intense that it positions the territory in concern as a 'dispute'. Then China uses all its diplomatic and military might to resolve the dispute by avoiding a forceful intervention. This is the larger approach of what is known as "two steps forward and one step backward".

CLAMOUR FOR 'BOYCOTT CHINA' (FROM HINDI–CHINA BHAI–BHAI TO HINDI–CHINI BUY–BUY TO HINDI–CHINI BYE–BYE!)

China and India have a 77.9 BND bilateral trade and the Chinese are our second largest trading partners after the US as the first (at 83 BND). China constitutes 10.6% of our total trade (with 235 Chinese firms in India since 2003 with majority in the telecom business) but India accounts for a fraction of trade at 2.1% only. After the Galwan valley incident, a clamor to boycott Chinese goods gained momentum. Such a clamour is good for optics (to please the domestic BJP political constituents), but the harsh reality is that such a slogan, if executed, will be disastrous for India in the long run due to various reasons. Firstly, India has a very limited export to China and such a slogan will not impact China much, but harm India more as we have no substitutes. Secondly, India is dependent upon the Chinese, for a wide array of imports that range from construction equipment to electronics to fertilisers and 'Made in China' often helps in 'Make in India' too. The implications of such a clamour, on the other hand, would be serious for India and would play at multiple levels. Thirdly, if India uses the tariff and non-tariff barrier route to reduce Chinese imports, then it will not only lead to higher price of goods for the Indian consumers (who are already suffering due to income erosion caused by job losses due to COVID-19) but will also affect our domestic manufacturing competitiveness (as we import capital goods and intermediate products also from China). Fourthly, it will be very difficult for the government to entangle the Chinese investments that have entered India's start-up space that ranges from Byju's to PayTM to Ola to Zomato etc. Thus, it is imperative for the government to understand that any policy architecture at the economic level with respect to Chinese should not be driven by knee-jerk reactions but by careful cost–benefit analysis. Also, the growing clamour for banning imports could have attracted the fire of WTO and India has done well to not resort to such a tactic. This Galwan standoff should also act as an eye opener for the government to scrutinise the bottlenecks that prevent the domestic players to undertake manufacturing. The government should push for legislations that will address such bottlenecks and strive to increase India's share in global trade as a long-term proposition.

In our discussion here, one thing is certain that a blanket ban on the Chinese imports is not feasible. However, can the tone set by Atmanirbhar Bharat and Make in India campaign lead to a mass movement where the masses individually resort to boycott any good having a Chinese component? In India, despite pesticides in Coke and neural disruptors in Maggi, mass movements have failed. Also, boycotting the Chinese goods in the age of globalisation will lead to China routing their goods from Hong Kong, Taiwan and Vietnam. In this case also, it will become difficult to trace the origin as the economies are too deeply coupled.

As India itself aspires to be a part of the global value chains, where the Chinese are already strong, banning imports from China can hurt India more than China. China will be happier to see a weak Indian economy as such a policy suits the Chinese grand strategy. Thus, India rightly resorted to the non-military option.

INDIA'S DIGITAL STRIKE AGAINST CHINESE

Queen Victoria rightly said, "The important thing is not what they think of me, but what I think of them." Even though the clamour for a military retaliation against the Chinese grew after the Galwan valley moonlight massacre, India decided to resort to a cool head, non-military digital strike and on grounds of privacy and security, banned 59 Chinese apps in India ranging from ByteDance Tik Tok, UC Browser and Club Factory etc. (Section 69-a of the Indian IT act allows such blocking of apps if they violate the sovereignty of India, a clause used in this case). This is a live proof that India finally seems to have evolved a strategy to tackle China and it has a blend of three components, namely military, economic and diplomatic.

Sir Colonel Qiao Lang and Wang Xiangsui, two officers of the Chinese army had written a book called *Unrestricted Warfare*. The book has a chapter called "Ten thousand methods combined one". In the chapter, it is stated that the war fought beyond the battlefield is an effective war and the app ban is certainly one of the ten thousand methods we have selected to respond. This approach of India is a strong signal to the Chinese that India can respond in other ways as well and is a token of India's will to impose an economic cost on the Chinese. The action of Beijing on the app ban was predictable, but laughable. Beijing immediately asserted that India should uphold the rights of "international investors" in a legitimate manner and while calling the app ban discriminatory, it threatened India that while banning the apps, India must remember the overall interests of the bilateral Sino-Indian relationship.

While some argue that how can ban on Tik Tok be an upfront to Indian sovereignty? These critics often miss the point. The Tik Tok is owned by a firm called ByteDance. This company has a strong relationship with the Chinese intelligence. Also, as per the cyberspace laws of China, every technology company operating in China has a legal obligation to "cooperate with the intelligence agencies of the state". In February 2020, Tik Tok update their security policy and categorically stated that the data of Indians, including data related to their location, mobile browser and browsing history etc. shall be shared with law enforcement authorities of the Chinese. This is a clear example of waging a war by other means where the sovereignty of India is being challenged on every day basis.

Cutting off Chinese at the economic trade level is also not feasible because India is striving to be a globally competitive economy and knows that economic strength is only the true security because economic strength is the fuel for military strength. However, the ban on these apps may have been a short-term strategic move, but, in the long run, this will have repercussions in Chinese investments in the digital start-ups of India and will impact job creation in India and the development of the mobile hardware sector of the country. Many experts assert that India should use this space created to allow the Indian app makers to flex muscles and compete at the global level, considering the irony that no Indian app today features in top 50 globally downloaded apps but the top 50 have mostly Indian developers only. This is the time for India to demonstrate the free market trend of cyberspace and allow Indian app makers to go for a wider reach, sync with the message of 'vocal for local'. But, the app ban action is an Indian tactic from the leaf of Sun Tzu that unless certain demands are met, serious harm could be on way for the Chinese. Even though India has not banned the Huawei 5G testing in India, but it does hold the 5G levers for future in China does similar aggression. The app ban also sends a positive message to other nations in Asia and Southeast Asia, who are also peeved with the brazenness of the Chinese. The app ban has been seen positively by many Southeast Asians who believe that India standing up to Chinese bullying has given them a sense of sigh and relief that they can too resist Chinese hegemonic assertions if needed. Through the app ban, the Chinese have rightly understood that the situation in 2020 is not what it was in 1962. Now, the contest is multidimensional and if the Chinese are going to use their economic, military and technical clout against India, then even India can respond to non-linear options to hit China where it hurts them the most. The mercantilist tendencies of Chinese have been certainly checked. After all, Sun Tzu rightly said, "It is more important to out-think your enemy, than to outfight him".

DISENGAGEMENT TO DE-ESCALATION TO BUFFER ZONES

After intense negotiations by the two sides, finally, from July 2020, the two have initiated a process of disengagement and de-escalation. India has been very clear that disengagement is the starting point of going back to status quo ante and de-escalation is the destination. The two sides also decided to create buffer zones in prevent clashes in the Western sector. Both sides have agreed that Indo-Tibetan Border Police would man the buffer zones from the Indian side and Border Defence Regiment from the Chinese side. The rational of using the police forces from the two sides to man the boundary is to avoid potential escalation. Also, in the buffer zones, there would be no use of carrying weapons, a job more suitable to the police, not for the army which, is trained in combat activity. While dis-engagement means going back from the forward areas to pre-established posts, this is where India favours a phased and step-wise disengagement and Chinese favour complete disengagement of frontline troops. Also, the Chinese are silent on de-escalation and for them, any de-escalation is only a shift to normalcy in the relationship. One reason why the Chinese are silent of de-escalation is because they know that they can deploy the troops at the LAC in Ladakh at a much faster pace than India. This is why India states that disengagement without de-escalation will not work. By advocating its position, India has hit the right notes. Firstly, it has lived up to the sanctity of the 1993, 1996 and 2013 agreements that assert that there should be tranquillity and peace at the LAC. Secondly, India has not hit any anti-China camp by its position, thereby asserting that it gives primacy to trust, that stands breached by unilateral behaviour of China. This is why China has been caught in a sticky situation now and wants to divert the tone of the standoff to the larger India–China relationship and seek its normalcy. But, a long and a cautious watch waits because India is not willing to oblige to it. The disengagement process has been initiated but India has adopted a new policy of "Distrust until fully and comprehensively verified". Thus, India has decided to ensure that it is not two steps forward and one step backward but two steps forward and two steps backward. It is not wrong to assert that the era of Chinese expansionism seems to be over.

THE HEART OF INDIA'S CHINA DILEMMA

It is not difficult to understand that why did Chinese under Xi Jinping behaved the way they did in 2020 Ladakh standoff. The father of Xi was a member of the communist party and when Mao was the leader, he was charged with disloyalty and sent to harsh labour in camps. This incident seems to have cemented the idea of Xi that the only way to ensure security is to seek absolute power. And, it is rightly said, power corrupts and absolute power corrupts absolutely. In 2020, there was a lot of criticism against Chinese for their failure in tackling the spread of COVID-19, which eventually emerged as a global pandemic. In this backdrop, the veterans of the Communist Party of China called a meeting to replace Xi. This came as a surprise to Xi and he responded by unleashing YingPais, a hawkish military cum political coterie on the dissenters (the veterans). To ensure that the people do not question the 2020 purge and give Xi an opportunity to reassert himself in the era of growing opposition, Xi needed an outward projection. This is where one of the loyal generals of Xi, Zhou Zhonqui, the head of the Western Theatre Command was brought in to flare up a nationalistic cause, leading to the Ladakh standoff. This emerged as a miscalculation and a strategic blunder for Xi.

One thing is certain that China would not want an escalated full-scale war with India because that does not fit into the political and strategic roadmap of China. However, by resorting to limited scale military defeats on India leading to chunks of territorial grabs will convey the message deeply to India. In any such minor escalation, India will try to overlook minor territorial losses by asserting that it prevented larger escalation. This is precisely what Chinese aim is. They want to undertake minor territorial grabs and push India where politically, the ruling party in India, dismisses the territorial grab as a minor loss that prevented a larger escalation. This policy will tempt Beijing to repeat such tactics again and this consideration lies at the heart of India's China dilemma today. Thus, India needs to have a blend of strong political direction, coupled with mature deliberation and a coherent strategy as key elements of its new China policy. Ladakh is a part of the 'New Great

Game' where China has unleashed a war psychology officially and India needs to realise that nibbling off the territory is not the real game of China because the real game is to condition Indian mind and tie Indian hands.

POSTSCRIPT OF LADAKH STANDOFF AND THE CHINESE 3M POLICY

China is a satiated power in Ladakh because they already have the control of Aksai Chin. Their prime driver in Ladakh assertion is to prevent India to try to change any situation on the ground by creating new infrastructures. It is important for India to differentiate between the objectives of Pakistan and China. China does not wish to alter status quo in Kashmir because its CPEC project passes through Kashmir and CPEC, a part of BRI, is a critical node of Chinese global power aspirations. However, China does not want India to make statements on altering the status quo either (as India in recent times has reiterated its old commitments of having back the control of every inch of PoK and Aksai Chin one day, something which has infuriated Chinese recently). This is where China differs from Pakistan as Pakistan aims to alter status quo in Kashmir and for Pakistan, Kashmir is a zero sum game. Thus, it is imperative for India to clearly distinguish between the objectives of Beijing and Islamabad on Kashmir and not get into the temptation of conflating the two at tactical level because doing so will make it difficult for India to adopt rational policy choices. It is important to understand that Chinese are not largely interested in occupying any Indian territory. They want to teach India a lesson for deepening ties with the US and refusing to sign the BRI. The larger message that they are trying to convey through the salami slicing with India is to force India to go for a political settlement, which shall involve India to re-orient its policies to suit the pattern of Chinese global policies (including dropping of India's stance on not joining the Chinese BRI, because Indian stance has given strength to many others to oppose China, which they frown upon). China once rightly maintained since the time of Mao that in Asia, only one sun rises (meaning, they have to keep India, a rising power and a Chinese competitor to global power status, bogged down). Xi Jinping is practicing this statement, said at the onset of the Cold War. The Chinese are guided by a policy of 3M. China today believes that they are on the path of recreating the Middle Kingdom identity again and being at the centre of the world, the Chinese think that no rules apply to them in their global and domestic behaviours as they rise on the world. The other two are Modern tools of engagement and Medieval mindset. These two mean that while the Chinese might have acquired technological prowess and might have even modernised their military with modern tools, their mindset remains medieval, which is reflected in state control of innovation, enterprise and individuals. The medieval mindset is seen in action too frequently as it partners with authoritarian regimes all over the world and use iron rods with nails, baseball bats with barbed wires in clashes and committing that it will not use weaponry to attack.

CHINESE GEOPOLITICS, WATER, GLOBAL POWER AND TERRITORIAL DEPTH

Michael Beckley has rightly stated that when rising powers suffer economic slowdowns (which China is witnessing due to its debt-based Belt and Road Initiative and now, COVID-19), they tend to become aggressive and especially aggressive in territorial disputes to divert the attention of its people. The recent incidents at Galwan Valley and Pangong Tso have occurred with highest strategic direction from Chinese government.

The question here is why? There are various plausible reasons. The first is that Beijing is interested to reassure its camp followers that it has muscle flexing capacity after receiving bad press globally for their poor handling of their designed coronavirus. This is in larger sync with Chinese wariness of India shifting to American orbit of influence and also the argument proposed by Michael Beckley.

Secondly, the Chinese are driven with a motive to undertake maximum land grabs as possible in Ladakh because they wish to increase their depth at National Highway G-219, the highway that connects Kashgar in Xinjiang to Lhasa in Tibet because, these two Western regions of China (Xinjiang and Tibet) are Achilles Heels of China. However, the larger design is·to extend their presence up to Galwan Valley and push India below Shyok River, which will enable them to have access to a huge territory, up to the Shaksgam Valley, that can give the Chinese access to abundance water (as Indus originates from Tibet and flows into Ladakh and goes to PoK) which they can use to manufacture microchips (as a 30 centimetre of a silicon wafer needs 10,000 litres of water and this is what Chin also wants from Pakistan, in the form of complete control of Indus). From 2018 to 2020, Chinese have imported 230 billion dollars worth microchips from the US, Japan and Taiwan. Now, it intends to make these microchips by itself and that can be only facilitated by water from Indus and melting of glaciers in Shaksgam Valley (also proven by the fact that they had decided to sponsor construction of five major dams in PoK in 2020). Thus, water, global power status and territorial depth are the larger geopolitical strategic designs of China in Kashmir. The incidents are nothing but an attempt by the Chinese to deny respectable parity at LAC, the same way it did with India at the nuclear level in its diplomacy with the Nuclear Suppliers Group. It is time for India to end pussyfooting Chinese intimidation and checkmate China by playing the real game in the real theatre, the Indian Ocean. India needs to augment power to develop key technologies and acquire critical infrastructure. India has rightly focused on the dynamic of QUAD (a security arrangement sponsored by the US in the Indo-Pacific region), which emphasises on the democracy and security dimensions. Now, India should behave like Arjun and only focus on the eye of the fish. This is possible by only enhancing India's economic capability (to expand India's Comprehensive National Power, which today is two and a half times less than Chinese) by forming a Middle Power Coalition under the American umbrella because an ambitious rising democracy and an economically powerful India is a death knell for all rising ambitions of China, that aims to design one unipolar Asia.

THE RISING MIDDLE KINGDOM WITH MEDIEVAL CHARACTERISTICS

The easiest argument that New Delhi South Block has always advocated is that the Indians deepening ties with the US drive the Chinese behaviour against India because China is trying to say that do not join any structure that sees our containment, else we will show you that you are a paper tiger. This argument is not always the case and one has to see the larger picture. There is another argument that Chinese have become more involved in Ladakh after India abrogated Article 370 in 2019 and made Ladakh a Union Territory and Chinese assertion that Indian action poses a threat to the sovereignty of land claimed by China. There is a belief in certain sections of India's strategic community that the chest thumping by BJP rulers of abrogation of Article 370 and unnecessary polarising statements related to Aksai Chin have been perceived by the Chinese as "continued damage to the territorial sovereignty of China by unilateral modification of a domestic law". It is ironical that these statements by the Chinese of unilateral changes by India (read Article 370 issue) come from someone that has made the South China Sea as Chinese administrative districts in the recent times. It is a pity to see that the debate on the crisis in Ladakh was being fixated on Indian constitutional changes, when in reality, it was the debate about the growing capabilities of the PLA and the political will to use the PLA against India. Chinese attempts to do assertion in Ladakh and elsewhere along the LAC will continue to grow as the military balance continues to favour China. It was for Delhi to take the larger message and build up its military power as Chinese would continue to loom larger than ever before on the entire Kashmir. This is the real message that the Chinese are affirming that it is now part of Kashmir question.

Today, Chinese are becoming more assertive in territorial gains against India because there is a shift of regional balance of power in favour of Beijing (with Philippines, Indonesia and Pakistan firmly with China). This shift in the balance of power is the driving force of all territorial assertions. They have to now be placed in the larger psychology of China. The skirmishes along the boundary with India are natural now because the CCP has been thumping its chest by asserting that 'Xi Jinping Thought' is the essence of '21st Century Marxism' and 'Socialism with Chinese Characteristics' has won over 'Western Capitalism'. The Chinese are too confident today that they can confront all powers, including India, because of their economic interdependence and political influence. The regime of Xi Jinping believes that using a combination of economic and political power, they can break and potential hostile power that might emerge as a challenge to the unstoppable Chinese. This behaviour of the CCP from their insensitivities from Himalayas to South China Sea to Indian Ocean to Belt and Road Initiative are driven by narcissism in the same way as behaviour of Imperial Japan and Imperial Germany acted prior to World War II (same behaviour was displayed by the Soviet in the 1970s when they perceived America as a declining power after their defeat in Vietnam, leading the Soviets to do social revolutions from Afghanistan to Cambodia). The tide eventually turned against Imperial Japan, Imperial Germany and Soviet Union and all the three were eventually thrown into the history's dustbin. The Chinese behaviour today thus reflects in what Thucydides stated, *The strong do what they can and weak suffer what they must*. The Chinese behaviour in Hong Kong (where Xi Jinping has abrogated the treaty of China with Britain on Hong Kong) and Taiwan (where Xi stated in 2020 that Taiwan should be incorporated with China) reflect Chinese desire for Akhand China. The border war with India revived by Xi is based on the same logic of Hong Kong and Taiwan. Xi has apparently told his population that when the Chinese were weak, the British took advantage and seized the Chinese territory of Tibet (read Aksai Chin and Arunachal Pradesh) and incorporated the same within India and Chinese have been asking the Indians to give them the territory back, which they have been refusing, thus, necessitating the violent action. All this is driven by a concept of nationalism that Xi has promoted in China. He has asserted that China has to regain its independent position of Middle Earth Pole in the world, the position the Chinese enjoyed in the 17th Century. Xi understands that to do so, China needs to have technological and economic prowess, which they seem to have achieved now. Thus, Chinese can be a regional and global disruptor and can even disrupt India, if it becomes a pawn in its global rise. This attitude of CCP is a grave mistake by CCP, which has neither carefully understood India's strategic resilience and nor analysed India's political culture, that produces an extraordinary degree of unity at the time of the crisis. Thus, by underestimating the 'non-cooperation' value of India, if China does not end up retreating from the illegally occupied India territories, then it should be noted that such a Chinese posture would compel India to resort to a radical reorientation of its Chinese policy, which may be detrimental to the interests of China, covertly and overtly. It is time for Chinese government to reign in their 'wolf-warrior' nationalists and cooperate and follow the dictum "he who tied the knot should untie it' because the sun may have reached its zenith.

GLOBAL DECOUPLING OF CHINA AND STRATEGIC CHURN BY INDIA

Francis Fukuyama rightly asserts that a grand political and economic decoupling between the West and China has finally begun. The strategic turn against Chinese has begun globally. The US has initiated complete decoupling with China through three steps. Firstly, the US has ended its special status with Hong Kong. This will financially hurt the Chinese very deeply because the businesses of China use Hong Kong for all international dollar business. Secondly, the US has tightened their curbs for entry of research students above undergraduate level to the US. For many years, the Chinese have been sending their PLA officers and members of MSS (Ministry of State Security, the Chinese intelligence agency), disguised as students, to the US for research studies, with an intent to get access to deep innovative technologies. The new US visa regime is likely to create an intense level of scrutiny into the inflow of Chinese students, thereby hurting the growing technological prowess of China in future. Thirdly, the US have shown strength by withdrawing from the World Health Organization in the wake of COVID-19. This withdrawal also takes away the ecosystem of scientific research of public health and medicine that US contributes globally. The Chinese in anyway cannot replace the US at WHO, and this would make G-7 or a G-10 (with Donald Trump proposed India as a participant) meeting significant without China. Xi Jinping often disdains the advise of Deng Xiaoping that "to keep your head low and bide your time", but Xi, this time with India, in the crisis of 2020, has refused to act responsibly. The 'China Dream' and 'Catching Up', the two key slogans of Xi to position China as a power to overtake the US by 2050, seem to be slipping out of hands now. Considering that Beijing was already pre-occupied by tackling COVID-19 origin issue, backlash by the European world, trade war with Australia (where China has stopped import of Australian beef when Australia insisted on a debate on probing Chinese links to suppression of COVID-19 information) and the US, crisis in Hong Kong and Taiwan; one would not have expected the Chinese to open another front with India at this juncture. But, by opening another front with India, the Chinese have tried to give a subtle message to the US that it has the capacity to handle pressure and is not going to shy away to display power, even if it is hard power. With its recent aggression at the LAC, China has pushed India to take a stand and initiate a reset of its ties with China. The question is that when India intends to reset, would India firmly remain non-aligned in its thoughts on managing China or would it join an anti-China alliance in the future. The Indian app ban is a public signal of strategic intent of India to decouple from China. A global decoupling effort now, with India as a global partner, will definitely lead to breaking up China economically.

INDIA'S TIBET POLICY AND IMPLICATIONS ON SINO-INDIA RELATIONS

India has a dual policy on Tibet. It accepts that the Tibetan Autonomous Region (TAR) is a part of PRC. India however sides with Dalai Lama to assert that historically Tibet has been autonomous politically and culturally. Therefore, India refuses to accept Tibet as 'inalienable and integral' part of China. If Kashmir is India's Achilles heal, Tibet is the same for China.

In April 2017, the Dalai Lama visited Arunachal Pradesh. The visit drew sharp reaction from the Chinese side. China has an uncomfortable relationship with the Dalai Lama and feels that he is a separatist whose prime intention is to create unrest in Tibet to seek an autonomous state. China has always harboured a feeling that India has been supporting the Dalai Lama to create unrest in Tibet. The Indian government's policy clearly signals the diplomatic cards India can play against

China. Ironically, the Dalai Lama has visited Arunachal earlier in 1983, 1997, 2003 and 2009 as well. China has been creating a diplomatic ruckus over such visits. What has irritated China in 2017 was that during the Dalai Lama's visit to Arunachal Pradesh, India's Minister of State for Home Affairs also accompanied him to Tawang. India has insisted that the visit of the Dalai Lama is purely religious and no political meaning should be attached to the same. China, on the other hand, enquired why, if the Dalai Lama's visit were purely religious, would an Indian Minister accompany him. A deeper analysis of the visit clearly signifies that the visit of the Dalai Lama is used by India to keep China in check.

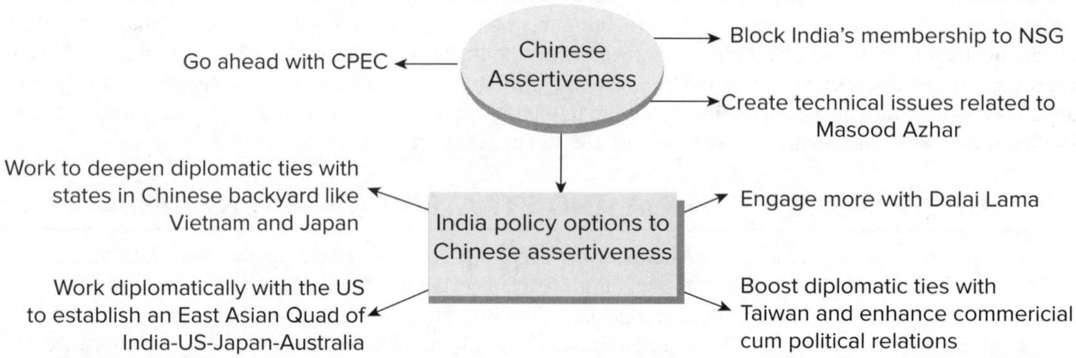

What motivates China to assert itself in Arunachal Pradesh is based in the region's history. In Tawang, there is a monastery called the Galden Namgey Lhatse. Lama Lodre Gyatso founded it in 1680 on the wishes of Ngawang Lobsang Gyatso, who was the Fifth Dalai Lama. The Tawang monastery is the seat of Karma–Kargyu sect and China knows that the Chinese legitimacy on Tibet will remain incomplete till it controls the Tawang monastery. This is the reason that China considers Tawang and Arunachal Pradesh as a part of Southern Tibet. In 2018, Dalai Lama celebrated 60th anniversary of flight to India from China. A leaked memo of the Indian government in 2018 mentioned that the government officials should stay away from commemoration event of Dalai Lama. Some in India began to say that this was an attempt by the government to 'appease China'. It is important to understand the changing reality in Tibet today. In the last two decades, China has invested tremendous resources for development of Tibet (at the cost of destroying the Tibetan environment), it has undertaken demographic re-engineering where Han Chinese are in rising. By convincing Nepal, China has clamped down the outflow of Tibetan refugees to India. Even at the cultural level, the Chinese film DVD's have replaced Bollywood. In India too, the Tibetan people living here are in a state of exile and disconnected from the developments in the Tibet. It is high time the government stops the wishful thinking that Tibetans in India are a strategic card. India needs to focus on evolving a policy to understand what the Tibetan people in India need and take required steps in the backdrop of these changing realities.

INDIA AND THE TAIWAN CARD AND ONE CHINA PRINCIPLE

In 1949, India recognised the PRC but not the Republic of China (ROC) India believed that it was important to recognise the fact that the PRC had been established. Thus, Nehru recognised PRC and also that Formosa is Chinese territory. As neither PRC nor ROC favoured any international mediation, Nehru also designed Indian policy appropriately and maintained that the civil war of China would end soon and the will of the Chinese people would be abiding. India refrained from playing any conciliatory role in ROC–PRC issue. During the initial years, as Nehru maintained this policy, leaders of the Hindu Mahasabha, namely N. B. Khare, and Jan Sangh's Madhok, felt that India had adopted a policy of double standards by not accepting a nationalist Taiwan while accepting a communist China. Post the 1962 Sino-Indian conflict, India and Taiwan began to witness a rise in military and media exchange which today manifests as rising parliamentary exchanges. But in the last 30 years, Taiwan–China relations have improved. A unique feature is that forces have not driven this improvement from top down but from bottom up. The Taiwanese businesses have invested heavily in China and as a result, the people-to-people ties have flourished. China has remained adamant on the One-China principle and has maintained that Taiwan is part of China, as ROC does not exist anymore. It is important to understand the One-China principle. As per China, there exists only one China in the present world. China asserts that Taiwan is a part of China and the PRC is the sole legitimate representative of China. As per the One-China principle, there is complete Chinese sovereignty over Taiwan and if any state in the world intends to undertake a diplomatic relationship with China, it needs to agree to One-China principle. Such a state is also to refrain any independent engagement with Taiwan. The One-China principle is a stabilising principle that helps China preserves the status quo over the political status of Taiwan. The One-China principle however allows Taiwan to operate as in independent administrative and economic entity. The One-China principle is different from One China Policy. The One China policy is used by the USA to assert that Chinese have claims over Taiwan, which is not recognised by the Americans. India follows One China Policy. India does engage with Taiwan, but under a different nomenclature. In 1995, India established an India–Taipei Association in Taiwan while Taiwan established the Taipei Economic and Cultural Centre (TECC) in India. The two sides don't have diplomatic relations and thus lack an institutional architecture. Today, the bilateral trade stands to be $9 billion as of 2020. India has received FDI from Taiwan. Taiwan has, however, faced difficulties in bringing FDI to India as in the official documents of India, Taiwan is mentioned as Chinese Taipei and the existing Indian rules that apply to China also apply to Taiwan, with no exception applicable. The Continental Engineering Corporation of Taiwan has been working with the Delhi Metro. It has often complained about the repeated RBI clearance it had to get for bringing investments to India. Taiwan somehow receives less support from the Indian political elites and its foreign bureaucracy. It is important for India to rectify this imbalance and boost ties with Taiwan. Taiwan has initiated a Go South Policy in 2019 and under this policy; it intends to establish representative offices in the states of SEA for economic engagement. The Go South Policy intends to use economic diplomacy to boost political relation. The new leadership of Taiwan under Tsai Ing-wen favours deeper economic ties with India.

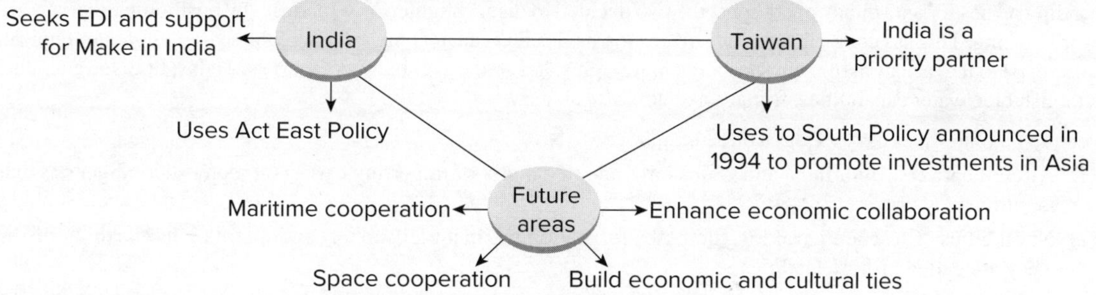

THE MYTHOLOGY OF SAMUDRA MANTHAN BETWEEN INDIA AND CHINA

The Samudra Manthan is one of the most enchanting episodes in the Indian mythology. Angels and demons, as per the myth, put a mountain on a tortoise and churned the oceans by spinning the oceans with giant reptile. Today, this Indian mythology has a direct relevance for the India–China ties.

FROM BEING INWARD TO INDO-PACIFIC RIVALRY

In the 21st century, the dragon and the elephant have started rising and their rise has altered the maritime environment of the region and the world. Initially, when the rise of modern India and China occurred, their focus remained primarily inwards. It is only after the two states began to globalise did the two realise the importance of the sea power. Because of globalisation, the two states have deepened their commercial ties with the states around them and this has resulted in the rise of a new maritime component in the psyche of the people. Because of the naval expansion, the two states are building blue water naval capabilities and projecting naval power. As they step into common waters together, the two are likely to step on toes of each other and of the US, the sole dominant power naval power in the region. The competition between the two at the naval level is immense and it requires deft diplomacy by the US in the Indo-Pacific (the new and rising geopolitical frame of future reference). Today, the two have developed a sense of rivalry with each other. At times, the two states have tried to put the rivalry at rest by asserting that the world has enough space for a peaceful rise of both; the reality is that the rising contradictions have only become irreconcilable today. Both today know that the sensitivity of the bilateral ties is more due to their relations at the global and regional level with other powers. As both engage with others, both believe that they are being encircled and this has led both to view their bilateral ties through the prism of a security dilemma. Thus, the Sino-Indian relations are a mixture of cooperation, competition and rivalry. It is in this backdrop we will explain this maritime competition in detail.

THE EVOLUTION AND ANALYSIS OF CONCEPT OF RESOURCE SECURITY

Since the two states have embarked growth through globalisation, the two have realised the importance to acquire minerals and resources to acquire from the outside states. This has led the two to focus on resource security for their domestic growth. As both have shifted their economy to outward globalisation, the sea power has become an important component in the strategic calculus. Consequently, the two have invested adequate resources to develop naval capabilities to protect the sea-lanes of communication. The dependence of India and China on hydrocarbons, resources and minerals from foreign states has been dubbed as vital and strategic. If China has historically followed String of Pearls and later the Belt and Road Initiative, then India too has responded from Look East Policy to Act East Policy and now Necklace of Diamond strategy.

COASTAL DEFENCE TO BLUE WATER NAVY

The sea that was used initially by both (India and China) for coastal defence is today an arena of power projection. The first instance of power projection by India and China happened in 2008 when the UNSC authorised navies of the world to take action against Somalia pirates, not only this provided the needed legitimacy for India and China to assert power; but by sending navies for anti-piracy operations, the two decided to display tremendous maturity by positioning their navies as outward looking. This has compelled the two to develop navies that can not only safeguard the sea-lanes of communication but also carry out evacuation of their Diasporas in foreign states in the eventuality of a crisis. Today, both have ambitions to establish blue water capabilities, frigates and aircraft carriers.

Developing a blue water navy requires three things:

1. Aircraft carriers: Both India and China have adopted a mix of importing carriers to domestic indigenous manufacturing.
2. Naval cities: These are naval logistic bases for stationing, material support and international birthing of ships. They are called inshore facilities.
3. Forward offshore bases: The two need islets for intelligence and reconnaissance operations. This is being developed by India as a part of its Necklace of Diamond Strategy and China as a part of their Belt and Road Initiative.

THE SIGNIFICANCE OF INDIAN OCEAN FOR CHINA AND CHINESE STRATEGY

As China is deep outwards in the sea, the Indian Ocean is important in the Chinese strategic calculus for three reasons.

1. It is a route to supply of energy, thus it needs to protect the sea-lanes of communication. As it uses the energy for its domestic growth and this energy is transported via the Indian Ocean, which has chokepoints, it needs to have presence in the Indian Ocean to check the adversaries.
2. There are Chinese nationals is states around the Indian Ocean and most of these states are unstable (Africa and Middle East). This may require China a space to carry out covert operations to evacuate its Diaspora, thus the need for presence.
3. China has undertaken massive investments in the region around the Indian Ocean and it needs to protect them.

China is trying to provide economic and security power to the states friendly to China in the Indian Ocean. It is undertaking military and naval modernisation to enhance its power projection capabilities and is resorting to security diplomacy. China deploys its navy globally in the name of anti-piracy operations and then makes the naval presence permanent. There is a shift towards developing capabilities for open ocean protection. This means that china is trying to vie for a sea control strategy. Under this, china aims to develop capabilities where it possesses the freedom for action for its own purpose while denying action by adversary. Sea control is only for a limited period of time and in a limited area and is different from sea denial, which is long-term, permanent and oceanic.

CHINESE GEO-ECONOMIC, GEOPOLITICAL TACTICS IN THE INDIAN OCEAN TO 'DEBT DIPLOMACY'

Firstly, China makes an offer to a state to boost the trade through investments. Secondly, China informs the state that the bilateral trade can further increase through infrastructure. This is a strategy to lure the state to seek enhancement of infrastructure. Chinese diplomats tell the government of the other state that creating infrastructure will create jobs and will help the political party or the head of the state in the long run in elections. Thirdly, this psychological strategy works and the state is induced to seek Chinese support for infrastructure. Fourthly, China uses this opportunity to create state of art Special Economic Zones and other infrastructure, thereby getting a hold on the economic possessions of the state. Fifthly, China strives to create a perception that China is a benefactor. This enables China to make provocative offers that states are unable to resist. Sixthly, when China succeeds in making massive investments and realises that the state is unable to repay the debt, China proposes to the state to make the debt an asset. This asset is then taken on lease by China for 99 years and so (reminiscent of colonial mindset) and the state falls into a debt trap.

CHINESE 'OVERSEAS STRATEGIC SUPPORT POINTS' AND 'MILITARY OPERATIONS OTHER THAN WAR' STRATEGY

It is important to note that firstly, China lacks a coherent strategy for Indian Ocean. Secondly, China has limited capacity for operations in far off waters. Thirdly, it does not have long-range air strike capabilities. Fourthly, it lacks massive logistical support at chokepoints. China does have capability where it can respond if there are any contingencies, but it does not have massive power projection capabilities. It has succeeded in crossing the Rubicon in 2017 and ended up in establishing a naval base at Djibouti (read about it more in India and Africa chapter). India and others assert that it is a naval base but china has clarified that they are 'places and not bases' as china asserts that in Djibouti (and Gwadar and Hambantota) there are no combat capabilities, which is an essential condition for a military base. Officially, China calls them as 'Overseas Strategic Support Points' (OSSP). India says that the Chinese OSSP at Gwadar in Pakistan is an attempt by China to bog down India in Chabahar (explained in India and Iran chapter), which will ease pressure for China from the Indian Navy in the east and help in mitigating the Malacca Dilemma. The strategy of China is not sea denial but MOOTW—Military Operations Other Than War. The MOOTW includes piracy prevention and evacuation of non-combatants including Diaspora.

INDIAN ASPIRATIONS IN INDIAN OCEAN AND INDIAN STRATEGY

India feels that it is a natural leader in the Indian Ocean and India is of the opinion that any presence of China or any other power in the Indian Ocean is extra regional and illegitimate. India feels that it is a net security provided and a regional security manager in South Asia and Indian Ocean. The problem arises when China refuses to accept this status and legitimacy of Indian claims in the Indian Ocean. China refuses to accept the Indian Ocean is India's Ocean. There is an Indian Monroe Doctrine amongst the strategic community of India. It asserts that India should establish a strong forward policy in the Indian Ocean to keep extra regional powers out of Indian Ocean, as Indian Ocean is the strategic backyard of India. However, this Indian Monroe Doctrine is only a preferred objective of Indian foreign policy and not a policy goal. Thus, as of now, India is trying to position itself as a net security provider in the Indian Ocean only.

THE UPA GOVERNMENT'S (2004 TO 2014) INDIAN OCEAN DIPLOMACY

The concern regarding Chinese presence in the Indian Ocean was visible for the first time in 2000s. In India, a narrative was born that China is trying to enter the Indian Ocean to seek access to larger nation states. Initially, the view was that china was trying to establish capabilities for protecting the SLOC (Sea-Lanes of Communication). In 2008, when China joined the anti-piracy operations in Somalia, a new narrative was born in India. It was asserted that China is trying to encircle India and Indian scholars and diplomats came out with a 'String of Pearls' theory. The UPA government had a different strategy to meet all these narratives. The entire strategy outlined below was based on a deeper understanding that India's Comprehensive National Power is two times less than that of China, thus the strategy has to accept this reality. Firstly, the government officially refused to accept the String of Pearls theory argument. It preferred to give China the space in Indian Ocean. In 2014, when the MH-370 Malaysian Airline plane disappeared, India did not powerfully come out to play any role in search and rescue operations, giving China primacy again. Secondly, as US–China rivalry was increasing, India asserted that in this rivalry, India should not take any sides; this is because for China, its territorial and maritime disputes are their own core issues. They are not the core issues for the US. So, India advocated that it should prefer to work with China than go against China. UPA government advocated a policy of cooperation and competition with China. The logic behind this policy was that China has legitimate interests in the protection of the SLOC and its concerns on Malacca Dilemma. So India should focus on engaging with China to explore joint protection of the SLOC in the Indian Ocean, rather than acting as an irritant. This led the UPA government to discount the idea of Indo-Pacific as it asserted that Indian Ocean and Pacific Ocean are two separate strategic spaces and there is no point in conflating the two as doing so would only antagonise China. Rather, the UPA government favoured that India and China should try to establish new security architecture to mitigate competition in the seas and evolve platforms similar to ASEAN Regional Forum and East Asian Summit.

NDA GOVERNMENT'S (2014 ONWARDS) INDIAN OCEAN DIPLOMACY

The NDA government brought about a radical shift in Indian Ocean diplomacy. The shift was natural due to the changed geopolitical circumstances. China had launched an ambitious Belt and Road Initiative in 2014, which had CPEC as a core irritant (both of which were perceived as expansionist by India). Secondly, China had refused to accept the verdict of the UNCLOS on South China Sea in 2016 and began to display assertiveness. This led the NDA to give high priority to the Indian Ocean. The strategy adopted by the NDA was a mixture of economic, political and military power relations in the Indian Ocean to negate the Chinese 'expansionist' approach. The logic behind the shift was based on two points. Firstly, it was believed that China through the CPEC will create massive infrastructure and this will legitimise the position of Pakistan in the disputed POK. Secondly, ASEAN and others lack aggressive power to halt Chinese expansionist behaviour. Thus, as per the new strategy, India decided to launch a new Necklace of Diamond strategy.

INDIA'S NECKLACE OF DIAMOND STRATEGY

1. Under this strategy, India aims to increase the bilateral diplomatic visits to maritime states in the Indian Ocean and acquire naval birthing rights. This will be a step towards checking the chokepoints from Chinese aggression.
2. The government has encouraged Para-diplomacy. The maritime Indian states will be encouraged to directly deal with state governments in India for non-security issues like trade etc. This has given a sense of assurance to the neighbouring states that their relations with India will not be held hostage to any geopolitics.
3. Surprisingly, India has started flexing its covert muscle to ensure that regimes in the littoral states are not involved in overplaying China card. This has been visible by India using Research and Analysis Wing to bring about regime changes in Sri Lanka (2015 and 2019), Bhutan (2018) and Bangladesh (2019).
4. India has opened a strategic playground in the KTM template. The KTM template is Kenya, Tanzania and Mozambique. In these states, India is adopting a mixture of aid and military diplomacy. This approach in Africa is done with intent to provide an alternative to China in Africa. (This is explained in the chapter on Africa.)
5. India has adopted a pan oceanic capability by engaging with Indian Ocean Naval Symposium and Indian Ocean Rim Association. This is visible in the government's blue economy and Sagarmala strategy. These initiatives are based on the logic that a state that is a resident power in the Indian Ocean has a higher responsibility for peace and stability. (This is explained in details in Indian Foreign Policy Doctrines.)
6. India has realised that connectivity today is a new yardstick that is used for measuring the geopolitical influence. Thus, it has adopted a strategy of enhancing connectivity via SAARC Satellite, BCIM-EC, Asia–Africa Growth Corridor and BBIN.

INDIA'S STRATEGIC BIND IN THE INDO-PACIFIC AND INDIAN OCEAN

India rightly understands that Indian Ocean as of now is second in priority for China as its first priority is Western Pacific. India favours an idea that if China is kept occupied in the Western Pacific; then India along with Japan, Australia, the US and Vietnam can continue to project power in the Indian Ocean. This will not deter China in the Indian Ocean but can at least delay China to come to Indian Ocean. This window can be used by India to enhance its naval capabilities. Some say that India today faces a strategic bind. This is so because India disapproves China in the Indian Ocean but is unable to tell China on its face that it is unwelcome in the Indian Ocean. The only way to mitigate this bind is by ensuring that India becomes a dominant power in the Indian Ocean. For this, it would need capacity support from the US and Russia and also predominance of the US in the Indian Ocean. It needs to work with the QUAD to ensure that China does not end up in misusing the Indian Ocean and leveraging its own geographical position in the Indian Ocean. India has a military advantage over China in the Indian Ocean. If China threatens India at the land level, India may suffer; but it can always do the same harm to China (through blockade of SLOC) in the Indian Ocean. This is what gives a strategic dimension to Sino-Indian maritime relationship. Indian strategy as of now stands to be a mixture of diplomatic engagement with China and countermeasures at the strategic level through hedging against China. India has enhanced its presence in the Indian Ocean and Bay of Bengal. It has resorted to naval exercises near the Strait of Malacca, to put psychological pressure on China. There is an element of great power diplomacy by India, as visible in the Malabar exercises. The government is actively pursuing the Act East Policy to play in the backyard of China, in the same way as China plays in our neighbourhood. India knows that Chinese presence in the Indian Ocean is not a part of any Grand Strategy of China to challenge India. Its presence in the Indian Ocean is more because of commercial reasons.

BALANCING MODEL BETWEEN INDIA AND CHINA IN THE INDO-PACIFIC

This is where an alternative strategy is being envisaged for the Indo-Pacific. This is based on the concept of concert of great powers, a model that was used in Europe to bring stability after the Napoleonic wars. There are experts on Indo-Pacific who argue that the region needs inclusive balancing to mitigate confrontation between India and China. They assert that there should be a concert of either the US and China or the US and Japan with India and Russia as partners. The idea of inclusive balancing favours that for Indo-Pacific, the US should cooperate with India, Japan, Russia and China. The underlying logic is that this nature of inclusive balancing will thwart any military adventurism and resist non-traditional security threats that may arise. This will ensure that the US does not contain or confront China, but strategically keeps it in check. This can be done by the US by deepening ties with India in Indian Ocean and Japan in the Western Pacific and simultaneously include China in international alliances for stabilising global politics. However, there is a view that concert system in Europe was a cathartic responsibility to systemic wars, which Asia has not seen till date. Also, the concert is successful only when it is based on shared interest and values.

COOPERATIVE MODEL BASED ON MULTILATERAL COOPERATION BETWEEN INDIA AND CHINA IN THE INDO-PACIFIC

As India and China are altering the Indo-Pacific theatre through their unique geopolitics, there is a need to debate and envisage models where the two can sync in future. One of the options for India and China in the Indo-Pacific is to establish a cooperative model on basis of multilateral cooperation. India and china apparently have been quite sceptical of the use of multilateralism in diplomacy historically. Since the end of the Cold War, a multilateral grouping like ASEAN has certainly helped in changing their historical perceptions. The two have used this ASEAN formula to carve out a niche of CBMs for naval exercises. But, the two have also become suspicious of each other's presence in the Indian Ocean and Indo-Pacific. Today, both states are experimenting multilateral naval diplomacy. For instance, India is pursuing diplomatic knitting through Indian Ocean Naval Symposium, Indo-Pacific, Quad and Indian Ocean Rim Association. But, these kinds of forums are not helping in reduction of diplomatic rivalry of India and China. Secondly, Indian Ocean Naval Symposium and Indian Ocean Rim Association, ASEAN Regional Forum and MILAN etc. have also not helped in reduction of stray instances of assertion in the South China Sea. Thus, any kind of a cooperative model on basis of multilateral cooperation will have to envisage elements of establishing a good order in the sea.

CHINA AS AN AUTISTIC SUPERPOWER AND A STRATEGIC TRIANGLE

All these strategies have only increased the concerns about China in the neighbouring states. China has taken no steps to reduce tensions through clarifications. All this proves that China is an autistic superpower. It suffers from a neurological condition where it is absorbed and happy in its own delusions and day dreaming fantasies. It has scant regard for understanding the emotional state of other states around it. The Sino-Indian relationship in the Indo-Pacific will largely depend upon the policies of the US. Though the US has remained a dominant power since the end of the World War II, the rise of China and India is going to affect the American power as the two are going to re-write the maritime power rules. This is where a possibility of a new strategic triangle emerges. The concept of strategic triangle asserts that a policy of one state in the strategic triangle will have an impact on the policies of the other two states in the strategic triangle. This is clearly visible in the Indo-Pacific. As china has started rising economically, its naval outreach manifests in its two-ocean strategy. As a part of this strategy, China has expanded its footprint in the Indian Ocean and Pacific Ocean. Though, as of now its strategy in the Indian Ocean is highly economic in nature, but this will manifest later deeply to reshape regional geopolitical dynamics. China aims to establish eighteen-pearls in Indian Ocean. China has adopted a strategy where it uses its economic diplomacy to create a favourable geopolitical condition for the states in the Indian Ocean that are favourably inclined to adopt a pro-China position. It is done through a well-established strategy outlined above. It is a truth that the power that commands the sea is a world power and any change in the world power is based on change in sea power also. The future of relations will depend upon the changing power equations in Indian Ocean.

CHINA–PAKISTAN AXIS AND ITS IMPACT ON INDIA

China and Pakistan's friendship has proved an all-weather friendship over time. In fact, despite the distinctive ideologies of both states during the Cold War, China followed Kautilya's Mandala theory (your immediate neighbour is your enemy but the neighbour's neighbour is your friend) with Pakistan. China has clarified that the Sino-India relations have nothing to do with Sino-Pak relations. However, India remains deeply concerned about Chinese supply of arms to Pakistan. China says it arms sale to Pakistan is based on an economic logic to make profit and is not meant to act against India and has reiterated that it is even willing to sell military equipment to India if needed. India, on the other hand, feels that China is arming nations around India to bring Pakistan on a strategic parity with India and maintains that Chinese weapons are used by Pakistan against India. India continues to feel that the Sino–Pakistan arms trade would impact the regional balance but China insists it would not. China has three interests in Pakistan. Firstly, there is a mutuality of Pakistan and China with respect to undercutting India. Secondly, it is the prevention of radical Islam from Afghanistan and Pakistan into the Xinjiang province of China to create a stir amongst the Uyghur Muslims. Thirdly, Pakistan is a gateway for China to Afghanistan and the Middle East. For Pakistan, China fits into the concept of borrowed power, to undercut India. China also serves the interests of Pakistan, be it regionally constraining India or globally vetoing decisions that are harmful to Pakistan like blocking India at the Nuclear Suppliers Group membership. Despite Kashmir and Tibet as core concerns between India and China, China has prevented India to achieve primacy in South Asia. Its engagement with Pakistan is to prevent 'hegemony of India' in South Asia. China has built nuclear level relations with Pakistan. Doing so has ensured that India remains bogged down to tackle Pakistan and its nuclear programme while it enjoys the space to project power without hindrance. Even though China joined the NPT in 1992, it exercised the 'grandfathering' clause to support Pakistan for its civilian nuclear programme and its missile development. This continues till today.

For china, Pakistan is

- A balancer to India
- A geopolitical bridge to the Middle East
- A champion of Sunni Islam
- A base for China to project power in the inner Asia
- A territory to prevent Chinese Malacca Dilemma
- An intelligence playground to prevent radicalisation of Uyghur Muslims in Xinjiang

INDIA AND CHINA AND NUCLEAR DIPLOMACY

After the Sino-India conflict in 1962, the globe witnessed Cuban missile crisis and to diffuse the global tensions came the Partial Test Ban Treaty (PTBT) in 1963. India signed the PTBT thinking it would help the diplomatic posturing of India in the context of a long-term disarmament policy but China refused its ratification. In 1964, China tested nuclear weapons and opened the nuclear dimension in security confrontation with India. India subsequently tested its PNE in 1974 but still shied away from developing further nuclear weapons. In 1998, India finally conducted nuclear tests and crossed the Rubicon to become a nuclear weapon state. The rationale forwarded by Vajpayee was Chinese threat and its clandestine support to nuclearise Pakistan. India effectively stated that the Chinese threat was the reason for India to go nuclear even when China, in contrast, had not resorted to citing the India threat as a reason for its own nuclear weapons programme. To understand the issue better, we need to revisit the Cold War. During the Cold War, what compelled China to go nuclear were the US and the Soviet Union having weapons. At any point of time even during that period, China never hinted it would use nuclear weapons against India. India, in contrast, believed that China could use the threat of nuclear weapons to coerce India and it is the nuclear weapon that had given China an international status that it may use to undermine India's attempt to increase its prestige amongst Asia and elsewhere. China further clarified that its nuclear weapon status is based on minimum creditable deterrence and also announced its 'No First Use' policy, thus nullifying the threat that Indian had envisaged. China went nuclear in 1964 but joined the IAEA in 1985. In this two-decade period, the media did prop up the issue of China proliferating to Pakistan. After China joined the IAEA in 1985 and the CTBT in 1996, it became an advocate and supporter of non-proliferation. However, the world is suspicious about China's claims due to its activities from 1964 to 1985 with respect to Pakistan, Iran and North Korea. Though China has accepted military ties with Pakistan, it has maintained that it has not given any ballistic missile capabilities carrying nuclear weapon to Pakistan. Despite Chinese refusal to accept that Pakistan had received nuclear weapon assistance from China, the international society continues to hold China responsible for proliferation to Pakistan. India has perceived all Chinese support to Pakistan at the military level, especially at the nuclear weapon level, as part of a strategy particularly designed to contain India. It is noteworthy, however, that China was merely one of the many important factors, not least of which was India's ambition to position itself as a great power and its domestic political compulsions. However, China took the Pokhran-II as part of an anti-China rhetoric. In fact, Vajpayee's letter to Clinton accentuated the Chinese threat theory as Vajpayee had clearly mentioned that what compelled India to conduct a nuclear test was the fact that it shared its borders with a nuclear weapon state that had indulged in aggression against India in 1962. Though China was not directly mentioned, it was a fairly unambiguous insinuation. Many in China had believed that India had a right to conduct a nuclear weapon test and there could have otherwise been no reason for China to oppose it until India's 'China threat' theory came to light. Consequently, officially China strongly condemned India's Pokhran-II and declared that India had resorted to immaturely blaming China for its urge to go nuclear. China said that it was never a threat to India as it had stated that it would never use nuclear weapon against non-nuclear weapon states. China also stated that India wanted to establish dominance over South Asia and its nuclear weapon test was a gesture to that effect. Thus, the Chinese threat theory became a major irritant in the relations as China clarified that a pre-requisite for a healthy relationship was an absence of fear from each other. However, after Pokhran-II, India did take steps to revive talks with China. India committed that dialogue was the only way out and even invited China to revive dialogues. An Indo-China Eminent Persons Group was established. Because India too has announced a 'no first use' policy, there is a high possibility that there will never be a nuclear conflict between India and China. However, China continues to be reluctant to accept India as a nuclear weapons state as it does not want India to emerge as a great power in its own neighbourhood. China observes that granting the status of a nuclear weapon state to India would jeopardise the international community's efforts for non-proliferation as it would be tantamount to admitting India's entry in the global nuclear order despite it being a non-signatory to the NPT and the CTBT. Even today, China is confident of its nuclear superiority over India and is concerned with a rise of Indo-US cooperation because of the possibility of the US using India as a hedge against China.

INDIA AND CHINA COMMERCIAL DIPLOMACY

In order to promote trade, there are various institutional mechanisms available.

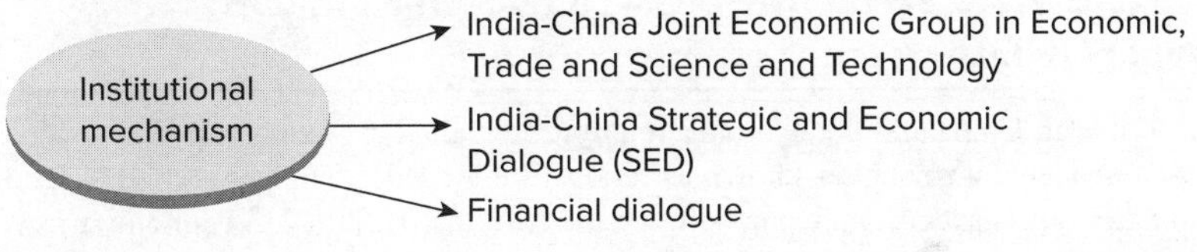

It was in 2005 when a pact was concluded and the financial dialogue was launched. The dialogue allows the two states to explore dimensions of commercial cooperation. India exports cotton yarn, copper, petro products andiron ore while importing telecom equipment, hardware, and industrial machines. Various Indian banks have presence in China while Indian firms such as Tata, Binani cements, Bharat Forge, TCS and NIIT, and so on, are present in China. Indian firms are primarily in IT, pharmacy, refractors and laminated tubes industry. The Strategic and Economic Dialogue is a mechanism for macroeconomic and strategic issues of cooperation, with infrastructure, energy, environment, high technology, railways and power generation being core areas of interest. India is an importer of Chinese goods but there is a trade imbalance as our imports from China are more than the exports. India has an edge in pharmacy, agro–bovine meat industry and textiles industry. India is seeking better market access to rework the trade imbalance. Chinese FDI to India is very less, and is surprisingly lower than the FDI India receives from Poland and Canada. It is not that the Chinese are not interested to invest in FDI in India. However, the Chinese investments are more in resource-rich areas of Africa and Central Asia, in oil and gas sectors, to fuel Chinese domestic growth. As India too is an energy importer, there is less possibility that Chinese FDI will rise in India in the near future. China does complain about red tape and delays in security clearances in India for Chinese projects while India complains that China gives preferences to its state undertakings, restricting Indian corporates' market access. We should not be overtly fixated with trade imbalance with China as India has a trade deficit with 16 out of top 25 trade partners. Because of a weak manufacturing sector, India is unable to produce goods to meet domestic demand and ends up importing heavily. Though India has a trade deficit with China roughly ranging from 54% to 56% its deficit is 90–91% with Iraq and 82–82% with Switzerland. Today, Chinese need India for 5G technologies, as it is a big market for 5G. The 5G technologies are the leverage with India and India has conveyed to China to address concerns that Indian players have while accessing Chinese markets as a quid-pro-quo.

THE QUANDARY OVER CHINESE 5G: KISS OF DEATH

The concept of 5G technologies produced by Chinese and pioneered by the Huawei, has to be seen in the larger strategy of Chinese four heavens. The four heavens include the BRI, Digital Silk Route of China, Made in China 2025 and Chinese Standards 2035. The 5G of Chinese are the mother lobe, coupled with AI, will give China the access of global data. This data will be used by 2025 to create products that the Chinese will manufacture under the Made in China 2025 and standardise under the Chinese Standards 2035 for global level dumping, making China the centre of earth in 2049. The 5G is the enabler, the trunk of the infrastructural cake, which, at its base has the BRI, Digital Silk Route of China and at the top, as icing has Made in China 2025 and Chinese Standards 2035. Thus, if Chinese progress with 5G, it will strengthen the cake and make China stronger. But, if the 5G is resisted by the world, then it will put an end to the economic and strategic dominance of Chinese at the global level and cause internal strife and disintegration of the Chinese state because it will degrade the social contract of "better life for Chinese people" that its government has been propagating. The world is already doing its bit to tackle the dominance of the Chinese in 5G. While the US and the UK have decided to look for players outside China for the 5G equipment, the Vietnamese have developed their own version of 5G. The Japanese and the EU are investing domestically to develop their own 5G technologies. This leaves the Chinese with the largest 5G markets in India. The Chinese will do everything in their might, from resorting to skirmishes on the border (Ladakh standoff 2020), to resorting to drone attacks on Indian oil installations in the western side of our country, to misusing the Chinese apps to gather data (for Made in China 2025 and Chinese Standards 2035 as explained previously) to cyber attacks on India. If India adopts a tough nose on 5G, the Indian telecom sector will be under stress to buy non-Chinese equipment from the EU. The signing of India–EU FTA can lubricate the process for the Indian telecom players. The creation of D10 club is being floated to channelise global expertise on 5G sharing and this D10 already excludes the Chinese. Thus, if India resorts to banning 5G, could India be able to contribute to the birth of rule of law and democracy in China?

US–CHINA TRADE WAR AND IMPLICATIONS ON TRADE RELATIONS WITH INDIA

Since the end of the Cold War, China and the US had a relationship called as 'neither friends nor foes'. This was a model of 'win-win economic engagement' or better known as 'cooperating rivals'. This situation changed after 2008 crisis as the crisis ended up in narrowing the economic gap between the two (in 2012, the US economy was two times bigger than

China, from four times in 2007). This has caused enormous differences in the perceptions. The Americans are anxious about the way the Chinese are flexing their economic (through BRI) and military muscle. The Chinese feel that Americans are a hurdle in the rightful place of China in the world order and does not prefer the world to be unipolar, probably what Americans want. Thus, the trade war is not just about trade centric issues but also, about global hegemony. Over the years, the US companies have taken the advantage of low costs of manufacturing in China. Most of these firms began to depend upon China for their needs of the supply chain. In fact, 50% of supplies of Apple, Dell, and IBM etc. come from China. Seeing the trade war, most of the firms have decided to de-risk their operations and supply chains. This is where India enters. The India and the US are 'natural allies' with a shared vision of democracy. As part of de-risking operations, the US firms have decided to switch over their supply chain requirements from India. But it is not going to be easy for India to replace China in the global supply chains. China has a tremendous infrastructure which India lacks. However, India can always leverage its position in automobiles and textiles apart from ICT. The government in India has to massively invest in not just low cost manufacturing but low cost logistics, which will enable the players to manufacture and export immediately. This is where India can leverage its unique position in the Indian Ocean as well. As the US keeps de-risking operations in the long run, India needs to use the situation to take a leap faith in its manufacturing.

BELT AND ROAD INITIATIVE AND THE CHINESE ASHWAMEDHA—THE INFLUENCE OF MYTHOLOGY

As Western hegemony wanes in the global village, China envisioned the One Belt, One Road (OBOR) project. At the heart of Chinese mythology is belief in the Mandate of Heaven. The Emperor of China has been given the divine authority to mirror heavenly order on earth. If the emperor fails to do so, he can be replaced. A successful revolution marks the shifting of this mandate from one king to another. Although communism sees itself as rational, and so anti-religion and anti-mythology, the communist revolution under Mao Zedong effectively marked the shift in the Mandate of Heaven from the old order to the new. The rise of China into an economic powerhouse under Deng Xiaoping also indicates yet another shift in the Mandate of Heaven. The current leadership of Xi Jinping in China is now expanding its Pax Sinica. Geography always plays a key role in Chinese mythology. At the centre is the Forbidden City (Beijing) around which is China and around which are the peripheral nations who look towards China for guidance to create heavenly order on earth. Beyond are the lands of chaos, whose people are best, kept out using projects such as the Great Wall of China. By contrast, time (kala) plays a key role in Hindu mythology. Buddhism, Jainism and Hinduism speak of a world that has no beginning (anadi), no end (ananta) and is always impermanent (anitya). Indian mythologies speak of great universal emperors (chakravartin) but these are more conceptual than historical. India thrives in dynamic diversity, with multiple kingdoms that rise and fall from Mauryas to Guptas to Vakatakas to Rashtrakutas to Kadambas to Gangas to Pallavas to Pandyas to Cholas to Nayakas to Mughals to British. There is no Beijing equivalent in Hindu mythology, though Delhi is often projected as such in post-Independence textbooks. India, known in Buddhist, Jain and Hindu texts as Jambudvipa or Bharata-varsha or Arya-varta, is bound not by politics but by religion; it has been united not by empires but by pilgrim routes, an idea that perplexes modern historians who try very hard to prove India is a creation of the British. In Chinese mythology, there is authority and bureaucracy in heaven too. The gods enable the living to be successful, and successful mortals such as emperors, military commanders and noblemen take the position of immortal gods. The highly formal, hierarchical and socially responsible Confucianism, with its great regard for authority, is balanced by the more mystical and occult Taoism, that speaks of harmony and flow. Essentially, the tone is highly materialistic and worldly in contrast to the otherworldly nature of Indian mythologies, where the psychological matters more than the physical. Jain, Buddhist and Hindu mythologies place great value on yoga, the un-crumpling of the mind crumpled by hunger and fear. In Chinese worldview, India is seen in two ways. Firstly, it embodies luan, chaos. This chaos threatens the Chinese sense of order. This makes India a perpetual threat. It makes the Chinese leadership nervous. Secondly, India is Sukhavati, the Western Paradise in Chinese Buddhism, source of great spiritual wisdom. It speaks about transcending materialism to be free of suffering, an idea that invalidates the promise of the material philosophies, be it communism or capitalism. Until the arrival of the Europeans, Buddhism was the only foreign idea that has had a dramatic impact on Chinese history. Since then, China watches with trepidation the rising tide of Christian evangelism in South Korea and Singapore, and Islam on its Western borders, and the hurricane of technology coming from the West. The Chinese way is eroding, unless the Emperor takes charge. Hence, Chinese heavenly emperor announced the Belt and Road Initiative. However, it is often stated that natural catastrophes are likely to be the sole causes for the end of Mandate of Heaven.

THE CONCEPTUAL DETAILS OF BELT AND ROAD INITIATIVE

China was initially a communist country and a closed economy. In 1978, China made a transition to open economy. This happened because in the 1970s, Chinese began to witness problems in leadership of Soviet. This crack in the leadership with Soviet was exploited by the US and in 1972, the US transformed their ties with the Chinese. In 1978, Deng Xiaoping adopted the 'Going Out' strategy and Chinese advanced to become an open economy. In 40 years, China transformed itself from an agricultural economy to the manufacturing powerhouse of the world. It has followed a unique model of producing commodities at home and exporting the commodities to developed global markets. However, the Chinese economy, in recent times, has witnessed a slowdown in growth, which has led the Chinese government to look for new avenues of growth within its developing neighbours who are witnessing a growing demand. The aim of the BRI project is to create an economic land belt and a maritime link to redirect Chinese capital to develop infrastructure and trade capacity of ASEAN, Europe, Central Asia, Europe and Africa. The idea of the Silk Road has been taken from the old Silk Road built by the Han Dynasty, connecting Xian to the Roman Empire. In this mega trade network, the Chinese used to trade in silk, which inspired the German geographer named Ferdinand von Richthofentoco in the term, 'Silk Road' in the 19th century. Now, as China has achieved global resurgence, we see the revival of the ancient Silk Road in the 21st century in the form of BRI.

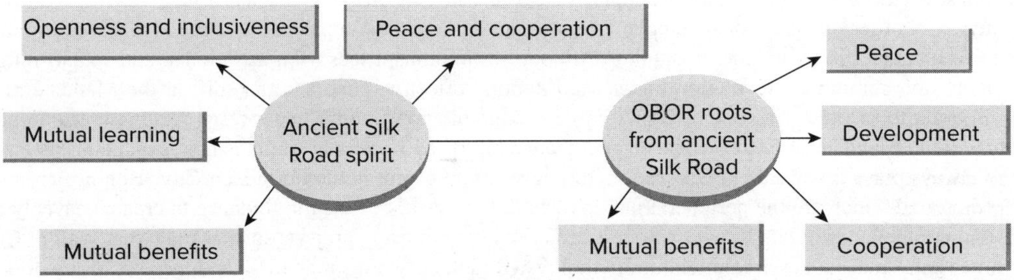

The concept of the BRI is based on certain principles where the broad aim is to establish a multi-dimensional and multi-tiered connectivity to tap the market potential of the region's leading countries to aggressively undertake job creation and promotion of consumption. The more important thing is that the BRI has a very strong cultural agenda to enhance people-to-people contacts, trust and understanding to promote harmony, peace and prosperity. Not only does the BRI rest upon mutual non-interference in each other's internal affairs, but also respect for the diverse development path adopted by a participating nation without any intention to change it. China does not want the initiative to be restricted to old Silk Road nations but rather proposes a global outreach for all to participate, as the basis of the Silk Road is to garner and channelise the market forces of demand and supply. China has a plan to involve more than 60 countries in the project and also plans to negotiate Free Trade Agreement with all of them along the entire BRI. Some studies done by the Asian Development Bank suggests that China would require around 8 trillion dollars' worth of investment for creating the needed infrastructure. China has created three financial institutions to support the BRI. In February 2014, China launched a 40-billion-dollar silk-road infrastructure fund, to be managed on the lines of China's sovereign wealth fund. In October 2014, the Asian Infrastructure Investment Bank was established as a global developmental bank for 21 Asian Nations, ranging from India to Laos to Oman to Uzbekistan, with a registered capital of 100 billion dollars. In July 2014, with a seed capital of 50 billion dollars, a new development bank was launched by BRICS nations.

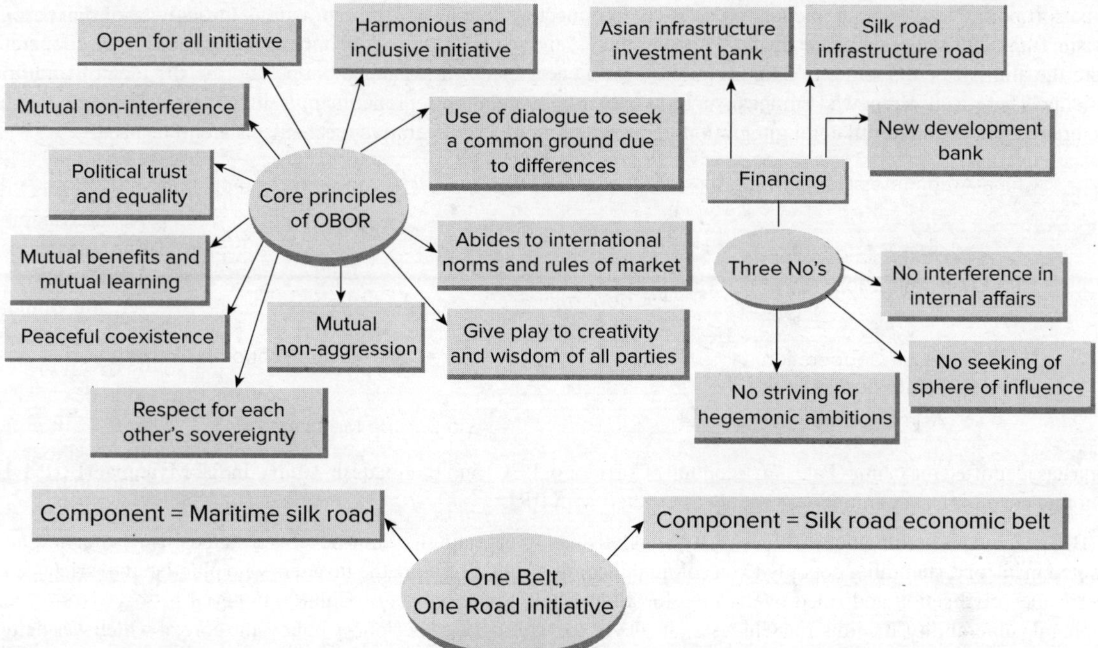

The BRI is designed in a way that it will also impact the domestic economy of China. China today has achieved an overcapacity in steel, cement and aluminium industry and would like to undertake exports to further stimulate its domestic economy. To do so, China has divided its domestic territory into five different regions. In each identified region, China will build infrastructure and use that infrastructure to establish connect with countries in the neighbourhood. For the BRI to succeed, China has decided to cooperate upon some core priority areas with participating states. At an initial level, China envisages policy coordination to be undertaken through multi-level intergovernmental macro policy exchange and communication mechanisms. The second priority is to strengthen sub regional and border infrastructure, with a strong focus on promoting a green and low carbon infrastructure creation.

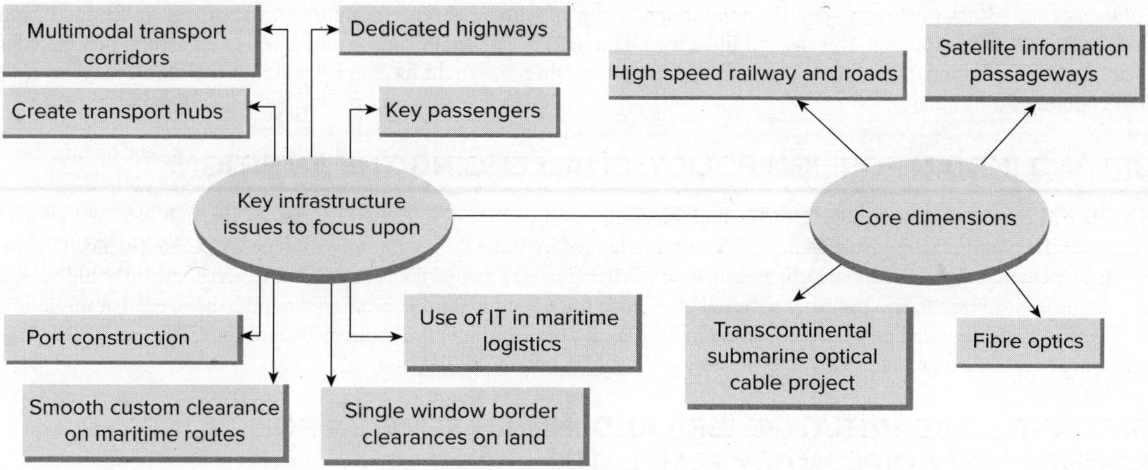

At the soft policy level, China intends to use BRI to connect to people of different nations through scholar exchanges, tourism, films, cultural years, art festivals, TV programmes, and so on. Another core dimension is health-based cooperation where the aim is to collaborate to address public health energies, with expanded cooperation in the idea of traditional medicine. There is also renewed emphasis upon youth employment, entrepreneurship training and skill development to accelerate regional and multilateral integration under which various cooperative mechanisms are to be used.

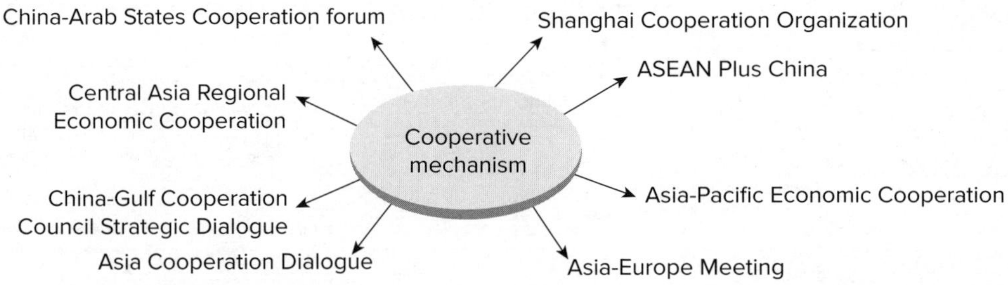

China has identified the China–Pakistan Economic Corridor (CPEC) and Bangladesh–China–India–Myanmar (BCIM–EC) economic corridor as key initiatives broadly associated with BRI.

The BRI of China is nothing but a Chinese territorial fetishism. Surprisingly, Chinese territorial fetishism is not new and it is rooted in history, stemming not only from colonial incursions but also nomadic invaders who plundered the rich Yellow River Valley civilisation and ruled over China for almost half of the period of Chinese imperial history. To overcome peripheral vulnerability, the imperial Chinese state devised a well-defined periphery policy, the core of which was defence through development and forced migration. The post-1949 Hanisation of Tibet and Xinjiang is therefore, a mere validation of imperial policy. Similarly, in the 1990s, to address the menace of ethnic separatism in the backward peripheral regions of Tibet and Xinjiang, China undertook the Western Development Strategy that was again laced with security measures, not economic amelioration, underscored in the five-pronged security policy of Hanisation, infrastructure development, resource extraction, military deployment and repression.

BRI AND INDIAN FOREIGN POLICY: BRAVE AND PRINCIPLED STAND

India has raised multiple objections to the BRI. India says the BRI is not a treaty-based concept and it does not conceptualise its rules and strategy at the outset. A core principle of the Indian foreign policy is its reluctance to accept anything that is not treaty based. Lack of a treaty specific commitment, coupled with an absence of mutual trust between India and China has compounded the problem. This has led India to call the BRI a 'national Chinese initiative'. India asserts that the BRI is not a true international initiative because had it been one, then, it would have conflated interests of all players. But, BRI is purely China centric.

BRI AND INDIAN FOREIGN POLICY: CHALLENGING THE AMBITION

India has a second objection to the CPEC, the core component of the BRI. The CPEC passes through disputed area of Jammu and Kashmir, the Pakistan Occupied Kashmir, claimed by India. Many initiatives of the CPEC are financed by the AIIB. The charter of AIIB very clearly asserts that if AIIB finances any projects in a disputed territory, it should seek a consensus of disputant states. India has asserted that China has not done this. This has given India the needed ammunition to eventually question that what exactly is the ambition of China and its core motives behind the CPEC and BRI? The investment in the disputed area only legitimises the illegal occupation of Pakistan.

BELT AND ROAD INITIATIVE (BRI) AND INDIAN FOREIGN POLICY: INDIA'S CONNECTIVITY DIPLOMACY TEMPLATE

India says that the key issue of BRI is the concept of connectivity envisaged by China. At this place, India has distinguished between connectivity projects that are unilaterally decided and one that is established via consultation. India has always supported consultative connectivity projects, which defuse rivalries at national level, in contrast to ones unilaterally, decided, that often adds to regional tensions and create unnecessary element of competitiveness. For India, if multi-polar world is the world of the 21st century, then multi-polar Asia is a passport to this multi-polar world. India has linked the creation of multi-polar Asia that is based on the system of consultations for benefit of all rather than unilateralism and for the benefit of one.

INDIA ON CHINESE PERCEPTION OF SOVEREIGNTY

India has asserted that Kashmir is an integral part of India, which is partly illegally occupied by Pakistan. Any initiative in a disputed territory affects sovereignty of India. India has asserted that as China is sensitive towards its own sovereignty, it needs to display the same sensitivity towards India too. All the above points clearly assert that the Chinese conceptualisation of BRI is contrary to Indian perception of any multilateral project. India per se does not have any problem with BRI.

PHILOSOPHY OF INDIA'S APPROACH FOR BELT AND ROAD INITIATIVE

Any project that entails massive investment in a disputed area (like POK through which CPEC passes) will only legitimise the illegal occupation of the territory by Pakistan. Also, India feels that Chinese maritime forays in Myanmar, Bangladesh, Maldives, Sri Lanka and Pakistan and its port creations in these states will give china an upper edge in the Indian Ocean, denying India options to play in Indian Ocean, which it considers its own backyard. India feels that due to ports created in the states above, china will cause massive dumping of goods and saturate their markets, which will put India in a tough situation where it will be left with only little scope for exports. This means, India feels that CPEC affects India's economic diplomacy. India feels that as BRI will give a competitive edge to Chinese corporations to do easy business in states around India and it would reduce the participative space for Indian corporate to leverage these markets. India has analysed that the objective of the BRI is to export the top-down, debt-driven Chinese development through government-to-government deals that are devoid of an element of competitive bidding. Thus, India's policy can be best termed as a muted response with unaddressed concerns.

INDIA'S PERCEPTION: BELT AND ROGUE INITIATIVE

As a strategy, China is using BRI to export its excess capacity, which will expand the Chinese market base and consequently its political clout. During the time of Mao, China initiated 'Red and Expert' initiative. This was an initiative where Red signified the communist China and Expert signified the technical and economic expertise. The Red and Expert initiative aimed to perfectly blend the politics, economics and technology for the benefit and growth of China. Few years later, Mao initiated the Cultural Revolution, where politics (Red) took over economics and technology (Expert), leading to a disaster. This is where the genesis of the BRI lies. After the death of Mao, Deng Xiaoping took all efforts to bring Chinese intellectual power to the forefront. As Chinese economy grew, Xi Jinping brought about the BRI. The backdrop of its launch was the Chinese assertiveness in the South China Sea and a constitutional order that removed presidential term limits for the Chinese Premier. In 2020, six years after the launch of BRI (2014), states are cancelling the projects of BRI. This raises questions on the legitimacy of the strategy of China. It is in this backdrop that India is proud to emerge as a leader of the new intellectual movement unleashed against the financial and security risks associated with this rouge initiative. India has rightly stated that BRI is a non-transparent and a neo-colonial enterprise of China. The prime objective of the BRI is to use cash-strapped states as targets and engulf them in a debt trap, thereby helping China to advance its geopolitical interests. The BRI clearly signifies the rise of a 'new imperialist China' and is 'reminiscent of European colonialism' (practices being followed by China like leasing for 99 years and so). The IMF too has advised caution to the states with respect to the 'predatory' practices of debt traps by China that can seriously undermine the national sovereignty and self-respect of the states. The case of China taking over Hambantota port for lease of 99 years is reminiscent of a farmer in debt handing over his daughter to the cruel moneylender. The same strategy was applied by China in Djibouti, where the debt and cash strapped state had no other option but give away the land on lease to China for a military base. All this proves that BRI is a geo-economic tool to promote geo-political objectives of China. The BRI is a strategy to remake the terms of global commerce on the terms dictated by China.

SHOULD INDIA JOIN THE BRI? REVERSING THE PRISM

It is imperative for India to join the BRI as India may accrue strategic and economic benefits of the same and also because joining BRI makes historical sense as Kautilya has often emphasised that to decapitate a rival, hug him tight. Various studies have pointed out that CPEC component of BRI have witnessed bottlenecks and the CPEC is no more a river of milk and honey but rather a millstone around the neck. The issues in CPEC range from opposition to infrastructure by Baloch people to that of the US–Pakistan rapprochement. This is where India can take advantage and offer China with Kandla to Kashgar connectivity. If China aims to develop Kashgar to Gwadar as part of CPEC, then India can offer this alternative space as a sweet revenge to Pakistan. Establishing a strategic corridor from Kandla to Kashgar will also weaken the bargaining power of Pakistan with China and enhance India's bargaining power with China. While rejecting the BRI, India has stated that connectivity projects should follow principles of financial responsibility and ensure that projects do no create unsustainable debt burden for communities. This is the place for India to act smart and use the BRI to internationalise these principles. This would also contribute to India position itself as a leading power. Thus, India should join the BRI for the strategic and economic sense it makes.

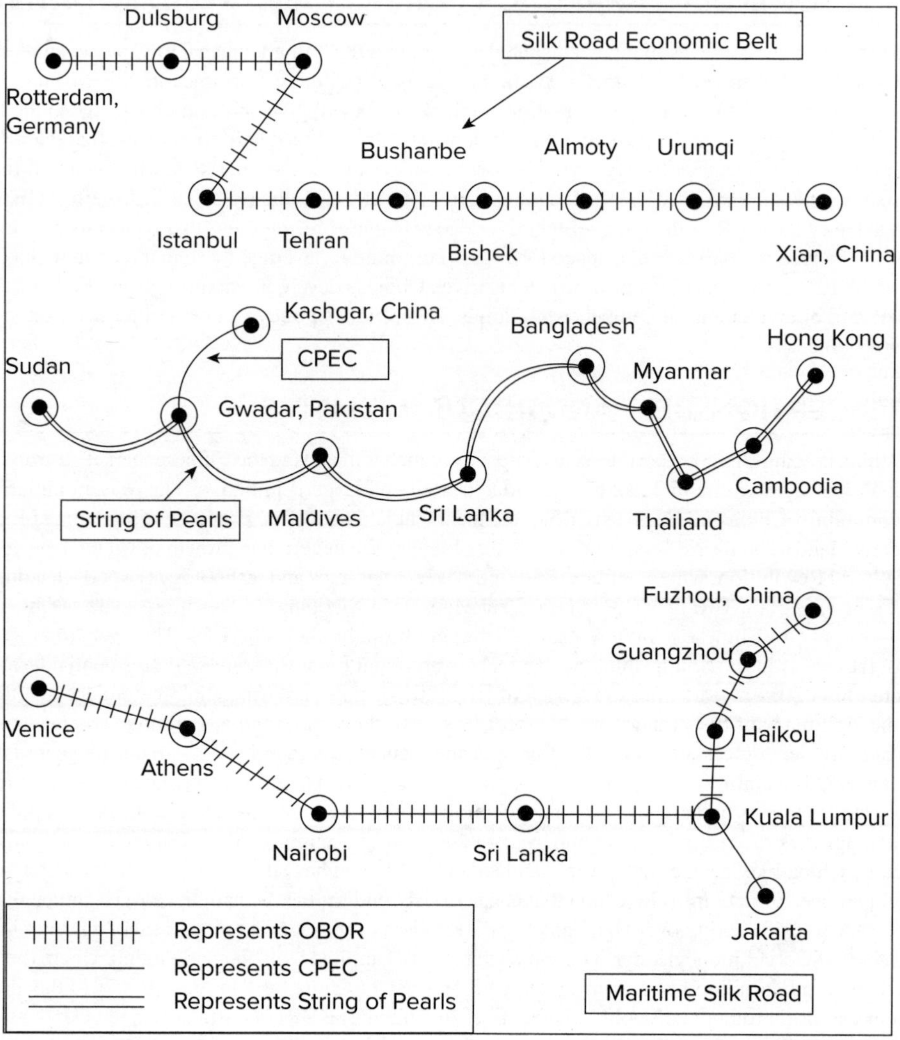

CONTEXT OF THE INFORMAL RENDEZVOUS OF WUHAN AND CHENNAI

Both China and the US see India as a swing state. This means that the US wants India to swing in favour of Washington in their grand strategy to counter China; while China does not want India to swing in favour of Washington to counter China; thus, the need for informal summits. The Indian Prime Minister and the Chinese Premier had an informal summit at Wuhan (a city in the mid of Yangtze is a symbol of economic might and resilience of China) in 2018 and Chennai in 2019. Informal summits do not have any pre-decided agenda for discussion and at the end of such summits there is no formal statement, no MoU announced and no joint press conference occurs. The only problem with an informal summit is that parties are not bound by their words. The advantage of an informal summit however is that it allows a relaxed atmosphere for the leaders of the two states to exchange views on things they cannot otherwise formally discuss in formal meetings and they are tools for trust building. India deliberately went for informal setting knowing that China does not have acquiescence in this kind of diplomacy. However, the two states, through their diplomats, do announce the core points of understanding achieved during the summit. The two sides have decided to institutionalise this concept into an 'Annual Summit' from 2020 onwards.

WHY WUHAN AND THEN CHENNAI SUMMITS?

The 2018 summit was significant as it happened in the backdrop of the Doklam crisis. But there were other factors. The US has unleashed a trade war on China. Xi felt that the confrontationist approach with the US would dent Chinese economy, so Xi looked at India as a possible balance in the trade war. Secondly, Modi in India was not keen to enter into the last year of his tenure with 2019 polls with a 'Doklam hangover', thus Wuhan. The summit was planned to resolve differences between the two sides so that both could respect each other's concerns, aspirations and sensitivities so that the two can rebuild the 'trust' and avoid rubbing against each other and prevent friction that can touch off a fire. The 2019 summit was a continuation of the positive energy generated at Wuhan and happened in the backdrop of differences in Kashmir (over abrogation of Article 370) and Indian military exercise in Arunachal. The 2019 summit happened in Mamallapuram. Chinese Buddhist monk Xuanzang had visited Kanchipuram during the Pallava dynasty. Bodhidharma, who spread Zen Buddhism to China, had set sail from the coast of Tamil Nadu and landed in present-day Guangdong (Canton) province. There was a major trade link between the Pallava and Chola kingdoms of south India with the southeast coast of China, particularly the province of Fujian and city of Quanzhou. The discovery of coins and potteries of China's Song dynasty are a testimony to that. Mahamallapuram is regarded as the city of Mamalla or Narsimhavarman-I of the Pallava Dynasty. It is the same site where 63 years earlier, Zhou Enlai and Ho Loung had visited in 1956. Mahamallapuram and China also have the oldest security pact on earth. In the 8th century, the Chinese sought help from the Pallava king Rajasimhan to counter Tibet, which had emerged as a strong power and a threat to China.

ANATOMY OF INDIA'S RESET OF CHINA POLICY AND WHY INDIA WENT FOR WUHAN AND CHENNAI

The reason for the summit was no doubt to diffuse the tensions, which had emerged because of Doklam crisis and Kashmir crisis but there exists three deeper logics. Today, in Indian strategic community, there is an understanding that conflict and any adversarial relationship with China will not be beneficial for India. Secondly, a consensus also exists that no external power is also interested to deflect China from its forays in Indian Ocean or India's neighbourhood. Thirdly, there is a belief that any acrimony between India and China only gives leverage to Pakistan to shape Chinese South Asia policy, which will be detrimental to India. Not only that, but India has also seen that the US and Japan too wish to maintain their ties with China, despite verbal conflicts. At one place the US has unleashed a trade war on China and simultaneously is engaging with China over de-nuclearisation of North Korea. Even Japan, which has a USD 300 billion trade with China, has asserted that it will engage with China on a 'case by case' basis for the BRI.

THE WARMTH AND CHEMISTRY AND THE MUTUAL INTEREST IN SERENITY IN WUHAN AND CHENNAI

1. The two sides decided to provide strategic communication at the highest level. This strategic communication is needed to identify vistas of cooperation in overlapping regional and global interests.
2. There shall be strategic guidance to the forces on the ground level between the militaries (to build trust and understanding) to facilitate flow of constant communication to avoid crisis in future by prudently managing differences with mutual sensitivity.
3. To reduce the trade deficit, the two sides decided to enhance cooperation in boosting agricultural and pharmaceutical exports.
4. To bridge the trust deficit and induce a spirit of positive cooperative competition, the two identified to undertake joint economic projects in Afghanistan. This is based on the understanding that overall geopolitical stability is crucial for economic growth. This led to the birth of an idea called the 'Two Plus One' format (an integrated approach for trilateral development), where Two are India and China and Plus one envisaged is Afghanistan (which as a model can be in future extended to Africa as China has been asserting that India and China are 'like-minded partners' in Africa).
5. At the international level, the two decided to sync their efforts on multilateral issues like climate change and seek reforms of international intuitions that affect developing states.
6. The two decided to cooperate in resolving the irritants like Indian membership to NSG.
7. A new strategic objective was agreed upon which included the early settlement of the border issue.
8. The Indian side asserted that China has adhered to (in Chennai) the 'Political Parameters and the Guiding Principles' signed between the two in 2005. This is important here because in the 2005 agreement, India made claims to disputed areas in the Eastern sector of the border.
9. The leaders have decided to "brighten up each other" by learning from each other how they can realise the true potential of two great ancient civilisations.

The core points of understanding at Wuhan and Chennai can be summarised into five words—shared vision, better communication, strong relationship, shared thought process and shared resolve. In the Wuhan Summit, to build people-to-people ties, the two have emphasised on STRENGTH—Spirituality, Tradition, Trade and technology, Relationship, Entertainment, Nature conservation, Games, Tourism and Health and healing. The Indian Prime Minister gave five principles of Soch, Sampark, Sahyog, Sankalp and Sapne.

ANALYSIS OF WUHAN AND CHENNAI AND IMPLICATIONS ON BILATERAL RELATIONS

The summit level diplomacy is a new feature of the 20th century. The advent of travel through airlines allows meetings can be planned at a short notice (as Wuhan). Secondly, the mass media making a spectacle of such summits for domestic political constituencies is another factor for such meets. In case of India and China, it is worth noting, that the first such summit happened in 1954 between Nehru and Zhou Enlai, at a time when China did not even have an aircraft to fly its leader. Eventually, an Air India plane brought Zhou to India for the summit in Delhi. Today, China has built an alternative domestic passenger aircraft, in competition to Boeing and airbus. In this changed ground realities, we need to look at the Wuhan Summit. At a time when the two have been distrustful of each other due to the bruising caused by Doklam standoff, the Wuhan Summit can be seen as an attempt to achieve entente cordiale between India and China. The summit ensured that the two sides comeback to the negotiating table even though they had no prefixed agenda of negotiation. This also means that such an informal meet was relevant for domestic messaging as well, which otherwise would have given domestic Indian opposition parties the chance to assert 'failed China policy' to the electorate. More important is that this time in Chennai, there was mention of 'our common interests outweigh our differences', which is different from 'our commonalities outweigh our difference' as always in the past. There was however no mention of any measures to reduce the tensions between the two to CPEC, proving that tension between India and China still runs 'along the spine of

Asia'. The distrust still remains. India still views Chinese 'encroachments' into its neighbourhood and Indian Ocean as an upfront challenge to Indian authority, while China views deepening of India's ties with the US and Japan as a challenge to its security. But a journey of a thousand miles begins with a single step.

Dimension	Border	Terrorism	Economy	Disputes	Strategic communication
Wuhan (2018)	Asked Special Representatives to intensify border settlement	Opposed terror of all forms and decided to cooperate	Promote bilateral trade and explore complementarities	Promote peace and stability in times of global uncertainty	Advocated the concept of strategic guidance and strategic communication
Chennai (2019)	Respect political parameters and guiding principles agreed in 2005	Decided for 'Joint Efforts' to strengthen global framework on terror	High Level Mechanism for Trade and Economic Cooperation created for mutual investments	Reiterated Astana Commitment of 2017 that difference should not become disputes	India formally adopted strategic communication and leader driven mechanism. The two have decided a sea voyage as part of 70 activities to celebrate 70 years of diplomatic ties.

INDIA AND CHINA: WATER WAR NARRATIVE AND CHINESE STRATEGY OF HYDRO-HEGEMONY

Water covers almost 71% of the earth's surface. Yet, only 3% of that water is potable, out of which 2% is held in glaciers and ice caps. Even this percentage is rapidly shrinking due to growing human population, increased economic activity and rapid pollution. When increase in population is read together with demands arising from prevalent consumption patterns, it presents a bleak future scenario. It has been projected that two out of three people in the world will live in water-stressed conditions by the year 2030. The indispensability of water combined with scarcity creates a fertile breeding ground for potential conflict. The fact that rivers, which are an important source of fresh water, do not follow political boundaries and are more often than not trans-boundary in nature makes the situation more complex. In this context, it becomes imperative to explore the unique advantage China has as a complete upper riparian power. China's bid to achieve water security as well as ambitions to establish itself as a hydro-hegemon in the region, through the case of mighty Yarlung Tsangpo/ Brahmaputra River, especially focusing on the implications for India. Asia comprises 60% of the world's population (4.4 billion in 2016) and also has the highest growth rate today, with its population almost quadrupling during the 20th century.

The upper and lower riparian nations often make incompatible claims about their rights over river waters. The upper riparian nations base their claim on the principle of 'absolute territorial sovereignty', meaning the right to use the river waters unilaterally regardless of lower riparian concerns. This is often called the Harmon Doctrine. According to this doctrine, an upstream nation can freely utilise a river's flow within its boundaries without considering the effect on a downstream state. The lower riparian states, on the other hand, base their claims on 'absolute territorial integrity', which argues that upper riparian actions should not affect the water flowing downstream. China has been seen to act in a manner typical of an upper riparian nation. Its distinctive position as a completely upper riparian nation allows it to act as a hydro-hegemon in the region. China's hydro-hegemony is made possible by its control over Tibet. The Qinghai-Tibetan Plateau extends over a vast area spanning 2.5 million square kilometres. This Plateau, often referred to as the 'third pole' and 'roof of the world', is home to the largest fresh water reserves outside north and south poles. It is the source of some of the Asia's most important river systems including the Indus, Ganga, Brahmaputra, Irrawady, Slaween, Mekong, Yangtze and Huang He. All these rivers are trans-boundary in nature, with the exception of Yangtze and Huang He. As per the estimates of the Chinese ministry of water resources, the Tibet Autonomous Region (TAR) has 448.2 billion cubic metres of water, which is strategically important since it gives China an enormous edge over India in terms of control over water resources. Chinese scientists have discovered that Tibet has 40,000 times more water resources than China. The Chinese occupation of Tibet, wherein the most important rivers originate, *de facto* assures China's hydro hegemony. The *de jure* control over water resources is aided by the fact that China has made huge investments in dams and has not entered into any water sharing agreement with India. China is no stranger to massive dam projects. The Three Gorges Dam on Yangtze River is by far the biggest in the world. However, unlike the Three Gorges Dam, where impact is restricted to areas within China, the several dam projects on Yarlung Tsangpo assumes significance since India (as well as Bangladesh further down) are directly affected and have to bear externalities emanating from it. The Yarlung Tsangpo enters India after passing the Great Bend, through Arunachal Pradesh where it is known as Siang/Dihang, then onto Assam where it is called Brahmaputra, and thereafter to Bangladesh where it is named Jamuna. China completed the Zangmu Dam (510 MW capacity) built on the upper reaches of Brahmaputra in 2010. Three more dams at Dagu (640 MW), Jiacha (320 MW) and Jeixu are at present under construction in 2020. The work on Zam hydropower station, which will be the largest dam on Brahmaputra, too commenced in 2015. Although the Indian allegations about Chinese dam building activities on Brahmaputra date back to more than a decade, Beijing admitted to the construction of Zangmu Dam only in 2010 and that too after a series of denials. China has not yet officially communicated anything about the construction of the other three dams—Dagu, Liacha and Jiexu —on Brahmaputra. Lack of communication by China has created an atmosphere of suspicion and mistrust in India, especially in its Northeastern region. China seems to have chosen a policy of absolute sovereignty rather than one of national integrity over shared water resources (where states have the right not to be negatively affected by activities of upper-riparian countries). China has been repeatedly invited to participate in multilateral consultations by downstream states comprising the Mekong River Commission (MRC), which it has refused to join. Chinese reluctance to participate in MRC could be attributed to growing water scarcity within the country and the possibility of similar demands by other downstream states. However, back in 2010, a severe drought in the country had pushed China to participate in MRC discussions and data sharing. China has also been reluctant to ratify the 1997 UN Convention on the Law of the Non-navigational Uses of International Watercourses that provides a framework for multilateral cooperation on water. Article 11 of this UN Convention mentions the need for states to share information regarding use of international watercourses. Articles 21 and 23 elaborate on pollution, prevention and protection of the marine environment. China believes that the Convention does not adequately consider the interests of upstream states. India too has not ratified it probably because the Convention has no force over non-party countries such as China. Geopolitical and strategic imperatives do not justify a state becoming a party to the Convention unless other states with trans-boundary water associations also become parties. China had refused to sign and ratify the Helsinki Rules too. In 1966, a codification of the principles of international law relating to trans-boundary water resources was completed through the International Law Association's (ILA) Helsinki Rules on the Uses of the Waters of International Rivers. The gist of the Helsinki Rules is that each state within an international drainage basin has the right to a reasonable and equitable part of the beneficial use of the basin waters. The two basic principles can be briefly summed up as reasonable usage and an obligation to do no harm. However, the enforceability of the Helsinki Rules is undermined by the ILA's status as an unofficial organisation. Thus, these resolutions cannot be legally binding in international law unless they are adopted in the form of a multilateral convention or followed by states as state practice. The Chinese decision to build more and more dams on Yarlung/Brahmaputra and continued evasiveness on its long-term plans, the number and kind of dams it intends to build, has been an issue of major concern for India. China, on its part, insists that the dams are and will continue to be run-of-river projects, wherein water will be returned to the river after use. As such there ought to be no fears of diversion, hoarding, and release of water later. The Indian Government has taken this claim with a pinch of salt. Government, in close cooperation with various State Governments including Government of Assam, which are users of the waters of river Brahmaputra, continues to carefully monitor the water flow in river Brahmaputra for early detection of abnormality so that corrective and preventive measures are taken to safeguard livelihood of peoples of these States of Union of India. What further adds to India's concerns is that these dams are large enough to be converted and used as storage dams, especially if the purpose is flood control and irrigation (as is the case with Zangmu Dam). In the absence of a water treaty, China depriving India of water during lean seasons becomes a possibility. Chinese hydropower projects could convert Brahmaputra into a seasonal river implying water scarcity in India. Another risk is the release of floodwaters during the monsoon season, which could inundate the already flooded Brahmaputra river basin in Assam. There is much apprehension that the Brahmaputra may lose the silt, which makes the plains in its basin fertile, because of sediment trapping in the dams.

Additionally, all hydropower projects, particularly around the Great Bend, are located in a highly volatile tectonic zone. Their proximity to known geological fault lines, where Indian Plate collides with the Eurasian Plate, makes them extremely earthquake-prone. In building its dams, China has also polluted its rivers. The disruptions of natural flood cycles of the river have adversely affected the rich geo-environmental and biophysical settings in India's Northeast. China has priority rights since it was the first to build dams on Yarlung Tsangpo. By building dams especially near the Great Bend, after which the river flows into India through Arunachal Pradesh, China could be seeking to leverage its position over the Indian state of Arunachal Pradesh. Around the time China started working on this dam project, India too decided to commence construction of 14 hydropower projects in Arunachal Pradesh, most of which were located lower down on Brahmaputra. This might be viewed as India's effort to establish its 'lower riparian right' to counter China's first use priority rights. The idea might be to ensure a strong bargaining position to detract China from building hydel projects on the river's upper reaches. However, except for one project, all other projects are currently stuck due to lack of necessary environmental clearance. The only project cleared so far is the 2000 MW Lower Subansiri hydroelectric power project, which too is languishing due to scarcity of funds. Some experts have pointed out that the volume of precipitation varies across the Brahmaputra sub-basin substantially. It receives primarily two types of precipitation, rainfall and snowfall. In this respect, the Tibetan part of the basin along the stretch of Yarlung, being located on the northern aspect of the Himalayas, receives much less rainfall as compared to the southern part of the basin, that is, the stretches in India and Bangladesh. The total annual outflow of Yarlung from China is about 31 billion cubic metres (BCM), while the annual flow of Brahmaputra at Bahadurabad, the gauging station near the end of the sub-basin in Bangladesh, is 606 BCM. Around 80% of the flows of Brahmaputra emerge within the Indian boundary. According to some Indian experts, the Brahmaputra gets mightier as it flows downstream because of the flow contribution of tributaries such as Dibang, Lohit and Subansiri. In terms of sediment flow, the flow volume and discharge is not sufficient to generate and transport the large sediment load that is characteristic of Brahmaputra downstream. Despite China having 50% spatial share of this 3,000 km-long water system, low precipitation and desert conditions mean that Tibet generates only 25% of its total basin discharge, while India, with 34% of the basin, contributes to 39% of the total discharge. This refutes the thinking that the flow of a river is proportional to its expanse within the country. Even then, the fact that intentional flooding and degradation of water upstream remain serious issues of concern for India cannot be summarily dismissed. As of now, there is no institutionalised mechanism on water cooperation between India and China. China has signed no such treaty with India or any of its neighbours and continues to act in a unilateral manner in the region. However, in 2002, India and China had entered into a Memorandum of Understanding (MoU) wherein China agreed to share hydrological information about Yarlung Tsangpo (Brahmaputra) including its discharge at Nugesha, Yangcun and Nuxia stations from June 01 to October 15 every year. This was helpful in the formulation of flood forecasts by the Central Water Commission. When this provision ended in 2007, it was renewed for another five years. In 2006, a Joint Expert Level Mechanism was set up between the two countries in order to exchange hydrological information and ensure a smooth transmission of flood season hydrological data. In 2013, this provision was renewed with the change that 2014 onward sharing of data would take place twice a day from May 15 to October 15. However, China had refused to share hydrological data during the Doklam standoff. Although hydrological data sharing resumed in 2018, the Doklam face-off showed how China could use water for political leverage. By refusing to share data which is crucial for flood control and planning during the monsoon period in India, China demonstrated that it is not averse to using water as a political weapon to control and force compliance on its downstream neighbours. Any forward movement on ensuring hydro security in the Brahmaputra basin would require a long-term understanding between the two countries. India's hydro-diplomacy thus faces the daunting challenge of engaging China in a sustained dialogue and securing a water sharing treaty that serves the interests of both the countries. To meet its surging energy demand, China itself seeks to utilise its huge hydropower potential of the Brahmaputra but on other hand, China has to maintain a stable relation with India and Bangladesh. Therefore, China follows the desecuritisation policy to deal with the water sharing conflicts. Desecuritisation refers to the process of "moving issues off the security agenda and back into the realm of political discourse and normal political dispute and accommodation. Desecuritisation is therefore about 'turning threats into challenges and security into politics' China's desecuritisation moves have primarily been of a reactive and short-term nature. Whenever there are concerns raised about the Chinese activities on the upstream of the river, Beijing resorts to a volley of rhetorical comments.

CORE IRRITANTS BETWEEN DIPLOMATIC RELATIONS OF INDIA AND CHINA

History is alone not the biggest reason for India and China to be where they are. Had history been the sole factor, today the world would have been Dar-ul-Harb (House of war). There have new sources of frictions in the 21st century, but history is obviously one of the factors, not the sole one.

1. Unresolved border between India and China
2. Regular border standoffs and incursions at the borders
3. The strategic American shift to Indo-Pacific that makes China uncomfortable
4. Revival of Quad by the US and attempts to position it as an Asian NATO
5. 'Deep Pocket' diplomacy of China in India's neighbourhood
6. Differences at international for Indian membership to the NSG and permanent membership at UNSC
7. Chinese contests Dalai Lama and his presence in India
8. Lack of transparency on water sharing by China, especially the rivers in East
9. Sowa-Rigpa, a traditional form of medicine in Himalayas is a newly emerging source of friction as both India and China strive to seek its enlisting at UNESCO as intangible cultural heritage
10. Rising trade deficit apart from the existing trust deficit

AREA OF FUTURE COLLABORATION-1: DEMOGRAPHY AND URBANISATION

India is witnessing a massive rise in its population whereas the population growth in China has slowed down, due to the One-Child policy adopted. However, both the states continue to witness population growth. The growth of the population directly impacts the urbanisation. In India, the urbanisation problem is more because of rise of urban population, whereas, in China it is more due to induced migration. Despite the differences, the problems caused by urbanisation ranging from slums, traffic congestion, sanitation, housing pressures and pollution, are common to both. This provides an incentive to collaborate. The first factor is to learn from the other how are they solving the problem? This requires experts to open up a channel of communication. Secondly, both can evolve an indigenous home grown strategy to solve these challenges that can eventually present a new alternative to the existing 'western' paradigm. Collectively, the states in the future can become a harbinger for change and development in other developing states.

AREA OF FUTURE COLLABORATION-2: HUMAN DEVELOPMENT AND GROWTH

The quantifiable data suggests that India and China are the two topmost fastest growing economies in the world. But, there is a catch. The two also have a low performance on human development indices. This proves that growth and development have not been commensurate in the two states. This is surprising because globally states that have expanded economic growth have also widened and improved on developmental indicators. This means that India and China are part of their own league where they differ from the global practices. This itself is a condition for collaboration where the sides can strive to understand why the human development indices have not improved despite both witnessing higher trajectories of growth. They can then strive to find a common ground to collectively improve their human development indices as well.

AREA OF FUTURE COLLABORATION-3: MEDIA AS A TRUST BUILDER

Despite the fact that in the last two decades the two sides have witnessed higher trade, one factor that plagues the relationship is 'trust deficit'. This is historical and has been deep rooted in the Indian psyche since the 1962 military conflict. On top of this, the media in the two states has often played a role in only strengthening this deep bilateral suspicion. In 2010, when the Chinese premier visited India, he urged the media in India to play a more constructive role in positioning a more positive image of China including on issues that are sensitive like the border issues. Despite pragmatism to move forward diplomatically (starkly visible in Wuhan Summit 2018 and Chennai in 2019), the clouded suspicion will remain an irritant. This provides an area of collaboration. The state-owned medias of the two states could take the lead. They can start having regular programs consisting of experts from both the states. These programmes can discuss various themes of bilateral cooperation and can play a positive role in addressing the 'trust deficit'. This will have a spillover effect and jointly with diplomatic pragmatism, can help the two states to change the psyche of the people.

AREA OF FUTURE COLLABORATION-4: CIVILISATIONAL POWER

The two states are civilisational powers. They have connected histories. However, the people to people engagement remain the lowest. This is one important pillar of collaboration. In the Wuhan and Chennai summits, India asserted the need to strengthen civilisational ties through cultural exchanges, sports, yoga and films. The two sides can jointly cooperate to emerge as spiritual world powers and redefine the concept of international power, which till today is dominated by pure military power only.

AREA OF FUTURE COLLABORATION-5: SOCIAL DEVELOPMENT

India is creating massive infrastructure. This ranges from highways to rail infrastructure to developing sustainable agriculture. China has investment liquidity and it can invest in Indian infrastructure projects. Secondly, to mitigate rural–urban disparity, India is focusing on enhancing agricultural productivity. This is one area where China can again be of direct help to India. As India is a pioneer in services while China in goods manufacturing, this is a potential area of high cooperation. India can try to deepen its 'Make in India' programme through a deep collaboration with China and through experts learn how China became a manufacturing powerhouse. China can do the same in services. This directly opens up a new area of joint cooperation, energy. This takes the two states to deepen their cooperation further in climate change. Both India and China can explore joint collaboration in development of shale gas. The shale is available in Tarain, Tuha, Sichuan and Ordos in China, while Godavari, Krishna and Cauvery in India.

AREA OF FUTURE COLLABORATION-6: SECURED ENVIRONMENT FOR BECOMING GLOBAL POWERS

India and China today face common three common threats of extremism, terrorism and radicalisation. If China witnesses them in Xinjiang, India witnesses the same in Kashmir. Even though the two sides have different views on the three threats as India believes Pakistan to be the factor causing the three while China not, the two sides can develop a common understanding on these threats. This can enable the two to further explore possibilities of joint cooperation in the Indian Ocean as well.

INDIA'S OPTIONS ON MANAGING CHINA: PLAYING A ZERO-DIM-SUM GAME

Be Patient, Be inscrutable, be Deceptive and keep your plans unfathomable

Just as nature abhors vacuum, same way, the international politics abhors an imbalance of power. This statement by Kenneth Waltz, further states that when a state faces hegemonic threats, it can either increase its own power, ally with another power to restore the power balance or jump on hegemons bandwagon. Keeping this in mind, India has to articulate a strategy on how it will manage a two front war if it occurs.

GIVE THE CHINESE A 'BLOODY NOSE"

The famous poet Maya Angelou rightly said, 'when someone shows you who they are, believe them'. Nations empower their militaries to deter war, and should they fail, fight to win wars. India's approach has to be firm and the country has to display a resolve to protect its territorial sovereignty. By displaying a firm resolve against China, India, which is not even under the US security umbrella can demonstrate to kill two birds with one stone. India is trying to resolve the matter via talks. The best way to resolve the matter is via talks only but if Chinese do not happen to retreat the occupied lands, then a military solution cannot be imposed on them owing to technological, military and economic asymmetries between the two, but, India can give the Chinese a 'bloody nose' in select locations if the matters aggravate.

GO FOR BOUNCING-IN APPROACH

If talks fail and Chinese refuse to retreat, then India can resort to the strategy of "bouncing-in" where India can use air power and boats on the Pangong Lake beyond Finger-4 and occupy the territories claimed by India. In case of Ladakh, the

Chinese may have the advantage of mobilising their troops faster as they have better infrastructure, but, the Indian side has better experience of mountain warfare, both in terms of skills and quality of human resources. The Mountain Strike Corps (MSC) and India's Special Frontier Force (a covert operation arm of RAW) will provide India the required deterrence and enable India to launch defensive operations if necessary to forcibly evict the Chinese from the Indian Territory they are occupying. Manmohan Singh and George Bush had developed a tacit understanding that if Chinese ever resort to a violent threat against India, then, the US would provide India with air support.

CHOKE THE CHINESE IN WATERS

If any military response by India snowballs into an all-out war with China and if Pakistan happens to open a second front, then India can always open up the dreaded maritime frontier for China and use Indian Navy to choke the sea routes crucial to Chinese.

WORKING MECHANISM FOR CONSULTATION AND COORDINATION ON BORDER AFFAIRS

However, to avoid such violent clashes as one happened in Galwan Valley in 2020, it is imperative for India and China to conclude Comprehensive Border Management Engagement Agreement between Indian Army and Chinese PLA which shall subsume all established mechanisms of confidence building, border personnel meetings, meetings of the Working Mechanism for Consultation and Coordination on Border Affairs (WMCC) and other diplomatic channels. When a disease is not cured permanently, any temporary palliatives do not work. This statement reiterates the fact that the long-term wisdom lies in permanently demarcating the LAC. If the situation persists, India can play five cards.

INDIA'S INTERNATIONAL OUTREACH

As part of a global campaign to tackle an expansionist China, India should expand Malabar and has rightly added Australia, join the Five Eyes Network and ban Huawei to access Indian market and 5G services.

HONG KONG CARD AND TAIWAN CARD

India till now has avoided any comments on internal situation of Hong Kong. However, if Chinese tactics continue, then India can try to support the US in siding with the aspirations of youngsters of Hong Kong (who are anti-China) at the domestic and international level. As explained in the chapter ahead, India can rightly use the Taiwan card by deepening economic and strategic ties.

INDIA'S XINJIANG CARD

India till now has refrained from commenting upon the human rights violations in Xinjiang regionally and internationally, despite the Chinese supporting the Pakistanis on human right violations in Kashmir. India can always leverage its deep relations, economic and strategic, with the Gulf to isolate China on blatant human rights violations on Uyghur Muslims in Xinjiang.

INDIA'S TIBET CARD

India, being sensitive to the Chinese concerns, has always allowed Dalai Lama to remain confined to religious and spiritual activities only. But, India can always leverage Dalai Lama by encouraging him to do political activities on behalf of the Tibetan people if needed. India can try to assist Dalai Lama in grooming his successor. In 1999, when Jiang Zemin, the then Chinese premier visited the Swiss Parliament, he was greeted with pro-Tibetan protestors. The Chinese Premier became so angry with this that he commented, "Swiss have lost a good friend". This is what Indian Prime Minister and Indian establishment can do, by displaying solidarity with Dalai Lama and communicate to the Chinese, "You have lost a good friend" (read India here). Maybe, India can try to open up the Historical Division in the MEA, which was shut down in the 1990s, to enable its officers and bureaucracy to learn what Chinese have done in their past.

DO MORE TRADE WITH CHINA TO MANAGE CHINA

At a time when emotional sentiment in India is against China and also trying to promote boycott Chinese goods; let us prove that how more trade with China can actually hurt them more. My suggestion here is let China do more business with India. Instead of being concerned that China will exploit the weak situation of Indian businesses hit due to COVID-19 and acquire stakes in Indian firms, it would be better if Indian government liberalises the FDI rules and actually allow the Chinese to take up such stakes. The Chinese corporate sector is controlled and financed by the Chinese government. So, if China invests in India, it effectively means money is of Chinese government in India. Such investment will increase interdependence between India and China. As the economic interdependence grows, India will happen to yield more leverage over the Chinese firms. How is that possible? In 1970s, when the Chinese began to open up their economy, the US was over willing to help Chinese acquire stakes in American businesses. Over a period of time, the economies of China and the US became so integrated and interdependent that today, the Americans have the right levers to arm-twist the Chinese because economically they enjoy a symbiotic relation. The core driver of the ongoing the US and China confrontation is seen here. The Americans have so much of economic leverage over China that they can ruin the Chinese firms like ZTE by denying them components made in the USA. This has the potential to hurt the 5G ambition of Huawei and break the Chinese monopoly in global telecom, which is their strategy to achieve superpower status. While most of the international relations theorists may be busy articulating the decline of the US and rise of global Chinese power, the US intelligence community knows that this leverage with America is only possible today because the US cleverly articulated to create this intricate interdependence while no such linkage was possible in the early years of the Cold War because the US and Chinese were de-linked. This is a real lesson for India. Rather than being jingoistic about seeking a military revenge with Chinese, it should encourage Chinese businesses and leverage economic diplomacy because economy triumphs military in case of China and Nehru was a live proof. This is where another argument is made that India should shed off its inhibitions, face a domestic loss for a short run, join the RCEP and hurt China economically by siding with like-minded powers like Australia and New Zealand that aim to teach Chinese a lesson for the global and regional mess ranging from COVID-19 to assertion in the South China Sea.

RESURRECT INDIAN FRONTIER ADMINISTRATIVE SERVICE

In the 1950s, to manage NEFA, the government pilot Indian Frontier Administrative Service (IFAS), which consisted of a bag of officers from Indian Foreign Service, Indian Administrative service and Indian Police Service, who were rotated and sent to tribal areas of NEFA. The government also created a separate desk in MEA for NEFA to spur its development. The IFAS made a lot of recommendations to spur up the border infrastructure. The IFAS was wound up in 1968 and Border Roads Organisation and Indian Army today do its role. There is a need to revive the idea of IFAS once again in the wake of recent border activities. In 2019, the governments of Arunachal Pradesh and Mizoram had written to the Central government that resurrecting the IFAS can rectify the neglect of frontier today by the Union.

POSTSCRIPT AND IGO: INDIA'S NEW GAME

While the leaders change and tactics may also change, but strategies and doctrines are embedded in the culture and mindset of a nation and they are far better predictors of their actions. For China and India, both have a rich culture and several texts explain the mindsets of the two states but an easier way to explain the difference is to study the strategy games of the two nations. In China, they play a game called "igo". This game is similar to the Indian chess and is played on a board with 19 x19 sides with 361 points, unlike 64 in chess. The difference from chess is that in igo, the stones, black and white, are positioned in this manner that they deny liberty to the stones of the opponents. The game is not played like chess, where the objective is to capture the king, but to surround a large area of the board by own stones and deny the opponent to do the same. The game is designed in this manner that the players build positions with stones to map out larger formations and territories. Whenever there is an opposing formation, it leads to expansion of number of stones, capture of number of stones or reduction and loss of stones also. The winner is the person who has the maximum captured territory and the highest number of captured stones. For long, the Chinese have been playing igo and not chess with Indians and is being played by the Chinese on a multi-dimensional canvas, bigger than the Indian landmass and at various spectrums that range from economic, military to that of blocking Indian liberty and manoeuvrability. While at one place China has coaxed the inveigled neighbours of India into one camp, on the other hand, it has penetrated deep into India's infrastructure, from health to economic to technological value chains, to this extent that India finds it difficult to disengage its dependence from China meaningfully. The western and southern neighbours of India have been made into surrogate pincers by China that beautifully ties down a large part of Indian military assets and strategic mindshare. In Mandarin, the word igo means encircle and Chinese, through their stones called Belt and Road Initiative, String of Pearls, have constricted Indian manoeuvrability from every direction. It is this encirclement India needs to break and it cannot be broken internally alone. India must cooperate with Japan, Australia, Taiwan, Malaysia, South Korea, Singapore and Vietnam which, are increasingly threatened by China's hegemonistic moves and should strive to expand the 'board". This will require India to think like a Go player and appreciate that unlike chess, the stones in Go do not possess any relative power. This requires India to divorce its national security from politics and enable long-term indigenous capacity building and strengthening of external alliances. Even though Mao said that political power may grow from a barrel of a gun, but national power emanates from a strong and vibrant economy. This requires internal peace, cooperation, and harmony to inspire confidence in the customer and investor.

SECTION 5

India's Relationship with Central Asia

- 1. The Strategic Importance of Central Asia in Global Politics
- 2. Chinese Foray into Central Asia: Concerns for Indian Foreign Policy
- 3. The SCO: Aims, Objectives and Importance for India's Foreign Policy
- 4. India's Relations with Central Asia: Regaining Strategic and Security Centrality
- 5. India's Hunt for Energy, Commerce and Connectivity with Central Asia

AN OVERVIEW

In 2001, the UPSC asked a question on strategic and economic importance of Central Asian countries for India. In 2002, there was a question on the opportunities and bottlenecks India faces while engaging with these countries. In 2018, the commission asked a question on what role could India play in Central Asia where other countries had entrenched themselves and this had to be analysed with reference to Ashgabat Agreement.

Potential foresight We should note that the UPSC's pattern of asking questions on Central Asia is block-centric and not bilateral. This implies that the commission is not interested in asking any bilateral questions with individual Central Asian Republics but wants to assess one's general understanding on how we engage with the region. Keeping this in mind, we can infer that the foresight should be strategic significance of Central Asia for India. This is said so because India has reconnected with Central Asia again with the coming of Taliban in Afghanistan. Also, in the past, the UPSC has asked questions on economic importance and bottlenecks, the strategic and security significance emerge as potential areas for the future. Keeping that in mind, this chapter will equip one with relevant knowledge needed to answer such questions.

CHAPTER 1

The Strategic Importance of Central Asia in Global Politics

THE REGION RE-EXAMINED FROM ANCIENT TIMES TO NEW GREAT GAME AND POWER DILEMMAS

Significance of Ancient Silk Route

Silk Route indicates an ancient trade network that was established during the rule of Han Chinese Dynasty and was used for commercial trade from 130 BC to 1453 AD. Apart from trade in silk and other commodities, the route was renowned for spread of cultural, religious and philosophical ideas that helped nations along the route to develop civilisational synchronisation.

India's relationship with Central Asia goes back to 2500 years old historical connection. The ancient Indian texts do mention about the challenges that India had to confront from nations that existed beyond the Himalayas and Hindu Kush. However, the links between India and Central Asia have remained uninterrupted since the time of Sakas or Indo-Scythians. In fact, the Sakas, Yavanas, Kambojas, Pahlavas and Pardas have all come from Central Asia and have been successfully absorbed in the Jat and Kshatriya communities in India. The great trade route, known as *Uttarpath*, that connected the Indo-Gangetic plains with Eurasia has been frequently mentioned in multiple ancient Indian texts. The ancient texts also frequently mention how Central Asia had remained the biggest artery for spread of culture, religion and philosophy. In fact, the famous silk route in the ancient times was less about silk and more about the cultural diffusion of Buddhism and Hinduism. The ancient Indian texts have also highlighted the security and strategic importance of Central Asia for India. This has been highlighted in Mahabharata and other Pali texts where Central Asia has been referred to as a region bringing relentless security threats to Indian land frontiers on the northwest boundary. In fact, all military ventures over land into India, from Greeks, Turks to Mughals, have come from the steppes region of Central Asia. The security threats from Central Asia did not subside in medieval times and Genghis Khan, who emerged from the Fergana valley came to create a havoc in India.

In the 16th century, Babur established the Mughal rule and its origin lies in Central Asia. In the 18th and 19th centuries, the British and Russians were involved in great game in the region and this great game phenomena brought the strategic importance of East Turkistan and Afghanistan into the minds of Indian leaders. After the World War I, the region of Central Asia was brought under the imperial control of Soviet Union (which was established after the Russian Revolution in 1917). The Soviet Union, throughout the Cold War, exercised deep influence over the five countries that constituted the block of Central Asia. The strategic establishment in India perceived the Soviet presence in Central Asia during Cold War as a positive outcome and this was a point of comfort for India. Since the end of Cold War, Russia has considered India as an important player in region of Eurasia and Central Asia and this has been exemplified with the fact that Russia has supported India to be a part of Shanghai Cooperation Organisation (SCO).

The region of Central Asia is seen in Indian history textbooks as a region that has significantly contributed in developing India's strategic thought. The region of Central Asia is looked through the security prism but Central Asians have been viewed in India with immense fondness. Since the time of globalisation, the view of the globe of Central Asia has changed. The withdrawal of Soviet Union in the post-Cold War period has been seen as a contributory factor, the energy resources available with Central Asians have made them strategic in the eyes of many nations. With its proximity towards Afghanistan and presence of enormous resources, the Central Asia is seen as a region where a great power rivalry is again unfolding, but in the domain of energy and security and this is often known as 'New Great Game' by strategic scholars. Russia, after re-emerging from the ashes of end of Cold War, has tried to revive its presence and hold over Central Asia by creation of Collective Security Treaty Organisation (CSTO) and Eurasian Economic Union (EEU). The main contestant in the region is China. The Chinese economy has been propelling and is in dire need of resources from Central Asia. The geographical proximity with Central Asia has compelled China to turn every challenge with Central Asia into an opportunity. Chinese had border disputes with Central Asians after the end of Cold War. The Chinese, who are reluctant to solve the border issue with India, displayed an extraordinary zeal in solving the disputes with Central Asian. In 1996, the Chinese conceptualised Shanghai-5, a regional grouping of China and Central Asia, to resolve the boundary issue and once the border issue was solved, the Shanghai-5 was transformed into SCO. The creation of SCO is an attempt by the Chinese to offer the republics of Central Asia with security so that Chinese have no security concerns while undertaking resource trade with Central Asians. In recent times, the Chinese have invested heavily by creating roads, infrastructure and rail projects to connect Central Asia and China, which has facilitated the trade of oil, gas and uranium. The Russians have not objected to Chinese forays into the region because the Russians have continued to support the dictators in Central Asia. The Chinese and Russians, with their autocratic rules, have found comfort in engaging with Central Asians.

> **What is the New Great Game?**
>
> The Central Asia, owing to its geographic location between East and West, has now emerged as a region witnessing geoeconomic and geopolitical competition. The search for strategic space by the US, Russia's unwillingness to leave its historical strategic legacy, Chinese attempt to penetrate the economic space in Central Asia without challenging Russia and India–Iran and Afghanistan forays into the region to create their own strategic spaces for regional cooperation has created a renewed thrust for new strategic and regional rivalry, which often is known as new great game.

> **What is the SCO?**
>
> It is a transcontinental, permanent, inter-governmental organisation created on 15 June 2001 by China with members of Central Asia and Russia to maintain mutual trust amongst neighbours, promote cultural, trade, political, scientific and technological cooperation so that there is peace, security and stability in the region, which shall manifest in the future as a new template of international political and economic order.

THE US, CHINA, RUSSIA IN CENTRAL ASIA

The US has seen the region only as a support and logistical hub for its operations in Afghanistan. The US has understood its own limitations that it cannot venture into Central Asia where Russia and China have established deep inroads and have treated the region as their own strategic and commercial backyard. The US is, however, concerned about China and Russia trying to 'impose' their will on Central Asians. This 'imposition' is seen by the US with Russia conceptualising EEU and Chinese focusing on SCO. The US has become more insecure seeing that through EEU and SCO, the Russians and Chinese are trying to institutionalise their presence and strategic depth in the region. Politically, the Russians, since the Cold War, have tried to nurture the dictators in the region of Central Asia. These dictators have, since the end of Cold War, continued their engagement with Russia and China. In order to counter the Russians and Chinese, the US is often seen supporting the Islamists in the countries of Central Asia. This is why in recent times, the countries of Central Asia are witnessing political instability because the US-backed Islamists are insisting on establishing the ties of Central Asians with rulers in the Middle-East, a region where the US exercises considerable influence over the Sunni states. The US believes that the only way it can weaken the presence of Russia and China in Central Asia is by supporting Islamists in the long-run. This support will create internal political chaos in Central Asia and as a result, the Central Asian states will remain 3 in internal conflicts, thus preventing the rise of EEU and strengthening of the SCO as a potential security provider. The Central Asians have deterred any attempts by Turkey, Pakistan and Arab states to impose their versions of Islam in their countries because these variations of Islam, backed by the US, are seen as sources of instability in the region and go against the quest for regional stability and commerce which all Central Asians strive for. It is in this backdrop that the strategic community of India also understands that the much talked about thought of 'Islamic Fundamentalism' in Central Asia is a hype and has no relevance for Central Asia as the region also sees the 'Islam under threat' theory as a myth. The main objective of US policy is to use Islamists to win energy contracts in Central Asia and thereby reduce and neutralise the attempt of Russia to sell gas and oil to Europe. The Russians have time and again thwarted the attempts of the Americans and Central Asians have been convinced to sell their oil and gas to Asia than to Europe. Such a tactic also ensures that Russia continues to be the main supplier of oil and gas to Europe whereas the Central Asians become suppliers to Chinese and Asia. The American options of using Central Asia to emerge as new suppliers of oil and gas to Europe are also limited by their own isolationist policies with Iran, uneasy relationship with Taliban and Pakistan in recent times. This has compelled the Central Asians also to not explore any regions and have been forced to accept the designs of Russia. This has not gone down well with the countries of Central Asia because they believe that since the end of Cold War, the Russians have prevented the Central Asians to assert their own independence in thoughts and actions of foreign policy. Russia under the leadership of Putin has seen Central Asia as a region where Russia will remain the key player in designing the destiny of Eurasia. This thinking of Putin has led Russia to defeat the 'Third New Force' in Central Asia, which is visualised as a secret society in connivance with West trying to seek the ruin of Russia. This is why the Russian actions in Central Asia today are not ideologically driven but driven with a goal to keep the West out of a region which has been a strategic lake of Russia. This explains why Russians have never seen Cold War also as an ideological struggle but have seen the fight with the West as a fight of Atlanticism and Eurasia. This explains why Russian historians have viewed the Cold War as 'a stage of great war of continents'. For Russia, Central Asia is a zone to assert the 'Eurasian capitalism' model as a counter to 'American capitalism' model. This thinking of Russia explains why Central Asia is seen as an important sophisticated block in tactful clash of Russia with the West. The Russians in early 2000s did not have the resources to counter these threats on their own. They welcomed the US and even supported them to use Central Asia as base territories to launch counter-offences against the extremists. In this sense, the American presence in the region close to strategic space of Russia was actually seen as a net-gain by the Russians and what really the Russians lost was ego. The Russians decided that under the drastically altered security environment post-9/11, it is better to live with a lesser ego, considering that it is transitory and will help Russia bounce back in the long-term. The Central Asians engaged with the US under the war on terrorism by establishing Central Asian Cooperation Organisation (CACO) in 2001. The logic that drove Central Asians to embrace the West in post-9/11 scenario was that if you need peace, you must prepare for war. They found that engagement with West would free the region from the clutches of terrorism and subsequently, foreign investment would flow into Central Asia. To ensure that Central Asia does not completely slip into the embrace of West, Putin played his cards in post-9/11 period in Central Asia. Putin started making forays into oil, gas, defence and mineral industries of Central Asia when the US was busy fighting Taliban and Al-Qaeda. This enabled Russia to develop long-term economic and defence presence in the region yet again and Russia began to re-assert itself as a dominant power in Central Asia, with a motive to steer away Central Asia from the embrace of West. In this context, Russia unveiled CSTO in 2003 that transformed Central Asian republics and Russia into a military alliance to drive away aggression. Russia now allowed the member states to serve into Russian armed forces, a novelty that was warmly welcomed by the republics of Central Asia as the youth found this as an interesting military employment opportunity. The creation of SCO has enabled Russia and China to establish a permanent security architecture in the region that has neutralised the West completely, especially at the security level. The entire region of Central Asia is witnessing acute ecological crisis because of depletion of its water reserves. In this backdrop, Russia has positioned itself as the core supplier of this basic necessity to the Central Asians, thus cementing Russian altruistic and development narrative in the minds of locals. In this backdrop, the US trying to make a renewed push for an entry into Central Asia. It conceptualised C5 + 1 Dialogue process in 2015 in Central Asia with the US as the core driver. The US is now driving the C5 + 1 initiative to visualise security, economic connectivity and trade projects with Central Asia. In this backdrop of rapidly changing political, strategic and commercial discourses within Central Asia, the Indian strategic community has evolved its own strategy. India is not only aggressively trying to re-establish a connection with the region to revive the historical and civilisational connectivity, but is looking to revive strategic relationship with modern content. The full membership of India in the SCO is now India's launch pad for engagement with Central Asia.

2 CHAPTER Chinese Foray into Central Asia: Concerns for Indian Foreign Policy

THE ENTRY OF DRAGON IN CENTRAL ASIA

When the Cold War ended, Chinese were very cautious in engaging with Central Asia. They knew that the region was an erstwhile territory of Soviet Union. However, the Chinese were able to see that at the end of Cold War, Russia did not have adequate economic and military muscle to prevent Chinese to fill the vacuum they left. The Chinese responded with aggression and launched a mega diplomatic initiative to cultivate ties with Central Asians. Initially, the Chinese were again concerned that how would the Central Asians react to Uighurs in Xinjiang province. The Chinese were suppressing the Uighur uprisings in Xinxiang and they knew that the suppression of Uighurs could be perceived negatively by the Central Asians because the Uighurs were of Central Asian descent. However, the Chinese were quite surprised to see that the Central Asians did not condemn the Chinese suppression of the Uighurs because the Central Asians knew that Uighurs were restive people and their uprisings could act as hurdles to the Central Asian dream of global engagement after they were free from the shackles of Cold War. In this backdrop, the leaders of Central Asia and Chinese leaders found a new point of security convergence and the Central Asian leaders decided to cooperate with the Chinese to keep the Uighurs in check. When the Chinese decided to impose bans on separatist movements in Xinxiang, the Central Asians supported the bans because they knew that separatism by Uighurs could have implications on ambitions of Central Asia. The Chinese were quick to wrap the new design of security cooperation with Central Asians with elements of trade, commerce and connectivity. Sensing rising opportunities, the Central Asians decided to cooperate with the Chinese in economic diplomacy because they found this dynamic commercial cooperation a shield to counterbalance any potential Russian or Islamic interference in their internal affairs. The Central Asians were also enthusiastic in engaging with the Chinese because this engagement gave high-spirits of independence in thinking and decision-making, something which was curtailed since 1925 when the Central Asians were under the control of Soviet Union. The Central Asians now emerged a new laboratory for the Chinese to experiment post-Cold War border negotiations and use the successful resolutions as templates to claim its responsible power status. However, it is important to note that the Chinese had many other motives in mind while resolving boundary issues with the Central Asians. After the disintegration of Soviet Union, the Chinese worried that the new Central Asian republics could become a new playground of Western powers and that would bring the West at the doorsteps of China. This is something the Chinese dreaded and this is why they decided to step into the shoes left by Russians. Secondly, the rising instances of instability in Afghanistan, Pakistan and terrorism in Kashmir in the 1990s was seen by Chinese as a security threat to their western frontiers. In this backdrop, the Chinese were clear that they had to secure their western periphery from extremism externally and separatism internally (by Uighurs, as explained previously). Thirdly, the Chinese were aware of that leaving Central Asia without a power dominance would leave space for either Russia or the US to resort to subversion within Chinese territory and that would be counterproductive for territorial integrity of China. The fact that the US could support the Uighur separatists to break Chinese was a threat that loomed large on Chinese security planners. So, the Chinese adopted a clear cut strategy to engage with Central Asia. They decided that keeping Central Asia stable would largely be in sync with the security and stability of western China. Secondly, they realised that any endeavour of the Chinese in Central Asia would elicit a Russian counter response. Thus, to mitigate a counter response from Russia where it might feel Chinese foray as an attempt to gain strategic presence in Russian strategic backyard, the Chinese decided to go for economic diplomacy.

THE THICKEST PIECE OF CAKE GIVEN TO MODERN CHINA BY HEAVEN

Chinese immediately designed a 'Go-West Policy'. The idea was to engage economically with Central Asia and make the region dependent upon China. The Go-West policy was a beautiful blend of incentives and coercion where economic incentives were provided to the countries of Central Asia in the realm of trade and commerce and in return these economic incentives were designed in a way that they would have sufficient heft in muting Central Asian response on Chinese management of Uighur separatism. In this way, the Chinese succeeded in not only bringing the Central Asians within the galactical economic orbit of China but also forestalled any potential support of Central Asians to Uighur separatists in Xinxiang. The border negotiations were designed by the Chinese in a manner that enthused the Central Asians while symbolically benefitting Chinese. They even made border negotiations in some cases intertwined with multi-million dollar trade and commerce projects so that the newly independent republics could be lured to close the border deals in return for upcoming economic benefits. The Chinese decided to bury their ego and were willing to accept territorial losses till the time the Central Asians were given adequate confidence that negotiations on border and engagement with Chinese were in their interest. The entire approach of the Chinese explained here was managed through the Chinese initiative known as Shanghai-5, which it conceptualised in 1996. The core driver of the entire Chinese diplomacy was to make sure that their forays neither elicit response from Russia nor invoke suspicion in any Western power. Some argue that the Shanghai-5 was a quick invasion by Chinese into the region of Central Asia, which enabled the Chinese to glide the relationship to strategic levels under the SCO. The Chinese were able to achieve all their objectives set in Shanghai-5 by the end of 1990s. When the world entered the dynamism of the 21st century, now was the turn of China to add strategic element to the newfound relationship with Central Asia. At the onset of the 21st century, the strategic planners in China analysed the strategic interests in Central Asia. They realised that Central Asia is strategically important because it is critical for Chinese energy security, territorial security, trade and commerce, ethnic balancing and military defence. The core driver that bound all these interests of China were economic resources and it is in this context General Liu Yazhou of People's Liberation Army of China stated that Central Asia is the thickest piece of cake given to modern China by heaven. Through a package of skilful diplomacy and economic inducements, the Chinese have been successful in breaking Russian economic monopoly over Central Asia. The Chinese have aggressively opened mandarin speaking institutes in multiple locations of Central Asia to ensure that they train the next generation Central Asians for future jobs in China. The fact that Russia, under Putin, is more busy in establishing 'Russian World' as a counter-challenger to the West has allowed Beijing more space in Central Asia.

WHEN CHINA SPITS, WE DROWN: THE CENTRAL ASIAN DISDAIN OF CHINA

The above discussion from the Chinese perspective makes it clear that Chinese have succeeded in achieving every stated objective. However, it is equally interesting to know that the Chinese are hated and disdained beyond limits in Central Asia. This is so because the Central Asians are historically conscious people and they know that in the past, the Chinese have always looked at Central Asians as vassal states. They know that a day is not far when the Chinese will display similar disdainful thinking again. There is a popular old saying that dominates Central Asia today that 'if Russian bridle is made of horse leather, the Chinese is made of iron' and 'when a black Chinese comes, a yellow Russian will appear to be farther'. Ablai Khan succinctly captured the disdain Central Asians have for Chinese when he stated that 'when China spits, we drown'. The people of Central Asia are willing to cooperate with the Chinese, but they are equally cautious of Chinese lebensraum designs. Despite all economic cooperation and security cooperation under the SCO, the Chinese have not succeeded in erasing the historical insults that Central Asia are still haunted by. The Central Asian states clearly know that there are limits to their Uighur policy. This is so because the local populations are sympathetic to Uighurs, whom they perceive as people of Central Asian descent. The leaders of Central Asia know that in future, the possibility of an armed confrontation with the Chinese on Uighur issue is imminent. The Chinese are also encouraging as many Uighurs to migrate to Central Asia as possible because this is in sync with the Chinese policy to alter demography of Xinxiang by influx of Han Chinese. However, what the Chinese are not able to grasp is that if these Uighurs go to Central Asia, then the Western powers are likely to use these Uighurs to carry out subversion on the western flank of China, thus nullifying all objectives that Chinese have intended to achieve till date. This is why the Central Asians are in a dilemma today. The dilemma is that they love Russians and Indians but can live without them and the economic dependency that Chinese have created in Central Asia is such that even if the Central Asians dislike the Chinese to their core, they cannot live without them. Under the new silk route gambit, as part of the Chinese Belt and Road Initiative (BRI), the Chinese have strategically outsmarted the Americans. What the US could not achieve by grand strategy in Central Asia, the Chinese have achieved through capital markets. From Central Asia, under the BRI, the Chinese plan to go all the way till Europe and in Poland, Belarus and Ukraine, it intends to carry out commercial farming; thus, cementing their strategic presence all the way deep in Europe. Hence, one thing is clear from the analysis that the strategy of China is not just a game of resource exploitation, it is of copying the game of Western imperialism in the world, step by step and the BRI is a process actualising the same for the Chinese.

SNAP INSPECTIONS IN CENTRAL MILITARY DISTRICTS AND RUSSIAN REBOUND IN CENTRAL ASIA

The Russians have been playing a different ball game in Central Asia. They have been using the vast swathes of land in Central Asia to carry out military drills. While these military drills are done to prepare Russians for launching full-scale offensive operations against Ukraine and other flashpoints in Europe where Russia is likely to come in confrontation with the West; the Central Asians seem to be mute in allowing their lands to be used by Russians for such snap inspections. Russians have always argued that snap inspections in Central Asia, which involve mass level military drills with a combination of air and ground power, are conceptualised to create self-sustaining strategic operational forces and ensure strategic mobility capabilities for Russian troops. These snap operations, as interpreted by strategic communities in Asia and India, are Russian strategies to prepare for any offensive with West in Central Asia. The Russian operations in Central Asia are an indicators to the West in particular and China tacitly that Russia will resort to use of instruments of national power to defend its strategic backyard of Central Asia. Russian operations are driven with certain concerns. Firstly, Russia is trying to display military prowess and send a message to the West that they will not tolerate any regime changes in Central Asia. Secondly, Russia is also trying to convey that they will use military means, if required, to safeguard ethnic Russians in the region defined by Russia as 'Near Abroad', which stretches from Ukraine to Central Asia. Thirdly and importantly, the Russians are giving a message to the Chinese that they will not accept any attempts of China to thwart Russian ambition of EEU. The Russian intervention in Ukraine in 2014, 2022 and its game in Crimea has actually emerged as a blueprint for Central Asians that to what extent Russia is willing to intervene if their interests are harmed. However, Russia has time and again asserted that its intervention in Ukraine in 2022 is to protect the interests of ethnic Russians. These Russian interventions, more specifically the war in Ukraine in 2022, have increased the fears amongst Central Asians that they are susceptible to regime changes from external quarters. Collectively, there are more than 10 million ethnic Russians living in Central Asia and fears of Russian operations loom large in Kazakhstan, in particular, which has highest chunk of Russian ethnic communities, where they fear that they could be next Ukraine. The problem is aggravated by the fact that many Central Asian nations have territorial claims in each other's territories and they fear that in case Russia starts salami slicing, as it did in East Ukraine in 2022, then other nations of Central Asia will start raking up the claims and this would eventually lead to balkanisation of Central Asia. The question that arises here is that what does this Russian reassertion mean for India? India is greatly concerned about the rising resurgence of Russia and militarisation of the region because it has looked at Central Asia through the prism of energy and economic resources. The biggest dilemma that confronts the strategic community of India is that if Central Asia descends into any chaos, it will have serious security implications on India's western front. The chaos will also affect India's economic rise and prevent India to have access to resources from the region of Central Asia, which it perceives as India's extended neighbourhood.

3

CHAPTER

The SCO: Aims, Objectives and Importance for India's Foreign Policy

THE SCO: AIMS AND OBJECTIVES

The SCO has been established by the Chinese as their pet multilateral project in the region of Eurasia. The SCO has gained significance in recent times owing to resurgence of Russia (as examined previously) and because of expansion of Chinese economic presence in the region. As examined earlier, the Chinese had multiple aims while establishing the SCO. Firstly, they wanted to resolve boundary disputes with Central Asians when the Cold War ended in terms that inspired confidence in the republics so that Chinese got coalesce them into their economic orbit. Secondly, the Chinese wanted to take the Central Asians into confidence to prevent any rise of separatism in Xinxiang, thus Central Asia was seen as a grand neutralising buffer. Thirdly, the Chinese established their own version of a grand strategy and wanted to exploit the resources of Central Asia in the post-Soviet space. When the Cold War ended, the initial motivation of China was to establish a steel wall that would prevent the crumbling of disintegrating Soviet Union to fall upon the Chinese. However, as the decade of 1990s unfolded, the Chinese began to play their cards well. They realised that the Russians are going to be occupied in tackling the West and this leaves a power vacuum that Chinese can fill in Central Asia. The fading away of Russia immediately after the end of Cold War also exposed the rising asymmetry in power which Chinese thought could be exploited for their own advantage. This is why the Chinese attempts of resolving the border, which began under the orbit of Shanghai-5, eventually manifested as bringing Central Asia into their strategic foothold, thus the SCO came and Chinese envisaged a leadership role for themselves. The Russians found themselves naturally allied to the Chinese endeavours of SCO. This is so because since the end of Cold War, there was a constant pressure by NATO to expand eastwards and add the East European nations, once a part of Soviet Union, into the American security embrace. Russia was neither able to control nor able to effectively offer security the eastern European region. This led the Russians to embrace Chinese and SCO as a counter-balancer. Similarly, what also motivated the Russians to embrace SCO and China was the luring potential of supplying oil and gas to markets in Asia, which now represented new centres of growth in the post-Cold War world order. Thus, Putin, leading Russia decided to achieve the common goal of ensuring unity and striving for working with friends in Asia. The Central Asians since the end of the Cold War also struggled to stand up on their own feet. During the Cold War, the Central Asians were comforted with security guarantee by Russia; the same immediately vanished when Soviet Union disintegrated and as a result, the Central Asians felt a security void which the SCO tried to fulfil and in this respect, the SCO became the driver of Chinese grand strategy in Central Asia.

The Chinese, as explained earlier, decided to solve the boundary disputes with Central Asians after the Cold War ended. To do this, the Chinese created an institutional mechanism known as the Shanghai-5. Apart from developing a consensus on boundary dispute, the Shanghai-5 also devoted enormous diplomatic capital to resolve the irritants of separatism, extremism and fundamentalism. As the Chinese began to diplomatically work on the agenda of Shanghia-5, it almost became clueless on how to respond to 9/11. The 9/11 came as a full-blown blot of fundamentalism on face of China and Central Asia. The SCO, which was created in 2001, was almost redundant when the US launched the global war on terror.

After the 9/11, the SCO could not establish a coherent response because it lacked resources, institutional mechanisms, intra-political conflicts in Central Asia and lack of experience of Russia and China to work in multilateral frameworks. Thus, the Chinese decided to infuse a new set of energy in SCO to make it appear relevant to Western presence in the region post-9/11. The Chinese came out with the concept of 'Shanghai Spirit' to signify the new energy that would coalesce Central Asia, China and Russia. A great sense of optimism was displayed by the Chinese and Russians to make SCO relevant in the wake of presence of Western troops in the region, something that both of them resented. The West saw the Shanghai Spirit as an attempt to salvage the assortment of Central Asians with the West. The Russians and Chinese began to spread a narrative that the American presence in the region in the pretext of war on terror is an attempt to re-impose the Western hegemony. This trick worked effectively in mobilising insecure Central Asians into the tighter grasp of SCO. The West was using the territories and air bases of Central Asians to launch offensive operations in Afghanistan and Iraq. This use of territory was converted into a fear by Russians and Chinese who spread a narrative that the US will soon seek regime changes in the Central Asia. The American attempts to foster democracy in Kyrgyzstan through the Tulip revolution confirmed the fears of Central Asians. Thus, the SCO decided to pass a resolution that members of the SCO will firmly reject the interference in affairs of other countries' internal affairs and reject any models of social development that are imported into the region, an indirect reference to the US and their attempts to promote democracy.

What is Global War on Terrorism?

It was an American grand project to bring together a host of friends and allies after the devastating 9/11 attacks to dismantle the roots of terrorism emanating in the world. The narrative built was that the terrorism in all forms globally would be dismantled. However, as the war unfolded, the US only removed Al-Qaeda and Taliban from Afghanistan and launched an offensive invasion of Iraq to remove Saddam Hussein.

The question also arises is how does India benefit from joining the SCO. For India, the SCO provides an opportunity to protect its own interests in Afghanistan, especially after the takeover of Taliban in 2021. With entry of Pakistan into SCO and growing convergence of Russia and Pakistan means that Pakistan will now become an important player in Eurasia and Indian presence in the SCO as a full member can help keep a check on nefarious designs of Pakistan. The presence of India will allow its access to intelligence reserves of RATS of SCO and this will help India develop better understanding of potential fundamentalist movements in Central Asia. While maintaining a bilateral road to engage with Central Asia, the SCO will also bestow India an opportunity to engage with Central Asians at a multilateral level. By being in SCO, India can also provide valuable growth levers for the Central Asian region by offering them solutions of information technology and banking. Also, India's wide experience in engaging with multi-institutional settings at the global level will contribute in strengthening the institutional settings of SCO. India will also be able to better understand the rising non-traditional security threats of Central Asia and devise effective solutions and thereby make SCO a futuristic platform for tackling non-traditional security threats, a novel contribution of India in SCO and a counter to Chinese security layers. Thus, India in SCO is definitely seen coming out of the tight geopolitics of managing a confrontationist China and hostile Pakistan. However, it must be noted that India's journey in the SCO is not going to akin to flying with a flock of 'wild geese'. India's interests in the SCO will invariably come into a clash when either Pakistan or China props up some connectivity initiative. If India develops rigidity and initiates a stance to oppose the proposals, then India will portrayed as an obstructionist and Pakistan will seek more sympathy. This will also allow China and others to balance off India in the SCO by asserting that other Asian states such as Nepal, Bangladesh, Sri Lanka etc. be given memberships in SCO. Thus, navigating this regional diplomacy will be a bigger challenge for India than any other multilateral institution it has engaged in the last 76 years.

THE SCO: PAX SINICA OR ASIA'S OWN MULTILATERAL GROUPING

The West perceived the SCO as an 'informal league of dictators', protected by the Chinese and Russians. The West began to see the SCO as a block where the innocent Central Asians were lured into a trap and have become victims of high-handedness of China. To challenge the tag of being an informal league of dictators, the SCO decided to open up their membership and brought India as a member in 2017. The presence of India was seen by Russia and China as an attempt to counter the American narrative of the grouping. If the things did not end here, a new rivalry began to emerge. The Russians gradually began to see SCO as an upfront threat to their EEU. A new Cold War seems to have opened up between Russia and China where the two are aggressively trying to assert themselves over resources, energy, oil and gas. This new quest of competitiveness for regional diplomacy is eroding the SCO today and making the cooperation more difficult. The main problem today is that both China and Russia view the SCO differently. The Russians wanted the Chinese to treat the SCO as a grouping to provide regional security only. The Russians were willing to allow this strategic space to be built by the Chinese. However, the Chinese, on the other hand, have seen SCO as a template to visualise an international order based on Chinese characteristics. For China, the SCO offers it an opportunity to display to the world a new form of international relations they would like to envisage in counter to the US. This is why China sees India in SCO as an attempt to balance off the US. This is because the Chinese today believe that SCO is used by the US to encircle them and prevent them to display any global role. The Chinese are more driven by building engagements with like-minded countries in the region by bringing them on the SCO to ensure that they act as bulwarks to American plan. This is why the SCO is seen as Pax Sinica and not a new multilateralism in Asia. It is in this backdrop that the Russians are extending the engagement with Japan to ensure that China does not venture deep into the heart of Eurasia, which Russia feels is its own strategic backyard. As Russia focuses more on EEU, China focuses on BRI, and the contradictions in the future are imminent. Given the complexities in the SCO we have analysed, tagging SCO as Asian-NATO is a pure misnomer. Despite all attempts to showcase military readiness in SCO, the military might of the regional grouping stands nowhere near NATO. This also explains why the SCO is unable to establish a coherent response to any security concerns in the region. With India and Pakistan joining the SCO, the security cooperation is all the more difficult not just because of serious diplomatic differences between India and Pakistan but also because of military skirmishes between India and China that have taken their bilateral relationship to the lowest ebb. In this backdrop, the presence of India in SCO, while seen from a balancing and democratic perspective does make sense, but till the time SCO itself lacks a coherent strategic congruity, the presence of India is not likely to make much of a difference in the regional architecture. Though it has often been stated that presence of India, China, Pakistan and Russia on a common platform such as SCO can help the conflicting parties resolve their differences; but in reality India has always clarified that it will prefer to resolve the bilateral issues at a bilateral and not at a multilateral level. The SCO is thereby seen as a weak institution for conflict resolution platform for bilateral disputes also weak. For that matter, it was quite ironic to even observe that Central Asians were not comfortable in having India and Pakistan as members of SCO because the coming of the two would lead to the group becoming hostage to geopolitical rivalries of South Asia. The discussion clearly points out that the objectives and aims of SCO and role members such as India can play in SCO remained ill-defined till date (a detailed discussion on India and SCO lies in the next chapter). India has received support from Moscow in SCO and the US too. The Americans favour Indian participation in the SCO to keep a check on Chinese. This has created a lot of ambiguities on what role can the grouping play in the post-pandemic world order considering that the SCO had hardly any cooperative achievement to showcase in the two years of pandemic. The future of the SCO obviously hinges upon how Russia–NATO–China decide their understanding of Central Asia and how India–Pakistan and China display maturity in keeping their Asian rivalry baggage back home and coming together to foster the growth of Central Asia and Eurasia as a region. Most importantly, it can be concluded that the SCO in its present form does provide for a delicate equilibrium for members of the region to navigate the post-pandemic and post-Cold War world order.

FUTURISING CENTRAL ASIA UNDER THE UMBRELLA OF SCO IN POST-PANDEMIC GLOBAL ORDER

As the things evolve in Central Asia in the post-pandemic world, there have been notable changes in regional power games. The Americans have understood that they will not benefit anything by having a narrowly focussed policy on Afghanistan alone. They are also sensitive to Russian presence in Central Asia and have decided to let go promotion of democracy and human rights in Central Asia for the time being and have decided to nurture Central Asia at the levels of commerce and connectivity and bring Central Asia at the fulcrum of Asian and European growth stories. The Chinese under their BRI have decided to use SCO as a platform to achieve their infrastructural and energy security goals. The experts argue that with this thinking, there is a possibility of Central Asia falling into a 'resource curse' because Central Asia is being viewed by the Chinese and Americans as transits for growth of Asia and Europe. The history has been a proof that any power in Central Asia, which is an outside power in the region, has never achieved any monopoly and attempts for dominance in Central Asia have gone against regional integration and unity. With rising ecological stress, non-traditional security threats not being addressed and excessive focus on resource exploitation; the local populations are becoming restive and SCO is not able to respond to these challenges, which have the potential of making these Central Asian states vulnerable to the external subversions. It will be interesting to see that how CSTO of Russia and SCO of China will offer security in the era of these rapidly changing security dynamics. The other game being unfolded is that at a covert level, the Americans seem comfortable to promote and push SCO because they prefer a weakened security control of Russia in Central Asia. The American ambition is driven by the fact that with Chinese at the security helm, the Americans can tilt Central Asians towards Europe, away from Russia. This is also likely as an outcome because the Chinese focus on using SCO is only to ensure that there is no restive activities in Xinxiang as Chinese are not interested in offering a broad spectrum of security to Central Asia. The Chinese also do not consider the idea of Russian floated Eurasia and EEU because both go against the Chinese ambition of BRI. The Russians, aware of the American and Chinese plans, are appearing to counter the same by courting Pakistan and Taliban in Afghanistan. If Russia succeeds in legitimising Taliban, then with the support of Pakistan, Russia will be able to counter the strategic designs and ensure that it remains a crucial security provider in Central Asia even with SCO at the helm.

4 CHAPTER

India's Relations with Central Asia: Regaining Strategic and Security Centrality

THE INTERRUPTED PERIOD OF RELATIONSHIP

The ancient relations between India and Central Asia were deeply nourished during the medieval period. As stated earlier, the foundation of the Mughal rule in India owes its origin to Central Asia. However, with the coming of the British and the advent of the 'great game', the civilisational connection between India and Central Asia witnessed an interruption. The trade and expeditions did continue in the period but the historical and civilisational values that were core binders of India and Central Asia, were lost all together. Much of the writings explaining Indian and Central Asian relations during the 20th century have Soviet Union leanings. This is so because the relation between India and Central Asia were guided by Soviet Union during the Cold War. The Central Asians had also participated in the first Asian Relations Conference and they also fondly remember the visit of Jawaharlal Nehru to Central Asia in 1955 with his daughter Indira Gandhi. The visit left such a deep imprint in the minds of Central Asians that many families, for many successive decades, named their daughters Indira, which remains a localised name in Central Asia till date. During the period of Cold War, India continued to exercise considerable cultural influence in the region through films and music. The Indian films were the only scope of cultural outlet for the people of Central Asia. Despite the entry of Western films since the end of Cold War, Indian films in Central Asia continue to exert enormous cultural influence in Central Asia.

BUDDHISM AS A NEW SOURCE OF INFLUENCE

In the preceding chapters, it has been argued that Buddhism came to Central Asia because of the silk route. The Central Asians were initially Buddhists and Islam was a late entrant in Central Asia. The Central Asians, in this context, have rejected any radical versions of religious interpretations because they have been nurtured in co-existing with Buddhism. In recent times, Buddhism is emerging as a new source of influence and connection because the nations are interested in reviving the past-historical legacy. The most important role in this regard is apparently being played by the Chinese who are trying to position themselves as the biggest patron of Buddhism in the region. The Chinese are not just using Buddhism to boost their regional influence but also use the soft power advocacy to pump their global ambitions. The Buddhism has emerged as a new psychological foreign policy tool of the Chinese in engaging in the region today. In this backdrop, India, which for some time has lost this emotional space of Buddhism to China, needs to reconnect. The Indian government today is conceptualising a strategy on how it can use academic exchanges as a new source of influence. The focus of New Delhi is to re-invigorate the past linkages with Central Asia by focusing on intellectual aspects of Buddhism, an element not worked on by the Chinese today. India is poised to resort to an Asian renaissance through promotion of living heritage of Buddhism with Central Asia. An important element of this strategy is inviting the scholars and historians of Central Asian nations to India to assert an academic discourse. The end objective of India in this regard is to start working with Central Asia in excavation of Buddhist sites and re-assert a new element of soft power play.

INDIA'S LOOK NORTH POLICY

As the Cold War ended, the five Central Asia Republics gained independence from Russia, giving them the needed strategic and autonomic space to explore relationships with other countries independent of the Russian yoke. India, on the basis of its historical and cultural proximity to Central Asia, now began making overtures again unlock potential alliances. India concluded fresh diplomatic treaties with all the five Central Asia Republics. Domestically, India made a transition from closed to open economy, and also began to feel the need of acquiring resources for sustaining its own economic growth. Thus, Central Asia became all the more significant for India as the region was a highly resource-rich one. But as the Central Asia Republics had just gained independence, one of the foremost concerns for India was to ensure that the region should not get engulfed in any form of religious extremism due to the US Mujahedeen campaign in Afghanistan. There was a high possibility of a spill over of these extremist elements from Afghanistan into Central Asia in 1989 (after USSR withdrew from Afghanistan) as a majority of the Central Asian states were Islamic. India feared that if Central Asia were to be engulfed by this extremism, it would give Pakistan an edge in maintaining strategic depth against India. Thus, India realised that it has to ensure that the region did not become a security concern for India. It began to realise that its own democracy, secular outlook and its own multicultural polity are its assets which it can use for promotion in Central Asia as the newly independent Central Asians would look for some role models to emulate. Since Central Asia was a cultural and a religious mosaic of multiple groups, India could use the modalities of democracy, secularism and multiculturalism as core ideals for Central Asia to take lessons from. In 1995, P. V. Narsimha Rao visited Turkmenistan and reiterated the common cultural legacy of the two nations to re-establish relationships. In his visit to Turkmenistan, Rao unveiled India's Look North policy.

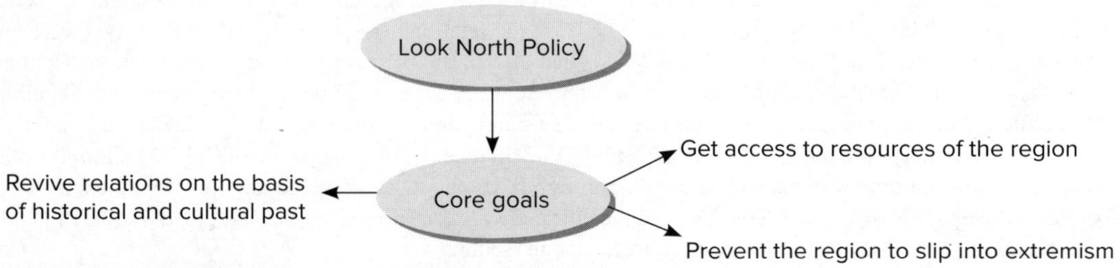

CHALLENGES IN LOOK NORTH POLICY

As time progressed, the security situation in the Central Asia region deteriorated. Afghanistan fell into the hands of the Taliban in 1996. Indian fears were exacerbated as Pakistan recognised Taliban rule in Afghanistan. The extremism from Afghanistan also spilled over into Tajikistan, which saw a civil war taking place. From the Pakistani side, there was an aggressive attempt to revive militancy in Kashmir in 1990s. India, Russia and Iran supported a group known as the Northern Alliance. India built a hospital near the airbase of Farkhor in Tajikistan. The military hospital provided medical assistance to the Northern Alliance. India also used the Ayni air base for the purpose of providing humanitarian assistance and aid. In the process, India–Tajik security cooperation strengthened over bilateral relations. However, as the region was in the grip of extremist forces, assertion of Look North Policy goals became increasingly difficult. In 1999, India's security vulnerabilities were woefully exposed when IC-814 was hijacked. The situation in the region changed after 9/11. The US invaded Afghanistan in 2001 and Iraq in 2003. The US began to develop airbases and military logistic centres in Central Asia for its global war on terror. India also realised the difficulty in the promotion of the goals planned under the Look North Policy and began to understand that Look North Policy could never be a successful policy to engage with Central Asia. By this time, around 2000–2001, the Indian economy, which had made a transition from a closed to an open economy a decade back, had begun to bear fruit. India was in dire need of resources to propel its economic growth. Thus began the search for Indian foreign policy tools, which would help it, look at Central Asia in a different way.

ASSESSMENT OF LOOK NORTH POLICY

As outlined above, the deterioration of the security of the region was a colossal concern. The civil war in Tajikistan, the takeover of Afghanistan by Taliban, Pakistan-sponsored militancy in Kashmir and support to Taliban were all noteworthy factors. However, many diplomats today agree, that apart from these reasons, India itself did not aggressively prioritise this region at the end of the Cold War. When the Cold War ended, the foremost priority of India was to improve relations with the US to fill the vacuum left by its past proximity to the erstwhile USSR. Thus, a mixture of all these factors made the implementation of Look North Policy weak.

Why did Look North Policy Remain Weak?

India initiated the Look East Policy, where the majority of its focus was directed to its Eastern neighbours. India not only neglected due attention to Central Asia, but the deteriorating security situation of Central Asia also made India to think of it from a purely security point of view than from the perspective of any economic significance.

INDIA'S CONNECT CENTRAL ASIA POLICY

As the Indian economy began to show signs of growth, India's hunger for resources also began to grow. For India, rebuilding a relationship with Central Asia using different parameters became important. India now realised that in order to get resources from Central Asia, it needed a reorientation of its policy. The new policy had to be based on economic diplomacy. As the region continued to remain fragile, however, India understood that the security component has to remain a part of the new engagement. India also found that the space for economic engagement with Central Asia was very limited by the pre-existing inroads China had made into Central Asia. China had been engaging with Central Asia republics economically since the end of Cold War. Thus, the challenge for India now was to chart out a balanced engagement in Central Asia. In order to do this, the Indian Council of World Affairs undertook a Track-II initiative called India– Central Asia Dialogue. On 12th June 2012, the Minister of State for External Affairs of India, during an address (at the first India– Central Asia Dialogue) in the city of Bishkek in Kyrgyz Republic, announced the Connect Central Asia Policy (CCAP). The new policy has the following goals:

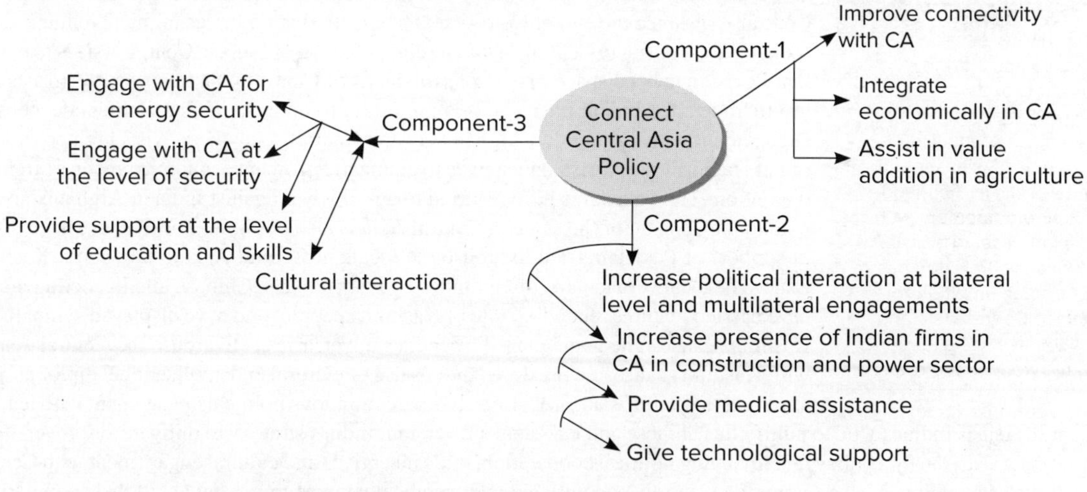

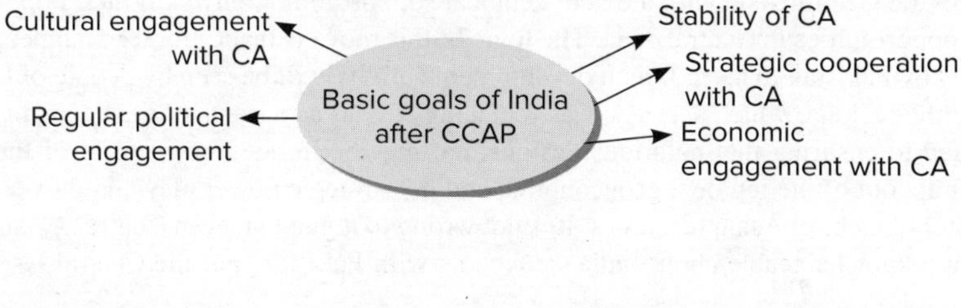

INDIA–CENTRAL ASIA SUMMIT 2022 AND INDIA'S 4C FORMULA

It was a ministerial level summit that was attended by the External Affairs Ministers of India, Afghanistan, Kyrgyz Republic, Tajikistan, Turkmenistan and Kazakhstan. To improve coordination on economic- and policy-related matters, a new Regional Development Group has been established between India and Central Asia. As Pakistan has been an obstruction between India and Afghanistan, in 2017, the two had established an air corridor to transport goods including perishable items. On the basis of the tremendous success of the air corridor, India has decided in the Dialogue to establish a similar air corridor with Central Asian Republics. The major focus of the dialogue was how to interlink India–Iran–Afghanistan to Central Asia to enhance trade and commerce. There was thrust on promoting connectivity and also cooperate on tackling terrorism. An important announcement by India was to provide for a two-week training for diplomats of the five Central Asian States at the Foreign Services Institute in New Delhi. To enhance the developmental diplomacy, India has decided to extend Line of Credits to Central Asia in the dialogue. India also signed an agreement with Uzbekistan for supply of uranium (second state to do so after Kazakhstan). On the lines of the European Schengen visa, Kazakhstan has proposed the silk visa. This will enable India to seek a role in enhancing people to people ties with the region, eventually enhancing the connectivity. In this backdrop, India announced the 4C formula of enhancing Connectivity, Commerce, Capacity enhancement and Contacts.

Outcomes of India–Central Asia Virtual Summit 2022

In 2022, the virtual summit between India and Central Asia aimed to focus on connectivity and security. The Central Asians have reposed faith to engage with India after takeover of Taliban in Afghanistan because they were worried of return of Islamic terrorism in their territories.

STRATEGIC AND ECONOMIC IMPORTANCE OF CENTRAL ASIA FOR INDIA

The region of Central Asia has enormous strategic and economic interests for India. The region is already witnessing a host of external powers that are contesting for geoeconomics. In this backdrop, India is not interested in any sort of clash of interests but has defined its posturing with the region in more strategic terms. The primary driver of India to deepen political relationship with Central Asia since the end of Cold War is to ensure that no forces inimical to interests of India have a free run in Central Asia. The chief concern of India in Central Asia is to ensure that Pakistan gets no space in using fertile lands of Central Asia to nurture terrorists and use them against Indian interests. It is important to understand that as India deepens its engagement with Taliban-led Afghanistan and Central Asia, there exists high possibility of Pakistan using terrorist launch pads to dismantle growing economic profile of India in the region. The Pakistanis have resorted to a proxy war against India in Afghanistan and potential extension of the same in Central Asia is also possible. The Chinese have often, in support of Pakistan, tried to arouse the locals in Central Asia to talk about Kashmir issue. The local vernaculars, often funded by Pakistani and Chinese intelligence agencies, have carried features related to 'fate of Kashmiri people' and have displayed sympathy to Kashmiri cause. The game played by India's adversaries is to arouse the Central Asians with Kashmiri cause and pin down India's use of cultural and civilisational diplomacy by asserting that India is anti-Muslims. India's continuous political engagement with leaders of Central Asia is Indian tactic to nullify the Chinese and Pakistani subversion. India's strategy to mitigate any adversity in Central Asia is driven by a policy mix involving political cooperation, trade incentives and cultural engagement with Central Asia. India's key policy is also to provide Central Asia with aid and technical support to not only skill their populations but also create ample amount of job opportunities in Central Asia. The logic of this move is that Central Asian people are busy in livelihoods, then any attempts by Pakistan to harm Indian development activity will be seen by people of Central Asia as inimical to their interests. Unlike China, which sees itself as replacing Russia as a security provider in Central Asia, Indian interests are more related to ensuring that nefarious designs that may be inimical to security of India are neutralised. This policy also keeps India out of the regional geoeconomic and geostrategic power play and thus prevents India from being tagged as an exploiter of Central Asian resources. It is not wrong to argue that even Central Asians have preferred to engage with India and are knowledgeable about India's concerns with Pakistan; but the Central Asians do

What are Pakistani Interests in Central Asia and how are they Anti-India?

Pakistan has tried to support proxy war against Indian economic interests in Afghanistan and Central Asians fear a similar tactic in their land as their engagement with India increases. This is so because, Pakistan has nurtured an ambition to Islamise Central Asia and position itself as a leader of Islamic world in the region.

not look at engagement with India as a counter-balancing force to any external player in the region. An issue in India's Central Asia outlook is that India continues to look at Central Asia from the Western prism and despite a deep historical and civilisational link, no effort has been made to evolve an understanding of social, cultural and language aspects of Central Asians; which unfortunately have created void spaces in India's strategic outlook for the region. However, India has looked at the region as an extended neighbourhood and security, energy, connectivity and political engagements remain the fulcrum of Indian policy.

INDIA'S UIGHUR POLICY AND INDIA'S OPTIONS FOR XINXIANG

In 1950s, many people from East Turkistan (the present day Xinxiang region) escaped the persecution of People's Republic of China (born in 1949). These people came in huge numbers to Ladakh and Leh. When China saw this, they sent their agents via Aksai Chin to Indian Leh and these agents massacred 2000 Uighurs by food poisoning. This created a deep shock in the Uighurs who had crossed over. Some decided to stay back in Leh but some managed to seek asylum in Turkey and Germany. The political and foreign policy practitioners in India have started working upon this fact in raising a counter to Chinese Uighur suppression. The Uighurs are once again in news. The 9/11 has highlighted that how restive Uighurs could create an arc of instability in the region. The proximity of India's Kashmir to Xinxiang is a cause of worry for India because any Uighur mass uprising will have security concerns for India's Kashmir. Pakistan, driven by its cross-purposes with India, has an active role to play in shaping Uighurs. Pakistan would do everything possible to make Xinxiang an area to pin down Indian aspirations. While Chinese are certainly concerned about Uighurs and want to use SCO to convince Central Asians and others to resist them; but Chinese use double speak tactics. At one place they call Uighur uprisings as acts of terror and on the other hand, they support Pakistani groups that attack other states. This strategy of China is in sync with their approach of using terrorism to expand their geopolitical interests. The repeated confrontation between India and China on Pakistani-sponsored terrorist groups such as Lashkar-e-Toiba and Jaish-e- Mohammad compelled India to allow a group of Uighur political activists to speak at a gathering in India. By conceptualising an issue to grant a visa to Uighur human right activist Dolkun Isa, India conveyed to Chinese in clear terms that they will not buy the Chinese definitions of selective terrorism and India reserves the right to hit the Chinese where it hurts them the most. By the issue of Dolkun Isa, India has communicated indirectly to the Chinese that India has considerable assets in hand and can choose to up the ante in Xinxiang at the time and place of its own choice. India had maintained a consulate in Kashgar till 1950s and continues to have enormous historical, cultural and religious inklings with Uighurs in Xinxiang. India must utilise these assets to establish listening posts and some hard ground assets to neutralise any Chinese adventures against India. India continues to nurture those Uighurs who came to India in 1950s and has supported their families. India must continue to nurture their contacts in Kashgar, Khotan and Turfan. India is also devising diplomatic strategies to clearly delineate the Uighur and Turkic nationalism and Islamic fundamentalism. The Chinese are conveniently wrapping the Uighurs as Islamic fundamentalists while leaving the real Islamic Wahhabi Islamic fundamentalists nurtured by Pakistan. This division of streams will help India diplomatically checkmate the Chinese.

THE CHINESE BRI IN CENTRAL ASIA, SECURITY CONCERNS OF INDIA AND INDIA'S POLICY OPTIONS

The Chinese and Central Asians are having deep levels of economic enmeshments. Any stance of cooperation of Central Asia with China or confrontation with China will have consequences for India. Today, the Chinese are undertaking mass diversion of waters from Ili and Irtysh Rivers of Central Asia to Xinxiang. This water is diverted to maintain the huge inflow of Han Chinese into Xinxiang. This water diversion has created ecological stress in regions that are proximate to India's northern borders. Any future confrontation of locals on water crisis with China will have security implications on India. The continued economic cooperation between Central Asia and China under the Chinese Belt and Road Initiative is a cause of concern for India. This is so because the Chinese are investing very heavily in creating rail–road and infrastructure projects in regions that border India's Kashmir. This will allow the Chinese to mobilise troops against India in case of a future confrontation with India and this will have military implications for India because India is nowhere a part of these global level transport corridors built near our frontiers. In this backdrop, India has to reconfigure the way it looks at Central Asia. It has to understand that in any policy foray India does in Afghanistan, it should involve Uzbekistan,

Turkmenistan and Tajikistan. The conference of National Security Advisors of Central Asian states, Afghanistan and India in 2022 was an attempt to achieve this objective. The Central Asian states bordering Afghanistan must be brought in by India in forging a regional consensus as that will reduce the influence that the Chinese could exercise. India must invest considerable diplomatic capital to develop ties with Ismaili Shias and Nur–Bakshia–Sufis who reside in Pamirs, Hindukush and Gilgit-Baltistan region. There is one school of thinkers in India who argue that India can explore options by engaging in the Belt and Road Initiative. They assert that doing so will enable India to reconnect with the northern axis, which has been prevented to India by the loss of Gilgit-Baltistan to Pakistan by the British through the operation Datta Khel (Refer to *Internal Security* by Pavneet Singh, published by McGraw Hill Education, for more contextual analysis of the operation). In this sense, any logical connectivity initiative must cross through traditional India and Central Asian routes and be via Xinxiang. India can use the BRI to champion the 'energy highway' that may start from West Siberia to north India, cutting via Central Asia and coastal China. The proponents here argue that this is an immediate option which India can work upon by engaging with Russia and Central Asia and prevent any attempts of encirclement by China. One school of thought even asserts that India can work on establishing India–China Silk Route Corridor (ICSRC) where India can champion a mega connectivity plan driven by energy, trade, connectivity, fibre optics and communication highways. In any scenario, it is imminent for India to widen the security lens and broaden the conceptual parameters to include Central Asia and Eurasia in its strategic thought.

CHAPTER

5

India's Hunt for Energy, Commerce and Connectivity with Central Asia

INDIA'S ENERGY DIPLOMACY IN CENTRAL ASIA

India has been pretty aware of the enormous energy stock that Central Asia continues to hold. In recent times, India has been making concerted attempts to dive into the energy reserves of Central Asia but the actual materialisation of the same will take many years. India has made three recent forays into the nuclear and oil sector which shall unlock India's deep presence in Central Asian energy markets. The first is India's long-term agreement with Kazakhstan to supply uranium for India's nuclear programme. The second is oil drilling contract for ONGC Videsh Limited (OVL) in Satpayev and the third is progress on a transformational, regional economic TAPI (Turkmenistan–Afghanistan–Pakistan and India) pipeline. The Russians are deeply interested in the TAPI pipeline project because they envisage the pipeline as not just an entry into Asian markets but also a counter to Chinese in Central Asia.

THE KAZAKHSTAN DILEMMA OF INDIAN FOREIGN POLICY

Turkmenistan and Kazakhstan, which are both geographically proximate to the Caspian Sea, possess enormous hydrocarbon potential. These nations have tremendous scope to fulfil India's hunger for energy. This explains why in 1990s, OVL opened its office inside the Indian Embassy building in Kazakhstan and has been relentlessly pursuing oil exploration in the Kazak territory. However, the Indian oil diplomacy in Kazakhstan failed miserably. There are various factors that explain Indian failure. Firstly, India's aspirations in the region were built on misplaced conceptions. India was of the belief that its historical and civilisational ties will enable India to make these forays easier as the nations would give India a priority. However, since the end of Cold War, there have been Americans and Chinese who have entered these energy markets in a big way. While the Americans have been led by their corporate giants, the Chinese oil diplomacy is state driven and India's OVL is miniature in terms of corporate profile in front of these big sharks. The Indian experience in Kazak is a clear indication that the cultural rhetoric need not always materialise into strategic considerations and has shown India the limits of civilisational diplomacy. The deeper reasons for the setback for India were that India never tried to take Russians onboard, despite knowing that Russia remains the dominant player in the region. India tried course correction in 2009 by inviting the Kazak Head of the State to India as the chief guest of the important Republic Day celebrations. Indian negotiators wanted to clinch deals on oil and atomic energy supplies. However, unfortunately, the PM, who often receives the State Guests, could not make a visit because he had to undergo an immediate coronary surgery. This caused immense diplomatic awkwardness and put the incoming Head of the State, who often was known for self-aggrandising character, in an ostentatious scenario. India has also understood that instead of pursuing oil from Kazakhstan, it should focus on cheap gas supplies from the state. Because, firstly, Kazak is a big supplier of oil to Europe and China is reluctant to allow India to have access to cheap oil as it makes enormous profit in existing sales. Thus, India may not enjoy any preferential treatment here. Secondly, Kazak has tremendous gas reserves and as of now, it does not have much gas buyers. As India tries to diversify its energy mix and switches over to gas as a cleaner fuel than oil, Kazak can play an important role in supplying unsold gas to India. The other area where Kazak is interested in engaging with India is nuclear realm. Kazak has tremendous reserves of uranium and India in 2015 signed the deal for a supply of 5000 metric ton uranium annually from Kazakhstan. The Kazaks also follow a no-strings attached policy and do not require India to be part of international nuclear agreements such as Nuclear Non-Proliferation Treaty (NPT). The nuclear cooperation can also be seen through the Russian prism because Russia is a big player in India's nuclear industry and Russia will be more comfortable to see Kazak supply nuclear raw material to India. Secondly, Russia also has a deep control over the Kazak nuclear mining, production, enrichment and reactors. In this sense, the Russians are direct beneficiaries in the nuclear commerce between Kazak and India. This is one of the lessons we have identified above, which was missed by India's diplomacy with Central Asia earlier.

CHALLENGES FOR INDIA'S ENERGY DIPLOMACY IN CENTRAL ASIA

India's experience in navigating energy diplomacy in Central Asia has given an important lesson for our policy makers. India has learned that any energy diplomacy in Central Asia cannot be done on historical or civilisation reasons but will be influenced by geopolitical considerations. India has also understood that the best way to navigate the Central Asian energy quagmire is to seek Russian support because directly or indirectly, Russia continues to have a strong hold on Central Asian energy and this factor is crucial how India approaches energy diplomacy in Central Asia. India would always be a net gainer if it takes Russia into consideration because Russia too wants to limit the Chinese influence in energy markets of Central Asia. In this backdrop, Russia can always support India and India will be a net gainer in this strategic balancing of geopolitical equations of Russia and China. Thus, the valuable lesson for India is that it cannot discount Russia in any of its future policy endeavours in Central Asia. Russia and Kazaks do consider India as a reliable and a trustworthy partner than China, but often assert that India is not a good performer. This 'good performer' is a term often mentioned in private conversations between Indian and Russian diplomats and Russians intend to convey that India must not seek any preferential treatments owing to historical connection and must be decisive enough to bid for resources in open markets and compete with Chinese and Americans. This is a serious cause of concern for India because even under its developmental diplomacy, India has not been able to do anything which is a game-changer. This implies that despite a paltry developmental assistance that India often grants to Central Asia, the Central Asians still remain economically and socially dependent upon China and Russia. This has been viewed by Central Asians as a negative point because they opine that India is not serious enough to help Central Asians gravitate outside the dependencies of Russia and China and help them stand on their own feet. The other problem is that Central Asia is merely a subject of continual intellectual curiosity in India and no serious efforts are made in India to understand the regional culture, language, political system, business rules and taxation policies. Despite the much touted and hyped TAPI pipeline, it is surprising to see that both India and Pakistan are willing to take economic losses in return for political and strategic gains. The Indian side is apprehensive that if the TAPI pipeline is built, Pakistan will not allow smooth passage of pipeline in its territory. India believes that the transit fees that Pakistan will generate for allowing the passage of oil through their territory will be routed to fund terrorism against India. Thus, despite Russian enthusiasm to materialise the pipeline and score some brownie points globally in helping the conflict resolution, India and Pakistan remain apprehensive of the fate of pipeline. In ultimate analysis, it can be stated that while some successes have been achieved in sourcing energy from Central Asia for India but Central Asia will not remain the last solution for India's energy needs for the time being. In this backdrop, the present Union government in India is approaching Central Asian theatre by looking at the larger geopolitical angle. It has understood that focusing on Kashmir and development of infrastructure within the country will become pathways that would allow India to integrate to Central Asia in future more easily and the abrogation of Article 370 in 2019, must be seen in this larger geopolitical context.

INDIA'S EURASIA POLICY, CONNECTIVITY DIPLOMACY, ASHGABAT AGREEMENT AND INSTC CORRIDOR

The biggest hurdle for India to reach Central Asia is access to direct land connectivity. On the other hand, the recent Chinese Belt and Road Initiative (BRI) has put India in a quandary. The China–Pakistan Economic Corridor (CPEC), a part of BRI, which India has opposed citing violations of territorial sovereignty, has been hushed aside by Chinese who call the corridor as a livelihood project for the region. When India opposed BRI, the Chinese tried to build a narrative that India is against connectivity diplomacy. This narrative is quite surprising because India has had its own Eurasian outreach plans. In fact, India has often communicated at multiple platforms that it is willing to take part in BRI-related projects provided the Chinese show sensitivity to divert the CPEC through the non-disputed areas. India needs to perform some creative diplomacy. India must support Gilgit-Baltistan and Ladakh, which together constitute 82% of Kashmir, at the centre-stage of its connectivity diplomacy as doing so can potentially blunt the Chinese narrative on Kashmir and CPEC. Parallely, India must work on raising assets to support the pro-freedom leaders in Baluchistan, Khyber-Pakhtunwa and Gilgit-Baltistan. Also, as mentioned earlier, India must make an entry into Gilgit-Baltistan and northern territories so that it can start leveraging some economic heft in Sinkiang and Wakhan regions and this is where India can press the right Russian buttons in the SCO to let India enter the zone. India's philosophy needs to be clear. It must travel on the road. Though it is unlikely that Chinese will re-draw CPEC because for China the CPEC is a quid pro quo for India's Act East Policy; however, its participation in Indo-Pacific and the QUAD has its own connectivity strategic thinking. In any case, exposure of Kashmir to the larger strategic discourse of Central Asia has to become the core driver of Indian foreign policy. In 2016, India inaugurated the Zaranj- Delaram highway that connects Afghanistan and Iran. In 2017, the Ministry of External Affairs (MEA) in India held a multi-stakeholder seminar with Federation of Freight Forwarders Association of India to highlight the significance of road transport in reaching Eurasia. The same year India formally acceded to Transports Internationaux Routiers (TIR) Convention. Apart from this, since 2002, India, Iran and Russia have been jointly working on the International North-South Transit Corridor (INSTC), a multi-modal connectivity project that intends to fuse Indian Ocean, Persian Gulf with North Europe. India has been very keen on the INSTC, as it will help it in integrating itself deeply in Central Asia without Pakistani logistical support, a regional obstructionist. It also helps India counter the Belt and Road Initiative of China. The trade costs shall be lowered and it will take less time circumventing many regions along the way. In May 2013, the Indian Shipping and Road Transport Minister signed an agreement with Iran to develop Chabar port. The construction of the Chabar port is a step towards the operationalisation of the INSTC. In September 2015, at a meeting in Delhi, a legal framework for transit and customs had also been agreed upon. The Indian Foreign Trade Policy 2015–2020 also made a pitch for INSTC.

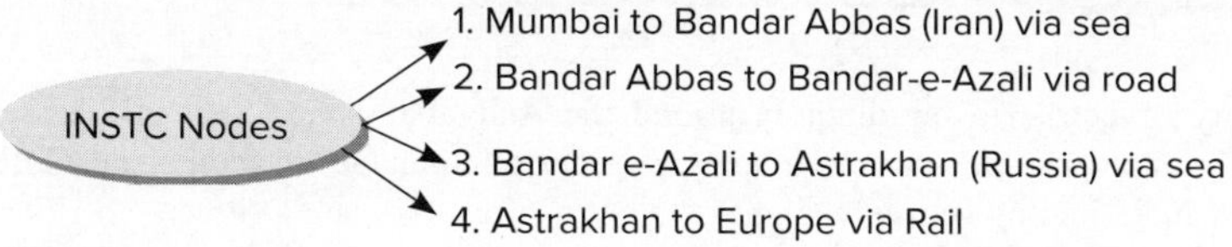

The INSTC links the Indian Ocean, Persian Gulf, and Caspian Sea to the Russian Federation. Studies by various transport experts have proven that the INSTC could provide multiple benefits to all players, especially to Russia and India. Strategically speaking, the INSTC has multiple benefits for India. The first is that the corridor provides India with viable surface transport connectivity to the Eurasian region. A study by the Iranian Ministry of Road Transport suggests that the corridor will reduce transport costs by 30% and shall provide a 40% shorter route as compared to the route passing through China and Europe to reach Russia from India. With the Sagarmala initiative of India and the India–Myanmar–Thailand highway, the corridor will connect Europe and Russia to the ASEAN states. From the Indian point of view, the INSTC and India–Myanmar–Thailand highway could transform India into a potential transit hub. There are lots of factors that constrain the full utilisation of the corridor.

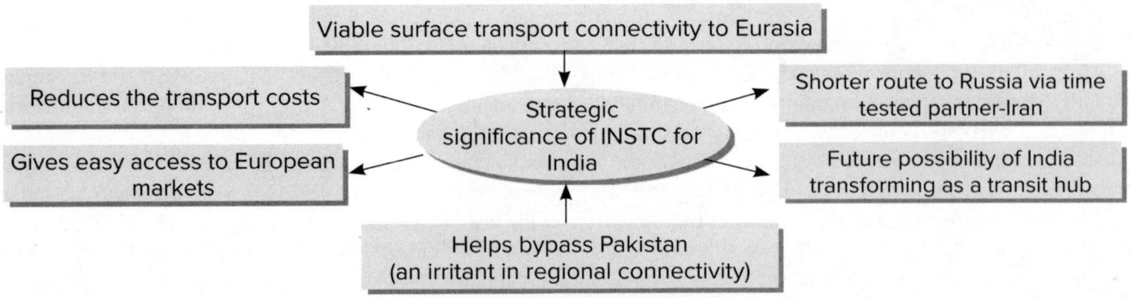

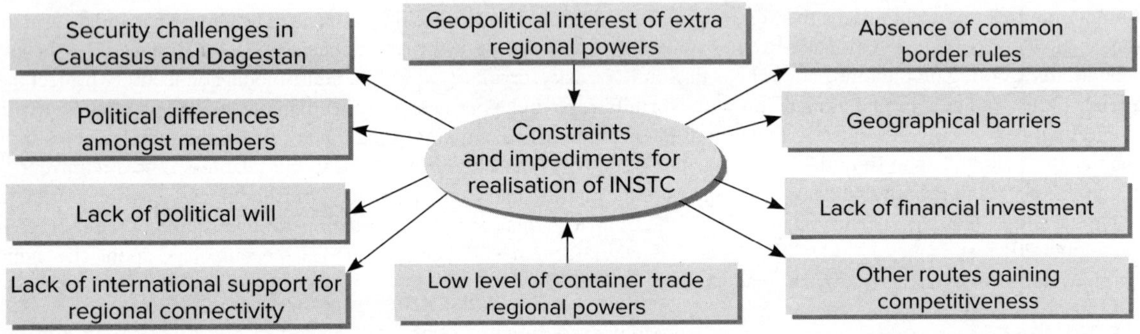

Keeping the connectivity objective in mind, India joined the Ashgabat Agreement in 2018. The agreement was conceptualised in 2011 as a multi-modal connectivity project to bring Indian Ocean and Persian Gulf together via Central Asia. The significance of India joining this agreement is that it aspires to create a 'green' corridor for vehicles, reduce time for transit by speeding works at railway checkpoints, create infrastructure for storing and transit of cargo and upgrade sea jetty facilities for maritime cargo. The entry of India into the agreement will now facilitate the trade between India and Eurasia, under the umbrella of Russia. The agreement also opens enormous connectivity potential for India to reach out to Central Asia. India now will not restrict its engagement under the agreement with Central Asia for trade but can look for concluding Free Trade Agreements (FTAs) with Central Asians. The accession of India to the TIR convention, as mentioned above, will provide security for transit of goods and help in reduction of insurance costs during transit for traders.

SECTION 6

INDIA'S RELATIONSHIP WITH AFRICA

AN OVERVIEW

In 1997, a question was asked on the analysis of India's Africa policy. In 2009, the UPSC asked question on NEPAD and its objectives. In 2011, question was asked on the salient features of political and economic relationship between India and Africa. In 2012, there was a question on why the African countries are rich with resources yet poor. In 2015, a question was asked on increasing interest of India in Africa. In 2018, a question was asked on how ITEC programme has achieved goodwill in Africa. In 2021, the UPSC asked a question on India's interests and influence in Africa.

Potential foresight A basic analysis of the previous years' questions suggests that the UPSC has often asked questions on what India is doing in Africa. A common theme that also emerges is that there are questions on Indian interests and influence in Africa. On the basis of this trend, it can be easily inferred that the questions in the future are likely on commercial, security and strategic dimensions. The reason is that these three dimensions are now emerging as new arenas of cooperation with Africa and these are the areas where India's interests also sync well. In this backdrop, this section on Africa has been redesigned by incorporating the new arenas of cooperation as separate chapters to equip the readers with adequate knowledge needed to write effective answers.

CHAPTER 1

India and Africa: Key Drivers of the Relationship

INDIA'S HISTORICAL BOND WITH AFRICA

The trade relations between India and Africa owe their origin to the monsoon winds. Sailors from India sailed in South East monsoonal winds to reach Africa (from June to September) and used the North Eastern monsoonal winds (from December to March) to sail back. During ancient sea trade, Indians used to trade rice, wheat, cloth, incense, palm oil, ivory and gold from Africa and they settled in East and South Africa. In 1497, when Vasco da Gama reached Malindi, he also noted the presence of Indians in Mombasa/Kiliwa. Trade opened up people-to-people contacts, which, in medieval times, saw one of its manifestations during the Mughal rule when Africans were placed in the Mughal army and they were mainly the Siddhis (people who are descendants of Bantu tribes). They were also found in the army of Muhammad Bin Qasim.

SCRAMBLE OF AFRICA AND INDIA

After the commencement of the imperial age in Europe, Africa became a colonial battleground. The British, French and Portuguese were the leaders in this race for colonisation and the 17th century period also saw slave trade beginning in Africa who were taken from Africa along with resources to sustain the Industrial Revolution back home in Europe. The French colonised Mauritius and Reunion and there was a need of masons, blacksmiths, carpenters and so on and perceiving these as opportunities, the Indian traders in Africa also brought skilled persons who fit the role from various parts of the west coast of India. A lot of Indians began to settle down to these jobs in Mauritius, Reunion and other East African States. Gradually, the British also emerged on the African scene. In 1833, slavery was abolished in Britain and they evolved a new indentured labour system. The British brought bonded labourers from India to work on sugar plantations, railway establishment in Africa and cotton plantations. Thus the link continued with Africa starting from maritime trade.

GANDHIAN FACTOR IN INDIA–AFRICA RELATIONSHIP

During British colonial rule in India, three important factors were Mahatma Gandhi, Jawaharlal Nehru and the Indian National Congress (INC). The Congress, since its inception, showed support to and solidarity with the African cause. In 1890, the British sent Indian soldiers to Sudan to fight—a move that the INC opposed vehemently as Indian soldiers in Sudan and Ethiopia did not fight for any cause that ultimately had any benefit for India. Rather, they were used by the British to suppress the natives. In 1893, Gandhi went on an assignment to Africa. During his study in Africa, he witnessed severe racial discrimination. During his stay in Africa till 1913–14, he evolved and practised the concept of Satyagraha, which eventually emerged as a technique of mass mobilisation. The success of Satyagraha in Africa affirmed its utility as a tool of non-violence and it went on to be later used as one of the core tools of Indian national movement. During the early 20th century, when the Indian national movement gained momentum, India did not lose touch with Africa. India always felt that Africa, like India, had also been a victim of imperialism and that India needed to assist Africa in its fight against imperial powers. In 1927, the INC, at its Calcutta session, took a decision to open offices overseas. Offices by INC were opened in Africa to assist Africans. In 1927, Nehru had already participated in the Brussels Conference of oppressed Nationalities and had advanced an idea of India being a kingpin in the process of liberating the world from imperial powers. The conference moulded our foreign policy thought from 1928 onwards as far as Africa was concerned—we began to link our freedom struggle with the imperial struggle of Africa. India evolved a thought that its own freedom struggle and Africa's struggle against imperial powers as well as its fight against apartheid were in natural continuation with the idea of one world, free of imperialism and oppression. This Afro-Asian solidarity also moulded our foreign policy that emerged after independence as the core pillar of policy of non-alignment.

INDIA'S RELATIONSHIP WITH AFRICA DURING THE COLD WAR

After India became independent, from 1950s to 1970s, it supported decolonisation in Africa. India believed that it became independent because of Gandhi's Satyagraha. Satyagraha was a technique that Gandhi had conceptualised and implemented successfully in Africa. So, India believed that it was their moral responsibility to teach Africans the idea of Satyagraha and support decolonisation over there. During this period, Nehru played an instrumental role in implementing this policy. The non-alignment became a crucial factor that acted as a bridge. India used non-alignment not only to reach out to Africans to support their decolonisation but also used it as a tool to promote non-alignment in Africa.

The instance of South Africa provided the necessary ammunition to India to build a constructive Indian foreign policy towards Africa based on its opposition to all other racial regimes in that continent. Thus, Indian policy in Africa introduced anti-racialism as a new tool along with anti-colonialism and anti-imperialism. India taking up the fight against apartheid in the UN in 1964 also resonated well amongst Africans, all the while India's intense and sole focus being on non-violent modes of protest.

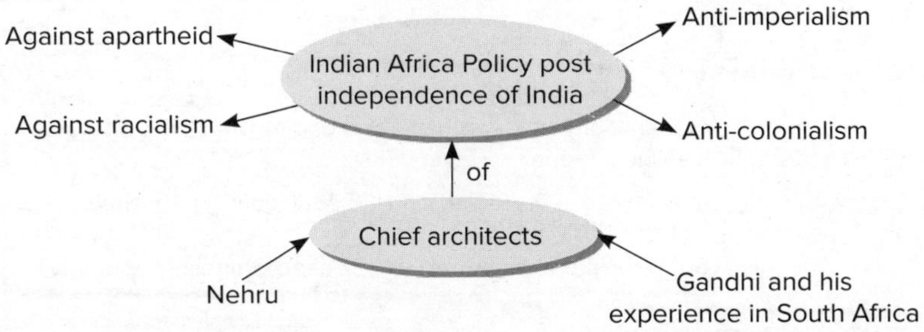

India advanced support to Africa against colonialism but it did not insist on fixing a date to end colonialism in Africa. This upset many African leaders as they deemed that India might not be serious about supporting the African struggle against colonialism. Things began to change for India after the 1962 conflict with China. Firstly, after the conflict, India became busier to counter an aggressive China at every forum. In contrast to the precepts of non-violence championed by India, China, on the other hand, preached armed struggle amongst Africans. This appealed more to some African leaders who were not happy with the results that the slow approach advocated by India brought about. For instance, Algeria, a French Colony in Africa, resorted to an armed struggle against France. Because of these reasons, support for India gradually began to decline amongst the African nations. The decline was visible prominently after the death of Nehru. Support for China began to grow and China began to make inroads into the African territory. The two case studies ahead aptly summarise the decline of support for India.

India and South Africa Relationship

South Africa was an important trading partner of India during the times of the British Raj. In 1946, South Africa came out with a Ghetto Act that aimed to aggregate resistant colonies in South Africa as per racial differences. This move irked India, and in 1946, Nehru, the interim PM took up the issue of the Ghetto Act in the UN by invoking Articles 10 and 14 of the UN Charter. Despite flourishing trade, India decided to cut ties with South Africa after its insistence on maintaining status quo. India not only broke off its diplomatic ties with South Africa but also did not revive the same till 1994, when apartheid in South Africa officially ended.

Divergences in India and Africa Ties

After the death of Nehru, Lal Bahadur Shastri led the NAM summit held in Cairo, Egypt. During the Summit, India wanted a resolution urging China on renouncing the use of force. There was hardly any support from African nations for this cause. Similarly, towards the end of the Summit, India wanted a resolution compelling China not to take the nuclear route. India thought that due to its disarmament credentials, there would be support for it from the African states, but initially only Cyprus supported it. This clearly signalled a situation of declining support for India amongst the African nations.

India and East Africa Relations

East Africa was one such area where there was a sizeable presence of the Indian diaspora. Nehru wanted to support East Africa against colonialism and sent his trusted aide, Apa Saheb Bala Saheb Pant, a respected Gandhian, writer, freedom fighter and diplomat, as India's ambassador to East Africa. His home had become a nerve centre for all efforts coordinated against colonialism. The British were alarmed upon seeing this. They pressurised Nehru to recall Apa Saheb Pant. Nehru was forced to recall Pant, leaving the East Africans disillusioned.

Reconnecting to the Indian Diaspora in Kenya

With a renewed focus on the diaspora from the 1970s, India and Kenya, in 1990, established the Africa–India Development Association. Apart from boosting bilateral economic engagement, the association aimed at integrating the Indian diaspora in the economic life of Kenya. This reflects the new importance attached to the diaspora acting as a bridge in the relations between the two nations.

The next phase (1970s to 1990s) began with India opening its relations with Africa due to its historical connection, bolstered by a common colonial legacy. As the African decolonisation was completed, the African nations were looking for a role model for development. India made strategies to regain the lost path, using Non-Aligned Movement (NAM) as a tool to rework its relationship with Africa. To seize the new opportunity in Africa, from 1970s, NAM became economy-oriented and India was in a place where it could flex its muscle because domestically things were in better order. The Green Revolution had succeeded in improving the food security situation. A military conflict with Pakistan succeeded in India's favour in 1971. India, then, decided to become economically assertive in Africa. The most important policy, however, was with respect to the Indian diaspora. During the Nehruvian era, Nehru insisted that the diaspora of India in Africa should place interests of the host nations they reside in over and above their own interests. More so, due to strategic concerns of the NAM, India gave less preference to the needs of the diaspora at that time.

During this phase of reconnect (1970s till the end of the Cold War), the importance of the Indian diaspora increased. The success of India's Peaceful Nuclear Explosion in 1974 also contributed to the rise of India's international image from 1970s. India began to use NAM Summits to economically integrate diplomacy with Africa and focused on strengthening the South–South Cooperation a term used by the policymakers to denote development and economic cooperation between developing countries of the global south.

In 1970, at the NAM conference in Lusaka, India outlined its new approach for Africa. India encouraged Africa to undertake vigorous domestic growth and pledged technological and economic support in this endeavour to strengthen the idea of SSC. India encouraged its Heads of Missions in Africa to focus on economic assistance to Africa and told the diplomats to promote economic engagement. A special role for the diaspora was envisaged in this by the new relationship as Indira Gandhi called upon the Indian diaspora to act as ambassadors of India.

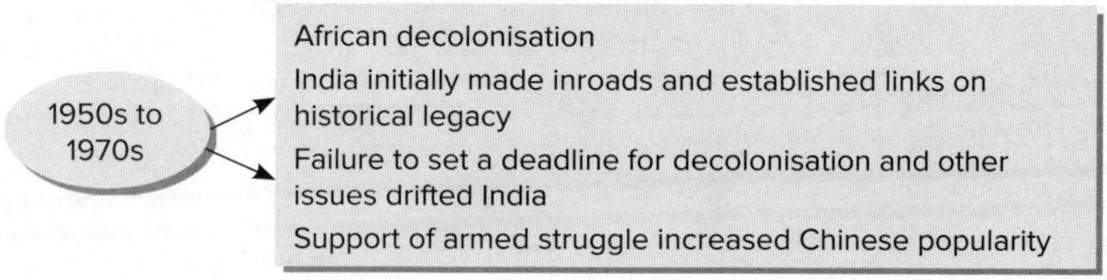

This renewed thrust gave India an opportunity to re-establish its link with Africa. Its economic diplomacy, however, was certainly not as aggressive as that of Western powers. Whatever assistance India gave was limited but had a positive impact in the African thought process as all assistance was provided without any conditionality, and driven with an intention of helping Africans grow.

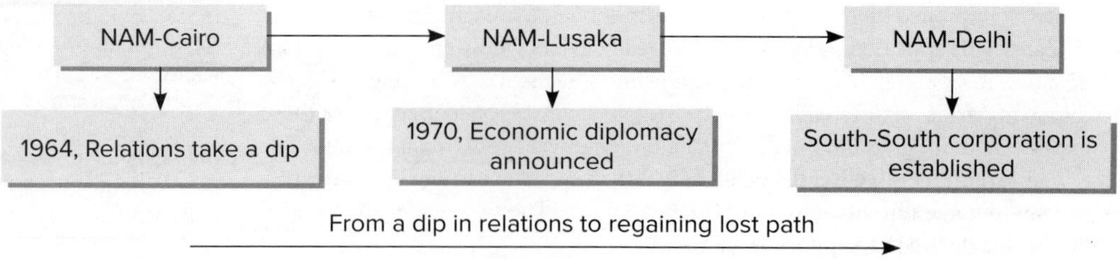

In 1986, India, at the NAM summit in Harare, established the AFRICA fund which acted as material assistance by India in the fight against Apartheid in South Africa and Namibia. The economic engagement continued with Ethiopia, Kenya, Tanzania, Uganda and Ghana re-established its ties more aggressively with Africa and continued to deepen the engagement in the post-Cold War period.

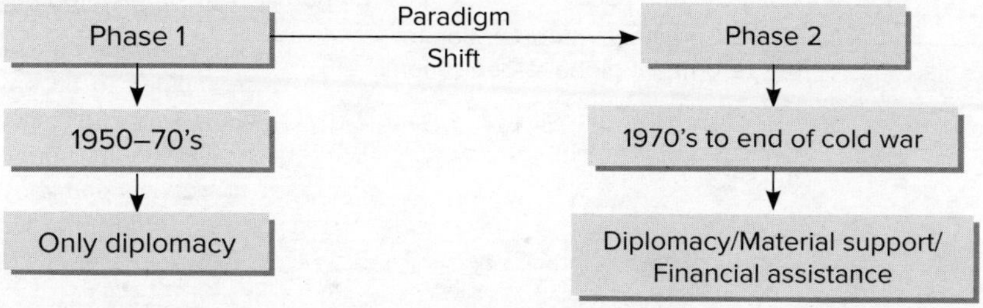

India and South West Africa People's Organisation (SWAPO) Diplomacy

The Namibian territory was under the control of South Africa. The South Africans continued with their illegal rule. When this illegal rule of South Africa, in Namibia, reached the International Court of Justice in 1972, the court deferred the decision of ending or termination of South Africa rule. In 1982, after enormous deliberation, India proposed a global level meeting and accorded full diplomatic status to SWAPO, while also providing it monetary and material assistance. In 1990, Namibia gained independence, which opened up diplomatic relations again.

INDIA'S RELATIONSHIP WITH AFRICA IN THE POST-COLD WAR PERIOD

India's engagement in the post-Cold War period owes its base to its Cold War engagement where energy concerns dominated. Economic diplomacy pushed the relationship. India realised the importance of Africa to ensure energy security in the future. In 2017, India organised the fourth India–Africa Hydrocarbons Conference. The conference again provided India an opportunity to showcase its expertise in oil exploration, oil refining and drilling technology. The new strategy of India's engagement with Africa is rightly called as ABBA–Africa for Bharat and Bharat for Africa.

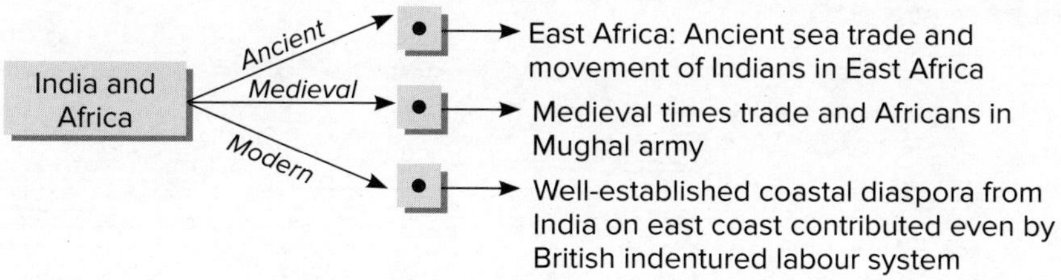

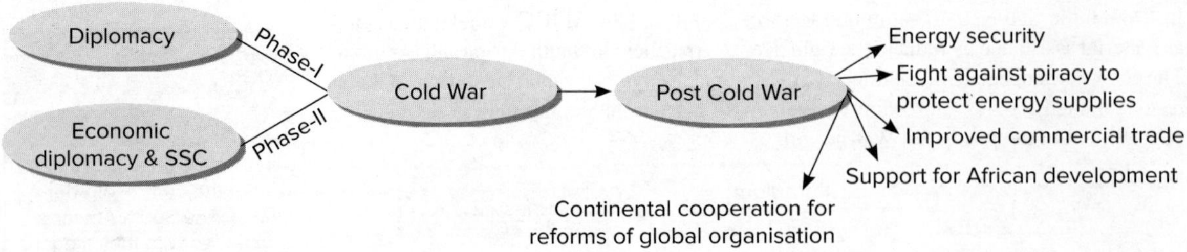
Diplomacy
Phase-I
Economic diplomacy & SSC
Phase-II
Cold War
Post Cold War
Energy security
Fight against piracy to protect energy supplies
Improved commercial trade
Support for African development
Continental cooperation for reforms of global organisation

2

CHAPTER

India's Africa Policy: Interests, Influence and Diplomatic Strategies in Africa

INDIA AND AFRICA OIL DIPLOMACY

The core tenets of Indian interests for Africa can be summed up in one word—OIL where O stands for oil, I for investment and L for location. The time that the Cold War ended was also the time when Indian economy made a transition to an open economy. To sustain the open economy, India needed oil, which it already had from its supply from the Middle East. Over a period of time, as India diversified its import basket, Africa came in the picture. India began to forge oil-based relations in Africa for energy security. India intends to obtain ownership in oil blocks in Africa. This strategy of going for equity oil is better than buying oil from open spot market because ownership in an oil block gives India a very deep exposure of the African markets. For India, Africa is a rising continent and offers multiple opportunities for our private sector, which can help bring India and Africa closer to each other. The location of Africa is strategic as it helps India to connect to Central and South America through the Cape of Good Hope and to West Asia through the African Maghreb. There are many drivers to India's Africa policy. First, we need to understand that India's intention is not only limited to harnessing African resources but goes much beyond. India has always kept it clear that due to our historical relations with Africa, it is in our interests to assist the entire African block in overall development. While assisting the African development process, India does not follow the white man's burden approach, but rather intends to share its own knowledge and developmental experiences with Africa for the mutual benefit of both. PM Narendra Modi himself has defined what lies at the heart of India–Africa partnership when he said India's priority is not just Africa, India's priority is Africans. Since the time of Nehru till the present, India has initiated multiple programmes in its bid to aid to African development. A brief mention of the programmes will ease our understanding of India's foreign policy towards Africa.

INDIA'S INFLUENCE IN AFRICA THROUGH ITEC PROGRAMME DIPLOMACY

The acronym ITEC stands for Indian Technical and Economic Cooperation. The Nehruvian foreign policy envisaged the idea of 'one world', which led to an interdependent world where countries cooperate in socio-economic and developmental well-being. After independence, India received tremendous assistance from international agencies and forums (for example, India played an important role in The United Nations Conference on Trade and Development (UNCTAD) in its developmental endeavour. India thereby reached an understanding that it would be important for India to share the development lessons and its experiences with other nations. Nehru had this dream of ensuring that other developing countries learn from India's own learning. This envisaged India to position itself as a trainer for the developmental need of other Third World Countries. Keeping this in mind, on 15th September 1964, India launched this bilateral initiative for Africa known as ITEC. India envisaged giving training to other countries for their overall development. For Africa, ITEC had three parts. First, ITEC as a programme continues to be one of the most important diplomatic tools for India abroad. Second, ITEC is now multilateral in nature and is linked to initiatives under the ASEAN. Third, the Development Partnership Administration Division, a division in the Ministry of External Affairs (MEA), manages the ITEC.

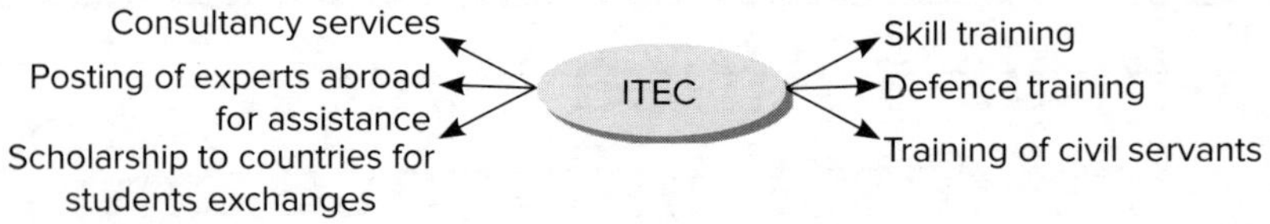

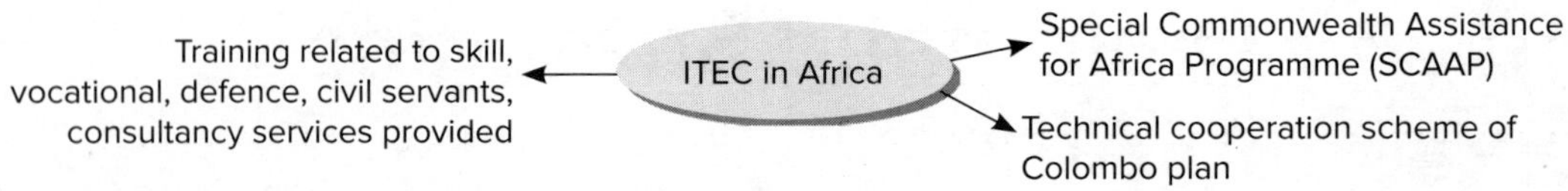

INDIA'S INFLUENCE IN AFRICA THROUGH SOUTH–SOUTH COOPERATION (SSC) DIPLOMACY

The origin of SSC goes back to Bandung Conference in 1955. In the conference, the African nations decided to initiate a partnership with each other at the development level. Since 1961, this partnership became a part of the NAM. Initially it had two components, namely, technical cooperation amongst developing countries and economic cooperation amongst developing countries. The idea was that the participating countries should undertake developmental cooperation, which would involve multiple stakeholders including national governments, civil societies, public–private partnerships and individuals. It envisaged the sharing of knowledge, developmental experiences, technical assistance and so forth. India always believed that North–South cooperation is important and it would act as a supplement to SSC. India approached SSC without any conditionality, and with full respect for the sovereignty of the other participating countries. In contrast, economic diplomacy is an economic engagement by countries for self-benefit through trade. In fact, SSC is also different from North–South cooperation as SSC is a demand-driven, voluntary, horizontal programme with no conditions attached. In the 21st century, India, under SSC, promotes sustainable development, inclusive growth, infrastructure and energy as goals. India assists Africa in SSC in all the parameters above.

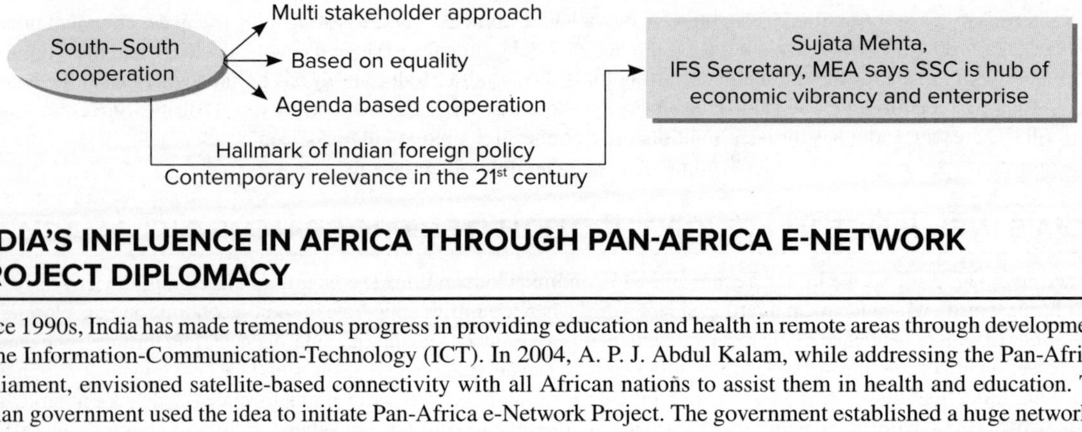

INDIA'S INFLUENCE IN AFRICA THROUGH PAN-AFRICA E-NETWORK PROJECT DIPLOMACY

Since 1990s, India has made tremendous progress in providing education and health in remote areas through developments in the Information-Communication-Technology (ICT). In 2004, A. P. J. Abdul Kalam, while addressing the Pan-African Parliament, envisioned satellite-based connectivity with all African nations to assist them in health and education. The Indian government used the idea to initiate Pan-Africa e-Network Project. The government established a huge network to provide services in consultations with Telecom Consultants India Limited. The project was officially inaugurated in 2010.

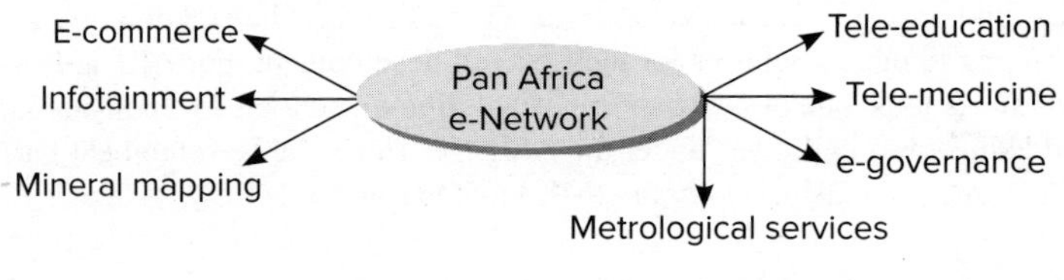

INDIA'S INFLUENCE IN AFRICA THROUGH TEAM-9 INITIATIVE

In 2004, the India government launched the Techno-Economic Approach for Africa–India movement. This is a regional initiative exclusively meant for eight West African States. India feels the need to establish a connection with West Africa as it is a resource-rich region. India, through TEAM-9, intends to help development in this resource-rich but underdeveloped region with assistance for infrastructure and low-cost technology. The aim here is to provide assistance to specific projects and give a thrust to the private sector of India so as to promote trade. India has earmarked 500 million dollars line of credit here. The West African region does not have large India diaspora but the Gulf of Guinea is certainly a new hotspot of oil in Africa.

INDIA'S INFLUENCE IN AFRICA THROUGH INDIA–AFRICA FORUM SUMMIT (IAFS) DIPLOMACY

Continental level engagements with Africa are not new for India. The origin of such interactions goes back to 1993, when Japan initiated the first ever Tokyo International Conference on African Development (TICAD). This was followed by China initiating the Forum on China–Africa Cooperation (FOCAC). On similar lines, to open up continental level engagement, India launched its first ever IAFS in 2008 in New Delhi. The forum concluded with the New Delhi Declaration that reaffirmed the shared vision of vibrancy and resurgence in India–Africa relations. The declaration set an agenda for India and Africa to collaborate on sustainable development, climate change and UN reforms. Subsequently, a second such summit was organised in 2011. The second IAFS was held in the Ethiopian Capital, Addis Ababa in 2011. The Addis Ababa Declaration adopted a new cooperative framework based on capacity building, peace and security. India envisaged the creation of institutions such as the Indian Institute of Technology and the Indian Institute of Foreign Trade in Africa. In the second IAFS, India also committed to creating a two-million-dollar fund for the African Union Mission in Somalia to curb piracy. The third IAFS was held from 25th to 28th October in 2015. The third IAFS is unique in multiple aspects. The first aspect is the issue of participation in the IAFS. This is because, in 2006, the African Union (AU) in the city of Banjul (capital of Gambia) announced the Banjul Formula. In the first IAFS, there was participation by 14 states, while in the second IAFS, there were 11 states that participated. In IAFS-3, India decided to do away with limited participation (as per the Banjul formula) and invited all 54 Head of the States from Africa. This was done because India had decided to launch the 'Outreach to Africa Programme' in the third session of the IAFS. Second, the IAFS-3 opened up on the cultural note. For the first time in the history succeeding the Cold War, India organised a successful event, hosting 54 nations at one place. The IAFS-3 concluded with the Delhi Declaration 2015, which articulated the India–Africa relationship as 'Partners in Progress' and pledged to work 'towards a dynamic and transformative development agreement'. India officially pledged support to the African Agenda 2063 and committed resources to Africa to help achieve goals of the agenda. India also announced

Western Sahara, Morocco and IAFS-3 in 2015

The region of Western Sahara was under the colonial control of Spain till 1975. Spain liberated Western Sahara in 1975. Immediately after this, Morocco and Mauritania began to claim West Sahara as it is a region rich in phosphate and has the largest phosphate reserves in the world. Over a period of time, Mauritania gradually went out of the picture but Morocco did not. In 1976, Sahrawi formed Sahrawi Arab Democratic Republic and established it as a sovereign state under the Polisario Front. In 1985, India gave recognition to Saharavi Republic as it thought Polisario Front was fighting a struggle for self-determination. However, as the UN took over efforts to resolve the issue, India, in 2000, withdrew its recognition. This recognition of SADR by India had created a deep resentment in Morocco–India relations as Morocco considered SADR a part of its territory. In IAFS-3, India had invited 54 African nations including Morocco with no representation officially from SADR/Western Sahara.

What is Banjul Formula?

According to the Banjul formula, (adopted in 2006), India would extend an invitation to 15 African Head of the States to participate in the India–Africa Forum Summit which would include five participating states of NEPAD (New Economic Partnership for African Development—A programme of African Union to seek global support for the development of Africa) programme, 8 member states to be identified from Regional Economic Communities of African Union and the Chairperson of the African Union Commission. These 15 nations would participate in IAFS.

10 billion dollar line of credit for projects, along with thirty thousand scholarships. What also makes the Delhi Declaration 2015 unique is that the areas in which Africa and India are going to collaborate were broadened to now incorporate solar technology, food security, blue economy, rural housing, skull development, use of social networks to enhance people-to-people cooperation and sustainable development. Delhi Declaration has also adopted a monitoring mechanism to implement the agendas envisaged. They have also adopted the India–Africa Framework for Strategic Cooperation.

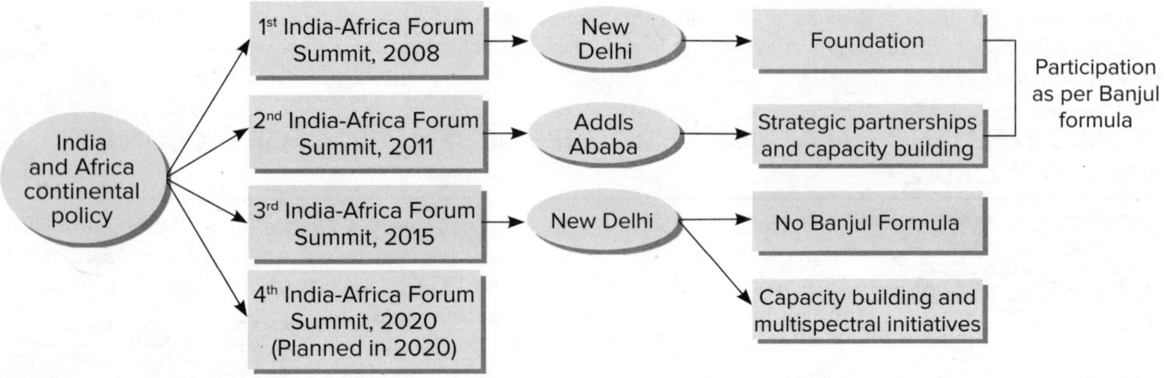

INDIA'S INFLUENCE IN AFRICA THROUGH INDIA'S AFRICA POLICY OF MODI GOVERNMENT

Since the coming of the new government in India in 2014, it has given tremendous importance to reaching out to Africa. India's outreach to Africa began in early 2015 when senior ministers were sent to visit all 54 nations in Africa to invite them to India for the third IAFS in October 2015. This spectacular diplomatic achievement later also saw India doing away with the Banjul formula. After the success of the summit, the second component of outreach began. As discussed above, the second component witnessed the Indian President and Vice President visiting African nations to strengthen bilateral ties. In the third component, we see the Indian Prime Minister reaching out starting July 2016. Thus, through this unique format, India was able to reassert people-to-people as well as government-to-government ties, along with building business link.

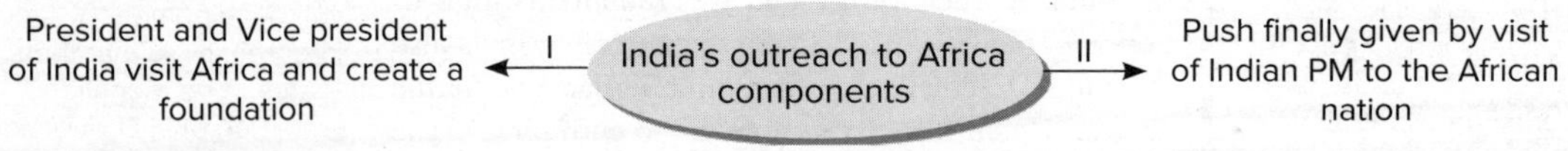

MODI'S TEN GUIDING PRINCIPLES FOR INDIA'S ENGAGEMENT WITH AFRICA

India has announced ten guiding principles that will enable us to engage with Africa. These principles are our vision for Africa.

Intensive and deep engagement	Development and skill enhancement of Africans
Support to African industry and intensive trade	Combat terrorism, extremism and ensure cybersecurity
Support digital revolution in Africa	Cooperative and inclusive Indian Ocean security
Improve agricultural output of Africa	Joint efforts to ensure Africa nurtures its youth
Jointly ensure just international climate order	Jointly create a just, representative and democratic global order

INDIA'S INFLUENCE IN AFRICA THROUGH HEALTH DIPLOMACY, PHARMACEUTICAL COOPERATION AND VACCINE MAITRI

The Indian pharmacy sector has recorded vibrant growth. It has not only shown noticeable progress in generic drugs but also quality medicines for TB, Malaria and so forth. In the time of COVID-19, India has sent consignments of Paracetamol and Hydroxychlorquine to 25 African states, with initial beneficiaries being Mauritius, Comoros, Seychelles and Madagascar as immediate beneficiaries even under 'Project Sagar'. India has also launched e-ITEC COVID-19 Management Strategies Training Webinars to provide training to health professionals in Africa to tackle COVID-19. While both India and China may be trying to provide health-based support to Africa in the times of COVID-19, their strategies are markedly different. For Chinese, the key influencing drivers of their health diplomacy are money, political power and elite level wealth creation. The Chinese are keener on developing state-to-state relations than people-to-people relations, because their larger interests are hard infrastructure for resource extraction. Thus, the Chinese are more concerned about pleasing the African elite. This is where India differs, because our focus is on building local capacities with African states on an equal partnership. The COVID-19 has proven that as India and China rise in Africa, two distinct models are available for the Africans to select their long-term partners ahead.

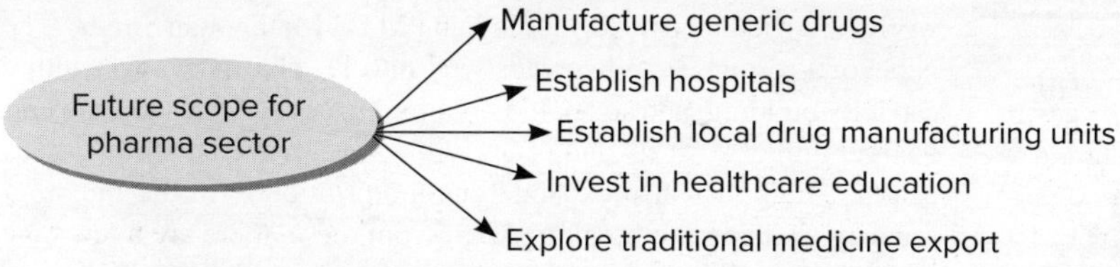

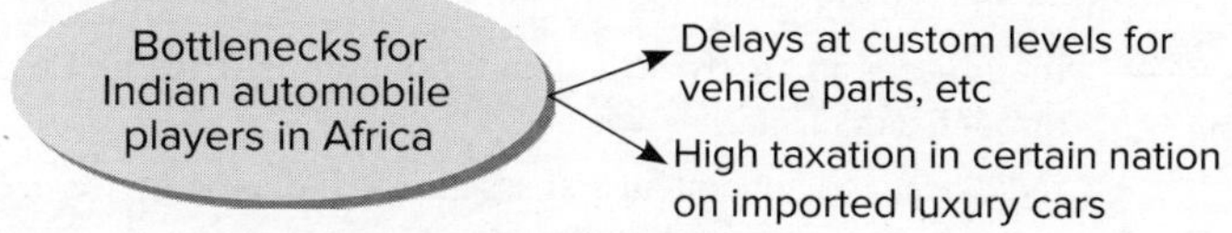

INDIA'S INFLUENCE IN AFRICA THROUGH EDUCATION DIPLOMACY

Africa has been receiving tremendous support from UN for its Millennium Development Goals and Education for All initiative. The focus of both is on universalisation of primary education and reduction of poverty and gender disparities. Due to special attention, Africa has made progress in school education but is struggling to arrange gainful employment for its school pass outs since Africa lacks institutions for skill development and higher education. It is in this context that India steps in. India has been focussing on skill development and scholarships in Africa. The prime interest of India is to skill the youth of Africa and enables them to play an aggressive role in the future development of the continent. In the second IAFS, in 2011, India entered the fray on continuous skill development through capacity building initiatives by building IIT and IIFT. India had, by 2015, provided more than 20,000 scholarships for higher education. The third IAFS, in 2015, has envisaged 30,000 scholarships for the future. Considering India has made noticeable advancement and tapped the skill and higher education market, it would be imminent for India at this stage to enhance this effort to become a global leader. The MEA needs to make this area its special focus and announce a properly planned HRD policy for African markets. India has not only invited African students to India for higher education but also offers courses with a special focus on skilling the African youth through vocational training. To ensure that India is able to attract the global student community, India needs to focus upon four things:

- Enhance the university curriculum capabilities to support cultural diversity in university campuses.
- At the diplomatic level, enhance academic partnerships.
- Ensure that the African students who come to India get hands on training in Small and Medium Enterprises in India as part of academic partnerships.
- Design special curriculums on climate change for African students.

INDIA'S INFLUENCE IN AFRICA THROUGH PAN-AFRICA E-KNOWLEDGE NETWORK

In 2019, India launched the Pan-Africa E-knowledge network. The programme aims to provide 4000 African students free tele-education annually. In addition to this, India will provide 1000 candidates of Africa medical education, which will include courses in nursing and paramedics. The new project is likely to act as a digital bridge of knowledge and health. The most crucial part of the project is that it is applicable to French speaking region of Western Africa also where India has a minimal presence. This programme is based on the vision of Indian Ocean security rooted in inclusivity, cooperation and growth for all. The programme will transform African youth into a nursery of aspirations in the future. Due to COVID-19, as the movement of African students to India has been affected, Indian government has decided to extend e-Vidya Bharti (tele-education project) to Africa. India is aiming to establish an India–Africa Virtual University by 2021.

HURDLES IN INDIA'S ENGAGEMENT WITH AFRICA

Fourth India–Africa Forum Summit 2022

The fourth summit was actually planned in 2020 but got delayed due to the pandemic. The fourth summit occurred in 2022 in Mauritania and the focus was on skill- and capacity-building initiatives, health care, agriculture, maritime security, climate change and nurturing Africa's digital revolution.

India has harnessed its historical relations with Africa and envisages a bright future ahead. India also acknowledges that Africa is a vibrant continent and the next 'growth pole' in the world (as articulated by former Indian PM Dr. Manmohan Singh). The Indian engagement is beyond resources and spreads well into IT, pharmacy, agriculture, skill, training and capacity building, and so on. India's aim is to assist Africa in its overall development, with a larger aim of security and peace with convergence on global issues. In the twenty-first century, India has also expanded its footprint aptly in the Indian Ocean owing to new security challenges emerging. Apart from these, there are a few other areas where India and Africa need to cooperate more which require changes in diplomacy from the Indian side. Some salient points are given below:

- India needs to firstly articulate a policy on Africa and engage with the continent through a doctrine.
- India needs to appoint an ambassador of India for Africa in the MEA who would act as a nerve centre for all policies in Africa.
- India should widen the discussion dynamics at the IAFS level and bring the private sector and the civil society in the IAFS platform rather than restricting it only to government-to-government interactions.

Despite various kinds of developmental assistance provided by India, some of the key obstacles in enhancing trade with Africa are as follows:

- Political instability in Africa and absence of stable regimes and rule of law.
- Corruption in African governments acting as a deterrent for private firms.
- Lack of regulatory framework and regime architecture.
- Lack of access to institutional finance to promote trade.
- Logistical concerns and poor connectivity in the hinterland.

AREAS OF FUTURE COOPERATION BETWEEN INDIA AND AFRICA

It would be the best for India if in cooperation with Africa it announces a skill development policy and helps African skill development through quantitative target setting. The MEA can designate the Indian diaspora as unofficial ambassador in its endeavour of soft power export and publicise the good work done in India to mould a framework public opinion. India has to accelerate engagement with Africa by injecting bilateralism in the diplomatic processes. This will give India an opportunity to have one-on-one interaction with African nations. For example, Morocco in the recent times as initiated a moderate Islamic programme that is exclusively designed for tackling radicalisation. India can enhance its cooperation with Morocco at this level. India has to spend more diplomatic capital to popularise the projects it is funding and executing in Africa. For example, in the recent times, after the outbreak of COVID-19, India has emerged as one of the top donors to Africa but our efforts have not received adequate publicity. India needs to evolve a suitable soft policy strategy with Africa that can yield bilateral mutual benefits. For example, India can envisage a tie up between film industries of both the countries. India can improve direct flight connectivity between India with Africa, which remains very poor till date. Africa presents numerous opportunities for cooperation in healthcare due to the presence of widespread diseases such as HIV, TB, Malaria, and so on. India can share all the effective measures it has followed to tackle COVID-19, with Africa as it lacks effective healthcare delivery and has scarce public resources. India can share all the effective measures it has followed to tackle COVID-19, with Africa as it lacks effective healthcare delivery and has scarce public resources. The COVID-19 crisis can be used to explore new partnerships in QUAD Plus format where QUAD states can propose cooperation with selected African states by creating mechanisms for exchange of views.

Boosting India's Exports by Linking LDCs into India's Potential Global Value Chains

This recent paper has shown that India intends to sharpen its presence in the global value chains by leveraging SSC and Africa is looking for partners to support their growth. The paper asserts that India is in need of dyes and leather, which it can source from African countries and enable them to become a part of the global value supply chains.

INDIA'S COMMERCIAL INTERESTS IN AFRICA

Africa is a land of resources. As per estimates, Africa is endowed with 10% of the world's oil and 40% of the world's gold. Different regions of Africa have different resources and the continent, in totality, is beneficial for India in multiple aspects. As the economy of Africa grows, there will be new demand for projects and goods. Indian private sector, in this regard, intends to play a key role in meeting African needs. Before we study the trade dynamics, it is important to briefly have a look at different regions in Africa.

Name of the region	Important commercial centres for India	Core competencies of the commercial centre and region	Miscellaneous information
Western Africa	Nigeria, Ghana, Ivory coast	Crude oil	Piracy problem
Southern Africa	Angola and South Africa	Crude oil (Angola only) Non-oil such as gold, diamonds, steel	Market access is absent
Northern Africa	Egypt, Tunisia	Oil, chemicals, phosphates and fertilisers	Arab spring and political instability
Eastern Africa	Kenya, Mozambique, Mauritius, Seychelles	Leather products, bags and islands are strategic importance	Need to augment skill and technics
Central Africa	Chad, Congo, Uganda, Malawi, Rwanda	Vegetables and coffee	Transport and reach is an issue

INDIA'S FOCUS AFRICA PROGRAMME (FAP) AND TRADE DIPLOMACY

To promote trade, India has used instruments such as lines of credit, FAP and duty-free trade preference systems. The CII and FICCI from India also play an important role in this regard. They regularly organise platforms in consultation with African forums, giving India an opportunity to leverage its private sector. The private sector appropriately uses these forums to create business in Africa. A brief mention here of the duty-free quota-free (DFQF) market access; the FAP and Indian firms in Africa will aid our understanding. The Doha round of negotiations in 2001 for the first time envisaged DFQF market access to least developed countries (LDC). It was only in 2005, in the Ministerial Conference (of WTO) in Hong Kong, the decision was taken that the developed countries would be allowed to undertake DFQF market access to LDCs. On the sidelines of the first IAFS in 2008, India went on to formally initiate duty-free trade preference scheme (DFTPS), designed to boost bilateral trade. The scheme has got further impetus in its effort to boost trade after its modification in 2014. The measures by India have further strengthened SSC. In 2002–2003, India also launched its FAP. This programme is underway in twenty-four African nations. Within this programme, heads of the Indian Missions in these 24 nations act as commercial sales agents. The diplomatic machinery does extensive research and outlines opportunities available for Indian exporters. The Indian exporters then undertake market access and market development. This helps India to boost its exports in Africa and opens up opportunities for the private sector of India. A lot of Indian companies are doing tremendous business in Africa. The role of private sector is analysed better when we study bilateral relations but broadly the picture is as given below:

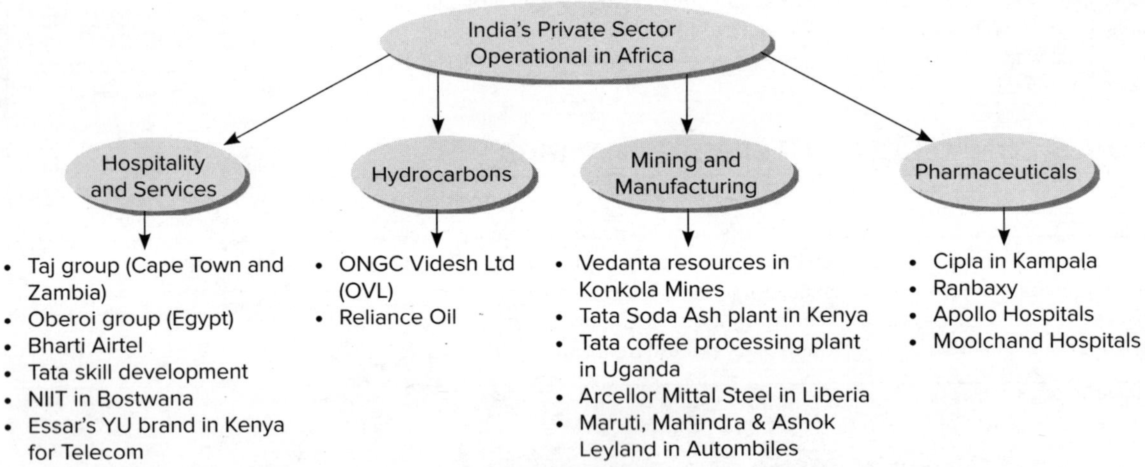

AFRICAN CONTINENTAL FREE TRADE AGREEMENT (AfCFTA) AND COMMERCIAL SIGNIFICANCE FOR INDIA

In March 2018, the heads of 55 African states gathered at Kigali, Rwanda, and signed the AfCFTA (it needs ratification of 22 signatory states to come into effect). Brokered by the African Union, the AfCFTA is a continental free trade agreement. As per a study of the UN Economic Commission, by 2022, the AfCFTA will boost the intra-Africa trade by 52% (from 2010 levels). The three core aims of AfCFTA include the following:

- Abolishing the import duties on 90% goods that currently average at 6%.
- Raising the internal African trade by 50%.
- Scrapping non-tariff barriers.

In 2020, the bilateral Indo-Africa trade stood at US$ 60 billion (an increase from US$ 11 billion in 2005). AfCFTA will be beneficial for India, as it will give an edge to the Indian exporters. The Indian exporters would now be able to access a unified and a robust market in Africa. Various economic think tanks have carried out studies to assert that if AfCFTA is established, Indian trade with Africa will increase by 10%. This rise in Indian trade will have geoeconomic and geostrategic consequences as well. This increased trade can help India balance out rising China–Africa trade. As China follows a more resource-centric extractive strategy, AfCFTA can be a boost to Indian development-centric strategy. As India looks at Africa for energy security, AfCFTA can help India potentially leverage the concept of blue economy. This will enable India to diversify its resource base and the trade basket. AfCFTA can be synchronised by India with the Africa Asia growth corridor and can help India leverage the overall trade dynamics. There has been 12% increase in India–Africa trade in 2019. India has become the fifth largest investor in Africa with cumulative investments of US$ 54 billion, creating thousands of jobs for local citizens. Over two-thirds of India's LOCs in the past decade directed to African countries. Currently 189 projects in 42 African countries at US$ 11.4 billion under implemented with Indian LOCs, the Foreign Secretary informed. For over half a century ITEC has offered training and skill development to countries from Africa. At the India–Africa Forum Summit in 2015, India announced a doubling of the number of scholarships to 50,000 befitting people across Africa.

Prime Minister	View of Africa	Policy Paradigm for Africa
Jawaharlal Nehru	Historical engagement	Non-alignment to connect
Indira Gandhi	Economic roots to historical policy	NAM became a tool of economic engagement
Rajiv Gandhi	Economic roots to historical policy	NAM became a tool of economic engagement
Narsimha Rao	Economic roots to historical policy	NAM became a tool of economic engagement
I. K. Gujral	Economic roots to historical policy	NAM became a tool of economic engagement
Atal Behari Vajpayee	No special significance given	Diplomatic engagement
Manmohan Singh	Development diplomacy	Focused on development of Africa
Narendra Modi	Development-cum-security diplomacy	Africa to be developed by India and its geopolitical location will be an advantage to the security of India in Indian Ocean.

3

CHAPTER

Asia–Africa Growth Corridor, Reflections on Indo-Pacific, SAGAR and Maritime Diplomacy

ASIA–AFRICA GROWTH CORRIDOR

At the 52nd Annual General Meeting of African Development Bank in Gandhinagar in May 2017, the Indian PM, along with his Japanese and African counterparts, propounded the idea of an Asia–Africa Growth Corridor (AAGC). Under this initiative, a mega sea corridor based on ancient sea routes connecting Africa with India and South East and East Asia is being envisaged. The idea is to create a low-cost, environment-friendly sea corridor to boost investment, transport, trade and connectivity. India and Japan are going to play a major role in developing the infrastructure. The creation of AAGC will be akin to making an investment corridor where Japan will contribute its expertise in infrastructure creation while India will bring its core diplomatic expertise. The priority areas of AAGC include projects related to health, pharmaceuticals, agriculture, food processing, disaster management, skill development and technology. Some scholars have theorised that the AAGC is a counter proposal to the Chinese Belt and Road Initiative or the BRI. The AAGC is unique in many aspects. Firstly, in contrast to the BRI, the AAGC is a purely sea-based corridor, which means that it ensures a lesser carbon footprint. Secondly, in AAGC, the process is more democratic and consultative as the focus is to assist the African states in the ways they want. Thirdly, the AAGC is a corridor where the private sector will be playing a major role in contrast to the BRI, which will be completely State funded. The corridor will have four components: Development and cooperation projects, Quality infrastructure and institutional connectivity, Capabilities and skill enhancement and people-to-people partnerships.

Reflections on Indo-Pacific: Perspectives from Africa

The Indo-Pacific is a vast maritime zone with geopolitical, geoeconomic and geostrategic significance but the concept unfortunately excludes Africa, which has a vast maritime frontier. In this backdrop, neglecting Africa in this vast maritime realm will deprive them of developmental benefits. Thus, India must take the leadership role and push for bringing Africa on board, thereby making Indo-Pacific truly inclusive.

INDIA'S PEACEKEEPING MISSIONS IN AFRICA AND DIMENSIONS OF SECURITY DIPLOMACY

Since independence, India has been consistent in sending peace keeping forces (PKF) to assist the UN in the process of decolonisation. The decisions of participation in UN activities through the PKF not only helps India achieve its foreign policy goal of maintaining peace but also increases India's prestige. In a very strategic sense, India does not achieve any goal related to national interest in the purest sense, as the PKF undertakes no combat roles on the ground. The PKF is primarily responsible for peace keeping. The participation gives Indian agencies exposure to the different kinds of conflict, which provides important lessons for logistics and military diplomacy. The participation of the PKF is overall in sync with Article 51 of our Constitution, which aims to promote peace and security at the international level. There is a Permanent Mission of India (PMI) in New York at the UN office. An officer of the rank of colonel in the Indian army receives requests by the UN for the PKF. The PMI forwards the application to the MEA. The file is then forwarded after clearance at MEA to the Ministry of Defence. A tri-services board under the Director General of Staff reviews the request, takes the necessary decision and hands the file back to the MEA. The file is then presented by the MEA to the Cabinet Committee on Security (CCS) and after approval, the MEA announces the decision in the Parliament to send forces. Thus, the decision to send the PKF is at the sole discretion of the Union Executive. Till date, India has sent PKFs in Namibia, Mozambique, Liberia, Sierra Leone, Rwanda, Congo and Sudan. In Africa, the PKF focuses primarily on peace and humanitarian assistance. For example, in Congo, our officials have provided medical treatment in the UN hospitals. One of the most important contributions of Indian PKF in Africa has been the promotion of gender equality. In 2004, India stationed its first ever all-women battalion of 125 (RPF) officers in Liberia.

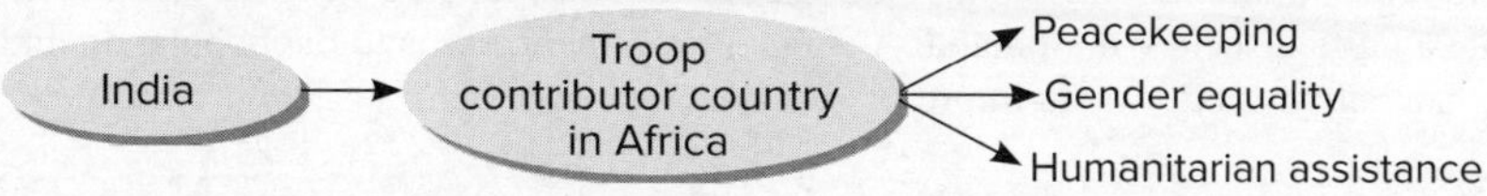

INDIA'S NAVAL POWER PROJECTION AND PIRACY MANAGEMENT WITH AFRICA

In the early modern times, the territory of Somaliland was occupied by three colonial players. One part was occupied by British, the second by Italy and the third by the French. The part occupied by the French became a new state known as Djibouti. The rest of Somaliland gained independence in 1960. In 1960, there was a coup by Siad Barre wherein took over the control of the state. Opposition rebels began to fight against Siad Barre. Two prominent opposition groups emerged, namely, the Somalia National Movement (SNM) and the United Somalia Congress (USC). The two parties, SNM and USC, started controlling the northern and southern territories and succeeded in ousting Siad Barre in 1991. Despite the ousting of Barre, no united government emerged as factionalism grew to the extent where tribal warlords began to assert control over their clans, creating a situation of complete anarchy. The tribal clans turned to piracy to sustain themselves. Absence of a stable centralised government since 1991 has aggravated stability issues making Somalia politically fragile.

Piracy as an exercise has been flourishing in the Horn of Africa region. It is primarily based in Somalia from where it spreads out in the seas affecting many nations in the Indian Ocean. Somalia is an easy base for piracy due to the absence of a stable government in the country. The US Office of Naval Intelligence has undertaken a deep study to understand the modus operandi of Somali pirates. The office is of the view that Somali pirates undertake piracy mainly for ransom money. The pirates have a well-established system of informers in foreign ports. When the ship passes through the Horn of Africa, the pirates, through well-established, specialised teams on ground and sea, launch pirate attacks. The pirate teams on the sea have in-depth knowledge of the sea and possess other maritime skills. As the pirates in Somalia have established a good network with terrorist groups operating in the Maghreb region, availability of arms is not a difficult task. Unlike pirates in the seas of South East Asia who also loot the goods from the merchant vessel and sell it in black markets, Somali pirates are only interested in taking ships hostage and demanding ransom. The merchant firms operating vessels in the region pay ransom money to get the ships released and this emboldens the pirates. At times, Somali pirates disguise themselves as coast guard and naval agencies and are able to fool the merchant vessels.

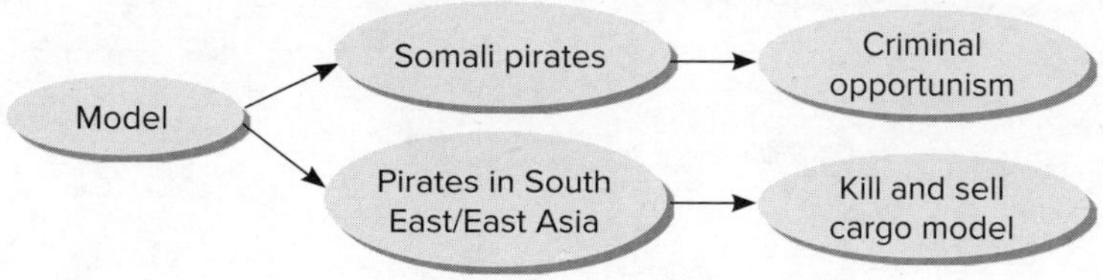

Because of rise in piracy, the cost of transporting goods has increased. The ships have started circumventing the area in favour of a longer route in deep sea to avoid piracy. Shipping firms have increased security on board of ships. The insurance firms have hiked the premiums. All this has led to an increase in the cost of trade. Nations have resorted to resolutions at the UN level. These UN level resolutions have legalised naval presence in Somali water. Countries have stationed their navies to protect the sea-lanes of communication. India has also likewise increased its naval presence in the Horn of Africa. India has urged the UN to track the ransom money being paid by help of international agencies like Interpol. India has been advocating that all Joint Anti-Piracy Operations (JAPO) be brought under the UN ambit and domestically, all nations create laws to criminalise piracy. Indian navy has been protecting sea lines of communication since 2008. The Indian coast guard has established new district head offices in Kavarati and in Minicoy. Through naval presence in Mauritius, Seychelles and Maldives, India has been able to keep the pirates in check. India has also clarified in an annual report released by the Ministry of Defence that the Indian Ocean region is central to Indian interests and piracy in the region is a cause of serious concern, to combat, which the Indian navy is ready to play a critical role in the region. The long-term solution lies in international collaboration to criminalise ransom payment and undertake adequate social engineering to create a unified society in Somalia. A stable government, skills to the population and creation of jobs in the fishing industry can help in a big way in future.

AFRICA'S INTEGRATED MARITIME STRATEGY 2050, INDIA'S SAGAR DOCTRINE AND BLUE ECONOMY

What is SAGAR Doctrine?

SAGAR is a geoeconomic construct that retains a balance between maritime security and economic development which focuses on cooperation in Indian Ocean region as the core philosophy.

Today, India is in sync with Africa's Integrated Maritime Strategy 2050 which has identified the threats Africa will face in the maritime domain. In this backdrop, India's 'near term plan' is to offer Africans resources, assets and technology to their navies and coast guards so that they can guard their coasts on their own. In the long-term India is assisting the Africans in establishing an African maritime system that will enable optimal utilisation of resources of Africa. The SAGAR Doctrine of India has committed Africa assistance for capacity building and maritime infrastructure creation. India is presently working on building a coordinated, focused and institutionalised security cooperation.

4 CHAPTER

China as a Factor in India and Africa Relationship and India's Defence Diplomacy

CLIMATE DIPLOMACY AS NEW ARENA OF INDIA–AFRICA STRATEGIC COOPERATION

The climate problems are not restricted by national boundaries but are global in nature. The solution to such problems must be transnational. The situation of Africa is that of being one of the lowest contributors of pollutants but one of the biggest sufferers of climate change. As Africa is resource-rich, the depletion of natural resources causes the continent immense anxiety. Degradation of land and environment has been at the core of a majority of the conflicts seen in Chad, Sudan-Darfur and Ethiopia. The drying up of the Nile, Orange, Zambezi and Kunene has sparked violent clashes amongst groups. If the sea levels increase, Lagos and Banjul, along with Seychelles, Mauritius, Reunion and Madagascar would be threatened. Climate change offers India a lot of opportunities to assist Africa in mitigating these challenges and helping the peace process. India has committed to the development of solar technology in IAFS-3 (2015). India may, in future, also plan assistance in wind and tidal energy. This can help the private sector of India to fetch more opportunities. Because of fluctuations related to the climate change in India and the rise in demand for agricultural commodities in 2015–16, a lot of private firms have started purchasing land in Africa. The land in Africa is under state control and is far cheaper than land in India. The private sector has undertaken mechanisation of agriculture in Africa to tide over climate change and supply agriculture commodities. From 2020, the Government of India has undertaken cultivation in Africa to mitigate domestic food shortages.

CHINESE STRATEGIC DIPLOMACY IN AFRICA AND IMPLICATIONS ON INDIA

One of India's main competitors in Africa is China. Our aim in this part is to analyse Chinese presence in Africa and scrutinise the Chinese approach in the continent. Chinese presence in Africa goes back to the Cold War times. It was during Mao's era that the Chinese began to promote armed struggle in Africa against decolonisation, which appealed to many African states. This also gave China an opportunity to provide economic aid for decolonised nations, thereby making inroads in these states. However, the Chinese engagement in Africa emerges aggressively after the end of Cold War. As Chinese economy began to grow by the 1990s, it also began to search for resources. Africa, being a resource-rich region, was a natural choice for China. China also found Africa to be a favourable market for its goods. In order to develop Africa as a sustained supplier of resources and a market for goods, China began to undertake creation of infrastructure in Africa so that it gives China an easy route to transport resources back home. Apart from this, China has been giving a lot of economic aid to Africa. However, many are dissatisfied with the aggressive Chinese resource-centric policy towards Africans. The scholars assert that the Chinese model in Africa is based on its greed for resources. A simple algorithm lies at the heart of its policy: China goes to an African nation, sets up industries and factories, exports Chinese labour to Africa, digs out resources from the nation, brings the resources back using infrastructure they have created to connect the industry to the port. De Soysa (a scholar) remarks that in this entire Chinese model, the African country does not stand to gain anything except very little pecuniary profit in the form of taxation. The lives of ordinary Africans in that country does not change as the people receive no skill development from China so that they are absorbed in the industry. This leads to a lot of disenchantment in the local people, leading ultimately to a kind of hatred against the Chinese presence. However, the state, instead of supporting the people, supports the Chinese in their endeavours, ultimately becoming a rentier state. This ultimately weakens institutional development in Africa. China has, as per its 'going out strategy', tried to link its domestic development to its global aspirations. The going out strategy is reflected well in Africa where China has diplomatic relations with more than 48 African nations. The basic strategy is to give Africa aid and undertake trade and diplomacy to establish a market for goods. We also need to note that Africans have an inclination for China as, firstly, African states are motivated by the Chinese state-led economic development model that has made them a regional hegemonic power. They take pride in how China, under Deng Xiaoping, started from a scratch to reach where it is today. This state directed capitalism, despite China being a communist regime, has earned it respect in Africa. Secondly, the Africans to some extent are disillusioned with lack of development of their domestic economies despite proximate ties with West and Europe since a very long time. But the most important connecting factor between Africa and China is how the Africans are portrayed. The West has always been pessimistic about the future of Africa, partially due to deeply entrenched habits of racial profiling a feeling of racial superiority. For example, in one of the covers of *The Economist* magazine, it went on to brand Africa as a hopeless continent. In contrast, China has always appreciated African dynamism, winning a lot of confidence amongst Africans. The Chinese model is unique in Africa in the sense that China allows poorly performing corporates back home to take up opportunities in Africa. If a corporate has not been performing well, the Chinese government would encourage that company to re-emerge and prove its worth by giving it support in exploring the African market. It has been seen that, with state support, these companies are able to re-emerge powerfully. This kind of an exercise also boosts the domestic corporate sector. The networking for corporate sectors is enhanced further by interaction undertaken by China at the Forum for China–Africa Cooperation (FOCAC). All this gives China an opportunity to play a deeper role in Africa and gain the needed diplomatic weight at international forums. China has created Tanzania–Zambia railway line, Addis Ababa–Djibouti railway line, Mombasa–Nairobi railway line. It is developing the East Africa Master Railway Plan, Trans-Maghreb Highway and Walvis Bay Container Terminal in Windhoek to name a few. In 2018 FOCAC meeting, the Chinese have committed 60 billion dollars for development of Africa and 1 billion dollar for BRI Fund for Africa.

What is a Rentier State?

A rentier state is a state, which derives all, or a substantial portion of its national revenues from the rent of indigenous resources to external clients.

CHINESE DONATION DIPLOMACY AMIDST COVID-19

In the wake of COVID-19, China has initiated "donation diplomacy" in Africa. Under this, Chinese aim to provide all sorts of medical assistance to African countries. By doing so, the Chinese are trying to position themselves as a leading provider of humanitarian support and 'public goods' in the global public health sector. Chinese, by resorting to donation diplomacy, aim to achieve three things. Firstly, this will enable the Chinese to divert attention from discussing the origins of COVID-19. Secondly, it will enable the Chinese to develop a strong amount of goodwill. Thirdly, it will support an image makeover for China. This three-point strategy enabled the Chinese to win the African support for supporting Chinese candidates as heads of FAO and WHO. Thus, Chinese have been able to use a blend of their economic heft and political influence in Africa at the time of a pandemic.

STRATEGIC IMPLICATIONS OF CHINESE NAVAL BASES IN AFRICA ON INDIA

China has established the first ever naval base in Africa in Djibouti. An authoritarian regime of Djibouti is quite comfortable to diplomatically deal with an authoritarian regime of China. This is an attempt by China to enhance its international clout. The base is located in the Indian Ocean and is perceived by Indian strategists as an attempt to encircle India as a part of Chinese String of Pearls Alliance network (which already includes naval bases in Bangladesh, Myanmar and Sri Lanka). In the recent times, Chinese are also investing in ports in Sri Lanka (Hambantota port) and Pakistan (Gwadar port) and these ports are being designed to accommodate naval vessels of China. This means that there will be an enhanced naval presence of China proximate to India. Though China has asserted that it would be using the Djibouti naval base for anti-piracy and humanitarian relief operations, but India's Research and Analysis Wing has clearly asserted that the port will have a permanent Chinese troop presence (of Chinese Marine Corps with nearly one lakh soldiers). Thus, such a strong naval presence in Indian Ocean has raised alarm bells in the South Block.

INDIA'S DEFENCE DIPLOMACY WITH AFRICA

The recent Indo-Africa ties are marked with rise in defence cooperation. In 2015, when African leaders visited India, there was a joint call by the leaders to provide defence and security-specific cooperation for Africa. Even though India has decades of cooperation with Africa in UN Peacekeeping operations and has been providing training to African defence officials, its defence diplomacy has remained very low profile. A part of the reason is that India does not have material and defence capabilities to offer deeper defence cooperation. China has taken aggressive steps to bolster its presence in this dimension where India has been providing space. Even though China does not have some exceptionally high quality conventional weapons to boast off in Africa, it is still making a dent in training where India has an edge. For instance, in 2018, China has established a Comprehensive Training Centre (CTC) in Bagamoyo in Tanzania. It is now using the CTC to provide defence training to Kenya, Uganda, Rwanda and Burundi. To cope up with regional crisis, China has announced the establishment of a US$ 100 million African Rapid Response Force. Along with all this China has identified a few new areas of defence cooperation that include:

- Arms sale
- Military assistance
- Political mediation
- Conflict resolution

However, in 2019, China stepped into the internal security of African states which is regarded as the most important dimension. Also, in the same year it initiated 'law enforcement diplomacy'. As part of this, China is enhancing bilateral cooperation in internal security. To do this, it is exporting artificial intelligence (AI) software and new technologies such as facial recognition to boost surveillance and law enforcement capabilities. Chinese firms such as Cloud Walk Technology and Hikvision are selling face recognition technologies and CCTV cameras to Zimbabwe. There is a deep motive behind this. By entering into law enforcement and internal security, China will be able to ensure political stability and also use these states as markets to improve its algorithms. The Chinese use of big data in Africa is a starting point where China is headed in future. All this proves that India cannot ignore the defence sector as lesser engagement by India here will only give China the much needed space to pace up defence ties with Africa.

INDIAN OCEAN REGION DEFENCE MINISTERS CONCLAVE 2021

In 2021, India hosted a conclave of Defence Ministers of states in the Indian Ocean region. In the conclave, India focused on how it has developed doctrines for humanitarian assistance and disaster relief, non-combatant evacuation operations, search and rescue operations and expansion of maritime domain awareness. India announced that as a part of blue economy, it intends to solely focus on peace, security and cooperation in the region.

What is Blue Economy?

The blue economy is a paradigm of sustainable development for oceanic resources with maritime security at its fulcrum. Its core focus is on security productivity and sustainability based on a participative framework.

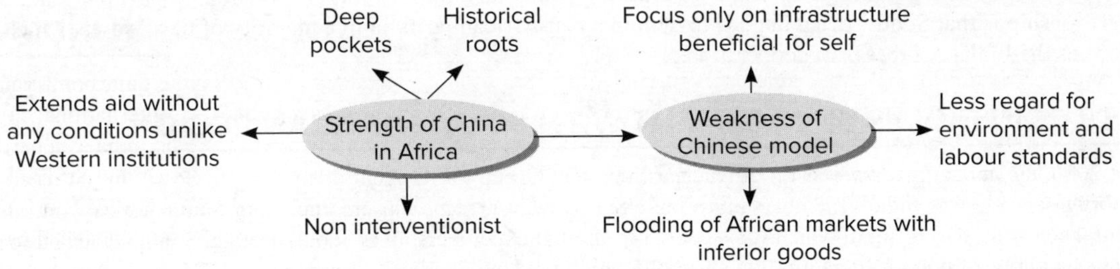

5

CHAPTER

India's Regional Diplomacy with Africa

INDIA'S INTERESTS IN SOUTH AFRICAN REGION

British took indentured labour to South Africa. Gandhi lived in South Africa and conceptualised Satyagraha. Satyagraha became a connector during freedom struggle. India supported South Africa against apartheid by not having diplomatic ties till it was abolished in 1994. India led a global crusade against apartheid, imperialism and colonialism of Africa. Since 1994, relation became pragmatic and economic-centric. India's core interests are as follows:

- Piracy, peace and maritime security
- Enhanced economic cooperation
- Global engagement via BRICS, IBSA and BASIC group (at climate change level)
- UNSC permanent membership aspiration

INDIA'S DIPLOMATIC STRATEGY TO ENGAGE WITH SOUTH AFRICAN REGION

South Africa is a strong naval player but is reluctant to project naval power as it lacks a maritime strategy. India uses Indian Ocean Rim Association as a forum to enhance maritime cooperation with South Africa. One of the most pragmatic moves has been to include South Africa in BRICS and align with the emerging economies than being dependent solely upon the West. The impact of pragmatism is visible on India–South Africa trade that has gone to reach almost 15 billion dollars at present. There is a huge demand of gold in India, and South Africa is one of the leading suppliers of gold to the country. Even the Indian private sector is quite keen to make use of South Africa as a base for sub-Saharan engagements. South Africa has a well-established financial market system, proper infrastructure and a stringent rule of law. Ranbaxy, Cipla, Tata, Mahindra are just some of the Indian firms to have made South Africa their base, to name a few. The relation between the two nations is equally strong at the multilateral level. Both are represented at IBSA (India, Brazil, South Africa) framework and undertake broad cooperation. At the level of WTO and climate change negotiations through the BASIC group, both are known to undertake multilateral cooperation. A peculiar feature in their relationship is that South Africa intends to uphold a pan-African position in a majority of these cases, which, at time, strains the India–South Africa cooperation.

HURDLES IN INDIA'S ENGAGEMENT WITH SOUTH AFRICAN REGION

In June 2016, the annual plenary session of Nuclear Suppliers Group (NSG) held its meeting in Seoul. In the meeting, an important agenda was India's membership to the NSG. However, some players, including South Africa, had raised procedural concerns, as a result of which India could not attain the membership in Seoul meeting. South Africa has been an ardent supporter of non-proliferation. Its non-proliferation credentials are so strong that in 1994, when South Africa ended apartheid, it went on to destroy its entire nuclear arsenal.

POTENTIAL AREAS OF FUTURE COOPERATION BETWEEN INDIA AND SOUTH AFRICA REGION

1. BRICS—Both have used BRICS as a platform to facilitate intra-BRICS trade, investment and cooperation at the financial level.
2. IBSA—Both have used IBSA as a platform to share expertise in development initiatives and SSC.
3. G-20—It has been used as a forum by the two sides to open cooperation in preventing illegal financial flows and promotion of trade.
4. India–South Africa Business Summit (ISABS)—The first summit happened in 2018 and the second one in 2019. In the summit, skill development, health services and digitisation of governance have been identified as core areas.

INDIA'S INTERESTS IN EAST AFRICAN REGION

India engages with Mauritius, Madagascar, Kenya, Uganda, Rwanda, Mozambique and Comoros in East Africa. India's interests include:

- Maritime security for trade which is strategically crucial for India's investment
- Indian naval power projection
- Protection of Indian diaspora
- Minerals for India's growth
- Petroleum and hydrocarbons supply
- Cultural relationship
- Development template for India abroad

INDIA'S INTERESTS IN MAURITIUS: THE STAR AND KEY OF THE INDIAN OCEAN

Mauritius has a crucial location and is known for the genius of its people. As early European explorers sailed around the African continent and ventured eastwards to India, they used to call Mauritius, the 'Star and Key of the Indian Ocean'. If the Portuguese and the Dutch were the first to gain a foothold in Mauritius, it was the French who gained effective control over the island in the early 18th century. A French soldier and colonial official, Félix Renouard de Sainte-Croix, described the island as 'a central geographical point between every other place in the world'. The British who gained control over Mauritius during the Napoleonic wars and turned it into a garrison island that would help secure the sea lines of communication between Europe and India. The enduring value of its location is reflected in the fact that Diego Garcia, once part of Mauritius, today hosts one of America's largest foreign military bases in the world. The French description of the island as a 'central geographic point' holds equally true for commerce and connectivity in the Indian Ocean. As a member of the African Union, Indian Ocean Rim Association and the Indian Ocean Commission, Mauritius is a stepping-stone to multiple geographies. Mozambique, Madagascar and Comoros together constitute the Mozambique Channel, a critical waterway in the Indian Ocean, that has shaped the strategic evolution of the Indian Ocean over the centuries. It is worth recalling that Vasco da Gama, in his search for a sea route to India, sailed through the Mozambique Channel in 1498 after coming round the southern tip of Africa. Since then, the Mozambique Channel had been a major choke point in the sea lines of communication from Europe to India and further east. That might be changing as a number of factors draw international attention to the Mozambique Channel in the 21st century.

THE THREE ISLAND CHAINS OF GEO-POWER AND INDIAN DIPLOMACY

The rise of China and East Asia as well as the slower emergence of India has deepened economic interdependence between Asia, the Middle East and Africa. The sea lines of communication between the east coast of Africa and the Far East have once again acquired some weight and importance. As old and new powers jockey for influence in the Indian Ocean littoral, every little island is becoming a contested terrain. Access to critically located islands has always been an important part of the maritime jousting between great powers. In the Pacific, the contest is best understood as the competition to dominate the so-called island chains as a springboard for either power projection or as a defensive line against potential naval aggression. Both the American and Chinese strategic communities agree on the existence of three island chains running in concentric Pacific arcs around Asia. As great power rivalry returns to the Indian Ocean, the concept of island chains helps us understand the new regional dynamic. Three Indian Ocean island chains are coming into view. One is the Andaman Island chain that bisects the Bay of Bengal. The Great Nicobar Island at the southern tip of the chain is well placed to dominate the western gates of the Malacca Straits that link the Indian and Pacific Oceans. A second chain runs from Gwadar in the northern Arabian Sea along the Laccadives–Chagos ridge to Diego Garcia island that hosts a large American base. A third island chain flows down from Djibouti in the Horn of Africa, down along the East African coast to the Mozambique Channel through the island of Zanzibar. The islands in the South Western Indian Ocean, including Madagascar, Comoros, Seychelles and Mauritius, can be seen as part of this chain. China's deepening security ties with the littoral countries of the Bay of Bengal could begin to undermine India's geographic advantages arising from the ownership of the Andamans. On the second island chain, Delhi warily watches China's expanding naval presence on Pakistan's Arabian Sea coast and is battling to retain India's primacy in Sri Lanka and the Maldives. Meanwhile, US naval presence in Chagos is coming under stress, as sovereignty over the archipelago has become the subject of an international dispute. Once dominated by the European powers, the third island chain running along the east coast of Africa to the South Western Indian Ocean has seen the dramatic expansion of Chinese economic and strategic influence over the last decade. Besides the establishment of its first military base, China has an ambitious agenda of port construction, infrastructure development and defence diplomacy. During its first term, the Narendra Modi government had done much to put Africa and the third Indian Ocean island chain on Delhi's mental map. This included decisions to enhance the diplomatic presence in Africa, initiate sustained high-level political contact and beef up security partnerships in the littoral of the South Western Indian Ocean. But the scale of the challenge confronting India in the three island chains continues to expand, amidst China's rapid strategic advance in the Indian Ocean.

INDIA'S VANILLA ISLAND DIPLOMACY DOCTRINE

A group of Exotic Island states in the South Western Indian Ocean, the Comoros, Madagascar, Mauritius, Mayotte, Reunion, Seychelles, joined hands a few years ago to promote tourism to their corner in the Indian Ocean. That many of them grow vanilla, which gives us the popular ice cream flavour, was a good enough reason for calling themselves after it. Comoros has been eager to step up its engagement with India. Delhi is finally showing up; and there is much to do. As part of the growing interaction with the island states, India hosted a meet of leaders of the Caribbean Community (CARICOM) and the Pacific Islands Forum (PIF) on the margins of the UNGA in 2020. Together they account for more than 40 members. Their large numbers and impact on the voting patterns in the UN and other multilateral forums had always made island states of interest to major powers. Today, a number of other factors lend them additional significance. Immediate vulnerability to rising sea levels has made island states the most active champions of urgent global action to mitigate climate change. Island states have also taken the lead in developing the concept of 'blue economy' focused on sustainable use and development of ocean resources. Modi's activism on countering climate change and promoting blue economy has made the island states special partners for India. Many of the island states are also beginning to see themselves as more than specks of land in the vast blue sea. Some of them are calling themselves large 'Ocean States'. India would want to build on the multiple lines of connection with the Comoros. The island nation is a founding member of the International Solar Alliance launched by Modi in 2018. It is a member of the Indian Ocean Rim Association that Delhi has sought to revive in recent years. The Comoros is also a member of the Arab League that India always had strong ties with and the Organization of Islamic Cooperation that India has begun to reach out in recent years. In the colonial era, the Vanilla Islands were very much the object of rivalry among the European powers. With all the sea lines of communication between Europe and the Indian Ocean came round Africa and went through the Mozambique Channel, the Vanilla Islands became attractive way stations. The Comoros was of special importance as it sits at the northern end of the Mozambique Channel and provided a strong base from which to control the channel. In the 18th century, France gained the upper hand among the European powers in the Vanilla Islands. The construction of the Suez Canal linking the Mediterranean and the Red Sea in the mid-19th century obviated the need for European shipping to go round Africa. This, in turn, reduced the strategic significance of the Vanilla Islands. As African resources become important for Asian powers such as China, Japan and India, the

SLOCS from Africa's east coast and the Vanilla Islands that straddle them have once again become important. As they appreciate their renewed salience, the islands are looking to develop partnerships with the major powers. As elsewhere in the region, India can contribute significantly to the security and prosperity of the Comoros. Although India has had strong ties with one of the Vanilla Islands, Mauritius, Delhi has long seen it through the prism of the Indian diaspora. It is only recently that Delhi has begun to pay attention to the strategic dimensions of the relationship with Mauritius. During PM Modi's first term, the Indian Foreign Office set up a separate Indian Ocean Division with a focus on the island states. It clubbed Maldives and Sri Lanka with Mauritius and Seychelles, but left out the other Vanilla Islands. To be effective in the southwestern Indian Ocean, however, Delhi must begin to treat the Vanilla Islands as a single strategic space. It can build on its traditional presence in Mauritius to launch substantive economic and defence cooperation with the littoral.

HURDLES IN INDIA'S DIPLOMACY WITH EAST AFRICA

Since long, Delhi has viewed states of East Africa through the prism of diaspora. This was, perhaps, natural since communities of Indian origin constitute a significant majority in the states of East Africa. But the time has come to reimagine states of East Africa in much larger terms.

FUTURE AREAS OF COOPERATION BETWEEN INDIA AND EAST AFRICA

As new investments pour into Africa, states of East Africa are where a lot of it gets serviced. States of East Africa can be the fulcrum for India's own African economic outreach. Second, until now India has tended to deal with the so-called Vanilla Islands of the south western Indian Ocean, Comoros, Madagascar, Mauritius, Mayotte, Reunion and Seychelles, on a bilateral basis. If the Indian establishment thinks of them as a collective, it could make states of East Africa the pivot of Delhi's island policy. Third, the states of East Africa pivot can facilitate a number of Indian commercial activities in the southwestern Indian Ocean as a banking gateway, the hub for flights to and from Indian cities and tourism. Fourth, India could also contribute to the evolution of states of East Africa as regional centres for technological innovation. India has not really responded so far to the demands from states of East Africa for higher education facilities from India such as the IIT. Fifth, climate change, sustainable development and the blue economy are existential challenges for states of East Africa and the neighbouring island states. The states of East Africa will be the right partners in promoting Indian initiatives in these areas. They could also become a valuable place for regional and international maritime scientific research. Finally, if Delhi takes an integrated view of its security cooperation in the southwestern Indian Ocean, states of East Africa are the natural node for it. The office of a defence adviser in Mauritius (2020) and defence attaché in Madagascar (2020), for example, can service the demands of all the island nations as well as the East African states. All this and more would be possible if Delhi takes a fresh and more strategic look at states of East Africa. One way of getting there is to have an early Indian summit with the leaders of the Vanilla Islands.

India and Agalega Islands—Strategic Asset Development Diplomacy

The Agalega islands are almost 110 km away from Mauritius, close by to Southern coast of India. The island has a very small population but the presence of Indian diaspora is quite evident. The islands are very strategically located. In 2015, during the Indian PM's visit to Mauritius, the government of Mauritius had granted permission to India to undertake infrastructure development rights on the Agalega islands. As per the agreement, India will refurbish an existing airstrip in Agalega and develop a new jetty. There is a possibility of India installing radars in Agalega. Though the bagging of IDR does not mean that India is going to develop Agalega as a naval base, as a purely strategic investment, this certainly helps India to increase its footprint in the Indian Ocean.

INDIA'S INTERESTS IN WEST AND CENTRAL AFRICA

In West and Central Africa, India engages primarily with Nigeria, Angola and Ghana. India's interests include the following:

- Crude oil and energy security
- Defence and security diplomacy
- Education diplomacy

- Science and technology diplomacy
- Civilian nuclear cooperation
- Health partnership
- Trade in diamonds

INDIA'S DIPLOMATIC STRATEGY TO ENGAGE WITH WEST AND CENTRAL AFRICA

India and Nigeria have a defence-based relationship. The components in defence cooperation are those of training and capacity building. India offers training to defence officers of Nigeria at the National Defence Academy and the Indian Military Academy in India.

In 2015, India decided to provide defence hardware to Nigeria to enhance military cooperation. Nigeria is a resource-rich country and is in possession of a lot of crude oil. India today imports anything between 8–12% of Nigerian crude oil. Nigeria, in the recent times, has tried to modify its oil selling and contract policies. Before this modification, the buyers of Nigerian oil had to purchase oil from spot markets. The problem of purchasing oil from spot markets was that it was vulnerable to price shocks. Nigeria has now started encouraging term contracts. As per a term contract, a fixed quantity of oil is to be supplied to contracting party at a stable price. Nigeria has also decided to sell oil directly to oil suppliers. In this context of a modified policy architecture, the Indian Oil Company (IOC) stands to gain as it had decided to agree for a term contract import of three million tonnes per annum crude from Nigeria in 2016. India has 700 plus firms operating in Ghana and it is the second largest investor in Ghana with investments in nuclear power development, rural electrification and agriculture research as core areas. India and Ghana have a robust defence relation because both states cooperate in UN PKF. Ghana is a victim of terror from ISIS and Boko Haram. Angola is one of the largest suppliers of oil to India. India's major items of export to Angola include transportation equipment, tractors, agricultural machinery and rice; and imports include majorly crude oil. The state-owned SONANGOL is the oil regulator and supplier in Angola. Apart from oil, Angola is also rich in diamonds.

HURDLES FACED BY INDIA IN DIPLOMATIC ENGAGEMENT WITH WEST AND CENTRAL AFRICA

Oil purchase from spot market versus oil purchase from term contract issue was the key hurdle in the ties. In 2017, at the 4th India–Africa Hydrocarbon Conference in New Delhi, India had committed to double its oil imports from Nigeria and this is yet to happen. As per R. Ghanshyam, IFS and India's High Commissioner to Nigeria, there is immense trade potential between India and Nigeria, which can be significantly enhanced if both nations try to guarantee investment protection. Ghana is looking for trade in small arms and does not find a reliable player in the region to support its requirements. The population of Ghana is growing and it needs energy availability, but as it is a signatory to African NW Free Trade Zone; this prohibits it to export Uranium to India and has emerged as a hurdle in nuclear cooperation. Angola is a rural economy, so not much scope for trade exists. This means India will find it difficult to explore Angola as a market.

FUTURE AREAS OF COOPERATION

Because of the diversification of the Nigerian economy, tremendous scope for Indian investment in infrastructure, and energy education, financial inclusion and poverty alleviation can be envisaged. In Nigeria, healthcare is a neglected area. The Nigerian government has not yet equipped Nigerian healthcare with the needed capacity. This provides an opportunity for India. More so, in Nigeria there is an attitude amongst people to give preference to anything which is foreign. This attitude is most visible in healthcare. Every month, more than 5000 people on an average fly abroad for treatment. A lot of Nigerians also come to India as treatments in India are cheaper than in the US and Europe. However, the lack of connectivity via direct flights between India and Nigeria creates a difficulty in mobilisation of patients. Thus, two things can be done to leverage the opportunity. First, to take medical tourism to its full potential, we can enhance flight connectivity with daily, regular direct flights; and secondly, encourage Indian hospitals to open up hospitals to cater to the market in Nigeria itself (for instance, Apollo hospital has opened a hospital in Nigeria lately). India is looking for defence exports in West Africa and Ghana is a potential future player. Sharing of intelligence and technical information can enable both to open up a new chapter in terrorism prevention. As Ghana is looking for players for nuclear energy in West African Power Pool Project, which aims to integrate national power system to a unified market; India, with its nuclear credentials can be a potential player. Angola is refurbishing its colonial railway and RITES India is providing technical assistance for this. India has provided locomotives and wagons. Lately, a lot of Indian companies are showing interest in rural and urban housing as the housing and construction industry in Angola is witnessing a boom.

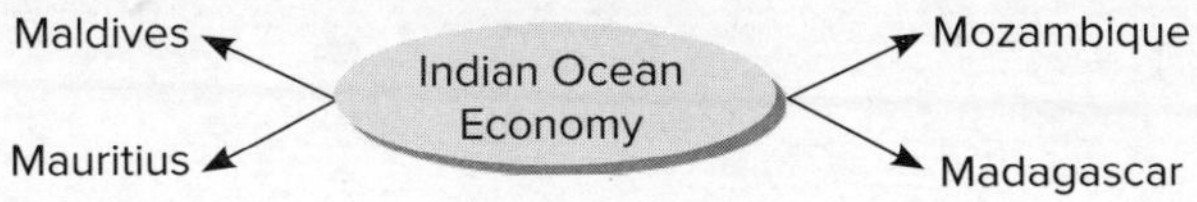

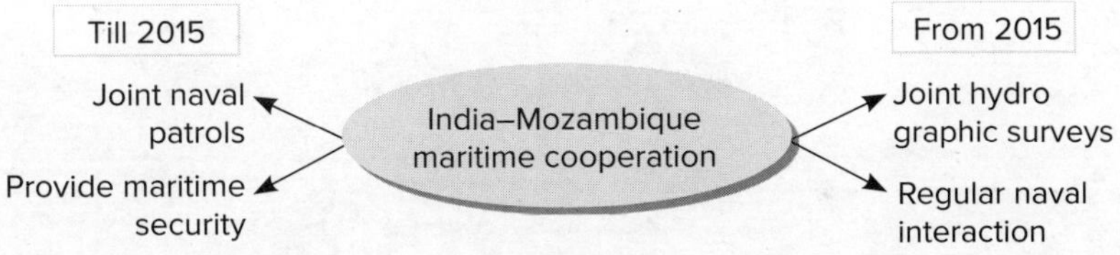

QUESTIONS FOR PRACTICE

S. No.	Questions for Practice
1.	A far wider cultural engagement with the continent is necessary to combat the latent racism among Indians. Examine the statement in the light of racial attacks on Africans in India.
2.	India's attitude towards Africa cannot remain imprisoned in the 'dark continent' stereotype. Neither can it be defined solely by the legacy of the colonial era. Our language of engagement needs to create a new edifice defined by an aspirational Africa's quest for a good life. Sketch your argument.
3.	Indian interests in Africa will benefit from timely implementation of projects. Examine the statement in the light of key hurdles in implementation of projects by India in Africa.
4.	The Chinese naval base in Africa is likely to have consequences on India's security interests in the Indian Ocean. Examine.
5.	Sustained India–Japan cooperation in Africa can match China's substantial outreach to Africa. Examine this statement in the light of the vision of the Asia–Africa growth corridor.
6.	From the age of colonialism to age of globalisation, India and Africa have done much together but there do exist challenges and frontiers that need to be crossed. Discuss.

SECTION 7

India's Relationship with West Asia

1. West Asia: Islam, Repression, Resistance and Great Power Games
2. Key Drivers of India's West Asia Policy
3. The Modi Doctrine for West Asia, India as Net Security Provider Policy and QUAD-2
4. Arab Spring, Crisis in Libya, Syria, Yemen and Strategic Significance of Abraham Accords
5. India's Relationship with Saudi Arabia and Iran: The Doctrine of Sunni–Shia Balancing
6. The Israel–Palestine Conflict, India's Relationship with Israel and India's Palestine Policy

AN OVERVIEW

The section on Middle East has gained prominence in recent times. The UPSC has asked questions related to India's Look West Policy many a times. Repeated questions have been asked on India's relationship with Israel and India-Palestine policy. The changing nature of India's policy in balancing shia and sunni powers with the engagement of jews is an engaging topic.

Potential foresight In the recent years, with Israel shifting the sands in Arab world and improving ties with the Sunni nations, the implications of such policy on Indian foreign policy is a favourite arena of UPSC. The students also need to prepare the dimensions of de-hyphenation of Saudia Arabia's policy for India and Pakistan. I2U2 alliance, India's Israel and Palestine policy and India's shift on east Jerusalem diplomacy, well analysed in this section, will be important for years ahead.

CHAPTER 1

West Asia: Islam, Repression, Resistance and Great Power Games

ORIGIN OF ISLAM

The rise of Islam is intrinsically linked with the Prophet Muhammad. He was born to Abd Allah Ibn Abd al-Muttalib (father) and Aminah (mother). Abu Talib, who belonged to the Banu Hashim clan of the Quaraysh tribe, raised him. He got married to Khadija. Muhammad was a worker. In his mid-forties, he took retirement. During his prayers at the Mount Hira cave, he received revelations from the Angel Gabriel, which was the God's message transmitted to Muhammad. These revelations became the foundation of the religion today, known in the world as Islam. Muhammad faced a lot of difficulties to convince people about the revelations of God but he succeeded in creating the foundation of Islam.

THE CALIPHATES AFTER PROPHET MUHAMMAD

After the death of Muhammad, Abu Bakr became the new successor. Abu Bakr established the first ever caliphate institution and became a Caliph after Muhammad. Nearing his death, Abu Bakr desired that Umar would be his successor as the Caliph. Umar established a committee of six to decide his successor. The committee arrived at a unanimous decision that the Caliph after Umar would be chosen from the six members. The committee chose two successors—Uthman and Ali. During the times of Umar as the Caliph, Islam grew into a huge empire. Now, the empire needed a Caliph who would be a politico-military genius-like Uthman, while Ali was a religious man and he was also the son-in-law of Muhammad. Uthman belonged to Umayyad clan that was wealthy and eventually succeeded Umar as the Caliph. The period of Umayyads saw a dynastic rule. Ali, who had been side-lined, did not appreciate the idea of Uthman as a Caliph and he advocated that someone hailing from the lineage of Muhammad would hold that caliphate. Thus, there was a growing rebellion against Uthman as a Caliph. During the reign of Uthman and Umar, Islam had spread outside Arabia to Egypt, Syria, Palestine, Iraq and Persia. However, after a few years, Egyptian Muslim rebels killed Uthman. After the death of Uthman, the caliphate now came under Ali who ascended the caliphate as the fourth Caliph. Ali faced a lot of challenges as a Caliph. Many people felt Ali was ineffective in punishing the killers of Uthman and some even suspected Ali's involvement in the murder. Uthman's cousin Muawiyah was a member of Umayyad clan and the Governor of Syria. At the time of Ali's reign, Muawiyah claimed the caliphate for himself. Ali refused to accept Muawiyah as a Caliph and advocated the need to get Islam back to the ethical path. A group of people known as Kharijites, who first appeared during the time of third Caliph Uthman were the followers of Ali. To manage Muawiyah, Ali began to bargain with the Umayyads. The Kharijites felt that Ali betrayed them by talking to Umayyads and subsequently assassinated him. Meanwhile, after the death of Muawiyah, his son Yazid succeeded him as a Caliph and defeated Hussein, son of Ali, at the Battle of Karbala, marking the full schism in Islam. Abu Muhammad Hasan ibn Ali succeeded Ali and the successors of Ali came to be known as Imams, while the Umayyad and Muawiyah adopted a caliphate monarchy.

THE SCHISM AND RISE OF SHIITE AND SUNNI ISLAM

In 638 AD, the faith was split into two main sects namely, the Shias and Sunnis. The Sunnis believed that the leader of Islamic faith would be elected from the successors of Prophet Muhammad whereas the Shias believed that the leaders would come from the descendants of the Prophet.

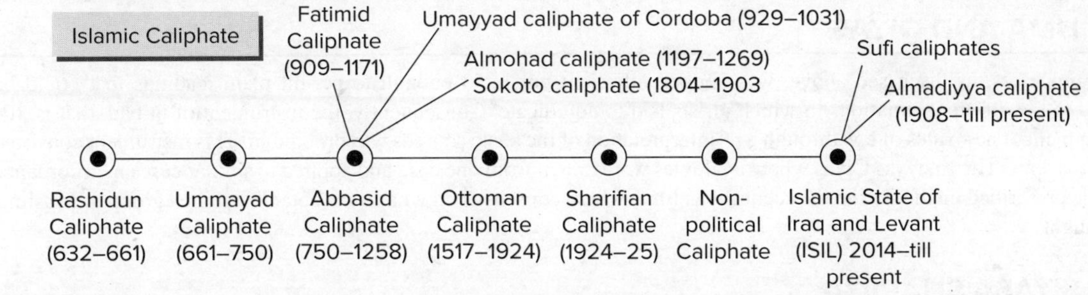

The Shia Muslims believe that Ali was the first Imam and Abu Muhammad Hasan ibn Ali was the second. For Shias, the eleventh Imam was Hasan Al Askari. Today, amongst the Shia Muslims, one school of thought believes that Hasan Al Askari had no surviving sons but another sect known as the Qatiyyas believes that Muhammad al-Mahdi is the son of Hasan Ali Askari and he is in hiding somewhere and shall come to guide the Shias.

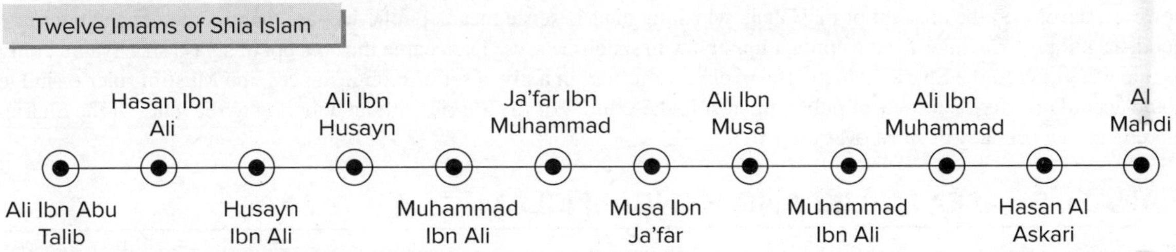

Broadly speaking, Muslims are divided into four branches, namely Shias, Sunnis, Kharijites and Quaranists. The Quaranists are those who hold Quran to be the authentic source of Islamic faith and reject different recorded oral traditions or Hadith. The Shias and Sunnis are further divided into various sub-groups.

POLITICAL ISLAM AND SHARIA

Political Islam is an assertion and promotion of beliefs, prescriptions, laws and policies which are Islamic in nature. The proponents of political Islam argue that their precepts aid restoration of authentic and original Islam which is cleansed from various innovations that have crept in Islam over the years. The society consequently created would be one which is the closest to the order envisaged by holy Prophet in Medina and the first four Caliphs.

The origin of political Islam in the modern times can be traced back to the colonial period when Arab states and other Muslim-dominated lands were overtaken by colonial powers. The loss of dignity at the hands of Western imperial powers compelled the Muslim intellectuals to look within and ascertain a path of reform. The concern of intellectuals in the 19th and the 20th century was how to implement Sharia, Islamic rules and institutions determined by Prophet Muhammad of which he was a part of.

The initial source of Sharia was the revelations of Allah to his Prophet, Muhammad, who was enshrined in the Quran, and the sayings and conduct of the Prophet, based on the testimony of his contemporaries, which were collectively the Sunna. In terms of Islamic law, the Quran and the Sunna are part of the 'revelation' and both enjoy an equal status.

The Sharia has evolved over several centuries and in the early period, the text of the Quran was finalised along with Prophet's traditions, known as Hadith, by the efforts of the scholars, called ulema, labouring on their own or in schools across the Muslim empire which was witnessing expansion. An effort was subsequently made to standardise the understanding of these texts in the Muslim realm by 'traditionalisation' of the revelation by tracing all legal principles and rules back to the revealed texts.

THE IJMA AND QIYAS

These processes, as discussed above, was neither sufficient nor lucid enough to permit plain readings that could be applied to the different situations in which jurists had to adjudicate. Consequently, the instrument of ijtihad, that is, the development of new rules of law through a re-interpretation of the basic sources was brought in. This instrument consisted of two systems. The first was Qiyas where analogies were drawn from one case and applied to similar cases in accordance with the prescribed methods, and the second was Ijma, where consensus on what is acceptable within a group of Muslims was sought.

THE SIYASA SHARIIYA

Since the earliest times, it is interesting to note that the commentators made a basic distinction in the content of the revealed sources, called Ibadat, which means the relation of man to God, and muamalat, which means relation of man with other men. While the former was seen as eternal principles for the sole purpose of worship which could not be changed at all; the latter were used for the good of man and society and a change was permissible in the same with times. Scholars, however, developed the concept of maslahah, which in generic sense means public welfare, public interest and common good, as guiding principles for the application of law in specific cases. Then came the concept of siyasa shariiya meaning to rule according to the Sharia, which effectively meant that, in a given set of circumstances, the Muslim ruler or judge could accord priority to notions of public interest in the "spirit" of the Sharia without adhering to the letter of the Sharia, thereby giving primacy to spirit over the letter.

HANAFI, SHAFEI, MALIKI AND HANBALI ISLAM

The scholars in different parts of the Islamic world attempted to understand and explain the meaning of the revealed texts called fiqh, meaning law and applied them in different situations, leading to the rise of four schools or madhhabs of Sunni Islam. Each of these schools took a few decades to concretise primarily on the basis of their writings, founders and students associated. They were fully developed by the early 11th century, and each school had their own adherents in geographical areas of Islamic world. The four schools that emerged were Hanafi, Shafei, Maliki and Hanbali and each had much in common in terms of the application of their legal precepts, while they did differ with respect to their methodology and their emphasis placed on certain concepts over others. The authoritative or established views of a school were collectively known as taqlid.

MIDDLE EAST OR WEST ASIA? UNDERSTANDING TERMINOLOGY DILEMMAS AND INDIA'S ARTICULATION

There is always a debate on what exactly constitutes Middle East or West Asia and how do we exactly address the region. It is important to remember that there exists no official or scholarly consensus on the terms and the terms used are based on how different nations have viewed the constructs. In 1902, Alfred Thayer Mahan, a distinguished writer on sea power, used the term Middle East for the first time, but till date no clarity exists about territories that should be included in the construct. India never accepted this Eurocentric conception where Europe was placed at the centre of the world affairs. India, after independence, preferred to use terminologies to define regions that were based on an objective geographic criteria. After independence, India created "West Asia–North Africa Division" in Ministry of External Affairs (MEA) which was mandated to look after region extending from Iran in east to Sudan in south. In the mid-1980s, after rising influx of Indian nationals in Gulf, India conceptualised a separate "Gulf Division". However, it was believed that since the Gulf Division would also be looking after the Hajj section, Iran would feel isolated and thus, the MEA decided to put Iran under the "Pakistan, Afghanistan and Iran" division.

THE INSECURE REGIONAL BATTLES AND IMPLICATIONS ON INDIAN FOREIGN POLICY

The region of West Asia has been dominated by a power play of Arabs, Jews, Turks and Persians. These four power centres have not just interacted commercially but have shaped the civilisation of the region through philosophy, art and wars. This civilisational narrative had been disrupted by invasions of Romans and Greeks to begin with, then British and French and finally by the Americans in the modern times. When Europe began to witness Industrial Revolution, the Arabs, Turks and Persians were colonised and the colonisers erected local puppet rulers who would help the imperial powers to crush local rebellions whenever they arose. This eventually weakened the people, the natives, who began to feel so helpless that they began to think that they had no control over their destinies. The colonial rulers did not just stop here but also brought thousands of Jews from Europe to settle in Palestine and later created the Jewish state of Israel. These Zionist settler colonialism ignored the existence and rights of the indigenous people and left a legacy of bitterness and outrage, which has poisoned the region till date. Today, this bitterness between the Arabs and Jews has manifested as racial discrimination, abuse and has unleashed a culture of violence.

The other issue with West Asia is that the region has produced two political models and none have successfully created strong nation states. On one side of the spectrum is a group of states that display republican form of government where coups have led to rise of rulers who have tried to claim legitimacy by rhetoric of nationalism, socialism and revolution. On the other side of spectrum is the six Gulf states that show monarchical form of governments which claim legitimacy through authoritarian rule. The republican states are led by strongmen who have failed to enforce economic development strategies while the monarchical states are equally weak but supported by the West for oil and gas sales in global markets. In this sense, the West is not just an entity that ensures global sales of their resources but also acts as a guardian of the royal families. In either case, we see the West Asian states as 'fierce states' or states that control the destiny of their citizens through coercion.

MIND MAP

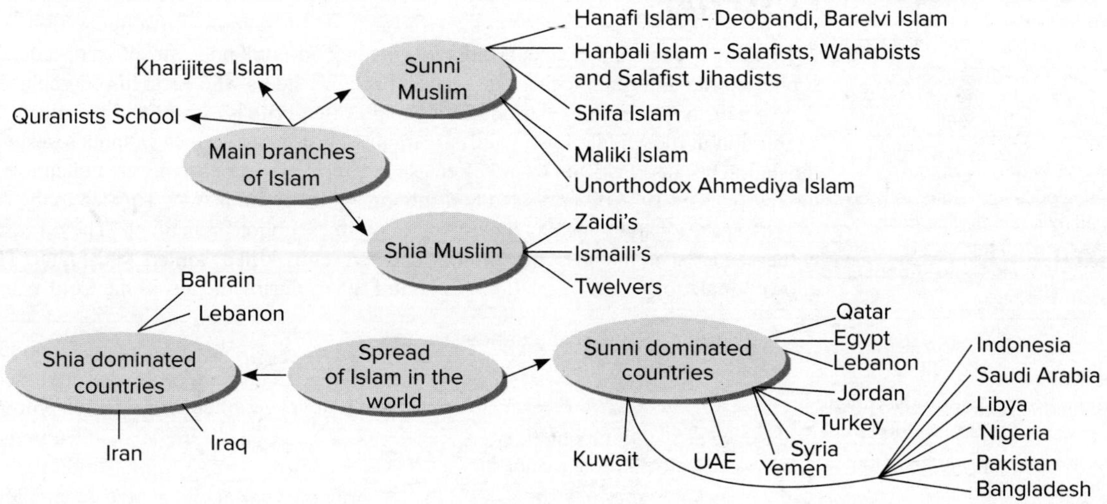

CHAPTER

2 Key Drivers of India's West Asia Policy

HISTORICAL RELATIONSHIP OF INDIA AND WEST ASIA

India and West Asia (hereafter referred to as WA) have a civilisational link with the ties going back to Indus Valley civilisation, when trade in turquoise, copper and spices were common. Indian merchants were present in WA even before the coming of Islam and the Indian merchants had trade with Mecca. Since 6th century BCE, Indians also undertook trade with Jews, who were the only community to trade along India's west coast. The coming of the British added a new geostrategic outlook to the Indo-West Asia trade. For the British, WA acted as a land bridge to Asia, Afghanistan and Europe and was strategically located with links to the Mediterranean Sea, Red Sea and access to Arabian Sea. The East India Company controlled India and the WA region through the Persian Gulf Residency (PGR). The PGR remained a subdivision of East Indian Company till 1857. After the 1857 revolt in India, the British crown assumed all responsibilities. The British Indian empires subsequently built outposts in the Gulf to safeguard marine trade. The British used the Indian rupee in Qatar, Kuwait, Oman and Bahrain. The RBI continued to use the rupee in the above states till 1959.

What is 1973 Oil Crisis?

The crisis occurred after the Yum-Kippur War in 1973 when Arab states, after their defeat in the war, decided to impose an oil embargo on West, putting the US economy on the verge of collapse due to no availability of oil. The crisis was defused through deft diplomacy and an oil boom followed.

INDIA'S RELATIONSHIP WITH WEST ASIA DURING THE COLD WAR

After India became independent, India followed a two-point policy in WA. It politically supported the Arabs and enhanced support to their leaders who focused on secularism and socialism. During this period, India would often criticise Israel and censure it for aggression in the Middle East. Pakistan remained a stumbling block in India's ties with the region because Pakistan would often use Islamic connections to negate Indian role in the region. The 1973 oil crises led to a subsequent oil boom in WA. This led to the rise of pro-West monarchs such as Saudi Arabia, with exceptions remaining. The oil boom witnessed a rise in the migration of unskilled and semi-skilled workers to the Gulf. This allowed India to sustain its relations with Gulf States during the rest of the Cold War.

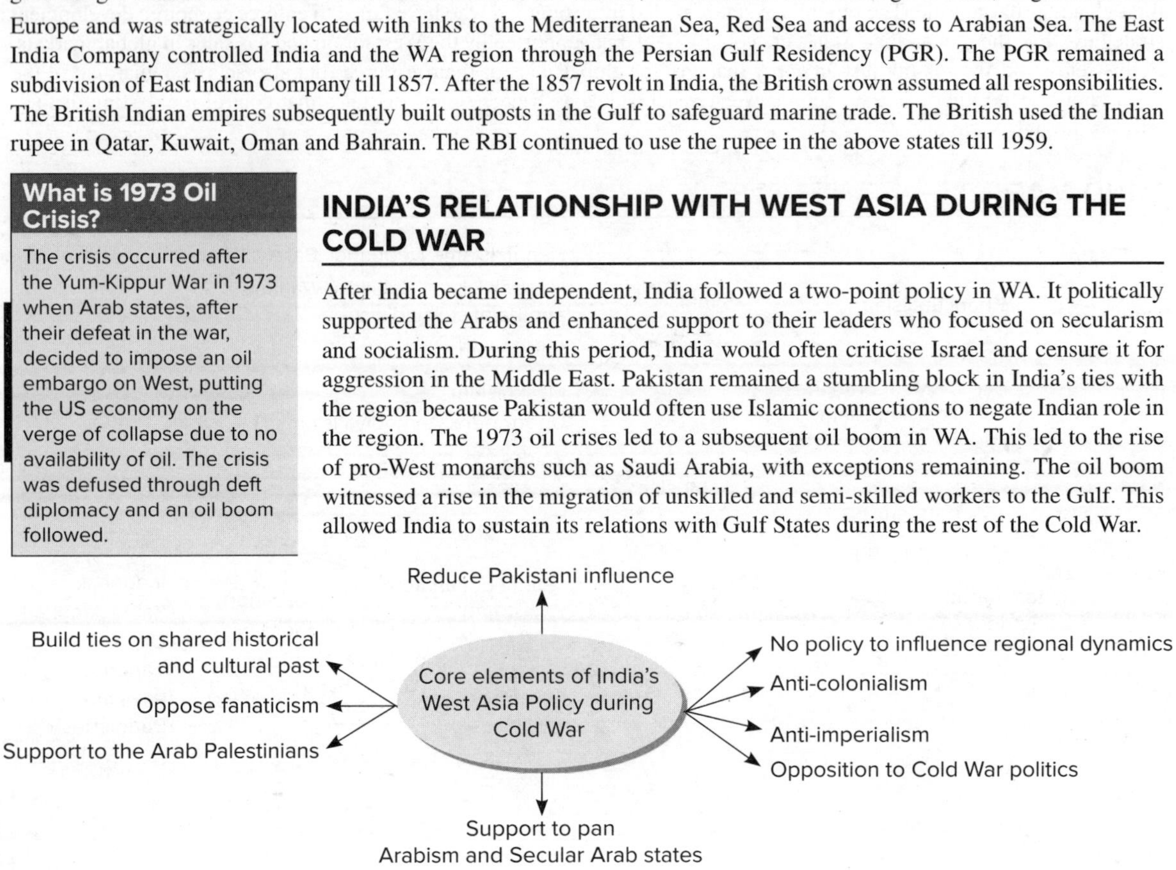

INDIA'S RELATIONSHIP WITH WEST ASIA SINCE THE END OF COLD WAR

At the end of the Cold War, India realised the significance of remittances from its diaspora in the Gulf. As India embraced globalisation at the end of the Cold War, the Indian diaspora began to witness a shift. The earlier unskilled diaspora now began to be complemented by a new while collar diaspora that specialised in IT and the services sector. The tenets of the policy in the post-Cold War period are summarised in the diagram below.

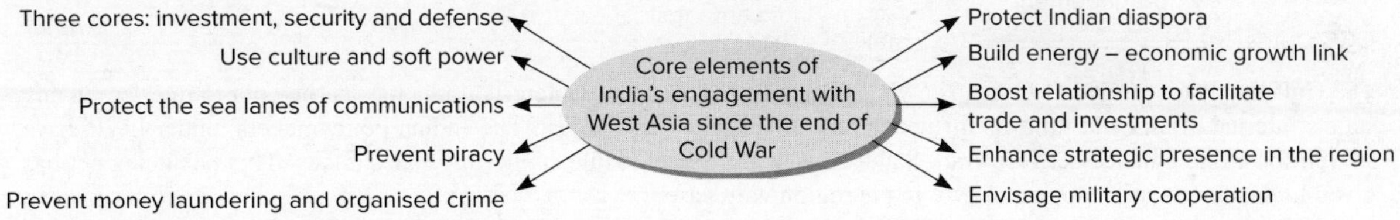

INDIA'S LOOK WEST POLICY

For India, there are three broad regions to engage in West Asia. The first is the Gulf Cooperation Council (GCC) region. The core dimensions of engagement here are trade, the Indian diaspora, oil and prevention of terrorism. In the second region of Mashreq (Turkey and Central Asia), trade and connectivity are crucial dimensions. The third is the Maghreb region, which is crucial for oil, trade and prevention of piracy. In 2005, Dr. Manmohan Singh announced a Look West Policy (LWP) and stated that West Asia is a part of India's extended neighbourhood. He advanced the idea of pursuing economic relations with the Gulf. India also shed-off the anti-Israel rhetoric and has enhanced ties with Israel. India has realised that West Asia is not a region to display power but to augment power and this compelled India to announce its Look West Policy. The policy has the following goals as given below.

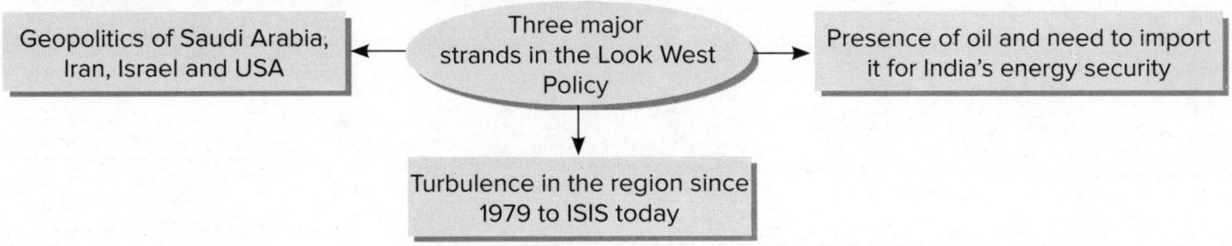

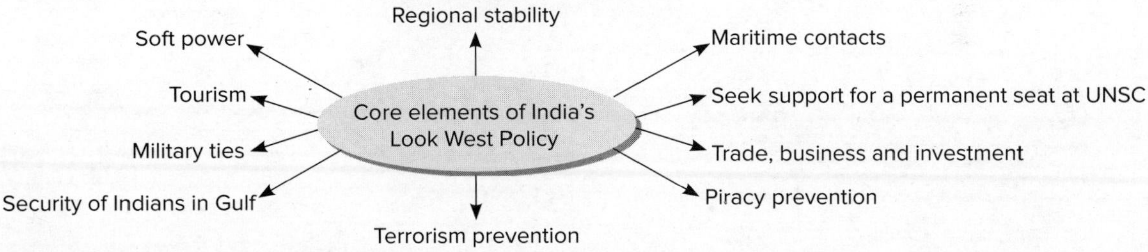

India's LWP got a new momentum with Narendra Modi's recent visits to the region. As global energy markets witness the turmoil due to shale revolution, the Middle Eastern states are keen to explore dimensions other than oil. The failure of the West to emerge as a reliable player has led the GCC to adopt "Look at India" policy. In order to achieve this, many Middle Eastern states initiated a Look East Policy and it is in this context that India assumes more significance.

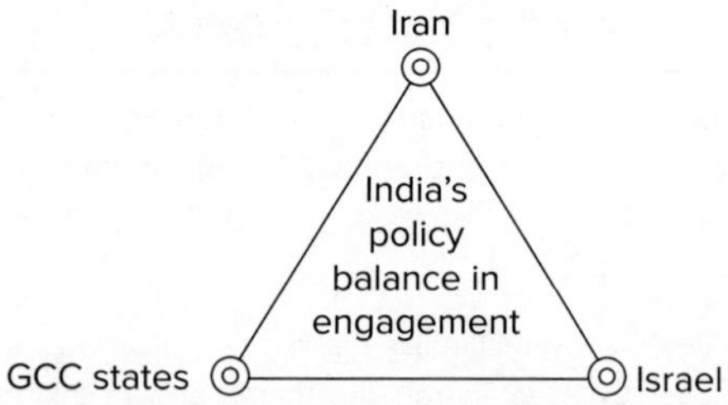

The Gulf has also emerged as Indian Navy's primary area of maritime interests. India has learned not to interfere in any state's internal affairs and limit its influence only to achieve self-interest. The Indian policymakers, under LWP, have striven for a fine balance between Iran, Saudi Arabia and Israel, while supporting Palestinians. This balancing act has given India a larger space to manoeuvre in the region with ease.

3 CHAPTER

The Modi Doctrine for West Asia, India as Net Security Provider Policy and QUAD-2

THE MODI DOCTRINE FOR WEST ASIA

The foreign policy of Modi in West Asia is driven by two drivers. Firstly, Modi is outdistancing his predecessors by going beyond the ties of energy, trade and investment to explore new and untapped areas of collaboration. Secondly, his focus is to add more strategic content to the relationship in every dimension. In pursuit of this thinking, today India and states in West Asia, especially GCC, are exploring engagements in dimensions that range from renewable energy to desert ecology to communications technology to support for start-ups. Also, each of the engagements has a strategic element of cooperating jointly in shared perceptions and approaches on security issues. Today, India has identified that shared threats to peace, security and stability are the core areas where a shared endeavour must be created to address the concerns. There is gradual realisation between states of the Gulf and India that they can cooperate together to promote regional peace, reconciliation and stability in Gulf and Indian Ocean region.

NARENDRA MODI'S WEST ASIA STRATEGY

India, under Modi, as part of LWP, is adopting a three-point strategy. First, it is expanding its domestic biofuel programme. Second, India has drastically expanded its strategic petroleum reserves. Third, India is striving to diversify its oil imports from West Asia. The core elements of India's engagement in West Asia under Modi government are economy, counter-terrorism and defence. A new element under Modi government has been of positioning India as a net security provider. It has the following ingredients: Conditions of peace and stability in individual littoral states; freedom to all states of the Gulf littoral to exploit their hydrocarbon and other natural resources and export them; freedom of commercial shipping in international waters of the Persian Gulf; freedom of access to, and outlet from, Gulf waters through the Strait of Hormuz; prevention of conflict that may impinge on the freedom of trade and shipping and prevention of emergence of conditions that may impinge on any of these considerations.

INDIA'S NET SECURITY PROVIDER POLICY IN WEST ASIA

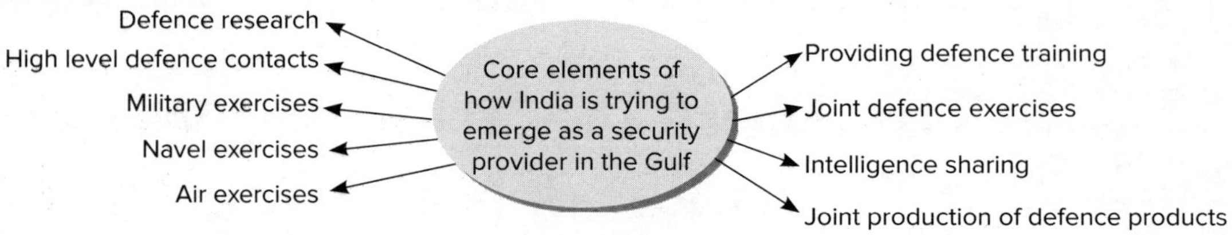

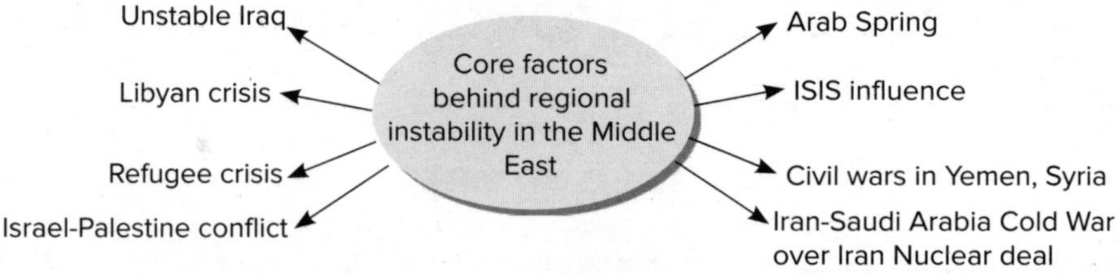

THE QUAD-2: A STRATEGIC GAME CHANGER

In 2021, the Indian Minister of External Affairs met with his Israeli, UAE and American counterparts. This meeting led the media to instantly signal the birth of a new 'minilateral' called QUAD-2. This is called QUAD-2 because the QUAD-1 comprises the US, India, Australia and Japan. The QUAD-2 is a new buzzword in the regional geopolitics and it is likely to focus on climate change, energy, maritime security and trade. The nations of this new minilateral have focused on establishing new joint working groups to take the cooperation further in the stated dimensions. While there does appear to be a lot of enthusiasm for this new grouping, but there is no clarity on what does the QUAD-2 mean for regional politics and what is the role for India in the same. As of now, there appears to be no strategic interest in the quartet that binds it because most of the issues identified for cooperation are already being discussed bilaterally. In this sense, the term appears more of a public relation exercise of Biden Administration to showcase to the American audience a new foreign policy buzz in the region by a new President.

QUAD-2: Will it help Indian Foreign Policy?

There exists a lot of concern on the role that India is likely to play in the new minilateral. This is because India has historically remained non-prescriptive, non-intrusive and non-hegemonic in engagement with West Asia. With the US and Israel in the grouping, both of whom have followed the policy approaches of prescriptions, intrusions and fight for hegemony; defining how India will play its cards is not clear. Also, India does not view QUAD-2 as anti-Iran while the other members do view it as anti-Iran. In this sense, India is not in a position right now to choose between Sunnis or Shias as it needs both.

INDIA AND UAE COMPREHENSIVE ECONOMIC PARTNERSHIP AGREEMENT (CEPA): AN ANALYSIS

The Modi government has accelerated India's economic diplomacy in the Middle East and this is visible with India and UAE signing a CEPA in February 2022. The CEPA was enforced from May 2022 and signifies a new dimension of strategic economic cooperation. India and UAE enjoy a deep historical relationship which has been nurtured by exemplary civilisational ties. The trade between India and UAE, which was 180 million in 1970s, has increased to 60 billion in 2019–2020. Apart from being a key partner in helping India with energy, UAE has also emerged as a crucial partner in sustaining India's infrastructural growth. To deepen their economic cooperation, the CEPA has been concluded in the recent times by the two states. The CEPA will now provide India and UAE greater market access through preferential tariff rates. This is so because the two sides have identified a list of goods where they will not just reduce but even eliminate customs duty on originating goods. A careful analysis of the CEPA tells us that a large amount of goods have been brought down to zero per cent tariffs and the two sides have decided to eliminate tariffs on the remaining goods in the next five to seven years. For trade in services, India has decided to provide market access to 100 sub-sectors of UAE. Indian service providers will now have access to engineering, communication, business, health, financial and social services etc. The CEPA also focuses on digital trade and the two sides have decided to maintain a legal framework that will govern digital transactions and these transactions will also be in compliance with the UNICTRAL Model Law on Electronic Commerce, 2006. To prevent the misuse of the CEPA, the two sides have developed a framework that will mention rules of origin and origin criteria which shall be used to obtain certificate of origin for goods. Export promotion is the philosophy that guides the thought from the side of the Indian government. This will be a valuable tool for India to allow the Indian industry to make inroads into UAE. Over the next five years, the quantum of the bilateral trade will rise to 100 billion USD and the CEPA will generate one million jobs in India in sectors that range from agriculture, leather, footwear and pharmaceuticals.

4 CHAPTER

Arab Spring, Crisis in Libya, Syria, Yemen and Strategic Significance of Abraham Accords

ARAB SPRING AND LIMITS ON INDIA'S WEST ASIA POLICY

Islam, after its origin, has spread as an ideology or religion to places and had a lot of interaction with different cultures all over the world. However, after 1453, the Fall of Constantinople led to subsequent Renaissance, Reformation, Enlightenment and Industrial Revolution and this saw the rise of Christianity in Europe. Islamic scholars perceived the rise of Europe as the rise of Christianity. This time also coincided with the beginning of imperialism. The western intrusion in the body politic of states led to a new discourse. Many scholars of Islam sensed a feeling of defeat and began to introspect. Some believed that the reason Christianity flourished was because of advancements in science (fuelled by the Renaissance and geographical discoveries) while others believed it was because of military superiority. Some Islamic scholars advocated deep introspection within and presented an idea of going back to pristine Islam as they felt that Muslims have deviated from their true faith. They felt that going back to pristine Islam would lead to Islam present a counter to rising Christianity. In the modern times, British and the French decided to control the Middle East for oil to sustain their Industrial Revolution. The World Wars also led to redrawing of the boundaries of the Middle East, done in a manner to suit the imperial interests than the interests of the natives. This territorial demarcation at the end of World Wars created a deep sense of resentment amongst the Arabs. The period after World War II and the Cold War saw the US emerging as a new power. The Cold War period in the Middle East witnessed a rise of military dictators and dynastic dictators (as in Saudi Arabia, Iraq etc.). In 1973 there was an oil crises (explained in the chapter of India and Israel Relations). It led to the oil embargo. When the embargo was removed, the lifting of the embargo financially strengthened the dictators but the financial benefits did not percolate to the Arab citizens. The population at large was still left out and felt humiliated to see how their leaders (authoritarian rulers) co-opted by the West.

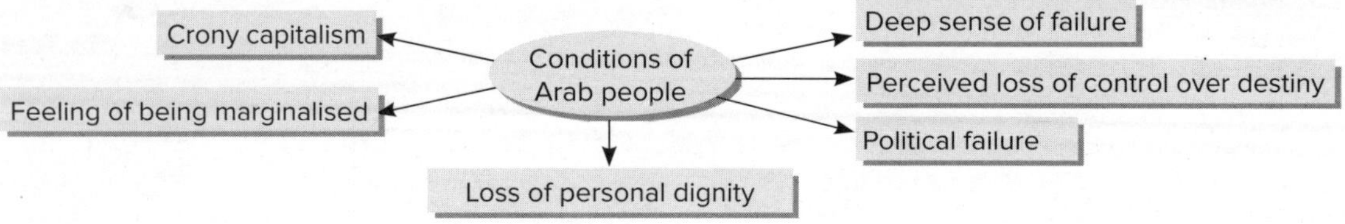

Some Islamic scholars in the Arab world decided to reassert the influence of Islam, and they decided to use Jihad as a tool for the same. The US, Saudi Arabia and Pakistan played a key role in revival of Jihad when Soviet invaded Afghanistan in 1979. The US used Jihadis to contain the Soviet influence in Afghanistan while Saudi Arabia spread Wahabism through Jihad and began to urge people in Pakistan and Afghanistan to return to pristine Islam. The Islamic scholars believed that the Americans are genuinely here to help the Muslims in their rejuvenation. The Salafism Jihadism that emerged during the Cold War was perceived as the first response to regain control over destiny. In this process, the religious fighters or

Mujahedeen were created to fight Communism in Afghanistan as the US had propagated to these Islamic scholars that they witness a threat to their existence from Russia. However, the Americans and Saudis, who had supposedly created these religious monsters, rapidly lost control over them because after Communists in Afghanistan were defeated, Mujahedeen began to realise that they were used by the Americans to fight Cold War and the Americans had no intention to help rejuvenation of Islam. The Soviet episode strengthened the anti-West fault lines amongst the Islamic scholars. Islamic scholars decided to seek revenge against the US and that revenge manifested as 9/11 attacks. Post-9/11 we saw the US invasion of Afghanistan (2001) and Iraq (2003). The 9/11 was used by the US to create a narrative of Islamophobia in the Christian world. The Arabs again were fatigued with increased violence and consequences caused by the Holy war or Jihad. It was now well accepted by the Muslims in the world that radicalism was not the answer. There was a huge intellectual vacuum felt by Arab citizens who had legitimate grievances against their leaders and realised that violence certainly was no answer. What contributed to more frustration in the Arab world was a series of Arab Human Development Reports that emerged from 2002 onwards till 2009. All these Arab Human Development Reports pointed out to lack of social development of Arab citizens. These reports also contributed to a deep sense of loss of dignity amongst the Arab people. The common Arab citizen was frustrated due to brutal suppression by their leaders, high prices of commodities, rising unemployment and rampant corruption. It is in this backdrop of historical suppression that the spark came from Tunisia in December 2010 when a street vendor, Mohamed Bouazizi, self-immolated himself due to suppression by Tunisian police. Self-immolation in Islam is a forbidden act, as it is believed that a person indulging in immolation will find no place in heaven. This act of self-immolation became a political statement leading to mass agitations in Tunisia against the ruler Ben Ali, who promptly ordered his forces to militarily suppress the protestors. The military forces refused to act on orders and rather joined the masses against him. This ultimately led to the downfall of Ben Ali. The revolution that happened in Tunisia was called Jasmine revolution because jasmine is culturally important for Tunisians—in the month of December, a lot of vendors in Tunisia sell jasmine flowers. The Tunisians appreciate the purity and the scent of the jasmine. It was called Jasmine revolution, as the idea was to purify Tunisia and clean it up from the corrupt government held by Ben Ali, thus led to the beginning of the Arab Spring. Because of this Jasmine revolution in Tunisia, on 20th January 2011, the Democratic Constitutional Rally, the party under Ben Ali was banned. On 1st March 2011, the Nahda Party in Tunisia was legalised to contest future elections. Ben Ali was convicted for embezzlement of public funds even though he had lived in exile in Saudi Arabia since his ouster. The unrest from Tunisia spread to Egypt. Egypt, since 1980, was under the rule of Hosni Mubarak, another corrupt dictator. The protestors occupied the Tahir Square in Cairo to demand the ousting of Hosni Mubarak. Post-Arab Spring, Egypt witnessed a power tussle between Muslim Brotherhood (a socio-political organisation in Egypt) and the Egyptian army.

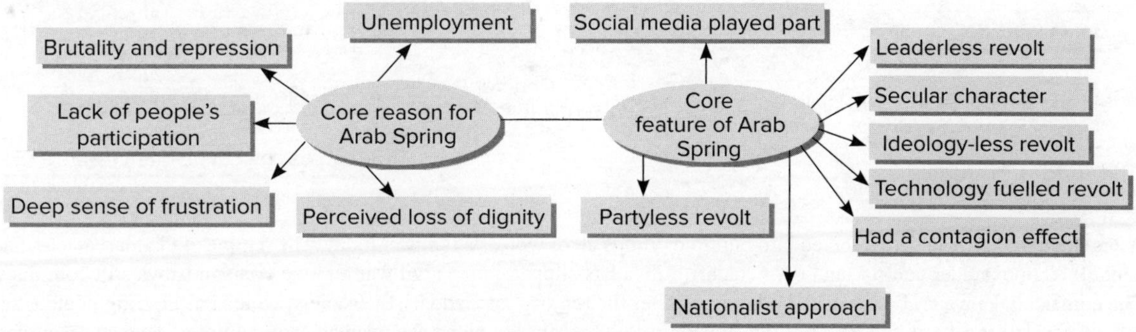

WHY IS THE REVOLUTION IN THE ARAB STATES CALLED ARAB SPRING?

Spring is a new season when normally the ice melts, winters end and new beginnings happen. The term at political level was first used in 1968, in Prague, when it achieved political liberalisation. The winter in political connotation signified a controlled society with a high degree of oppression exercised by a ruler and no freedom for the people. The spring signified a change from the winter. This is what the Arab Spring that began in December 2010 in Tunisia signified.

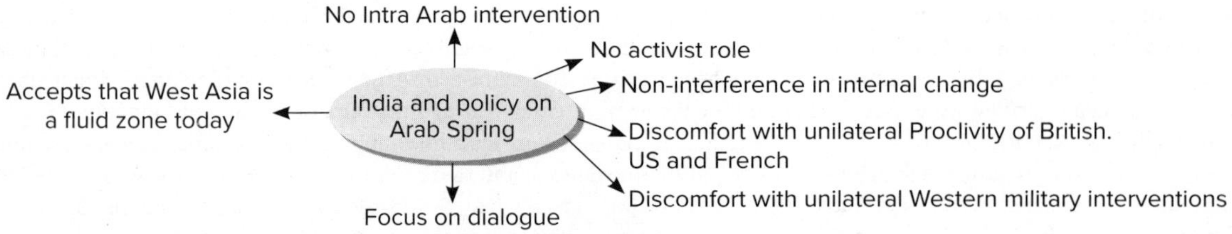

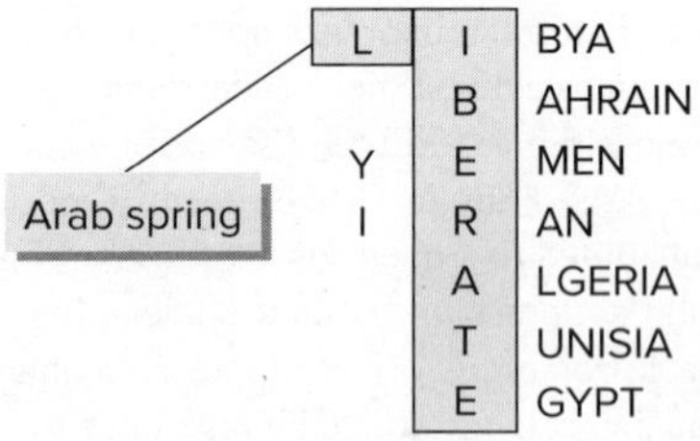

INDIA'S POLICY ON ARAB SPRING

India has followed a pragmatic approach and has evolved its view on a case-by-case basis. India has advocated the policy of non-enmeshment in sectarian conflicts. Broadly, India has followed hands-off approach of not interfering in internal transition. As some countries have slipped into civil wars post-Arab Spring, one priority that has emerged in the Indian foreign policy is the protection of Indian expats in this region. A bigger concern for India has been to protect the sea-lanes of communication to sustain oil supplies. Our policy is that as the Arab Spring favours democracy and has a secular outlook, India favours the changes brought about by it in the Arab World.

LIBYAN CRISIS AND LIMITS ON INDIA'S WEST ASIA POLICY

In 2011, the Arab Spring started against the Muammar Gaddafi regime in Libya who refused to leave the Libyan scene. Libya then subsequently saw a NATO intervention, which led to a forced removal of Gaddafi. Libya became the first state that underwent civil war after the Arab Spring.

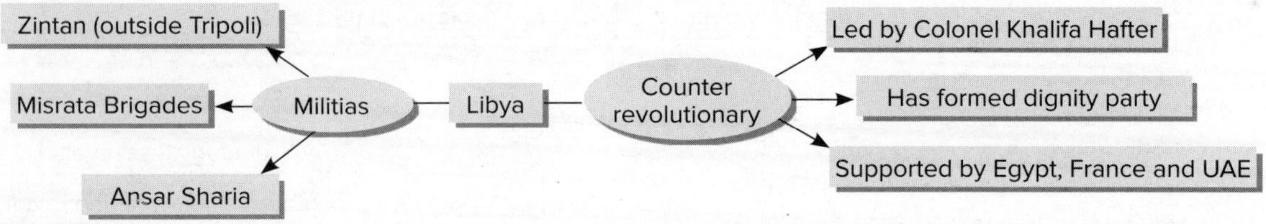

After Gaddafi, Libya has fragmented into multiple groups all of who assert power today. The regime of Gaddafi at least had kept all factions under control but post-Gaddafi, Libya has slipped into a civil war and the crisis in Libya still continues. The conflict in Libya is about wealth and power. After the removal of Gaddafi, the society, which has got fragmented, has seen the rise of local militias. The militias are controlled by tribes, which have been asserting dominance over resources. In 2012, the General National Congress was elected but each major city still has a dominant militia. The GNC elected in 2012 had to give power to House of Representatives in 2014, which has not happened till 2022. The Arab Spring has seen protests against Ali Abdullah Saleh in Yemen and also against the ruler in Bahrain. In Morocco, King Mohammed VI has agreed to transition. Elections have happened and people want the monarchy to stay in Morocco as well as in Jordan.

SYRIAN CRISIS AND LIMITS ON INDIA'S WEST ASIA POLICY

The Arab Spring created protest even in Syria but Assad refused to leave the scene. This has plunged Syria into a situation of civil war as the opposition favours his removal. This issue of the Syrian conflict has become all the more complex with foreign participation. Russia supports Syria as Russian Black Sea bases are not very far away from Syria and Syria is an important nation in Russia's West Asia Policy. The civil war in Syria has caused enormous damage to its civilian population, which has led to the population to seek refugee outside Syria. The year of 2015 saw colossal refugee crises when people began to leave Syria for Germany, Greece, Sweden and Turkey.

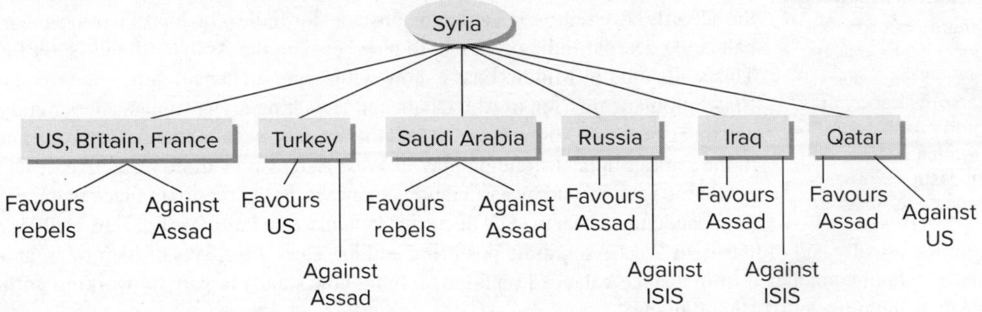

THE CRISIS IN YEMEN AND LIMITS ON INDIA'S WEST ASIA POLICY

Yemen is an Islamic nation with 65% Sunni and 35% Shia population. It is a fertile territory that also receives adequate rainfall due to its mountainous terrain. The population of Yemen is relatively poor as the natural resources of Yemen are declining. Historically, Yemen had a Zaydi Mutawakkilite kingdom from 1918 to 1962, which ended with the reign of Muhammad al-Badr. The conflict in Yemen is primarily between Houthis and Abdrabbuh Mansur Hadi. Houthis belonged to a Shia sect called Zaydis and were organised as the Jund Ansar Allah.

The problem in Yemen began for the first time in 2004 when Hussein Badr-al-Houthi began an uprising against the Ali Abdullah Saleh government in Yemen. The root cause of the uprising was the demand by Houthi for more autonomy with an aim to protect Houthi Shias from cultural invasion by Sunni Muslims. This conflict lasted from 2004 to 2010. In 2011, as the Arab Spring gripped the entire Arab World, the Houthis participated against the Saleh government, which was being led by Abdrabbuh Mansur Hadi as a de facto head. In 2012, Abdrabbuh Mansur Hadi came to power. In February 2014, National Dialogue conference happened in Yemen. Houthis also participated in the conference. The conference spoke about dividing Yemen into a federation of six regions. The Houthis opposed the idea, saying that with the formation of such a federation, violence would begin all over again. Houthis, being Shias, receive support from Iran and at present, control Northern Yemen and the capital Sana. In the southern part of Yemen, since 2007, there has been a secessionist movement called al-Hirak or South Yemen movement, which also poses threat to Yemen's sovereignty. In the southeast part of Yemen, Al-Qaeda in the Arab Peninsula and Ansar-al-Sharia are active as Sunni extremists and they are supported by Saudi Arabia. The conflict, at the regional level, can be perceived through the prism of the Shia–Sunni axis, with groups supported by both Iran and Saudi Arabia.

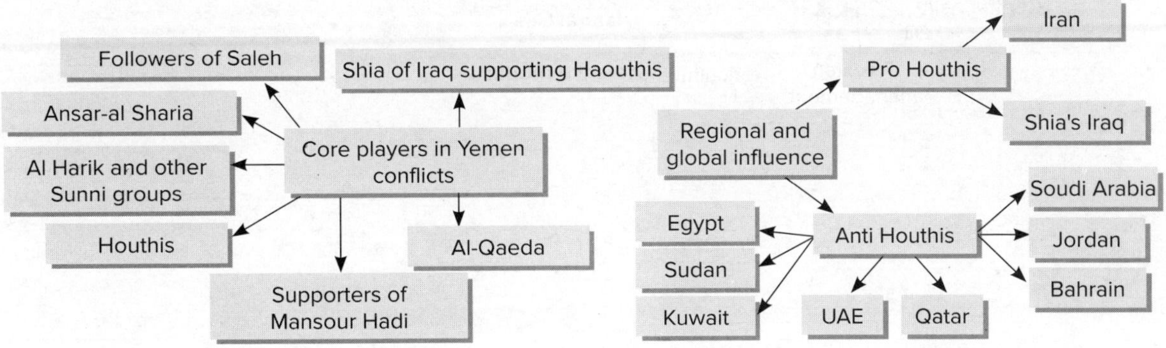

ABRAHAM ACCORDS AND THEIR STRATEGIC SIGNIFICANCE FOR INDIAN FOREIGN POLICY IN WEST ASIA

Why did the Abraham Accords Fail?

The Abraham Accords did not enjoy popular support. The state of Israel is still seen as an outsider by the people of the Arab states and will remain so till Israel settles the issues with Palestinians peacefully.

Abraham Accords were signed between the US, Israel and a consortium of Arab states led by UAE to normalise diplomatic relations. The signing of the accords is significant as the accords have removed a strategic obstacle for India which is of a trapeze wire delicate balancing act that India often had to play between the Arab Gulf and Israel for decades. This status quo in Middle East is now witnessing a change with Israel inaugurating its first diplomatic mission in Abu Dhabi and launching direct flights, encouraging business and tourism. New Delhi has welcomed the accords, because they offer peace and stability in the region. India's strategic play in West Asia is now more reflective of its emerging economic growth, and by association, an increasingly important place in the global order after pandemic. From the UN Security Council to the Indo-Pacific, New Delhi is now more assertive, diplomatically and militarily in West Asia, in its posturing and has shed the cloaks of its foreign and strategic policies are now being conducted from a stage balanced on a fence. India now stands to gain by working with the West Asian QUAD of India, Israel, UAE and the US.

MIND MAP

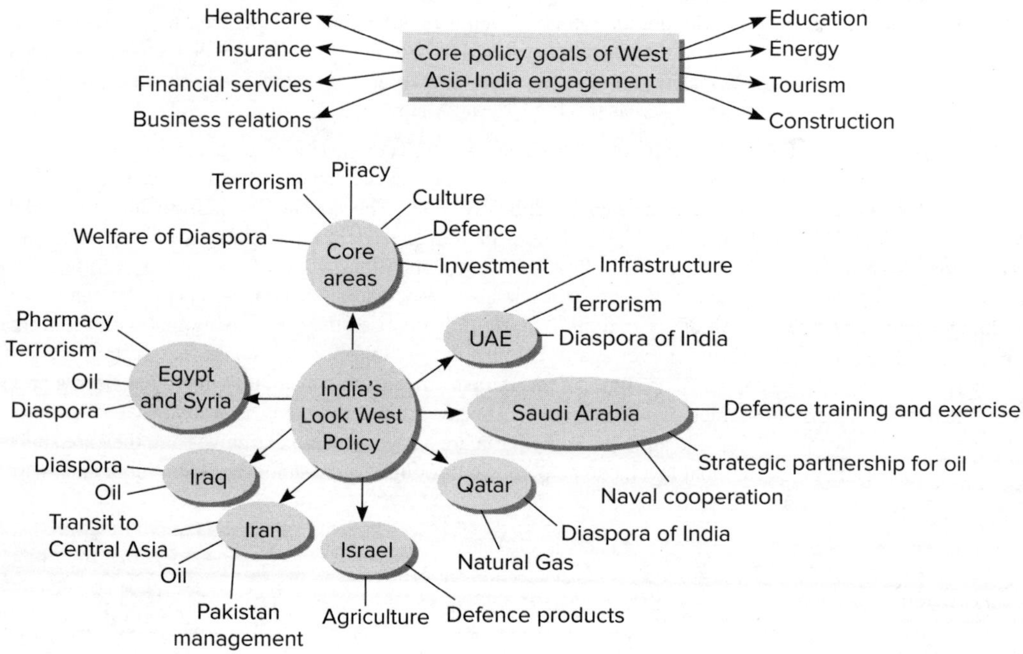

5 CHAPTER

India's Relationship with Saudi Arabia and Iran: The Doctrine of Sunni–Shia Balancing

FOUNDATION OF INDIA'S RELATIONSHIP WITH SAUDI ARABIA

India and Saudi Arabia established diplomatic relations in 1948. However, the relations with Saudi Arabia have not been very smooth during the Cold War. In the aftermath of independence, India and Pakistan had a war in 1948. Pakistan was able to garner Saudi support owing to its religious foundation and its emergence as an Islamic state. In 1953, Saudi king Al-Saud visited Pakistan and supported Pakistan on the Kashmir issue. However, Saudi–Pakistan relations deteriorated when, in 1955, Pakistan joined the US alliance brokered by the Central Treaty Organisation or the Baghdad pact. Saudi then used this opportunity to cultivate relations with India. In 1955, Saudi Prince Faisal visited India and later, King Saud also visited India. In 1956, Nehru paid a state visit to Saudi Arabia. Again, this bonhomie was not long lasting as in 1957; Saudi itself announced a pro-west alliance. Saudi Arabia used its alliance with the US to assert hegemony in the region. During the early decades of the Cold War, Egypt had propounded an idea of Pan-Arabism and Arab unity. However, Saudi began to weaken the influence of Egypt and Syria in the Middle East by using Pan-Islamism as a tool. As India was pro-Egypt, a weaker Egypt also meant weaker Indian influence in the Middle East. As Saudi succeeded in tilting the balance of power of the Middle East in its favour, it gave Pakistan an increased leverage to side with Saudi Arabia. In 1965, in the Indo-Pak war, Saudi supported Pakistan as Egypt supported India. Even in the 1971 war with Pakistan, the Saudis continued to support Pakistan. Saudi even refused to give diplomatic recognition to Bangladesh after its creation in 1971. After the 1973 oil embargo, as more money flowed into Saudi Arabia, it gave Saudi the option to undertake aggressive arms race with others. However, three events in late 1970s and 1980s drastically changed the landscape of the Middle East. The Soviet invasion of Afghanistan in 1979, the Islamic revolution in Iran in 1979 and the beginning of Iran–Iraq war in 1980 were defining moments of the time. In the recent times, the US are no longer a reliable supporter of Saudi as it has explored Shale gas as an alternative to oil. This has reduced the strategic significance of Saudi in the thought of the US. To make the matters more complicated, Saudi is occupied in fighting its arch-rival Iran. Turkey supports Iran by propping up Sunni radicals that threaten the House of Saud. All these geopolitical events have compelled Saudi to undertake massive social and economic transformation with Asia. This brings India into the strategic calculus of Saudi.

Kashmir irritant between India and Saudi Arabia

Pakistan was successful in mobilising the support of Saudi Arabia for Kashmir. They convinced Saudi Arabia that Kashmir being a Muslim province, under 'illegal occupation' of India, is detrimental to Muslims in general and Islam in particular. The Saudis during the Cold War period were embraced in the American umbrella and they bought this argument and went on to criticise India. They insisted that Kashmir issue be resolved through UN resolutions, plebiscite and even favoured third-party interventions. All these became major irritants between India and Saudi Arabia during Cold War.

JASWANT SINGH FACTOR IN INDIA AND SAUDI ARABIA RELATIONS

When the Cold War ended, Saudi Arabia wanted to re-look at the relations with other nations and India became a priority country. The prime importance attached to India was due to the presence of Indian nationals in the kingdom and a huge Indian workforce assisting the Saudi government. In January 2011, the Indian Minister of External Affairs, Jaswant Singh, paid a visit to Saudi Arabia. The Saudi Foreign Minister Prince Saud Al Faisal made a press statement at the end of the meeting where the issue of Kashmir was spoken about. There was no reference by the Prince on plebiscite, third-party mediation and UN resolutions. The Saudi kingdom emphasised that Kashmir is a bilateral issue and must be resolved by India and Pakistan bilaterally. The kingdom went further to announce in the statement that Saudi Arabia feels that India is a valuable partner and will not view its ties with India through prism of a third country. Thus, in response to the visit of Jaswant Singh, the Saudis decided to not just de-hyphenate India and Pakistan but also opened up a new chapter in the relationship where no third-country influence would be a deciding factor of bilateral relationship.

PRACTICING DIPLOMATIC POLICY OF DE-HYPHENATION OF INDIA–PAKISTAN

In the recent times, an important point mentioned in the joint statement between India and Saudi Arabia was that Saudi policy on Chinese BRI syncs with India's position on the BRI. The statement says that regional connectivity projects should respect international law, sovereignty and territorial integrity of states. A peculiar feature of the visit of Mohammed bin Salman (MBS) to India in 2019 was that not only MBS de-hyphenated India and Pakistan, but also condemned Pulwama attack and decided to increase all possible pressure (through intelligence sharing with India) on countries that offer support to terrorism (an indirect reference to Pakistan). Saudi has shown a 'positive understanding' on India's abrogation of Article 370, despite Malaysia and Turkey being negative. As Saudi Arabia is trying to diversify its economy, India sees this as a positive attempt as India feels that if Saudi focuses more on economy and eventually returns to moderate Islam, then it will have a positive impact on global Muslim community and weaken ideological moorings of radical Wahhabi Islam, which is currently inflaming Kashmir valley.

STRATEGIC SIGNIFICANCE OF SAUDI ARABIA FOR INDIA

In 2006, King Abdullah visited India. This visit marked a new chapter in Saudi Arabian foreign policy as Saudi decided to now strengthen its relations beyond the US. In the same year, King Abdullah was made the Chief Guest of the Republic Day parade celebrations. India and Saudi Arabia, in 2006, concluded the Delhi Declaration. This was the first ever-comprehensive document bilaterally signed to envisage a deep relationship between the two states. The components are explained below.

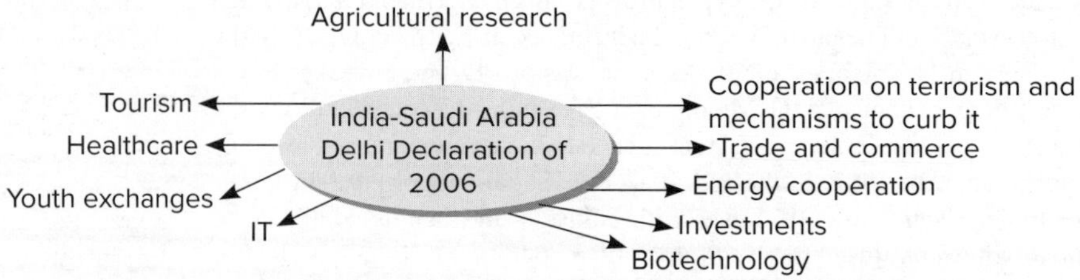

As the Delhi Declaration of 2006 opened up the cooperation, Indian PM Dr. Manmohan Singh visited Riyadh in 2010. The aim of the visit was to build cooperation on a platform beyond the Delhi Declaration. During PM's visit to Riyadh, not only did he conclude the Riyadh Declaration, but also the partnership was now taken to the level of strategic partnership. The components are explained below.

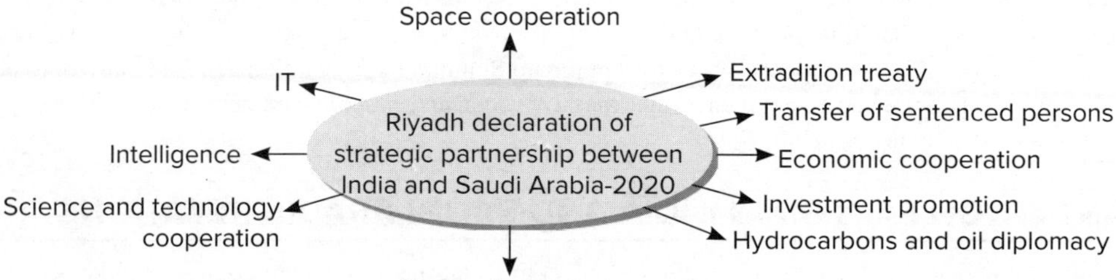

In 2019, a Strategic Partnership Council has been established between Indian PM and Saudi Crown directly where the two head of the states engage and set agendas for political, economic, security and socio-cultural matters. Under the Council, multiple working groups are created to ensure that matters are dealt with in an institutionalised manner.

INTER-GOVERNMENTAL AGREEMENT FOR COOPERATION IN OIL, GAS, DEFENCE AND CIVIL AVIATION BETWEEN INDIA-SAUDI ARABIA

In 2019, during the visit of Indian PM to Saudi, both sides have signed an Inter-Governmental Agreement for Cooperation in Oil, Gas, Defence and Civil Aviation. India has become the fourth country after Germany, Russia and Japan to have such an agreement. India has also been an active participant in the Saudi-led Future Investment Initiative (an initiative of Mohammed bin Salman), also known as Davos of the Desert, where India pitched for five trends in India for the global investors to remit. They include infrastructure, HRD, innovation, environment and business friendly governance.

NUCLEAR DIPLOMACY BETWEEN INDIA AND SAUDI ARABIA

Because of the recent global downturn, the oil prices have fallen and as a result, Saudi deficits are necessitating diversification and movement beyond oil. This has created opportunities for India to strengthen its strategic presence and outreach in Saudi. A new dimension of India–Saudi Arabia relation that has emerged is cooperation in science and technology. Saudi Arabia has announced the setting of 22 nuclear reactors by 2023 as a priority goal. India has decided to assist Saudi Arabia in manpower training, thorium supply, nuclear research and nuclear waste management. The strategic relations, which till date were oil based, are set to diversify and are likely to have a nuclear component.

STRATEGIC IMPORTANCE OF INDIAN DIASPORA IN SAUDI ARABIA

There is a 2.6 million strong Indian diaspora in Saudi Arabia. Wherever the Indian PM has travelled in recent times, he has made sure to address a mega gathering of the Indian diaspora, be it in a stadium in the UAE or massive crowds in the USA and Australia. However, no such thing was visible in Saudi Arabia. The Saudi Arabian law prohibits any assembly of people for political reasons. It is this point of the Saudi law that compelled the PM to visit and address the diaspora at the residential complex in 2016. This also gave an opportunity to the diaspora to have a much closer touch with their leader and helped establish a different level of connect. To assist the Indian diaspora, in 2020, Saudi Arabia decided to launch RuPay cards for payments. Saudi Arabia has emerged as the third state after UAE and Bahrain to do so.

STRATEGIC AND DEFENCE DIPLOMACY BETWEEN INDIA AND SAUDI ARABIA

India has evolved security interaction through the security engagement with West Asia having the following pillars:

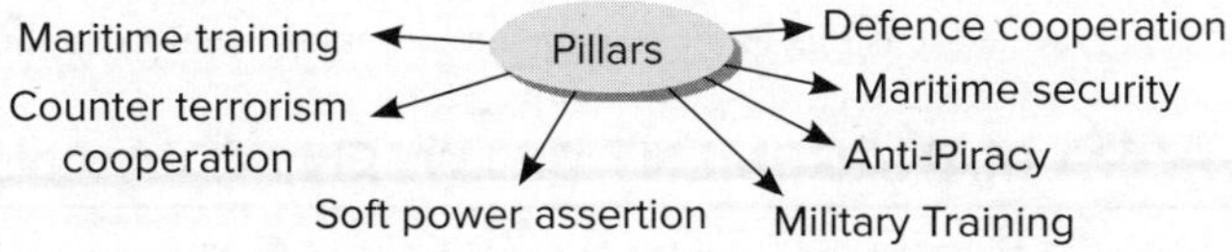

The two are cooperating in defence training and defence exchanges as the fourth Joint Committee on Defence Cooperation happened in 2019 where they decided to collaborate for joint naval exercise and joint production of naval spare parts and maritime security.

COMPREHENSIVE SECURITY DIALOGUE BETWEEN INDIA AND SAUDI ARABIA

In 2020, India and Saudi Arabia established a 'Comprehensive Security Dialogue', in which National Security Advisors of the two states participated. In that dialogue, a Joint Working Group Terrorism had also been established.

OIL AND ENERGY DIPLOMACY BETWEEN INDIA AND SAUDI ARABIA

Saudi Arabia, as part of its Vision 2030 (where Saudi Arabia aims to diversify from oil into manufacturing, technology and services; with an objective to link Saudi Arabia to global value chains and prepare Saudi women and men for the 21st century workplace), has identified India as one of the eight strategic partners. It has identified four areas to deepen its partnership with India. These include security, trade, investment and culture. India is one of the second largest buyers of oil from Saudi Arabia, after the first being Iraq. MBS decided to invest USD 100 billion in India and a Saudi firm Aramco (in partnership with Abu Dhabi National Oil Company) will invest in the Ratnagiri refinery and other petrochemical projects. Now, the question arises why is Saudi Arabia undertaking these investments in India? The reason is that Saudi Arabia is building a refinery in Gwadar, which was being built also to help China seek oil from the refinery. But, as per recent reports, China is increasing its shale oil output from Xinjiang and also importing shale from Kazakhstan. This is likely to make the refinery at Gwadar less attractive, thus Saudi Arabia is investing in India. This does not mean that Pakistan will lose relevance in Saudi Arabian strategic thought. Saudi Arabia will continue to use Pakistan to bleed Iran (through Jaish al-Adl terrorist group, supported by Saudi Arabia, based in Pakistan that attacks Iran). Bringing Saudi Arabian investment in our western periphery can deter Pakistan to launch any offensive against India. This is so because they will never attack any strategic location of India where there is Saudi Arabian investment. In 2020, Saudi Aramco decided to partner in strategic petroleum reserve with India and would setup a reserve in Karnataka, under the India–Saudi Arabia Strategic Partnership Council.

PAKISTAN FACTOR IN INDIA AND SAUDI ARABIA RELATIONS

A scholar named Harsh V. Pant asserts that when the Indian PM visited Saudi Arabia in 2016, the visit did not succeed in de-hyphenation (to convince Saudi Arabia to act tough on Pakistan and stop the export of terrorism). He asserts that although the joint statement did assert concerns over rising terrorism and offered condemnation, it felt short to name Pakistan. In 2019, Mohammed bin Salman (MBS) visited Pakistan and appreciated Pakistani role in the fight against terrorism.

HURDLES IN OIL AND ENERGY DIPLOMACY AND APPROACH OF GULF COOPERATION COUNCIL

As far as the region is concerned, unfortunately, due to the sectarian divide in the Middle East, evolving a consensus on regional security has become difficult. Iran prefers the idea of bilateral cooperation with its suppliers for guaranteeing regional security, though it does not have any successful model worth emulating. Within the GCC nations, there is no consensus. The GCC prefers the international community's engagement that is not agreeable to Iran, which wants to evolve regional security interactions in the region keeping its own national interests in mind. Also, in the recent times, due to conflict between Iran and Saudi Arabia, manifesting attacks on oil tankers, has added up as a new headache for India, which is struggling to ensure stable supplies of oil from the region. The killing of Qasem Soleimani in 2020, the chief of Quds force of Iran has aggravated tensions in the region and has put the region on the brink of a new Cold War.

HURDLES IN DIASPORA MANAGEMENT BETWEEN INDIA AND SAUDI ARABIA

Saudi Arabia has announced labour reforms and has committed to establish a unified standard contract for domestic workers. For female domestic workers, under contract, the Saudi employers have to deposit 2500 US dollars in the Indian embassy, which is refundable to the employer if there is no issue of abuse or non-payment of salary. There is a new minimum wage of 1500 SR to be paid to the workers. In 2016, the Indian PM gave approval to the MOU on labour cooperation signed one during his visit for the necessary changes and the new format of labour categorisation.

DIPLOMATIC DIMENSIONS OF FUTURE COOPERATION WITH SAUDI ARABIA

The two countries identified solar power and satellite technology as new areas of cooperation for the future. Economically, India can offer Saudi Arabia software and human capital for their economic transformation, thereby creating a new regional geopolitical template of cooperation as both sides know that this entente cordiale is not only positive for their bilateral potential but also enables the two to widen their geostrategic options. Riyadh wants to use Pakistan as a valuable asset to counter growing influence of Iran from Syria to Yemen.

HISTORICAL DIMENSION OF INDIA'S RELATIONSHIP WITH IRAN

The relations between India and Iran began in 1950 when they signed a treaty of Friendship and Perpetual Peace. However, Iran became a part of the US alliance via the Baghdad pact in 1954 and the Cold War separated the budding allies. During the Cold War, Iran due to its affiliation to CENTO also developed proximity with Pakistan. During the 1965 and 1971 war, Iran provided military assistance to Pakistan. In 1979, there was an Iranian revolution and this brought Ayatollah Khomeini to power and he established the theocratic Islamic Republic of Iran. Post-1979, India and Iran began to establish proximity. During the Iran–Iraq war, which began in 1980 and lasted till 1988, India remained neutral and continued economic diplomacy for oil imports. In 1983, they established an India–Iran Joint Commission (JC). The aim of the JC was to promote economic cooperation and organise foreign minister level meets. In the 1980s and 1990s, the dialogue on trade and economy continued. In 1993, Narasimha Rao visited Tehran while in 1995, Akbar Hashemi Rafsanjani visited India. In 2001, Vajpayee and Khatami signed the Tehran Declaration while, in 2003, Khatami, on his visit to India, signed the New Delhi Declaration.

STRATEGIC DIMENSION OF INDIA'S RELATIONSHIP WITH IRAN

The relation dipped due to the nuclear programme of Iran in 2005–06. In 2005, India and Iran had signed an agreement to supply 5 million tonnes of LNG per year from 2009 and this 32-billion-dollar deal got affected due to nuclear sanctions. In 2008, Ahmadinejad, on a visit to Pakistan and Sri Lanka, halted in India for refuelling and this stopover was transformed into a state visit to patch up relations. During the US–Iran confrontation, India maintained that Iran had the right to have its own nuclear programme. India and Iran's strategic diplomacy is based on the Tehran Declaration and the New Delhi Declaration. The following are the components of the two countries.

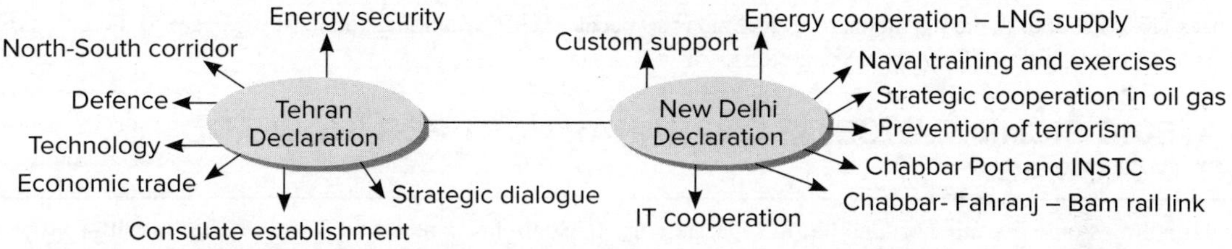

IRAN–PAKISTAN–INDIA PIPELINE DIPLOMACY TEMPLATE

The IPI (Iran–Pakistan–India) pipeline was conceived by a Pakistani engineer Malik Aftab Ahmed Khan in mid-1950. In 1989, R. K. Pachauri conceptualised the project. Different Prime Ministers in India have followed different approaches to the IPI pipeline.

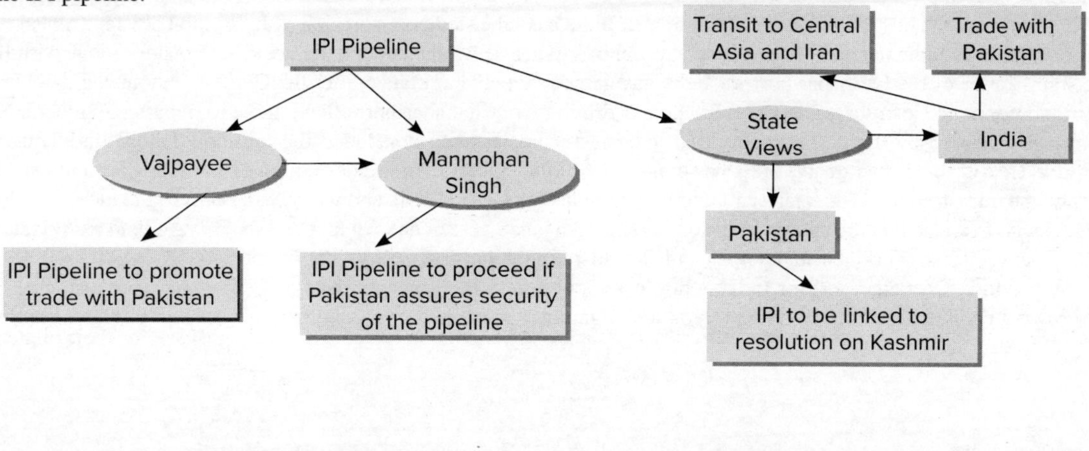

Because of the US sanctions on Iran, India since 2008 has abandoned the pipeline. However, in 2017, a Parliamentary panel in India has recommended that India should revive the work on the IPI pipeline. The panel has asserted that India can import 60 million standard cubic meters per day from South Pars Gas field from Iran to Pakistan and India. India fears the safety of IPI pipeline passing through Pakistan and India favours that Iran takes the responsibility for the security of the pipeline.

KASHMIR ISSUE AS AN IRRITANT BETWEEN INDIA AND IRAN

On 26th June 2017, during the Eid sermon, Ayatollah Ali Khomeini equated conflict in Kashmir at par with one in Yemen and Bahrain. In 2019, when India abrogated Article 370, Ayatollah Ali Khomeini advocated that India should protect Muslim interests. It is not the first time Iran has done this as it had made similar statements in 2010 also. Since 1979, Iran and Saudi Arabia have been engaged in a proxy war where both have used religion as a tool to pursue power. India has tried to balance Iran and Saudi Arabia but Iran does not appreciate India's tilt towards Saudi Arabia and the recent utterance of Khomeini must be seen in that context. Iran through the statements has asserted that it is a crucial player in the Islamic world and India cannot ignore Iran. Though India has ignored the provocation by Ayatollah on Kashmir, India needs to rework its economic engagement with Rouhani. For India, Iran remains a strategic economic partner to cooperate in Chabahar Port/International North South Transit Corridor.

ENERGY AND OIL DIPLOMACY BETWEEN INDIA AND IRAN

India has been buying oil from Iran since the Cold War time. Russian Gazprom and Chinese National Petroleum Corporation have emerged as new potential players. Iran has been visibly upset with India, which allied with the US during the sanction period and reduced oil imports from Iran. As per the Indian policy, today only Indian carriers can import oil from foreign countries. India is going to amend the policy to allow a foreign shipping container firm to import oil. India, at the energy security level, is making a shift to gas resources and in the process is planning to hire very large container carriers (VLCC) from Japan to import gas from Australia, Russia, Iran and Mozambique. Iran is an irreplaceable supply partner for gas. India has also initiated a diplomatic dialogue with Iran to discuss the possibility of Iran–Oman–India pipeline in the future. India uses UCO Bank to make payments to Iran. This is so because UCO Bank has the least exposure to the US and this makes it less vulnerable to US CAATSA sanctions.

STRATEGIC SIGNIFICANCE OF CHABAHAR PORT FOR INDIA AND PORT DIPLOMACY

Chabahar is Iran's only oceanic port and has to separate ports of Shahid Kalantari and Shahid Beheshti with five berths. Chabahar port is a part of the regional economic strategy of India. Since the end of the Cold War, Chabahar port is a component of India's grand strategy. After 1991, the core objective of Indian foreign policy was to seek foreign support for economic development of India, engage with middle and great powers, normalise India's engagement in the neighbourhood and raise India's profile in external neighbourhood (this is the point where Iran's Chabahar port comes into play) and finally to improve India's international standing. The idea of Chabahar port came up in 2003 when Iranian President Khatami visited India and a deal was signed between the two states. For India, Chabahar port remains the most important tool that can alter the hostile regional geography that India has inherited post-partition of India and Pakistan. As Pakistan continued to deny India overland transit access to Central Asia and Afghanistan, India decided to make a move with Iran. The significance of the Chabahar port for India has gained higher importance after the Chinese announced the China–Pakistan Economic Corridor under the Belt and Road initiative. Chabahar port allows India to bypass the geographical limitations imposed by the partition. In 2016, India–Afghanistan–Iran concluded the trilateral Transit and Transport Corridor Treaty. Under this treaty, India has committed 500 million dollars to develop the Chabahar port and establish railway line infrastructure. The treaty will allow India to access Central Asia and will give a boost to the idea of regional connectivity. Iran also favours India's inclusion into the Ashgabat Agreement. Under the Ashgabat Agreement (concluded in 2016 between Iran, Turkmenistan, Oman and Uzbekistan), the Persian Gulf will be connected to Central Asia through a direct corridor. Chabahar port for India is not just about access to energy markets of Central Asia but also access to fast growing economies of the Eurasian region and a gambit against history. India may witness some challenges in the endeavour of developing the Chabahar port. Firstly, India has to convince private players to use Iran as a transit route to reach Central Asia than China, which is the presently used route. Secondly, to access the future markets of Central Asia and Eurasian region, Indian exports need to become more competitive. In 2016, India decided to refurbish Shahid Beheshti and reconstruct a 600 m long container handling facility. The 2016 agreement allows India Ports Global (a joint venture of JNPT and Kandla Port trust) to develop two berths. India is also constructing a railway line to connect Chabahar and Zahedan and on Iran–Afghan border. This helped India to bypass Helmand province of Afghanistan that is a hot bed of Taliban. If berths are developed then the trading capacity rises from 2.5 million tonnes to 8 million tonnes and will give India access to Eurasia and Afghanistan. To develop Chabahar India Ports Global has got 500 million dollars from India. The pioneers in the construction are Swiss firm Liebherr and Finland's Konecranes. Because of Trump's withdrawal from JCPOA, India Ports Global has not been able to proceed to take help. In 2016, a deadline of 18 months was set up but the uncertainty prevails even today. James M. Dorsey is of the view that the USA seems to work with Saudi Arabia and UAE to destabilise Iran and check Qatar and this would affect Chabahar and India. However, in February 2018, a part of the Chabahar became operational. In 2020, the US gave India a 'written' assurance that it would seek support of global banks to mobilise money to support India for the development of the port.

FARZAD-B OIL FIELD IRRITANT BETWEEN INDIA AND IRAN

In 2008, ONGC Videsh Limited (OVL) discovered gas in Farzad-B offshore field. Farzad-B is the biggest gas discovery in Iran. To secure rights over Farzad-B, IOC and OIL consortium have been established. India sought preferential treatment in development rights of Farzad-B as it explored and gas found as per exploration agreement of 2012. Iran was not keen to give India any preference. Iran was not happy with India supporting the US during sanctions against Iran. After 2015 Lausanne framework, India offered 6 billion dollars for developing the gas field and 5 billion dollars for LNG export terminal. Post sanction removal, Chinese National Petroleum Corporation and Russian Rosneft Gazprom have offered interest in Farzad-B. India has cut oil imports from Iran since 2017 due to not getting preferential access but no effect happened on Iran. Iran says that India should sell gas from Farzad-B it discovered at current international rates which India feels is low as global demand is not high as there is enough supply in the market. India asserts that gas exploration at Farzad-B is tough as gas is impure and extracted gas has to be cleaned which increases the cost and selling this gas after incurring additional cost at current international prices will lead to a loss to India. The Consortium of India feels that it may affect the returns to investors of the Consortium this way. Energy expert Deepak Mahorkar says that India needs Iranian gas as Iran being geographically close to India and India running short of gas resource. Iran had asserted that India explored gas, process it and setup an LNG terminal to sell and export it. India committed 11 billion dollars investment for it. Iran has now asserted that India's Consortium can explore the gas and deliver it to an offshore field at a landfall point in the gulf island. India need not to process the gas of impurities such as sulphur or do marketing as both will be done by Iran. This has reduced the overall cost for India as India will not establish an LNG terminal, thereby India will save 5 million dollars and also save money in processing impurities. India needs to establish a development facility for exploring gas that will not cost 6 billion dollars as planned earlier, but around 4 billion dollars. The rate of return Iran is offering for delivery conditions could be just around 5% to 6%.

THE INSTEX METHOD—INDIA'S OIL PAYMENT MECHANISM IN THE ERA OF SANCTIONS ON IRAN

India could be helped by the alternative trade system that the European Union has been putting together after the US sanctions prevented countries from using a dollar-led SWIFT to trade with Iran. European Union, which is still committed to the nuclear deal signed in 2015, attempts to mollify an enraged Iran resulted in the creation of a system, INSTEX, which is nothing but a complicated barter system that side steps the dollar route. European countries that began its usage in July 2019 have confined it to humanitarian goods only so that they do not antagonise Washington. Iranian authorities claim that goods worth $14 billion have been lined up for trading, which excludes oil. Many countries including India that want to disengage from the US controlled trading order also want to explore INSTEX. Washington sees in INSTEX beginning of a revolt of against its hegemony of the financial world order and is keen to smother it.

ORIGIN OF IRANIAN NUCLEAR ISSUE

In 1953, the US president Eisenhower gave a speech at the UN General Assembly entitled 'Atoms for Peace' (AFP). The US was determined to use atomic technology for peaceful purposes within and amongst developing counties for civilian nuclear programmes. The recipient states were to use the nuclear technology only for civilian and peaceful purposes. The Iranian Nuclear programme (INP) began in 1957 when Mohammad Reza Shah of Iran entered into an agreement to cooperate on civilian use of atomic energy. In 1959, in the University of Tehran, the Iranian Shah established the Tehran Nuclear Research Centre (TNRC) and initiated negotiations with the US under AFP for civilian nuclear support. In 1967, the US established a 5 megawatt nuclear reactor with highly enriched uranium fuel to fuel the reactor at the TNRC, which had the capacity to produce 600 grams of plutonium per year in the spent fuel. Akbar Etemad was the father of the INP. Under the AFP, Iranian scientists also got an opportunity to get trained in the US. In 1974, Iran created the Atomic Energy Organisation of Iran to achieve the target of training manpower for 20 reactors in the next 20 years. Subsequently, in 1975, the Atomic Energy Organisation of Iran and MIT entered into an agreement to train Iranian nuclear scientists. Things changed after the 1979 Iranian revolution. When the rule of the Shah came to an end in 1979, the US suspended all nuclear cooperation with Iran. Iran, on the other hand, continued to receive support from Russia, China and Abdul Qadeer Khan's nuclear arms bazaar. Initially, Ayatollah Khomeini reduced the intensity of the INP but the 1980 Iran–Iraq war brought about a rethinking in Iran about its nuclear programme. In 1983, Iran asked the IAEA to provide Iran assistance for technical help in setting up of a plant to provide uranium hexafluoride (UF6) required for enrichment. With assistance for France, Iran had established a home-grown facility to develop nuclear fuel at Esfahan Nuclear Technology Centre (ENTEC). The IAEA, under Article X1-A of its statute, was obligated to help a member state with such a project. In the same year, a team from the IAEA visited ENTEC to assist Iran with local expertise. Finally, due to the US pressure, however, the IAEA did not initiate any support. From 1976 to 2003, as per the subsidiary arrangements of the safeguards agreement between Iran and the IAEA, Iran had to report any new facility to the IAEA within 180 days along with providing information on any new location or outside facility. Since 1992, the subsidiary arrangement, which was part of the safeguard agreements, began to change but Iran was not a party to change in the safeguard agreements till 2003. The Iranian opposition party, Mujahedeen Khalaq Organisation (MKO), revealed that Iran had established a secret facility at Natanz. As Iran was not a party to the changing safeguard agreements till 2003, by not declaring the Natanz facility within 180 days, it did not violate any legal obligation of the IAEA.

NUCLEAR DIPLOMACY OF IRAN AND SIGNIFICANCE OF SADABAD DECLARATION

Since 1992, the Board of Governors at the IAEA began to accept the subsidiary arrangement known as Modified Code 3.1 that required a member state to notify any decision to setup a new facility immediately. In 2003, Iran agreed to abide by the Modified Code 3.1, but as the US sanctions continued, Iran refused to finally ratify the Code. Iran began negotiations with the EU-3, that is, Britain, France and Germany. The talks led to the adoption of Sadabad Declaration between Iran, Britain, France and Germany, whereby Iran decided to suspend all uranium enrichment. This was followed in 2004 with the Paris agreement. Under this, it was agreed that Iran and EU-3 would look for a long-term agreement to ensure an INP for peaceful purpose. The Sadabad Declaration and the Paris Agreement failed, as Iran could not get a security guarantee for any attack on Iran. Iran said that it got a box of chocolates out of the deals, which was empty.

THE JOINT COMPREHENSIVE PLAN OF ACTION

Since 2006, Iran resumed enrichment at its facility in Natanz. The belligerent policy of the US on Iran gave rise to a hardliner in Iran, Mahmoud Ahmadinejad, who became the next president. The refusal of Iran to ratify the Modified Code 3.1 led the US to send the Iranian dossier for sanctions to the UN Security Council. In 2009, Iran sent a letter to the IAEA declaring that it is constructing a second uranium enrichment facility at Fordo under the mountain. As the Iranian Majlis had not ratified the Modified Code 3.1, it was not bound to follow. Tensions between the US and Iran continued. In 2006, China, Russia and the US joined the group of EU-3, becoming the P–5+1. Germany was a key trading partner of Iran and its nuclear programme depended upon German products and services. German firms such as Siemens, Mercedes, Lurgi,

Krupp and Volkswagen were also heavily operational with Iran. The negotiations of P–5+1 did not yield any results due to the presence of the hardliner Ahmadinejad. In 2012, with the election of Hassan Rouhani, things began to progress further. The first success was achieved in 2013 as per the Geneva Accord, where a joint plan of action (JPOA) was achieved. It was further negotiated upon, leading to a final JPOA in June 2015. The 2013 Geneva deal acknowledged that Iran has to accept that it would not enrich uranium for a nuclear bomb. The deal accepted the fact that it is a step-by-step solution where actions by Iran in good faith shall gradually lead to a comprehensive solution, and would finally involve an integrated whole, where nothing would be agreed upon until everything would be agreed upon. Under the Geneva agreement, Iran was not to enrich uranium beyond 5%. Iran would make no advances of activities at facilities in Natanz, Arak and Fordo.

THE PROVISIONS OF THE LAUSANNE FRAMEWORK

In 2015, under the Lausanne Framework joint comprehensive plan of action (JCPOA), Iran had agreed not to enrich uranium beyond 3–6%. It retains the right for a peaceful nuclear programme. Iran would cut centrifuges from 19,000 to 6,104, with 5,060 centrifuges for enrichment. This makes it tough for Iran to make a bomb. Iran would also reduce its stockpile from 10,000 kg to 300 kg, ensuring transparency in its peaceful use of nuclear technology. The IAEA will access all nuclear facilities of Iran and there will be gradual lifting of sanctions. Iran has to address the concerns of the IAEA related to possible military dimensions of its nuclear programme and has to redesign the heavy water facility at Arak and transform the Fordo facility into a physics research centre. The Middle Eastern states had a mixed response to this arrangement. Hezbollah leader Hassan Nasrallah and the Lebanon's speaker Nabih Berri welcomed the deal, along with the Syrians. Saudi Arabia felt that the Iran deal allowed Iran to maintain a nuclear threshold and that the elimination of sanctions would economically revive Iran. A strong Iran will allow it to assert its hegemony over Lebanon, Iraq, Yemen and Syria. Though Israel has criticised the deal, we must note that Israel has actually never witnessed any existential threat from Iran. It has, however, faced regional competition post-withdrawal of sanctions. For Israel, the real issue, therefore, is not the bomb but the regional balance of power. A nuclear Iran, even for civilian use, threatens the decade-old strategy of allowing Israel to be an unrivalled military power of the Middle East. Israel knows that allowing Iran to have a civilian nuclear facility means that Iran too shall have the flexibility to turn military in nature at a short notice. Such a situation would severely delimit the ability of Israel to be the only player in the Middle East to establish regional hegemony with 200-plus unmonitored nuclear warheads. For Saudi Arabia, the revival of the regional GCC to prepare for a long-term confrontation with Tehran is the only option. Iran had decided to follow the Chinese model. The idea is to get the sanctions removed and get rich and then use the wealth to establish Iran as a regional hegemony. Both Israel and Saudi Arabia fear the dominance of Iran stretching from Beirut, Damascus to Bagdad and Aden. This fear is disturbing the balance of power in the Middle East post the 2015 Nuclear Deal.

NUCLEAR POLICY OF JOE BIDEN FOR IRAN

Trump said Iran was violating the spirit of the deal if not violating the deal in letter as it continued to work against the USA interests in Syria and Yemen and support to Hezbollah. Obama signed the deal on a balance of give and take relations where the idea was too curb nuclear ambitions of Iran but allow Iran a limited space to test ballistic and other missiles. Trump says that the nuclear deal does not restrict Iranian missile testing. This is despite the fact that JCPOA did not mention missile-testing point. The JCPOA mentions that Iran, which would reduce the centrifuges for enrichment from 19000 to 5060, will be for 10 years till 2025 but after 2025, these restrictions will be removed and limits on use of centrifuge ends in 2025 and limits on enrichment ends after 2030. So, Trump feels that by 2030 and afterwards Iran can go nuclear, thus the deal lacks comprehensiveness. Thus the US sanctions were re-imposed on Iran. Trump wanted a better deal where missile testing is curbed (ballistic missile testing) and Iran facilities are fully transparent for inspection. He wanted removal of 2025 and 2030 deadlines (also called sunset clause) and wants that sanction money that got released after the removal of sanctions on Iran is not used by Iran for proxy war in Yemen and Syria. Though Iran has asserted that its ballistic missiles cannot be used to carry nuclear warheads as Iran possesses no nuclear warheads and its ballistic missiles are only for conventional warfare, but this does not affect Trump who unilaterally withdrew from the deal. India has maintained that despite the US withdrawal from JCPOA, it will continue to engage with Iran for oil trade and development of Chabahar port for the purpose of transit development to Central Asia and Afghanistan and has maintained that Iran has a right to peaceful use of nuclear energy.

INDIA'S STAND ON NUCLEAR ISSUE OF IRAN

At the international level, India at the time of signing its nuclear deal with the US in 2005, had to confront Iran. The US and Iran did not have a comfortable relationship as the US was deeply concerned about the Iranian nuclear programme. India was, on the other hand, reluctant to undermine its relations with Iran although it could not jeopardise a growing strategic partnership that had begun with the US in favour of Iran. India voted against Iran in 2006 at the IAEA voting. India clarified that when India had conducted a nuclear test in 1998, Iran had favoured a UNSC resolution asking India to put a cap on its nuclear capabilities and had urged India to sign the NPT and the CTBT. There are many things about Iran, which caused discomfiture to India. India, however, did not turn aggressive towards Iran and maintained that Iran was a great friend to India, while pushing for resolving the Iranian nuclear issue through diplomacy. India used the IAEA and Iran's programme to highlight the role of A. Q. Khan and of Pakistan as a proliferator state. India sponsored the US/EU-favoured resolution, recommending Iran to be examined as a case by the IAEA. India clarified that its vote was to prevent vitality in the Middle East and had no relation with Indo-US cooperation. However, since 2015 Iran nuclear deal, India has consistently maintained that Iran has a right for a 'peaceful' nuclear programme and its enrichment should remain with the ambit of civilian use.

MIND MAP

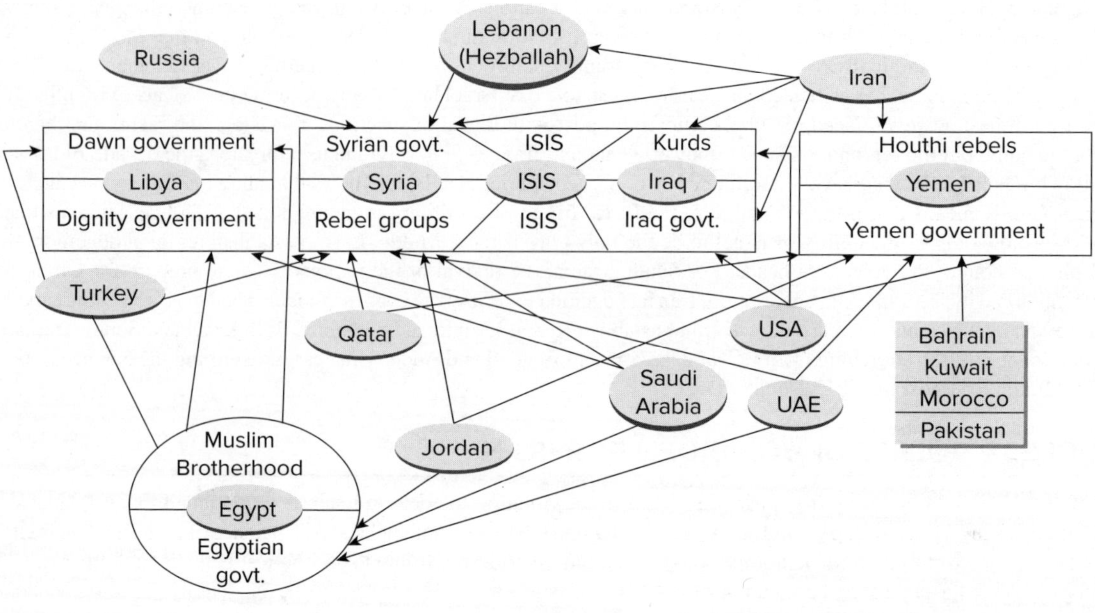

CHAPTER 6

The Israel–Palestine Conflict, India's Relationship with Israel and India's Palestine Policy

JEWISH ZIONISM, INDIAN PERCEPTION OF ZIONISM AND PALESTINE PROBLEM

When the Industrial Revolution began in Europe, it also brought about the spirit of nationalism amongst the Europeans. The British and the French emerged as two major European powers. After the unification of Germany by Bismarck, even Germany emerged as a strong power. This period of nationalism in Europe also was coupled with a period of colonisation. The British and the French resented the rise of Germany, as they perceived it as a serious competitor. As the World War I broke out, in 1916, the British and the French secretly signed the Sykes–Picot Agreement. Also known as the Asia Minor Agreement, the agreement had the British and the French decide the division of the Ottoman territory amongst themselves after the World War I. As the war ended, the British and French emerged victorious and Germany, Austria–Hungary and the Ottomans lost. The victorious powers of the World War I now decided to curb German ambitions and also divide the Ottoman territory. The establishment of the League of Nations after the World War I, the Mandate System and the Balfour Declaration gave effect to the ambitions of victorious powers. The British got the Mandate of Iraq, Trans-Jordan and Palestine while the French kept Syria and Lebanon as mandates. In order to curb German ambitions, the Treaty of Versailles was designed and signed in 1919. The wars also created a sense of nationalism in the Jews. The Jews were also inspired to have their own national home in the land they believed had been 'promised' to them by God. Theodore Herzl, in 1896, established the World Zionist Organization in Basel in Switzerland as a political movement to take Jews from Europe to Zion. (Zionism subsequently emerged, as a political movement of Jews; Zion or Jerusalem is where the temple mount is located in Palestine.) The basic idea of Theodore Herzl was that first, rich European Jews would go to Palestine and purchase lands and over a period of time; other Jews would go and settle in Palestine. Zionism, which emerged as a political movement, ended up being a movement to colonise Palestine. As the number of Jews in Palestine began to increase, the Arabs did not appreciate the move. After World War I, as the Mandate of Palestine had come under British control, the Arabs complained to the British about the rising number of Jews in Palestine. The British subsequently controlled the entry of the Jews into Palestine but did not impose a complete halt. This sowed the seeds of the Arab–Palestine disenchantment. During the inter-war period, Germany began to defy the Treaty of Versailles and also began to uproot the Jews in Germany. Hitler blamed Jews for the problems of Germany and in 1940 unleashed the horrific Holocaust as a 'final solution to the Jewish Problem'. The mass massacre of Jews led to a wave of deep sympathy for the Jewish people all over the world. America also convinced its ally Britain to allow entry of one lakh Jews from Europe to Palestine and ease the entry restrictions. As a greater number of Jews began to enter Palestine, it upset the Arabs in Palestine. The situation in Palestine was very volatile.

BIRTH OF ISRAEL, PARTITION OF PALESTINE AND INDIA'S POLICY

As the Jews and Arabs fought for the claim of Palestine, the UN was created as a successor to League of Nations on 15th May 1947. The British decided to hand over their Mandate of Palestine to the UN for deliberation. Subsequently, the UN established United Nations Special Commission on Palestine (UNSCOP). The UNSCOP deliberated upon the Palestinian issue. During the UN debates, one group advocated that Arabs have been controlling Palestine but Jews also have a rightful claim on the territory and therefore, the territory of Palestine should be partitioned for Arab Palestinians and Jews, creating a plan which came to be known as the Majority Plan. On the other hand, the other group advocated that there should be a Federal Palestine and Jews can be accommodated in a unified Federal Palestine without the need to partition. Thus, this group created this plan, which came to be known as the Minority Plan. On 29th November 1947, the UN voted on both the plans. As per the vote, the Majority Plan received the maximum votes. The Palestine territory was to be partitioned and it was decided to establish an Arab Palestine and a Jewish Palestine while keeping the city of Jerusalem under international control. As per the decision of the UN, with support of the US, on 14th May 1948, the Jewish Palestine got established on the demarcated territory and Israel, as a state, was born.

GANDHIAN AND NEHRUVIAN DOCTRINE OF PALESTINE

Gandhi initially developed his views about Jews and Zionism through his early interaction with Jews in South Africa, whereby he developed a substantial understanding of Jewish nationalism and their demand for a national home. Though he sympathised with the Jews for their horrific persecution in Germany at the hands of Hitler but he did not find much legitimacy in the demand of Jews to establish a national home. In the initial years after the World War I, Gandhi insisted that Palestine should not be a Jewish state but should remain under Muslim control. There were two reasons for Gandhi to espouse this view—first, Gandhi had kept domestic Indian Muslim community and their participation in the national movement in mind while forming his opinion; and second, Muslims had ruled Palestine for many centuries and it would have been a wrong strategy on the part of the British to accede to Zionist demand for the creation of a homeland in Palestine. He clarified that he believed Christians and Jews should freely go and worship in Palestine but should not acquire any sovereign jurisdiction over Palestine. But after the dissolution of Ottoman Empire in 1923, Gandhi argued that Zionists should not nurse territorial or political aspirations but rather, realise the Zionist ideas internally and spiritually. Gandhi also was very critical of Zionist cooperation with the British to achieve their demands of a national home as India was fighting British Imperialists. Indians began to perceive Zionist cooperation with British as Zionist intention to colonise Palestine. However, during this period, the Jewish Agency for Israel continued to work in close association with Gandhi and kept him abreast of the developments in Zionist political thought and goals. Nehru, who became the Prime Minister and Foreign Minister of India in the immediate period after Indian independence, was also opposed to the idea of a national home for Jews but did develop affinity with socialist Jewish leaders. The first reference by Nehru to the issue of Palestine can be seen in 1933 when he wrote a letter on the issue from a prison to his daughter Indira. In the dialogue, Nehru appreciated Jewish achievements and their contribution to the improvement of living standards of Palestinians through modern industry. He did not, however, support the cause for a Jewish national home. He also did not appreciate the Zionist cooperation with the British for a colonisation of Palestine as he held forcible colonisation to be morally and ethically wrong. Nehru favoured the idea of a united Palestine and not one divided by religion. Nehru articulated his views on the Palestine in a different manner. For Nehru, the Palestine issue was a fight by the Arabs against British imperialists. Nehru inferred that the Jewish issue was a deliberate creation of the British—similar to the divide and rule tactic of British in India—where the British pitted Jews against Arabs in Palestine. Nehru was extremely moved by the plight of the Jews in Germany and Eastern Europe, and after witnessing their persecution first hand during his visit to Central Europe in 1938, he advocated asylum for Jews in India. In 1937, when the Peel Commission report recommended the partition of Palestine, the Indian National Congress (INC), in its 1938 Haripura session, condemned the partition scheme and extended sympathy to the Arab cause. The INC was sympathetic to Jewish persecution in Central Europe but did not favour any partition or support for a separate home for Jews. India played a key role in supporting anti-imperial struggles in Syria, Egypt and Palestine and expressed solidarity with their nationalist struggles while refraining from quoting any Jewish organisations. India abstained from developing relations with any Zionist movement as it intended to promote a secular outlook of nationalism.

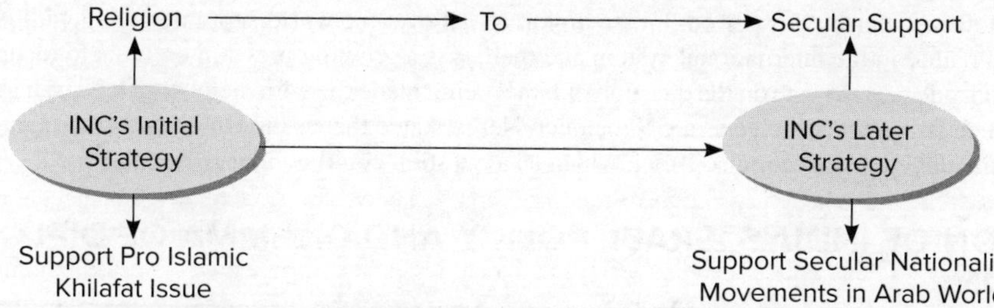

The INC in India maintained a policy in favour of Arabs while the Muslim League had severely criticised the Zionist movement. The aim of the INC was to show solidarity with Palestine Arabs as also to reassure the Indian Muslims on which side they were. However, the INC and Muslim League differed in the sense that the INC was supportive to Arabs but was not hostile to Jews like the Muslim League was. The Muslim League vehemently opposed the creation of a Jewish Palestine and had also condemned the Balfour Declaration in 1917.

INDIA'S ISRAEL POLICY AND UNITED NATIONS DIPLOMACY

In 1947, New Delhi organised a conference of the Asian Relations Organisation called the Asian Relations Conference (ARC). In the conference, both Arabs and Jewish delegations were invited. This was in sync with the earlier policy of the INC that had evolved support for Arab Palestinians, with conciliatory accommodation of Jews. A 10-member delegation of Jews headed by Samuel Hugo Bergmann, also known as the Hebrew University delegation, participated in the conference. Ironically, the Arab states declined to participate owing to Jewish invitation and this gave an opportunity to the Jews to present their case to India. During the ARC, the Jewish delegation again presented their idea of partitioning Palestine for accommodating Jews, which did not resonate well with the Indian leadership. Through the ARC, India also undertook a fine foreign policy manoeuvre by maintaining that Palestine belonged to Arabs, but simultaneously showing sympathy with the Jews. When the British placed the Palestinian issue before the UN General Assembly, Nehru appointed Asaf Ali as the Indian representative to the special session at the UN. Asaf Ali was instructed that he should not commit India to any situation that may affect India's relations with other nations but ensure that India would support the termination of the British Mandate of Palestine. Nehru asked Ali to play a cautious game as India wanted to support Arabs but not upset Jews as doing so would consequently affect India's relations with Western powers. The idea was to remain friendly to both the parties. The UNSCOP presented a final report in September 1947. The majority of members supported partition of Palestine but India, Iran and Yugoslavia advocated a Federal Palestine with both Arabs and Jews as a part of the territory. Thus, India continued to stick to its pre-partition policy of supporting Arabs and accommodating the Jews. As the partition plan won at the UNGA, it was clear that the partition of Palestine was inevitable. The question before India was what to do once a Jewish state in Palestine was born. On 14 May 1947, Israel as a state was born and both the US and the USSR recognised the existence of Israel. The task for Israel now was to seek diplomatic recognition from the world. It decided to seek the same from India too.

INDIAN CONSTITUENT ASSEMBLY DEBATES ON PALESTINE QUESTION

On 17 May 1948, Israeli Foreign Minister, Moshe Sharett, sent a letter to Nehru seeking diplomatic recognition of Israel from India. The Indian established decided not to make any hurried decision and adopted a wait-and-watch policy. In August 1948, H. V. Kamath enquired about the Indian position on Israel in the Constitution Assembly Debates where Nehru reiterated the wait-and-watch stance. There were two important reasons for India to adopt a wait-and-watch policy. The first was that after Israel got created, hostilities broke out in the region and the situation turned rapidly volatile with the outbreak of the 1st Arab–Israel War in 1948. In 1948, after the creation of Jewish Palestine or Israel, Syria, Lebanon, Iraq, Egypt and Jordan collectively attacked Israel. This led to the first Arab–Israel war in 1948. The UN immediately stepped in and by 1949, an Armistice Agreement was achieved. Secondly, the Indian Muslims had gone through the traumatic experience of partition and making a statement on Israel was not warranted at this stage. Further, during this period Pakistan began to establish proximity with Arabs to ignite the idea of Pan Islamism, which they could use against

India in Kashmir. However, during this period, Indian diplomats all over the world kept interacting with Israeli diplomat. Israel had become a reality in the international system and there was a growing pressure on India to recognise Israel. On 11th May 1949, UNGA decided to vote on the question of Israel being made the 54th member of UN. India voted positively on this question. When Israel got accepted as a UN member, Nehru stated that as the UN has accepted Israel as a member, India is moving in the direction to recognise Israel, which as a question could no longer be postponed.

ARTICULATION OF INDIA'S ISRAEL POLICY AND DILEMMA OF DIPLOMATIC RECOGNITION

Between 1948 and 1950, Turkey and Iran too had recognised Israel. There was a direct pressure on India to recognise Israel, as it could no longer play the domestic Muslim population card. Nehru announced India's recognition of Israel in February 1950 in a statement made in the Indian Parliament. But this declaration was verbal. Neither was there any official document that recognised Israel nor was any step taken to establish diplomatic ties. Finally, on 17th September 1950, a press communiqué was issued to recognise Israel after 28 months of requests from Israel. India thus removed the main obstacle in the recognition of Israel. The delay in Indian response was attributed to the diplomatic backlash India may have had to face from the Arab states. India clarified that the recognition to Israel in no way meant a change to Israel–Palestine policy of India and that it would continue to promote Arab cause. Other factors played a role in the diplomatic shift undertaken by India. India, through the recognition of Israel, made it clear that its support to Arabs was not unconditional and that India did expect reciprocity. India did not appreciate Egyptian vote at the UN against India on the issue of Hyderabad and its abstention at the UN vote on the Korean issue.

NEGATIVE STRAINS IN INDIA'S ISRAEL POLICY

Even though India had recognised Israel, it did not lead to the establishment of diplomatic ties instantly. India made a distinction between legally recognising Israel and the political act of establishing diplomatic relations. India made the right choice in maintaining a balance in the diplomacy related to West Asia. In September 1951, a consular office was opened in Bombay and F. W. Pollock was made honorary Consular Agent of Israel to India. An Indian Friends of Israeli Society was formed and it continued to interact on various occasions. This was no doubt appreciated by Israel but the society had a limited influence on foreign policy. Israel perceived all these steps to be important because countries, which had declared war on it, surrounded it. Its neighbours isolated Israel and the only option for Israel was to engage with the West. In Asia, Israel perceived India as a springboard to the other part of the world. From 1949 to 1956, there was truce in the region but in 1956, Nasser nationalised the Suez Canal and prevented Israel from accessing the Suez Canal. This led to a tripartite agreement between Israel, Britain and France in Sevres, France after which, Ariel Sharon of Israel attacked Egypt and captured the Gaza Strip and Sharm el Shaikh. The subsequent intervention of the US to diffuse the crisis led to peace again. But the Suez crisis firstly led to a big blow to the supremacy of Britain and France while boosting the image of Nasser in the Arab world. India condemned Israeli aggression in Suez Canal in 1956, with Nehru branding the military operation of Israel on Egypt as a clear, naked act of aggression.

INDIA'S DIPLOMATIC POLICY FOR PALESTINE LIBERATION ORGANISATION

Israel did invite Nehru in 1960 for a state visit but he declined the invitation as such a visit at this juncture could complicate matters. In 1963, in the Parliament, India clarified that due to less consular work between the two states; it is not appropriate to establish diplomatic missions with Israel. The awakened Arab world, after 1956 Suez crisis, began to ponder as to why the Arabs could not succeed in establishing the Arab Palestine. The Arabs realised that it was because they lacked an organisation such as the Jews and recognised the fact that splinter groups advocating for Arab Palestine have to be brought under a unified umbrella. In 1964, the Arabs established the Palestine Liberation Organization (PLO). The PLO emerged as an organisation of the Arabs fighting Israel military for supremacy in the Palestinian region. After the death of Nehru in 1964, Lal Bahadur Shastri continued the Nehruvian legacy with regard to India's Israel policy. In 1964, India accorded recognition to the PLO. India continued cooperation with Israel in the field of technology and agriculture.

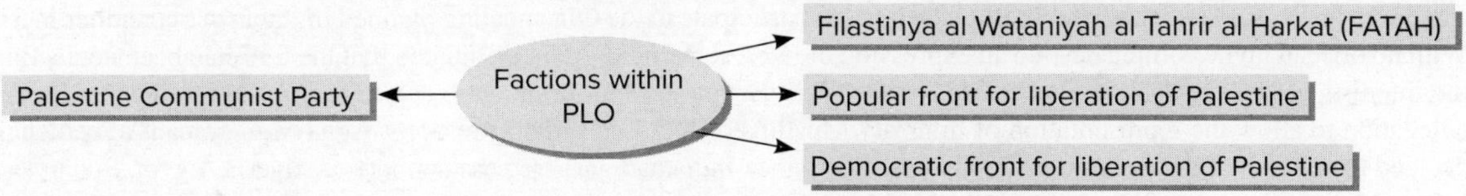

INDIA AND ISRAEL DIPLOMACY DURING THE COLD WAR

During the 1962 Indo-China conflict, India asked for military assistance from Israel and it agreed, considering that this may provide an opportunity for Israel to put in place diplomatic ties with India. In January 1963, top-level officials of Israel and India had a meeting and this became the first ever-proper contact between the two forces. In the 1965 India–Pakistan conflict, Pakistan succeeded in garnering the support of Arabs. The only Arab state standing with India was Egypt, which offered mediation in the Casablanca Summit of Arabs in September 1965. India had again requested for Israeli assistance for heavy mortar and ammunition. Israeli Foreign Minister Golda Meir was non-committal, but Prime Minister Levi Eshkol sent shipments of ammunition to India. Despite the support, no steps were taken by Shastri regime for modifying Israel–India ties. However, the lack of Arab support during 1965 war for India and outright support to Pakistan led the opposition in India to heavily criticise India's West Asia Policy. The coming of Indira Gandhi saw a resurgence of the hardcore pro-Arab policy. In March 1966, Israeli President Zalman Shazar, while on his way to Nepal, requested a 24-hour halt in India. The MEA requested the halt to take place in Calcutta and somehow no official greeting of the Israeli head of the state took place. This reflected the absence of depth in the relations. In 1966–67, the Arab–Israel conflict began again, with the situation becoming volatile along the Syria–Israel and Jordan–Israel border. India was affected when, in 1967, Egypt asked the UN Emergency Force (UNEF) to withdraw from Egypt-controlled areas near the border. India was a significant contributor to the UNEF. But due to Israeli aggression, many Indian UNEF officials and soldiers had died. India, at that time, was a non-permanent member of UNSC and again condemned Israel for escalation of conflict and strongly objected to the pre-emptive attack of Israel on Egypt. The opposition in India blamed the Indian government for supporting Arabs without reciprocity and stated that India should not favour Arab world as they supported Pakistan. There was a gradual rise in India of this new orthodoxy, which was not anti-Israeli but lacked assertion as they were out of the power structure. In 1967, Egypt was mobilising its military units along the Sinai and also closed the Gulf of Aqaba to Israel. Israel decided to attack Egypt and this war lasted for six days (also known as the Six Days War 1967) and Israel captured the Gaza Strip from Egypt. Israel also snatched the West bank from Jordan and Golan Heights from Syria during the war and expanded its area by 200%. Arabs took the matter to the UN and urged the UN to compel Israel to vacate the occupied territory and go back to accept the borders that existed before the 1967 war. The UN passed the UN Resolution 242, urging Israel to vacate the territory and immediately resort to holding of borders as existed before 1967. The state of Israel refused to comply with UN orders. The refusal of Israel to comply with UN Resolution 242 came as a big shock to the Arab world. The PLO subsequently became more radical to tackle Israel. In the Six Days War in 1967, India blamed Israel for escalating conflict and showed support to Egypt and the Arab states. As Israel expanded its territory in 1967, India advised that Israel should follow UN Resolution 242 and go back to pre-1967 borders. However, the government toned down the anti-Israel rhetoric and began to attribute its pro-Arab policy to energy and economic considerations. India also began to use UN Resolution 242 as a new benchmark for Indo-Israel rapprochement.

COVERT DIPLOMACY AND INTELLIGENCE COOPERATION BETWEEN INDIA AND ISRAEL DURING COLD WAR

After the creation of Research and Analysis Wing (RAW) in 1968, India opened up lines of communication with the Israeli Mossad and thus began intelligence cooperation. The RAW officers in Geneva acted in collaboration with Mossad and collection of intelligence on Pakistan and thereby began a new phase of cooperation, albeit low in tone. In August 1969, the Al Aqsa mosque in Jerusalem witnessed a fire. The mosque is the third holiest site in Islam after Mecca and Medina. The Arab states blamed Israel for lack of protection of Islamic sites and Saudi King Faisal called for the convening of an Organisation of Islamic countries (OIC) Conference. The criteria were that only countries that have Muslim majority population or a Muslim head of State would be able to participate. Pakistan long used the OIC as a forum to propagate anti-India feelings related to Kashmir. India decided to participate in the OIC meeting planned in Rabat in September 1969. With no official invite coming despite an expression of interest by India, India insinuated that the OIC had been neglecting the interests of Indian Muslims. India also lobbied with Egypt and Indonesia, who convinced Faisal to allow an Indian delegation to allow the representation of minority Muslims of India. Pakistani President Agha Muhammad Yahya Khan decided to walkout of the Summit on 23rd September since India had garnered the support of Algeria, Egypt, Sudan and Libya. Morocco and Saudi Arabia convinced Yahya Khan to attend the last session after it was agreed that India would not be a part of last session. The final declaration by the Islamic Muslims condemned Israel for its actions. The issue caused public embarrassment for India but the government tried to justify its participation asserting the need to block Pakistan from using the OIC for its anti-India propaganda. The Arabs again stood by Pakistan in the 1971 war and showed inadequate appreciation of the refugee crisis India faced. In contrast, Israel supported India and recognised Bangladesh. The factional group called Fatah was one of the most radical groups, which began to gain popularity for its aggressive stance to Israel. In 1969, the leader of the Fatah, Yasser Arafat, became the head of the PLO and began to vouch for an armed struggle against Israel. The Arabs continued to support the aggressive tactics of the Fatah, which now dominated the PLO.

CHANGING DYNAMICS OF INDIA AND ISRAEL RELATIONSHIP AFTER YOM-KIPPUR WAR

On 6th October 1973, as the Jews were busy celebrating the holy festival of Yom Kippur, Egypt, Syria, Jordan, Iraq and Libya attacked Israel. This took Israel by surprise, but with support of the US, Israel succeeded in defeating each Arab participant in the Yom Kippur War. Subsequently, the Arab countries of OPEC imposed an oil embargo upon the US. The efforts of the Nixon administration led to the lifting of the embargo by 1974 but also caused an upward spiral of oil prices. For the first time, the global financial balance of power tilted in favour of the Middle East. The US responded domestically with Project Independence (a project for energy security) and also decided to use the comfortable situation to advocate for peace. Post the oil embargo; PLO also shifted its original maxima list position of advocating for liberation of Palestine under Israeli control to advocating the two states theory. It pressed for the creation of Arab Palestine in the Gaza Strip and West Bank. In 1973, when the Yom Kippur War started with Egypt and Syria attacking Israel, India blamed it on Israel, citing its refusal to vacate territories captured in 1967 as a cause of Arab frustration, leading to aggression.

BIRTH OF HAMAS AND INDIA'S HAMAS POLICY

The US in 1978, invited the Arab nations for talks at Camp David. The PLO rejected the call for talks organised by the US. However, Egypt, led by Sadat Anwar, responded positively and went ahead with the talks. The Camp David Talks of 1978 led to the Israel–Egypt Peace Treaty and Egypt agreed not to use violence against Israel while Israel agreed to more autonomy for Palestinians, with the possibility of sovereignty in future. However, the Arab world and the PLO denounced the Israel–Egypt rapprochement. In 1979, the Soviets invaded Afghanistan and all Arabs condemned it. India did not condemn the Soviet invasion owing to proximate ties with Soviets but to prevent ostracisation from Arabs, India immediately granted full diplomatic status to the PLO and allowed it to establish a diplomatic mission in New Delhi. In 1980, Indira Gandhi came to power. When Israel objected to Indian criticism of Israeli attack on Iraq in 1981 and Lebanon in 1982, the Israeli counsel Youssef Hassen, who had criticised India, was expelled. This again took Indo-Israel relations to their lowest point.

However, in the second half of the 1980s, India witnessed a change in political leadership as Rajiv Gandhi was elected as the Prime Minister of India on 24 December 1984. Rajiv Gandhi, educated at Cambridge University, signalled a fresh Indian approach towards Israel and though unable to reverse the traditional Indian pro-Arab foreign policy completely, initiated a number of moves in favour of Israel. He also held a meeting with Shimon Peres, his Israeli counterpart, at a UN session in 1985. The PLO was based in Lebanon. When Israel attacked Lebanon, the PLO's headquarters moved to Tunisia. In 1985, Israel bombarded the PLO offices in Tunisia. India condemned the Israeli attacks. In October 1985, the UNGA session began. The Arabs sponsored a resolution for seeking the expulsion of Israel from UN. India abstained at the vote. Later, India allowed an Israeli Vice Counsel back in Mumbai. Rajiv Gandhi, in 1987, allowed the Israeli Tennis team to play in India at the Davis cup. This event became a diplomatic move much appreciated by Israelis who, since 1960s, had not been granted visas by India to attend sports events. Later the government allowed the Israeli consulate to have jurisdiction over

Kerala. Despite a breakthrough at Camp David talks with Egypt, there was no big achievement overall as the PLO did not participate while Israel refused to give effect to the UN Resolution 242. The frustration amongst Arabs for their failure to make Israel vacate territory and the intense disenchantment in Palestinian people led to the first Intifada. The first Intifada culminated with rise of Harkat-al-Muqawama al-Islamiya (HAMAS), led by Sheikh Ahmed Yassin.

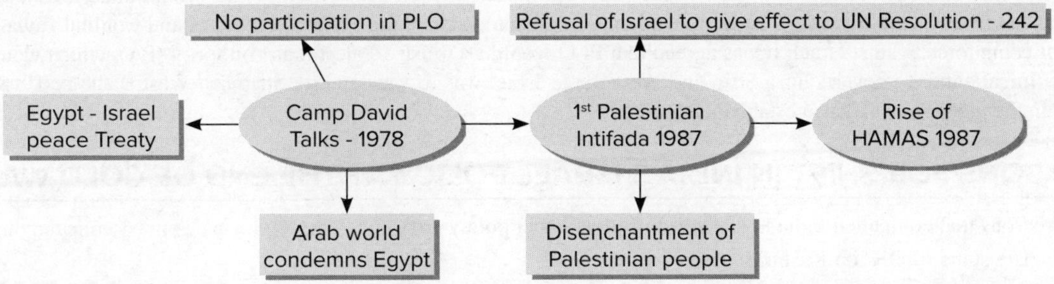

HAMAS emerged as an organisation in Gaza Strip and vowed to eliminate Israel by force. At this time, the response of the Fatah was different and it proposed that as an organisation, its focus would remain on establishing the Arab Palestine in Gaza Strip and West Bank.

INDIA AND ISRAEL DIPLOMACY AT THE END OF COLD WAR

After the assassination of Rajiv Gandhi, the Congress staged a comeback, with Narsimha Rao as Prime Minister. Rao formed the government in a coalition and was not constrained by the Muslim vote bank politics of the INC. In 1990–91, Rao steered the Indian foreign policy based on regional and domestic developments. In 1990–91, there were internal divisions in the Arab world related to the Gulf War. In the Kuwait crisis, PLO supported Iraq while Arabs supported Kuwait. Saddam Hussein too sided with PLO to position himself as a leader of the Palestinian cause. The support of PLO to Iraq led to isolation of PLO in the Arab world. Domestically in India, the economy needed a push and the USA was the only country that could give India the needed financial muscle. India understood that the US financial assistance is tied to India opening up its relationship with Israel.

POST-COLD WAR POLICY OF DE-HYPHENATION BETWEEN INDIA AND ISRAEL

Since 1987, Pakistan had been using the US-trained Afghan Mujahedeen's to create unrest in Kashmir. India began to suppress this externally sponsored insurgency in Kashmir; Pakistan successfully used the OIC forum to internationalise the Kashmir conflict by highlighting the human rights violation by India in Kashmir. OIC even decided to send a fact-finding mission to Kashmir, which was strongly protested by India. India asserted that Kashmir was an internal conflict of India and OIC had no jurisdiction on an internal issue related to India. India felt that its pro-Arab policy during the entire Cold War did not serve any strategic support to India for Kashmir. On 23rd January 1992, in a cabinet meeting, discussions on diplomatic relations with Israel were undertaken. In July 1992, India extended the consul relations to full diplomatic relations and Ephraim Duek presented his credentials to Indian President as the first Israeli Ambassador to India. India asserted that there was an economic logic to India's improved ties with Israel. India wanted to use the scientific and technical expertise of Israel for its domestic development. The change happened in 1992 because Narsimha Rao was convinced that a rehaul of our West Asian engagement was long due. The domestic political repercussions no longer guided our policy now. The realisation that India can gain from security relations with Israel by engaging strategically, also acted as a factor. As the Cold War ended with the disintegration of the Soviet Union in 1989, the US emerged as a superpower. In 1991, the US invited the Arabs again at Madrid as a follow up to the Israel–Egypt Peace Treaty. In the Madrid conference in 1991, Israel, Jordan, Lebanon, Syria and some influential Palestinian people participated, although the PLO had not been invited as a representative of the Palestinian people. The only success of the Madrid Conference was the Israel–Jordan Peace Treaty. Syrian insistence on reclaiming Golan Height delayed the Syria–Israel truce. Israel did propose, however, that it would hand over Golan Heights back to Syria if Syria concludes a Peace Treaty. The talks with Lebanon in Madrid could not proceed as Iran exercised influence on Lebanon, through Hezbollah. The US followed up the Madrid talks of 1991 with the Oslo Accords in 1993. For the first time in the history of the Middle East crisis, the US succeeded in bringing Israel and the PLO at a common platform for talks. HAMAS continued with its military position and therefore was not a part of Oslo talks. The Oslo talks saw the 'Land for Peace' proposals. It was decided that Israel would undertake a phased withdrawal from Gaza Strip and West Bank while the PLO would accept the existence of Israel and would do away with idea of using force against Israel. It was agreed that PLO would establish a Palestinian Authority (PA), which would act as a political entity to govern Gaza Strip and West Bank. Israel was to vacate Gaza Strip and West Bank by 1998. The PLO, in the meantime, had also established the PA.

REASONS FOR SHIFT IN INDIA'S ISRAEL POLICY AT THE END OF COLD WAR

Core reasons that compelled India to make a shift in its Israel policy are:

1. The stand of OIC on Kashmir issue.
2. Internal divisions within the Arab world on the ongoing Gulf war.
3. Jordan (Madrid Conference 1991) and Egypt (Camp David Accord 1978) had already signed a peace treaty with Israel.
4. PLO and Israel initiated peace talks in 1993 in Oslo leading to the tectonic Oslo Accords.
5. Indian economy needed a push from the USA, which made financial assistance as a precondition to rapprochement with Israel.
6. India needed a defence partner (which the USA eventually became) after the disintegration of the Cold War and demise of the USSR.
7. China too gave diplomatic recognition to Israel at the end of the Cold War prior to West Asia peace talks, thereby making a shift in its own policy of the Cold War.

FROM LOW OCTANE RELATIONSHIP OF INDIA TO STRATEGIC PARTNERSHIP WITH ISRAEL

Narsimha Rao opened up diplomatic relations with Israel but preferred to have a low-level engagement, which analysts attribute to the Congress government's desire to not compromise Muslim votes. He allowed only two cabinet ministers of his government to travel to Israel. The government resorted to a cautious approach of allowing the private actors and bureaucracy to be used to clearly identify areas where both would cooperate. India also clarified there was no change in Palestine policy and India would continue to support Arabs in the Palestine issue. Indian government instructed J. N. Dixit to make a case to Ambassadors of Arab states about India's Palestine policy. Dixit asserted to the individual diplomats that India expected reciprocity from Arab states in cases of issues pertaining to Pakistan. Post-1991, India decided to embark upon a journey to focus on self-reliance in military technology. In this context, Israel became a core partner for India as it had vast experience in the Military Industrial Complex it had established in collaboration with the West. Israel had technology, which they had developed indigenously and therefore was not bound by End User Licensing Agreements (EULA). Israel too expressed willingness to work with India through joint ventures. Though the relationship between the two states did pick up, but remained short of a genuine strategic partnership. After 1991, as India adopted the policy of diversification in defence industry, it began to forge a new alliance with Israel. Israel not only had a large military–industrial complex but through arms support in 1962, 1965 and 1971, had proven its mettle. Moreover, the disintegration of the Soviet Union and Indian defence industry's reliance on Soviet equipment became a factor since Israelis had developed special skills in upgrading Soviet era equipment. Thus, both defence and economic ties between the nations improved. Even though a strong case was made for defence deals with Israel, the Indian government decided not to publicly talk about the same. In 1998, when the BJP came to power, there were high-level visits from India by L. K. Advani (Home Minister) and Jaswant Singh (Foreign Minister) to Israel. The rise of a right wing government in Israel by 1998 created an issue. In 1998, the

Israeli government refused to vacate Gaza Strip and West Bank (as per Oslo Accord 1993). Subsequently, Israel's PM Ariel Sharon visited the Al-Aqsa Mosque in Jerusalem (the third holiest site in Islam after Mecca and Medina) and this move provoked the Palestinians. This provocation manifested as the second Intifada in 2000. The second Intifada caused heavy violence in the region again.

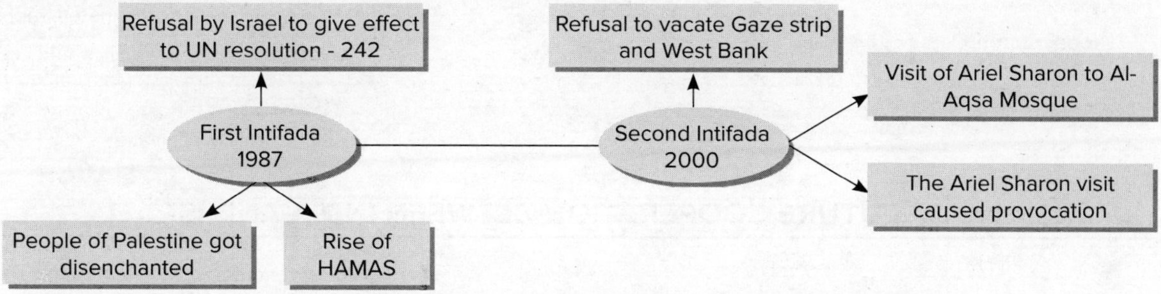

STRATEGIC DEFENCE DIPLOMACY BETWEEN INDIA AND ISRAEL

The volatile situation came under control in 2003 when Ariel Sharon announced the Disengagement Plan. Israel agreed to vacate Gaza Strip and West Bank by 2005. However, in 2004, Yasser Arafat died and was succeeded by Mahmoud Abbas. In 2005, Israel vacated Gaza Strip and West Bank and elections were organised on behalf of the PLO. Both PA and the HAMAS decided to contest elections. The US and its allies extended their support to PA in the election. As the results of the election were announced, it stunned everybody as HAMAS won the election in Gaza Strip while Fatah won a few seats in the territory of West Bank. This sowed the seeds of subsequent Fatah–HAMAS conflict. In 2007, after Saudi Arabia brokered negotiations, HAMAS and Fatah formed the National Unity Government (NUG) where Khaled Mashal led HAMAS and Mahmoud Abbas led PA. The violence still continued due to ideological differences. The NUG collapsed in June 2007, after which the HAMAS took control of the Gaza Strip while the Fatah took over the control of West Bank. As Fatah enjoyed the support of the US, in 2014, it succeeded in making Palestine a non-member state of the UN and in 2015, a member state of International Criminal Court. Hamas as an organisation continues to deploy military tactics and remains committed to eliminate Israeli military. In December 2016, the US abstained at the Security Council resolution related to a resolution sponsored by New Zealand on the settlement issue in the Palestinian territory. This was the first time in the history of creation of Israel that the US, instead of supporting Israel, abstained from a resolution and came down heavily on Israel. However, Israel since 2007 has been trying to illegally occupy territories in Gaza Strip and West Bank and has been creating 'settlements' in these lands. This illegal occupation of territory is a violation of the Hansell Memorandum and Geneva Conventions. The Trump Administration in 2020 has supported Israel in illegal occupation of these lands. This is primarily an attempt by Trump to appease the Jewish lobby in the US prior to US elections. Biden has followed a hands off approach till date.

Negev Summit 2022

In recent times, there has been a concerted attempt by the Sunni world to patch up ties with Israel. In May 2022, UAE, Morocco, Egypt and Bahrain held a summit with Israel in a resort in Negev desert. The Sunni world and Jews are collaborating now to tackle the rising hostilities unleashed in the region by Iran.

INDIA'S POLICY WITH PALESTINIAN AUTHORITY AND HAMAS

The Indian President visited Israel in October 2015 in the first ever Head of State level visit to Israel. The President was honoured by Al-Quds University and was hailed as the 'Knight of Peace'. He decided to strengthen cooperation in agriculture, defence and technology sectors. There were MoUs in avoidance of double taxation, culture, academic and student exchange.

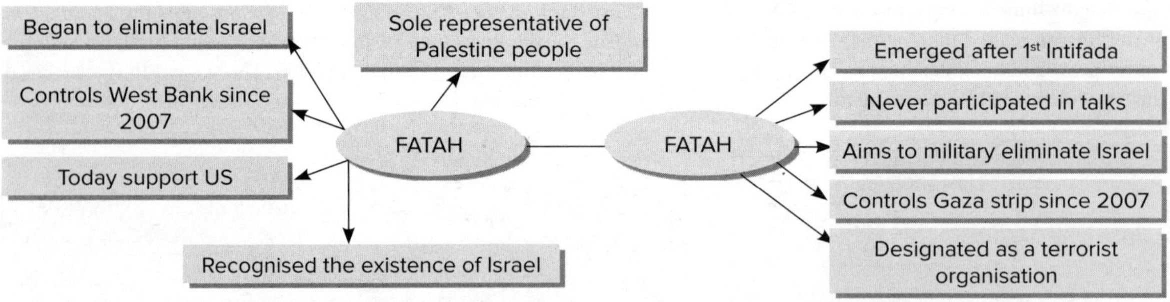

DIMENSIONS OF FUTURE COOPERATION BETWEEN INDIA AND ISRAEL

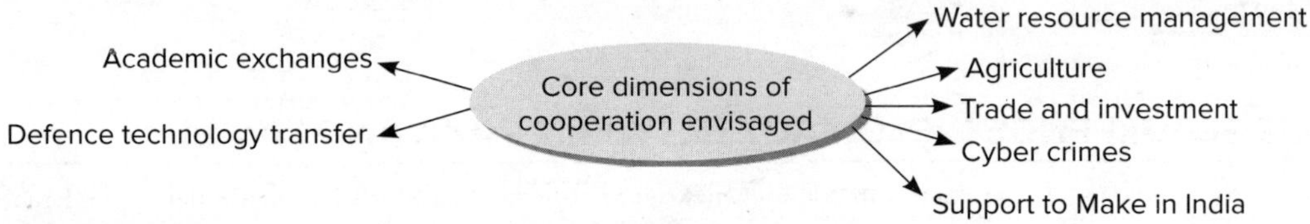

HISTORICAL ASPECTS OF INDIA'S PALESTINE POLICY

Since the Indian National Movement, India has been positively inclined towards Arabs and India has rejected Zionism. India believed Zionism is a colonial movement of the Jewish people to try and eventually colonise Palestine. India did not harbour any negativity towards Jewish people, but it rejected the ideology of the Jewish people to colonise Palestine. After India became independent, India recognised the creation of Israel at the UN, yet extended no diplomatic relations with Israel. In the 1956 Suez crisis, India blamed Israel for escalating conflicts. After the 1967 war, India favoured the UN Resolution 242 and advocated that Israel should vacate the territory captured in the 1967 war. In 1974, India allowed the PLO to establish an office in New Delhi and also accepted the PLO as the sole representative of the Palestinian People. In 1981, Yasser Arafat paid a state visit to India. In 1988, India recognised the state of Palestine and opened a representative office in Gaza Strip, which in 2003 was shifted to the city of Ramallah. Post the Oslo Accords of 1993, India has supported the Fatah or the PLO or the PA. India does not support the HAMAS. In 2011, India supported the membership of Palestine to the UNESCO. The Representative Office of India in Ramallah started issuing Visas since 2013. In 2018, Narendra Modi was the first ever-Indian PM to visit Palestine state.

MODI DOCTRINE ON PALESTINE AND INDIA'S POLICY SHIFT

Since 2017, there is a subtle shift in our policy for Palestine. The shift was visible from the fact that when Modi visited Israel, he did not visit Ramallah. The first sign of a change in the policy by Modi was seen in 2015. In 2015, at the UN Human Rights Council vote against Israel on war crimes in Gaza, India abstained along with Kenya, Ethiopia, Macedonia and Paraguay as the resolution related to International Criminal Court, to which India is not a signatory. In 2017, Modi government announced the new policy of India towards Palestine by making a statement that India supports

- Sovereign
- Independent
- United and
- Viable Palestine
- Co-existing peacefully with Israel

This statement, which is highly loaded, has far reaching implications on the way India now looks at the issue. India has always supported an independent and a viable Palestine. The concern is with respect to the word called "United Palestine", announced by India for the first time. The United Palestine involves Gaza Strip and West Bank territory. The unification of Palestine has not happened because Gaza Strip is still occupied militarily by HAMAS. Internationally recognised Palestinian Authority, led by Mahmoud Abbas, controls the West Bank. By advocating for a United Palestine, India has collided with Israel that today advocates for a one state solution (in contrast to the two state solution, which India too favours) that is an Israel without Palestine. This is where the catch lies. The major shift has been made silently by India with respect to East Jerusalem. Till now, India had always asserted the need to have a sovereign Palestine state that will have its capital at East Jerusalem. On various past occasions of diplomatic engagement with Palestinians, India asserted East Jerusalem should be the capital of Palestine state. This is surprising because the UN Security Council too never mentioned till date that East Jerusalem would be the capital of Palestine state.

INDIA'S NEW EAST JERUSALEM POLICY UNDER AND MODI DOCTRINE

The Modi government made the silent shift. During Modi's meeting with Mahmoud Abbas in 2017, the statement made a mention of a united Palestine with no mention of East Jerusalem as the capital. The change in Indian policy on East Jerusalem has to be seen with respect to India's policy shifts in UNESCO over East Jerusalem. East Jerusalem is an area with intense historical, theological and political contestations. The major contestation in the East Jerusalem is with respect to claims by Islamic states and Israel. Jerusalem is a holy city with Mount Moriah and Mount Zion (collectively known as the temple mount, located in the Eastern part of the city of Jerusalem) being the two most crucial mounts in the history of humanity. According to the Jews, in 957 BCE, King Solomon built a temple on the temple mount. The Babylonians destroyed the first temple. In 516 BCE, Zerubbabel built the second temple on the ruins of the first temple, which was eventually sacked by the Romans. Many years later, Umayyad clan (a Muslim rule) decided to superimpose the Al Aqsa Mosque and Dome of rock on the ruins of the second temple. The objective of the Umayyad clan was to assert the Islamic supremacy over the non-Islamic lands. Since then, as the time progressed, the Christians, Jews and Muslims have made contesting claims over the Eastern part of Jerusalem. Historically, one thing is clear is that the Temple Mount is a Jewish site. Islamic states assert that the area of East Jerusalem belongs to the Muslims. The Jews, however, make a contesting claim that the East Jerusalem historically had two Jewish temples built and the area belongs to the Jews. India feels that these claims and counterclaims need to be archeologically identified and resolved through mutual respect, negotiations and accommodation. In 2016, in UNESCO, 58 Members endorsed a resolution that exclusively endorsed Islamic narratives and out rightly dropped any reference to the Jewish temples. The resolution declared that the Temple Mount is an Islamic structure. Ironically, in the 2016 resolution, India voted against Israel. This led to massive protest by Israel on the Indian decision. There is a belief that the Indian decision was done by the foreign policy bureaucracy that was rooted in the historical legacy of support to the Palestinians against Israel. However, with the intervention of the PMO, when the similar resolutions were taken up in 2017, India abstained from the vote. The decision to abstain was a clear signal of the shift in Indian policy towards East Jerusalem. Since then, till today, India asserts now that India stands by a united Palestine (with no reference to East Jerusalem as the capital). What began in 1992 with Rao calling it 'balancing' between India and Israel is now de-hyphenation by Modi.

MIND MAP

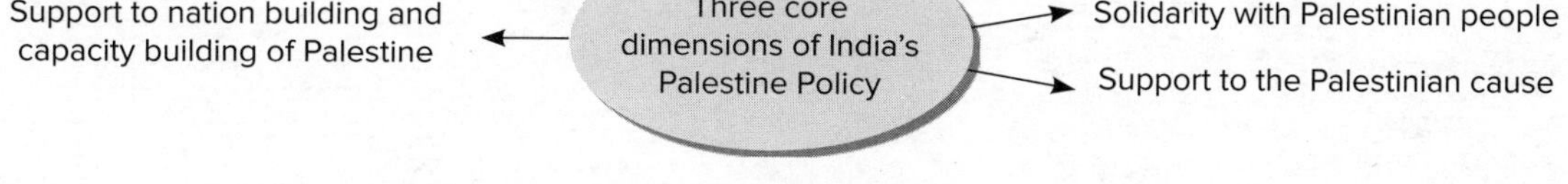

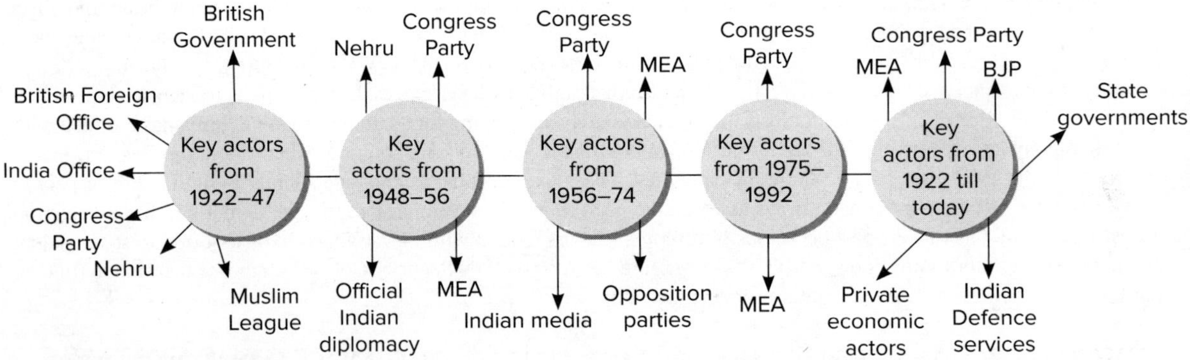

QUESTIONS FOR PRACTICE

S. No.	Questions for Practice
1.	How does India seek to gain from Saudi Arabia's Vision 2030? What are the options for India in energy and strategic defence partnerships? Do you think Saudi Arabia must cease India–Pakistan hyphenation for win–win partnerships with India? Examine.
2.	A strong partnership is taking shape between India and Israel. Examine how it can change India's stakes and status in West Asia.
3.	By skewing its policy towards Saudi Arabia in pursuit of short-term goals, India runs the risk of antagonising Tehran. Do you think India needs a balanced West Asia policy?
4.	As Gulf jobs and remittances decline, India must re-orient the Look West Asia policy to attract investments from the region. Examine the statement in the light of instability in West Asia and opportunities for India.
5.	The joint statement of India and Israel during Prime Minister Modi's visit reflects changed geopolitical realities on India's Palestine Policy. Examine.

SECTION 8

India's Relationship with Southeast, East Asia and Indo-Pacific

AN OVERVIEW

This is one of the most important areas from where questions are regularly asked by the UPSC. The questions are of two types. Firstly, we have bilateral questions on India's relationship with Vietnam, Japan and Australia. Secondly, we have questions that relate to India's participation in QUAD, Indo-Pacific, ASEAN, ASEAN Regional Forum, Asia-Pacific Economic Forum and its trade and security interests in South China Sea and Pacific Islands Forum.

Potential foresight In the recent times, India has deepened its presence in this part of the world through FTA with ASEAN, participation overtly in Indo-Pacific and QUAD. The Act East Policy and India's military dimensions of diplomacy through Malabar and Milan are visible. The author is certain that this area will continue to be important in the years ahead.

CHAPTER 1

India's Idea of East: From Antiquity to the Cold War

INDIA'S EASTWARD ENGAGEMENT: CORRECTING THE PROBLEMATIC NARRATIVES

For long, amongst the historians, diplomats and research scholars, there has been a feeling that India has not adequately engaged with the countries in the region of Southeast Asia and East Asia. The narrative was strengthened by certain Indian diplomats using the documents of Indian Ministry of External Affairs, thereby endorsing this criticism. Such a criticism is unwarranted because there is no rhyme or reason that actually explains India's neglect of the region. However, there may have been disruptions in India's diplomatic engagement, but in this section we will learn that these disruptions were not unilateral but were driven by factors not in India's control. A common understanding is that Indian interests in the region arose in 1990s when India announced the Look East Policy. This is a misplaced notion because the engagement is more than two millennia old and India, in reality, has never stopped looking the East. The matters of neglect were highlighted when President Obama, in 2010, told the Indian Parliamentarians that India needed to engage with the region more actively and Look East was not creating the zeal that was expected of India. This avoidable intellectual provocation hit India's long cultural and civilisational connect since antiquity and was used again by the academic community to assert that India was in an era of disruption. The then UPA government ignored the advice of Obama and the subsequent Modi government implicitly endorsed the American narrative by changing the Look East Policy with Act East Policy (we will elaborate both terms and analyse later in the section).

The purpose of re-writing the entire section of India's relationship with Southeast and East Asia in this edition of the book is to correct the perceptual narratives and offer the civil services aspirants the story of India's eastward engagement from antiquity till now. The narrative of this section is designed to help the readers understand that the phases of low-key engagements were explained because of India's British colonial experience and subsequent economic inability to sustain the vitality and vigour in the relationship after independence. Also, the period of the Cold War brought in a host of ideological factors that constrained Indian engagement since the end of the Cold War. India deepened the outreach and displayed a new enthusiasm. This section will also carefully analyse if changing the name from 'Look' to 'Act' East Policy has brought about any radical shift in the way India looks at the region or not.

THE LAND OF SUN WORSHIPPERS: THE IDENTITY BINDING INDIA AND EAST

India is a land that worships the rising sun. This worship is ingrained in Indians since the Indus Valley Civilisation. As per this rationale, India has always looked at the East with a sense of reverence and devotion. Because the sun is not just seen as a source of light but energy that drives life. India has integrated this relationship into its cultural and civilisational philosophy. The importance of sun as the centre of human philosophy was subsequently nurtured by the Vedic literature where the four Vedas talk about different energies and virtues of sun. The Sun Temple at Konark on the east coast of India is a testimony of how the reverence of the sun is institutionalised in India. The health system that India stands for, Yoga, also has a series of postures where the human body bowing to the sun in the form of Surya Namaskar. The civilisational and cultural diffusion is explained by adoption of Hinduism and Buddhism in countries of Southeast Asia. The process of cultural diffusion that began in the first millennium of the Christian era continued non-stop till the seventh century. The coming of Mughals did not stop the cultural diffusion but only slowed down the momentum of the process because even during this period the trade and voyages did continue. In fact, during the Mughal period, the Indian people on Indian coasts acted as intermediaries in spread of Islam to the East. The South Indian Muslims, especially from the region of Malabar, played an important role in taking Islam to the region. The Islam that got transferred to the region was a version that adopted coexistence with Buddhism and Hinduism, as visible in Indonesia and Malaysia even today. The British are responsible for introducing a strategic factor in India's relationship with the East. The spirit of engagement that India had nurtured during the pre-colonial era was now replaced by territorial expansion consolidation and control of the British. This was accentuated by the use of Indian natives in the British army to fight the French and Portuguese in the region. The use of Indian soldiers by the colonial army distorted the idea of India in the perception of the East and added a military dimension that never existed till date. The perception of India was dented again when Subhash Chandra Bose demanded liberation from British by joining hands with aggressor Japan during the World War II.

TRANSITIONS IN INDIA'S ENGAGEMENT AND RISE OF THE INDO-PACIFIC THINKING

After independence, the security threat from Southeast Asia to India never dominated Indian policy discourse. A minor hiccup was seen in 1965 when Indonesia had threatened India that it would block Indian access to Andaman and Nicobar islands. This was because Indonesia displayed an overt tilt to Pakistan during the war and the move was driven primarily by an Islamic identity, imposed by Pakistan on India via Indonesia. In the 1980s, another hiccup was visible when an Indian naval officer made a statement that India should aspire to become a blue-water navy (a naval force that has capabilities to do power projection in foreign waters). The statement was perceived as aggressive by Australians who thought that India could not be given the liberty to dominate a huge swath of waters of Indian Ocean. However, the controversy died out soon because India neither had financial capacity nor had an aggressive design for any neighbour in the East. Contrary to such scares, Lee Kuan Yew, the head of Singapore was quite favourable for a role for India in the East in security realm. He advocated that not only India offer security training to the armed forces of nations of the region but also wanted India to develop capabilities to stand up to China. India did not respond to the initiatives of Lee because it was not interested involving in regional disputes of the region as it had always followed the policy of non-intervention and non-intrusion. However, when the Cold War ended, India's economy embarked upon a path of expansion and Indian foreign policy acquired a new strategic vision. The future discourse was set by India through the Look East Policy and later by the Act East Policy.

The India's idea of the East has expanded to include a new thought called Indo-Pacific. The idea of Indo-Pacific was first visualised by the India's first Prime Minister Jawaharlal Nehru. In his book 'Discovery of India', he mentioned that Atlantic in future would not be more relevant and Pacific Ocean would take the place of Atlantic Ocean. In this context, Nehru asserted that India would have adequate influence to exercise in the region and Indian Ocean once it would develop economic prowess. This would allow India, stated Nehru, to position herself as an economic and strategic player in the development of world. Building on Nehruvian though, it was in 2004 that the Indian Maritime Doctrine had proposed the idea of shift from Atlantic–Pacific to Pacific–Indian Ocean region. This idea of Indo-Pacific was raised for the first time by Shinzo Abe, the Japanese Prime Minister in 2007. Abe was inspired by the book written by Aurangzeb's brother Dara Shikoh titled 'Confluence of Two Seas'. He envisaged the need for India and Japan to come closer by forging a geostrategic space of Indian Ocean and Pacific Ocean to create Indo-Pacific as a new geostrategic reality. Today, India looks at Indo-Pacific as a geopolitical construct that offers a new vision of world order where there is unbridled commitment to build confidence, resolve disputes by following international law, promote peace and ensure security and growth for all. The Chinese have not perceived the concept in a positive sense.

What is meant by Indo-Pacific?

Indo-Pacific is a driver of global politics that replaces the old concept of Asia-Pacific where Indian and Pacific Oceans are seen as a seamless link to promote trade, growth and well-being of humanity by ensuring the protection of sea lanes of communication. As an operational concept, it links the Indian Ocean and Pacific Ocean, the two dynamic oceans of the future to sustain global growth.

There has been no official response by Chinese of the concept but the Chinese academia has debated the concept and has found it vague, underdeveloped and an idea driven by the West to contain the rise of China in the region. In any case, the Indo-Pacific is seen by India as a cultural, economic, political and security continuum that stretches from Indian Ocean and Pacific Ocean with common opportunities, intersecting maritime and security interests and challenges for the region. Today, the term Indo-Pacific is given enormous strategic weight in official circles and the government in India looks at the term rooted in historical and civilisational experiences of India and an emerging geostrategic reality. The expansion of culture of India into Pacific world is a grand chapter in the human history. In 2017, India initially hesitated to embrace the concept when Donald Trump, the then US President, proposed the idea in modern avatar. This was because India had reservations that by accepting the American definition of Indo-Pacific, it would strategically become close to the US and this would cost India her 'strategic autonomy'. However, since then, India had shed off these concerns because when India introspected, it found that the concept of indo-Pacific was rooted in its own cultural and civilisational past and had been nurtured by its long historical traditions. Indo-Pacific for India is a new powerful instrument for cultural and strategic diplomacy and India now openly embraces the idea of a shared vision for maritime cooperation in the region.

SEVEN WAVES OF INDIA'S ENGAGEMENT WITH SOUTHEAST AND EAST ASIA

When we analyse India's engagement with the region, we can distinctly fit it into seven phases.

Phase	Distinct feature
First	Hindu–Buddhist influence
Second	Islamic influence
Third	British era and national movement
Fourth	Nehruvian era
Fifth	Post-Nehruvian era
Sixth	Look East Policy era
Seventh	Act East Policy era

The first and second waves offer a fascinating picture of India's cultural engagement that has left a deep imprint on the region. In the first phase, we observe the relations going back to the pre-historic era. The history is more distinct from the second century AD where we find names of Indian kings commonly used by kings in the East. This period also sees a distinctness in practices related to religion, customs, manners and language (with Sanskrit having an impact on their languages even today). A great amount of royal patronage was provided during this time to keep up the trade and cultural engagement. The Mahayana Buddhism, dominant in the region in Korea, Japan, China and Taiwan, till date uses Sanskrit for religious texts and rituals. Empress Wu in China took steps to even promote Buddhism as a 'state religion' in the seventh century. The significant contribution of this phase was that it manifested in emergence of world class centres of learning, as seen in Nalanda and Vikramshila universities. The Cholas played an important role in adding a strategic dimension to India's engagement with the East. In 1050 AD, the Chola king Rajendra Chola, as per an inscription in Thanjavur, used a powerful navy deployed in the Andamans to challenge the might of Sri Vijaya rule in the East and after defeating him, established Chola power in the Malaya peninsula. This is a proof of how Indian kings not only explored and navigated the Pacific islands but also dominated the region with display of hard power. However, the Islamic phase was different from the first phase in the sense that it was devoid of any royal patronage. This period saw Indian rulers becoming obsessed with north-western borders considering that the primary threats arose from the region. This led to a reduced vision for Southeast and East Asia. Even though Akbar had an impressive navy, but the navy was designed to deter Arakanese and Portugal from Myanmar and Indo-China. With rise of Muslim rulers in India, two things happened. Firstly, the state patronage for promotion of Buddhism and Hinduism was replaced with patronage for Islam. Secondly, the Muslim rulers did not stop the ongoing cultural and economic engagements with the region but trade was relegated to common people than state. The third phase saw British designing the imprint colonially while the actors of national movement countering the British thought with India's civilisational legacy. The third phase was interesting because it offered a glimpse of how contrasting waves, working with different objectives and even led by different actors, contributed in leaving an imprint. The British, as explained previously in the chapter, used the native Indians to suppress the societies in the East. They used the British Indian capital in Calcutta till 1911 to develop colonial and strategic presence in Southeast Asia. In this sense, the Indians were gradually perceived by people of the region as local tools of oppression. So, when the British took labours from India to work in plantations in colonies in the East, the labours were seen as an alien community and a threat to the local poor strata of the colonial society. This has had a repercussion till today because the Persons of Indian Origin (PIOs) living in the East till date are looked as outsiders. The British awakened the strategic dimension that was initially created by Rajendra Chola. During the World War II, India was exposed to an invasion from Japan and this Japanese invasion opened the eyes of Indian national movement leaders on the importance of Southeast Asia as a maritime compact. It was during this British period only when the nationalist leaders of India established a direct contact with political leaders of the region. Dr. Sun Yet-Sen, Nehru, S. C. Bose, Chiang Kai Shek, Gandhi, Sukarno and Mohammad Hatta had frequent deliberations. The Congress often passed resolution against the use of British force in colonising Southeast Asia and this allowed Indian leaders to open a parallel yet diametrically opposite engagement with the region. The most important individual who played the crucial role in India's eastward engagement during this period was Tagore and he often emphasised the cultural and civilisational links between the regions. On the 2nd April 1929, Tagore even wrote a poem 'Lamp of East' in the Korean newspaper 'The Dong-A Ilbo'.

THE NEHRUVIAN WAVE AND INDIA'S EASTWARD IDEA: HOPES BELIED

The two core drivers of Nehruvian thinking in the East were India's civilisational and cultural connect with the East and Nehru's passion in struggle against colonial oppression. He designed a vision for Asia which was not only free from colonialism but also was resurgent, culturally homogenous and politically harmonious. On the basis of the context of national, regional and international political realities of the time, the Nehruvian thinking for the East can be seen in three layers. The first layer is the period before Indian independence. In this period, Nehru as a leader of Indian national movement witnessed not only the two world wars but also anti-imperialistic struggles in Asia and Africa and these events enabled Nehru to articulate his vision of foreign policy. These events were followed by imprint of India's civilisational legacy on Nehru which enabled him to use the historical linkages to support anti-colonial and anti-imperial struggles in the region. This is why when Nehru participated in Indian participation in Brussels International Congress Against Colonial Repression in 1927, he announced that India, on attaining independence, would leave no stone unturned to assist the countries of the region in their struggle against imperialism. In 1936, a foreign department was established within the Congress to reach out to states in the East and grasp their situations. In 1945, Indonesia, during the World War II was under the Japanese control declared independence but it was neither accepted by Britain nor by Dutch. The Dutch in fact tried to re-colonise Indonesia compelling India to take the matter to the United Nations. At the UN, India linked the colonialism of Indonesia by Dutch as a security threat to Asia. Nehru stated that if colonialism continued to linger on in the region around India and other nations of Asia, they would have no freedom to carry out independent foreign policy. This led India to equate the independence of Indonesia as a case for security of Asia. The UN intervened and ensured in 1949 that Indonesia was not colonised and became independent under the leadership of Sukarno and Mohammad Hatta. Sukarno visited India and called Nehru as his political father and Indonesia decided to become a non-aligned state, but with an open economy, and worked for maintaining peace and equilibrium in Asia. The success of India and Indonesia eventually led to the birth of the Bandung Conference in 1955. In this conference India was able to champion the idea of decolonisation and independence of states. The conference also marked the zenith of India's multilateral diplomacy and was a grand success of India's eastward diplomacy. This conference was also seen by Nehru as a launching pad for Indian vision of Asia in world affairs.

Nehru's Enthusiasm and Indonesia

Nehru was very enthusiastic in letting Indonesia organise the Bandung Conference. He went into minutest of the details in organisation of the mega event. While micro-observing the preparations for the conference, Nehru told his counterpart that adequate provision of bathrooms and lavatories is essential in any mega event. While Indonesia was prompt to take the instructions of Nehru seriously but they were slightly uncomfortable on the remarks because they saw the remarks as a reflection of their inability to organise an international event. It is stated that Sukarno did not communicate the discomfort upfront but felt humiliated.

INDIA AND INDONESIA RELATIONS: FRIENDS TURNED FOES

Even though the Bandung Conference is seen as a positive event, ironically India and Indonesia turned out to be the biggest losers. There are several reasons attributed for this. Firstly, the Western countries were certainly not comfortable in seeing a rising Asian solidarity as they found this solidarity as an upfront threat to their world view. Secondly, the Western media deliberately tried to highlight the internal differences amongst Asian leaders in the conference. For instance, during the conference, Sri Lanka insisted that countries of the East Europe were under the colonial rule of Soviet Union. This definition of colonialism was in sharp contrast to the definition of colonialism Nehru promoted because he wanted to advocate a generic condemnation of the Western colonialism. Eventually, the conference agreed to 'condemn colonialism in all its manifestations and forms' as a trade-off; a narrative picked up by the Western media. Even though the Western nations had tried their level best to keep China out of the conference, but China did participate. The participation of China was an opportunity for China to cultivate their relationships with Southeast Asians. After the Sino-Indian conflict of 1962, Chinese used a narrative that Indian arrogance was responsible for the conflict and they used this narrative to build their relationship with Southeast Asians while pushing India down in its desires for a role in Asian leadership. Thirdly, post-1962, the Southeast Asians became uncomfortable with both India and China because they perceived that these Asian giants were trying to vie for supremacy in the region. This compelled them to shed off engagements with both and explore regional minilaterals and thus ASEAN (Association of Southeast Asian Nations) was born in 1967 as a consequence.

After the Bandung Conference, India's relationship with Indonesia also began to get adversely affected. For instance, India and Indonesia began to have differing perceptions on their territorial identities. The Indonesians were upset that Dutch decided to chip away West Papua, which was a territory that Indonesia claimed. While India asserted that West Papua belonged to Indonesia, it added a caveat that Indonesia should resolve the territorial dispute of West Papua as per wishes of people in a peaceful manner. After the Bandung Conference, Indonesia was keen to organise another version of the Afro-Asian Conference. However, Nehru was non-committal in letting Indonesia organise such a conference because the Afro-Asian Conference of 1947 was designed to seek decolonisation of Asia and Africa only. By 1955, Nehru had conceptualised non-alignment and was not keen on limiting the participation only to Asia and Africa but also wanted participation from Latin America and Europe. Indonesia perceived the lack of interest of India in the second Afro-Asian Conference as a softening stand of colonialism and imperialism. In Belgrade Conference in 1961, Nehru articulated that colonialism was 'not an immediate threat'. This assessment was made by Nehru because the world was under the Cold War and was witnessing great power rivalry which was taking the world on the brink of a nuclear confrontation. For Nehru, the Belgrade Conference in 1961 was an opportunity to portray non-alignment as a balancer to the rising tensions of the Cold War. Nehru also was not very comfortable with the rising political crisis in Indonesia where Sukarno had proclaimed himself as the 'president for life' as this was perceived by Nehru as a great setback to democratic and federal credentials that Indonesia committed earlier. The India and Indonesia relations began to lose warmth and reached their lowest ebb in 1965. Even during the 1962 conflict with China, Malaysia became a competitor to Indonesia. Indonesia remained neutral in 1962 but Malaysia, led by Tunku Abdul Rehman, decided to support India and even created a 'Save Democracy Fund' and contributed one million rupees to India. This was perceived by Indonesia as a direct challenge and threat for regional power play.

THE LIGHT OF ASIA AND THE GREATEST FIGURE IN ASIA

The second layer of engagement began from 1947 till mid-1950s. This was a phase when India established relations with the East as an independent nation. This was the time when Winston Churchill, the British Prime Minister, described Nehru as the 'Light of Asia' and asserted that Nehru would now play and important role in promoting dignity and freedom of the people of the East. The Nehruvian policy in Indonesia as seen above got him the title of 'The Greatest Figure in Asia'. During the second layer, India's engagement was now built on three paradigms. The first was the Asian Relations Conference of 1947 where extensive personal interactions were done with political leaders. Secondly, the paradigm focused on getting freedom for Indonesia, Burma and the region of Indo-China. Thirdly, there was focus on ensuring that peace and stability was promoted in the region at a time when the Cold War had arrived deep in the East. The third layer was from mid-1950s to 1964. In this period India, being a non-aligned state, was picked up by the UN to resolve the crisis in Korea. The crisis in Korea had begun in 1950 when the northern Korea invaded Southern Korea to unify the Korean peninsula. The attempt of North was seen by the US as an attempt to impose communism, leading to the US stationing troops in South Korea. On behalf of the UN, India as head of the UN established Korean Commission, peacefully negotiated a settlement between the conflicting Koreas and a boundary was drawn in 1953 as the 38th parallel. In 1954, South Korea and the US signed a mutual defence treaty and became allies while the North drifted towards communism and embraced China. While Philippines became independent in 1946, India became independent in 1947, Burma in 1948, Indonesia in 1949, Malaya in 1957 and Singapore in 1965; all these nations were vulnerable with respect to their external security. They all had to focus on economic restructuring and financial stability to promote growth. This was the time when India decided to use non-alignment to keep the states away from the politics of the Cold War. The things took an unfortunate turn due to Sino-Indian conflict in 1962. The nations of Southeast Asia were in a state of shock and disbelief to see violence used by India and realised that something had gone drastically wrong in India's diplomacy that things reached this level. The change in the perception of Southeast Asians was understandable. This was so because many of the Southeast Asian nations, if not all, after independence had gravitated to adopt a capitalist economic model. Although they were ideologically and personally attached to India, their economic models were at contrast. Also, by early 1960s, the nations of the East were discussing on coming closer to establish an economic platform to deepen their economic ties with each other and also with the rest of the world. This economic platform eventually was born in ASEAN in 1967. The Sino-Indian conflict of 1962 came as an egg on the face for India's eastward engagement because there was a loss of reputation for India and countries became worrisome of hegemonic ambitions of China, thus compelling the nations of the region to look at both India and China in a negative sense. In assessment, Nehru tried to fight colonialism in the East but the roots of colonialism were way too strong for him to realise his vision of Southeast Asia. The intra-Asian rivalries were exploited by the leaders of the Cold War politics and India's lack of economic and military prowess prevented it to play a significant role, thus allowing the Cold War players to immerse themselves with ease. Thus, the factors that Nehru was subject to in realising his dream were international and regional factors and they were beyond his control. The Sino-Indian conflict of 1962 was the final nail in the coffin that ripped apart the diplomatic profile that India had nurtured. Nehru eventually left a legacy that his successors had to now pursue under different circumstances.

AFTER NEHRU: DID INDIA GET DISCONNECTED IN EASTWARD ENGAGEMENT?

In the previous discussion we saw that while Nehru was one of the chief architects of the modern Indian engagement with Southeast and East Asia but his dream to shape the dynamics of the region the way he wanted were belied. While India was successful in building a narrative of decolonisation in the region, it could not succeed in the narrative of Asian solidarity because there were external cold war factors that hindered India's dream. In the period that followed after the death of Nehru, India was not able to re-connect with the region with the same vigour but also was not completely detached from the region. It did try to remain in touch with major players in the region and continued to react to important developments in the Indo-Pacific. The India–China conflict of 1962 and demise of Nehru in 1964 ultimately ended the era of world politics where foreign policy was dominated by the Prime Minister. The subsequent period after Nehru was followed by internal political struggles. Initially, Lal Bahadur Shastri succeeded Nehru but his tenure was short lived. India at the time of Shastri had faced two full-scale threats from its neighbours and the country was in a state of food insecurity. After the death of Shastri, Indira Gandhi succeeded as the Prime Minister but the senior leaders of the Congress formed a 'syndicate' and tried to develop their own hold over the party and the government, something not amenable with Indira Gandhi. The ongoing internal political struggle led to a split in the Congress in 1969 and eventually Indira Gandhi emerged victorious. Once the internal political struggles were controlled, India now devoted energies under the leadership of Indira Gandhi at the foreign policy level. The first few years of 1970s helped India regain confidence. The successful dismemberment of Pakistan in 1971, peaceful nuclear explosion by India in 1974 and merger of Sikkim in 1975 came dominant foreign policy achievements of the regime. Indira Gandhi and later Rajiv Gandhi continued to engage with Southeast and East Asia based on same principles and tenets as laid down by Nehru. After the death of Nehru, the strategic community in India was now keen to identify countries that supported or sided with Pakistan in the India–Pakistan war of 1965. Singapore was identified as a nation that supported India and same was the case of Malaysia. The tilt of Malaysia towards India was perceived negatively by Pakistan which decided to sever its diplomatic ties with Malaysia but renewed them when Reza Shah Pahlavi of Iran acted as a bridge between Malaysia and Pakistan. During this period, Thailand and

Philippines remained neutral while India was deeply irked by the change of stance by its most trusted friend, Indonesia. The Indonesian leadership had been paying multiple visits to Pakistan before the 1965 war and had been comforting Pakistan to wean Kashmir away from India. Indonesia went to the extent of sending secret missions to China to provide Pakistan with military assistance. Indonesian navy chief even stated that Andamans were an extension of Indonesia and India had no right to claim the islands and to put military pressure on India in 1965, even decided to block the access of India to the islands. India realised the rising strategic triangle of Jakarta–Rawalpindi and Beijing and understood the rising security threat that this new strategic triangle could pose. It is important to note that Indonesia displayed such a behaviour owing to certain reasons. Firstly, Indonesia was not comfortable with India's support to independence and formation of Malaysian federation. Secondly, Indonesia and India relationship had been deteriorating post-Bandung Conference and the 1965 was the final nail in the coffin.

THE TRIPOD TO QUAD AND INDIA ON POWER VACUUM THEORY

In this backdrop, Indira Gandhi and Rajiv Gandhi decided to conceptualise an approach towards the East with five key drivers. Firstly, the idea was to offer resistance to great power interventions and military groupings in the region. While offering strong resistance to the Cold War players in the region was an outcome of Nehruvian thinking; the situation now was different. Now, the US and the UK were on a withdrawal mode from the region and there were rising fears that China could step in and fill the vacuum left. Intellectually, the scholarly community began to articulate that as the US and the UK retreat, the space in the Southeast and East Asia should not be filled by China but by India, Japan and Australia. It is interesting to note that this tripod that was being argued for the region of Indo-Pacific saw a manifestation of the Quadrilateral Security Dialogue (QUAD). India was not immune from the discussions regarding the power vacuum theory but was clear that it would not be keen to join any military-centric alliance for regional security. India had categorically rejected the power vacuum theory and stated that it would support any endeavour which focused on nationalism, regional economic cooperation and building of strength and capabilities. India placed a lot of emphasis on nationalism because it stated that the European had to shun colonialism in Asia and Southeast Asia not because of any altruism or caprice but because of rising presence of Asian nationalism. This is why India asserted that this power vacuum theory was nothing but a continuation of colonial outlook by the West in another garb. In 1968, in her visit to Southeast Asia, India offered a nationalistic narrative in contrast to the power vacuum theory. It stated that the Southeast Asians and Indians must come together to forge a common understanding on regional cooperation and economic development and growth. India was not in favour of any security or military dimension in regional cooperation because it explained that India was already busy with its own troubles by its neighbours. It stated that it has already deployed its troops in managing its own boundaries and any deployment of forces outside its immediate territory would not only weaken its own defences but also unnecessarily provoke others, thus creating greater tensions in the area when India was striving for regional peace.

INDIA'S REGIONAL COOPERATION STRATEGIC THINKING AND INDIA'S ASEAN DILEMMA

In the above framework of mind, India decided to approach the idea of formation of ASEAN in 1967. It is important to note that ASEAN was not the first grouping that the Southeast Asians tried to materialise. They had tried to make unsuccessful attempts earlier and Association of Southeast Asia (ASA) was one in 1961 and the other was Malaysia, Indonesia and Philippines (MAPHILINDO) Federation in 1963. However, in 1967, Indira Gandhi sent Indian Foreign Minister on a tour to Southeast Asia. During his trip, the Minister officially outlined India's thinking and he stated that India would be happy to open trade and commerce-centric cooperation with Singapore, as demanded. Also, India would be happy to support a regional economic cooperation initiative if other states wanted and even clarified that India would also be equally satisfied in staying out if the other states did not demand so. In any case, India asserted that it had no interests in dominating any regional grouping. The Southeast Asian nations in 1967 were witnessing subversion by communist China and very visibly upset at such interference. India was almost in a dilemma on how to welcome the creation of ASEAN because the founding members had come together to create a group that was only for non-communist states. Though India happily shared the value of peace and stability that ASEAN stood for, but it failed to articulate an effective response because India knew that ASEAN was being backed by the Americans and any attempt by India to align itself during the Cold War with

ASEAN could damage its credentials of non-alignment. The reason why India was actually in a dilemma was because India wanted the US as a power in the region as the US was the only effective bulwark against the subversion of China, but being proximate to Soviet Union, India could not officially take such a stand publicly. Even if we look within ASEAN, Indonesia, which was one of the founding members of ASEAN was not keen to have India as a member because it saw India as a rival in its own regional ambitions which it wanted to materialise in ASEAN. In this backdrop, when ASEAN was officially formed in August 1967, there was no invitation extended to India. India's idea of a regional organisation was very different. Firstly, India in 1960s had accepted that regional cooperation was not a remote idea anymore. This was quite contrast to India's stand on regional cooperation because since Nehruvian times, India had a firm belief that only a global platform like the UN would significant in a turbulent post-World War. Secondly, India in 1960s clarified its own vision of how it saw regional cooperation. After accepting the idea of regional cooperation as a diplomatic necessity of the times, India clarified that a regional grouping should complement development in the member states, engage on basis of mutual benefit and equality and not have any political undertones or military undertones. This was significant because India was not keen on having a grouping that would emerge with camp follower leanings or become satellites of bigger power. Thirdly, in reference to ASEAN, India stated that it would welcome a broad-based regional grouping that would have economic and developmental agenda as core binder and would prefer the name to be 'Asian Council' or 'Council of Asia', as that would imply a more inclusive meaning. This point was significant because India wanted to, in a subtle way, discourage an American-backed ASEAN and were in favour of recasting ASEAN as an inclusive grouping. In 1973, ASEAN created ZOPFAN or Zone of Peace, Freedom and Neutrality and this, to some extent, did reduce India's dilemma if relating itself to ASEAN because the ASEAN through ZOPFAN tried to position itself as an organisation independent of American thinking. By ZOPFAN, the ASEAN also effectively asserted a greater independence from the US, dominance of the Chinese and displayed opposition to any form of military approach for regional security. India showed tremendous appreciation for the ZOPFAN initiative of ASEAN because the idea was in sync with Indian efforts to establish a zone of peace in Indian Ocean. While India definitely did not succeed in achieving its version of ASEAN during the Cold War, but when the Cold War ended, ASEAN eventually expanded, added communist nations, autocratic nations and conceptualised the East Asia Summit (EAS) as a regional grouping. All these developments in ASEAN since the end of the Cold War added credibility to India's approach in the long-run and enabled the members of ASEAN to deepen engagement with India effectively since the end of the Cold War. In essence, one can assert that India's idea of regionalism and sub-regionalism was based on common interests that would bring people together. India never envisaged regionalism which contradicted nationalism or internationalism but supported any instrument of regional diplomacy which came up as a genuine and legitimate instrument of cooperation. After all the ups and downs, India, as seen with respect to its ASEAN diplomacy, was well-placed in the Indo-Pacific region after the death of Nehru. India's regional cooperation diplomatic posturing and its ASEAN policy helped India consolidate its bilateral relationships with Singapore, Vietnam, Japan and South Korea during the Cold War. With Rajiv Gandhi trying to normalise relations with China, the stage was set for India to take advantage of the regional economic dynamism. When the Cold War ended, India was ready to integrate with region economically and strategically.

CHAPTER 2

Streamlining and Restructuring India's Eastward Engagement and India's Look East Policy

THE CHANGE OF FOREIGN POLICY DISCOURSE AND MYSTERY AROUND LOOK EAST POLICY

In the previous chapter, we have analysed that India's engagement with Southeast and East Asia, after the death of Nehru had become ad hoc, reactive and unfolding in a differentiated manner based on a country-wise approach. Since the end of the Cold War, India's eastward engagement was given a new direction under the term Look East Policy (LEP). While the term LEP was credited to Narsimha Rao, the larger concern was on how did the term come into usage? There were different schools of thought that explained the different originations of LEP. One school of thought argued that the term was used in 1992 when Southeast and East Asia found a new presence in the discourse of Ministry of External Affairs. This view was even endorsed by the then Secretary in the Ministry, A. N. Ram. However, a considerable scholarship argued that the term LEP was used by Narsimha Rao when he delivered a lecture in Singapore on 8th September 1994 and since then began the articulation of the term. This school argued that the term LEP was eventually used in the annual reports of the Ministry of External Affairs of 1995–1996 and this was a justification that Rao brought about this shift in the orientation in policy thinking. At this juncture, it must be mentioned that when Rao delivered his lecture in 1994 in Singapore, he never used the term Look East Policy. The absence of usage of such a term and its subsequent use in annual report of the ministry the next year again created a mystery on who actually coined the term. The former foreign secretary of India, Salman Haidar, gave his own opinion. As per his argument, the term LEP was a cut-off slogan that was devised by ministry officials for the visit of Rao to South Korea in 1993. He argued that when the Prime Minister visited Seoul, there was a need felt in the ministry to have a catchy phrase that would give a distinctive focus to his journey to Southeast and East Asia and set the visit to the region as a pioneer visit, in contrast to other visits around the globe. In this view, the term LEP was thus a deliberate inversion of long dominated westward direction of Indian policy making.

ECONOMIC CONTEXTUALISATION OF LOOK EAST POLICY

The LEP was brought in during the 1990s and this period saw uncertainties and anxieties because of rapidly changing global and domestic environment. Globally, the Soviet Union had disintegrated, the Cold War came to an end and the military-bloc politics that had dominated the international discourse came to an end. The onset of globalisation presented the Southeast Asian economies as the new rising jewels of the region. While the ending of the Cold War did open up new opportunities for the Indian foreign policy, India also had constraints in managing the post-Cold War world order because India was now left with only a unipolar US. India, during the Cold War, with its tilt towards the Soviet Union, saw a shrinking global environment. In this sense, it was imperative for India to redefine not only the old strategic relationships but also discover and identify new friends. Domestically, India was witnessing economic and political crisis. The foreign exchange reserves of India were depleting at a time when the country was politically unstable. The wave of globalisation was gradually weighing heavily on the inward looking Indian economy and India was in dire need of economic reforms, which were eventually initiated by Manmohan Singh, the then Finance Minister of Rao government. In pursuance of this domestic situation, India decided to go for opening up its economy and seek investments, trade support and technology to boost economic growth. The LEP, in this sense, had been seen by many scholars as an economic initiative that would be a driver of India's own economic growth. However, this is not true because the LEP was not just driven by economic considerations but also strategic considerations. Let us examine how the strategic considerations drove the LEP.

STRATEGIC LEANINGS OF INDIA'S LOOK EAST POLICY

The next bigger challenge for India was China. China, since 1949, had a closed economy and followed communism. In 1979, the Chinese began to change their orientation and started to tilt towards capitalism. The various factors attributed to the shift in the Chinese outlook were a part of discipline of world history and beyond the purview of this book, it was imperative to note that one of the core factors was power. The Chinese and Soviet Union were locked in a perpetual power contestation since 1950s and the contest was that who would be the leader of the communist world. While the Soviet Union wanted to assert their supremacy in leading the global communism, the Chinese felt that they were frontrunners for the same. This power contestation eventually led the Chinese to come out of the embrace of communism and join hands with the US during the Cold War. In 1970s, the Chinese joined hands with the US and tried to checkmate Soviet by drastically increasing their own power. Since 1978, when China was led by Deng Xiaoping, the state made a turn towards a capitalist-based growth model. The Americans were eager to assist the Chinese because initially they thought that if Chinese were supported, then the Americans could weaken the Cold War by checkmating Soviet. Secondly, the Americans aided the Chinese growth because they were of the belief that in the long run, the Chinese would eventually embrace democracy in the future. However, the only thing that eventually happened was that the Chinese hugged the Americans tightly, took out all capitalist support, enhanced their economic and military power to the extent that they developed global power ambition to now undercut the US as the sole superpower in the world. When the Cold War ended, the biggest challenge for India was not just on how to adjust in a world which was a unipolar world led by the US but also how to adjust to an economically powerful China in the neighbourhood and an economically assertive China in the region. The third worry for India was the growing military relations between China, Pakistan and Myanmar. India was of the belief that there appeared to be a deliberate attempt by the Chinese to militarily arm India's neighbours as this would allow Chinese the space to keep India bogged down in regional affairs while having a clean space to explore for global power ascendency. The countries in Southeast and East Asia were also alarmed to see the rise of China and were concerned that the Chinese were likely to resort to aggressive posturing in the region in future. In this backdrop, the smaller countries in the region such as Philippines, Vietnam, Singapore and Malaysia decided that they must open up deeper engagement with India as they believed that India can be an effective regional strategic option. Thus, India, during the Cold War was not perceived as a prominent player in the region by many was now seen as a player that could strategically balance the power equations in the region. Thus, a clear analysis helped us to understand that LEP was not just economic but also had strategic overtones. The compulsion of the government to announce the LEP was a comprehensive and systematic approach which was nothing but a continuation of previous approaches. The LEP was, in this sense, a re-casted and redefined thinking as per new and emerging trends in strategic environment. Thus, the strategic impetus to the LEP was driven by three factors, the rise of China, its attempt to militarise India's neighbours to bog down India regionally and transformation of ASEAN states to use India as a balancer.

How did India Strategically Manage China under the Look East Policy?

Since 1988, when Rajiv Gandhi paid a visit to China, the successive governments, even though at times with different political complexions, have tried to manage Chinese through a coherent strategy. India has tried to maintain peace and tranquillity with China while engaging with other countries in Southeast and East Asia to strengthen its economic and strategic profile. India has ensured that it strived for balancing rivalry and always used incentives for good behaviour with China. The hardest task in Indian diplomacy in managing Chinese has been to carefully articulate balance as it manages the competition, cooperation and rivalries.

ARTICULATION OF INDIA'S LOOK EAST POLICY: FUSING STRATEGIC AND ECONOMIC DIMENSIONS

With the changing domestic and international environment, India now embarked upon the role of establishing relations in the East on a firm footing. The cognitive thinking of Narsimha Rao was driven by two factors. Firstly, Rao wanted that

India's domestic economic situation must improve and for this, building an economic engagement with the world in general and the Southeast and the East Asia was imminent. Secondly, Rao wanted to ensure that India had a multi-dimensional level of engagement with the East and this manifested in the thought that India would engage at the multilateral level (meaning India would deepen engagement with ASEAN) and bilateral levels with the Southeast and the East Asia. India was very keen to open up engagement with ASEAN because it was inspired by their model of development and were keen to emulate the economic policy, procedures and delivery systems of ASEAN. However, India was also very clear of the thought that investing strength in the bilateral relationships in the region with mutually beneficial content would advance India's policy. This is why Rao decided to place a significant interest in engaging with Indian diaspora, not just in the Southeast and the East Asia, but also abroad. Rao placed emphasis on engaging with influential Indian community which comprised of Indian intellectuals and academicians, which today under Modi government have been broadened to include the Indian public at large. In 1994, when Narsimha Rao addressed a lecture in Singapore, he made it clear to articulate the relevance of the region for India. He began his lecture by stating the economic reforms India had domestically undertaken and reforms that were envisaged. He explained the gathering that their investments in India were not only help the money grow but their investments would help a billion Indian people to grow. Narsimha Rao tried to link the economic investments with social investment because he stated that if Indian people grow, then these people would act as a force of stability in Asia-Pacific. The facts also justify the thinking envisaged in the LEP. From 1991 to 1994, approximately 20% of the total foreign investment that flowed into India came from the region of Asia-Pacific. India decided to utilise majority of the investments from abroad to create infrastructure, which would become fulcrum of India's growth story. Thus, India was not just positioned as a vast market and a reliable partner but the involvement of investments in Indian development story were to usher in a renaissance of a great and noble civilisation. It is equally important to note that the LEP was well aware of the strategic challenges that were likely to arise in the region of Asia-Pacific. India clearly articulated that while the Cold War had ended, the Cold War attitude still persisted and the persistence has nothing to do with inevitability of such thoughts but the fact that removal of such thoughts was a time taking process. India was aware that once the US became a unipolar power and Chinese rose in Asia, the region of Asia-Pacific was likely to witness a new confrontation. The confrontation would no more be ideological in the post-Cold War because the Cold War had dismantled the ideological diaphragms. But the confrontation would be over the new centre of economic gravity, that is Asia-Pacific. In this sense, India articulated under its LEP thinking that the region would witness challenges pertaining to security of waterways, piracy, navigational challenges, disputes over colonial islands, maritime zones and resources. This is because these disputes had existed in the region historically and they had been defused many times but never dispelled and were likely to reoccur. In this backdrop, India had clearly articulated that the nation would also play a crucial role in maintaining peace, security and stability. India also clearly mentioned that in no way India was asserting that it would have any expansionist role in the region and nor would like to alter regional security. This is because India's sole concern was to focus more on its regional defence, Indian Ocean region, but not shy away to exercise a prominent role in global affairs if needed. It is important to note why India had to make a statement to clarify that it had no expansionist mindset. In 1971, during the India–Pakistan war, the US tried to intimidate India by sending a nuclear-powered aircraft carrier, USS Enterprise, in the Bay of Bengal. The Soviet was effectively able to defuse the existential crisis upon India during the course of war but the event had set alarm bells ringing in Indian security establishment. An immediate need was felt, after the war, to rebuild Indian naval forces.

Maharaja Diplomacy

In 1992, India sent the former Maharaja of Jaipur to court the Sultan of Brunei. This is because both the individuals had a close rapport and India wanted to use the personal proximity as a bridge between India and Brunei. The Maharaja reached Brunei and often played polo matches with Sultan and build up a bridge of oil diplomacy between India and Brunei.

Why Myanmar became the Fulcrum of India's Look East Policy?

Myanmar, in 1990s, was transitioning to democracy but the Tatmadaw acquired power. This led the Chinese and Pakistanis to court the Tatmadaw. The Pakistanis began to supply arms to insurgents in Indian Northeast from Myanmar while the Chinese established listening posts to keep a check on India's military movements in Northeast. In this backdrop, India realised that cooperative and congenial relationship with the Tatmadaw was essential not just for India's outreach to the Southeast and the East Asia under the LEP but also to effectively manage India's internal security concerns in the Northeast. India thus adopted a new Myanmar policy which was based on two fundamental thoughts. Firstly, it would extend moral and political support to the supporters of democracy in Myanmar; and secondly, it would envisage a relationship with the military regime, thereby accepting the new geo-political realities and yet maintaining a value-based foreign policy.

India embarked upon massive naval modernisation and this had raised suspicions in the Southeast Asians who thought that India was developing a naval force with an expansionist mindset. This, however, was never the case. India only wanted a naval force that would secure its own regional defence and wanted to engage with other nations without endangering anyone's security. The role envisaged by India would always be devoid of any military alliance or multilateralism but one where India would be able to determine its own destiny, its own national interests and ensure international consensus on matters that confront the world. India's estimation of strategic challenges in the Asia-Pacific region were apt and today, in the 21st century, the region is actually witnessing every challenge which India had articulated in the LEP.

THE IMPLEMENTATION OF INDIA'S LOOK EAST POLICY

The discussion above clearly helps us to understand that India's relationship with the Southeast and the East Asia improved due to various factors. The initiation of the LEP was not a knee-jerk event because the global strategic environment had a crucial role to play. The Cold War had ended, the US was withdrawing from the region, there was rising China and apprehensions amongst the regional nations of a possible Chinese dominance. In this backdrop, the regional players were also inclined to look elsewhere and India, with which these states had historical and civilisational ties since antiquity, was a crucial player to ensure supremacy of a harmonious regional balance. India was envisaged as an important player in the regional thinking. As explained, India too decided to look at the region for its growth and an attempt to expand its global footprint, which till now had been constrained owing to the Cold War. The member states in the region not only decided to work with India economically (which was a core dimension of India's national interest) but also they envisaged to work with India in the arena of security and defence interoperability (an arena of national interest of many Southeast and East Asian nations). Singapore, Vietnam, Malaysia and Laos emerged as leaders in embracing a security relationship with India and consequently a host of defence exercises, defence training and deeper security cooperation opened up. In 2004, in a significant departure from its long standing policy, India even allowed Singapore to have access to Indian training facilities at the Air Force and Army levels under the bilateral Defence Cooperation Agreement (signed in 2003). The security and defence relationships between India and the region were more intensified and institutionalised and this was over and above the deepening economic relations under the LEP. In this sense, one thing was clear that India's engagement with the East would not have been possible had the regional states not showed an equal inclination to engage with India. Thus, India's LEP can be seen to have gone through phases of exploration, articulation and pursuance of engagement. The first phase of exploration and articulation lasted till the end of the decade.

The phase of pursuance of engagement was given a new shape with the coming of the NDA government in 1998. On 29th September 2003, the Indian External Minister, Yashwant Sinha, in a speech at Harvard University explained the new phase of engagement. He stated that in the phase of exploration and articulation, India's prime focus on looking at the East was trade, investment and security linkages. He further explained that under the NDA regime, an attempt had been made to widen the definition of 'East' and the fulcrum now defined was from Myanmar to Australia, having ASEAN at the core. Sinha asserted that in this widened geographical outlook of the LEP, the focus was on not just economic cooperation but also building joint capacities to tackle emerging strategic concerns such as protection of sea lanes of communication and counter-terrorism. In this new approach now outlined, the focus was on engaging with Australia to build a regional grouping in the Indian Ocean Region. The idea of India in conceptualising such an organisation was preventive in nature. This means that the idea was to prevent any bigger power to dominate the Indian Ocean region by ensuring that India took the lead and secured its own stakes in the region. It is also important to note that counter-terrorism entered into the policy discourse of India's LEP because of the altered global security environment caused due to the 9/11. The 9/11 had brought India and the US closer at the security levels and the US had finally accepted that terrorism was a global menace, something which India had been asserting since long. Thus, by bringing the US under its embrace successfully, India tried to use the American engagement to deepen ties with American allies such as Australia, Japan and South Korea.

CONCEPTUALISATION OF THE FREE AND OPEN INDO-PACIFIC UNDER INDIA'S EASTWARD POLICIES

As the relations with the US were not just confined to economic matters but also security and defence; India decided to deepen ties with the US and develop credible capabilities to manage security in the Indian Ocean. At the security level,

India had integrated itself well with the region and it was a participating state in ASEAN Regional Forum (a platform for security and defence cooperation) and ADMM Plus (ASEAN Defence Ministers Meeting Forum). India's attempts to position itself as a Net Security Provider (see the meaning in the next sentence) have helped its evolving defence diplomacy. Under the LEP, India is today focusing on assistance and supplies of defence equipment, ensuring safety and security in the region by resorting to direct deployment tasks (meaning of Net Security Provider), resort to participation in defence exercises (with a potential for future defence sales of military equipment) and Humanitarian Assistance and Disaster Relief (HADR). The larger security diplomacy of India as visible in its LEP is driven by two factors. The first is to counter terrorism and piracy in the region and the second is to ensure that the region is free and stable for navigation. At the level of terrorism, while every nation might have differing national priorities on how to view terrorism, but there appears a general consensus that radicalisation and terrorist violence must be nipped in the bud. The countries in the region of Indo-Pacific and India have a broad consensus that freedom of navigation must remain central policy of security engagements. India is gradually working to evolve a security architecture where Indo-Pacific is free, open, plural, flexible and where ASEAN remains the bedrock.

ASSESSMENT OF INDIA'S LOOK EAST POLICY

As the LEP evolved from exploration, articulation and pursuance, one thing is clear that India was able to renew, reactivate and reinforce the relations with the Southeast and the East Asia. The intensification of political dialogue was an ample demonstration of successes achieved by India. The bilateral ties with players in the region had acquired myriad facets ranging from cooperation in diverse areas such as fisheries to defence to space technology to combating international terrorism. However, when we make an assessment of India's LEP in the region, we see that India's relationship unfolded in a way that can be described as a 'differentiated engagement'. This term means that when India engaged with the region, there were different drivers in everywhere that ranged from security, economic and strategic. Thus, a coherent engagement was not seen across the region. For instance, an assessment of the LEP tells us that India's engagement could be identified across three or four categories.

Category 1	India's engagement with the Southeast Asia region
Category 2	India's engagement with the Indo-China region
Category 3	India's engagement with the East Asia region
Category 4	India's engagement with the ASEAN region

India created a separate unit in the Ministry of External Affairs for deepening engagement with countries in the Indo-China region. The countries in this region included Cambodia, Laos, Vietnam and Myanmar. These countries were geographically proximate to India and not as Westernised as other nations in the Southeast and the East Asia. Also, these countries were closer to the Soviet Union during the Cold War and thus India had a different idea of engagement with these states. The most important gain for India in LEP was engagement with ASEAN. In 1992, India became a sectoral dialogue partner with ASEAN and identified trade, investment, tourism and science and technology as core areas of cooperation. Eventually, India progressed later to become a full dialogue partner and this enabled India to deepen cooperation in the four areas identified above. The US had worked quietly behind the scenes to enable the rise of India in ASEAN. In 2002, India and ASEAN Annual Summit was finally institutionalised and now India was able to law down new areas of cooperation, innovative delivery mechanisms and methods and accord special priority down the line with ASEAN. The member states of ASEAN found a congruence of shared interests with India. The sophisticated diplomacy of India, its regional security imperatives outlined for the Southeast and the East Asia juxtaposed the regional security environment and thus ASEAN and India became natural partners. The key to India's success in engaging with the region is its ability to persuade the regional partners that India is a non-threatening and a supportive nation. This voluntary acceptance of Indian posturing is an achievement of Indian diplomacy and this delicate fruit will require sensitive and careful nurturing in the decades ahead. India's approach to LEP is also visible in its search for institutional integration beyond ASEAN and this has manifested in Indian diplomacy in BIMSTEC (Bay of Bengal Multi-Sectoral Initiative for Technical and Economic Cooperation), Mekong–Ganga Cooperation (MGC) and East Asian Summit (EAS).

INDIA AND BIMSTEC, MEKONG–GANGA COOPERATION AND EAST ASIAN SUMMIT DIPLOMACY

The BIMSTEC was conceptualised by Thailand when they announced their Look West Policy and envisaged a connect with South Asian states to boost economic integration. The organisation, owing to political and economic factors, had not been able to perform well but India was trying to re-energise the BIMSTEC and wanted to position it as a parallel to SAARC, which apparently had become defunct due to Pakistani refusal to go ahead with initiatives of regional connectivity and abandon use of terrorism as state policy. In November 2000, the Mekong–Ganga Cooperation was formed with India representing the Ganga basin and Myanmar, Thailand, Laos, Cambodia and Vietnam representing the Mekong basin. The idea was to envisage a regional grouping which strengthens the civilisational and historical connect and harness economic potential. The other countries of ASEAN which were not members of the MGC had welcomed it because it focused on building a strong regional economic and strategic culture by emphasising diplomacy around tourism, culture, education, transport and communication. The idea of EAS was proposed in 1990 by the Malaysian Prime Minister Mohammad Mahathir in presence of Chinese premier Li Peng. Mahathir proposed creation of an East Asia Economic Group (EAEG) akin to trading blocs established by the West. It eventually concretised in 2005 as EAS when the Kuala Lumpur Declaration was finally signed. The EAS has a wide spread geographical membership and includes India, the USA and even China. The idea of inviting India and the US was of Japan and Singapore who wanted to ensure that EAS is not dominated by the Chinese. The EAS, BIMSTEC and MGC have no conflict with ASEAN and are normally seen as part of a broader regional economic and strategic architecture with ASEAN at core driving force. The trade between India and ASEAN had prospered after India and ASEAN signed the Free Trade Agreements in Goods (2009) and Services (2014) and India–ASEAN Investment Agreement (2014).

Hurdles in India and ASEAN Trade Diplomacy

Even though trade has prospered between India and ASEAN, the shortfall is attributed to a few factors. Firstly, from Indian side the biggest barrier is non-tariff barriers, procedures and trade-related paperwork. From ASEAN side, the biggest hurdle is connectivity. India must enhance the domestic business environment, reduce corruption, improve performance on rule of law, provide speedier project clearances, boost manufacturing, simply tax procedures, focus on easing FDI norms, promote awareness of its domestic cities in ASEAN states and be more flexible with Public–Private Partnership contracts.

CHAPTER 3

India's Act East Policy, RCEP Diplomacy and Stand on South China Sea Dispute

THE ACT EAST POLICY: INDIA'S SEVENTH WAVE OF EASTWARD ENGAGEMENT

In the preceding chapters we had seen that India's eastward engagement can be seen through seven waves and in that context, the Act East Policy (AEP) is the seventh phase. The AEP was announced by Prime Minister Modi on 12th November 2014 during the opening remarks of the India–ASEAN Summit in Myanmar. The Indian Prime Minister asserted that India was witnessing a new era of economic development, industrialisation and trade and in this context, the India's Look East Policy is now the Act East Policy. The Prime Minister asserted that India has decided, under the AEP, to push a great sense of priority in engaging with the East and the East Asia Summit was now identified as an important pillar in the new thinking. In this context, it is important to note that in the previous chapter we saw that India under the LEP had identified the ASEAN as a central pillar and under the new AEP, the fulcrum was the EAS. At this juncture it is equally important to note that India did not announce the AEP on 12th November 2014 but had been dropping prior hints. In 2014, prior to the India–ASEAN Summit, the Indian External Affairs Minister had travelled to Vietnam and she too had asserted that India's visit to Seoul was a part of India's intention to 'Act East'. This proposition was later elaborated by the official spokesperson of the Indian MEA when he stated that the term 'Act East' means 'Action', 'Dynamism' and 'Proactive India'. Later, the Prime Minister in the India–ASEAN Summit, officially announced the policy. The AEP was now the flagship policy of the government and India was now moving Eastward under the AEP at a wider level through a highly multi-dimensional and action-oriented policy architecture. The policy was also elaborated by the officials of the MEA in 2015–16. The officials stated that AEP was a continuum of the LEP and was now beyond the traditional dimension of ASEAN, the focus of LEP has acquired strategic, political and cultural dimensions to leverage opportunities for peace, prosperity and security. They even argued that the objective of the policy was to leave a larger Indian imprint in the region and complement the regional approaches of security with an intention to integrate their approaches to our security and strategic agendas. The policy was given three objectives namely political–security, economic and cultural diplomacy (with an aim to leverage Hindu–Buddhist links). The AEP was to drive India's deepening engagement with ASEAN, ASEAN Regional Forum (ARF), EAS, BIMSTEC, MCG and Indian Ocean Rim Association.

CORE PILLARS OF INDIA'S ACT EAST POLICY

The AEP focuses on integrating India's Northeast with neighbouring countries of the region. It intends to go beyond ASEAN centrality, which has been achieved by the LEP, and focus on the realm of Indo-Pacific by including other regional and multilateral organisations. The AEP is also not just purely commercial- and economic-centric but also intends to deepen cultural, people-to-people ties, civilisational links and more importantly, political-strategic cooperation. The hyphenation of political-strategic in the policy needs elaboration. This means that India will not only be a net provider of security in Indo-Pacific but will also set the agenda and strategy for being a net security provider at the highest political level (Prime Minister's level). This is also a reflection of how India intends to cooperate at security level in Indo-Pacific through a democratic thinking. A close look at the pillars of the AEP clearly tell us that the changes in the AEP from the old LEP are more quantitative than qualitative. This means that firstly, the only thing that the AEP has done is to focus more on continuity with a new name than bring about any thematic changes. In the previous chapter, we analysed at length how the LEP was conceptualised by Narsimha Rao with economic focus and NDA government added another layer to the LEP with a strategic focus. In fact, the two layers of the LEP had already captured the larger Indian thought on engagement Eastwards. The LEP had focused on the connectivity and people-to-people ties but never made an official statement of the same and nor did ever highlight the religious dimension. While the AEP has highlighted the religious dimension, it has focused on Hindu–Buddhist civilisational links and has ignored Islam. While it is true that Islam did not originate in India and has been absorbed in India with Deobandi, Sufi and Barelvi strands as syncretic strands; but so is the case with Buddhism, which actually originated in Nepal and not India. By omission of Islam in the AEP, some concerns have been raised and India is finding it difficult to have an all-encompassing engagement in Indo-Pacific. This is so because Indonesia, Malaysia and Brunei are dominant regional players and they feel neglected by India's AEP. The Indian Prime Minister tried to rectify the policy inadequacy by paying a visit to Istiqlal Mosque in Indonesia and Chulia Mosque in Singapore in 2018.

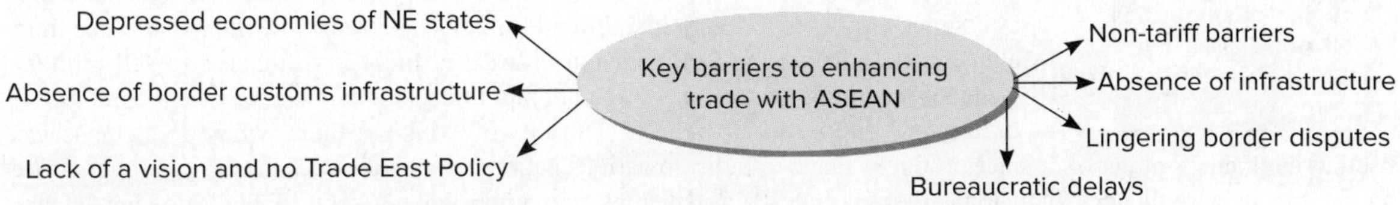

ACT EAST POLICY: NEW INITIATIVE OR RE-PACKAGED INITIATIVE?

Many Indian scholars have been trying to label the AEP as a brand new initiative of the government while some argue that the initiative is a re-packaged LEP and has nothing new to offer. While the previous analysis in this chapter does point out that there have been natural elements of continuity in the AEP, but it will also be wrong to assert that no new change was visible when India transitioned from LEP to AEP. The LEP did achieve a lot of intended outcomes but was falling short of trade and investment targets. At the levels of connectivity, even countries of Indo-Pacific agreed that India was creating a delivery deficit. In this sense, a need arose for India to reassert its role in the region and the AEP was Indian answer that outlined Indian vision to play a more constructive and meaningful regional role. The urge to change the name in 2014, in this sense, was based on a strong desire of the new government, to differentiate its foreign policy approaches from that of the predecessor governments. However, it has also been argued that the change in the name of the policy was not a major factor because there is no evidence of any systematic discussion in Indian foreign policy establishment circles for the name change. Many officials of the Indian MEA accept that there has been no beforehand assessment of implications of name change, terms of planning and discussion of policy options under the AEP. This is evident from the fact that the Annual Report of MEA of 2014–15 also argues that with AEP, India wanted to generally convey that it would have to be more active and effective in tackling the rise and assertion of China while trying to be pragmatic in concretising cooperation at political, economic, strategic and cultural levels with the Southeast and the East Asia. The period of 2014 to 2022–2023 of AEP does see an active and intensive political engagement of India in Indo-Pacific region. This engagement is driven by India's new great self-confidence where at the foreign policy level, India aspires to be a leading power and not just a balancing power. It intends to shoulder greater global responsibilities. This new approach has been even noticed by the Chinese and Chinese think-tanks have often stated that India is now more vibrant, assertive and has a higher risk-taking ability. A personal rapport is built through intensive high level visits now. Besides visits, regular discussion on issues of mutual interests have now been institutionalised. In 2016, India institutionalised the Forum for India-Pacific Islands Cooperation (FIPIC) that now constitutes a Pacific community. Secondly, there is a thrust by India to invite Singapore and Japan to create infrastructure in India's Northeast. Simultaneously, India is working with private sector to create manufacturing hubs in Cambodia, Laos, Myanmar and Vietnam. The initiatives such as Kaladan Multimodal Project and India–Myanmar–Thailand Trilateral highway have to be seen in this context. Domestically, there has been a concerted attempt to neutralise the insurgent groups and the Naga Peace Framework is a testimony to stabilisation efforts. The linking of India's Northeast under the AEP has to be seen in the larger context of regional initiatives such as Security and Growth for All (SAGAR) and India's mega port infrastructure initiative known as Sagarmala. The idea of the AEP is to link India's Northeast as a land-bridge to ASEAN and use the Indo-China nations to stabilise Northeast so that it can emerge as vibrant

How does India define a strategic partnership?

Indian concept of the term strategic partnership is not how Europeans and West normally define it. In Indian foreign policy, the term is more generically used to signify economic, political, defence, security, technological and civilisational toes. In any case, Indian conception of strategic partnership is not a formal alliance but an urge to deepen ties at a privileged level.

economic hub. Under the AEP, India is also encouraging the neighbouring countries to open consulates in Guwahati, a city which forms fulcrum of Indian AEP. In this backdrop, the government of Assam has also set up an 'Act East Ministry' at the State government level and is pursuing the objective of deepening culture, commerce and connectivity. New centres to study Southeast Asian studies have now been opened in Assam to create a new culture of academic and intellectual debate under the AEP. Similarly, at the security level, the AEP has not just continued with security paradigms and architecture created under the LEP, but also deepened and expanded cooperation in security wherever possible. India has adopted a multi-path strategy to achieve this. Firstly, it has decided to reinforce and upgrade the strategic partnerships with the countries in Indo-Pacific. Under the AEP, the strategic partnerships have been reinforced with Australia, Japan, Vietnam, Singapore and Indonesia. An important aspect of India's growing security cooperation, apart from strategic partnerships, under the AEP, is India's participation in QUAD and Indo-Pacific, as counter responses to the Belt and Road Initiative and Maritime Silk Route. The third element of India's security dimension of AEP is India's willingness to sell military weapons to Philippines in 2021 as an attempt to deepen the defence ties. A vital aspect in this new diplomacy of India is centrality of 'Make in India' where India envisages itself as a reliable supplier of defence products, made in India, to various nations, so that they develop capacities to tackle regional security challenges. India today looks at Indo-Pacific nations as an important market for India's growing defence products. The fourth element of security under AEP is India's willingness to counter-terrorism, though an element of LEP, but in a new way. Under the AEP, India is trying to look at countering terrorism by mobilising support from Indo-Pacific nations to contain the threats of cross-border terrorism and also build a larger consensus to tackle threats by jihadi tanzeems to security of India and the Indo-Pacific. This is implemented under the AEP through deepening cooperation in information sharing, intelligence sharing, law enforcement-based cooperation and building of security capacities under the existing architectures laid down by the ASEAN. In this backdrop, the fifth element is maritime security with a thrust on freedom of navigation, in general, and South China Sea in focus. At the bilateral and multilateral forums, India is now more vocal on ensuring that it is able to express concerns related to Chinese assertiveness in the South China Sea, the issue will be elaborated in the next segment.

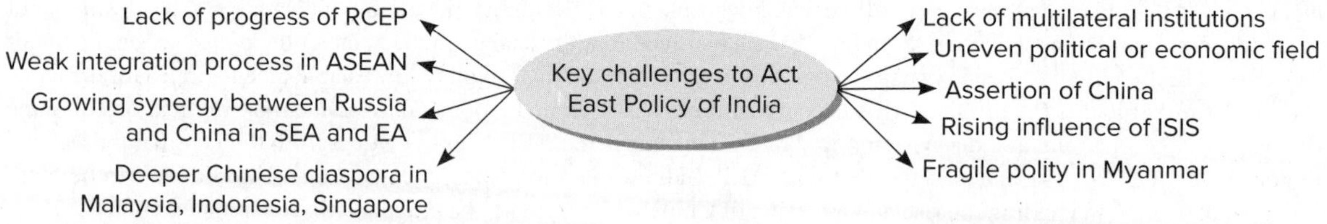

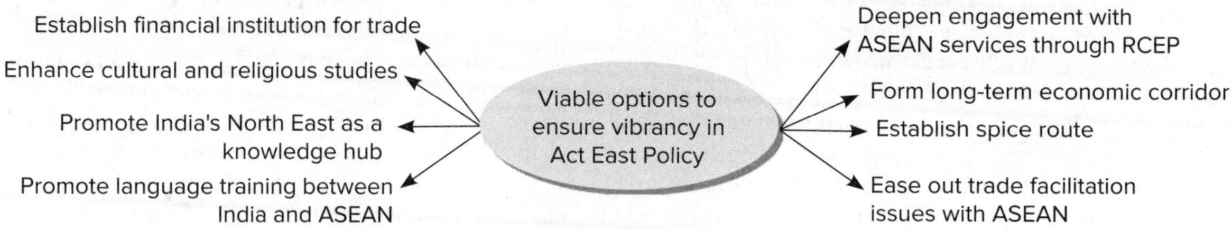

INDIA'S RCEP DIPLOMACY UNDER THE ACT EAST POLICY

One of the major thrusts of the AEP has been deeper economic integration with the region at trade and investment levels. In 2011, the ASEAN countries had conceptualised the Regional Comprehensive Economic Partnership (RCEP) and India too joined the discussions. In the same year, a framework for evolution of the RCEP was adopted by the negotiating parties. The RCEP was envisaged as a modern, comprehensive, high-quality agreement which will be mutually beneficial to forge economic partnerships by achieving a balanced instrument to boost trades in goods, services and investments. The RCEP was also an ambitious project because it decided to bring India, Japan and China on a regional forum in a single regional trading agreement that would be the largest trading bloc in the world. The RCEP was given a tremendous amount of centrality in negotiations by players of ASEAN because it was a step in realising the ASEAN economic community vision. Since 2014, India decided that under its AEP, it would negotiate in the RCEP because India would get an opportunity to expand and diversify its exports markets and become a part of regional value chains. As the agreement was about to be enforced, India decided to back out of the RCEP. RCEP was the world's most ambitious trade proposal comprising 16 states (10 members of ASEAN and 6 FTA partners). It brings together India, China and Japan, the three largest economies in Asia along with ASEAN members and South Korea, Australia and New Zealand. Once established as an agreement with sixteen chapters, it shall be the largest trading bloc in the world with a trade area covering 49% of global population and a 22 trillion USD combined GDP. It will truly make Asia the factory of the world, a genuine reflection of the Asian century. More importantly, it will address the 'noodle bowl' syndrome by reducing the overlap amongst the FTA's operating in Asia. The international multilateral trade is in flux today. The Americans who established the global trading system and nurtured the free and liberal trade today feel victims of their own creation. As the WTO remains sluggish to prove its stature, it is the regional trade agreements that have emerged a new game in the town, thus the RCEP. As RCEP is a mixture of wealthy states, large economies and low-income economies, all of which have different visions of world trade, it is indeed difficult to achieve a consensus on the basics of a free trade agreement. There has been tremendous difficulty for the states to evolve a common architecture for eliminating tariffs. The negotiations are proving difficult in areas that range from intellectual property (where India is reluctant to commit over and above the TRIPS commitments) to e-commerce. All this is because of two major reasons. First, there is mistrust amongst the member states. Second, this mistrust is enhanced due to differential economic size of the member states. At a time when the WTO is sluggish and is struggling to deliver its promises, the RCEP has a prospect to recharge the global trade and act as a 21st-century template of an inclusive group that accommodates a wide diversity of states in terms of economic strength. Broadly, India had two core objections. In general, India has a trade imbalance with China and a trade deficit with all member states. Market access and differential market access: India has a massive trade deficit with China. China is one of the core members of the RCEP. India does not have an FTA with China. So, India feared that the RCEP would give China an access to Indian markets (and an advantage in sectors such as steel, plastics, copper, aluminium, textiles and pharmacy etc.), which will further enhance the trade deficit. So, to mitigate this, India proposed 'differential market access'. Most of the RCEP members have accepted this proposal of India. Since the 2018 Wuhan Summit, China has allowed India to export pharmacy and agrarian commodities to address the trade deficit. Most of the RCEP members want India to lower the custom duties on various products and want India to liberalise its market by allowing a greater market access. India is still reluctant to open up the markets as demanded. This is because India seeks a liberalised access to the services sectors along with free mobility for the workers of India in Australia and Singapore, both of whom are reluctant. Many of the member states have often stated that India is an obstruction to the RCEP. However, such India bashing is wrong because any power will bargain hard to negotiate a deal that maximise its exports if they were to make similar concessions in imports. The conventional logic in any trade deal is that imports are a cost while the exports are a benefit. But in pure economics, the true gains a state will accrue are from imports while exports are the cost to pay for those imports. India has had many concerns with the RCEP. This is why Milton Friedman rightly stated that we can eat imports but we cannot eat exports, as once shipped out, they are not consumable. An analysis of India's negotiating behaviour suggests that our negotiators are concerned that a larger access of China to Indian markets will widen the trade deficit. However, it is important to note that Indian concern here is a good bargaining chip that can be used to seek better access to Chinese markets, but such a chip should not become the guiding behaviour of Indian policy. It is always important for a state to export its products to states that offer a higher price and import from partners that offer products at a lower price. Such a strategy is bound to create an imbalance in bilateral trade. It is this logic India needs to keep in mind while it negotiates the RCEP. The deal will allow multinational enterprises to have large-scale movements in India. The large-scale of labour pool coupled with a huge domestic market would be an inducement for the multinational enterprises to set up production bases in India, thereby giving a flip to the 'Make in India'. It will be beneficial for these multinational enterprises, as through production bases in India, they would get market access to the larger RCEP. Firstly, the free movements of inputs with no tariffs will make the multinational enterprises doubly competitive. Though India has made liberalisation of services and free movement of IT workers a key issue; India needs to remember that its services exports will have a limited market in the RCEP states because of language and cultural barriers. These are things that surprisingly a free trade agreement cannot overcome. Secondly, if India makes these two issues as make or break deal issues, it will undermine the larger benefits India stands to accrue from the deal in the manufacturing sector, which anyway has lagged behind in Indian economic development story. India needs to think of itself as a major production base that shall supply the larger products to the vast markets of RCEP states.

Reasons why India pulled out of RCEP

- Inadequate protection against the surges in imports and a fear that China might flood Indian markets.
- India wanted an auto-trigger mechanism that would enable India to raise tariffs on products in case imports crossed a certain threshold, but the demand was rejected.
- India was unable to seek credible assurance over use of non-tariff barriers by states as such barriers prevent the growth of Indian exports.
- Rules of origin in trade mean criteria used to determine the national source of a product. India wanted certain measures to check possible circumvention as certain countries try to route products from states where India would maintain higher tariffs.
- India also could not get a favourable base year that would be used to reduce tariffs on products that would be traded as a part of the deal.

THE SOUTH CHINA SEA DISPUTE AND INDIA'S STAND ON THE ISSUE

In 1949, when the People's Republic of China was born, they began to issue passports to their citizens. In these passports, China on the background showed a map. In this map, China showed the Mainland China and some islands in the South China Sea (SCS).

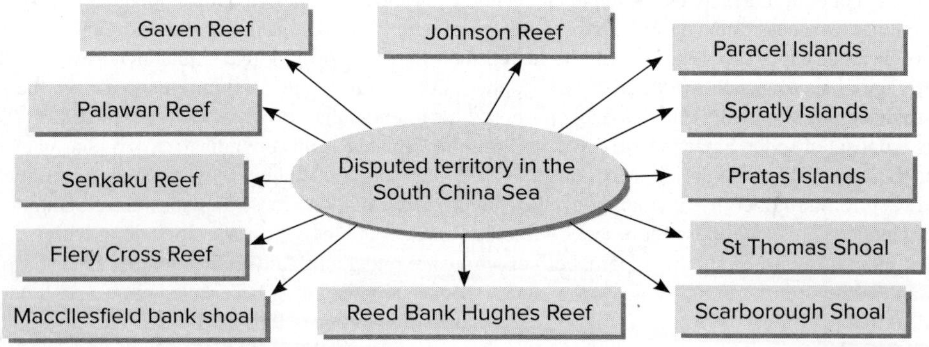

These islands belonged to other countries such as Brunei, Vietnam, Philippines etc. The citizens of China used their passports to travel to these states. In 1970s, these states began to observe the cartographic aggression of China in the maps. They showed the islands belonging to others as a part of China by drawing a hypothetical U-shaped line around the islands. The U-shaped line, a hypothetical dotted line, was found to be a 9-dash line by the South East Asians. They took up the matter with China and sought explanation as why did China try to claim the islands that belong to them as a part of its own territory? China did not issue any clarification and this upset the South East Asian states. In 1982, as the time progressed, UNCLOS (UN Convention on Law of International Seas) was born. When India became independent, it extended sovereign rights over the continental shelf without mentioning the depth or distance of the territories. Gradually by 1956, it claimed a 'fisheries zone' up to 100 miles away of territorial waters. At the international level, the US and the USSR were negotiating the width of territorial waters but were not able to reach consensus. In 1958, the first UNCLOS meeting adopted a codified law known as the Geneva Convention, which accepted freedom of navigation of the seas and sovereignty of a state in territorial sea. It worked to adopt immigration rights for contiguous zones but the first UNCLOS could not evolve consensus on the issues regarding the width of territorial waters and economic fisheries zones. In 1960, the second meet of UNCLOS was held, in which there evolved the idea of having territorial waters up to six miles. It was also proposed that an additional six miles beyond territorial waters be considered as economic fisheries zone, but a two-thirds majority could not emerge and eventually this idea failed once again. In the first UNCLOS meeting, India proposed that any warship should get authorisation from the state. There was no consensus on this issue in the UNCLOS meeting and the proposal, therefore, could not be added. Consequently, India refused to ratify the Geneva Convention, which emerged after the first UNCLOS meet. In 1967, as Pakistan extended its territorial waters from 3 to 12 nautical miles (NM), India also did the same on 12th September 1967. During the 1960s, as the technologies progressed, nations began to use modern technology to explore oil and gas in the seabed. This advancement in seabed technology led the countries to take steps to safeguard their interests. Some advanced nations deployed submissions with ballistic missiles. This compelled the UN to find a solution. In 1968, the General Assembly established a Seabed Commission of 42 UN members to discuss how nations can peacefully use the seabed. In 1970, a Declaration of Principles was accepted whereby the areas of seabed and resources in the seabed were to be considered the common heritage of humanity and the seabed and resources were declared to be subject to a global regime through a treaty. This was the time when the Indian government had authorised the mining of polymetallic modules from the seabed and had also discovered oil and gas in Bombay and Andaman Islands. On 25th August 1976, India passed the Maritime Zones Act. The act stated that up to 12 NM would be territorial waters, 24 NM would be contiguous zone and up to 200 NM would be EEZ and to enforce its compliance, the government established coast guard as an armed force of the Union of India in 1978. The Indian coast guard was to enforce the act and assist the fishermen in distress, in addition to providing back up to customs in anti-smuggling activities and prevention of marine pollution. In 1973, at the global level, began the third meeting of UNCLOS or UNCLOS-3. India participated in UNCLOS-3 and proposed 'Freedom of Navigation' and free mobility of naval ships. It also advocated the idea that Andaman and Nicobar Islands be declared as archipelago islets. India further advocated division of waters as per its own maritime zone act. India was included as a pioneer investor for seabed mining. Most of what India advocated was agreed in the UNCLOS-3 declarations. But there was an opposition to the idea of notifications being needed by foreign warships in the territorial waters of a foreign state. Moreover, Andaman was not accorded the status of an archipelago as UNCLOS-3 granted the status only to those islets that had a distinct political entity. This was done to ensure that off-lying islets are not used by states to restrict freedom of navigation. The UNCLOS-3 also held that 500 metres around any artificial island should be a safety zone. India's proposal for a bigger buffer area was not accepted. India has, since then, peacefully concluded agreements with Pakistan, Bangladesh, Sri Lanka, Myanmar, Thailand and Maldives and Indonesia over a period of time. The UNCLOS-3, after negotiating for nine years, adopted the draft of UNCLOS in 1982. It adopted five zones, as given in the table below:

S. No	Zones	Area	Rights	Indian Agencies
1.	Internal waters	Within	Full sovereignty	Law and order agencies
2.	Territorial waters	0 to 12 NM	Full sovereignty	Marine police and coast guard
3.	Contiguous zone	12–24 NM	Full sovereignty	Coast guard, customs and CISF-Marines
4.	Exclusive economic zone	24–200 NM	Mining, fishing and oil exploration only	Indian navy
5.	High seas	200 NM and above	Open zone	No domestic agency

UNCLOS said that a country in its territorial waters and contiguous zone can create artificial islands but cannot extend its zones further from the islands because the zones remain as they were measured in 1982. It said that there is a possibility of two nations and their zones overlap. The overlap will occur when a country can draw a 200 NM EEZ in any direction from its coast. When it draws that 200 NM line, such a line, which can be in any direction, can overlap with another maritime neighbour. In such a scenario, the two nations have to bilaterally identify a Common Zone of Activity (CZA). The CZA will enable both maritime neighbours whose zones are overlapping to identify where to do fishing, explore oil and minerals. If two states are unable to bilaterally demarcate the CZA, the aggrieved party can approach the Permanent Court of Arbitration—PCA (established in 1899 by the Hague Convention; it is a permanent international bureaucracy to

> **From 11-dash line to 9-dash line**
>
> In 1947, when China took control of some islets in the South China Sea occupied by Japan, they created a map with 11-dash line to show them as a part of China. In 1949, the People's Republic of China (PRC) established presence there and the KMT regime fled to Taiwan. Since then the PRC became the legal legitimate representative of China and decided to control the entire maritime claims of the region. As the Republic of China government fled to Taiwan, the PRC government allowed the North Vietnam regime to establish a radar station and a transit point for goods in the South China Sea. This was done on the basis of spirit of comradeship and brotherhood with the communist North Vietnamese regime. In 1957, China ceded Bailongwei island to Hanoi. Thus, the two dashes were removed by China to bypass the Gulf of Tonkin as a gesture to North Vietnam.

arbitrate disputes brought to them by the states. The PCA is not a court and is in no way related to the International Court of Justice, ICJ, which is a court of the UN). China not only created an arbitrary 9-dash line but also began to create artificial islands and began to extend their zones further (prohibited by UNCLOS). Thus, keeping in mind the strategic significance of the South China Sea, India firstly feels that the fact distortion strategy of China is similar to the fact distortion strategy it has adopted in Himalayas where it sends army officials disguised as grazers, villagers and road engineers. In the South China Sea, China has been sending coast guard personal, fishermen and militias to make historic claims in the region. As the Cold War ended, there was a sense that the US would withdraw from the South East and the East Asia as its strategic goals to contain the Soviets had ended. As the debate on a power vacuum left by the US was raging, China became possible filler. In 1995, the Chinese had built upon an artificial island on Mischief Reef in Spratly, located very close to the Philippines. As Taiwan was gearing up for its first presidential election, during a military exercise by China in 1996 in the Taiwan Straits, it launched a few missiles. This incident brought the US back into the picture as it sent a US carrier force into Taiwan Strait to signal China that it would not tolerate any interference or restriction on its maritime activity in the SCS. In 1992, at a meeting of Foreign Ministers of ASEAN, all nations had agreed upon a joint declaration on SCS with a commonly agreed principle of not using any violence in the dispute settlement. As ASEAN expanded at the end of the Cold War, it brought Cambodia, Laos, Vietnam, Myanmar and Brunei within its fold. The 10-member ASEAN block had nations that had claims on territories in the SCS. In the first decade since the end of the Cold War, China, however, insisted that it would resolve all disputes in SCS bilaterally with the states. In 1999, ASEAN adopted a Draft Code of Conduct putting an end to more occupation of reefs in the SCS. China again proposed that joint cooperation be the core value in dispute settlement. In 2002, the Draft Code of Conduct was finally adopted as a Declaration of Conduct of Parties as conflicts had flared up repeatedly due to China's assertiveness and territorial claims in the SCS due to the presence of oil and gas region. In the recent past, we have witnessed China asserting itself over the "nine-dash line" to virtually claim the entire South China Sea. Countries in the region and the US have blamed China for aggressively militarising the SCS. China has been resorting to a passive–aggressive strategy to state claims.

In fact, in September 2015, Rear Admiral Yuan Yubai of the Chinese Navy stated that the South China Sea also belongs to China as the name itself has 'China' embedded in it. China has made a shift from its earlier strategy of invasions to creation of new facts by confounding, bullying and bribing its adversaries. In 2010, China said that Tibet, Xinjiang province and

South China Sea are part of 'Core National Interests' of China. China has clarified that Core National Interest signifies that the issue will be significant enough for China to go to war. Despite the fact that China, in 2002, in the 8th ASEAN Summit, agreed upon a Declaration of Conduct to solve issues in South China Sea peacefully with no use of force, its strategy to distort facts continues. Since 2010, China has been converting uninhabited islets into artificial islets to bring it under UNCLOS (examples would include Haven Reef, Johnson South Reef and Fiery Cross Reef). China has been changing the size and structure of the reefs by modifying their physical land features. It has also established airstrips on Parcel and Spratly. In 2012, China snatched away Scarborough Shoal. In 2019, it used swarming tactics with fishing boats in the Thitu Islands against Philippines. The scramble of SCS by China is for

- Fishing rights
- Natural resources
- Domination of trade route
- Energy and oil

After years of undertaking futile negotiations at a bilateral level with China, the Philippines, decided to take the issue to the Permanent Court of Arbitration (PCA) in January 2013. China opposed it, advocating that the issue needs to be resolved bilaterally.

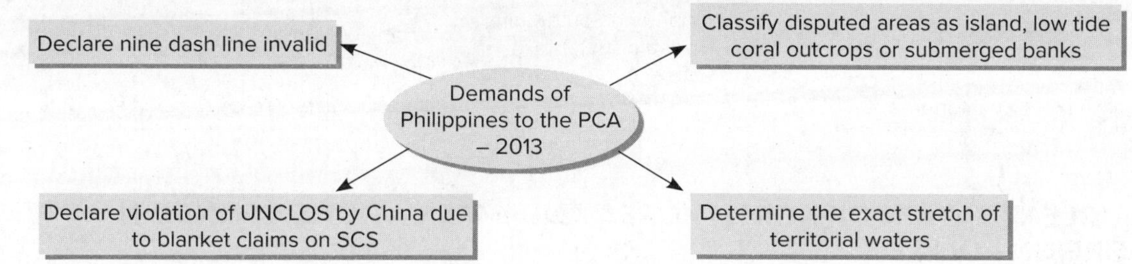

The reason for the Philippines suddenly dragging China to the PCA was that China had escalated the tension by taking control of the disputed Scarborough Shoal in 2012. Tensions further got aggravated in 2012 when Chinese vessels began to poach marine species at Scarborough Shoal and Chinese surveillance strips prevented the authorities of Philippines to apprehend them. In July 2016, after three years of intense deliberations on the SCS, the tribunal came out with a 501-page award in favour of Philippines.

However, China has refused to follow the verdict of the PCA. Considering the fact that PCA lacks an enforcement mechanism, nothing on the ground is likely to change, though the verdict is a morale booster for Philippines. The award is, however, likely to heavily affect diplomatic and economic ties between China and Philippines.

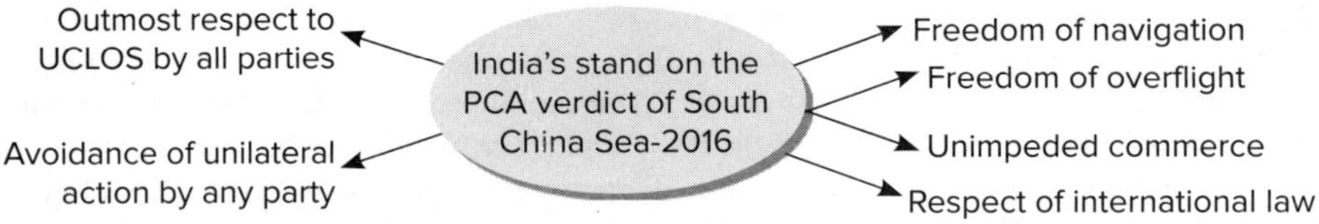

India is not a party to the dispute in the South China Sea. However, as it explore soil jointly with Vietnam and also uses the sea-lanes of communication for commerce, in the recent times, it has evolved a stand based on the points above. India's Act East Policy has made India more sensitive to the concerns of its ASEAN friends. India's stand to endorse Freedom of Navigation in South China Sea is a prerequisite for India to meet its rising military ambitions. India has also conveyed to China that if non-proliferation rules cannot be bent for India (for instance, in case of India's membership to NSG) then UNCLOS cannot be bent for China.

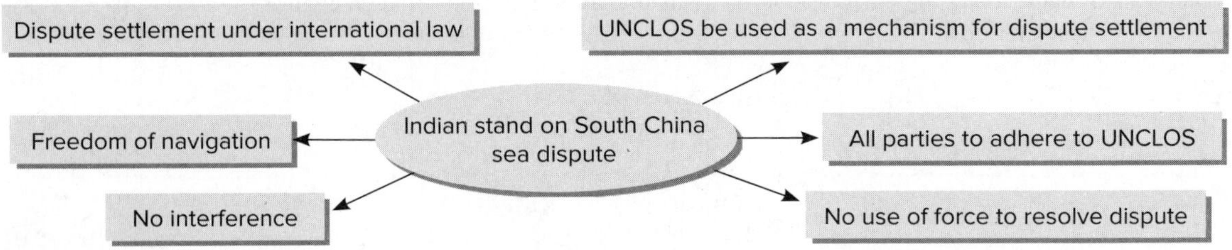

NUCLEARISATION OF NORTH KOREA AND IMPLICATIONS ON INDIAN FOREIGN POLICY

The Biden Administration has inherited a specific problem of a nuclear North Korean (which has capacity to make 10 bombs due to possession of 50 kg plutonium). The US has demanded a complete, verifiable and irreversible denuclearisation of North Korea. It adopted deft diplomacy to tackle it as visible in the first ever rapprochement between North Korea and the US, first in Singapore in 2018 and then at the Hanoi Summit in 2019. The antecedents of this denuclearisation deal have several historic dynamics attached to them: Firstly, the US decided to relegate the core tenet of the American policy of denuclearisation of North Korea based on Libyan model. Tracing the history of this model, back in 2004, Col. Qaddafi, the then leader of Libya had relinquished the nuclear weapons in return for economic integration with economies of the West only to be toppled down and killed in the wave of Arab Spring that began in 2011. This American relegation of the Libyan model, as seen in Singapore Summit, was primarily due to the fact that Pyongyang had issued threats that it will not negotiate unless there is a guarantee that Americans will not resort to the Libyan model. The Americans have sought total disarmament and have devised a policy to exert 'maximum pressure' on North Korea. However, in the Hanoi Summit in 2019, the Americans had explicitly acknowledged that total disarmament would not be possible unless there were many rounds of negotiations. Secondly, and most importantly, at the Hanoi Summit, the Americans had adopted a new approach where they decided to not put new sanctions on North Korea, while retaining the existing sanctions, and thereby promising to not cripple North Korea further. This, according to the Americans, would give window to North Korea to negotiate while maintaining deterrence. In return, Pyongyang would cease nuclear and missile tests. The Chinese and Russians favoured this idea too. The sticky issues however remained, as North Korea had insisted that the only possibility for it to undertake complete denuclearisation would occur when the US would withdraw nuclear capable forces and armament from the region including an additional security guarantee to the North Koreans by America. So far, the United States has refrained from any discussions on these pertinent concerns. As the Libyan model is not to be used by the Americans anymore, North Korea has insisted on the South African model. In the South African model, South Africa dismantled their six nuclear weapons and also destroyed all documents related to nuclear weapons. But South Africa still maintained weapons grade enriched uranium and then allowed the inspections from the international community. Today, as North Korea has refused to allow international inspections, probably they too insist on the South African model as they want denuclearisation but without monitoring by international agencies. This will enable North Korea to keep covert sub-regional capabilities. If the South African model is applied by the US in North Korea, North Korea will give up long-range capabilities but may still be allowed to possess atomic assets, thereby giving North Korea the potential to become the new Pakistan on the global nuclear map. Unlike Pakistan that could have established nuclear weapons after India vivisected East Pakistan in 1971, as a tool to conduct a low-intensity military conflict against India in Afghanistan and Kashmir, for North Korea, the nuclear weapon is a harbinger of peace, which is the greatest distinction between these two scenarios of nuclear-war possessing nations. The debate of the Korean crisis offers an important lesson to Pakistan—that nuclear weapons are not the end in them and can always be traded for greater causes such as peace with adversaries and economic benefits. India has asserted that the nuclearisation of North Korea is a threat to the sovereignty and security of India. India continues to press on the need for an in-depth investigation by the international community on how North Korea could acquire nuclear weapons in the first place (India suspects this was through covert support of China and Pakistan). Any attempts towards denuclearisation of North Korea will help India in two ways. Firstly, it will end the unholy nexus between Pakistan and North Korea, thereby bringing more strategic stability in the region. Secondly, it will allow New Delhi a window to boost trade and commercial ties with North Korea. There is one lesson for India from the Korean crisis, that is, there is always room for creative diplomacy for the strong will states (should be read in reference to Pakistan).

4

CHAPTER

The Era of Minilateralism: The QUAD, Indo-Pacific, AUKUS and Indian Diplomacy

THE RISE OF MINILATERALISM IN THE INDO-PACIFIC

What Exactly does Minilateral Stand for?

While there is no scholarly consensus on how to define a minilateral, the experience in Indo-Pacific suggests that minilaterals is a group that consists of three to nine nations that come together exclusively to concretise a flexible and functional policy objective. They follow the critical mass approach, which implies that they only comprise nations that are relevant to addressing the issue in question that defines the creation of the platform. Some of the examples include the Trilateral Strategic Dialogue of Japan, Australia and the US created in 2002, the Quadrilateral Security Dialogue (QUAD) of Australia, the US, India and Japan created in 2007 and Malacca Strait Sea Patrol group created in 2004 between Indonesia, Malaysia and Singapore. The Lancang–Mekong Cooperation (LMC) established in 2015 between China, Cambodia, Laos, Myanmar, Thailand and Vietnam also are a part of the same.

In the preceding chapters, we have understood that the regional security architecture in Indo-Pacific during the Cold War was dominated by two primary axes of security cooperation and they were bilateralism (where the US and the Soviet Union had bilateral ties with nation states of the region) and multilateralism (which was dominated by ASEAN architecture since 1967). At the bilateral levels, the focus of the US was to forge a network of alliances with Australia, Japan, South Korea, Thailand and Philippines and this was called during the Cold War as the San Francisco System. Through these alliances, the US was able to establish its complete presence in the Indo-Pacific. Initially, as analysed previously, the attempts to forge multilateral cooperation were relatively difficult because the member states in the Indo-Pacific had a lot of mistrust with each other. However, with the creation of ASEAN in 1967 and later the East Asian Summit and ASEAN Regional Forum, the things began to change. Since the beginning of 2000s, the region had started to witness a new more of regional cooperation and the Indo-Pacific was seeing rise of minilateral platforms that were specifically designed to achieve security objectives. The rise of LMC and revival of the QUAD in 2017 were a testimony of how minilaterals were making a re-entry in Indo-Pacific in the era of Sino-US rivalry. The issue to understand here is that the rise of minilaterals in Indo-Pacific is primarily driven by two factors. The first is due to rising doubts of sustainability of the US leadership and alliances of the Cold War to solve regional issues. The second is the failure of existing bilateral (alliances) and multilateral (ASEAN) to address the growing regional security concerns. In this context, the rising regional cooperation in the Indo-Pacific under the minilaterals is driven by an urge to establish a new 'coalition of the willing'. Today, the region of Indo-Pacific is witnessing a new and a strange phenomenon of ASEAN-centric multilateralism, minilateral–multilateralism and bilateralism nexus-based diplomacy.

CONCEPTUALISING MINILATERALISM IN INTERNATIONAL RELATIONS

If we have to define what a minilateral is, we must first understand what multilateralism is and how is minilateralism different. Firstly, the concept of minilateralism draws from the literature of multilateralism only and both involve cooperation involving indeterminate number of parties. Thus, speaking purely in the numerical sense, the minilateralism is a subset of multilateralism. What differentiates minilateralism from multilateralism are two factors and they include the numerical strength and the qualitative dimension of engagement. In contrast to a multilateral group, numerically speaking, the minilateral will involve a smaller group of participants. While there may be no consensus on a 'magic number' to define a minilateral, but based upon the issues such as climate change, nuclear proliferation, protection of sea lanes of communication etc.; the magic number for effective action can be up to twenty. In the context of Indo-Pacific, the numbers involved in minilaterals are even smaller. The second dimension is the qualitative dimension and that means that in a minilateral, there is more focus on functional exclusivity than a multilateral. Generally speaking, a multilateral works on indivisibility and generalised organising principles which require a broad and an inclusive approach. This makes consensus making on a multilateral platform relatively difficult. This is where a minilateral differs. Here, the conceptualisation involves an acknowledgement of discriminatory nature of power, which means that there is an acceptance that only a few nations have the potential to resolve a particular issue. In contrast to multilateralism, there is more realistic assessment of driving action for solving problems with select handful players. In this sense, there is a general perception that because minilaterals promote power asymmetries, thus they are undemocratic and exclusionary. The primary reaction of China to the QUAD is principally driven by this rationale. The Chinese believe that QUAD is an Asian NATO and divides the Asia-Pacific (the Chinese refuse to use Indo-Pacific because they call it an American conception) into hostile armed blocs. Practically speaking, the minilaterals in this sense can either maintain the regional balance of power or end up fuelling security dilemmas in the region. The third distinguishing feature of a minilateral from a multilateral is that it is more nimble and targeted in its approach because the governance is more informal and focused on functional objectives that are clearly articulated. The multilaterals have a more delayed decision making and sometimes interests of the states are generally not served. Thereby, a minilateral that way offers states a sense of an additional middle-ground for their security interests which are not fully served at the bilateral and multilateral levels. As the commitment to multilateralism declines, the minilaterals today buttress the global multilaterals by supplementing their existing inadequacies. The creation of Malacca Strait Sea Patrols, Sulu Sea Trilateral Patrols and Our Eyes Initiative (intelligence sharing initiative of Southeast Asian states) are concrete operationalisations of minilaterals under the multilateral ASEAN. Functionally, the nature of minilaterals suggests that these arrangements are flexible enough that they form and disband without any institutional legacy. This is a classic feature which distinguishes minilaterals from multilaterals where the focus is on rules and long-term reciprocity. While such a tactic appears good for driving a collective action but the lack of institutional legacy also means that the sustainability of the minilateral is pretty much contingent upon interests of parties that are participating. For instance, the QUAD was initially formed in 2007 but then faded into obscurity when Shinzo Abe, the Japanese Prime Minister had resigned and Kevin Rudd, the Australian Prime Minister to withdrew because it was not interested in provoking the Chinese. Its revival in 2017 was a testimony to the assertion made in the previous statement. Having understood the conceptual underpinnings, we can now proceed to analyse the minilateralism in practice in Indo-Pacific in more detail.

SHIFTING CENTRE OF GRAVITY FROM ASIA-PACIFIC TO INDO-PACIFIC

Since the end of World War II, the East was always called the Asia-Pacific. This was also because the countries in the region were underdeveloped, yet to come out colonial hangover and struggling to stand up economically. This period also coincided with the period of the Cold War where the Atlantic occupied prominence in global trade and resurgence of West. Since 1980s, the centre of gravity seemed to shift eastwards. With rise of China, the end of the Cold War, rise of the post-Cold War, globalisation and economic dynamism reflected by the Southeast and East Asians, the power centres of the East began to become prominent and Atlantic power centres witnessed stagnation. Taking a positive cue of the changed geo-economic and geo-political realities, the Japanese and Indians began to champion the idea of Indo-Pacific. With increased interactions, shared strategic concerns and rising economic interdependencies between Indian Ocean and Pacific Ocean, the Indo-Pacific concept started gaining strategic currency. The re-scaling of Asian region indicated a fundamental shift in core drivers of regionalism. Various factors today drive the shift towards Indo-Pacific and they include emergence of economically significant Japan and India, rising an economically powerful China, Sino-US rivalry because of Chinese attempts to displace the US as a global power, rising maritime assertiveness of China in South China Sea and increased threats of piracy, terrorism and natural disasters to the most important sea lane of communication that carries the bulk of global oil shipments and cargo. India has openly embraced the concept of Indo-Pacific because it accords India, a self-consciously rising power, the status of a regional power, which it was not offered under the Asia-Pacific framework. The Quadrilateral Security Dialogue as a new regional minilateral must be seen in this perspective. But before we analyse the QUAD, it is important to place the origin of QUAD as a minilateral in a proper setting.

INDIA'S SIX-LAYERED POLICY AND SEVEN PILLARS FOR INDO-PACIFIC

For India, Indo-Pacific is part where it is adopting an interlocked six-layer strategy. These six layers are based on India's own ability and its global aspirations. They include

1. Mutual prosperity-centric development of blue economy and a Free and Open Indo-Pacific (FOIP)
2. Enhancing the capabilities at the naval level and seeking interoperability at naval and defence level
3. Linking connectivity and infrastructure
4. Seeking presence in informal groupings that range from dimensions like security (QUAD) to humanitarian assistance
5. Leveraging the centrality of ASEAN through Act East Policy
6. Building up cultural and religious relations through faith diplomacy

India has focused on six pillars of Indo-Pacific. They include

1. Maritime domain awareness
2. Marine environment
3. Humanitarian assistance and disaster relief
4. Sustainable use of maritime resources
5. Science and technology
6. Capacity building

MINILATERALISM OF QUAD IN INDO-PACIFIC: LEGACY, VIABILITY AND DEFICIENCIES OF NEW SECURITY ARCHITECTURE

The region of Indo-Pacific in recent times has been witnessing a host of security challenges. At one place, the region is a witnessing nuclearisation by North Korea and on the other side, there is an attempt of China to display assertiveness in the South China Sea. The Chinese are also locked in contestation of maritime waters of Vietnam and claiming islands of Japan, the Senkaku/Diaoyu islands. The sea lanes of communication are constantly under a threat and there are dangers to the maritime commerce at a time when the world is recouping from the ills of pandemic and disrupted supply chains. In this backdrop, while the nations in the Indo-Pacific have always seen the US as a reliable security provider, but with diminishing interest of the US to provide reliable security, its domestic 'America First' thinking, its reluctance to cooperate with nations during the pandemic, its inability in rebuilding disrupted supply chains of Indo-Pacific have compelled the nation states to seek refuge in concretising new minilaterals for ensuring their own security. The history of minilaterals, as examined in the previous sections, clearly prove that they have been often successful in climate change, arms control, institution building, trade and nuclear non-proliferation but the venturing of minilaterals in the arena of security in Indo-Pacific is a new phenomenon. Throughout the history that has unfolded after the World War II, it has been seen that the US has adopted a different policy for security in Europe and Asia. In Europe, the US has provided security to all states under the umbrella of NATO and in Asia, the US has tried to provide security through bilateral alliance agreements with Australia, Japan, Philippines and South Korea. The US has explained this divergent approaches to security by stating that the entire theatre of Europe was witnessing a common threat of Soviet Union and the ground realities in Asia are different because here, no single entity has ever posed a threat which is commonly faced by all. This is why the US asserts that the region of Indo-Pacific requires a country by country approach. However, this rationale of the US does explain the regional security concerns in the Cold War period. Since the end of the Cold War, there has been an aggressive attempt of China to grow its economy. As Chinese have grown economically powerful and have integrated their economy with the economies of the Southeast and the East Asian states; Chinese have started to use their economic power to become militarily strong. They have started using military tactics to stake claims over islands and blanket claims over oceanic waters in South China Sea. Similarly, North Korea today is propped up by the Chinese as a laboratory of power assertion. The Chinese have been secretly funding the North Korean nuclearisation because North Korea will then keep regional powers such as Japan, Australia, Thailand and South Korea bogged down in Indo-Pacific while allowing the Chinese the space to assert global power. In 1999, as a response to North Korean nuclearisation issue, the US, Japan and South Korea came together to form Trilateral Cooperation and Oversight Group (TCOG). The TCOG was an inter-alliance approach of powers in Indo-Pacific to have a coordinated response to a new regional security challenge. However, the TCOG failed to establish any credible response because the Americans wanted to use the TCOG to bring about a regime change in North Korea, on lines with their policies in Iraq and Libya, and this is what precisely concerned the South Koreans and the Japanese because they felt that any such power vacuum brought in by the Americans through a deliberate and forcible regime change in North Korea would only end up opening more space for the intervention of China and make South Korea and Japan more vulnerable to Chinese adventurism. In 2001, the US tried to then create the Trilateral Security Dialogue (TSD) as a mechanism to solve North Korea issue and now brought the Japanese, Australians and Americans on one platform. The TSD was envisaged as a complementary instrument to the TCOG in driving a collective minilateral policy response to North Korea. The TSD became a confused grouping because the Australians insisted that Chinese also be brought in to play a constructive role in the management of the regional security threat pose by North Korea. Since 2001, the subsequent meetings of the TSD have only displayed an urge to manage a host of threats that range from traditional to non-traditional security and the minilateral again lost its purpose. In this backdrop, the third minilateral grouping that unfolded in the region of Indo-Pacific in 2007–8 was the Quadrilateral Security Dialogue (QUAD or QSD) with Australia, the US, India and Japan. A revised edition of the QSD was launched in 2017, with democracy as a common binding factor reasserted. Since 2017, all the four partners of the QSD have outlined their own conceptual underpinnings of the QSD. For the US, the QSD is clearly a new minilateral that will be used to contain the rise of an aggressive China. This thought, though shared by Japan and Australia, but is articulated differently. For Japan, the QSD is an attempt to seek American assurance in protection of its islands under dispute with China while for Australia, it is an attempt to rebalance power equations and re-assert its own role in Indo-Pacific. India has clearly articulated that it does not see QSD directed against any country (especially China here) but is focused on ensuring freedom of navigation and a free and open Indo-Pacific. India is not keen to see beyond Indian Ocean today. It is certainly concerned about the muscular policy of Beijing in South China Sea but is reluctant to expend resources under the QSD for a coordinated response to security challenges. India has time and again clarified that its conception of Indo-Pacific is not a club limited to a few members and India asserts that it sees the Indo-Pacific as an open, free and inclusive space which is driven by the ASEAN centrality to seek a common, rules-based order for regional states. At one place, the Indian establishment is part of American-led QSD which is aimed at containing China outside ASEAN mechanisms and here is India which has been asserting that QSD is neither anti-China nor outside ASEAN centrality. The deliberate reason for India to assert the centrality of ASEAN here is because India's Act East Policy looks at engagement with ASEAN and EAS as the fulcrum of its eastward thinking and not an outright embrace under the orbital policy architecture spearheaded by the US. In this sense, India has a 'non-bloc' vision of regional security in the new conception of Indo-Pacific. In this context, one thing is very clear that the new minilaterals in the region of Indo-Pacific are yet to articulate coherent responses to regional security. The QSD members do not have any procedural roadmap and a consensus on operational preferences. There is not a single national interest that is shared by the four participants of QSD, thereby making the grouping less significant operationally and more prominent for mere optics. The players that are kept outside of these new minilaterals such as QSD have tried to develop a disdain and have continued to use existing ASEAN mechanisms and champion 'ASEAN way' and ASEAN centrality in resolving regional concerns. This confusion over the minilaterals in the Indo-Pacific has allowed the Chinese to continue to be assertive and mould state behaviours as per their interests.

PHILOSOPHY OF QUAD AS MAKE CHINA RESPONSIBLE FRAMEWORK

In the years ahead, the QUAD will become a high strategic grouping. It will not just be stuck with existing four members but include other like-minded players that range from South Korea to Singapore etc. The QUAD will ensure the delivery of public goods through open, secured and uncontested sea lanes of communication and create passages for free movement of people, energy supplies and trade. The QUAD in future will replace the Pax Americana that for long had been writing security in different regions of the world. The second thing QUAD will ensure is that it will open up spaces for infrastructure creation in realm of Indo-Pacific through big investments that till now were only dependent upon China. In this sense, QUAD will not just bring finances for physical infrastructure but technology instruments that have never been shared by the Global North with Global South. More importantly, the QUAD will ensure that we do not create a "No China" world because the entire world wants China and has benefitted from its low-cost manufacturing skill. But the QUAD will ensure that China is kept honest in its economic and political engagements when all players engaging with China collectively put up a combined front. In this sense, the QUAD must be seen as a "Make China Responsible" framework designed to keep Chinese honest and a responsible actor in the global economic system. The pandemic has created a situation where Captain America is missing in action and an irresponsible new power with no regard for democratic opinions of others is put in charge. Seen through this lense, the QUAD is a coalition emerging under the American patronage, of middle powers which is not a luxury or choice in international relations but an existential reason to invest into.

THE LANCANG–MEKONG COOPERATION AND COMPETITIVE DIPLOMACY

In this backdrop, the Chinese attempts to conceptualise the Lancang–Mekong Cooperation (LMC) is interesting. The LMC was launched in 2015 between China and its neighbouring region and had a focus on political-security issues, economic affairs, social affairs, people-to-people ties and sustainable development. The LMC in the recent times is a new attempt of the Chinese to strengthen their presence and influence in the Mekong region. The deliberate attempt of the Chinese to mention sustainable development in LMC is to display a new template of hydro-diplomacy. Today, the Chinese are an upstream state in case of Mekong river and the LMC offers the Chinese an opportunity to improve living conditions of people in the downstream region. There is a growing perception in the ASEAN states that China wants to project LMC as a new version of 'Asian Security and Development' architecture, akin to the Shanghai Cooperation Organisation (SCO) of Central Asia. The ASEAN members argue that while the Indo-Pacific is gradually witnessing the rise of new minilaterals, these groupings must not compete with ASEAN but compliment ASEAN. This is where India is able to score brownie points by asserting that its vision of Indo-Pacific and QSD both put ASEAN at the centre of fulcrum but the Chinese through their LMC appear to go on a divergent path. This way the Indo-Pacific seems to witness a host of competitive and cooperative minilateral architectures.

THE AUKUS ALLIANCE, POTENTIALITIES ON ECLIPSING QUAD, THE RELEVANCE OF NPT AND INDIA ON AUKUS

In September 2021, the US, Australia and United Kingdom outlined a new historic security pact called the AUKUS, taking initial letters of the participating states. This announcement came after the US withdrew from Afghanistan the same year. The attempt of the US to share sensitive technologies and nuclear technologies came as a big relief to American friends and allies in the region who were awry to see a declining power of the US in Asia. The US through AUKUS has sent a clear and strong signal to the regional friends and allies that the new centre of gravity for the US is Indo-Pacific and this region will now be a theatre of new strategic contestations and the US is willing to play a crucial role. Under the alliance, the US and the UK are going to share sensitive nuclear technologies with Canberra and enable the Australians to develop eight nuclear-powered submarines. It is important to note that since 1957, the US, New Zealand and Australia had partnered under the ANZUS alliance. This made the Australians a part of the larger American security umbrella during the Cold War. However, since the Chinese transitioned to an open economy since 1978, there has been a concerted attempt by China to seek deep economic relations with resource-rich Australia. The relationship between Australia and China economically deepened after the end of the Cold War to this extent that almost every Australian Prime Minister since the end of the Cold War was fluent in mandarin language. The deepening of economic relations of Australia and China on one hand and strategic relations of the US and Australia on the other hand was always a bottleneck in Australian identity. The Australians were witnessing a dilemma on announcing whether they are with the US or with China. They could neither leave China as Chinese sustained Australian economic growth and they could not leave the American embrace as America was a part of rebuilding of Australia in the post-World War twice. In this backdrop, the COVID-19 pandemic brought about the clarity in Australian identity. The Australians insisted that China must allow a thorough investigation by WHO on origins of COVID-19 that had killed millions of people globally. The reluctance of China to allow open investigations soured the relations between Australia and China and the Americans took advantage of this sourness to bring back the Australians into the American fold once again. By offering support of sharing of sensitive nuclear technologies to aid the development of nuclear-powered submarines, Australia will be economically able to balance off the support it was contingent upon from China. However, just because the submarines are nuclear-powered does not mean that they are going to have nuclear warheads. The technology is sensitive because not every country in the world possess the technology to power submarines by nuclear grade fuels. The move of AUKUS is also seen by the US to counter China in Indo-Pacific. Under the NPT, the Australians are prohibited to manufacture nuclear warheads. However, the NPT has a shortcoming as it exempts the naval reactors. The US has used double standards here and has not allowed India to access this technology by stating that it is a classified technology. However, the message to India is very clear. The Americans will help India with most advanced and sensitive technologies only if India shuns strategic autonomy and embraces the American alliance system and helps the US counter China in Indo-Pacific, which at the moments is certainly not a priority for India. The Chinese have blunted the AUKUS by discounting it and have mocked at the Americans for sharing obsolete cold war technologies of 1970s with its allies. It has used the occasion to humiliate the Australians by pushing a message amongst the Indo-Pacific region that on embracing America, the member states will only get old American junk technologies. However, the Chinese have also cautioned that the AUKUS will revive a new cold war in the region and stated that this new zero sum game mentality will only create narrow geopolitical spaces in Indo-Pacific that would hinder the growth prospects of Indo-Pacific. The responses from India are quite different. India is of the belief that AUKUS will now keep the Australians, Americans and British busy in building yet another minilateral nuclear architecture. This will allow India the space in Indo-Pacific to up the game of development diplomacy by focusing on vaccine diplomacy, infrastructure building, technology and supply chains. India is however not happy in the way the Americans have displayed negativity in rejecting France as an important player. This negation of France in AUKUS and American preoccupation with British as the only reliable ally after BREXIT has confirmed to many that America does not consider other European states as valuable allies. While France is certainly angry, it provides India and France an opportunity to conceptualise their own developmental blueprint in Indo-Pacific. India is no doubt happy to see that Australia, which is a traditional friend and a close partner of India in QSD, is getting nuclear-powered submarines. India is worried that the Eastern Indian Ocean will not only get crowded with submarines that would erode India's influence and authority over the Indian Ocean but it would also compel China to resort to more adventurism in Eastern Indian Ocean. While China will be away from the Indian waters and deploy submarines and warships in Eastern Indian Ocean, but the presence of these warships in littorals of Indian Ocean will put pressure on Indian naval assets. The other game of AUKUS is of technology supremacy. By integrating the defence industrial supply chains, the Australians, the US and British will now be able to beat China in the race for high-tech supremacy. The QSD and AUKUS members are likely to expand cooperation in quantum technology, artificial intelligence and this will shift the power balance in Indo-Pacific. In this sense, India sees the AUKUS as a pact that will bolster the QSD to search for open-minded and creative solutions for upcoming regional security challenges. India however feels that QSD till now was a non-military and non-security minilateral that was struggling to outline an identity of its own. The coming of AUKUS has taken away the aura of QSD and India feels that the sheen of QSD will be lost. But QSD is not a military alliance and a minilateral of like-minded states to cooperate on regional challenges and uphold international rules and values that will strengthen peace, stability and security of Indo-Pacific.

TRADE INTEGRATION, SECURITY RIVALRIES AND DILEMMA DIPLOMACY

Since the end of the Cold War, there has been a growing economic integration of states in Indo-Pacific. This integration, it must be clarified is driven more by trade and investments and less by movement of people. The core drivers of this trade integration include rise of China as manufacturing power, regional trade mechanisms such as ASEAN and the recently concluded Regional Comprehensive Economic Partnership (RCEP). The intra-Asian trade integration in the Indo-Pacific has a serious geopolitical significance because the important driver is the rise of China and in this backdrop, the US will find it difficult to isolate China. The Americans cannot afford to use the same strategies of the Cold War because in the Cold War, they were able to contain Soviet as they never created economic interdependences. This is what makes the rise of China different as a strategic and economic challenge for the Americans to tackle. The strategic dilemmas are compounded in Indo-Pacific in the absence of an all pervasive security treaty or a regional cooperation agreement such as the NATO. As examined in the preceding chapters, the US in Asia has resorted to a hub and spoke model of regional security driven by the San Francisco System where it has prioritised individual security treaties with nation states. This security architecture concretised by the US during the Cold War continued even at the end of the Cold War. It failed to factor in the rise of China and strategic consequences of the same on nations of Indo-Pacific. The Chinese took advantage of absence of a regional security architecture and began to become aero-navally assertive in Indo-Pacific and on land with India at the Line of Actual Control. The region of Indo-Pacific is in a dilemma. The dilemma is that how is the political economy of Indo-Pacific going to unfold in coming years. The question before many Indo-Pacific nation states is that whether the growing economic interdependencies of nations with China will provide a ballast for establishing political, security cooperation and thus leading to a regional and pan-Asian security consensus as a new treaty or a minilateral or a multilateral? Or will the absence of a regional security architecture, which is all inclusive, and not exclusive such as QUAD and AUKUS accentuate the strategic rivalries, distrust and prevent any political integration, which normally is the outcome of economic integration? These questions are likely to shape the future responses of India in Indo-Pacific and define its identity in the Indo-Pacific.

COLD POLITICS AND HOT ECONOMICS IN INDO-PACIFIC

In the preceding section we argued that economic integration will lead to political integration. In Europe, the democracy had been a binding factor in bringing the NATO as a force to counter the communist regimes. In this sense, the US was able to use NATO as a tool to counter the Soviet Union. In Asia, while many countries are democracies and they are well aligned to the democratic agenda of the US, there are many nations such as Thailand and Brunei which are autocratic and are aligned with the US. Then there is an autocratic China which is on opposing side of the US, its friends and allies. The biggest challenge that the US is facing today can be seen on two fronts. Firstly, it does want to be a dominant player of providing regional security in the Indo-Pacific. But the challenge for the US is that none of the nations in the Indo-Pacific have economic interdependencies with the US as they have with China. In this sense, the US is quite reluctant to build a security architecture where it can gain and offer regional security like in Europe. The biggest advantage that the US had during the Cold War in Europe was that they were able to forge NATO with economic components and aid the rebuilding of states after the World War II. However, in case of Indo-Pacific today, the countries here are way too deeply integrated with China and thus, there is little economic incentive for the US to provide regional security. Secondly, as argued previously, the motivating factor for the US in NATO in Europe was that the nations were bound by the framework of democracy and the US found it more conducive to engage with democratic regimes than with non-democratic ones in Europe in particular. Today, in order to cover up for the economic incentive logic the US often states that the reason why it is unable to offer a regional security architecture of NATO types in Indo-Pacific is because of differing political systems in nation states of Indo-Pacific. This however makes no sense because despite differing political systems between the US and the Middle-Eastern states, the Americans during the Cold War had created regional security architectures like Baghdad Pact. In this sense, what clearly explains the reluctance of the US to build an all pervasive regional security architecture in Indo-Pacific, despite the rise of China as a strategic threat to the US, its friends and allies, is the absence of an economic incentive for the Americans because the nations of the Indo-Pacific are economically intertwined with China. A benevolent hegemon that can act as a nucleus of regional security in Indo-Pacific will remain missing for the time being.

IMPLICATIONS FOR INDIAN FOREIGN POLICY IN INDO-PACIFIC AND NETWORK MODEL OF BALANCING

In the security, strategic and economic scenario outlined above, the question arises that what are the implications of this state of flux in Indo-Pacific on Indian foreign policy. Since the 1990s, there has been a concerted attempt of the US to improve its relationship with India. During the Cold War period, owing to ideological differences and American insistence on hyphenation of India and Pakistan and their overt tilt to Pakistan acted as serious hindrances between India and the US. The relations between India and the US began to improve since the end of the Cold War and defence cooperation was one of the first dimensions. The Americans positioned themselves as a reliable defence equipment supplier to India after the decline of Soviet. This enabled India to use the American umbrella to build up ties in Indo-Pacific with Japan, Australia and South Korea. In 2000s, after the 9/11, there was a growing realisation in the American strategic thinking that the rise of China is likely to alter balance of power of Asia. In this context, the Americans, in 2005, decided to give India a nuclear deal and enhanced the defence, security and nuclear cooperation. The American policy was driven by an attempt to rebalance the power equations by enhancing the capacities and capabilities of its own friends and allies in Indo-Pacific. The American policy was touted as the 'Pivot to Asia' or 'Rebalancing Initiative'. This policy has seen more deepening of India and the US ties under the recently concluded agreements such as LEMOA, COMCASA and BECA. It is equally important to understand that the US rebalancing had accepted the rise of China as matter of fact and all its generosity to its friends and allies was more driven by the attempt of maintaining its own strategic position of a global hegemon through economic opportunities in Indo-Pacific. The US, in its 'Pivot to Asia' programme not only strengthened bilateral capacities of its friends and allies but also encouraged them to build a network of proximity amongst themselves so that there can be higher levels of interoperabilities. The US since then has created a new network model of balancing to tackle the rise of China. This network model (see the diagram below) incorporates minilateral, mini-networks such as QSD and AUKUS, as analysed in preceding sections.

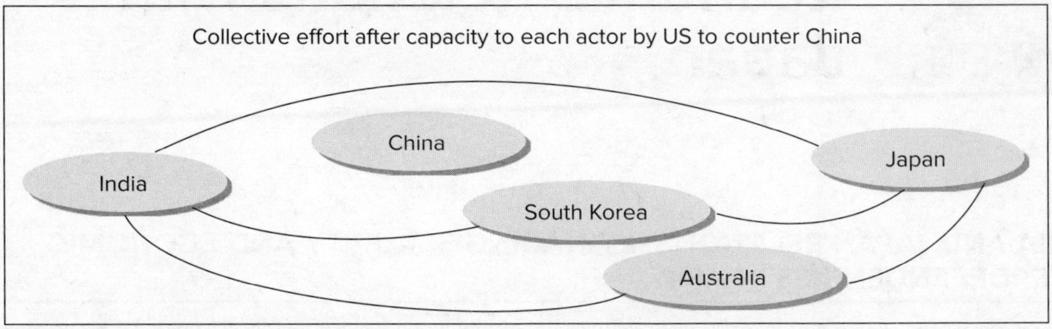

In this new network model of minilaterals, India is rising as a new middle power with aspiration of playing a bigger role and achieve a higher international status in the world. From the discussion here, it is now clear that implications of the US network model on Indian foreign policy is clear. India will continue to deepen relations with states in the Indo-Pacific to seek capital, technology and partners that will support India's growth so that India can achieve a leading power status. As the US, after AUKUS, is now going to be a dominant power in Indo-Pacific, India is likely to enter the embrace of the US and the gaps between India and the US relations will melt down even further. The Chinese will be difficult to isolate in the region. But with AUKUS, as the US will now be more deeply present in the Indo-Pacific, the Chinese will use their Belt and Road Initiative to reduce their sea-borne presence and focus more on seeking energy and resource supplies from Middle-East (and then via CPEC to China through land route and thus avoid maritime routes) and Europe. India's engagements with the US will also have its own limitations because the Chinese will use Pakistan and precarious border issue with India where it resorts to salami slicing to bog down India. The US will not be able to do anything if Chinese divert the waters of Indus and Brahmaputra for their use and create ecological security threats for India or resort to salami slicing and territorial grabs, an ongoing strategy in Ladakh since 2020. Thus, even in case of a US-dominated scenario in the Indo-Pacific, there would be limitations of India and the US engagements. India would try to balance out these limitations of the US policy on Indian security by taking independent stands on international issues under the garb of strategic autonomy, as visible in India's stand on Ukraine crisis in 2022. In any scenario, the only logical strategy for India to follow without being confrontational to China, Pakistan and without becoming upset of the full US support is to grow its economy aggressively. As the Indian economic pie will grow, India will have to divert the economic resources to resort to modernise its military and narrow down the military gaps with China and thus balance off a future full-scale military confrontation with China. The government of India's thrust on an Atmanirbhar Bharat and subsequent economic policy architecture has to be seen in this strategic perspective.

5

CHAPTER

India's Strategic and Economic Relations with Japan

INDIA AND JAPAN RELATIONS: MANAGING SECURITY AND ECONOMIC INTERDEPENDENCIES IN ASIA

The new canvas and cauldron of international relations and economic diplomacy is Asia. The parallel economic rise of India and China has renewed debates on geopolitics in Indo-Pacific. The active presence of Japan in the region has added an additional element of peace and direction in the international relations unfolding in Indo-Pacific. In the newly unfolding multipolar world and Asia, the fault lines are seen in the maritime and littoral realm and the linking of Indian Ocean and Pacific Ocean under the Indo-Pacific realm is resurrecting the geopolitics. Consequent to the rise of Indo-Pacific is rising dependence on sea trade, resources and communication which has transformed the perceptions of traditional military threats to environmental dimensions as well. Although the economic rise of Asia is multidimensional and promising, the intersection of geopolitical and geographic risks associated with unchecked models of economic growth pose new challenges for the Indo-Pacific. In this sense, the Pacific century is focussed on littoral states and securing freedom of navigation is the dominant focus. The difference between the 20th and the 21st century lies in the heart of geography because the 20th century Europe was a landscape and the 21st century Asia is a seascape. In this backdrop, the strategic space for India to navigate the Indo-Pacific has not only grown wider but also more complex. The India and Japan relations have to be traced in this emerging context.

INDIA'S CORE INTERESTS IN ENGAGING WITH JAPAN

Japan and India have an ancient relationship, with Buddhism acting as a common connecting factor. During the era of the ancient Silk Route, Buddhism spread to China from India. From China, Buddhism also spread to Korea and Japan. There was a dip in Indo-Japan relations during medieval times. Yet, the cultural engagement at the level of Buddhism continued. During the World War II, Subhash Chandra Bose formed close ties with the Japanese in his bid to wage a war on the British army. Bose's Indian National Army (INA) was the brainchild of Japanese Major (and post-war Lieutenant General) Iwaichi Fujiwara, head the Japanese intelligence unit Fujiwara Kikan and had its origins, first in the meetings between Fujiwara and the president of the Bangkok chapter of the Indian Independence League, Pritam Singh Dhillon. Through Pritam Singh's network, the recruitment by Fujiwara of a captured British Indian army captain, Mohan Singh on the western Malayan peninsula in December 1941 also contributed to the cause as Fujiwara's mission was "to raise an army which would fight alongside the Japanese army". After the initial proposal by Fujiwara the Indian National Army was formed because of discussion between Fujiwara and Mohan Singh in the second half of December 1941, and the name chosen jointly by them in the first week of January 1942. The INA's first commitment during the the World War II was in the Japanese thrust towards Eastern Indian frontiers of Manipur. INA's special forces, the Bahadur Group, were extensively involved in operations behind enemy lines both during the diversionary attacks in Arakan, and the Japanese thrust towards Imphal and Kohima, along with the Burmese National Army led by Ba Maw and Aung San. The Japanese also took possession of Andaman and Nicobar Islands in 1942 and a year later, the Provisional Government and the INA were established in the Andaman and Nicobar Islands with A. D. Loganathan appointed its Governor General. The islands were renamed Shaheed and Swaraj. However, the Japanese Navy remained in essential control of the island's administration. However, Japan's funding for the INA gradually dwindled and the army was forced to pull back, being defeated in crucial battles and finally capitulating to the British army. This was followed by Japan's defeat and eventual capitulation in the World War II after the US dropped nuclear bombs at Hiroshima and Nagasaki. Post-independence, it was in the year 1952 that India and Japan concluded a Treaty of Peace and Friendship, laying the foundation of India's new diplomatic relations with Japan. However, we need to remember that relations between the two during the Cold War were not warm. One of the key reasons was the ideological difference, which separated the two. India, during the Cold War, was an advocate of non-alignment. Japan, on the other hand, after the World War II, concluded the Treaty of San Francisco with the USA and tilted towards the capitalist orientation as Japan was economically weak and was undertaking economic reconstruction after the war. India supported Japan with the supply of iron ore. In return, India regularly got economic aid from Japan in the form of ODA (Overseas Developmental Assistance, also at times called Official Developmental Assistance). In fact, by 1986, Japan emerged as the largest economic aid donor to India. During the Cold War, when India faced conflicts with China in 1962 and Pakistan in 1965 and 1971, the foreign policy stance of Japan towards India remained very neutral. The Japanese never supported India, nor supported its opponents, and chose to not take sides. But somehow, Japan being a follower of the US camp in the Cold War, was always uncomfortable with India's tilt to the USSR post-1971. Because of the domestic ferment and problems India had during the Cold War, Japan always perceived India as a chaotic and desperately poor nation, having no potential to be a partner in the near times. Because of successive conflicts between India and its neighbours between 1962 and 1971, the Southeast and the East Asian states branded India as needlessly aggressive. In 1967, when the Southeast Asians created the ASEAN (Association of Southeast Asian Nations), they did not include India to be a part of the group, which also contributed to India's larger exclusion from that part of the world. However, things did improve between India and Japan after the end of the Cold War. The ending of the Cold War brought about a radical shift in the world policy as also Indian Foreign Policy. India began to improve its relations with the USA. This also led India to improve its relations with other allies of the USA, including its most important partner in the East, Japan. In the first few years in the post-Cold War period, India began improving its relations with Japan, but the progress was short lived as in 1998, India carried out another nuclear test and positioned itself as a nuclear weapon state. After the test, Japan became a vocal critique of India at the regional and international level. Japan even went on to cut its economic aid to India. It was natural for Japan to condemn such foreign policy behaviour as it had been the only nation in the world to have witnessed the horror of an atomic bomb attack first-hand. Post-World War II, Japan has become a very peaceful nation with an acute abhorrence of atomic and nuclear bombs. It perceived the Indian nuclear test as an insult to the growing relationship. Thus, post-1998, India saw a dip in its relations with Japan. However, the US, which was also initially upset about India's nuclear testing, saw the test as an opportunity to improve its relationship with India at the level of nuclear commerce. The USA also convinced its allies, including Japan, not to be negative about the Indian nuclear tests. Consequently, in 2000, of the Japanese Prime Minister Mori Yoshiro conducted a state visit to India. Mori asserted that India and Japan would become Strategic Partners in future. This visit led to the birth of a new partnership between the two that has continued from 2000 to the present. The beauty of the Indo-Japan relationship has been that it is moving in an upward trajectory reaching new heights, which we can now explore in themes ahead. The core interests of India today include

- Domestic diplomacy
- Systemic diplomacy
- Individual diplomacy
- Nuclear diplomacy
- Defence diplomacy
- Checkmate China diplomacy
- Development through two plus one diplomacy

DOMESTIC FACTORS AND PERSONALITY POLITICS IN INDIA AND JAPAN

In Japan, many studies had been conducted which said that approximately by 2050, Japan may be pushed on the verge of zero per cent economic growth because of an aging population that is moving towards a demographic disadvantage. To mitigate this challenge, Japan has, in recent times eased up its immigration policies, allowing the entry of skilled professionals.

Therefore, this is one area where India and Japan have an interaction as a lot of skilled members of the Indian population are now looking at Japan as a viable option to support Japanese economic growth. Further, with coming of Shinzo Abe in Japan, we have a unique Japanese economic revival happening under a conceptual framework called Abenomics (Abe + economics). Abenomics is a unique blend of fiscal, monetary and structural reforms, which Shinzo Abe is aggressively pursuing in Japan. It is again in this context that India and its corporate sector today sees a vibrant opportunity in Japan. This is also coupled with a perception, which Japan has of India as a knowledge superpower, while perceiving China to be a cheap commodity superpower. The Japanese ODA is put to use in infrastructure projects in India such as the Delhi Metro, the Delhi–Mumbai Industrial Corridor, the Dedicated Freight Corridor and the Bangalore–Chennai expressway. Thus, at domestic levels, India and Japan collectively complement each other. Foreign policy experts have commented that India–Japan relations are classic example of Prime Minister-driven relationship. In recent times, both Manmohan Singh and Narendra Modi have infused enormous political energy in the relations with Shinzo Abe. Both leaders from India have jointly emphasised upon the establishment of a Single Seamless Asian Whole and the creation of 'Arc of Freedom,' leading to an alliance of these two leading democracies. The idea is to establish a seamless paradigm for free movement of navy, trade capital, finance and people between India and Japan.

COMMERCIAL AND DEVELOPMENT DIPLOMACY OF INDIA AND JAPAN IN ERA OF INDO-PACIFIC

India and Japan had limited commercial ties during the Cold War. The rise in bilateral commercial relations is a post-Cold War phenomenon. However, relations at the commercial level had existed even before the World War II. At the end of the Edo Era, the Japanese ports were opened for commerce and its trade relations with India began. With the opening of the ports Japanese industries began to import Indian cotton yarn. The trading merchants in Bombay opened more shipping lines with merchants in Yokohama. As the World War II ended and India became independent, Japan began to export machinery and metal products to India while importing iron ore from India. The imported iron ore was used by Japan to mitigate material shortages it was facing in its domestic steel industry. Though Japan had been also providing ODA to India, during the Cold War its overall quantum had got reduced. Japan gradually started importing more iron ore from Brazil and Australia than India. It was in 1981 that India initiated partial economic liberalisation, with the process completed in 1992. In 1984 Japanese Prime Minister Nakasone visited India and doubled the total amount of ODA. In the 1980s, Japan began to import diamond and prawns from India. As the Cold War ended and India embarked upon full economic liberalisation, a new chapter in the bilateral trade opened up. In November 2004, India and Japan established a Joint Study Group (JSG) to explore the possibility of a CEPA (Comprehensive Economic Partnership Agreement). The JSG held four meeting from July 2005 to April 2006. In December 2006, it was decided to establish a negotiation mechanism. From January 2007 to September 2010, 14 rounds of negotiations were held and in September 2010, an agreement in principle was arrived upon. On 16th February 2011 India and Japan concluded the CEPA. The CEPA gives India access to a 5-trillion-dollar GDP while giving Japan an access to more business opportunities in India. India feels the CEPA is an alliance between Japanese technology and Indian labour force. As per the CEPA, by 2012, for trade in goods 94% tariffs were eliminated between India and Japan on a trade value basis.

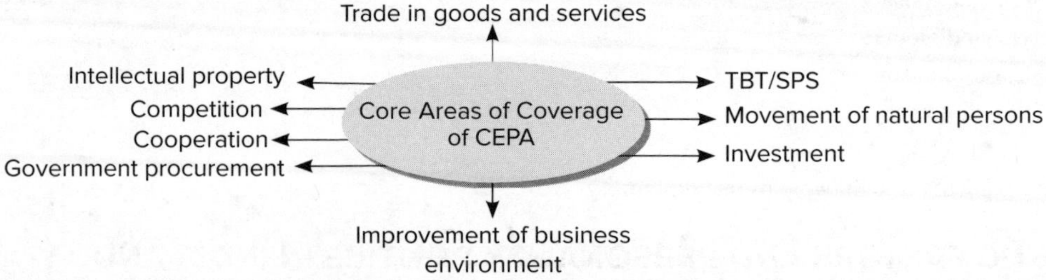

During Indian Prime Minister's visit to Japan in 2014, the Japanese Prime Minister Shinzo Abe committed 35 billion dollars' worth investments to India till 2019. India exports petroleum products, chemicals, fish, clothing and machinery to Japan while it imports electrical machinery, transport equipment, plastic materials and precision instruments. Japanese

FDI to India is mainly limited to the automobile and pharmaceutical sectors. With a red carpet for Japanese investors under the Modi government, the trade relations are bound to increase in future. The Indian Prime Minister, along with his Japanese counterpart, visited the FANUC Corporation in 2018. The visit to FANUC was very significant as India was gearing up to the Industrial Revolution 4.0 where it intended to leverage IoT, Artificial intelligence, robotics and 3D printing for industrial enhancement. Despite the fact that India and Japan have a CEPA (signed in 2011, a comprehensive deal covering trade in goods and services along with IPR and movement of persons), the trade is sluggish (due to inadequate infrastructure, land acquisition issues in India confronted by the Japanese and complex taxation mechanisms in India). There are cultural and punctuality issues that hinder India and Japan economic cooperation. India imports machinery and iron and steel while exporting petroleum products and non-metallic mineral ware.

In September 2017, the Japanese Prime Minister Shinzo Abe visited India for the 12th India–Japan Annual Summit. During the visit, the two countries discussed a Maritime Security Pact and decided to institutionalise a Maritime Security Dialogue to take forward the Maritime Affairs Dialogue (signed in 2013). The Japanese Prime Minister officially launched Asia–Africa Growth Corridor and inaugurated the Mumbai–Ahmedabad High Speed Rail (MAHSR) project. The project heralds a new era of safety, speed and service and will help the Indian railways craft a pathway to becoming a global leader in scale, technology and skill. The MAHSR works on an attractive low-cost long-term financing model. Japan will be providing a soft loan of 90,000 crore rupees to India at an interest rate of 0.1% over 50 years. The re-payment of the loan is to begin after 15 years of receiving the loan. There have been criticisms that such a high-speed train in a poverty-stricken India is elitist and India can do without it. Such criticisms were there even in 1969, when the first ever Rajdhani Express was launched from Howrah to Delhi. However, leapfrogging technology and development with elitism is unwarranted at this stage.

THE INDO-PACIFIC STRATEGIC BINDERS BETWEEN INDIA AND JAPAN

The origin of the defence diplomacy between India and Japan could be traced back to the year 2000 when Japanese Prime Minister Yoshiro Mori visited India and envisaged a global partnership with India. In 2007 Shinzo Abe envisaged the confluence of the two seas and establishment of an arc of freedom and prosperity, which saw its final culmination in 2014 in a Special Strategic and Global Partnership.

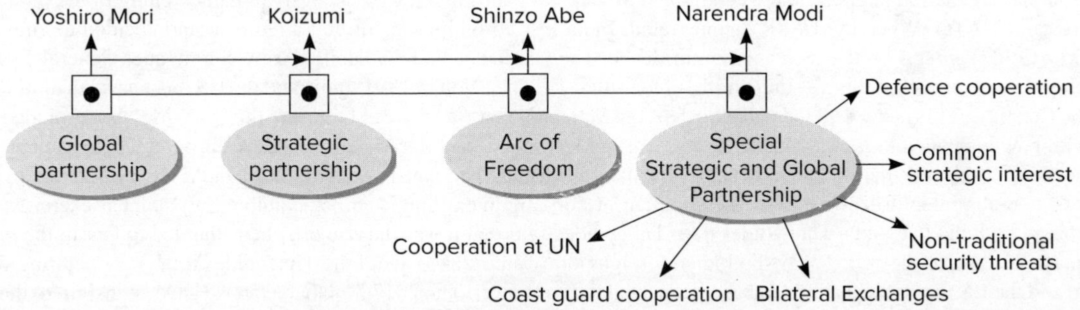

Under the Act East Policy, the most crucial connector between India and Japan has been maritime cooperation. The two sides have a Maritime Security Dialogue since 2013. The most unique feature of this maritime cooperation is that it incorporates not only naval cooperation but commercial maritime activities as well. In 2015, India and Japan concluded Agreement on Transfer of Defence Equipment and Technology Cooperation. This agreement would provide India with advanced defence technology for the purposes of research and development. As the Indian defence market opens up, Japanese defence players will see rising presence in India. India has declared Japan as a privileged market partner in Make in India programme.

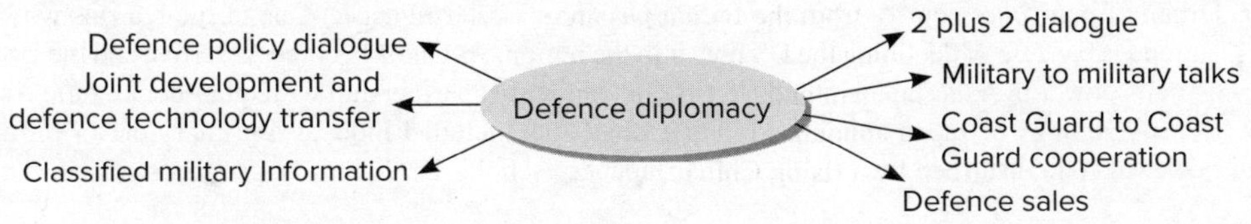

Japan has opened up its defence sector, as envisaged in the 2018 National Defence Programme Guidelines (NDPG). The recent past has seen bilateral military exercises, the 'Dharma Guardian-2019' (between the Indian Army and Japanese Ground Self-Defence Forces), the 'SHINYUU Maitri-2019' (between Japanese Air Self-Defence Force and the Indian Air Force) and also the trilateral Malabar exercise by India, Japan and the US. India and Japan concluded their maiden '2+2 Foreign and Defence Ministerial Meeting' (started in 2014) in New Delhi on November 30, 2019, and it was just ahead of Japanese Prime Minister Shinzo Abe's visit to India in mid-December for the 14th India–Japan Annual Summit (which got postponed due to anti-CAA protests in India).

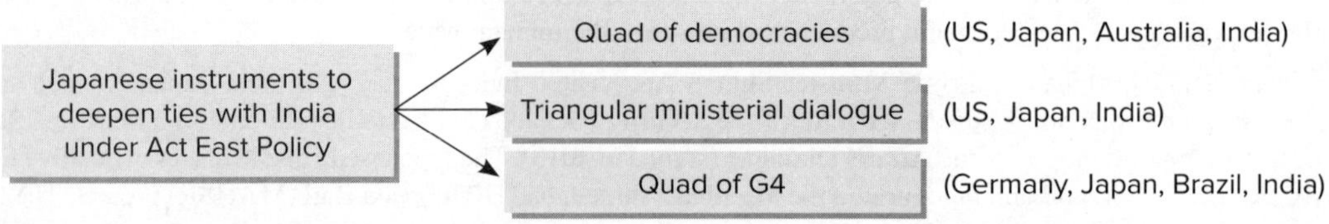

Japan has effectively used multiple 'minilateral' forums (as visible in the diagram above) to boost its ties with India. The Quad of G-4 has been used to collectively seek a UN Security Council Seat. Similarly, the Triangular Ministerial Dialogue was used as a mechanism not only to promote public opinion and dialogue but also to foster maritime cooperation. The reinterpretation of Article 9 of the Japanese Constitution allows Japan to boost strategic cooperation with India. The amended Article 9 (since September 2015) allows Japan to send military aid to friendly states (that includes India) if they come under attack from another state. This amendment has opened up new avenues of strategic diplomacy between India and Japan.

MALABAR EXERCISE—A CONCERT AT THE SEAS TO AVOID THE THUCYDIDES TRAP

In 2017, Indian Navy (IN) collaborated with Japan and the US to carry out the Malabar exercises. During the Cold War, IN remained isolated due to the non-alignment. Though Soviet Union did provide India with naval hardware, but, no professional interaction happened between IN and Soviet Navy during the Cold War. IN remained clung to the outdated doctrines of NATO. When the USSR disintegrated, India lost all inhibitions of non-alignment and decided to embrace the post-Cold War world order with a new confidence. The US dispatched the Pacific Army commander General Claude Kicklighter who proposed the US–India military to military cooperation in 1991. India and the US did a naval drill in 1992 for the first time. This naval drill led to the birth of the Malabar exercise between India and the USA. Malabar provided the IN with new insights into tactics, doctrines and warfare techniques. As the Malabar exercises progressed, Japan entered the scene in 2016 and thereby made Malabar a trilateral format. The naval cooperation of India has moved out of the orbit of non-alignment to enter into the new mutant of non-alignment that is strategic autonomy. Malabar exercises are an attempt by India to avoid a Thucydides trap. Thucydides said that it was the rise of Athens that led to fear in the mind of Sparta, leading to the war. Today the Indian foreign policy, in order to avoid the Thucydides trap is cooperating with Japan and the US to establish a favourable regional balance of power. The 2017 Malabar exercise gave an insight to the IN to benefit from the diverse operational expertise. As China acquires bases in the Indian Ocean and enhances its presence in India's backyard, the Malabar exercises provide the IN an opportunity to establish a triad which could manifest as a mega trilateral balancer in the region.

DEMOCRATIC SECURITY DIAMOND IN INDO-PACIFIC

Shinzo Abe has also proposed a 'Democratic Security Diamond' involving Japan, India, the US and Australia. The Diamond shall be the guardian of maritime security from the Indian Ocean to western Pacific. One of the reasons why Japan has proposed the Diamond is because of declining the US power in the region. As China becomes assertive and the US witnesses a gradual decline in its power in Asia, Japan intends to fill the void with a partnership with other democratic Asian states. The National Security strategy of Japan announced in 2013 had also included India as a primary driver in maintaining the balance of power in Asia disturbed by a rising China. Japanese scholar Dr. Satoru Nagao has stressed that countries in the Indo-Pacific region are in the midst of a security dilemma regarding their maritime projection and are countering this by up scaling production of submarines, which are considered symbols of tackling statist threats. He emphasised that the coastal countries around the East China Sea have increased the number of submarines in their naval arsenal in the light of the changing power balance between the US and China. Speaking at the conference on 'India–Japan Partnership in the Changing Asian Strategic Scenario', organised on March 18, 2016, he further asserted that to mitigate the threat of assertiveness China, Japan should cooperate at the defence level with India, which is also another rising power in Asia. One of the key areas of identified cooperation is at the maritime level. India has decided to buy 12 US–2 Amphibian aircrafts from Japan. The defence cooperation, while being on the rise, has also brought some concerns. Japan is concerned about its intellectual property in defence technology transfers. India has convinced Japan of its stellar reputation in preventing breaches of intellectual property. Though the US will remain the nucleus of Japan's security policy, India has emerged in the ambit of Japan as a crucial player for Asian security.

NUCLEAR DIPLOMACY BETWEEN INDIA AND JAPAN

In November 2016, at an annual bilateral summit, India and Japan concluded a nuclear deal, which was being negotiated since 2010. The successful conclusion of the deal will provide India access to the Japanese nuclear market as well as their technology. During the negotiation stage, Japan had been insisting that India sign the NPT and the CTBT. India, on the other hand, convinced Japan of its good track record in non-proliferation as well as a self-imposed moratorium on further nuclear testing. India, thus, concluded the deal without being a signatory to the NPT. They have signed an additional document called a 'Note' on views and understanding as per which if India violates its self-imposed moratorium, and then Japan has the right to terminate nuclear cooperation with India. The termination of the deal shall not be up-front. There will be a joint security assessment to analyse the reasons that compelled India to undertake the nuclear testing in the first place. This would be followed by a safety assessment where they would determine the impact on the safety of the facility in case supplies are stopped. This would be followed by the clause of right to return. As per the clause, Japan, at its own cost, will seek a return of the material supplied to India. As per the deal, Japan will give a one-year notice to India before ending nuclear cooperation if India tests a nuclear weapon. India has already signed deals with France, Russia and the USA. As a majority of the nuclear parts were made by Japan, in the absence of a deal with Japan, India found it tough to order nuclear technology from the US, France and Russia. As firms like GE, Westing house and Areva have stakes in Hitachi, Mitsubishi and Toshiba, the Indo-Japan deal will now open up business opportunities in India for all of them. India used the Indo-US nuclear deal as a template while designing the clause related to reprocessing. India has the right to reprocess at sites, which are under the safeguards put in place by the IAEA by signing the nuclear deal with Japan. Japan not only has some very advanced nuclear technologies but also is a reliable player, as it is known for not imposing additional ties. As the two countries take their relations to global strategic partnership level, the nuclear deal will help the two achieve the dream of Asian G-2.

TOKYO DECLARATION AND TWO-PLUS-TWO DIALOGUE BETWEEN INDIA AND JAPAN

The Indian Prime Minister paid a visit to Japan from 31st August to 3rd September 2014. During the visit, the two nations concluded the Tokyo Declaration. The two sides decided to strengthen bilateral cooperation through various dialogue mechanisms and to use 'two plus two dialogue' involving their foreign and defence secretaries to strengthen security cooperation. The Prime Minister announced establishment of India–Japan Investment Promotion Partnership where the two sides decided to double the inflow of FDI to India over the next five years. Japan also decided to invest 3.5 trillion yen ODA to India in specific sectors. The visit of Indian Prime Minister to Japan in 2014 led to the birth of Tokyo Declaration. The two leaders have taken the bilateral relations to the level of special strategic and global partners. At the defence level in 2014, the leaders had further decided that:

- There shall be regular military and naval exercises between the two nations.
- There shall be a trilateral defence meeting between India, Japan and the USA.
- Japan has lifted the ban on sale of products of defence companies they had imposed after 1998 PNE.
- Japan would sell US-2 amphibian aircrafts to India.

Similarly, Japan has affirmed investments in the 'Plus Five Segment', namely infrastructure transport, smart cities, Ganga cleaning, manufacturing and clean energy. Japan shall also be creating Industrial townships in India. The two have decided to name Varanasi as Kyoto's sister city in the near future.

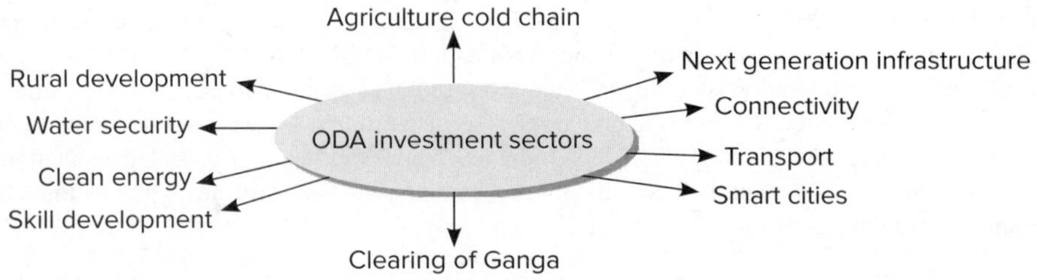

Japan has committed to develop

- Electronics parks and Japanese-style industrial townships in India
- Various projects in infrastructure, investment, energy and natural resources
- Cooperation in the field of civilian nuclear energy for peaceful uses
- Japan in the next 10 years would train 30,000 Indian youth by setting up a Japan–India institute for manufacturing
- Transfer of defence equipment and technology
- Agreement on protection of classified military information
- To create an infrastructure that would boost connectivity, the two sides decided to synergise the Act East Policy and Japan's partnership for quality infrastructure

WILL JAPAN LEAVE AMERICAN MONOGAMY AND DRIVE INDO-PACIFIC ORDER WITH INDIA?

Considering that NITI Aayog has given a big push to use IoT, Artificial intelligence, robotics and 3D printing for development in India, the Indo-Japan cooperation can help in leveraging the sectors together. In the summit, India has decided to integrate Ayushman Bharat and Japanese Asia Health and Well-being Initiative to leverage cooperation in medical equipment and hospitals. During the Cold War, India and Japan could not envisage a strategic relationship due to ideological differences. As India followed non-alignment, it emerged as a big tree that gave no shade while Japan focused on economic reconstruction after the World War II and earned a reputation of an economic giant but a political pygmy. In the post-Cold War period, the growing assertiveness of China and the decline of the US power in Asia has prompted proximity between India and Japan as both have realised that they have to defend themselves to tackle China. Both also fear a possibility of G-2 (the US and China) as a new threat. Shinzo Abe has demonstrated capabilities to position Japan as a leading power in Asia while Modi has driven India away from the ideological burden of non-alignment to position India as a leading power by building wide ranging partnerships. The bilateral economic cooperation too has got enhanced under the Act East Policy of India and Expanded Partnership for Quality Infrastructure in Asia (EPQI) of Japan. The newness in the India–Japan relationship is a bilateral decision of the two to form a minilateral coalition to jointly develop Africa (by pooling human and financial capital) under the Asia–Africa Growth Corridor. A strong alliance between India and Japan will not upset the US as both favour Indo-Japan proximity. As the depth in the bilateral diplomatic ties enhance, three questions remain:

- Whether India will enter into an alliance with Japan to promote a stable balance of power in Asia?
- Whether Modi will overcome the bureaucratic inertia to go for an alliance?
- Will Japan leave the monogamy of its alliance with the US and embrace India?

Japan, being a nation in need of rare earth metals, is eagerly exploring the same in China despite the fact that India has a lot of rare earth metals. However, India lacks adequate technology to explore them. This is certainly one area where Japan and India can work jointly in the future.

CHAPTER 6

India's Strategic and Economic Relations with South Korea

LOCATING THE STRATEGIC SIGNIFICANCE OF SOUTH KOREA IN INDIAN FOREIGN POLICY

In 1929, in a poem, Tagore wrote "In the golden age of Asia Korea was in of its lamp bearers, and that lamp is waiting to be lit once again for the illumination of the East." These evocative lines by Tagore clearly reflect the vision of the Republic of India about the Republic of Korea (ROK). The connecting factor between India and ROK has always been Buddhism. Ashoka is known to have sent iron and gold from India to Korea to establish Buddhist statues there. In 1947, the UN Temporary Commission on Korea consisting of nine member states was established to hold elections in Korea in May 1948, with India as the Chairman of the Korean Commission.

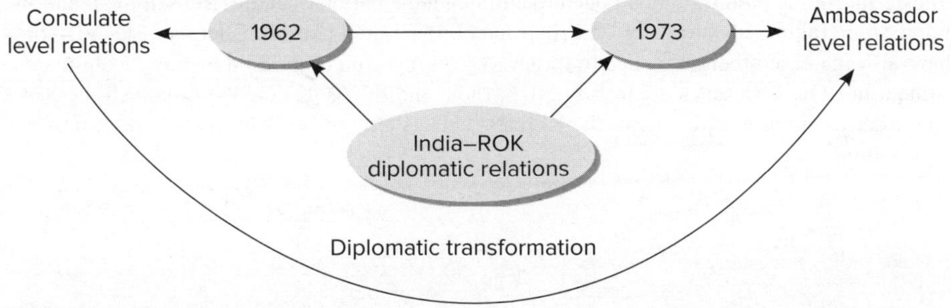

India played an important role during the period from 1950 to 1953, with North and South Korea finally accepting the Indian-sponsored ceasefire on 21st July 1953. India's diplomacy in 1954 Geneva Conference that officially ended the Korean crises was highly appreciated. As the Cold War entered Asian theatre in the 1950s, India announced non-alignment while ROK chose an alliance with the US and in 1953 signed a mutual defence treaty with the US under the leadership of Rhee Syngh Man.

COMPREHENSIVE ECONOMIC PARTNERSHIP AGREEMENT AND KOREA PLUS DIPLOMACY WITH INDIA

The Foreign Policy and Security Dialogue envisaging long-term cooperative partnership and matters related to defence and terrorism and so forth were discussed in the dialogue. As the negotiations went on, the two diversified into trade, science and technology, IT and infrastructure. Gradually textiles, oil and gas also came up in energy negotiations and economic cooperation. ROK recognised that India has ready availability of cheap and skilled labour. The ROK began to envisage India as an emerging as a destination where the ROK can invest, manufacture and boost exports to the rest of the world. ROK identified, as per the Indian skill set, automobiles and shipbuilding to work upon.

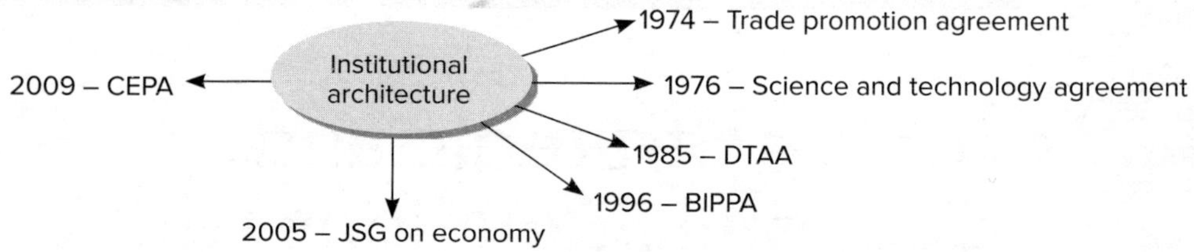

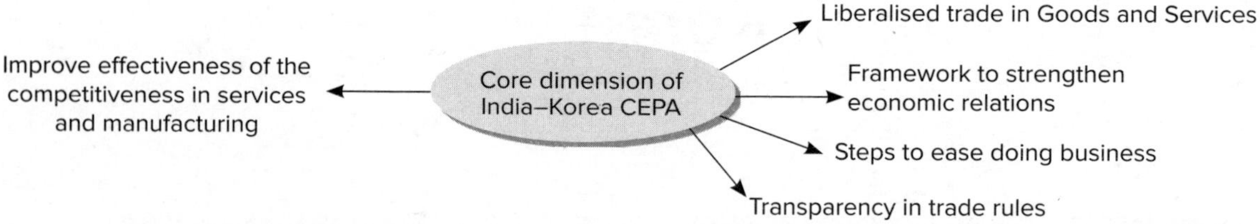

To enhance economic cooperation, a Joint Study Group (JSG) was established in 2006. The JSG began to explain the potential of a future Comprehensive Economic Partnership Agreement (CEPA) between India and ROK. The CEPA was concluded in 2009 and came into effect in 2010. As a result of the CEPA, bilateral trade has increased and India has become a top exporter of IT and ITES exports. On the other hand, India is taking advantage of the high-quality steel and heavy machinery imported from Korea. The CEPA has classified 11,200 tariff lines of Korea and 5200 tariff lines of India, which are, put under six broad categories for tariff reduction and elimination. As textiles and agriculture are crucial and sensitive to both, they have been excluded. The CEPA has also led to India expanding in telecom and construction sectors, apart from IT. It also allows movement of professionals, especially at the IT and engineering levels. In 2014, the Ministerial Joint Commission had been recommended creation of India–ROK Joint Trade and Investment Promotion Commission. Taking advantage of CEPA, Honda has set up a plant in Chennai. LG, Visteon Automobiles and Hyundai have also increased their presence in India. Korean investment in India mostly lies in manufacturing just as Indian investment in ROK is in services. In July 2016, India and the ROK decided to launch the Korea+ Platform to boost trade. In order to promote investment, the Korea + acts as a platform that hosts representatives from Korean industry and energy ministries.

INDO-PACIFIC AS BINDER OF STRATEGIC COOPERATION OF INDIA AND SOUTH KOREA

The origin of India–ROK Strategic Partnership (SP) owes itself to the visit of Roh Moo Hyun to India in 2004. India and the ROK signed Agreement for Long-Term Cooperation Partnership for Peace and Prosperity in 2004. In 2010, when South Korean President Lee Myung Bak visited India, the relations were transformed and upgraded to the level of strategic partnership. Over a period of time, both had realised the need to cooperate at the strategic level due to the changing balance of power in Asia, thanks to a rising China. The commitment of both for a multipolar and a democratic Asia strengthened their need to cooperate at the strategic level. In 2015, the Indian Prime Minister visited South Korea and upgraded the relation to the level of a Special Strategic Partnership.

A unique factor of the Special Strategic Partnership is that now the two nations shall undertake a 2+2 dialogue at the Foreign and Defence Ministers' level regularly.

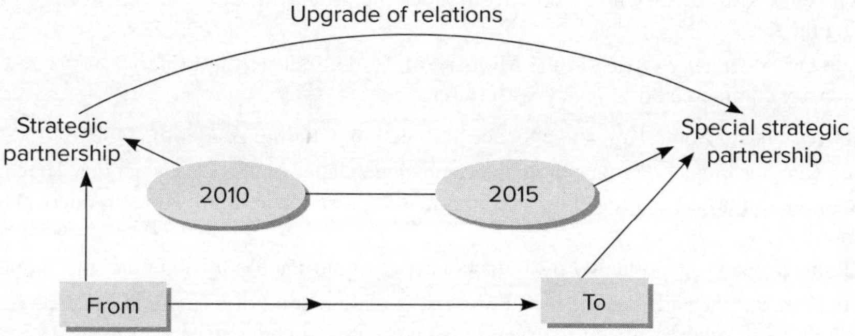

DEFENCE AND NUCLEAR DIPLOMACY IN THE INDO-PACIFIC

In 2011, India and the ROK signed a nuclear deal. Korea is a market leader and is also building nuclear reactors for the UAE. South Korea has been working on fourth generation fast reactors and is making progress in that area. The ROK wants to build reactors for India but India plans to first undertake nuclear research jointly with the country. It would be important to note that India has adopted a wait-and-watch policy over nuclear commerce with the ROK since 2011 as India wants to witness the success of Korean reactors in the UAE (Korean reactors are already very successful in Jordan). Most of the Korean nuclear technology is indigenously manufactured and Korea has successfully used nuclear diplomacy in its foreign policy amongst global players. The year 2005 saw India–ROK sign Agreement on Defence Logistics and Supplies. This increased the bilateral defence visits. In 2010, both signed Agreement on Humanitarian Assistance and Mutual Interest in the defence sector. There is a permanent diplomatic post of a defence attaché in Indian Embassy in Seoul. In 2014, the South Korean President visited India and signed an Agreement on the Exchange of Classified Military Information. This clearly reflects the growing strategic convergence between the two nations. Now, sensitive intelligence and defence information would come to be regularly shared. Since 2014, cyber security has emerged as an important dimension. Korea is a pioneer in shipbuilding and naval combat technology and India has expressed interest to cooperate in this regard. The strategic partnership and defence cooperation are destined to lay down a deep future cooperation.

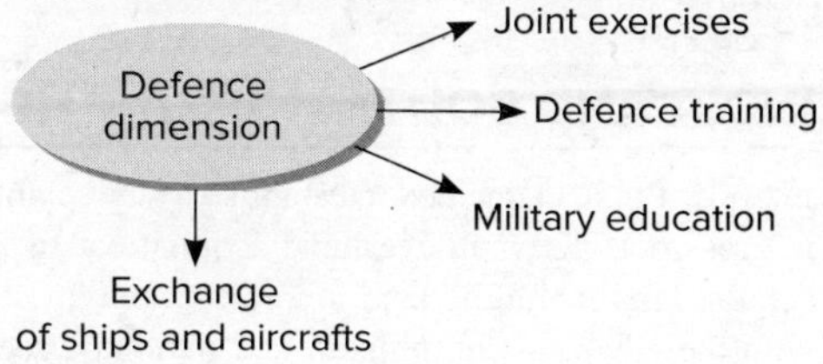

SOUTH KOREA: INDIA'S NEW 'SEOUL' MATE IN INDO-PACIFIC REALM

Because of a rising China and its own southbound policy titled as Belt and Road Initiative, the Asian states are witnessing a rise on new nomenclature of policies today. India has initiated 'Act East Policy', South Korea 'New Southern Policy', Japan has initiated 'New Southward Advance' and Taiwan has 'New Southbound Policy'. In the recent times South Korea has attached greater significance to India in its foreign policy. The recently announced New Southern Policy (NSP) is a testimony to the fact. The NSP is designed to enhance strategic and economic relationship with South East Asian states and India. This is the first ever South Korean official endorsement and documentation of deepening ties with India. The NSP has to be seen in the larger context of the New Northern Policy (NNP). The NNP has been established with the objective of engaging with Russia. The NNP and NSP together is a new cosmic power unleashed by South Korea to engage with states that were never under the radar of South Korea and build a 'balanced diplomacy'. The major difference between India's Act East Policy (AEP) and NSP is that while NSP is purely economic in nature, the AEP has both geostrategic and economic components. For India, South Koreas is a shining economic example. In 1960s, South Korea was one of the poorest economies and was able to enter into the wealthy club of OECD in 1996. It is a remarkable transformation where it underwent a movement from poverty to prosperity in one generation, thereby avoiding the 'middle income trap' in which India is stuck as of now. Under the NSP, South Korea, for India, has carried out certain important actions.

1. In the Korean National Diplomatic Academy, South Korea has established a research centre on India.
2. The research centre will identify and theoretically does the ground work for the President on the core areas of strengthening the ties.
3. A New Trade Order Strategy Office in the Ministry of Trade, Industry and Energy has been created by South Korea to intensify commercial diplomacy with India.

There are four major reasons for South Korea to enhance partnership with India under the NSP.

1. Firstly, South Koreans intend to reduce their economic dependence on the US and China. They have realised that India is one of the important centres of economic gravity that can help South Korea reduce their dependence on the US and China.
2. Secondly, South Korea wants to tacitly push the concept of Indo-Pacific by aligning with India.
3. Thirdly, at the heart of the shift lies the threat of a rising China. South Korea does not perceive the rising China as an opportunity but rather a threat (a survey of South Korean people affirmed this as 41% of the population agrees China is a threat). The recent Chinese forays in the South China Sea; its assertive behaviour on maritime issues and its reluctance to respect international laws of seas has increased fears in South Koreans who perceive that China is an expansionist state.
4. Fourthly, there is domestic reason. South Korean President Moon Jae-In came to power on the promise of democratising the businesses that apparently are owned by large business families in South Korea (called as chaebol). The chaebol have assumed a characteristic of crony capitalism and have been involved in political scandals. Moon was elected on the promise of pushing up bottom up jobs and that is possible only through wider diplomacy with new states, thus NSP and India.

This new approach of South Korea has put India on a strategic footing. It already has a CEPA with South Korea. The NSP of South Korea and Act East Policy of India can now synchronise with each other easily. The two sides can now evolve an understanding to deepen ties from commerce to strategic constructs like the Indo-Pacific to become genuine 'Seoul Mates'.

INDIA AND SOUTH KOREA: THE NEW SECURITY PROVIDERS

In 2005, POSCO decided to establish a steel plant in India. However, the project, since its inception, has gotten entangled in grassroots activism over land acquisition. In 2008, the Indian Supreme Court also gave a green signal to POSCO to acquire land including land in a forest area for steel plant construction. But the project was further entangled in hurdles with the environment ministry and national green tribunals. Because of the ongoing issues, in July 2015, POSCO had announced its decision to put the project on hold citing an internal decision of the management. The project may not be operational as of now but POSCO still continues to be in India. The prosperity seeks to enhance cooperation for mutual economic growth and economic integration. The peace refers to a denuclearised Korean peninsula that will be conducive for regional and global stability. In order to strengthen the cooperation under the rubric of 3P (People, Prosperity and Peace) for civilisational and cultural tie, the two sides have diplomatic cooperation under the Korea plus initiative, New Southern Policy and India South Korea CEPA.

CHAPTER 7

India's Strategic and Economic Relations with Vietnam

STRATEGIC SIGNIFICANCE OF VIETNAM FOR INDIAN FOREIGN POLICY

The relations between India and Vietnam go back to the second century BC when Indian traders used to sail from India to the Indo-China region. The trade also led to a spread of Indian culture and ideas to Vietnam. The biggest manifestation of Indian culture is visible in Central and South Vietnam where the Champa Temples stand as testimony to cultural diffusion. The two countries also have commonality at the level of a National Liberation movement for independence. During the World War II, both India and Vietnam (a colony of the French) were able to establish a solid foundation on a common anticolonial plank and non-alignment. During the Cold War, the US–Vietnam War broke out; India showed support and solidarity with Vietnam and condemned the US presence in Vietnam. In June 1966, India advocated an end of bombing by the US in Vietnamese territory and favoured conflict resolution through the Geneva Accords. The US–Vietnam War finally ended in 1972 with the conclusion of the Paris Accords.

India expressed happiness and satisfaction on the conclusion of the US–Vietnam conflict by making positive statements on the floor of the house of the Indian Parliament. In 1972, India and Vietnam established ambassador-level relations and opened up diplomatic ties. Post-unification of Vietnam in 1975, India even supported the Vietnamese Cambodian invasion. It also supported the Vietnamese in their War with China in 1979. During the Cold War period, India and Vietnam remained committed to each other bound by a common ideology of non-alignment. However, they also had their adverse attitude towards the US as another commonality during the Cold War. As the Cold War ended, India initiated a new policy paradigm at the economic and foreign policy level. India also made an internal economic transition of open economy. At the foreign policy level, in 1993, India initiated the Look East Policy (LEP). Under this policy, India decided to integrate itself with South East Asian states. Vietnam was not only an important South East Asian economy but also became a member of the ASEAN. As under the Look East Policy, India began to initiate a dialogue with the ASEAN, and began to use it as a platform to economically engage with Vietnam. In the Ministry of External Affairs of India, a separate division was created for CLMV countries (Cambodia, Laos, Myanmar and Vietnam), which provided the needed impetus to propel Indo-Vietnam cultural relations. As India and Vietnam began to explore the commercial dimension in their bilateral diplomacy, a new feature that came up into the Vietnamese foreign policy was its gradual rapprochement with the US. Because of an increasingly powerful Chinese presence, the US has realised the strategic significance of Vietnam in keeping an eye on China. As the US initiated the rebalancing of Asia-Pacific through its Pivot to Asia Policy, Vietnam found its presence in the new strategic calculus. Vietnam is not only a part of the USA's Pivot to Asia, but was also one of the twelve Trans-Pacific Partnership states. Since the end of the Cold War, India–US ties have also improved and the two have even explored a strategic dimension in their bilateral diplomacy. In the context of India and Vietnam, the strategic dimension signifies a strong defence partnership. If India and Vietnam are developing proximity at the strategic level today, then apart from India's Act East Policy, a common factor has been the US need to check a rising China. Thus, India and Vietnam relations have transformed over a period of time from being ideological in nature to economic-cum-strategic in nature today. The diagram below captures the shift in Indo-Vietnam diplomatic ties. India's Act East Policy and Vietnamese Look West Policy seem to be converging at the right point to reshape the Asian Balance of Power.

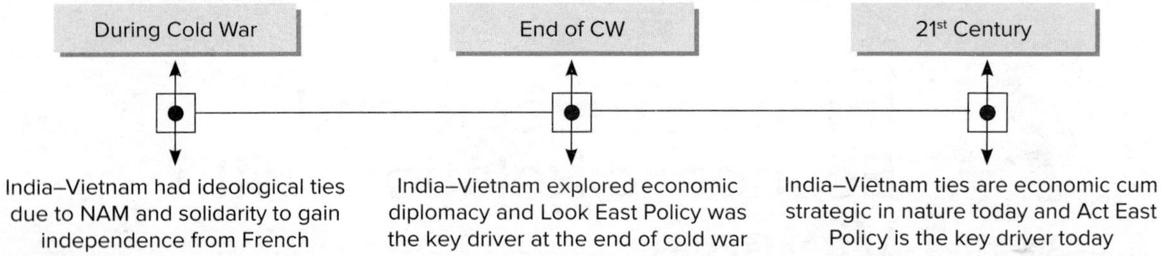

BUILDING OF STRATEGIC AND SECURITY DIPLOMACY STRUCTURES

In 2007, both sides had signed Strategic Partnership Agreements. The Indian Prime Minister Narendra Modi visited Vietnam in 2016 and held talks with his counterpart Nguyễn Xuân Phúc. During the Indian Prime Minister's visit, both sides elevated their Strategic Partnership to the level of a Comprehensive Strategic Partnership. Whenever two states intend to explore their relationship in a particular dimension, there are multiple diplomatic mechanisms available. Normally the ties move in the direction as depicted below.

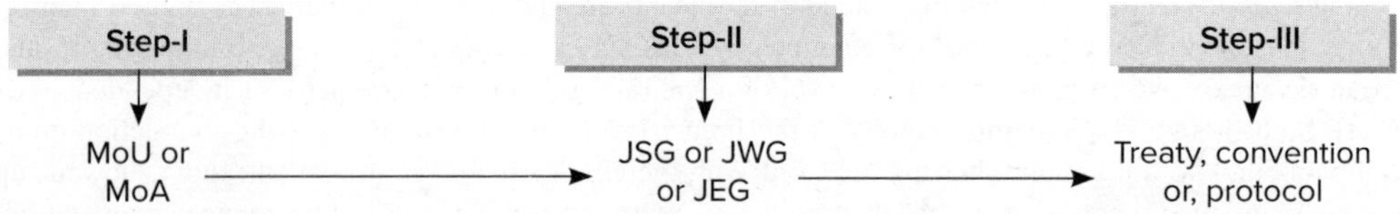

However, practically, in diplomacy, it is found that countries do not usually follow the three steps chronologically and often jump from one step to the other directly. India and Vietnam signed MoU on Defence Cooperation in 1995. This MoU led to the conclusion of India–Vietnam Defence Protocol in the year 2000. There are multiple dimensions in the strategic diplomacy between India and Vietnam.

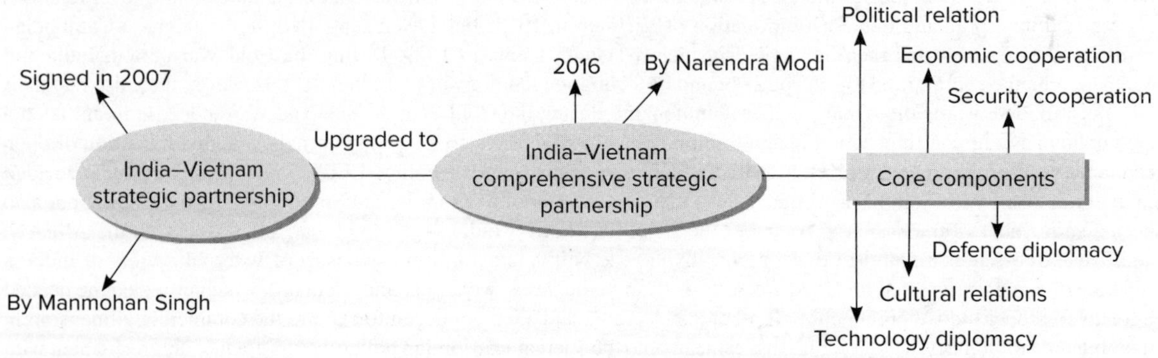

INDIA'S COMMERCIAL DIPLOMACY TEMPLATE IN INDO-PACIFIC AND VIETNAM MODEL OF COOPERATION

During the Cold War as both India and Vietnam were closed economies, which rendered the commercial angle in diplomacy pretty weak. The end of the Cold War ushered in a resurgent commercial dimension. India and Vietnam almost undertook economic liberalisation simultaneously. This opening up of the economy in Vietnam was called the Đổi Mới. A unique feature shared between India and Vietnam is that both the countries in the post-Cold War era have adopted a socialist economy with a tilt towards capitalism. Vietnam cited lack of finance as a reason that hindered bilateral trade with India. As finance became a hindering factor, India decided to assist Vietnam. When a country needs to boost trade, it can use two instruments, that of a loan or a line of credit. Let us take a hypothetical example. Let us say India decides to give Vietnam a loan of 100 rupees. In case of a loan, the purpose once defined cannot be changed. Thus, loan at times becomes a rigid instrument. It cannot use the unused amount for any purpose other than the stated purpose. But when it comes to the interest repayment, Vietnam shall pay an interest to India on the entire 100 rupees even if it has not used or been able to use the entire amount. Thus, loan becomes a commerce-centric instrument. That is why another instrument used for promoting trade ties is the line of credit. Now, the nation receiving the LOC has the flexibility to use the money for whatever purpose they want. The nation extending the LOC can recommend to the recipient nation on the potential use of the money but the recipient nation has the freedom to use the money for any purpose. Let us assume Vietnam used the 100 rupees LOC to buy a machine for the same purpose as stated above. Let us say, that the machine costs 80 rupees. Now if 20 rupees is the unutilised amount, Vietnam has the flexibility to use it for any purpose, which is not true in case of a loan. In an LOC, the interest is always paid on the amount utilised by the recipient state (that is on 80 rupees). The LOC is a very flexible instrument because if the recipient nation feels that it cannot utilise the entire amount, it has the flexibility to give back the unutilised amount back without the interest. If Vietnam feels that it cannot use the remaining 20 rupees at all, it can return 20 rupees back to India without an interest on the same. Since India had the option of extending a loan or an LOC to Vietnam, India chose to grant Vietnam LOC. India since the end of the Cold War has given 20 lines of credit to Vietnam. It is due to these lines of credits that the bilateral Indo-Vietnam trade is approximately 8.3 billion dollars. India imports machines, phone components, computers, electronic hardware, rubber, chemicals and coffee while it exports meat, fish, corn, cotton and pharmacy products. India has 93 projects going on in Vietnam totaling about one billion dollars. In 1982, India also extended the 'Most Favoured Nation' status to Vietnam. Tata Power is investing 1.8 billion dollars in a 1320 megawatt power project in Nha Trang Province. At the level of capacity building, India, in 2007, established a centre for English language training in Technical University in Nha Trang and a centre for Software development in Ho Chi Minh City. India has been taking FDI to Vietnam primarily in the oil, tea and sugar industries. As India and the ASEAN have an FTA, this forum is also utilised by both India and Vietnam to deepen their engagement at the commercial level. To enhance the bilateral economic ties, achieving trade target of 15 billion dollars by 2020 has been declared as a strategic objective.

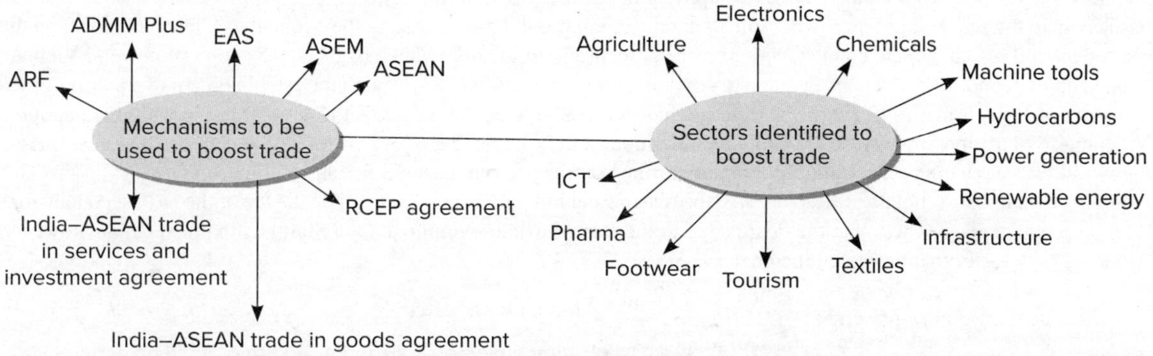

INDIA'S OIL INTERESTS IN VIETNAM, STRATEGIC CLASHES WITH CHINA IN SOUTH CHINA SEA AND INDIA'S STAND

India's presence happened in 1978 when Petroleum minister K. D. Malviya had shown interest in oil from Vietnam. Vietnam privatised their oil and gas sector in 1988. Since then, India's ONGC Videsh Limited (OVL) has been undertaking oil cooperation with Vietnam. To facilitate deeper oil cooperation, India's OVL has set up a joint venture with Petro Vietnam primarily for oil exploration. Vietnam has invited India into its exclusive economic zone and continental shelf for oil exploration. India is undertaking oil exploration in offshore blocks number 128, 152 and 153. Indian efforts for oil exploration in South China Sea has not been appreciated by China, which has objected to Indian endeavours in oil exploration in the disputed territory. India has countered Chinese claims by asserting that its presence in South China Sea is legal and it falls within the ambit of Vietnam's EEZ. India has also asserted that its oil exploration in South China Sea is as per India's maritime interest. One of the key maritime interests of India is to retain a favourable geostrategic position.

India has maintained that its presence in the South China Sea is not to contain China but for its own economic interests, especially that of its energy security needs. As per United Nations Convention on the Laws of the High Seas (UNCLOS), countries in their EEZ can explore oil, mineral resources, living and non-living natural resources including resources under the sea, seabed and subsoil. Vietnam says that by inviting India to explore oil in its EEZ, it has not done anything illegal. In the South China Sea, the executive economic zone of China and others overlap. The Paracel Islands are claimed by China, Taiwan and Vietnam. The Spratly Islands are claimed by China, Taiwan, Vietnam, Brunei and Philippines. The Scarborough Shoal is claimed by Philippines, China and Taiwan.

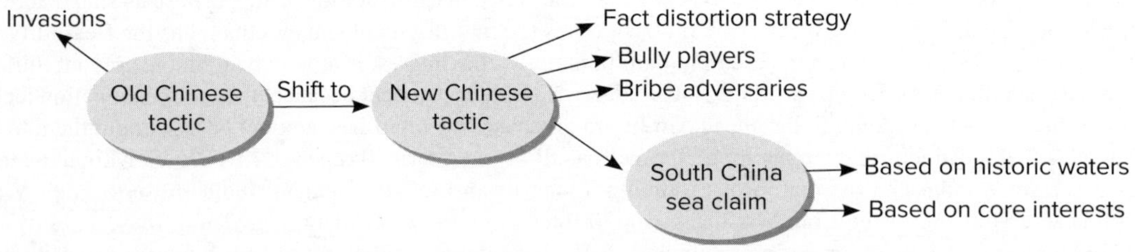

Thus, China's increasing ability to decide and expand its role in the South China Sea has not only made the region strategically significant but has also compelled India to re-evaluate its approach on the issue.

INDIA AND VIETNAM STRATEGIC COOPERATION MODEL IN INDO-PACIFIC

In recent times, defence diplomacy has gained significant acceptance in Vietnamese foreign policy discourse. Historically, Vietnam, due to its geopolitical location, has always been of maritime significance. The western part of Vietnam is hilly, meaning that the people of Vietnam have to majorly look towards the east for economic development. The east of Vietnam has access to the sea. Out of 64 provinces in Vietnam, 28 are coastal provinces. As the Vietnamese depend heavily on the sea for oil and resources, the countrymen are very susceptible to the dominance of the sea by foreign powers. Vietnam opened up its economy in 1991 and decided to go for economic modernisation through the establishment of a marine-based economy in 1997. Since 1997, maritime thinking has dominated Vietnam. In 2007, the Vietnamese government adopted Vietnamese Maritime Strategy 2020. Vietnam has a modest defence budget of 3.6 billion dollars but in 2007, it surprised the world by announcing a 1.8 billion dollar submarine contract (to purchase 6 kilo class submarines) with Russia. This landmark deal led the scholars of IR to analyse the reasons behind the Russia–Vietnam deal. One of the easiest conclusions that the scholars reached was that the deal is due to the fear of Chinese dominance in South China Sea. China, however, is not the only factor that prompted the deal.

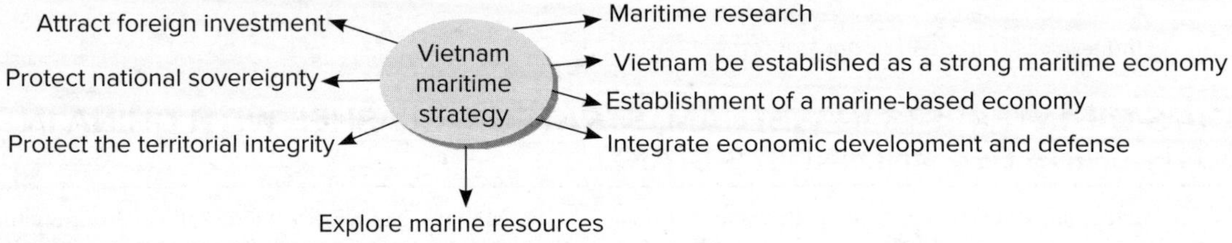

As it is clear from Vietnamese maritime strategy that Vietnam wants to achieve a perfect blend of economic and defence development, as each component is deemed crucial to achieve growth in the other. The government of Vietnam adopted a White Paper on Defence in 2009 where it had identified certain hotspots in Asian security. Larsen and Toubro would work with Vietnam Border Guards for offshore high-speed patrol boats. Vietnam would use the 100 million dollars line of credit provided by India in 2014 for defence procurements.

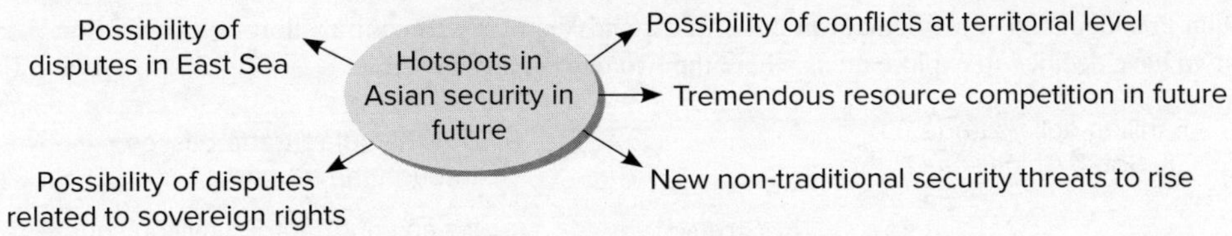

This understanding of hotspots in Asian security in future has compelled Vietnam to undertake a shift.

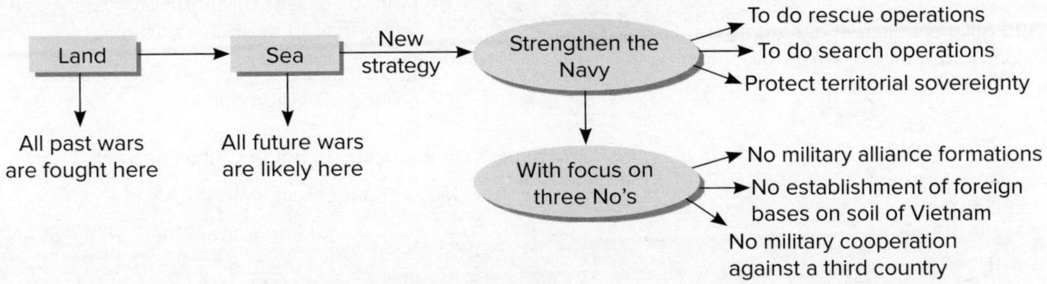

Thus, Vietnam has clarified that its naval modernisation is linked to its domestic economic development. It does not favour any arms race and has no desire or ambition to develop its navy against any third country. It has, however, kept the option open to cooperate with Russia, Japan, the US, India and Australia to assist in its defence modernisation. It is in this context that India has opened up defence diplomacy with Vietnam. In December 2016, India and Vietnam agreed on cooperation in defence and cooperation in peaceful use of atomic energy. The India–Vietnam Defence Cooperation is likely to establish a new Asian Balance of Power. The future Asian security order is therefore likely to differ from old Asian security order.

The old system was based on the US-centric alliances but over a period of time the bilateral alliances have not flourished. This means that, despite the US being a common ally to South Korea, Australia, Japan and Vietnam, it has not yielded much cooperation between these countries. One factor for the absence of such security cooperation is a lack of the US resources to tackle problems in the region. Thus, with changing ground realities, new alliances have to be built up. These new alliances are emerging as minilateral security networks which may culminate as a futuristic collective security-centric system. Thus, a new minilateral India–Vietnam alliance at defence level is on the rise in future.

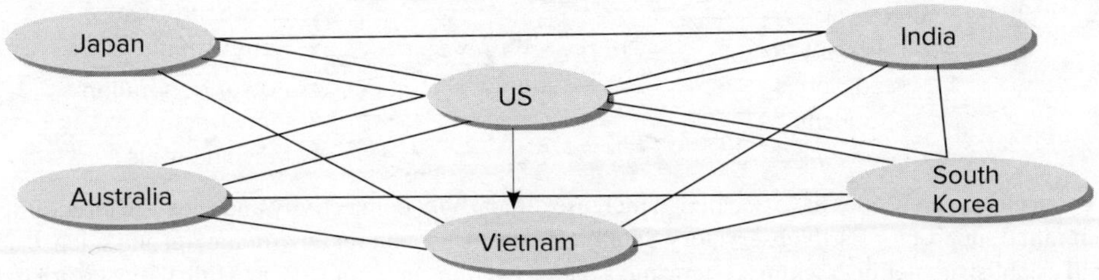

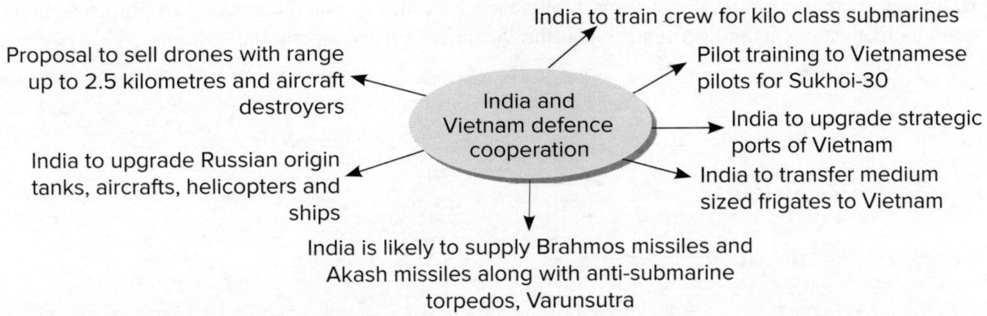

During Indian Presidents' visit to Vietnam in 2018, India and Vietnam agreed to explore a 'cooperation model'. In this model, the two have decided to explore areas where the two can achieve synergies.

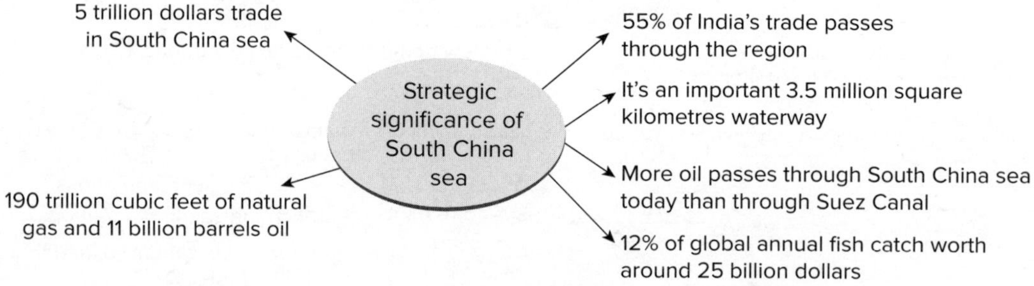

FUTURE DRIVERS OF INDO-PACIFIC REALM

The two sides have identified priority areas of cooperation.

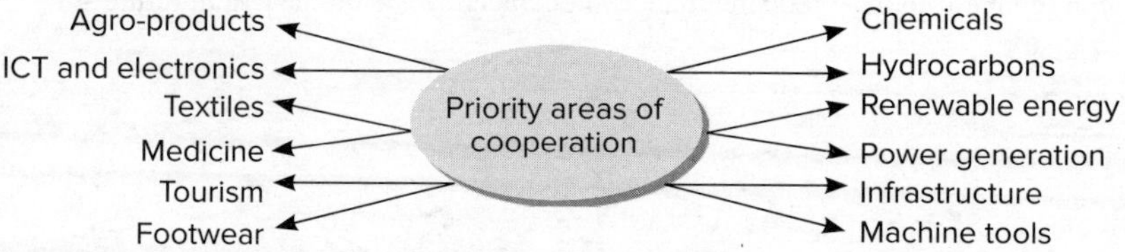

To improve connectivity, both sides have decided to increase direct flight connectivity and even use direct shipping routes. India has committed support for Earth observatory Satellite Tracking System for environmental and science needs of both. The ISRO will establish a satellite tracking system and a data reception centre in Ho Chi Minh City at a price of 23 million dollars. The images are to be used by Vietnam for intelligence, surveillance and reconnaissance purposes. India will also assist Vietnam with quick impact project funds under the Mekong–Ganga cooperation.

CHAPTER 8

India's Strategic and Economic Relations with Australia

CRICKET, CHICKEN TIKKA AND SAMOSA DIPLOMACY

The land of cricket champions, Australia has loomed large on Indian consciousness. Australia was an erstwhile British colony like India and their relation started unfolding during the colonial period. During the British era, Indian labour was used in the plantations and cane fields in Queensland. India, after its independence in 1947, established a mission in Australia and the relations can be subsequently seen in three waves. From Owen Dixon (the Australian-born UN mediator in Kashmir) who once wrote to his daughter, Anne, in Melbourne that "India is a place I hope never to trust and never wish to see again" to a virtual summit between Indian and Australian Prime Minister in 2020 reflects that India now stands high on the radars of Australia.

Australia for long has been one of the neglected countries in the Indian foreign policy despite the country having a strong international weight. Australian intelligence community is globally reckoned with while its armed forces have global recognition in the field of professionalism. With its deep security and economic connections with ASEAN, Australia have a limited but a powerful sphere of influence in the East Asian world. Despite all these strengths and Nehruvian perception of Australia as an extended part of Asia (he even invited Australia in the Asian Relations Conference, 1947), the relationship in the rest of the 20th century remains alienated. India continued to neglect Australia throughout the Cold War because of its obsession with either the neighbours or striving for a seat at the global table. It is not wrong to say that for India, the guiding factor of its 20th century diplomacy with Australia was ideology over interests. This is where Chinese had gained, who promoted an engagement with Australia on the basis of interests over ideology and targeted to engage with the Middle Power (Australia) and tried to weaken its influence with the superpowers (explained later in the strategic diplomacy section of the chapter). Now, there has been a concerted effort in Indian foreign policy to liberate it from the ideological prejudice and focus on interests over ideology. India has now realised that the key to the changing global geopolitics is held by a middle power like Australia. The common member ship of India and Australia in QUAD, G-20, the East Asian Summit and Indian Ocean Rim Association has increased possibilities for the two to cooperate in regional security and global diplomacy dimensions. The two sides have rightly identified cooperation in themes that range from reforms of WHO in the wake of COVID-19, to climate change to development of critical technologies. The geopolitical churn in the Indo-Pacific, due to Chinese assertion in South China Sea, has brought the two to explore a security dimension in the relationship.

India and Australia have a relationship based on shared values, shared interests, shared geography and shared objectives and both are committed for an open, inclusive, prosperous Indo-Pacific. In fact, India can propose a new concert of maritime cooperation with the UK, Malaysia, Singapore, Australia and New Zealand; for the larger purpose of keeping the international waters, a global common good, free for navigation for all. This will be in sync with India's rising leading power aspirations. As Britain wants to return to the orient seas, India can propose a Five Power Defence Arrangement (FPDA) to limit the global geopolitical imbalance in the waters. A promising future plurilateral is the idea of G-11, of Trump, that incorporates both India and Australia; a newly emerging construct to tackle emerging threats to global rules-based order. India and Australia seem to have taken the plunge now and both sides are determined to build an ambitious template for geo-economic and a geopolitical dynamic. The two are finally connected by the Indian Ocean and united by Samosa (a reference by Scott Morrison, the Australian Prime Minister, who have made Samosa to eat over the weekend prior to his engagement with the Indian Prime Minister in a virtual summit in 2020). Indeed Samosa Diplomacy at practice!

THREE WAVES THAT DEFINE INDIA'S ENGAGEMENT WITH AUSTRALIA

Wave 1: Foundation, Initiatives and Apprehensions The relationship of Australia and the US goes back to 1900–1901 when both cooperated for the first time to suppress the Boxer Rebellion in China. The US and Australia fought the World War II together. India had already had its mission opened in 1944 and took this opportunity to convert it to an Indian High Commission in 1947. In 1951, the ANZUS alliance was formed between Australia, New Zealand, and the USA as a Treaty for Pacific Security. In 1954, when the SEATO was created, ANZUS was brought within its ambit but the ANZUS per se continued to be the bedrock of the US–Australia relation. Because of the ideological difference, India and Australia drifted apart.

Wave 2: Attempts to mitigate apprehensions In 1971, India and Australia envisaged cultural cooperation. After the Indo-Pak war of 1971 and the subsequent conclusion of the India–Russia Treaty of Friendship, the relationship began to slowdown. The dip in the Indo-Australia relations came in 1975 when Malcolm Fraser, Australian Prime Minister criticised India's proximity to the USSR. He also took a dig at India's condemnation of the US base in Diego Garcia and refusal of India to condemn Soviet presence in the Indian Ocean region.

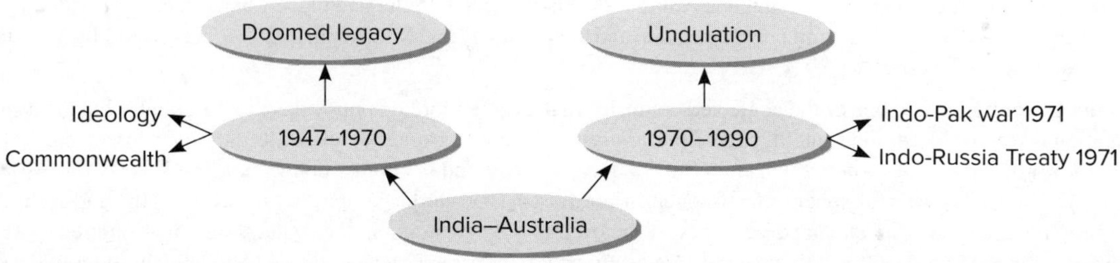

Wave 3: Confluence of ideas, inertia and strategic convergence As the Cold War ended, a growing cooperative spirit began to emerge between the two nations. Both nations began to recognise shared ideals of democracy and peace. The ending of the Cold War also made India improve its relations with the US and its immediate neighbours. Both countries identified economic cooperation as an area for strengthening bilateral relations. An Australia–India Council to promote long-term interests in India was established and in 1992, a Joint Working Group on Coal was formed. In 1994, a report called 'India's economy at the Midnight Hour' was prepared. The report examined trade and investment opportunities in India and identified areas of future investment for Australia. This report acted as a strategy document for Australian businesses. In 1995, the Australian Trade Minister Bob McMullan visited India and developed Government-to-Government ties for the institutionalisation of trade. Australia has a unique way of undertaking research to fill the gap in awareness of a target market for future. Thus, the East Asia Analytical Unit in Department of Foreign Affairs and Trade prepared the above report to guide future action. It also outlined education as a core area and encouraged Australian education industry to tap India on priority as a market for higher education.

KNOWLEDGE DIPLOMACY BETWEEN INDIA AND AUSTRALIA

Australia has come out with a White Paper Plan in Education that places Hindi as one of the four priority languages along with Chinese, Japanese and Indonesian. Australia aims to equip their children with Asian languages. Australia is promoting higher education and skill development for foreign students. If we compare Australia vis-à-vis Europe in post-study work permit, part time work permit and permanent residency permits, Australia stands positive on all three areas over and above Europe. However, with relation to Indian students, Australia saw some racial attacks in 2010–2012 where Indian students were targeted on Australian territory. Australia subsequently amended its domestic laws to make punishments very stringent for racial attacks. This created the needed impact. Australia has also undertaken a severe crackdown on fake and non-recognised universities in Victoria and other cities making education highly controlled through stringent norms. In 2014, during the visit of Tony Abbott, the Australian Prime Minister to India, he unveiled the New Colombo Plan for education. Under the plan, 1800 students from Australia will pursue internship and short programmes in India. Australia shall be training Indians in vocational skills to make them job ready in India. In 2020, Australia has abolished the 457-visa programme. Under the 457-visa programme, the Australian businesses could employ skilled foreign workers for up to four years to meet the shortage of skilled workers in Australia. Under the 457-visa programme, the employers were free to employ any number of foreigners, as there was no cap in the programme. The Turnbull administration has replaced the 457-visa programme with a Temporary Skill Shortage (TSS) visa, which would allow Australian firms access to foreign workers in a limited way. As walls turn around us everywhere, India should not fall for the hype of herds but turn the walls into an opportunity. As the future would be such where Indian workers may find it tough to work aboard, India should build up an ecosystem to incentivise foreign firms to relocate to India. To tackle rising protectionism all over the world, India should innovate its economy and ensure India emerges as a knowledge hub in the future.

COVID DIPLOMACY AND ROADMAP TO GLOBAL RECOVERY

In an effort to promote bilateral cooperation during the time of COVID-19 pandemic, the two sides have committed a new phase of engagement. The two have signed India–Australia Strategic Research Fund. This fund will enable both the parties to jointly identify innovative solutions to respond and treat COVID-19 and other determined priorities. The two also subsequently organised a Special COVID-19 Collaboration Round, a joint platform to discuss a joint response.

Australia is one of the few countries that have managed to combat COVID-19 so far through "controlled adaptation" by which the coronavirus has been suppressed to very low levels. Two of the leaders of this great Australia-wide effort are Indian-born scientists. Shitij Kapur, of the University of Melbourne, led a community of academics to produce a path breaking report, "Roadmap to Recovery", while S. S. Vasan has led efforts to develop a vaccine in a Commonwealth Scientific and Industrial Research Organisation (CSIRO) facility in a dangerous pathogens facility in Geelong, near Melbourne. One of Australia's richest businessmen, Anthony Pratt of Pratt Industries, and first patron of the Australia–India Leadership Dialogue, has described the promise of DTC–CPG (direct to consumer; consumer packaged goods) that could transform global supply chains.

NUCLEAR AND STRATEGIC DEFENCE BINDERS OF INDIA AND AUSTRALIA UNDER AUKUS

The India–Australia nuclear issue has always revolved around the NPT. Australia has a lot of uranium that India needs. However, Australia had been reluctant to supply for a long time on the basis that it was a signatory of NPT while India was not. Australia has always insisted that its nuclear supply would be conducted and in accordance to the NPT and supplies would only be granted to NPT signatories having proper safeguard agreements in place as per the IAEA. India is a non-signatory to the NPT despite having acknowledged good non-proliferation credentials. If India and Australia had any nuclear commerce, then it would mean that Australia had tried to reward non-compliance to global regimes. However, post the 2005 nuclear deal between India and the USA and Australian support to India at NSG, it has initiated a rethink. In 2011, a Joint Nuclear Group announced a policy shift for uranium exports to India for civilian use. Australia has made it clear that strict safeguards need to be negotiated upon. The change is attributed to economic gain and fear of being isolated as the US, France, Canada have already concluded nuclear deals with India. In addition, Australia has given uranium to China, which does not have a good non-proliferation record. In September 2014, Tony Abbott visited India and concluded a nuclear deal. The basis of this 2014 nuclear deal was 2005 Indo-US nuclear deal. Australia finally concluded the deal based on Indian commitments in 2005.

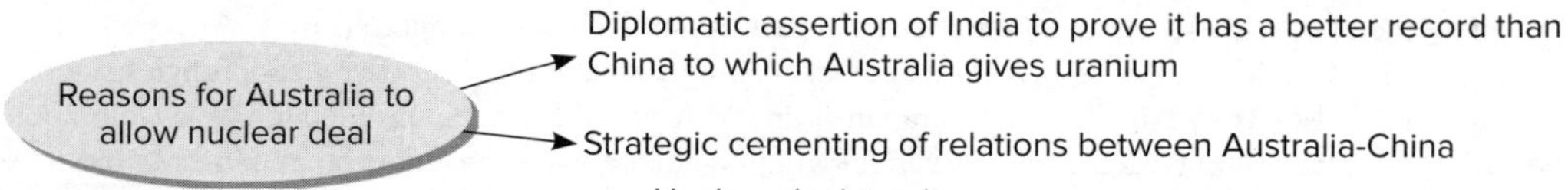

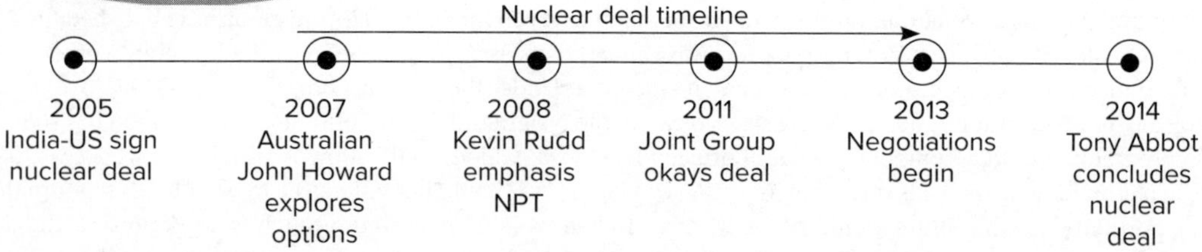

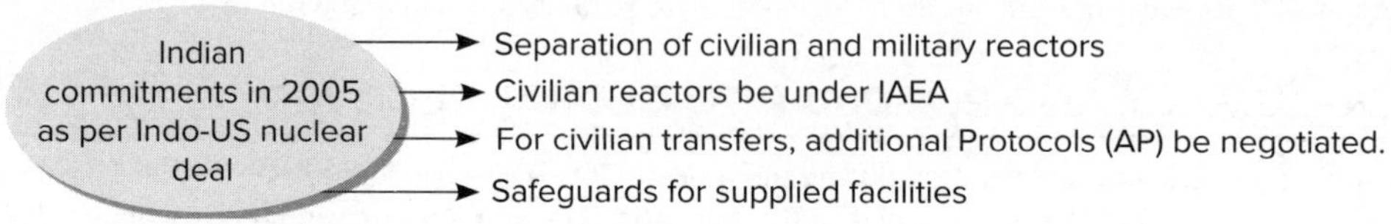

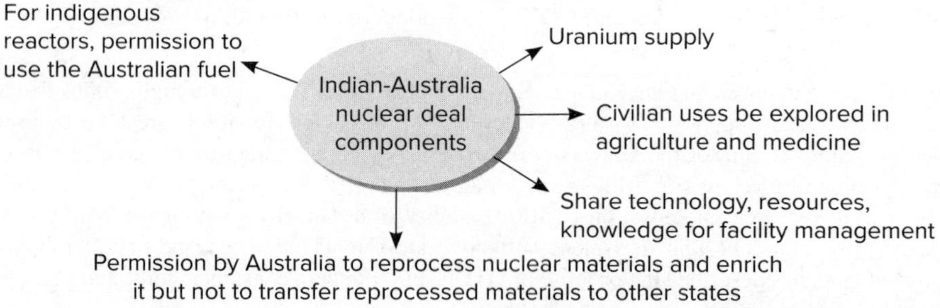

In 2009, India and Australia announced their Strategic Partnership Agreement (SPA) when the then Australian Prime Minister, Kevin Rudd, visited India. One important reason is an increased assertion by China in the South China Sea. Both India and Australia felt the need to cooperate at multiple strategic levels to ensure protection of sea-lanes of communication. Australia in 2012 had announced a White Paper on Defence. The title of the paper was 'Australia in the Asian century'. Australia says that the centre of gravity has shifted to the Indo-Pacific as the new theatre of commerce and power. Hence, Australia intends to explore opportunities in Asia.

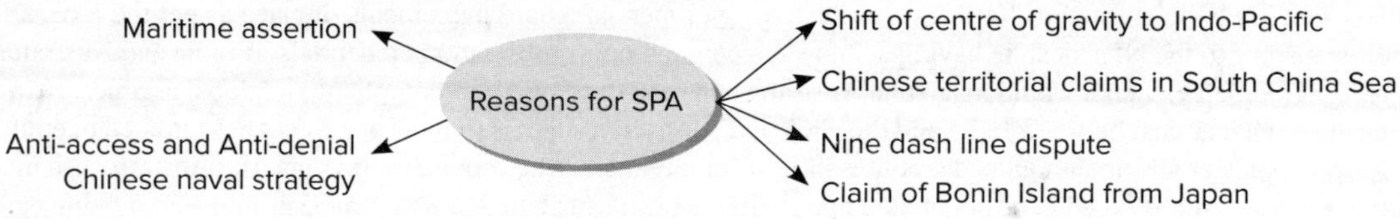

Thus, the cooperation at strategic level between India and Australia can stabilise the region and both have a shared concern for China in the strategic sphere. But the more Australia undertakes commerce with China and continues to remain a US ally, the more will be the Australian dilemma in choosing a long-term relationship with India.

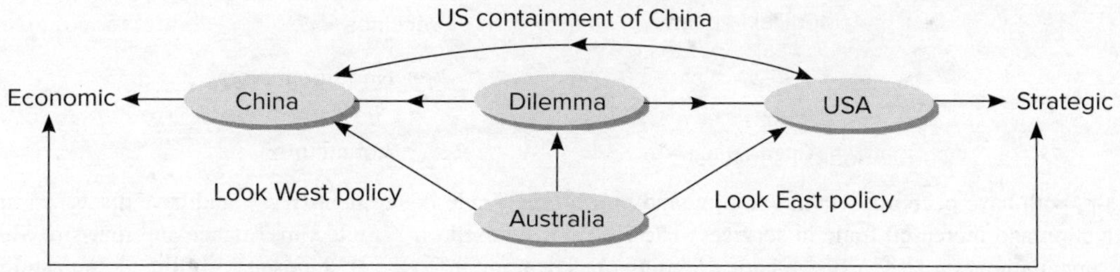

India–Australia signed a Framework for Security Cooperation in 2014. The first edition of joint naval exercise called AUSINDEX happened in 2015 in Vishakhapatnam. In June 2017, India and Australia carried out the second edition of the same in the West coast of Australia. This helped both sides lay down a foundation for a professional culture of future war fighting. Australia and India want to ensure that the dynamic Indo-Pacific region remains a region of prosperity and both sides are able to uphold a rules-based order which is challenged by unilateral action of some states (*indirect reference to China* and its assertion in the region). Both Australia and India are democracies where the leaders are accountable to the people. When democratic principles are translated and applied to foreign policy and international engagement, it gives rise to a rule-based international system based on cooperation, transparency, predictability, peace and security; which both states intend to uphold. In 2020, during the time of ongoing global COVID-19 pandemic, India and Australia held a virtual Prime Ministerial Level E-Summit. An important outcome of the summit was that the two sides decided to elevate India and Australia ties to Comprehensive and Strategic Partnership Level. The two have also decided to go for ministerial level two plus two dialogue from earlier Foreign Secretary and Defence Secretary Level, bringing Australia at par with the US and Japan now. The future for the two lies in exploring dimension common to both, that range from, marine research to joint development of strategic islands to building of underground domain awareness at the maritime level. The two sides also concluded a pact on cooperation in cyber-enabled critical technologies in 2020. The two also concluded the Mutual Logistics Support Agreement, which shall facilitate interoperability in the defence services and allow each other to use their bases (India has similar agreements with the US, South Korea, Singapore and France). This agreement will enable Indian military aircrafts to use the Cocos Islands (an Australian island located at choke point of Indian Ocean and South China Sea) that are located between Australia and Sri Lanka. In the 2020 Summit, Australia went to recognise India as "a preeminent maritime power in the Indian Ocean and a front rank partner of Australia". This growing realisation of India in the psyche of Australia is driven by China factor. The interference of Beijing in Australian politics, the Chinese strategy of using trade for geopolitics have compelled Australians to have a rethink of long-term engagement with China.

AUSTRALIA'S NEW ECONOMIC STRATEGY AND ECONOMIC SIGNIFICANCE OF INDIA IN AUSTRALIAN STRATEGIC THINKING

As the diplomatic ties between India and Australia began to normalise, trade as a dimension picked up. India exports to Australia pearls, medical instruments and IT services and imports gold, coal, copper and vegetables.

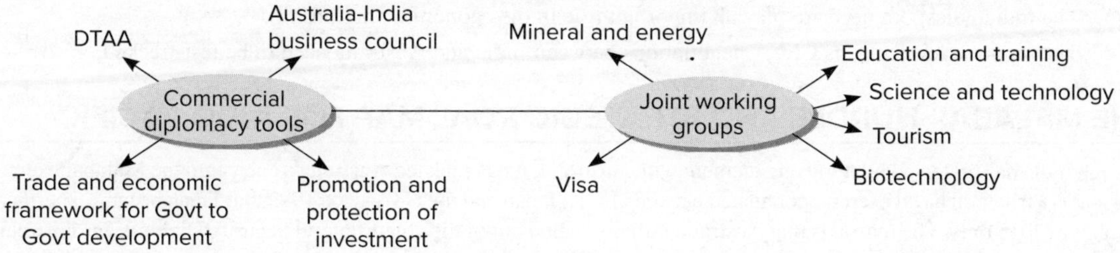

In 2006, the Australia–India Research Fund was founded with an aim to promote bilateral research in sectors to enhance science-based collaboration. In 2014, Tony Abbott donated 20 million dollars for four years to Australia–India strategic Research Fund that had identified five support areas.

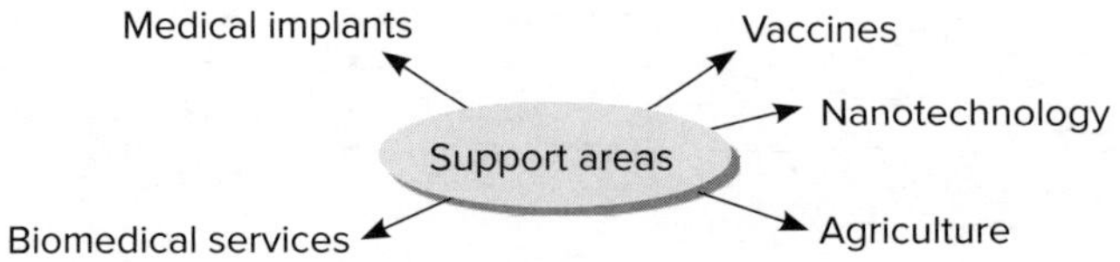

Since 2008, both have been undertaking a joint study for a Free Trade Agreement (FTA) and have discussed impact of tariff reduction and increased trade in services. The FTA has focused on IT, telecom, finance and tourism. Since May 2011, the negotiations for CECA began and still going on. The trade in 2020–21 stands at 21 billion dollars and needs to grow in the future.

Australia shall provide India with a stable source of minerals in the future and two sides during the 2020 Prime Ministerial Virtual Summit decided to conclude a new pact on Cooperation in Mining and Processing of Critical and Strategic Minerals. This agreement will enable the two parties to work together for future technological demand. The premise of this agreement is an understanding on working jointly on exploring new technologies for exploring and extracting minerals. With shared challenges and similar economic conditions, the two sides, in 2020, have also identified agriculture as a new challenge and have concluded India–Australia Agreement on Grain Management to reduce post-harvest losses, facilitate development of advanced logistics, rationalise costs and ensure farmer incomes are not affected at the time of COVID-19.

The New Economic Strategy adopted by Australia accepts that India is a rapidly growing economy. The geostrategic compulsion behind the strategy is the rising profile of the two states in the Indo-Pacific. With centre of economic and strategic priority shifting to the Indo-Pacific, the strategy makes an entry point at the right moment. Australia has already asserted that it will cooperate with India in 2019 in Indo-Pacific Endeavour (IPE), a maritime engagement under AUSINDEX. The report acknowledges that despite diplomatic relations between the two states have entered the first tier; the economic diplomacy is stuck as second tier. With its rising economic weight, India cannot be neglected. The strategy has asserted that Australia needs to press the reboot button to have a renewed and fresh look at India with stress on people-to-people ties and geopolitical congruence (on factors like rising China, rules-based maritime order to prevent buy or bully behaviour of hegemons, and desire of India to bring democracies together).

The report makes certain recommendations:

1. A new trade target for twenty years has been set. The target is to take the bilateral trade to 45 billion USD (which was 15 billion USD in 2020).
2. To undertake transformation in the relationship, Australia needs to increase investment in India to 100 billion USD in twenty years (from 11 billion USD today).
3. The strategy has identified 10 sectors and 10 states where Australia has a competitive edge and where it needs patience and strategy to implement.
4. The core sectors include education, agribusiness, resources, and tourism and energy, health, financial services, infrastructure, sport, science and innovation. In education, agribusiness and tourism, Australia has appointed Ministerial Champions to leverage ties with India.
5. The Indian diaspora needs to play an important role in the economic relationship.
6. The report asserts that, as CECA negotiations between India and Australia need to be fast-tracked.

THE MALABAR HURDLE AND STRATEGIC ROADMAP FOR INDO-PACIFIC

Though India has preferred bilateral engagement with Australia, it has rejected Australia's entry into the Malabar exercises. Malabar is a trilateral naval exercise conducted between India, Japan and the USA since 1992, but Japan became a permanent member in 2015 only. The reason is that Australia initially pulled out of the Quadrilateral Security Dialogue, as it perceived that engaging in such a dialogue could upset Australia–China relations. Australia and China have a deep strategic and economic relationship (with the bilateral trade approximately 60 billion dollars between the two). Australia and China also signed a Free Trade Agreement in 2014. India remains concerned about strategic clarity form the Australian side vis-à-vis China. India feels that if Australia tilts more towards China at the strategic level, then by deepening its bilateral engagement with the USA and Japan in Malabar, India will be able to counter balance the influence of China. Addition of Australia in the trilateral Malabar, India feels, will not give it any tactical gain on the ground. In the near future, Australia may enter Malabar, but, as of now, India–Australia prefers bilateralism to gain strategic value.

Despite the reluctance of India to add Australia in the Malabar format, in 2020, during the Virtual Prime Ministerial E-Summit, the two sides decided to break the ice. India and Australia have signed an India–Australia Roadmap for Cooperation in the Indo-Pacific Region to Harness Opportunities and Meet Challenges as Comprehensive Strategic Partners.

INDIA AND AUSTRALIA: THE NEW PLAYERS OF ASIAN CENTURY

In September 2014, Tony Abbott visited India and created a roadmap for future cooperation. Australian cultural diplomacy bolstered India's faith the moment he returned idols of Chola dynasty including a Natraja idol and the sculpture of Ardhanariswara.

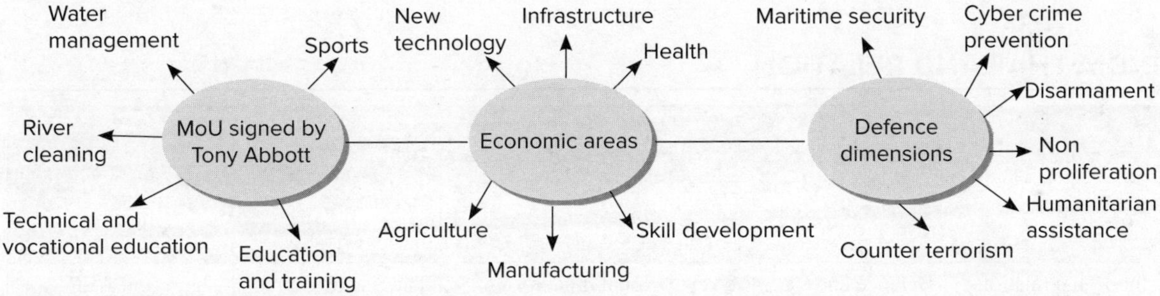

Australia is an energy resource-rich country. India also expressed interest in LNG, uranium, coal and gold. To enhance strategic cooperation, the two have decided to work together on 'two plus two' format of dialogue where Defence and Foreign Ministers of both states will interact. As the Australian parliament has passed the Civilian Nuclear Transfers to India Act, India has received the first batch of uranium from Australia starting 2019.

The weakest link in India's exports to Australia is in merchandise. India needs to look at three broad areas. First, despite globalisation, markets are country-specific and culturally sensitive. Indian companies will need to invest a little more in market research on Australian consumer expectations and lifestyles before their products can successfully penetrate the Australian market. Second, Australia is a brand-conscious market while India has not created a single consumer brand of international acceptance. Only when India's textiles, leather products, cars and two-wheelers, kitchen equipment and other products are visible across the world's shopping malls and supermarkets displaying their own brands that India will be recognised as a major player in the global markets. Third, innovation is emerging as the single-most important factor for sustained success in every sphere. Cricket, for instance, has incorporated the 20/20 format. Such innovations have kept the game alive and popular. Global trade cannot be different.

CHAPTER 9

India's Strategic and Economic Relations with Regional Powers

INDIA-THAILAND RELATION

Historical Engagement between India and Thailand	India's core interest in engaging with Thailand	India's diplomatic strategy to engage with Thailand	Shortcomings or problems that India faces in engaging with Thailand	Future areas of potential cooperation
Indo-Thai relations go back to the ancient times when Ashoka sent a mission to Swarnabhumi to spread Buddhism. This led to a rise of cultural exchanges between India and Thailand. In 1947, the two states established diplomatic ties and Thailand became an integral part of India's Look East Policy.	Defence and security Strategic cooperation Economic cooperation	A key regional binder for India and Thailand is the BIMSTEC. The relations have been deep at the economic level between the two states as they signed an Early Harvest Scheme in 2003 that ultimately culminated into an FTA. The rise of China in the region has altered the security dynamics of the region. However, the recent Chinese assertion in South China Sea has opened up a new space of cooperation for India and Thailand. In 2012, India and Thailand concluded an MoU on defence cooperation. Its core elements are summarised in the diagram below.	The rise of China has compelled Thailand to seek cooperation in maritime security. However, India, under Look East Policy was unable to fill the space. The Act East Policy of India has positioned India as a net security provider in the region. The diagram below helps to summarise the same.	The recent AEP signifies India's strategic interest in injecting the strategic dimension into the relationship. India has already enhanced strategic control of its relationship with Vietnam, Japan, Singapore and South Korea. Thailand has emerged as the next destination, along with Indonesia, where relations can be taken to a strategic level.

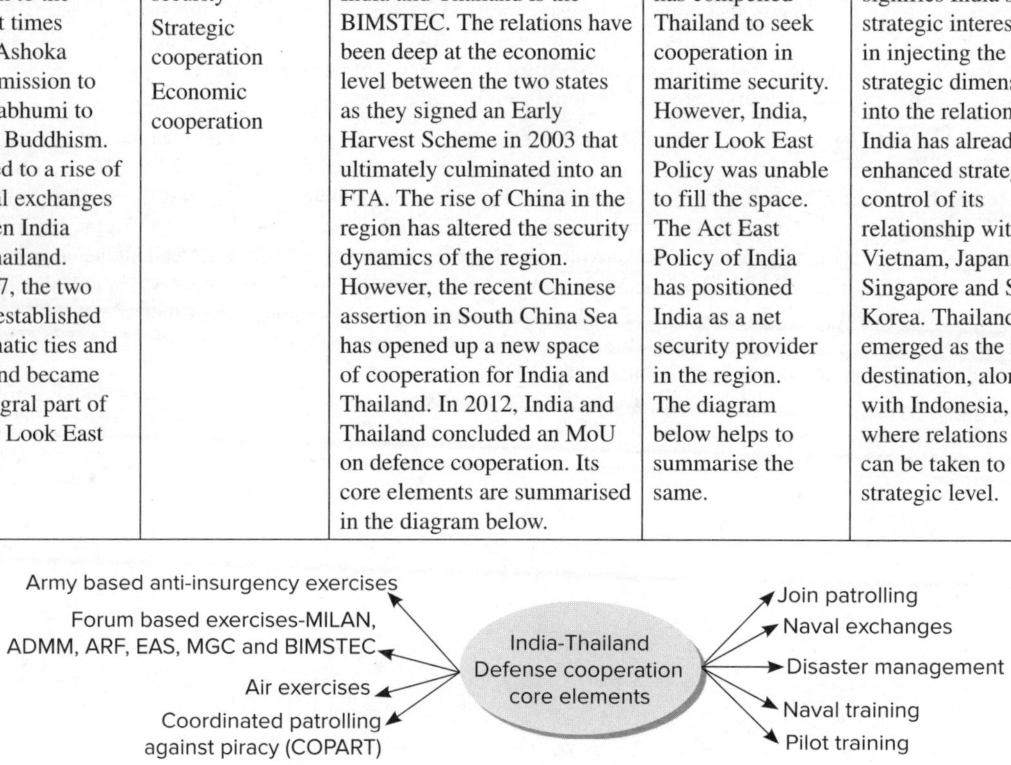

INDIA-MALAYSIA RELATION

Historical engagement	India's core interest in Malaysia	India's diplomatic strategy to engage with Malaysia	Shortcomings or problems	Future areas of potential cooperation
India and Malaysia have historic and civilisational ties. The two sides established diplomatic relations in 1957.	Defence and security Strategic cooperation Economic cooperation under Enhanced Strategic Partnership	In 1993, the two sides concluded an MoU on defence cooperation. Apart from the regular meetings of the defence secretaries of the two countries, there are regular air level and naval exercises. In 2010, the two sides concluded a CECA. As Malaysia is a member of the ASEAN, the two sides also benefit commercially due to the India–ASEAN FTA. In April 2017, the Malaysian Prime Minister visited India. He addressed a conference of Indo-Malaysia CEO forum. To further enhance the strategic partnership, the two sides have decided to augment cooperation in multilateral affairs and economic issues. In 2019, the two organised Malaysia–India Defence Cooperation Committee and defence, security and strategic port use are its components. The Malaysia–India Business Council is a permanent forum to discuss the trade centric issues.	India imports palm oil from Malaysia and 900 million USD worth of palm oil is imported every year. In 2019, Malaysian President Mahathir voiced critical notes against India at the UNGA on India's abrogation of Article 370. This tirade against Kashmir has led India to shift over palm oil imports from Malaysia to Indonesia as a retaliatory measure.	India is concerned over shifting oil import to Indonesia because Malaysian farmers adjusted their regular cropping patterns to cater to Indian demand. However, after the Indian shift, a desired impact was visible. In 2020, Imran Khan of Pakistan visited Malaysia and during the visit, Malaysia made no mention of Kashmir. In 2020 February election, RAW ensured the defeat of Mahathir and M. Yassin won the election.

INDIA-INDONESIA RELATION

Historical engagement between India and Indonesia	India's core interest in engaging with Indonesia	India's diplomatic strategy to engage with Indonesia	Shortcomings or problems that India faces in engaging with Indonesia	Future areas of potential cooperation
India and Indonesia have a common thread through Hinduism, Buddhism and Islam. The depth of the cultural unification is seen from the fact that Indonesian stories base themselves on Ramayana and Mahabharata President Sukarno and Nehru played an extremely crucial role in the birth of NAM. India and Indonesia have a Masala (spices in India) Bumbu (Bhasa in Indoneisa) relation. There is need of imaginative diplomacy to revive the links between Nalanda University and Muara Jambi.	Necklace of Diamonds: Indonesia is a strategic pearl of India Maritime diplomacy Commercial diplomacy Cultural diplomacy	In 2018, Indian Prime Minister visited Indonesia and the relation was taken to strategic partnership level. A Shared Vision on Maritime Cooperation in the Indo-Pacific was announced by India and Indonesia where investment, disaster risk reduction cooperation and tourism were identified as core themes. To tap the economic maritime potential, a link between Andaman and Aceh has been envisaged. The recent decision of Indonesia to provide India with investment opportunity in the Sabang port strengthens Indian case for positioning itself as a Net Security Provider. There is synchronisation of Indian SAGAR initiative and Indonesian Global Maritime Fulcrum. In bringing Indonesia in the QUAD, the two sides can further strengthen the construct of Indo-Pacific. Core five sectors where Indonesia will invest in India under Make in India: airports, ports, hospitals, power plants and mining.	China factor: Indonesia has a close proximate relationship with China. The two have a comprehensive strategic partnership as well. The Cold War historical baggage: India still is unable to come out of the Cold War hangover that in 1965 Indonesia supported Pakistan. Border problems: India and Indonesia have not been able to settle a maritime border in the Andaman Sea. Lack of connectivity: The two sides lack air and marine connectivity, thereby a hindrance in people to people ties.	The strategic location of Indonesia provides India the apt opportunity to position itself as a Net Security Provider. Two have political differences in how they look at China, Belt and Road Initiative and OIC participation of India (to which Indonesia is not positive). As Indonesia is looking for recognition of its capabilities and joint ventures in defence, India can position itself as an appropriate supplier. India has sought strategic cooperation in Sumatra port.

INDIA-SINGAPORE RELATION

Historical engagement between India and Singapore	India's core interest in engaging with Singapore	India's diplomatic strategy to engage with Singapore
The India–Singapore relations began during the Chola period who even named the island Singapore. Singapore was later colonised by the British and governed from Calcutta till 1965. India Singapore relations paced up since the end of the Cold War and in 2005 the two sides concluded a CECA In 2015, India and Singapore celebrated 50 years of diplomatic relations. In the same year, Indian Prime Minister also attended the funeral of Lee Kuan Yew. The foundation of the economic relationship between the two is the Double Taxation Avoidance Agreement (DTAA) signed in 1994 (with protocols signed in 2011).	Necklace of Diamonds: Singapore is a strategic pearl of India Maritime diplomacy Strategic Commercial diplomacy Cultural diplomacy	In 2003, the two sides concluded India–Singapore Defence Cooperation Agreement and established a Joint Working Group on intelligence cooperation. Today, the two sides cooperate in defence at the level of maritime security and defence technologies. There have been frequent bilateral army and naval exercises under MILAN and SIMBEX formats. At the strategic economic level, to enhance strategic commercial diplomacy with India, Singapore follows a three-point strategy. Firstly, it encourages private investment to India. Secondly, it collaborates with countries like Japan and South Korea to invest in India and thirdly, India and Singapore jointly explore possibilities of investing together in other countries (mainly Africa, Latin America, and Central Asia). Singapore has complained about bureaucratic hurdles, procedural hassles and lack of transparency as some of the hurdles in commercial diplomacy. In the recent times, under the leadership of Narendra Modi, India has decided to attract global investment to make India a manufacturing hub of the world. Just like China has used Hong Kong as a collaborator to access international investment community, India has decided to use Singapore in the same way to access global finances. India is taking steps to integrate to the global economy by integrating the India Rupee through Singapore to make it an international currency. The RBI has allowed Indian firms to raise Rupee bonds abroad. Such bonds are raised in the local currency and can be settled in US Dollars. Singapore can play an important role to allow India to internationalise the Rupee. Singapore is the second largest FDI provider to India. In 2018, India and Singapore signed a bilateral naval cooperation agreement. The agreement allows India to seek naval re-fuelling (and logistical access) at the Changi naval base of Singapore. The Changi naval base is strategically located in proximity to the disputed area of South China Sea. The bilateral naval agreement focuses on increasing cooperation in • Maritime security, • Joint naval exercises, • Temporary deployments in each other's naval facilities, • Mutual logistics support Changi is a critical choke point for global marine trade. The presence of India in Changi (plus Chabar on the other side) expands India's spectrum and enables India to position itself as a 'Net Security Provider'.

INDIA-NORTH KOREA RELATION

Historical engagement between India and North Korea	India's core interest in engaging with North Korea	India's diplomatic strategy to engage with North Korea
The relations between India and Democratic People's Republic of Korea (DPRK) are not usual diplomatic relations, though; during the Cold War some commonalities did exist. The origin of the relations goes back to Korean crisis in the 1950s when the Northern part of Korea invaded the South. The South as also by India condemned this invasion by North of South. The DPRK joined NAM in 1976 and thereafter requested India to raise the Korean issue at the NAM Summit and take up the issue of Korean reunification. In 1988, DPRK Prime Minister LI Gun Mo came to India for a good will visit.	Prevention of nuclear proliferation Access of rare earth metals Checkmate China Ensure strategic stability in East Asia	India advocated that the Korean issue be resolved bilaterally between ROK and DPRK and that the upcoming NAM Summit of 1977 was not an appropriate forum for the matter. DPRK accepted India's request and trusted upon advice rendered by India. At the UN Security Council, India supported action through the UN Security Council resolution (UNSCR)–82 and 83. It is interesting to note India did not support UNSCR–84, which advocated military assistance to ROK against DPRK. India aptly invoked NAM and maintained that it would not ally with any military commitments but would prefer the UN action. In April 2015, North Korean Foreign Minister Ri Su Yong visited India and met his Indian counterpart. India conveyed an intention to improve bilateral relations.

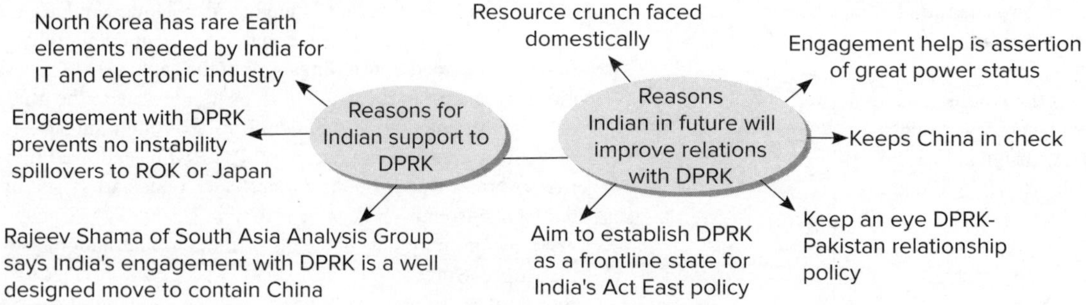

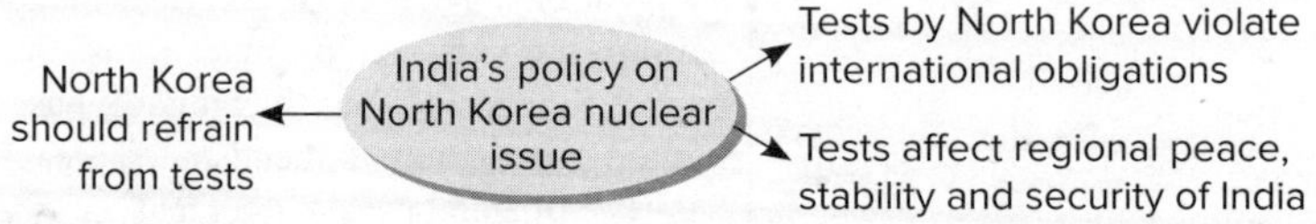

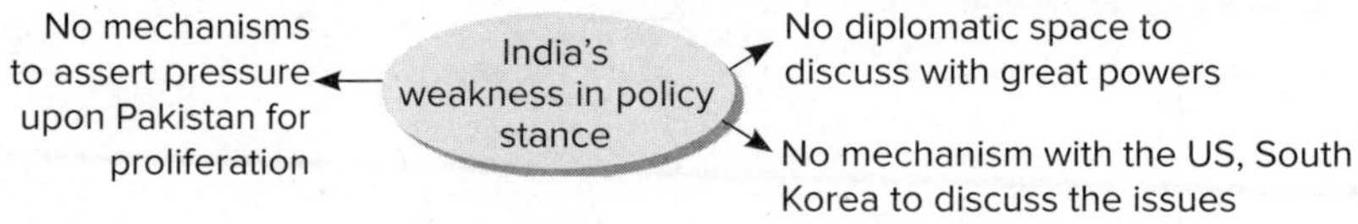

For comprehensive analysis of India and Taiwan relations and issues related to US-China and Taiwan standoff, please refer to the YouTube channel of the author:
https://www.youtube.com/c/PavneetSinghUPSC

SECTION 9

India and the European Union Relations

AN OVERVIEW

The EU is not a very favourite area for the UPSC. There were questions related to trends in India and the EU, hurdles in India and the EU and areas of general engagement. A micro question on India's engagement with any regional European power is yet to be asked.

Potential foresight EU is going to be the dark horse in the UPSC in the coming years. Firstly, there is a recent rise in Indian governmental thinking for the EU and we are engaging with them on issues of national interest. Secondly, India is prioritising engagement with central and eastern European powers because till now it has only engaged with the Western Europeans and this has caused imbalanced engagement. Thirdly, with India playing an important bridge between the West and Russia in recent Ukraine crisis (for which the author has designed a separate chapter in this book), the author believes that Europe will gain dominance in the UPSC questions in the times ahead. The new design of this section with freshly written chapters will ensure one's success.

CHAPTER 1

India and the European Union—Key Drivers of the Relationship

EVOLUTION OF INDIA AND THE EUROPEAN UNION RELATIONS

India and the European Union (EU) are natural partners as both belong to multilateral order founded on democracy. A very unique connector is both having a foreign policy on the basis of aspirations of their citizens, which also is a source of their legitimacy. India–EU relations have been historically cordial with diplomatic relations going back to 1962. The relationship had evolved only in the period after the Cold War ended. In 1996, the EU and India signed an Enhanced Partnership Agreement, leading to the first India–EU Summit in 2000 in Lisbon. India is one of the few select countries in the world with which the EU has regular summit level meetings. The 2004 Hague summit was important because here India and the EU decided to elevate the relations to the level of strategic partnership, and in 2005 agreed to a Joint Action Plan (JAP). The JAP had laid down the foundation of India–EU Strategic Partnership Agreement. Indian foreign policy views the EU as a successful block of economic and political integration but at times some policy makers in India view the EU through the lens of NATO and they feel that the EU lacks concrete multilateral commitment for India's permanent membership candidature at UNSC. This is because the EU states do not have consensus with India's candidature. They feel that there is time for India to assume global responsibilities as poverty and inequality in India is a wall against its global aspiration. The EU does recognise India as a middle-income emerging market economy where transfer of technology and trade can be a foundation of India–EU relationship.

REFLECTIONS ON INDIA–EU SUMMIT: TOWARDS UNREQUITED LOVE

India and the EU have been holding regular annual summits. The latest summit was driven by a social media hashtag of #euindiaeksaath. The hashtag summarises the substance India and the EU have evolved in cooperation. The table below presents an analytical glimpse of stands taken by India and the EU on various dimensions of diplomatic engagement and asserts the new positions that reflect growing propensity of India and the EU as natural partners.

Dimension of engagement	Old position held by India and the EU	New position evolved by India and the EU
Democracy	Joint statements only talked of democracy	Joint statements now talk of democracy, freedom, rule of law and human rights
Growth	The EU only wanted India to do inclusive growth	The EU wants to engage with India on climate change and sustainable growth
Global institutions	The EU stated that global institutions have stood the test of time	Post-pandemic, the EU urges WHO to be more transparent in functioning

Dimension of engagement	Old position held by India and the EU	New position evolved by India and the EU
Healthcare	The EU focused on urging India to provide adequate health to its people	The EU today focuses on stepping up cooperation in medical supplies and ensure vaccine availability
Digitalisation	The EU asserted India to adopt the Western standards because Global North would set standards for all	The EU looks at setting global standards and realising that Global North has no preserve on standard settings
Indian ocean	Enhance maritime cooperation in the region with no direction	Ensure safety and stability in Indo-Pacific region

Today India attaches great importance to Europe because India realises that Europe can be an important partner to drive imperatives in green energy, technology and digitalisation. In this new world after pandemic, the old Europe still matters for India and trust remains a binding factor.

INDIA'S DIPLOMATIC ENGAGEMENTS WITH EUROPE

India has often looked at engaging with Europe through big powers of Europe. This policy of India has made it neglect potentialities in engagement with certain states of central Europe, namely Czechoslovakia, Hungary, Poland and Slovakia (also known as the Visegrád group). Central Europe is an area for India that it is prioritising today. From Indian perspective, we have not yet evolved continental policy for Europe and the European states do not have clarity as to what India seeks from them continentally, regionally and bilaterally.

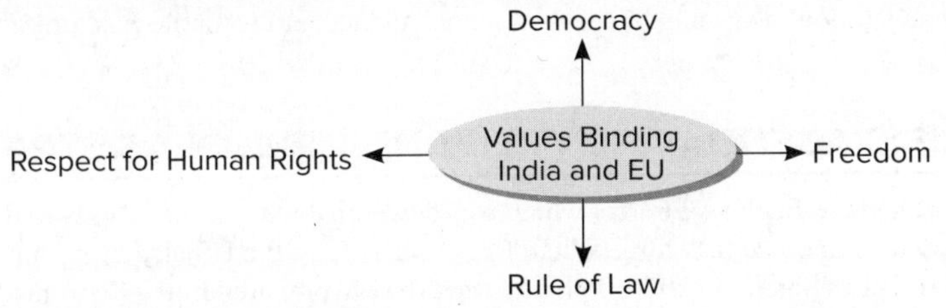

SHARED VALUES BINDING INDIA AND THE EU

The shared values that bind India–EU are as follows:

- Cooperation based on the shared values and democracy
- Significant contributors to peacekeeping initiatives under the UN
- Face threats of terrorism, piracy, cyber-attacks and climate change
- Have natural convergence in Afghanistan and Indo-Pacific as an external realms of threats of foreign policy

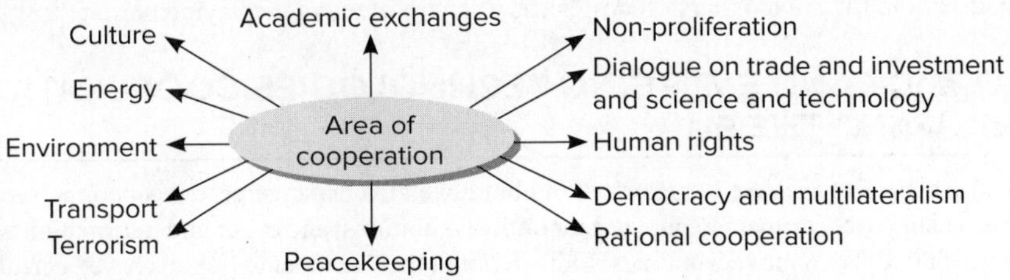

NON-TRADITIONAL SECURITY THREATS DIPLOMACY AND CHALLENGES BETWEEN INDIA AND THE EU

Non-Traditional Security (NTS) threats are people-centric challenges that threaten their survival and well-being and range from food security to health security to energy security etc. In 2008, India–EU Joint Action Plan was adopted. India and the EU recognised the need to cooperate on peace and comprehensive security. The cooperation in peace and security did not talk about NTS. However, the NTS has been a part of the bilateral relations of the two. The reason why the Joint Action Plan of 2008 did not out rightly mention the NTS was because the concept of NTS has remained uncertain in the minds of the EU officials. In 2011, at the 10th Asian Europe meet (India has been a part of ACEM since 2007) the EU explained that NTS had been perceived vaguely by the EU. But in the 10th ACEM meet (in Hungary), the EU diplomatically accepted the need to analyse NTS in detail to boost diplomatic cooperation. After 2011 meet, consensus began to develop over NTS in the EU. The EU began to define NTS as threats related to climate change, food security, water security, energy security, inclusive growth, poverty, science and technology, cultural dialogues etc. In 2011, India expanded the EU definition of NTS to add terrorism and non-state actors' threat in marine security. India, on the other hand, has a limited definition of NTS threats but does not believe that it encompasses a holistic view of food security, security policy and other challenges. India has tried to link a strong domestic economic framework to achieve objectives to tackle NTS. So, India has tried to be pragmatic in its foreign policy and tried to engage at the foreign policy level for inclusive growth, energy security, education, infrastructure etc. India also used pandemics such as H5N1, AIDS and COVID-19, as part of NTS and all this has opened up its cooperation with the EU.

However, both India and the EU do have challenges in ensuring NTS collaboration.

a. The definition of NTS threats is still vague of the two sides and both still have not identified NTS areas of synchronisation.

b. The Joint Action Plan has no concrete steps of cooperation. Some Indian and the EU diplomats assert that the two sides have cooperation in sustainable development, science and technology, culture but there is no mention in the JAP.

EU'S INDO-PACIFIC AGENDA AND FREE AND OPEN SEAS STRATEGY

In 2008, the EU had launched the EU Naval Force, which was developed with the capability to deter and prevent piracy. It was designed to work with combined task force where Russia, India and the US also have ships and they all cooperate with the NATO Operation Ocean Shield. In 2016, both India and the EU prepared India–EU Agenda for 2020 document in which the two sides decided to cooperate on maritime security, countering piracy and promotion of freedom of navigation. Because 90% of India's trade is via sea, the EU also requires freedom of navigation for market access. However, the two sides do witness common threats that range from piracy problem to Pakistan–China power politics that could lead to blockade of key marine routes. In 2014, the EU released its first maritime security strategy. The strategy stated that 90% of the EU's external trade and 40% of internal trade is dependent upon sea and the EU does witness threats to marine trade from piracy to attack on marine infrastructure to state aggression on choke points. In 2015, India announced the Indian Ocean Strategy where it had defined that protection of marine territory and countering maritime terrorism was India's interest and it aimed to enhance economic, security cooperation with marine neighbours, island states to promote collective action for peaceful and a cooperative future. Today, the EU intends to play a greater role in maintaining a free and open Indo-Pacific and states of the EU are looking at Indo-Pacific as a new arena of displaying power.

CYBER DIPLOMACY AND EMERGING TECHNOLOGIES COOPERATION BETWEEN INDIA AND THE EU

The advancements in the field of IT have helped mankind but have also endangered the economic security. Today, the nation states have been using cyber domain to pursue geopolitical ambitions, and cyber and information war have emerged as new non-kinetic warfare tools. In the recent times, India–EU and their computer systems have been affected by cyber-attacks. In 2007, websites of Estonia were targeted by distributed denial-of-service attack. In 2017, WannaCry ransomware affected both states. The 2015 Paris attack investigations found that the weapons used in the attack sourced from deep web. In 2022, explained in a separate chapter in this segment, the Russians have resorted to use of cyber weapons against Ukraine. In 2010, India and the EU in the Annual Summit at Brussels initiated a Dialogue on Cyber Security and in 2015 a Bilateral Cyber Security Dialogue was established where

- CERT-EU and CERT-India would have operations-based dialogues.
- Counter Cyber Terrorism dialogue was established.
- India has Bilateral Security Dialogues with Germany, France and the UK.

In 2016 India–EU summit, both had decided to cooperate on Internet Governance under Digital India Programme and EU Digital Single Market Initiative. However, there are two gaps that remain to be addressed in cyber cooperation.

Guilty by association This means that both India and the EU have negative perceptions about each other that prevent India–EU power play. For example, India has anti-EU sentiments on cyber issues but the EU also is suspicious of India's real agenda at data localisation level. This means that both are guilty by association of each other.

Principal policy gap EU–Indian policy architecture is the reason for lack of India–EU cooperation as the policy has certain misunderstandings. This is why it has been suggested that both should shift to pragmatic idealism-centric diplomacy where local authority-based collaboration (means individual states) and establishment of research community can sort out differences between the two and address the policy gaps.

GENERAL DATA PROTECTION REGULATION OF THE EU AND IMPLICATIONS ON INDIA

The General Data Protection Regulation (GDPR) was ratified by the EU in 2016 and came into effect from 2018. The GDPR replaces the 1995 regulations of the EU on data protection and comprehensively addresses the concerns related to transfer of personal data at the international level. The GDPR is targeted to give more power to the users in Europe. It empowers the residents of Europe to give and withdraw their consent for use of their personal information. Any company that holds information of the users now needs to seek their consent to retain the user data. In case of a data breach, the company has to inform the user within 72 hours so that the user can ask the company to delete the data. In case of non-compliance, the GDPR places a fine of 20 million Euros or 4% of the annual global revenue of the firm (whichever is higher). In case of children under 16, the consent of the parents is required. The GDPR applies to all 28 nations in the EU, irrespective of where the company is located and collecting the data. This means that if there is an Indian firm handling data of any EU client, it is liable for laws. More importantly, the companies based in the EU have to comply with GDPR while offering services to even those citizens who are not residents of the EU. Free flow of data is a unique feature of the globalised economy. In the last one decade, the free flow of the data has increased the global GDP by 10% and India is one of the important beneficiary states. With the GDPR in place now, it does impact India majorly. In the past few years, India has been an exporter of IT products and services that range from financial services to health analytics to the EU. While India offered these services, it collected a lot of data from the EU citizens, thus making Indian firms liable to GDPR. As per GDPR, data transfer from the EU to a non-EU state is permitted only when the non-EU state enacts national privacy legislation, which is equivalent to the law of the EU. States such as Argentina and Uruguay do have national laws but the problem is that they have same standards for all companies operating in the home country also. This hampers the development of domestic markets because if a state does not have a law at par with the EU, then there will be a limit to access financial and other services in the EU. Enacting the EU-type laws also will affect the cost of doing business for firms, which would hurt services at domestic level. India's data protection law does not pass the adequacy test in the EU. As a result of this, the Indian firms either have to accept corporate rules that bind global operations or they have to go for a special model contract agreement needed in each specific business deal with the EU. Both options require Indian firms to provide data protection as per European standards and establish a data controller who will be held liable for breach of data in the member state of the EU. All this leads to higher operating costs for small firms. This is where the question arises. If the EU has a legitimate right to protect data, can it do so without hurting interests of India? In the recent times, the EU and the USA cooperation model for data protection has a model for India. After the EU enacted their first law to protect data, the national laws of the US became inadequate. To ensure safe transatlantic data flow, the US and the EU negotiated an agreement. Under the agreement, the American firms will protect the data of the EU citizens and also as per the EU standards but in return for unrestricted data flows. The Federal Trade Commission and American Department of Commerce will monitor the commitment of the firms. As per the laws related to trade in services (under WTO), the EU has to offer other states a comparable arrangement. India needs to take advantage of this opportunity and first create a credible institution like the one in the US. Doing so will ensure that Indian firms would not require to have any presence in the EU states and also India would not require a national privacy law which has to be stringent as per international norms. India will be free to establish a domestic standard to cater to domestic needs and also follow foreign standards to export to specific foreign markets. This will ensure that there is no conflict between developmental goal of accessing foreign services markets and improving services access to the citizens.

EVOLUTION OF TRADE DIPLOMACY BETWEEN INDIA AND THE EU

In 2020, the EU had urged India to negotiate a Bilateral Investment Protection Agreement or BIPA, as the BIPA would delink the stalemate on FTA. The EU has recently signed a BIPA with Singapore and wishes to adopt the similar model for India. The EU feels that if BIPA is carved out of the FTA, then the commercial engagement with India can be enhanced, even if the BTIA (Bilateral Trade and Investment Agreement) or FTA is not signed. Till now, the position of the EU was that it wanted BIPA to be a part of BTIA. But now, based on its experience with Singapore, the EU wants the BIPA to be separate from the BTIA. India is yet to respond for the same. It is important to note that on 31st March 2017, India terminated all its Bilateral Investment Treaties (BIT) with the EU members and urged them to sign fresh BITs with India as per the new BIT model the Union Cabinet adopted in 2017. The EU has communicated that it will sign the BIT now as a bloc of Wuropean Union as a single unit and does not allow states of EU to individually sign BITs and this has emerged as another strain today. In 2015, India came out with a new Bilateral Investment Treaty (BIT). The new BIT of India adopts protectionist standpoint that the preference for dispute settlement as per BIT used for domestic judiciary. The BIT says that investors should litigate for 5 years in India before approaching a foreign tribunal. The EU is not happy with this due to a tardy image of Indian judiciary. Recently the EU and Singapore signed a Free Trade Agreement (FTA). For Investor State Dispute Settlement (ISDS), the FTA asserts through a provision that an investor can bring the dispute to a state's National Court where investment is made or submits the dispute to an international arbitration. Now, when the EU–Singapore FTA was to be ratified the issue erupted was who would ratify the FTA—the EU member states or the EU. This issue erupted due to ISDS provision. The European Council Judiciary pronounced that the EU could ratify the FTA except ISDS provision, which would be ratified by member states. This decision impacts India because if ISDS provision of India–EU is to be ratified by member states, then India has an edge and it can negotiate the same bilaterally. The EU can also make ISDS part of India through free trade agreement as a provision of optional protocol and facilitate this. India also does not enjoy Generalised System of Preferences Plus (GSP+) tag and that will make it difficult for India to keep its exports competitive. Because of enormous bureaucratic apathy and red tape India is not a preferred destination for the EU for trade. In 2015, the EU banned sale of 700 pharmacy products from India over quality of data from clinical trials obtained by GVK biosciences. The drugs have been sold in the EU markets without any adverse report, but in 2015, the EU regulatory agencies from France inspected GVK biosciences manufacturing plant in South India. It found data manipulation ranging of electrocardiograms for last 5 years. So, France decided to suspend drug sale as a precautionary measure. But this upset India, as its pharmacy is a flagship sector.

INDIA–EU BILATERAL TRADE AND INVESTMENT AGREEMENT: ISSUE, CHALLENGES AND WAY AHEAD

The EU is India's largest trading block today. India–EU commercial diplomacy can be seen through the following instruments. In 1971, the EU started Generalised System of Preferences (GSP) to India enabling India to export Indian manufactured products at preferential tariff. In 1974, India–EC Commercial Cooperation Agreement was signed. In 1981, Indian–EC Commercial and Economic Cooperation Agreement was concluded. In 2004, India–EU Annual Summit began. In 2005, India–EU Joint Action Plan was signed. There has been significant Indian FDI to Europe as well. However, the European economic crises in the recent times have led to a slowdown between the two at the level of trade. Since 2007, India and the EU have been negotiating a BTIA or the FTA. However, the BTIA/FTA negotiations have not yet delivered the results as of now. Even up till 2020, the BTIA had been stuck on a number of issues and no final agreement was reached. The tables below give us a better picture of issues confronting the BTIA.

Serial number	What does the EU want in BTIA/FTA?	What is India's position?	Present status
(1)	Reduced tariffs in automobiles, wines and spirits	Reluctant on tariff reduction specially in automobiles	Automobiles sector is under negotiation
(2)	Higher market access in banking, retail, telecommunications and accounting services	Reluctant to grant market access in banking and retail	Banking and retail are being negotiated
(3)	Modifications in IPR in pharmacy	Totally opposed to grant only concession	Deadlock prevails

Serial number	What does India want from the EU in BTIA/FTA?	What is the EU's position?	India's present status
(1)	India wants data secure status from the EU as that will make it easy for the EU firms to outsource business to India	The EU is not keen on the same due to lack of data protection laws in India	Under negotiation
(2)	Freedom of movement of skilled professionals in the European service sector	Reluctance on opening up to skilled Indian immigration	Under negotiation

TECHNOLOGY DIPLOMACY TEMPLATE BETWEEN INDIA AND THE EU

The origin goes back to 1958, when Germany assisted India with the development of IIT Madras. India is also a participant in International Thermonuclear Experimental Reactor (ITER) project. Under the Joint Action Plan, a Centre for European Studies has been opened in India. India has also opened Institutions for contemporary Indian Studies in Europe. The level of academic collaboration is also high due to the EU's support to India under an initiative for the development and integration of Indian and European research since 2009. The most robust science-based partnership India has is with Germany. A lot of German institutions have academic cooperation with Indian institutions, with Germany also offering vocational training to Indians.

EU'S DEVELOPMENT DIPLOMACY AND INDIA

India and the EU have a development partnership where many of the EU nations have been providing aid to India to assist in developmental initiatives. Germany, for instance, has been giving developmental aid to India for energy efficiency and renewable energy while the UK, post-2015, has focused more on technological collaboration. More so, at a macro level, the EU supports India to help it achieve the Millennium Development Goals and at a sectoral level, advances support in health and education sectors.

COUNTER-TERRORISM COOPERATION BETWEEN INDIA AND THE EU

Terrorism and security are two areas where India and the EU have tremendous convergence. Both sides want that terrorism, at the international level, be tackled within the larger framework of the UN. India has been a victim of terrorism for a while, and the resurgence of the ISIS in the recent times has led to Europe becoming its latest victim. In 2016–2020, attacks in Paris, Nice, Brussels, and London have made Europe extremely vulnerable to attacks. The European Security Strategy document clearly outlines the threat India and the EU face at both global and regional levels. At the bilateral level too, India's defence relations with France, the UK and Germany have improved while Russia remains the top-most players for arms supply. Both India and the EU undertakes use of multiple instruments to promote democracy and human rights, ranging from conditionalities in the Official Development Assistance (ODA) to election observer missions, both of which India refrain to use at the international level. As of now, Europe lacks a strong policy to tackle Pakistan problem while India favours strong EU policy.

EU–INDIA CONVERGENCE ON MULTILATERALISM AND DIVERGENCES IN GLOBAL GOVERNANCE

Issues in the EU's Envisaged Role for India as a Global Power

The EU asserts in various Joint Statements that it has 'noted' India's intense engagement with multilateral export control regimes. What is puzzling is that the EU has used the words like 'noted' and not 'support'. Despite this, in the conceptual terms, India and the EU have transcended their rhetoric into natural partnership today to contribute to global growth

At the level of global governance and multilateralism, both India and the EU do have convergence in acceptance of an idea of a multipolar world but have different approaches to engagement with other states. While India emphasises national sovereignty, the EU on the other hand is in favour of a rule-based multilateralism model. India does not interfere in internal affairs of other nations but the EU is in favour of a rule-based multilateralism interference model. India and the EU have evolved a common platform of interaction, which is, however, not stable when it comes to global forums. For example, both India and the EU have adopted different parameters based on their respective national interests while interacting at the level of climate change, WTO and so on.

CHINA FACTOR IN INDIA AND THE EU RELATIONS, EU'S INDO-PACIFIC FORAYS AND ROLE OF INDIA

Geographically, the EU today is the most important political actor on earth because it has the potential to drive the global political trajectory. The Europeans have always attached importance to values of democracy, freedom, rule of law and human rights and all these values have made Europe the champion of the liberal order. Today, there is a concerted attempt by the Russians and the Chinese to break this European liberal order and pierce the ethical paradigm that defines the identity of Europe. The game began with Chinese engaging with the EU under their Belt and Road Initiative. Initially, the Europeans embraced the BRI with the hope that BRI would change the authoritarian Chinese. The Europeans were tempted by the materialism offered even at the cost of the Atlantic Project. The Chinese drive the same vehicle and use the same phones as Europeans but they do not share the same values and same principles because a convergence in the world views does not exist. The perverse conduct of masked diplomacy and wolf warrior doctrine have ended up in disturbing European sensibilities. The engagement of Europeans with the Chinese was based on the premise that European engagement with China will create a political consensus of change in Beijing but the reality is that Beijing is not interested in politics but only control of European markets. Today, if Europe splits between north, south, east or west; it will swing in some direction and what will be interesting to see is that when Europe swings, will it be an actor or will it be acted upon. Today, the Chinese through their BRI have attempted to change the shape of Asia by making Asia model on the Confucian hierarchical order with China as a middle kingdom. The only way that Europe can prevent their change of shape is by embracing India, Indonesia, Australia and Japan. This explains why many European states today are announcing strategies to engage with Indo-Pacific and this strategy is an explanation of how India can position itself as a new fulcrum of trust amongst the heart of Europeans. The Indo-Pacific is not just a frontline for the European safety and stability but also a theatre for Europe to practice the ethics of an open, rules-based order it stands for. Since the 2008 financial crisis, the world has no superpower but more of quasi-superpowers with the US, Russia and China behaving like quasi powers sometimes. This period has also seen centre of gravity shifting towards the Indo-Pacific realm. The French and British too realised that Indo-Pacific is one area when a century ago they dominated power. Today, the British and French have realised that as the US and China are locked in their own hegemonic contests, they both need to go back to Indo-Pacific, rework engagements with regional players and bring back Europe in the new arena of power contestations.

CENTRAL EUROPEANS: THE KEY DECIDERS OF FUTURE GLOBAL ORDER

The Central Europeans are going to be the key deciders of the future here because they are the swing states and history tells us that swing states decide the global order. This is because the Central Europeans are being showered love by Chinese and military assurances by the US, while they continue to remain economically weak. India is playing a very different game in Central Europe because it is asserting that it intends to see the region to be a rule driver of Fourth Industrial Revolution and not a rule taker. Even though India is not economically as powerful as China and the US but has a million plus digital platform architecture and laboratories for AI, Machine Learning and Big Data. The technology will make the distance barrier between India and Central Europe disappear because land routes and shipping lanes are to be replaced with bits and bytes. In this backdrop, India presents in front of Europe, in contrast to China, a room to manoeuvre. The choice for Europeans are no more binary, of the US and China, but an emerging India. The COVID-19 has unleashed a spirit of reshoring and de-coupling and exposed the fragility of globalisation. The Europeans have realised the need to de-couple and move towards developing supply chains with countries where political trust is utmost. The countries do not have to have an alignment on every dimension of engagement with others but at least need to operate on a common political and ideological spectrum and India definitely takes the lead here. As the societies now become more digitalised, individual data and individual spaces will assume centrality and countries would not prefer to engage with states they do not enjoy political trust because values will become a core binding factor in future industrial growth after the pandemic.

EU'S ENGAGEMENT WITH INDIA IN RESPONSE TO CHINESE BELT AND ROAD INITIATIVE

The Chinese Belt and Road Initiative and its Maritime Silk Route component has implications for India and the EU because we see China trying to secure strategic Sea Lanes of Communication and setting up bases in Djibouti and claiming ownership in Sri Lankan ports of Colombo and Hambantota and disturb a rules-based order. This is where India and the EU can together uphold the rules-based order under stress. In South China Sea, the challenge for India and the EU is to accommodate a rising China in Indo-Pacific as China is threatening the balance of power in the region and is projecting power in Indian Ocean. During the UPA regime, Italy acted as a roadblock to India–EU cooperation over the Italian marine issue. The NDA government favoured the policy to resolve the Italian marine issue through arbitration procedures as per international tribunals.

KASHMIR ISSUE AND HUMAN RIGHTS VIOLATION AS AREAS OF DIVERGENCE BETWEEN INDIA AND THE EU

Initially, the EU wanted to ensure that the UK and the USA handle Kashmir dispute. After 1972 Simla Agreement, the EU has changed its Kashmir policy and today is not supportive of Pakistan-sponsoring terrorism in the valley but also is not very positive about Indians handling of the issue. India has urged the EU that the 9/11 has exposed the true nature of Pakistan and expects the EU to strongly condemn Pakistan but as Pakistan is a frontline ally of the US against Global War on Terrorism, the EU avoids strong condemnation. The human rights is another disagreement. The EU feels that Indian security forces are responsible for human rights violations in Kashmir but India reminds the EU that security forces are operating in a space where terrorists are doing harsher security-centric killings.

INDIA'S OUTREACH TO THE EUROPEAN PROGRAMME AND MODI DOCTRINE FOR THE EU

India has realised today that Europe is a source of economic capital and being the world's second largest economic entity, it is indeed India's natural partner in progress. The Modi government has initiated a new outreach to the European programme in 2016. The Prime Minister visited Germany, Spain, Russia and France. India has decided to present itself as an attractive partner to Europe. This will allow India to check China, which is trying to reach out Europe through its Belt and Road Initiative. India is trying to position itself as a balancer in Europe. As Trump has reduced the relevance of NATO in Europe by insisting that the EU should also contribute to evolve its own security; the Europeans are looking at partners to re-write their destiny. As the EU witnesses a new reordering of power structure, it provides an opportunity to India. Though China is trying to deepen its engagement with the EU due to its economic heft, but the EU may not be comfortable in embracing China due to authoritarian values. At the ideological level, India is well-positioned as a defender of liberal values and a counter narrative to China. In this age of uncertainty, India is constructing relations with the Middle

Powers in the East and the West. The world has changed in the last three centuries. The Anglo-Americans are looking at their navel whereas the Hans and the Slavs are constructing a new Eurasian coalition. It is time for India to look beyond the Anglo-Americans and the Slavs and embrace Eurasian alliances. India has taken positive steps to bring back Europe at the centre of its global consciousness. The depth in the cooperation can be judged from the fact that the Joint Statement in India–EU engagement mentions 53 paragraphs in contrast to standard 30 paragraphs since 2004. The new approach to reach out to Europe has multiple strands. First and foremost was to show the Indian flag. There have been many European states where no Indian leaders have ever visited and this is specifically true for Central Europe. In 2018, the Indian President had a state visit to Cyprus, Bulgaria and Czech Republic. Surprisingly, there are states where even senior officers of the MEA too never visited. In 2018 during the President's visit to Greece, India outlined its new diplomatic outreach to Europe. Thus, the first step, to infuse political diplomatic capital has succeeded. Secondly, the government adopted a strategy to resolve the unresolved contentious issues with the European states that had injected negativity in the ties. For instance, the long-pending Italian marines issue was a drag in India and Italy ties, which through direct diplomacy was resolved. This eventually led Rome to support India at various multilateral export control regimes and lift the political hold on Indian participation in the India–EU Annual Summit in 2016. Thirdly, the government has identified certain states in Europe and decided to strengthen the strategic hold with them. France and Russia are two core examples of this approach. Taking advantage of the change, the EU has developed 'India Strategy' document. This strategy focuses on deepening the relationship with a new strategic salience by identifying areas such as trade liberalisation, educational exchanges, and climate change and defence and security diplomacy. The strategy also seeks India–EU cooperation in the international realm from stability in Afghanistan to anti-piracy operations in Horn of Africa to food aid in Somalia under World Food Programme. Fourthly, the government has injected a new political will to break away from the colonial hangover that always affected India's relationship with Britain. The Indian Prime Minister's enthusiastic participation in bilateral diplomacy and Commonwealth has opened a new chapter of cooperation with London. Fifthly, as India reconnects with Europe it has understood the multiple forces such as religion, ethnicity and politico-economic difference that shape the destiny of various European states. For instance, as India engages with states in Central Europe, it acknowledges the complexity involved in Central Europe's relations with Germany and Russia. Similarly, when India reached out to the Nordic states, it again acknowledged their deep-seated suspicion with an assertive Russia. These perceptions in Indian foreign policy are new as none existed during the Cold War, where Europe was perceived as a singular variable. Sixthly, India is gearing up to take advantage of the changing security and strategic situation in Europe. The Trump administration has asserted that the European states need to be responsible for their own security. The European states are coming out of the security shell of the USA. Now is the time when they would be looking forward to cooperating with new partners from Eurasia to Indo-Pacific, thereby opening up new lines of strategic advance for India in the times ahead. The European states in their EU–Asia strategy have identified security as a new dimension of cooperation. The EU has identified capacity building, defence training, UN peacekeeping cooperation and joint defence exercises as a new area to cooperate. The aim of the EU is to use security cooperation with Asia to collectively emerge as a new engine for world politics and global stability.

MODI DOCTRINE OF INDIA'S NORDIC OUTREACH AND NORDIC SUMMIT DIPLOMACY

In the last thirty years, for the first time India has prioritised the Nordic region in its foreign policy. In 2018, Indian Prime Minister held the first ever India-Nordic Summit and held engagements with heads of Denmark, Iceland, Finland, Norway and Sweden. India's initial diplomatic focus was primarily on the West and four core European powers such as Britain, Germany, France and Russia. Despite having complementarities at the political and economic level, the Nordic region remained disconnected from Indian foreign policy. The Bofors scandal also played an irritant in India to explore the relations with Sweden again. Even from the Nordic states perspective, their priority remained on trying to manage their identity with the EU and India was not a priority for them too. The world order is witnessing a massive change now. China and Russia are trying to re-write the rules of global governance to influence geopolitics as per their advantage and India in the meantime has emerged as a new powerhouse with renowned democratic credentials. This changing global narrative has compelled the Nordic states to establish a strong partnership with India. In India's outreach to Nordic, Sweden is the centre of gravity. The two sides have decided to re-work their relationship in the defence sector. Sweden has proposed Saab Group's Gripen-E-Single engine jet fighters for the Indian Air Force. Sweden and India have explored a bilateral agreement for three core areas—cyber security, exchange of classified information and private sector supply chains for defence and aerospace equipment for small and medium enterprises. The two sides have adopted a Joint Action Plan and Joint Innovation Partnership Pact (to establish an innovation ecosystem for climate change and sustainable development). The government of Sweden is going to provide 59 USD million for smart cities and sustainability through innovation. The first India–Nordic Summit 2018 has explored dimensions of cooperation that range from health, skill development energy, global security and sustainable development. The Nordic countries have also decided to voice their concerns on challenges that emanate from the changing global order. To uphold rules-based international order, the Nordic states have supported India's membership at the NSG, despite the fact that these Nordic states sometime back had strong opposition to India's nuclear programme.

The 2nd India Nordic Summit 2022

India and Nordic states organised a summit in 2022 and identified new areas of cooperation that ranged from multilateral cooperation in the post-pandemic economic recovery, climate change, sustainable development, innovation and digitalisation and green and clean growth. India's Arctic Policy announced in 2022 provides India with a new framework to engage with Nordic states and establish cooperative diplomacy models centred around blue economy.

GREEN ENERGY, EMERGING TECHNOLOGIES AND CIVIL SOCIETY-BASED DIPLOMACY AS FUTURE TEMPLATES

At the trade level, India has two strategies to adopt in the future. First, India can continue to liberalise the other areas of cooperation while it may freeze the talks on data localisation issue. Second, India must sign the BIPA immediately and conclude the FTA or BTIA soon. This will require India to look at the FTA from a strategic perspective, especially when India is already out of the RCEP and lacks a trade deal with the USA. India should take this opportunity because even the EU is looking for alternatives to China. At the level of technology, both sides have identified four areas of cooperation that range from 5G technologies, Artificial Intelligence, Big Data and Internet of Things. To promote cooperation in NTS, a study by Carine Barbier and Ritu Mathur says that India–EU should involve civil society organisations while establishing cooperation for funding of India–EU Joint Partnership Projects in climate and energy science. The India–EU need to evolve cooperative framework under India–EU Strategic Partnership where the EU can provide its expertise to tackle NTS threats jointly. This cooperative framework will help the two sides synchronise their cooperation. India follows a careful policy of Balance of Interest amongst major Powers and not Westphalia Balance of Power. This means that India believes that international and regional security can flourish only if all nation states converge on areas of common interest. For India and the EU, the Balance of Interest Theory helps convergence at NTS threats such as climate change, food security and inclusive growth. India and the EU need to evolve a joint understanding of marine governance and freedom of navigation from Indo-Pacific to Mediterranean. The two have to increase their navel coordination to ensure Maritime surveillance, anti-piracy operations and evolve EU–India High-Level Dialogue on Maritime Cooperation. There is a need for the two to synchronise the EU Blue Growth Strategy with India's Blue Economy Strategy to promote multilateral framework for cooperation. To foster cyber cooperation the two need to establish Joint Working Group on cyber threats. They should foster cooperation between investigation agencies and intelligence of each state. Instead of the EU pushing EU regulations as benchmarks, the EU should understand India's privacy laws and bridge data adequacy differences. They should establish a Dialogue on Internet of Things.

THE IMPORTANCE OF INDIA AND THE EU PARTNERSHIP IN POST-PANDEMIC WORLD

The preceding discussion tells us that India and the EU have common values, which for both are indeed a way of life, but they must also use these values to script a future together which is today challenged by rising authoritarianism knocking at their borders. The Chinese attempt to expand globally under the Belt and Road Initiative was not seen by the EU as a big threat because they thought that the BRI is likely to create economic opportunities for the EU states which had been struggling for finances since 2011. The BRI led the EU states to keep mum on Chinese military adventurism in Asia, its misuse of multilateral trading systems and human right violations and crackdowns on Tibetan and Uighurs. However, the recent invasion of Ukraine by Russia in 2022 has sent alarm bells ringing across the capitals of the European states on the potential dangers of dictators. The fears of technocrats and bureaucrats of the EU have become more exacerbated after Russia and China announced a "no limits" partnership in early 2022. India too has been in a tight spot with repeated border stand-offs with China. In these times, when the largest democracies in the world are witnessing increasing threats, it is imperative for India and the EU to script a new chapter of engagement. For that to happen, India and the EU have to iron out the differences in negotiations of climate change, trade and geopolitical issues. As analysed previously, India and the EU have been struggling to conclude on a trade deal. India's trade with the EU is 1.8% and India is at the tenth position as a trade partner with the EU whereas the Chinese trade with the EU is 16%. The limits in trade partnership are not just restricted to commercial figures but stringent emphasis on labour and environment standards in production chains that India is reluctant to work upon. At the level of climate change, in Glasgow Summit in 2021, India and China together compelled the world to adopt "phasing down" than "phasing out" of coal plants, much to the annoyance of the EU. The divergences are even further exemplified on questions of geostrategy and positions held by India and the EU on Ukraine crisis of 2022 in UNGA are a clear reflection of the same.

EXPLAINING THE CLUMSY TANGO IN TRADE DIPLOMACY BETWEEN INDIA AND THE EU AND WAY AHEAD

If India and the EU have an unfulfilled partnership, then both sides are to be blamed. The EU wants to have a business-type partnership with India. Since 2014, India's foreign policy has acquired commercial overtones and India too is open to business with all. Whenever the two sides negotiate trade, the EU instantly slides down the realm of social and environmental standards. The tone in which the Europeans discuss these appear to Indian negotiators as if they are being preached on the importance of liberal values. India does not find the tone useful in building trust because Indian negotiators believe that the EU does not respect India's civilisational status. India also does not like the deliberate hypocrisy of the Europeans who happen to turn a blind eye on authoritarianism in China and human rights violations in Xinxiang but frequent lambasting of human rights violations and weak democracy in India. The problem is compounded further because the Europeans have done no research into negotiation styles and behaviours of India as a potential market and continue to look at India in a judgmental sense. These factors today impede India and the EU to script a new relationship based on depth and trust. India too has been complicating the story today. During the Cold War, India remained a champion of values in foreign policy. Now, India seems to place more emphasis on pragmatism in foreign policy over values. Firstly, the Europeans, being historical states, have always attached greater importance to values and this pragmatism by India is perceived by them as an incoherent policy response because pragmatism is seen by the EU as value erosion exercise. Secondly, the EU is not happy with India's multi-alignment posture because they feel that India must truly embrace the West, liberal values and join alliances. This kind of philosophical posturing is not acceptable to India. In this backdrop, how can India and the EU script a new future? The EU must accept that the West is not the sole guardian of liberal values. The Global South also has some traditions of liberalism which are rooted in the ancient past of nation states. For this, India needs to become more explicit in owning the liberal traditions rooted in its past and must drive a narrative to support the same. Geopolitically, it is imperative for the EU to realise that India's stand will be based more on pragmatism and national interests than on values because India is an emerging market economy and sometimes has to engage with states (like Russia for oil and arms) because of not just a historical legacy but reluctance of the Europeans and the West to support India's developmental endeavours. Rather than being critical, it would be better for the EU to look for new avenues of cooperation with India and reduce its dependence on others and help India become self-reliant in energy through green diplomacy.

2

CHAPTER

India's Relation with France

THE HISTORICAL BACKGROUND

India and France had a limited relationship during the colonial times, with the French having colonial settlements in some parts of India, such as Chandannagore, Yanaon, Karikal, the Coromandel and Malabar coasts and Pondicherry. However, today, it is one such country in Europe with which we have a very well-defined foreign policy. The relations between India and France are not only limited to economic interaction but are also based on other broad areas of defence, nuclear technology, strategic partnership and global partnership. Diplomatic relations between India and France have existed since 1947. The French have been old supporters of India's entry to the United Nations Security Council (UNSC). What is equally interesting is that the French have been ardent promoters of a nuclear pact with India. France supports India in Nuclear Suppliers Group and other export control regimes. Though France was not a follower of Non-Aligned Movement, Charles de Gaulle, the French President, ensured national independence and strategic autonomy in the national decision-making process of France, which was independent of the US–UK axis. In 1948, the Department of Atomic Energy in India was established. Homi J. Bhabha decided to look for foreign cooperation. Amongst the foreign players, France was the first with which India opened up nuclear cooperation. In 1960s, France helped India establish a heavy water production unit in Baroda. In 1979, the French again helped India with the establishment of a Fast Breeder Reactor at Kalapakkam. After India's peaceful nuclear test in 1974, when other nations suspended nuclear commerce with India, French continued to supply India with fuel for the Tarapur plant and continued the supply till 1992. The 1962 Indo-China conflict saw the French condemning China for its military moves along the border as they chose to side with India. In 1980, the French President Valéry Giscard d'Estaing saw India as a future potential power. In 1982, Giscard's successor, President François Mitterrand, visited India, leading to the opening up of a new partnership. Mitterrand encouraged French firms to do business with India but the French firms had an image of Indian markets being based on excessive regulation and state control. The French firms found India a difficult place to do business and thus the governments of both countries began to undertake cultural promotion to gradually ease the process. It was decided that India would promote its culture in France, enabling the French people to know more about India, which would, in turn, open up business collaboration. In 1988, I. K. Gujral was an interim Prime Minister, but he had not been able to prove his majority in the house. Jacques Chirac, despite the absence of a stable government, visited India. Later on, a new government headed by Atal Bihari Vajpayee replaced I. K. Gujral. Chirac visited India again in 1998, after the Indian nuclear tests and went on to establish a strategic partnership with India. An important dimension that emerged in the strategic partnership agreement was of defence dialogue and defence cooperation. The origin of this strategic partnership lies in a shared common history of the two nations and in France's colonial involvement with India in a limited sense. After the 1998 tests by India, UNSC condemned India while the US and Japan imposed sanctions on it. But the French did not resort to imposition of sanctions, unlike other powers. This was viewed by India very positively and also ensured that 1998 nuclear test did not emerge as an obstacle in the Indo-French relations. However, after the nuclear tests by India, a new thinking emerged in the foreign office of France. A small minority group did feel that India should not have crossed the threshold and undertaken the test. However, the majority asserted that it was better to accept India as a de facto nuclear weapon state and initiate cooperation at a civilian nuclear level. The French knew that any nuclear cooperation with India would be difficult till the time there were to be a consensus on ending India's nuclear isolation. Consequently, the French adopted a wait-and-watch policy with a clear tilt towards envisaging a favourable civilian cooperation at the nuclear level in future. After the US negotiated a nuclear deal in 2005 with India, Jacques Chirac decided to engage with India, and in 2006, he declared in favour of nuclear cooperation with India. After Jacques Chirac, Nicholas Sarkozy, François Hollande and present President Emmanuel Macron have continued to deepen economic, defence and strategic ties.

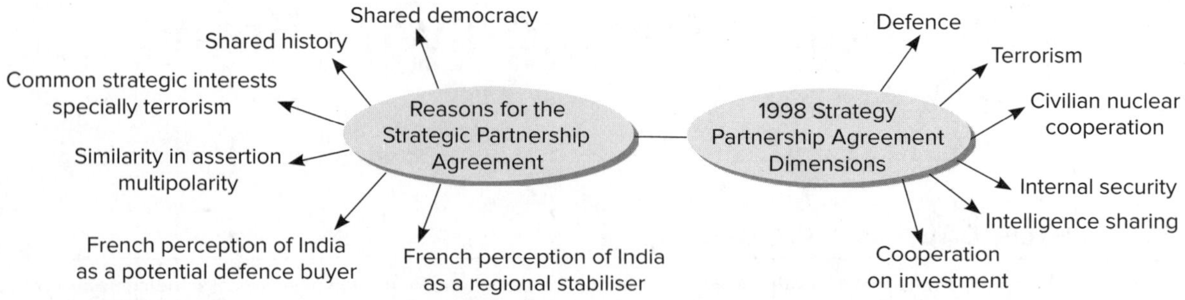

STRATEGIC DIPLOMACY—FRANCE AS INDIA'S GOLDILOCKS OPTION

Emmanuel Macron has opened up new domains of cooperation with India at three levels, which include, maritime cooperation and oceanographic research, climate change cooperation and terrorism prevention through improved interoperability of forces-based cooperation. In the recent times, with the United Kingdom acting more negative towards India over Indian abrogation of Article 370 for Kashmir and Germany not having a political weight as it had earlier; France emerges as India's new all-weather friend not only in Europe but also the larger international scenario. The ability of the French to resist the US, and stand up for strategic autonomy is something that resonates with India making the two natural partners. French follow a unique policy of 'singularities' despite being a part of the Western alliances. In this case, France is India's Goldilocks option. In Europe, India does engage with Russia majorly; but, with its expulsion from G-8 and complete breakdown of Russia and its ties with the West; France emerges crucial for India as a partner in Western-dominated forums. France has called Indian abrogation of Article 370 for Kashmir as India's internal matter. This decision of France is crucial because it can help prevent any misadventure by the US or China in the UNSC. At the international level, India and France have a common identical position on issues that range from stability in Afghanistan, Iranian nuclear deal and freedom of navigation in the Indo-Pacific. One can conclude safely that after a long period of time, India has decided to shed off its Anglo-Saxon bias in foreign policy and has moved beyond a myopic Russia, the USA and China engagement to appreciate that Europe broadly and France specifically can play an important role in transforming India's position internationally. As US continues to breakdown the Cold War world order; China continues to adopt a muscular foreign policy and Russia re-emerges as a world leader; both India and France have collectively decided to work on multiple things. France, with India, is working as a bridge between Russia and the West and such a role of will enhance the global stature of the two players. Firstly, India and France have worked to construct a new coalition that can provide some strategic stability in the unstable world. Secondly, both have decided to deepen cooperation in strategic technologies that range from civilian nuclear cooperation, digital technologies and artificial intelligence under Indo-French roadmap on cyber security and digital technologies. Both will jointly protect the economic information infrastructure impacting national security as they have recognised cybercrime as a transnational crime.

INDIA AND FRANCE TERRORISM PREVENTION DIPLOMACY

India and France have decided to cooperate on terrorism prevention by launching the "No Money for Terror" International Conference on Fighting Terrorism Financing. There is cooperation between the intelligence agencies of the two states on preventing online radicalisation. Both nations support the Christchurch Call (an action plan developed by the West to eliminate violent extremist content online).

INDIA AND FRANCE SPACE DIPLOMACY

Since 1960s, India and France have undertaken space cooperation and the Indian Space Research Organisation (ISRO) has been deeply associated with the French. Since 1981, the ISRO has been using French-made Arians rocket facilities in French Guiana. France has emerged as a partner with ISRO to send a manned mission to space and the ISRO's attempt to reach Venus. This has emerged as a new area of cooperation in planetary exploration and human space flight. France will train Indian astronauts for Indian manned space mission planned in 2022.

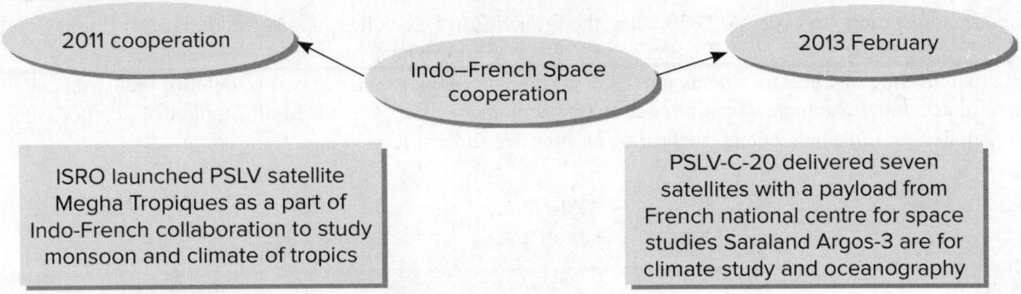

INDIA AND FRANCE COMMERCIAL DIPLOMACY

J. R. D. Tata had developed the commercial link between India and France to a large extent. He had a unique French connection. He was born and brought up in France. Later on, he went on to become the bridge of modern Indo-French relations and after his death he was buried in Paris. The institutional architecture of the commercial structure is as follows:

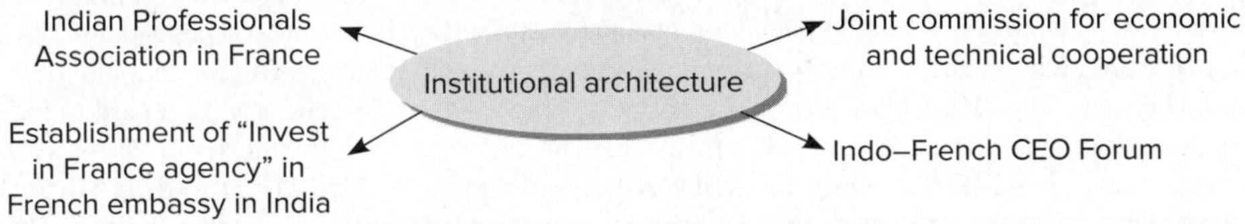

INDIA AND FRANCE NUCLEAR DIPLOMACY

In 2008, India and France concluded an agreement where Areva (the French firm) would work with the Nuclear Power Corporation of India as per a signed MoU to build 6 European Pressurised Reactors (EPR) for 10,000 MW electricity in Jaitapur to give nuclear fuel to India for 25 years.

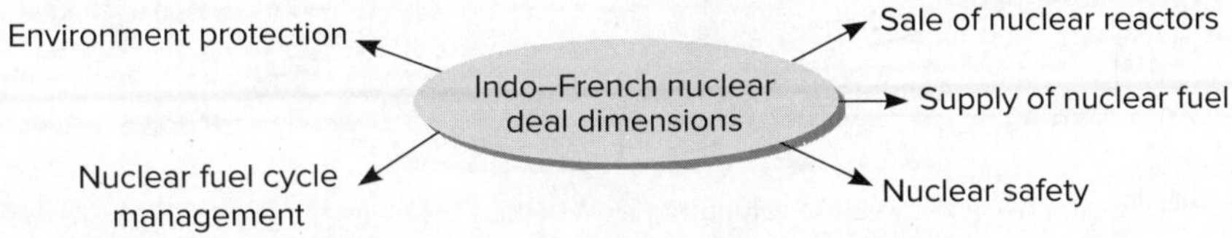

INDIA AND FRANCE TECHNOLOGY DIPLOMACY

The International Thermonuclear Experiment Reactor (ITER) project was envisaged in 1980s. A final agreement was signed in 2006 at Elyse Palace while it was enforced from 2007. The ITER site is in Aixen Provence in France where India is an important partner country along with France. The ITER is environment-friendly and evergreen due to the fact that it uses nuclear fusion instead of nuclear fission. In a nuclear reactor, the atoms are split and power is generated. When we split atoms, it generates radioactive waste. The nuclear wastes have to be managed. In contrast, the ITER fuses the atoms.

The fusion generates waste, which is either helium or water. In the project India is contributing in is creating the largest refrigerator in the world that would work at –269° Celsius. The need for such a refrigerator is a part of the project. In the process of fusion at the ITER, a huge steel frame will be heated to a high temperature and then giant magnets would be used to release atoms that would fuse with the steel frame, generating more heat which would be used to rotate the turbine. The magnets are special super-conducting magnets, which will operate only when kept cold. The fridge would ensure the same.

INDIA AND FRANCE DEFENCE DIPLOMACY

The defence cooperation goes back to 1953 when the French firm Dassault equipped the Indian Air Force with hundred Toofani fighter jets called the Mystere IV. Since the 1960s, the French have been helping Hindustan Aeronautical Limited (HAL) in manufacture of Cheetah, Chetak and BDL's Milan anti-tank missile as part of defence industrial collaboration. India and France undertake large weapon procurement diplomacy. France is a leading supplier of defence equipment to India. It supplies aircrafts, helicopters, surface-to-air missiles and artillery.

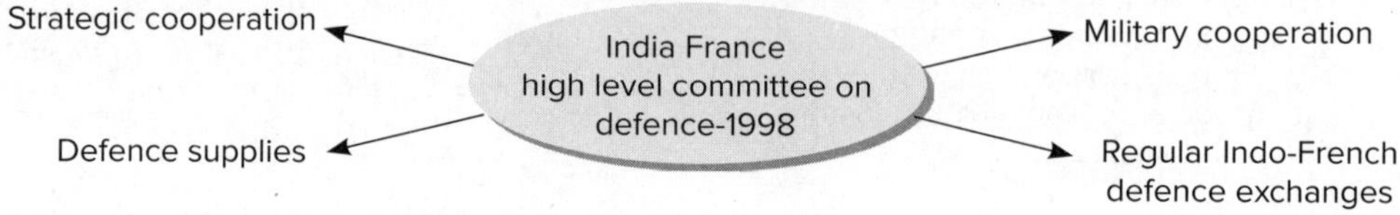

India and France have established Joint Working Group on terrorism in 2001. There are more than 60 events at various levels of defence interactions between India and France. In the recent times the two sides have decided to develop IN-FRA, a joint development of new generation jet engine.

At the defence level, what works between India and France is the level of diplomatic and political trust each has on the other. Moreover, although France has been supplying some weapons to Pakistan, it has never tried an Indo-Pak hyphenation. France has always adopted the policy of dehyphenation in defence diplomacy. France also accepts that India has a defence foreign policy of diversification and shall drive its policy as per its national interests. Russia undoubtedly remains a big supplier, but the US, Israel and France are also major partners. France has no insecurity with regard to India's policy of diversification. India had signed a pact with a French firm named DCNS for technology transfer to Mazgaon Docks Limited to build Scorpene submarines. Mazgaon Dock Limited was designated as the builder. The pact with DCNS included Indo-French collaboration for six Scorpene-class submarines. A Scorpene-class submarine is known for its stealth features and can be used to launch guided attacks with torpedoes and tube-launched anti-ship missiles. In May 2016, Kalvari became the first Scorpene-class submarine that went into operation. An understanding between India and France is that France would not halt spares supply and weapon supply in war, though with respect to the US and Germany, a lot of uncertainty prevails on this point. India prefers to envisage joint development and production with players to emerge as potential partners for the future. France has accepted India's policy of co-production and development of defence equipment.

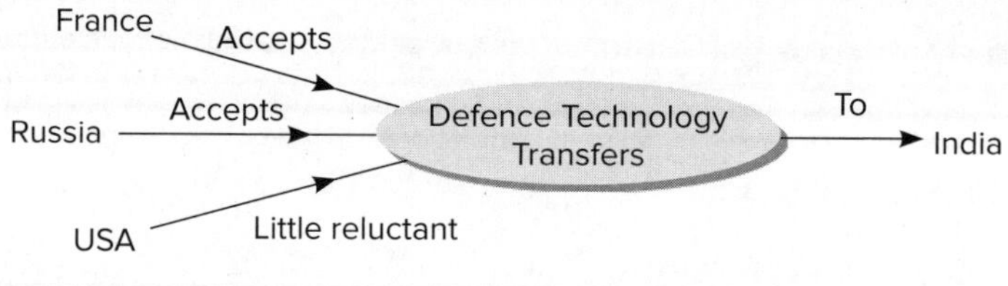

THE RELEVANCE OF DASSAULT RAFALE FOR INDIAN AIR FORCE AND DIPLOMACY WITH FRANCE

The Indian Air force (IAF) had both heavy and light fleet. In 2001, the IAF decided to procure medium-range fleet. A major part of the plan was to introduce the Medium Multi-Role Combat Aircraft (MMRCA) as part of the medium fleet. In 2007, the Defence Acquisition Council started a bid through Request for Proposal (RFP) for 126 MMRCAs. In the contract to bid for the MMRCA, six manufacturers participated. Dassault is a French firm that manufactures aircraft. Rafale is one such Omni role aircraft (MMRCA), which can perform multiple functions. It can perform nuclear deterrence, carry out in-depth strikes and can also function as an anti-ship strike aircraft.

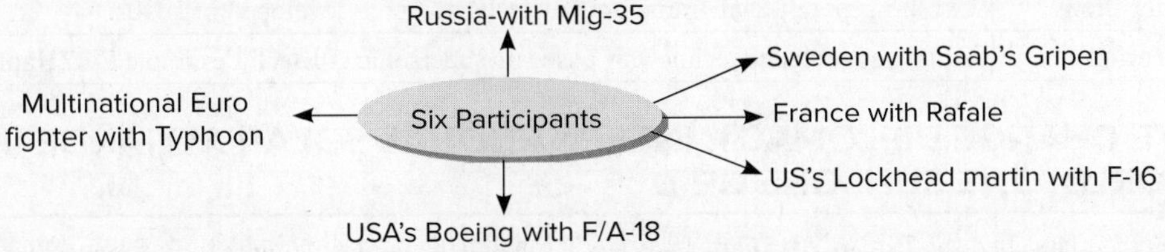

The IAF tested the aircrafts of all six participants and shortlisted Rafale and Euro fighter. In the final bid in 2012, Dassault won the contract for the supply of 126 Rafale MMRCAs. As per the deal, it was decided that 18 Rafale aircrafts would be purchased in a fly-away condition and the HAL in India would manufacture the rest of the 108 and France would undertake a technology transfer. The negotiations with Dassault began in 2012 and got completed in 2015. In the four years' interval, the price was being negotiated. In 2015, the earlier plan of 126 Rafale was declared economically unviable and India finally decided to take 36 Rafale jets in a fly-away condition. One of the reasons for the delay in negotiations was a disagreement on assembling the aircrafts in India. The offset clauses also emerged as an irritant. As per the Defence Procurement Policy of India, offset clause means that any foreign firm doing defence business with India has to bring some portion of the investment of the agreed amount of the deal back to India for investment here. The policy says that any defence deal above rupees 300 crores by a player means the player should invest 30% of the value in India. During the negotiations, India had been pitching that France has to participate in Make in India and thereby demanded 50% offset clause and also that France establishes two bases for Rafale in India. The French were willing to participate in Make in India but alleged that the establishment of two bases and other helmet-related modifications may escalate deal costs and finances. The French are also unwilling to agree to the demand for a 50% offset clause. India on 10th April 2015, finally announced the decision to buy 36 Rafale fighter jets which would boost for India's air power to deter China and Pakistan. In September 2016, India finally inked the Inter Government Agreement (IGA) and other associated commercial protocols with France. The Indian government has also cancelled the MMRCA project to acquire 126 fighter aircrafts in 2015 citing Indian Air Force's critical operational necessity and the need to cut time and costs to go for direct acquisitions of 36 Rafale aircrafts. As per the new deal with France, France will have to plough 50% of the contractual value back to India as per the offset clause. The 36 aircrafts will add power to the IAF, which as of now has only 31 flight squadrons against 42 sanctioned. By the 2022, Dassault and Reliance will jointly manufacture Falcon 2000 business jets together.

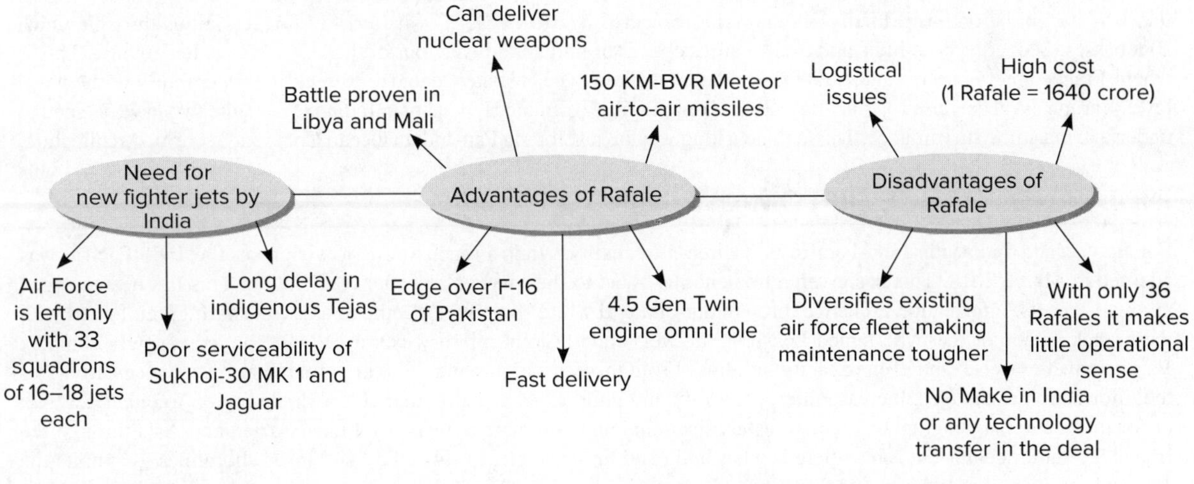

4th Generation	Technology and design is based on 1980s. They use avionics and basic radars and are used globally.
4.5th Generation	Use 4th generation airframe but advanced avionics developed in 1990s.
5th Generation	Cutting edge stealth technology based on supersonic cruise, for example F-22 Raptor of the US.

CLIMATE CHANGE DIPLOMACY: INTERNATIONAL SOLAR ALLIANCE (ISA)—ONE WORLD, ONE SUN, ONE GRID

India and France launched the ISA in 2015, after the UN Climate Change Conference in Paris. In November 2016, it was opened for signatures at Marrakesh, Morocco. An International Agency for Solar Policy and Application has been established as the headquarters in India. The deliberate reason of launching the ISA at Paris climate meet was to signify the intent of the developing states to tackle climate change. The target of India is to install 100 GW solar power by 2022. This would reduce emission intensity by 3–35% by 2030. The objective of the ISA is to develop solar energy through world cooperation by focusing upon 121 countries between Tropic of Cancer and Tropic of Capricorn. As of today the ISA is an international treaty-based organisation; it has geopolitical advantages for India, as India is able to display its global leadership commitments. ISA will transform India into a technical hub with manufacturing of solar technologies and syncs well with Make in India. The ISA and One-Planet Summit of India have enabled India to create a space to engage with major powers and leverage the intent and scale of technologies. The ISA is a clear example of India's leading power ambitions.

INDIA AND FRANCE COOPERATION IN MARITIME SECURITY

In the recent times, due to rising global trade, Indian Ocean has acquired a new strategic significance in Indian foreign policy. Even though India is striving hard to position itself as a reliable player in the region, its entire Indian Ocean policy suffers from one deficiency. India does not have a reliable partner in Indian Ocean that can help India to advance its national interests. The Joint Vision statement between India and France (signed during the Indian Prime Minister visit to France in 2018) seeks to address the concern. The statement has identified information sharing and naval exchanges as a new component in the bilateral ties. The statement is not only a consequence of India's long-term defence diplomacy with France but also a natural desire of the two states to assert themselves as states in Indian Ocean. In the absence of security architecture in Indian Ocean and the failure of ASEAN to enhance security, France has its own concerns regarding finding a reliable defence and security player in Indian Ocean. There are larger geopolitical considerations bringing India and France closer at the maritime level. They include recent reservations of France on Chinese Belt and Road Initiative (BRI) that BRI cannot be one-way. Firstly, India too has objected to BRI because of its territorial reservations through which BRI passes. Secondly, both India and France are sceptical of unilateral behaviour of the US, which is hegemonic. This is where France enters into oceanic-strategic calculus of India. The two have decided to seek interoperability at the naval level. Varuna naval exercise is a step towards interoperability. To enhance security in Indian Ocean, the two have decided to undertake maritime surveillance. This will go a long way in developing Pan-Indian Ocean Coherent Security Architecture.

INDIA AND FRANCE DIPLOMACY IN INDO-PACIFIC

For France and India, the Indo-Pacific is a three-fold reality. Indo-French strategic vision on the Indo-Pacific was adopted in March 2018. This has given a tremendous boost to their navies' decadal cooperation. This has been stepped up in all aspects: information exchange through our bilateral white shipping agreement; analysis sharing, reinforced with the French liaison officer who joined IFC-IOR this very month; joint military exercises, with the increasingly complex Varuna naval exercise; and even capacity building. From this very high point, both are looking to raise the sensitivity of the information exchanged, increase interoperability and build synergy with other actors in the region to either act with or for them. First, a geographical reality, as civilisational and commercial ties have linked Africa and Asia through the Indian Ocean for centuries. Today there is what India and France collectively call a 'culture of shorelines' that unite the regional countries. Second, a national reality, as France, like India, is an Indo-Pacific rim nation and an actor in the region. Third, the Indo-Pacific is above all a strategic reality, with security, economic and environmental dimensions. Not only is the region exposed to the threats of piracy and illegal maritime trafficking, terrorism and the security consequences of climate change, but it also lies at cross-roads of global maritime trade and digital flows, and harbours fish stocks and energy reserves that are vital for humanity. This multi-dimensional reality calls for a dedicated global approach that will enable India and France to preserve their sovereignty, protect their exclusive economic zones, guarantee respect for international law and promote multilateral solutions. The French vision of the Indo-Pacific has three pillars. The first pillar is security and it involves collectively ensuring the security and stability of this region by sharing French analyses of the maritime situation, carrying out surveillance missions, and strengthening the capacities of the region's countries. The second pillar is environment and blue economy in particular and focuses on developing marine economy in a way that is sustainable and resilient to global warming. Protecting marine biodiversity is crucial for both coastal communities. The third and last pillar is connectivity that aims to meet the region's huge needs in terms of infrastructure and harmonisation of standards. This would involve strengthening transport and digital links as well as people-to-people ties. Connectivity must be economically sustainable and respect the sovereignty of states. On blue economy, France and India have much common ground, which both need to translate into further action. Given their shared principles and values, their mutual strategic trust, their excellent cooperation already underway in several domains, France and India are ready to build and develop their Indo-Pacific agenda together for the coming years.

THE SHORTCOMINGS/PROBLEMS OR HURDLES INDIA FACES IN ENGAGING WITH THE STATE DIPLOMATICALLY

Issues in nuclear cooperation: The Jaitapur nuclear power plant is in Madban village of Ratnagiri district in Maharashtra. The plant has witnessed some protests in recent times. The area on which the plant is to be established is very close to the sea. A lot of fishermen depend upon the sea for their livelihood. Once the plant is operationalised, it is expected to release a lot of hot water in the sea. The fishermen fear that this release of hot water will raise the sea temperatures, which would, in turn, affect fishing. The fish catch of Ratnagiri is exported to the EU and Japan. The release of the hot waters will affect their exports. In 2003, the region of Ratnagiri was also declared as a horticulture district and is famous for Alphonso mango. The National Environment Engineering research institute, in its report, has branded large tracts of land as barren land. This is viewed by the locals as dichotomous to the claims of government of Maharashtra. The site of Jaitapur being in a highly seismic zone adds to the existing concerns.

Issues in ISA Firstly, the cost of installations of the solar technologies is high. The developing states find coal plants to generate electricity cheaper. Secondly, as the US has held monopoly over the solar cells, the countries need to import them from the US. The US charges high tariffs and this increases the cost of solar energy. The research and development in the solar technologies still remains very low. The storage of solar energy remains a problem due to common and wide use of lithium batteries.

3

CHAPTER

India's Relations with the United Kingdom

EVOLUTION OF HISTORICAL RELATIONS: FROM COLONIAL ERA TO INDO-PACIFIC COOPERATION

Great Britain or the United Kingdom (UK) was India's colonial ruler. As India became independent, the British allied with the US during the Cold War. India advocated for non-alignment and decolonisation, which did not augur well with the British. India did not favour joining any military alliances. Thus, at the international level, the two were at loggerheads with each other both politically and ideologically. The most important issue that came up was India joining the Commonwealth. When India decided to join the British Commonwealth, there was a strong reaction from the opposition in India. The opposition asserted that doing so would contradict India's non-alignment policy. However, Jawaharlal Nehru clarified that India would, firstly, join the Commonwealth as an independent nation. Secondly, it would not accept the British monarch as its head of state, but would join the body as an independent Republic. Thirdly, Nehru clarified that India, even after joining the Commonwealth, would continue to maintain its own strategic autonomy in decision-making. Indian diplomats worked tirelessly to change the rules of the game in the British Commonwealth. India ratified the Commonwealth Agreement in 1949 and joined it as a representative after 26th January 1950. Since the 1940s, the British and Indian economies were linked financially. The British had agreed that after the World War II, it would reimburse the money spent by the Indian government in the war. The amount was about 13 million Pounds, and an agreement was made that the British would return the money from 1947 to 1957. The businesses run by British firms also had to adapt to the new policies of the Indian government. The British firms and their subsidiaries that preferred to stay back faced severe competition from Indian firms and Indian Public Sector Undertakings. The British also continued to provide aid to India, both at the bilateral level and also through the Colombo Plan (launched in 1971 to provide development aid to South Asia). One concern on the foreign policy front that emerged was the question of Pakistan and Kashmir. The British approach was to maintain good relations with both nations and go for the UN-based mediation but India was visibly upset with the British for not supporting her. After Indian defeat in the 1962 conflict, India decided to go for defence modernisation. The British and the US saw it as an opportunity to make India lean towards the West. India's focus was on technical support so that suppliers could provide it arms under a licence, helping India to diversify its suppliers' range. The Russians offered what India demanded while the British linked supplies to the revival of Kashmir talks with Pakistan. India rejected the British conditionality and went ahead with its arrangement with the Russians, thereby costing the British a supply market. The 1965 war was a game changer. When India witnessed Pakistani infiltration, it retaliated with an attack on Pakistan. The attack affected the Punjab region of Pakistan. The British branded India as an aggressor and began alienating India. In 1966, India faced economic crisis. The US took it as an opportunity to advise India to undertake devaluation and adopt the International Monetary Fund (IMF) reforms package. The Bank of England did not toe the US line on this and in fact declined IMF support. It also dissented with the World Bank when it advocated India to go for devaluation. The Indo-British divergence was especially visible when India signed the Friendship Treaty with the USSR in 1971.

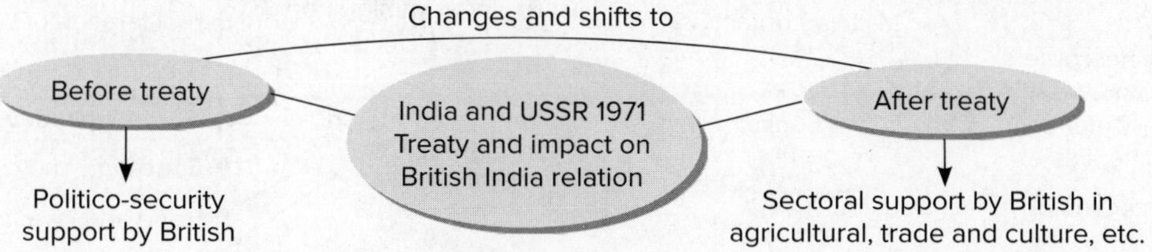

In 1968, the British decided to reduce its presence in Indian Ocean at the military level. It continued to maintain control on the Chagos Archipelago in Maldives territory. In 1966, the British had given the Chagos Archipelago atoll to the US. The US decided to establish a military base the island of Diego Garcia. The British decided to remove the residents of Diego Garcia to free it up for US use. This move gave the US a higher degree of presence in the Indian Ocean. India resented the move strongly. However, seeing strong reaction of India, the approach of the British towards Kashmir changed. The change was visible from 1979 to 1990. The British favoured bilateral negotiations. The opening up Indian economy and the end of the Cold War opened up an ocean of opportunities between India and the British. The British seized the opportunity to establish business relations with India. In 2004, the two nations concluded a Strategic Partnership Agreement while, since 1995, there has been a Defence Consultative Group formed between the two.

INDIA'S FINANCIAL PARTNERSHIP WITH BRITAIN

In 2014, India and the UK financial partnership was announced. The aim of the partnership was to examine priority areas of financial coordination between India and the UK. The thrust area was professional financial services industry. The UK has decided to commit financial training as a new component of financial partnership and impart work stream professional training for Charted Accountants and other financial professionals. The UK has tied up with India's First International Financial Centre—GIFT City in Ahmedabad to train Indian professionals. The Indian diaspora in Britain is largely a supporter of the Labour party but in recent times, conservatives have made some incursions in the diaspora. An important contribution is of the BBC (British Broadcasting Corporation), which continues to promote British values to its listeners. The BBC has a well-defined audience in India and broadcasters like Mark Tully have been awarded with Padma Bhushan. The relations had improved during David Cameron's term as his idea was to approach relations bilaterally rather than taking a South Asian perspective. He also stayed away from intruding on India's internal matters, like the Kashmir issue. However, in the present reign of Boris Johnson, there has been hyphenation of India and Pakistan again. The British MPs have been negative towards Indian abrogation of Articles 370.

DEFENCE AND INTERNATIONAL SECURITY PACT BETWEEN INDIA AND BRITAIN

A new Defence and International Security Pact was agreed in 2015.

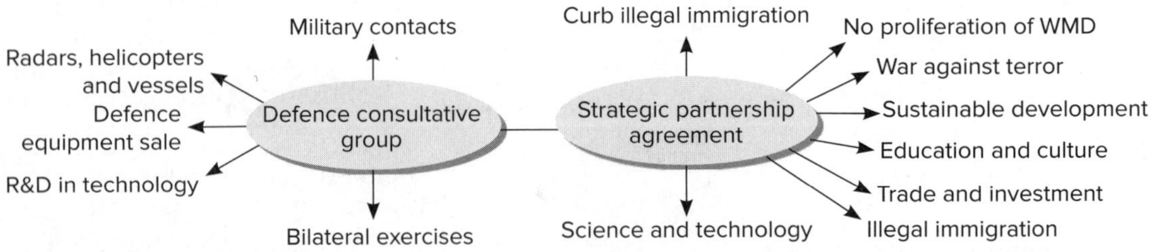

JOINT VISION STATEMENT ON ENERGY AND CLIMATE CHANGE BETWEEN INDIA AND BRITAIN

The Joint Vision Statement between India and Britain was signed in 2015 to ensure cooperation to reduce fossil fuels consumption and focus on clean energy.

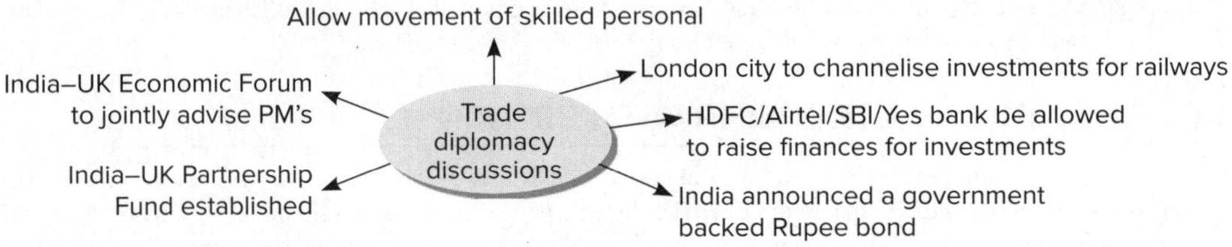

COMMERCIAL DIPLOMACY BETWEEN INDIA AND BRITAIN

Information and communications technology, critical engineering and healthcare products are identified as areas of cooperation. The two sides agreed to use the India–UK CEO Forum to enhance cooperation in the three identified sectors. The issues related to market liberalisation and market access that may arise after Britain's exit from the European Union (EU) are to be negotiated at the Joint Economic Trade Committee (JETCO). The British firms will use JETCO to enhance their businesses with Indian partners. The London Stock Exchange has emerged as a pioneer exchange to raise offshore rupee financing instruments. There is an agreement to support the development of corporate bond market of India was agreed upon between the SBI and the London Stock Exchange group's index business, i.e. FTSE Russell. The private sector in London will contribute 500 million Pounds in the India–UK Sub Fund to support infrastructure financing under the National Investment and Infrastructure Fund. Britain has committed support for redeveloping the Varanasi Railway Station. Also, it has committed 20 million Pounds for the Start-Up India Venture Capital Fund. Over and above the 160 million Pounds has already been committed by Britain to fund 75 start-ups across India. The two sides concluded an MoU on Intellectual Property.

DEFENCE AND INTERNATIONAL SECURITY PARTNERSHIP OF INDIA AND BRITAIN

To enhance bilateral defence cooperation, in November 2015, India and Britain had concluded Defence and International Security Partnership (DISP).

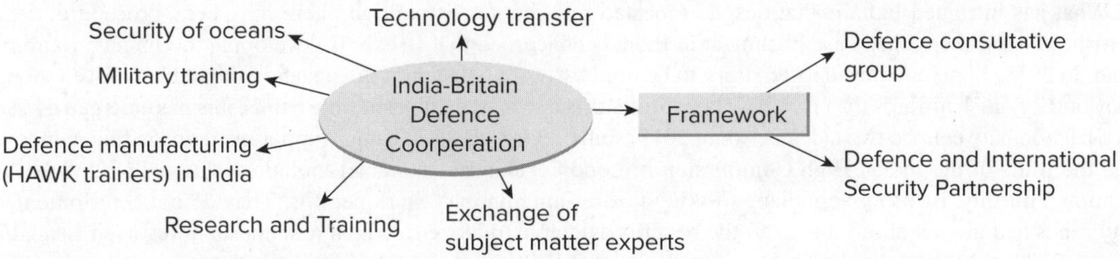

PAKISTAN FACTOR IN INDIA–BRITAIN RELATIONS AND KASHMIR ISSUE AS DIVERGENCE DIPLOMACY

Britain's conduct with regard to developments in Jammu and Kashmir is unacceptable as it played a dubious role in the United Nations Security Council's (UNSC) closed-door meeting on Kashmir which was prepared to support a press statement by the UNSC based on a consensus, which did not emerge (China and Pakistan would have wanted it). The British were fully aware of Pakistan Prime Minister Imran Khan's declared plan to launch an intensive international campaign against India's step to nullify Article 370, which included mobilising Pakistani communities abroad to stage abusive and hate-filled demonstrations against India. Britain's foreign secretary, Dominic Raab, had made a totally unacceptable statement in Parliament on the Kashmir issue, reflecting an enduring imperial hangover. Lecturing India on respecting internationally recognised human rights showed disrespect for India's democracy. Raab has disregarded India's compulsions to take preventive steps to protect the lives of innocent Kashmiris from Pakistan-sponsored jihadis who have caused terrible mayhem in Kashmir for three decades now. The restrictions imposed by India prevent violence, not inflict it. With the Internet and social media, terrorists can promote violence through rapid mobilisation, exhortation and fake news. The British themselves are grappling with this new tool of radicalisation and instigating violence. Why does Raab think that India, with a much graver ground situation than what Britain faces, should not have these concerns? Raab sermonises, "The issue of human rights is not just a bilateral issue for India and Pakistan or a domestic issue, but an international issue". We have never claimed or accepted that the human rights issue is a bilateral one between Pakistan and us. We have all the domestic instruments of a functioning democracy to deal with human rights issues, and we do not accept international interference. Unlike Britain, and other Western countries, we have no historical baggage with regard to barbaric violations of human rights through external conquests, colonialism, racial discrimination, slavery and genocide of indigenous populations. Currently, Britain has participated in the destruction of Iraq, Libya and Syria, inflicting untold miseries on local populations. It should be careful in taking the moral high ground on human rights issues with India. Worse, Raab has insidiously introduced UNSC resolutions on the Kashmir issue in his statement by claiming that "as recognised in the UN Security Council resolutions and the Simla Agreement", India and Pakistan have to fundamentally resolve the Kashmir "dispute", forgetting that the UNSC resolutions were structured around the UN mediation; that even as late as 1961, Britain formally intervened in the Kashmir issue along with the US, and that the Simla Agreement excludes the UN or any third-party role. How does Raab mention the UNSC resolutions and the Simla Agreement in the same sentence, when they are contradictory? His unwarranted reference to the UNSC resolutions only confirms its mischievous role in the UNSC closed-door meeting. Britain seems ready to internationalise the Kashmir issue, as Pakistan wants, when it says that while Britain wants to respect India's constitutional arrangements in Kashmir, they do "have implications internationally as they touch on internationally respected and recognised human rights". This boosts Pakistan's plans to raise this issue in the Human Rights Council.

FIVE HURDLES IN DEEPENING OF INDIA AND BRITAIN TIES

There are five major irritants. Firstly, Britain in 2018, refused to put Indian students into a special category for the visas. Even though India is not pleased with the latest stance, the British government has countered the fact by saying that in the last few years, the success rate for Indian students to seek visas was 89%. The British government exempted the Indian doctors and nurses in Tier-2 category, facilitating their easy recruitment in Britain. Secondly, India is not pleased with British decision of not proactively taking up support for extraditing economic fugitives such as Vijay Mallya and Nirav

Modi. What has intrigued India is that despite repeated requests for extradition, there have been procedural delays by the British. Thirdly, the security establishment in India is concerned that Britain is developing too much proximity with Pakistan. In 2018, London allowed its territory to be used by pro-Khalistani militants and Sikh radicals. Even though the leniency of the British towards the pro-Khalistani militants is to woo the domestic vote banks, this has emerged as a serious point of friction between the two sides. Also, in 2019, some 10,000 pro-Khalistani supporters damaged the windows and defaced the walls of the Indian High Commission in London. This was a blatant violation of Article 22 of the Vienna Convention. Fourthly, British give Indians working in Britain temporary work permits. They do not contribute to social security funds and are not allowed to avail the benefits available to citizens, which remains an unresolved issue. Fifthly, in January 2020, a Member of the European Parliament (MEP) Shaffaq Mohammad (hailing from Pakistan-Occupied Kashmir), belonging to the UK (bestowed with Order of British Empire Award 2015 for 'political service' as a councilor of Sheffield City Council), drafted a resolution for discussion in the European Parliament against the Indian Citizenship Amendment Act (CAA). The ISI of Pakistan was behind Shaffaq and they drafted the resolution which used words like "CAA could trigger the largest statelessness crisis in the world and cause widespread human suffering", despite CAA being an internal affair of India.

BREXIT—A PROOF THAT DIVORCES ARE MORE COMPLICATED THAN MARRIAGES?

After the World War II, Germany and France began trade with each other following a mechanism that reduced trade duties. Later Germany, France, Belgium, Luxemburg and the Netherlands joined the group and began to deal in coal and steel. In 1957, the trade between the above states saw the rise of a comprehensive framework governing the trade. In the same year, the Treaty of Rome was signed, setting up the European Economic Community (EEC) as a common market. Gradually, the EEC kept on expanding and became a union of 28 states. In 1990, a meeting of the European Council was held in Rome, which initiated an inter-governmental conference on establishment of a monetary union. In 1992, the Maastricht treaty on the EU was concluded, which established the EU, aiming to ensure the free movement of people, goods, services, and capital within the internal market, enact legislation in justice and home affairs, and maintain common policies on trade, agriculture, fisheries and regional development. The British had joined the EEC in 1973 and had been a part of the EU since its inception.

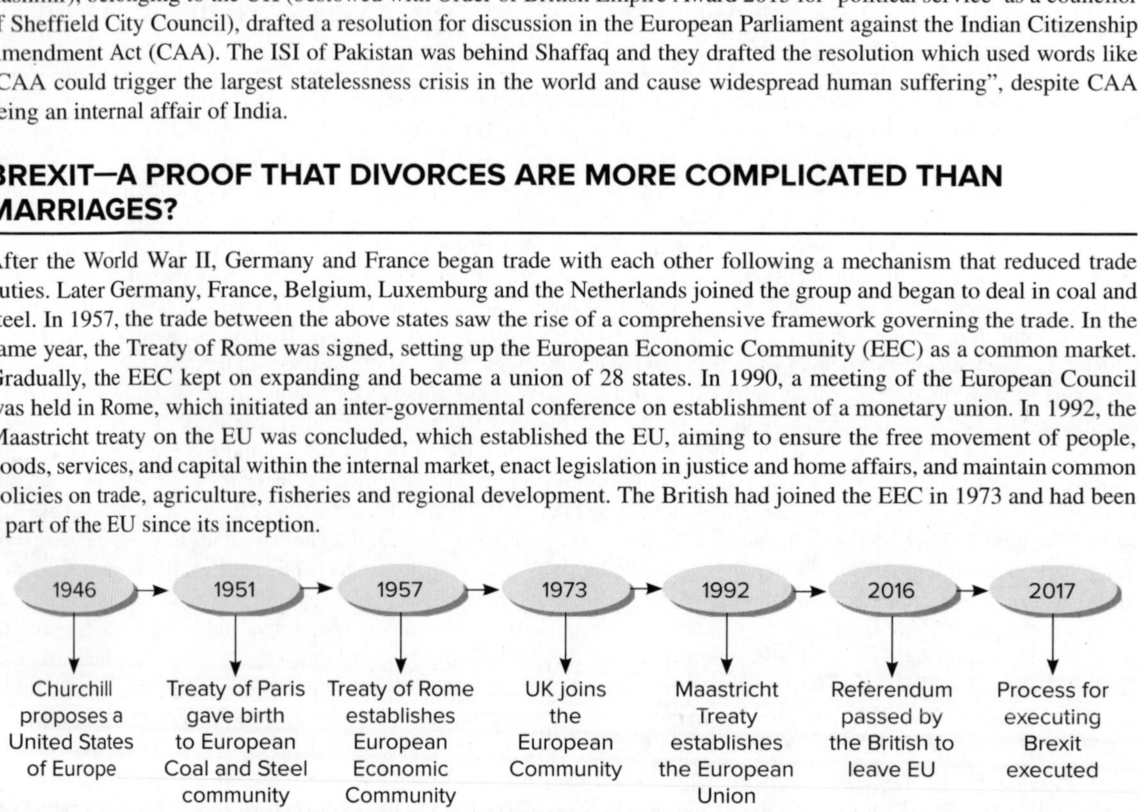

On 23rd June 2016, there was a Brexit referendum where 51.9% of the voters in the UK voted in favour of leaving the EU. One of the big reasons for a 51.9% UK vote to leave the EU was the free movement of labour in the UK. The intention to take back control on immigration was a key factor. Foreign firms would be impacted as, under the erstwhile passport scheme, a financial service firm could use another member EU state to carry out business without any extra cost that were normally associated with foreign entities. This feature will be lost now and it will create an impact.

IMPLICATIONS OF BREXIT ON INDIA AND SPACES OF NEW COOPERATION WITH BRITAIN

Many firms used to favour the UK and over a period of time, London had become a trade hub. The procedure to leave the EU began from March 2017 and the British formally left the EU on January 2020. The British and the EU would now work out how the future relations of Britain and the EU would be by 31st December 2020. The impact of Brexit on the

Indian economy on the immediate level would be comparatively less due to a rise in agricultural production in India. The consumer industry demand in India did slow down due to demonetisation but it picked up due to the ratification of the 7th Pay Commission. The exports to and from India have fallen in the UK due to a weak demand in the Euro zone and Britain, since the Eurozone crises. Post-Brexit the possibility of dip in exports may rise as currencies will fluctuate and the real picture will only emerge upon the basis of appreciation of other currencies with the Pound. The process will also create an impact on outbound FDI from India to the UK, which today stands to be at 8% of the total FDI. As India export automobiles, it will affect our exports to the EU and the UK. The deeper impact is to be on IT exports, which constitutes the core of Indian exports to the UK. Other commodities such as metals, pharmacy, garments and financial service will also feel the pinch. As the number of the EU applications for education to the UK will fall, it will be favourable for Indian students for outbound education seekers. A depreciation of the Pound will lead to short-term gain for Indian students as the cost of education will decrease.

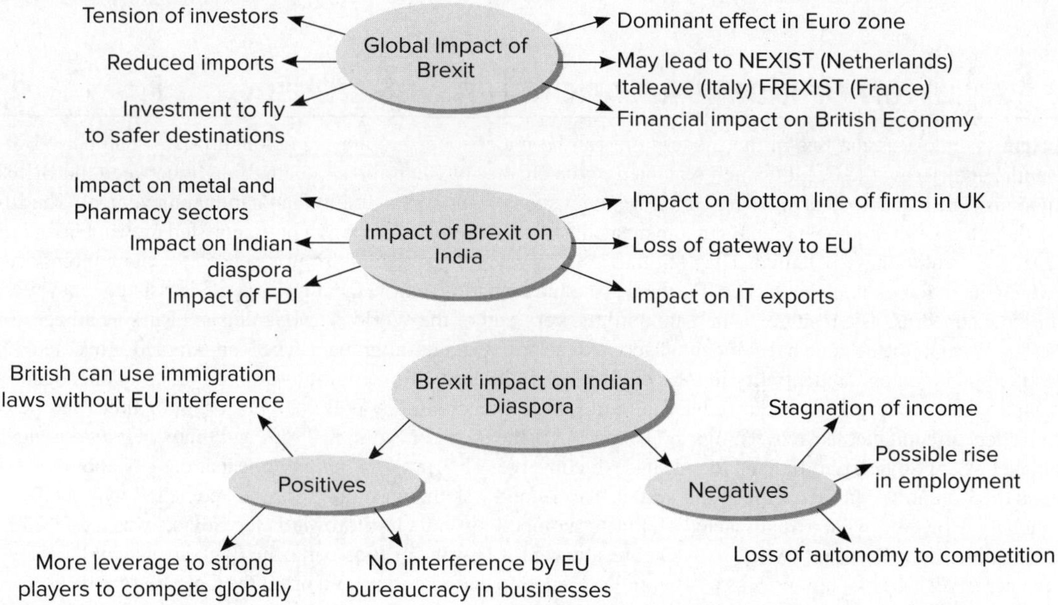

CHAPTER 4

India's Relations with Russian Federation

THE EVOLUTION OF INDIA'S RELATIONSHIP WITH RUSSIA

The origin of Indo-Russian ties in the modern era can be understood through the colonial prism. The period of early nineteenth century saw the Great Game (explained in the chapter of Central Asia) being fought between the British and the Russians. The leaders of early Soviet Union were not keen on supporting the Indian national movement. The Russian leaders thought that the Indian national movement against British colonialism was a bourgeois-led movement and did not have a strong revolutionary potential. They felt that a strong revolutionary impulse was needed for fight against imperial rule, which the Indians somewhat lacked. Further, as the Indian national movement progressed, Russia got busy with their own internal concerns, as a result of which, up until the very end of the World War II, India and Russia had very limited interaction. When India became independent, it adopted the policy of non-alignment. The Non-Aligned Movement (NAM) tried to maintain ideological neutrality in the exciting era of bipolarity. In the initial years of Indian independence, up to 1953, Stalin was not very keen about India. Stalin did not appreciate the non-aligned posturing of India and perceived Indian leaders as capitalist lackeys. Things did change after the death of Stalin in 1953, and there were two issues at the global level where Soviets and Indians found space to converge. The first was Indian protest at the UN about its decision to extend the Korean War north of the 38th Parallel. The second was Indian support for the People's Republic of China to enter the UN. However, what actually acted as a factor compelling India to tilt towards the Soviets was the US. In 1954, the US established the Southeast Asia Treaty Organisation (SEATO) and in 1955 came the Baghdad Pact or CENTO. India began to perceive these two alliances as an attempt by the US to encircle India and bring the Cold War to the doorsteps of India. After the death of Stalin, with the coming of Nikita Khrushchev to power, Soviets began to view India favourably as a counterbalance in the East West confrontation. India also responded to the changing Soviet posturing. India offered strong condemnation of Anglo-French aggression of Egypt during the Suez crisis in 1956, but did not up the rhetoric in the case of Hungarian invasion by the Soviets in 1956. Nikita Khrushchev favoured the improvement of ties with the US while Mao tried to criticise it and promote his own image as a sole representative of revolutionary movements. This difference between the Soviets and China led to Soviets favouring India during the 1959 Chinese aggression. Soviets stood along the Chinese theory that the border between India and China is a colonial legacy. After the 1962 conflict, the Soviets gave an aggressive push to defence ties with India and emerged as one of the top-most defence suppliers for India by the late 1960s. In the 1965 Indo-Pak war, India appreciated the role of the Soviets during mediation through the Tashkent Declaration. This also led to India and Russia's convergence on global issues such as the Vietnam War and Czechoslovakia. As the US explored options of undertaking rapprochements with China, India began to fear a Beijing–Washington–Islamabad axis. Henry Kissinger tried to make it clear that a future Indo-Pak conflict could also involve China. India acted hastily. Since 1969, India and the USSR were negotiating a diplomatic and strategic engagement. India speeded up the negotiations and in 1971, concluded a twenty-year India–Soviet Treaty of Peace and Friendship. The treaty gave India the needed strategic support from Russia in any eventuality of conflict. After the creation of Bangladesh in 1971, the India–Russia Treaty acted as a great strategic stabiliser for India and the region as it deterred any Chinese or American intervention unfavourable to India. In 1974, India conducted the nuclear test and the Soviets did not condemn it, in fact, it went on to support India with the supply of heavy water for the nuclear programme, which got halted when American and Canadians took back their supplies. In 1979, when the Soviets invaded Afghanistan, India at that time in the UN General Assembly abstained from voting which had advocated that Soviets stop military intervention in Afghanistan. Domestically, within India, cutting across party lines, all parties had an understanding that relations with Russia were serving the Indian national interest and thereby needed to continue. After the disintegration of the USSR and subsequent birth of the Russian federation, the years of Boris Yeltsin in Russia saw Russia undertook rapprochements with the West again, which, in turn, affected the Russian tilt to India. However, in January 1993, Boris Yeltsin visited India and concluded the Twenty-Year Indo-Russia Friendship and Cooperation Treaty. In 1989, when Soviets withdrew from Afghanistan, it not only paved way for the rise of the Taliban in Afghanistan but also, due to Pakistani support to extremists in Afghanistan, succeeded in creating a rift in Kashmir. From the 1990s began the rise of Kashmiri extremism. Problems erupted in 1996 when the Taliban took over Afghanistan. India and Russia, along with Iran, began to support the Northern Alliance. This convergence of interests of India and Russia in Afghanistan from 1996 paved way for warming up of bilateral relations, ultimately cultivating in Strategic Partnership in 2000 which has been elevated to Special and Privileged Strategic Partnership in 2010. India and Russia share a multi-diverse partnership that is multicomponent in nature and is gradually moving into non-traditional spheres now. The relationship is wide and deep in areas that range from military cooperation, trade, space cooperation, energy sector, regional balancing and international cooperation to cultural engagement.

CORE DRIVERS OF INDIA AND RUSSIA RELATIONS IN THE POST-COLD WAR TIMES

In the Post-Cold War period, there are four key drivers of Indo-Russia ties. The first is India's assertion for a multipolar world. The logic here is that the resurgence of Russia in the world and its attempt to project itself as an independent pole in the international system suits India as it will prevent any form of unipolar assertion by either the US or China. Thus, India's multipolar assertion is in sync with Russian resurgence. The second driver is that Russia is comfortable with a strong India in South Asia and this attitude of Russia gives India more space to manoeuvre its strategic policy. The third is an understanding in India that there is very little obligation to deepen ties with Russia in contrast to the US because Russia has served Indian national interests well and would continue to do so in the future. The fourth is the China factor. Indian establishment has understood two things. Firstly, that Russia has a strained relationship with the West; and secondly, it does not have the capacity as of now to punch above its weight in Europe. Thus, due to these two things, Russia is compelled to go close to China. But India knows that growing Russia and China proximity is not a threat to India because Russia uses India to balance the growing ambitions of China in Central Asia and Eurasia. As the US focuses on 'de-globalisation' and China focuses on 'Globalisation 2.0 with Chinese characteristics', for the Russian foreign policy, India has emerged as a potential geopolitical, geo-strategic and geo-economic balancer to regional and global ambitions of China.

RUSSIA AND INDIA IN THE POST-PANDEMIC WORLD ORDER

The preceding analysis clearly tells us that strategic legacy is one of the strongest binders of India and Russia relations. In the post-pandemic world, the two sides have understood that a multipolar Asia and a multipolar world are in interests of both. Today, the multipolar Asia is under a threat with rising hegemony of China in Asia and American attempts to counter the same. While Russia is definitely interested in endorsing the strategic vision of multipolar Asia in the post-pandemic times; it would not favour a situation where the Chinese influence is curtailed, only to be replaced with an American influence in Asia. While Russia and India differ on relative roles of poles shaping the order, there will be a bigger picture of convergence on a multipolar world. India knows that Russia is not going to sit in the court of Emperor Beijing as a junior partner and would establish an independent worldview that will create space for India and Russia to cooperate.

RUSSIA'S PERCEPTION OF KASHMIR ISSUE AND DIPLOMACY OF CONVERGENCE THINKING

Russia has consistently supported India on the Kashmir issue. In November 1955, Soviet leader Nikita Khrushchev referred to the decision taken by the Kashmir Constituent Assembly in 1953, to join the Indian Union. He remarked, "The people of Kashmir had already decided to join the Indian Union". Russia's 100th veto in the UN Security Council on June 22,

1962, was against a resolution moved by Ireland, duly backed by the US and its allies, seeking selective implementation of parts of past UN resolutions, alluding to a plebiscite in Kashmir. Interestingly, this came a year after a Soviet veto of a US-led resolution in December 1961, seeking to reverse the liberation of Goa, by India. The Soviet Union vetoed three Security Council resolutions directed against India, during the December 1971 Bangladesh conflict. Some non-permanent members, duly backed by a virtual Sino-American alliance, initiated these resolutions. The UK and France abstained from backing these resolutions. A little-known fact is that the Russians warned the Chinese against any involvement in the Bangladesh conflict, with a huge deployment of their mechanised forces and air power, along the Kazakhstan border. In 2019, when India abrogated Article 370, Russia maintained that it was an 'internal matter' of India.

INDIA'S ACT FAR EAST POLICY: THE VLADIVOSTOK MOMENT IN INDIA–RUSSIA RELATIONS

The city of Vladivostok has a special place in the hearts of Indian. This is so because in 1971, when navy of Britain and the USA threatened Indian security, Russia dispatched nuclear armed naval fleet from Vladivostok to support India. In 2019, Indian Prime Minister participated in the 20th India–Russia Annual Prime Minister Summit and 5th Eastern Economic Forum Summit in Vladivostok, Russia. The visit gave a new direction, new energy and new speed to the bilateral ties. The Far East region of Russia, which lies in Asia part of Russia, has enormous scope in deep-sea exploration, oil and gas and minerals. The region is extremely resource-rich but is underdeveloped and Russia is very keen to take advantage of shifting of centre of gravity to Asia and seek support of the Asian powers to develop the region. As of now, this region is dominated by Chinese investments as it borders China. Russia is seeking to lessen its dependence on China by diversification as part of Russian pivot to Asia strategy. One reason for Russia to invite India in Far East is also the 'Indo-Pacific'. Russia feels that India's foray into the American Indo-Pacific concept can deprive Russia of an old-time ally at the defence and strategic level, even though India has conveyed to Russia that its engagement with the US is not against Russian interests. It is important to note that Americans look at the concept of Eurasia as an attempt of the Chinese and Russian to marginalise the US in the continental space of Eurasia. This has created opportunities for India, which has announced the 'Look East, Act East Policy' and India has stated that Far East of Russia is the 'takeoff point for Act Far East'. During the visit of the Indian Prime Minister, the two sides have decided to explore direct connectivity between India and Far East region of Russia. Now, Chennai and Vladivostok cargo ships will run and this will help India bypass Europe to reach Russia. The Chennai and Vladivostok cargo ship will take only 24 days in contrast to the 40 days route via Europe. This route will require a stable South China Sea and can open up trilateral cooperation between India–Russia and Vietnam. Indian oil firms have decided to invest in Russian upstream projects in the Far East. In the Far East, India has decided to focus on oil- and gas-based energy (enabling India to bypass unstable West Asia for oil), tourism, agriculture, coal (the region has metallurgical coal, which India lacks, but is needed by the steel industry), gold and diamond mining and alternative energy. India has decided to provide 10,000 USD to fund study of Indology at the Centre of Regional and International Studies at Far Eastern Federal University. To assist the development of Far East, India has decided to commit 1 billion USD line of credit and also send doctors, engineers and teachers as the region faces the problem of lack of manpower. The presence of Indian manpower can also balance off Chinese migration in the region. From the Far East, India is going to import timber and can undertake joint collaboration with South Korea and Japan. One unique feature of Indian diplomacy in Far East is 'para diplomacy', where Indian states such as Gujarat, Uttar Pradesh and Goa have collaborated with provinces in the region to increase bilateral trade through cooperation of mid-sized and small businesses.

STRATEGIC SIGNIFICANCE OF RUSSIA IN INDIAN DEFENCE MARKET AND DIPLOMATIC STYLES OF NEGOTIATIONS

The origin of defence diplomacy between India and Russia began since 1962 and since then is based on mutual trust. Today, more than 70% of Indian defence equipment is of Russian origin. These weapons have also proved their worth at a time when India needed them in conflicts. During the Cold War, to save forex, the two sides have used Rupee–Rouble agreements, which significantly contributed helping India save forex. Russia has always helped India with technology transfers. Crisis of vast Military Industrial Complexes of the Soviet after the disintegration of the USSR and their failure to sustain the complexes led India to seek alternative routes through a policy of defence diversification. India diversified and explored the possibility of Israel and France, along with the US, acting as potential suppliers. In the first decade, following the end of the Cold War saw Russia trying to consolidate its military industrial complexes. Indian reliance on Russia will not decrease despite diversification and delays in projects because Russia remains committed to defence technology transfer and co-production, which India feels it needs for the development of its domestic defence industry. Russia and India continue to have joint development of weapons and continue to interact through institutionalised mechanisms of cooperation. The Indo-Russia defence ties have also witnessed a transformation to a model of cooperative production on shared risk partnership from the erstwhile model of a supplier–consumer relationship. Since 2007, the two are working on developing a fifth-generation combat aircraft. The MiG-35 has had India embark upon a mega defence modernisation programme. India is undertaking domestic co-production of BrahMos missile, T-90 tank and Sukhoi aircrafts. The Chinese too were not very far behind in importing Russian technology. However, the Chinese imports were not only lesser in value but also in quantity as China favoured to import only those technologies that it could clone in China. Uniquely, the cooperation with India led to no possibility of creation of unlicenced clones whereas such possibility continues to remain high for transfers done to China.

Defence has been a vital pillar of the relationship. Unlike other nations, Russia has never invoked arms sanctions on India and at critical times such as the Kargil conflict, Russia supplied items to India from their own military reserves. Indian requirements of defence products made Russia technologically more productive as it enabled creating a system of innovation that pushed Russians to produce half-a-generation more advanced equipment. There was an overall improvement in Russian aviation and missiles technology industries. This development was taken positively even by Russian defence corporate houses as it enabled them to establish long-term strategies to meet Indian requirements. The Russian corporate houses in the avionics industry used Indian orders as a springboard to spearhead innovations in engines (thrust vector controls) and radars (phased-array radars).

RECIPROCAL EXCHANGE OF LOGISTICAL SUPPORT AGREEMENT AND PROJECT 11356

In the 1990s and early 2000s, the Indian-side placed multiple defence orders from Russia that ranged from Talwar-class frigates under Project 11356 to MiG-29K shipborne aircrafts. Indian demands spearheaded a culture of innovation in the Russian defence industrial complex to cater to advanced needs India and Russia in 2019 had signed a 3 USD billion deal where Russia would refurbish and supply an Akula-class nuclear powered attack submarine (Chakra 3) to India. In 2021, India and Russia concluded military logistics support agreement known as Agreement on Reciprocal Logistical Support (RELOS) that gives Russians the right to refuel ships and enhance sub-conventional preparedness in the waters while India gets access to Russian military facilities in the Arctic.

THE ASSAULT RIFLE-BASED COOPERATION FOR INTERNAL SECURITY

The Indian government signed an agreement with Russia in 2019 to manufacture the AK-103 rifles for the Indian Army. Russia will manufacture the AK-103 in India. Even though Russia had sent the proposal for AK-103 to India in 2018, the deal could not be finalised because the requirement of the army was not fulfilled in the Russian proposal. In 2019, the army announced a new proposal. The army wanted to purchase 7.62 caliber assault rifles along with an import of a small bag of 'hi-tech rifles' for frontline troops on the border. The hi-tech rifles can be imported and the rest can be manufactured in India. The AK-103 is to be manufactured domestically and would be used for hinterland and counterinsurgency operations (with a preferred caliber of 5.56 mm and a 500-meter range). The Army would also use AK-103 for paramilitary forces and also export in the long run.

THE MINESWEEPERS, S-400 TRIUMF, SOVEREIGN GUARANTEES AND CAATSA TANGLES

What is a Sovereign Guarantee?

Sovereign guarantee means that the company that won the contract has to by law provide a guarantee from an international bank which can be encashed by the purchaser of the product in case a delivery of the product does not happen on time despite the payments being made.

A minesweeper is a specialised warship, which is used to clear harbours and critical areas of mines, which are laid, by the submarines and vessels of the enemy states. For Indian Navy, the minesweepers are a critical deficiency as earlier it had twelve but now only one, that is, INS Kozhikode. In 2019, India's response to seek minesweepers had met with a positive response from Russia. In 2018, India and Russia signed a 5 USD billion deal with no sovereign guarantee but as a government-to-government deal where India will purchase Russian S-400 Triumf (five units) long-range surface-to-air missile system. India has decided to purchase the missile defence system, which will shield any incoming ballistic missile directed towards the soil of India. To create a layered defence, the S-400 Triumf can be deployed in five minutes and fire three types of missiles within an altitude of 30 km and a range of 400 km and the S-400 Triumf can engage aerial targets, aircrafts, UAVs and ballistic and cruise missiles. It has the potential to target 100 airborne targets simultaneously including F-35 of the US. Russia has been using the S-400 Triumf since 2007 and in 2015 deployed them in Syria to guard Russian and Syrian naval and air assets. There are some S-400 Triumf units in Crimean peninsula as well. China in 2015 purchased S-400 Triumf and has been using it since 2018. With coming of S-400 Triumf, India will be able to tackle air and missile threats from Pakistan. The NATO calls S-400 Triumf as SA-21 Growler which is a Modern Long-Range Surface-to-Air Missile (MLRSAM). The S-400 Triumf (a fourth generation MLRSAM and a successor to S-200 and S-300) is more sophisticated and effective than the American Terminal High Altitude Area Defence (THAAD) system. The two sides have developed their own systems of transactions including a national currency swap for payments. In 2017, the US President signed the Countering America's Adversaries Through Sanctions Act (CAATSA). The legislation was for Russia, Iran and North Korea. As per Title II of the Act, because of Russian intervention in Ukraine and meddling into the US Presidential elections in 2016, any dealings by any state with the Russian gas, defence and security industry would invite sanctions. Section 235 of the Act talks about 12 sanctions that can be imposed upon persons engaging in significant transactions (39 Russian entities identified by the US State Department, which includes Space Defence Cooperation JSC, the manufacturer of S-400 Triumf) with the defence and intelligence of Russia. Section 231 gives powers to the US President to invoke five out of the twelve sanctions in Section 235. However, India, Indonesia and Vietnam were granted a waiver under CAATSA, which conveys that India retained its strategic autonomy. Russia, similarly, will not reduce its dependence on India as India acts as the biggest testing ground for Russian weaponry. As China goes on to supply arms to developing nations in future, it will try to undercut the Russian influence, thus necessitating Russia to stay with India so as to be able to use India as a springboard to other developing markets despite an Indian tilt to the US.

Core Defence Projects where Russia is Engaging with India

S-400 Triumf	MANGO ammunitions
Frigates for Navy	VSHORAD systems
AK-203 Assault Rifles	Drone technologies
T-90 Tanks	Cyber technologies
Sukhoi-30 MKI	Doctrinal coordination
MiG-29	Minesweepers

RUSSIAN TILT TOWARDS PAKISTAN, INDIAN PERCEPTIONS AND IMPLICATIONS ON BILATERAL RELATIONSHIP

The post-Cold War era has seen a shift in India's armament policy, inducting France, Israel and the USA, in a field that had always been dominated by Russia. As France, Israel and the USA increase their presence in India's armament supply, it shrinks in space for Russians. On the other hand, Russia wants to explore new markets for its arms and energy. It is the shrink of Indian space for arms supply that has motivated the Russians to look at Pakistan. The US–Pakistan relations have not been very smooth lately under Trump. Because of a number of strains in the US–Pakistan relations, Pakistan does not want to be dependent solely upon the US in future. Pakistan too has demonstrated an openness to explore a relationship with Russia. The world is witnessing not just a multipolar world, but a huge spectrum of multiple alliance building based upon linkages and dependency. Russia has been quite cautious and it is carefully exploring whether the Chinese Belt and Road Initiative is actually Chinese foray into the Russian backyard of Central Asia. One of the key motivations of Russia is to keep China in check, which has compelled Russia to balance China by improving relations with Pakistan, which is in the backyard of China. There is potential re-alignment of power structure witnessed where a Russia–China–Pakistan axis could also emerge. Such an axis could use its combined effort to challenge the unipolarity of the US in global affairs. The Trump administration is undertaking more assertion of the US power in the world and it could meet the China–Russia–Pakistan axis as a potential challenger. The Russia–China axis has been a channel to promote strategic cooperation to resist the US hegemony but the inclusion of Pakistan in the matrix of Russia–China makes a compelling case for the commencement of a New Cold War. Russia is not only trying to re-balance the region but is positioning itself through a new diplomatic space to project Russia back on to the centre stage in global affairs. The new geo-strategic goal of Russia is to check the USA hegemony. What feeds the Russian matrix is the entry of Pakistan. Pakistan has been a core ally of the US but the sanctuary of Osama bin Laden in Pakistan and its support to terrorist groups has brought the US and Pakistan on two opposing sides of a continuum. As the number of players of the West and their support to Pakistan dwindles, the entry of Russian on the scene opens a new strategic front for Pakistan. In 2016, Russia and Pakistan undertook a military exercise known as Druzhva 2016 or Friendship 2016, between Pakistan army and Russian ground forces, at the special force-training centre in Cherat in North Pakistan. It lasted as a drill for two weeks where the two sides worked together on combat preparedness at high altitudes. Despite the fact that Russia and Pakistan have been rivals during the Cold War (the USA used Pakistan to breed Mujahedeens against the Soviet invasion of Afghanistan), the defence exercise marks a new shift in the ties. In 2014, the arms embargo on Pakistan imposed by Russia was removed and in 2015, Pakistan purchased four MI-35 helicopters from Russia. This should act as a wakeup call for India to not take Russia for granted. The US also refused the sale of F-16 jets to Pakistan. This compelled them to purchase military aircrafts from Jordan. Pakistan is also trying to build up a hedge against the USA by developing proximity to Russia.

BRAHMOS EXPORT DEAL WITH PHILIPPINES, RUSSIA FACTOR AND INDIA'S PROVOCATIVE DIPLOMACY

The BrahMos is a jointly developed supersonic cruise missile developed by India and Russia. In recent times, India has been engaging with the US quite aggressively in Indo-Pacific under various minilaterals like QUAD. The Russians were not very comfortable with the same and have been looking for spaces for engagement in Indo-Pacific. The Chinese have not given the Russians any space in the region because they consider Indo-Pacific their own strategic playground. This has frustrated the Russians. India, with a historical legacy of deep engagement with Russia has come to Russian rescue. India too does not intend to put all its eggs in one basket and thereby sees Russia as a neat balancer to hegemony of the US in the region. In this backdrop, India through its bilateral diplomacy with Philippines has convinced the state to purchase three batteries of supersonic missiles with each battery comprising two missile launchers, a radar and a command-and-control centre which can fire two missiles within 10 seconds. The deal with Philippines not only gives Russia an indirect space in Indo-Pacific but also enables India to position itself as a defence manufacturer and an exporter of defence products and also strengthen the capabilities of India's Act East Policy. From the perspective of Philippines, the deal is significant because it bolsters their capacity to ensure their coastal defence when Chinese are staking claims in South China Sea at Mischief Reef and Scarborough Shoal. The defence acquisition by Philippines is explainable through the philosophy that smaller countries (Philippines here), by calibrated acquisitions of state-of-the-art and asymmetric capabilities (read BrahMos) can develop this overall minimum deterrence.

THE CHINA FACTOR IN RUSSIA AND INDIA RELATIONS AND IMPLICATIONS ON BILATERAL TIES

Russia and China have a defence and energy-based relationship. It is important to locate the reason why the two cooperate. Russia, in the recent times, has a very strained relationship with the West and till the time Russia is isolated by the West, it will continue to embrace Chinese. Also, the US has exercised a tremendous influence on the EU to cut short their engagement with the Russians. This is why Russia is looking for an alternative market. China in this regard is a promising market in Russian neighbourhood for arms, oil and gas. With strained ties of Russia and China and China and the US, it makes all the more sense for the two to combine together and counter the US. This relationship of Russia and China does not affect India in any way for a simple reason. Russia is not interested in being positioned as a player subordinated to the Chinese in the global architecture. Also, India is not a factor in Russia and China partnership, as the US prominently is. This is testified by the fact that the Russians have been ardent supporters for India to play a role in both SCO and BRICS. The two may hay a strategic partnership, which is a state level defence arrangement, but the partnership does not enjoy much support. The Russians have only 110 USD billion trade with China (in contrast to 230 USD billion Russia–EU trade). In fact Russia supplies more gas and oil to the EU that it does to Chinese. The Russians have also not gained much from the Chinese BRI as of now that can act as a great connector of the two. In 2020, when India and China were locked in a standoff in Ladakh, there was Russia–India–China trilateral meet organised by Moscow. In the meeting, the Indian side advocated that Russia should speedily deliver the pending arms that India has purchased. However, during the standoff, the Chinese tried to apply pressure on the Russians by reaching out the strategic community of Russia. They informed the community to defer any sale of defence products to India. This tactic of the Chinese was largely in sync with the Chinese information war. However, Russia and India ties are time tested. Russia knows that India did not succumb to the American pressure while purchasing S-400 Triumf from Russia; thus, the Chinese request to Russia to not yield to Indian arms request stands no ground. India remains a stable market for Russian arms and energy. Even though the Russian arms market in India may have shrunk to 56%, it still remains a core supplier, despite India's quest for diversification of defence imports. In any case, Russia will strike a neutral posture between India and China as it continues to have stakes in both the states and in any case, Russians will never swing sides.

SPACE DIPLOMACY, GLONASS AND COOPERATION IN GAGANYAAN

In 1963, with the UN assistance, India launched a satellite from Thumba equatorial launch site. On 19th April 1975, India's Aryabhatta was launched on a Soviet Kosmos-3M rockets from Kapustin Yar range. In 1979, Bhaskara-I was launched from Kapustin Yar range once again. In 1984, Indian astronaut Rakesh Sharma visited space in the Soyuz T-10, which was an issue of great political prestige for India. Today, Russia is the most important strategic space power for India. In 1992, Russia agreed to provide India cryogenic rocket engines but due to India being a non-signatory to MTCR at that time, the deal was later suspended. The sudden suspension of the deal came as a serious setback to Indian space programme. At the end of the Cold War in 1994, both countries signed a space cooperation agreement and have been working in collaboration over GLONASS and the Indian Moon Mission. Russia is going to train Indian astronauts at Star City, near Moscow, which is being used by Russians since 1960s, for Gaganyaan in 2022, which will strengthen India–Russia space cooperation. Russia will also be training the crew of Gaganyaan for the International Space Station (ISS). The ISS is habitable satellite orbiting at the low-earth orbit.

TRADE AS A NEW CONNECTOR BEYOND DEFENCE BETWEEN INDIA AND RUSSIA

A very peculiar feature thus observed in India–Russia trade relationship is that the relation is more like old relatives who have warm feelings for each other in their hearts and not in actions and the moment either side receives a new relative, it is the new relative who gains more attention. Today, the two have created the India–Russia Inter Governmental Commission on

Trade and the India–Russia Forum on Trade and Investments, which are core institutional mechanisms available to oversee trade. There have been regular interactions of CEOs through the India–Russia CEO's council. The trade target has been 30 billion dollars by 2025, when the bilateral trade at present is only around 8 billion dollars. Russia–China trade is at 66 billion dollars, with a target to take it to 100 billion dollars. The economic relations also suffered when the Supreme Court, in 2012, declared 2G licences in telecom as null and void after Russian AFK Sistema had teamed up with Shyam Telecom services. Russia has decided to setup six additional reactors for India and agreed to undertake localisation of equipment to promote Make in India. To safeguard the bilateral investments, the two sides in 2020 had signed a Bilateral Investment Protection treaty. To promote cooperation in science, both sides have agreed to work together under the framework set by the Arctic Council with the Russian Scientific Centre in the Spits Bergen Svalbard Archipelago.

India is negotiating a CEPA with Eurasian Economic community presently on railways, fertiliser production and aircrafts construction. A Joint Study Group has been studying the possibility of an FTA and both sides affirmed to early conclusion and preparation of a report. A special notified zone at Bharat Diamond Bourse is to be created soon to promote diamond trade. Textiles, jewellery, fruits, pharmacy, dairy and IT products are areas for future cooperation. The two sides have identified four core focus areas for future cooperation—energy, digital economy, start-up and infrastructure.

ENERGY DIPLOMACY AND INDIA'S OIL AND GAS TRADES WITH RUSSIA

Russia is an energy supplier while Indian demand for energy is increasing as it inches to become a five trillion-dollar economy. As India is a net importer of energy, Russia is in a strategic position to cooperate in this regard. At the energy level, India follows a two-point strategy. The first is to increase India's assets into the regions of the world where oil is available and the second is to enter into reliable energy security pacts. The second point of the policy is at work with Russia. India has been importing coal and oil from Russia and in future it might also look for import of gas. Russia has tremendous amount of oil in East Siberia. Both China and Japan are keenly interested in importing East Siberian oil through a pipeline. This pipeline route via Kozmino Bay could also be explored by India. If India collaborates with the Chinese One Belt One Road initiative, it will give India access to rail and road networks in Mongolia and Daqing, a route that will be used by Russia to export oil to China. The OVL already has a 20% stake in Sakhalin-I and is in a joint venture in Sakhalin-III with Rosneft. More OVL participation will be required to meet India's growing energy needs. In the recent times, petrochemicals have emerged as a new area of cooperation and in 2020 both sides signed India–Russia roadmap for cooperation in the hydrocarbons till 2024, which focuses on joint development of oil and gas fields in Russia and offshore facilities in India. In 2020, due to rapidly expanding electric vehicle manufacturing industry, India has emerged as one of the largest markets of butyl rubber and halogenated butyl rubber. Sibur and Reliance Industries have established a joint venture called Reliance Sibur Elastomers Private Limited in Jamnagar, Gujarat, to manufacture butyl rubber in the butyl rubber halogenated plant that will manufacture 120 kilo tons per annum of butyl rubber and 60 kilo tons per annum of halogenated butyl rubber. In addition to this, Sibur will also train people in India and share butyl rubber technology to India by bringing polymerisation reactors. India has decided to cooperate with Russia in the arctic shelf and undertake joint exploration and development of oil in shelf of the Pechora and Okhotsk Seas. India has decided to continue to invest in Vankorneft and Taas-Yuryakh Neftegazodobycha. H-Energy and Petronet LNG, the two Indian firms, shall also be buying LNG from Russian firm called Novatek on a long-term basis. In 2017, Rosneft completed the 12.7 USD billion acquisition of Essar oil. In the recent times, Russia is taking a lot of steps to allow Indian companies to do business in

Food Security and India–Russia Relations

In recent times, food security has emerged as a new area of diplomatic cooperation. India is leasing lands in Far East regions of Russia and cultivating the same with Indian labour. It offers a tantalising prospect for cooperation because the Russians are witnessing demographic crisis and human resource deficits. While Chinese too are cultivating in the region; what makes India different from China is that whatever produce Indian labour cultivate in the region, it is sold only in Russian markets, while whatever China cultivates, only a part is sold in Russia and rest is imported to China. The Indian government has negotiated an enabling agreement with Russia where private sector Indian players are executing the food security diplomacy. Bringing India is a win-win situation because India in Far East can help Russia balance off China and reduce Russian dependence on China while India can horn its skills on cultivation in this region and can later explore similar templates with other Europeans.

oil-rich zones. They have started developing port infrastructure, developed an incentive-based taxation system, developed the North Sea Route and has opened up space for firms to invest in the Arctic. India expressed hopes for cooperation in natural gas in fields at Gydan Peninsula and Gulf of Ob.

THE NUCLEAR ELEMENT IN BILATERAL RELATIONSHIP

India–Russia nuclear cooperation goes back to 1960s. In 1961, India had concluded research and development agreements with Russia in Hungary for the Rajasthan Atomic Power Station (RAPS). India concluded a contract with the USSR in 1976 for supplying of heavy waters. During the Cold War period, Russia also supported India by supplying fuel at Tarapur in 1982 and in 1988, agreed to help construct reactors and supply light water for reactors at Koodankulam after Pokhran-II. In October 2013, Russia succeeded in operationalising the first unit of the reactors at Koodankulam but the construction of subsequent units got delayed and India's nuclear liability law-related issues had acted as constraints. In 2020, India and Russia had explored joint development of nuclear power in Rooppur in Bangladesh.

AFGHANISTAN, RELATIONSHIP WITH TALIBAN AND INDIA–RUSSIA RELATIONS

The first thing to analyse is the Russian position on Afghanistan. Russia is supporting Taliban and asserts that Taliban is a legitimate force in the future of Afghanistan. Russia feels that if Taliban is integrated into the political setup of Afghanistan, it will be conducive for the stability of the region. Russia has an interest in negotiating with Taliban as it feels that if Taliban comes to power in Afghanistan, it will help keeping the rise of Islamic extremism in Russia under check. India feels the Russian–Taliban policy of Afghanistan could deflect pressure on Pakistan because if Taliban is given any leverage in Afghanistan, then it can provide immunity to Pakistan to provide a safe haven for terrorists. India feels, this is the reason why Russia and Pakistan have done a military exercise (and even supplied it with offensive defence equipment) as Russia intends to use Pakistan (also seen in 2017 Six Nation Speakers Conference in Islamabad where Russia supported the Pakistani line on Kashmir issue, where historically it had tilted towards India) to reach out to Taliban. In 2020, Russia had done a course correction in its Afghanistan policy and stated that Indian involvement was crucial for the long-term stability of Afghanistan.

INDIA'S CONCERNS WITH DEFENCE EQUIPMENT OF RUSSIA AND INDIAN QUEST FOR DIVERSIFICATION

Indian armed forces often complain about problems in spare parts and issues in the maintenance of Russian equipment. Part of the blame is on Indian defence and foreign policy negotiations that failed to develop a deeper perspective on the life cycle of products. When they were negotiating contracts and agreements, they often do not take care of products' life cycles. At times, Indians ended up taking some equipment, which became obsolete after a few years and its production plants also shut down, thereby making spare parts availability a huge concern.

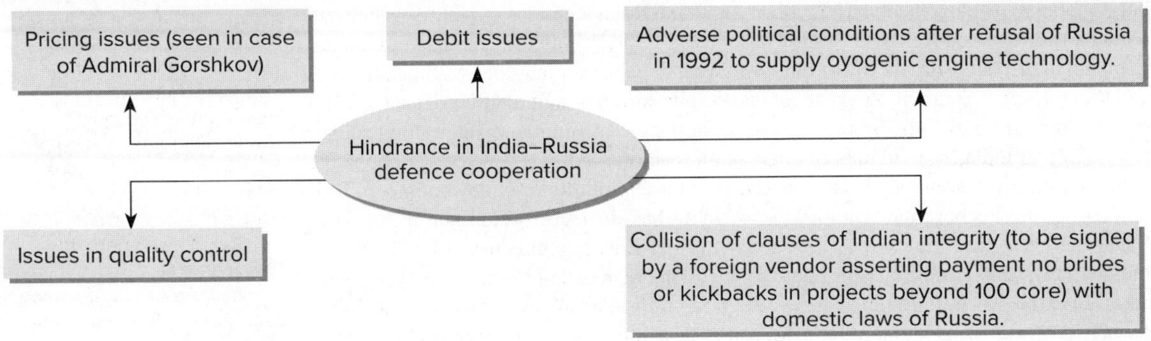

CHALLENGES IN TRADE AND COMMERCE DIPLOMACY

- Overdependence on arms trade has shadowed other items
- No direct land access to Russia
- Inadequate information about business potential (can be mitigated with establishment of media outlets that would advertise the business potential in each other's country)
- Poor knowledge of Russian language
- Bureaucratic delays
- Lack of access to institutional finance to boost exports

INDIA–RUSSIA INTERGOVERNMENTAL COMMISSIONS ON MILITARY–TECHNICAL COOPERATION

Russia created the Rosoboronexport in 2000, which is a state intermediary body that monopolises arms export. India raises the issue of after sales support at almost all India–Russia Intergovernmental Commissions on Military–Technical Cooperation (IRIGC–MTC) and this platform helps us to resolve our issues.

LOCATING RUSSIA IN INDIAN OCEAN AND INDIA–RUSSIA INDO-PACIFIC ORDER

Russia has displayed interest in coming to the Indian Ocean (IO). During the colonial times, IO was one area where the British were a dominant power. At the onset of the Cold War, the British were replaced by the USA. Throughout the Cold War, the USA remained a key security provider to the littoral states of the IO. However, in the recent times, we observe Russia trying to make forays into the IO. In 2019, Russia, China and Brazil had carried out joint naval exercises with South Africa in the Cape of Good Hope called Moris. This was the first time that Russia had entered into the security calculus of Africa and it tried to fill the vacuum in South Africa, which in the recent times is drifting away from the West. Even though Russia may never be able to dominate the IO, but with its recent forays, it definitely can alter the dynamics of the IO. This is proven by many facts. First, Russia has displayed credibility in Syria to prevent the fall of Assad regime. Second, Russia already has a deep relationship with Iran and both have naval cooperation in the Persian Gulf. Third, as Russia is a permanent member of the UNSC, some African states such as Mozambique and Libya have developed proximity with Russia to prevent the Western pressures on human rights issues in the UNSC. This has enabled Russia to play a significant role in security of littoral states of IO through African states, which can enable Russia in the future to develop a naval base. Fourth, as most of the African states are mineral-rich, Russian energy and mineral exploration firms can offer options to these states to develop their capacities further. All these instances prove Russian activism in the IO and from the Indian point of view; it should be welcomed, as it is an addition to the assertion of multipolarity in the IO. But this is where India should initiate a deep dialogue with Russia and identify how can India's Indian Ocean strategy fit into the framework of Russian–Indian Ocean framework, as this can be a potential future area of cooperation. However, Russia looks at Indo-Pacific as an American strategy to counter China and is quite negative about the participation of India in the Indo-Pacific. India has clarified that it does not look at Indo-Pacific as an effort to contain China. India rather prefers a more inclusive, open and multipolar Indo-Pacific and would even welcome Russia in the same ahead.

RUSSIAN PERCEPTION OF INDO-US RELATIONS AND INDIA IN QUAD AND INDO-PACIFIC

Russia in the recent times has become a little concerned with India tilting too much towards the US. Russia feels that as India tilts to the US (for arms sale and architectures like QUAD), it will end up in losing a defence market, thus, compelling Russia to shift towards Pakistan as an emergent market. Also, a point of constant reticence between the two sides is surprisingly terrorism. India has been trying hard to ensure that the Joint Statement mentions Pakistani supported proxy groups like LeT, JeM etc., but Russia has stuck to 'condemnation of all forms of terrorism including state-sponsored terrorism and cross-border terrorism'. India feels that this does not strengthen Indian case of isolating Pakistan.

However, it is imperative to understand that there are many cracks in the way Indo-Pacific are perceived by India and the US and these cracks are actually spaces where India and Russia can cooperate.

Element	American perception of Indo-Pacific	Indian perception of Indo-Pacific	Space for Russia and India in Indo-Pacific
Geographical expanse	Starts from the West Coast of India	Starts from the West Asia at Iran	Russia–Iran–India can explore this space left by the US
Importance	Only maritime component	Land and maritime component	Russia–India can explore land space and fuse with maritime
Significance	Pacific Ocean	Indian Ocean	Arctic–Indian Ocean realm
Strategic weight	Through AUKUS, the US envisages Australia to be the fulcrum in Indo-Pacific and wants it to play lead role	India envisages itself as a claimant for Net Security Provider and Preferred Security Partner	Russia and India defence cooperation and the historical legacy can ensure achievement of Indian ambition with strategic autonomy
Polarity thesis	The US aspires hegemony through allies	India favours multipolar Indo-Pacific	Russia favours multipolar Indo-Pacific
Vision	Augment military power through alliances and minilaterals	Augment geo-economic and geo-strategic power	Greater Eurasian Partnership intends to counterbalance China
Vladivostok city	Does not figure into importance	Russia dispatched armed flotilla in 1971 for India from here	City was a part of China till 1860 and Russia allows India here to pinch China
Identity	No role envisaged	Asian and Indian values	Bring Russia in Indo-Pacific to invoke Russian–Asian identity

5

CHAPTER

Ukraine Crisis, Inflection Point in Global Order and India's Diplomatic Posture

EXISTENCE OF UKRAINE AND DEBATES ON UKRAINIAN INDEPENDENCE SINCE 13TH AND 14TH CENTURIES

Ukraine has never existed independently and its existence has always been vacillated between Europe and Russia. In the 13th and 14th centuries, the centre of gravity in the region shifted to Moscow and since then, Russia has been a force on the global scene. In modern times, Ukraine had an independent existence only for a limited period in the 17th and 18th centuries. In the post-World War II European order, Ukraine had the second largest area and next to it was the Crimean peninsula. In the period from 1853 to 1856, the region witnessed the Crimean War, in which the Russian Empire lost to an alliance of the Ottoman Empire, France, Britain and Sardinia. The immediate cause involved the rights of Christian minorities in the Holy Land, which was a part of the Ottoman Empire. The French promoted the rights of Roman Catholics, while Russia promoted those of the Eastern Orthodox Church. The long-term causes involved the decline of the Ottoman Empire and the unwillingness of Britain and France to allow Russia to gain territory and power at Ottoman expense.

UKRAINE FROM THE RUSSIAN REVOLUTION TO THE END OF THE COLD WAR

From 1917 to 1921, Russia witnessed the Russian revolution, during which Ukraine vacillated and drifted under the control of Austria–Hungary Empire and the Polish empire. Post-1921, Ukraine again came under the control of Soviet and remained there for some time. Crimea, a region next to Ukraine was controlled by Soviet but in 1954, there was transfer of power of Crimea to Ukraine. Soviet ruler Nikita Khrushchev decided to hand over Crimea to be controlled by Ukraine because Crimea was dependent upon Ukraine for all its basic needs including food, oil and gas. Khrushchev was of the opinion that such a mechanism would be useful for the administration of Crimea and would not create an issue for the Soviet because Ukraine was still under the Soviet control. This mechanism prevailed till 1991 when the Soviet Union disintegrated.

THE POST-SOVIET UKRAINE AND ORANGE REVOLUTION

After the disintegration of the Soviet Union, the erstwhile Russian satellite states began to assert independence. Ukraine too asserted independence but was vacillating between having a pro-Russian or pro-European regime. In the period after the disintegration of the Soviet Union, in a referendum in Ukraine, 90% people voted in favour of a separation from Russia. Since then, till 2004, Ukraine remained a state with lose control and a vacillating identity. In 2004, Ukraine witnessed elections in which a pro-Russia leader, Yenukovich, won and initiated his rule. The election of Yenukovich was challenged by his opponent and a pro-US, Yushenko, who launched a protest against Yenukovich, which came to be known as Orange Revolution. The Orange Revolution led to a re-election in Ukraine in which Yushenko won in 2004. In the next election in 2010, Yushenko lost while Yenukovich won.

UKRAINIAN FLIRTATIONS WITH THE EUROPEAN UNION AND BLACK SEA GEOPOLITICS

In 1994, Russia and the North Atlantic Treaty Organization (NATO) entered into an agreement that neither would resort to expansionism in Europe. In 1998, Russia and Crimea entered into an agreement where Crimea agreed to allow Russia to station 25,000 Russian soldiers in Crimea near the Black Sea. Russians today have Black Sea as the only warm water port available for navigation. This led NATO to initiate expansion and the US extended NATO memberships to Poland and Hungary. In 2004, NATO expanded further by offering memberships to Slovakia, Slovenia, Estonia, Lithuania and Latvia, thus violating the 1994 agreements. In 2008, the US initiated the process to bring Ukraine into the fold of NATO. In 2008, Ukraine was led by Yushenko, who was a pro-US leader. As a consequence, the Russians entered into an agreement with Crimea where Crimea offered Russia access to a part of Sevastopol port in the Black Sea region. As per the agreement, Russia would maintain a Black Sea Fleet in Sevastopol and the Russian presence would remain undisturbed till 2042.

THE EUROMAIDAN PROTESTS, ANNEXATION OF CRIMEA AND NORMANDY FORMAT

As this expansion and counter-expansion by NATO and Russia unfolded, in 2013, the US offered Ukraine a membership to the European Union (EU). This offer was made to Yenukovich, a pro-Russia leader, in power since 2010. Russia saw this offer as an indirect attempt by the NATO to reach Russia borders. As Yenukovich rejected the deal to allow Ukraine to be a part of the EU, a crisis began to unfold. In the independence square in Kiev, the Ukrainian capital, massive protests took place to seek a pro-EU decision for Ukraine. Russia supported the counter-protests and this led to violence in Ukraine leading to the beginning of the Ukraine crisis in November 2013. As the crisis intensified at Euromaidan where protestors thronged in huge numbers, in February 2014, Yenukovich fled the country, signalling a victory for the rebels supported by the US. Witnessing the situation turning in favour of the rebels, Russia, in March 2014, instigated Crimea to undertake a referendum. On 16th March 2014, Crimea ordered a referendum and 95% people in Crimea voted in favour of Crimea joining Russia. On 19th March 2014, Russia took over Crimea and used Crimea to assert power in Ukraine. The 5% people who did not vote in favour of Crimea joining Russia were the Tartars. The Tartars are ethnic Muslims in Crimea who have always been at the receiving end of repression by the Russians. In 1950s, Stalin had crushed the Tartars and even deported them to Bulgaria, Turkey and Romania because he perceived them as outsiders who had settled in regions belonging to the ethnic Russians. Post-Soviet disintegration, the Tartars settled back in Crimea again where they had been living for many centuries. Since 19th March 2014, Crimea has been under the Russian control. France, Russia, Ukraine, Germany came together in 2014 to establish Normandy format of talks to find a peaceful resolution to the crisis. The US and the other Western states alleged that Russia has illegally annexed Crimea. Since then, the Russians have come under sanctions of the West. In October 2014, when fresh elections were held in Ukraine, Petro Poroshenko won the election. Poroshenko favoured an equidistance policy and had maintained distance from both Russia and the US. Over a period of time, the US too had realised its mistake of stirring up controversy in Russian backyard.

RUSSIAN GEOSTRATEGIC INTERESTS IN UKRAINE AND PROTECTION OF ETHNIC DIASPORA

Russia has tried to assert dominance in Ukraine and Crimea. For Russia, Crimea and Ukraine are strategically important. The Russians get an access to the warm waters of the Black Sea only through Ukraine and Crimea. Russia's northern stream and southern stream pipelines pass through these states. These pipelines are lifelines for the European states of Germany, France and others. Russia supplies oil to the European states through these pipelines. The violence in Kiev, Luhansk and Minsk, along with other regions, has been under control since a 2015 ceasefire agreed upon between the rebels and others. However, firstly, the rebels were armed by the Central Intelligence Agency (which had pumped 5 billon USD in the region) continued to possess arms as there had been no mechanism to take back the arms from the rebels. Secondly, the eastern regions of Ukraine have a significant population of ethnic Russians and Russia has been assertive on ensuring that their diaspora is protected at all costs from any psychological tactics of the West to dilute their ethnicity.

THE MINSK-I, MINSK-II AND QUESTIONS ON STABILITY

After the 2014 crisis, Russia and Ukraine had concluded a 12-point ceasefire deal, known as Minsk-I Agreement, in Minsk, the capital of Belarus. The deal broadly talked about prisoner exchanges, delivery of humanitarian aid and withdrawal of heavy weaponries. The Minsk-I broke down immediately because there were violations by contracting parties. In 2015, France and Germany mediated and a Minsk-II Agreement was signed with 13 points. The Minsk-II was also negotiated by Organisation for Security and Cooperation in Europe.

The Minsk-II asserted the need for a comprehensive ceasefire, restoration of state borders by Ukrainian government, withdrawal of foreign mercenaries and military equipment. In Minsk-II, the most important provision was that Ukrainian government would carry out constitutional reforms and decentralise powers in Luhansk and Donetsk regions bordering Russia.

Organisation for Security and Cooperation in Europe

It is the largest security-oriented intergovernmental organisation on earth, conceptualised in 1975 as Conference on Security and Cooperation in Europe and renamed in 1994, but presently based in Vienna with 57 members from Asia, Europe and North America, but India is not a member. Its mandate includes discussion on matters pertaining to arms control, promotion of human rights and freedom of press and organisation of free and fair elections.

THE FLAREUP IN 2022 AND RUSSIAN USE OF NON-KINETIC MEANS OF INFORMATION MANOEUVRES

The Luhansk and Donetsk regions are collectively known as the Donbass region. In 2022, the Russians declared the independence of Donbass and thus the Minsk Agreements virtually died. Firstly, the Russian interests in the Donbass region are not only based on Russian ethnic diaspora but also excessive deposits of coal in the region. Secondly, the incumbent Ukrainian President Volodymyr Zelensky (who assumed power on 20th May 2019) had started flirtations with Europe for the EU membership and the US for NATO membership for Ukraine. This led Russia to use force in Donbass region and proclaim independence. The Russians launched a well-planned campaign in Ukraine with usage of non-kinetic means such as cyber wars to disrupt the Ukrainian economy. Secondly, after the cyber-attacks crippled Ukraine, the Russians launched a full-scale invasion in Donbass region.

THE R2P DOCTRINE OF THE US AND THE SWIFT ISSUE

The West and the US adopted a two-point policy based on the concept of Responsibility to Protect (R2P). Firstly, they decided to arm Ukraine with weapons and trainings so that Ukrainians develop capacity for resisting Russia. Secondly, the West and the US decided to counter-cripple Russian economy by suspending Russia from SWIFT payments architecture.

What is SWIFT and why it Matters?

SWIFT stands for Society for Worldwide Interbank Financial Transaction and is a Belgian cooperative society, not an intergovernmental organisation, which provides services that execute financial transactions and payments between banks at global levels. Being a financial messaging network, SWIFT provides a network where banks can send data from the branch of one bank to another through a secured communication. The SWIFT does not manage any individual or institutional accounts or holds funds nor does it perform any clearance or settlement functions. It is a highly secure network for global transactions with encryption and decryption technologies.

ENTRY OF FOREIGN FIGHTERS, THE UN CHARTER AND CRUMBLING WESTPHALIAN ORDER

A very peculiar scenario seen in 2022 crisis is the inflow of foreign fighters into the fighting scenes. The foreign fighters have come from both sides and the newly unfolding verbal gymnastics unleashed by the West against Russia only weakens the morality the West has been trying to uphold in international politics. The problem with this new nomenclature of foreign fighters is that they argue that they are fighting for a 'just cause' of Ukraine. The 'just cause' theory is exactly similar to the logic advanced by the Islamic fundamentalists during the Cold War and 9/11. The narrative is even more problematic because since the Westphalian order, it was argued that national armies and professional militaries would fight wars. The Cold War period saw use of paid mercenaries mobilised into tanzeems for fighting on models of plausible deniability. Such tactics were not just costly but also extremely devastating for global peace, security and stability. In this backdrop, the Ukraine crisis now offers a new insight into evolving security scenarios where Russian and American companies are resorting to agile, flexible bunch of foreign fighters which are armed to fight for a specific 'just cause'. The UN Charter asserts that in the face of external aggression, every member in the comity of nations has the right to take help from outside and outsiders. The significant word in the UN Charter is 'outsiders'. There exists no clarity on international law defining these 'outsiders' and no clarity even exists if they would be called illegal combatants or combatants, would they be absorbed in armies, would they support armies as first line of defences. In the context of Ukraine, the foreign fighters are disparate, unconnected individuals cutting across ideological echo chambers and one of the key takeaways from the Global War on Terror since 9/11 is that those who pick up arms are governed not just by ideology and money, but also by a sense of tribalism that overrides any civic or social identity, as clearly visible in Ukrainian contexts. In this sense, the Ukraine crisis is a watershed event with seismic consequences for the international order and has consequences for national security of various states.

GEOSTRATEGIC ASPECTS OF WAR AND SOUL SEARCHING BY CHINA

The war between Russia and Ukraine has not just mobilised the world but also digitised it. The war has widened the gaps between how the countries perceive what is right versus wrong, how they view democracy versus authoritarianism, globalisation versus protectionism, and more importantly, victory versus defeat, thus making the world more polarised in post-pandemic scenario.

What Does the Ukraine Crisis Tell Us?
Nuclear Russia is a deterrent for the West.
Economic sanctions do not deter aggression.

China has had a deep introspection of the war and done its own bit of soul searching. The most valuable lesson for the Chinese is to see how the Americans crippled Russia economically for their failure to uphold the international rules-based order. The Chinese have not called the Russian act an invasion but "special military operation". Calling it by name is not the concern, the lesson is that there must be respect for territorial sovereignty and integrity. While for a country such as China, the crisis is seen from its BRI and urge to dominate European markets; for Europeans, it is a battle between the ideology of authoritarianism and democracy. China knows that if Russia falls, they will be the next, thus explaining why the West is keen to use Ukraine as a battle of ideology.

THE CORE DEMANDS OF RUSSIA AND THE WESTERN COUNTER-RESPONSES

Russia has been under sanctions since 2014 and now SWIFT sanctions since 2022. It has kept the tensions high at the eastern borders of Ukraine to seek sanction relief from the West. However, even though West has intensified their sanctions, the Russians have been compelled to develop deeper proximity with China to bypass the sanctions.

Russian Demands
No membership of NATO to Ukraine
No membership of the EU to Ukraine
Halt to NATO expansionism in the East European theatre
Halt to balance of power politics and maintain status quo
No long-range missile deployments in the region
No NATO cooperation with the erstwhile Soviet republics

Western Response
NATO's open door policy to continue or NATO will continue to bring new members in Europe
The US to continue to offer training and weapons support to Ukraine
New economic sanction on Russia to continue with the objective of global isolation of Russia

EFFICACY OF ECONOMIC SANCTIONS AND IS ECONOMICS THE NEW NUCLEAR BOMB?

The economic sanctions unleashed by the West on Russia in 2022 are more focussed, stringent and strong enough to cripple the Russian economy. The economic sanctions have been in use for a long period of time but there have been constant debates on their effectiveness. Even though economic sanctions have often been used by stronger states to deter and punish the belligerent states, there are concerns that continue to remain.

Broad Trends in the Use of Economic Sanctions in International Relations

Objective of sanctions	Challenges involved in achieving the objective
Uphold an internationally accepted rules-based order	The sanctions are designed to uphold the rules-based order but their practical implementation, even visible in Ukraine issue, proves that they actually serve geopolitical interests of select few. The more so, they act as punitive measures on 'sender' countries (countries that send money to country such as Russia) and lack of coordination to ensure alternative supplies in trade raise doubts on a uniform mechanism of response. The excessive use of sanctions by the developed world without respecting sensibilities of the developing world make upholding rules-based order an undemocratic process, thus piercing it from within.
Belligerents improve resilience against standards	The biggest lesson of imposition of sanctions is on other belligerent such as Chinese who draw crucial lessons on how to develop systems that bypass economic sanctions. The promotion of counter currencies to the US dollar and establishing parallel secured financial communication systems weaken the overall impact envisaged by sanctions and fail to bring behavioural changes.
Diversification of currency baskets and end of dollar hegemony	If the West continues to use sanctions, then countries will be compelled to diversify their currency baskets and consequently will strive to establish a multipolar currency basket. This will weaken sanction imposer in the end.

ENERGY POLITICS IS AT THE HEART OF UKRAINE CRISIS

The Ukraine issue is a geopolitical conflict for dominance. The West has expanded the NATO aggressively and is at the doorsteps of Russia, something that Russians do not like. An indirect attempt was made by NATO through the EU to penetrate into Ukraine thereby leading Russia to lose its patience over NATO expansion. Some scholars have observed that the crisis is only a beginning of a new energy war in Europe since the US is desperately looking for a shale gas market in Europe and wants to end the dominance of Russia in the Western Europe. However, an assertive and rising Russia, as visible in Ukraine, Iran and Syria, is a pointer to the fact that the future could see a commencement of a new Cold War. The implications of the Ukrainian crisis on global politics is that Russia has tried to assert multipolarity and has conveyed to the US that it should learn to respect the opinions of others.

INDIAN POSITION ON UKRAINE THROUGH THE PRISM OF MULTIPOLARITY THESIS IN INTERNATIONAL RELATIONS

Though India has not been a direct party to the dispute over the crisis in Ukraine, it has still maintained that it favours Russian assertion of multipolarity. Multipolarity itself is a goal that the Indian foreign policy stands for. The idea of distribution of power and co-dependency are at the heart of multipolarity today but this in anyway does not mean there is equal and favourable co-dependency. India has realised that in a multipolar world, middle powers (that includes India) become crucial actors in the international system to define and shape the arguments of the bigger powers. This is because in a multipolar hierarchical and anarchial world, if a great power wishes to retain its hegemonic position, it ought to take the middle powers and their opinions into consideration. In a globalised world, India realises that the interconnectedness unleashed allows it the space to pursue its own goals in international system because it widens the scope of negotiations and allows India the space to reconfigure certain dynamics in international political order. But the same multipolarity is a threat to multilateralism because there is no coherent and collective response against aggressors because multipolarity creates unignorable dependencies that bind nations through global supply chains. This explains that why India has been able to solicit support from the West for its oil and gas deals with Russia even when Russia is under an umbrella of economic sanctions. India has not condemned the Russian intervention in Crimea like most of the Western powers as it believes that there are legitimate Russian interests in the region that need to be taken care of by Russia. However, India has not openly supported the Russian invasion as it stands for conflict resolution through positive dialogue.

6

CHAPTER

India and Germany, Sweden and Portugal Relations

INDIA AND GERMANY RELATIONS

Historical engagement	India's core interest	India's diplomatic strategy	Shortcomings
Germany, after the World War II, was divided into two parts—the Federal Republic of Germany (FRG, or West Germany) and the German Democratic Republic (GDR, or East Germany). India supported diplomatic relations with the FRG and stayed away from recognising the GDR till 1970s.	Technology diplomacy Commercial diplomacy Skill generation Security diplomacy Global-order stability Sustainable development	India–Germany Inter-Governmental Consultations (IGC) was established by the strategic Partnership Agreement in 2000, which provides the framework for cooperation of the two. The two sides have a High Technology Partnership Group (HTPG) for technology cooperation. German engineering economy is driven by small companies and India aims to engage with them to seek their expertise (Make in India Mittelstand Programme). A new chapter of cooperation in Industry 4.0 has started and the two have identified automation, big data and AI as dimensions to cooperate. Both have a pact on mutual recognition of qualification which helps India in quality manpower skilled by Germany. Urban mobility, river cleaning, manufacturing clusters, climate resilience and renewable energy have been identified as areas for cooperation in 2020–2021.	German firms have raised certain issues in doing business with India such as Corruption IPR-related barriers Absence of legal provisions for business grievances Absence of a framework for investment

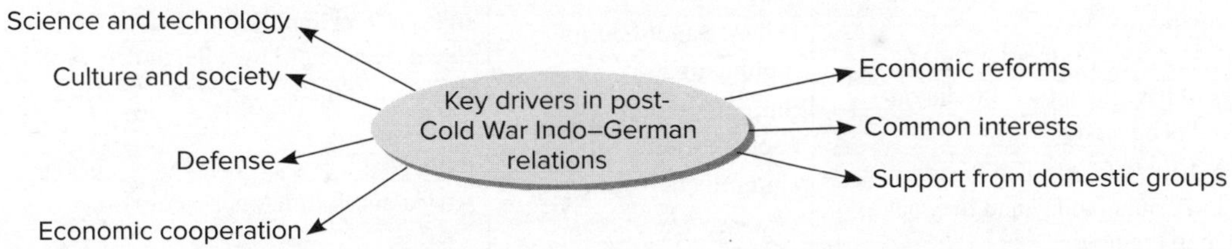

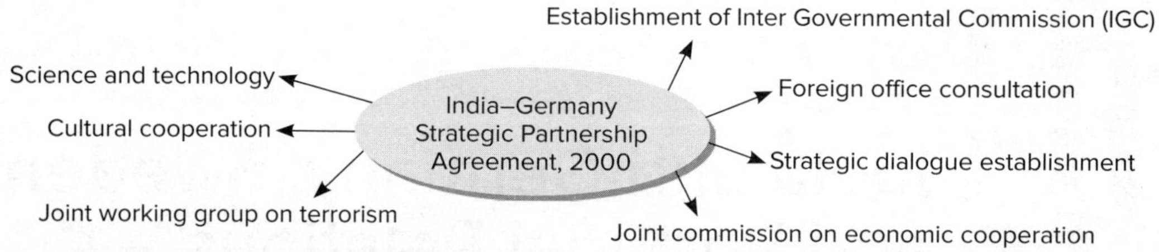

INDIA AND SWEDEN RELATIONS

Historical engagement	India's core interest	India's diplomatic strategy to engage with Sweden
In 1903, L. M. Ericson delivered the first manual switchboard to India. Diplomatic ties began in 1949. #SwedenIndiaSambandh has emerged as a new hash tag of the ties in 2020.	Strategic commerce Healthcare diplomacy Defence diplomacy Green technology diplomacy Maritime cooperation in Polar Science	India has sought manufacturing expertise of Sweden and they follow "In India for India" strategic framework for India as a market. Atlas Copco, Sandvik and Alfa Laval are firms in India since 1960s and have created two million jobs till date. Swedish firms such as IKEA and H&M have identified retail as a space of growth in India. In 2020, India used a Swedish tech TORREFACTION (made by BIOENDEV, a Swedish firm), which can convert rice stubble (by heating it to 350 degrees) into bio-coal pellets, which can be used for industrial use in steel and cement production. India since 2020 is seeking Swedish support for clean technologies, healthcare, green tech and defence. Bofors scandal, over 410 field Howitzer guns, did emerge as a drag in the ties as it affected the then Prime Minister Rajiv Gandhi, but, now, Saab, the largest defence manufacturer of Sweden, is providing support for Make in India. India is looking at purchasing Swedish Gripen fighters for IAF as Gripen is powered with American engines.

INDIA AND PORTUGAL RELATIONS

Historical engagement between India and Portugal	India's core interest in engaging with Portugal	India's diplomatic strategy to engage with Portugal
Goa was under the Portugal rule and liberation of Goa emerged as a sticky point. In 1974, the two concluded a diplomatic treaty. Portugal is one of the first European states to have a pact with India on Nalanda University. More than 70,000 Indian diasporas live in Portugal today and they act as a bridge in the ties.	Strategic alliance Technology diplomacy Start-up-based cooperation Defence and security diplomacy Shipping-based cooperation Cultural cooperation	India looks at Portugal as an economic gateway to Europe. Portugal wants India to be a part of a multilateral strategic alliance of democratic states to tackle problems that range from freedom, rule of law, tolerance to social justice and act as an alternative to non-democratic models. India also looks at Portugal as a bridge to Africa and Latin America diplomacy.

SECTION 10

India's Nuclear Diplomacy, Disarmament Policy and Nuclear Posturing

- 1. The Fundamentals of Nuclear Diplomacy
- 2. India's Nuclear Policy: Changing Perceptions and Policy
- 3. Nuclear Security Challenges for India in the Post-Pandemic World Order

AN OVERVIEW

In the past, the UPSC asked questions pertaining to India's stance at NPT and CTBT. Questions on India's nuclear doctrine and its assessment have been asked repeatedly. The questions asked are not complex and are relatively straight forward. But they do give us an insight on what lies ahead.

Potential foresight Analysing previous years' questions, we can infer that the commission may not shy away from asking questions on changing dynamics of India's disarmament policy. There could be potential questions on the need for India to change its nuclear doctrine especially after the recent Ladakh standoff with China. This chapter is constructed succinctly to align one's thoughts in the analytical fashion.

CHAPTER 1

The Fundamentals of Nuclear Diplomacy

THE NUCLEAR FUEL CYCLE

Mining → Milling → Conversion → Enrichment → Fuel Fabrication → Storage → Reprocessing

The uranium that exists in nature is extracted from the ground. The naturally occurring uranium is called the Uranium-238 isotope. In this isotope, the fissile material Uranium-235 0.7% that is just enough to sustain a nuclear reaction. Because Uranium-235 only constitutes a meager percentage of the fuel, more amount of fissile material is required. The naturally occurring uranium is leached using chemicals to prepare the yellow cake. The transformation of yellow cake is brought about using uranium hexafluoride gas. As the concentration of Uranium-235 increases, it becomes ready for generation of nuclear energy. The enriched uranium is grinded into power form. The powder is further processed to produce ceramic pellets. These pellets are put inside the fuel roads to power the reactor core. After the usage of Uranium-235, Uranium-238 and plutonium thus generated are then kept in the spent fuel pool separately. The plutonium and Uranium-238 are then further used thereby competing the fuel cycle. Uranium enriched up to 3–5% is civilian grade uranium and is used for generation of electricity. Uranium enriched up to 20% is called highly-enriched uranium and is used for medical isotopes. Uranium enriched up to 90% is called military grade uranium and is used for nuclear weapons.

ATOMS FOR PEACE

It was a programme that had its origin in the speech of the US President Dwight Eisenhower at the UN General Assembly in 1953. In the speech, Eisenhower not only highlighted the dangers of nuclear weapons but also proposed peaceful use of nuclear technology. During the Cold War, the US began to use the programme to win allies in the global order. The US declassified nuclear documents and began to transfer nuclear technology to other states for peaceful use. India, Pakistan and Iran took advantage of the declassified knowledge to build up peaceful nuclear programmes. The logic behind this declassification was that countries in the world would seek the US support at the nuclear level and such American support will give the US the leverage to prevent states to gravitate towards the USSR and thus make the capitalist camp more powerful. The US also stated that to facilitate the civilian transfer, an international body would be subsequently established. To execute the transfer of civilian nuclear secrets with nations, a body was proposed called the International Atomic Energy Agency (IAEA).

INTERNATIONAL ATOMIC ENERGY AGENCY

It is an international body, proposed under the Atoms for Peace initiative that was to assist other nations in peaceful use of civilian nuclear technology, that they would receive from the US and other Western powers. The IAEA had three objectives. First, it would ensure peaceful use of civilian nuclear technologies by member states. Second, it would establish safeguards to prevent the diversion of civilian technology by states to military use. Third, it would establish nuclear safety standards for the countries to follow. To implement the third point, the IAEA conceptualised safeguard agreements and additional protocols (APs).

NUCLEAR NON-PROLIFERATION TREATY (NPT)

The NPT was announced in 1968 and was implemented in 1970. It was a treaty that was designed to prevent proliferation of nuclear technologies to other states.

What is meant by Proliferation?

Proliferation means spreading. In the nuclear context, it means spread of nuclear technologies for uses other than stated purposes.

SAFEGUARD AGREEMENTS

To ensure that countries receiving nuclear assistance use the assistance only for civilian use, the IAEA conceptualised the safeguard agreements. The IAEA under the safeguards could carry out inspection for unauthorised activities only at designated or specified sites declared by a country. This basically left an option open for states to carry out covert nuclear programmes.

ADDITIONAL PROTOCOLS AND MODIFIED CODE 3.1

Additional protocols are basically safeguard agreements. After it was revealed that Iraq had violated the IAEA safeguards, a need was felt to have extra safeguards. Under the old IAEA safeguards, all NPT signatories would specify their nuclear sites and IAEA would carry out inspections in the specified sites. Thus, in 1993, the IAEA-designed APs, under a programme called Modified Code 3.1, to tighten the existing safeguarding regime. Under the APs, now the IAEA can keep a check upon the entire nuclear fuel cycle of a state. For instance, as per the APs, if a state mines uranium or thorium, it has to report it to the IAEA. If a state uses uranium or thorium, it needs to inform the IAEA. Similarly, if a state disposes off the nuclear waste, then it needs to inform the IAEA. Thus, under the APs, IAEA is empowered with stringent levels of intrusive checks to prevent any covert diversion of fissile materials. But the AP was kept voluntary for a state. India, as part of the Indo-US nuclear deal, signed the AP with IAEA. Indian-specific APs do not give IAEA the right to hinder or interfere with activities which are outside the scope of India's safeguard agreements, thus recognising that India reserves a right to a military nuclear programme outside IAEA agreement.

NUCLEAR FIRST STRIKE

First strike is a nuclear strategy of identifying and completely destroying enemy countries' nuclear forces. The attacker needs to have complete idea as to where the enemy has kept its nuclear weapons (to destroy them) and some additional reserve of nuclear forces to prevent any devastating reprisal in case of an unsuccessful first strike. The first strike should not be seen as same as the first attack. A first attack would be a limited attack that may not destroy the enemy's nuclear forces.

POSTURE OF FIRST USE

If a state is not able to defend itself with conventional military forces or feels that there is uncertainty in its capacity to defend itself through conventional forces, it may reserve a right to the first use of nuclear weapons. Normally, when a state feels that its adversary may possess significantly superior conventional forces, it may be compelled to adopt first use. But first use does not mean early use, as states having first use may still resort to use of nuclear weapons as last resort. India has No First Use (NFU) doctrine.

CONFERENCE ON DISARMAMENT

It is a disarmament-negotiating agency with its headquarters in Geneva. Five members from NATO and five members of Warsaw Pact in 1960 in Geneva had established the Ten Nation Committee on Disarmament or the TNCD. To encourage further dialogue between the US and Soviet Union, the UN, in 1961, established Eighteen Nation Committee on Disarmament (ENCD). The ENCD added eight members from the third world and the ten from TNCD. The ENCD, in 1969, was rechristened and reconstituted as Conference of the Committee on Disarmament (CCD) and finally the CD replaced CCD in 1979. The CD has been instrumental in negotiation of CTBT (Comprehensive Test Ban Treaty) along with acting as a forum to negotiate First Missile Cut-off Treaty (FMCT) and prevention of arms race in outer space treaty.

FISSILE MATERIAL CUT-OFF TREATY

FMCT is a treaty being proposed to prohibit production of highly-enriched uranium and plutonium. Regarding the scope of verification procedure, there is unanimity that the procedure should be strong, effective and also politically acceptable. Many countries have advocated that the procedure should not be the same as prescribed under NPT. Some sections in the Indian establishment are of the view that FMCT should have mechanisms whereby all states comply with all obligations. India's ambassador at the CD has reiterated that India will only favour a treaty if it intends to ban future production of fissile material only.

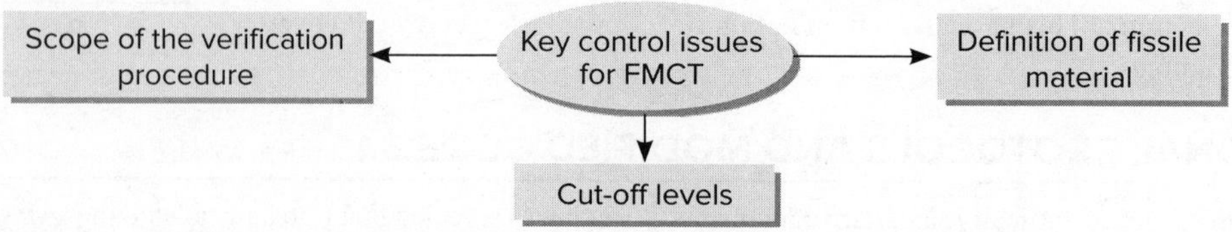

PEACEFUL NUCLEAR EXPLOSION (PNE) AND NUCLEAR WEAPONS TEST

When a nuclear explosion is carried out for non-military purposes, it is called a PNE. Such explosions are permitted by the NPT. Theoretically, characterising a test as peaceful is very difficult. In 1974, India undertook a PNE, Operation Smiling Buddha at Pokhran. It is also called as a technology demonstrator test. A nuclear weapon test is a test of nuclear weapons where the state achieves the sub-critical position. This means when a state conducts a nuclear weapon test, the yield of the weapon detonated is so high that it generates enough data which the state can use to improvise the yield of the weapon through computer simulation and no further physical testing is needed. India achieved this honour in 1998. Testing of a nuclear weapon makes a state a nuclear weapon state. The 1998 test was called Operation Shakti.

2

CHAPTER

India's Nuclear Policy: Changing Perceptions and Policy

BUILDING INDIA'S NUCLEAR INSTITUTIONAL ARCHITECTURE

The Indian nuclear issue can be traced back to the time of Nehru. He had exercised tremendous influence on India's nuclear thought and policy. He laid down the foundation of India's nuclear programme and its nuclear behaviour. The person other than Nehru who created a deep imprint on the Indian nuclear programme was Homi J. Bhabha. In 1939, Bhabha came back to India to establish the Nuclear Research Institute. He sought financial assistance from the Sir Dorabji Tata Trust to further Indian nuclear research and to establish a nuclear research project. He was able to convince him about the role that nuclear technology could play in the development of modern India. In 1945, the Tata Institute of Fundamental Research (TIFR) was established, with Bhabha as its director. He based his idea of nuclear technology and energy resources on the basis that as India would progress, there would be a demand for more energy and India's conventional energy resources would not be able to meet that demand. Thus, nuclear energy as an alternate and affordable option needed to be developed. To explore the nuclear option, nuclear reactor technology had to be understood and built upon. The government, after independence, established an institutional architecture for further nuclear research. The Indian Atomic Energy Act was modelled on the act of Britain that created British Energy Generation Limited. The British Act advocated tremendous secrecy over nuclear materials and the nuclear programme overall. India openly advocated for peaceful use of nuclear technology and yet the bill was adopted upon conditions of stringent secrecy on the lines of British act.

CONSTITUENT ASSEMBLY DEBATES AND NUCLEAR QUESTION

Dr. B. P. Sittaramaiah and S. V. K. Rao raised the matter regarding nuclear issues in the Constituent Assembly Debates (CAD). Both advocated the need for clarification whether India could apply secrecy for the peaceful programme or whether India should harbor intentions of running a secret military programme. Nehru, under pressure, conceded in CAD debate on 6th April 1948 that he did not know how to distinguish between a civilian and a military programme.

In fact, S. L. Saksena argued that India should and must have nuclear weapons to prevent war. Nehru, while addressing both the CAD and the Parliament, agreed that India needed nuclear energy for peaceful purposes whereas Saksena asserted that the association of atomic energy and nuclear weaponisation is unavoidable.

However, Nehru certainly did not clampdown the option for subsequent heads of state to establish the initiatives for nuclear weapons and intimately linked nation building to power assertion. It was in 1948 that India passed its first atomic legislation to establish a framework to manage the Indian nuclear sector. The Atomic Energy Act 1948 modelled on the British Atomic Energy Act, established the Atomic Energy Commission (AEC) as the main regulatory body. In 1962, the Atomic Energy Act 1948 was superseded with a new Atomic Energy Act of 1962. Both the legislations have only centralised the Indian State Control over nuclear-related activities.

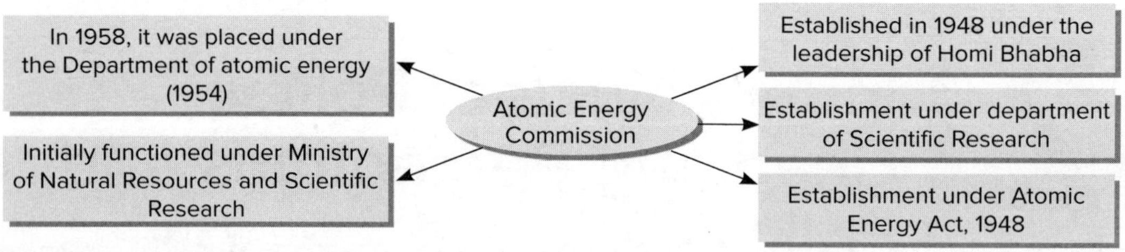

THORIUM NITRATE ISSUE, INDIA–US AND CHINA RELATION

In 1951, the US passed Mutual Defence Assistance Act. The US, in 1953, launched the Atoms for Peace programme. India became a partner country in the Atoms for Peace initiative. The US provided thorium nitrate (a nuclear fuel) to India under Atoms for Peace and Mutual Defence Assistance Act of 1951. The US Mutual Defence Assistance Act stated that if the US supplies any nuclear materials to any country, then the recipient country could not trade materials given by the US with Soviet Union, its satellite states or any communist state. In 1953, China demanded thorium nitrate from India. India saw this sale as an opportunity to boost bilateral cooperation with China. India decided to send a shipment to China. The US, therefore, opposed India's bid to sell thorium nitrate to China saying that such a sale will violate the US Mutual Defence Assistance Act 1951. India asserted that American laws do not bind India and such laws have no jurisdiction over the territory of India. India stated that as a sovereign state, it reserves the right to decide about commercial diplomacy.

This emerged as a friction between India and the US but the matter was diplomatically resolved. The US allowed the existing shipment to be sent to China on the condition that India in future would not transfer the US material to any communist state. After India became independent it began to seek assistance from foreign nations.

EXTERNAL SUPPORT FOR INDIA'S NUCLEAR POWER STRUCTURES

In 1955, Canada provided a 40-megawatt reactor, which used natural uranium and heavy water. In 1956, the British helped India to build the Apsara reactor. The heavy water was provided by the USA under a partnership called CIRUS. India chose Canadian reactors because India possessed very limited foreign exchange and used this limited foreign exchange to purchase the only affordable reactors, which Canada offered. Canada further attached a no-strings policy on how the plutonium was to be used.

INDIA'S PLUTONIUM BANK NEGATION DIPLOMACY

In 1957, Eisenhower Administration, which had proposed the Atoms for Peace Initiative in the UN General Assembly announced establishment of the International Atomic Energy Agency (IAEA), as an international body to assist other nations in peaceful use of civilian nuclear technology. The IAEA decided to establish tight safeguards over nuclear materials given to states. One of the points was plutonium generation. The IAEA asked that plutonium generated by states be given to IAEA, which would, in turn, allow some quantity to be kept with a country for non-military use. Bhabha opposed this policy and advanced that it was an inalienable right by a state to retain plutonium or any other fissionable material. Ultimately, India won on this point at IAEA. A decision was arrived at that such safeguards would not affect socio-economic development of a country and India retained its right to have plutonium for future use. In 1958, a plant named Phoenix was established at Trombay to extract plutonium. In 1958, the government adopted a three-phase power production plan. India would first take assistance from Canada and develop uranium-fueled reactors. As these reactors would operationalise, they would generate plutonium as a by-product. In the second stage, India would develop reactors, which would use plutonium and burn plutonium with thorium. The burning of plutonium and thorium would create uranium (U-233). In the third stage, India would use U-233; burn U-233 and thorium to produce more U-233 and nuclear energy.

PRINCIPLES OF INDIA'S DOMESTIC NUCLEAR POLICY

The foundational ideas that dominated our development discourse after independence were a heavy industrialisation model and import substitution. It was believed that this model would push India to the next stage of growth. In this model, nuclear energy was to have a core role in providing electricity. Nehru and Bhabha had a confluence of ideas at this level as they both agreed that nuclear energy can take the country forward and help in achieving its developmental goals. Thus, Indian policymakers understood that nuclear energy can be an alternative to conventional energy and can be produced at a cheap price to achieve socio-economic goals. This plan of using nuclear energy for the stated purposes was institutionalised in the second Five-Year Plan.

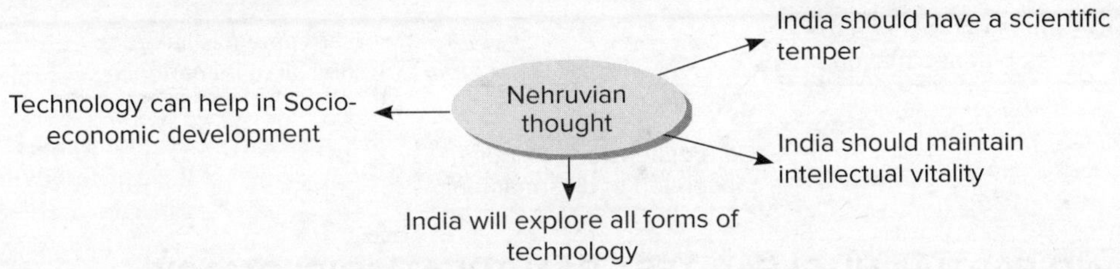

The Indian scientists, by 1960, created fuel rods and used them for the first loading of CIRUS in 1960. The use of self-made fuel rods gave India the claim to use the resultant plutonium for future use.

PRINCIPLES OF INDIA'S DIPLOMATIC NUCLEAR POLICY

India used 1958 to 1960 to articulate its Disarmament policy. After India became independent, the world was witnessing Cold War. India stated that Cold War is a situation where there is an ideological confrontation between the Americans and Russians. This confrontation is not just ideological but also military. This is so because both superpowers are living in a constant state of fear that the other opponent might attack. This is the reason why both superpowers are undertaking development of arms. They are developing arms to prevent an attack from the opponent. Such development of arms has caused an arms race between the superpowers. This arms race has adopted a nuclear component also and both superpowers are even trying to develop nuclear arms. All this arms development or armament is ironically happening when both superpowers have already stated that they will not fight militarily. India stated that such an arms race, which is a nuclear arms race, is a threat to the world and wastage of resource, preventing the development of the world. India stated that as a non-aligned country, India would contribute to maintenance of world peace.

INDIA'S STAND ON COMPLETE DISARMAMENT DIPLOMACY

As a non-aligned state, India favoured to advocate for disarmament. It is important to keep in mind the difference between disarmament and complete disarmament. If disarmament is about reduction of weapons, then complete disarmament is reduction and complete elimination of weapons. India stated that if states in the world start doing disarmament and eventually resort to complete disarmament, then there would be a nuclear weapons free world. In such a world, the states would be able to save a tremendous amount of resources and these resources saved can be channelised for development of humanity. This is why Indian strategy of complete disarmament was linked to development and well-being of humanity.

What is Disarmament?

Disarmament is exactly opposite of armament. If armament is about increasing the number of weapons to prepare oneself for a potential attack from an adversary, then disarmament is about reduction of the weapons.

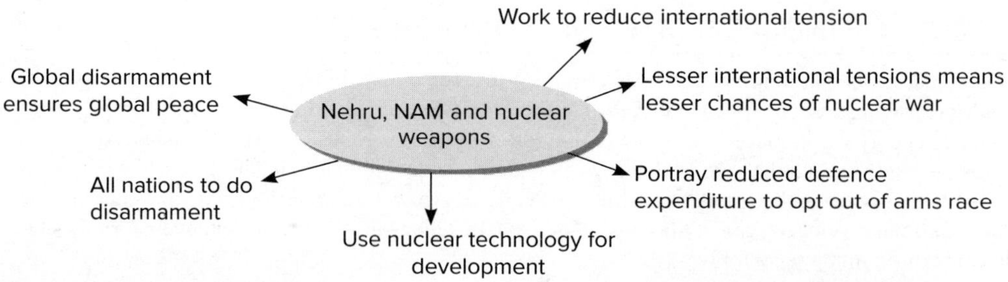

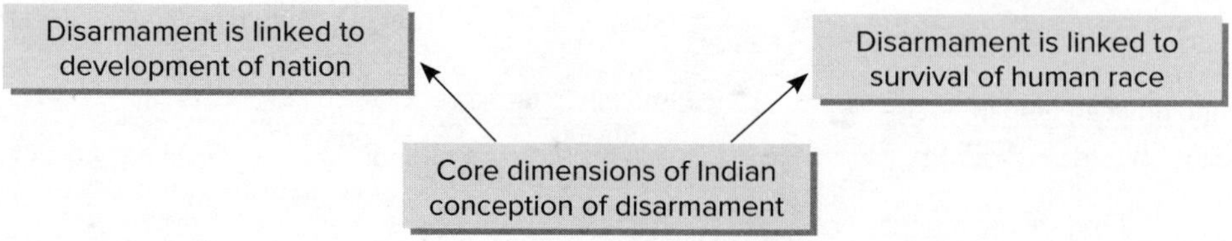

INDIA AND PARTIAL NUCLEAR TEST BAN TREATY DIPLOMACY

Two remarkable events happened in 1962. First was the Cuban missile crisis and second was India–China conflict. The US, the USSR and Britain decided to work towards the reduction in nuclear escalation Cuban missile crisis. In 1963, they drafted a Partial Nuclear Test Ban Treaty (PTBT or LTBT). India found PTBT a favourable draft. The PTBT asserted that there should be complete prohibition on underwater, atmosphere and outer space nuclear testing. India ratified the PTBT, thinking that the PTBT is a step towards complete disarmament. However, China refused to conclude the PTBT, which aggravated tensions in India. India was unable to understand that what could be the rationale as to why did China not ratify the PTBT? China conducted a nuclear test in Lop Nur in 1964 and proclaimed itself as a Nuclear Weapon State.

PUGWASH CONFERENCE

In 1964, there was a Pugwash Conference organised by world powers in India. Bhabha attended the Pugwash Conference in Udaipur in 1964. He presented that a country such as China having nuclear weapons can threaten India, and India had to either go for development of a nuclear weapon or collective security. Two things emerged here. Firstly, India was trying to articulate a collective security pact with the US or the USSR for security guarantee, which especially became more relevant post-1962. Secondly, India explored the option of going nuclear. At the Pugwash Conference, Bhabha gave a clear understanding of the problems lying ahead for India with a nuclear China around and effectively presented a likely course of action for India. Russians and Americans refused any collective security for India. The first nuclear test was conducted by China on 16th October 1964.

LAL BAHADUR SHASTRI AND INDIA'S SUBTERRANEAN NUCLEAR EXPLOSION AUTHORISATION

A six-week debate in India from 16th October 1964 to 27th October 1964 brought a major shift in the Indian nuclear thought. After the nuclear test of China in 1964, days later, a pitch by Jan Sangh and Samyukta Socialist Party to allow India to possess nuclear weapons began. The debate saw tremendous pressure being exerted from the opposition parties. Though Shastri continued to follow Nehruvian line, he also continued to accelerate military rebuilding of India. As domestic pressure grew, Shastri, on 27th November 1964, announced the authorisation of subterranean nuclear test or a peaceful nuclear explosion in the Parliament. The period till 1965 saw Indian scientists debating costs and financial implications for the same. Bhabha also believed that a nuclear India would serve as a triumph for the third world and would strengthen democracy in Asia. The initial idea of a security guarantee could not work out as the US continued with its alliance with Pakistan and India's own non-aligned credentials would not have favoured an active relationship with either the US or the USSR.

INDIA'S NUCLEAR DIPLOMACY AT EIGHTEEN NATION DISARMAMENT COMMISSION

In 1965, Eighteen Nation Disarmament Commission (ENDC) was established to negotiate a nuclear Non-Proliferation Treaty (NPT). India was one of the eight non-aligned nations, along with the five US allies and five Russian allies that were part of the commission. India, at the ENDC, advocated that all 18 nations freeze nuclear weapon production and halt production of delivery systems, which would be the only move that would ensure that Non-Nuclear Weapons States (NNWS) would not go nuclear. India also clarified that a security guarantee could not deny nuclear weapons to NNWS and that only a complete disarmament by Nuclear Weapon States (NWS) can give assured satisfaction to NNWS. India also pitched that a global approach to disarmament is needed. This stance of India at the ENDC alarmed the US. On 24th January 1966, Homi J. Bhabha was travelling to Vienna on Air India flight number-707 (flight was from Mumbai to New York). The CIA of the USA had planted a bomb in the cargo panel of the flight. The bomb exploded midair and the plane crashed into Mont Blanc Mountains in the Swiss Alps.

INDIA AND NUCLEAR NON-PROLIFERATION TREATY

The ENDC was concluded by the NPT in 1967. The provisions of the NPT were:

- The NPT as a treaty stated that the world would be divided into NWS and NNWS.
- The NPT said that the countries that have tested a NW (nuclear weapon) before 1st January 1967 were to be called NWS.
- The countries that had not tested a NW before the date fixed were thereafter labelled as NNWS.
- The NPT stated that NWS would not increase their nuclear arsenal and would undertake gradual disarmament.
- The NNWS, on the other hand, would not procure nuclear weapons. The NPT clarified that there shall be a review of NPT 25 years from the date of its enforcement.
- The NPT also said that in order to prevent any diversion of nuclear energy from peaceful to military use, the state parties to the NPT will accept the IAEA safeguards.

REASONS FOR INDIA'S REJECTION OF NUCLEAR NON-PROLIFERATION TREATY

After looking at the draft, India refused to sign the NPT. India gave the following reasons for refusal.

- India asserted that NPT was a *discriminatory treaty*, which had divided the world into nuclear haves and nuclear have-nots.
- India held that this distinction in the treaty was *highly arbitrary* in nature.
- India also said that the NPT as a treaty was *unfair* because it placed no obligation on nuclear weapon states to destroy their nuclear weapons and the gradual disarmament advocated therein was nothing more than eyewash.
- The NPT had set no time frame for complete disarmament and it was clear that the gradual disarmament advocated was not happening in the foreseeable future unless a timeline was adhered to by the states. Thus, NPT is *vague*.
- India clarified that under the NPT, if NWS were allowed to have a nuclear weapon, the NPT would be a *threat to India*.
- India aptly understood that NPT intended to augment *nuclear apartheid*.

The NPT was opened for signatures in 1968 and finally was enforced in 1970. The NPT created an impression that the emerging powers would not be allowed to have nuclear weapons and the monopoly over nuclear weapons was being legitimised by the superpowers.

THE EXISTENTIAL THREAT TO SECURITY OF INDIA FROM US AND INDIA'S RETHINK

Indira Gandhi focused largely on domestic economy but certain events furthered India's urge to think about nuclear weapons. In December 1971, when the Indo-Pak war in East Pakistan broke out, the US dispatched a nuclear-powered aircraft carrier called USS Enterprise in Bay of Bengal to support Pakistan and threaten India. This made India rethink its post-war situation.

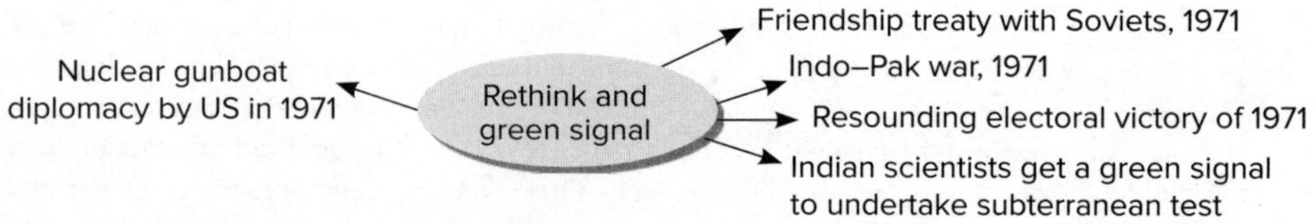

India had established a plutonium reprocessing facility at Trombay that had generated a huge stockpile of plutonium, which was weapon grade in nature. The operation of the Purnima reactor designed by the Bhabha Atomic Research Centre had provided Indian scientists the data needed for designing nuclear explosive devices. The scientists pressed the government to grant permission to conduct a nuclear explosion at the subterranean level for use in civil engineering purposes. The US and the USSR, during the Cold War period, conducted many Peaceful Nuclear Explosions (PNE). Indira Gandhi finally approved the PNE for Indian scientists in October 1972. One of the immediate factors that motivated Indira Gandhi to give a go-ahead for the PNE was the Bangladesh war.

INDIA'S PEACEFUL NUCLEAR EXPLOSION, 1974 (OPERATION SMILING BUDDHA)

After the visit of Henry Kissinger to China, he told the Indian Ambassador to Washington, L. K. Jha, that if there is an Indo-Pak war over East Pakistan and in case the Chinese intervene in the war to support Pakistan, the US would not be able to support India. This incident was perceived by India as outright intimidation. Though no paper records exist for Indira Gandhi's decision to give a green signal for PNE, it is widely believed that this was one of the reasons that influenced her decision. Another reason was the continuous Chinese nuclear testing from 1964 onwards, which was certainly important in the security calculus of India.

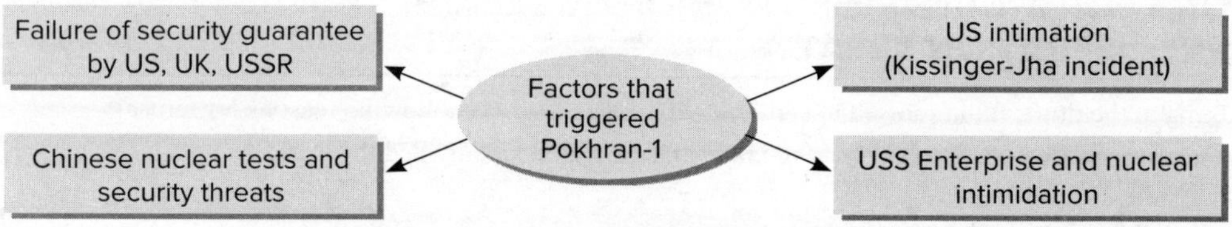

India conducted Pokhran-I, a PNE, and codenamed as Operation Smiling Buddha. The US and Canada suspended all support to India and the Nuclear Suppliers Group (NSG) was formed in 1975. Domestically in India, emergency was imposed, which was followed by the Janata Party government in 1977 led by Morarji Desai till 1980. Desai reviewed India's nuclear policy.

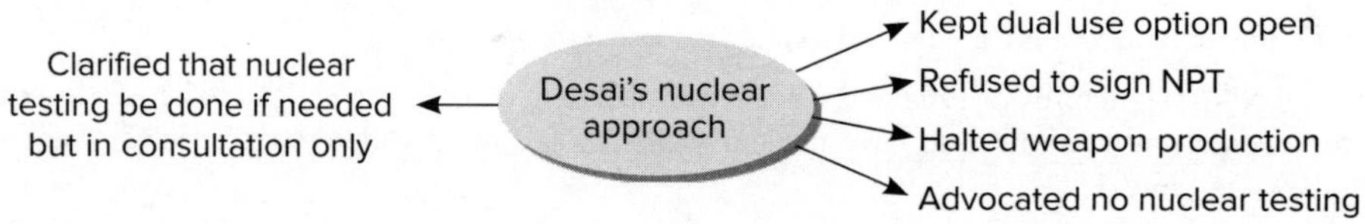

EATING GRASS TO MAKE NUCLEAR BOMB: PAKISTAN'S NUCLEAR FORAY

During the time of Janata Party government, RAW was able to gather intelligence about Pakistani nuclear activities at Kahuta. It is the site of the Khan Research Laboratories (KRL), Pakistan's main nuclear weapons laboratory as well as an emerging centre for long-range missile development. The primary Pakistani fissile-material production facility is located at Kahuta, employing gas centrifuge enrichment technology to produce highly-enriched uranium (HEU). Dr. A. Q. Khan was a German-educated metallurgist, who until 1975 was employed at the URENCO, uranium enrichment facility in Almelo, the Netherlands. A year after India's 1974 nuclear test, Dr. Khan departed URENCO with stolen blueprints for the uranium centrifuge, and information on URENCO's key suppliers. A. Q. Khan founded the Engineering Research Laboratories (ERL) on 31 July 1976, with the exclusive task of indigenous development of uranium enrichment plant. On 1 May 1981, ERL was renamed as Dr. A. Q. Khan Research Laboratories (KRL).

RAW'S OPERATION KAHUTA

To gather intelligence related to Kahuta, Indian Research and Analysis Wing (RAW) launched Operation Kahuta. It was one of RAW's most ambitious and daring covert operations overseas, inside Pakistan. Kahuta was the answer to Zulfikar Ali Bhutto's silent prayers, who as Pakistan's Minister of Foreign Affairs had passionately vowed that Pakistan would build a nuclear bomb, even if the people had to eat grass (as he said in an interview with The Guardian in 1965). Under the leadership of Dr. A. Q. Khan (often colourfully referred to as the "rogue scientist") was born the "Islamic bomb". RAW actually found the answer lying on the floor of a barbershop. By analysing the hair samples (which were sent by RAW agents to BARC, New Delhi) of the scientists (collected from the barber shop near the plant where the scientists would go for getting a haircut), RAW discovered they had indeed developed the capability to enrich uranium to weapons-grade quality. The RAW managed to infiltrate the Kahuta plant in 1977.

INDIA'S DIPLOMACY AT SPECIAL SESSION ON DISARMAMENT

The United Nations General Assembly, on request of the developing countries, launched a Special Session On Disarmament (SSOD) to achieve global disarmament. The first SSOD meet happened in 1978 and reaffirmed the need for disarmament. At the end of the first SSOD, the General Assembly established a Disarmament Commission comprising all UN members. The second SSOD happened in 1982 but failed to establish consensus despite an urgent need for disarmament. The third SSOD in 1988 also failed to establish a consensus.

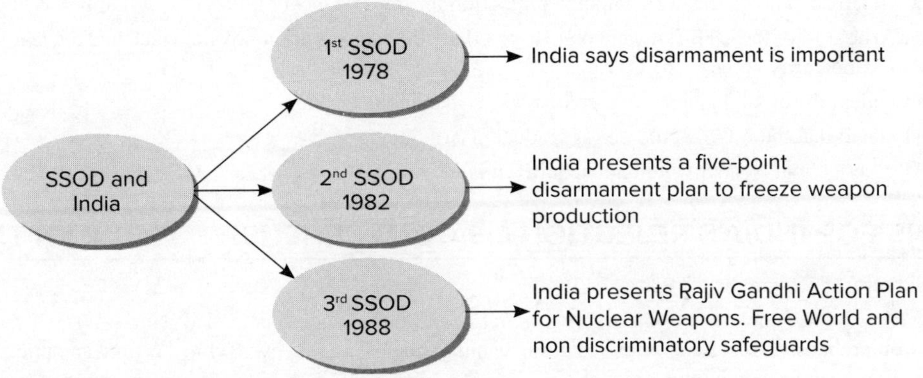

INDIA PREPARES FOR NUCLEAR WEAPONS TEST IN 1982

By the time Indira Gandhi came back to power in 1980, reports of Pakistan having acquired nuclear capability were going around. Zulfikar Ali Bhutto, then head of state of Pakistan, acquired Saudi Arabian financing for nuclear weapon. The most important reason for Pakistan's going nuclear was India's already having done so. Pakistan perceived its nuclear capability as a bargaining chip in the Kashmir in future. Indira Gandhi in the Parliament accepted Pakistan's right to go nuclear but maintained that India had an edge on "all aspects" over Pakistan.

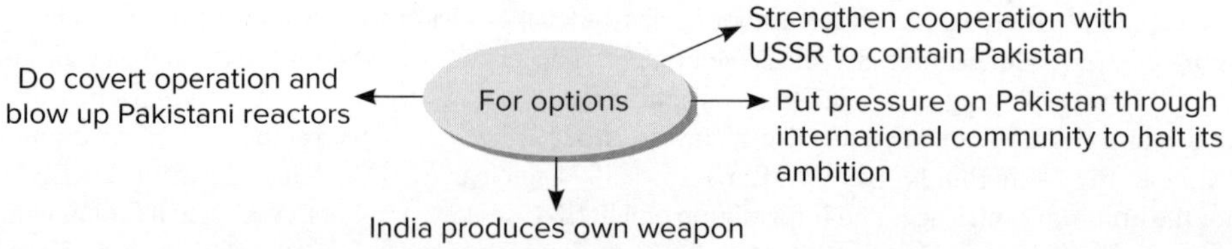

Indira Gandhi adopted a wait and watch policy. Though reports do suggest that she planned to test nuclear weapons in 1982, when the US satellites captured images of the nuclear test preparations by India, the idea was immediately dropped.

LAUNCH OF INTEGRATED GUIDED MISSILE DEVELOPMENT PROGRAMME

In 1983, India launched the Integrated Guided Missile Development Programme (IGMDP) to establish five guided missiles (Nag, Trishul, Akash, Prithvi and Agni). After India tested Prithvi in 1988, the MTCR was established. During the times of Rajiv Gandhi, Pakistan continued nuclear weapon development. As Pakistan had opted for a military programme since the beginning of their nuclear programme, money was judiciously used and, unlike India, did not divert the resources for civilian use.

INDIA'S DIPLOMACY AT CONFERENCE ON DISARMAMENT

As the Cold War ended, in 1992, IAEA had also come out with a safeguard agreement and had stated that only full scope countries be entitled to get technology. The Nuclear Non-Proliferation Treaty (NPT) Review Conference was slated to happen in 1995. The end of the Cold War also saw the Indo-US rapprochement. In 1993, the Conference on Disarmament (COD) began. India participated in the COD and pitched for complete disarmament. The COD culminated in 1996 in a draft of the CTBT.

The provisions of CTBT are as follows:

- The CTBT firstly banned all forms of nuclear testing, including underground testing which, as an option, had been left open by the PTBT.
- The CTBT made allowances for computer simulation for improvement of the yield of bomb.
- Under Article 14 of the CTBT, it went on to assert that all countries of the world, which had nuclear technologies, were to mandatorily agree to the CTBT.
- A subsequent list of 44 nations was prepared which also included India.
- CTBT stated that the NWS would go for gradual disarmament.
- CTBT asserted that NNWS would not acquire an NW.

REASONS FOR INDIA'S REJECTION OF COMPREHENSIVE TEST BAN TREATY

In 1996, India refused to sign the CTBT.

- India asserted that the *name of the treaty was faulty* and that it should be called 'Nuclear Test Ban Treaty' and not 'Comprehensive Test Ban Treaty' as it was banning nuclear testing even while keeping an option of computer simulation open for bomb improvement.
- India also asserted that Article 14 of *CTBT violated international law* as no treaty can compel a state to sign a treaty that the state had not intended to sign.
- India urged for removal of Article 14 and also refused to sign CTBT for its lack of commitment to complete disarmament and asserted the treaty to be *vague in commitments*.

- India asserted that *CTBT aims to promote global discrimination* by allowing NWS to keep their weapons intact and preventing NNWS to acquire weapons.
- India stated that *CTBT is arbitrary* because NWS do not need to undertake tests and for them, the point of computer simulation makes sense and they can improve their weapon yield; but for NNWS, who have no data, it makes no sense to have computer simulation.

INDIA TESTS NUCLEAR WEAPON, 1998 (OPERATION SHAKTI)

The NPT Review Conference of 1995 also decided to continue the NPT in the same format without any change and advised no more reviews in future of NPT. Thus, in 1996, India refused to ratify both the NPT and the CTBT. Perceiving the trend of discriminatory global practices, India conducted Pokhran-II in 1998. From 11th May to 13th May, India carried out three nuclear tests in an underground format. After conducting the nuclear tests as Operation Shakti, India subsequently announced a nuclear doctrine and proclaimed itself NWS.

ANNOUNCEMENT OF INDIA'S NUCLEAR DOCTRINE

Indian Nuclear Doctrine (IND) was announced on 4 January 2003. Its features are as follows:

- Seek a credible minimum deterrence
- The policy of no first use
- Undertake massive and unacceptable retaliation on first strike
- Civilian nuclear command be under the control of civilian political leadership
- Non use of nuclear weapons against non-nuclear weapon states
- Usage of chemical or biological weapons by any state against India or Indian armed forces anywhere will lead India to respond with nuclear retaliation
- Self-imposed moratorium on further nuclear testing
- India is still committed for nuclear weapons free world

ASSESSMENT OF INDIA'S NUCLEAR DOCTRINE

The phrase, Credible Minimum Deterrence, means that India has not developed a weapon to be used in a war. It has developed a weapon (which is a credible tool) to prevent states to blackmail India with nuclear retaliation. The word Minimum Deterrence means that India shall not keep its weapon in the state of readiness all the time as the possession of the weapon itself is a sufficient condition for deterrence to others who may blackmail India.

India clarified that on first strike, it will resort to massive and unacceptable retaliation against the adversary state. This was India's concept of credible minimum deterrence. India's nuclear posture is defined not by the number of weapons in its total arsenal but how it will inflict damage on an adversary as a retaliatory strike of first use by others. India has tactical nuclear weapons launch capability. The weapon launch system is called Prahaar and has a range of 150 to 300 kilometers and it can be used for conventional and tactical nuclear use. Though India is not interested in projecting any tactical nuclear fighting posture (despite Pakistan having tactical capabilities), because India's posture is of massive retaliation in response to nuclear use against its forces or territory.

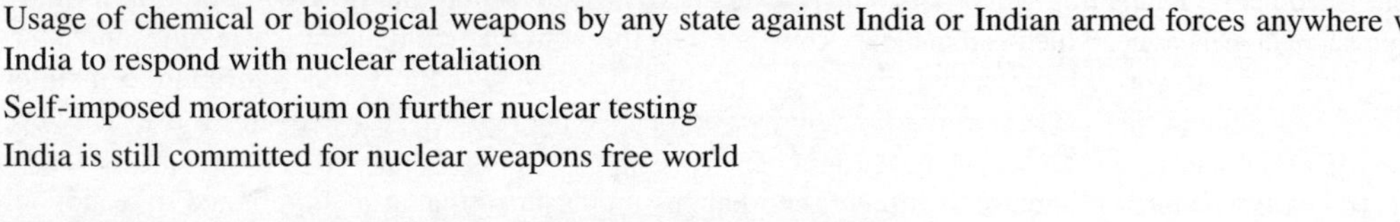

INDIA'S NUCLEAR FIRST USE POSTURE

The core purpose of India to have nuclear weapons is to have them for national security in a world of anarchy and blackmail. India has not acquired its nuclear weapons to rectify military imbalances or assert regional superiority but serve the purpose of deterrence. However, debates have arisen about the efficacy of the NFU Policy. Some scholars assert that the Indian NFU is a pious hope without covering other Nuclear Weapon states. In this case, assuming that India might shift to first use policy, the question arises, would it serve any purpose? The answer is no. Because a first use policy does not prevent blackmailing threats and more so, is destabilising in nature. In this case, India's NFU is at least deterring the use of weapons of NWS. There could be a situation, however, where a NWS could threaten India with a nuclear strike and an assessment by India could establish that the threat was imminent. In this scenario, would India resort to a first strike? The nuclear doctrine is silent on this and this remains a grey area. Thus, Indian NFU and its deterrence have provided the needed protection to India. The nuclear choice of India may have been couched in moral terms but has been expressed in realistic terms.

INDIA'S DISARMAMENT DIPLOMACY FROM 1947 TO 1998

The time period from 1958 to 1960 was also used by India to articulate its disarmament policy. After India became independent, the world was witnessing Cold War. India stated that Cold War is a situation where there is an ideological confrontation between the Americans and Russians. This confrontation is not just ideological but also military. This is so because both superpowers are living in a constant state of fear that the other opponent might attack. This is the reason why both superpowers are undertaking development of arms. They are developing arms to prevent an attack from the opponent. Such development of arms has caused an arms race between the superpowers. This arms race has adopted a nuclear component also and both superpowers are even trying to develop nuclear arms. All these arms development or armament is ironically happening when both superpowers have already stated that they will not fight militarily. India stated that such an arms race, which is a nuclear arms race, is a threat to the world and wastage of resource, preventing the development of the world. India stated that as a non-aligned country, India would contribute to maintenance of world peace. India stated that the best way to maintain world peace is to go for disarmament. It is exactly opposite of armament. If armament is about increasing the number of weapons to prepare oneself for a potential attack from an adversary, then disarmament is about reduction of the weapons. India stated that as a non-aligned state, not only would it favour disarmament as an immediate step, but in the long run advocate for complete disarmament. It is important to keep in mind the difference between disarmament and complete disarmament. If disarmament is about reduction of weapons, then complete disarmament is reduction and complete elimination of weapons. India stated that if states in the world start doing disarmament and eventually resort to complete disarmament, then there would be a nuclear weapons free world. In such a world, the states would be able to save a tremendous amount of resources and these resources saved can be channelised for development of humanity. This is why Indian strategy of complete disarmament was linked to development and well-being of humanity.

INDIA'S DISARMAMENT DIPLOMACY SINCE 1998 AND THEORY OF PROPORTIONATE DISARMAMENT

India tested the nuclear weapon in 1998 and proclaimed to be a nuclear weapon state. Does that mean India has switched over from its goal of disarmament? It is important to remember that India remains committed to a verifiable, global, non-discriminatory disarmament and a nuclear weapon free world. But India has stated that till the time nuclear weapons remain in the world, India will continue to use its deterrent capabilities for 'credible deterrence'. It is true that large military and nuclear capabilities cannot bequeath India with a tag of a 'Great Power', but a grand strategic vision that amalgamates military power with a doctrine of national security can advance its march towards such a status certainly. India has clarified that if the world goes for complete disarmament and establishes a nuclear weapon free world, and then India shall also undertake complete disarmament. But, even if one state in the world continues to have a weapon, India shall reserve the right to use its deterrent capabilities for 'credible deterrence'. This means that today, India's disarmament is proportional to the disarmament of the world. Since the end of the Cold War, India has become an ardent supporter of a multipolar world. A multipolar world is possible only if it is non-hegemonic, and by extension, non-nuclear. India has stated that possession of nuclear weapons is antithetical to the achievement of a non-hegemonic international order. Since the two states are non-compatible, the only logical step India favours is a complete nuclear disarmament. A more equitable international order is possible only if the nuclear weapons are eliminated. India has tried to link democratisation of the international order as a core principle leading to the evolution of national domestic democracy. India has pitched for complete elimination of nuclear weapons by all states in the world as a pre-requisite for its own national security.

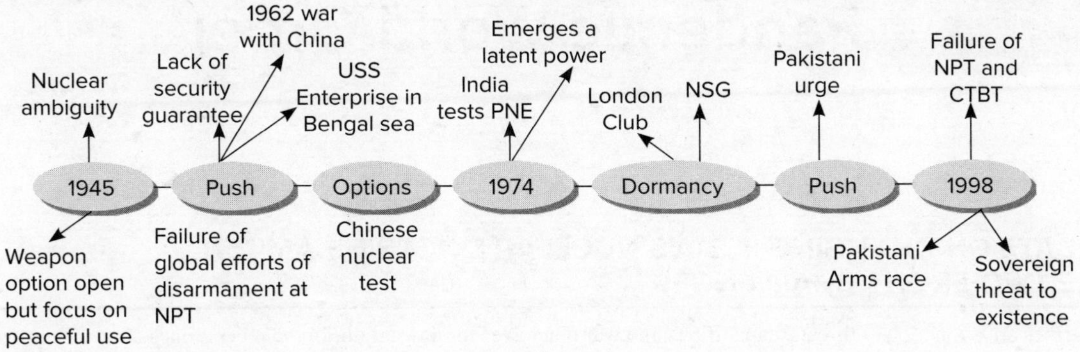

3

CHAPTER

Nuclear Security Challenges for India in the Post-Pandemic World Order

DEBATE ON CHANGING INDIA'S NUCLEAR DOCTRINE AMIDST THE TWO-FRONT CHALLENGES

Doctrines are a function of threats, capabilities and war objectives for any nation. In the recent times, there is a growing clamour amongst the political circles, intellectual class and the general public in India seeking a review of the Indian Nuclear Doctrine (IND). Let us first understand the scenario under which we are debating a possible shift in our nuclear doctrine. Nuclear first use usually refers to the first use of tactical nuclear weapons against conventional forces of the adversary, which threaten to break the adversary. Nuclear first strike means the use of nuclear weapons to attack the other side's nuclear arsenal to pre-empt an imminent nuclear strike or to prevent a nuclear strike sometime in a longer-term but foreseeable future. Pre-emption and prevention go against current doctrine of India. Contemplating a nuclear first strike posture implies moving policy from the threat to use nuclear weapons against population centres (in a retaliatory strike) to the threat to hit the other side's nuclear weapons (before they hit us). Unless India's military is incompetent, there is only one theatre in which it is possible, Kashmir. One could imagine a situation where deeply alienated Kashmiris in the Valley combine with jihadis and militants with support from Pakistani irregulars (as in 1948) and later Pakistani regulars to encircle Indian forces. Is the situation in Kashmir, after revocation of Article 370, that dire? A second first-use circumstance is if China attacked India in strength. Given force numbers, terrain and infrastructure in Tibet, Chinese forces could push Indian forces back to some depth along a broad front. Or China might make a more localised grab; say, for Tawang (given that the monastery there has significance for Chinese control of Tibet). Or worse, China might push past the border to the plains of India. Let us leave aside whether these scenarios with China are at all likely. Certainly, a Chinese thrust into the plains would be military madness given the logistical challenges and India's ability to devastatingly counterattack. In confronting a more powerful China, India will find roles reversed: China will have escalation dominance in relation to India. Would India choose first use against the PLA in this situation? A third circumstance is a two-front war in which India fights Pakistan and China simultaneously. A first-use strike against either Pakistan or China (or both) could give India breathing space or jolt Islamabad and Beijing into terminating hostilities. The problem here is that if China by itself has escalation dominance against India, how much worse would the situation be for India in a two-front war? The strategic uncertainties of first use against either adversary or both in a two-front war are so great that it boggles the mind. What kind of strategic calculations about first use would make any sense? Is it even likely that hostilities would be confined to India, Pakistan and China? Would it ever get to the point of a two-front war given the interests of the US and Russia? This is based on certain threats being perceived from Pakistan and China along with a generic perception of weakness of India to tackle these threats due to No First Use (NFU). It is very clearly known that Pakistan developed nuclear weapons to seek parity with India. Pakistan has since then used nuclear rhetoric to prevent India to retaliate using conventional weapons. According to many scholars, this has limited India's options to hit Pakistan. There is a hardliner constituency that asserts that India needs to give up NFU. This is because Pakistan has developed tactical nuclear warheads and hardliners are of the opinion that India should develop such warheads and prepare for nuclear escalation if needed. Similarly, even though China maintains the policy of NFU; still China has not clarified weather it applies this policy against states possessing a nuclear weapon or is it universal NFU against NWS and NNWS.

This is why Indian strategic community feels that an ambiguous nuclear doctrine of China has heightened the security concerns for India; thereby, growing the clamour for revisiting the IND. Even though, the Indian government has time and again clarified that Indian nuclear weapon is only for deterrence and not for usage in war, the clamour is still growing.

STRATEGIC, DIPLOMATIC AND ECONOMIC CHALLENGES IF INDIA REVISITS ITS NUCLEAR DOCTRINE

The government can try to keep the public confidence high by periodic statements about up gradation of the nuclear arsenal. This will instill confidence in the public and help mitigate concerns in the society of lack of commitment of India in using the nuclear weapons. However, there is counter current to this debate that asserts there is no need to revisit the IND. This group asserts that any attempt to tamper the IND will fritter away all gains enjoyed by India in the international community as part of our restraining posture. This will only complicate India's integration into the multilateral export control regimes. Also, it increases government expenditure to maintain the command and control. In fact, by changing the no first use to first use, there is a high possibility that India will weaken its possibility for a conventional war due to nuclear overhang. Most importantly, South Asia will be painted as a nuclear flashpoint and will encourage foreign meddling, affecting strategic autonomy of India. In all instances, from Kargil to 2001 Parliament attack and 2008 Mumbai attacks, India demonstrated extraordinary restraint and did not cross over the LOC to retaliate. Pakistan, without any fear of retaliation from India, continued to sponsor terrorism. In 2019, Pakistan breached the red lines again when Jaish-e-Mohammad (JeM) resorted to a suicide bombing attack on a CRPF convoy in Pulwama. This time, India resorted to massive air strikes inside Pakistan. Not only did India breach the LOC, but also hurt Pakistan deep inside their state. Many assert that such postures of India have shifted Indian strategy of restraint. However, the reality is that all these Indian responses only assert that India is trying to recalibrate its doctrinal strategy to militarily respond to Pakistani adventurism. This has brought the idea to revisit the IND and accept the new challenges. As the clamour for this grey area in IND grows, it causes more uneasiness in the West regarding massive doctrinal shift in the IND and its impact on the Asian strategic stability.

INDIA'S READINESS TO TACKLE THE THREAT OF NUCLEAR TERRORISM

India has been a victim of state-sponsored terrorism by Pakistan for a long period of time. Over a period of time, through various approaches and strategies. India has managed the threat of tanzeem-centric terrorism emanating from Pakistan. However, with changing dynamics of terrorism, the possibility of Pakistan resorting to nuclear terrorism always remains high. While it is next to impossible for tanzeems of Pakistan to get hold of a nuclear weapon off the shelf and use against India, but the tanzeems can use two potential strategies. First, they can resort to a cyber intrusion into India's nuclear facilities. Secondly, the tanzeems could use a conventional weapon and infuse nuclear material into it to cause a low-intensity detonation and a psychological blow to the public. Out of the two, the first one seems more prominent and Indian security agencies must enhance cyber capabilities. An important aspect for India to work on would be to evolve a framework on how to respond if the adversary resorts to a nuclear catastrophe.

CANISTERISATION OF INDIA'S NUCLEAR ARSENALS AND INDIA'S NEW NUCLEAR SOPHISTICATION CURVE

In 2021 and 2022, India has tested Shaurya hypersonic missile and Agni-P missiles. These missile tests have triggered a flurry of analyses by strategic experts who assert that India has made improvements in the nuclear and hypersonic arsenal's level of readiness and argued that dangerous prognostications exist about these missile developments for strategic stability between India and Pakistan. While there is no official change in India's nuclear doctrine and policy of NFU, the operational posture of India's nuclear readiness has undergone a drastic shift with these tests. With the Agni-P test, India has officially entered the realm of canisterisation of missiles, which will now enable India to undertake rapid deployment because the warheads could now be mated with missiles and placed climate-controlled tubes that would prevent further damage. The canisterisation will enable India to use an ambiguous posturing against Pakistan which refuses to go for NFU doctrine and eventually nullify the asymmetric escalation posture of Pakistan.

QUESTIONS FOR PRACTICE

S. No.	Questions for practice
1.	Given the fact that both India and Pakistan are equipped with a nuclear deterrent, does not India realise the danger of cold start?
2.	Why is the nuclear and conventional arms control a 'non-issue' in the current and past talks between India and Pakistan?
3.	How do we define 'minimum' in India's nuclear doctrine of minimum credible deterrence?
4.	How far is Chinese nuclear commerce with Pakistan a violation of Chinese membership of NSG and what steps have other NSG members taken to check this?
5.	Indian disarmament policy has changed post-India's nuclear testing in 1998. Discuss the major shift in the Indian disarmament diplomacy.
6.	We must not be frightened by the bogey of foreign designs upon India and not allow the forces to turn into an octopus bleeding daily for support. Analyse words of Sardar Patel in reference to the debate of INS Arihant.

SECTION 11

India's Relationship with America

1. India's Relationship with Latin America
2. India's Relationship with the United States of America

AN OVERVIEW

The US is one of the favourite areas of the UPSC from where regular questions are asked. The questions range from defence to commercial to nuclear dimensions of diplomacy.

Potential foresight The content in this section is extremely exhaustive for readers to grasp the minute details of every aspect of diplomacy from where questions can be asked.

CHAPTER 1

India's Relationship with Latin America

LATIN AMERICA: HOW THE TERM WAS COINED

Spain and Portugal have been colonial rulers of the entire Latin American region. In fact, Spanish is the most commonly spoken language in the region. Brazil is the only Portuguese-speaking nation, surrounded by other Spanish-speaking nations. These European languages, namely Spanish, Portuguese, French, Romanian and Italian, are derived from Latin during the time of the Roman Empire in Europe. The Europeans who speak these languages are known as Latin people. In the 1860s, the French Emperor Napoleon III tried to extend his imperial control over the region. It was during his administration the term 'Latin America' was coined. Today, it is widely referred to as South America.

LOCATING LATIN AMERICA IN INDIA'S NATIONAL INTERESTS

Latin America (hereafter referred to as LA) is an emerging growth pole in the 21st century. India exercises deep cultural influence in LA. The Indian influence is seen in arts, dance, philosophy and yoga. In Brazil, yoga is very popular and yoga centres can be seen in almost every nook and corner. The Indian films resonate very well with the LA population. Initially, LA used to view India as a land of magic and mysticism, whereas today it views India as a rising power and an emerging market economy. When India became independent in 1947, it propounded the idea of non-alignment in the era of bipolarity. India, in the initial years of its independent existence, faced crises situations because of its hostile neighbours and hence, neglected LA. Thus, firstly, the Indian policy, in the initial two decades, focused on curbing threats emanating from the neighbourhood. Secondly, India also tried to use non-alignment to reconnect with countries where it had some interaction due to the presence of British in India. During this period, LA was completely neglected. India, under the British, never had extensive interaction with this region. Also, in the strategic calculus that emerged in the aftermath of its independence, LA never acted as a threat to India. Both these factors to some extent were responsible for a lack of initiative from the Indian side to pitch up the relations. Though India did establish diplomatic relations bilaterally with the countries in LA in the early 1950s, the tone of foreign policy remained low. For India, executing the ideas of decolonisation and non-alignment was a priority, but the ideas did not resonate well with the LA nations. Jawaharlal Nehru visited only one LA nation, that is, Mexico, in 1961, during his term as Prime Minister. The improvement in the relationship with LA began in 1960s. The establishment of G-77 and the United Nations Conference on Trade and Development (UNCTAD) brought about resurgence. The G-77 and UNCTAD challenged the existing global model of development dynamics and gave thrust to South–South Cooperation. These two platforms provided India and LA a common base to interact and evolve new development dynamics. As the interaction between India and LA increased, the two evolved mutual interests and this marked a new phase of cooperation moving away from the erstwhile neglect. The cooperation that began then continued to deepen and its manifestation was seen finally in the non-aligned movement (NAM). By 1983, at the NAM Summit, there was participation of fifteen states from the LA and Caribbean. Initially, the LA nations were not keen on the NAM ideas; however, what brought them into the orbit of NAM was the internal change in NAM itself. The NAM, in 1960s, began to mold itself as a platform to initiate an economic diversification in foreign policy and gradually increased its global economic assertiveness. In India, in 1960s and 1970s, there was a growing rhetoric to tilt towards leftism. The domestic campaign of Garibi Hatao, nationalisation of banks etc. and conclusion of the 1971 Treaty of Friendship and Cooperation with the USSR championed the wave of Third-Worldism and a revisionist agenda for a new dynamic of development. This led to attempts at the international level to establish a New International Economic Order, which consequently brought India and LA closer to each other. India's relations with LA states have improved in the post-Cold War period. The Indian private sector has become an immediate connector in the region. India exports tons of raw materials to LA. This helps LA to use its own private sector to use the raw material import to make finished goods and thus participate in the global supply chain. The trade quantum of India is less in comparison to China, though, a significant difference being that China exports finished goods to LA, while India provides raw material that gives it an edge to produce its own goods to sell at the global economic level. LA has also emerged as a continent of hope in Indian energy security thought. The Indian PM met his Brazilian counterpart in 2014, when he visited Brazil to participate in the BRICS Summit. Since 2014, the government of India has prioritised the development of its economy through foreign policy maneuvering, LA can hold tremendous significance for India ahead.

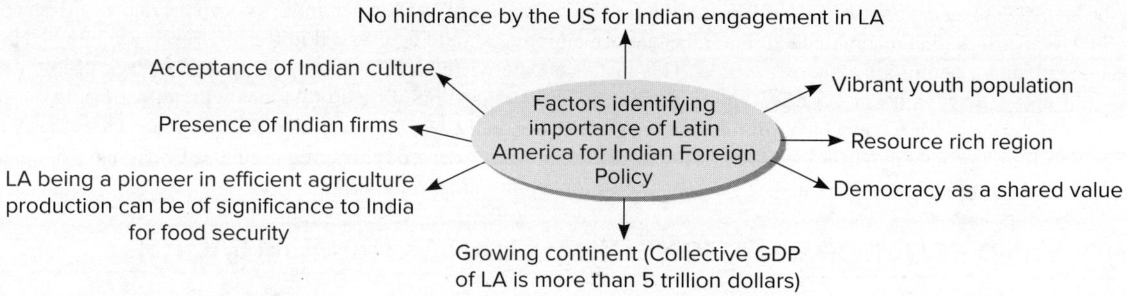

INDIA'S MERCOSUR AND FOCUS-LAC DIPLOMACY

As the Cold War ended, India attached greater significance to LA nations. It has increased bilateral political visits with the individual nations of the region. This has led to rise in bilateral trade. In 1997, the government initiated the FOCUS-LAC (Latin America and Caribbean) Project. The aim of the project was to enhance the presence of the private sector in the region. Over a period of time, a lot of Indian firms have made their presence felt in the region. Most of the countries in the region, namely Chile, Brazil and Argentina, are rich in oil and copper. They are also all pioneers in agricultural production. India has made its presence felt in not only hydrocarbons but also in IT, corporate governance and the consultancy sector. India has an FTA with Mexico, Columbia and Peru and PTA with Chile, Brazil and MERCOSUR.

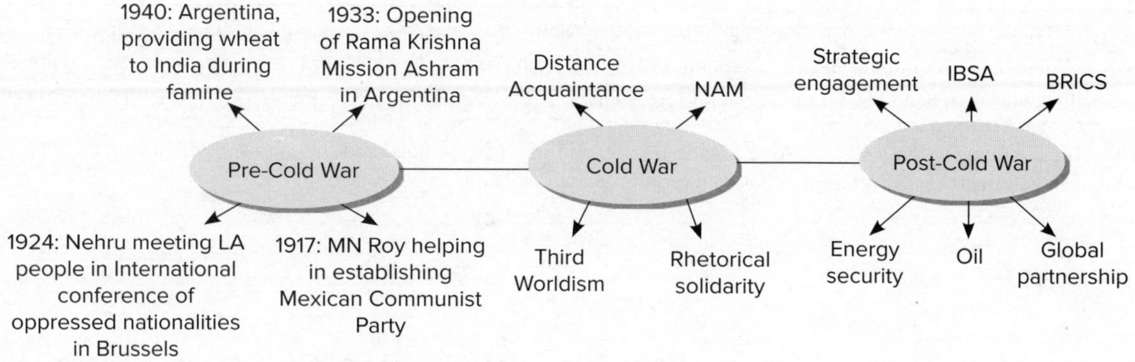

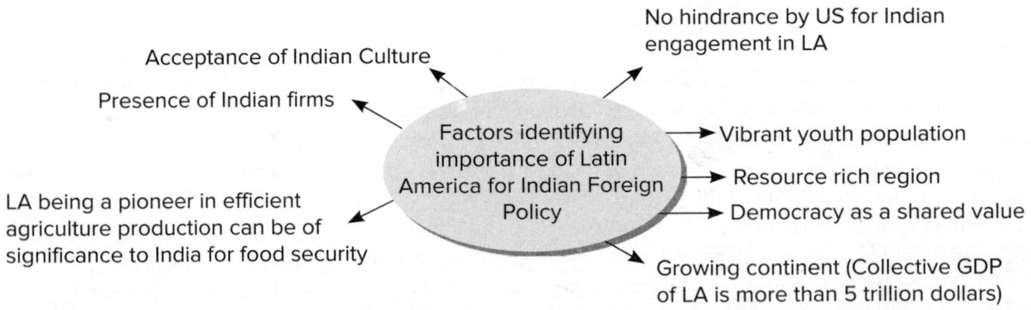

INDIA AND ARGENTINA RELATIONS: THE PAKISTAN AND KASHMIR THORN

As India marginalised LA during the Cold War, it faced two consequences for its neglect. The most immediate price was at the UNSC vote on the issue of Kashmir. After the first Indo-Pak war in 1948, when India took up the matter of Kashmir at the UNSC, Argentina recommended that Pakistani armed forces should be allowed in Kashmir even when the UNSC was negotiating a demilitarisation of the area. This instance exposed India to the consequences of its lack of initiative to build up relations with LA. As a learning measure, India prioritised building up relations with all nations to garner support for the Kashmir issue, which, till then, was neglected. Secondly, when India used military force in Goa to seek its liberation from Portugal in November 1961, it led to Brazil showering severe criticism on India as Brazil had sided with the Portuguese on the same. This instance also marked a low point in the relationship.

INDIA AND ECUADOR RELATIONS: KHALISTAN EXTREMISM FACTOR

In 1984, India closed its embassy in Quito, Ecuador. It cited lack of finances as the reason behind the decision to close down the embassy. However, in July 1985, some reports began to emerge from Ecuador. This period of 1985 was a troublesome period for India because of the 1984 Sikh riots and Khalistani extremism. Reports from Ecuador suggested that an Ecuadorian delegation had met Khalistani extremists in London and Ecuador was on the verge of giving recognition to a Khalistani government in exile. India was deeply concerned about the issue. Within a few days of India taking up the matter, the Ecuadorian administration announced that the team of people meeting Khalistani leaders in London was a private affair with the Ecuadorian government having no say in it. The issue gradually dissipated but because of the closure of the embassy in 1984 and subsequently weak bilateral relations, India could not exercise any leverage over the issue that was about to challenge Indian sovereignty on an international scale.

FUTURE CONNECTORS FOR INDIA AND LATIN AMERICA

In 2010, Argentina imposed restrictions on Chinese goods. Up till 2010, the China–Argentina trade relation never saw any swing. China had been importing a huge amount of soya oil from Argentina, which was its major export commodity. As Argentina imposed restrictions on Chinese goods entering its economy, China, in retaliation, stopped soya oil import. The Argentinean economy was badly affected, and India seized the opportunity and tripled its soya oil imports from Argentina. Thus, India coming to the rescue of Argentina in the soya oil import case bolstered the Indo-Argentina ties. Even today, a lot of Indian firms can be seen establishing their presence in Argentina.

2

CHAPTER

India's Relationship with the United States of America

COLONIAL ELEMENT OF INDIA'S RELATIONSHIP WITH THE US

As India was a British colony, the communication between India and the US, at an independent level, was impossible. It was F. D. Roosevelt who realised that India could play an important role in the World War II. According to Roosevelt, India could act as a block to resist Japanese aggression in South Asia and provide the needed resistance for war efforts. To ensure that India participates in the World War II, the nationalist leaders of India were to be taken into confidence. The nationalists stuck to one particular point—that India would support war efforts provided the British give them independence in return. Roosevelt, for that matter, took up the Indian issue with Churchill. The British did not appreciate the US prodding their affairs, which resulted in some tension in the US–British alliance. As far as the US was concerned, it was of the opinion that as the Allied powers are fighting for independence and right to self-determination (RTSD), they should also in turn liberate their colonies, which were fighting imperialism for the same reasons. In fact, the fundamental disagreement over India can be best elaborated if we look at how the US and the British viewed the Atlantic Charter (AC), which was a pivotal policy statement issued during the World War II on 14 August 1941, which defined the Allied goals for the post-war world. The leaders of the United Kingdom and the United States drafted the work and all the Allies later ratified it. The Charter stated the ideal goals of the war—no territorial aggrandisement; no territorial changes made against the wishes of the people; self-determination; restoration of self-government to those deprived of it; reduction of trade restrictions; global cooperation to secure better economic and social conditions for all; freedom from fear and want; freedom of the seas; and abandonment of the use of force, as well as disarmament of aggressor nations. Adherents of the Atlantic Charter signed the Declaration by United Nations of Allies on 1 January 1942, which became the basis for the modern United Nations. The Article 3 of the Charter advocated the idea of RTSD. The Atlantic Charter mentioned that all participating allies in the war needed to ensure that once that war would over, the people belonging to the lost territories after the war would have the RTSD. Churchill's view was that this Atlantic Charter point of RTSD held exclusively for Nazi areas won in the war. However, for Roosevelt, the Atlantic Charter was a universal proposition and also applied to territories under colonial rule. Thus, for the US, India was a rightful claimant to RTSD.

IDEOLOGICAL DIVIDE BETWEEN INDIA AND THE US DURING THE COLD WAR

The period of the Cold War subsequently remained a low phase in the Indo-US engagement. This is so because India adopted non-alignment and the US became the spreader of capitalism. As they became ideologically opposite, the relationship tensed. The ties became strained as the US brought the Cold War at the doorsteps of India by making Pakistan a member of CENTO and SEATO. This made India tilt towards USSR, which eventually made the US more suspicious of India. The US, throughout the Cold War, still tried to provide India with assistance at the economic and social level. This was due to the fact that they found synchronisation with India, as India was a democracy; which since the end of the Cold War became a 'shared value' between the two. Also, such assistance would allow the US to have presence in India and enable them to keep a check on China and prevent India to gravitate completely towards USSR. This is the reason why the US displayed willingness to support India with arms when India made a request at the time of Sino-Indian conflict in

1962. The US, however, threatened India in 1971 with nuclear retaliation in the India–Pakistan war. This has remained a scar on the bilateral ties till today with many in the 'establishment' of India remaining skeptical of the US. After 1974 Peaceful Nuclear Explosion, the US isolated India by creating the Nuclear Suppliers Group (NSG). All these prove that ties remained low in the Cold War.

INDIA AND THE USA: THE 'NATURAL ALLIES' SINCE END OF THE COLD WAR

India on Ukraine Crisis

In recent times, India has been criticised by certain segments in the US for having an independent and neutral stand on Russian invasion of Ukraine. India's stand is apparently based on a four-point agenda of respect for territorial integrity, sovereignty of states, UN Charter and international law. Today, these four points are at the core of the Indo-Pacific strategy and in this backdrop, India's strategy on Ukraine is a mirror of the Indo-Pacific thought.

The Indo-US ties have strategically deepened since the end of the Cold War. There have been three core factors that have facilitated the strategic convergence. First, when the Cold War ended, the international strategic environment changed because of the disintegration of USSR and it shifted the global and regional realities. This led the two to explore a new depth. Second, at the end of the Cold War, India opened up its economy, compelling the American businesses to look at India as a vibrant market. Third is a three million strong diaspora of India, which acts as a bridge between India and the US. The upward trajectory of the Indo-US ties began with Atal Bihari Vajpayee's era in India, which called India and the US as 'natural allies' while Obama hailing India and the USA relations as a 'Defining Partnership in the 21st Century'. The US has realised the importance of India in the Indo-Pacific region and is keen to integrate India into the new strategic space.

THE STRATEGIC ELEMENT OF INDIA AND THE US RELATIONS

India and the US relations today are determined by a new sense of strategic cooperation. A true strategic cooperation is never a relation of complete convergence but one which manages differences through dialogue and channelises the differences to create a new realm of opportunities, a realm that fits India and the US. The new areas of opportunities, the two sides identified are summed up below and elaborated in the chapter ahead.

Strategic and defence diplomacy	Energy and climate change diplomatic cooperation	Science and technology diplomacy	Health and innovation diplomatic cooperation	Education and development diplomatic cooperation

INDIA'S DEFENCE NEGOTIATION BEHAVIOUR WITH THE UNITED STATES

The first ever step of defence diplomacy between India and the US was seen in 1962 when India had a conflict with China. At that time Nehru, in a letter to John F. Kennedy, had sought US military help. The then Foreign Secretary of India, M. J. Desai, had conveyed categorically to the then US Ambassador to India, John Kenneth Galbraith, that India would seek military aid from the US provided that the US does not insist on alliance formation. When China came down the Himalayas in 1962, President Kennedy sent Ambassador Harriman and Carl Kaysen to see whether they could get Pakistan to withdraw its forces from the Indo-Pakistan border, so that they could be sent to the Chinese border. Prime Minister Nehru was supposed to have told Harriman and Kaysen that Pakistan would not oblige whereas, amusingly, Finance Minister Morarji Desai told them that they should not worry because "even if the Chinese occupied India", that would only be "for maybe a thousand years" and that eventually "India would throw them out". The US agreed to provide military support to be airlifted to India. However, the two sides perceived this initial cooperation very differently. The US saw the Sino-Indian conflict as an exercise that would allow the US to explore a common working ground with India. For the Indians, it was limited assistance and much lesser than what they expected, which also eventually was stopped in 1965 when another war with Pakistan broke out. For India, the cooperation was insignificant in contrast to Indian cooperation with the USSR. Since the end of the Cold War, both India and the US have steadily improved their security cooperation and both sides have signed many security agreements over time. In 2020, the US blocked the attempt of Pakistan to place the name of an Indian engineer, Venu Madhava Dongara, before the UNSC 1267 Sanctions Committee.

INDIA'S DEFENCE AGREEMENTS WITH UNITED STATES AND FOUNDATION OF DEFENCE DIPLOMACY

Agreement Number 1: Kicklighter Proposals 1991

In 1991, the commander of the US Army Pacific, Claude Kicklighter, sent a proposal to the chief of Indian Army General Sunith Francis Rodriguez. These proposals were known as the Kicklighter proposals and envisaged bilateral visits, training and conferences between India and the US. An important dimension also was the participation of India in regional conferences sponsored by the US. A new defence policy group was also established. The approval for the Kicklighter proposals had to come from Indian Ministry of Defence. The clearances came very slowly and painfully.

Agreement Number 2: Agreement Minute on Defence Relations 1995

In 1995, the two sides concluded an agreement called the agreement minute on defence relations or framework for defence cooperation. The US officials were again puzzled as this agreement too was negotiated by the civilian bureaucracy in India and was again slow in process and was just concluded a month before the visit of Secretary Perry from the US to India in 1995.

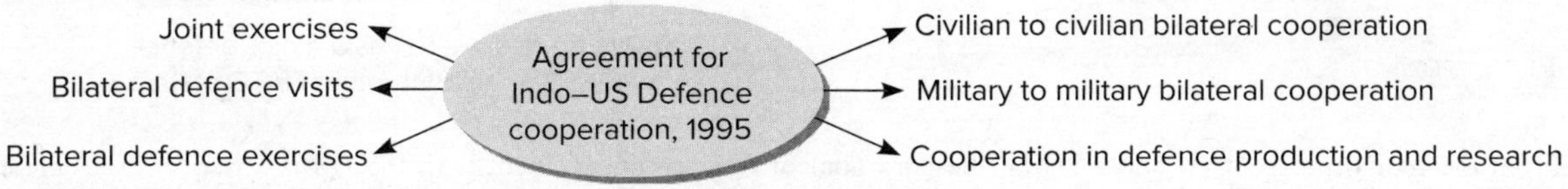

Agreement Number 3: General Security of Military Information Agreement (GSMIA) 2002

In 2002, GSMIA was signed. In Indian Ocean, a tsunami occurred in 2004 and it struck Sri Lanka, Indonesia, Maldives and other areas, compelling the Indian Navy to launch a mega disaster relief operation. The US appreciated the Indian Navy's swiftness while India appreciated the American Navy's professionalism and logistics. The two decided to work together to provide immediate post-disaster relief.

Agreement Number 4: Bilateral Security Cooperation 2004

The joint experience of 2004 tsunami gave rise to emerging bilateral security cooperation, which had never been witnessed before. This led the two sides to establish cooperation at the dimension of naval diplomacy with humanitarian applications.

Agreement Number 5: India–US Defence Agreement 2005

Though framework for defence cooperation had been established in 1995, at the time of implementation there was a perceived gap in the objectives that each side intended to achieve. For the Indian civilian bureaucracy, technology access was the core objective while the Indian military envisaged access to specialised courses and equipment. On the other hand, the US officials wanted military contacts with future interoperability as the objective. The defence relations were further enhanced in 2005 when the two sides concluded a framework agreement where both, for the first time, accepted common interests and shared beliefs in values such as freedom, democracy and the rule of law. There was a decision taken to give a public character to the emerging bilateral relationship. The 2005 agreement identified thirteen broad activities that both sides decided to envisage bilaterally. A dimension of cooperation in missile defence was added in the 2005 agreement.

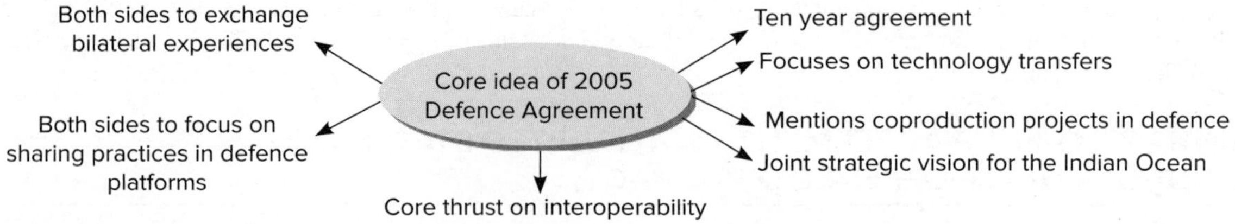

Agreement Number 6: Defence Technology and Trade Initiative 2013

In 2013, the US Deputy Secretary of Defence, Ashton Carter envisaged a defence technology initiative (DTI) with India. India perceived it as majorly a DTI; while for the US, it was more a defence trade initiative. The initiative was finally called the DTTI or defence technology and trade initiative. The DTTI enabled the US to develop insight into Indian defence negotiation behaviour.

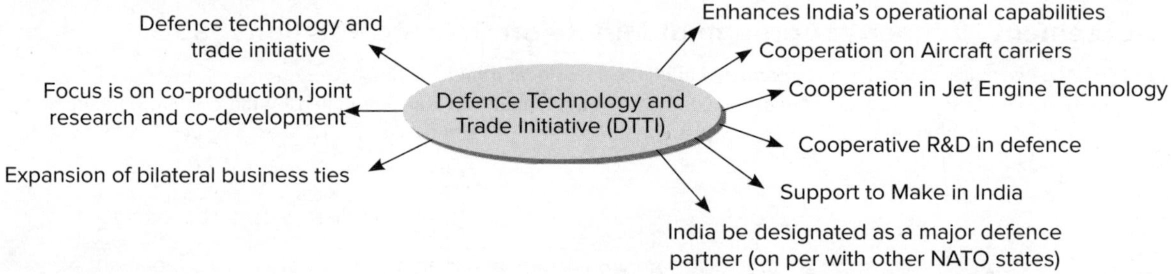

From the Indian perspective, under DTTI, the core goal of defence engagement with the US is based on transfer of sophisticated military technology from the US to India for supporting domestic development of defence equipment. India believes that any military diplomacy with a foreign state should assist the Indian defence industry to undertake production of technology in India. For India, the maintenance of a credible strategic autonomy is possible only if India develops a capable defence industry domestically. For the US, its defence diplomacy with India is to establish a long-term relationship that would allow both India and the US to jointly address contingencies in the region that may arise in the future. For the US, if India purchases defence products from them and uses their equipment, then interoperability gets drastically enhanced. For this, the US favours more bilateral military exercises to establish technical interoperability. The DTTI provides for a fulfilling attribution in cyberspace in areas of artificial intelligence, cyber security and 5G technologies. India, in recent times, has started positioning itself as a net security provider in the Indian Ocean region as an extension to India's quest of regional supremacy. Indian officials believe that any interoperability with the US will be an unwanted intrusion into sovereign Indian space. Indians favour a one-time transaction over establishing a partnership with the US, as they still perceive the US as an unreliable supplier. This is because, as per the US laws, the US Congress, even before the transaction is consummated, can block or amend a sale agreement through legislation. A precedent can be cited in the way, after the 1974 nuclear test by India, the US halted fuel supply to the Tarapur Plant despite a thirty-year supply agreement. Though the bilateral Indo-US defence trade does not require licensing anywhere, there is a perception amongst the Indian side that the US Arms Export Control Act will act as a burden on defence purchases made by India.

The DTTI is driven by a shared commitment to defence trade, elimination of bureaucratic obstacles, promotion of a collaborative technology exchange, strengthening of cooperative research and enablement of co-production and co-development of defence systems for sustainment and modernisation of the military.

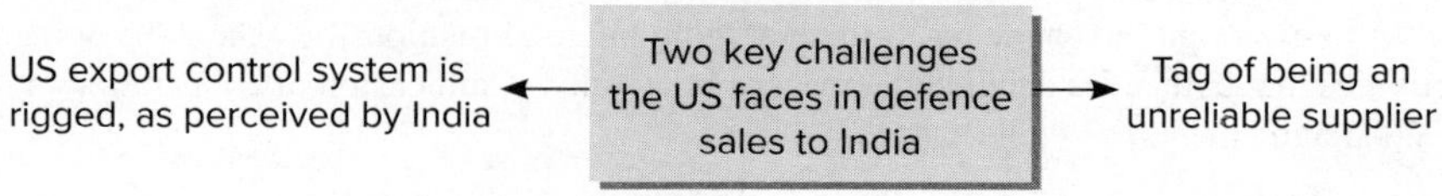

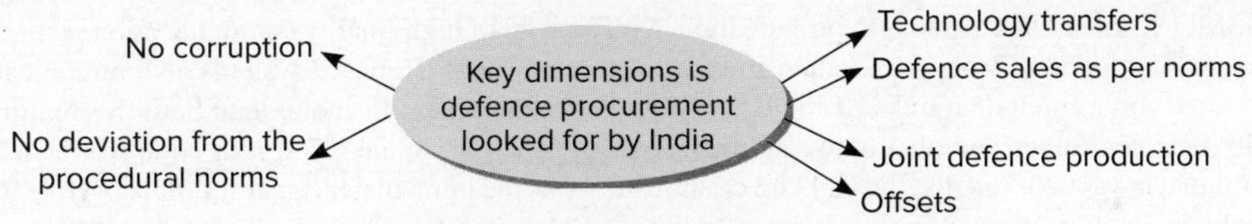

Agreement Number 7: Strategic and Commercial Dialogue

The Obama administration started it and the focus of the dialogue was to create synergies at defence and foreign diplomacy level. The strategic and commercial dialogue (SCD) was eventually replaced by the two + two dialogue in 2018.

Agreement Number 8: India–US Defence Agreement 2015

With the coming of the Modi government in 2014, India and the US concluded a ten-year framework agreement for defence cooperation in 2015. What makes the 2015 agreement different from the 2005 agreement is its focus on more areas of cooperation. The diagram below shows the 2015 India–US defence framework.

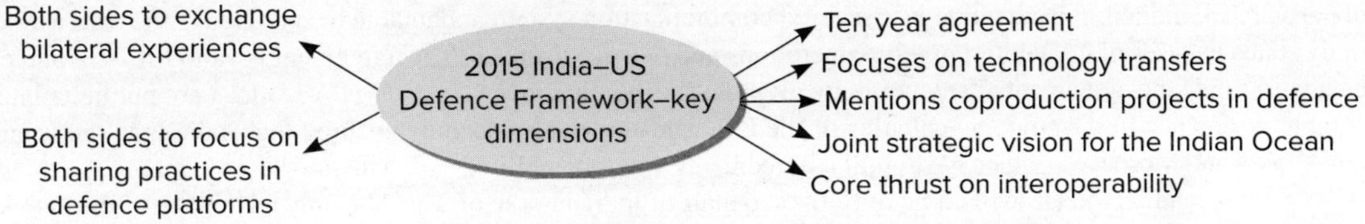

Agreement Number 9: Foundational Military Agreements 2016

The strategic convergence is designed as part of functional military relationship and foundational military agreements of the US. In 2016, the US proposed India to sign these agreements. The defence products from the US come with their own set of obligations for security requirements. The foundational military agreement is one of the forms of these obligations. The US has four of them. The first is General Security of Military Information Agreement (GSMIA) which India and the US signed in 2002. The second is Logistics Exchange Memorandum of Agreement (LEMOA). The third is Communication Compatibility and Security Agreement (COMCASA). The fourth is Basic Exchange and Cooperation Agreement for geo-spatial cooperation (BECA), for which negotiations have begun since 2020.

Agreement Number 10: Major Defence Partner Tag to India

The Obama administration designated India as a 'Major Defence Partner' in 2016, which makes India eligible to access US defence technologies at par with the closest allies of the US of NATO plus five. This put India into an elite club of the US allies (of NATO and bilateral alliances) that are allowed to access premium US technology, along with co-production and collaboration.

Agreement Number 11: Logistics Exchange Memorandum of Agreement 2016

The LEMOA is an agreement that is broadly related to cooperation in naval logistical exchange and troops stationing. For India, the LEMOA has been modified to keep in mind Indian concerns; for instance, the agreement ensures that it warrants no foreign troops of the US to be stationed in India. The agreement only envisages refueling and birthing facilities for aircrafts and naval ships without a huge rigmarole of clearances being involved from different ministries. This will enhance joint cooperation in humanitarian relief of the two at the naval level.

Agreement Number 12: Communications Compatibility and Security Agreement

Americans feel that Communication Interoperability and Security Memorandum Agreement (CISMOA) will facilitate interoperability in defence communications. Though the US preferred to sign CISMOA, India had raised objections to its name and as a result, the US changed the name to Communications Compatibility and Security Agreement (COMCASA).

The aim of CISMOA, now COMCASA, is to provide India with transfer of high-quality communication security equipment that will facilitate interoperability between Indian and the US forces. These US based systems of communication security equipment are used for secured data links. If the US will give this equipment to India, then both the countries can seek interoperability between forces and also between other countries that use same US origin equipment. In the strategic community of India, it was believed that the Doklam crisis (2017) was the immediate trigger for India to go for COMCASA. During the Doklam crisis (explained in the chapter "India and China Relations"), India had no intelligence on the troop movement by China. It was only after the troops came close to the sight of the soldiers on the border did India got to know. This was the time when Indian strategic community realised the significance of the US intelligence on the Chinese troop movement had such an arrangement was in place. India has been using less secure communication security equipment and the US feels that because of such lesser secure requirements, a functional military relation with India will be difficult to build. As the US has granted India a tag of 'Major Defence Partner' where it will sell high-end defence technology to India. The US realises that absence of COMCASA can be a hurdle for it to sell MH-60R multi-role helicopters and twenty-two MQ-9 Sea Guardian (which will create 2000 jobs in America), High Altitude Long Endurance (HALE) drones (a weapon sold previously to NATO allies only) which India wants (to prevent any misadventure by China in Indian Ocean and another repeat of 26/11) as they are dependent upon very high-quality secure data and communication systems. The main purpose of the US to push India to go for COMCASA and to ensure that its technologies at the military level are not leaked to any third party. Also, India is dependent on less secured communication system and unable to share real-time data with other friendly states in cases of humanitarian relief operations and defence exercise. The agreement is valid till 2028 and either side can terminate the agreement at any point, by giving a six-month notice. The COMCASA does not put India into any high table of defence in the strategic calculus of the US. The agreement has only ensured that India is in the league of states—Egypt and Morocco—which have similar agreements. Interoperability is just a natural by-product of the agreement. This does not mean that the US will come to fight on behalf of India in case of war. The only advantage of the agreement is that it will facilitate the information sharing that will help in the war exercises of the two states. Secondly, the US will share real-time sensitive operational information used from ground to air communication. The arrangement will also allow India real-time access to US intelligence and real-time imagery. As per some military officials of India, the singing of COMCASA has compromised India's strategic integrity. This is because the US has always pushed COMCASA as an attempt to balance China, compelling India into 'anti-China' logic, which India is not comfortable with. However, India will now be in a position to have access to real-time intelligence on troop mobilisation by its adversaries, which it did not have during Doklam crisis. India realises that US communication equipment is intrusive. It violates Indian sovereignty, as US inspectors, under COMCASA, will have a right to inspect Indian bases that will install such communication equipment. The US have a similar agreement with South Korea and the language of the agreement with South Korea is highly intrusive. Thus, some experts in India feel that India has implicitly accepted the extraterritorial application of American laws. This is at variance with end-user monitoring agreement (EUMA) between India and the USA in 2009. The EUMA stated that US inspectors would not inspect Indian bases about the status of both. The government has not clarified anything. India also feels that COMCASA equipment will not be compatible to Russian and indigenous Indian military platforms. India's concern is that if they use COMCASA equipment, then the US could monitor Indian activities and this may violate India's sovereignty. Thus, India favours checks and balances to be inbuilt which address Indian concerns. The US has modified the CISMOA to COMCASA where it has categorically asserted that the COMCASA communication links will apply only to the weapons that the US supplies. The US will not be able to share Indian data, from Indian platforms, with any other country and will not access data without permission. The US is also concerned that as India has purchased Russian S-400 Triumph air defence system—a system so advanced that it can track all aircrafts, UAVs and missiles—it may conflict with the US as S-400 can allow Russia to access US information as S-400 Triumph is a mega complex of radars, control systems and missiles. The US has reasons to worry because S-400 can map America's superior F-35 fighters (which have a unique feature of low observability character). The third concern is that if the US installs any communication system in India under COMCASA, it would affect and compromise the secrecy of military installations in India. Some experts have raised a question that as the US is not going to anyway stand behind India in case of a future conflict, why is such an agreement even needed? The US will ensure that if it provides any equipment under the agreement, such equipment will be operational all the time. This is an important point for India because it ensures that in future, if it has a conflict with another state, then the US will not shut off COMCASA equipment. The data encryption and decryption codes of equipment under COMCASA will be of the US origin. Technically, this means that the US will be able to access Indian data. But the Indian negotiators in RAW were able to bargain that the US would not share data they generate from Indian platforms with any third country or entity without the authorised consent by India. In fact, India has requested the US to devise encryption and decryption codes exclusively for the use of India.

Agreement Number 13: Indo-US Strategic Trade Authorisation (STA): From STA-2 to STA-1

Since 1974, after India conducted the Peaceful Nuclear Explosion (PNE), the US tried to deny India with high technology. This changed after the 2008 Indo-US nuclear deal, under which the US decided to provide high technology to India. Whenever US exports defence technologies of (civilian and military) dual use (present in the commerce control list and munitions list maintained by the Department of State) to any state, there are two factors looked into. The first is 'regional stability' of the state. The second is 'political determination' to provide the technology. In 2011, to ease out transfers of defence technologies of dual use and create jobs, the Obama administration carried out a comprehensive review of the US export control systems. The Obama administration created a new concept known as STA that was aimed at a license free and license exempt regime. This led to creation of STA-1, STA-2 and commerce control lists (dual use list). The states that were not a part of these lists could apply for a license for the items that were mentioned in the commerce control list. STA-1 (36 states) and STA-2 have created hierarchies of states under which the US would certify a state as a 'good country' (one which would not contribute to proliferation). STA-1 includes those states that have an impeccable non-proliferation record and are trusted allies of the US who are exempt from licensing regime for dual use technologies from the US. STA-2 states do enjoy licensing exemptions but cannot access dual use technologies from the US. India was in the STA-2 list till 2018 before being elevated to STA-1. Then there are states that are outside STA-1 and STA-2 and cannot access American high technologies. There are exceptions like Albania (NATO ally in STA-2), Israel (not in STA-1), Philippines and Pakistan (non-NATO allies of the US is in no list). The jump from STA-2 to STA-1 is a great leap for India, which will provide India with access to high technology and commerce. There are two major benefits for India. First, the industries can setup manufacturing bases in India and need not worry about licenses anymore. Second, a third country can come to India; setup a manufacturing unit in it with import of high technology from the US, with great ease. The designation of India in the STA-1 category is a 'reaffirmation' of India's 'impeccable record' of being a non-proliferator and both states through this have been able to overcome a 'long arc' of 'hesitation of history'.

Agreement Number 14: Indo-US Two Plus Two Dialogues of 2018

The strategic and commercial dialogue (SCD) was replaced by 2+2 dialogue. Initially, India was reluctant to go for 2+2 dialogue because it perceived such a format alien to any diplomatic or strategic intercourse. The 2+2 dialogue, between the defence and the foreign ministers of the two states, is a mechanism to deepen strategic, defence and security cooperation. During the first meeting in 2018, the two sides concluded various agreements, as mentioned in the 'Joint Statement on the Inaugural India–US 2+2 Ministerial Dialogue'.

1. COMCASA (as explained above).
2. Memorandum of Intent (MoI) was signed between the US Defence Innovation Unit and the Indian Defence Innovation Organisation.
3. Agreement for Industrial Security Annex was contemplated. It is an agreement that will allow the US government to share classified information to boost defence manufacturing in India.
4. Agreement to bring India in the Counter ISIS Finance Group (CIFG), which is an international group to degrade and defeat the ISIS. This will involve cooperation at the level of intelligence sharing, counter terrorism and cyber security. The Indian Intelligence Bureau is the nodal agency to coordinate with the US Terrorist Screening Centre, administered by the FBI.
5. India was able to secure a waiver under CAATSA (*an American law which sanctions countries in the world that deal in financial transactions with Iran, North Korea and Russia*) for its dealings with Russia and Iran.

The 2+2 dialogue has indeed opened up a 'new era in defence and strategic engagement between India and US' and the outcomes are rightly touted as two plus two turning five. The US has established US Naval Forces Central Command (NAVCENT), which is in Bahrain and India has been included as an official member state.

Agreement Number 15: Indian Ocean Cooperation and Training Exercise 2019

In December 2019, the signing of the MoI between the US Defence Innovation Unit (DIU) and the Indian Defence Innovation Organisation–Innovations for Defence Excellence (DIO–iDEX) had also set the roadmap for possible defence research on a sustained basis. To strengthen cooperation in the Indo-Pacific region, the two sides had launched Indian Ocean Cooperation and Training Exercise in 2019. It would enable India and the US to jointly strengthen the capabilities of the states in the Indian Ocean to combat regional issues ranging from piracy to trafficking to terrorism.

Agreement Number 16: Indo-US Two Plus Two Dialogues

In 2019, during the 2+2 dialogue, the US announced that India would be stationing an Indian Liaison Officer in NAVCENT. The NAVCENT is responsible for anti-piracy operations and counterterrorism in areas ranging from Red Sea to Arabian Sea and the Persian Gulf. The presence of India in NAVCENT would enable India to play a larger role in the Indian Ocean region. In the dialogue, the two sides decided to make tri-services exercise Tiger Triumph an annual event. In the dialogue, the two sides agreed to undertake greater information sharing, expand defence trade, place defence liaison officials in each other's territories and conclude defence-enabling agreements. Till now, India engaged with the US Pacific Command on maritime issues. Since 2020, India has expanded the naval cooperation and included cooperation with the US Centcom and Africa Command as well. This has given India a wide access on multilateral engagement from West to East.

Agreement Number 17: Industrial Security Annex 2020

The two sides also concluded Industrial Security Annex (ISA). The Modi government had initiated the 'Make in India' programme. Under this, India wanted the US to transfer technology to India and manufacture defence products in India under license or other mechanisms. This required the US to bring to India the complete military industrial ecosystem. Such an ecosystem would not only support the nascent Indian defence-manufacturing sector but also help ease pressures on overburdened Indian defence public sector; which are overburdened in meeting past orders and receptive to embrace any new technology. The ISA provided the momentum for collaboration because it would facilitate a regime for technology transfer and facilitate domestic capacity building. The ISA would facilitate exchange of classified military information between the two states. It would provide protection to the American firms involved in defence manufacturing and create a positive regime for harnessing and developing technology in India. Tata Boeing Aerospace Ltd. and Tata Lockheed Martin Aerospace structures Ltd. are positive templates for a successful ISA ahead.

Defence Sales from the US to India

Just before the visit of Donald Trump to India in February 2020, the two sides signed 3.5 USD billion worth defence deals. India decided to purchase 30 heavy-duty armed helicopters. This included 24 MH-60 Romeo multi-mission helicopters, armed with MK-54 torpedoes and precision kill rockets, for the navy (which would arm the navy to check Chinese forays in Indian Ocean) and 6 Apache attack helicopters for the army. By 2022, army would get six choppers armed with stinger air-to-air missiles and Hellfire Longbow air-to-ground missiles. India had already purchased 22 Apache attack helicopters for the army in 2015. In 2020, the US also sold Integrated Air Defence Weapon System (IADWS) worth 1.8 USD billion to India.

Agreement Number 18: Basic Exchange and Cooperation Agreement for Geo-spatial Cooperation 2020

The Basic Exchange and Cooperation Agreement for Geo-spatial Cooperation would allow India to access advanced satellite and topographical data for long-range navigation and missile targeting. The agreement was under negotiation and India signed it in 2020.

STRUCTURAL PROBLEMS AND ISSUES IN INDIAN DEFENCE NEGOTIATION STYLE WITH THE US

Structural Problem The difference in the structure of defence establishments in India and the US often create different worldviews, thereby, at times, causing friction in the process of security cooperation. In India, the civilian bureaucrats, often with no experience in national security, have an upper hand; while in the US, it is the military officials who have an upper hand in military diplomacy.

Negotiation Strategy Problem The US officials face difficulty in negotiating prices with Indians. Indian Defence Procurement Policies have no concept related to life cycle costs. The US equipment is costly. While the pre-bid phase of acquiring technology is on, India favour deals on the basis of fixed costs. The US suppliers, on the other hand, assert that they do offer expensive equipment but later, the costs can come down when it comes to contracts for long-term maintenance as they see a product through its complete life cycle. Thus, the US suppliers favour 'life cycle costs'-based bidding whereas the Indians are skeptical about such moves. Furthermore, India favours more customisation of equipment owing to the broad variety of conditions in which the Indian military operates. The Israeli and French bidders excel in coordination over their US counterparts. India is also very particular in ensuring that bidders meet all specifications at the evaluation stage—even if one specification is not complied with, India rejects the bidder.

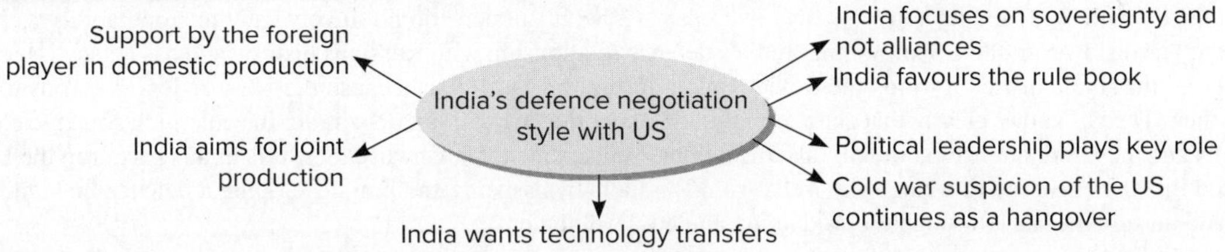

AREAS OF FUTURE DEFENCE COOPERATION

There is one-way India and the US can deepen their defence cooperation, which can also help address certain deep-rooted fears Indians have of the US. The F-16 aircrafts are manufactured by an American firm called Lockheed Martin. Today, the US military is no longer requiring F-16 aircrafts. The US Air Force will only require servicing of existing F-16s till 2040. The Lockheed Martin F-16 aircrafts are highly needed by Indian Air Force. They are also used by 25 other states, including Pakistan. India and the US can explore a new opportunity here. As Lockheed Martin does not have much business left in the US, it is planning to shift out its entire F-16 production line to India. Tata Advanced Systems have shown an interest in collaborating with Lockheed Martin. If the two states can reach an understanding where Lockheed Martin shifts the production line to India, this will be a game changer. India will not only produce Lockheed Martin F-16s (a boost to Make in India), but also would become a global hub for manufacturing and services of the same. As of now, India is one of the biggest buyers of American defence products. However, the US should note that the defence relation cannot only be a buyer–seller relationship and India cannot be a junior partner in the Indo-Pacific region. The US has to undertake technology transfers and focus on aggressive co-production, possible after ISA-2019, to ensure that India emerges as a hub of defence products for buyers in Asia and Africa.

India and the US 2+2 Dialogue 2022

India and the US defence diplomacy has now acquired a new character. The two sides have identified new opportunities that extend the operational reach of bilateral militaries across the expanse of the Indo-Pacific region. This is significant because an analysis of agreements of bilateral defence cooperation till now indicated an urge of India to strengthen its own defence segment but now India aims to develop its military for a larger role in the indo-Pacific realm. The 2022 Dialogue saw India and the US concluding MoU on space situational awareness that would strengthen the bilateral engagement in outer space cooperation. The two have also concluded agreements to enhance warfighting capabilities in cyber domain.

RUSSIA FACTOR IN INDIA–US RELATIONS AND ANALYSIS OF THE CAATSA CONUNDRUM

For India, the S-400 offers an unmatched long-range requirement for its air force. It has the capability to constrain the air operations of the adversary within their own airspace and can destroy high-value air assets of adversary with a secondary missile capability, which is way beyond the capability of the US Patriot PAC-3. The issue with the US is not just a technologically advanced S-400 with its friends and allies but such technologies having capabilities to impede American technology transfers and joint operations. The CAATSA law has been a deadlock between India and the US for a long time. The US has not been happy with India's decision to purchase S-400 from Russia and general defence engagement with Russia. The law is not designed to punish countries that have maintenance requirements from Russia but to prevent addition of significant high-end technologies from Russia. The law does provide for exceptional waivers that its friends and allies might require but not a blanket ban that India seems to expect from the US. It is equally important to understand that CAATSA does not only apply to S-400 but even other procurements of India from Russia. They include multiple agreements that India has signed with Russia since 2016 such as supply and local production of four Project 11356 frigates for navy, procurement of 21 Mig-29 and 12 Sukhoi-30 fighters and domestic production of Russian AK-203 assault rifles. While fighters and frigates do come under the "capable contemporary platforms" which are prescribed under CAATSA, but India seems to exercise the "grey area" to argue that the acquisitions of fighters and frigates only add on to capacities of existing platforms built by Russia and are not under any contemporary platforms criteria. The point is further explained by India when it argues that the defence exercises done by India and Russia are not just lesser in number than they do with West and its allies but also that exercises with Russians do not involve any interoperability as it does with the West. However, the US knows that India's defence relationship with Russia is historic and has legacy issues. The US agrees that India drifted towards the Soviet Union during the Cold War because the US was less generous towards India then. The US knows clearly that sanctioning India under the law will not only strain the emerging strategic element of India and the US relationship but will take the strategic engagement back by decades. It is in this backdrop the US has realised that the only way to wean away India from Russia is by assisting India in developing a defence manufacturing base and nurture the same through co-production and co-development.

TOWARDS AN INDIA AND US CONVERGENCE IN COUNTERTERRORISM

The counterterrorism cooperation between India and the US has been a new chapter in the relationship and can be traced to end of the Cold War. In 2000, the two signed the Indo-US Statement on Joint Working Group on counterterrorism. This was further built in 2010 when the two concluded Strategic Dialogue and in 2011, conceptualised a Homeland Security Dialogue. In 2011, an Indo-US Counterterrorism Cooperation Initiative was launched and in 2015, a Declaration on counterterrorism was eventually signed. In 2019, an Indo-US counterterrorism in Table Top Exercise for QUAD Countries was envisaged. Even though the two nations have clearly articulated the areas of convergence but the convergence has not seen any policy outcome because the security environment in which the two countries operate are different. One plausible reason that explains this divergence is ambitions of state. The US is a global hegemon and looks at security threats from the globe that emerge to challenge the American hegemony. The Indian side, on the other hand, does aspire to be a global superpower but is presently focused on becoming a regional hegemon first. In this sense, the Americans are driven by a normative approach and favour to create broad global norms that prevent hegemonic threats but India is more concerned on tackling terrorism sponsored by Pakistan in Kashmir and rest of India. In recent times, India and the US have tried to achieve cooperation and synergy through a bilateral approach that includes designating Hizbul Mujahedeen as a Foreign Terrorist Organisation, oversee the designation of Masood Azhar under UN 1267 List and designation of Pakistan in grey list of the FATF. The US, however, remains more concerned on not isolating Pakistan, which remains the fulcrum of anti-India terrorism. In this backdrop, as the US fixation on Pakistan weakens gradually, India must focus on exploring counterterrorism consensus in the Indo-Pacific region and the Indo-US Counterterrorism in Table Top Exercise for QUAD Countries should be seen as the beginning of a new norm.

JOE BIDEN'S INDO-PACIFIC STRATEGY

After being appointed as President, Joe Biden announced his Indo-Pacific strategy. The strategy reflects the geopolitical shifts in the region and importance America attaches for regional security and prosperity. The document unveiled reflects how the US views regional complexities, opportunities, challenges and how it, intends to maintain a rules-based order with its friends and allies. In the document, China has assumed the most significant presence owing to its material capabilities and expansion of capacities in South China Sea, East China Sea, border with India and Pacific Island presence. The document assesses that the Chinese have a desire to solidify their regional sphere of influence in the Indo-Pacific region and aspires to become the most influential power in the world; however, the US seeks to limit the assertive behaviour of the Chinese through creation of minilaterals in the Indo-Pacific region with like-minded countries and strengthen the norms, rules, institutions in the region than adopting any confrontational approaches. Such a strategy, which is not confrontational but seeks to compel Chinese to adopt a rules-based behaviour is a normative strategy built on multilateralism. In this backdrop, it is clear that the larger approach is not to change China but shape the strategic environment in which the Chinese operate. The advantage of such a normative approach is to create spaces where cooperation with the Chinese in non-traditional security arenas such as climate change, terrorism and non-proliferation is an open domain. The Indo-Pacific Action Plan is built on certain elements like...

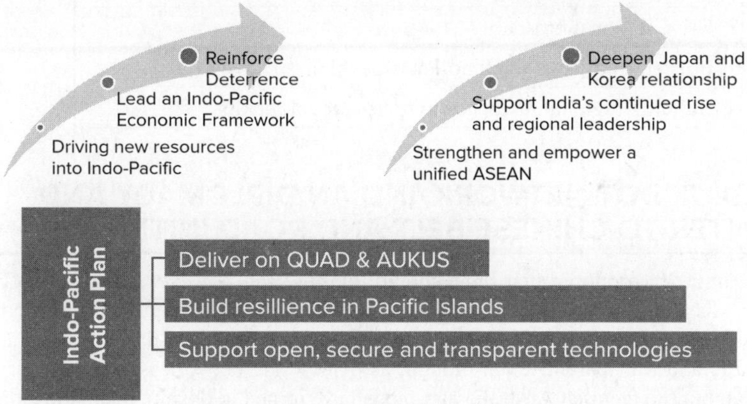

Indo-Pacific Economic Framework

It is one of the action plans of the Indo-Pacific strategy of the US which focuses on facilitating high-standards trade, governing the emerging digital economy, improving supply–chain resiliency and security, catalysing investment in transparent and high-standards infrastructures, and building digital connectivity with the ultimate aim of doubling down the economic ties to the region while contributing to broadly shared the Indo-Pacific opportunity.

In this sense, the approach of Biden is different from Donald Trump and the difference can be succinctly captured in the table below.

Element	Donald Trump's Indo-Pacific Strategy	Joe Biden's Indo-Pacific Strategy
Indo-Pacific Strategy	Calls out Chinese as an authoritarian state that resorts to unfair practices to achieve economic dominance and exploit vacuums left by the US since end of the Cold War. In Trump's view, the US must enhance its own military capabilities to tackle China.	Engage with allies and friends in the region based on shared values and improve their levels of interoperability, information sharing, capacity building and preparedness across the spectrum of conflict.
Role envisaged for India	India to emerge as a counter to Chinese assertions in the region.	India to emerge as a net security provider first and a preferred security partner eventually in the region.
India's perception	Welcomed the relevance of India but reluctant to play a counter to Chinese.	Positive embrace of the idea as it reflects India's global power aspirations.

STRATEGIC RELEVANCE OF INDIA IN THE INDO-PACIFIC STRATEGY UNDER BIDEN ADMINISTRATION

With a vast population, large economy and a robust military, after China, India has occupied a significant mention in the Indo-Pacific strategy of Joe Biden as India has cemented its position as a country with a capacity to stand up to China. India also is a natural partner in American thinking of the Indo-Pacific region because of its emphasis on a rules-based order and a deep willingness to rise in the new world order being shaped in the geographical realm. Given India's shared values and concerns with the US, its friends and allies in the region, India stands to complement the momentum the US intends to conceptualise in the Indo-Pacific region. In this backdrop, the strategy of Joe Biden not only realises the importance of India in the Indo-Pacific region but also supports the leadership of India to position the country as a net security provider and then a preferred security partner. This explains that the US is willing to engage with India in Quadrilateral Security Dialogue, despite announcing AUKUS because it sees the QUAD as a plurilateral grouping that envisions a free, open, transparent and inclusive the Indo-Pacific region. In any case, the Indo-Pacific region will remain a realm of strategic contestations.

India is engaging with the US in the Indo-Pacific region at five levels.

Level	Dimension of Engagement
1.	Advancing free and open the Indo-Pacific region
2.	Building diplomatic connections within the region and beyond
3.	Drive regional prosperity
4.	Bolster security of the Indo-Pacific region
5.	Building regional resilience to transnational threats

Challenges to Biden's Indo-Pacific Strategy

Biden's strategy in the Indo-Pacific does reflect the relevance the US attaches to the region and the power plays here but the events in Eastern Europe, Russia–Ukraine crisis and declining relevance of NATO in Europe have raised questions on how the US would maintain consistency to realise this vision in the Indo-Pacific region. An analysis of history has shown that whenever the US has become pre-occupied with other theatres, the Chinese have exploited the US vacuum and enhanced its military and economic capacities. There are murmurs in the global intelligence circles that the entire Russia–Ukraine crisis in 2022 could have been scripted at the behest of Beijing and executed by Russia to divert the focus of the US from the Indo-Pacific region.

THE BLUE DOT NETWORK, INDIAN DIPLOMACY AND COUNTER TO CHINESE BELT AND ROAD INITIATIVE

The US, in 2020, proposed that India should join the Blue Dot Network (BDN). The network was announced by the US in 2019 and was designed to certify infrastructure projects. It would provide certification of projects being market-driven, financially sustainable and transparent. Even though, as of now the network is merely a vision statement, but the fact that Australia and Japan have joined it, despite being the largest trading partners of China, reveals something about the network. The prime idea of the network was to mount a multilateral pressure on Chinese Belt and Road Initiative (BRI). The BDN is only a certification authority and unlike the BRI, it does not extend loans or finances for projects. The BDN remains focused on assessing the sustainability and fiscal prudence of the projects. India has not responded on its willingness to be a part of the network but was likely to join the BDN in 2020. The reason why India should join the BDN is important to be understood. The US Build Act has started improving the American performance in the projects overseas. As India has overseas developmental projects, the US firms can give Blue Dots to Indian firms involved in the projects and this can enhance the sustainability of the projects in future.

DIEGO GARCIA: A CONUNDRUM BETWEEN INDIA AND THE US

The Diego Garcia is in Chagos archipelago in Indian Ocean and a base of the US military since the Cold War. Mauritius has claimed the rights of the Chagos and the same have been upheld by the International Court of Justice and United Nations General Assembly. In the resolution at the UNGA, the US and the British had hoped that as a regional player in Indian Ocean, India would side with the US but India unequivocally supported "people striving for decolonisation" and favoured the claims of Mauritius. The behaviour displayed by India over the issue has created ripples in the Euro-Atlantic circles but India has championed itself as a leader of decolonised world once again as it did in the Cold War. The Indian behaviour has also asserted that India would prefer to champion South–South cooperation over the Euro-Atlantic cooperation. However, the issue is also a debilitating dilemma for India because at one place it has to demonstrate its closeness to an important Indian Ocean player, Mauritius, and on the other hand, cannot derail the strategic convergences with the US, which have been witnessing an upward swing. For India, one thing is clear that it cannot favour an American military presence over the choice of indigenous people.

INDIA'S NUCLEAR DIPLOMACY NEGOTIATION STYLE WITH THE US

The nuclear deal signifies a quantum leap in the relations from suspicion during the Cold War to strategic partnership in the 21st century. One of the key structural determinants of the US–India Entente has been the economic regeneration of India since the end of the Cold War. The US did not envisage any comprehensive alternative to the goal of nuclear non-proliferation yet wanted to improve relations with India.

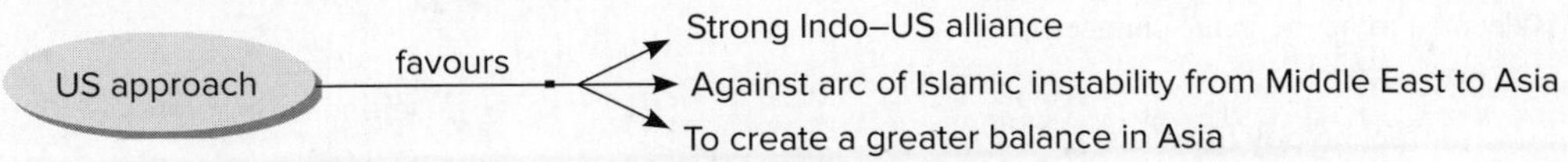

To tackle this challenge, the Bush administration, by giving India the nuclear deal, had successfully incorporated India into the global nuclear order and encouraged India to emerge as a great power in the future. Thus, shifts in the global balance of power have encouraged the US and India to reorient their foreign policies and the nuclear deal is the most important symbol of this new partnership. Let us try to analyse how did the nuclear deal eventually happen. The entire deal can be broken down into 26 steps.

EVOLUTION OF THE INDO-US NUCLEAR DEAL AND GREAT POWER POLITICS

Step 1: High-Technology Cooperation Group

The Bush administration created a High-Technology Cooperation Group (HTCG). The aim of the HTCG was to agree upon principles that would expand exports from the US industries to India. The group and the principles adopted were agreed upon intense negotiations between the US (under the Secretary of Commerce, Kenneth Juster), and India (Foreign Secretary, Kanwal Sibal). The agreement spelled out possibilities of the export of dual-use technologies from the US to India.

Step 2: Next Step in Strategic Partnership proposed

Subsequent to the HTCG, in 2003, during further negotiations, the US presented Next Steps in Strategic Partnership (NSSP) to India. In January 2004, a basic framework for the NSSP was proposed.

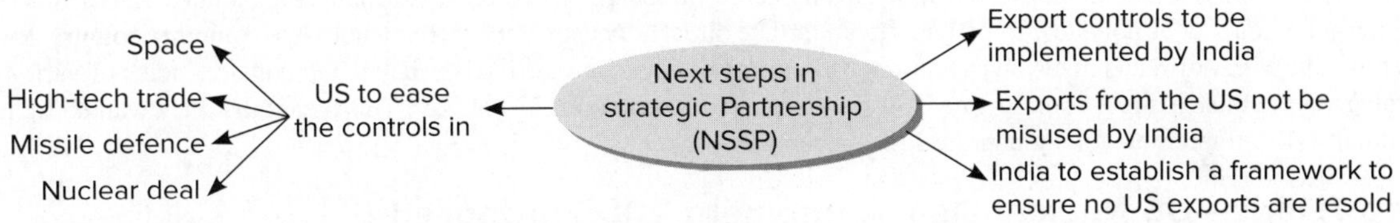

Step 3: Thirty issue list negotiation of India

The coming of the UPA government in 2004 led to renewed push. Prime Minister Manmohan Singh appointed J. N. Dixit as the new National Security Advisor. J. N. Dixit wanted a complete transformation in the Indo-US relations. He picked three Indian Foreign Services officers to work with him at the task. They were Ronen Sen, S. Jaishankar, IFS (now the Foreign Minister of India) and Raminder Jassal. The Indian side sent a list of thirty issues to the US to be considered. These issues represented an ambitious push from India for strategic cooperation. Initially, the US negotiators rejected the list and asserted that for them, the NSSP is the agreed framework. Dixit had instructed the Indian negotiations not to return until negotiations on the list were initiated. Finally, in September 2004, the US began to pick up issues from the list and began addressing them. Taking advantage of the progress, in March 2005, the US Secretary of State, Condoleezza Rice visited India and agreed to start nuclear negotiations, as it was one of the items in the list.

Step 4: Next Steps in Strategic Partnership concluded

In 2005, Condoleezza Rice visited India and the NSSP was signed. This took India by surprise but the Bush administration eventually announced civilian nuclear cooperation with India to help India emerge as a world power. After 9/11, Bush redefined how the US saw non-proliferation. The idea was that some states could not be trusted with nuclear weapons due to their unstable political regime domestically, while states like India, which have an impeccable non-proliferation policy to restore readability at the level of global non-proliferation norms, could be allowed nuclear access. The announcement of NSSP is deemed to be the game changer.

Step 5: The US Proposes India–US nuclear deal

On 25th March 2005, the White House announced that the US was going to help India emerge as a 'major player of the twenty-first century'. Both sides decided to conclude the agreement on nuclear cooperation by mid-July 2005, during the visit of Manmohan Singh to the US.

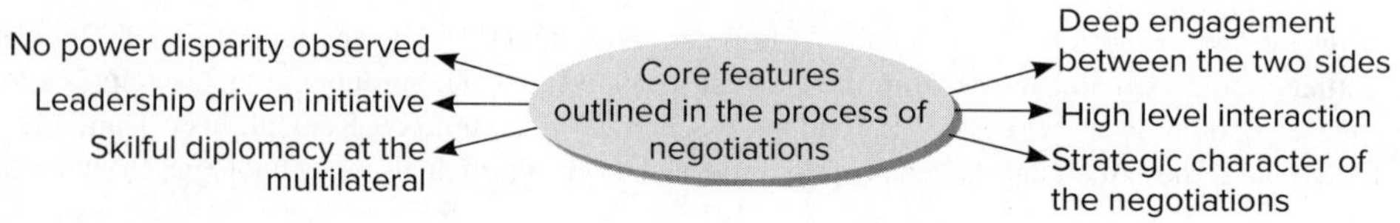

Step 6: India initiates direct advocacy with parliamentarians of the US to resolve nuclear issues

To resolve further issues, the Indian side resorted to an intense campaign of advocacy. Normally, the Indian MEA (Ministry of External Affairs) does not allow its officials to undertake direct advocacy with parliamentarians of another country. But this time, the MEA officials made an exception. More importantly, many officials even visited constituencies of various members to establish a direct contact. The US Congressmen often stated '123 for 126'. This meant that they wanted India to purchase 126 fighter jets for signing the 123 Agreement.

Step 7: India–US Nuclear Deal Agreement 2005 proposed

Bush realised that marginalising India would not benefit the nuclear non-proliferation order as he believed that the character of the regime was a more important determinant than a stand on a treaty to decide nuclear technology transfers. A nuclear deal would successfully de-hyphenated India and Pakistan and would give India the de facto status of a nuclear weapon state. In 2005, the nuclear deal was eventually proposed.

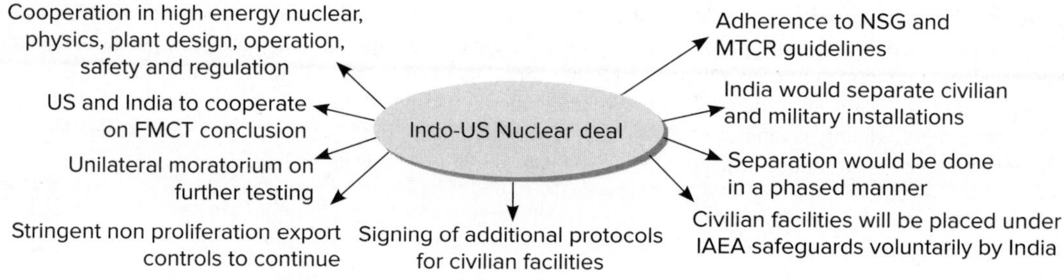

Step 8: BJP raises opposition to the separation plan

At the national level in India, BJP criticised the deal by advocating that separation of civilian and military installations (as committed by India under the deal) would compel India to incur huge costs. The Left parties, which were in a coalition with the government of the day, criticised the deal for renunciation of India's long held policy of nuclear disarmament and of non-alignment.

Step 9: Scientific community of India raises concerns on fast breeder reactor (FBR)

The starkest criticism of the deal came from the scientific community. The department of atomic energy strongly resisted putting of FBRs under the civilian list.

Step 10: Government addressed the concerns of the scientific community

To placate the concerns of the Indian scientific community, the then Indian Prime Minister Manmohan Singh declared in the Indian Parliament that India's FBR would not be put under international inspections of the International Atomic Energy Agency (IAEA) and the FBRs would not constitute elements under the civilian list. India succeeded in this hard bargain with the US.

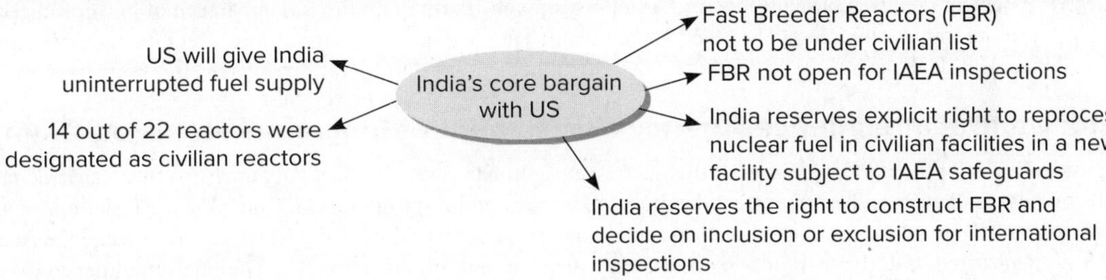

Step 11: India and the US sign Nuclear Deal agreement on 1st March 2006

With the bargain successfully undertaken, India signed the agreement on 1st March 2006, achieving a judicious balance between the energy security and national interests.

Step 12: US signs the 123 Agreement to execute the deal

The signing of the 123 agreement (based on section 123 of the US Atomic Energy Act) becomes the touchstone of the Indo-US partnership. The 123 Agreement refers to the section 123 of the US Atomic Energy Act, 1954 under which the US undertakes nuclear commerce with various countries. The US used this section to enter into agreements with various countries pertaining to nuclear cooperation. In 1963, India and the US had signed the 123 Agreement for Tarapur Atomic Power Station. The US, after passing the Hyde Act in 2006, signed a 123 agreement with India in July 2007, thereby making an exception by allowing the US to permit nuclear commerce with India despite India being a non-signatory to the NPT. The 'US–India Nuclear Cooperation Approval and Non-Proliferation Enhancement Act' was subsequently passed.

Step 13: India makes an exception to future nuclear testing and solves other issues

In the deal, India has not made mention of any provision related to the testing of a nuclear weapon which is likely to impact the deal, but the US President, under the Atomic Energy Act, is bound to ask for a return of nuclear technology if India tests a nuclear weapon. The major issue of disagreement on the Indian side was related to India's nuclear weapon programme testing. Indian Prime Minister Manmohan Singh assured the Parliament that the Indo-US deal no way affects Indian deterrence potential. India made it clear that the core issues while negotiating the 123 agreements that had to be taken into consideration were as follows:

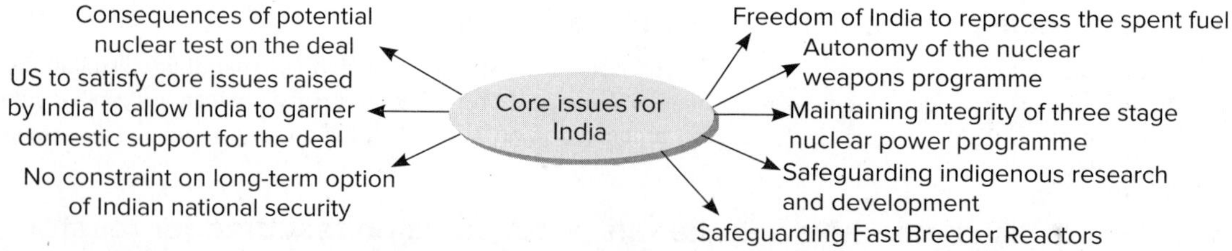

As intensive negotiations happened on these core issues, the terms of 123 agreements were finally accepted. The US agreed to assist India in the development of a strategic fuel reserve and ensure uninterrupted supply of nuclear fuel. India was allowed to establish a new facility subject to the IAEA safeguards to reprocess the spent fuel from the civilian reactors. The US president, as per the Atomic Energy Act of the US, remains bound to seek complete return of nuclear material in case of any violation, but the Indo-US deal did not make any reference as such for the same. However, the US would not hamper or create any hindrance in the growth of the nuclear weapons programme of India. In fact, India undertook aggressive diplomacy to ensure that if India tests a nuclear weapon, the US would not suddenly stop supplies of fuel and technology and demand a return, but would analyse the circumstances that led India to test the weapon. The plan to separate eight reactors for weapon or military use would now allow the use of domestic Uranium ore reserves for these separated reactors. This would allow the eight reactors to produce fissile material needed for credible minimum deterrence. The nuclear deal was basically viewed as an instrument in reshaping the Asian balance of power rather than affecting non-proliferation architecture. However, since the nuclear weapons programme was brought under the aegis of the IAEA, the nuclear deal has overall strengthened the global nuclear non-proliferation order.

Step 14: Central Intelligence Agency assessment of Indian nuclear programme

The biggest concerns for the US Congress were that such an exception in case of India would open up other states' demands to such technology and would adversely affect the global safeguard of non-proliferation. Under the NPT, there is no such clause where an NPT signatory cannot sell nuclear technology to non-NPT signatories. The Central Intelligence Agency of the US was entrusted with the task of assessing the nuclear programme of India. The National Intelligence Council also gave briefings to the US Congress in the same regard. As the US tried to tackle the dissidents within, the hearing that happened in the US Congress on the issue of the nuclear pact revealed that a majority of the members testified before the House International Relations Committee that such a pact would weaken the overall international non-proliferation regime that the US had spent decades building.

Step 15: Senator Richard Lugar raises concern in the US Congress

Senator Richard Lugar outlined the vocal criticism in the US Senate Foreign Relations Committee and he opened his statement by urging to the Senate that India does not have a very satisfying nuclear record. He also made references to Indian violation of bilateral pledges in 1974. He outlined a four-point benchmark for the US Congress's consent to the pact.

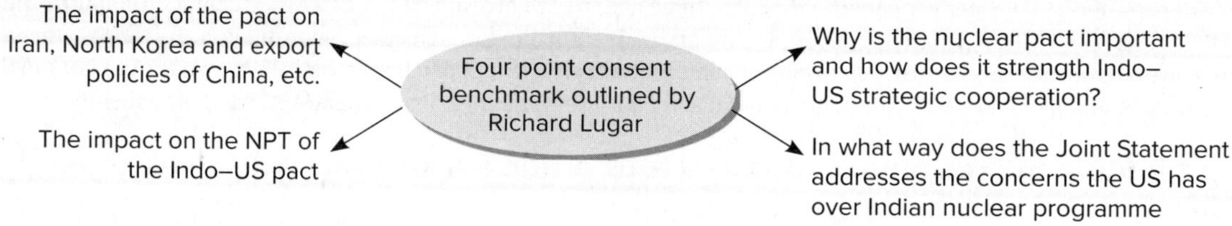

Step 16: Bush Administration resolves concerns of Richard Lugar

The Bush administration, in its response to the Foreign Relations Committee, admitted that the US could not establish a clear cut link if CIRUS reactor had violated the US–India contract of 1956 on the use of heavy water. The administration asserted that deriving a conclusive answer to whether the plutonium generated by India happened from heavy water supplied by the US for the CIRUS reactor was not possible. The biggest reason for such criticism in the US Congress and the foreign policy bureaucracy was the reluctance of Bush to consult the two before embarking upon the nuclear deal with India. The Bush administration understood that taking an incremental approach to the deal, in sync with the bureaucracy and the US Congress, would have knocked down the initiative. This is the reason that Condoleezza Rice resorted to the 'Big Bang' announcement and compared the deal with India at par with Nixon's opening to China. However, all opposition was managed when the Republicans lost majority in the Congress and the Senate signed the nuclear deal, thereby culminating in the three-year process.

Step 17: The US makes a case for NSG-specific waiver for India in 2008

The US subsequently pressed for an India-specific waiver at the NSG. The NSG was created by the US in 1975 to isolate India for its PNE of 1974.

Step 18: China raised concerns for India-specific waiver at NSG

China raised concerns in 2008 at the NSG that making a special waiver for India would affect the credentials of the NSG. It also advocated that such a waiver for India, which is not a signatory to the NPT and CTBT, would weaken the global nuclear architecture.

Step 19: The US resolves the concerns of China and NSG-specific waiver for India is passed

The US was able to assuage the China and other NSG members and succeeded in the NSG-specific waiver for India. The administration asserted that India has good non-proliferation credentials and such states should be rewarded than being kept out of the global architecture. The US asserted that a specific waiver for India would strengthen the global nuclear architecture. On 8th October 2008, the US President signed the US–India Nuclear Cooperation Approval and Non-Proliferation Enhancement Act. Great power politics and nuclear non-proliferation are the two competing imperatives of the US foreign policy that created such difficulty in the negotiation of the Indo-US nuclear deal. Both India and the US perceived the deal very differently. For the Bush administration, the deal was a bridge to establish a strategic partnership with India; while, for Indian establishment, it was a mechanism to reach the global nuclear mainstream and a step towards great power status. However, from our analysis of the nuclear deal in this section, we can clearly infer that the Indo-US nuclear deal is not just about nuclear technicalities but the emergence of a new global balance of power, which highlights the strategic considerations of great powers, related to nuclear non-proliferation. The Bush administration clearly perceived the nuclear deal as a means towards helping India emerge as a global player and therefore, the institutional imperatives of the non-proliferation regime were once again trumped by the global political realities.

Step 20: India commits to ratify convention on supplementary compensation for nuclear damages and also prepare a nuclear liability law

When India and the US concluded the nuclear deal, to operationalise it, India had to ratify the convention on supplementary compensation (CSC) for nuclear damages and also prepare a nuclear liability law. The Paris Convention on Third Party Liability in the Field of Nuclear Energy was established in 1960 and aims to limit liabilities to a fixed amount in case of nuclear accidents. The Vienna Convention also relates to liability-related matters in case of nuclear accidents. The third is the CSC for nuclear damages that came up in 1997 and aimed to not only establish a global liability regime but also to ensure that in case of a nuclear accident, the victims get increased amounts of compensation. Now if a country wants to join CSC, it has to be a part of the Vienna Convention. The CSC has a clause, which says that if a country is not a party to Paris or Vienna Conventions, it can still become a part of CSC if it establishes a national law, which synchronises with the CSC provisions and its annexes.

Step 21: India passes the Civil Liability of Nuclear Damages Act in 2010

India prepared the Civil Liability of Nuclear Damages Act (CLNDA) in 2010. On 29th October 2010, it signed the CSC on the basis of its CLNDA. The aim of the CLNDA is to ensure that in case of a nuclear accident, the victims get quick compensation without having to prove negligence by operator or supplier. The liability was capped at 1500 crore rupees.

Step 22: Section 17B and Section 46 of the Civil Liability of Nuclear Damages Act emerge as irritants preventing the execution of the nuclear deal

There are two issues raised by equipment suppliers in CLNDA. The first issue of CLNDA is section 17B, which states that the plant operator in India, NPCIL, can claim compensation from the supplier of equipment if the nuclear accident will happen due to faulty equipment or material supplied by the supplier. The second issue is related to section 46. As per this section, the accident victims can sue both operator and material supplier over and above the amount capped. Now equipment suppliers, which are foreign players, say that these clauses (section 17B and section 46) put the supplier in a vulnerable situation and unnecessarily drag them into open-ended criminal action and tort law compensation. The suppliers say that the operator and not the supplier has to identify defects and get them rectified and in case of the failure of the operator to do so, the operator is to be held liable. The suppliers also say that India's CLNDA violates the Paris Convention of 1960 and the Vienna Convention of 1963 as well as the CSC for nuclear damages.

Step 23: India proposes Nuclear Insurance Pool in 2015 to resolve issues related to Section 17B and Section 46 of the Civil Liability of Nuclear Damages Act

The government has tried to give some assurance to the suppliers by saying that as per section 7 of CLNDA, if the liability exceeds 1500 crore cap, the central government will establish a nuclear liability fund to protect the suppliers from any claims made by the operator. However, suppliers have pointed out that section 7 of the CLNDA still does not protect a supplier from claims made by accident victims under the law of torts. In 2015, during the visit of the US President Obama, the two sides finalised administrative arrangements to execute the nuclear deal. This was built upon the Indian Prime Minister's visit to the US in 2014 when a contact group to implement the deal had been established. After the successful completion of negotiation in the contact group, India agreed to establish a nuclear insurance pool formed by General Insurance Corporation of India (GIC) and 4 different PSUs, which would contribute 750 crore rupees out of a total of 1500 crore rupees while the government would contribute the rest of the amount. The insurance pool would provide cover to suppliers under section 17 of the CLNDA. Now under the pool, the operators and suppliers would become partners in risk management rather than eyeing each other as adversaries. The compensation amount would be three hundred million in special drawing rights (SDR) and CLNDA has capped maximum liability for an operator to 1500 crore rupees. In case if value of SDR increases and goes beyond 1500 crore rupees, the government would bridge the amount. On 12th June 2015, the General Insurance Company of India had launched the Indian Nuclear Insurance Pool with a capacity of 1500 crore rupees as envisaged under CLNDA.

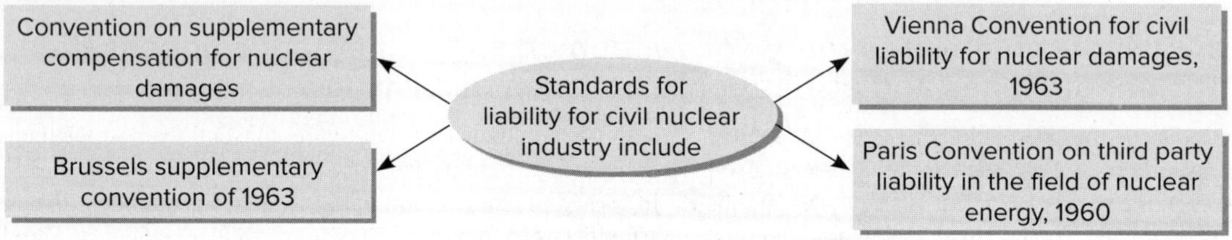

Step 24: India ratifies CSC for Nuclear Damages in 2016

The Indian CLNDA follows the CSC and its annexes and India finally ratified the CSC through Instrument of Ratification and became a state party to CSC on 4th May 2016.

Step 25: Nuclear diplomacy with the US and other states is fully operational

The CLNDA and ratification to CSC eventually operationalise the nuclear cooperation.

Step 26: India becomes a member of MTCR, Wassenaar Arrangement, Australia Group and strives to be a member of Nuclear Suppliers Group

There are four multilateral export control regimes. They are Australia Group (AG), Wassenaar Arrangement (WA), Missile Technology Control Regime (MTCR) and Nuclear Suppliers Group (NSG). All these four are informal regimes and they are not treaty-based. They are a club of like-minded states. The keenness of India to join these multilateral export control regimes can be seen from the perspective of India and NPT. India feels that as NPT will not accept it today as a 'nuclear have', it realises that the only logical way it can legitimise its nuclear status is to make NPT irrelevant. To achieve this objective, India has adopted a two-point policy. Firstly, it favours to join the multilateral export control regimes such as NSG and MTCR (as both require accession to NPT as one of the membership 'criteria'). India feels that by joining NSG and MTCR, it can make NPT redundant. Secondly, India, after its nuclear test in 1998 had focused on civilian aspect of nuclear technology and its trade rather than a nuclear weapon. This is the reason why 11th May (1998 was the day when India carried out its nuclear tests) is celebrated as a National Technology Day.

INDIA'S DIPLOMACY AT NUCLEAR SUPPLIERS GROUP AND ISSUES IN NSG MEMBERSHIP

NSG was formed in response to India's PNE (1974) in 1975 and was initially called London Club. Its aim was to manage export controls and nuclear proliferation issues which were outside the framework of NPT. Till 1991, NSG remained a dormant group. At the end of the Cold War, with the disintegration of the USSR, the threat of nuclear war was replaced with the threat of nuclear proliferation, which re-energised the NSG, to tackle those matters that were left out of the scope of NPT. The decisions in the NSG are taken by consensus, making memberships difficult for new member states. At the end of the Cold War, Belarus, Ukraine and Kazakhstan possessed weapons of Soviet era. Both USSR, through proactive diplomacy, and the US decided to de-arm them and made the three states join the NPT as NNWS. Since 1991, with the advent of Gulf War-1, and situation of proliferation in Iran and North Korea, there was a growing belief that NPT would not sufficient to tackle nuclear proliferation. The NSG made attempts to rectify such shortcomings of NPT. To reposition NSG as a serious grouping to tackle nuclear proliferation and not merely position as a club; NSG in 1991 stated that it would not use member states as a term, which could be replaced with PG. Subsequently, in 2001, a new 'procedural arrangement' was adopted that talked about admitting a new PG to NSG. The procedure has five-point criteria.

1. State should have the ability to supply or produce items mentioned in the control list of NSG.
2. State should adhere to the guidelines of NSG.
3. State should legally enforce the guidelines of NSG.
4. State should support global efforts to seek non-proliferation of weapons of mass destruction.
5. State should adhere and comply with one or more obligations of the NPT.

It was clarified that the above points were only 'considerations' to be used for membership and were not mandatory as a criteria. As part of an attempt to operationalise the India–USA nuclear deal, in 2008, India was given NSG-specific waiver. In 2010, India expressed an interest to become a member of the NSG. From 2010 to 2016, there was a political and diplomatic void in India taking up the issue with the NSG. This was primarily out of concerns arising out of India's Civilian Liability for Nuclear Damages Act. In 2016, when India made a formal attempt to join the NSG, after resolving the concerns in the liability law, its membership was blocked by China.

CHINESE OBJECTIONS TO THE INDIAN MEMBERSHIP AT NUCLEAR SUPPLIERS GROUP

1. China asserts that there needs to be 'broader consensus' to evolve a technical, legal and political criterion to admit new states to NSG as PG.
2. China asserts that let there be a two-step process for admitting a new PG to NSG. First, let there be a formula developed for admission of non-NPT members to NSG. Second, after such a formula is developed and adopted, only then NSG should admit new PG.

3. China asserts that in the absence of such a formula there will be serious effects of admitting non-NPT member states (like India) to NSG as PG because such states in NSG (without being a member of NPT) will affect the integrity of the non-proliferation architecture in the world. Indian strategic community believes that this is used by China as a cover to push the case for Pakistan along with India for admission to NSG.

Because of obstructive and non-cooperative attitude of China, Indian membership to the NSG remains a hurdle till date. In the June 2016 Seoul Plenary Session, India applied for membership, but China objected to India's entry to the NSG and raised procedural concerns. However, China is also not a member of the MTCR, of which India is a member, the whole issue of membership came down to a quid pro quo bid. China objected stating the NSG is based on the NPT, of which India is not a part, and thus, pushed back the Indian case. The Indian membership now depends upon the diplomacy and cooperation with China.

THE AUSTRALIA GROUP AND INDIA'S NUCLEAR DIPLOMACY

In 1980, during Iran–Iraq war, Iraq legitimately and legally procured chemicals and began to develop chemical weapons. This emerged as a new threat to international security. In 1985, in a meeting in Brussels, a list was developed which maintains chemicals, which were to be subjected to export control. Doing so, as believed, would prevent the proliferation of chemical weapons. The annual meetings to evolve the list happened in the Australian Mission in Paris. Once the list was developed by 15 Western states, a group called AG was born. Over a period of time, biological agents were added to expand the list and more technical and other equipment were added to expand the scope to incorporate chemical and biological weapons. In 2018, India joined the AG as a 43rd member state. Joining AG proved that India had safeguards and export controls for chemical and biological weapons, which met the benchmark standards of the international community. As India's chemical industry has emerged as a global exporter of chemicals; its trade has increased in dual use chemicals. Joining the AG would harmonise India's export controls as per international standards.

THE WASSENAAR ARRANGEMENT AND INDIAN DIPLOMACY

In 1950s, the US had established Coordinated Committee for Multilateral Export Control (COCOM). It was an attempt to block the export of strategic materials and technologies to Soviet Union and its satellite states. After the end of the Cold War, COCOM was replaced with WA. In WA, the member states have to harmonise their national policies. They are harmonised to control transfers of conventional munitions list and dual use goods and technical list. WA covers an area of strategic materials and technologies where no international treaty exists. WA is very important in the globalised world as ICT technologies (of encryption and surveillance etc.) are developed by private players for commercial use. This makes it tough for the governments to regulate dual use. WA aims to foster transparent practices with respect to sales and transfers of arms, materials and technology, which aid buildup of nuclear capabilities. It has mechanisms to prevent falling of such technologies into the hands of non-state actors. In WA, member states share and exchange information related to transfer of technology or denial of technology (conventional and nuclear) to states not a part of WA. India joined WA in 2017. It can now access dual use technology that is proscribed for non-members. India can also sell nuclear reactors that are indigenously built without any restrictions from states.

INDIA'S MISSILE TECHNOLOGY CONTROL REGIME DIPLOMACY

In 1987, to prevent the proliferation of unmanned delivery vehicles for nuclear weapons, an informal agreement had been established called as MTCR by the US, United Kingdom, Canada, France, Germany, Italy and Japan. As per the MTCR, it places a ban on the transfer of such missiles that can carry more than 500 kilogrammes or have a range beyond 300 kilometres. In 1992, the MTCR expanded its mandate to add unmanned aerial vehicles.

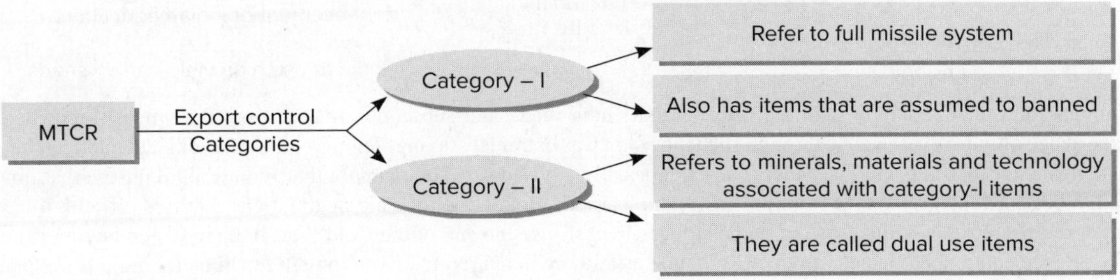

India joined the MTCR in June 2016. In 2015, India's membership to join the MTCR was blocked by Italy (because of Italy's objection to the investigation of Italian Marine fishermen killing issue). China is not a member of the MTCR. It has been blocking Indian membership to NSG, as informally China wants a quid pro quo. It wants India to support Chinese candidature to MTCR and in return China would support Indian candidature to NSG. The members of MTCR object to Chinese inclusion to MTCR as China has a dubious record of proliferating missiles to Pakistan (in violation with certain stated aims of MTCR).

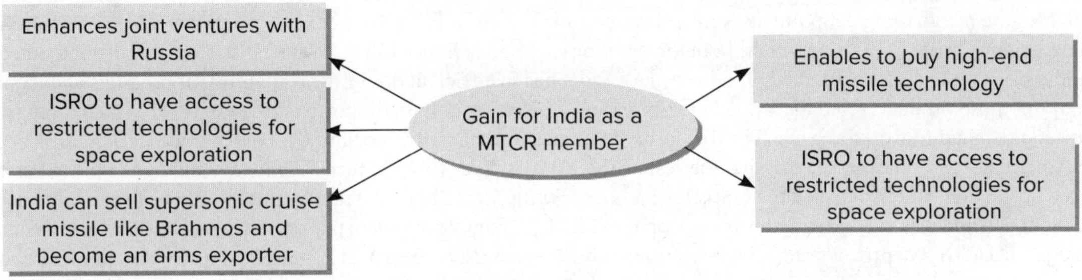

INDIA'S TRADE NEGOTIATION STYLE WITH THE UNITED STATES

In 1949, Nehru paid his first state visit to the US. Domestically, at that time, India was suffering from a famine and severe grain shortage. Instead of directly asking for food aid from the US, Nehru dropped hints about the willingness of India to accept an offer. The US awaited a proper request. Nothing came out of the visit. One of the peculiar behaviours of the Indian foreign policy mandarins is that they never ask for aids directly, which reflects distaste for asking. However, with repeated failures of monsoons and successive famines, in December 1950, the Indian Ambassador to the US, Vijaya Lakshmi Pandit, requested the US to supply two million tonnes of wheat. The US conveyed to India that such a proposal would require Congressional approval. As the Congress was debating the matter, India conveyed to the US that it needed assurance that no conditionality would be imposed on wheat supply and the aid would not affect India's foreign or domestic policy. Further, the US would not interfere or influence the sovereign domains of India. The US, however, asserted that it would observe the distribution of the wheat they would donate. On 11th June 1951, the US Congress as a long-term loan to be released for India approved a bill authorising 190 million dollar. The next line of the Indo-US offensive came up in 1965, when India witnessed a severe famine and food shortage. India requested 10 million tonnes of food grains under the two-year food aid programme. This time the US President Lyndon Johnson announced a 'short tether policy'. As per the policy, Johnson stated that all food aid shipments to India would require his personal approval. India found the policy very offensive. The US began to insist that India should undertake aggressive agricultural reforms. To work out an agreement, the Indian Agriculture Minister, C. Subramaniam, held meetings with his American counterpart in Rome. India agreed to a very intrusive programme by November 1965 and brought changes in its agricultural policy.

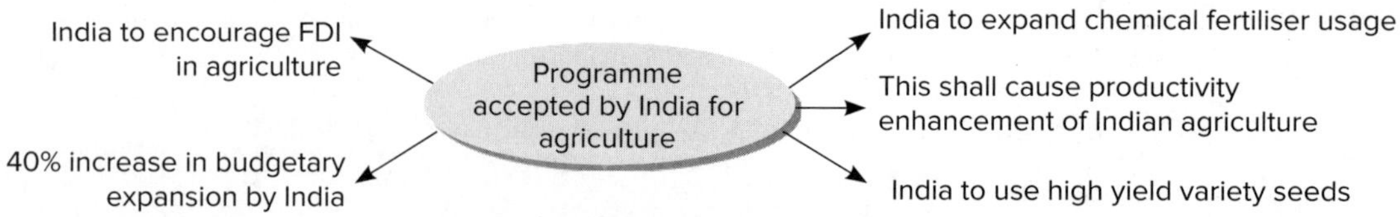

Though Johnson was happy with the reforms that India made and subsequently eased out the wheat shipments, the experience of India to have gone through such intrusion was extremely taxing. Though Indira Gandhi had publicly thanked Americans for their aid and assistance, she categorically advised C. Subramaniam that India should ensure that it never had to beg for food grains ever from the US. India learned through the food aid negotiations that it is difficult to accept any foreign control over the usage of domestic resources. Since the end of the Cold War, India has been buying from the US defence equipment, nuclear products, oil and gas and civilian aircrafts. Even though the bilateral trade has expanded since the end of the Cold War, it is important to note that the majority of the trade consists of 're-exports'. This means that India imports raw materials and exports a finished product back to the US and that seems to be the case in gems, jewellery and petroleum (the core items of Indian export). Thus, the net gain to India is the value-added or the labour costs only.

ISSUES IN INDIA AND THE US TRADE DIPLOMACY

In 2002, the US Ambassador to India raised the issue of a weak trade with India and stated that American trade inflows to India are "flat as a chapati". The US since then has often raised the issue of trade deficit with India, as with other allies as well. Despite the growing geopolitical, strategic and regional convergences between India and the US, the trade deficit is a new irritant. Trade deficits are natural outcomes of buying and selling of the two states, and not engineered outcomes. If India has a trade deficit with the US, it is because India has insufficient domestic availability of products and it ends up in buying those products from the US. There are various factors why India imports more than it exports that range from domestic demand to workforce etc. This brings us to a question that why does the US have a trade deficit? It is because the Americans consume more than what the rest of the world collectively produces. To rectify this, Trump was seeking a forced correction, which defeated the market principles. Trump wanted other states (including India) to forcibly buy what US produced and was encouraging his own people to buy less from what other states produced. This distorted the market principle because it deprived states to buy cheaper substitutes and also deprived Americans to buy cheaper alternatives.

The US under the Trump administration had raised several trade issues with India. They are as follows:

1. Selective access available to the US in many sectors in India.
2. FDI not permissible in many sectors.
3. The US want India to change IPR laws and cloud computing laws.
4. At the level of pharmacy, the US wants data exclusivity (explained below) to which India is opposed.
5. Trump had raised concern of India charging high-duties on import of Harley Davidson motorcycle.
6. He had justified the withdrawal of the GSP (explained below) by classifying India as a developed nation.
7. Trump had demanded access to Indian agriculture sector including almond and dairy products.
8. Trump had imposed duties on India under Section 232 of National Security Act for steel (25% tariff imposed for imports from India) and aluminum (10% tariff imposed). Ironically, Trump had used national security legislation measures; normally used against countries with which the US was at war; against its strategic partner.
9. Trump had tightened the H1-B visas (explained later separately) and that had affected Indian firms doing business in the US as they found it difficult to renew visas for existing staff or send new staffers for projects.
10. The US asserts that India lacks the requisite regulatory, legislative and bureaucratic apparatus to ensure sensitive technology is not given to rogue nations.
11. The US wants lower tariffs for American ICT goods and mutual withdrawal of WTO disputes.
12. The US also wants markets access for American berries in India.

THE US RECIPROTARIANISM OF THE DIMINISHED GIANT SYNDROME

Jagdish Bhagwati, has rightly called the policy of Trump as reciprotarianism of the diminished giant syndrome. The US is pressurizing India to allow greater market access in foods and automobile industry, of which India is reluctant. Even though India's trade surplus with the US is 20 USD billion (while China has a 400 USD billion trade surplus with the US, which caused the US–China trade war); still US is adamant on reducing it. In fact, an ideal scenario for the US would be to collaborate with India and tackle the trade deficits both have with China collectively.

THE REVOCATION OF GSP STATUS, IMPLICATIONS ON TRADE AND END OF STRATEGIC ALTRUISM

The generalised system of preferences or GSP system came into force in 1974. It is a preferential trade programme of the US under which the US waives off import duties on many products from around 120 countries. Devised in its own interest, the lack of imposition of import duties on these products meant that the US industries often got inputs at a cheaper rate. According to the website of the US Trade Representative, the GSP spurs sustainable development in beneficiary countries by helping them increase and diversify their trade with the US. The programme also supports tens of thousands of jobs in the US. The Trade Representative says the GSP is important to the US small businesses, many of which rely on the programme's duty savings to stay competitive. President Trump had called India the 'import tariff king'. One of the conditions of GSP on beneficiary countries is that it requires assessment on whether it will provide equitable and reasonable access to its market to the United States. The idea is grounded in a strong belief in reciprocity trade agreements executed by the US, as seen by the Trump's economic policies with other nations. The US Government pointed out specific instances of Indian policies that tantamount to a violation of the access to market condition. To eliminate extortion by hospitals and medical practitioners for foreign-manufactured heart stents, India announced an upper cap to the pricing of these stents. The Advanced Medical Technology Association complained to the US Trade Representative to withdraw India's GSP as they believed that this caused foreclosure to their entry into the Indian markets and many were made to do 'forced sales' at low prices. Historically, India has been the largest beneficiary of the GSP programme. However, President Trump in a tweet proclaimed that the US was being used by other countries and announced his intention of putting the American worker first. In fact, this was one of the reasons for the trade war between USA and China, which began in 2018 and continues. Under GSP, as many as 1,900 Indian products from various sectors such as chemicals and engineering equipment, leather, textiles, gold, building materials and dairy items got duty free access to the US market. While there may be no substantial effect, as India's Commerce Secretary announced that it would only impact around $190 million annually. However, there is no denying that it has critically affected on sales and employment of Micro, Small and Medium level enterprises that are solely export-oriented units. Since the landed price (that is, cost plus shipping, insurance, freight) would become higher, the US consumers and businesses might be able to find cheaper alternatives by other countries that would continue to enjoy the GSP benefits. However, it was not solely Indian manufacturers that would be hit. For exclusive Indian exports, such as high-quality gemstones, Basmati rice etc., for which ready alternatives were not available, the negative effect would be felt by industries in the US relying on these imports. Moreover, this could give India, a good opportunity to levy higher taxes on imports from the USA, such as Harley Davidson, which enjoyed a 50% duty, which was lowered from 100% after Trump had expressed a want for zero-duty on these motorcycles. While negotiations between India and the USA are important, with issues of commerce and economics requiring diplomacy and adequate advocacy at the World Trade Organization, the Indian government has decided to step in to protect interests of small manufacturers that are likely to be worst hit, as the GSP stands withdrawn. Mechanisms for alternate employment and exploring the new market opportunity for Indian exports have been initiated by the Indian state. Moreover, since the benefits of GST are not available for fuel costs (since petrol and diesel are kept out of the purview of GST), the government is likely to offer financial benefits to such manufacturers to compensate for the increased duties that may follow.

INTELLECTUAL PROPERTY RIGHTS (IPR) ISSUES AND BILATERAL INVESTMENT TREATY (BIT)

In 2009, India and the US started negotiating a treaty to protect foreign investment that flows from one state to the other. The negotiations were slow because both sides updated their model BIT template in 2015, replacing the 2003 template. A BIT protects the investments of the investors by allowing them extra rights against unlawful actions of host states and thereby boosts investors' confidence, leading to more FDI. As per the 2003 BIT of India, the treaty offered investors fair and equitable treatment based on reasonability and due process. The 2015 treaty has replaced it with customary international law. Now the investment by an investor shall not be subjected to any measures that violate existing customary international law. The Indian BIT of 2015 grants full security and protection to the foreign investors and their investment. More importantly, the BIT clearly states that the state will not discriminate the foreign investor from the nationals of the host state and shall not act in a discriminatory manner against foreign investors. The new BIT also talks about the provisions related to expropriation. According to the provisions, any investment shall be done with adequate compensation and under due process in accordance to the laws of the host states. The compensation shall be in freely convertible currency on the basis of the market value. Under the new BIT, for dispute resolution the investor needs to exhaust all local remedies available in the state up to five years. The investors get a choice to arbitrate disputes either under International Centre for Settlement of Investment Disputes (ICSID) arbitration rules or the additional facility rules of ICSID or the United Nations Commission on International Trade Law (UNCITRAL) arbitration rules. However, India not being a party to ICSID convention, the ICSID arbitration rules mechanism shall not be available to the investors. The new BIT does not mention the need for the 'most favoured nation' status tag for each other. There is no provision for an umbrella clause, which means there is no requirement to observe contractual obligations by the parties. An absence of the umbrella clause means that the domestic courts may not pursue claims, as there are no direct contractual obligations involved. The Modi government at the centre has declared a need for 1 trillion dollars' investment in the infrastructure sector. If India and the US conclude a BIT, this is one area where the US firms will stand to have an edge over other competitors. A future BIT can also lead to a grand collaboration between India and the US in retail and business services sector. The stringent environmental and labour concerns in the US BIT are irritants perceived by India. One reason why India and the US have not been able to conclude a BIT till date is because of the issues related to investor–state arbitration. India's emphasis in the new BIT, as stated earlier, is that the investor should first exhaust local remedies in the state up to five years. The US firms are not very enthusiastic about this provision due to a fairly poor image of Indian legal system as being overstretched. The Indian BIT does not bring taxation within its purview. The US firms are of the view that an absence of such a provision enhances the tax leverage in the hands of the Indian authorities.

THE SPECIAL 301 REPORT OF THE US, INDIA'S CONCERNS AND ISSUE OF EVER-GREENING OF PATENTS

Moreover, the Indian BIT has no mention of matters related to the insurance of compulsory license (CL) and in the absence of the same, the US firms would not get the power to sue an Indian firm for issuance of CLs or revocation of IPR. The two nations have differing perceptions on IPR despite both being compliant to the Agreement on Trade-Related Aspects of Intellectual Property Rights (TRIPS) agreement of WTO. The matter was aggravated in 2014 when the Office of the US Trade Representative put India under priority watch under the 'Special 301' Report. The US stated India has inadequate IPR protection in IT, pharmacy and publishing industries. The US also alleged that India is a major source of counterfeit drugs. India has not been pleased with this allegation since it is a generic drug exporter, and such an allegation could hurt the country's global image of being a pharmacy supplier. Since 2012, patent disputes have emerged as a sticky issue because India has refused the US firms the right to patent, due to firms resorting to ever-greening. Ever-greening means that the company makes a mirror amendment to its already patented product and seeks to expand patent life further after a minor modification. India has invoked Section 3(d) of the Indian Patent Act often.

INDIA–US TRADE POLICY FORUM AND INDIA–US KNOWLEDGE SHARING AGREEMENT

To resolve the IPR issue, a high level working group has been established under the India–US trade policy forum. As the negotiations progress, India should focus on protection of its national interests. India needs to give some space to the principle of eminent domain where, in public interest, the state can subordinate the IPR of private entities. The working groups should lay down a set of boundaries in case of 'eminent domain' being used for health-related issues. As the US is trying to reduce the drug prices in their own country and India is trying to develop its secondary and tertiary healthcare; the potential the two have for collaboration is intense. In 2020, India and the US signed a pact on IPR. The pact is called as the India and the USA Knowledge-Sharing Agreement, which shall enrich the IPR systems between the two states. The pact involves no legal commitment by either side but shall facilitate training sessions for experts and officials to help understand and study each other's IPR laws. This is an important step because the US wants India to drop Section 3(d) of the Indian Patent Act and also denies patents to items that are not very significantly different from older versions (explained below). The US is also opposed to compulsory licensing for drugs. In this context, the pact shall focus on the entire IPR regime of the two states and is sector-agnostic, means it will cover patents, copyrights etc. and will not be limited to specific sectors.

PHARMACEUTICAL DIPLOMACY, TIERED PRICING AND IPR ISSUES BETWEEN INDIA AND THE US

There has been a deadlock on pharmaceuticals between the Indo-US. The main issue here is that American firms want India to adopt a strict IPR regime while India, being a signatory to TRIPS of WTO is not keen on the same. This is where the two parties are at a deadlock. India is a developing state. It has to take care of a huge population and their health. American companies manufacture medicines. These medicines are produced after enormous research and innovation. These medicines help in curing rarest of rare diseases. But these American firms then sell these medicines at a very hefty price. The firms are justified in high price as they assert that they spend a huge amount of money in innovation to create that drug. Now, in India, the IPR laws are weak. So, Indian pharmacy firms (under state patronage) tweak the formula of the American-produced drug and come out with a generic product. This generic product does not require enormous field trials and innovations. It only involves minor restructuring of the product already innovated (where American firms have invested thousands of billions of dollars). As India is able to produce this generic drug, it helps in providing the drug to Indian patients at an extremely low price. India being a signatory to TRIPS of WTO also exports these generics to other developing states. This is where the issue for the American firms is. They say that they do not get compensated in developing markets (which are the markets that will use their drugs most) financially. So, these American firms try to pressurise the US administration to push India to go for stringent IPR laws that can prevent generic production by tweaking components. This is also a reason why the US pharmacy firms are not interested to set up a manufacturing base in India. The US has often categorised India as a state of concern and is often criticised under Special 301 Report (which it publishes under Section 301 of the US Trade Act of 1974). India always says that the Special 301 Report is a unilateral American report to unduly pressurise India to go beyond IPR measures outside the ambit of WTO. India also has concerns that are legitimate. Indian firms assert that the American firms go for ever-greening of patents. This means that they introduce cosmetic changes in the drugs when its patent is about to expire. With these cosmetic changes, the American firms continue to maintain a monopoly over the patent. India thus complains that these firms in the US do not have any concern for social responsibility and are primarily governed by greed of profits. As the US administration supports the ever-greening, the conflict never gets resolved. The solution to the deadlock is tiered pricing. In tiered pricing, a mechanism can jointly be achieved between India and the US. The firms can develop, say, a three-tier pricing strategy. Those at the bottom-most strata can legally get access to the product at a set price. This helps in sales maximisation and brings cash inflow to mitigate the financial concerns of the American firms from developing markets. The other two tiers of pricing can be used for the customers of the developed world who have the pockets to pay for the product as well. Such a tiered pricing can help protect national interests and profits collectively.

THE DATA EXCLUSIVITY CHALLENGE IN INDIA AND THE US RELATIONS

Let us understand the concept of data exclusivity. A pharmaceutical company, which is into manufacturing of drugs, has to prove the efficacy of the medicine. It also has to ensure that the manufactured medicine is safe for use. To do so, a pharmacy firm undertakes clinical trials on humans and animals. The trials lead to generation of data. By generating this data and keeping it exclusive for its use, the company that has innovated the medicine can prevent its competitors from obtaining license to manufacture a low-cost version of the drug. The pharmacy company or the innovator wants to mostly maintain exclusivity of their drug. Despite deepening of the Indo-US ties since the end of the Cold War, there have been few perceptual hurdles between the two.

THE STENT PRICING, KNEE IMPLANTS AND ISSUE OF TRADE MARGIN RATIONALISATION

India imports 80% of medical devices and the US have a share of 30% in this. The US is unhappy about the ever-greening of patents by India and also with Indian decision to control the prices of cardiac stents and knee implants. India's National Pharmaceutical Pricing Authority found that the US stent makers are making huge profits and huge margins by selling stents and implants to India at a high price. They found a discrepancy between the manufactured price and retail price. This led India to impose a high tariff on import of stents and implants. This led to a loss to the US stent producers. In 2020, India and the US had decided to replace the blanket price caps for high-end medical devices with an option of trade margin rationalisation (TMR) as the TMR will use landing price as a base for trade margins; which will bring more affordable medical products to India. Under the TMR, the trade margins can be capped at rational levels and then added to the selling price indicated by the overseas manufacturer at the first point of sale; which is import-landed price when the product lands in India and GST becomes applicable. This would rationalise the profits for the retailers and traders. Even though the US have been a significant player in our medical industry, Indian players are restricted to access the US markets due to non-tariff barriers. This is where the US should make future concessions for India. India should also ask the US to make concessions on import fees because Indian pharmacy exporters have to pay very high fees to the US regulators and this restricts India's entry to the US markets.

CHICKEN NATIONALISM AND DARK MEAT IMPORTS BETWEEN INDIA AND THE US

The US are the biggest exporter of poultry in the world. As per American dietary habits, the people in the US consume chicken breasts and legs and thighs are considered as 'dark meat' because it is believed that they are tough to chew and have a stigma associated. The poultry producers of the US have adapted to the American preferences and have started exporting the thighs and legs to other countries in the world. India is one of the markets where legs and thighs have no stigma and more so, are in high demand than the chicken breasts. Citing avian influenza as a concern, India in 2007 stopped importing American poultry. The US took the poultry dispute to WTO in 2012 asserting that a countrywide ban cannot be resorted to by India. The WTO in 2012 ruled against India and asked India to allow the US imports. In 2015, the US again complained to WTO for non-compliance by India. In 2018, reluctantly, India allowed the imports in a limited manner. Indian concern was that if the US dumps the 'dark meat' in India, then, Indian domestic poultry producers would not be able to withstand American competition. The Trump administration had not raised poultry as a priority with India.

CHALLENGES IN DAIRY INDUSTRY BETWEEN INDIA AND THE US

Today, India cannot export meat products to the US while it does to Japan and EU because the American inspection standards are different. The US cannot export dairy products to India because their suppliers cannot certify that their products do not originate from bovine animal fed ruminants while the EU and Japan do provide India with this certification. This is a religious issue in India. Both can resolve these issues for mutual advantage of each. A future possibility is quota-restricted imports where labeling regarding the cattle feed is specified. India simultaneously can open up imports of blueberries and cherries. India can further liberalise the FDI norms and seek the US FDI in building storage plants and agro-processing units.

FUTURE ELEMENTS OF DIPLOMACY IN TRADE BETWEEN INDIA AND THE US

Trade level India wants the US to grant market access for grapes and mangoes, removal of duties on iron and steel, single digit duty on high-end bikes, revocation of GSP status and easy norms for visas and free movement of people.

Service export India continues to provide the US with world class IT exports; an area where the US is supply constrained. India should work to strengthen cooperation here.

Big data India is generating the new oil called big data. It has 800 million plus users with mobile phones. American firms ranging from Facebook to Google are already making substantial profits from Indian data. In the future, as the US firms move on to AI, data analytics, Internet of things, cloud computing, nanotechnology and 5G technologies, they will need more of Indian data to fuel their growth and big data will be a future area of cooperation.

Data protection Similarly, as data protection issues have arisen recently, India has to choose between business-friendly and competing rules of EU or the US. India has to select either on the basis of whichever offers India stronger data privacy. In the recent times, e-commerce has emerged as an irritant. The e-commerce firms like Amazon and Walmart is facing restrictions in India, which can be easily removed and India should strive to promote more competition. The grand goal for India is an FTA with the US.

Leverage diaspora It is imperative for the US to offer India, a smaller economy, with favourable trade terms than cribbing about a small trade surplus. India should rather calculate the cost of 4 million Indians in schools, colleges, laboratories and offices working day in and out trying to 'Make America Great Again'. In such a case, India will run a massive trade deficit with the US.

DE-INDUSTRIALISATION TEMPLATE BETWEEN INDIA AND THE US

A deeper association in the future can provide Indian companies with deeper market integration and the US firms will get a better alternative to China. Partnership with the US firms can provide Indian firms also with greater competitiveness and develop attractive capacity building options in industries that range from AI to renewable energy to education to healthcare. This partnership is going to be beneficial because India is currently witnessing de-industrialisation. This means that there is a waning impact of manufacturers in textiles, leather, iron and steel etc. on the GDP of the nation via contribution to wage growth mobility, value add to the GDP and employment. In common economic parlance, de-industrialisation is natural because over a period of time, the manufacturing sector shows an inverted U-shaped curve; allowing the service sector to pick up. As India currently witnesses de-industrialisation, a partnership of Indian firms with the American firms in areas where cooperation can expand not only in bilateral but also in global domain can be a template for the future. The US and India can jointly collaborate on testing of 6G and 7G technologies and can jointly emerge as leaders in the technology, considering China is a master of 5G technologies.

INDIA–US FOREIGN TRADE—TRUMPED UP OR DOWN?

In the era of 'Make in India' and 'America First', there are a few steps India can take to enhance its exports.

State market mapping The USA has 50 states, all of which have different consumption patterns. The Indian government needs to authorise a study of market of each state and there behavioural economics. This data can be given to Indian exporters to enhance the leverage. As of now, only 1 state out of 50 is dominated by India, leaving a potential of 49 to be explored. To do this, the government should follow a three-step classification. Firstly, it needs to identify hot spots. These are states where India can be a top importer to some states. Secondly, identify warm spots, which are those states where India can concentrate to develop market access. Thirdly, develop cold spots that are those states that require efforts by Indian government to cut competition from existing players and create a niche.

Sector domination The Chinese have adopted a unique strategy. They have mapped the product requirements of American states and have dominated the product industry. Today, an American product is unable to bear the competition from a Chinese product in the American market. India has been a back end IT services provider to the US for long now. Nut, as there is a backlash to this strategy now, it is imperative for India to identify a new sector to dominate. India can build from its IT legacy. It now needs to shift to new IT products, of high-technology value, and position itself as an IT service provider in the US.

Radical is the new normal India has to establish a body similar to USTR. This body has to be manned by diplomats and trade specialists. Such a body has to work with their counterpart bodies in the US and identify common grounds for mutual benefit. India has to be positioned as a trade hub for products. It has to improve infrastructure, strengthen corporate governance mechanisms, encourage global branding and establish robust legal frameworks.

INDIA'S ENERGY DIPLOMACY WITH THE US

In 2018, India signed the US–India Strategic Energy Partnership and India had started importing oil and gas from the US. The Strategic Energy Partnership has four pillars. They include oil and gas; power and energy efficiency; clean and renewable energy; and sustainable growth. Though it may not be the cheapest option but is definitely one where India stands to be a gainer. India favours a deal between Tellurian Inc. and Petronet LNG in the future. In 2020, Exxon and Chart Industries had collaborated with Indian Oil Corporation to provide India with LNG. This is important because India is presently focusing on building gas pipeline infrastructure and that process will take time. So, in the meantime, in its push towards renewable energy, India is planning to import gas through containers as an alternative. In 2020, the US International Development Finance Corporation would setup an office in India and started with a financing facility of 600 million USD for renewable energy projects in India.

INDIA'S EDUCATION DIPLOMACY WITH THE US AND 21ST CENTURY KNOWLEDGE INITIATIVE

In 2009, the Obama–Singh 21st century knowledge initiative was launched. It is now a part of the Indo-US strategic partnership agreement. In 2011, the India–US Education Summit was held. It has subsequently held dialogues in 2012 and 2013 and had organised a road trip to promote strategic institution partnership. The aim of the Obama–Singh knowledge initiative was to promote R&D, vocational training and junior faculty development. As of 2016, it had been renamed the Indo-US 21st century knowledge initiative awards. India and the US have had Fulbright programme since 1950 and in 2008; it was renamed as the Nehru–Fulbright programme for science, technology and agriculture. India, under its latest government, is trying to emulate the concept of community colleges in the US to enhance vocational education and skill development in India.

THE H1-B AND F-1 VISA REGIME ISSUES BETWEEN INDIA AND THE US

Trump was in favour of 'merit-based' immigration in contrast to 'chain migration' in the existing format. The US government has the provision of an H-1B visa. It is a non-immigrant visa for temporary workers. It is given for select special occupations. The issue is that in the US, if a company like an IT firm cannot find a skilled US worker, it can attract skilled workers under the H-1B programme. The US population is skeptical about the majority of the jobs being given to outsiders as they allege that firms hire from abroad to cut costs as labour is cheaper if imported and this undermines the employment to the US citizens. Indian citizens are one of the largest H-1B users in the US. In 2015, the US administration under Obama signed the Consolidated Appropriation Act 2016. As per the law, the visa fee would be increased and the rise in cash flow to government coffers will be used for financing Obama's healthcare and biometric tracking system.

The hike in the fees is going to offset IT and BPO exports of India. With the coming of Donald Trump as the new US President, India and the US had some irritants in their bilateral diplomacy. The H-1B visa issues had emerged as one of the greatest sources of friction between the two countries. An employer had to apply for an H-1B visa for the employee with the US immigration department. At the same time, there was one L-1 visa category, which was an inter-company transfer category where the foreign worker could be temporarily transferred to the US in an executive or marginal position in the office of the same employer or its branch or subsidiary. Donald Trump had advocated changing the immigration system of the US and had asserted to make it more merit-based. The main logic of merit-based immigration was to ensure that the immigrants entering the US were highly skilled and contributed to the American economy. The goal of the new system was to have less low-skilled immigrants. In March 2017, the Trump administration decided that the government should not undertake fast track processing of H-1B visa applications from 3rd April 2017, for the next six months so that the US immigration authorities could analyse the H-1B extension applications of visa holders whose visas were on the verge of expiry. India has been an aggressive advocate of a fair and a rational approach to be adopted on visa-related issues. India's Foreign Minister S. Jaishankar had conveyed to the US lawmakers to treat the H-1B issue as a trade and service matter than treating it as an immigration issue. The private US firms can pay a premium of 1225 US dollars per application. The payment of the premium ensures that the immigration department expedites the H-1B application and processes it in 15 days in contrast to the normal process of six months. The government of the US has now stopped this practice. Under the Obama administration, a new H4 visa programme was launched that enabled the spouse of the H-1B visa holders in the US to undertake jobs in the US. Trump administration had signaled a roll back of H4 visa as well. The Trump administration placed the High-Skilled Integrity and Fairness Act of 2017 in front of the House of Representatives. The legislation had advocated for a market-based allocation of visas. The legislation introduces mechanisms where companies can attract foreign talent by making it mandatory for a H-1B visa holder to have a minimum salary of 1,30,000 USD. This figure is double of what existed since 1989, that is, 60,000 USD. The legislation thus reduces the incentive to outsource jobs yet allowing an option to outsource jobs if the company expresses a willingness to pay. The legislation intends to promote fairness in hiring skilled workers globally by removing the per country cap for immigrant visa policy. To plug the loopholes in H-1B and L-1 visa programmes, the H-1B and L-1 visa reform acts were also envisaged. In January 2017, the Protect and Grow American Jobs Act envisaged an increase in the minimum salary of H-1B visa holders and removal of the master's degree exemption. The H-1B reforms will affect Infosys, TCS, Wipro and so forth. More so with the hike in the minimum salary for visa holders, the smaller firms may find it difficult to incur costs, thereby affecting their growth. The profitability of the Indian IT sector would be affected as profits were maintained on the off shoring model. India has officially conveyed its concerns without taking up the matter through diplomatic channels. Indian firms in the US have now started recruiting domestic Americans as per the new requirements.

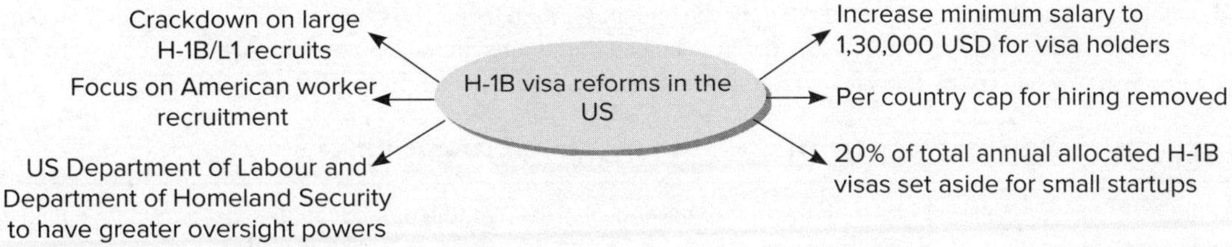

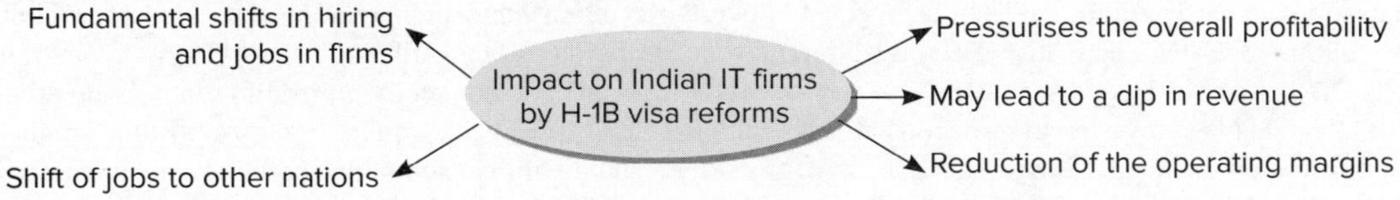

THE COVID-19 AND IMPACT ON THE INDO-US VISA DIPLOMACY

The US offers F-1 visa to the students that allows them to study for one year with a paid optional practical training, which usually leads to a job on the H1-B visa (the H-1 Visa regime began in 1952). A huge chunk of white-collar professionals apply under the H1-B category separately and migrate over to the US for short- and long-term projects. In most cases, these projects lead to lifelong employments. Over the last few decades, a combination of these two streams has formed the core of the 4 million strong Indian communities in the US. However, the COVID-19 pandemic is likely to not only disrupt the annual migration but threatens to dismantle the template, which has led to the formation of this vibrant cohort. The COVID-19 has led to 36 million Americans being unemployed and this has destroyed the American Dream of many Indian immigrants. As the US under Trump had announced in June 2020 that the US government was cancelling H1-B visas for one year, this move was likely to affect the American economy because the US did not churn out adequate number of graduate in Science, Technology, Engineering and Medicine field for needs of the US industries and corporates. The reason why prominent American firms prefer immigrants is not because of a fiction that they are cheap labour (despite the US Labour Department certifying that they are well-paid) but because the global giants need global talent and this highly internationalist workforce also gives these American firms an opportunity to expand their presence in global markets and these firms know well that brain drain is better than a brain in a drain (implying leaving the global talent at places of origin where they cannot explore international opportunities due to lack of global standard businesses). No doubt, the great physicist and futurist Michio Kaku had rightly called the H1-B visa programme the secret weapon of America. The American Immigration Council has rightly advocated that H1-B workers are critical in responding to public health emergencies in the US and they are the driving forces of the COVID-19 vaccine development programme as well.

THE NAFTA TEMPLATE FOR H1-B DIPLOMATIC COOPERATION

For instance, when Trump voiced his concerns on NAFTA, the Canadian PM realised that Canadian interests were at stake. He adopted a unique approach where the two parties could find a common ground rather than any confrontation. The strategy worked and a renewed NAFTA was finally adopted in 2018. The lesson for India here was a principle that came out. India needed to focus on collaboration and not confrontation with Trump. The idea of India would be to find a common ground mutually beneficial for both. The Trump administration had been very critical of H1-B visa issue. The administration had introduced some changes in the visa policy as well on the basis of Buy American and Hire American policy. Trump was concerned about what he called 'chain immigration' (where existing immigrants seeks permanent residencies for their relatives in the USA). It is important to note that Trump was not against immigration. All he had emphasised was that there needed to be immigration of highly skilled people to the US, who could help in the growth of the US and not of those who had limited skills. India had adopted a right approach in dealing with the issue. India had not raised the H1-B issue at a very high level in the administration except asserting that certain segments of the policy were discriminatory. The reason was that India had understood that there was no point adopting a confrontationist attitude because there were other green shoots available where a common ground could be achieved. India also knew that the protectionist strategy of Trump (compelling him to cut down H1-B visas and encourage states to go for domestic hiring) would make business tough for the American firms in the long run and they would themselves lobby for H1-B relaxations soon. Also, India knew rightly that in the last decade, the Indian who had immigrated to the US were 'highly skilled', thereby meeting the requirement of what Trump had emphasised upon. So, India had done precisely what Canadian PM did for NAFTA.

KASHMIR ISSUE AND DIVERGENT STRANDS OF DIPLOMACY

Upon the insistence of the US, India took the matter to the UN in 1947. India opined that the UN would urge Pakistan to halt aggression and withdraw forces. In the meantime, India sent an extensive combat operation in Kashmir. By the time Indian troops entered Kashmir, Pakistan had occupied two-thirds of Kashmir. India continued to advocate a diplomatic solution through the UN. The British certainly did not favour escalation and they tilted to support Pakistan out of its own interest. The British decided to seek the US assistance. The US itself was not keen on meddling into Asian affairs and was initially reluctant. However, to respect its alliance with the British, the US began to develop a position similar to the British position on the matter. They also advocated a plebiscite and a political solution. The US even warned India that if India did not cooperate, it could have consequences for the Indo-US relations. India, in contrast, insisted that it did not need goodwill of any nation and it could anyway develop proximity to the Soviets. India resented the Anglo-American axis and perceived the US policy on Kashmir as an extension of the colonial legacy. Thus, Kashmir has been one of the core dimensions of the American policy since the Cold War. Both Obama and Trump administration had tried to add Kashmir into the US equation. Both had a common objective of doing so and that was to appease Pakistan. Both followed this appeasement policy to ensure that they get honorable solution to the American nemesis in Afghanistan. For the US,

Pakistan is very crucial because he needs their support to ensure that Taliban does not attack American interests in future when they become a credible player in Afghanistan.

AMERICAN OBJECTION TO CITIZENSHIP AMENDMENT ACT AND INDIA'S LAUTENBERG AMENDMENT

The Indian Citizenship Amendment Act has been criticised by the US House Foreign Affairs Committee (HFAC). A quasi-official body called US Commission on International Religious Freedom (USCIRF), dominated by Christian fundamentalists advocated that there is a need to sanction principal leadership of India for the CAA. As a counter to CAA, India has raised Lautenberg Amendment of US (which was spearheaded by US Senator Frank Lautenberg in 1989), which allows certain persecuted religious minorities in the erstwhile Soviet Union to get the US citizenship. The amendment was extended to include 'persecuted minorities' from Iran in 2004, through the Specter Amendment. For India, the Lautenberg Amendments of the US are a strong response for Indian CAA because the amendments recognise that some refugees of specific religions from specific countries could be identified as 'historically persecuted groups' and, hence, given refugee status without requiring them to show that they individually had been persecuted. The template of the Indian CAA is quite similar.

THE US COMMISSION ON INTERNATIONAL RELIGIOUS FREEDOM REPORT AND DIVERGENT DIPLOMACY

The USCIRF in its 2020 Report has added India as a country of particular concern (CPC), a tag that India got the second time after 2002 Gujarat riots under the able leadership of Narendra Modi. The USCIRF was established in 1998 under the International Religious Freedom Act as an independent US Federal Government Commission to monitor the freedom of religion all across the globe minus the US. The body has nine commissioners, of which three are appointed the President of the US, two by the party of the President of the US, four by opposition leaders in Congress. The report has branded India as a CPC due to various factors that range from a discriminatory Citizenship Amendment Act to that of violation of civil liberties in the aftermath of abrogation of Article 370 to that of Supreme Court playing a subjugated role of siding with the Executive in overlooking the implementation of a divisive and exclusionary NRC in Assam. Many true hate-filled orange coloured nationalists in India were too concerned about India being placed as a CPC along with Saudi Arabia, Pakistan, North Korea, Syria, China and Myanmar on religious freedom. They became more upset when certain West Asian countries tweeted them to remind them of the civilisational commitment of tolerance India always stood for, which stands to be eroding now due to state-sponsored terrorism unleashed in the country. From being a country of special concern (CSC), where India stood par with Scandinavian states, to now a CPC, which engages in severe violations of religious freedom is a domestic achievement of the ruling regime. This global blot on India has only proven the systematic, on-going and egregious violations including torture, degrading treatment, prolonged detention without charges and other flagrant denial of right to life and liberty of the minorities. A nation where occupants to highest constitutional offices, with complete patronage from the highest political office of India, proclaim, "revenge for anti-CAA protestors be fed with bullets and not biryani" have been contributors for India to be tagged a CPC. Even though the government might have diplomatically rejected the report by branding the report as "prejudiced, inaccurate and full of misleading observations", but the report does present an opportunity for India to introspect on the status of religious freedom being violated with a culture of impunity and state patronage.

SHARED VALUES, SHARED DEFICITS BETWEEN INDIA AND THE US AND CULTURAL MULTIPOLARITY

Democracy and pluralism have been the greatest shared values that bind India and the US and have been a core driver of bilateral convergence. In any global posturing, the role of values in foreign policy seem to be declining today. This decline is traced back to the Cold War when the US tried to break the Sino-Soviet axis, aid the Chinese growth and eventually claim victory of the Cold War by defeating the Soviet. However, in this victory of the US was sown the seeds of decline of American predominance as the aid to Chinese growth eventually manifested as global ascendence of China. While aiding the Chinese growth story, the Americans displayed no interests in human rights and democratic values, both of which were absent in China till the time China was a willing partner in breaking the Soviets. Even though the US has often used values and democracy as per their own convenience in the international system; it has left no opportunity in highlighting a 'democracy deficit' in India whenever possible. In recent times, through murmurs on India's religious freedom, democracy and human rights record, the Americans have often tried to corner India and portray it as a dark player in the international system. Despite the US using this as a faultline, the way India has handled these faultiness reflects that the two democracies can manage divergences quite maturely. India is well aware that the legacy of civil war continues to haunt the US and the recent event like Black Lives Matters, White Supremacy, Capitol Hill riots are showcasing to the world that the very foundation of trust, which binds American democracy, appears to be on shaky grounds. In this backdrop, both India and the US know that having multi-cultural and multi-ethnic societies will compel the two to often look at larger forces of history as they both realise that the world is not just politically and militarily multipolar but even culturally multipolar. In this sense, both India and the US know that the issue of democracy is not a challenge but a way to open a new space of cooperation between India and the US.

THE ROAD AHEAD FOR INDIA'S DIPLOMACY WITH THE US

As analysed above, there are a lot of irritants that happen to exist as the relations are not between equals, as India is a post-colonial state while the US is a mature hegemonic power; thus, a situation where even small things can have large consequences. There is absence of mutual trust and high respect deficiency. The establishments of the two sides are often disappointed for non-achievements of short-term objectives. The two sides do not have adequate understanding of the potential of the bilateral economic ties. Unfortunately, the two sides till now have not developed meaningful and pragmatic ideas that can be applied realistically to enhance their strategic partnership. More so, the Americans till today suffer from the 'chained elephant' symptom. Despite India making tremendous economic progress, the Americans still feel that India is a land of snake charmers and illiterate people. There is no strategic convergence on many issues. India feels that at the international level, the US is a protector of the rich and the US feels that India is a manipulating nation that is a representative of the poor. India feels that the US has not been able to realise that India has a mind of its own. India says that the US is not able to understand that as India was colonised by the British because of trade practices, it is this why India is reluctant to be too open on issue of trade, like the US. The Indians till today are unable to come out of the hangover of American support to Pakistan during the Cold War. A huge segment of Indian strategic community feels that the US is not a reliable partner. In the present times, the India and the US have very divergent views on Russia, China and Iran. For India, Iran is a valuable partner not just for oil but also access to Afghanistan and the larger Eurasia. The US views Iran as an evil and wants India to reduce its oil dependence from Iran. This is ironic as historically American West Asia policy has been also dependent upon energy from the region. In the era of Trump, the entire American society was divided in Russia. Half of the society in the US feels that Russia needs to be constrained through sanctions and isolation to prevent a revival of the Cold War (Trump falls here), while the rest half believes the need to cooperate with Russia for stalling China. India is caught in this crossfire, despite having a deep relationship with Russia, which India is not willing to forgo, despite its growing proximity to the US. Thus, India has to negotiate carve-outs, sanction waivers and exemptions. Even though there is consensus in India and the US that China is the 'Banquo's ghost' and is a threat in Asia owing to its attempt to position itself as an Asian hegemon; there is no understanding on how India can share burden and responsibilities to check China. In fact, India has adopted a layered strategy where it is okay to engage in the Indo-Pacific and Quad (designed as per Americans to check China but perceived as just other 'multilateral arrangements' by India). Only if these deep-seated perceptions change, can the two sides enable to evolve a deep geopolitical and strategic relationship, based on 'shared values'.

QUESTIONS FOR PRACTICE

S. No.	Questions for Practice
1.	Do you think the India–US nuclear deal was an attempt to balance China? Discuss.
2.	Examine the major irritants between India and the US relations.
3.	India and Latin America have low octane ties? Discuss.
4.	Explain the major features of India and the US strategic convergences.
5.	Do you think that the trade war between the US and China is an opportunity for India? Discuss.

SECTION 12

Important International Institutions, Agencies and Fora—Their Structure, Mandate

1. India in the United Nations: Negotiation Styles and Aspirational Status
2. India's Diplomacy in Global International Organisations

AN OVERVIEW

UPSC has asked macro questions from this area. For instance, in 2021, a question on QUAD was asked while in 2020, the question was related to the role of WHO in managing the pandemic. In 2018, one question was on Ashgabat Agreement while another was implications of trade war. It is observed that questions can be divided into two parts. Sometimes the questions are related to institutions associated with the United Nations and sometimes, the questions are related to other institutions outside the UN system like BRICS, AIIB etc.

Potential foresight On the basis of the trend observed, it is clear that questions are likely to be more related to macro agreements, India's participation and growing profile in G-7, G-20, India's permanent candidature in the UNSC, experience of India as a non-permanent member of the Security Council and India's global agendas. There must be a careful study done of the reforms India is seeking in international institutions and methodologies associated. Also, one must carefully analyse institutions where India is able to break the ice and act as a bridge such as OIC and BRICS.

CHAPTER 1

India in the United Nations: Negotiation Styles and Aspirational Status

HISTORICAL ORIGIN OF THE UNITED NATIONS

The origin of the United Nations (UN) can be traced back to the period of enlightenment in the eighteenth century, which inspired the concept of rationality in the conduct of international affairs. The manifestation of this rationality culminated in the birth of first, the League of Nations, and then of the UN. The age of enlightenment gave birth to modern liberal democratic nationalism and introduced concepts such as democracy and international law. In the period preceding the eighteenth century, the international relations between states were based upon mutual treaties to maintain peace and force as an instrument was used only when any principle of a treaty was violated. The hierarchical imperial administrations maintained public order through dominance. The Peace Conference of Westphalia in 1648 was the first instrument of modern times that established the idea of balance of power. The Peace of Westphalia addressed issues related to the reorganisation of Europe after the conclusion of the Thirty Years' War. The Peace of Westphalia was followed by another landmark event—the Vienna Conference in 1814–15, where the participants of the conference aimed to serve peace to the world by organising regular meetings of the great powers. The Vienna Conference or the Concert of Europe ultimately established a peaceful Europe. It initiated the System of Congress in European affairs where consultation was used as a mechanism to resolve disruptive rises. Though the Concert of Europe had helped in supporting international cooperation, World War I caused a serious disorder to the existing system. At the end of the World War I, the USA entered the club of the great powers. Woodrow Wilson, the President of the USA, in his famous 'Fourteen Points' speech[1], envisaged the creation of a new body called the League of Nations. The basic aim of the League was to strive for collective security and eliminate chances of a future war. The formation of the League as an international body made sense because there had been tremendous bloodshed during the World War I. Leaders at the time were determined to establish a world organisation to prevent another conflict on the same scale. In 1919, at the Paris Peace Conference, Wilson tried to include the clause detailing the establishment of the League of Nations as part of the Treaty of Versailles. The Covenant for the League of Nations finally came into force on 10th January 1920 and the League held its first meeting in Geneva.

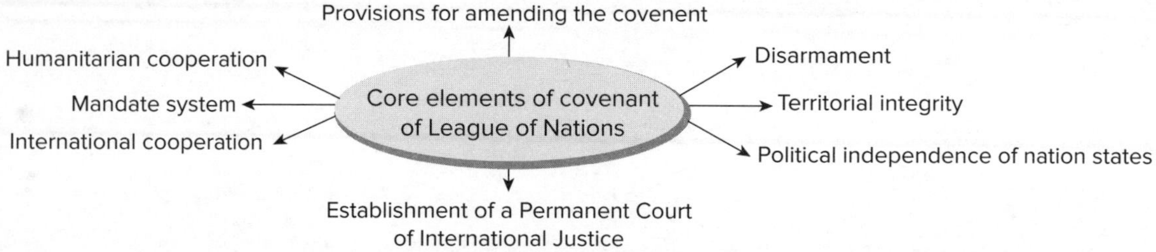

[1]Fourteen Points is a blueprint for world peace that was to be used for peace negotiations after World War I, elucidated in January 8, 1918, speech on war aims and peace terms by the US President Woodrow Wilson.

The USA, which had proposed the creation of the League in the first place, did not join the same as the USA Senate had refused to ratify the Treaty of Versailles. The entire cause of the League of Nations got diluted because of the absence of the USA as a power in the League. Over a period of time, the League as a body became ineffective and inoperative. The Atlantic Charter of 1941 planted the seeds for a future global organisation for 'general security'. In 1942, the Foundational Declaration of the UN was announced. Franklin D. Roosevelt coined the term UN for the first time. The new organisation was envisaged under the Atlantic Charter and it advocated the idea of general security and not collective security as envisaged under the League of Nations. Roosevelt, Churchill and Stalin laid the foundation of the new body called United Nations (hereafter referred to the UN) at 4.50 p.m., on 24th October 1945. A total of 51 original members (or founding members) joined that year. Fifty of them signed the Charter at the UN Conference on International Organisation in San Francisco on 26 June 1945, while Poland, which was not represented at the conference, signed it on 15 October 1945.

BASIC PRECEPTS OF THE UN

As mentioned in the previous section, the UN emerged as a second attempt by the world to create a new inter-governmental organisation (IGO) after the creation of the League of Nations.

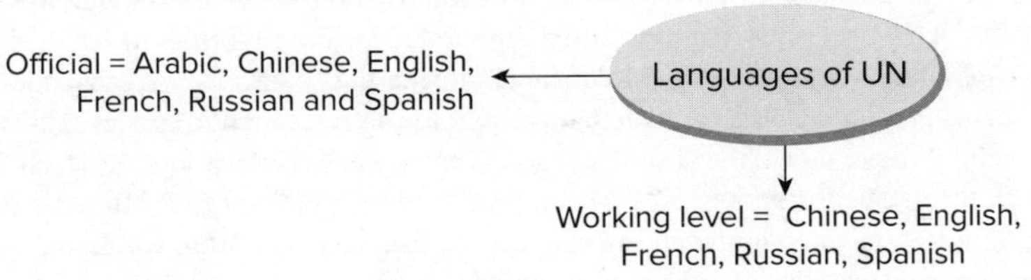

India is a founder member of the UN as it was one of the parties, which signed the charter establishing the UN in 1945 in San Francisco. The UN presently consists of 193 sovereign member states that have equal representation in the UN General Assembly. The UN is the world's largest intergovernmental organisation, ahead of the Organisation of Islamic Cooperation. The UN can suspend a member if a member violates the UN Charter. No country has ever been suspended from the UN till date. The UN has not achieved universality because Vatican City and Taiwan have not become members of the UN till date. The criteria for admission of new members to the UN are set out in Chapter II, Article 4 of the UN Charter:

1. Membership in the UN is open to all peace-loving states, which accept the obligations contained in the present Charter and, in the judgment of the Organisation, are able and willing to carry out these obligations.
2. The admission of any such state to membership in the UN will be effected by a decision of the General Assembly upon the recommendation of the Security Council.

A recommendation for admission from the Security Council requires affirmative votes from at least nine of the council's fifteen members, with none of the five permanent members using their veto power. The Security Council's recommendation must then be approved in the General Assembly by a two-thirds majority vote.

The primary responsibility of the UN, which lies in maintaining global peace and security, rests with the Security Council (SC). The UNSC has five permanent members namely, the USA, the UK, France, Russia and China. The five permanent members have special voting rights. This special voting right, which they may also exercise against or for each member, is called veto power. Using a veto power, any of the five member states can defeat a decision. Abstinence from a voting by a permanent member is not tantamount to the use of veto. While solving international disputes, the SC has the responsibility to take decisions. To maintain peace and security, the SC can setup fact-finding missions, observation missions and may even advocate a case for mediation, conciliation and assistance.

CONCEPT OF RESPONSIBILITY TO PROTECT (R2P) AND PREVENTIVE DIPLOMACY

The functioning of the UNSC is not open to the public. The global community is apprised of the decisions of the UNSC through announcement of briefings. What goes into the making of these decisions by the five permanent members is not disclosed. Knowing how UNSC takes decisions is crucial as it is the sole global body vested with the authority to determine if a threat to international security exists or not. Indian diplomat Hardeep Puri asserts that at times, UNSC decisions have been perilous interventions causing more destabilisation in an already volatile situation. According to Puri, who has served as the Permanent Representative of the UN, when India was elected to be a non-permanent member of the SC in 2011–12, the recent UN interventions in Syria and Libya have been perilous. Puri moreover insists that the perilous and unnecessary interventions in Iraq have led to the rise of non-state actors and terrorist groups such as ISIS. Such interventions are largely made on the logic of 'Responsibility to Protect' (R2P) to prevent genocide and seek support at the humanitarian level. Since the end of the Cold War, the idea of preventive diplomacy has emerged in the form of R2P. Some scholars who have analysed the R2P have developed a view that *R2P is a code that gives the international community unbridled powers that often lead to interference in the internal affairs of nation states.* Such scholars feel that R2P could be a phenomenon that could potentially give rise to a new era of colonialism. The main idea of preventive diplomacy is to cure the conflicts before they emerge in their fiercest forms on the international scene. Dag Hammarskjöld, who was then the Secretary-General of the UN, used the term preventive diplomacy for the first time in 1960s. He proposed that the basic idea of preventive diplomacy was to keep local conflicts outside the superpower rivalry and prevent the two superpowers from escalating conflicts. Though the view of Hammarskjöld was relevant during the Cold War period, it lost its relevance during the post-Cold War era due to the absence of active rivalry between power blocks. The sixth Secretary-General of the UN, Boutros Boutros-Ghali propounded a new approach in the post-Cold War times in 1992. According to him, preventive diplomacy was not only about preventing disputes that already exist from escalating into conflicts, but also about taking action to prevent a dispute itself from arising. The idea was based upon the logic of common good of the entire humanity. The eighth UN Secretary-General, Ban Ki-Moon, also asserted that preventive diplomacy should involve all the stakeholders to strengthen the UN partnerships between all regional and international actors. He emphasised that any preventive diplomacy, when applied, should be under the larger umbrella of the UN Charter and should not violate the sovereignty of a state.

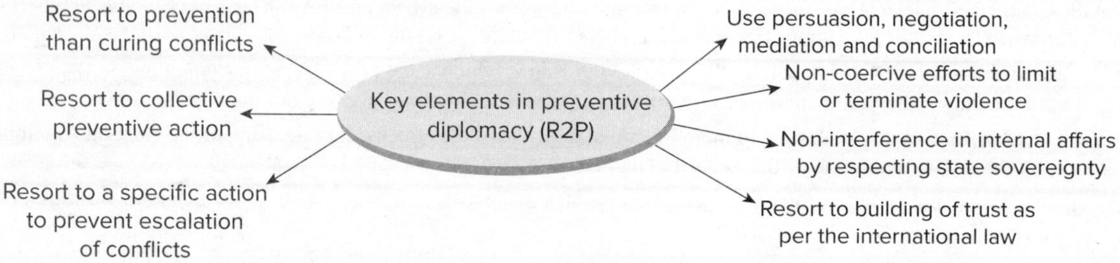

Preventive diplomacy is not concerned with solving every problem in the world, as it is a special response in a situation, which warrants interference to avoid escalation into any form of violence. It may not even always prevent a conflict, but as a tool may promote peace by preventing escalation of the conflict. According to Article 51 of the UN Charter, if there is an armed attack upon a state, the state can resort to use force in self-defence while informing the UNSC immediately. Article 51 further asserts that the SC can also initiate steps to restore peace and security in the international system. Under the Chapter VII of the UN Charter, the determination of the existence of a threat to the world peace would be taken only by the UNSC and under Article 41, steps would be taken to maintain peace without the use of force. However, under Article 42, the UNSC is empowered to use air, sea or land power to restore peace through blockades and operations. A lot of questions remain unanswered. The most important question is on what criteria the UNSC would get to decide that an issue in a state is ripe for international intervention and is not an internal matter. There are, however, international situations where a concept such as the R2P actually helps. The idea of R2P is that a state actor should take steps to protect people and if a state, in some extreme scenario, is unable to protect its people, then the responsibility to protect its citizens falls upon the international community. The R2P was endorsed by the UNGA in 2005 and the UN resolutions 1694 (in 2006) and 1894 (in 2009) also affirmed the same. The states are quite worried, as some have developed a feeling that R2P would be used to interfere in the internal affairs of a state and may lead to regime changes.

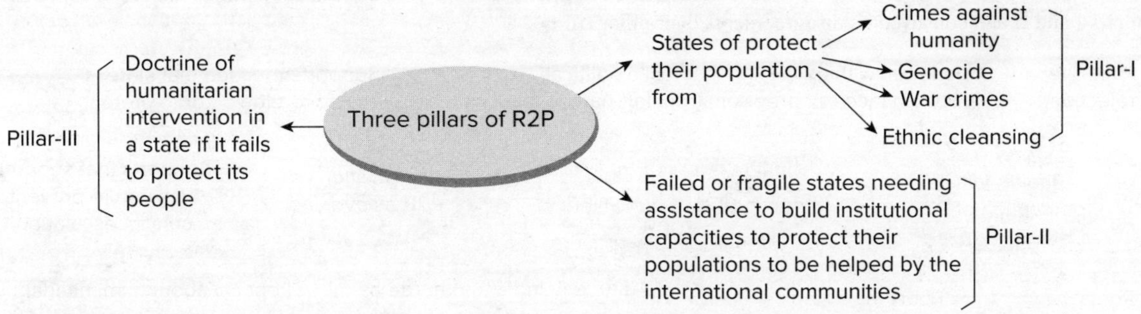

PRINCIPLES OF INDIA'S PREVENTIVE DIPLOMACY AND R2P DIPLOMACY

During the Nehruvian times, India evolved the principles of non-interference and non-intervention. However, in 1971, when Indian troops helped sliced off East Pakistan, India cited the logic of right of self-defence provided under Article 51 of the UN Charter (as explained above). At the global level, whenever India has engaged at UN level, it has favoured the idea of using non-violence as a tool of conflict resolution. India's political perception of not viewing the world in completely black and white is rooted deep in its psyche. This perception owes its origin to 2000-year-old Indian epic called *The Mahabharata*. India often dictates openness, tolerance and non-violence to all states as a value irrespective of a domestic regime. In 2001, the International Commission on Intervention and State Sovereignty (ICISS) prepared a report on R2P. India, during the initial phase of evolution of the concept of R2P, showed some skepticism. It, initially, did not even send official representatives for a discussion. The reason it did not officially participate in ICISS was because ICISS was an NGO and India normally does not officially interact with NGOs by sending its diplomats. More importantly, the Indian perception about R2P was that it was largely, as explained and discussed by the ICISS, just a new name for humanitarian intervention where Western states wanted to resort to some sort of force to achieve their own interests. All these years, India had formed a group called G-4 in 2004 with India, Brazil, Japan and Germany, and used the G-4 to advocate for the UN reforms. As the debate on R2P progressed, India initially stated that it would not accept right of humanitarian intervention or idea of military humanism in any form, as was under discussion. In fact, India's Permanent Representative to the UN at that time asserted that only a reformed and enlarged UNSC should be authorised to undertake any decision on any such issue and that it should also include the regional organisations. India constantly exhibited recalcitrant opposition to the idea of R2P in the initial years. The initial document of the R2P followed the idea of coercive solidarism[2]. However, as there was a staunch opposition to the idea, the idea of 'consensual solidarism' was added by replacing the idea of coercive solidarism. However, two events in the times ahead brought about a shift in Indian perception of the R2P. Let us have a look at the two events. In 2007, the military Junta of Myanmar suppressed peaceful protestors. All Western states condemned the suppression and even resorted to sanctioning Myanmar. India, on the other hand, stated that such issues were domestic issues of a state and that India would remain neutral to its neighbour's internal squabbles and continue to engage with Myanmar. In 2008, Cyclone Nargis caused heavy devastation in Myanmar. India immediately resorted to an engaging approach of closed-door diplomacy and provided immediate relief supplies. Similarly, in 2009, as the Sri Lankan civil war was in its final stages, India maintained a diplomatic rhetoric of no harm to the civilians (this was due to domestic political compulsions and the upcoming elections in 2009), but refused any sort of intervention

[2]Solidarism is the social theory of a combined solidarity of interests.

in the affairs of Sri Lanka. These two instances of 2007 and 2009 gave India an option to evolve its position on R2P. In 2009, when the UNGA debated the R2P, India asserted that it favours the idea that protecting its citizens is the sovereign responsibility of the state. India supported the pillar I of the R2P. India also supported the idea that weak states would be provided international assistance to prevent conflicts from escalating. India, thus, also supported pillar II of the R2P. India showed resistance to the idea of international humanitarian intervention in case a state failed to protect its people. India asserted that this measure should be used as a last resort and only exercised on case-specific basis. India maintained that if international humanitarian intervention is used (as a last resort) it should be used in compliance with the Charter of the UN and regional organisations operating in the region of intervention should be consulted. India, therefore, supported pillars I and II and conveyed its disagreements over pillar III.

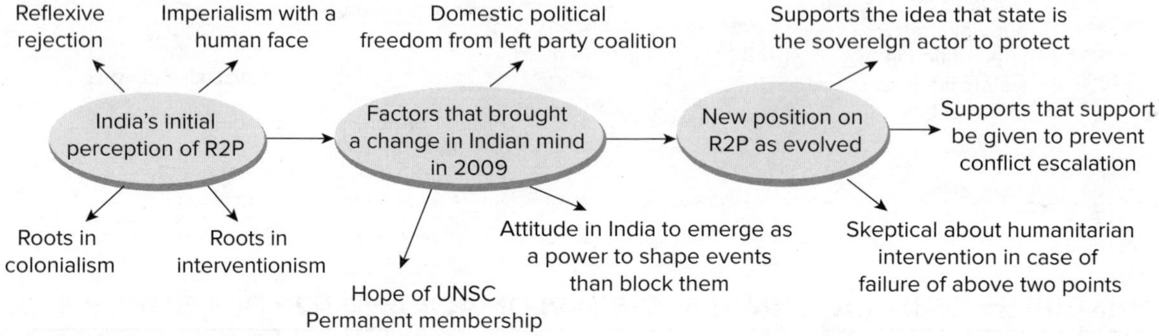

In 2010, India was elected to the UNSC as a non-permanent member for two years. India witnessed its first challenge in February 2011 when the Libyan crises took place. The UNSC passed a resolution (resolution number 1970) urging for an immediate halt of violence and advocated that the Libyan case be referred to the ICC. India voted in favour of the UNSC resolution 1970. As the situation in Libya worsened, the UNSC passed another, more stringent, resolution (resolution 1973) and urged the member states to take all possible actions to protect civilians. India abstained in the vote of the UNSC resolution 1973 as it stated that there was no clarity on the ground situation in Libya and the action advocated under the UNSC resolution 1973 violates Libyan sovereignty. The NATO immediately launched Operation 'Unified Protector' in Libya. India vocally criticised the NATO operation as, when the NATO began its operations, it began to fund the rebels for a regime change. India was alarmed to see that instead of focusing on making peace on the ground, NATO was making no attempts for a ceasefire. India asserted that the way the UNSC resolution 1973 was adopted and implemented on the ground brought a bad name to the idea of R2P. India began to press the idea that there needed to be a broad debate upon the third pillar and the circumstances in which it will be used. Brazil also promoted the idea of Responsibility While Protecting (RWP) and India advocated that R2P should be anchored in RWP. India further asserted that imposing the idea of a regime change from outside is a dangerous path to be followed.

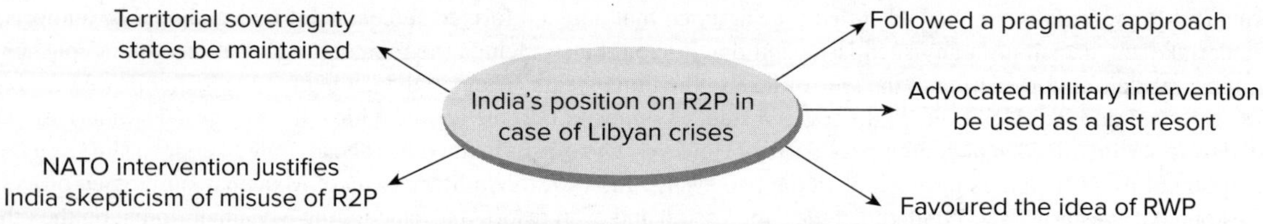

In October 2011, the Syrian crisis became the second area of contention for India. India again abstained from voting in the case of Syria, as it did not want a 'second Libya' situation to be perpetrated in Syria. India emphasised that it would favour a dialogue in Syria and not a threat of sanctions as advocated by the West. India, during its tenure as a non-permanent member of the UNSC, succeeded in getting statements passed that not only condemned the Syrian atrocities on civilians but also proposed a negotiation and a national solution amongst the parties in the civil war. In February 2012 and July 2012, India supported two more resolutions, which favoured a regional attempt by the Arab League to find a solution and use of non-military sanctions on the Syrian regime led by Assad. The analysis of Syria and Libya clearly prove that India favoured its own interpretation of R2P rooted in its own historical past. Our analysis of India's behaviour from 2005 to 2012 on R2P shows that India does not want to be a power that obstructs but instead wishes to be an emerging player that shapes international norms, while preferring to play a rule-based game.

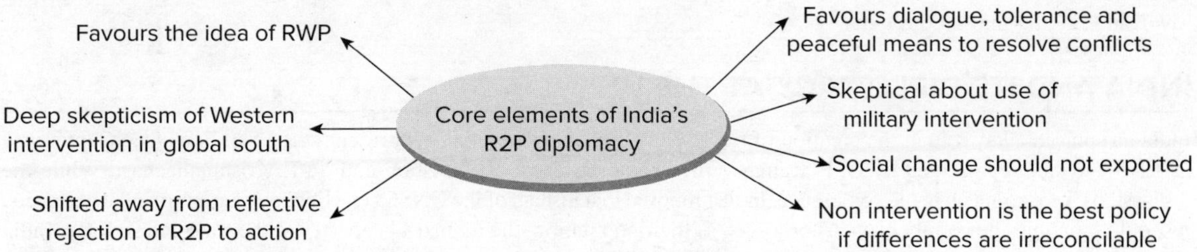

KEY ELEMENTS IN INDIA'S MULTILATERAL NEGOTIATIONS IN FOREIGN POLICY

India has realised that multilateral forums offer India necessary platforms to exercise global influence. India always attaches greater importance to global organisations as it helps in measuring the rise of India as a major player in the international system. Indian diplomats also consider postings in the global organisations as prestigious as it enables them to inculcate some serious negotiation-related skills in themselves. In the initial period of the Cold War, India used to be a rule taker at the global level. Since the end of the Cold War, India has shifted its position to that of a rule maker today. Keeping in sync with growing Indian capabilities and a rising international profile of India, India has decided to partake in the exercise of shaping norms today. What puts Indian diplomats in a place of advantage in international organisations is their proficiency in English and deep knowledge about the history of core issues vested in the international scene. Instead of formal training, Indian diplomats work upon building their historical knowledge database by working with senior diplomats and such skill comes handy in international organisations. Many countries in the world, at different times, have appreciated this quality in Indian diplomats. At the international level, Indian diplomats strive to act as a bridge between conflicting parties. A unique feature of Indian diplomacy at the multilateral level is that they may refuse firmly to accept a deal which may be unfavourable to India. This aspect of India's policy is visible at forums discussing climate change, trade and nuclear deals such as NPT and CTBT and so on. Because of such a behaviour, at times, India often puts to risk the support of powerful countries that may have helped her play a larger role in shaping norms at the global level. India's traditional multilateral policy began from the way it rallied countries under the rubric of non-alignment and G-77. These groups were used by India to reject the ideas propounded by the West against the interests of the participants. The non-aligned states and G-77 collectively worked as a coalition in the UN to block any initiatives that might hurt the interests of the coalition. At the end of the Cold War, non-alignment became more of a forum. India gradually began to shift to seek solidarity with smaller groups that could advance Indian interests. As India searched for smaller groups, it remained confined to developing states only. According to Aruna Narlikar, the coalition was not issue-based but still a bloc-style concept. India has, however, found it difficult to obtain recognition for new groups. India, for instance, found it difficult to establish a group called 'Development Agenda Group', comprising twenty-two states. India has, in the meantime, launched a massive bureaucratic campaign for a permanent seat to the UNSC. In fact, whenever there has been a state visit of any leader, India makes the pledge of support by the visiting Head of the State as a part of the Joint Communiqué. Despite support pledges from the USA, the UK, France and Russia, India has not been able to succeed effectively. In fact, India has become a part of the G-4 to seek a coalition-based support for a permanent UNSC seat. One of the important reasons for these unsatisfactory results till date regarding the campaign is the lack of a powerful push from the Indian political leadership and relatively less resources available to the diplomatic corps for the campaign. India, in the last two decades, has become unsuccessful in mobilising foreign states, based on compelling arguments, to push for India's candidacy at the UNSC. Also, there has been no realisation amongst the P-5 states of anything of India's inherent power structures that may compel them to add India in the group. The P-5 has still not had the feeling that the absence of India at the P-5 states may have led to a missing link in adequate representation of all states equally in the world. The bureaucratic lethargy was visible in 2006 when Shashi Tharoor entered the fray to be appointed the UN Secretary General. Tharoor lost out to South Korean Ban-Ki Moon, as Indian foreign bureaucracy could not powerfully assert at the level of closed-door negotiations with all states in the world while South Koreans made Ban-Ki Moon's appointment one of the core priorities of their foreign policy. In 2007, India rectified the shortcomings in Tharoor's campaign when it came to the appointment of a Secretary General of Commonwealth of Nations. India's MEA and political leadership launched an elaborate and a massive campaign that saw Kamlesh Sharma sail through.

INDIA AND ITS DIPLOMACY AT THE UN

India has played a key role in the creation of the UN. An Indian delegation was present at the San Francisco Conference in 1945 and was represented by C. P. Ramaswamy Mudaliar, Feroz Khan Noon and V. T. Krishnamachari. While the discussions were going on in the conference, India proposed that instead of the UNSC 'electing' six non-permanent members, it should 'appoint' the members on criteria such as their population, the industrial capacity of the state and so forth. India also asserted that six members be 'appointed' to the UNSC to participate in the discussions of the UNSC without a right to vote. Though India's suggestions were not accepted, India also raised concerns over veto powers. India became one of the founding members of the UN. As India began to engage with the UN as an independent country, it first focused on decolonisation. India believed that the UN, as a platform, could be used to expedite the process of decolonisation of the world and this would also provide India an opportunity to showcase its global leadership at a world platform. Throughout the period of the Cold War, India began to use the UN platform for spearheading disarmament and solicited the support of the UN for development. The 3-D formula of India at the UN (Decolonisation, Disarmament and Development) worked well for India. However, at present, India has been seeking reforms in the UNSC. India aspires for a permanent seat at the UNSC. In 2015, an Intergovernmental Negotiation adopted a formal document at the UN for the UN reforms. A text-based negotiation process has been launched for reforms of the UNSC from 2015.

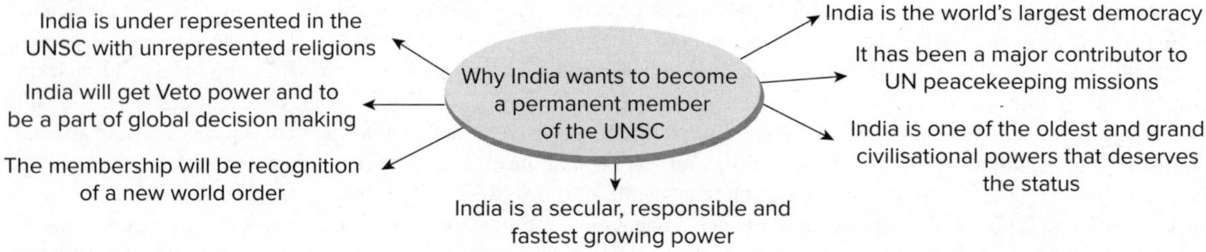

China has been one of the primary hurdles in India's accession as a permanent member to the UNSC. China does not want to share the status of being the only Asian power in the UNSC with India. More so, although India has received vocal support from the USA, the UK, France and Russia for its permanent candidacy to the UNSC, these powers have been quite reluctant to undertake the UNSC reforms to add India. There is a general perception that the powers intend to maintain a status quo in the arena of international relations. Also, as permanent membership to the UNSC requires two-thirds majority of the UN General Assembly, seeking a consensus on the same shall be another challenge for India. Some permanent members of the UNSC have argued that India's contribution to the budget of the Security Council does not match its claims to be at the higher table. However, with the beginning of the text-based reforms since 2015 for the first time in the modern history of the UN, the situation has reignited hopes for India's permanent candidacy once again.

INDIA'S AGENDA AS A NON-PERMANENT MEMBER OF THE UN SECURITY COUNCIL

In 2021, India was appointed as one of the non-permanent members of the UNSC for 2021–22. India was elected unopposed from Asia-Pacific seat with 183 of 193 votes in favour. Prior to its selection, India initiated a brochure campaign to highlight its agenda that India intends to put at the global table as a member. India's Foreign Minister S. Jaishankar asserted that India shall highlight international terrorism, reforms of the UNSC and its expansion, streamlining the peacekeeping operations of the UN and technology initiatives India intends to undertake. India, on becoming a member, highlighted that the processes of international governance have come under a severe strain because the traditional and non-traditional security threats have remained unchecked and one such egregious example is of terrorism. India also asserted that the COVID-19 caused economic crisis and unreformed and under-represented SC are global challenges. Thus, Indian foreign minister has asserted that as a non-permanent member, India shall be pushing for New Orientation for Reformed Multilateral System (NORMS). To achieve success in the objectives India has set for herself, it is imperative that India does not go for a transactional diplomacy at the global table, but rather adopts a value-based leadership and position itself as a voice of the weaker nations.

INDIA AND CLIMATE CHANGE DIPLOMACY

The debate of climate change owes its origin from 1970s. The UN Conference on Human Environment was held in 1972 in Stockholm. Twenty years later, in 1992, the world achieved consensus to establish UNFCCC (United Nations Framework Convention on Climate Change). Over a period of time, the UNFCCC along with IPCC (Intergovernmental Panel on Climate Change) worked out some dedicated scientific research on the issues relating to global warming. The newfound euphoria for climate sciences culminated in the birth of the Kyoto Protocol in 1997. The Kyoto Protocol, however, ended in 2012 (as its compliance period was from 2008 to 2012) and since then the leaders of the world have been struggling to come out with a new successor agreement, despite the Paris Agreement available as a rudimentary framework since 2015. In the same time period, however, the leaders of the world were able to achieve a consensus on Montreal Protocol to tackle issues pertaining to depletion of ozone layer. India has participated in the global climate change diplomacy since the 1980s. India was one of the most forceful voices in 1972 at the UN Conference on Human Environment that was held in Stockholm. India asserted that the fixation of the Western world on industrialisation and aggressive economic growth has been the most important reason for rise of environmental concerns at the global level. Indira Gandhi at Stockholm emphasised that over-consumption of resources in the West was a major cause for the degradation of environment. She refuted the claims of the West that exploitation of natural resources by developing world was the major reason for the environmental mess. Indira Gandhi asserted the right to development of the developing world as a strategy. She advocated that the Western world provide assistance to the developing world in its quest for development, as they were responsible for the injustices perpetrated upon the third world due to colonialism and imperialism. In 1988, the UN asserted that climate change is a common concern for mankind and decided to setup an IPCC to deliberate upon the issue of climate change. The UNGA, in 1989, urged members to establish a 'framework convention' to address climate change. In 1992, this led to the birth of the United Nations Framework Convention on Climate Change (UNFCCC) in Rio at the Earth Summit. India was a part of the intergovernmental negotiating committee, which negotiated the conduct of the convention. India understood that climate diplomacy could affect its national interests and hence, became a part of the climate change negotiations. India began to outline its position on climate change that the GHG (greenhouse gas) emissions were majorly caused by the developed world, as the emissions of the developing world were miniscule in comparison. India also said that as developing world will have to work to remove poverty and undertake development, their GHG emissions would rise. Therefore, in this prevailing scenario, a legally binding target upon the developing world could not be advanced. India advocated that any convention in future should establish a bridge of technology transfers from the Western world to the global south to help them meet developmental challenges. India advised that an equitable solution to tackle GHG emissions is that the developing world reduce their emissions per capita and converge them with the per capita emissions of developing world.

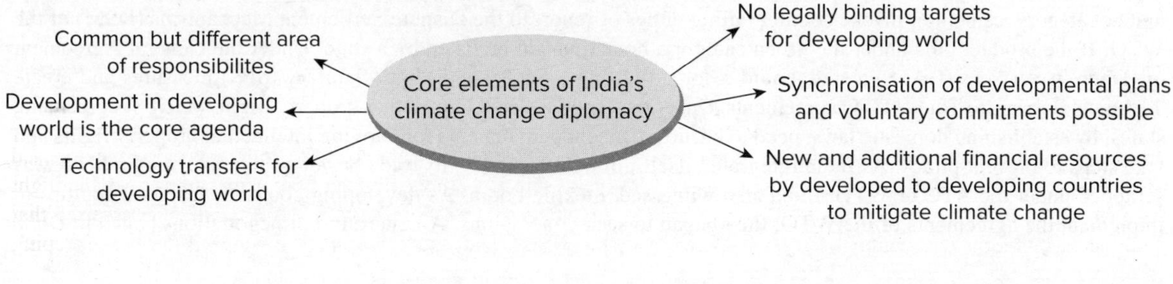

At the CoP-1 (Conference of the Parties) in Berlin, in 1995, India advocated that Annex-I parties accept legal targets to reduce emissions in a time-bound manner through a protocol. India succeeded to get the idea of 'differentiated responsibilities' endorsed in the Berlin mandate. India, during the CoP-3 negotiations in Kyoto, pressed for the removal of any voluntary commitments for developing world. The CoP-3 agreed upon the same but introduced mechanisms such as joint implementation, clean development mechanism (CDM) and emissions trading and so on. Over a period of time, India accepted that it would ensure (through a voluntary pledge) that its emissions do not exceed the emissions of the developed world. In the Bali Action Plan, India successfully ensured that its domestic measures for mitigation are not placed under external scrutiny as doing so would have violated India's sovereignty. In 2008, India announced its National Action Plan on Climate Change. India pledged that it will resort to mitigation actions domestically and by 2020, would voluntarily reduce India's emission intensity by 20–25% of its GDP. India follows a two-point strategy. It has joined hands with the G-77 to ensure that no legally binding commitments are imposed on developing states. It has also worked with the BASIC group (Brazil, South Africa, India and China) at the global level. When the Modi government came into power in 2014, it continued with the same policies as it had espoused earlier. India is still following a bilateral policy to garner financial and technical support for clean energy; its recent deals with France and the USA are testimony to that fact. India in the recent times has shown a great resolve at the Paris Agreement of Climate Change. The Paris Agreement focuses on developing the capabilities of developing countries to combat climate change in sync with their national priorities that each state has to define under the Intended Nationally Determined Contributions (INDCs). India has announced its INDCs and is trying to play a crucial role in global climate debate. When Donald Trump assumed the Presidency of the US in 2017, he passed an order withdrawing the US from the Paris Agreement. This provides India yet again an opportunity to lead the global climate negotiations. Under its INDCs, India has indicated that it will achieve about 40% cumulative electric power installed capacity from non-fossil fuel-based energy resources by 2030 with the help of transfer of technology and low-cost international finance including the Green Climate Fund. The contributions under INDC have to be achieved by 2030. India has set renewable power deployment target of 175 GW by the year 2022, which includes 100 GW from solar and 60 GW from wind energy.

INDIA AND ITS DIPLOMACY AT THE WORLD TRADE ORGANISATION

Before the World Trade Organisation (WTO) came into existence in 1995, there was a General Agreement on Tariffs and Trade (GATT). India was one of the members of GATT but could not achieve much success as GATT was dominated by the quad of Canada, the USA, Japan and the EU and was a rich man's club. Before the WTO was born, the world witnessed heavy protectionism. There were tariff barriers, which were imposed by states that restricted trade, but, when the WTO was formed, its primary focus was removal of tariff barriers to integrate the economies of all nations in the world. The WTO came out with 19 agreements (with each having an annexure) to achieve its objectives. In 1986, multilateral negotiations began under the Uruguay Round. The negotiations under the Uruguay Round ended in 1994, with a recommendation to create the WTO. Uruguay Round advocated that there should be a gradual reduction of tariffs and a timeline to dismantle Multi Fibre Arrangement (MFA) which governed the textile trade under the Agreement on Textiles and Clothing (ATC) as well as the Agreement on Agriculture (AOA). Though the process to dismantle the tariffs competed by 2005, textile products still continued to have high tariffs. When the WTO was formed, it advocated non-discriminatory free trade through negotiations by ensuring predictability and transparency in global trade. The WTO came out with an Agreement on Subsidies and Countervailing Measures (SCM), which, in turn, came out with three product categories. Under the red category, if one state gave a subsidy on a product for its manufacturing and then exports it to the other state, then the importing state can ban the import of the product. A state in this case, under the amber category, can either invoke countervailing duties or report to the Dispute Settlement Mechanisms (DSM) of the WTO. If the product falls under the green category, no action can be taken by a state. Under the General Agreement on Trade in Services (GATS) a state could resort to setting Sanitary and Phyto-Sanitary (SPS) measures and create Technical Barriers to Trade (TBT) agreements. Under the Trade-Related Intellectual Property Rights (TRIPS) agreement, states, by establishing domestic laws, need to ensure stringent punishments for copying intellectual property rights and take steps to prevent piracy. As India integrated itself through the WTO, its trade began to increase. As the MFA was scrapped under the ATC of WTO, India also witnessed a textile boom. As developing countries faced difficulties to implement the agreements of the WTO, they began to seek concessions. A new round of negotiations began in Doha in 2001. The negotiations were known as the Doha Development Agenda (DDA). As the DDA negotiations began, India raised concerns over the Special Safeguard Mechanisms (SSM), which was essentially a tool that would allow developing countries to raise tariffs temporarily to deal with import surges or price falls. Issues related to Non-Agricultural Market Access (NAMA) too emerged in the DDA. During the DDA, the developing countries asserted that they had not been granted sufficient trade concessions, while developed countries argued that developing countries have not eliminated tariffs in agriculture and services sectors. During the DDA negotiations, the developed countries advocated that through a Trade Facilitation Agreement (TFA), the developing countries should open up their markets. Because of many differences between the developed and developing states at the DDA, the negotiations collapsed. After the failure of Doha negotiations, to make a breakthrough on agriculture subsidies and SSM, the next debate began in 2013 in Bali where again issues related to agriculture erupted. The Bali negotiations decided to focus on TFA, as it would facilitate border trade. For India, the priority with respect to TFA was to clarify that if it was unable to fulfill some complicated provisions of TFA, then it should not be made to go through proceedings related to dispute settlements. As the USA realised that TFA could again become an issue with the developing countries, if they started making concessions in agriculture. The issue in agriculture was of stockpiling and challenging stockpiles of developing states. Members at the WTO agreed that if a developing country maintained a stockpile over 10% of its agricultural produce, then other WTO members could challenge it. But the WTO said that for a certain length of time, the developing countries, in order to provide food security to its population, could maintain excess stockpile (over 10% limit) without any member challenging the decision. The issue was to decide what interval would be allowed for such a limit to remain unchallenged by other member states. India wanted unlimited and indefinite timeframe while the USA favoured a two-year 'peace clause'. After intense negotiations, the Ministerial Decision on Public Stockholding for Food Security Purposes that a four-year peace clause will be followed and the TFA has to be concluded and implemented agreed it. However, when the Modi government came into power in 2014, it asserted that it would not accept the agreements related to TFA and public stockholding as they are against the interests of India. India asserted that a new agreement should be worked out where stockholding restraints are removed for developing countries and they be given an indefinite exception. Later, in 2014, during a meeting with Obama, Modi announced his support for the Bali Agreement with a tighter language and the Bali Agreement was then taken to the next step. Many negotiators theorise that India always adopts a hardline policy in trade negotiations as it always suffers a feeling that any blanket trade treaty may put India in a disadvantage. Thus, India has this culture of resorting to either a flat-out refusal or, at times, taking a long time to negotiate. However, India also has to understand and consider the consequences of the costs involved with such an attitude on other member states in the times ahead.

DEATH OF THE APPELLATE BODY AND COLLAPSE OF WTO

WTO has a dispute settlement body. It is also known as the crown jewel of the WTO. It allows member states to seek action against others in case of violation of rules of WTO. In WTO, the dispute settlement is a process that begins by allowing the domestic parties to engage and resolve the dispute themselves. If such bilateral consultation fails, the complainant can seek the formation of a panel to resolve disputes. The established panel receives submissions from both parties involved and prepares a final report. This report can be challenged in the Appellate Body (AB) of the WTO. The AB hears appeals and makes a final decision, which is binding on the parties. The AB has a strength of seven judges. In 2019, two American judges retired and the then president blocked new appointments to the AB asserting that the AB had often overstepped their jurisdiction. This has brought the entire WTO on the verge of collapse. If the AB and WTO collapse, it would hurt India as all the 30 disputes India has pending in the AB (ranging from the US steel and aluminum tariffs to H1-B visa issues) would be in a limbo.

INDIA AND ITS DIPLOMACY AT THE WORLD BANK AND IMF

The World Bank was formed in 1944. It was then called the International Bank for Reconstruction and Development (IBRD). The idea initially was to support economies devastated by the World War II with economic aid. It began to shift to reconstruction from development. In 1956, the International Finance Corporation (IFC) was formed and it began lending to private firms of developing states. In 1960, when the International Development Association (IDA) was formed, it began to focus upon poverty eradication amongst the poorest countries in the world. In a bid to connect the need of developing states with the financial resources of the world, the International Centre for Settlement of Industrial Disputes (ICSID) and Multilateral Investment Guarantee Agency (MIGA) were launched. India is a member of World Bank, IBRD, IFC, IDA, ICSID and MIGA. The World Bank has been assisting the Indian government through the Country Partnership Strategy (2013–2017) with a vision of faster and more inclusive growth. The focus is on reducing poverty in the special category states by supporting projecting of state governments with priority for integration, transformation and inclusion. India is one of the largest recipients of loans from the World Bank with projects ranging from Prime Minister Gram Sadak Yojana to social sector initiatives to dedicated freight corridor funded by the bank. In the recent times, the NITI Aayog has been undertaking monitoring and evaluation of the World Bank projects in India. In 1944, at the Bretton Woods Conference, along with the IBRD, the International Monetary Fund (IMF) was established. India has been a founding member of the IMF and since 1993, has never taken any financial assistance from the IMF till date. By 2000, India had repaid all the loans from the IMF. The IMF works on the concept of quotas. The Executive Board decides the quotas of states based upon inner tariff barriers and GDP. The voting rights are automatically higher if a state has a higher quota. After the USA sub-prime crises, a process of quota reform was spearheaded by the developing countries. However, we need to remember that for any IMF reform, nations collectively with 70% quotas have to vote in favour of the reform. In December 2015, after approval from the US Congress, the quota reforms were executed. India's quota share has increased from 2.3% to 2.6% now and this pushes India into the top 10 members of the IMF.

INDIA, WORLD HEALTH ORGANISATION AND COVID-19

The COVID-19 pandemic has brought to for the misuse of biology at the centre stage of global politics and along with the Chinese, the World Health Organisation (WHO) is today at crosshairs. The world has criticised WHO under the International Health Regulations, (an international agreement adopted by the WHO in 2005 on infectious diseases and other disease) which empower the body to take actions that can challenge how governments exercise sovereignty by collecting information from the NGOs, verifying the information from the governments and sharing the same with other states, something which WHO did not do at the right time of the outbreak of COVID-19 (leading the US to label the WHO Director General (DG), Tedros Adhanom Ghebreyesus, a former foreign and health minister of Ethiopia, as "puppet of China"). There have been various calls for the organisation to reform and bind Chinese, the global challenger of the world order. Such a reform will be good for the humanity and for the organisation itself. In the G-20 video call by the Indian PM in 2020, India reiterated the commitment to seek reform of the global body. In 2020, India also became the chair of WHO Executive Body (EB) for three years period at the 147th session of the World Health Assembly. Though, the EB only meets twice a year and has no significant role than electing the DG of WHO, it is now the time for India at EB to initiate a process of systemic reform of WHO and rewrite the global health architecture. India has prepared a draft of WHO reform. In an interaction with Dr. Manjeev Singh Puri, IFS (India's Deputy Permanent Representative to the UN), the Indian diplomat told the author of this book that India should focus on four core points. First is the reform in the governing structure of the body from its current intergovernmental format. The EB has 34 members, who are elected on the basis of geographical representation. India intends to urge the WHO to replace this with creating Standing Council of World Health Council, which shall only consist of government representatives. India asserts that the council should have only 20 members, balancing regional representations and states with greatest healthcare capacities, including states from the developing world. These 20 members should be provided with executive oversight and powers to ensure action at the WHO. Second, India should push for a legislative action. This means that there should be a legally binding mechanism with WHO to notify a virus or pandemic outbreak at the earliest. Such legislation should be beyond the existing International Health Regulations and the world can negotiate a Convention for the same. Third, in the global compact, there needs to be mechanisms established within the Biological and Toxic Weapons Convention to ensure legal and binding bio-surveillance, verification and compliance in case a possibility of misuse of biology occurs. Fourth, looking at the World Bank's Consultative Group on International Agriculture Research (CGIAR) and its yeoman service in food security, it is important for the WHO to come together and establish research on virus to facilitate vaccine development. It is imperative for the India to establish good diplomacy with the world and seek reform of the body. It is time that India plays a global leadership role in getting the world rid of "de-politicising the health agenda" idea. India must also lead a global ban on trade and consumption of wild animals, with sole exception of species needed for scientific research.

2

CHAPTER

India's Diplomacy in Global International Organisations

INDIA AND ITS DIPLOMACY AT THE INTERNATIONAL CRIMINAL COURT

The idea to have an International Court to judge political leaders accused of international crimes was proposed for the first time in 1919, at the Paris Peace Conference by the Commission of Responsibilities after the World War I. However, no such court could be established at that time. Similar proposals were made even after World War II, as well as in the early 1990s, during the Cold War. However, the following three events gave a strong push for the idea again in the late 1980s and 1990s. Firstly, in 1989, the then Prime Minister of Trinidad and Tobago A. N. R. Robinson proposed the creation of an International Court to deal with issues related to drug trafficking. After the proposal of Robinson, an International Law Commission (ILC) was tasked by the UNGA to draft a statute to establish a permanent court. Secondly, atrocities in Yugoslavian wars by the armed forces of Yugoslavia led to the formation of an International Criminal Tribunal for trying cases related to the former Yugoslavia in 1993. Thirdly, following the genocide in Rwanda, an International Criminal Tribunal for Rwanda was established in 1994. When these tribunals for Rwanda and Yugoslavia were established, there was a need felt to have a permanent International Criminal Court (ICC). In 1994, a final draft for the establishment of ICC was prepared by the ILC. The ILC urged the UNGA to convene a conference and negotiate a treaty to establish a statute for the court. The negotiations began to draft the statute and continued till 1998. The UNGA organised a conference in Rome to finalise the treaty that would act as a statute for the ICC. Subsequently, the Rome Statute of the ICC, or simply, the Rome Statute as it was commonly called, was adopted and the ICC was formally established, after ratifications by member states, on 1st July 2002. The headquarters of the ICC is in the Hague, the Netherlands. The ICC prosecutes leaders responsible for genocide, war crimes and crimes against humanity and is the court of last resort, which intervenes only if a national authority, could not prosecute the ones responsible for the crimes stated above. Till date, India has neither signed nor ratified the Rome Statute and is nor a party to the ICC. India has raised a lot of objections to the Rome Statute. India feels that under the Rome Statute, the ICC has been subordinated to the UNSC and such subordination would result in political interference by the UNSC in the decisions of the ICC.India asserts that as per the Rome Statute, the ICC can bind the non-state parties that approach the ICC to the report to the UNSC. This, India feels is a violation of the Vienna convention, because under the Vienna convention if a state has not accepted a treaty, it cannot be made to forcibly accede to it (veritably the same point of objection that India has in case of the CTBT). India feels that the Rome Statute has given extraordinary powers, in this regard, to the UNSC. Moreover, India takes issue with the fact that the Rome Statute has refused to accept terrorism and use of nuclear weapons as crimes under ICC, as proposed by India. India has also raised objections to the definition of "war crimes" under Article 8 of the Rome Statute as it has included in its ambit "armed conflict not of an international character". India feels this provision could be used against India by other states by making a case for Kashmir where India asserts it is tackling state-sponsored terrorism by Pakistan. India, thus, has not signed or ratified the ICC and remains an observer to the ICC.

INDIA AND ITS DIPLOMACY AT THE INTERNATIONAL COURT OF JUSTICE

The origin of the International Court of Justice (ICJ) can be traced back to the Permanent Court of International Justice (PCIJ). During the World War II, the PCIJ began to lose its relevance and was later succeeded by the ICJ. The UN Charter in San Francisco established the ICJ in 1945. The ICJ is in Hague, the Netherlands, and it has 15 Judges belonging to different nationalities. The ICJ helps in settling disputes between two conflicting states on the basis of international law. It also looks into legal matters referred to it and gives advisory opinions. The ICJ can only be approached by member states of the UN as private individuals and entities are not permitted to take up the matters at the level of ICJ. When a state may take up a matter at the ICJ, it can take up a case of an individual person with respect to another state in concern. It is on the basis of this point that India in 2017 took up the matter of Kulbhushan Jadhav (an Indian national, in the custody of Pakistan, arrested by Pakistan on 3rd March 2016 in Mashkel area of Balochistan on spying charges). Pakistan had arrested Jadhav in their territory and asserted that Jadhav was sent by India's external intelligence agency (RAW) to create destruction of the China–Pakistan Economic Corridor. Jadhav was arrested on the charges of espionage and terrorism. India and Pakistan both are signatories to the Optional Protocol of the Vienna Convention on Consular Relations (VCCR), Vienna, 1963. India has sought consular access to Jadhav many times while Pakistan has rejected the same every time. Jadhav was further tried in a military court in Pakistan and in April 2017 was awarded death sentence. India subsequently took up the matter to the ICJ. The ICJ has the jurisdiction to hear disputes if an aggrieved party asserts that there has been a different interpretation on the VCCR by the other party involved in the dispute. In May 2017, India requested ICJ to apply provisional measures to ensure Pakistan not to execute Jadhav. Under the provisional measures, ICJ under Article 41 of the statute can issue injunctive directions. Article 74 of the ICJ has given powers to the President of the ICJ to issue ad-interim directions when matters related to provisional measures are brought up. Under Article 74(4) of the ICJ Statute, the ICJ President issued orders to Pakistan to ensure that it does not execute Jadhav for the time being. India had put up to the ICJ that if Pakistan executes Jadhav, there would be irreparable damage caused to the rights which are claimed by India. The ICJ while ordering ad-interim relief to India in May 2017 asserted that Pakistan by denying consular access to India has violated the human rights of Jadhav despite it being a signatory of the VCCR.

INDIA AND ITS DIPLOMACY AT THE G-7 AND IDEATING THE G-11

In the 1970s, the Western world received an oil shock. Because of the 1973 oil crisis, the non-communist states witnessed inflation in their economies. In 1975, the industrialised and capitalist countries came together and decided to address ongoing concerns in their economies. In 1975, the USA, the UK, France, West Germany, Italy and Japan established a group of six countries (the G-6) to address concerns related to economy. In 1976, Canada joined the G-6, making it the G-7. In 1998, Russia too joined the G-7, transforming it into the G-8. We should note that the European Union (EU) is also a non-enumerated member to the G-8. Officially, to join G-8, there is no formal membership criterion. A cursory look at the member's profile suggests that the members are advanced industrialised economies. G-8 is neither an institution nor does it have any secretariat. However, it does hold annual summits. One of the most important values of G-8 countries is that they are believers in democracy. In this regard, Russia was an exception. In 2014, when Russia made advances on Ukraine, the G-8 countries decided to suspend Russia from the group, as its actions were not perceived in line with the democratic values propounded by G-8. In the 43rd G-7 summit in 2017 (in Taormina, Sicily, Italy), the Tunisian president Beji Caid Essebsi was a guest invitee. Neither India nor China has been a part of the G-8. There is a growing perception that the G-8 (G-7 as of now) is anachronistic as it lacks participation of states such as India and China, along with Brazil, South Korea and Mexico and so on, that have long surpassed the GDP of the G-7. Some scholars observe that absence of these countries of the developing world was an impetus to formation of BRICS as a platform. India asserts that being the largest democracy in the world, it has a rightful claim to be a part of the G-8.

During outbreak of COVID-19, there have been calls for restructuring the world order. In this backdrop, the US President made a far-sighted and a creative proposal in 2020 of enlarging the G-7 to G-11 as the current G-7 is outdated. President Trump proposed addition of India, South Korea, Russia and Australia in the new grouping. On predictable lines, Beijing immediately denounced the proposal by branding it "an idea doomed to fail". Once established in September 2020, the G-11 would rightly recognise the place of India amongst the world's rich nations. This would be nothing sort of an acknowledgement of India's global voice. India's adherence to the international law, its respect for human rights and Indian policy of multilateralism in trade and security are its strong credentials. It is high time the world accepts the reality of a changed India and gives India the right place it deserves in the comity of nations. The US President has also renewed a proposal of establishing Five Eyes along with G-11. The Five Eyes is a frequently used terminology in the intelligence community of the world and includes an Intelligence Alliance of the US, the UK, Australia, New Zealand and Canada, to decide on a strategy to manage China.

INDIA AND ITS DIPLOMACY AT THE G-77

When the first session of the United Nations Conference on Trade and Development (UNCTAD) ended in Geneva, in 1967, seventy-seven countries came together to establish an intergovernmental organisation called the G-77 in the UN to use it as a platform to collectively promote the economic interests of the Global South. The idea was also to use the platform to promote South–South cooperation. India has been one of the founding members of the G-77. India has been playing a leadership role in advancing the interests of the developing world through the G-77 at the UN. In the recent times, the G-77 has played an important role in climate change negotiations. India, China and G-77 have forcefully demanded that developed countries should provide adequate finances to the developing countries to tackle climate change. India has been negotiating at the climate change level with G-77, the Like-Minded Developing Countries (LMDC) and the BASIC group of countries (Brazil, South Africa, India and China). The G-77 and India have achieved some impressive feats globally. They have been able to assert that each individual sovereign state has sovereign control over its resources. They have also successfully asserted that the global wealth distribution should be equal. India has asserted under the G-77 umbrella that wealth should be reallocated on the principles of equality and equity. This has been India's core policy point even in the climate change negotiations. India has also asserted that all states, and more importantly, all developing countries need to have equal participation in global economic affairs. These points, stressed by India through G-77, also form a part of the basis of the G-20. However, the G-77, being a loosely knit organisation with no permanent research institution for propaganda, has a weak international response. In the climate change talks, many of the G-77 players have been found having differing positions and thereby G-77 has not been able to emerge as a united front.

INDIA AND ITS DIPLOMACY AT THE G-20

In 1999, with a focus on global economic governance the governors of the central banks of 20 states came together to promote international financial stability and established the G-20. The G-20 was basically formed as a group of 20 emerging market economies and developed countries to promote discussion on policy issues pertaining to the global economic governance. The G-20 held its first summit in 1999 in Berlin. The major difference between G-20 and G-8 is that G-8 only focussed on developed countries while G-20 has a broader participation with emerging market economies of the group. The chairmanship of G-20 is rotational, with one nation annually getting the chair. India has been a member of this powerful economic club. In 2019, India held the chair of G-20. The G-20 has no formal voting criteria. In the past G-20 summits in 2014, 2015, 2016, and 2017, India had advised that the global economic surplus wealth would be deployed for development of infrastructure. India, in the summit of G-20 in Hamburg in Germany in 2017, had also proposed that surplus wealth would be used to develop efficient energy technologies. In the 2017 summit, the G-20 nations congratulated India for taking steps to make it easy to do business in India. In this summit, India forcefully argued on issues related to terrorism. India asserted that states supporting terrorism should not be allowed to be a part of G-20 and sought early conclusion of the UN Convention on International Terrorism.

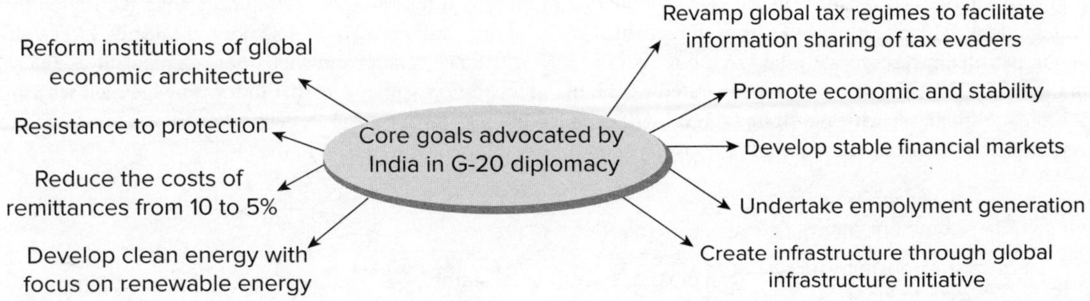

In 2017 Germany G-20 summits, India offered strong resistance to protectionist measures adopted by the states. India has pitched for free movement of labour and capital amongst the states to bolster up the global economy. India has further pitched for stronger action at the level of tackling black money and terrorism. A new element in India's diplomacy at G-20 has been to pitch for poverty eradication.

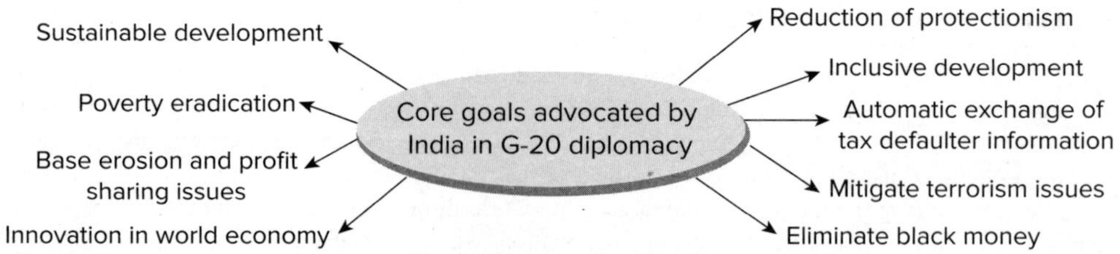

The G-20 is an excellent forum for interaction between developed and emerging market economies, but India has, over time, raised some concerns about the organisation. India believes that, in the era of global economic slowdown, if nations resort to quantitative easing due to injection of cash, in the advanced economies, the capital flows become volatile and the developing countries, in cases such as these, should be given a right to resort to capital control measures. India has also pointed out that although G-20 has spearheaded a discussion on reforms of global financial architecture, the progress has been slow. India has stated that having the US dollar as a reserve global currency has exposed the vulnerabilities of a systemic risk during crises. Thus, India asserts that a possible solution here for the G-20 could be to explore widening of the SDR basket and add more currencies.

INDIA AND ITS DIPLOMACY AT THE GULF COOPERATION COUNCIL

In 1981, Saudi Arabia, Oman, the UAE, Kuwait, Bahrain and Qatar came together to establish an intergovernmental regional politico-economic block known as the Gulf Cooperation Council (GCC). The GCC emerged as an alliance of six Gulf states to promote economic interaction. Western scholars believe that GCC is based on a foundation of a common security concern but the scholars of the GCC nations insist that it is a platform for economic, cultural, political and scientific integration. There was a proposal in 2011 to establish a Gulf Union and transform the GCC into a tight economic and military union. The proposal has met with certain objections from some member states. The GCC has also been negotiating a common currency named Khaleeji, but the progress on the same has been slow. India's relations with GCC have been on since 1947. Initially, as mentioned in the chapter of 'India–West Asia Policy—Key Drivers,' India politically supported GCC and other states in the region during the Cold War. By the end of the Cold War, as India's dependence upon energy from the Gulf increased, India began to hold the GCC as crucial for its energy security. In earlier chapters, we have mentioned that India decided to sign oil-based partnerships with Saudi Arabia, the UAE and Qatar. India realised that it can leverage its historically good political relationship with the GCC to develop energy security partnerships. As India's oil trade increased in the post-Cold War times, a lot of Indians began to work in the Gulf states as professionals. The post-Cold War times have witnessed a shift from the blue collar to the white collar Indian presence in the GCC states. In the recent times, India has realised that as the trade with the region enhances, it not only needs to protect the sea-lanes of communications but also ensure safety of its diaspora in the GCC. India, due to these two reasons, has started observing the region through a strategic lens. This is also visible from the recent high-level bilateral visits. India has not only decided to establish a strategic petroleum reserve with the UAE but also has added defence relationships as a new element in its interaction with the GCC. The GCC states have cooperated with India in the region as they feel that India's engagement with GCC at economic, political, security and strategic level will enhance India's global profile. A declining US presence in the region also provides India the space required to boost its economic and strategic footprint in the GCC.

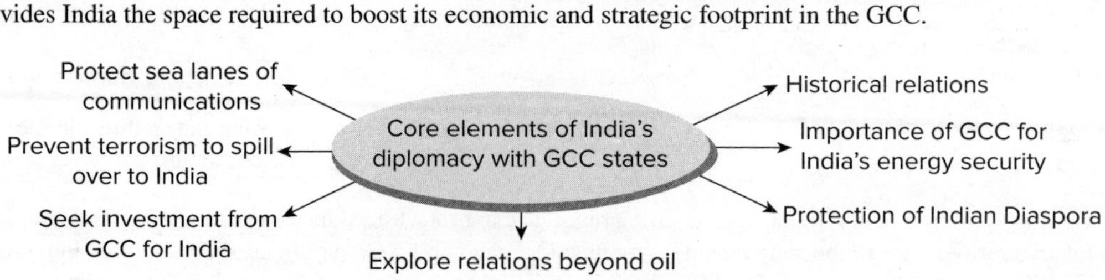

In the recent times, the perception of Gulf states about India has changed. The GCC no longer looks at India merely as a supplier of cheap goods and labour but a stable democracy and a vibrant regional economy with highly skilled manpower.

This change in perception of the GCC has contributed to their realising the need to build up strategic partnerships with India. As the GCC states have begun to look East, it has found sync with India's attempt to link West. The GCC, however, has been insecure about India's developing proximity with Iran and Israel. Pakistan, too, plays the Islamic card to assert to the GCC that India is an anti-Muslim state and therefore remains an irritant in the deepening India–GCC ties. Despite these issues, India has successfully decided to enhance strategic and defence partnerships with the GCC. Today, India has added dimensions beyond oil in its outreach to the region. India has committed support to GCC in dimensions such as food security, IT, pharmacy and consultancy services.

INDIA AND ITS DIPLOMACY AT THE BRICS[1]

In 2001, an economist with Goldman Sachs undertook an econometric analysis and asserted that by 2050, the economies of Brazil, Russia, India and China would constitute the largest economies of the world. In 2006, on the margins of the G-8 Outreach summit at St. Petersburg in Russia, the BRIC leaders (all countries except South Africa) held a meeting and formalised the BRIC group. In 2009, the first BRIC summit was organised in Yekaterinburg, Russia. In 2010, it was decided that South Africa would be added to the group. In 2011, in the 3rd summit in Sanya in China, South Africa participated and the organisation formally became BRICS from BRIC. Initially, the idea of BRICS was to use it as a platform to engage upon economic issues but over a period of time, BRICS summits have started discussing issues ranging from trade, health, technology, agriculture and so on. In 2016, India chaired the eighth BRICS summit and the meeting was held in Goa. In the very first BRICS summit, there was a severe criticism of Bretton Woods's institutions over their failure to reform their structures and processes and give a voice to emerging market states. India asserted that the existing global financial architecture is dominated by the West and does not give adequate voice to the emerging market economies. In the sixth BRICS summit in Fortaleza, Brazil, in 2014 through the Fortaleza Declaration, the BRICS members decided to establish the BRICS Bank or the New Development Bank (NDB). The NDB became operational from 2016, with its headquarters in Shanghai, China. The NDB shall provide loans to states to manage balance of payment crises and for projects related to infrastructure and sustainable development.

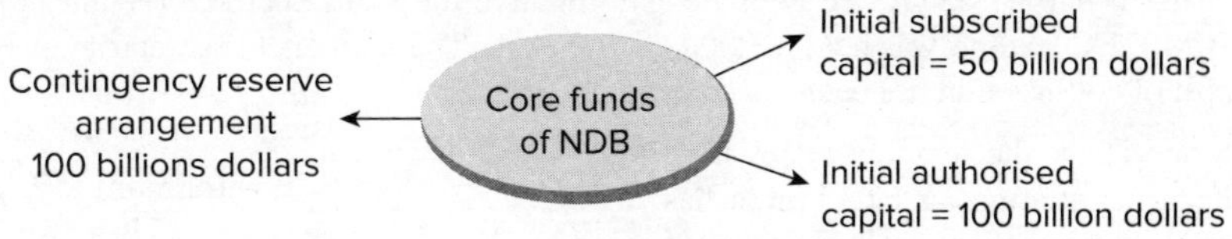

K. V. Kamath is the first President of the BRICS Bank or the NDB. What makes the NDB different from the World Bank and IMF is the fact that here, infrastructure has been identified as a priority sector by the BRICS. The NDB has prioritised areas such as education, healthcare and women rights, which are issues that all BRICS members face today. In 2016, the NDB had issued 3 billion Yuan bonds in China to finance projects related to clean energy. In 2017, NDB had decided to issue Masala bonds worth 300–500 million dollars for projects related to rural drinking water and infrastructure (rupee denominated bonds that are issued outside India are called Masala bonds). In 2017, the BRICS members also decided to launch their own credit rating agency in future. India held the chair for the eighth BRICS summit in Goa. The theme was building responsive, inclusive and collective solutions. The BRICS–BIMSTEC Outreach summit was held in Goa in 2016.

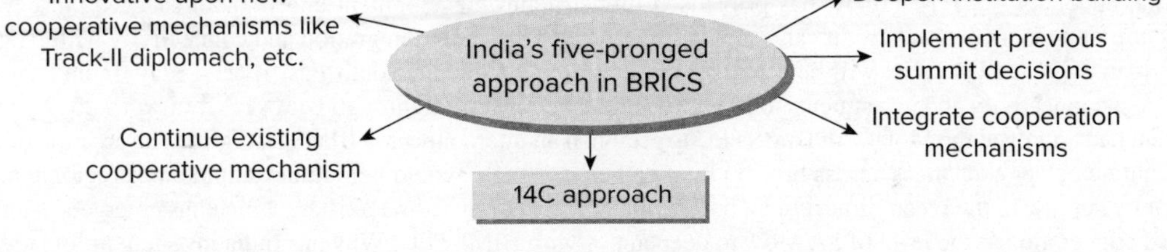

During the eighth BRICS summit, India also signed MoUs with Brazil on agriculture, pharmacy, investment cooperation, and facilitation treaty and assisted reproductive technologies. At the end of the summit, a Goa Declaration was adopted. The declaration reaffirmed a number of state commitments to tackle terrorism, advocate the UN reforms, facilitate

[1]Brazil, Russia, India, China and South Africa.

economic and investment partnerships and use policy tools to achieve inclusive growth. The ninth BRICS summit was held in China in 2017.

COVID-19 AND BRICS DRIVEN PHARMACY ALLIANCE

Despite the strong global criticism that Chinese have faced for COVID-19, it is interesting to see that the Chinese leveraged their position as the workshop of the world and announced their Health Silk Road Doctrine. Under this doctrine, the Chinese provided the two global hotspots, Italy and Iran, with the needed medical aid and PPE Kits. For that matter, India, as a BRICS member, was able to position itself rightly as world pharmacy player, by exporting Hydroxychloroquine to a dozen of countries. In fact, Russia too sent medical supplies and experts to the two global hotspots. In the African continent, another BRICS member, South Africa, also holding the chair of the African Union for 2020, has effectively worked to frame a Pan-Africa response. All the BRICS members have demonstrated their capacities of being providers of Humanitarian Assistance and Disaster Relief (HADR). This has aptly positioned them as global COVID warriors. The NDB of BRICS also allocated 1 billion dollar emergency loans and has positioned the NDB as a new template for addressing natural disasters. All these are templates for the BRICS nations to sit down and design a pharmacy alliance for the future.

INDIA AND ITS DIPLOMACY AT THE BIMSTEC[2] AND COMPARATIVE ANALYSIS WITH SAARC (SOUTH ASIAN ASSOCIATION FOR REGIONAL COOPERATION)

In June 1997, a meeting was organised in Bangkok and Bangladesh, India, Sri Lanka and Thailand decided to come together to establish an economic cooperation under the banner of BIST-EC. In December 1997, Myanmar joined the economic cooperation and the group now called BIMST-EC (Bangladesh, India, Myanmar, Sri Lanka and Thailand Economic Cooperation). In 2004, after Nepal and Bhutan were admitted to BIMST-EC, the name of the organisation was changed into BIMSTEC (Bay of Bengal initiative for Multi-Sectoral Technical and Economic Cooperation). The first BIMSTEC summit was held in 2004, in Bangkok. The permanent secretariat of BIMSTEC is in Dhaka and 32% of the cost of construction has been borne by India.

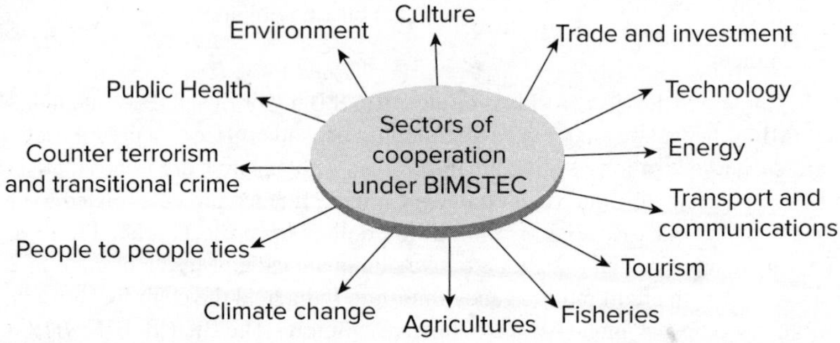

Since 2004, the member states have been negotiating an FTA. India has been pushing for an early conclusion of the FTA as it will facilitate trade in goods and services. Despite a framework agreement for the FTA in place since 2004, the FTA has not become operational as issues persist on agendas such as negative list, rules of origin, custom agreement and dispute settlement mechanism. Scholars assert that if India and Thailand can take some FDI to other BIMSTEC members, the investments can act as a push for the FTA. India, under its Act East Policy, has prioritised infrastructure development and if India succeeds in developing infrastructure in the north-east states, it can act as a springboard for deeper integration and connectivity with BIMSTEC. India has realised that BIMSTEC will be a bridge between South Asia and South East Asia. Today, India has initiated steps to boost connectivity and investments to promote regional cooperation through BIMSTEC. In April 2017, the Indian government had approved the MoU with BIMSTEC to establish an interconnected BIMSTEC grid. The creation of the grid would facilitate power exchanges across borders by member states and would help in development of regional networks for electricity supply. In the recent times, India has decided to shift away from Pakistan, which has emerged as an irritant in regional cooperation at the level of SAARC, to deepen ties with BIMSTEC. Why has India invested diplomatic capital in BIMSTEC? There are two reasons.

1. **SAARC and Pakistan factor:** The SAARC has almost become defunct because of non-cooperative behaviour of Pakistan. This has limited the role for India in regional governance. This is why India has adopted the strategy of

[2]Bangladesh, India, Myanmar, Sri Lanka, Thailand Economic Cooperation.

South Asia minus one (that is, keeping Pakistan aside and going forward with regional connectivity and governance). The failure of SAARC offers India an opportunity to revive BIMSTEC as a counter strategy. BIMSTEC has been rightly touted as an Indian rebound to pursue regional ambition in case of failure of SAARC. However, SAARC is a regional organisation of South Asia only while BIMSTEC is an inter-regional grouping that brings South Asia and ASEAN together.

2. **Drag prevention:** There is a growing realisation in India that unless the neighbourhood does not prosper economically, it will act as a drag for India's own economic growth. This has motivated India to link the neighbourhood to ASEAN.

In 2019, BIMSTEC celebrated its 21st anniversary. The significance of India for BIMSTEC is very high as it fits well in the strategic calculus of its 'Neighbourhood First' policy and 'Act East Policy'. It is an area of opportunity for India as BIMSTEC is the least integrated region in the world. In the recent times, India has taken a lead in the revival of BIMSTEC. In 2016, the BIMSTEC–BRICS Outreach summit in Goa created the foundation. The private sector and FICCI have been roped in to evolve a working strategy for BIMSTEC states. A renewed BIMSTEC is an opportunity for India to integrate the Northeast region and propel regional growth. The FICCI in 2018 prepared a document titled 'Reinvigorating BIMSTEC: An Industry Vision for the Next Decade' at the 4th BIMSTEC summit, Kathmandu, Nepal. The document has made certain suggestions. Firstly, to boost greater economic integration, the document has asserted that there needs to be timely availability of information and improvement in the regional multimodal connectivity. Secondly, to boost collective capabilities, the document suggested that member states can establish regional value chains that can be integrated into the global value chains. This will augment the MSME sector and thereby generating employment. Interestingly, the document highlighted that women can also play an important role in the supply chains through an innovative business strategy. This will help in establishment of the Brand BIMSTEC in the long run. Till now BIMSTEC has functioned on the basis of Bangkok Declaration 1997. In the 4th summit in 2018, it was decided to evolve a Charter for BIMSTEC. A decision was taken to establish a Permanent Working Committee which would provide directions between summits and establish rules of procedure. The summit has decided to enhance additional financial resources to facilitate groupings activities. The member states have decided to establish a BIMSTEC fund. The member states have decided to enhance the international outreach of BIMSTEC. This will be done through increasing its visibility on the international scene. In the summit, Thailand has proposed that the member states identify five core pillars to strengthen multilateral cooperation in them. They include connectivity, trade and investment, people-to-people ties, security and science and technology. India asserted to additionally focus on blue economy and counterterrorism. In Kathmandu, the states also singed an MoU on grid connectivity. An announcement was made for early conclusion of the FTA (something being debated since 2004) and establishes a Free Trade Zone by 2021. There are certain policy dilemmas for India to revive BIMSTEC. These challenges are both from within and outside the region.

1. Firstly, India's commitment to institution building. As of now, India stands to be the second biggest contributor (2 crores) for the BIMSTEC secretariat. If the outreach of BIMSTEC needs to expand, then it needs to enlarge its secretariat and incorporate officials from different states. This will require more budgetary contribution from India.
2. Secondly, there are growing fears of possible India domination in BIMSTEC. This is natural owing to India's rising economic profile. This was also a problem India faced in SAARC. It has to take concrete steps to mitigate these fears by being more sensitive to the concerns of the smaller states. The smaller states around India are keen to engage with India and seek benefits from the meteoric economic rise of India.
3. Thirdly, the strategic challenge in BIMSTEC is of China. China was brought in as an observer state in SAARC by member countries. This was done to balance fears of Indian domination. Today, India's neighbours are deeply embedded with Chinese infrastructure projects. Thus, India has to tread a careful path in the regional geopolitics emerging here.
4. Future areas of cooperation include conclusion of the FTA, Motor Vehicles Agreement and Energy Centre and a Coastal Shipping Agreement. The BIMSTEC also needs to ensure that the summits are held regularly.
5. The BIMSTEC is a catalyst for a peaceful and economically prosperous neighbourhood along with offering India an opportunity to counter China through its own unique infrastructure and connectivity model. For Bangladesh, BIMSTEC is a platform to position itself as a regional player in Bay of Bengal. Nepal and Bhutan find BIMSTEC as a platform for reaching out to the Indo-Pacific. Sri Lanka has used BIMSTEC to connect to South East Asia.

For Thailand and Myanmar, the BIMSTEC offers a platform for accessing the rising consumer markets. India perceives BIMSTEC an apt platform to bring the ecological landmass of Great Himalayas close to Bay of Bengal and the larger Indo-Pacific. Till the 20th century, BIMSTEC states were connected through sub-regional waterways and seaports. The present attempts by the member states seem to rediscover the lost past.

INDIA AND ITS DIPLOMACY AT THE BCIM CORRIDOR

In the 1990s, Bangladeshi economist, Professor Rehman Sobhan, proposed an economic corridor between India, China via Myanmar and Bangladesh. According to Sobhan, such a corridor would enhance trade and growth and contribute to reduction of poverty in the region. Sobhan's idea saw material action in the Kunming Initiative, which evolved into a regional forum for BCIM (Bangladesh, China, India and Myanmar) states. In 2013, in a meeting between the then Prime Minister Manmohan Singh and Li Keqing, the BCIM economic corridor (BCIM-EC) finally gained momentum. The entire BCIM zone was perceived as a sub-region where connectivity between South Asia, South East Asia and China was envisaged. As the sub-region has high resources but poor connectivity, the corridor will promote economic integration. Though the Modi government has shown enormous interest in the corridor, some challenges exist. There is no clarity whether the BCIM-EC should purely be economical in nature or widen to include cultural- and people-centric activities. People in India's Northeast and Myanmar have raised concerns about the environmental impact of the BCIM-EC. More so, there is a dilemma of whether BCIM-EC is promoted as a regional and geopolitical initiative or whether local communities along the borders should be used as stakeholders for benefit sharing under a sub-regional arrangement. How BCIM-EC works out in tandem with the Chinese Belt and Road initiative will be something to observe in the future.

INDIA AND ITS DIPLOMACY AT THE INDIAN OCEAN RIM ASSOCIATION (IORA)

The Indian Ocean is one of the most important trading routes of the world. To promote social, economic and political cooperation amongst the states in Indian Ocean region, in 1995, an Indian Ocean Rim Initiative was launched. Subsequently, in 1997, the Indian Ocean Rim Association–Association for Regional Cooperation (IORA–ARC) was formed. Today, the group, with 21 member states (including India) also has seven dialogue partners and is called IORA.

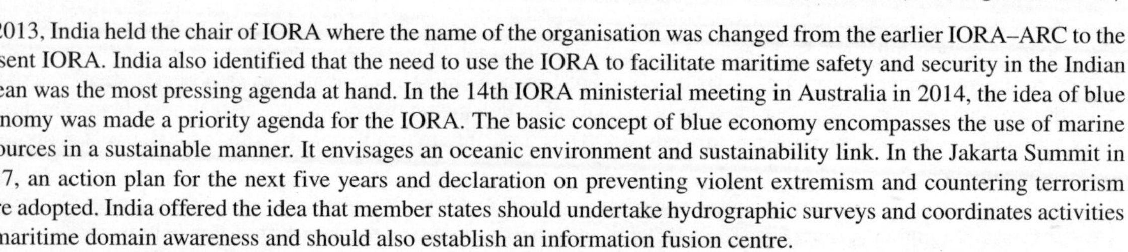

In 2013, India held the chair of IORA where the name of the organisation was changed from the earlier IORA–ARC to the present IORA. India also identified that the need to use the IORA to facilitate maritime safety and security in the Indian Ocean was the most pressing agenda at hand. In the 14th IORA ministerial meeting in Australia in 2014, the idea of blue economy was made a priority agenda for the IORA. The basic concept of blue economy encompasses the use of marine resources in a sustainable manner. It envisages an oceanic environment and sustainability link. In the Jakarta Summit in 2017, an action plan for the next five years and declaration on preventing violent extremism and countering terrorism were adopted. India offered the idea that member states should undertake hydrographic surveys and coordinates activities of maritime domain awareness and should also establish an information fusion centre.

INDIA AND ITS DIPLOMACY AT THE ASIA-PACIFIC ECONOMIC COOPERATION

The origin of the Asia-Pacific Economic Cooperation (APEC) can be traced back to the period of economic integration of South East and East Asia. In 1967, the Association of Southeast Asian Nations (ASEAN) was formed. ASEAN states began to develop deep trade with Europe and in 1979, began trade with China. Economic interaction was the key goal of the ASEAN states. In 1980s and 1990s, the EU was formed. This affected the ASEAN–Europe trade. As the US consolidated the North American Free Trade Agreement (NAFTA), this further dented the ASEAN's trade practices. In 1989, Australia suggested the creation of the APEC as an Asian version of an FTA comprising Northeast Asia, South East Asia and the Pacific Rim states. Similarly, even Malaysia proposed an East Asian Economic Group (EAEG). In 1989, Australian Prime Minister Bob Hawke met his South Korean counterpart and mooted an idea where ministers could meet to enhance regional economic cooperation. In November 1991, a Seoul Declaration was adopted that announced the scope of the APEC. The APEC was to promote trade, technology transfers and promote growth. The first APEC summit was held in 1993 and decided to focus upon liberalisation and economic trade. The APEC has 21 member economies today, and India wants to join this economic community as it wants to undertake trade promotion within the economies of the Asia-Pacific. Initially there was opposition to India's membership to the APEC as some members initially raised objections about India's economic reforms and its engagement with the WTO. In recent times, a lot of members feel that as India has undertaken economic reforms and it should be allowed to be part of the APEC. Many feel that India's maritime strengths and its clout, as a balancer will help the APEC. Currently, India holds the position of an observer state in the APEC. The US too has favoured India's accession to the APEC as a member. If India becomes a member of the APEC, it will be perceived as a serious economic power in Asia-Pacific and this will help in India's negotiations at the bilateral FTA's with states as India has left Regional Comprehensive Economic Partnership (RECP). Apart from improving trade volumes, joining the APEC will facilitate India's domestic growth and lead to job creation. The main reason as to why India is not yet a member of the APEC is geography. Geographically, India is not part of the Pacific region. Some APEC members also have reservations about India's high custom duties and stringent rules for FDI. India is not keen on shedding off protectionist measures prevalent in its domestic economy, which has not gone down well by other member states. Over a period of time, if consensus evolves, India might enter the APEC club.

INDIA AND ITS DIPLOMACY AT THE MEKONG GANGA COOPERATION

India, in order to enhance relations with states in the Mekong region (for example, Cambodia, Laos, Myanmar, Vietnam and Thailand), had formed the Mekong Ganga Cooperation (MGC) in 2000. Under the Act East Policy, India has decided to integrate India's Northeast with Mekong region.

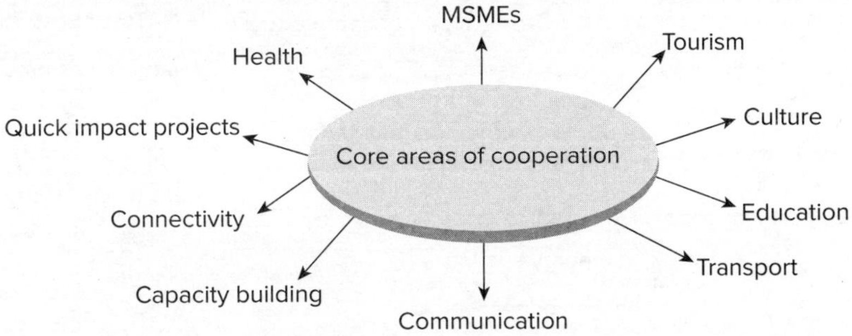

INDIA AND ITS DIPLOMACY AT THE SHANGHAI COOPERATION ORGANISATION

Henry Kissinger, the renowned US diplomat, in his book 'World Order' rightly stated that creation of the Shanghai Cooperation Organisation (SCO) allows new world powers to shape an alternative vision for global governance based on their themes of "divergent historical experiences and values". He asserted that such kind of architecture will not clash but break the monochromatic Western ideal.

At the end of the Cold War, the five Central Asian Republics broke away from the USSR and became independent. A lot of Uyghur Muslims lived in Central Asia (CA). China thought that the Uyghurs in China may begin to link with Uyghur's of CA and create unrest in Xinxiang province in China. In 1992, China, along with Russia, Kazakhstan, Kyrgyzstan and Tajikistan, began to negotiate a security pact. After 22 rounds of negotiations, a group called the Shanghai-5 was established in 1996. The aim of Shanghai-5 was to undertake confidence-building measures and demilitarise borders. In 1996, a Treaty of Deepening Military Trust in Border Region and an Agreement on Confidence Building in Military Filed in Border Areas were signed. In 1997, a Mutual Reduction of Armed Forces in Border Areas Agreement was concluded.

In 2001, Uzbekistan joined the group and it was renamed as SCO to emphasise its role as a body for regional cooperation. China, through SCO, wishes to fight the three evils of separatism, terrorism and extremism. The SCO decided to establish a Regional Anti-Terrorism Structure in Tashkent. India joined SCO as an observer state in 2005. In the year of 2011, a Memorandum of Obligation of SCO was approved to allow non-member states to join SCO as a member. India applied for membership. Initially, China was reluctant to add India to the SCO, but Russia favoured the induction of India as a regional balancer. In the Ufa summit in 2015, India and Pakistan were admitted as members. India has viewed SCO positively and wanted to use SCO to play a bigger role in CA. India feels that SCO being an Asian body will allow it to connect to CA and enhance its economic and security relationships in CA. India feels that SCO can be used as a regional platform to contribute to peace in Afghanistan. As a member, India can use SCO to augment its Connect Central Asia Policy and enhance connectivity and commerce with CA.

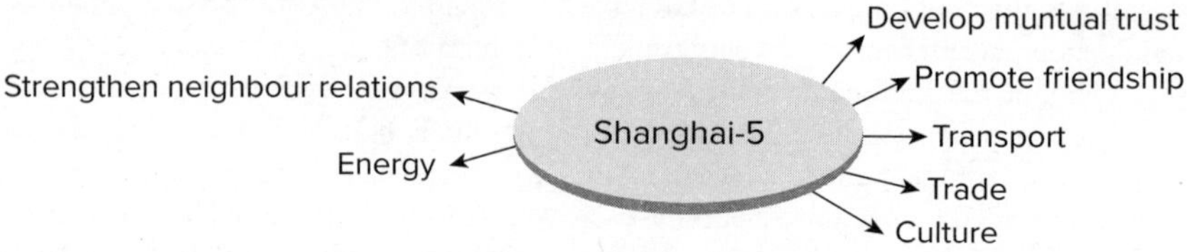

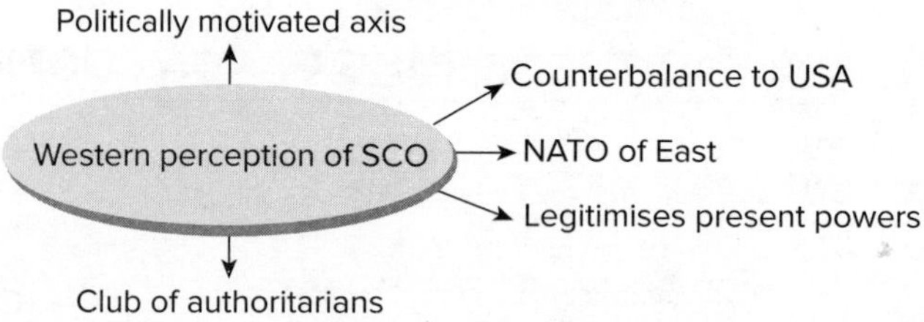

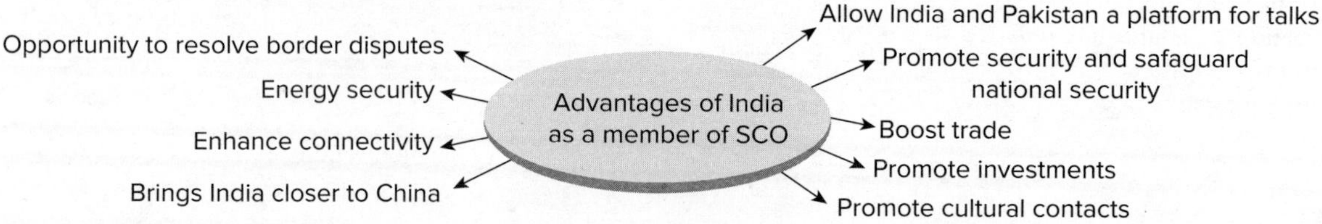

In 2018, India participated in the SCO summit in Qingdao for the first time as a full member of the organisation. There were 22 agreements in total signed by the two. A special agreement was signed on terrorism and de-radicalisation of youth. A three-year plan was adopted for combating terrorism and extremism. An anti-drug strategy was signed from 2018 to 2022. This was a veiled attempt to challenge the internationalisation of the US dollar. Indian Prime Minister evoked the legacy of Buddha and Rumi as a precursor to the ideology of SCO. The SCO also provided India and Pakistan an opportunity to discuss a two-way Pakistan–Central Asia connectivity project. If the project eventually materialises, the improvement of Indo-Pak relations can emerge as a subset of the rise of Eurasia.

INDIA AND ITS DIPLOMACY AT THE SAARC

Since the times of Jawaharlal Nehru, India favoured a deeper engagement with its neighbours. In 1980s, Zia Ur Rahman, the former Bangladeshi President, came up with an idea of knitting the South Asian (SA) states under a group. Initially, India viewed the proposal cautiously as it thought that such a body would be used by the SA states as an opportunity to resort to India-bashing. India also thought that if it does not accept the proposal, this move would be perceived by the SA states as an attempt by India to scuttle a mechanism for regional cooperation. In 1985, India, keeping these concerns aside, decided to go ahead and join the SAARC. Thus it was formed in 1985 with India, Bangladesh, Bhutan, Nepal, Pakistan, Sri Lanka and Maldives its members. In 2007, Afghanistan joined SAARC as a member. The SAARC wanted to promote economic cooperation amongst members and help each member facilitate economic growth, thereby contributing to the alleviation of poverty. Each member state was to respect the territorial integrity of others and no interference would be tolerated in each other's internal affairs. It was decided by members that SAARC as a forum will not be used by any member to raise any contentious and bilateral issues as such issues had to be resolved on a one-to-one bilateral basis. Since the end of the Cold War, there has been a renewed thrust towards regionalism but SA has not witnessed the same despite the presence of SAARC. Many believe that it has ended up in becoming a 'talk shop'. SAARC has had some achievements—for instance, the states have agreed on a Regional Convention on Suppression of Terrorism, a SAARC Audio-Visual programme in Dhaka and a SAARC Agriculture Information Centre; and the members have also agreed upon a social charter for poverty eradication and development of human resources. In 1993, the South Asia Preferential Trade Agreement was finalised (yet to be operational). The fundamental reason for the weakness of the SAARC as a platform is trust deficit amongst its core members. Unresolved border disputes and trade barriers erected by each member state too have contributed to weakness of the organisation as a whole, as well as its inability to achieve its goals. Scholars assert that a perpetual cold war between India and Pakistan has fuelled mistrust. For Pakistan, Kashmir remains an irritant for SAARC to flourish while India cites terrorism sponsored by Pakistan as a reason for the mistrust. The member states have viewed the borders more as security threats than a conduit for people-centric engagements. As India is one of the largest members of SAARC, other members perceive any initiative by India as an intention on India's part to assert hegemonic ambitions. Such perceptions are further cemented because of different political beliefs in the neighbourhood. There are three structural impediments in SAARC. Firstly, it flows from the SAARC charter. The charter mentions that steps would be taken to promote growth and self-reliance. But the ground reality is that these steps have not been institutionalised. Secondly, SAARC has concluded a lot of agreements and conventions but implementation on ground amongst states have been poor. Thirdly, SAARC bodies also prevent meaningful interactions, as these bodies have not contributed to the removal of suspicion and mistrust. For any form of regional cooperation to succeed, there are three necessary conditions and some sufficient preconditions. Regional cooperation can be successful if states, first of all, renounce violence. This renunciation leads to the birth of a pluralistic, secure community. Then, there should be an agreement that no state will question each other's territorial integrity, as doing so leads to possible conflict. Lastly, if there is a dispute, then it needs to be resolved mutually. The charter of the SAARC has all these three necessary conditions. The charter, as mentioned above, asserts that states will not use force, not interfere in each other's affairs and shall advocate for peaceful resolution of conflicts. However, Pakistan has not commented upon the non-use of force. Pakistan has always asserted that if political differences are not resolved (namely, the Kashmir issue), then there cannot be any meaningful cooperation. For Pakistan, SAARC is just another platform for furthering the cause of Kashmir. Despite the 1972 Simla Agreement between India and Pakistan that the two shall resort to bilateral mechanisms to resolve disputes, Pakistan is often keen on bringing foreign powers into dispute resolution. Geographically, since the ancient times, there is a belief that South Asia consists of a single compact unit and a common geographical space where people, culture and ideas have freely moved. India has always believed that SAARC, as a platform, can be used to gain the erstwhile geographical space and fuse SA yet again into a compact unit. This is the reason why India lays so much emphasis upon connectivity with its neighbours (the recent BBIN-Motor Vehicles Agreement is testimony to this). The rest of the South Asian states, however, perceive it differently. Pakistan feels that the Indus River separated its territory from SA and makes it closer to West Asia. Nepal feels that it has always had a separate existence while Sri Lanka too feels that it has had its own trajectory of historical evolution. India's neighbours find it tough to reinforce the idea of recreating the unity of past, favouring instead a unity of equals. It is for this reason that despite SAARC, Pakistan and Bangladesh are reluctant to allow their territories as routes for transit. India, through SAARC, visualises a homogenisation of the region while the other members see it as hegemonisation and resort to measures leading to dehegemonisation. Because of such differences of perceptions amongst the members of the SAARC, the body has almost been pushed into a morgue. Although many steps were taken by Atal Bihari Vajpayee and Manmohan Singh to revive the SAARC, but the perceived mistrust continued to hamper any meaningful interaction. The coming of the Modi government was seen as positive sign. In his swearing-in ceremony, Modi invited all the SAARC leaders and tried rehabilitating SAARC relationships. Modi launched India's Neighbourhood First Policy in 2014 and SAARC was destined to play a central role in the same. Modi attended the 18th SAARC summit in Kathmandu, Nepal, in 2014. He asserted that India would take all steps to remove the cynicism and skepticism associated with the SAARC. He proposed that a SAARC Union be formed where there is free flow of trade, people and investments. As things progressed from 2014, the cross-border terrorist strikes on Indian soil from Pakistan in 2016 brought the engagement to a halt. The 19th SAARC summit was scheduled in 2016 in Islamabad. After the attacks at Uri in India, India decided to cancel its participation in the summit. Citing Article X of SAARC charter, Pakistan has postponed the SAARC summit. India has also realised that its conflicts with Pakistan would remain an obstacle to regional integration. India has thus recognised that it needs to adopt a policy of 'SAARC minus one'. It has spearheaded regional integration with like-minded countries. The BBIN Motor Vehicles Pact, India's thrust to re-energise BIMSTEC and a possibility of a future Bay of Bengal Community or BOBCOM are shining examples of India's new 'SAARC minus one' diplomacy. To ensure that the rest of South Asia and India move ahead, in May 2017, India resorted to stratospheric diplomacy and gifted its neighbours a SAARC satellite. To ensure that rest of South Asia continues to integrate, we have now started witnessing a new form of sub-regional cooperation. This will go a long way in reviving the SAARC once again. In 2019, China had proposed CSACF (China South Asia Cooperation Forum). It is a new regional cooperative forum that includes the states of South Asia. It is an alternative to SAARC, which has become almost defunct due to 'jhappi' and 'katti' oscillation of Pakistan's relationship with India. It is at this level where India needs to assert itself as a consensus builder and then position itself as a net security provider. India can make SAARC relevant again by following the ASEAN model. India can take the lead in two things. First, it can encourage SAARC states to meet informally. This will help in reduction of suspicion. Second, as in ASEEAN, a large economy such as Indonesia allowed a small country like Singapore to take lead; the same can be done by India. India can take a back seat and allow other SAARC members to build a harmonious process.

COVID-19 DIPLOMACY AND SAARC

In 2020, during the outbreak of COVID-19, Indian Prime Minister resorted to a measure of imaginative diplomacy to leverage a crisis into a mechanism for regional cooperation, and decided to launch SAARC 2.0. The Prime Minister hosted the first ever Virtual SAARC Leaders Summit on 15th March 2020. All the participating nations decided to work together to tackle the virus by sharing their experiences and perspectives. They launched a SAARC COVID-19 Emergency Fund. The uniqueness of the fund was that it was not be managed by SAARC Secretariat or any nation, but by the member states themselves, who would be responsible for disbursals on request from other member states. All the SAARC members, minus Pakistan, have reposed faith in jointly collaborating in tackling the virus. The Indian leadership has rightly put Pakistan in a serious dilemma because Pakistan had refused any cooperation with India since the abrogation of Article 370. The revival of SAARC 2.0 was an added constraint on Pakistani recourse to state-sponsored terrorism. India the first nation in the world to respond to the crisis beyond the national concerns as the Prime Minister rightly said that "region can respond best to corona virus by coming together, not growing apart".

CAN COOPERATION IN ELECTRICITY DIPLOMACY BE A FUTURE TEMPLATE FOR SAARC?

The nation states of SAARC are witnessing rising demand of energy. Energy security means access of uninterrupted supplies of energy at an affordable price. Most of the member states are striving for energy security with the objective of providing electricity to the households. There are various challenges the states face. Firstly, the supply of electricity still remains poor in the region. Secondly, the public sector, which controls the distribution in South Asia, witnesses tremendous losses. Thirdly, the cross-subvention strategy where different groups receive electricity at different prices has contributed to the rise of inefficiencies. The political factors and climate change have caused structural transitions in the electricity markets of South Asia. This is where SAARC comes in. The member states are blessed with renewable resources. The parties can establish generation and supply agreements. A macro level institution with stakeholders of all states can pool electricity sources and establish a common market. With rising stress of climate change and large sections of people in the member states in vulnerable category, SAARC can establish a market for renewable energy. It is time to revive the SAARC Framework Cooperation Agreement on Energy signed in 2014 and facilitate the establishment of cross-border electricity grids.

SECTION 13

Indian Diaspora

- 1. Conceptual Paradigm of Diaspora Studies
- 2. Indian Diaspora Around the World: A Region-Specific Analysis

AN OVERVIEW

Indian Diaspora is a part of the syllabus our syllabus but no questions have been asked till date.

Potential foresight With recent operations by India to rescue its diaspora from Ukraine and Africa, there could be a question on Indian diaspora in Europe, its profile and the doctrinal approaches of India to safeguard its diaspora. The content in this section will enable one to write answers.

CHAPTER 1

Conceptual Paradigm of Diaspora Studies

CONCEPTS AND TERMS IN DIASPORA STUDIES

Operation Vanilla In January 2020, a cyclone hit Madagascar. The state instantly sought international mobilisation. The Indian Navy immediately responded with Humanitarian Assistance and Disaster Relief (HADR).

Analysis The assistance of India to Madagascar is in consonance with the Indian Navy's Foreign Cooperation initiatives in line with the Prime Minister's vision of 'Security and Growth for All in the Region (SAGAR)'.

Operation Sahayata In March 2019, a cyclone stuck Mozambique. They requested India for help. India dispatched Naval ships with the needed relief and support.

Analysis The support that India provides largely helps to position itself as a Net Security Provider.

Migration means movement from one place to the other. It can also mean movement from one country to another. **Immigration** is when a person comes to a foreign country as a permanent resident. **Emigration** is the act of settling in another country away from the home country. As per the Foreign Exchange Management Act, 1999, a **Non-Resident Indian (NRI)** is a person who has an Indian passport but stays outside India for business, employment, vocation for more than 182 days in a year. A **Person of Indian Origin (PIO)** is one whose parents or grandparents were Indian citizens by virtue of naturalisation. If an Indian citizen marries a foreign citizen, the foreign citizen married to the Indian citizen shall also be hold the status of a PIO. The indentured labourers taken by the British to foreign states from India settled in those lands and their offsprings in subsequent generations are now known as PIOs. If an NRI becomes a citizen of another country, he or she will hold the status of a PIO. A **Person Resident in India (PRI)** is an Indian citizen who is a citizen of India but may go abroad for a certain period for education purpose or medical treatments.

The entire phenomenon of human migration is presently captured in a term called 'Diaspora'. It originates from a Greek word that meant scattering or dispersion (of seeds). It was first used in sixth century BC to explain the Jewish exile from Babylon and later to describe the population of Jews living outside Palestine. Diaspora, therefore, signifies a movement and a spread of people outside their homeland. Earlier, such migration used to be in search of food, shelter and resources. In the post-World War II period, the migration was brought about with the movement of labour to the industrialised countries for jobs, and in search for better quality of life. The most recent trend of migration is influenced by globalisation and the demand of skilled expertise as well as large-scale political instability in certain regions of the world which occasions frequent refugee crises.

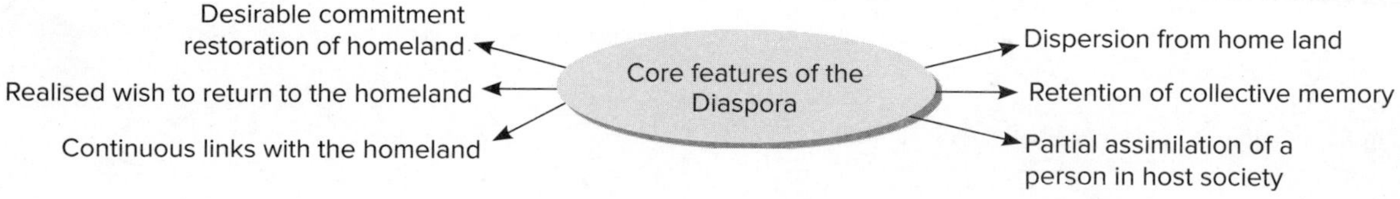

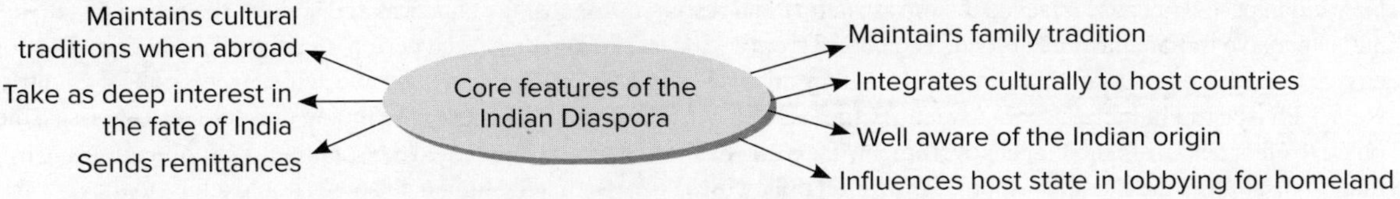

HISTORICAL ANALYSIS OF THE INDIAN DIASPORA

The first ever recorded migration of Indians abroad is during the time of the Greek and Mesopotamian civilisations. In the second century AD, during the reign of Kanishka, a group of people migrated from India to Eastern Europe. During the Chola period, people from the Chola kingdom migrated to South East Asian states as they had a powerful navy. Many Indians began to settle soon in the regions comprising present-day Indonesia and Malaysia. During the British times began the first wave of migration, which is referred to as 'Old Diaspora'. In 1833, the British abolished slavery and initiated the indentured labour migration system from India to meet the labour demand. Under this system, the labourers would enter into a contract for five years to work in a plantation or a factory. They were paid in cash and kind. After the expiry of the five-year period, the labourers could either leave and go back home or initiate a fresh contract. If the labourer decided to go back home, then he or she would have to testify before a magistrate that they had indeed finished their existing contract.

From 1834 began the export of bonded labour from India to the African states. This was also replicated by the Dutch and the French, which in turn led to a mass movement of Indians to other nations. The workers from India were mostly taken for plantation work. The labour was taken mostly from Bihar and the United Province to Mauritius, Suriname, Trinidad and Tobago and Fiji. From Punjab and Gujarat, the labour was mostly sent to Guyana and East Africa. The indentured system was abolished in 1916. This old diaspora constituted 60% for the Indian diaspora abroad and was majorly a pre-World War II phenomenon. During the Indian National Movement, delegations of Congress leaders comprising C. F. Andrews, V. S. Srinivasa Shastri, H. N. Kunzru and Gopal Krishna Gokhale would travel abroad to check the conditions of Indian workers and used to bargain for better conditions for the workers.

A section in the Congress wanted to safeguard the economic interests of the Indian diaspora in Britain. During this period, there was mass mobilisation of the Indian diaspora in Mauritius and Fiji, and consequently, the Indian diaspora began to be absorbed in local governments of these states. In some countries, the sections of the Indian community also pushed for Indian Independence. In 1927, a foreign policy document prepared by Jawaharlal Nehru advocated that Indians in foreign countries should adapt themselves to local countries and not seek special positions or provisions for themselves. The core idea propounded by Nehru was that the Indian diaspora should cooperate with the natives and support the anti-colonial struggles of their host countries. Nehru advocated that the interests of the natives should be paramount during the process. The post-independence period witnessed the rise of a new wave of migration known as 'New Diaspora'. A lot of Indians in the second phase began to move to the USA, Britain, Australia, Canada and Western Europe. After the World War II, Britain had formed a commonwealth immigration policy whereby citizens of commonwealth nations could work and live in Britain. This led to the movement of lot of skilled workers and students from India, and other commonwealth states, to Britain. The period of the 1960s also witnessed phenomenon of double migration by the Indian diaspora. During this decade, many newly independent African states initiated policies that affected outsiders. In Kenya and Uganda, there were anti-Indian discriminatory campaigns and this led the Indians to migrate from Africa (as well as the Caribbeans and Fiji) to Europe, Australia and North America. In the 1970s, began a movement of the Indian diaspora to the Gulf states. This happened largely due to the oil boom which resulted in the movement of semi-skilled workers to the Gulf states to assist Arab citizens. However, the Indian diaspora in the Gulf enjoys the status of mere second-class citizens. In the post-1990s period, globalisation led to a software boom, leading the US to introduce the concept of H1-B visas. A US firm, under H1-B visas, could hire the citizen of a foreign state if the citizen had a special occupation and set of skills. The software boom led to a huge wave of Indians entering the US as highly skilled workers in the IT industry. Since independence, Nehru had been of the idea that if India supports the Indian diaspora abroad, it would lead to more harm than good for India. He deliberately favoured a policy of disassociation as he wanted the Indian diaspora to serve native interest in their respective host nations. India also followed a policy of dissociation during the

Nehruvian period because it lacked the infrastructure and resources to meet the concerns and address the issues of a diverse and expansive Indian diaspora abroad. The period from 1950s to 1960s witnessed a period of active dissociation. The core advice to the diaspora during this time was that they adapt to their host countries and become active agents of host countries. Nehru advised the Indian diaspora to identify themselves with the locals. Whenever the Indian diaspora was in crises, they failed to elicit help from the Indian government. Thus, the Nehruvian period witnessed the suppression, subjugation and even marginalisation of the Indian diaspora. The overall policy till 1962 was that the Indian diaspora should adjust to the countries they reside in, even at great cost to themselves. Post-1962, the policy towards Indian diaspora began to change. In 1964, during Indira Gandhi's tour of Africa, she did emphasise that the Indian diaspora be loyal to their local communities but also began to address the Indian diaspora as ambassadors of India. The policy of Indira Gandhi was showing a shift away from the Nehruvian policy of active dissociation. When Indira Gandhi became the Prime Minister in 1966, the shift from dissociation began to visible as the Indian diaspora was gradually brought into the policy discourse. There was a further visible shift in the policy, in 1970s, when there was an oil boom in the Gulf. Due to this, a lot of low-income Indian workers began migrating to the Gulf to work in the oil services and construction sectors. These Indian expats began to send foreign remittances back home. The moment money started flowing to India, the government began to improve the banking system to ease out the repatriation of foreign exchange. The government also took up issues related to the welfare of the workers with host countries, primarily to protect the Indian workers from exploitation. In 1980s, the rise of IT-based diaspora that got fully established in 1990s in the USA, UK and Canada, also saw a rise in remittances back home. At the end of the Cold War, as India witnessed economic growth, it began to accept aid from the cash-rich NRIs abroad. The Indian government convinced the cash-rich NRIs to park their funds in branches of Indian banks abroad and rallied to have them invest their money in the industries in India. As India brought about structural reforms in the economy, the Indian diaspora too began to show faith in the future of the Indian economy, began to push their money into India. The government also embarked upon a proactive association with the diaspora abroad. The NRIs were allowed by the Narasimha Rao government to invest in stock markets and established industries. As India's priority was to usher in economic resurgence, the proactive diaspora policy began to focus more on the NRIs than on the old diaspora. The association with the old diaspora continued to be cultural in nature while with the new diaspora and the NRI, it became more economic and political. As the BJP government came in 1998, they brought about a radical rehaul in the diaspora policy. Their focus was now not only on transfer of investments and assets but also on using the diaspora as an instrument to make India a global power. The L. M. Singhvi committee was appointed during the BJP rule, which led to birth of a host of new initiatives of which the Pravasi Bharatiya Divas (PBD) and Pravasi Bharatiya Samman (PBS) were the most notable developments. The concept of PBD was launched in 2003 and has continued since then.

CONCEPT OF PRAVASI BHARATIYA DIVAS

The PBD was launched in 2003 as a platform to appreciate the access of knowledge, skills and expertise of the Indian diaspora. India organises the PBD from 7 to 9 January, every year. The date selected is significant as it was the very same date in 1915 that Mahatma Gandhi returned to India from South Africa. For those who cannot attend the PBD, the government organises regional PBD in New York, Singapore, Hague, Durban, Mauritius, Toronto and Sydney.

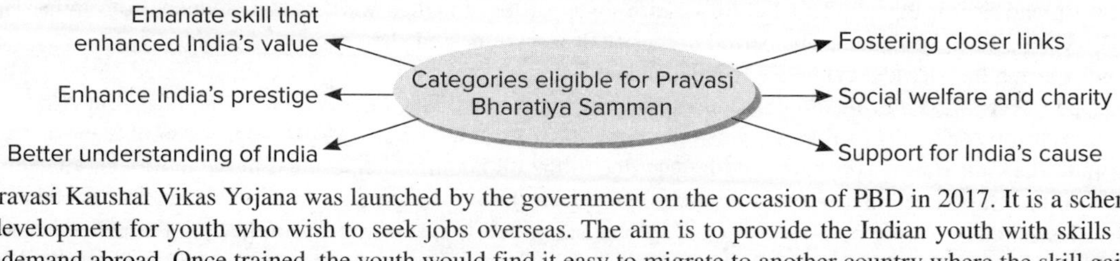

The Pravasi Kaushal Vikas Yojana was launched by the government on the occasion of PBD in 2017. It is a scheme for skill development for youth who wish to seek jobs overseas. The aim is to provide the Indian youth with skills which are in demand abroad. Once trained, the youth would find it easy to migrate to another country where the skill gained is high in demand. The Visiting Advanced Joint Research (VAJRA) scheme was also launched. The aim of the scheme is to allow NRIs to participate in research in India. The Science and Engineering Research Board has implemented VAJRA. The PBD 2020 was held in New Delhi on 9th January 2020 in which External Affairs Minister interacted with diaspora in eight countries through Video Conference. The event was webcast live to all Indian Missions and Posts abroad. The

UPA government also initiated multiple policies for the Indian diaspora during their rule from 2004 to 2014. A new women's helpline, a legal helpline for the diaspora in distress and various MoUs to safeguard Indians abroad have been their initiatives. The coming of the new government in 2014 has brought the diaspora back to focus. The Modi government has gauged that the diaspora is an important tool for economic development and has an important role as international influencer. The Modi government has made the diaspora a key driver of the Indian foreign policy. The various chapters of this book leading up to this chapter have also elaborated upon Modi's diaspora policy. To recap quickly, Prime Minister Modi addresses the diaspora in foreign countries to inform them about the programmes in India where the diaspora can be a stakeholder in India's development story. He usually addresses the diaspora in a huge gathering to convey to the host countries that there is a sizable chunk of Indian population in most nations, and that they are taken care of, they will, in turn take care of the local politicians in the elections.

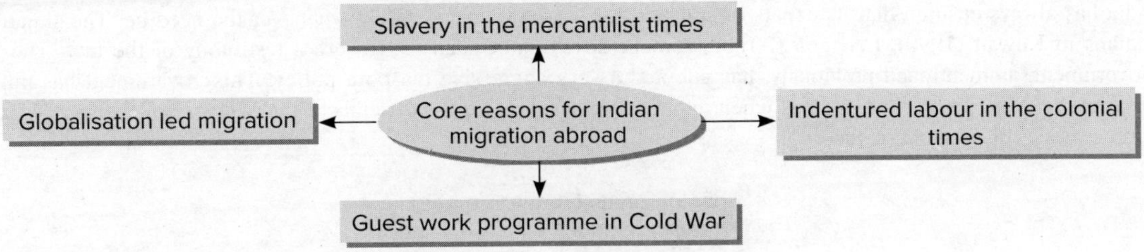

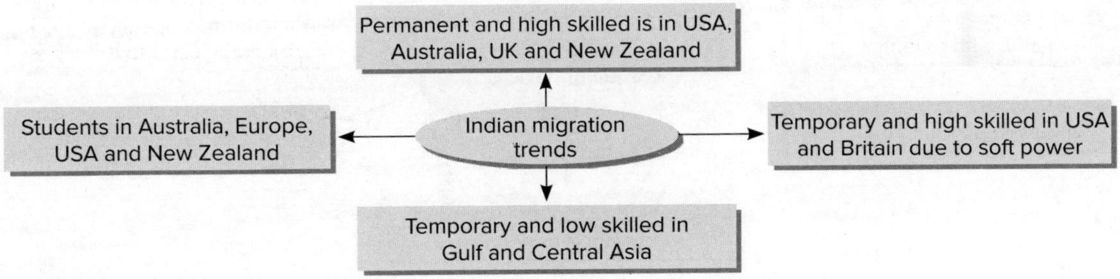

BRAIN DRAIN IN MODERN TIMES IN INDIA

Brain drain happens when there is an abnormal one-way flow of highly skilled workers to the advanced nations in search of better paying jobs, eventually leading to their resettlement in those countries. India has witnessed it in the case of the USA where skilled IT workers go to work with firms and eventually settle there. It is a loss to the parent country. The brain drain is majorly applicable in case of engineers, medicine practitioners and scientists. In India, lack of jobs and a stimulating research culture has bolstered the brain drain. Though brain drain explains the interdependence of all societies, the home country suffers as the skilled workforce settles aboard in large numbers. For the host country, it is a brain gain.

INDIAN DIASPORA—AN UNTAPPED ASSET GLOBALLY

The Indian diaspora has penetrated well into a range of countries with qualifications ranging from doctors, engineers to entrepreneurs. However, India has still not been able to capitalise upon this asset by taking advantage of the human and financial capabilities of the diaspora for the long-term development of India. The biggest area of our failure has been to create policies to halt the flow of spill workforce from India to other states. We have also not been to capitalise upon the diasporic workforce to make India into a global hub of knowledge that can act as a magnet for the diaspora of other nations. Our diaspora constitutes 2% of the total population but has a wealth approximately equal to one trillion dollars. It is this wealth that we tap for our domestic development. There is an immediate need of policy focus to attract the high achieving group of our diaspora. There is exodus of Indian students abroad for skill education. These students, post their education, stay back and this causes further brain drain. India has to take steps to reverse the brain drain into a brain gain. There is immediate need to create an ecosystem in India where we are able to attract the diaspora of other states.

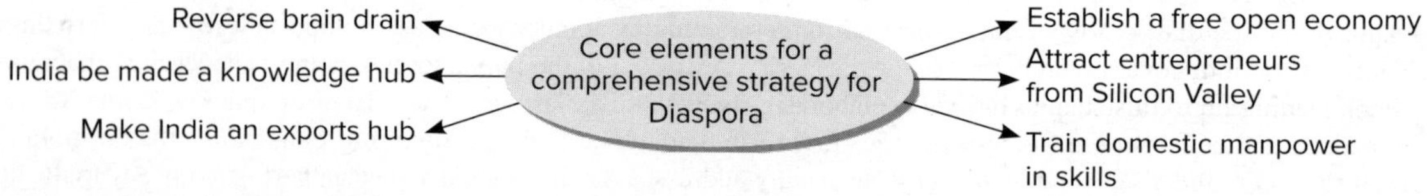

ENSURING THE SECURITY OF THE INDIAN DIASPORA

India has always ensured that its expats in conflict zones are evacuated safely whenever the need be. The situation of Indians in Kuwait (1990), Lebanon (2011), Yemen (2015) and Sudan (2016) are a testimony of the fact. The Modi Government, as mentioned previously, has adopted a very aggressive diaspora policy. This government has not only ensured the evacuation of the citizens when in need, but has directed the officials of the Ministry of External Affairs to address issues of diaspora on priority.

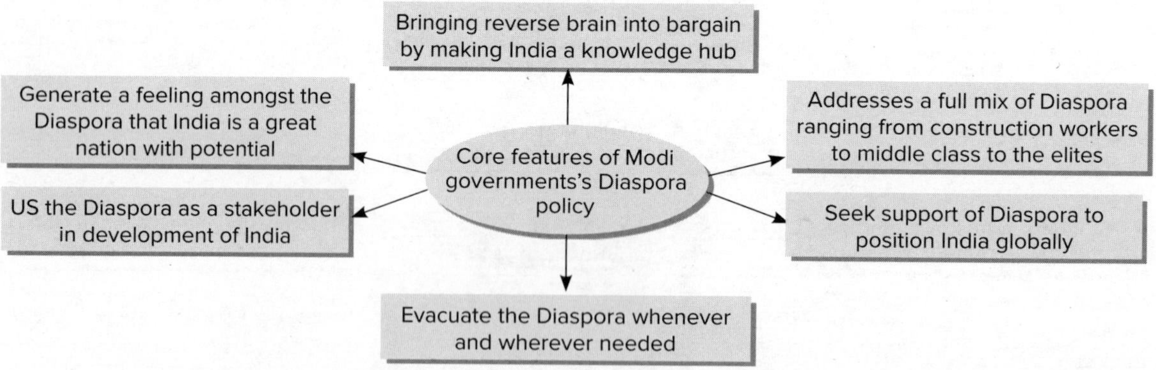

Talking about NRI interests does not upset foreign states but speaking about the interests of ethnic Indians who are no longer Indian residents may be viewed by a foreign state as an intrusion. Immense care needs to be taken at this level because addressing such sections could lead to risks at the bilateral diplomatic level. In 2007, when Malaysia used strong-arm tactics on Indian minorities, many Indian politicians made critical comments, leading to an intense backlash from Malaysian politicians. The PIOs have lived in territories abroad for a long time but have still been unable to completely integrate with host nations, which are, in turn, struggling with accepting citizens from a non-Western country. The host nations are still making attempts to reconcile with their citizens' national identities. In such circumstances, the PIOs have to be exceedingly loyal to the states they reside in since any possibility of the PIOs displaying multiple loyalties could be detrimental to their own interests. For example, when PM Modi attended a public event in Singapore, the government of Singapore mandated that only NRIs attend the event and not ethnic Indians in Singapore. In recent times, the security of the diaspora is a concern. RAW collects intelligence upon potential threats to the diaspora abroad. To secure the diaspora, steps at the military level are also taken.

RECENT OPERATIONS TO EVACUATE INDIAN CITIZENS ABROAD

Operation Vande Bharat 2020 and Operation Sạmudra Setu 2020 These two operations were launched by the Indian government via air and water to evacuate its diaspora that had been stuck in different countries due to the outbreak of COVID-19. However, owing to slow, tardy and arbitrary responses of the government in the operations, the government came under severe criticism from the stranded Indians. The COVID-19 crisis clearly asserts that if government needs to emerge as an effective rescuer in the future, then there is a need for government to adopt a **citizen evacuation policy** at the earliest.

Operation Sukoon It was one of the largest evacuation operations done by the Indian Navy since World War II. In 2006, Hezbollah attacked Israelis by launching cross-border raids. The Lebanese demanded release of the Lebanese prisoners from Israel. Israel responded to the cross-border raids by launching a full-scale invasion of Lebanon. This led to the 2006 Lebanon war. Due to this, around 2200 Indians, Sri Lankans and Nepalis in Lebanon got affected. The Indian government directed its Navy to launch the evacuation. The Navy pressed into services INS Brahmaputra, INS Betwa, INS Shakti and INS Mumbai.

Operation Safe Homecoming It was launched in March 2011, to evacuate Indian citizens stranded in Libya during the Libyan civil war. The Indian Navy and Air Force worked jointly to establish an air and a sea bridge. Due to the Libyan crisis, around 18,000 Indians were affected. INS Mysore, INS Aditya and INS Jalashwa, along with Air India aircrafts, were pressed into service for citizen evacuation from Tripoli.

Operation Raahat In 2015, Saudi Arabia launched attacks on Houthi rebels in Yemen. As the hostilities intensified, the Indian government decided to evacuate around 5000 Indians trapped in Yemen. During the crises, Yemen became a no-fly zone. India used Djibouti to evacuate its citizens. The operation for evacuation began on 1 April and was successfully completed on 11 April 2015.

Operation Sankat Mochan In 2016, a hostile war broke out between Sudan and South Sudan. As a result, around 600 Indians in South Sudan and the Indians settled there got affected. The Indian Air Force was pressed into service to evacuate the Indians.

RECENT SCHEMES, INITIATIVES AND PROGRAMMES FOR SAFEGUARDING THE INDIAN DIASPORA

SWADES (Skilled Workers Arrival Database for Employment Support) Because of COVID-19, a lot of Indians working in Gulf have come back. The government had created this database in 2020 that would capture the skill set of the workers and fed into a centralised database that would enable the Indian firms to access the skilled workers to assist in creating an Atmanirbhar Bharat.

Indian Community Welfare Fund This is a specialised fund established to assist workers in distress. The Indian Missions abroad will use the contingency fund for worker's welfare.

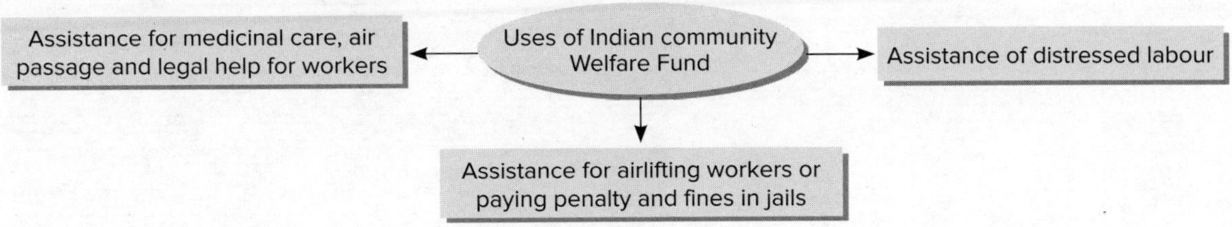

Mahatma Gandhi Pravasi Suraksha Yojana It was launched in 2012 to enable Indian workers to get life insurance. The scheme also encourages workers to save money for pension.

Pravasi Bharatiya Bima Yojana It is a compulsory insurance scheme for Indian workers with ECR (Emigration Check Required) stamped on passports.

Know India Programme It is a three-week programme for Indian expatriates in the age group of 18–26 years. One Indian state partners with the central government and the expatriate youths are introduced to Indian culture, education and so on. The youth is then made 'Youth Ambassadors' for Indian culture.

Study India Programme It aims to connect expatriate youth to educational institutions where the youth come to undertake short courses in India. The cost of the programme is borne by the Indian government along with 50% of the airfare of each participant.

Scholarship Programme for Diaspora's Children Under the scheme, there is provision for scholarship for engineering, law and science education for children of the Indian diaspora for higher education.

Overseas India Youth Club An initiative to keep the overseas youth in touch with the development of India by India Youth clubs abroad.

Tracing Roots Scheme Under this scheme, an Indian diaspora family can get its roots traced in any state in India on provision of paying a charge for the facility.

E-Migrate The Indian government has launched an online platform for foreign employers who wish to recruit Indian citizens. The foreign employees need to register in the online registration system as the registration once done shall be inspected by Indian missions abroad. The employers can use the platform to recruit Indian workers by giving them permits. The advantage of this system is that the worker will be informed about the terms and conditions online before employment.

Madad If Indian citizens living abroad wish to file any consular-related grievance, the new website launched by the Indian government called Madad may be used as a platform. The portal will act as a grievance redressal mechanism, allowing the Indian diaspora greater accessibility and reach. The authorities would now be more accountable and would have to resolve grievances more quickly and in a time-bound manner. The portal will use red, amber and green colours, signifying the official stand on the complaints.

CHAPTER 2

Indian Diaspora Around the World: A Region-Specific Analysis

INDIAN DIASPORA IN AFRICA

There exists a considerably large Indian diaspora in Africa, with most of it settled in Mauritius. Most of the Indians had reached Africa under the Indentured Labour System. Indians were taken to work in forests in East Africa to lay down railway lines. A lot of migrant Indians were also free passengers who were mainly traders from the West coast of India, especially Gujarat. The Indians faced difficulties in Kenya and South Africa and the Indian government did attempt to provide covert and overt support to the Indian diaspora whenever needed. In 1946, when South Africa had initiated segregation and discrimination of Indians, the Indian government took up the matter at the level of UN not just for Indians who were discriminated against, but for all communities that became victims of racial discrimination. Jawaharlal Nehru, in other parts of Africa, recommended integration of the Indian diaspora with the African cause but maintained a different policy towards the Indian diaspora in South Africa where there was outright support. With reference to South Africa, India tried to merge the issue of apartheid and Indian discrimination. India, post-independence, solicited economic support from all sources except South Africa, and Nehru decided to break up diplomatic ties with the former over racial discrimination. In East Africa, the Indian diaspora had visibility since ancient times. As the Indian diaspora in East Africa mainly comprised of trading community, it was visibly a rich diaspora. During colonial times, the British followed a nativity policy, thereby debarring the PIOs from any form of power sharing. In 1967, the government in Kenya initiated a process of Kenyanisation of the economy which affected the Indians as well. The Indian government encouraged the Indians in Kenya to apply for local citizenships. The government instructed the Indian diplomats stationed in Kenya to help PIOs get integrated, to which the Indian diaspora in Kenya showed a lukewarm response. The government launched an Africa–India development cooperation to help the Indian community in Kenya get economic support. India also faced a similar issue when Idi Amin, the third president of Uganda decided to outlaw outsiders from Uganda. Amin gave a 90-day ultimatum period for the outsiders to leave during his ongoing war of liberation. India, by diplomatically taking up the issue with Idi Amin, ensured that the Indian settlers with Indian passports would be given compensation for their business and properties held in Uganda. In Mauritius, the Indian diaspora is a majority. Since independence till today, India has used the Indian diaspora in Africa as its goodwill ambassadors.

INDIAN DIASPORA IN SOUTH EAST ASIA

The Indian diaspora is well represented in Singapore, Thailand and Philippines. The Indian diaspora in South East Asia (SEA) comprises NRIs, PIOs and stateless Indians. Some are affluent while others are striving for affluence. The local leaders of ASEAN states trust the Indian diaspora, thereby ensuring that the community plays a positive role in the development of SEA. In the chapter entitled 'India and South East Asia Policy—Key Drivers', we have discussed about the eviction of Indians belonging to the Chettiar community from Burma. As more Indians were evicted, the space was filled by the Chinese migrants. The inaction of India in Burma, which stands in complete contrast with the proactive stance of India in case of Sri Lanka, also became counterproductive. In the post-Cold War period, India brought about a shift in its Indian diaspora policy in SEA. India realised that its diaspora in Singapore, Thailand and Malaysia, is placed in strategic sectors such as trade, investments, engineering and textiles. The Sindhi community, in Philippines, is dominant in manufacturing while Punjabis are dominant in money lending. Singapore has a mixture of Tamils, Malayalis, Gujaratis and Punjabis who range from being in trade to civil services to education to pharmacy. The Sikhs and Sindhis are dominant in Thailand in textiles, IT and real estate.

INDIAN DIASPORA IN EUROPE

Import of spices, ivory and so forth, via other countries, do find a mention in the Old Testament of the Bible. King Solomon was gifted many spices by the Queen of Sheba from India. There is evidence of the *Panchatantra* being translated in the 6th century BC, in Latin, Spanish and Italian. India came in contact with Europe during the 15th century, when trade was undertaken via the sea route. Vasco da Gama was a Portuguese explorer and the first European to reach India by sea. His initial voyage to India (1497–1499) was the first to link Europe and Asia by an ocean route, connecting the Atlantic and the Indian oceans and therefore, the West and the Orient. Vasco da Gama's discovery of the sea route to India was significant and opened the way for an age of global imperialism and for the Portuguese to establish a long-lasting colonial empire in Asia. The Portuguese used the ocean route to avoid sailing across the highly disputed Mediterranean and traversing the dangerous Arabian Peninsula. The sum of the distances covered in the outward and return voyages made this expedition the longest ocean voyage ever made until then, far longer than a full voyage around the world by way of the Equator. With the advent of the colonial era, the Indian movement to Europe saw an upswing. In the initial year of the Cold War, the aggressive nationalism in Africa led to the migration of Indians to European states. The Indian diaspora in Europe amounts to nearly 8% of the total population of Europe with majority of it concentrated in Britain.

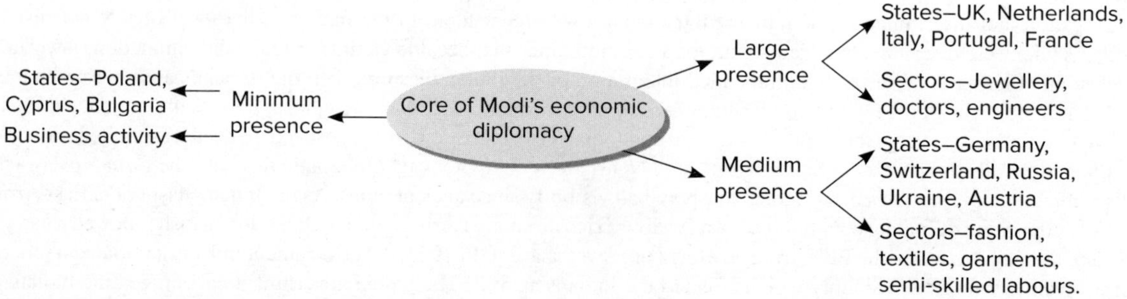

The Indian diaspora in European Union settled close to the capital cities and industrial towns than in the hinterland. After World War II, another wave of professionals working in IT, construction, medicine and engineering migrated to Europe. In 1990s, the European Union imposed restrictions leading to the entry of only teachers, nurses and scientists. From early 2000s, the migration of IT professionals has again been on the rise in Britain.

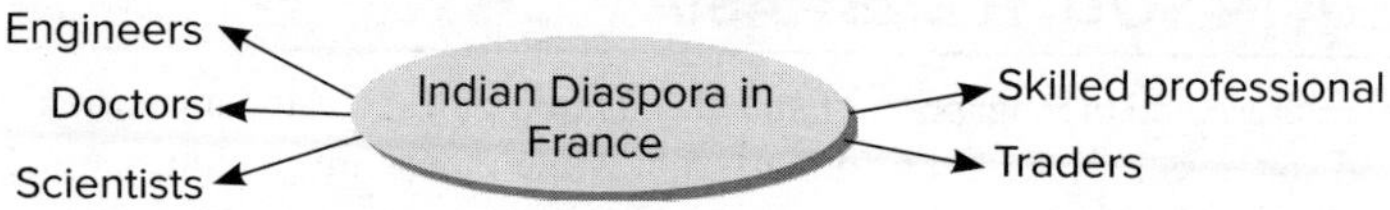

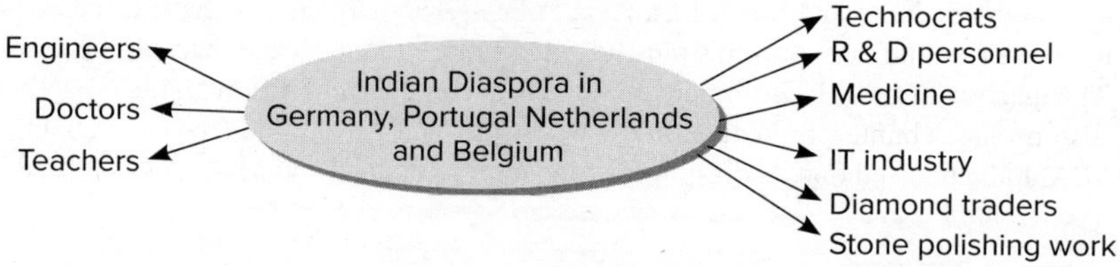

INDIAN DIASPORA IN NORTH AMERICA

There is a strong Indian diaspora in Canada, in Toronto and Vancouver. The Indian diaspora in Canada is majorly the Sikh population. The Sikhs in Canada consider the non-Sikh Indian community in Canada as outsiders, asserting the religious–regional bias. The Indian diaspora in Canada is politically influential as they have strong presence in the political and bureaucratic setup. In the USA, the Indian diaspora is composed mainly of the educated and professional class. The presence of the Indian diaspora in the USA has increased from 1970s, when amendments were made to local laws allowing entry of trained skilled personnel. A scholar named Jenson has argued that the migration of skilled workers to the USA has led to a brain drain in India. In 1990s, there were more amendments in the US laws allowing the US firms to build up human capital capabilities of the USA and this gave the US firms an option to open up the US labour market for Indians. The H1-B, a non-immigrant visa, also facilitated the transfer. Indian immigration to the US has been majorly in the professional category, including executives, administrators and managerial staff. Ethnic balancing of the population is, however, a concern that, at times, leads to hate crimes against Indian diaspora.

THE DIASPORA IN AUSTRALIA, NEW ZEALAND AND FIJI

Australia, an island continent and a former British penal colony, shares the shores of Indian Ocean with India and acts as a bridge in the movement of people. In the 18th century, Indians began to migrate to Australia, which was then known as 'New Holland'. Later, traders from Gujarat, Sindh and Punjab also landed up in Australia. A lot of Anglo-Indians in the post-1947 period had settled in Australia. In 1958, the Migration Act allowed settlement rights to Anglo-Indians from India to Australia. The Indian diaspora is largely involved in sugar plantations, taxi driving and security. These days, the number of members of the Indian diaspora working in IT, health, medicine and academics is also on the rise. In New Zealand, in the 20th century, a considerable number of Indians worked as halal slaughterers in the meat packaging industry. Presently, New Zealand has a skilled diaspora of professionals, doctors, geologists and academicians. The Indian diaspora in New Zealand is settled mainly in Auckland and Wellington. In 1879, the indentured labours were taken by British to work as coolie in the sugar and cotton plantations of Fiji. Later, Gujarati traders began trading cotton cloth while the Punjabis, began work in transport and money lending. In 1970, when Fiji gained independence, the Indians in Fiji accepted Fijian nationality. In the present day, Indians dominate the political system of Fiji and contribute to national development.

INDIAN DIASPORA IN WEST ASIA

India–West Asia relations go back to the ancient times that led to the birth of trade and cultural ties. The presence of Indians in the Gulf goes back to pre-Islamic times. During the medieval times, the merchants from India traded with the Gulf. In the 17th and 18th century, India traded with Iran through the land route. The trade extended up to Central Asia. The coming of the British in India saw a large number of Indians settling down in the Gulf region, especially in Muscat and Bahrain (due to a thriving pearl fishing industry). In the 19th and 20th century, pearl finishing was a dominant activity but when it gradually declined, Indians shifted to general trade and goods in ports from India and Europe. Since the discovery of oil, Indians have been actively working in the oil sector. The oil boom of the 1970s led to another major flow of migrant Indians to join the oil sector in the Gulf. As the political conditions of the Gulf witnessed a swing from 1990 to 1998, there was a general decline in number of Indians in the Gulf. About 70% of the Indian diaspora in Gulf is from Karnataka, Andhra Pradesh, Telangana and Tamil Nadu. Indian diaspora is also present in Israel and they are in agriculture work. Because of COVID-19, a lot of Indians working outside the country had to come back.

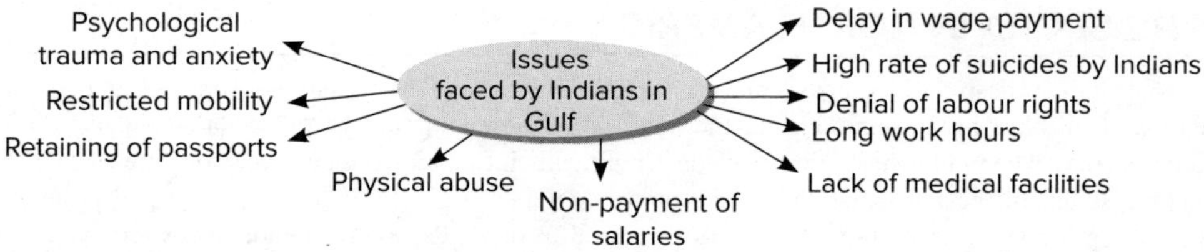

INDIAN DIASPORA IN THE CARIBBEAN ISLANDS

The islands from Mexico to Panama are known as Caribbean islands. Initially, the islands were under Spanish control. The Spanish were ruthless and were mainly interested in draining the resources of the area. The major economic activity in the area was plantation work and slavery was therefore quite rampant. The Indians were taken to the Caribbeans as part of the indentured labour system. As the islands gained independence from their colonial masters, the region became a strategic backyard for the USA, leading to a transformation of the region's economy from plantation work to industrialisation. As the nature of the society began to witness change, the Indian diaspora also evolved and began to adapt to a new, modern way of life. The Indian diaspora realised the significance of education and educated the younger generations. The period from 1880 to 1914 saw multiple strikes by Indian plantation workers, leading to an assertion of their identity and thereby giving birth to a new kind of political activism by the Indian diaspora.

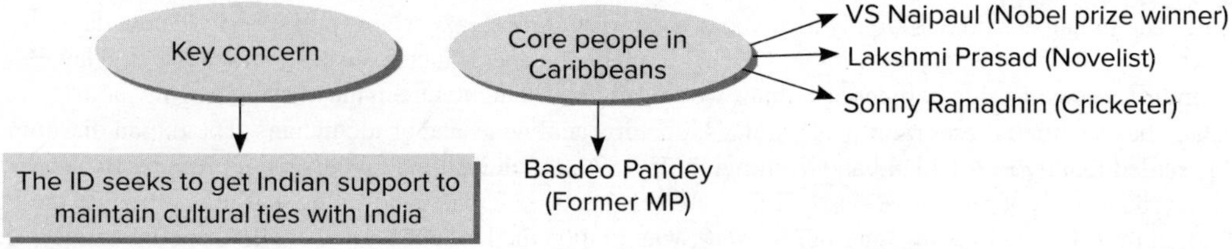

Bibliography

1. The New World Disorder and the Indian Imperative by Shashi Tharoor and Samir Saran
2. World Order: Reflections on the Character of Nations and the Course of History by Henry Kissinger
3. The Penguin History of the World: Sixth Edition: 6th edition by J. M. Roberts and Odd Arne Westad.
4. Sapiens: A Brief History of Humankind by Yuval Noah Harari
5. Mastering Modern World History by Norman Lowe
6. Glimpses of World History by Jawaharlal Nehru
7. World History 101: From Ancient Mesopotamia and the Viking Conquests to NATO and WikiLeaks, an Essential Primer on World History (Adams 101) by Tom Head
8. A History of the World by Andrew Marr
9. Indian Foreign Policy: Challenges and Opportunities (Foreign Service Institute)
10. Choices: Inside the Making of Indian Foreign Policy by Shivshankar Menon
11. Indian Foreign Policy (Oxford India Short Introductions Series) by Sumit Ganguly
12. Indian Foreign Policy: The Modi Era by Harsh V Pant
13. New Directions in India's Foreign Policy: Theory and Praxis by Harsh V. Pant
14. India's Foreign Policy: A Reader (Critical Issues in Indian Politics) by Kanti P. Bajpai and Harsh V. Pant
15. The Oxford Handbook of Indian Foreign Policy
16. The Agartala Doctrine: A Proactive Northeast in Indian Foreign Policy by Subir Bhaumik
17. Indian Foreign Policy by Chris Ogden
18. How India Sees The World: From Kautilya to Modi: Kautilya to the 21st Century by Shyam Saran
19. Staggering Forward: Narendra Modi and India's Global Ambition by Bharat Karnad
20. India-China Boundary Problem, 1846-1947 by A.G. Noorani
21. China-India Relations: Cooperation and conflict (Routledge Contemporary Asia Series) by Kanti Bajpai, Jing Huang
22. The China - Pakistan Axis: Asia's New Geopolitics by Andrew Small
23. The Great Game in the Buddhist Himalayas: India and China's Quest for Strategic Dominance by Phunchok Stobdan
24. India's China War by Neville Maxwell
25. China's India War: Collision Course on the Roof of the World by Bertil Lintner
26. JFK's Forgotten Crisis: Tibet, the CIA, and the Sino-Indian War by Bruce Riedel
27. The Elephant and the Dragon – The Economic Rise of India and China and What It Means for All of Us by Robyn Meredith
28. China: A History by John Keay
29. East of India South of China: Sino-Indian Encounters in Southeast Asia by Amitav Acharya
30. China and India: Asia's Emergent Great Powers by Chris Ogden
31. India China Relations: The Border Issue and Beyond by Mohan Guruswamy and Zorawar Daulet Singh
32. India's China Strategic Perspectives by Subramanian Swamy
33. Fateful Triangle: How China Shaped US-India Relations During the Cold War by Tanvi Madan
34. One belt, one road: China's global outreach by Srikanth Kondapalli
35. The China-Pakistan Economic Corridor of the Belt and Road Initiative: Concept, Context and Assessment (Contemporary South Asian Studies) by Siegfried O. Wolf
36. China's One Belt One Road Initiative and Private International Law (Routledge Research in International Law) by Poomintr Sooksripaisarnkit and Sai Ramani Garimella
37. Belt and Road: A Chinese World Order by Bruno Macaes
38. China's One Belt One Road: Initiative, Challenges and Prospects by Nivedita Das Kundu
39. The New Silk Roads: The Present and Future of the World by Peter Frankopan
40. Politics of Geo- Politics: Continuity and Change in India - Nepal Relations by Lok Raj Baral

41. Hindu Kingship, Ethnic Revival and Maoist Rebellion in Nepal by Marie Lecomte-Tilouine
42. India's Borderland Disputes China, Pakistan, Bangladesh and Nepal by Anna Orton
43. DO KALAPANI, LIPULEKH AND LIMPIYADHURA BELONG TO INDIA OR NEPAL? by LB THAPA
44. Indo Nepal Relations in Linkage Perspective by S. K. Chaturvedi
45. India- china major disputes; Nepal Bhutan and Tibet by Satish Kumar
46. China's Approach Towards Territorial Disputes: Lessons and Prospects (First) by Ms Sana Hashmi
47. India–Bhutan Relations: International Politics by Vaqar R. Shaikh
48. Transboundary Water Governance and International Actors in South Asia: The Ganges-Brahmaputra-Meghna Basin by Paula Hanasz
49. India Bangladesh Domestic Politics: The River Ganges Water Issues by Punam Pandey
50. The Blood Telegram: India's Secret War in East Pakistan by Gary J. Bass
51. Operation X: The Untold Story of India's Covert Naval War in East Pakistan by Captain M.N.R Samant and Sandeep Unnithan
52. Sri Lanka in crisis: India's options by Subramanian Swamy
53. Sub-Regional Cooperation in South Asia: India, Sri Lanka and Maldives by Venugopal B.
54. Sri Lanka by Nirupama Subramanian
55. Pakistan's Inter-Services Intelligence Directorate: Covert Action and Internal Operations by Owen L. Sirrs
56. Taliban: The Power of Militant Islam in Afghanistan and Beyond by Ahmed Rashid
57. Kashmir's Untold Story: Declassified by Iqbal Chand Malhotra and Maroof Raza
58. Fighting to the End: The Pakistan Army's Way of War by C. Christine Fair
59. The Unending Game: A Former R&AW Chief's Insights into Espionage by Vikram Sood
60. Descent into Chaos: How the War Against Islamic Extremism is Being Lost in Pakistan, Afghanistan and Central Asia by Ahmed Rashid
61. India's Afghan Muddle by Harsh V. Pant
62. The Wars of Afghanistan by Peter Tomsen
63. China Pakistan Economic Corridor Needs a Counter Strategy of India by Arlen Clemens
64. Afghanistan: A Role for India by Arun Sahgal
65. Mapping the Great Game: Explorers, Spies & Maps in Nineteenth-century Asia by Riaz Dean
66. South Asia's Nuclear Security Dilemma- India, Pakistan, Afghanistan and China by Aubree Penrod
67. Pakistan: A Hard Country by Anatol Lieven
68. India and Pakistan Pathways Ahead by Amitabh Mattoo
69. Pakistan's Tactical Nuclear Weapons: Giving the devil more than his due? by Inderjit Panjrath
70. Pakistan: Courting the Abyss by Tilak Devasher
71. Afghanistan Pakistan India: A Paradigm Shift by Shaida Mohammad
72. Kashmir in Conflict: India, Pakistan and the Unending War by Victoria Schofield
73. The China–Pakistan Axis: Asia's New Geopolitics by Andrew Small
74. Where Borders Bleed: An Insider's Account of Indo-Pak Relations by Rajiv Dogra
75. The People Next Door: The Curious History of India-Pakistan Relations by T.C.A. Raghavan
76. The People Next Door: The Curious History of India-Pakistan Relations by T.C.A. Raghavan
77. The People Next Door: The Curious History of India-Pakistan Relations by T.C.A. Raghavan
78. India and Pakistan: Neighbours at Odds by Avtar Bhasin
79. India vs Pakistan: Why Cant We Just be Friends? by Husain Haqqani
80. Dragon on Our Doorstep: Managing China Through Military Power by Pravin Sawhney and Ghazala Wahab
81. Future Oil Demands of China, India, and Japan: Policy Scenarios and Implications by George G. Eberling
82. The Future Of India and South-East Asia by K M Panikkar
83. India and South East Asia: Cultural, Economic and Strategic Linkages by Chandra
84. East of India South of China: Sino-Indian Encounters in Southeast Asia by Amitav Acharya
85. Competing Visions of India in World Politics: India's Rise Beyond the West by K. Sullivan
86. Integrating South and East Asia: Economics of Regional Cooperation and Development by Jayant Menon
87. Rivals: How The Power Struggle Between China India And Japan Will Shape: How the power struggle between China, India and Japan will shape our next decade by Bill Emmott
88. US Policy Towards China, India and Japan New Challenges and Prospects by Madhuchanda Ghosh
89. Asian Juggernaut: The Rise of China, India, and Japan by Brahma Chellaney
90. India Japan Relations in Emerging Asia by Takenori Horimoto and Lalima Varma
91. Emerging Horizons in India-Vietnam Relations by Shakti Sinha and Sonu Trivedi
92. India - Vietnam Enhancing Partnership by Jayachandra Reddy G and Nguyen Xuan Trng
93. India-Vietnam: Agenda for Strengthening Partnership by Rajiv K. Bhatia
94. India- Australia Relations: Evolving Poly- centric World Order by Darvesh Gopal
95. India-Australia Relations: Convergences And Divergences by D. Gopal
96. International Relations and Asia's Southern Tier: ASEAN, Australia, and India (Asan-Palgrave Macmillan Series)
97. Reimaging India and Australia: Culture and Identity by D. Gopal
98. The Politics and Culture of Globalisation: India and Australia by Hans Löfgren

99. Geopolitics, Security and Bilateral Relations: Perspectives from India and South Korea by B. K. Sharma
100. Conflict in Asia: Korea, China-Taiwan, and India-Pakistan by U. K. Heo and Shale A. Horowitz
101. Forty Years of India - Korea Relations and Looking Ahead by Rajat Kathuria and Sanjana Joshi
102. China-India-Japan in the Indo-Pacific by Jagannath P. Panda and Titli Basu
103. Rise of the Indo-Pacific: Perspectives, Dimensions and Challenges by Chintamani Mahapatra
104. Samudra Manthan: Sino-Indian Rivalry in the Indo-Pacific by C. Raja Mohan
105. Strategic Balance in the Indo-Pacific Region: Challenges and Prospects by M. H. Rajesh and Raj Kumar Sharma
106. The Indo-Pacific Axis: Peace and Prosperity or Conflict? by Satish Chandra and Baladas Ghoshal
107. The Indo-Pacific: Trump, China, and the New Struggle for Global Mastery by Richard Javad Heydarian
108. Scaling India-Japan Cooperation in Indo-Pacific and Beyond 2025 : Corridors, Connectivity and Contours by Jagannath P Panda
109. Asia's New Geopolitics: Essays on Reshaping the Indo-Pacific by Michael R. Auslin
110. The Quad Plus: Towards a Shared Strategic Vision for the Indo-Pacific by Walter Lohman, Lt General Ravi K Sawhney
111. Geopolitics of the Indo-Pacific by Kerry Bolton
112. Indo Pacific Region: Political and Strategic Prospects (Project of Indian Council of World Affairs) by Rajiv K. Bhatia and Sakhuja Vijay
113. Act East to Act Indo-Pacific: India's Expanding Neighborhood by Prabir De
114. The South China Sea Arbitration: Toward an International Legal Order in the Oceans by Yoshifumi Tanaka
115. Asia's Cauldron: The South China Sea and the End of a Stable Pacific by Robert D. Kaplan
116. The South China Sea – The Struggle for Power in Asia by Bill Hayton
117. The Politics of South China Sea Disputes by Nehginpao Kipgen
118. Global Power Revelry and South China Sea Dispute by Lester B Stone
119. Nine Dash Line : Deciphering the South China Sea Conundrum by Pooja Bhatt
120. The South China Sea Dispute by Lan Storey
121. Trade in Services and Trade Agreements: Perspectives from India and the European Union by Arpita Mukherjee
122. Privacy & Data Protection Laws in India, USA & European Union by Javid Ahmad Dar
123. India and European Union: Perceptions of the Indian Print Media and Elites by Shreya Pandey
124. India and the European Union in the 21st Century by R. K. Jain
125. Globalization and Intellectual Property Rights: A Comparative Study of the Patent Governance Systems of India and the European Union (EU) by Makhan Saikia
126. India-European Union Trade Prospects & Impact of Euro by Vibha Mathur
127. India–EU People Mobility: Historical, Economic and Regulatory Dimensions by Rupa Chanda and Pralok Gupta
128. India's Emerging Partnerships in Eurasia: Strategies of New Regionalism by Nivedita Das Kundu
129. The World Was Going Our Way: The KGB and the Battle for the Third World: Newly Revealed Secrets from the Mitrokhin Archive by Christopher Andrew
130. India-Russia Partnership: Kashmir, Chechnya & Issues of Convergence by Debidatta Aurobinda Mahapatra
131. India and France in a Multipolar World: Proceedings of the Seminar by Fondation nationale des sciences politiques
132. India and EU: An Insider's View by Bhaswati Mukherjee
133. Russia-India relations in the post cold war era: the China factor by Ajay K. Singh
134. Reinventing Indo-Russia Relations by Jitendra K Das and Hitesh Arora
135. China Russia India Relations in 21st Century by Deepak Yadav
136. India-Russia Post Cold War Relations by Chandra Rekha
137. Russia-India Relations: The Significance of Subjective Factors by Aubree Penrod
138. India and Central Asia: The Strategic Dimension by P Stobdan
139. India and Central Asia: Exploring New Horizons for Cooperation by Rajiv Bhatia
140. The Resurgence of Central Asia: Islam or Nationalism? by Ahmed Rashid
141. India and Central Asia: Geopolitics, Economy and Culture by Nasir Raza Khan
142. India and Central Asia: Two Decades of Transition by P.L. Dash
143. Developments in Central Asia: India-Kyrgyzstan Relations by Bal Krishan Sharma and Nivedita Das Kundu
144. India-Central Asia Economic Relations: Prospects and Challenges by Ishfaq Ahmad Malik
145. The Great Game by Peter Hopkirk
146. Eurasia and India: Regional Perspectives (Central Asia Research Forum) by K. Warikoo
147. China and India in Central Asia: A New "Great Game"? (CERI Series in International Relations and Political Economy) by Marlène Laruelle, Jean-François Huchet
148. India Africa Trade Relation by Tribhuwan Prasad, Shashi Shekhar
149. India in Africa, Africa in India: Indian Ocean Cosmopolitanisms by John C. Hawley
150. India and Southern Africa by Paramjit Singh
151. Security Dimensions in India- Africa Relations by Vimal Nayan Pandey
152. India in Africa: Changing Geographies of Power by Emma Mawdsley and Gerard McCann
153. No god but God (Updated Edition): The Origins, Evolution, and Future of Islam by Reza Aslan

154. Zealot: The Life and Times of Jesus of Nazareth by Reza Aslan
155. Children of Abraham at War: The Clash of Messianic Militarisms by Talmiz Ahmad
156. The Islamist Challenge in West Asia: Doctrinal and Political Competitions after the Arab Spring by Talmiz Ahmad
157. How to Win a Cosmic War: Confronting Radical Religion by Reza Aslan
158. Salafism: The History and Legacy of the Conservative Salafi Branch within Sunni Islam by Charles River Editors
159. ISIS: A Byproduct of Salafism? by Sadi Kose
160. Salafism: Oxford Bibliographies Online Research Guide (Oxford Bibliographies Online Research Guides) by Jonathan A. C. Brown
161. The Future of Salafism post-Arab Spring developments: The Future of Salafism by Dr Mohamed Ali Ahdash
162. And God Knows the Martyrs: Martyrdom and Violence in Jihadi-Salafism by Nathan S. French
163. Neo-Salafism: Rashid Rida and the Wahhabification of Salafism in the 20th Century by Mikhah Ben David
164. India-West Asia Relations: Understanding Cultural Interplays by M. H. Ilias and P. J. Vincent
165. Foreign Policy of India: West Asia & North Africa (WANA) by Faisal Ahmed
166. Foreign Policy of India & West Asia: Change & Continuity by Fazal Mahmood
167. India & West Asia in the Era of Globalization by Anwar Alam
168. The Gulf in Turmoil: A Global Response by A. K. Pasha
169. Contemporary Saudi Arabia And The Emerging Indo-Saudi Relations : by A. K. Pasha
170. Saudi Arabia and Iran: Power and Rivalry in the Middle East by Simon Mabon
171. India - Saudi Arabia : Implementing India's Look-west policy by A N Swamy
172. Saudi Arabian Foreign Policy: Conflict and Cooperation (Library of International Relations) by Neil Partrick
173. Nuclear Weapons and Indian Security: The Realist Foundations of Strategy by Bharat Karnad
174. Indian Nuclear Policy (Oxford India Short Introductions Series) by Harsh V. Pant and Yogesh Joshi
175. India in Nuclear Asia: Evolution of Regional Forces, Perceptions and Policies (Strategic Studies) by Yogesh Joshi and Frank O'Donnell
176. Sharpening the Arsenal: India's Evolving Nuclear Deterrence Policy by Gurmeet Kanwal
177. India's Nuclear Policy (Praeger Security International) by Bharat Karnad
178. Nuclear Strategy in the Modern Era: Regional Powers and International Conflict (Princeton Studies in International History and Politics Book 143) by Vipin Narang
179. India and the United States in the 21st Century: Reinventing Partnership by Teresita C. Schaffer
180. The US-India Nuclear Pact: Policy, Process and Great Power Politics by Harsh Pant
181. A Debate to Remember: The US–India Nuclear Deal by Chaitanya Ravi
182. Destined for War: can America and China escape Thucydides' Trap? by Graham Allison and Andrew Hastie
183. Open Embrace: India-US Ties in the Age of Modi and Trump by Varghese K George
184. Trump: The Art of the Deal by Donald Trump
185. Indian Foreign Trade: Trumped Up or Down by Amiya Chandra
186. India Latin America, An Alliance for Future by Soraya Caro Vargas, Geetali Baruah
187. Make it in India: Global CEOs, Indo-US Insights by Ranjini Manian & Joanne Grady Huskey
188. India in the United Nations: Interplay of Interests and Principles by C.S.R. Murthy
189. Perilous Interventions: The Security Council and the Politics of Chaos by Hardeep Singh Puri
190. India and the Responsibility to Protect (Rethinking Asia and International Relations) by Alan Bloomfield
191. The Responsibility to Protect and the Third Pillar: Legitimacy and Operationalization by D. Fiott and J. Koops
192. Bargaining with a Rising India: Lessons from the Mahabharata by Amrita Narlikar and Aruna Narlikar
193. The Oxford Handbook on The World Trade Organization (Oxford Handbooks) by Amrita Narlikar
194. The Indian Diaspora: Dynamics of Migration (Themes in Indian Sociology series Book 4) by Narayana Jayaram
195. The Indian Diaspora: A Political Need: Pravasi Bharatiya Divas Celebrations by Hiral Ravia
196. Indian Diaspora: Study of Emerging Sandwich Cultures by Surendra K. Gupta
197. Indian Diaspora in the Caribbean: History, Culture and Identity by Edited by and Rattan Lal Hangloo
198. The Rise of the Indian Navy: Internal Vulnerabilities, External Challenges (Corbett Centre for Maritime Policy Studies Series) by Harsh V. Pant
199. India's Quest for Energy Through Oil and Natural Gas: Trade and Investment, Geopolitics, and Security by Sanjay Kumar Pradhan
200. Air Power in the Indian Ocean and the Western Pacific: Understanding Regional Security Dynamics (Military Strategy and Operational Art) by Howard M. Hensel
201. India's Energy Security by Lt Col Vivek Dhal
202. India's Pursuit of Energy Security: Domestic Measures, Foreign Policy and Geopolitics by Ashok Sharma
203. Role of Pakistan in India's Energy Security: An Issue Brief by Maj Gen A K Chaturvedi